Part 1

Planet Earth

Earth in Space

Humans have always been fascinated by Earth's place in the universe. Earth (above) is just one of many planets, moons, and stars that form our solar system. We still have much to learn about how the solar system formed, and to predict about how it will end. An artist's impression of the surface of Earth (right) shows the land and water that cover its crust.

Ideas on the origin of Earth, other planets, the Sun and stars can be traced to the time of classical Greece. They range from an Earth-centered universe to one where the position of this tiny, life-generating planet is placed in a context of an expanding universe populated by billions of stars, with an unknown number of planets similar to ours in composition and structure.

It was late in the eighteenth century that the great early geologist James Hutton (1726–97), a Scot, captured in a few poignant words the vastness and the immensity of time over which Earth, the Sun, the solar system, the galaxies, and the universe have evolved. He noted that there is "no vestige of a beginning, no prospect of an end". This phrase challenged the established thinking of a very limited time for the creation of the natural world and opened up a new era of geological and cosmological thought.

We live on a planet that is circling a single star of apparently limitless energy. Yet we now know that the engine of nuclear heat driving the Sun has a birth and a stable phase, and, as it runs short of hydrogen fuel, will go through enormous cataclysms. This process will absorb the Sun's dependent planets, and eventually lead to its own slow "death".

Our views of Earth as part of the universe have varied over time. New concepts and theories, such as Einstein's general theory of relativity, have offered scientists different perspectives on the origin of the universe and all matter. New technologies ranging from telescopes to satellites have opened up vast vistas within and beyond our solar system. Now available to scientists are tools to measure the composition and structure of matter racing through space. We understand much better the characteristics of various forces at work, such as those driving the expansion of the universe, the clustering of stars, the condensation of gases, the orbits of planets, and the movement of meteorites.

The big-bang model for the universe is based on a number of observations. It is not speculation. Yet, as a model of how the universe evolved, it has been modified by cosmologists and scientists over time. New observations should lead to further changes as we continue to explore whether there is enough matter and energy in the universe to slow and stop the expansion started 10 billion or 15 billion years ago.

As gases condensed to form stars, there was a distinct tendency for these stars to cluster. The Milky Way Galaxy is an example of a large spiral galaxy or cluster of stars composed of a thin, circular disk surrounding a central bulge. Interestingly, new technologies show that many galaxies, including the Milky Way, have more mass than can readily be seen. There also appears to exist at the core of some galaxies a central powerhouse generating narrow jets of high-energy particles streaming outwards. Only more observations and theorizing will help us understand the significance of these phenomena.

Yet it is the stars themselves which offer so many clues to the origin of the universe and, ultimately, ourselves. They vary widely in size, color, and temperature. Stars are powered by nuclear reactions whereby hydrogen is fused to helium. We now possess knowledge of sequences through which stars may change from one state to another. Our Sun is no exception and can be seen as representative of an average star in the Milky Way Galaxy. It generates light and heat, which are transmitted through space to help transform life on the surface of one of its planets, Earth.

Radiometric dating of ancient rocks on Earth and its moon give some clue as to the age of the solar system—about 5 billion years. Cooling and consolidation under gravity of interstellar gases and dust created the Sun and progressively hardened objects accreted and condensed to form the nine planets and their moons. Early in the period of planet formation, the sweeping up of solar system debris led to bombardment of planet and moon surfaces, a phenomenon dramatically depicted today by photographs of the cratered surface of Earth's moon.

The Sun is the ultimate source of energy for life processes on planet Earth. As the Sun formed, it captured most matter in the Solar system, leaving only 0.1 percent to form the planets, their moons, asteroids, comets and dust. The Sun possessed sufficient mass to generate electromagnetic or radiant energy at various wavelengths. The hot Sun mostly radiates shorter wavelength energy, especially at visible wavelengths. There are also large sunspots caused by magnetic storms on the Sun's surface. They can be observed as visible dark patches and as areas of X-ray activity ejecting electrically charged particles, the solar wind. Sunspot activity is not constant but is cyclic in behavior. When these particles meet the Earth's atmosphere dramatic visual displays occur, especially in polar latitudes. Whether sunspots influence the weather is uncertain.

The spinning Earth orbits the Sun, traveling a distance of approximately 150 million km (93 million miles). Energy is received at a more or less constant rate, but is distributed unevenly because of the tilt of Earth's axis, yielding seasonal changes in temperature away from the equator. Yet Earth possesses its own heat engine: radioactive processes within its core help generate gases into the atmosphere and drive movements of its crustal plates. The presence of different gases, including water vapor, has provided that vital mixture of substances from which life has evolved, as well as the thin protective envelope high in oxygen and nitrogen which forms the atmosphere.

Thus spaceship Earth, spinning systematically around the Sun, receiving heat, generating gases and driving its crust into mountains, offers various life forms an environment for evolution. Over time these environments change. Ultimately the future of the planet itself is tied to that of its solar system and its Sun.

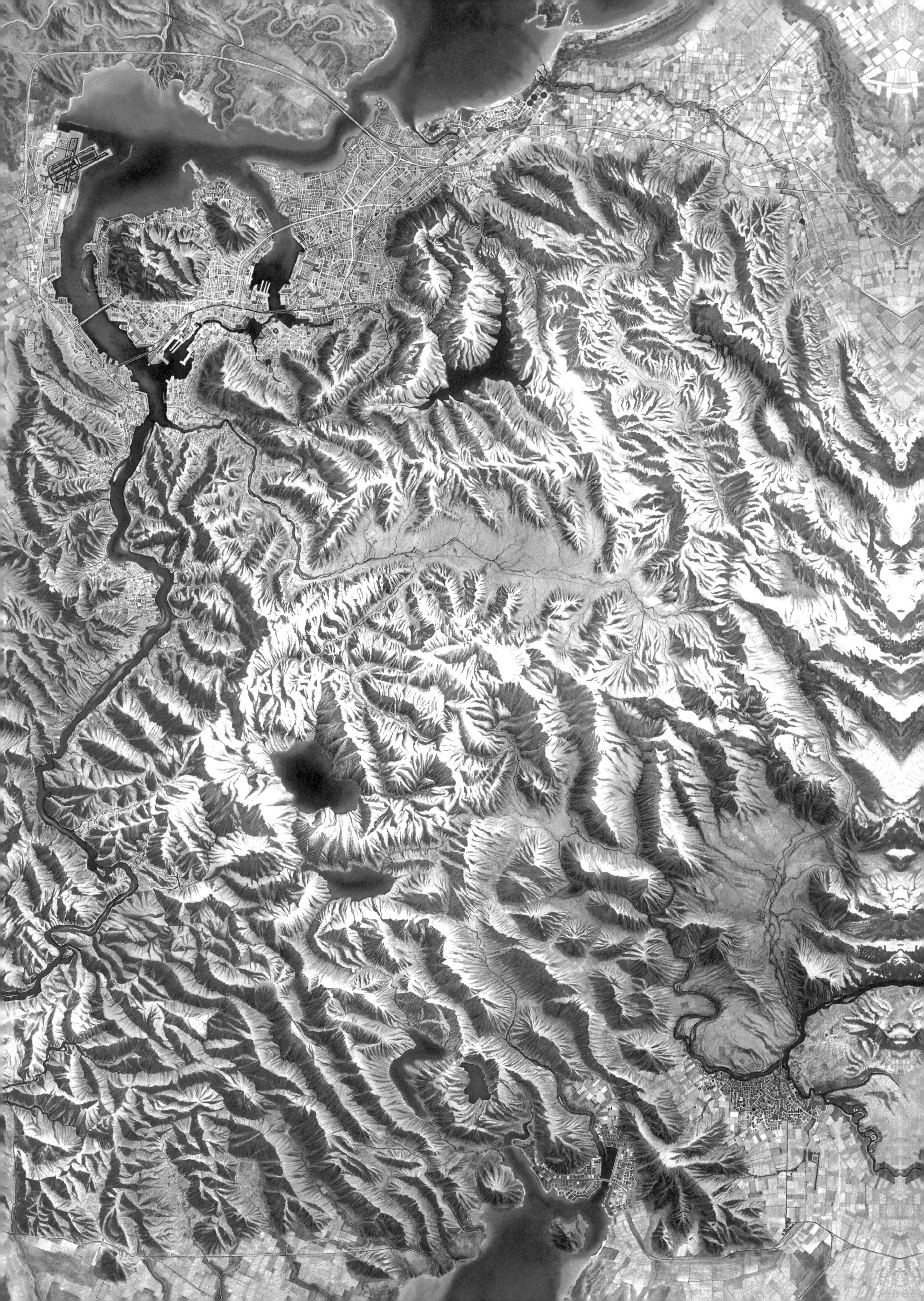

ORIGINS OF THE UNIVERSE

When we look out across the universe, we look back in time. Light traveling from distant galaxies, speeding across 300,000 km (186,000 miles) every second, has taken billions of years to reach Earth. We see the most distant galaxies across billions of light years, as those galaxies were when the universe was younger.

What is the universe really like? The modern view of the origins and future of the universe is based on the idea of a Big Bang that marked the beginning of the ongoing expansion of the universe. The popular view of the Big Bang, however, imagines galaxies flying away from one another out into empty space after a massive explosion. This naturally leads to questions about what happened before the Big Bang, and where it occurred. However, these questions arise from a misunderstanding of the Big Bang concept. Galaxies do not fly away from each other through space; rather, space itself expands, carrying the galaxies with it. The Big Bang was not an explosion *in* space, but an explosion *of* space and time. All of space and time arose in the Big Bang. There was no time before the Big Bang, and all of space was involved.

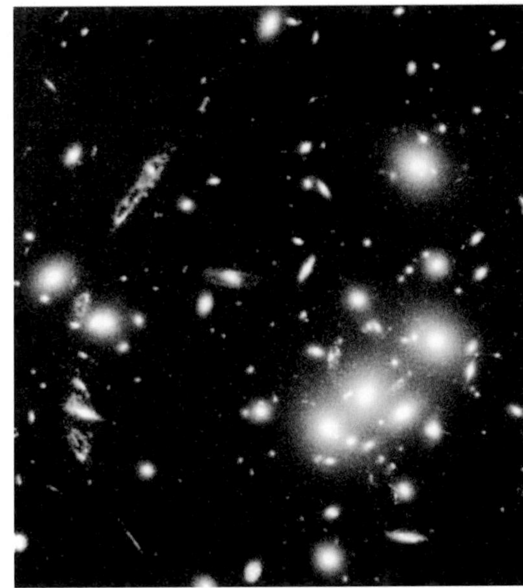

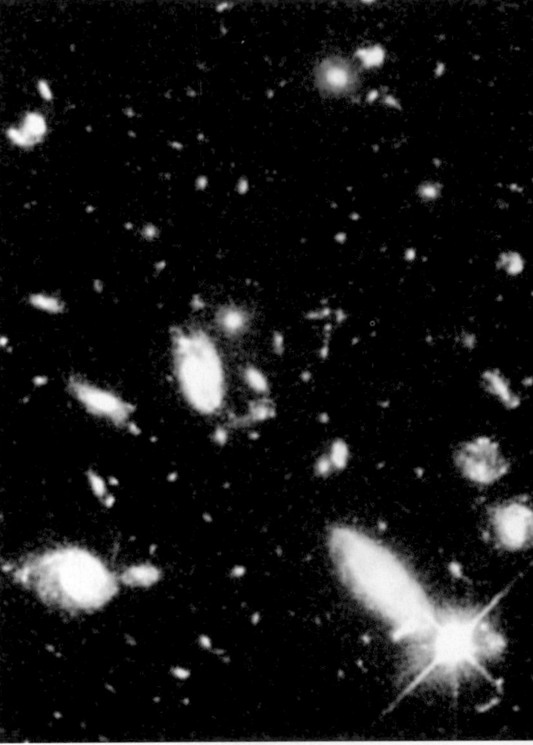

A brief history of the universe

Ten to fifteen billion years ago, the universe of space and time began, as a hugely hot cauldron of energy governed by physical laws that we do not yet understand. Within a tiny fraction of a second the expansion had moderated the conditions to a point from which (we believe) our current understanding of physical laws can begin to describe what happened. The universe was expanding and cooling, but there may also have been a brief spurt of dramatic inflation in size—this is critical to understanding today's universe. If this sudden growth spurt *did* occur, then the part of the universe that telescopes can survey today was merely a tiny fraction of the total.

After no more than 10 millionths of a second, the universe had become a sea of high energy radiation—gamma ray photons characteristic of a temperature well over 1 trillion degrees. At such energy, photons can produce a pair of particles, a matter particle and its anti-matter partner, which exist fleetingly before annihilating each other in a flash of gamma ray radiation.

As the universe continued to expand, the photons dropped in energy as the temperature fell. Particle production ended, first for the heavy particles and then for the light ones. Most of the particle and anti-particle pairs were annihilated, leaving only a small residue—the protons, neutrons, and electrons that we know today.

As the temperature dropped further, some of these particles combined to build simple atomic nuclei. Within half an hour this phase was over, and, for the next few hundred thousand years, the universe was an expanding gas of light nuclei and electrons in a sea of photons. It was an opaque fog until continued cooling allowed the atomic nuclei to capture electrons and form atoms of simple elements, mostly hydrogen and helium. Without the free electrons to scatter them, the photons streamed freely through space and the fog cleared.

Matter was then free to respond to the influence of gravity alone. The first generations of individual stars formed from small knots in larger gas clouds that became whole galaxies of stars. The galaxies formed into clusters and superclusters that are still scattered throughout the universe today.

Are we sure of this picture?

This view of the universe is rather different from earlier versions. Ancient Egyptian cosmology featured the sky goddess Nut arched over Earth, with the sun god Ra traveling across the sky every day. Greek thinkers removed gods from their cosmology, and constructed their world view largely on philosophical grounds. A more scientific approach to cosmology began to emerge after Copernicus, in the sixteenth century, discovered that it was the Earth that traveled around the Sun. The current view is the latest step in scientific cosmology, but can we be sure that the modern picture will not also be superseded?

Three important observations form the basis of the Big Bang model. The first emerged early in the twentieth century, when observations revealed the expansion of the universe. This fits into Einstein's theory of General Relativity, which describes the nature of space and time. The second key observation is recent measurements of the abundance of light elements, especially helium, in the universe. These observations agree with the amount that the Big Bang model predicts to have been formed in its first few minutes.

Perhaps the most compelling plank supporting the Big Bang concept was the discovery in 1965 of cosmic background radiation—an all-pervasive glow coming from all parts of the sky. It is our view of radiation from the era when the universe became transparent. It is the glow of the Big Bang itself, cooled by the universe's expansion.

Recent years have been exciting in cosmology, because new observations have begun to allow us to choose between variations of the basic Big Bang cosmology and some alternative concepts to the Big Bang itself. In particular, the Cosmic Background Explorer (COBE) satellite

In its first seconds, the universe was a dynamic soup of gamma ray photons and particles such as protons and electrons, which are the building blocks of atoms.

After about two minutes the temperature had dropped below 1 billion degrees—low enough for nuclear reactions to build some of the light elements, especially helium.

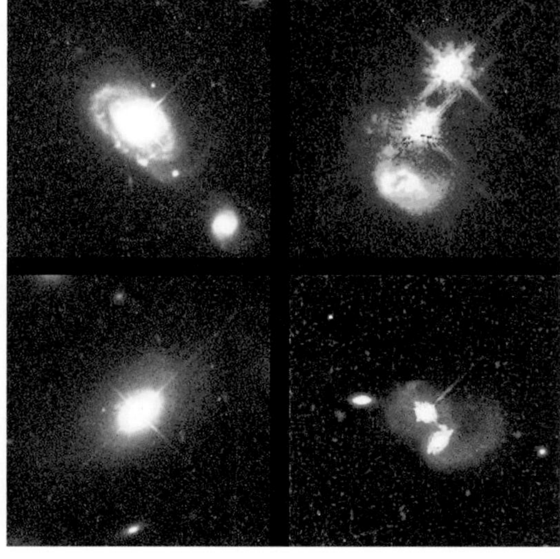

Far left: This Hubble telescope image shows a large galaxy. Its gravitational force is so strong it can bend light, changing what we see from Earth. The blue images are one galaxy, not scattered objects. Center: Each speck of light in this Hubble Deep Field picture is a distant galaxy. Above: These quasar images show events that happened more than a billion years ago.

revealed the incredible smoothness of the cosmic background radiation, in all directions, challenging us to explain how the clumpy distribution of galaxies we see today could have had time to develop. Exactly how much time has passed in building this pattern remains uncertain, since astronomers are only now beginning to agree on just how fast the universe is expanding. This is a time of dramatic developments in cosmology.

Will the expansion continue?

Will the universe go on expanding until all the stars have died? The force of gravity governs the fate of the universe, so the question becomes: is there enough matter and energy in the universe to slow and stop the expansion? In mapping the distribution of matter, it is now clear that there is more matter out there than is apparent. This "dark matter" must surround many galaxies, including the Milky Way, to explain the motions of stars within them. There is more in clusters of galaxies, helping to hold them together.

Studies are seeking further evidence of this matter, trying to determine what it is: small dark planets, star-sized bodies, or something less familiar.

Adding all this together, normal forms of matter appear to account for less than 10 percent of the matter needed to halt universal expansion. But many cosmologists think that less than 10 percent is quite close to 100 percent in this instance. Moreover, there are theoretical reasons for thinking the universe may in fact be on that balance point between eternal expansion and ultimate halt and collapse. It may be that most of the matter in the universe is in forms as yet unseen.

The history of the Sun and Earth play only a small part in this picture. Born long after the Big Bang, both will die long before the universe changes much from the way it looks today.

Gravitational lenses

In recent years astronomers have discovered a new way in which to probe further into the universe and at the same time seek out dark matter closer to home. Einstein's theory of General Relativity predicted that the straight line path of light across the universe is affected by gravity. This was first observed in 1919, when light from stars was observed to be minutely deflected as it passed the Sun.

Recent observations have revealed the gravitational effect of whole galaxies and even clusters of galaxies, which can act as a lens to bend and focus light coming from more distant galaxies. Although the images produced by these gravitational lenses are distorted, they do enable us to study light from galaxies that would otherwise be far beyond the reach of our telescopes.

This gravitational lensing has also been seen—on a smaller scale—when the light of distant stars brightens briefly; this is because of gravitational lensing caused by an intervening object. Knowing this allows us to study the lensing objects that are part of the halo of dark matter believed to encircle our galaxy. What is this dark matter? It seems that gravitational lensing may be able to tell us.

After several hundred thousand years, at a temperature of around 3000 °C (5450 °F), the electrons were captured by atoms and the universe suddenly became transparent.

Tiny bumps in the density of matter in the early universe grew, under the influence of gravity, to form the galaxies and clusters of galaxies that we see today.

One of the galaxies that formed over 10 billion years ago was the Milky Way. A mere 4.6 billion years ago the Sun was born within it.

GALAXIES

Many people today are city dwellers whose view of the night sky is hindered by the bright lights of the modern world. When we are fortunate enough to look at the night sky from a dark place, we see thousands of stars and the faint starry band of the Milky Way meandering across the sky. We now know that this is an insider's view of the vast collection of more than 100 billion stars we call the Milky Way Galaxy.

A dark sky will also reveal the Andromeda Galaxy, an even larger star system lying beyond the boundaries of the Milky Way. Both are members of the small cluster of galaxies called the Local Group, which lies on the edge of a supercluster of galaxies. Beyond lies the vast expanse of the universe—countless more distant galaxies.

The Milky Way

In 1785, William Herschel, the astronomer who discovered Uranus, counted stars in various directions across the sky and decided that the Sun lay near the center of a flattened disk of stars. In 1917, Harlow Shapley studied the distribution of globular clusters—clusters of hundreds of thousands of stars—and concluded that they clustered around the center of the galaxy in the direction of the constellation of Sagittarius. Herschel had been deceived by the clouds of dust which are scattered through the Milky Way and which obscure our view of more distant stars.

The modern view reveals the Milky Way to be a large spiral galaxy composed of a thin circular disk surrounding a central bulge, with a halo of stars and globular clusters. Light would take about 100,000 years to speed across the disk: a distance of 100,000 light years. Traveling as fast as the fastest spacecraft, a trip across the galaxy would take well over a billion years! The Sun lies in the disk, some 28,000 light years from the center, completing an orbit around the central bulge every 240 million years.

Around 95 percent of the visible mass of the galaxy is composed of stars, in particular the vast mass of faint Sun-like stars that contribute the yellowish background glow of the disk and bulge. Despite their vast numbers, the distances between the stars are immense, compared with their sizes. The nearest stars to the Sun are 4.3 light years away (40 trillion km; 25 trillion miles). Traveling on the fastest spacecraft, this trip would take some 60,000 years.

The heart of the galaxy is a mystery being slowly unveiled by observations using radio and infrared telescopes which can pierce the veil of dust which hides it from our eyes. Astronomers suspect that it harbors a black hole with the mass of more than a million suns.

The remaining mass we see in the galaxy is the thin interstellar medium of gas and dust lying between the stars. Most of this is compacted into dense, cold clouds of gas laced with traces of dust.

This spiral galaxy, above, has two prominent arms, showing red patches of ionized hydrogen where stars have formed. A barred spiral galaxy, right, showing the yellow color of old stars at its nucleus, with blue, young stars in its arms.

The Milky Way system originated in a vast condensation of gas, which began to form stars within a billion years of the Big Bang. Early generations of stars in this cloud included those that form the halo of stars and globular clusters surrounding the galaxy. Successive generations of stars had orbits much closer to the thin disk we see today. When the Sun was formed 4.6 billion years ago, the galaxy was already middle aged, and would have looked much as it does today.

New stars are still being born from clouds of gas. While they live, these beacons and their gaseous birthplaces trace out the

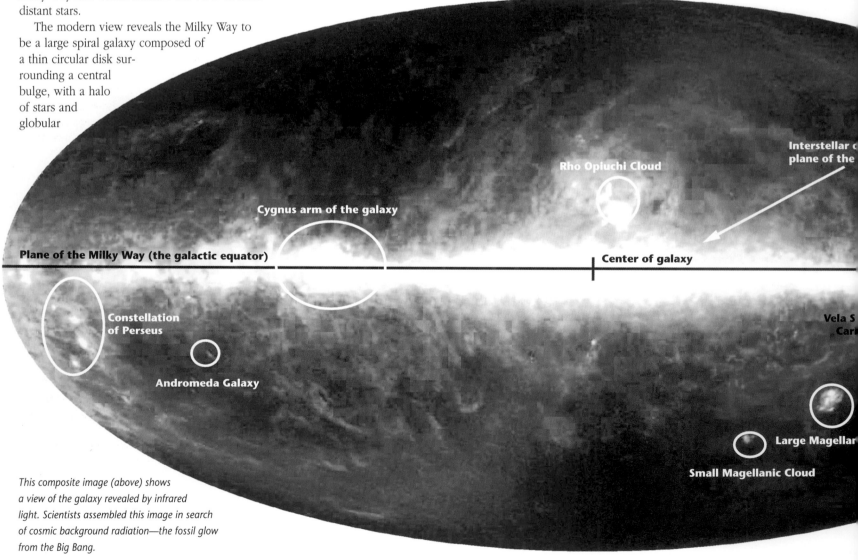

This composite image (above) shows a view of the galaxy revealed by infrared light. Scientists assembled this image in search of cosmic background radiation—the fossil glow from the Big Bang.

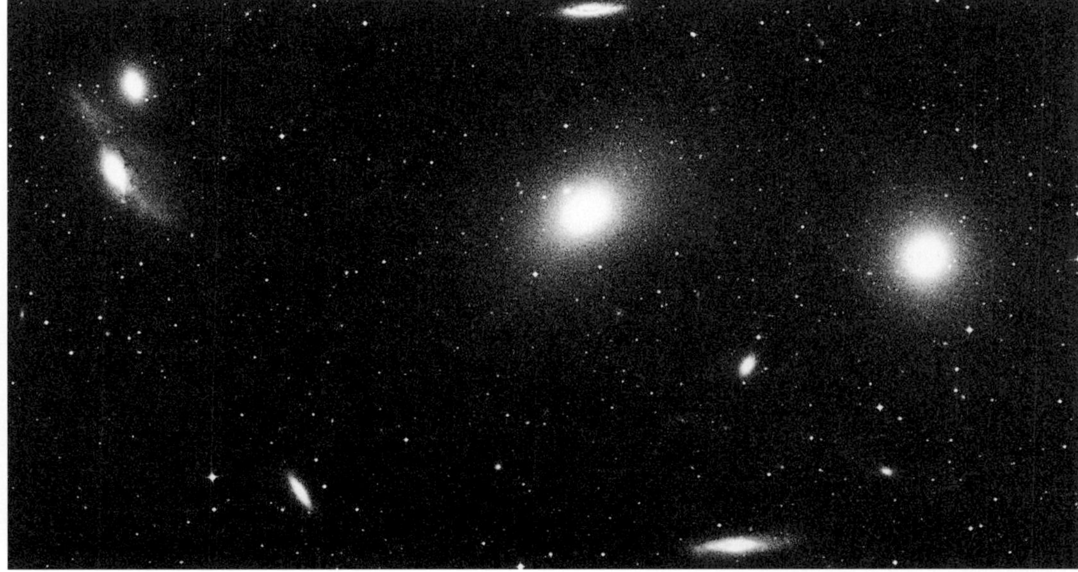

spiral arms within the background glow of the disk.

Individual stars will live and die, but the Milky Way will probably continue to look much as it does today for billions of years, until stars such as the Sun are long dead.

Other galaxies

The existence of galaxies other than the Milky Way was long suspected, but only became accepted in the 1920s, when Edwin Hubble measured the distance to some nearby galaxies. We classify galaxies according to their overall appearance, since only in the nearest ones can even the brightest stars be discerned individually.

Most familiar are the spiral galaxies like the Milky Way. Photos of these galaxies reveal that they are in beautiful spiral patterns, traced out by bright stars and gas, hiding the fainter background glow of the disk in which they lie. The spiral patterns range from loosely wound S-shapes to arms so tightly wound that the spiral cannot be discerned. The Milky Way falls midway in this range. Some spirals have a distinct bar across the nucleus from which the spiral arms trail.

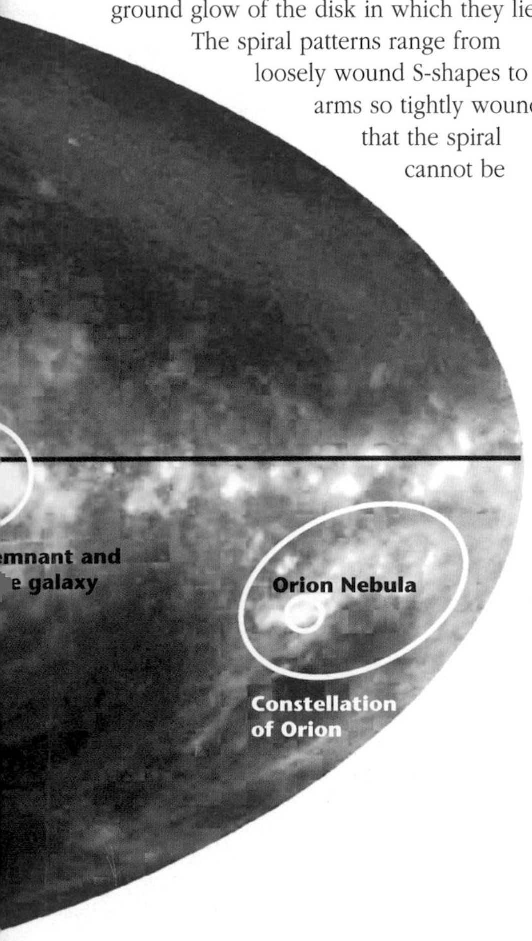

Other galaxies show no apparent structure beyond a smooth spherical or elliptical shape. Unlike the spirals, these elliptical galaxies usually lack any significant signs of recent star formation or the gas to promote it. Giants of this class are rare, but are the most massive galaxies known. On the other end of the scale, faint dwarf ellipticals, little larger than a globular star cluster, are probably the most common type of galaxy.

Perhaps a quarter of all galaxies are classified as irregular because they do not fit neatly into either of these categories. They are typically faint, but with a mix of old and young stars, gas, and dust.

Many galaxies, including the Milky Way, show signs of more mass than can readily be seen. Some galaxies hide another enigma—a central powerhouse at their core that generates narrow jets of high-energy particles streaming outward. These active galaxies are believed to be powered by matter swirling around a massive black hole. It may be that many large galaxies have a central black hole with a mass equal to millions of suns, but in most of them, as in the Milky Way, this lies dormant unless brought to life by an inflow of gas.

Clusters of galaxies

Galaxies, like some stars within galaxies, tend to exist in clusters. The Milky Way's Local Group is a small cluster, with 30 or so members, most of them small elliptical or irregular galaxies. The nearest large cluster of galaxies is the Virgo cluster, with some 2,500 members, lying about 60 million light years away. The Virgo cluster is a major component of the Local Supercluster.

Compared with the amount of space between the stars, galaxies in these clusters are relatively close together. As a result of this proximity, they sometimes run into one another, causing cosmic fireworks. The stars within the galaxies almost never collide, but the tenuous interstellar clouds crash together and form new stars, changing the appearance of the galaxy and possibly triggering the nuclear powerhouse into activity.

Some of the bright galaxies of the Virgo cluster, top. Above: This galaxy, Centaurus A, features an unusual obscuring dust cloud and is a powerful source of radio, X- and gamma rays.

Exploring space

Before the telescope, astronomy consisted largely of measuring and predicting the positions of stars and planets observed by eye. In 1609 a revolution began, when Galileo Galilei used a telescope to reveal mountains on the Moon, Jupiter's moons, and countless stars in the Milky Way. Despite these amazing discoveries, however, for the next 250 years astronomy was predominantly devoted to measuring positions and cataloging.

Almost 150 years ago, the first identification of a chemical element in the Sun was made using a spectrograph, which separates sunlight into its component colors. This marked the start of our ability to deduce the composition of the stars. The science of astrophysics was born.

Today, spectrographs are used on optical telescopes hundreds of times the size of Galileo's first instruments. One of these, the Hubble Space Telescope, views the sky from above the distorting effect of Earth's atmosphere. Optical telescopes joined by radio telescopes on the ground and in space can be used to form large radio arrays. Other observatories in space search for sources of infrared and ultraviolet light, X-rays, and gamma rays.

STARS

When we look at the stars in the night sky, it is easy to understand how people in ancient times imagined them to be flickering lights attached to the dark vault of the sky. It was not until 1838 that the first stellar distance was measured and the enormous distances of the stars from Earth and from each other were confirmed.

The first half of the twentieth century saw the development of the physics necessary to understand the composition and structure of the stars and the sources of nuclear energy that power them. As a result, astronomers today have an extensive understanding of the stars and the way they have evolved.

Types of star

While stars vary widely in size, color, and temperature, they are all essentially vast balls of hot gas powered by nuclear reactions deep in their cores. For most of the life of a star, these reactions fuse hydrogen into helium. Late in its life, a star leaves behind this main sequence phase and develops into a giant, converting helium into carbon and heavier elements. In both processes, a small fraction of the matter is converted into energy. The temperatures that are required in a star's core in order to achieve this are measured in tens of millions of degrees.

The main factor determining the characteristics of a main sequence star is its mass—how much matter it contains. Stars range in mass from less than one-tenth of the Sun's mass to perhaps more than 50 times its mass. At the top end of the range are the rare massive stars, which are a few times the size of the Sun but radiate hundreds of thousands of times more energy from their blue-white surfaces. The Sun itself has a slightly yellow color to its 6,000 °C (10,800 °F) surface. A less massive main sequence star will be somewhat smaller than the Sun, perhaps less than 1 percent as bright, with a cooler, red hue. Red dwarfs of this sort can only be seen from relatively nearby, but are the most common stars in the galaxy.

At the end of their main sequence lifetimes, stars swell to become giants and supergiants. The largest of these are cool red stars, which are more than a thousand times larger and a million times brighter than the Sun. Many of the giants will end their days as white dwarfs only as big as Earth—the faint glowing embers of old stars.

The nearest star

The Sun, which is the only star that we can readily see as anything other than a point of light, is representative of an average star in the Milky Way. Its surface displays a cycle of activity that

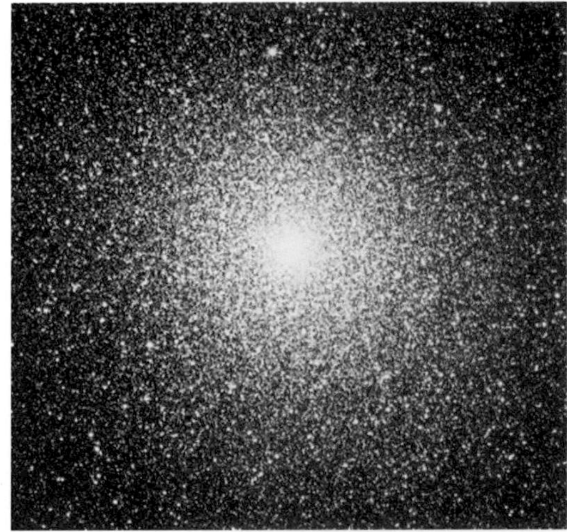

This globular cluster—47 Tucanae, above—is an enormous group of stars formed early in the life of the Milky Way Galaxy; it contains some of the oldest known stars. One hundred and eighty years ago, the massive star Eta Carinae experienced an outburst which created the lobes of gas now surrounding it, right.

is roughly 11 years long. The most obvious manifestations of the cycle are sunspots, the number of which rises and falls during the course of the cycle. Sunspots are often larger than Earth, and are relatively dark in appearance because magnetic effects make them slightly cooler than their surroundings. They are also centers of other activity—powerful solar flares, for instance, which last for a few minutes, glowing brightly and pouring hot gas into space. This gas is channeled by the solar magnetic field and sometimes strikes Earth, causing intense auroral displays near the poles and disrupting radio communication and, sometimes, electrical power systems.

The sudden outburst of a flare punctuates a more general outflow from the Sun's hot outer atmosphere, known as the corona. This solar wind is relatively mild when compared with the massive outflows from certain other stars. While the Sun will lose little mass through the solar wind during the course of its life, larger stars can blow away a sizeable proportion of their mass in this way.

Observations reveal that some other stars have cycles of activity that resemble those of the Sun. Although we are unable to see sunspots on their surfaces, we can detect the slight changes in brightness that accompany changes in activity.

The Sun's magnetism arises from the flow of electrical currents within its outer layers, but most of its material is packed closer to the core, where the energy is generated. In recent

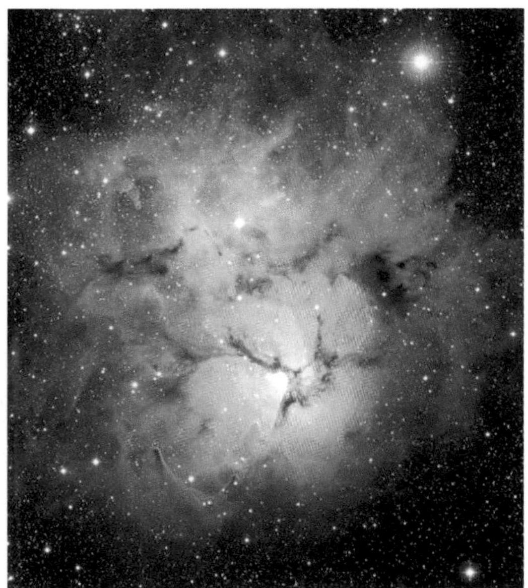

This pillar of gas, left, contains cool hydrogen gas and dust and can incubate new stars. It is a part of the Eagle Nebula, a star-forming region 7,000 light years away. The Trifid Nebula, above, contains hot young stars which cause the gas to emit red light, and cooler gas and dust reflecting blue light.

Star birth begins deep in a tenuous cloud of interstellar gas and dust. Perhaps triggered by the birth or death of stars nearby, the cloud begins to collapse.

As the gas falls in under the force of gravity, it heats up, becoming a protostar, glowing warmly with infrared light through an obscuring cocoon of gas and dust.

A star like the Sun takes millions of years to form. It then embarks on the main part of its existence, living for 10 billion years as a stable main sequence star.

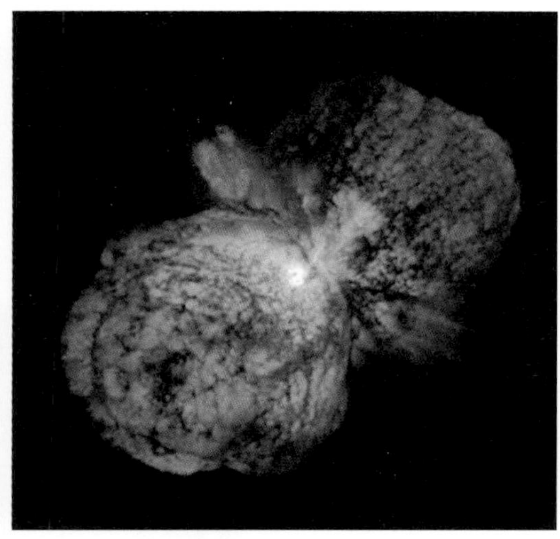

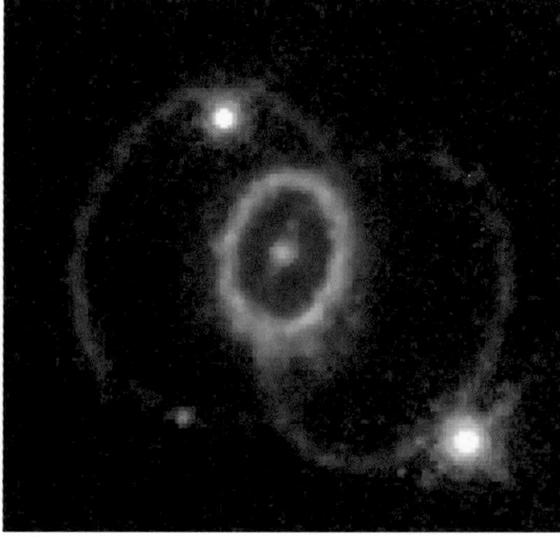

Left: These rings of glowing gas surround an exploded star which was first observed in 1987—a supernova. It is 169,000 light years away in the Large Magellanic Cloud, a nearby galaxy visible from the southern hemisphere.

years, astronomers have begun to probe beneath the surface of the Sun using a technique called helioseismology. This is helping to clarify our picture of the Sun's structure.

The life of a star

A constant battle takes place between gravity, which is attempting to pull a star inward, and the pressure of hot gas pushing outward. The battle starts when gravity begins to collapse a small part of an interstellar gas cloud. As the cloud falls in, the temperature at its core increases, and eventually hydrogen begins to fuse together to form helium. The collapse slows as the growing pressure of the hot gas resists the gravitational force. Finally the collapse comes to a halt; the protostar has become a stable main sequence star.

A star such as the Sun will remain balanced in this state for around 10 billion years, constantly converting hydrogen to helium at its core and by degrees growing a little bigger and a little brighter. The Sun is currently about halfway through its main sequence phase.

In approximately 5 billion years, after it has circled the center of the galaxy some 20 more times, the Sun will begin to grow quite rapidly. By the time it has doubled in size, the oceans on Earth will have completely boiled away. Eventually, the Sun will become a red giant, perhaps 100 times larger and 1,000 times brighter than it is at the moment. It will envelop Mercury, Venus, and Earth, evaporating Earth's atmosphere and eventually causing the planet to spiral inward to oblivion.

Cooler, lower-mass stars will follow much the same path, but over spans of time so long that not even the oldest of them has yet had time to complete its sedate main sequence life. In contrast, massive stars consume their nuclear fuel at a prodigious rate and become red giants in a matter of only a few million years.

Once it has become a red giant, the Sun will begin to fuse helium to carbon in its core. However, this new energy source will only delay the inevitable victory of gravity. Within about a billion years the Sun will peel off its outer layers to reveal a white dwarf remnant that will cool slowly, over billions more years.

Stars that begin life larger than about eight times the mass of the Sun will blow away much of their mass during the course of their lives, but will still end up too large to survive as white dwarfs. Instead, they blow up in brilliant supernova explosions, leaving neutron stars or black holes to mark their passing.

After a supernova

Massive stars die spectacularly in a supernova explosion. If the remnant after the explosion is less than about three times the mass of the Sun, a neutron star will result. Despite the intense force of gravity, the neutrons making up much of the star refuse to collapse any further than a dense ball 20 km (12 miles) across. Neutron stars are sometimes seen as pulsing sources of radiation—they are then called pulsars.

If the remnant of the star contains more than three solar masses of material, the strength of the gravitational force cannot be resisted, and the collapse produces a black hole. Not even light can escape from within a black hole. Any matter that falls within the boundary of a black hole is lost from view.

The importance of black holes and neutron stars to astronomy lies more in what happens in the intense gravitational field around them than in what is inside them. Gas falls onto black holes or neutron stars with tremendous energy, producing intense radiation. The largest black holes are believed to be millions of times the mass of the Sun, and reside in the nuclei of active galaxies. They are the powerhouses of these beacons that shine across the universe.

About 10 billion years after it formed, the Sun will run short of hydrogen fuel in its core, but it will actually increase its energy output and swell to become a red giant.

After perhaps 1 billion years as a giant, the Sun will eject its outer layers to form a short-lived planetary nebula surrounding the cooling core.

The Sun will live on as a white dwarf for billions of years, slowly fading from view, with little or no nuclear fusion to slow the cooling.

THE SOLAR SYSTEM

Among more than 200 billion stars in the Milky Way Galaxy, one is unique. It is the Sun—the only star that we know has a planetary system, including at least one planet which can support life as we know it. That planet is Earth, of course, although Mars may also be a candidate.

Until recently, the Sun's family was the only planetary system we knew of, but evidence that large planets circle several Sun-like stars is now accumulating. In time, observations may reveal that they also have Earth-sized planets.

The solar system's formation

A little less than 5 billion years ago, the Sun was formed in a cloud of interstellar gas. The infant Sun was surrounded by a cooling disk of gas and dust—the solar nebula—where knots of material were forming, colliding, breaking, and merging. The larger objects, called planetesimals, grew by accreting smaller particles, until a few protoplanets dominated. The protoplanets from the warm inner parts of the disk became the small rocky planets. Further out, in a cooler region where ices of water, ammonia, and methane could condense, the giant planets formed. These planets grew in mass more rapidly, forming deep atmospheres around rocky cores. The giant planets copied the Sun's accretion disk in miniature to create their moons.

As the Sun settled into its present stable state, the pressure of radiation and the gas of the solar wind streaming outward blew away the remains of the solar nebula. The newborn planets swept up the larger debris. In the process they were subjected to an intense bombardment, evidence of which we see in the craters on the rocky surfaces of the inner solar system and the icy surfaces of the moons of the outer solar system.

The solar system today has been largely swept clean of the debris of its formation. It is dominated by the Sun, at its center, which constitutes almost 99.9 percent of the solar system's mass. Most of the remainder is contained in the two giant planets Jupiter and Saturn, while Earth represents less than 0.0003 percent of the Sun's mass.

The region of space inhabited by the planets is a flat plane centered on the Sun and about 15 billion km (just under 10 billion miles) across. This is almost 50 times the span of Earth's orbit. Vast as this sounds, it is only 0.02 percent of the distance to the nearest star! The great void of interplanetary space is sparsely populated by debris orbiting the distant Sun, ranging in size from particles of dust to rocky asteroids and icy comets—these may be tens or even hundreds of kilometers across.

Above: An image of the Sun taken using the red light of hydrogen, showing a loop of gas, called a prominence, erupting from the solar surface.

The family of planets

The inner rocky planets and asteroids and Earth's Moon share a common heritage, yet visits by spacecraft have revealed their histories to be quite different. The smaller ones, Mercury and the Moon, are geologically dead worlds retaining little or no atmosphere. Mars has had more geological activity and features Olympus Mons, the solar system's largest volcano. The larger inner planets, Venus and Earth, are similar in size but differ geologically. Both show evidence of volcanic activity, but Earth's activity includes moving plates of rock causing active mountain building; this has not occurred on Venus.

The common thread in the surface histories of the rocky planets is the heavy bombardment they underwent early in their existence. Occasional impacts still occur, as was dramatically illustrated in 1994 when Comet Shoemaker-Levy 9 broke into fragments and crashed into Jupiter.

Of the inner planets, Venus, Earth, and Mars have significant atmospheres, although these are only thin veneers over their rocky surfaces. The atmospheres of Venus and Mars today are mostly carbon dioxide. Earth's atmosphere is unique in having only traces of carbon dioxide in an atmosphere consisting mainly of nitrogen and oxygen. A combination of oceans of liquid water, an active geological history and abundant plant life has stripped the atmosphere of much of its carbon dioxide, and released oxygen.

In stark contrast, the faces presented by the giant outer planets, Jupiter and Saturn, are clouds of ammonia compounds and water in layers riding high in deep atmospheres. These gaseous envelopes are believed to surround a mantle of liquid metallic hydrogen overlying a rocky core. The clouds are split into bands by high-speed winds circulating in regular patterns within the atmosphere. They are punctuated now and then by cyclonic storms, the best known being Jupiter's Great Red Spot, which has survived for at least 300 years.

The asteroid Ida, top, seen by the Galileo spacecraft; a tiny moon can be seen to the right. Comet West displays its tails across the sky, above. Above right: Jupiter, showing the short-lived scars of the impact of Comet Shoemaker-Levy 9. Right: The planets' relative distances from the Sun (see box opposite).

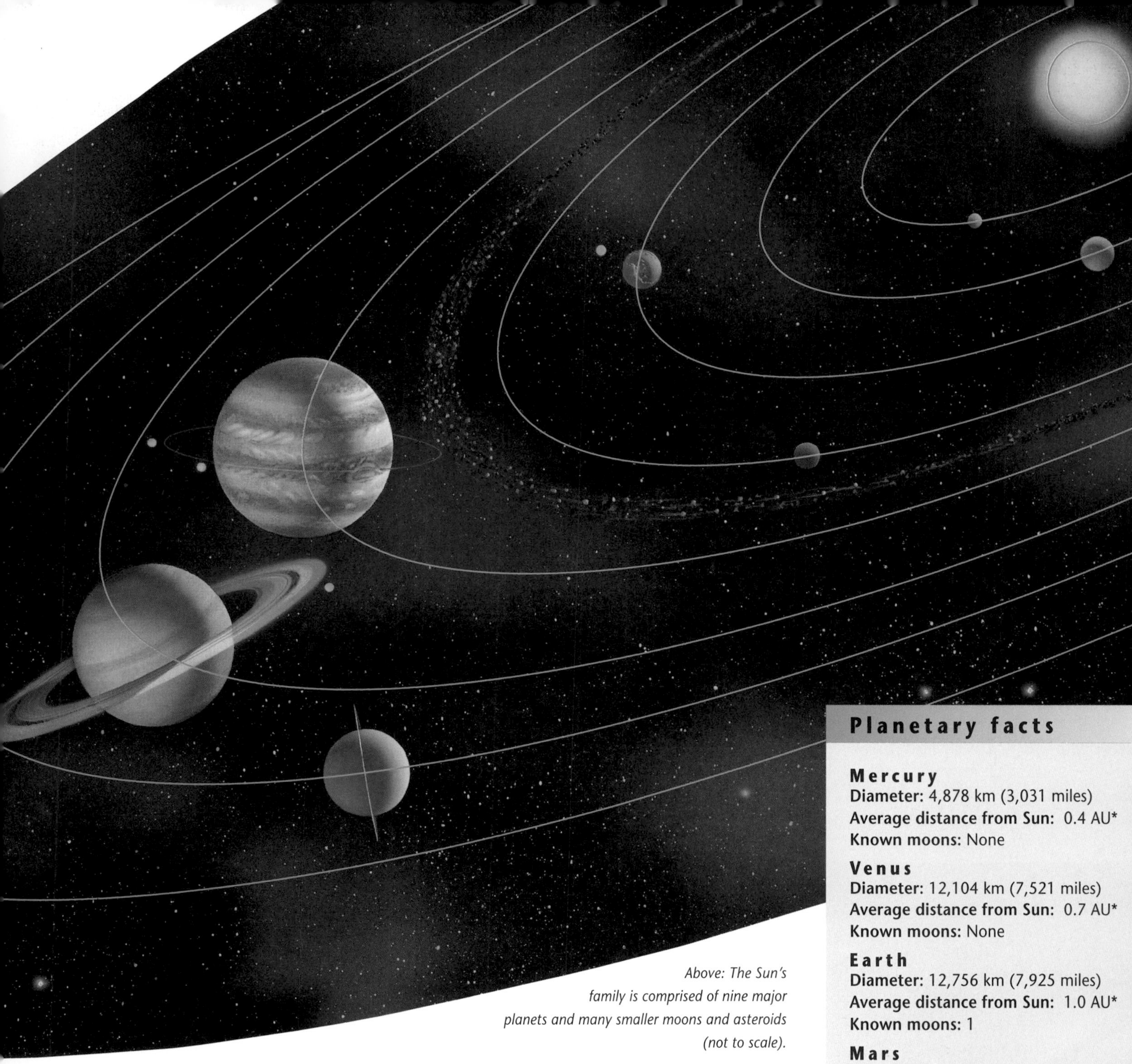

Above: The Sun's family is comprised of nine major planets and many smaller moons and asteroids (not to scale).

The smaller, colder giants, Uranus and Neptune, have few atmospheric features, and their blue–green coloring results from methane in the atmosphere. Their atmospheres overlie an icy core of water, methane, ammonia, and rock.

The giant planets all have large moons in orbit around them which were formed in their surrounding nebulae, plus smaller objects that are probably captured asteroids. The largest moons, Jupiter's Ganymede and Saturn's Titan, are larger than the planet Mercury. Most of the moons have thick, icy crusts pitted with craters that date from the heavy bombardment which scarred the inner planets. Distant Pluto and its moon Chiron are much like them, but Pluto's elongated orbit grants it status as a planet. The one exception is Jupiter's large inner moon Io, which has a surface covered in sulfur-rich rock. Io is locked in a gravitational embrace with Jupiter and its neighboring moons, Europa and Ganymede, which causes heating and results in it being the most volcanically active place in the solar system.

All four giant planets have systems of thin rings orbiting over their equators. Saturn's famous rings are by far the most substantial, but none of the rings is solid. They are composed of icy particles that range in size from tiny specks to blocks as large as houses, and their orbits are shepherded by the gravitational influences of nearby moons.

What the future holds

As in the past, the future of the solar system will be dominated by the evolution of the Sun. About 5 billion years from now, the Sun will suddenly increase in size and brightness, ultimately encompassing most of the inner planets, causing their orbits to decay and the planets to spiral into the Sun. The outer planets and their moons will be subjected to 1,000 times the current energy output from the Sun; this will melt icy surfaces and alter their atmospheres. Within a few hundred million years the Sun will decrease in size to become a white dwarf, only feebly illuminating the remains of its family.

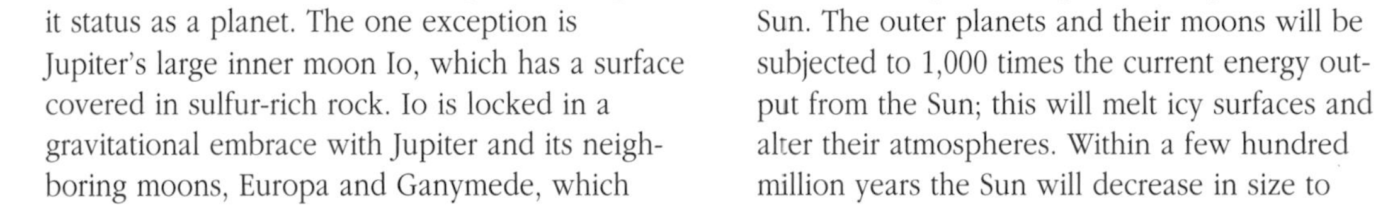

Planetary facts

Mercury 
Diameter: 4,878 km (3,031 miles)
Average distance from Sun: 0.4 AU*
Known moons: None

Venus 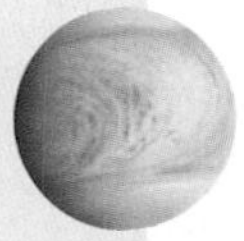
Diameter: 12,104 km (7,521 miles)
Average distance from Sun: 0.7 AU*
Known moons: None

Earth 
Diameter: 12,756 km (7,925 miles)
Average distance from Sun: 1.0 AU*
Known moons: 1

Mars 
Diameter: 6,787 km (4,217 miles)
Average distance from Sun: 1.5 AU*
Known moons: 2

Jupiter 
Diameter: 143,800 km (89,400 miles)
Average distance from Sun: 5.2 AU*
Known moons: 16

Saturn 
Diameter: 120,660 km (75,000 miles)
Average distance from Sun: 9.5 AU*
Known moons: 18

Uranus
Diameter: 51,120 km (31,765 miles)
Average distance from Sun: 19.2 AU*
Known moons: 17

Neptune
Diameter: 49,500 km (30,760 miles)
Average distance from Sun: 30.1 AU*
Known moons: 8

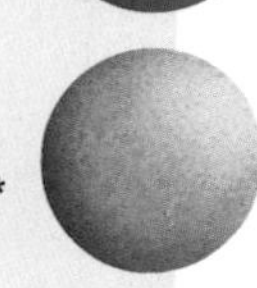

Pluto
Diameter: 2,360 km (1,466 miles)
Average distance from Sun: 39.4 AU*
Known moons: 1

*AU stands for astronomical unit: an AU is the average distance between Earth and the Sun—about 150 million km (93 million miles).

PLANET EARTH

With the exception of Pluto, all the planets in the solar system lie in almost the same plane. This reflects their common origin in the disk surrounding the infant Sun. Pluto wanders far from this disk, indicating a history we can only suspect, but clearly one that differs considerably from those of the other planets. Earth is a better-behaved member of the Sun's family but, like the rest of the planets, it has its own particular characteristics and history.

Earth's motion

The orbits of all the planets around the Sun are elliptical, but, like those of most of the planets, Earth's orbit is quite close to circular. The distance between Earth and the Sun varies between 147 and 152 million km (92 and 95 million miles), known as 1.0 AU (astronomical unit). The point of closest approach occurs on 2 January each year, during the southern hemisphere's summer. It is a common misconception that the small change in distance produces the Earth's seasons.

Apart from its revolution around the Sun, Earth also spins around a rotation axis which passes through the north and south geographic poles. Seen from above the north pole, Earth spins on its axis in a counterclockwise direction, and it circles the Sun in the same counterclockwise direction. Most of the other planets and major moons behave in the same way, which again points to their having common origins.

Earth travels around its orbit at 30 km per second (18 miles per second). At this speed, it takes 365.25 days to complete one circuit—that period defines our calendar year. The period of a day is defined by the rotation of Earth on its axis relative to the stars—once every 23 hours and 56 minutes. In that time, however, Earth has also advanced 2.6 million km (1.6 million miles) along its curving orbit, so it has to turn a little further to rotate once relative to the Sun. This takes about 4 extra minutes, and makes the time from midday one day to midday the next exactly 24 hours.

Changing seasons

The Earth's axis is tilted relative to the plane of its orbit by 23.5°. This axis remains pointed in the same orientation relative to the stars as Earth circles the Sun. As a result, Earth's northern hemisphere is tilted more directly toward the Sun in the middle of the calendar year.

From the ground, the Sun then appears higher in the sky and the direct sunlight leads to warmer weather—the northern summer. At the same time, the southern hemisphere has a more oblique view of the Sun, resulting in cooler winter weather. The situation is reversed six months later when Earth is on the opposite side of its orbit.

The direction of Earth's axis is not strictly fixed, but swings around in a circuit lasting 26,000 years. As a result of this precession, our seasons today would seem out of step to the ancient Egyptians, who lived some 5,000 years ago. Their seasons would have differed by around two months from ours, Earth's rotation axis having changed its direction somewhat since that time.

Other effects also operate over periods of tens of thousands of years to slightly change Earth's tilt and how close Earth gets to the Sun. Acting together, these effects produce changes in the amount of heat Earth receives from the Sun, and these changes may significantly affect Earth's climate. There is some evidence that these changes result in periodic ice ages, but the concept remains controversial. Links between the Sun's 11-year sunspot numbers cycle and the Earth's climate also remain speculative.

Earth's orbit, right: The Earth orbits the Sun in 365.25 days, or one calendar year. It also rotates in slightly less than 24 hours on an axis which is tilted relative to the orbit. This tilt leads to the progression of the seasons each year.

The largest rocky planet

The Earth is a ball of rock 12,756 km (7,925 miles) in diameter at the equator, but its rotation causes it to be slightly flattened at the poles. It is the largest of the rocky planets in the solar system and, as a result of its bulk, it retains a hot interior; the

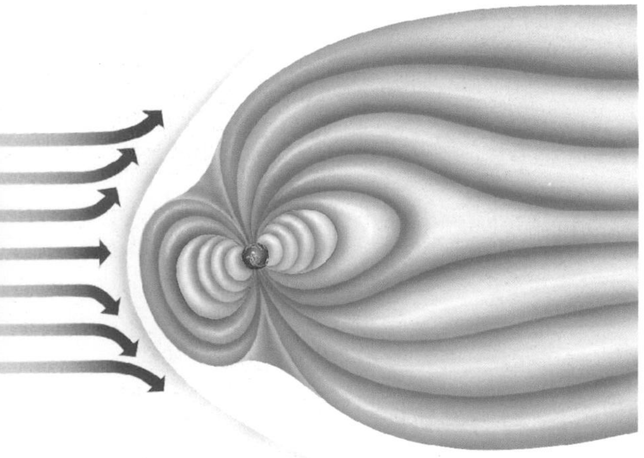

The Earth is surrounded by a protective magnetic envelope called the magnetosphere (in blue and brown, above). Some charged particles from the Sun (red arrows) tend to be channeled down onto the Earth's poles where they cause the air to glow as an aurora, as seen from a space shuttle (top).

Magnetic reversals

When molten lava from a volcano cools and solidifies, it captures the orientation and strength of the Earth's magnetic field at that time and place. This built-in compass needle has proved a powerful tool for studying the gradual drift of Earth's continents. It has also revealed periods, usually spaced by a few hundred thousand years, when Earth's magnetic field has briefly disappeared. Within a geological instant of only about 5,000 years, the field shrinks to zero and then reappears with magnetic north and south swapped. The magnetic imprint of this swapping is found in alternating bands of rocks along mid-oceanic ridges. Each band is made of rocks formed around the same time, and with the same magnetic signature. This provides dramatic confirmation of the picture of continents drifting apart with new crust forming between them. The origin of this change in magnetic directions lies in the electrical dynamo working in Earth's outer core to create the field. How it happens so quickly and why the interval is so irregular remain unknown.

How this change would affect those migratory animals that seem to use the direction of the magnetic field to navigate on their journeys, we do not know. And what if we lost the protective cloak of the Earth's magnetosphere? Cosmic ray particles from the Sun and interstellar space that are normally deflected or trapped by the magnetosphere would reach the surface of Earth. This would cause dramatically higher rates of genetic damage to animals and plants and lead to mutations and perhaps extinctions.

temperature may reach 6,000 °C (10,830 °F) at the core—as hot as the surface of the Sun.

The core is a mix of metallic nickel and iron split into a solid inner core and an outer fluid zone which reaches halfway to the surface. Enclosing the outer core is Earth's mantle. The dense rocks in this zone flow, over geologic time, under the intense heat and pressure. Overlying the mantle, Earth's crust is a skin of lightweight rocks: a mere 60 km (36 miles) deep at its thickest.

Its inner heat makes Earth one of the most seismically active objects within the solar system. On the surface, it causes volcanic activity, and at greater depth, it drives the separate plates of the crust into motion. This motion—folding the rocks of the crust—creates mountain ranges. At the perimeters of the plates, new crust is created or old crust destroyed. Atmospheric forces such as wind and water flow also reshape Earth's surface, by eroding rock and depositing weathered material to form new sedimentary rock strata.

All these processes together act to renew the planet's surface over hundreds of millions of years, removing or altering the ancient impact scarring that can be seen on the surfaces of so many other objects in the solar system. Only a few recent impact craters are visible, providing hints of Earth's turbulent early history.

Earth's atmosphere

Earth is surrounded by a thin atmospheric envelope which tapers off into space and is all but gone 100 km (62 miles) above the surface. This envelope maintains the surface at a higher temperature than it would otherwise be, permitting oceans of liquid water on the surface. The atmosphere is a unique mixture of nitrogen and oxygen, with only traces of carbon dioxide and other gases, and is certainly not Earth's primeval atmosphere. Oxygen only began to build up when primitive forms of life developed photosynthesis. Oxygen reacts to form ozone, which protects the surface of the planet from intense ultraviolet radiation. Life has crafted the environment of the blue planet to suit itself.

Above the atmosphere lies the protective cocoon of the magnetosphere—the domain of Earth's magnetic field. While most of the particles flowing from the Sun are deflected by the magnetosphere, some become ensnared and are channeled onto the north and south poles, forming the glowing aurorae.

The magnetic field originates in electrical currents within Earth's outer fluid core, and its axis is at a slightly different angle from the planet's rotation axis. As a result, Earth's magnetic and rotation poles are not quite the same, creating a difference between magnetic north, as measured by a compass, and "true" north.

Right, top: A total solar eclipse occurs when the Moon passes in front of the Sun and obscures it. As the Sun is finally eclipsed, rays of sunlight filtering through the hills and valleys on the Moon's edge create an effect known as Baily's beads, center. Right, bottom: A lunar eclipse—the Moon darkens as it passes through the Earth's shaaow.

THE MOON

A light in the darkness of night, the Moon was considered a deity in many ancient cultures and has provided humans with their calendar. The 29½ days it takes to go through its cycle of phases is close to the length of a month, the word "month" coming from the word "moon".

Galileo's telescopic observations in 1609 of mountains on the Moon played an important part in showing people that the Moon and planets were worlds something like Earth. But the greatest step in this process was the series of six Apollo landings on the Moon between 1969 and 1972. So far, the Moon is the only other world that humans have visited.

Phases of the Moon

The Moon orbits Earth in just under 27½ days relative to the stars. Earth moves appreciably along its curving path around the Sun in that time, however, so the Moon needs to travel for two more days to get back to the same position relative to the Sun and Earth and complete its cycle of phases. At the same time, the Moon is rotating on its own axis, but the strong gravitational pull of Earth has locked these two motions together. As a result, the Moon always presents the same familiar face to us on Earth: apart from a little around the edges, we never see the "far side" of the Moon. It also means that a "day" on the Moon is two weeks long!

Half of the Moon is always lit by the Sun, and the amount of that sunny half we can see from Earth depends on where the Moon is in its orbit. If it lies directly sunward of the Earth, the Moon's night side (not the far side) is presented to our view. It appears dark and invisible when it is near the Sun in the sky. This is New Moon. Over the following days the sunlight begins to illuminate one edge of the visible face and the Moon appears as a crescent shape in the twilight sky. The crescent expands through First Quarter and on to Full Moon, when the fully illuminated disk is opposite the Sun in the sky. Over the following two weeks the sunlit portion of the disk shrinks back through Third Quarter towards New Moon.

Solar and lunar eclipses

The Moon's orbit is tilted by just over 5° to the plane of Earth's orbit. As a result, the New Moon usually passes close to the Sun in the sky, but does not cross it.

About twice a year, however, the orbital angles converge—the Sun and Moon line up and the Moon's shadow is cast towards Earth. Sometimes the shadow only just reaches Earth, as a dark spot no more than 270 km (170 miles) across. As Earth turns underneath it, the spot draws a thin line of darkness across the globe.

The Earth-bound observer sited somewhere along the total eclipse track sees the Moon as just big enough to cover the disk of the much larger but more distant Sun. Day turns to night for a few minutes as the solar disk is covered, revealing the faint glow of the surrounding corona.

The Moon orbits Earth once a month, above, as the Earth itself orbits the Sun. We only see one face of the Moon, but how much is lit by sunlight depends on the Moon's position in its orbit. The lower illustrations show the Moon's changing phases as we see them, corresponding to the Moon's position in the upper illustration.

Observers usually find the few minutes of a total solar eclipse a remarkable experience, and some have felt compelled to travel around the world, chasing further opportunities to see one.

A wider swath of Earth's surface lies off the track of totality, and sees the Sun only partly eclipsed. Also, about half the time, the shadow falls short of Earth, causing the Moon to appear too small to cover the Sun in the sky; this is called an annular eclipse, and it lacks the darkness and magic of a total eclipse.

When the situation of Earth and the Moon are reversed, the Full Moon can be eclipsed by Earth's shadow. Sky watchers on the whole night side of Earth will see the Moon darken for several hours as it traverses Earth's wide shadow. The effect is somewhat less dramatic than a solar eclipse, but more commonly seen.

The motions of the tides

The most obvious effect of the Moon on Earth is the tides. These alterations in sea level twice a day are caused by the gravitational pull of the Moon on water and on Earth itself.

The water on the side of Earth nearest the Moon feels a stronger force from the Moon than does the center of Earth, which is itself more

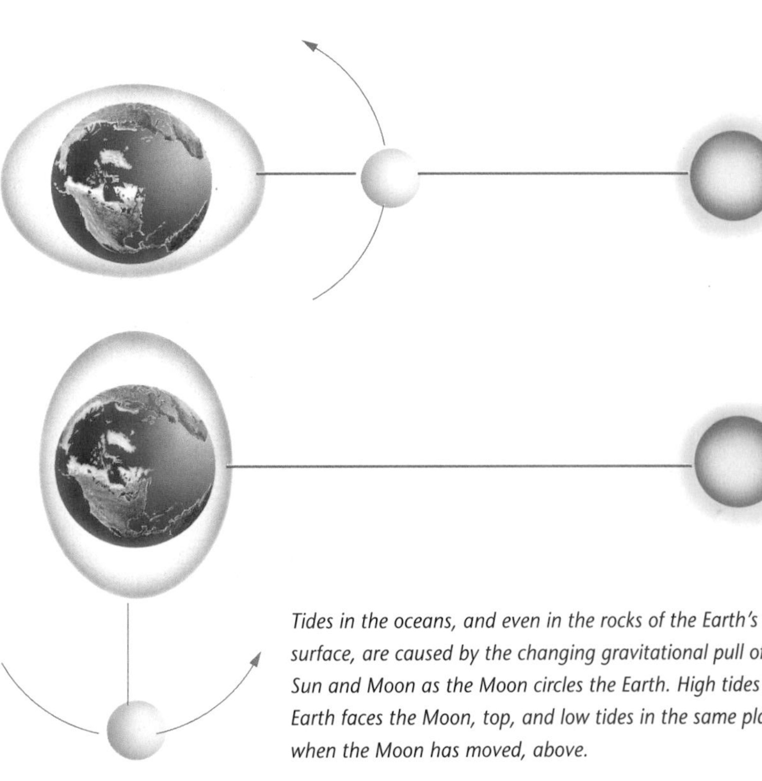

Tides in the oceans, and even in the rocks of the Earth's surface, are caused by the changing gravitational pull of the Sun and Moon as the Moon circles the Earth. High tides as Earth faces the Moon, top, and low tides in the same places when the Moon has moved, above.

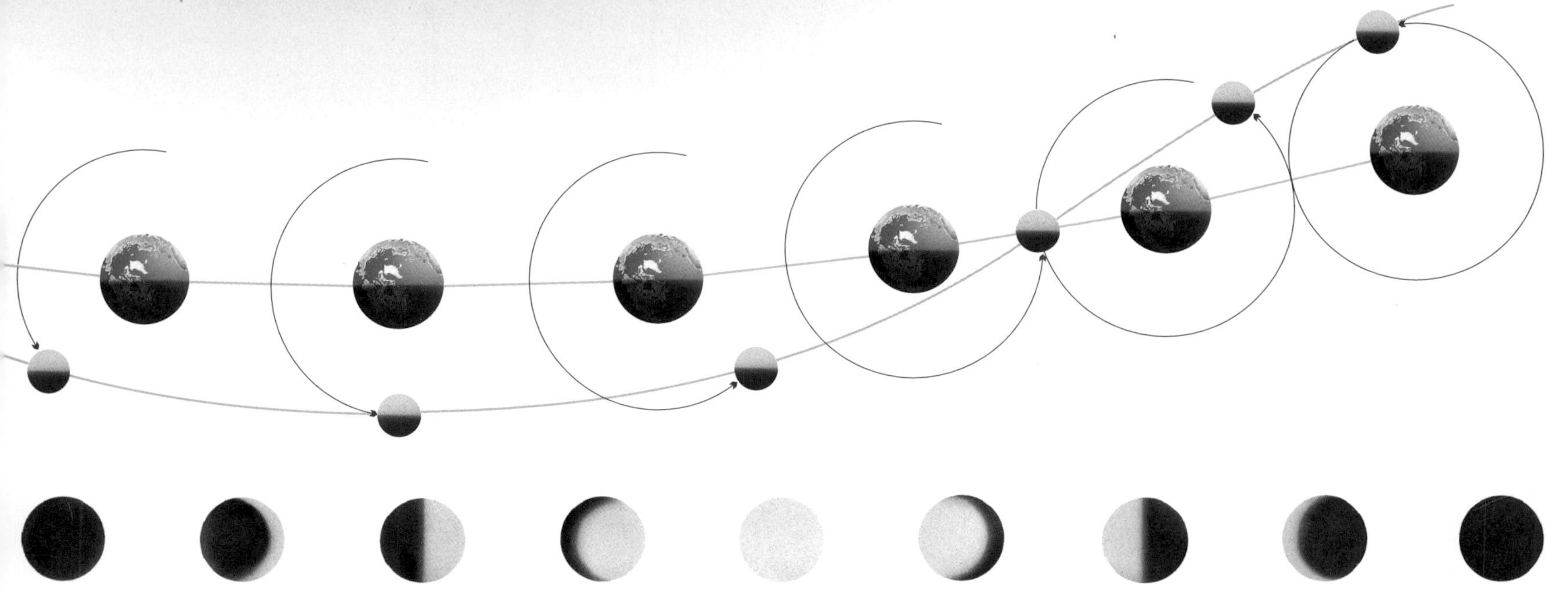

strongly attracted than water on the side away from the Moon. This results in water accumulating in two high tides: one on the side of Earth facing the Moon, and one on the far side. In between these regions of high tide are regions of low tide, where the water level is at its lowest. Tide heights vary greatly because of local effects, but they can range as high as 10 m (33 ft) in some locations. Tides of a few centimeters are also raised in the rocky crust of Earth itself.

But tidal forces have even more profound consequences. The Earth's rotation slows by 0.0023 seconds per century. This makes a day now four hours longer than a day was when the first complex life forms arose in Earth's oceans. The same effect on the smaller Moon has already slowed its rotation to make its "day" equal its orbital period. Tidal forces are also causing the Moon to recede from Earth by about 4 cm ($1^1/_2$ in) a year. As a result, solar eclipses will eventually all be annular, because the Moon will be too far away to ever fully cover the Sun's disk.

Lunar history

The origin of the Moon has long been a subject of debate, but current theory imagines a collision over 4 billion years ago between the infant Earth and another planetesimal as large as Mars. Some of the lighter debris then collected in orbit around Earth to become the Moon.

Both Earth and the Moon were subjected to intense bombardment early in their histories, as the solar system was swept clear of most of the debris of its formation. On the Moon, the last stages of this cosmic storm are still recorded in the bright highland areas of the surface, which are covered with impact craters. Other areas suffered large impacts late in the bombardment; these gouged enormous basins in the surface. Many of the basins on the side nearest Earth were soon flooded by dark lava flows from within the Moon. Rocks brought back to Earth by Apollo astronauts reveal that the youngest of these maria (singular mare, Latin for "sea") is over 3 billion years old, despite being marked by relatively few craters.

Since that time, the Moon has cooled to inactivity, with only occasional impacts changing the scene. The last large impact occurred perhaps 100 million years ago, creating the crater Tycho and splashing debris across the surface.

A new generation of spacecraft has recently begun to build on the legacy of the Apollo missions, by studying the Moon again. The most exciting finding from these recent studies has been the apparent discovery of water ice on the Moon's cold crater floors. These crater floors are shielded from the glare of radiation from the Sun, which bombards the rest of the surface unhindered by any atmosphere.

Man on the Moon

Man's first step on the Moon was taken on July 20, 1969, during the US Apollo XI mission, and was watched by millions around the world as it was broadcast live on television.

The excitement this event generated may seem extraordinary now, but man seems to have always dreamt of walking on the Moon.

Since that first landing, when Buzz Aldrin and Neil Armstrong both stepped onto the Moon, there have been six other Apollo Moon missions, all between 1969 and 1972. One was aborted, but on each of the others, two more astronauts walked on the surface of the Moon.

Below: Buzz Aldrin taking a historic step on the Moon, watched by millions of television viewers on 20 July 1969. Bottom: Earthrise—taken from Apollo 11, this picture shows the Earth coming up over the Moon's horizon.

SPACE EXPLORATION

Our view of the solar system and the wider universe has improved dramatically in recent years. The exploration of the solar system by robot probes has revolutionized our perspective on the planets and their moons. Closer to home, telescopes in Earth orbit have studied the universe using ultraviolet, X-ray and gamma-ray radiation which is invisible from the ground. Arrays of radio telescopes, including one in space, probe the radio universe at finer resolution than any single optical telescope can achieve. On the ground, optical astronomers are building a new generation of larger telescopes which will probe the visible universe more deeply than ever before, and scan the infrared radiation coming from the sky to study regions hidden from visible light.

Exploring the solar system

The space age began with the beeping voice of Sputnik 1 circling Earth in 1957. In retrospect, it seems a small step, but Sputnik led to a series of Soviet Luna and American Pioneer and Ranger spacecraft over the next few years; they sped past the Moon or deliberately crashed into it.

The exploration of the planets began with attempts to reach Venus and Mars in the early 1960s. In 1973, the US Mariner 10 spacecraft successfully flew past Venus and then continued to Mercury, where it captured what are still the only close-up images we have of the surface of that planet. The surface of Venus is hidden by perpetual clouds, but in 1975 the Soviet Venera 9 and 10 landers returned images of a rocky, desolate surface. More recently, radar maps of the surface have been produced by the Pioneer Venus and Magellan spacecraft.

The first spacecraft to orbit Earth was Sputnik 1 in 1957. Since then, Skylab and Mir have paved the way for the larger space station ISS to orbit the Earth.

While the Soviets explored Venus, the Americans were visiting Mars. In 1976, the Viking 1 and 2 orbiters arrived to map the surface from space for several years, while their accompanying landers studied two sites on the surface and tested, unsuccessfully, for evidence of life. This exploration of the surface was not resumed for another 21 years until, in 1997, the Mars Pathfinder landed, with its rover Sojourner. The exploration of Mars continues today with renewed vigor.

The exploration of the giant outer planets began in 1972 with the launch of Pioneer 10, followed soon after by Pioneer 11. They returned the first stunning images of Jupiter's colorful clouds and the surfaces of its major moons. Pioneer 11 continued on to a repeat performance at Saturn in 1979. By that time a new generation of explorers, Voyager 1 and 2, had already reached Jupiter. Both journeyed on to Saturn, and Voyager 2 then made a foray to the realms of Uranus and Neptune. All four of these interplanetary explorers are still journeying outward, reaching in different directions towards the edge of the Sun's domain. Meanwhile, the exploration of the giant planets continues, with the Galileo spacecraft surveying Jupiter and Cassini orbiting Saturn since July 9, 2004.

While the outer reaches of the solar system were being explored, objects closer to home were also under investigation. Comets, asteroids and the Moon have all recently been explored.

Humans in space

The exploration of the solar system by robot spacecraft has been paralleled by a program of human spaceflight closer to Earth. It began in 1961, four years after Sputnik 1, with the flight of Yuri Gagarin in a Vostok spacecraft. The Soviets continued with the Voskhod and Soyuz programs. After being beaten into orbit, the US rapidly developed the techniques of working in space in the Mercury and Gemini programs, with the ultimate goal of satisfying President John F. Kennedy's challenge of landing a man on the moon before the end of the 1960s.

A lunar landing was the objective of the Apollo program. It began disastrously with a fire in early 1967 which killed three astronauts. The first piloted mission was Apollo 7 in 1968, followed in rapid succession by Apollo 8, 9, and 10, which tested the equipment needed for the landing. On July 20, 1969, the program reached its culmination, with the landing of the Apollo 11 lunar module Eagle on the dusty floor of the Moon's Sea of Tranquillity. Soon afterward, Neil Armstrong became the first human to set foot on the Moon.

The Apollo program continued through five more successful landings, returning 382 kg (844 lb) of lunar rock and soil, plus photographs and other data which have shaped our current understanding of the history of the Moon.

The 1970s were the in-between years of US manned space activities: between the Apollo program and the advent of the reusable space shuttle. In 1981 the much-delayed space shuttle Columbia was launched for the first time, and a schedule of regular launches has continued since then, but with a break of more than two years after the loss of all seven crew members in the Challenger accident in 1986.

The Soviet human spaceflight program concentrated on learning how to cope with long periods in space aboard the Salyut and Mir space stations. The US program featured Skylab in the early 1970s and then lapsed until US and international astronauts began to visit Mir during the 1990s. Since November 2000,

Planetary science spacecra

PAST MISSIONS

Mariner 9 (1971, NASA)
The first spacecraft to orbit Mars. Carried out detailed photography of the surface and of Phobos and Deimos, Mars' two moons.

Apollo 11, 12, 14, 15, 16, 17 (1969–72, NASA)
Manned landings on the Moon and sample returns.

Pioneer 10 (1973, NASA)
First spacecraft to fly by Jupiter. Now about 10.6 billion km (6.6 billion miles) from the Sun.

Pioneer 11 (1974–79, NASA)
Followed Pioneer 10 in 1974; first probe to study Saturn (1979). Now about 7.6 billion km (4.7 billion miles) from the Sun.

Mariner 10 (1974–75)
Used Venus as a gravity assist to Mercury; returned the first close-up images of the atmosphere of Venus in ultraviolet; made three flybys of Mercury.

Venera 9 (1975, USSR)
Landed on Venus, returned pictures of the surface.

Pioneer Venus (1978, NASA)
An orbiter and four atmospheric probes; made the first high-quality map of the surface of Venus.

Viking 1 (1976, NASA)
Probe in Martian orbit and lander set down on the western slopes of Chryse Planitia; returned images and searched for Martian microorganisms.

Viking 2 (1976, NASA)
Arrived in Martian orbit a month after Viking 1:

lander touched down in Utopia Planitia; same tasks as Viking 1, plus seismometer.
Magellan (1989, NASA)
Mapped 98 percent of the surface of Venus at better than 300 m (1,000 ft), and obtained comprehensive gravity-field map for 95 percent of the planet.
Galileo (1989–2003, NASA)
While in transit to Jupiter, returned the first resolved images of two asteroids (951 Gaspra and 243 Ida), plus pictures of the impact of Comet SL9 on Jupiter (1994). Disintegrated in Jupiter's dense atmosphere. Atmospheric probe has studied Jupiter's upper atmosphere. Mission hampered by antenna problems.

ONGOING MISSIONS
Voyager 1 (1977–, NASA)
Flew past Jupiter (1979) and Saturn (1980). In early 2004, the craft was 14.5 billion km (9 billion miles) from Earth.
Voyager 2 (1977–, NASA)
Launched just before Voyager 1, Voyager 2 flew by Jupiter (1979), Saturn (1981), Uranus (1986), and Neptune (1989). In early 2004, the craft was 11 billion km (6.8 billion miles) from Earth.
Ulysses (1990–, ESA/NASA)
Launched to investigate the Sun's polar regions. Gravity boost from Jupiter in 1992 took it out of the plane in which the planets orbit and over the Sun's south, then north, poles.
SOHO (1996–, ESA/NASA)
Solar Heliospheric Observatory (for studying the Sun and its structure), in solar orbit 1.5 million km (1 million miles) from Earth.
Pathfinder (1996–7, NASA)
A low-cost planetary discovery mission, consisting of a stationary lander and a surface rover. Operated on Mars for 3 months in 1997 measuring wind and weather, photographing the surface and chemically analyzing rocks.
Mars Surveyor Program (1996–, NASA)
Mars Global Surveyor is the first mission of a 10-year program of robotic exploration of Mars. It entered polar orbit in September 1997 and is mapping surface topography and distribution of minerals, and monitoring global weather.
Cassini (1997–, ESA/NASA)
Consists of an orbiter to study Saturn's clouds and a probe to land on Titan, Saturn's largest moon. Used gravity to assist flybys of Venus, Earth, and Jupiter before arriving at Saturn in 2004.

NEW MISSION
Stardust (1999–, NASA)
Launched on February 7, 1999, Stardust flew within 236 km (147 miles) of Comet Wild 2 in January 2004, collected particles from its tail and is scheduled to return to Earth in 2006.

experiments with long-term human presence in space are conducted on the international space station ISS, in preparation for possible manned missions to Mars.

Exploring the universe

One function of an orbiting space station is to serve as an astronomical observing platform. However, most astronomical observations from within Earth's orbit are performed by unmanned telescope observatories controlled from the ground. The best known is the Hubble Space Telescope (HST), a 2.4 m (95 in) aperture telescope which offers views of unprecedented sharpness in infrared, visible, and ultraviolet light. It orbits at a height of about 600 km (375 miles) above the Earth's surface—well above the blurring effects of Earth's atmosphere.

Equally important is the range of astronomical satellites studying other radiation from space. Satellites such as the International Ultraviolet Explorer (IUE) and the InfraRed Astronomical Satellite (IRAS) have made major contributions in the past. More recently, the Cosmic Background Explorer (COBE) has probed the glow of the Big Bang, while satellites such as BeppoSAX have hunted down elusive sources of energetic gamma-ray bursts. The Japanese Halca satellite is a radio telescope which observes the sky in conjunction with Earth-bound telescopes to create a radio telescope thousands of kilometers across. The Solar Heliospheric Observer (SOHO) observes the Sun from a point 1.5 million km (1 million miles) closer to the Sun than Earth.

Bottom left: As part of the Pathfinder mission, the unmanned Sojourner rover took X-ray measurements of Martian rocks. Below: The nucleus of Halley's comet, taken by Giotto spacecraft in 1986. Bottom right: astronauts carrying out repairs on the Hubble Space Telescope, 1993.

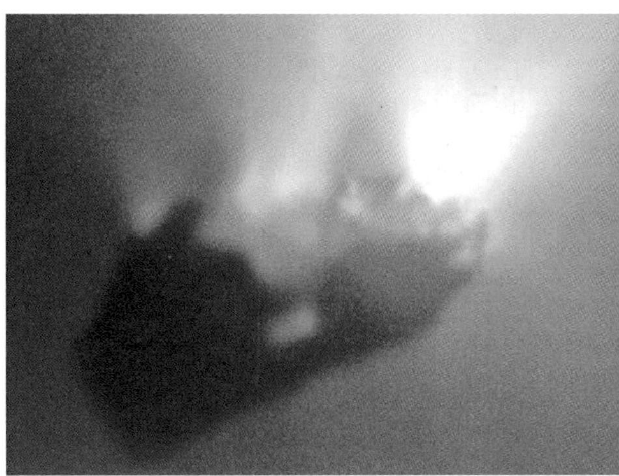

Search for life

One of the reasons for exploring the solar system is to search for life beyond Earth. The desolate surfaces of Mercury, Venus, and the Moon are not promising sites. Mars, historically the most popular source of alien neighbors, remains a far more likely candidate after the discoveries of the space age. Although the surface is cold and dry today, evidence indicates it was once warmer and water flowed on it. The Viking landers searched for life in 1976 without success. There is no evidence yet that life ever arose on Mars.

The Galileo mission to Jupiter has enlivened speculation that Europa (right) may have a warm ocean of water under its icy crust. Perhaps life could arise there. Cassini also examines Saturn's moon, Titan, and may show whether it has lakes or oceans of carbon compounds where some sort of life might have appeared.

Life elsewhere in the solar system is likely to be primitive, but its discovery may be within reach of interplanetary spacecraft from Earth.

The search for life among the stars is far more difficult. Current efforts are directed at listening with radio telescopes for signals from distant civilizations. This project is known as SETI—the Search for Extra-Terrestrial Intelligence.

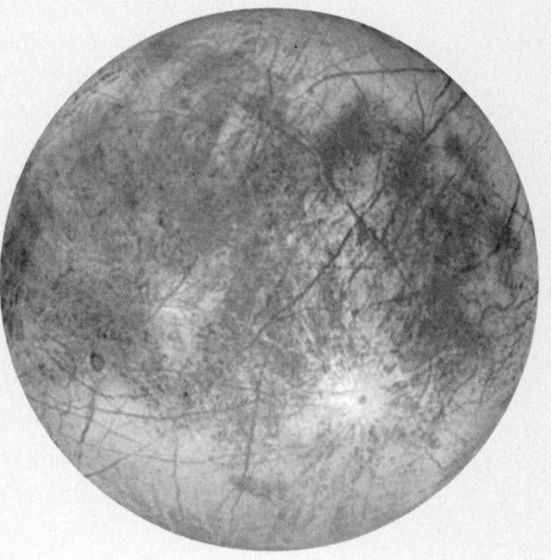

PLANET EARTH

Earth as a biophysical system

The plants and animals we know today—such as this Chinstrap Penguin in Antarctica, above—have evolved over thousands of years to adapt to their surroundings. Opposite: Volcanoes, such as this one in New Zealand, can provide geologists with clues to the puzzle of Earth's history.

There are many factors that make Earth a unique planet. Its atmosphere, oceans, moving plates, escaping gases, diverse life forms, soils, and the presence of humans all contribute to a distinctive biophysical system. Above all else, it is the dynamic, ever-changing ways in which the air, land, and oceans interact that create particular landscapes available for human use and abuse. From the equator to the poles, from mountains to the depths of ocean basins, plants and animals go through their life cycles nurtured by the climates and the nutrients in soils and waters.

Yet what we observe today has not always been present. The world humans inhabit has been transformed not once, but many times since the hard, rocky crusts of continents and the watery masses of oceans first formed, around 4 billion years ago.

Charles Darwin was one of many scientists who conceptualized patterns of evolution. Organisms did not immediately find their place in the world, he proposed; rather, there were countless histories of evolving life for the different plants and animals that have occupied space on land or in the sea over geological time. These patterns of evolution were not uniform. Past life histories show punctuated successions of periods dominated by particular organisms, followed by extensive extinctions of various species. The cause and meaning of such changes are often a mystery and remain to be explained.

It is very difficult to unravel Earth's history. Geologists and paleontologists are like detectives. They are required to piece together fragmentary evidence using their imagination, and their sense of adventure and curiosity, exploring the world and discovering for themselves what has happened in the past. Some geologists, such as Charles Lyell, have had the ability to synthesize masses of information and develop generalized histories from field observations and interpretations. Increasingly, new technologies, including the capacity to calculate accurately the age of rocks using radiometric dating methods, have opened new vistas of thought, allowing the testing of theories such as that of continental drift.

Discoveries of magnetic reversals in rocks on the floor of oceans, the volcanic character of mid-oceanic ridges, and the age of oceanic basalts covered by a veneer of geologically young sediment, have contributed to our understanding of the processes of sea-floor spreading and hence to the development of plate tectonic theory. This was one of the most remarkable scientific advances of the twentieth century. It formalized the grand dreams of those who could see evidence for the validity of continental drift theory in the rock record and in the distribution of plants and animals. Yet, for decades, these geologists and biologists were not able to convince the skeptics, because they had no mechanism to explain the movement of the relatively light continental crust over vast distances. New technologies in ocean research changed all that; with plate tectonics, it is possible to explain much more satisfactorily the formation of mountains, as well as the distribution of earthquakes, volcanoes and many life forms.

Plants and animals, or biota, occur in particular groups, reflecting their adaptation to each other and to the environment. Interaction of biota with climatic, soil, landform, and other conditions has been the subject of much ecological discovery. Competition and predation are just two of the ways in which species function—on a range of scales from microorganisms in the soil to whales at sea. On land and in the ocean, there are clear regional groupings of biota which contribute to the differences between places. But even these differences are not static—they too are subject to change.

Changes in climate, for instance, whether it be over millions of years or tens of years, require organisms to adjust. On a global scale, it is possible to document periods of Earth cooling and the consequent expansion of ice sheets and falls in sea level. Vast areas of Europe and North America were under 1 km (0.6 mile) of ice as little as 15,000 years ago. Yet Earth warmed, and the glaciers retreated. Today, these areas are home to millions of people.

Rising sea levels flooded continental shelves and river valleys, creating new habitats for plants and animals; in the fertile deltaic plains of many countries, for instance. Such changes have taken place many times over the past 2 million years, the so-called Quaternary period of Earth's history. Understanding why these and other, smaller-scale climatic fluctuations such as the El Niño phenomenon occur is still the subject of much scientific debate.

Against the background of natural variability in climate, another factor comes into play—the impact of humans disturbing the chemistry of the atmosphere and inducing global warming, or the greenhouse effect.

Plants, animals, and human productivity are highly dependent on the state of soils. Continental rocks are of varied chemical composition; on exposure to the atmosphere, they disintegrate or weather into different mixtures of mineral matter combined with decayed matter from plants and animals. The close inter-relationship between soils and climate, vegetation, landforms, and rock type is well known, and this knowledge has helped us develop crops which can be grown successfully in different soils. Again, however, we are confronted with lands that become transformed as soils are overused and exploited, losing their productive capacity and causing populations to decline and migrate.

Landscapes derived from the changing yet distinctive combinations of these biophysical factors constitute part of the human inheritance. Increasingly, we are recognizing our responsibility towards the management or stewardship of this heritage.

EVOLUTION OF THE EARTH

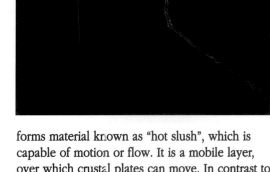

Earth is believed to have developed, along with the rest of the solar system, some 4,500 to 5,000 million years ago, when whirling dust aggregated to form the Sun and the planets. In the process, Earth may have attracted a primordial gaseous atmosphere around itself. The planet was then dominated by volcanic eruptions pouring out gases, including water vapor, onto its surface.

These gases gave rise to Earth's present atmosphere. As Earth's surface cooled, the water vapor condensed to form oceans. The oxygen content of the atmosphere was built up through photosynthesis by primitive life forms. Earth's plant life, through photosynthesis, gives off oxygen, which is then available to help sustain animals, including humans.

Earth's average density is about 5.5 g/cu cm (3.2 oz/cu in), but this is not uniformly distributed. Earth is formed of concentric layers, the innermost layers having the greatest densities. The density of Earth's crust is only about 2.7 g/cu cm (1.6 oz/cu in), about half its average density; the highest densities (around 12.5 g/cu cm—7.2 oz/ cu in) lie at the planet's core, which is believed to consist of iron and nickel, both of which are dense materials.

The surface of Earth

When compared to its diameter, Earth's crust is very thin—only 5 to 40 km (3 to 25 miles). Much of Earth's surface is covered by water bodies, such as oceans, inland seas, lakes, and rivers, and these constitute the hydrosphere. The atmosphere and the hydrosphere together sustain plants and animals, which form the biosphere.

Earth's crust is cool on the surface, with temperatures in most cases not exceeding 30 °C (86 °F), but its deepest parts have temperatures as high as 1,100 °C (2,010 °F). The material of which the crust is composed can be divided into light continental material and heavier oceanic material. Light continental material has a density of 2.7 gm/cu cm (1.6 oz/cu in), and is often granitic. Heavier oceanic material has a density of 3.0 gm/cu cm (1.7 oz/cu in), and is mostly basaltic.

The thickness of Earth's crust varies widely; it is much thicker under the continents (an average of 40 km [25 miles]) and much thinner under the oceans (an average of 5 km [3 miles]). The crust is thickest below young, folded mountains such as the Alps and the Himalayas. In places such as these, it can be as thick as 64 km (40 miles).

Below Earth's crust

Below Earth's surface lie the mantle and the core. The mantle is a thick, mostly solid layer. It is about 2,895 km (1,800 miles) thick, with temperatures ranging from 1,100 °–3,600 °C (2,010 °–6,510 °F). The upper mantle is about 670 km (420 miles) thick and contains pockets of molten material. In some places, this molten material finds its way to Earth's surface through fractures, causing volcanic eruptions such as those along the mid-oceanic ridges or in isolated hot spots. A feature of the upper mantle is the low-velocity zone, as defined by the decrease in seismic waves penetrating through the Earth. The rock here is near or at its melting point, and forms material known as "hot slush", which is capable of motion or flow. It is a mobile layer, over which crustal plates can move. In contrast to this, the much thicker lower mantle (2,230 km; 1,385 miles) is entirely solid.

Earth's core is divided into an outer liquid core (2,250 km; 1,400 miles thick) and an inner solid core (1,255 km; 780 miles thick). The outer core has temperatures ranging between 3,600 °C (6,510 °F) and 4,200 °C (7,590 °C). Its liquid nature has been deduced from earthquake information.

Earthquakes transmit seismic P- and S-waves. S-waves cannot pass through liquid layers and are therefore deflected from Earth's core. In contrast, P-waves, which can be transmitted through liquids, pass through the liquid outer layer and eventually emerge on the other side of Earth.

The core of Earth is made of solid iron, and has a temperature of 4,000 °C (7,230 °F). This is surrounded by liquid iron, and it is this layer that generates Earth's magnetic field. Above this is the mantle, made of rocks. This is topped by Earth's crust, which is made of lighter rocks.

Crust

Mantle

Outer Core

Inner Core

Above Earth's surface

Earth's present atmosphere and water make it unique amongst the other planets of the solar system. The atmosphere, however, has undergone many changes in its long history. If Earth still had an atmosphere of primordial gases, that atmosphere would resemble the gaseous mix which occurs elsewhere in the solar system. This mixture contains an abundance of hydrogen and helium, as well as of carbon.

These gases, however, occur in very small amounts in Earth's present atmosphere. It is very likely that those primordial gases were lost from Earth's atmosphere and that a secondary atmosphere developed around the planet from gases emitted by volcanoes and produced by chemical and biological processes.

It is significant that the elements which form Earth's atmosphere are also found in its crust and thus an exchange between the two can take place. For example, carbon occurs in carbon dioxide in the atmosphere and in the oceans, in calcium carbonate in limestones, and in organic compounds in plant and animal life. Both carbon dioxide and oxygen form part of the cyclic process that involves photosynthesis by plants and respiration by animals. Oxygen was actually absent or present only in very small

Active volcanoes, such as Volcan de Pacaya, in Guatemala (left) generally occur along fault lines between plates or along mid-oceanic ridges. Molten lava bursts through the Earth's crust and flows downwards, sometimes causing great loss of life and the destruction of entire towns.

amounts in Earth's early atmosphere, but became abundant much later. The abundance of plant life that had developed by about 400 million years ago must have boosted oxygen supplies to their current level in Earth's atmosphere. It now seems that oxygen levels which could sustain animal life may possibly have existed as early as some 700 million years ago.

The atmosphere, which rises above Earth's surface to 100 km (60 miles), is mainly made up of nitrogen (78 percent) and oxygen (21 percent), with the remaining 1 percent made up of small quantities of carbon dioxide (0.04 percent), hydrogen, water vapor, and various other gases such as argon. The atmosphere has a layered structure: the densest layers lie close to Earth's surface and the atmosphere becomes more and more rarefied as one moves upwards.

The layer of most concern to us is the troposphere. It is about 12 km (7.5 miles) thick, and contains 75 percent of all the atmospheric gases, including those essential for life. It is within this layer that all our weather occurs. The temperature falls as one rises in this layer.

The stratosphere lies above the troposphere and is about 40 km (25 miles) thick. It contains a narrow layer of ozone molecules. This ozone layer protects life on Earth by shielding it from harmful ultraviolet radiation from the Sun. This ozone layer is under threat from the emission of chemicals produced by human activities—especially chlorofluorocarbons (CFCs), which have been used in aerosol cans and refrigerators. When chlorine is released from CFCs, it rises to the ozone layer and destroys ozone molecules.

In 1985, a large hole (7.7 million square km; 3 million square miles) was discovered in the ozone layer over Antarctica. The depletion of ozone in the area where the hole is has been linked to the increase in skin cancers, especially in Australia. Damage to the ozone layer implies that human impact reaches out 15 to 55 km (9 to 35 miles) into the atmosphere. Worldwide concern about ozone depletion has led to government action; there are now international agreements relating to phasing out the use of CFCs.

Human contribution to Earth's evolution

The changes in the composition of Earth's atmosphere, and the damage to the ozone layer, vividly demonstrate that since the advent of industrialization, humans have had considerable impact on Earth's environment and, as a consequence, on its biosphere. Many of these adverse effects were not foreseen.

It is becoming increasingly clear that human behavior can have far-reaching consequences; not only on our own local environment, but on the entire evolution of Earth. Therefore, all proposed industrial, agricultural, and other developments need to be carefully evaluated in terms of their impact on the environment before they are approved and implemented.

The gaseous mix of the troposphere has also been inadvertedly altered by humans, particularly since the acceleration of industrialization in the nineteenth century. The principal change is the increase of carbon dioxide due to emissions from the burning of fossil fuels (coal, natural gas, and petroleum) by factories, power plants, railway engines, and automobiles.

Although carbon dioxide forms only about 0.04 percent of Earth's atmosphere, it is a critical component because, along with the other greenhouse gases, it acts as a blanket, trapping some of the heat of the Earth that would otherwise escape into space.

The emission of carbon dioxide and other gases (methane, nitrous oxide, and ozone) is believed to have caused global warming—the greenhouse effect. Global temperatures have risen by 0.3 °C to 0.6 °C (32.5 °F to 33.1 °F) since the mid-nineteenth century and, at the current rate of increase of greenhouse gases, this figure could double by the middle of the twenty-first century. Some predictions place the increase at between 1.5°C (34.7°F) and 5.5°C (41.9°F).

The weather patterns in the world have shown great disturbance in recent decades, according to some observers. This also is being attributed to the greenhouse effect. If global warming continues, it could result in the melting of polar ice sheets and the consequent rising of sea levels, which in turn would seriously threaten low-lying areas, including quite a number of major coastal cities.

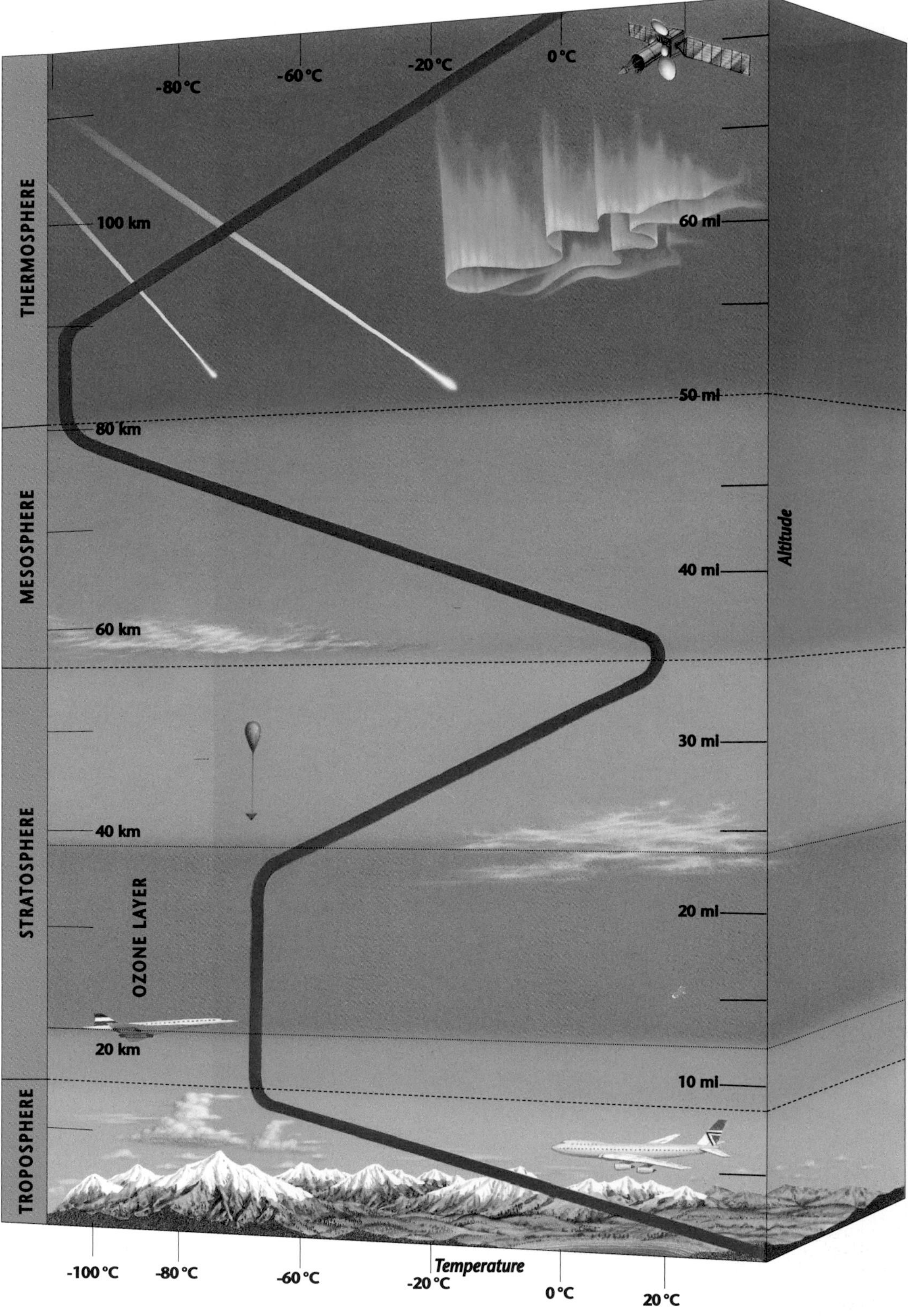

The troposphere is the layer of the atmosphere where life exists. The stratosphere is the next layer. The ozone layer, which absorbs most of the Sun's harmful ultraviolet rays, is in the stratosphere. The next layer is the mesosphere. The thermosphere is the outer layer of our atmosphere. Gases are very thin here, and this is where auroras and meteors are seen. The red line shows the decreases and increases in temperature through each layer of the atmosphere.

MOVEMENT OF PLATES

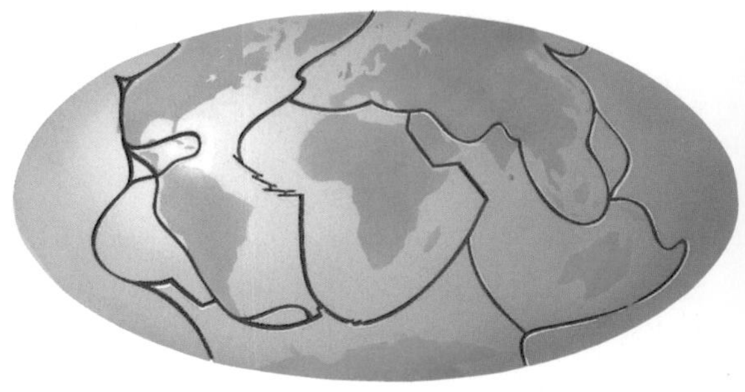

Earth's crust is made up of rigid tectonic plates. Their movement, over millions of years, has determined the structure of our continents and oceans, the formation of mountains and volcanoes, and the distribution of earthquakes.

Earth is a dynamic planet, and forces within it are continuously active. Continents and oceans have changed in position and shape over time. Earthquakes and other evidence prove that Earth's crust, which is a solid and rigid layer, is broken up into parts called lithospheric or tectonic plates. Plate boundaries coincide with major earthquake zones, many of which also have volcanic chains along them. Seven major plates (Pacific, North American, South American, Eurasian, African, Indo-Australian, and Antarctic), and perhaps twice as many minor plates, have been identified.

Over many millions of years, crustal plates have moved considerably. They have separated (divergent plates), giving rise to oceans, collided (convergent plates), forming the world's highest mountains and the deep oceanic trenches, and slid past each other along fault lines. Thus Earth's crust has spread at divergent plate boundaries and contracted at convergent plate boundaries.

Divergent plate boundaries

In the middle of the Atlantic and Indian oceans, and in the eastern part of the Pacific Ocean, long rifts exist where molten material has risen to form undersea chains of volcanoes. This molten material originates from magma pockets within Earth's upper mantle, and crystallizes as basalt on cooling. These oceanic volcanic chains, called mid-oceanic ridges, form an interlinked system about 60,000 km (37,300 miles) long. In some places, the volcanoes have erupted above the water level, forming islands such as Iceland and the Azores.

Mid-oceanic ridges are not continuous features, but are fractured at several places, with parts being offset by transform faults. Shallow-focus earthquakes, recorded by sensitive instruments, occur frequently along mid-oceanic ridges.

Each time a new series of volcanic eruptions takes place, the existing ridge is split in two and the parts are pushed apart, spreading the sea floor. The corresponding parts of the early ridges are now far apart, on opposite sides of the current mid-oceanic ridge. The separated bands can be identified on the basis of their recorded magnetic directions and age. When the basaltic bands crystallized, Earth's magnetic direction at the time of formation was imprinted in them. Such data proves that Earth's magnetic direction has reversed many times during geological history.

Sea-floor spreading is believed to have produced the Atlantic and Indian oceans, and to have enlarged the Pacific Ocean. Plates move very slowly—on average, only about 2–5 cm (3/4–2 inches) per year—with the spreading of the Atlantic Ocean having taken about 65 million years. Some plates are separating much more quickly—the Nazca and Pacific plates move at about 18 cm (7 inches) per year.

Compared with the continental crust, which is more than 1,000 million years old, most of the oceanic crust (at less than 65 million years old) is geologically very young, the youngest parts being those that lie along the mid-oceanic ridges.

The Red Sea is an example of new sea-floor spreading, whilst the elongated Great Rift Valley in Africa, which extends for more than 2,890 km (1,800 miles), possibly represents new continental rifting and splitting. There are several centers of volcanic eruptions along the Rift Valley; to the north and south of Lake Kivu, for example.

Convergent plate boundaries

Crustal plates may split and diverge on one side, and collide with other plates on the opposite side, giving rise to volcanic chains and oceanic ridges.

When plates collide, one plate slides under the other one in a process called subduction, the subducted plate being pushed deep into Earth's mantle. As a result of subduction, collision zones are marked by deep focus earthquakes, such as have occurred in recent times in Japan, Iran and Afghanistan. Subducted plates are dragged deep into the Earth, where they melt. This molten material later rises to form volcanoes.

The deep oceanic trenches lying parallel to the volcanic island arcs, which formed as a result of oceanic-to-oceanic plate collisions, are the deepest features on Earth's surface, ranging from 7,000 to 11,000 m (23,000 to 36,000 ft) deep. The Marianas Trench in the West Pacific is nearly 11,000 m (more than 35,000 ft) deep. There are several trenches in the western Pacific, along the coasts of Japan and the Philippines.

Where continental and oceanic plates collide, the continental plate is crumpled and the oceanic plate buckles downward deep into Earth, where it melts and mixes with the molten material inside the Earth. Lavas from this mixed molten material are lighter in density and color than oceanic basalt. The rock formed is andesite and it is found along

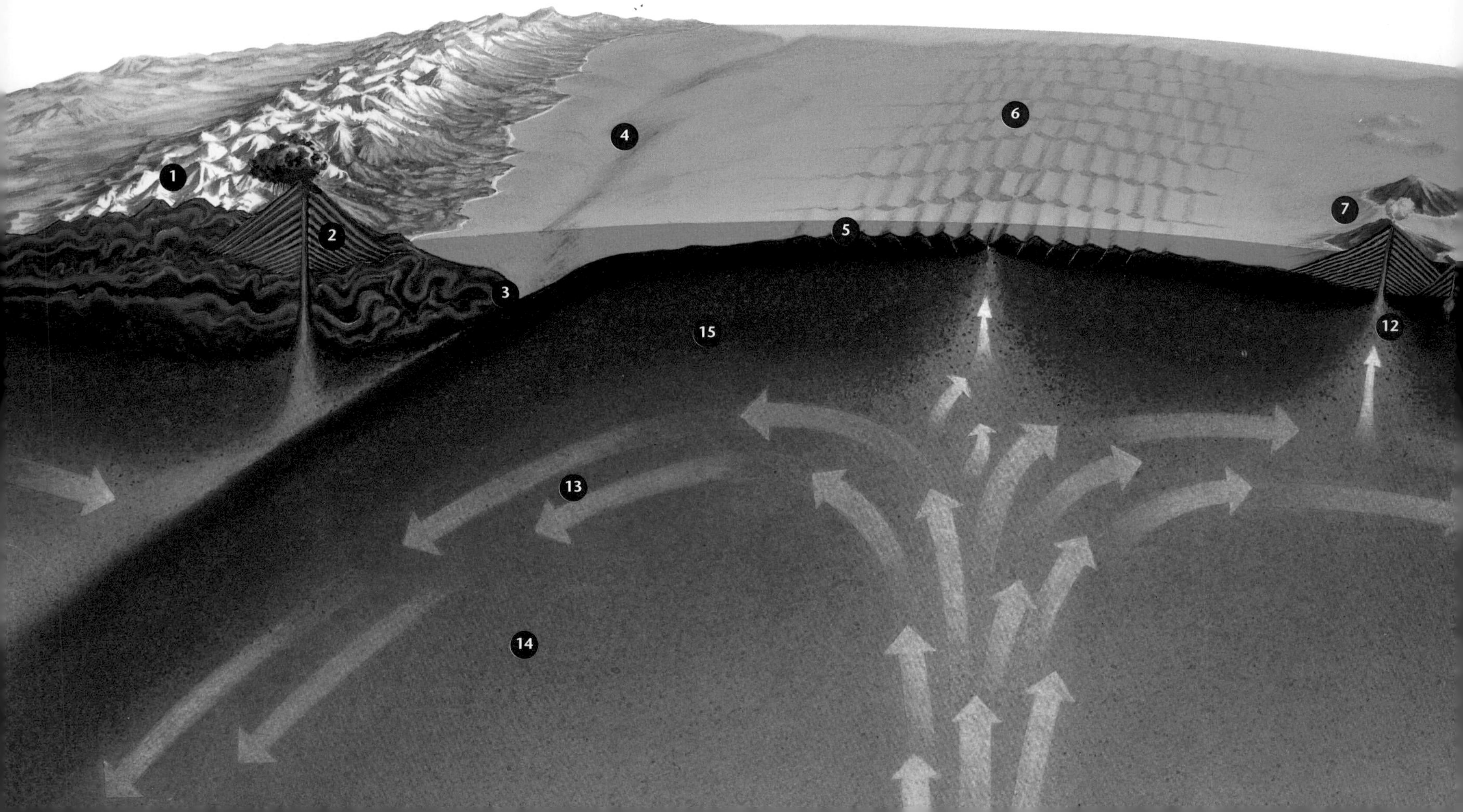

1
2
3
4
5
6
7
12
13
14
15

A panoramic view of the Himalayas, the world's highest mountain range (left). The Himalayas are actually made up of three ranges, formed at different times. The koala (below), unique to Australia, may be an animal that became isolated after the break-up of the supercontinent Gondwanaland.

a long chain around the Pacific Ocean. Several plates have collided with the Pacific Plate, giving rise to folded mountain chains, including the Cascade Range in the western USA, and the Andes in South America. This circum-Pacific zone is often referred to as the "Ring of Fire" because of the presence of active volcanoes.

Continent-to-continent plate collisions result in the formation of mountain ranges such as the European Alps and the Himalayas, in Asia. The process gives rise to crustal thickening.

The stupendous Himalayan range arose when the Indo-Australian Plate collided with the Eurasian Plate. The Eurasian Plate rode over the Indian side, pushing up huge sedimentary strata from the then-existing sea into great mountain folds, some of which were thrust towards the south and almost overturned.

Three parallel ranges were formed in successive geological epochs. The southernmost chain is the lowest, ranging from 900 to 1,200 m (2,950 to 3,935 ft) in height, whilst the middle chain rises 2,000 to 4,500 m (6,560 to 14,765 ft). The chain of highest elevation, lying in the north, has the world's highest peaks (topped by Mount Everest, at 8,848 m [29,028 ft]), which are about 8,500 m (27,885 ft) in height. Its average altitude is 6,000 m (19,685 ft). It adjoins the high Tibetan Plateau, which has an average altitude of 4,000 m (13,125 ft).

Transform fault boundaries

The third type of plate boundary involves two plates sliding past each other along a fault line. There is no collision or separation involved, but earthquakes result from the movement of these plates. The best-known example of this is the San Andreas Fault in California, which has been associated with major earthquakes in San Francisco and Los Angeles. Along that fault line, the Pacific Plate is sliding northwards in relation to the adjacent North American Plate.

Continental drift

It was in 1922 that Alfred Wegener first expounded his theory that the continents had drifted to their present positions. His hypothesis centered on the close jigsaw fit of Africa and South America. The English philosopher and essayist Francis Bacon had drawn attention to this much earlier, as did Snider-Pellegrini in 1858, who pointed to the similarities in the characteristics of plant fossils in coal deposits found in both continents.

Wegener marshalled evidence to show that the fit involved the juxtaposition of river valleys, mountain chains, and similar rock formations and mineral deposits. Those rock formations contained similar fossils. Wegener hypothesized that all the continents once formed a single landmass, which he named Pangaea, and which, he claimed, began breaking up in the Carboniferous Period (divided into the Pennsylvanian and Mississipian epochs in the United States) about 300 million years ago. That split first resulted in two continents: a northern one called Laurasia and a southern one called Gondwanaland. The various supposed parts of the southern continent (South America, Africa, India, Australia, and Antarctica) showed a much better geological fit than did the supposed parts of the northern one.

Wegener's theory was based on the premise that the light continents floated on a denser underlying crust, and that these continents thus drifted to their present positions. The absence of an acceptable mechanism for drifting was used as an argument against Wegener's ideas—it was thought physically impossible that the solid continents could have moved through an underlying rigid, denser layer.

Nevertheless, many scientists were inclined to accept that the continents had moved to their present positions because there was mounting geological evidence, such as that marshalled by Alex du Toit of South Africa, which proved similarities in areas which had been said to have once been joined together.

During the past 50 years, modern technology has provided much new information about the sea floors. In particular, evidence has emerged leading to the acceptance of sea-floor spreading. This, in turn, has led to the development of plate tectonics, which may be considered an update of Wegener's ideas about continental movement. As a result, his main ideas about the original juxtaposition of the continents have now been largely vindicated.

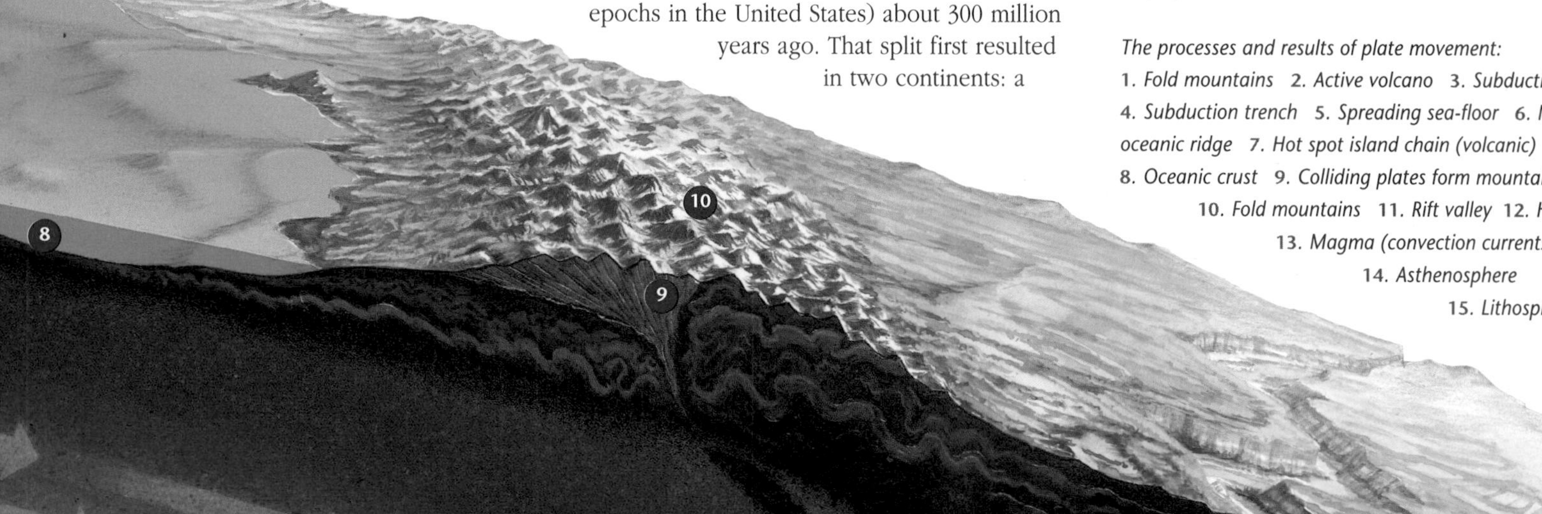

The processes and results of plate movement:
1. Fold mountains 2. Active volcano 3. Subduction zone 4. Subduction trench 5. Spreading sea-floor 6. Mid-oceanic ridge 7. Hot spot island chain (volcanic) 8. Oceanic crust 9. Colliding plates form mountain chain 10. Fold mountains 11. Rift valley 12. Hot spot 13. Magma (convection currents) 14. Asthenosphere 15. Lithosphere

ROCKS

Earth's crust consists of rocks. These rocks combine a variety of minerals that may or may not be crystalline, and which can form in several ways. Igneous rocks are made of crystalline minerals which originate during the cooling of molten material called magma. In contrast, sedimentary rocks result from the compaction or consolidation of loosened minerals, rock fragments, and plant and animal matter. Metamorphic rocks are formed when existing rocks are altered through pressure and temperature—they result either from compaction under pressure or from partial remelting, when new minerals can be formed from crystallization.

Minerals

Minerals are inorganic substances with defined chemical and atomic structures. When magmas cool, minerals crystallize. Each mineral exhibits its own unique crystalline shape. Minerals can also originate in the breakdown of pre-existing minerals, as in the case of clays, or from the reconstitution of existing materials, as in the case of metamorphic rocks.

A common mineral is quartz (an oxide of silica), which occurs as large crystals in some rocks and as sand on sea shores. It is a light-colored mineral. Other light-colored minerals include felspars, which are silicates combining silica, aluminum, potassium, sodium, and calcium. These light-colored minerals are commonly found in rocks of light density, such as granite. Dark-colored silicates, which are combinations of silica, magnesium, and iron (pyroxenes, amphiboles, olivine, and dark micas), predominate in dark-colored rocks such as basalt.

Era	Major geological events	Period	Millions of years ago
CENOZOIC	• Ice age • First humans	Quaternary	1.6
	• Rockies, Alps and Himalayas begin to form • First hominids	Tertiary	65
MESOZOIC	• First flowering plants • Extinction of giant reptiles	Cretaceous	145
	• Pangaea splits into Gondwanaland and Laurasia • First birds and mammals	Jurassic	208
	• First dinosaurs • Supercontinent of Pangaea in existence	Triassic	245
PALEOZOIC	• First amphibians	Permian	288
	• Extensive forests, which later formed coal deposits	Carboniferous	360
		Devonian	408
	• First land plants	Silurian	438
		Ordovician	508
	• Age of the trilobites, the first complex animals, which had hard shells and were marine	Cambrian	570
PRE-CAMBRIAN	• Oldest rocks on Earth's crust identified • First life forms: single cell forms like bacteria and algae • Continents and oceans formed • Extensive sedimentary rocks like iron ore deposits were laid down		4560

Igneous rocks

When molten material lying deep within Earth's crust cools, minerals form large crystals, because of slow cooling, producing plutonic igneous rocks. The most common plutonic rock is granite, which is also the rock that is most widespread in the continental crust. Granite is light colored and low in density because it contains silica and felspars.

When magma is extruded onto the Earth's surface as lava, faster cooling takes place, resulting in smaller crystals, even glass. The most common volcanic rock is basalt, which is dark colored and dense because of dark-colored minerals such as biotite, pyroxenes, amphiboles, and olivine. The ocean floors are largely made up of basalt.

Large pockets of magma inside the crust give rise to large rock bodies called batholiths, which are mostly made of granite and are often found in great mountain ranges. Smaller igneous intrusions may form in cracks and joints in other rocks. When these intrusions cut through sedimentary strata, they are called dikes; intrusions between the bedding planes of strata are known as sills.

The vapors emanating from igneous intrusions often crystallize in neighboring rocks as valuable minerals—gold, silver, copper, lead, and zinc. Such deposits are found in recent geological formations such as those around the Pacific "Ring of Fire," as well as in more ancient rocks such as those near the Kalgoorlie goldfields of Western Australia. A rare igneous rock called kimberlite, which occurs in pipe-like shapes, contains diamond deposits such as those found in South Africa.

Sedimentary rocks

Sedimentary rocks can be made up of either organic or inorganic particles. Organic sediments are the remains of plants and animals—one example of a sedimentary rock made up of plant remains is coal. Large deposits of limestone are mostly the result of the precipitation of calcium carbonate, but can also be the result of the agglomeration, or clustering, of sea shell fragments and the building of coral reefs. Inorganic sedimentary rocks include those made up of sand (sandstone), clays (shale), or pebbles cemented together (conglomerate).

The Grand Canyon, USA (right), with a color-coded strip added (see geological time scale, left) to illustrate the geological history of the area. The diagram shows geological eras from the origin of Earth (4,560 million years ago) until the Cenozoic Era, which began 65 million years ago.

Sedimentary strata deposited in large basins like the sea sometimes become exposed through vertical uplift, in which case the strata may remain horizontal. When strata are folded in the process of mountain formation, however, they form complex structures such as anticlines (dome-shaped folds) and synclines (basin-shaped folds). Anticlines have often become reservoirs for petroleum, while basin-type structures can often contain artesian water.

Several valuable minerals are found in sedimentary rocks: iron ores; oxides of aluminum (bauxite); and manganese. Coal deposits are sedimentary accumulations of transformed ancient forests. Building materials such as sandstones and materials for producing cement and fertilizers also come from sedimentary rocks.

Metamorphic rocks

When sedimentary rocks are subjected to high pressure they alter to become metamorphic rocks. Thus shale is converted to the more solid slate, sandstone to the very hard rock called quartzite and limestone to the crystallized rock known as marble. The presence of chemical impurities in limestone can result in marbles of a variety of colors and patterns.

When sedimentary and igneous rocks are subjected to high pressure as well

An area of the East Sussex, United Kingdom coast known as the Seven Sisters (far left) consists primarily of limestone, a sedimentary rock. The banded boulders (left) in the Canadian Rockies, and the Waitomo Caves in the North Island, New Zealand (below) are also limestone; its appearance depends on the depositional environment in which it formed.

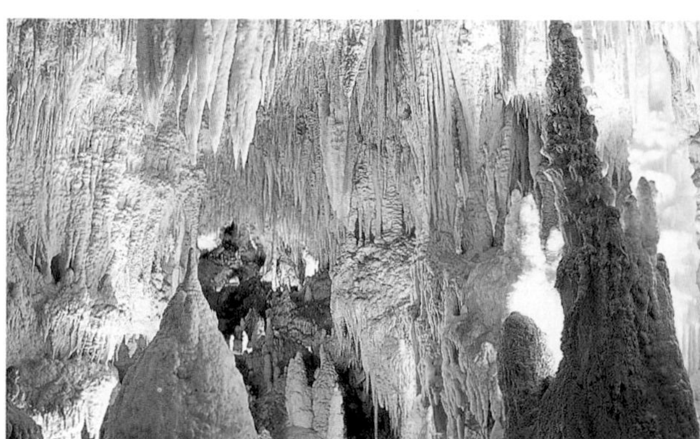

as high temperature, partial melting can take place. This partially remelted material gives rise to crystalline metamorphic rocks called schist and gneiss. Gneiss resembles granite in appearance, but it generally has a layered structure. Schists are made of platy minerals, including micas.

Large igneous intrusions often change the rocks into which they intrude to metamorphic rocks through the effects of the heat and the gases that they carry. Batholiths, the largest igneous intrusions, have created metamorphic aureoles in contact zones such as are found in the Alps.

Two important building materials, slate and marble, are metamorphic rocks. Other commercially valuable metamorphic mineral deposits include talc (used for cosmetics) and graphite (used for making pencils).

The rock cycle

In recent years, the concept of the rock cycle has proven useful. It represents the continuous recycling of rock materials and their conversion into different rock types, and helps link the various kinds of rocks found on Earth's surface.

When igneous rocks are exposed on the surface of Earth, they become weathered. Solar radiation, running water, ice, wind, and waves all weather rocks mechanically. Water acidified through the absorption of carbon dioxide and organic acids weathers rocks chemically. Over a long period, mechanical and chemical weathering produces pebbles, sands, and clays, which often consolidate into sedimentary rocks.

When these rocks are then dragged deep into Earth's crust by the process of plate subduction, they enter zones of very high pressure and temperature, resulting in partial melting and producing crystalline metamorphic rocks. If the rocks are carried still deeper into the Earth, however, where the temperatures are high enough to melt the rocks completely, a new magma is formed. This new magma may either crystallize deep inside Earth and form new plutonic igneous rocks, or be extruded as volcanic lavas.

Where volcanoes have erupted along zones of plate subduction, a rock named andesite has formed from lavas; this rock is a mixture of dark- and light-colored minerals, as it reflects the mixing of light continental and dark oceanic materials.

LANDFORMS

Earth's surface is constantly being transformed by falling rain, glaciers, rivers, underground water, wind, and waves. These constantly erode the land, transporting debris and depositing it elsewhere. The land is moulded into new forms through erosion, and new landforms are also created by the deposition of eroded debris.

Rainfall and water flow in creeks and rivers are the main agents of landform creation in humid areas; glaciers are the most important agents at high latitudes and in mountainous areas of heavy snowfall; and wind is important in arid areas.

Landforms of erosion

Glaciers, rivers, winds, and waves are powerful erosive agents. Glaciers pluck pieces of rock from valley sides, rivers carry rock fragments along in their current, and winds lift and transport particles of dust. Air and water velocities determine the erosive force of winds and rivers, and the rock fragments they carry with them make these agents additionally abrasive.

Rock fragments embedded in glaciers scour rock surfaces on the glacier's floor and sides; sand and gravel in fast-flowing rivers erode their floors and banks; and wind-borne sand blasts rock surfaces, creating intricate structures. Platforms, caves, and cliffs are formed by the action of waves carrying sand, pebbles and boulders and beating them against rocky coasts.

Rivers in mountainous areas flow rapidly because of steep slope gradients. Such streams may be highly erosive, and may cut their channels vertically, producing V-shaped valley profiles.

Glaciers are made of solid ice, and result from the compaction of snow. Some of the longest glaciers remaining, at 39 to 73 km (24 to 46 miles) in length, are found in the Karakoram ranges in the Himalayas. Although they generally move very slowly (2 to 3 cm [3/4 to 1 1/4 inches] per day), glaciers are powerful eroders, and can move 4 to 5 m (13 to 16 1/2 ft) a day.

Glaciers typically create U-shaped valleys called troughs. Glaciers at the head of sloping valleys give rise to basin-shaped features known as cirques. When cirques from two opposing sides meet through erosion, a pass, or col, is formed. Between glacial valleys, sharp ridges, known as arêtes, develop. At the top of glacial mountains, arêtes meet at sharp peaks called horns, such as those on the Matterhorn and Mt Everest.

Where glaciers have disappeared, troughs are exposed, along with tributary glacial valleys, and these form hanging valleys perched above scarps. They often have streams cascading over them as waterfalls, and are often used as sites for the generation of hydroelectric power.

Depending on their velocity, winds can lift loose rock particles or soils. Generally speaking, the wind transports particles which are dry and not protected by plant cover—so wind action is mostly restricted to arid and semiarid regions, and some coastal areas. Strong winds can scoop out hollows in loose, dry soil. This process is known as deflation, and the hollows formed are called blowouts. These can range in diameter from about a meter to a kilometer or more.

When waves approach a coastline made up of headlands and bays, they gather around the headlands and spread out in the bays. Wave energy becomes concentrated on the headlands, where the steady pounding carves platforms and cliffs. In bays, by contrast, wave energy is dissipated, and the waves deposit sand and other detritus. These may also be transported along the shore, depending on the angle of the coast in relation to the direction of the waves.

Rock debris—such as loose, unsupported material and waterlogged soil—tends to move down hill slopes through the action of gravity.

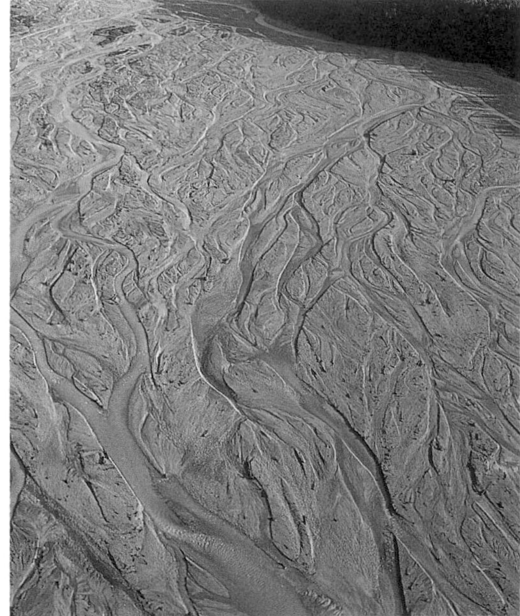

Slow movements known as soil creep are often imperceptible, and are indicated only by the changed position of fixed objects—trees, fences, and houses. The shaking of sloping ground by earthquakes can trigger a more rapid movement of loose materials. Fast movements such as landslides (or snow avalanches) tend to occur after heavy rains (or snowfalls) on steep slopes. In contrast to landslides, slumps are formed when slopes slip in a backward rotation, a phenomenon sometimes found in waterlogged soils.

Transportation and deposition of rock debris

The debris resulting from erosion is transported by glaciers, rivers, winds, and waves. A glacier carries assorted rock debris (boulders, pebbles, or finer materials) on or beneath its solid surface.

As a glacier moves, it plucks rocks from the valley walls, and the rock debris falls along the sides of the glacier to form what are known as lateral moraines. When two glaciers meet and coalesce, two lateral moraines join in the center of the new, larger glacier, forming a medial moraine.

As mountain glaciers reach lower, warmer levels, they melt and drop their debris, which forms terminal moraines. The resulting meltwater carries a fine glacial flour, which may be spread as a vast depositional plain. Rich soils have

The following features are those typically found in glacial areas, showing the close interconnection between current landforms and past glaciers: 1. *Cirque basin* 2. *Hanging valley in a glacial trough* 3. *Outwash plain from glacial meltwater* 4. *Terminal moraine of a valley glacier* 5. *Lateral moraine* 6. *Medial moraine* 7. *Ground moraine* 8. *Arête or sharp-crested ridge* 9. *Horn or sharp peak*

An aerial view of a braided river channel showing the build up of sediment on the river bed (far left), and a coastline dramatically eroded by wave action (left). The cirque (below) shows typically steep walls—carved by the movement of glacial ice—and a flat floor.

developed in such plains in both northern Europe and the northern United States.

The amount of rock particle rivers and winds carry is determined by velocity; in general, larger particle sizes need greater velocities. At lower speeds, rivers deposit their sediment load, which then forms fertile alluvial flats and broad alluvial plains. These areas may be periodically inundated by floods. Much of the sediment carried by rivers in flood is deposited at the coast as deltas. Several major rivers carry high sediment loads—the Huang River in China carries more than one and a half million tonnes annually.

Wind

Other landforms result from wind. Strong winds can lift and carry sands, while lighter winds lift and carry silts and clays. High winds rework sand masses into dunes of various types, depending on sand availability and wind direction. Sand dunes in deserts include crescent-shaped barchans, which have gentle windward slopes and abrupt leeward slopes—the crescent's horns point downwind. Silt-sized particles are transported by the wind to form thick, fertile deposits known as loess. Extensive deposits of loess are found on the edges of some deserts and in areas once glaciated (northern China and the Mississippi Valley, for instance).

Waves

Waves tend to approach a beach perpendicularly. The movement of the wave as it runs onto the beach is known as swash; the water, or backwash, then returns to the sea. Swash and backwash move sand along beaches, which contributes to littoral or longshore drift (when waves approach the beach at an angle). Along coastal plains, waves tend to build sand barriers by the shore. Lagoons develop behind these barriers, which are connected to the sea by tidal inlets. These lagoons can later fill with sediment, a stage in the gradual seaward extension of the coastal plain. The sea-level rise, on the other hand, along with storm wave erosion, can drive the sand barriers landward.

During the next several decades, because of global warming, the sea level may rise at rates up to 10 cm (4 inches) per year. This would cause the loss of sand barriers and adjacent lagoons and wetlands, and the loss of some islands on coral reefs.

CLIMATE

Just as weather is the day-to-day condition of the atmosphere, climate consists of the long-term average of weather conditions, including seasonal and year-to-year variability, and extremes. Many distinctive climatic types can be identified. These vary with regard to incoming solar radiation, temperature, wind, precipitation (rainfall and snowfall), evaporation, storms (type, frequency and magnitude), and seasonal patterns.

Solar radiation

Solar radiation (insolation) is received unequally in different parts of Earth. The equatorial belt receives strong solar radiation uniformly throughout the year, whilst places close to the poles, in contrast, have great differences between summer and winter solar radiation; perpetual ice climates exist at the poles. Along the equator, the lands are warm throughout the year, but, in the latitudes further away from the equator, seasonal variations become more discernible, with marked differences in the temperate zone.

General atmospheric circulation

The large amount of heat received at the equator means that air becomes heated and expands, and this air rises and flows towards the poles. Some of this air flows back to the equator in the form of trade winds as part of the Hadley Cell circulation. Flowing from the east, these winds are called easterlies. The subtropical belt (up to about 30° latitude), is the zone of large high-pressure cells from which winds move through more temperate latitudes towards the poles. Cold, dense air from the poles flows, as polar fronts, back through these latitudes towards the equator. These fronts clash with tropical air masses in the temperate zones, giving give rise to cyclones (low-pressure cells), which bring inclement weather and rainy days. Such weather conditions are more common in the northern hemisphere, where there are extensive landmasses. In the southern hemisphere, in contrast, there are more extensive oceans. In that belt, between 40° latitude and Antarctica, a westerly wind blows eastward along an almost unbroken stretch of seas throughout the year.

Climatic types

Of the several proposed climatic classifications, the best known is that devised by Köppen, who divided climates broadly into five classes: A, B, C, D, and E. The humid climates are A, C, and D, with A being the warmest and lying in the tropics, C being found in the warm temperate regions, and D covering cold climates with regular winter snowfall. Arid climates, both tropical and temperate, are classed as B climates. Ice sheets are represented by E climates.

Humid tropical climates (A)

Type A climates are found between 25°N and 25°S latitudes. These humid tropical climates receive abundant rainfall and have year-round high temperatures, with the areas further away from the equator having hot summers and mild winters.

These areas favor the abundant growth of vegetation, particularly rainforest. This climatic belt has extensive agriculture and often large populations. Heavy rainfall and high temperatures, however, leach soils of their valuable nutrients, which is detrimental for agriculture.

A typical A climate is the tropical monsoon climate that is found in Southeast Asia. It is characterized by a distinct season of heavy rainfall, preceded and followed by dry months; for example, large parts of India and Southeast Asia receive most of their rain between June and September, while March to May are typically dry months. Along the west coast of India, annual rainfall can be as high as 25,400 to 28,800 mm (9,900 to 1,123 inches).

Monsoon flooding in Vietnam (above). Monsoons are usually annual events, and deliver 85 % of East Asia's annual rainfall, but can also cause devastation to low-lying areas.

Desert climates (B)

Deserts are found in subtropical and temperate zones, and are classified by Köppen as B-type climates. Being areas of low rainfall, deserts have either few plants, or only small plants that are particularly well suited to dry environments.

Hot deserts lie in the subtropics—in the belt extending from North Africa (the Sahara Desert) and the Middle East to northwestern India (the Thar Desert)—and in the Central Australian Desert. These deserts have high daily temperature ranges; it can be very hot during the day and quite cool at night. The Gobi Desert, which lies in central Asia, is the best-known cold desert.

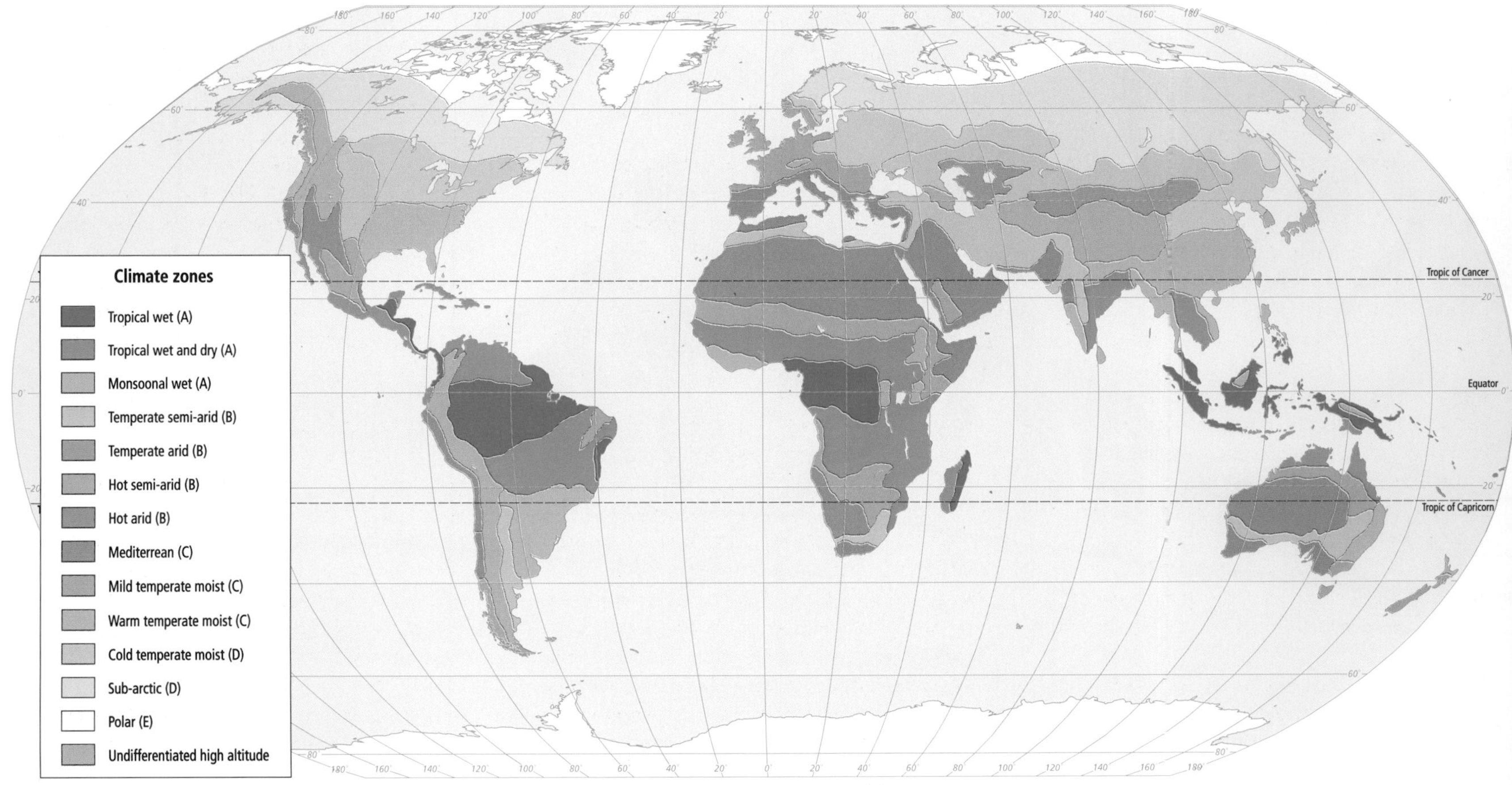

The Valley of the Moon, in the high-altitude Atacama Desert, Chile, said to be the driest desert on Earth (left). Lush mountainous terrain in Bolivia (below). An ice floe, with walrus, in Arctic Siberia (left, below). Productive agricultural land in a temperate zone—southern France (far left, below).

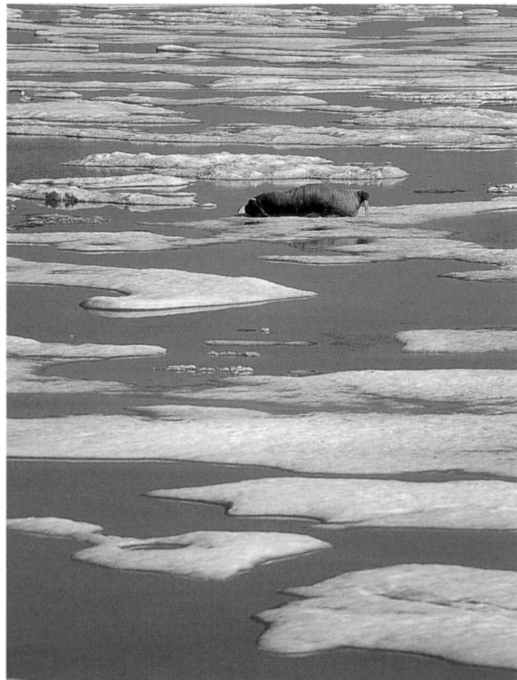

Humid temperate climates (C)

Type C climates lie between latitudes of 25° and 45°. They have marked seasonal variations, with temperature differences between summer and winter being quite large. The Mediterranean climate is a good example of a B climate; summer temperatures can on occasions soar to the mid-40s (110°F) in southern Greece and Italy, while winter temperatures can fall to 10°C (50°F). The Mediterranean climate is characterized by cold, wet winters and hot, dry summers.

The temperate zone close to the tropics (25° to 35° latitudes) is warm. It is now common to find that belt referred to as the subtropics. The subtropical areas lying along the eastern sides of the continents are particularly warm, as they receive the warm easterly tropical winds, and warm ocean currents flow along their coasts. This east coast climate is found in southeast China, eastern Australia and South America.

In contrast, the westerlies in the higher latitudes (35° to 60° latitudes) give rise to a cooler west coast climate. Year-round rainfall and adequate temperatures promote the growth of forests in both east and west coast climates.

Grasslands generally occur in the continental interiors of C climate areas, where annual rainfall is moderate (300 to 400 mm; 12 to 16 in), and water in the soil is not abundant. These areas lie in the rainshadows of major mountain ranges. Seasonal temperature ranges are usually sizeable.

Cold temperate climates (D)

Moving into the temperate zone close to the poles, temperatures fall because there is reduced solar radiation. This is exacerbated by cold polar winds. Polar winds are easterlies, although their directions can be variable in temperate latitudes. Such type D climates lie between 45° and 65° latitudes, and are only significant in the northern hemisphere—the equivalent belt in the southern hemisphere is mostly covered by the oceans.

The taiga climate is a good example of this climate; lying close to the Arctic polar region, the area is characterized by abundant snowfall and unique woodlands. Temperatures in winter commonly fall to -30 °C (-22 °F), and in some places can go as low as -40 °C (-40 °F). During midsummer, however, temperatures can rise to around 15°C (60°F) or higher.

Ice climates (E)

E-type climates are found between 65° and 90° latitudes, the principal examples being Antarctica and Greenland. These ice sheets cover about 10 percent of Earth's surface, and form an essential part of the system which regulates the global atmospheric circulation. These areas are subject to long periods of darkness, and temperatures rise above freezing level for only 2 to 4 months a year.

If global warming reduces the extent of these ice sheets, climatic conditions in the world will alter: ice melting would contribute to rises in sea level, with adverse effects on low-lying areas.

The El Niño phenomenon

Deviations from normal temperature patterns of the waters in the southern Pacific Ocean, between Australia and South America, result in the phenomenon called El Niño. Under normal conditions, eastern trade winds blow across the Pacific. These drive the sun-warmed surface water from the central Pacific to the coast off northern Australia. When clouds form above this area of warm water and move over Indonesia, Papua New Guinea, and Australia they bring rain with them.

Every two to seven years, however, this pattern is interrupted by the El Niño event. During El Niño, the Pacific Ocean off Australia does not warm as much as it normally does. Instead, it becomes warmer right up to the coast of Peru in South America. At the same time, the easterly trade winds that blow across the Pacific reverse their direction. This causes high-pressure systems to build up to the north of and across the Australian continent, preventing moist tropical air reaching the continent. These conditions in turn result in storms, and in rain falling in the eastern Pacific Ocean and in South America instead of in Australia, Papua New Guinea, and Indonesia, which then suffer drought conditions.

While the effects of El Niño are sometimes weak, at other times they are very strong. During a severe El Niño period, extreme drought conditions prevail, as in 1982–83 and 1997–98. In contrast, heavy rainfall and flooding occurred in parts of North and South America. In 1997, there were severe storms and floods in Mexico and further north along the west coast of the United States.

The converse of the El Niño effect is the La Niña effect, which is an exaggeration of normal conditions. This takes place when trade winds blow strongly and consistently across the Pacific towards Australia. This pushes the warm waters from the central Pacific, off the northern Australian coast, to build up into a mass that is bigger than normal. Thus, much more cloud develops than usual, and this brings considerably more rain to Australia and neighboring countries.

THE WATER CYCLE

Earth, in contrast to all the other planets in the solar system, has an abundant supply of water. Much of this, of course, lies in the oceans and seas (more than 97 percent), and is saline. The polar ice caps lock up slightly more than 2 percent of the remaining water, leaving less than 1 percent of fresh water to sustain life on Earth. Human needs are met by the water from rainfall, rivers, and underground supplies (plus a small amount from desalination plants).

Water falls as rain and snow, and flows as rivers and glaciers before ultimately reaching the sea. It also sinks into the ground to form underground water reservoirs, to emerge as springs or to seep into river water. Fresh supplies of water are continuously needed and nature provides this supply through the water cycle.

How the water cycle works

Solar energy evaporates exposed water from seas, lakes, rivers, and wet soils; the majority of this evaporation takes place over the seas. Water is also released into the atmosphere by plants through photosynthesis. During this process, known as evapotranspiration, water vapor rises into the atmosphere.

Clouds form when air becomes saturated with water vapor. The two major types of cloud formations are a stratified or layered gray cloud called stratus, and a billowing white or dark gray cloud called cumulus. Nimbostratus clouds and cumulonimbus clouds are the cloud types that are associated with rainy weather; nimbostratus clouds will bring steady rain, and cumulonimbus clouds will bring stormy weather.

Precipitation as rain, snow, or hail ensures that water returns to Earth's surface in a fresh form. Some of this rain, however, falls into the seas and is not accessible to humans. When rain falls, it either washes down hill slopes or seeps underground; when snow and hail melt, this water may also sink into the ground.

Rainfall also replenishes river water supplies, as does underground water. Snowfall may consolidate into glaciers and ice sheets which, when they melt, release their water into the ground, into streams, or into the seas.

Water in river courses

Rivers pass through several phases on their journey from hilly and mountainous areas to the seas and oceans. In their early phases—that is, close to their sources in the hills and mountains—they have steep slope gradients and, therefore, move with high velocities. They carry rock fragments and have high erosive force.

In these areas, the energy from streams provides the potential for hydroelectric development. This potential has been harnessed in many places, such as in the foothills of the Himalayas in Nepal.

On flat plains, rivers tend to wind their way in meandering courses. Here, the water flow has now lost most of its erosive capacity. Massive clay deposits may also give rise to fertile alluvial plains. During times of heavy rainfall, flooding can take place, and this is a serious issue along some of the major rivers of the world, such as the Mississippi in the United States, the Yangtze in China, and the Ganges in India.

The Arrigetch peaks and glacier, in Alaska (above). Water is released as steam into the atmosphere from electric power plants (right). A hot water artesian bore (far right).

Human interference in the water cycle

There has been considerable human interference in the water cycle throughout recorded history, but far more so since the beginning of the twentieth century. For centuries, humans have built dams across rivers to store water, which is then used for irrigation, or for domestic or industrial water supply. Dams have also been built to control river flooding, such as across the Huang River in China, and to produce electricity.

The Aswan Dam across the Nile provides arid Egypt with essential water. The two highest dams in the world, more than 300 m (985 ft) in height, have been built across the Vakhsh River in Tajikistan. The dam with by far the largest reservoir capacity—2,700 million cubic meters (3,530 million cubic yards)—is the Owen Falls Dam, across the Nile, in Uganda.

Hydroelectric power is generated in several parts of the world, such as at Itaipu, across the Parana River, in Brazil—this dam can generate

12,600 megawatts of power. The building of dams in areas prone to earthquakes, such as Japan, however, causes great concern because of the potential for serious damage.

Water is necessary for agriculture, industry, and domestic use. Agriculture depends on rainfall, as well as on irrigation from stored water. The provision of water for domestic use—particularly the need for clean drinking water—has become very important with the spread of urbanization. Reservoirs are often built to ensure urban water supplies and water is purified before being channelled to consumers.

The discharge of industrial, agricultural, and domestic effluents into streams and lakes (especially in the twentieth century) has reduced water quality and damaged aquatic life. These effluents include metallic substances. One of the most dramatic examples has been the discharge of mercury into rivers in Japan. This mercury has now entered the food chain through fish, creating serious health problems. The discharge of pesticides has also been detrimental to aquatic life, and excessive use of fertilizers, along with salts released into rivers and lakes by poor land use practices, have also altered the ecological balance.

Changes in air quality brought about by humans have also affected the water cycle. The use of fossil fuels to generate electricity and power transport has resulted in substantial sulfur dioxide and nitrogen oxide emissions. When these gases and water react, sulfuric and nitric acids are produced. These pollutants are present in clouds and fog, and fall with rain and snow as acid rain. A pH value of 5 in water is acidic enough to damage aquatic life.

This acid rain phenomenon is most likely to occur in dense industrial centers such as those in the United States, Canada, and Europe. The problem, however, is not confined to these areas, as winds blow polluting gases over long distances. Acids can become concentrated in still waters and threaten aquatic life. The entire ecology of affected lakes, including the natural food chains, can be very seriously harmed.

Artesian wells

When rain falls, some of it sinks into the ground and is held in the soil—this water is known as ground water. A layer under the ground becomes saturated with this seeped water; the surface of this layer is called the water table. Wells are mostly dug to tap water in the water table. There is another way, however, that water can seep under the ground to form water reservoirs. Some types of rock are porous, and this allows them to hold water; water can move through such permeable rock.

Sandstone is a permeable rock. If a sandstone bed is dipping at an angle, rainwater can penetrate the exposed part of the rock and travel along the stratum into the ground. The water will be retained by the sandstone layer if the rocks above and below it are impermeable. If this water reservoir lies well below the ground, it is held under pressure; if a well is bored to the reservoir, the water will gush out under this pressure. These reservoirs are called artesian wells. The permeable strata that carry the water are called aquifers; the impermeable layers which lie above and below the aquifers are known as aquicludes.

Artesian waters are important where rainfall is low and water supplies uncertain. Overuse of artesian water can result in the ground sinking, and if the reservoir is close to the sea, excessive removal of water can allow saline water to penetrate the reservoir, reducing water quality.

The water cycle (below): the sun heats water, which evaporates and rises into the atmosphere as water vapor, only to fall again later as rain and snow. The rain and snow then concentrate in rivers, or flow as ground water to the sea.

OCEANOGRAPHY

Earth is the only planet of the solar system with seas and oceans, and these cover more than 70 percent of its surface. The oceans lie in large and deep basins in Earth's crust. The seas, however, spread to the margins of the continents, drowning their shelves. The melting of the ice sheets following the end of the last ice age (about 15,000 years ago) resulted in a rise in sea levels and thus an increased area covered by seas.

Ocean currents

The waters of the oceans are in constant motion. This motion takes the form of ocean currents. These currents move at an average of 8 km (5 miles) per hour, and redistribute heat energy, thus influencing climate. Winds are the most important originators of ocean currents in the upper layers of the seas: they produce a frictional drag on the water which pushes it along.

As water is a fluid, it is subject to the Coriolis effect (caused by Earth's rotation)—that is, currents tend to move towards the right in the northern hemisphere and towards the left in the southern hemisphere. The resulting deflection is 45° to that of the direction of the wind. In the deeper parts of the oceans, it is water density that produces ocean currents. Water density depends upon two factors: temperature and salinity. The colder the water is, the denser it is; and the higher the salinity, the higher the density. The circulation which results from temperature and salinity difference is referred to as thermo-haline circulation.

There are broadly two types of ocean current: warm currents, which originate in tropical areas; and cold currents, which originate in polar areas. Warm currents are mostly located in the upper 100 m (330 ft) of the seas. Cold currents, on the other hand, are often encountered at greater depths. They move more slowly because of the overlying pressure exerted by surface water. The exchange of heat energy occurs as equatorial currents move towards the poles and polar currents move towards the equator. This exchange moderates Earth's heat patterns, preventing the equatorial belt becoming unbearably hot and the waters in the temperate zone becoming much colder than they are today.

Ocean water temperatures are a major influence on climatic conditions; warm currents bring warmth to the coastlines along which they flow and, likewise, cold currents reduce temperatures in the lands along which they flow.

Warm tropical ocean currents

Winds blowing westward along the equatorial belt generate west-flowing ocean currents called equatorial currents. When water from the equatorial currents piles up against land, the current reverses its direction and flows eastward, resulting in equatorial counter currents.

Equatorial currents turn towards the right in the northern hemisphere and towards the left in the southern hemisphere as a result of the

North Atlantic Drift
Canaries Current
Tropic of Cancer
Equator
Tropic of Capricorn
Benguela Current
Monsoonal Drift
Indian Counter Current
South Equatorial Current
West Australian Current
West Wind Drift
Kuroshio Current
North Pacific Current
Alaska Current
California Current
North Equatorial Current
Equatorial Counter Current
South Equatorial Current
West Wind Drift
West Wind Drift

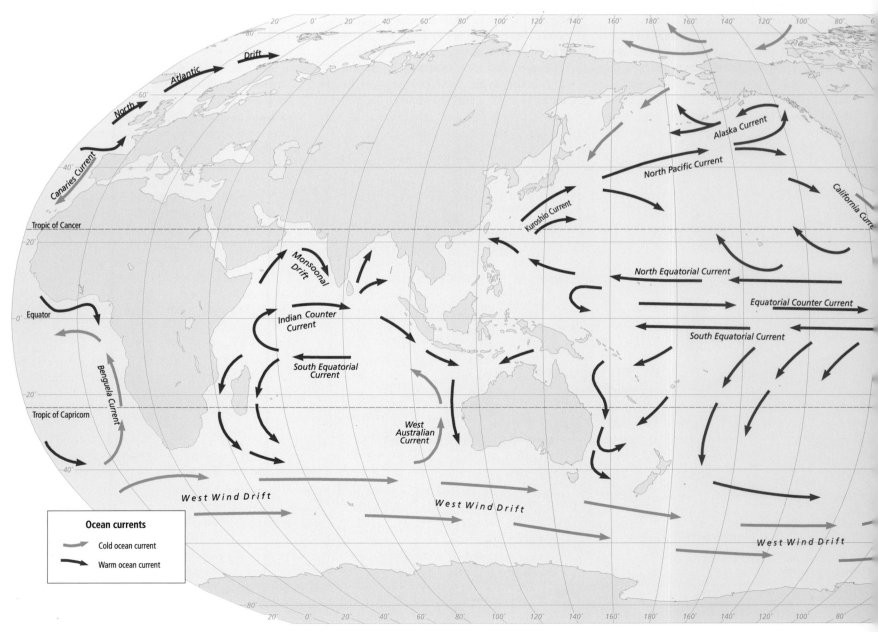

Ocean currents
Cold ocean current
Warm ocean current

Projection: Robinson Equatorial Scale approx 1:110 milliom

A sea whip in the warm waters of the Indian Ocean (far left). Coral islands (left) are at risk if sea levels rise because of the greenhouse effect. Polar bears in Arctic Siberia (below) survive on the ice floes, which are broken off icebergs by strong currents and winds. The southern right whale (far below) feeds off aquatic life that thrives in the nutrient-rich Antarctic waters, which are now threatened by ozone depletion.

Coriolis effect, and because of that motion, they develop into huge, circular, whorl-like rotating systems. These systems are known as gyres. Gyres rotate in a clockwise direction in the northern hemisphere and an anticlockwise direction in the southern hemisphere.

The distribution of the continental landmasses influences the size and shape of these gyres. There are major gyres in the northern and southern Atlantic and Pacific oceans, and in the southern Indian Ocean. There is also a gyre in the northern Indian Ocean, but it is restricted by the landmasses surrounding it, and so is much smaller.

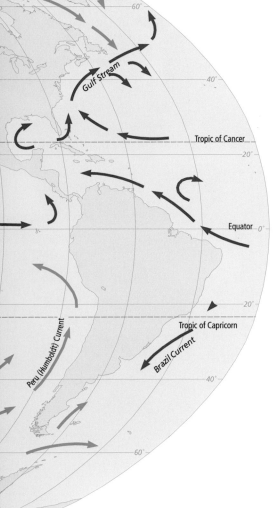

Gyres carry warm equatorial water into the temperate zone. These currents carry about 25 percent of all the heat that moves polewards from the equator. In the North Atlantic, the Gulf Stream or North Atlantic Drift, which flows from the Gulf of Mexico towards Western Europe, warms the seas around those countries, making their climates warmer. Thus London (51°32'N) is warmer than New York, even though New York lies at a much lower latitude (40°43'N), because of this warming effect.

The Japan Current, flowing from Southeast Asia, warms the eastern coasts of China and Japan. The west coast of Japan, on the other hand, is cooled by cold currents originating in northern areas. The magnitude of large ocean currents is demonstrated by the enormous amount of water they can carry—for example, the Gulf Stream carries more than 50 million cubic meters (65.5 million cubic yards) per second.

The build-up of warm waters can have significant effects on climate. For example, tropical cyclones or hurricanes or typhoons develop in the areas of warm water in Southeast Asia. These can have devastating effects on those areas.

Also, temperature changes in the waters of the South Pacific Ocean provide indications of the El Niño and La Niña weather disturbances. The onset of El Niño is heralded by unusually high water temperatures in the central Pacific, with the warm water spreading across to South America.

Cold polar currents

Cold ocean currents originate in polar regions. They flow deep in the oceans and only surface through upwelling—when winds blowing from the land drive warm surface water back out into the ocean. Cold water then rises to the surface.

Two well-known upwelling sites, both on the western sides of continents, are the Humboldt or Peru Current along the coast of South America and the Benguela Current in southern Africa. Their nutrient-laden waters are rich breeding grounds for fish.

Two important cold currents flowing on the eastern sides of continents are the Kamchatka Current, which flows alongside Siberia and Japan, and the Labrador Current, which flows along the east coasts of Canada and the United States.

Icebergs and ice floes

Seas in the polar zones can freeze, forming pack ice that covers the sea surface. If subjected to strong currents or winds, this pack ice can break into pieces, called floes. Ice broken from ice sheets can also be seen floating in the seas as icebergs. Ice floes are mostly less than 5 m ($16\frac{1}{2}$ ft) thick—much thinner than icebergs.

Icebergs can be very thick indeed—up to hundreds of meters in thickness—but only about one-sixth of an iceberg floats above water. The rest of it remains submerged or hidden below the water. This makes icebergs a major navigational hazard. There are always likely to be icebergs in the North Atlantic; they originate from the Greenland ice sheet and its glaciers.

The Antarctic zone

The waters around Antarctica flow in an unbroken band around the globe because there are no land areas to obstruct them. The West Wind Drift, as the winds blowing incessantly from the west to the east are called, results in some of the world's most turbulent seas. The seas in latitudes between 40°S and 60°S have been referred to as the "Roaring Forties," the "Furious Fifties," and the "Screaming Sixties."

In the Southern Ocean around Antarctica, between the latitudes 50°S and 60°S, cold currents interact with the warm currents coming from the tropics. The cold, nutrient-rich waters are driven upwards by this convergence, becoming the breeding ground for abundant oceanic life. These waters are thus a vital component of the food chain which depends upon that aquatic life.

PLANTS AND ANIMALS

Stromatolites in Hamelin Pool, Shark Bay, Western Australia.

Earth is about 4,500 million years old. After about 1,000 million years, most of the basic metabolic processes on which modern life depends were in place. The first eukaryote cells (cells that were capable of resisting oxidation) appeared about 1,500 million years ago. After about 4,000 million years, multicellular animals and plants appear in the fossil record. In the past 600 million years, life has exploded into a vast array of forms, but many of the animals and plants we are familiar with are relatively recent arrivals.

To deduce the history of Earth's life forms (collectively known as biota), and the prevailing environmental conditions, scientists primarily rely on physical evidence: the character of rocks or the fossils contained within them. Increasingly, however, biochemical evidence is also used.

The first life forms

Life is defined as a self-contained system of molecules that can duplicate itself from generation to generation. In Earth's early history, the elements that make up the vast majority of living tissues (hydrogen, carbon, oxygen, and nitrogen) were available in some form, and energy was abundant. Also, the concentration of atmospheric oxygen was low, which probably allowed a period of chemical evolution before the development of life. The earliest life forms may have resembled the bacteria-like organisms that exist today in hot springs associated with volcanic activity.

The first bacteria-like microfossils are dated at 3,500 million years old. Stromatolites, fossilized mats of cyanobacteria (a bacteria secreted by blue-green algae), first appear in the fossil record at about this time. These are the dominant fossils found in rocks older than about 550 million years. Between about 3,500 and 1,500 million years ago, cyanobacteria and blue-green algae were probably the main forms of life. Importantly, they slowly contributed oxygen to the atmosphere.

The build-up of free oxygen, hazardous to most life forms, may have stimulated the development of organisms with more complex cellular organisation (the eukaryotes) about 1,500 million years ago. The eukaryotes could reproduce sexually, thus allowing evolutionary change. They generated more oxygen and eventually (by about 1,300 million years ago) an ozone shield—this is probably what enabled further biotic evolution.

The earliest fossil record of protozoans, which are animals and so derive their energy from ingesting other organisms, is from about 800 million years ago. By about 680 million years ago, the protozoa were a highly diverse and complex range of multicellular animals—mostly coral- or worm-like life forms.

PROTEROZOIC EON
2,000 mya
1,000 mya
800 mya
680 mya
EDIACARAN FAUNA
600 mya
570 mya
PROTEROZOIC EON
PALAEOZOIC ERA
440 mya
544 mya
MESOZOIC ERA
245 mya
200 mya
MESOZOIC ERA

Invertebrates and vertebrates

During the late Proterozoic or early Paleozoic Era, the principal groups (or phyla) of invertebrates appeared. Trilobites were probably the dominant form of marine life during the Cambrian Period. The seas teemed with a huge diversity of animals, including a group with an elongated support structure, a central nerve cord, and a blood circulatory system—members of the phylum to which humans belong, the Chordata.

A major extinction event ended the Cambrian Period. The Ordovician Period (500 to 435 million years ago) is characterized by another increase in species diversity. The fossil record is dominated by marine invertebrates, but vertebrates also appear. The primitive jawless fish of 485 million years ago are the first ancestors of all advanced life forms: fish, amphibians, reptiles, birds, and mammals. Another major extinction event ended this period.

From ocean to land

The first land plants—probably similar to modern liverworts, hornworts, and mosses—seem to have arisen about 450 million years ago. The move onto land was a significant evolutionary step; life on land was very different, demanding innovation and evolutionary change.

The diagram (above) illustrates all the major stages in the evolution of plants and animals, from the first bacteria-like organisms, around 3,500 million years ago (mya), till humans, who first appeared in the late Quaternary Period.

During the Silurian Period (435 to 395 million years ago), algae diversified and all the major fish groups appear. Fossils of vascular plants (with specialized systems for moving nutrients, liquids, and so on) are found at about 430 million years ago. *Cooksonia,* a small moss-like plant common at this time, may have resulted in two distinct lines of evolution, one leading to all other higher plants. Floras of the late Silurian to early Devonian time are very similar worldwide, and may constitute evidence that the supercontinent Pangaea existed then.

During the mid-Devonian Period (395 to 345 million years ago), plants underwent a remarkable diversification, resulting in the development of Devonian "forests," which included giant clubmosses (lepidodendrons) and horsetails (calamites). The fossil record of the amphibians also begins here—animals were moving onto land—and the first fern-like foliage and gymnosperms appeared. The late Devonian was also marked by a mass extinction event.

Fossils from the Carboniferous Period (345 to 280 million years ago) suggest that the clubmoss forests teemed with spiders, scorpions, and centipedes. Amphibians gave rise to the first reptiles about 300 million years ago—vertebrates were no longer dependent on returning to water to reproduce. A trend towards an ice age occurred in the late Carboniferous Period, leading to low-diversity flora dominated by primitive seed ferns.

The Permian Period (280 to 245 million years ago) is dominated by the fossil remains of primitive members of the conifer line. By this period, reptiles with skeletal features characteristic of mammals were present.

The Age of Reptiles

The largest mass extinction event on record marked the end of the Permian Period. During the Mesozoic Era (245 to 65 million years ago), the "Age of Reptiles," flowering plants, dominated by cycads and gymnosperms early on, developed. Birds and mammals also appeared.

During the Triassic Period (245 to 200 million years ago), mammals, lizards, and dinosaurs appear in the fossil record. Some long-established reptiles were replaced by new groups, including the turtles, crocodilians, dinosaurs, and pterosaurs.

Dinosaurs date from early in the Triassic Period. From about 220 million years ago they dominated land habitats—for almost 160 million years. Mammals (initially small, perhaps nocturnal, shrew-like creatures) appear to have arisen from mammal-like reptiles. There was another mass extinction event (about 200 million years ago) in the late Triassic Period. Frogs and toads may have appeared around this time.

Pangaea began to break up during the Jurassic Period (200 to 145 million years ago). Ocean currents and the global climate were altered. The position of the continents and the break-up sequence determined the migration routes available and, therefore, the interrelation or common features of the plants and animals that we now see in the modern world.

Jurassic rocks include Earth's earliest fossils of flies, mosquitoes, wasps, bees, and ants; modern types of marine crustaceans were abundant. It was also a critical point in the evolution of birds, which evolved either from the dinosaurs or from an earlier group of reptiles. The Archaeopteryx, which existed about 150 million years ago, is perhaps the most famous early bird-like animal.

The early Cretaceous Period (145 to 65 million years ago) had a cosmopolitan flora. The first record of bats appears at this time. From about 80 million years ago, gymnosperms and angiosperms expanded at the expense of cycads and ferns. Mammals were also becoming dominant.

The Cretaceous Period also saw the apparent rise of the monotreme and marsupials and placentals, and the first predatory mammals. The diversification and spread of angiosperms provided the impetus for the co-evolution of animals.

The Age of Mammals

A great extinction event occurred at the end of the Cretaceous Period, causing the demise of the dinosaurs and the loss of about 25 percent of all known animal families. This change marks the beginning of the Cenozoic Era (65 million years ago to the present). This era saw the formation of the famous mountain systems of the world, the movement of the continents to their present positions, and a cooling trend that culminated in the ice ages of the Quaternary Period.

After dinosaurs died out, mammals quickly expanded into newly vacated habitats and roles, adapting and diversifying. Eventually, the warm-blooded animals came to dominate, so the Cenozoic Era is often called the "Age of Mammals." Late in the era, humans finally appear.

The Tertiary Period (65 to 1.8 million years ago) saw major new groups developing within pre-established plant families. Grasses appeared (about 50 million years ago), expanding particularly in the Miocene Period. The development of grasslands resulted eventually in a proliferation of grazing mammals. Hoofed, placental herbivores are first recorded as fossils 85 million years ago. The first horses appeared about 55 million years ago. A similar explosion in small rodents also occurred from about 40 million years ago.

Although birds have been essentially modern since the start of the Cenozoic Era, the first songbirds seem to appear at about 55 million years ago; all the major bird groups of the modern world had evolved by 50 million years ago. At about the same time (mid-Eocene Period), the carnivorous mammals split into two major lines: the dogs and the cats, basically. The first toothed whales are from the Oligocene epoch and the first plankton-feeding whales are from the Miocene.

The first primates seem to date from the end of the Cretaceous Period, though it seems that both monkeys and apes did not separate from earlier groups until the Oligocene epoch. The oldest biped yet found—usually taken as the start of the hominids—is from about 4.4 million years ago.

Nearly 2.5 million years ago, stone tool users—the hallmark of our own genus, Homo—seem to have arisen. Homo erectus, dating from about 1.8 million years ago, migrated from Africa as far as China and Southeast Asia. Our species, Homo sapiens, seems to have evolved in Africa within the past 200,000 years and to have migrated out of that continent only during the past 100,000 years.

EARTH'S BIOSPHERE

The biosphere is the zone where all living organisms on Earth are found. It includes parts of the lithosphere (Earth's crust and mantle), the hydrosphere (all the waters on Earth), and the atmosphere. The term "biosphere" can also refer collectively to all Earth's living organisms.

Imagine a sort of biological spectrum, arranged from the simple to the complex; it would start with subatomic particles, then move through atoms, molecules, compounds, protoplasm, cells, tissues, organs, organ systems, organisms, populations, communities, and ecosystems, to, eventually, the biosphere. Each stage represents another level of organization, and each level implies new attributes and different properties.

"Population" refers to a group of organisms of a particular kind that form a breeding unit. Not all individuals of a kind (or species) can mix—for example, due to geographic isolation—so a population is the functional group that is capable of breeding. A "community" is all the populations of plants, animals, bacteria, and fungi that live in an environment and interact with one another. Populations within a community are linked by their interaction and effects on each other, and by their responses to the environment they share.

"Ecosystem" is a shortening of "ecological system," the concept that the living (biotic) community and the non-living (abiotic) environment are a functioning, integrated system. An ecosystem involves transfer and circulation of materials and energy between living and non-living systems. There is almost infinite variety in the magnitude of ecosystems, from a global ecosystem that encompasses the entire biosphere to the ecosystem of a fallen log or of the underside of a rock, or even of a drop of water.

Environmental conditions influence the distribution of individual organisms. Limiting factors may be physical (such as temperature and moisture availability) or biotic (such as competition, predation, and the presence of suitable food or other resources). A limiting factor is anything that tends to make it more difficult for an organism to grow, live, or reproduce—that makes some aspect of physiology or behavior less efficient and therefore less competitive.

The distribution of organisms is strongly influenced by the fact that each kind can tolerate only a certain set of conditions. For many organisms, distribution is critically associated with, or determined by, relationships with other organisms. A community of organisms is thus likely to include a loose collection of populations with similar environmental requirements, and possibly another, tighter, collection of organisms that are dependent in some way on each other.

Due to genetic variation, individuals within a population have a range of tolerances around their ecological optimum, but beyond a particular tolerance limit, the species is unable to live. Importantly, this spread means a group may be able to cope with environmental change. A species must be able to complete all phases of its life cycle in a given region if it is to persist for a prolonged period, and different species vary in their tolerance of environmental factors.

The major biomes

Communities are strongly linked to their physical environment or habitat; this habitat is also modified by its communities. Since climate, soils, and biotic factors vary around the world, communities are bound to change. Vegetation is often the most visible aspect of communities, so they are often classified on the basis of vegetation. Communities recognized by their vegetation structure are termed "associations" or "formations;" when the definition also implies the consideration of animal communities, the term "biome" is used.

A biome is a grouping of communities or ecosystems that have similar appearances or structures (physiognomy). As physiognomy generally reflects the environment, the environmental characteristics of a specific biome on one continent will be similar to that same biome on any other. Furthermore, widely separated biomes are likely to include unrelated animals with a similar role and possibly similar morphology (form and structure), due to convergent evolution (animals evolving separately, but having similar characteristics).

At the global level, a number of distinctive features are generally recognized. There are several forest biomes, ranging in diversity and ecological complexity from tropical rainforest to the coniferous high-latitude forests of the northern hemisphere. In regions with seasonal contrasts in rainfall, trees become more widely spaced, species less diverse, and savanna grasses more characteristic of grassland areas develop. Other grassland biomes occur in temperate climates. Shrublands are dominated by shortish, scraggly trees or tall bushes, and may have an understorey of grasses.

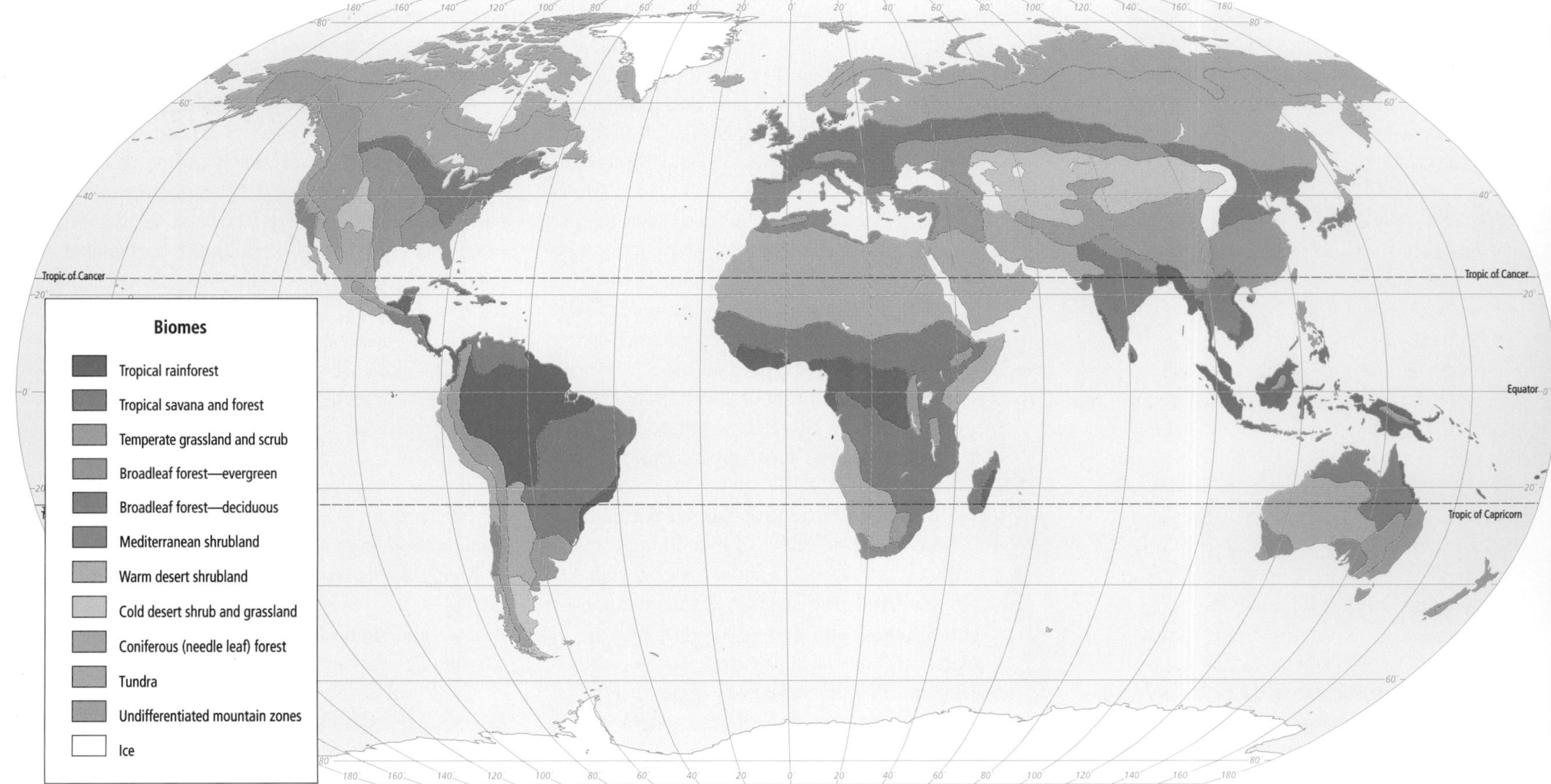

These monkeys have adapted to life in the trees in Lombok, Indonesia (left). They find their food there, sleep there, and can move quickly through the branches at considerable heights from the ground. The Weddell seal in Antarctica (below) has few predators, and finds plenty of food in the nutrient-rich waters of the Ross Sea.

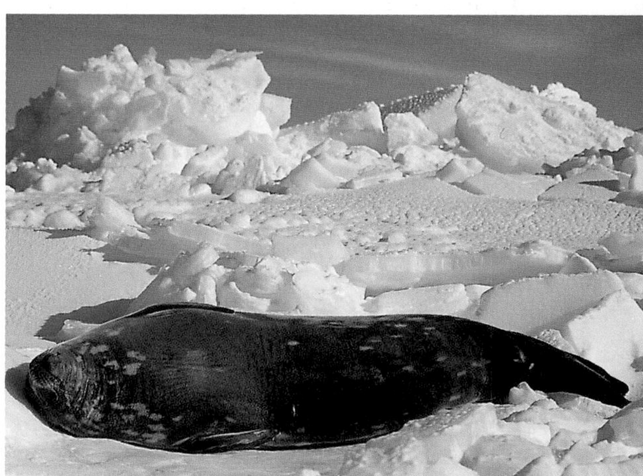

A frill-necked lizard from Australia (left) is well adapted to live in its dry environment, and giraffes in Tanzania (above) fill the large herbivore ecological niche of their environment.

In drier climates, scrub vegetation may be quite scattered and small in size.

The boundaries of Earth's biomes are rather blurred and maps can only show approximate distributions. Human activity has greatly disturbed natural ecosystems, often leaving mere remnants of once-vast areas of forest or grassland.

Energy in the biosphere

Most life on Earth is supported by the continuous flow of energy from the Sun into the biosphere. A tiny proportion of this radiant energy is used by plants, which are then able to maintain the biomass and the vital processes of the entire biosphere. Energy is eventually converted to heat and lost from the system.

Plants are capable of capturing and storing energy from sunlight. In the process called photosynthesis, plants absorb the radiant energy of the Sun and transform it into the energy of chemical bonds. The energy left after that used for the vital processes of the plant may accumulate as organic matter, and is available for harvest by animals and decomposition by bacteria and fungi.

As only plants can trap solar energy, their productivity determines the energy limits of the entire biosphere, and the total size of all consumer populations, including humans. The amount of this leftover energy is highest in regions with optimum conditions for plant growth.

On land, productivity is controlled primarily by water availability; in aquatic environments, nutrient availability is crucial. The most productive regions are found at the interface between the land and the sea. Generally, terrestrial communities are much more productive than aquatic systems.

The energy stored by plants as organic matter sustains other organisms. This transfer of energy, as food, from plants to herbivores, and from herbivores to carnivores, is a food chain. At each level of a food chain, a large amount of energy is degraded into heat and other forms of non-recoverable energy, so there is a steep decrease in productivity for each step up the sequence of the food chain. Correlated with this is usually a decrease in the number of organisms, and thus a decrease in total biomass.

The ecological niche

An ecological niche is the role that an organism plays in the ecosystem. Whereas habitat is the physical position of the organism, the ecological niche represents its functional position. For example, within grasslands, the kangaroo in Australia occupies the same niche as the bison in North America. They have the same role—large herbivores. Natural selection has often resulted in organisms adapting to their role, which means that the morphology of an animal can often be a good indicator of its niche.

Species vary in the breadth of their niche—some are specialists, others are generalists. Specialists are usually more efficient in the use of resources, due to adaptation, but they are also more vulnerable to change.

Importantly, two species with similar ecological requirements cannot occupy the same niche within an environment. This principle, called competitive exclusion, means that cohabiting organisms either use different resources, behave in such a way that resources are shared, or exist in a variable environment that favors each species alternately. Species that do have similar niches must compete for resources.

Specialization reduces this competition and, given time, adaptation to this new role may result in an altered morphology. Competitive exclusion is thus an extremely important evolutionary force.

The diagram below illustrates the food chain in the tundra. At the top of the chain is the wolf, who has no predators. At the bottom is the vegetation. In between are insects, small mammals (such as lemmings, ground squirrels, and Arctic hares) and birds, followed by other larger mammals such as caribou and Arctic foxes.

SOILS

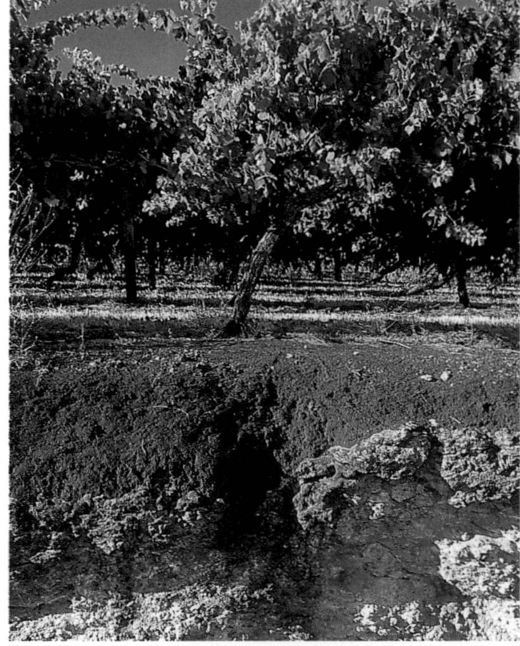

Soil formation is a very complex process. It involves the interaction of climate, type of rock, topography and biota (the total plant and animal life of a region). These factors operate over time, and the amount of time required for soil formation varies substantially from place to place—some soils and their associated weathered products have been forming for millions of years. Soils are formed from weathered materials, usually with the addition of organic matter. The disintegration or weathering of rocks is the result of both physical and chemical processes. Physical weathering breaks rocks down into fragments, while chemical weathering leads to the transformation of rock minerals into products of different composition.

Climate and soils

Weathering products are largely determined by climatic conditions. Mechanical weathering is particularly powerful in drier environments; in hot deserts, the heating of rocks induces expansion and subsequent breakdown of exposed surfaces; freezing has a similar effect. Salt crystallization in crevices mechanically disintegrates rocks. Root growth also leads to mechanical dislodgment.

In wet climates, moisture helps remove particles from exposed rocks, and provides a means by which minerals in those rocks can be attacked chemically to form clay minerals. Pure water is not a significant chemical agent; but the presence of dissolved carbon dioxide and complex organic substances in soil waters generates a chemical environment able to decompose, remove and redeposit rock (clay-rich) materials and salts.

Hot wet climates, plus the opportunity for plants to grow on stable surfaces for long periods of time, leads to extensive decomposition of rocks. In humid tropical climates, mineral decomposition results in the formation of oxides of aluminum and iron-producing red soils, sometimes cemented into a brick-like substance known as laterite. Such soils are much less fertile than those formed under somewhat drier grassland climates, where organic (or humic) matter and calcium-rich salts accumulate into a nutrient-rich soil capable of growing crops such as wheat and barley.

Rock type and soils

Within one climate area, soil type can vary as a result of the weathering of rocks of different mineral composition. Granites, basalts, quartz-rich sandstones and limestones are common rock types containing distinctive minerals. Chemical decomposition of these rocks over time will yield soils with different types and quantities of clays, varying amounts of precipitated salts, and different degrees of water retention and mobility (due to the existence of pore spaces and the capacity of minerals to absorb moisture).

Similar rock types in contrasting climate zones may also produce different soils. For instance, different rates and intensities of weathering can yield dark, organic-rich soils in grassland areas, underlain by basalt, whereas basalt soils in tropical areas are likely to be red and iron-rich.

Soil processes

The essence of soil formation is the breakdown and mobilization of mineral and organic matter in the presence of water. Living and dead organisms, both microscopic and larger (such as earthworms), assist in this process. The result is the formation of layers, or horizons. Each horizon has distinctive color, grain size (texture), chemical composition, organic matter content and pore space size (porosity). In some soils, binding agents such as organic colloids or iron oxides harden the layers. Over time, these layers may thicken, depending on slope position and the rate of landscape removal or deposition. Ground water movements can lead to precipitation of salts in soil layers, or even on the surface, leading to reduced soil productivity, as in lands bordering the Aral Sea.

Well-structured soils generally display "A," "B" and "C" horizons; A and B horizons are the real soil layers, known as the solum, while the C horizon consists of the weathered parent rock. The A horizon—the exposed soil—is often dark at the top because of the accumulation of organic material. A horizons are subject to leaching (eluviation). Leached material is transported to the B horizon, where it is deposited (illuviation); some B horizons are poor in organic material. Eluviation is assisted by the organic acids produced by decaying vegetation.

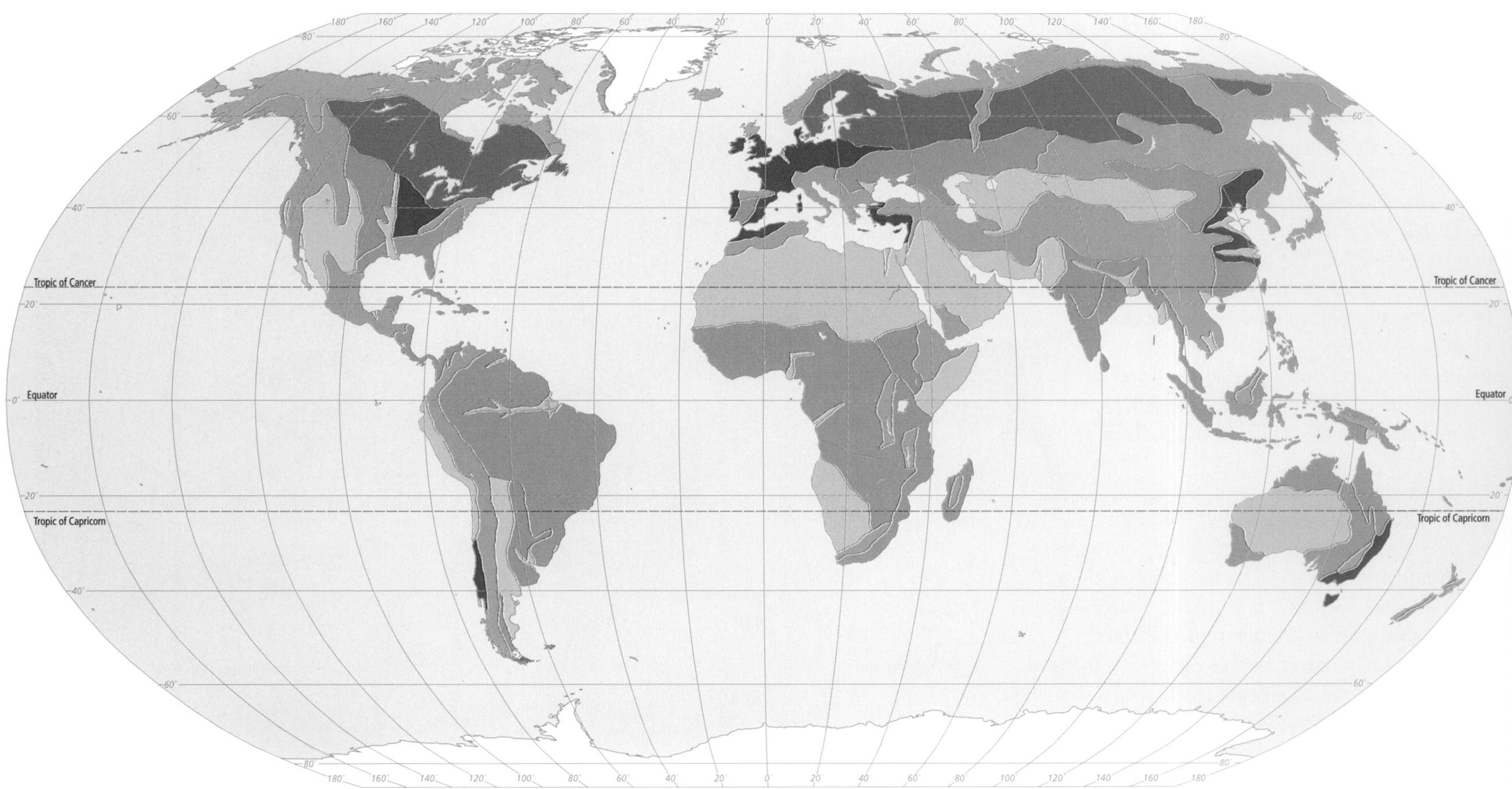

Layers of soil are exposed in this weathered escarpment, Australia (far left); parched, eroded ground leaves trees unable to tap into food and water in the soil, Papua New Guinea (left); this plant from the desert of Angola and Namibia has adapted to life in desert soil.

Soil nutrients

Soil texture and composition influence plant growth and therefore the suitability of a soil for agricultural use. Chemical and organic materials form colloids. Colloids are negatively charged, and attract plant nutrients such as calcium, magnesium, and potassium, which are positive ions (or cations). These nutrients are essential to the existence of all life on Earth.

Gray sandy soils of temperate regions are generally acidic; these soils are not rich in plant nutrients such as calcium and potassium, but this can be corrected by adding lime and fertilizers. On the other hand, some dry desert soils, which often contain mineral accumulations such as calcium carbonate and salts, are alkaline. Whilst many such soils have excessive salt levels, some are quite fertile and, irrigated, can be used for agriculture.

Soil types

Many attempts have been made to classify soils. Properties such as color, texture, composition, horizon thickness and porosity are used to define soil types. But even locally there can be considerable variation in soil type, given changes in elevation, slope angle, rock type and vegetation. In mountainous or hilly areas, for example, many different soil types may exist within short distances over a range of altitudes and slope positions.

At the global scale, soil types largely reflect climatic conditions. However, the history of a land surface may also be significant. The "fresh" deposits of recently deglaciated places in North America and Europe contain relatively poorly leached minerals, contrasting markedly with ancient unglaciated tropical plateaus, from which nutrient-rich minerals have long been removed.

Any world map of soil types must be a broad generalization. Iron-rich weathered soils can occur in areas where past climates have had a significant effect (for instance, southwest Western Australia). Alluvial soils, on the other hand, are constantly forming and reforming as new sediments are deposited in flood plains. Yet soils in both areas may be extremely rich in nutrients and thus of great agricultural significance. By way of contrast, the sparsity of moisture and biota in desert regions, or the presence of ice on the ground, will greatly inhibit soil development.

Soil zones

- Warm to cool temperate forest soils, moderately to highly leached, moderate to low in mineral bases and organic material, well developed horizons [Alfisols, Gray-brown podzolics].
- Cool temperate forest soils with highly leached upper profile, acidic accumulation of humus, iron and aluminum in illuvial horizon [Spodosols, Podzols].
- Grassland soils of subhumid and semiarid areas, often mixed with shrubs, organic-rich in upper profile in more moist regions, also rich in mineral bases, fertile [Mollisols, Chernozems, Vertisols].
- Latosolic soils of tropical and subtropical climates with forest and/or savanna cover; highly to moderately leached profile, low in mineral bases but high in oxides [Ultisols, Oxisols, Red Podzolics, Laterites—some relic of past climates].
- Desert soils of arid areas with little soil profile development and very low organic material but may contain abundant salts [Aridisols].
- Alluvial soils in all climates especially in deltas, subject to frequent flooding and new deposition of river silt, fertile (only major areas shown) [Entisols].
- Tundra soils in subpolar areas with permanently frozen subsoils; subject to mass movement on slopes (solifluction) [Inceptisols].
- Mountainous areas: soils are typically shallow and stony and highly variable in profile and thickness depending on climate and slope position; includes localized areas of fertile soils especially in mountain basins and near volcanoes.
- Ice sheets

A soil section, showing horizons enriched by organic matter (A1), and leached of humus and minerals (A2). A horizon of accumulation (B) contains mineral matter leached from above. The bedrock (D) is decomposed into a weathered horizon (C).

Earth as a home for humans

All humans live by exploiting Earth's natural resources, whether by small-scale fishing in Malawi (above) or employing modern farming techniques to farm cattle in Australia (opposite).

As humans, we dominate our planet. There are very few places where our impact is not felt. Even the atmosphere has now been altered by gases produced by humans, and some of these—such as chloroflurocarbons (CFCs)—are the result of chemical processes alien to natural systems. Many who travel or work at sea are aware of human debris in our waters. Lakes are drying up and are often heavily polluted, as are rivers. Much of the forests and grasslands of Earth have been disturbed. Over the past 200 to 300 years, in particular, we have transformed this planet in ways which at times enhance our welfare, but at others threaten the existence of societies.

As the human race evolved, so did its capacity to utilize natural resources. The mineral uranium was of little use to societies for much of human history, but, from the end of the Second World War, its value as a destructive force and as a source of power has grown immensely. In contrast, the fertile soils of river floodplains and deltas have long been utilized in some areas, and civilizations such as those of Egypt have depended upon their richness. But as a resource, soils need nourishment. Without appropriate care, their ability to maintain the levels of productivity necessary for agriculture will decline. History is full of accounts of battles waged to maintain social structures and population levels in the face of soil degradation. On the other hand, other societies, such as in China, Japan, and Western Europe, have carefully nurtured their soil resources.

For the early humans, the vast forests of Earth were largely avoided. There is some evidence that forests displaced human activities during the period of global warming immediately following the Ice Age in Europe. Progressively, however, forests in tropical, temperate and high latitude areas have been removed or exploited to create new land uses. Today, fires sweep across vast areas of Amazonian and Indonesian rainforests as more timber is removed and land is cleared for cattle grazing and crops.

Marine life has long provided food for humans. Fishing in shallow waters using primitive lines and spears has developed into sophisticated technologies enabling large ships to roam the oceans capturing fish over a vast range of depths. Fears of exploitation and the reduction of stocks to levels at which particular species will not survive have resulted in international agreements on resource use, although the effectiveness of these agreements is in question, with countries such as Japan and Norway still actively hunting whales, for example. Other forms of more sustainable fishing have been developed to feed societies which are heavily dependent upon food from the sea. This includes various forms of aquaculture at sea, in sheltered bays, and on reclaimed land.

Pressures placed on natural resources are closely linked to population growth. One of the most amazing and environmentally significant aspects of the twentieth century has been the rate of increase in population. With nearly 6 billion people alive at the moment and perhaps close to 10 billion by the year 2050, it is no wonder that environmental managers, planners, and scientists are deeply worried about the consequences. Also, population increases are not distributed evenly across the world; it is often in developing countries already suffering from depleted resources that the impacts of many new mouths to feed will be most harshly felt. The effective and equitable distribution of food to those in need will become increasingly important. Unfortunately, major health problems also arise in countries where food supplies are threatened. The impact of poverty and disease, and the capacity of international aid and economic organizations to support developing countries, create further uncertainties in a world beset with environmental and other problems.

Higher standards of living using available natural resources have been made possible through human inventions, including those designed to increase food production and to resist the ravages of pests and diseases in plants and animals. Many areas of high population have benefited from the so-called "green" revolution, but the ability of pathogens and parasites to undergo genetic change and therefore develop resistance to controls reminds us of the need for constant vigilance and research. Undertaking this research and acting on knowledge gained from other countries remain issues of global concern.

What has changed dramatically in recent years is the ability of individuals and groups to communicate quickly across vast distances. In one sense, space has "shrunk". Geographical isolation—such as that imposed by mountain ranges—no longer impedes the information flow; in the past, such barriers meant that separate languages developed in Papua New Guinea (for instance) in regions which, although physically close, were separated by their inaccessibility. Today, satellite television communications, electronic mail facilitated by fiber optic networks, and 24-hours-a-day business transactions are part of a global economic system which enables information to flow within and between nations.

The ability of societies to respond to natural hazards is another issue of great concern to international aid agencies and governments. Natural hazards may be insidious (droughts) or virtually instantaneous (earthquakes). Great loss of life and property can ensue; the impacts do not respect national economic strength (for example, the number of deaths as a result of tornadoes in the United States). Yet some areas are subject to frequent disasters of a scale which disturbs the economy. Floods in Bangladesh are of this category. Greenhouse-effect-induced rises in the sea level are another more insidious hazard which potentially threatens the futures of coral island nations such as the Maldives in the Indian Ocean.

LAND RESOURCES

Humans meet their principal needs—for water, minerals, and plants—from the land. Inorganic resources include minerals, water, and various elements in soils, whilst organic or biotic resources include plant and animal life. Fossil fuels (coal, petroleum, and natural gas) are of biotic origin. Both mineral and biotic resources are unequally distributed throughout the world—while some countries have abundant plant and water resources, others do not.

The presence or absence of water is often reflected in population densities, with high rainfall areas generally attracting, and being able to support, greater concentrations of people. China, for example, lacks water in its western half, but has a water surplus in its eastern half, and this is reflected in its population distribution.

Mineral resources are also very unevenly distributed. Some countries possess abundant reserves of certain minerals (such as petroleum in the Middle East), and others have gold reserves (Russia and South Africa).

The fact that resources are unequally distributed means that countries must trade what they have for what they need. The highly industrialized countries of Western Europe and Japan, for instance, import raw materials to run their industries. Also, many countries depend upon fossil fuel imports for their energy supplies.

Climate

Climate can be considered a resource because agriculture is so highly dependent on climate. The world's industries and urban centers are mostly located where there is a favorable climate—in areas which have comfortable temperature ranges and adequate rainfall.

Agricultural products can, generally, only be grown economically in suitable climatic conditions. Since the middle of the nineteenth century, plantations in the tropics have produced sugar, tea, coffee, and rubber for international consumption—these areas have been exploited for the production of crops that do not grow elsewhere and are much in demand. Likewise, wheat and other cereals are produced in temperate climates and exported internationally.

Landforms

Human settlement concentrates along river plains and deltas because of fertile soils and available water. In Japan, flat land is prized because of its scarcity. In some places, such as in Japan and on the island of Java in Indonesia, hillsides have been terraced for agriculture. In Europe and North America, deposits of sediment, encrusted with ice age glaciations, form fertile plains.

A beef cattle feedlot in California, USA (above). This is a method of intensive agriculture; less land is needed per head of cattle, but cattle lead a more restricted existence.

Agriculture

A long-established agricultural practice is "slash-and-burn." This involves clearing a forest patch, then burning to fertilize the soils; cultivation only

Tropic of Cancer
Equator
Tropic of Capricorn

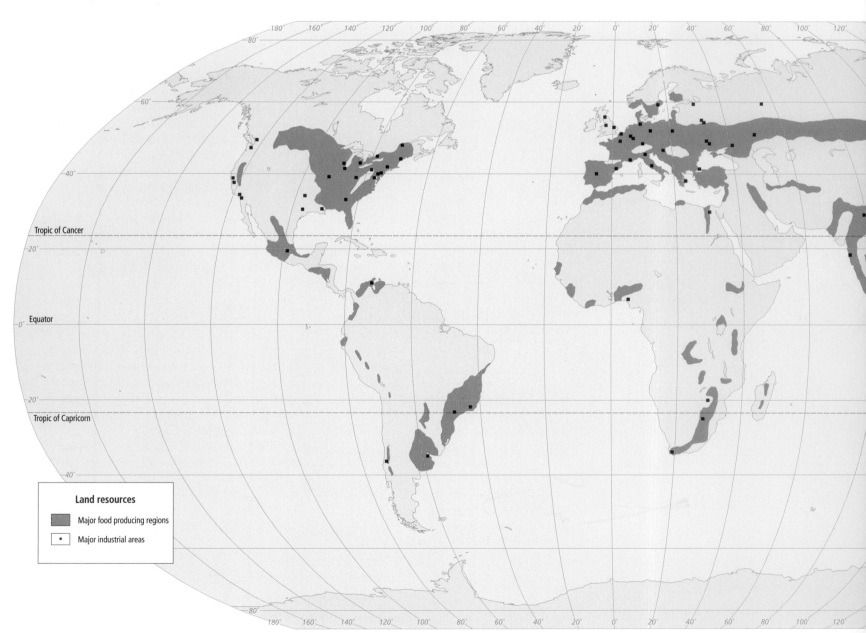

Land resources
- Major food producing regions
- Major industrial areas

Projection: Robinson   Equatorial Scale approx 1:155 million

Vast wheatfields like these in Saskatchewan, Canada (left) and the "Super Pit" in Kalgoorlie, Australia (below) both show human interference with the environment, and depend on high levels of mechanization. Near Beijing, China (bottom), people still use donkeys to plow—a pre-industrial farming method still practiced in less developed countries.

lasts a few seasons as the soils become depleted of nutrients. The exhausted patches are then abandoned and a new patch of forest is cleared. Secondary forests grow in these abandoned sites and, after some years, the reafforested areas can be used again. This rotating system can only support small numbers of people. It is not suitable for the type of food production that is needed for large, or growing, populations.

The development of grain farming, some 10,000 years ago, ensured food production for large populations. It led to sedentary settlements and, ultimately, to some of the great ancient civilizations such as Egypt, northern China, and the Indus Valley. Since the nineteenth century, agriculture has seen the development of mechanization, the use of fertilizers and pesticides, and improved varieties of both plant and animal species. These new developments paralleled the great milestones in industrialization, such as the invention of steam engines, the internal combustion engine, electric power and, more recently, the silicon chip.

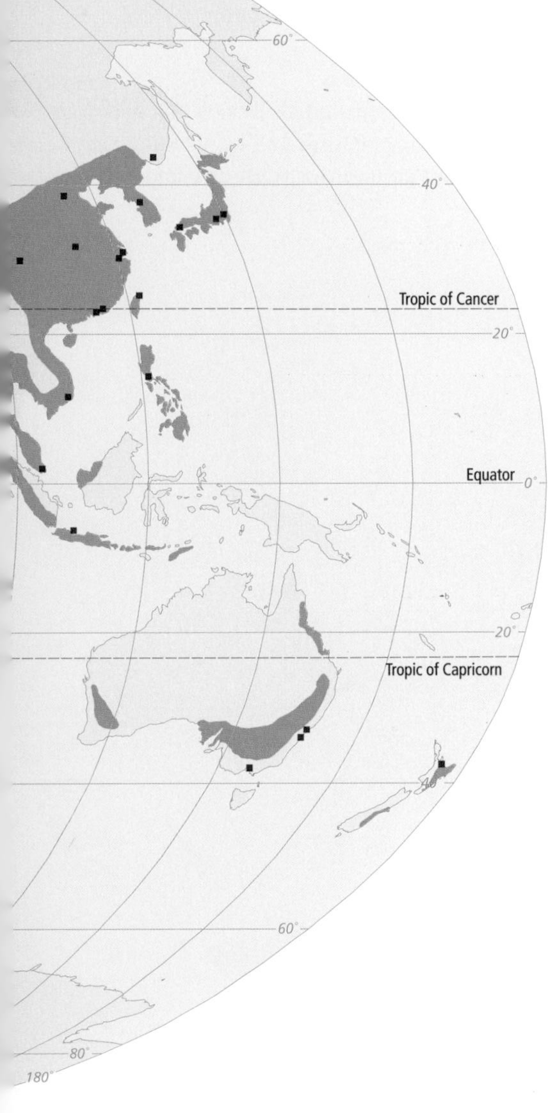

The population explosion in several developing countries within the past 50 years greatly increased their demand for food, and it became necessary to increase crop yields per unit of land. This ushered in the so-called Green Revolution, which involved using high-yielding seeds, fertilizers, and pesticides. Although these products increased grain output, the increase has been at some environmental and social cost.

Brazil is a good example of changing uses of the land. Before becoming a colony, its agriculture was of the slash-and-burn type practiced by forest Indians. Colonialism brought in plantation agriculture. The development of coffee plantations boosted Brazil's economy. Great increases in population have placed pressure on its once largely untapped resource, the Amazon rainforest. Large tracts of the Amazon are being transformed by people wishing to establish farms; forests are being burnt down to clear land for agriculture. Large areas are also being cleared to raise beef cattle for export; this also, of course, results in the large-scale loss of forests.

Tropical rainforest clearance cannot easily be reversed. Currently, more than 10 million hectares (24.7 million acres) of forests are being lost each year. These large-scale clearances have adverse effects globally—they accelerate global warming and its effects on climate.

Minerals

Minerals supply the raw materials for several major industries: for the extraction of metals (primarily iron); for fuels such as uranium, coal, and petroleum; and for manufacturing fertilizers and cement. Minerals are valuable resources because they only occur in some places and are finite in nature: once extracted, they cannot be renewed. Minerals are very important for sustaining modern civilization and, as standards of living continue to rise on a global scale, so too does the demand for minerals. In fact, more minerals have been mined in the twentieth century than in all previous centuries combined. As demand for minerals increases and they become more scarce, their strategic importance to industry—including, especially, the defence industry—also increases, placing even greater strain on already vulnerable finite resources.

The principal metal in demand is iron for making steel; steel forms the basis of much of the world's manufacturing, and every major industrial country produces steel. Other important metals include aluminum, copper, lead, and zinc.

Coal, petroleum, and natural gas provide energy supplies, and, in recent decades, uranium has provided the basis for nuclear energy. Coal is used for electricity generation and in the manufacture of steel. The ever-growing use of automobiles ensures continuing demand for petroleum, while natural gas is being used extensively for heating. Nuclear energy is currently the subject of much controversy because of dangers associated with nuclear power generation, the problems of nuclear waste disposal, and the potential for using nuclear materials from such plants for nuclear weapons.

The greatly increased use of minerals by the developed countries, and the increasing use by newly industrializing countries, has led to concerns about there being adequate mineral supplies for the future. Substitution of new materials for metals and the search for new or renewable energy sources—such as solar power or wind generation—are amongst the developments aimed at conserving our mineral resources.

OCEAN RESOURCES

The oceans, covering more than 70 percent of Earth's surface, are the source of enormous amounts of valuable resources. These broadly fall into two main categories: marine life and minerals. Marine life can be divided into pelagic forms and benthic forms. Pelagic forms move about in the waters—these resources include fish and marine mammals. Benthic forms, which live on the sea floor, include corals, molluscs, and crustaceans. There are also marine plants such as kelp that are harvested and used by humans.

The oceans also contain mineral deposits, including petroleum and gas, and mineral nodules. These resources are generally more difficult and expensive to obtain than marine life, but they are of great economic importance.

Within the past 50 years, modern technology has meant that detailed mapping of the oceans has become possible. Recent studies of the oceans, using this technology, have revealed some well-defined physiographic patterns: close to the land lie continental shelves which often end in steep continental slopes; these are followed, further from the shore, by gently sloping features called continental rises, which end in deep ocean basins; and the latter are intersected by mid-oceanic ridges. There are different marine resources commonly found in the different zones where these physiographic features are found.

Many nations, realizing the potential riches of the oceans, have declared resource boundaries under the United Nations' Law of the Sea Convention. Territorial seas are normally set at 12 nautical miles (22 km) from the coast, whilst exclusive economic zones extend to 200 nautical miles (370 km). These mostly include the resource-rich continental shelves.

Continental shelves, however, can vary in width from 110 to 170 nautical miles (200 to 320 km); the shelves in the Atlantic Ocean and the Gulf of Mexico are exceptional in being up to 260 nautical miles (480 km) wide. A nation can legitimately claim all its adjacent continental shelf, even if that shelf extends beyond 200 nautical miles (370 km), as is the case with the United States and Australia. As a result of this law, some small island nations, such as in those in the South Pacific, have maritime claims that far exceed their land areas.

Fishing

Fishing is the most important resource-gathering activity from the seas. In recent decades, however, overfishing of the seas has reached, in some places, crisis proportions. For example, the North Pacific haddock catch dwindled in 1974 to less than 10 percent of what it had been a decade earlier, and the once highly productive cod fishing industry in Canada, employing an estimated 40,000 people, collapsed in 1992.

Several nations grant licenses to foreign fishing fleets to fish in their waters, and this can exacerbate the situation, as has been the case with the southern bluefin tuna from the waters of Australia, New Zealand, and the Southern Ocean. Overfishing is threatening the very existence of this tuna species; the numbers of this species have fallen, it is estimated, to just 2 to 5 percent of its original population.

Until recently, whales were one of the most threatened species of marine life, but a huge international outcry against whale hunting has resulted in most whaling nations giving up whaling altogether and international agreements for whale protection being enacted. The outcry was generated not only as a result of concern for preservation of whale species, but also because of the horrific nature of the hunting itself.

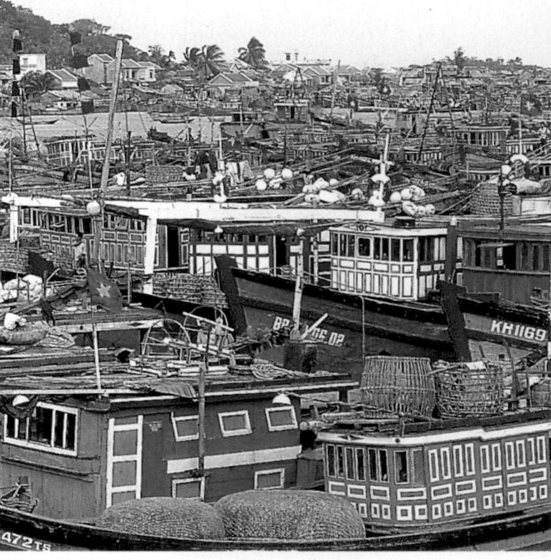

Brightly colored fishing boats docked at Nha Trang, Vietnam (above). During the late twentieth century, fishing has been affected by changes in technology and by ocean pollution.

By the time that whale protection measures were agreed upon, however, several species—including the bowhead, gray and right whale species—had been hunted almost to extinction.

An extensive whale sanctuary in the Southern Ocean now covers the territory of more than 90 percent of the world's whale population. Japan and Norway, however, continue to hunt whales. Japan justifies its whaling operations on the grounds of scientific research, but this explanation is not generally accepted by conservation groups, many of which continue to campaign against all forms of whale hunting.

Coastal fishing

Seas close to shore are usually rich in a wide variety of marine organisms, and have traditionally been fishing grounds for coast-dwelling commun-

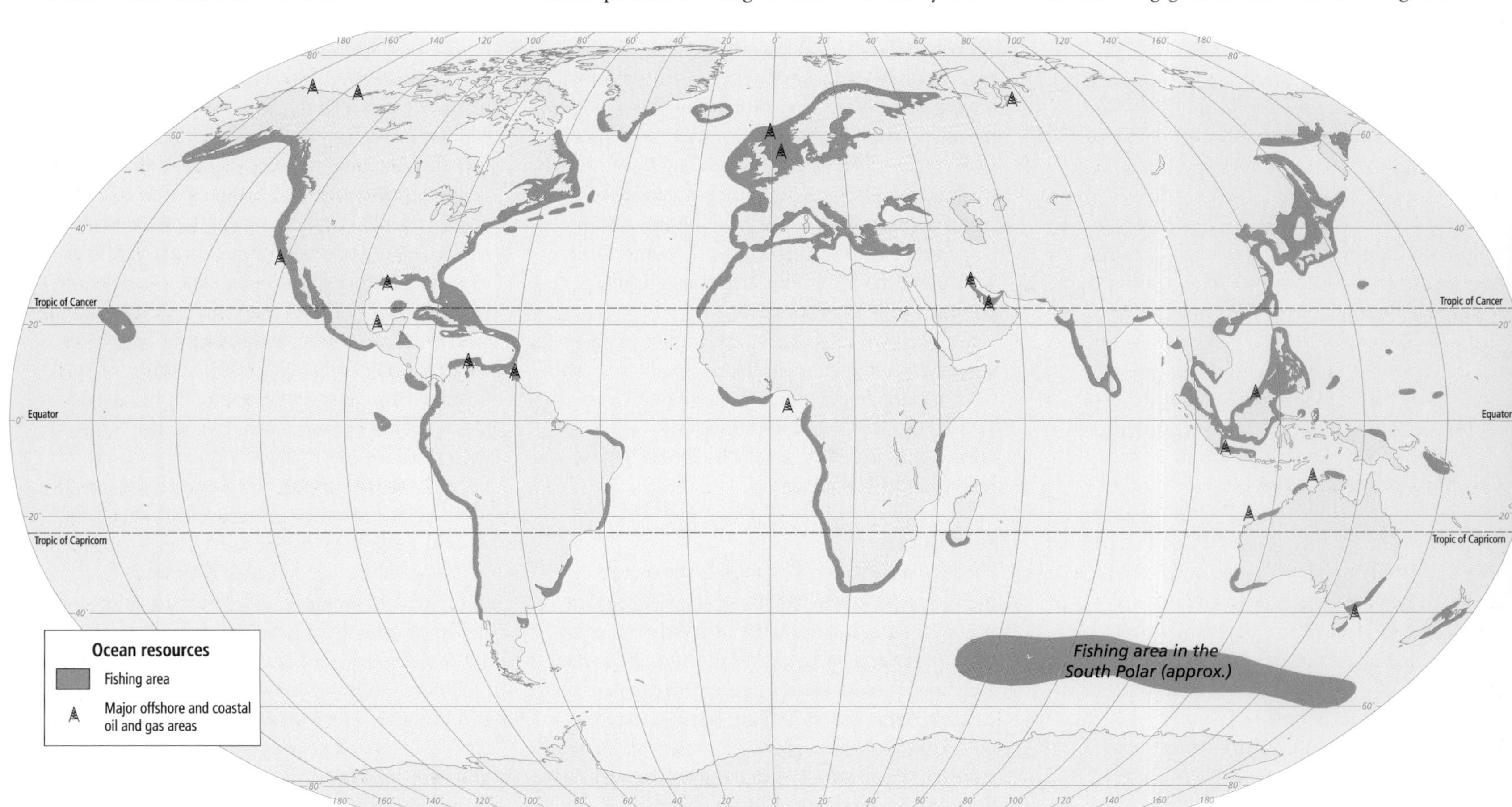

This busy container port in Singapore (left) and fish farming (of Atlantic salmon in Australia, below) are relatively new commercial uses of ocean resources. Human predation has seriously affected creatures like the humpback whale (bottom), though international agreements aiming to reduce commercial hunting of whales may help to restore numbers.

ities. These are also the areas, not surprisingly, where shellfish farming, aquaculture (fish farming), and salt extraction have, more recently, been widely undertaken.

Kelp, which is rich in both potash and iodine, is another product harvested from the seas in coastal areas. It is used for both food and fertilizer.

Fish breeding and shellfish farming, such as oyster breeding, are carried out close to the land. Aquaculture can provide reliable and convenient fish supplies, in contrast to fishing—it is no longer possible to depend upon the ever-dwindling supplies from the seas. Fish farming has been practiced for a long time—the breeding of fish in freshwater lakes in China, for instance, has been carried out for a great many years.

Modern aquaculture is a high-technology industry, as it requires meticulous monitoring of water conditions (such as salinity, oxygen levels, and water temperature) and nutrition. Only a limited number of species—salmon in the Outer Hebrides of Great Britain, for example—are being farmed at present.

In the Inland Sea of Japan, an arm of the sea has been completely cut off by metal nets, thus creating a confined space in which fish can be bred. In Japan particularly, seaweed is another important product of aquaculture.

Coastal countries that do not have sufficient supplies of fresh water can extract fresh water from sea water. However, the capital equipment required to establish these desalination plants is costly. There are several such plants for producing fresh water from salt water in the oil-rich countries bordering the Persian–Arabic Gulf—Kuwait, for instance, has desalination plants.

Continental shelves

These shallow, gently sloping features range in depth between 120 and 180 m (400 to 600 ft). When surface sea water is blown away from the land by offshore winds, colder nutrient-rich water rises to the surface. Where such waters are sunlit—these are known as epipelagic or euphotic zones—they make excellent breeding grounds for the minute marine organisms known as plankton. Plankton are tiny plant (phytoplankton) and animal (zooplankton) organisms that provide nutrition for other larger marine organisms.

Although sunlight can penetrate as far as 1,000 m (3,300 ft) below the ocean surface, photosynthesis can only take place in depths of up to 200 m (660 ft). As a result, phytoplankton can only survive within this shallow layer of ocean water. Small zooplankton feed on the phytoplankton in this layer and they, in turn, are preyed upon by larger organisms such as anchovies and squid. Larger fish such as tuna feed on the smaller marine life, only to be, in turn, consumed by still larger fish. This marine food chain extends even beyond the seas, to the seabirds which are the predators of fish.

The cold and extremely nutrient-rich waters in the continental shelves surrounding Antarctica are the breeding ground for small crustaceans known as krill. Species including seals and whales, as well as penguins, feed on krill.

In recent decades, rich petroleum and natural gas deposits have been discovered in the continental shelves. The petroleum deposits originated from the debris of marine organisms in oxygen-free shelf bottoms millions of years ago. Amongst the well-known deposits that are currently being exploited are those in the North Sea, the Gulf of Mexico, and off the city of Bombay on India's west coast.

Improvements in drilling technology have enabled exploration in ever-deeper seas; drilling for natural gas deposits is currently being carried out at depths of more than 1,700 m (5,600 ft) in the Marlim field, off Brazil.

Ocean basins

The ocean basins are made up of large, flat areas called abyssal plains. These abyssal plains lie at depths of about 4,000 m (15,000 ft). In these dark and cold areas, temperatures are low, perhaps only 4 °C (40 °F), compared with around 20 °C (68 °F) at the ocean surface.

These deep ocean basins lack plankton and are, therefore, not rich in marine life. Large parts of these plains, however, are covered with minerals, the most important of which are manganese nodules in the Pacific, Atlantic and southern Indian oceans. These nodules could be exploited at depths of up to 5,000 m (16,500 ft) using technology that has already been developed, but this is currently not economically viable.

The ocean basins are intersected by mid-oceanic ridges, which are formed by volcanic eruptions. The sea water and sediments around them often contain concentrations of zinc, lead, copper, silver, and gold. While these minerals are of considerable economic value and, therefore, importance, no method has yet been devised to extract them economically.

Ocean pollution

The seas have, unfortunately, long been considered convenient dumping grounds for waste—anything from urban sewage to nuclear materials. Chemicals from factories, fertilizers and pesticides from agricultural areas, and oil slicks from ships are also being released, often illegally, into the seas. Ballast water taken on by large ships on one side of the world is released on the other, with all its attendant marine organisms thus finding their way into other environments. The effects of such pollution are quite severe already in some areas, particularly in the semi-enclosed waters of the Mediterranean Sea.

Pollution threatens the existence of marine life, and thus, because marine ecological systems are entwined with land-based ecological systems, it will eventually affect life on land, including human life. There are more immediate effects, too, in some cases: dangerous oil spills such as that from the Exxon Valdez in Alaska threaten the livelihood of the nearby fishing communities who depend on the sea for their economic existence. Fishing communities in the Gulf of Mexico have also experienced this threat following oil spills from offshore petroleum wells.

COMMERCE

The movement of goods and services from place to place has long been a characteristic of human endeavour. The exchange of products, information and ideas within an economic system extends beyond subsistence societies, and into the "global village" of today. The scale of transactions has changed, though—it now ranges from village or tribal bartering to the almost instantaneous transfer of vast sums of money on the international foreign exchange market. The size and bulk of trade also varies with the commodity, and there are great contrasts—camel trains range across deserts and huge bulk carriers roam the oceans.

Trade is the transport and/or communication of commodities from place to place, and is generally measured in terms of the monetary value of the items moved. Until the advent of steam-driven trains and ships and the extensive use of iron and steel for the manufacture of such carriers, the time taken and capacity to move large volumes of materials was limited. These technological limitations helped determine what could be traded, and what could be traded economically.

The volume and scope of trade, the movement of people, and the flow of information increased enormously in the nineteenth century, and will continue to do so. The effects of the increasing numbers of roads, cars, and trucks since the Second World War, for example, are so all-encompassing that it is difficult for many people to imagine life without these relatively recent transportation innovations. Add to these changes the enormous advances in electronic communication technology, and it is easy to see why today's modern suburbanites have become almost completely dependent upon their cars and their electronic communication devices.

The communication of information (ideas, images, audio signals, and written texts), especially as it converges with computer technology to produce information technology (IT), is undergoing another technological revolution. Information technology, combined with cable, satellite, optical fiber, and other technologies, can now transmit digitized information (including money) over cyberspace from one part of the globe to another instantaneously, and with potentially staggering effects. Entire national economic systems can suffer very quickly as a result of currency crises facilitated by the use of such technologies—this happened in parts of Asia during 1997 and 1998.

International trade imbalances

To appreciate the effects of recent changes in transportation and communication technology on trade, it is useful to compare trade between highly industrialized nations (such as the United Kingdom) and other parts of the world in the 1950s with that today.

An international division of labor existed then. Some countries produced manufactured goods in factories, using a highly skilled and well-paid labor force. These goods were traded for primary commodities (coffee and gold, for instance), which were produced by poorly paid and relatively unskilled labor. This unbalanced market system generated an unequal exchange: wealth accumulated in the industrialized areas, leading to unprecedented levels of development, while the other regions remained underdeveloped, largely because of these trade imbalances. That is, the Western world became richer and the Third World remained underdeveloped and poor.

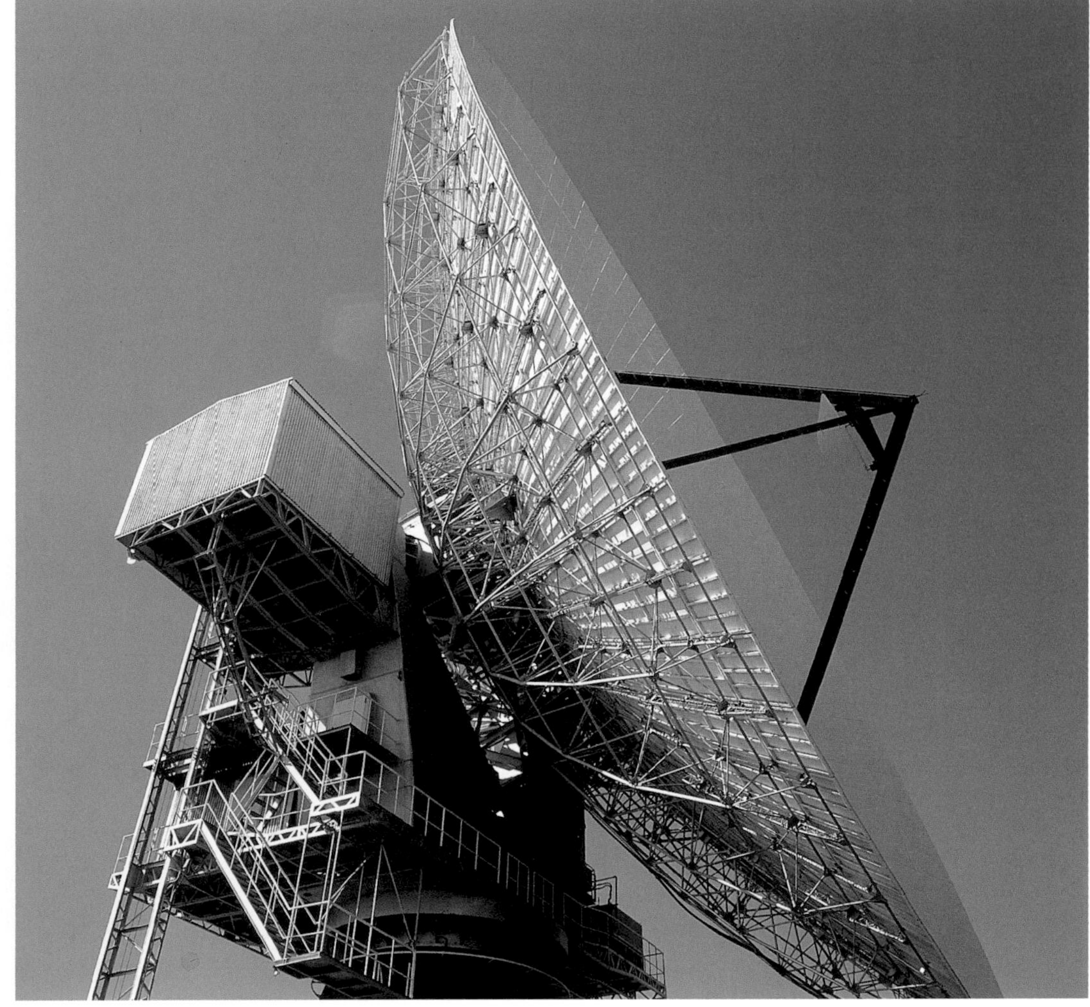

Recent developments

In the 1960s, manufacturing jobs began to move to selected sites in the so-called developing countries, resulting in deindustrialization in the center, and selective industrialization in the periphery, of the global economy. The textile industry was an early industrial sector to move to the periphery, so some "banana" republics became "pajama" republics. The term "newly industrialized nation" applied to former peripheral nations such as Singapore, South Korea, Taiwan, Mexico, and a dozen or so other countries that were undergoing sustained, rapid growth in manufacturing.

The term "economic tiger" also arose, to describe the performance of some countries in the Pacific Rim. Their economies grew faster than those of the USA or Europe during the 1980s and early 1990s, but as those economies were export-oriented, they suffered greatly as a result of the withdrawal of foreign funds after 1987.

International commerce is led by the wealthy economies; it increasingly involves service industries based on innovation and technology—finance, insurance, transport, marketing and information flow. Trade in raw materials, including those from countries heavily dependent on agriculture or mining, today accounts for little more than 20 percent of total world trade.

Satellite receiving dishes like this one (left) are more common now, as international trade becomes increasingly dependent on satellite communications.

Container ships like the Katie (left) transport all manner of goods worldwide today. Increased freeway traffic (in San Diego, California, US, below) and the pollution it causes are a result of increased technology use in many countries. Simpler forms of transport, such as those that are used in Agra, India (bottom), are still used in developing countries.

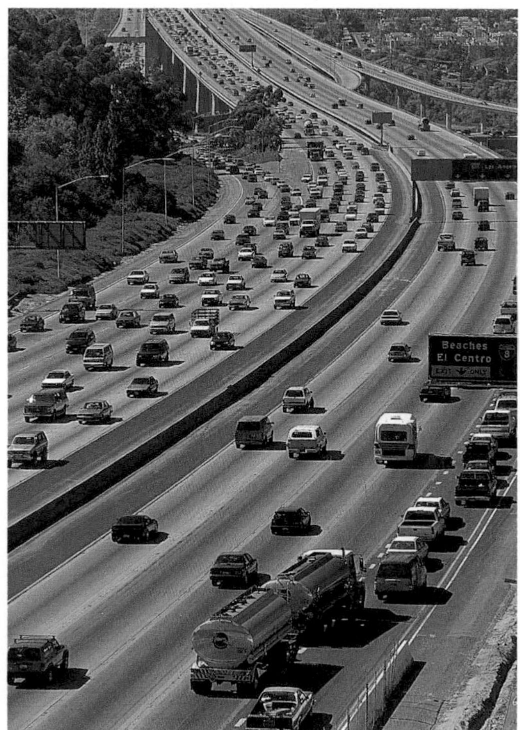

Manufactured goods are now produced and supplied by a range of developed and developing countries with former closed economies—China, for instance, is becoming more market-oriented and is contributing significantly to world trade.

Multinationals and trade blocs

Another major trend is the spread of multinationals in an ever-widening global process. This is occurring in a number of fields that are engaged in world trade. This process is epitomized by the internationalization of stock markets—they operate around the clock and now even penetrate countries such as Russia.

A further feature of world commerce has been the emergence of powerful trade groups or blocs. These represent collections of countries which, as groups, have accepted rules and regulations that permit a freer exchange of goods and services between the countries in the group. Three main trade blocs are the European Union (EU), the signatories to the North American Free Trade Agreement (NAFTA), and the Association of South-East Asian Nations (ASEAN). The release of a single currency, the Euro, in parts of the EU in 1999 signalled another major development in the concept of trade between and within blocs.

Adverse effects of the global economy

Despite the benefits which have arisen from the growth and development of international trade, there are many areas where market liberalization and the availability of funds for investment and growth have created problems.

The replacement of subsistence agriculture by a limited range of "cash" crops is one. This change has placed many societies at the mercy of declines in commodity prices, or the failure of the crop itself, due to climatic or other factors.

The need for capital has raised debt levels in countries such as Thailand, Mexico, and Indonesia to amounts which, at times of crisis, may induce political and social instability. International funding agencies such as the International Monetary Fund (IMF) and the World Bank, as well as aid agencies operating through the United Nations (UN), have become critical in sustaining these economies in the face of changes in technology and the global marketplace, which they may not have survived or been able to exploit.

"E" stands for "electronic"

E-mail and e-commerce (electronic mail and electronic commerce) are still quite new to many, but they represent changes in the way business and communication are conducted, worldwide, that will soon affect everyone.

E-mail allows people to write messages on their computer screens and then, via a phone connection, and for the cost of only a local telephone call, send those messages instantaneously to any person (or group of people) who has the equipment to receive them. It is therefore cheaper (and, of course, faster!) than mailing a letter, cheaper than faxing written material overseas, and cheaper than telephoning overseas. And it is user-friendly—a genuine revolution in communication.

E-commerce means the buying and selling of goods and services via the Internet. It is even newer than e-mail, and has not yet won the acceptance that e-mail has. There are issues—credit card security (the majority of purchases made on the Internet are made by credit card), censorship and copyright, to mention just three—that are as yet unresolved. These issues are particularly difficult as the Internet does not reside in any country; it exists only in "cyberspace", and it is not clear who has jurisdiction to regulate behavior on it, nor how, in practical terms, such regulation could occur effectively. Despite these uncertainties, e-commerce is growing.

The attractions of e-commerce are many: the buyer can, from home, view and compare a range of alternative products; there are web sites that specialize in comparison shopping, so the purchaser can find very low prices for some products; and consumers can buy products that are not available locally at all. The sorts of things that are succeeding in this brave new market range from groceries to clothes, books and compact discs, computers, airplane tickets and shares.

While it is claimed that at present only 1 % of commercial activities take place on the Internet, online consumer sales will soon reach $US 20 billion, and online commerce between companies will reach $US 175 billion. A 1998 US survey found that 46 % of commerce-related web sites were currently profitable, and an additional 30 % were expected to be within two years. Consumers will determine, as time passes, what sorts of products can be successfully sold this way.

POPULATION AND HEALTH

The growth of the human population in just the last 50 years has been staggering. In 1950, the global population was 2.5 billion, and it is currently 6.4 billion. It is projected that 8.5 billion people will live on the planet in 2025 and perhaps 10 billion people by 2050. If you are 30 years of age or less by the year 2000 and living in a developed country, according to current life expectancy figures, you will probably live through the final exponential surge in the human population—it is estimated that the total number of people may start to decline in the second half of the twenty-first century.

Exponential growth refers to the doubling of a population over a given time period. The growth of the human population is of deep concern, as 6.4 billion people at current levels of resource consumption and waste generation are already causing major environmental problems.

Factors causing population growth

How is the growth in population explained? Demographers and population geographers generally begin explaining world population growth by discussing its two immediate causes: increased fertility and changes in mortality. Fertility refers to the number of children born to women of childbearing age. Mortality refers to various aspects of death, including how long people tend to live (life expectancy) and the causes of death (viruses, cancers, accidents, etc.).

Other factors that play a part in any explanation of population growth include the level of economic development of a given place, the availability of birth control, and the way people in different societies think about children.

Before the Industrial Revolution, the world's population grew slowly or did not grow at all. Although fertility was high in pre-modern societies—women commonly gave birth to between 8 and 12 children—mortality was also high. One out of four children died before reaching its first birthday (infant mortality) and perhaps another one out of five died before reaching 5 years of age (child mortality). Infectious diseases and poor diet were the major causes of high mortality, including infant and child mortality.

Why was the fertility rate so high then? If a family wanted or needed six children, mortality rates alone would require them to have ten or more. Families required the children for agricultural and domestic labor, and as a source of support when a parent grew old—children were the only pension fund available.

The early exponential growth of population resulted from a substantial improvement in the health of populations, especially with respect to control of infectious diseases and the improvement of nutrition, both of which reduced the mortality rate without a corresponding decline in the fertility rate. Infant and child mortality plummeted, and population growth surged.

As economic and social development moved into a more advanced stage, the economic meaning of children also changed. As children began attending school, they were no longer available for labor, and children became an expense rather than an asset. Raising a child today in a developed country may now cost between $US 250,000 and $US 750,000. Thus, fertility rates have declined with advanced development because of the increased survival rates of children (increased health) and because parents become economically poorer by having many children (though not necessarily socially poorer) today, as against the past, when children labored for their parents for a substantial portion of their lives.

The advent of modern birth control has also played an important role in the decline of fertility. Most, if not all, developed countries have fertility rates below that required for maintaining current levels of population; immigration is the major factor responsible for continued population growth within developed countries.

Life expectancy—the individual

Looking at changes in health in greater depth, the health of a population has three components: mortality, morbidity (sickness), and disability. Life

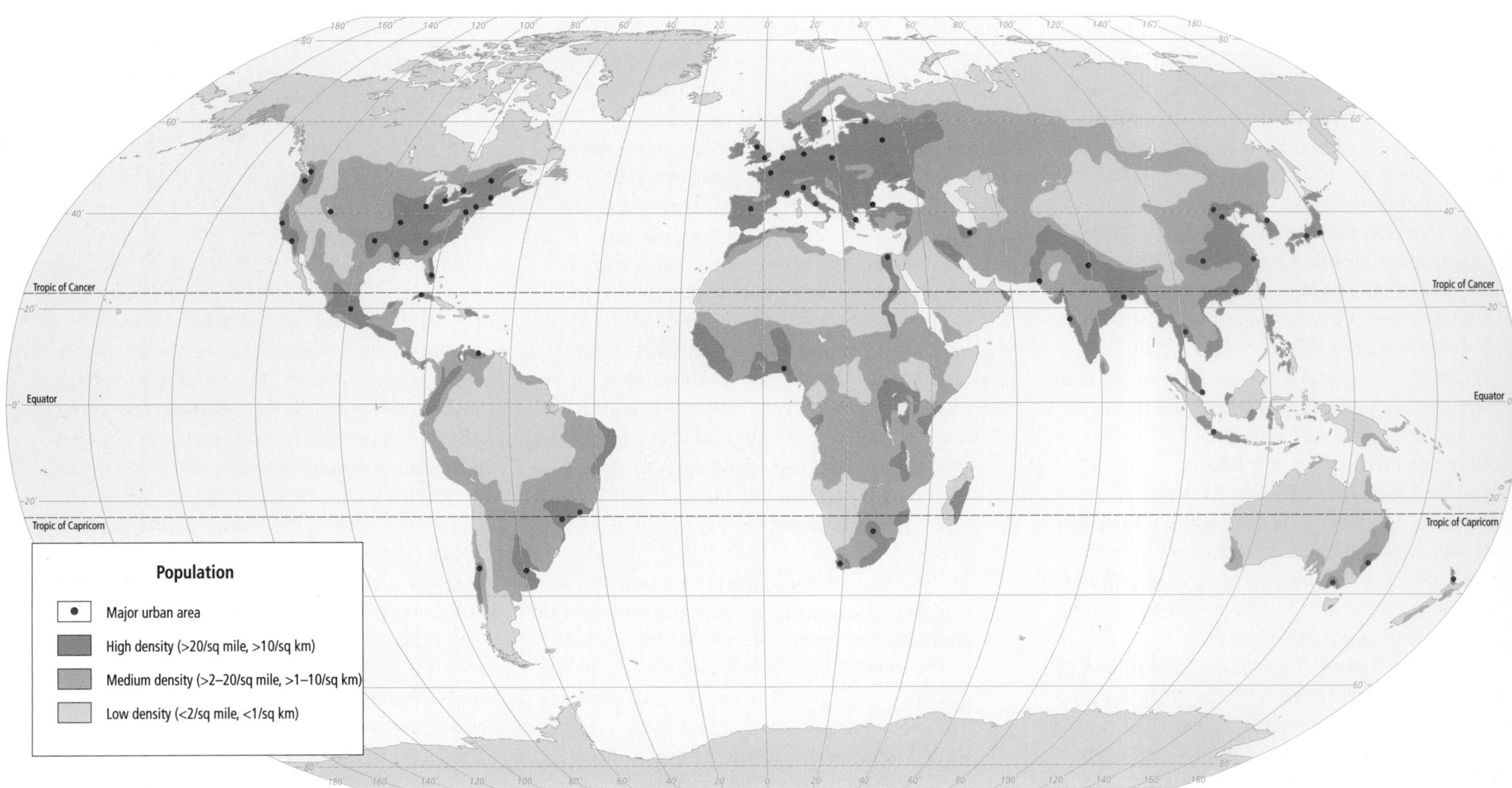

Exponential population growth occurs when rising prosperity coincides with high fertility rates, as in Bangladesh (above). Communities in Zimbabwe (above right) work to improve their health, while some countries such as India (right) continue to suffer low life expectancy.

expectancy is commonly accepted in demography and development studies as a good general index of the health of a population. In fact, many see life expectancy as the single best index of the development of a nation or population, but it is important to remember that life expectancy specifically measures only the effects of mortality changes; it does not relate to the sickness and disability aspect of human health.

Life expectancy was generally low before the Industrial Revolution. If life expectancy is expressed in terms of years a population as a whole lives, then life expectancy was low (between 45 and 55 years), mainly because of the prevalence of infectious diseases (measles, pneumonia, polio, and malaria, for instance), poor nutrition, lack of family planning, and the like.

Substantial advances in the reduction of a range of infectious diseases, coupled with improvement in nutrition, represent what the United Nations Children's Fund describes in their annual publication *The Progress of Nations* as simply that—the progress of nations. Life expectancy increases by 10 to 15 years because of these improvements to health.

Further increases in life expectancy—when compared with, say, life expectancy in the late 1960s and into the 1970s—are the result of advances in the reduction of death due to degenerative diseases (strokes, cancers, and heart attacks, for example) and the greater emphasis on improving lifestyle—a healthy diet, regular exercise and a reduction in smoking.

For a few nations, life expectancy is slightly more than 81 years at present. On the global scale, life expectancy at birth was 46 years in 1950, 64 years in the late 1990s, and is projected to be 77 years in the year 2050.

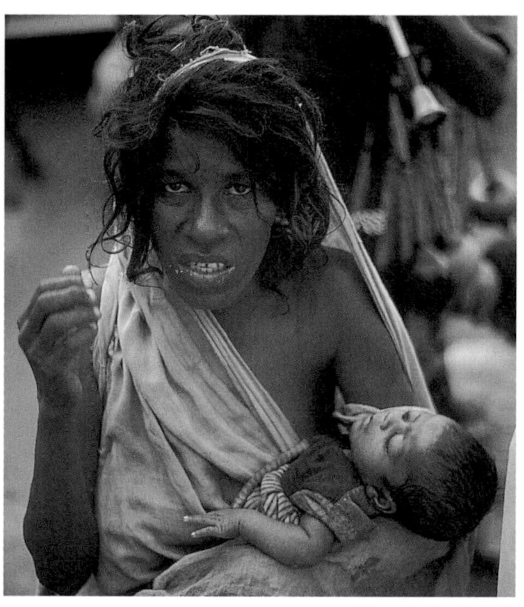

Life expectancy—the global view

Considerable regional diversity in the causes of population growth and life expectancy is evident in the late 1990s. Generally speaking, North America, Australia and Europe have high life expectancy and have internal growth rates below population replacement; South America and East and Southeast Asia are not far behind; and Africa south of the Sahara has low life expectancy, but population growth remains explosively high.

Many of the countries in the former communist world are experiencing deterioration in health, and life expectancy is actually declining in some of those nations, including Russia. It is interesting to compare the two most populous nations, China and India. Changes to population growth and life expectancy in China resemble those in other East and Southeast Asian nations, whereas India continues to have a very high growth rate and a moderately low life expectancy.

The future for life expectancy

Is there a limit to life expectancy? This is a most controversial topic about which there is no agreement. Under natural conditions, all life forms have a limit, called senescence: the point where an organism simply wears out. For the human population, senescence was believed to be roughly 85 years; however, a few population groups live into the low 90s. Genetic and other medical research, however, may well change the upper limit of life expectancy during the first half of the twenty-first century.

Of course, all of this optimistically assumes that improvements in health will continue. It remains to be seen whether or not the impact of diseases such as AIDS will retard or even reverse the historical improvement in human health, the resistance of some forms of bacteria to antibiotics, in particular, will give rise to deaths from diseases or infections previously thought to be under control, and whether the advances that come through medical research will be affordable to a sizeable proportion of the world's population.

Famine

Famine can be defined as a high degree of lack of food within a population, and it often goes along with widespread mortality. Malnutrition, on the other hand, refers to levels of nourishment that are below those needed to maintain health, and can apply to a whole population or part of a population.

Both are thought to be results of population pressure —the pressure that builds, in developing countries particularly, between the size of the population and the economic resources (especially food) of the country. Falling living standards can be an early sign, in countries with rapidly growing populations, of this pressure. Many societies have suffered famines; in modern times, famine has most often affected societies in Africa.

The links between famine and malnutrition and mortality and fertility now seem not nearly as clear as may previously have been thought. Investigations into mortality in developing countries have found that it is the combination of malnourishment and infectious disease that is responsible for high mortality among infants and children, not simply lack of food.

It seems that populations are able to maintain their rates of fertility despite quite large reductions in nutritional levels—metabolic rates actually appear to readjust.

NATURAL HAZARDS

Natural events which cause damage and loss of life are classified as natural hazards. These hazards are generally unpredictable—they strike suddenly and can therefore leave the affected populations traumatized. Natural hazards can result from movements taking place inside the Earth or on its surface, or in its atmosphere.

Movements within the Earth result in volcanic eruptions and earthquakes. Changing weather conditions generate wind storms, cyclones, tornadoes, heavy rainfall, and snowfall, as well as lightning strikes, which can trigger forest fires. River floods and tsunamis can cause loss of life and serious damage to property.

Earthquakes

Plate collision along the Japanese archipelago makes that area vulnerable to earthquakes and to tsunamis generated by earthquakes on the ocean floor. Plates sliding past each other can also cause earthquakes, such as along the San Andreas Fault in California, where earthquakes have occurred in San Francisco and in Los Angeles.

Earthquakes strike suddenly, and if they are of high intensity, buildings can be toppled and life and property lost. The famous San Francisco earthquake of 1906 was devastating to that city and its people—hundreds of buildings were destroyed and the resulting fires swept through the city center, leaving about 3,000 people dead and many thousands more homeless.

An intense earthquake in 1995 toppled and wrecked the tall buildings and infrastructure of Kobe, in Japan, killing more than 6,000 of its inhabitants and injuring more than 35,000 others. The worst scenarios involve earthquakes located close to inhabited areas, notably cities.

On the Richter scale, earthquakes are serious when they exceed a magnitude of 4, cause damage when they exceed 5 and are intensely destructive when they are between 7 and 8.6. Although more than a million earthquakes occur every year, most of these are of low magnitude, and cause no loss of life or damage to property. High-intensity earthquakes, on the other hand, are capable of causing great damage and therefore receive the most publicity, particularly when they are centered on densely populated areas.

Tsunamis

Earthquakes taking place on the sea bed can trigger tsunamis (tidal waves) which, on reaching land, can assume enormous proportions and result in great damage. Such waves may be less than 1 m (3 ft) in height where they begin, in the deep oceans, but they can reach the enormous heights of more than 30 m (100 ft) as they approach land, and they cause devastation to low-lying areas. Worse still, within seconds, more than one such giant tidal wave can strike.

In 1983, a tsunami resulted in the deaths of 30,000 people in Japan. On 17 July 1998, a tsunami struck the northern coast of Papua New Guinea, sweeping over the village of Arop and others nearby, which lay on a low-lying sandy spit; entire villages and their populations were swept away, and it is estimated that the death toll could be as many as 4,000 people.

Volcanoes

Volcanic eruptions are common along certain paths, which are also seismic zones. Here, crustal plates separate and collide. Volcanoes erupt where molten material (magma) accumulates just below

Earth's surface and then rises to the surface. A volcanic explosion ejects ash and superheated steam into the atmosphere and cascades very hot lava along the sides of the volcanic cones. Volcanic eruptions are another natural disaster that can be devastating to life and property.

In AD 79, lava and ash destroyed the ancient city of Pompeii in southern Italy when Mt Vesuvius erupted. Mt Pelée, in Martinique, erupted in 1902, destroying the city of St Pierre and killing most of its inhabitants. Mt Pinatubo, in the Philippines, erupted in 1991, ejecting steam, ash, and lava, and threatened hundreds of thousands of people just 27 km (17 miles) away in Angeles; its ash even blanketed parts of Manila. Volcanic eruptions are also common in Bali and Java (Indonesia).

Volcanic eruptions are rated on the Volcanic Explosivity Index. The Krakatoa eruption of 1883 in Indonesia, one of the most spectacular on record, is rated at 6. No recorded eruption has

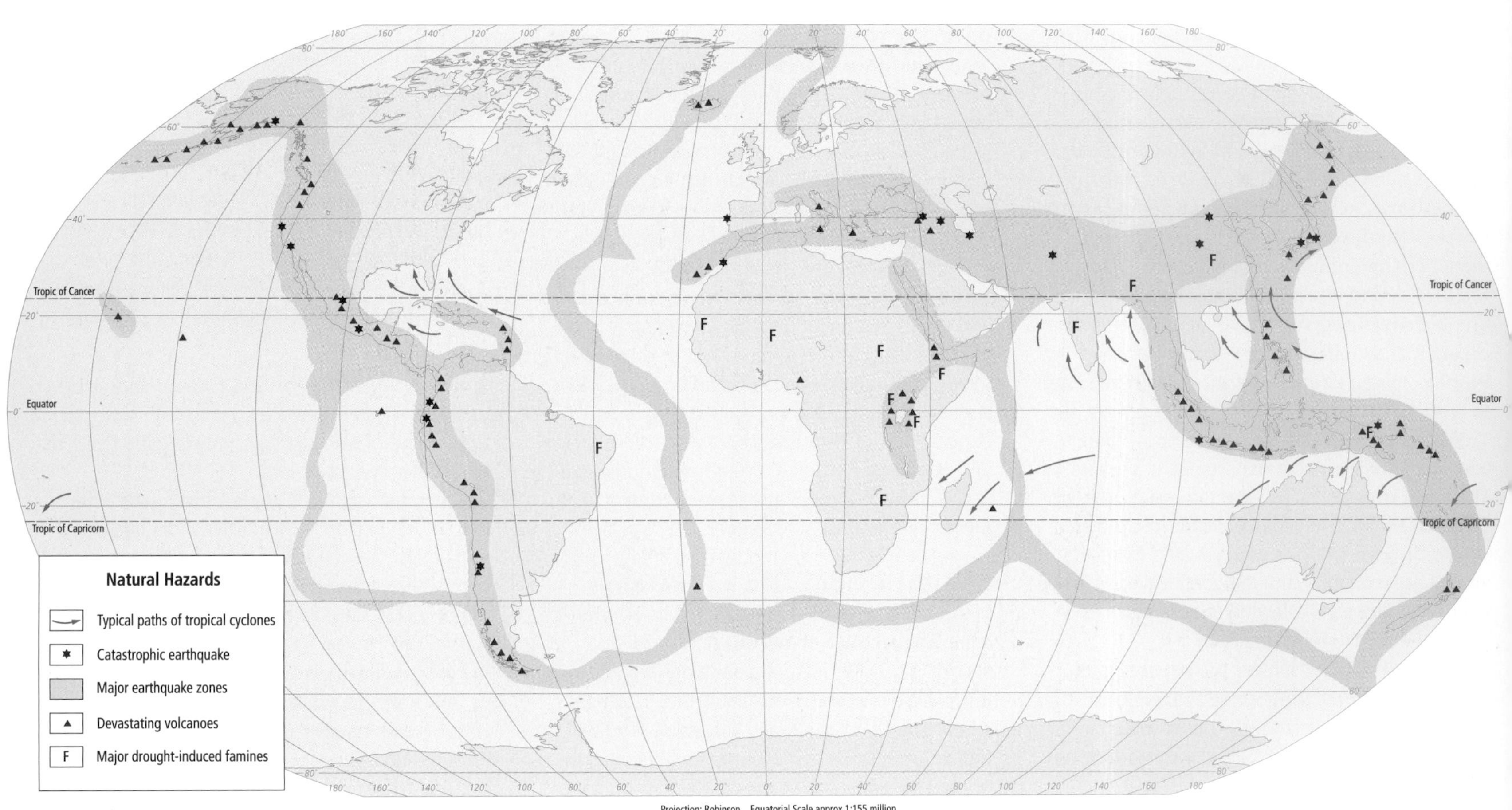

Projection: Robinson Equatorial Scale approx 1:155 million

Wildfires (bushfires, far left) consume large tracts of forest in many countries every year. Often lives are also lost, and millions of dollars worth of property is destroyed. Mt Pinatubo in the Philippines erupted in 1991 (left), causing widespread damage with devastating mud slides which swamped a large area including the town of Lahar (bottom). Drought (below) is a more predictable natural hazard.

reached 8, which is the highest possible rating. The Krakatoa eruption was heard more than 4,500 km (2,800 miles) away; it generated tsunamis, and more than 30,000 people are believed to have perished as a result.

Tropical cyclones and tornadoes

Tropical cyclones, known as typhoons in East Asia and hurricanes in the Caribbean, are also very destructive atmospheric hazards. Tropical cyclones are whirling, low-pressure vortices that can be up to 500 km (310 miles) in diameter and have wind speeds reaching more than 200 km (125 miles) per hour. They can pick up trees, rooftops, light boats, and planes and destroy them. This flying debris is enormously dangerous to people, too.

In coastal areas, large waves, or surges, which sweep the land may be generated, resulting in considerable damage. These cyclones have a calm center, called the "eye" of the cyclone; when the eye passes over an area there is a period of calm, after which the storm returns in all its fury, but with the winds now reversed in direction.

The coastal areas of Southeast and East Asia, the Bay of Bengal, the Pacific Ocean west of Mexico, the Caribbean and Florida, plus island groups of the Pacific Ocean such as Fiji, and northern Australia, are amongst the areas most prone to tropical cyclones.

Cyclones have struck with great fury along the coast of Bangladesh, a small country which mostly consists of the combined deltas of the Ganges and Brahmaputra rivers. That low-lying deltaic area is particularly vulnerable to the surges which cyclones can generate. This has resulted, on several occasions, in considerable loss of life and damage to property.

In contrast to tropical cyclones, tornadoes are small low-pressure cells, not more than 0.5 km (3/10 mile) across. They are, however, very intense, and their wind speeds can exceed 400 km (250 miles) per hour. They thus have the potential to inflict sudden and serious damage. Their vortices become vividly visible as they whip up soil and other debris. The most damaging tornadoes occur in the central parts of the United States, although mini-versions are also found in parts of eastern Australia.

River floods

River floods are a common hazard in floodplains. Spectacular floods, covering thousands of square kilometers, often occur over the immense plains of the major rivers of China, India, and Bangladesh. These areas are often densely populated because of the fertile soils and abundant water supplies.

The Huang River in China flows along a course which is elevated over the surrounding plains; this is because levees have naturally built up on its sides. These levees have been further reinforced by human action. The bursting of the levees in 1887 inundated more than 130,000 sq km (50,000 sq miles) and resulted in a million deaths.

In the case of the Ganges River in India and Bangladesh, the deforestation in the Himalayas has resulted, at times, in water from heavy rainfall and snowmelt rushing onto the vast plains through which the Ganges runs and flooding them. In 1988, 90 percent of Bangladesh lay under water when the Ganges flooded.

Floods regularly bring human and economic disasters to many parts of the world—in 1998 alone, 250 million people were affected by the flooding of the Yangtze River in China—and dams and irrigation networks have been built across many flood-prone rivers in an attempt to mitigate and control flood damage.

Wildfires

Wildfires or bushfires strike when forests are dry. These fires can cause serious damage and result in significant air pollution. The 1997 wildfires in the tropical forests of Sumatra, Indonesia, for instance, released a dense pall of smoke over a large area, including parts of Malaysia and Singapore. These fires were lit by humans clearing land for agriculture or woodchipping. Normally, rains ensure that wildfires are temporary, and restricted to a small area. In Sumatra, however, the prolonged drought, blamed on the El Niño effect, resulted in the uncontrollable spread of the wildfires.

The naturally occurring eucalypt forests of Australia and the eucalypt forest plantations of California are also particularly prone to wildfires, as the volatile oil the eucalypts contain makes them highly flammable. Every year, wildfires wipe out large areas of these forests and damage human settlements or property in the process.

Remote sensing, using satellites and highly sophisticated monitoring techniques, is now being used to track possible natural disasters. It provides data to ground centers about the development of tropical cyclones, the spreading of flood waters from rivers, and the build-up of lava in volcanoes. Such advance warning systems have already helped save lives and limit damage.

People and Society

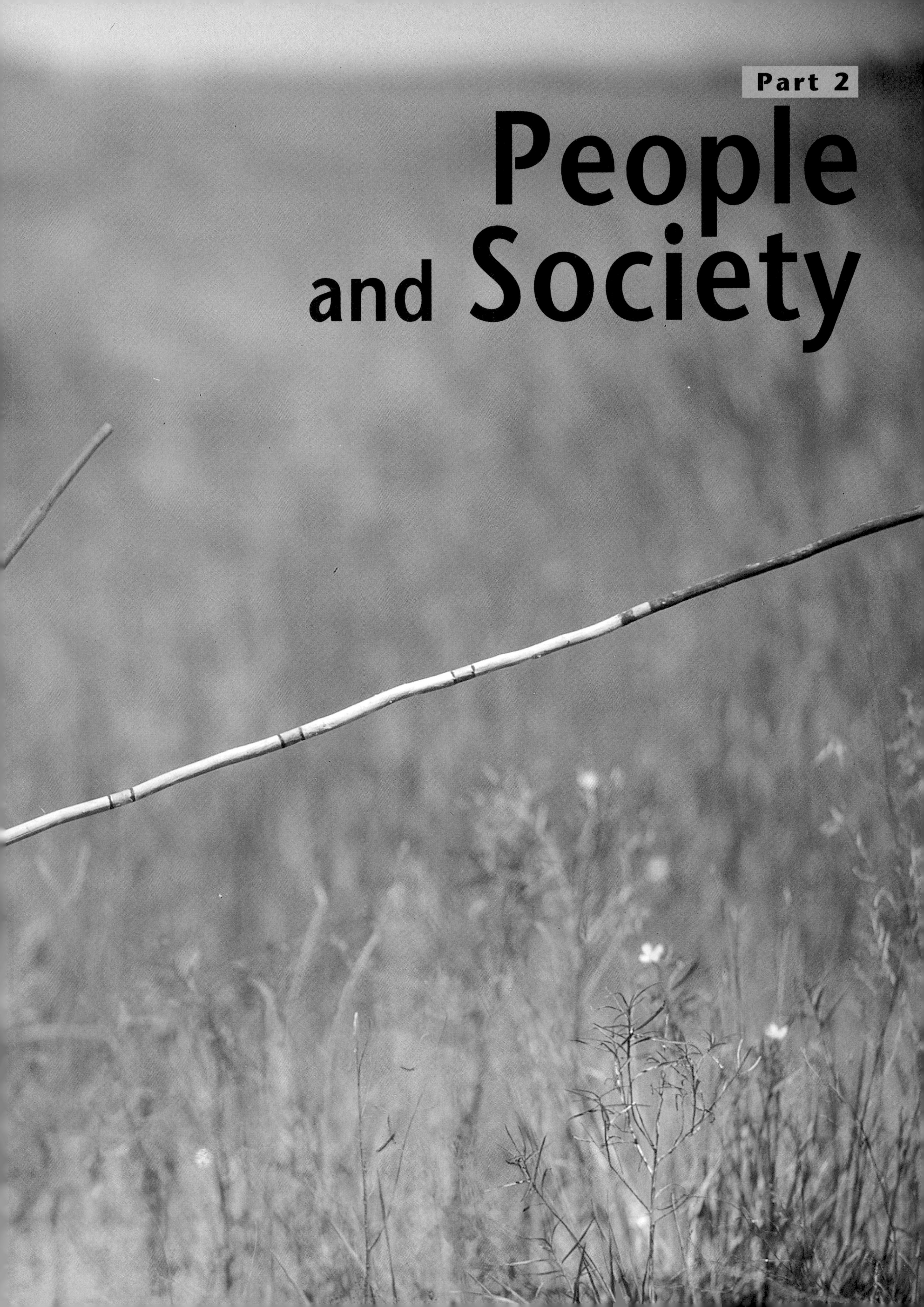

PEOPLE AND SOCIETY

The Changing Scene

Human societies have changed more during the 20th century than in any previous one, but mechanized facilities are not yet available to all—no running water for these Indian women in Varanasi, opposite. Conversely, highly sophisticated cultures developed thousands of years ago without modern conveniences, leaving treasures such as this floor mosaic, above, from Cyprus.

Today's global pattern of peoples and nations rests on a long process of social evolution, going back about 2 million years. It was then that humanity began to clearly distinguish itself as something special on the planet—and unlike the great apes—by physical and mental changes such as a fully upright way of walking, and much bigger brains than the apes possessed. Then, some time in the past 40,000 years, the great evolutionary breakthrough occurred: a fully developed capacity for language, an ability to create new tools for new purposes, and a talent for forward planning. Previously nomadic, hunting wild animals and foraging for seeds and fruits, humans now chose to live a more settled existence. People began to live in regular campsites and used shelters they made themselves. In some places they dug pits for food storage, and had well-built, regularly used fireplaces as far back as 20,000 years ago. Art and religion also appeared, with remarkable cave paintings and evidence of ritual associated with the burial of the dead.

It is thought that *Homo sapiens sapiens* (the technical name for modern humans) originated in Africa. From there waves of migration carried people to every corner of Earth: to distant Australia perhaps 50,000 years ago, to North America across a land bridge (where the Bering Strait is now) perhaps 20,000 years ago. As they moved, they took their languages with them, and when they settled, their languages continued to evolve, many soon becoming mutually unintelligible. Then, around 10,000 years ago came a major development—the rise of agriculture and permanent settlements. In Turkey and Iraq, in China, and in Mexico, farmers began to grow wheat and barley, or rice, or maize. At around the same time, the first farm animals were domesticated: pigs and cattle, goats and sheep, and llamas in South America.

Permanent farming settlements transformed human life economically, and on this foundation civilizations arose in different parts of the world. In Egypt and Iraq, in China and India, in Mexico and Peru, some towns became cities, with centralized political systems, strong rulers, and monumental buildings. The buildings were often religious temples associated with a class of priests, and in Egypt they were tombs for divine kings, built to preserve their bodies and effects for the afterlife. These social and political developments were accompanied by equally significant developments in science and technology.

The Stone Age, which for millions of years had provided stone implements for hunters, and then stone adzes and reaping blades for the first farmers, came to an end. First bronze was invented, then people found out how to make iron—by 500 BC, iron tools and weapons were spread throughout Europe and Asia. Metals and metallurgical science gave those who had them a huge military advantage over those who did not, as did the wheel, when it appeared around 3,500 BC. Horses harnessed to chariots changed the nature of warfare in ancient times.

War and conquest were normal conditions of life. Other things being equal, victory went to those whose weapons were most advanced. Some dominant cities developed into empires, subjecting other cultures to their rule. The Roman Empire, at its height, included large areas of Europe, North Africa, and the Middle East. By 206 BC, China was united under the Qin Dynasty, while by AD 1,520 the Incas controlled some 2,000 miles (3,330 km) of territory west of the Andes in South America. The military advantages of steel weapons and guns were demonstrated by the easy victories of Cortez over the Aztecs (1521) and Pizarro over the Incas (1533) against vastly greater numbers of ill-equipped Amerindian forces. The consequences of empire were that the knowledge, ideas, religion, technology and language of the dominant civilization were spread far and wide. Trade, both private and state-sponsored, also played a major role in this. The Han Empire in China (206 BC to AD 220), for instance, traded its silks with the Syrians of the Roman Empire far to the west. Arab trade spread round the Indian Ocean, and by AD 1200 had reached as far east as Java.

The spread of the main world religions has also been of major importance in the last two thousand years. These religions have been responsible for the most enduring examples of the art, literature, and architecture of civilization. A major distinction can be made between proselytizing religions, which actively seek to convert people to their beliefs (such as Chistianity, Islam, and Buddhism) and those which do not, such as Hinduism and Judaism. The world's three major religions are Christianity (33.0 percent), Islam (19.6 percent), and Hinduism (12.8 percent), the first two being derived from early Judaism (0.3 percent).

In the past 200 years, industrialization has been the biggest force for social change. Beginning in England with textile manufacturing in the 1780s, then progressing to manufacturing based on iron and steel in the nineteenth century, industrialization now combines science with technology in an unending cycle of invention and discovery. What began in Europe has now spread to every country in the world. Industry, which takes raw materials and then turns them into products to be traded, has provided millions of jobs for peasants who would otherwise be tied to the land. But in order to take those jobs they have moved into the cities. Urbanization has created huge concentrations of people in Asia and in South America, and while raising incomes, it has brought social problems too.

Political changes have come thick and fast. The nation-state arose as a political movement in Europe in the nineteenth century, where it superseded an earlier pattern of city-states such as Venice, Antwerp and Amsterdam. After the Second World War it spread through Asia and Africa during the process of decolonization, and since 1989 it has disrupted the domains of the former Soviet Union. Endemic conflicts born of nationalism continue to plague troublespots in Africa, Indo-China, the Balkans, and the Middle East. However, there has been at the same time a balancing move toward large, over-arching international organizations. The European Union steadily moves toward greater political and economic unity. Meanwhile, the United Nations, its resources and abilities increasingly overstretched, its goals more honored in the breach than in the observance, endeavors to keep international peace.

HUMAN EVOLUTION

The oldest primate fossils found in Africa and Asia date from between 45 and 50 million years ago. Around 15 million years ago, Asian and African hominoids (the earliest known ancestors of both humans and apes) diverged. The African hominoids adapted to woodland and savanna habitats and developed the ability to walk on two legs, while the Asian hominoids continued their tree-climbing existence. Although the fossil record is incomplete, a later divergence probably occurred among African hominoids between gorillas and the common ancestors of humans and chimpanzees.

Early hominids

The first hominids (the earliest ancestors of modern human beings not also related to modern great apes) developed about 5 to 6 million years ago. During the earliest phases of their evolution, hominids underwent anatomical changes that resulted in an erect posture, allowing them to walk habitually on two legs. Other changes included the reduction of canine teeth and the development of a comparatively vertical face. Features that are widely accepted as hominid hallmarks, such as a larger brain and the capacity for cultural life (indicated by stone or bone tools), appeared later.

The earliest hominid fossils have been found in southern and eastern Africa. The Olduvai Gorge in the Great Rift Valley of Tanzania has proved to be a rich source. In the 1930s, the anthropologist Louis Leakey began excavations there, and in the ensuing years he and others found a large number of hominid fossils and stone tools. The most famous find occurred in 1959 when his wife Mary uncovered a hominid fossil she called *Zinjanthropus*, believed to be 1,750,000 years old. Most scholars now believe that *Zinjanthropus* is an example of *Australopithecus* (specifically *Australopithecus boisei*), the earliest group of hominids yet found.

Handy man

Other hominid fossils found at Olduvai Gorge were more clearly identifiable as members of our own genus, *Homo*. These hominids were tool users and have been classified as *Homo habilis* ("handy man"). Tools similar to those found at Olduvai have been found at sites elsewhere in Africa and dated at between 1,800,000 and 2,340,000 years old.

Fossils of species that are more recognizably like ourselves have also been found in Africa and dated at about 1.9 million years ago. The best example is a nearly complete 1.6-million-year-old skeleton found in northern Kenya and known as Turkana Boy. The boy died in adolescence, but, had he lived to maturity, he would have been tall (about 1.8 m [6 ft]), with long, slender limbs, and well adapted to living on the open savanna.

Turkana Boy and other similar fossils found in Africa were originally thought to resemble specimens discovered in Java and China. All were classified as *Homo erectus* and it was believed that *Homo erectus* had evolved in Africa and then migrated to Asia about 1 million years ago. Discoveries in China in the past decade, however, together with the application of more sophisticated dating methods to previously excavated Asian sites, have pushed back the date of the first appearance of early hominids in Asia to about 2 million years ago. Hominid fossils found in Longgupo Cave in Sichuan province in China, dated at around 1.9 million years old, more closely resemble the earlier hominid species *Homo habilis*. This suggests a much earlier migration out of Africa. As a result, some scholars now believe that *Homo erectus* evolved independently in Asia and was not an African species. African hominid fossils of a more modern appearance, such as Turkana Boy, are now classified as a separate species, *Homo ergaster*.

Although there are a number of early hominid sites in Europe, they have yielded few fossils. Sites containing tools have been dated at around 1 million years old, with the earliest being about 1.5 million years old. Until recently, some of these were classified as *Homo erectus* sites. Since this species is now considered to be an Asian evolutionary sideline, however, the fossil record is being reassessed. In 1994, excavations in northern Spain produced numerous simple stone tools and some hominid fossils subsequently classified as a separate species, *Homo heidelbergensis*. This find has been dated at more than 780,000 years old and may provide evidence for the European ancestors of the Neanderthals.

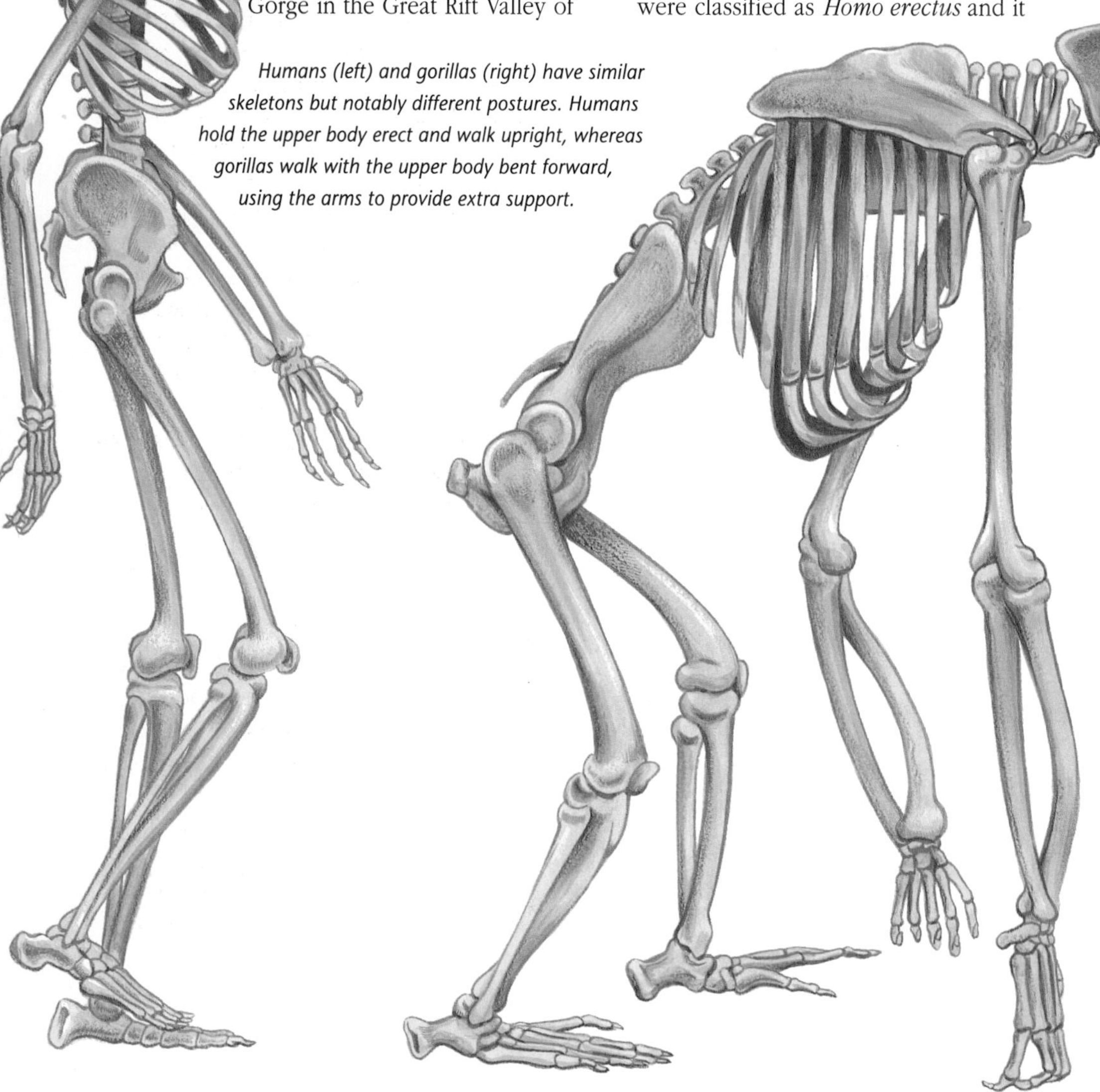

Humans (left) and gorillas (right) have similar skeletons but notably different postures. Humans hold the upper body erect and walk upright, whereas gorillas walk with the upper body bent forward, using the arms to provide extra support.

Archaic *Homo sapiens*

The earliest archaeological discoveries made in Europe were fossils of archaic *Homo sapiens*. The fossils were named Neanderthals, after the Neander Valley near Düsseldorf in Germany, where they were first discovered in 1865. This find caused widespread excitement as it was the first discovery of an extinct ancestor of modern humans. Since then, numerous Neanderthal sites have been found throughout Europe and the Middle East. The Neanderthals are generally considered to be a subspecies of *Homo sapiens*, known as *Homo sapiens neanderthalensis*. However, some scholars believe that the Neanderthals' less evolved physical characteristics and less sophisticated technology indicate that they were a separate species, *Homo neanderthalensis*.

The Neanderthals lived in Europe and Western Asia approximately 35,000 to 130,000 years ago, overlapping with the modern human species (*Homo sapiens sapiens*). They had larger brain cases and smaller back teeth than earlier populations, but differed from modern humans in their receding forehead and large, protruding face with front teeth and forward-projecting jaw. The Neanderthals had a relatively short, bulky stature and considerable strength, and showed evidence of complex cultural traits and social organization. For example, they used planning and cooperation to hunt large mammals. They also buried their dead and seem to have had some knowledge of art, demonstrating a capacity for symbolic behavior. Their vocal apparatus and neurological structure provide indirect evidence that they may also have developed speech.

Neanderthals disappear from the archaeological record around 40,000 years ago in the Middle East and about 35,000 years ago in Europe. It may be that they slowly evolved into modern humans, contributing to the gene pool of the present-day inhabitants of Europe and the Middle East. However, many scholars now think that they were gradually overwhelmed and replaced by incoming populations of a more advanced species classified as *Homo sapiens sapiens*, or modern humans.

Out of Africa

The early history of modern humans is still uncertain, as the fossil record is far from complete. Some scholars argue that *Homo sapiens sapiens* developed independently, in a number of different geographical locations. Others consider that what is popularly called the "out of Africa" theory better reflects what is now known about the process of evolution. This proposes that modern human populations are all descended from a single ancestral population that emerged at one location between 150,000 and 100,000 years ago. Increasing archaeological evidence suggests that the place of origin of modern humans was somewhere in Africa. From this homeland, *Homo sapiens sapiens* migrated northward into Europe some 40,000 to 100,000 years ago, and then spread throughout the world, gradually replacing more archaic populations wherever they encountered them.

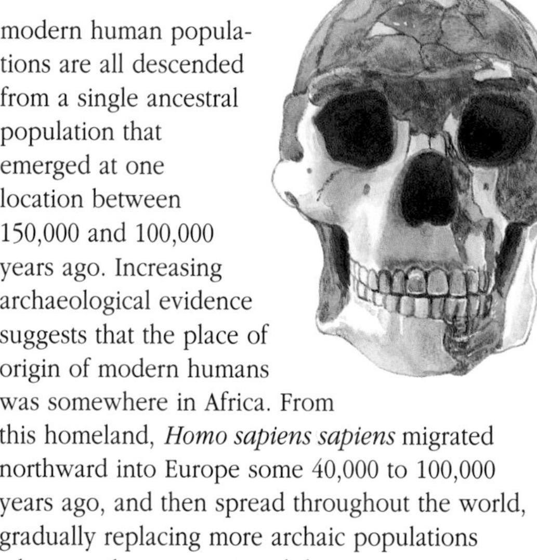

Human fossil skulls: 1. Australopithecus boisei 2. Homo habilis 3. Homo ergaster 4. Homo erectus 5. Homo sapiens neanderthalensis 6. Homo sapiens sapiens. *Note the gradual disappearance of the thick brow ridges, and the growth of the cranium—indicative of increasing brain capacity and intelligence.*

The classification of primate fossils

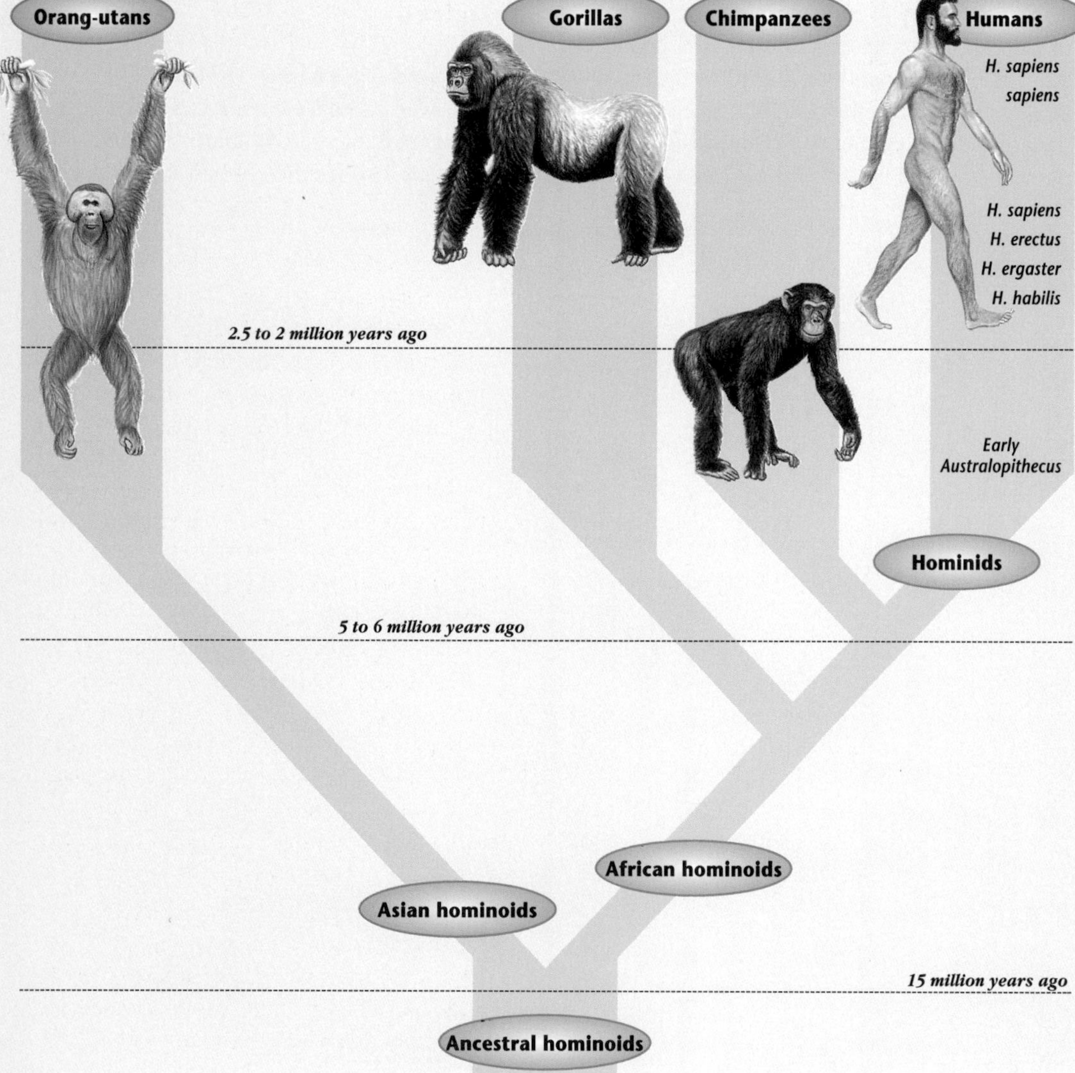

In 1735, the Swedish naturalist Carl Linnaeus caused a public outcry when he classified human beings as part of the animal kingdom. Today, however, his taxonomy—which has been extensively revised and expanded—is the accepted way of classifying all forms of plant and animal life.

The human species, *Homo sapiens sapiens*, belongs to the genus *Homo* (which includes our hominid ancestors) in the family *Hominidae* (which includes the apes). This family is in turn part of the Primate order. The relationship between humans, apes, and early hominid fossils is problematic. Recent studies by molecular biologists have shown that there is a much closer genetic link between humans and the African great apes (especially chimpanzees) than might have been predicted from comparing their anatomies. This has led some taxonomists to place humans, gorillas, and chimpanzees in one family, *Hominidae*, and Asian apes such as the orang-utan in another, *Pongidae*.

The currently accepted classification of hominid fossils establishes a chronology for modern humans from the development of the first australopithecine species (appearing around 5 million years ago), to early *Homo* species such as *Homo habilis* and *Homo erectus* (from around 2 million years ago), through to later *Homo* species (around 1 million years ago) and archaic *Homo sapiens* such as the Neanderthals (about 130,000 years ago). Both the classification and the chronology are likely to be revised as new fossil discoveries are made.

THE FIRST MODERN HUMANS

The success of modern humans, *Homo sapiens sapiens*, in colonizing Earth's landmasses owes much to the evolutionary changes that occurred in the physical form and mental capacity of hominids. Although the basic hominid anatomy changed little, the features that distinguished hominids from other hominoids, such as their erect posture, ability to walk habitually on two legs, vertical face, smaller teeth and enlarged brain, were refined in each successive species and subspecies. By far the most significant change, and the one that signaled the emergence of *Homo sapiens sapiens*, was the progressive enlargement of the brain, which was out of all proportion to changes in body size. In absolute terms, the average brain capacity of modern humans is three times that of the great apes.

Increased brain capacity allowed *Homo sapiens sapiens* to develop greater intelligence and problem-solving capabilities. This led to the appearance of tools as well as speech and language (although full language capacity emerged less than 40,000 years ago). It also enabled modern humans to develop strategies for coping with harsh environments, such as camp fires, clothing, natural food storage facilities, and primitive cooking methods. Further intellectual development resulted in a flourishing cultural life and increased capacity for social organization, which in turn stimulated the growth of civilizations and led to the evolution of modern society.

Making and using tools

Many people believe that it is the presence of tools that distinguishes early humans (*Homo* spp.) from other hominids, but a number of other animals also make and use tools. Chimpanzees, for instance, have demonstrated an ability to make and use tools for digging for food. More specifically, some scholars have argued that it is the power and complexity of human tool assemblages that distinguishes humans. However, the simplicity of the tool assemblages of archaic humans and certain hunter-gatherers of the recent past makes this explanation inadequate. What *is* unique about human tool making and tool use is that the tools were made for particular purposes. Moreover, they were constantly improved and adapted for new purposes, to the extent that tools eventually pervaded all aspects of human life. This is not the case among chimpanzees.

The first hominid fossils associated with handmade tools were those of *Homo habilis*, found at Olduvai Gorge in Tanzania, and dated at about 2 million years old. Tools have been found in older East African sites, but without any fossil remains. Although earlier hominid species knew how to make and use tools, it was probably only with the emergence of the genus *Homo* that tools became part of daily life.

The early *Homo habilis* tools were crude, stone hand-axes. Unsurprisingly, stone and some bone tools dominate the archaeological record. Tools made of perishable materials such as wood are found occasionally at waterlogged, frozen, or arid sites, but such finds are rare. From about one million years ago, tool assemblages became more specialized, but it is only in the past 40,000 years that there has been a proliferation of designs.

The simplicity of early tools clearly indicates that hominids obtained their food by foraging and scavenging. The traditional view that the hunting of animals accompanied and influenced the evolutionary development of modern humans has been reassessed in the light of this evidence. Regular

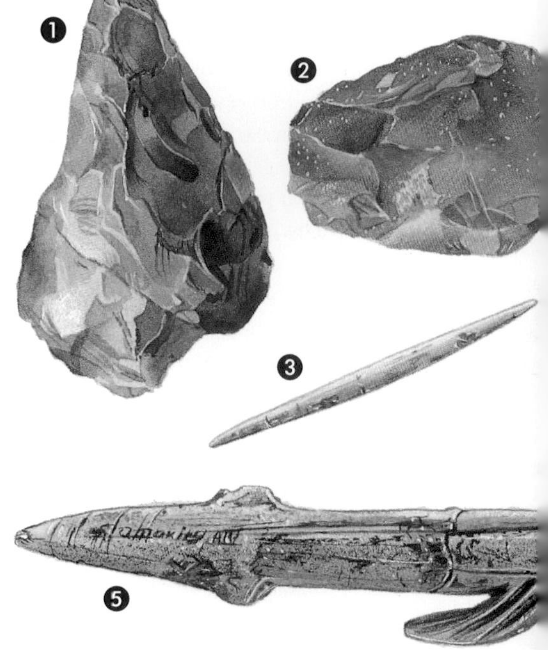

hunting, particularly the killing of large mammals, probably began later. Far more important at this stage in the evolution of modern humans was the development of an ability to plan ahead. Although this would become essential for organizing hunts, it was also required at an earlier stage to enable humans to forage for food and store supplies for lean times.

Art and cooking skills

There seems to have been a watershed in the development of modern humans around 40,000 years ago. This is reflected in a dramatic world-

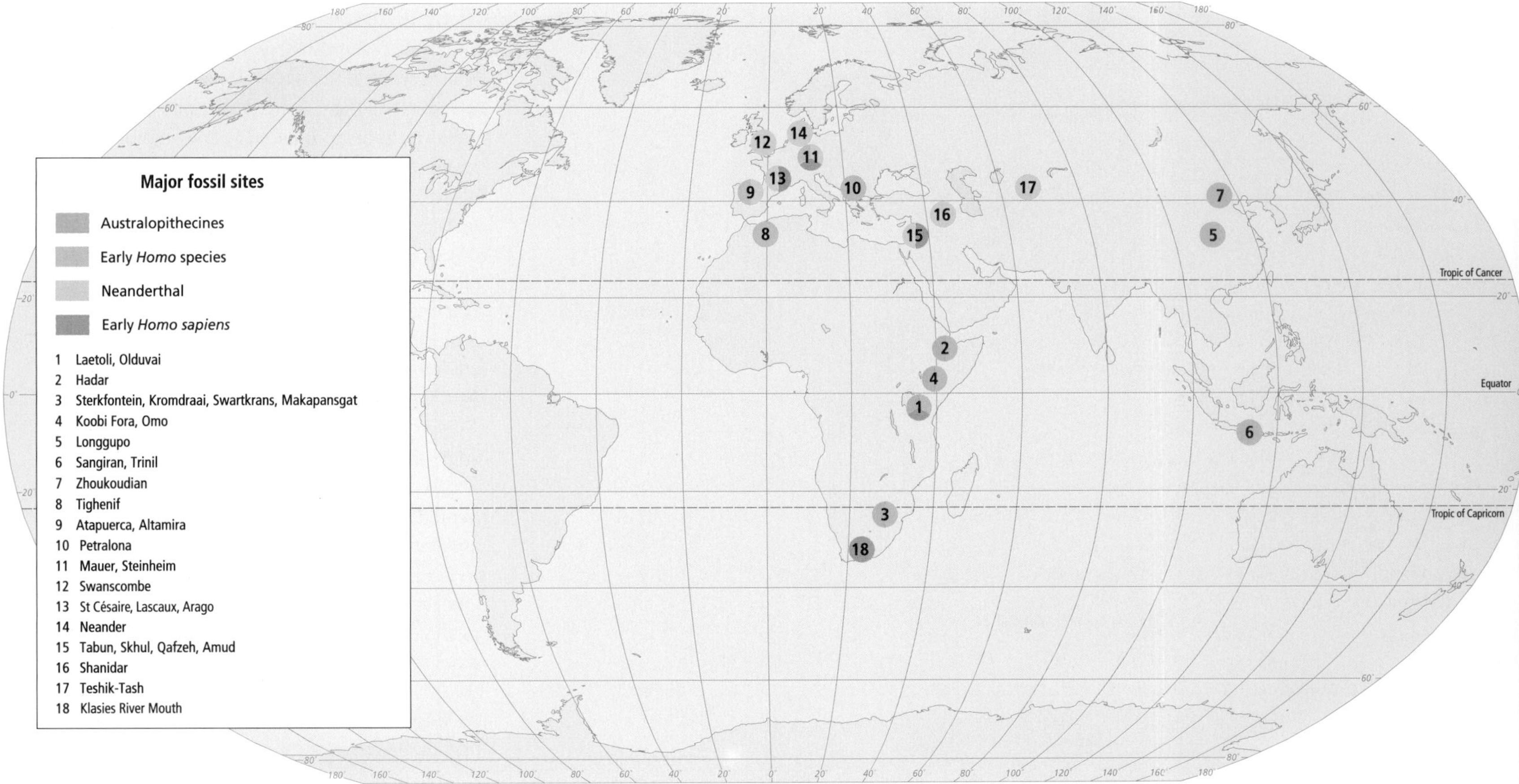

Projection: Robinson Equatorial Scale approx 1:155 million

Many people believe that the invention and use of tools distinguished the early humans from other hominids. The development of human technology is reflected in these tools (below):

1. *Scraper from Swanscombe, England; 300,000–200,000* BP
2. *Sidescraper from Le Moustier, France; 70,000–35,000* BP
3. *Bone point from Aurignac, France, 35,000–23,000* BP
4. *Bifacial stone knife from Solutré, France; 20,000–17,000* BP
5. *Bone harpoon from Le Morin, France, 16,000–8,000* BP

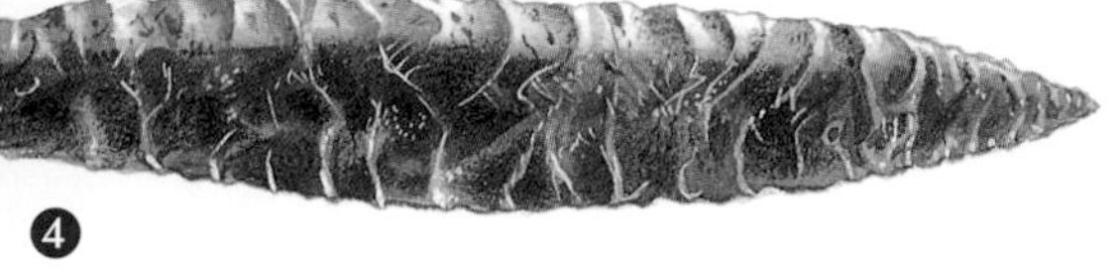

wide change in the archaeological evidence. Not only did tool assemblages become more sophisticated, but art, in the form of jewellery, figurines, paintings, and engravings (often depicting hunting scenes), also become prevalent. The widespread use of raw materials that could only have been obtained from distant sources suggests that trade networks had expanded. Camp sites show evidence of more settled living, including artificial shelters, food storage pits, and well-built, regularly used fireplaces. Burial sites become more elaborate, containing ornaments and other cultural objects. The disposal of the dead clearly involved some form of ritual, reflecting metaphysical concerns and symbolic behavior.

There also appears to have been a "culinary revolution," with stone knives being used to cut up food. This allowed for more thorough cooking, which may in turn have resulted in changes in the cranial structure of humans, as large teeth would no longer have been necessary for tearing raw or partially roasted meat.

These cultural and physical changes occurred during the last ice age, which culminated about 15,000 to 20,000 years ago, when glaciers covered large areas of the world. Successful strategies developed by modern humans to cope with the deteriorating climate gave them a clear advantage over more archaic forms of *Homo sapiens.* Despite the spread of hostile environments during the ice age, *Homo sapiens sapiens* succeeded in colonizing the world far more rapidly and extensively than earlier hominid migrants.

Colonization on the scale undertaken by *Homo sapiens sapiens* required all of the species' newfound technical and social skills. Its success depended not just on tools and an ability to plan ahead, but also on the existence of extensive social structures which could provide the support and cooperation necessary for the completion of long, hazardous journeys into unknown lands.

The art of early hunter-gatherers

Art is widely believed to have originated during the last ice age and appears to have flourished mainly in Europe and the southern hemisphere (southern Africa and Australia). Little has been found at ice-age sites in North Africa, China, or elsewhere in Asia. This does not mean, however, that art did not exist in these areas—it may simply be that the forms of artistic expression were more temporary or that the materials used did not survive.

Ice-age art is linked with major innovations in tool technology, including well-crafted and highly efficient blades, and hafted spears. With the rapid evolution of hunting techniques, obtaining food would no longer have been as difficult and, consequently, more effort could be expended on the development of art, language, and spiritual interests. No record remains of stories, songs, or dances of these pre-literate cultures, nor of artworks made out of perishable materials. The art that has survived can be divided into two main types: moveable objects and rock art.

Moveable objects comprise small figures or decorated weapons made of stone, bone, antler, ivory, or clay, which were sometimes placed in graves to accompany the deceased in the afterlife. Rock art, such as engravings and paintings, is often found in caves. While drawings of human figures have been found, most rock art depicts game animals such as bison, mammoths, deer, and bears, which were important sources of food, clothing, tools, weapons, and ornaments. Outstanding examples of cave art were discovered in the nineteenth century at Altamira in northern Spain and at Lascaux in southwestern France.

This ancient cave painting (above) was found in Rhodes-Matapos National Park in Zimbabwe, Africa. Fertility figures, such as the 20,000-year-old Willendorf Venus from Austria (left), are among the earliest indications of a human concern with rituals and symbols.

HUMAN MIGRATIONS

Recent research undertaken on fossil and genetic evidence suggests that hominids migrated "out of Africa" on many occasions, probably beginning with *Homo erectus*, *Homo habilis*, or the taller and more slender *Homo ergaster* more than 2 million years ago. Changes in the climate may have been a major factor in these early migrations. One theory suggests that between 2 million and 3 million years ago, a widespread drop in temperature led to the replacement of the tropical woodlands in eastern Africa by savanna grassland. This change in vegetation favored the *Homo* species over the australopithecines. With their larger brains, more generalized diets, and greater tool-using ability, the *Homo* species adapted more readily to the open terrain and soon began to roam widely. Initially, they probably followed the land mammals on which they scavenged, as the animals moved north and east following the expansion of the grasslands.

To date, early *Homo* sites have been discovered at several Asian sites in the Republic of Georgia, in China, and on the island of Java in Indonesia. Early humans did not make an appearance in Europe until some time later (around 1 to 1.5 million years ago), and this region remained sparsely populated until 500,000 years ago.

During their migrations, early *Homo* species would have crossed various land bridges that appeared during the recurring ice ages of the past 2 million years. However, to explain the presence of 800,000-year-old stone tools on the Indonesian island of Flores, which would have remained at least 20 km (12 miles) offshore even at the height of the ice ages, scientists have tentatively suggested that *Homo erectus* made use of simple vessels such as bamboo rafts to cross short stretches of sea.

Migrations by modern humans

Compared with the migrations made by archaic populations, the spread of modern humans during the last 100,000 years occurred remarkably rapidly. Furthermore, *Homo sapiens sapiens* ventured much farther than earlier hominids, eventually reaching the Americas and Australia. These more extensive migrations were made possible by this species' greater adaptability and by the exposure of numerous land bridges during the last ice age.

Scientists are still debating when and how the Americas were colonized, although it is generally accepted that hunting groups crossed into Alaska via a land bridge in the Bering Strait. This could have occurred either between 63,000 and 45,000 years ago or between 35,000 and 10,000 years ago. Although some argue that the earlier crossing is more likely because the Alaskan ice sheet would not have been as extensive as during the later period, the earliest reliable dates for archaeological sites in North America are no more than 20,000 years old. Consequently, the more widely held view is that the crossing occurred between 12,000 and 20,000 years ago, with people gradually drifting south down the continent. Recent evidence suggests that Monte Verde in southern Chile may have been settled as early as 12,500 years ago.

The question of whether there was one or more crossings is also unresolved. Some researchers believe that genetic variations among the indigenous peoples of the Americas are so great that they suggest three or four waves of migration. A more recent assessment cautiously suggests that there were no more than two waves—one arriving about 20,000 to 25,000 years ago and the other around 11,300 years ago. These early settlers were probably of more diverse origins than previously

thought, and some may even have arrived by sea rather than across the land bridge.

Debates of a similar nature surround the colonization of Australia. The earliest direct evidence of humans is about 40,000 years old (claims that various artifacts and sites in the Northern Territory date from around 60,000 years ago have not been confirmed). Since some of these sites are in the south of the continent, dates of up to 50,000 to 60,000 years ago for the initial arrival of humans from Southeast Asia have been proposed to allow for the settlement of large areas of the continent by 40,000 years ago. The absence of Asian fauna in Australia indicates that there must

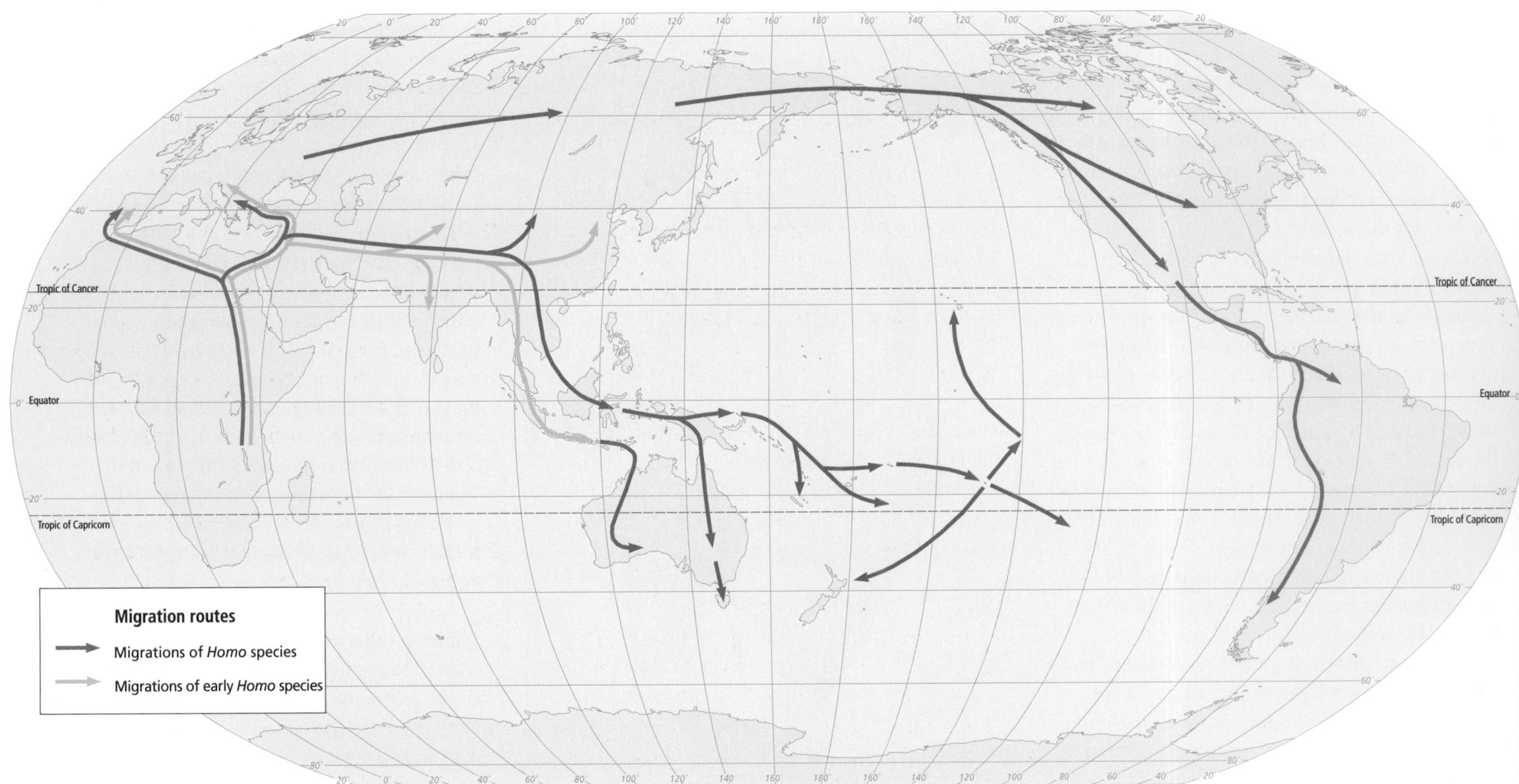

The expansion of African grasslands (left) as a result of climatic changes assisted early migrations. The first people to settle in North America would have had a lifestyle similar to that of present-day Inuit (below). Early Polynesian watercraft may have resembled this canoe from the Solomon Islands (bottom).

have been a substantial stretch of sea between the two continents for millions of years.

Colonizing the Pacific

The islands along the western rim of the Pacific were probably colonized around the same time as Australia and New Guinea, when sea levels were sufficiently low for them to be linked to the Asian mainland. Of course, *Homo erectus* may also have occupied these islands while they were linked to the mainland during earlier periods of glaciation, but the earliest signs of human occupation in Japan have been dated at around 30,000 years ago. Based on the evidence currently available, it appears that other islands on the western Pacific rim, such as most of the Philippines, were probably occupied 10,000 to 15,000 years later.

By the time European explorers reached the Pacific region in the early sixteenth century, virtually every inhabitable island was populated. Exactly when and how all the islands of the Pacific were first settled, however, is not entirely clear. The archaeological evidence is still meager, and there is considerable speculation about early migrations.

Not long after the Second World War, in an attempt to prove that the population of the Polynesian islands originated in South America, the Norwegian ethnologist and adventurer Thor Heyerdahl and his small crew sailed from the Pacific coast of South America to Polynesia on a balsa raft named *Kon-Tiki.* Although Heyerdahl showed that such a voyage was possible, most scholars still believe that the great bulk of linguistic and botanical evidence suggests that the populations originally came from Southeast Asia rather than South America.

The Pacific Islands are customarily divided into three ethnogeographic areas: Melanesia, Micronesia, and Polynesia. Melanesia includes the predominantly dark-skinned peoples of New Guinea, the Bismarck Archipelago, the Solomons, Vanuatu, New Caledonia, and Fiji. Micronesia comprises the very small islands and atolls in the northern Pacific, including the Marianas, Carolines, and Marshalls. Polynesia forms a large triangle in the eastern Pacific, from Hawaii in the north, to New Zealand in the south, and Easter Island in the east. Despite these classifications, however, archaeological evidence, linguistic studies, and blood group analyses all suggest similar origins for the people of the three areas. The physical and cultural differences between modern-day peoples may result from the fact that the islands were occupied by successive waves of migrants.

The Lapita people

The earliest dates for settlement of the Pacific Islands in Micronesia and Polynesia go back no further than the second millennium BC. As they moved eastward, these early settlers took with them a well-developed agricultural tradition based on taro, yams, and pigs. This agricultural tradition was associated with a coarse, finely decorated pottery known as Lapita ware. By studying the distribution of this pottery, archaeologists have been able to trace the movement of this people across the Pacific.

One theory suggests that the Lapita people began to make their way eastward from eastern Indonesia or the Philippines about 4,000 years ago and then spread farther eastward through New Guinea to the southwestern Pacific. It is thought that they may have been forced to keep moving as a result of pressure from incoming groups of rice-growers. As they moved, they gradually developed distinctive Polynesian characteristics, which included complex hierarchical social, political, and religious systems.

The last region of the Pacific to be settled by Polynesians was New Zealand. Colonists probably arrived there by canoe from the Hawaiian islands some time around AD 1,000, although many scholars now favor a date closer to AD 750.

LANGUAGES AND WRITING

As with many other questions about human evolution, there is still no consensus about the origin of speech and language. A number of scholars have suggested that art and language must be closely intertwined because they both require the ability to understand abstract ideas and symbolic concepts and to share these understandings with others as part of a cultural system. According to this theory, fully fledged languages would not have existed before the appearance of art—which first emerged about 40,000 years ago. If this argument is correct, archaic *Homo sapiens* such as the Neanderthals, who coexisted for some time with *Homo sapiens sapiens* and also created primitive art, would have possessed some form of language. Certainly, no one doubts that the Neanderthals were able to communicate with each other, although changes to the brain and facial structure would have meant the linguistic ability of *Homo sapiens sapiens* was markedly superior.

The complexity of human language and speech is dependent on a number of neural and anatomical mechanisms found only in *Homo sapiens sapiens*. These include a vocal tract that permits a wide range of speech sounds, areas of the brain that control and interpret these sounds, and an efficient memory that can use past experiences as a guide to the future. Although scientists believe that earlier hominid species were able to communicate both vocally and by gestures (just as animals do), their use of words, concepts, and sentence construction (syntax) would have been limited. Even chimpanzees can be taught to use words when placed in a human-like environment, yet they never progress beyond the vocabulary or grammatical ability of an average three-year-old child. Humans alone are able to talk to each other, rather than just transmit words.

Although fully fledged linguistic ability would have been found only among *Homo sapiens sapiens*, it is still possible that language of some sort existed among the first anatomically modern humans in East Africa as early as 130,000 years ago. Some scientists even argue that *Homo habilis* may have been able to communicate vocally, albeit in a much simpler fashion. In other words, early humans may have had speech, but not a complete language.

Further evidence that early hominids were able to communicate verbally has recently emerged from what may at first seem an unlikely source: scientific research into the evolution of dogs. Studies in molecular biology suggest that wolves evolved into domestic animals more than 130,000 years ago, and wolf bones have even been found with 400,000-year-old hominid bones. These facts suggest that the association between humans and canines goes back a very long time. Some scientists now think that the domestication of canines had a profound effect on human evolution. The close association with dogs would have made it less crucial for early hominids to have a keen sense of smell that would alert them to other hominids or animal predators. In turn, this would have allowed the development of the facial and cranial modifications necessary for speech.

Languages of the world

Thousands of languages are spoken in the world today. Populations that share similar cultures and live only a short distance apart may still speak languages that are quite distinct and not readily understood by neighboring populations. For example, the inhabitants of New Guinea and adjacent islands speak approximately 1,000 different languages, or about one-fifth of the world's total.

At the same time, similarities exist between languages used in different parts of the world, which suggests that they developed from a common source. Scholars group such languages in families on the basis of similarities in vocabulary, sound systems, and grammar. English, for example, is part of the Indo-European family, which includes languages of antiquity, such as Sanskrit and classical Greek, as well as contemporary languages in both Asia and Europe, such as Hindi and Russian. Other geographically dispersed language families are Malayo-Polynesian (also known

The world's major languages

Language	Speakers (millions)
Mandarin (Chinese)	885
English	322
Spanish	266
Bengali	189
Hindi	182
Portuguese	170
Russian	170
Japanese	125
German	98
Wu (Chinese)	77
Javanese	75.5
Korean	75

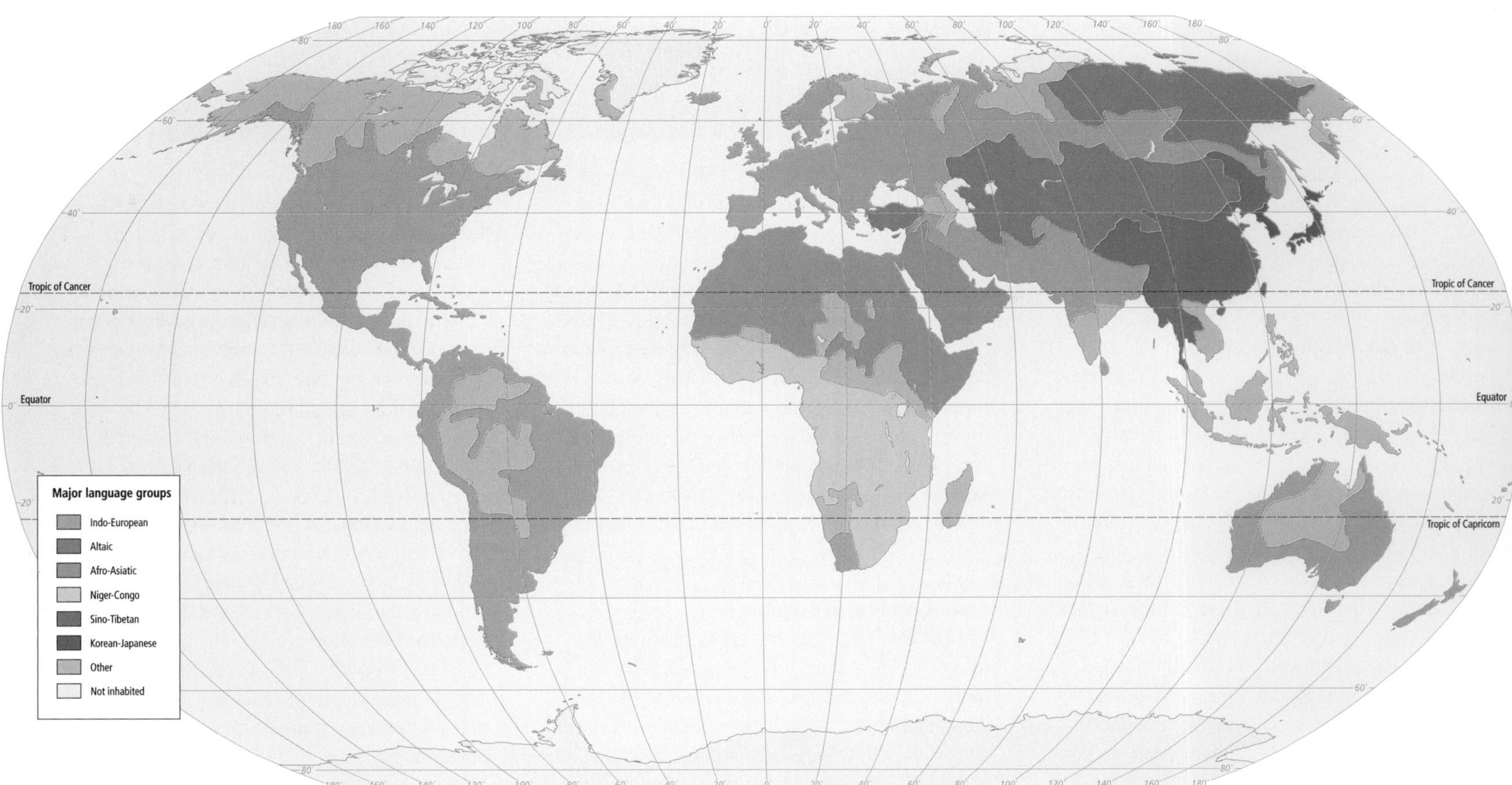

As a result of geographical isolation, the Papuan tribes that gather at traditional sing-sing ceremonies (left) may speak many different languages. Egyptian hieroglyphs (bottom) are a form of pictorial writing, whereas the Latin script on this tablet from the Coliseum (below) illustrates alphabetic writing.

as Austronesian), which includes Hawaiian, Javanese, and the languages of Madagascar, and Uralic, which includes Finnish, Hungarian, and the Samoyed language of Northern Siberia.

The first languages were disseminated in a number of ways. The most obvious was migration. As they spread out across the globe, early peoples carried their languages into uninhabited territory. Languages would also have spread as a result of contact between different peoples. For example, the invention and adoption of food production would have encouraged agricultural peoples to migrate into territory occupied by hunter–gatherers, who may then have adopted both the cultivation techniques and language of the immigrants.

A third form of language dissemination involves the replacement of an existing language by one spoken by a dominant group. The development of complex societies allowed incoming minorities with some form of centralized organization to dominate larger populations, who, in many cases, subsequently adopted the language of the elite. For example, the adoption of the Chinese language family in southern China in historical times occurred as a result of the military expansion of the Chinese empire.

The origins of writing

Writing is thought to have arisen around 5,000 to 6,000 years ago in Sumeria (southern Mesopotamia), and to have appeared shortly afterward in widely separate parts of the world, including Egypt (3000 BC), the Indus Valley (2500 BC), and China (2000 BC). Writing may have spread from Sumeria to the Indus and probably also to Egypt, but it was almost certainly independently invented in both China and, later, Mesoamerica, where it first appeared in the third century AD. Writing was unknown elsewhere in the Americas, even in the highly developed Inca civilization of the central Andes which flourished in the fifteenth century.

Scholars usually distinguish three broad kinds of writing systems, although in practice some systems combine elements of more than one kind. They are known as logographic, syllabic, and alphabetic writing.

In logographic writing, separate symbols are used to represent single words. This can complicate the representation of even simple statements. Because most of the symbols in logographic writing have, or originally had, a pictorial basis, it is believed that this is the earliest form of writing. Examples of logographic writing include early Sumerian cuneiform, Egyptian hieroglyphs, and modern Chinese characters.

In syllabic writing, symbols represent syllables. Examples of this type include later Sumerian cuneiform and the remarkable Cherokee syllabary developed by a Native American called Sequoyah in Arkansas in the early nineteenth century.

The third, and now most common, form of writing is alphabetic, in which symbols represent units of sound, or phonemes. Widespread alphabetic systems include Arabic, Roman (which is used for English and most other European languages), and Cyrillic (used for Russian and some other Slavic languages).

It has been suggested that these three types of writing reflect an evolutionary progression, from logographic to alphabetic; however, most scholars now regard this view as too simplistic. For instance, in a number of writing systems, logographic elements have been adopted, discarded, and then reintroduced.

The development of writing is closely associated with the rise of hierarchical societies. Literacy contributed to the formation of more complex state structures and bureaucratic institutions. In its early stages, it was often closely linked to religious activities and authorities. In Sumeria, for instance, the recording of economic transactions was controlled by religious officialdom. Writing also arose as a religious practice in Mesoamerica, remaining the preserve of the elite until the Spanish conquest in the sixteenth century.

THE RISE OF AGRICULTURE

Humanity's transition from a mobile life of hunting and gathering to a sedentary farming lifestyle in settled communities was not a sudden "revolution". It took place by degrees, with the dependence on cultivation increasing slowly as selective breeding modified wild plant species. Nevertheless, in terms of the prehistory of modern humans (100,000 years or so), the emergence of full-scale agriculture, which includes the development of both plant cultivation and animal husbandry, was relatively rapid.

It is probable that the cultivation of plants developed independently in a number of different regions, including the Fertile Crescent (a region stretching from present-day central Turkey southeastward through Iraq to the Persian Gulf), China, Mesoamerica (roughly present-day Mexico and Guatemala), and the Central Andes. Some scholars suggest that food production also originated in other centers such as New Guinea and West Africa.

Plant cultivation first occurred in the Fertile Crescent, where evidence for the domestication of grains such as wheat and barley, and other foods such as pulses and olives, begins to make an appearance in the archaeological record around 11,000 years ago. Flax was also cultivated as a source of fiber for making cloth. Although much of this area was then, as it is now, rocky and rather arid, the fertility of the river floodplains probably encouraged an increasing reliance on cultivation. In the region between the Tigris and Euphrates rivers in present-day Iraq, the development of canal-based irrigation allowed farming centers to flourish. From there, agricultural methods spread throughout the Mediterranean, across the Balkans, and along the Danube River into central Europe. By 7,000 years ago, farming was also firmly established in Egypt's Nile Valley.

Recent archaeological finds have indicated that plant cultivation may have begun in Asia not long after it began in the Fertile Crescent. For example, it is possible that rice was cultivated along the middle Yangtze of central China as early as 9,500 years ago. In northern China, there is evidence that millet and rapeseed were grown around the same time. Farming practices spread along the fertile floodplains of Chinese rivers, where many early sites have been found. At about the same time, local people also began to domesticate animals, including pigs, cattle, sheep, dogs, and chickens.

Food production may have arisen independently in at least two parts of the Americas. One of these is the Peruvian Andes, where beans were cultivated perhaps as early as 7,000 years ago. At around the same time, people in Mesoamerica also started to grow beans, together with squash and pumpkins. Maize, which became the most important staple, may not have been cultivated until more than a thousand years later. The early archaeological record is sparse in South America, but it appears that plants such as manioc, amaranths, peanuts, potatoes, cotton, and chili peppers were slowly domesticated in different parts of the continent.

Agriculture may have begun earlier in New Guinea. In the island's central highlands, archaeologists have discovered evidence of irrigation ditches in areas of swamp which date from around 9,000 years ago. They remain uncertain about the types of crops grown there, although taro and other native noncereal plants are likely candidates.

Foods and their origins

Most agricultural products were native to one part of the world and then spread gradually to other regions. The following list shows the origins of selected foods.

wheat	Fertile Crescent
potatoes	Central Andes
rice	China
maize	Mesoamerica
sugar	New Guinea
coffee	Ethiopia
tea	China
apples	Western Europe
oranges	Southeast Asia
sheep	Fertile Crescent
turkey	Mexico

The domestication of animals

Although the dog was domesticated somewhat earlier, the process of rearing animals for food—and later for clothing and as draft and pack animals—began at around the same time as plant cultivation. Many animals hunted by humans were unsuitable for breeding as a result of such factors as their diet, growth rate, ability to breed in captivity, or behavioral disposition. Domestication therefore had to proceed by trial and error, and gradually it modified many species.

Some animals, such as the wild pig and the auroch (a large, long-horned wild ox), were distributed over a wide area of Europe and Asia, and were probably domesticated independently in a number of places. Others, such as goats and sheep,

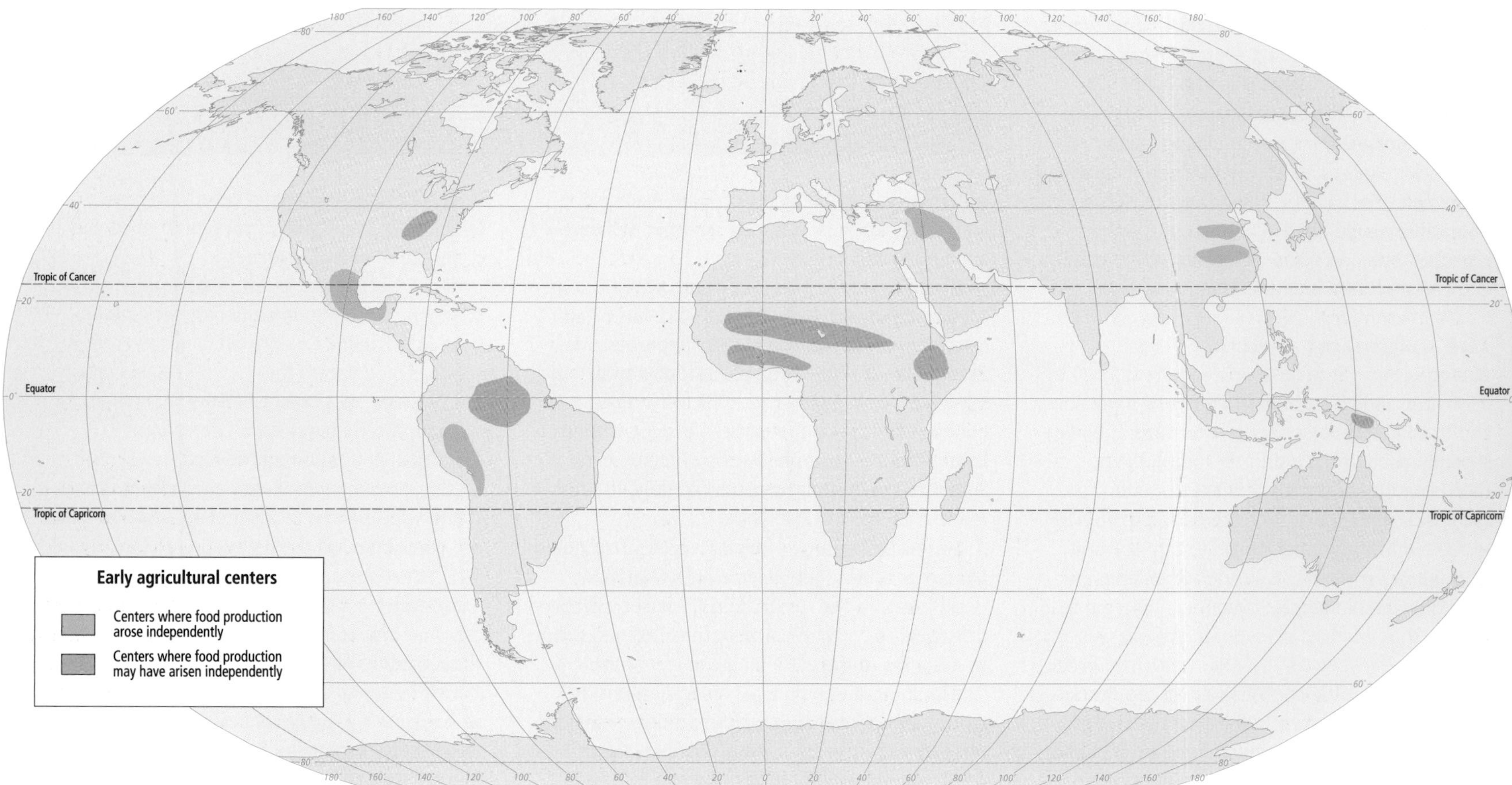

Food production began independently in China when rice was cultivated about 9,000 years ago in the valley of the Yangtze River. From there, rice cultivation spread throughout Southeast Asia, reaching Indonesia (left) about 4,000 years ago. The shift from hunting-gathering to agriculture resulted in the development of new technologies, including animal-driven pulley systems like the one on this well in Egypt (below).

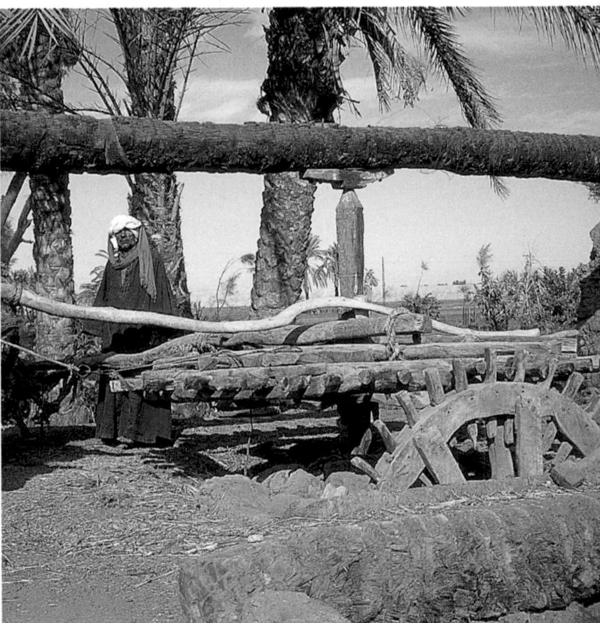

were confined largely to the Middle East and western Asia, and were later introduced into Europe. The people of the Andes domesticated llamas for use as pack animals and guinea pigs for food. The earliest evidence for the domestication of cats has been found in Greece. Cats were subsequently domesticated in many areas, usually to protect grain stores from rodents.

Why choose agriculture?

Not all communities switched to agriculture as soon as they came into contact with it. Many early peoples remained dependent on food collecting and hunting, and hunter-gatherer societies continue to exist to this day. These communities may modify their environment—for example, by burning vegetation to encourage growth that attracts game—and some also undertake minimal husbanding of plant resources, such as replanting rootstock cuttings and protecting fruit-bearing trees. But despite this and the fact that they may have often come into contact with people practicing agriculture, they have chosen not to switch to a sedentary lifestyle based on farming.

The reason for this is that subsisting as a hunter-gatherer usually requires less work than subsisting as a farmer. As long as population densities remain low, a food-collecting lifestyle can be more attractive and efficient, and provide a more balanced and diverse diet. In fact, scientists find it hard to explain why certain populations ever became totally dependent on farming. However, once the switch had been made, the demographic and social consequences of an agricultural lifestyle would have made it difficult to reverse the trend.

The consequences of agriculture

Agriculture transformed both human societies and landscapes. The need to make cultivation more efficient encouraged rapid technological innovations. The use of clay, which was already known in pre-agricultural times, became widespread and people began to make large receptacles for food and water. In turn, these receptacles transformed diets, as grains and pulses could be soaked and boiled, making them easier to eat and digest. Other innovations that emerged in agricultural societies were metalworking, the wheel (which improved the making of pots and stimulated progress in transport), and the use of sails on boats. Small copper objects have been found at early agricultural sites in the Middle East, but extensive metalworking and purification techniques were not developed until a few thousand years later.

Early agricultural societies were based on small village communities. As the range of domesticated plants and animals grew, the village economies became increasingly diverse and food production techniques improved. These developments enabled communities to create surpluses which could be used to support full-time craftspeople. Specialization led to internal barter and to trade with other communities. Items and commodities that were found or produced in only certain localities were traded over considerable distances. Social divisions also increased and, in many areas, complex hierarchies, headed by hereditary leaders, came into existence. In some societies, elite classes emerged who were able to devote their time to religious, cultural, and military pursuits while living off the surplus produced by subordinate groups.

Agriculture and demographics

Some scholars believe that population growth encouraged the adoption of agriculture, while others think that it was agriculture that triggered an increase in population. Although there is no firm demographic evidence to decide the question, archaeological research suggests that the number and size of settlements usually increased following the appearance of food production in a region.

Despite the attractions of new technologies, many communities, including the San of the Kalahari Desert in southwestern Africa, rejected agriculture and continue to follow a hunting-gathering lifestyle to this day (above right).

The rapid expansion of agriculture affected the environment, in some cases quite catastrophically. For example, archaeologists have found that the barren landscape of modern Greece is the result of more than 5,000 years of farming, during which deforestation and land clearance led to the loss of topsoil and severe soil erosion.

EMERGING CIVILIZATIONS

The first civilizations arose on the fertile alluvial basins of major rivers such as the Tigris-Euphrates in Iraq, the Nile in Egypt, the Indus in Pakistan, and the Yellow (Huang Ho) in China. These regions shared many common features, including arid environments that made agricultural communities dependent on irrigation, and readily available supplies of raw materials such as stone, metal, and wood. The Tigris-Euphrates, Nile, and Indus regions were probably linked by trade well before the appearance of the early cities, but Chinese civilization developed in relative isolation.

The first urban societies

Cities emerged in all four regions during the third millennium BC as villages and towns slowly grew into cities with large public buildings and developed specialized and well-organized production and trade, forms of writing, hierarchical social structures, and centralized political systems. This process of evolution varied, although the cultural attributes of emerging cities were similar.

In most cases, cities arose following the emergence of a social elite. As a class or family became dominant, it usually sought to create a power base in one region. This power base attracted immigrants and businesses, resulting in the rapid growth of the urban community. Scholars have suggested various reasons for the emergence of social elites. Some propose that the construction and maintenance of the large-scale irrigation works needed to support a growing population would have required considerable organization and encouraged the development of a managerial class. Others emphasize the role of specialized production and trade in creating a dominant commercial class. Another explanation is the growing influence of warfare: as settlements were overrun by invading peoples, their inhabitants were often forced to become the subjects of their conquerors. It was probably a combination of all these factors that led to the development of the first "upper classes" and the first sophisticated urban societies.

The pyramids at Giza in Egypt (below) were built during the Fourth Dynasty to house the remains of the rulers Khufu, Khafra, and Menkaure.

Cradles of civilization

In the region between the Tigris and Euphrates rivers known as Mesopotamia, farming gradually became more productive, canals were built, large temple platforms (called ziggurats) were erected, and the cuneiform script was simplified and standardized. Crafts, such as pottery and metalwork, became more specialized and production more organized, leading to greater social divisions in society. The city-states had their own monarchs, and were often heavily fortified. Their ascendancy came to an end, however, around 2350 BC, when Sargon, a military ruler from Agade in central Mesopotamia, forcibly amalgamated them into the Akkadian empire.

In Egypt, by contrast, it was the unification of the cities and towns of Upper and Lower Egypt at the beginning of the third millennium that caused civilization to flourish, giving rise to a well-developed political and administrative system, writing, and a complex religion. During this period, the massive stone pyramids of Giza were constructed to preserve the bodies, knowledge, and wealth of the Egyptian kings in the afterlife. The pyramids also symbolized the structure of Egyptian society, with the god-king at the apex, officials in the middle levels, and the mass of the population at the bottom.

The emergence of the Indus civilization was marked by the appearance of distinctive artistic styles in pottery, copper, and bronze (a copper-tin alloy). These objects were traded with nomadic pastoral peoples who, in turn, transported the merchandise into central Asia and along the coast of the Arabian Sea. Around 2400 BC, the different cultural traditions of the Indus merged into one, called Harappa by archaeologists after the first city to be excavated in this region. Harappa culture had writing, a form of centralized control for administration and commerce, and large buildings made out of baked brick. In contrast to other early civilizations, however, Harappan society does not seem to have included a priest-king class, nor did its spread depend on military conquest.

In China, it is likely that villages merged to form states in several areas, but legend and archaeological evidence locate the first civilization, that of the Xia, in the middle and lower valleys of the Yellow River, from about the end of the third millennium BC. Texts written much later suggest that the Xia united a number of groups in a loose confederation. One of these was the Shang, who gained ascendancy in the second millennium BC. They developed an early form of Chinese script and expanded their territory through military campaigns. They were defeated by the Zhou, another Xia confederate, at the end of the second millennium BC.

Culture and trade

The expansion of civilizations was assisted by trade and migration as well as conquest. Trade routes in particular allowed knowledge and practices to be dispersed across sometimes vast distances. They were particularly significant in the expansion of Chinese culture into Southeast Asia, and in the

These bas-reliefs (left), which date from about 500 BC, decorate the walls of the ancient Mesopotamian city of Persepolis. Greek city-states such as Athens (bottom) emerged around 750 BC. At that time, Teotihuacán (below) in Mesoamerica was one of the largest cities in the world.

spread of Egyptian and Middle Eastern traditions as far as North Africa, southern Asia, and Europe.

The first major European civilization emerged in Crete at the end of the third millennium BC. The Minoans, whose powerful navy controlled the Aegean Sea for much of the second millennium BC, constructed large cities centered on elaborate palaces including those at Knossos, Malia, and Phaistos. Later, urban societies also sprang up on the Greek mainland, the most notable being the Mycenean civilization, which came to prominence during the late second millennium BC. Classical Greek civilization emerged during the first millennium BC in a number of self-governing cities such as Athens and Sparta. These urban societies were distinguished by the formal constitutions that directed their political life and by the increasing power held by the male citizenry at the expense of a centralized leadership.

Civilizations also developed independently, but much later, among the agricultural communities of Mesoamerica and the central Andes. Mesoamerican civilizations emerged during the first millennium BC. The most important was that of the Maya, who developed a form of writing around AD 300. The Maya maintained commercial ties to city-states developing elsewhere in the region. One of these, Teotihuacán, in central Mexico, was an important trade center with a population that peaked at more than 100,000 around AD 600. During the same period, several interrelated civilizations existed in the central Andes, with territories that are now in present-day Peru and Bolivia. These societies created monumental buildings and elaborate crafts, but left no evidence of any written languages.

The meaning of "civilization"

In eighteenth-century Europe, "civilization" meant cultural refinement—the opposite of barbarism. Nineteenth-century social philosophers found this meaning too restrictive, so they used the term in the plural sense to refer to large-scale societies. This usage is followed by present-day sociologists and anthropologists.

Human societies can be classified in terms of their size and complexity. Small-scale or tribal societies comprise small bands loosely coordinated by kinship relations. These groups often live together at permanent settlements, although some may be nomadic. Medium-sized communities are usually made up of clusters of villages or small towns united under some form of confederation or chiefdom. In large-scale societies, at least some of the inhabitants live in large urban societies which are linked by a network of social, economic, and cultural ties, and normally unified under a centralized political organization.

Early Mesopotamian artworks such as this ivory carving often include portraits of members of the ruling elite.

THE IMPACT OF CIVILIZATION

The main impetus for rapid progress over the past few thousand years was the development of large-scale urban societies. Their benefits in enriching human experience through technological innovation, scientific knowledge, and diversity in social life appear obvious. Certain consequences of civilization were less benign, however. These include the increasing destructiveness of warfare, the spread of disease, and the life-long bondage imposed on certain classes of people.

Innovation and adaptation

Many thousands of years elapsed between the development of specialized stone and bone tool assemblages and the beginnings of food production. After the adoption of agriculture and a sedentary lifestyle, however, the widespread diffusion of the latest innovations occurred remarkably rapidly. This was partly due to the obvious usefulness of the technology. Many inventions were developed in one location and then rapidly dispersed because of their immediate utility. The wheel, for example, appears to have been invented near the Black Sea around 3400 BC, and within a few hundred years, it was being used throughout Europe and Asia.

Another reason for the exponential growth of technology was that new inventions were rapidly adapted to diverse local needs. For example, shortly after the emergence of the wheel, innovations based on this technology—such as pulleys, water wheels, and windmills—appeared and then spread quickly along ever-expanding trade routes.

Some innovations, however, did not travel as extensively as may be expected. For example, the wheel was probably also invented independently in Mesoamerica, where it was used in children's toys, but it was never adopted for transportation in this region due to the lack of draft animals. Nor did the wheel spread from Mesoamerica to South America, even though the people of the Andes had the Americas' only beast of burden—the llama—and despite the fact that technologies such as metallurgy had already spread northward from the Andes to Mesoamerica.

Technology and warfare

New technologies led to the expansion of production and, consequently, an increase in the size of urban populations. As cities grew in size, conflict over land with neighboring agricultural and pastoral peoples often led to warfare. In turn, this stimulated the manufacture of weaponry.

Early weapons were made of bronze, but by the beginning of the first millennium BC, iron weapons were being widely produced in the Fertile Crescent, and smelting techniques, which produced an early form of steel, were already well understood there. By 500 BC, iron tools and weapons were widespread throughout Europe and Asia. However, ironworking did not appear in the Americas until after the Spanish conquests of the sixteenth century. The devastating effectiveness of steel weaponry was demonstrated by the Spanish conquest of the Incas. In 1532, the conquistador Pizzaro, with an army of only 168 soldiers, was able to defeat the Inca army of more than 80,000 soldiers and capture their emperor Atahualpa.

Monuments to royalty, such as the massive temple of Abu Simbel in Egypt (above) built during the reign of Ramses II (1279–1213 BC), reflect both the development of technology and the emergence of complex social hierarchies.

The Spanish soldiers had chain mail, helmets, steel swords, lances, daggers, and horses, whereas the Inca army was protected by quilted padding, armed with blunt clubs, and traveled on foot.

Science and disease

Although many advances in the domestication of plants and animals and in technology were the result of accidental discoveries or trial and error, written records indicate that early civilizations were making careful observations of natural phenomena. For example, the Maya developed a calendar based on the solar year and lunar month, and could predict eclipses—a feat that required advanced mathematical skills. The Egyptians acquired considerable medical knowledge and surgical skills. Among the sophisticated techniques they developed was the practice of trepanation. This involved the cutting of bone in the skull to relieve pressure on the brain resulting from a skull fracture, or to treat headaches or epilepsy.

A sedentary lifestyle enabled ailing individuals to receive better care than

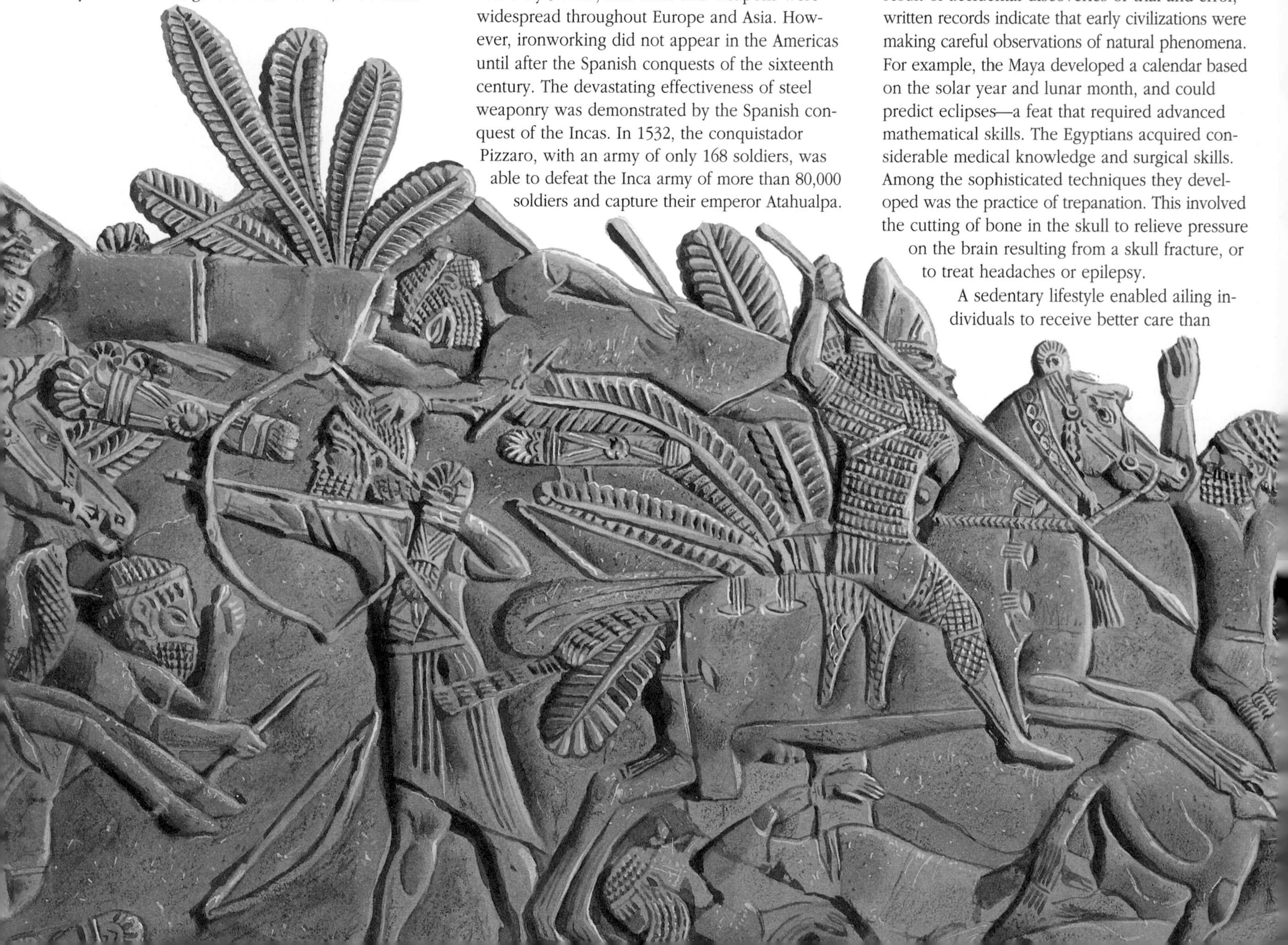

Invented in western Asia, the wheel was rapidly adapted to create devices such as the water wheel (below). As a result of their preference for cooler climates, llamas (left) never spread northward to Mesoamerica. Sophisticated socieities such as that of the Maya (bottom) thus remained without pack animals.

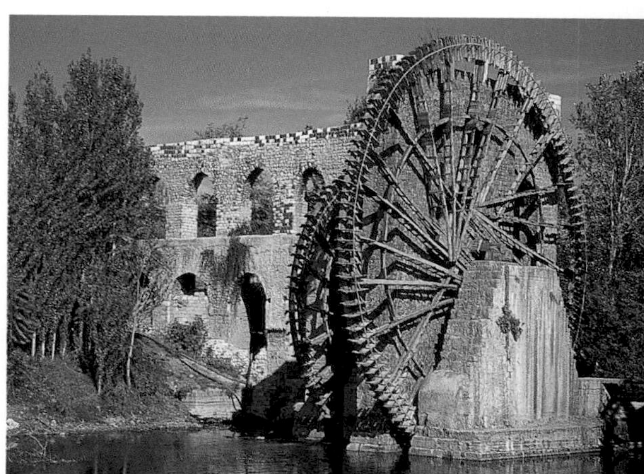

they would receive if they remained nomadic. However, large concentrations of people living in close proximity to domestic animals and (initially, at least) dependent on a relatively limited range of foods created the perfect environment for the spread of disease. When human populations are small and move frequently, the opportunities for parasitic infections to spread are limited. Urban lifestyles, in contrast, with their permanent housing and large refuse dumps, attract disease-carrying vermin and insects, and allow parasites to spread more quickly. Land clearance, irrigation, and the use of natural fertilizers would also have encouraged certain diseases in sedentary communities, particularly where diets were deficient and the population less resilient. Even more significant was the domestication of animals. Today, people associate animals with diseases such as rabies, anthrax, and parasitic worms, but domestic animals were also the original source of infections that are now commonly transmitted by humans, such as smallpox, measles, and influenza.

The spread of disease was encouraged by trade, migration, and conquest. For example, bubonic plague is thought to have been restricted to Asia until it was spread to other parts of the world by traders. When it reached Europe in the mid-fourteenth century, it wiped out one quarter of the population. Diseases carried by conquering armies were often more destructive than their military campaigns. For example, in 1520, the Spaniards under Cortés inadvertently brought smallpox to the Aztecs, causing a massive epidemic that killed more than half the population and led to the demise of the empire.

As civilizations grew and technology spread, warfare, as depicted in this bas-relief from Nineveh in Assyria, became more sophisticated and more commonplace.

Social hierarchies

The increasing division of labor and the steady enhancement of specialized skills in urban communities led to the development of ever-more sophisticated social hierarchies. People directly involved in food production—the commoners—were often obliged to provide tribute payments to a centralized authority. This did not necessarily mean that commoners were physically separated from the elite—in many early cities, they lived in close proximity to each other and even shared in decision-making. But as urban populations increased and relationships became more complex, so the social distinctions became more marked.

In China, for instance, the Shang, and later the Zhou, administered a feudal system of vassal states. Members of the royal clan, and others who assisted the king, were granted fiefdoms over parts of the kingdom. Below these nobles and loyal administrators were the farmers from whose ranks the soldiers were recruited. At the lowest end of the social scale were the slaves, who were usually nomadic pastoralists captured by the ruling elite. This pattern of enslaving captives was common in these evolving nation-states, probably because mass production and large-scale public works provided many uses for slaves in menial occupations.

Domestic horses

Today's domestic horses are descended from wild species native to southern Russia. Horses were first domesticated there around 4000 BC—much later than most other domestic animals—and before long had become the principal means of transportation throughout much of Asia and Europe. Horses transformed warfare, providing formidable military advantages when yoked to battle chariots or ridden. At the same time, however, they transmitted several diseases to humans, including tetanus and the common cold.

Mongolian horses are the only surviving relatives of the species from which all domestic horses are descended.

FROM CITY-STATES TO EMPIRES

There is no doubt that warfare was a part of human experience long before historical records were kept—even the small-scale societies of Melanesia that existed at the time of the first European contact were involved in frequent and violent tribal conflicts. However, the scale, range, and destructiveness of war increased significantly with the development of the first states. High population density, advances in transport and weapons technology, centralized decision-making, and a new fervor among troops willing to die for a powerful leader allowed extensive resources to be mobilized for warfare. This in turn meant that military engagements could take place much farther from home. Whereas war had previously involved only the annexation of adjacent territories from enemies who had either been chased away, killed, or enslaved, now they could lead to the amalgamation of entire societies into larger political units. Furthermore, the subjugated peoples could be forced to pay tribute, thereby increasing the ruler's resources for further campaigns. In this way, empires were born.

The rise of empires greatly enhanced the diffusion of knowledge, ideas, technology, languages, and cultural traditions. It also expanded trade links and imposed administrative and political unity on previously dispersed communities, laying the foundations for future nation-states.

There are three broad reasons why rulers of small city-states and medium-sized kingdoms ventured into empire-building. One was to create alliances that would provide protection against an external threat—the formation of the Chinese Empire is a good example of this. Another reason was to subdue a persistent enemy—this is why Alexander the Great began his conquests. The third was to acquire control over desired commodities, trade routes, and other resources—Roman expansion can be explained in this way. All three reasons influenced most expansionist ambitions, but one tended to be more dominant than the others in the building of individual empires.

The threat from the north

By the third century BC, the Zhou kingdom of northeastern China was breaking up, having been weakened by years of attacks perpetrated by warring tribal peoples to the north and northwest. Following the collapse of the kingdom, wars broke out between rival states and various alliances were formed and severed. Eventually, one of the Zhou vassal states, the Qin (221–206), gained ascendancy and brought the other states under their control. They then set about uniting the states into a single Chinese empire. The principle objective of this policy was to secure Qin territory against the foreign invaders that had plagued the Zhou. To ensure the protection of the empire, the Qin began to construct an enormous physical barrier to invasion by linking defensive structures originally built during the Zhou period. The Great Wall, as this barrier came to be known, would eventually stretch 3,000 km (1,860 miles) across northern China. The Qin also built an extensive network of highways and canals to improve communications throughout their empire.

Following the death of the first emperor, the Qin Empire was taken over by the Han in 206 BC. The Han expanded their empire further south beyond the floodplains of the Yellow (Huang Ho) and Yangtze rivers, and also defeated tribes to the west. This helped silk merchants to create a new trade route through central Asia which eventually extended all the way to Europe.

Alexander the Great

The rise of the Persian Empire in the sixth century BC posed a significant threat to Greek city-states such as Athens and Sparta. They responded by forming strategic alliances, which they managed to maintain long enough to defeat the Persians during the following century. However, subsequent disputes between the cities allowed Philip II of Macedon to take advantage of their disunity and unite Greece with Macedonia in 338 BC. In the following year, Philip declared war on Persia to revenge the Persian devastation of Greece, but before the war could begin he was assassinated.

Philip was succeeded by his son, Alexander, who realized his father's plans to crush Greece's formidable enemy. He successfully engaged the Persian army in Turkey and the eastern Mediterranean, moved westward to Egypt where he founded the city of Alexandria, and finally crushed the Persians in a decisive battle at Gaugamela in Mesopotamia in 331 BC. His conquests continued to the Indus River before he turned back, only to die suddenly at the age of 33 in Mesopotamia in 323 BC. Alexander's vast empire was divided up between his generals, and, without a strong leader, it soon disintegrated, although the kingdoms of Egypt, Persia, and Macedonia persisted.

Despite his short reign, Alexander left a long-lasting legacy. His decision to take scholars and scientists on his campaigns ensured that Greek learning, language, and cultural traditions were disseminated widely. He founded a number of Hellenic cities with Greeks and Macedonians, the most notable being Alexandria, which became a renowned center of learning.

Although the Greek city-states had previously established trade centers throughout the northern Mediterranean, they had largely left the southern shore to the Phoenicians. Alexander's conquests extended Hellenistic influence into North Africa and the Middle East. In this way, Alexander imposed a cultural unity on the Mediterranean region which stimulated trade and learning and which later played a significant part in the advancement of the Roman Empire.

The Roman Empire

In the seventh century BC, Rome was one of several small towns in the Tiber Valley that were situated on a strategically important road leading to saltworks at the mouth of the Tiber River. During the following two centuries, Rome gained control of neighboring territories, including the valuable saltworks, and became a potent force in local politics and commerce. Like other Mediterranean cities in that era, Rome was strongly influenced by Greek culture, but it never came under Greek control.

In the fifth century BC, Rome became a republic ruled by a Senate formed by an aristocratic clique. From that time, Rome gradually expanded its territory to encompass the whole of the Italic peninsula—while Alexander was conquering Persia, Rome was winning decisive battles for the control of southern Italy.

Success in southern Italy encouraged the Romans to seize Sicily, which was then under the

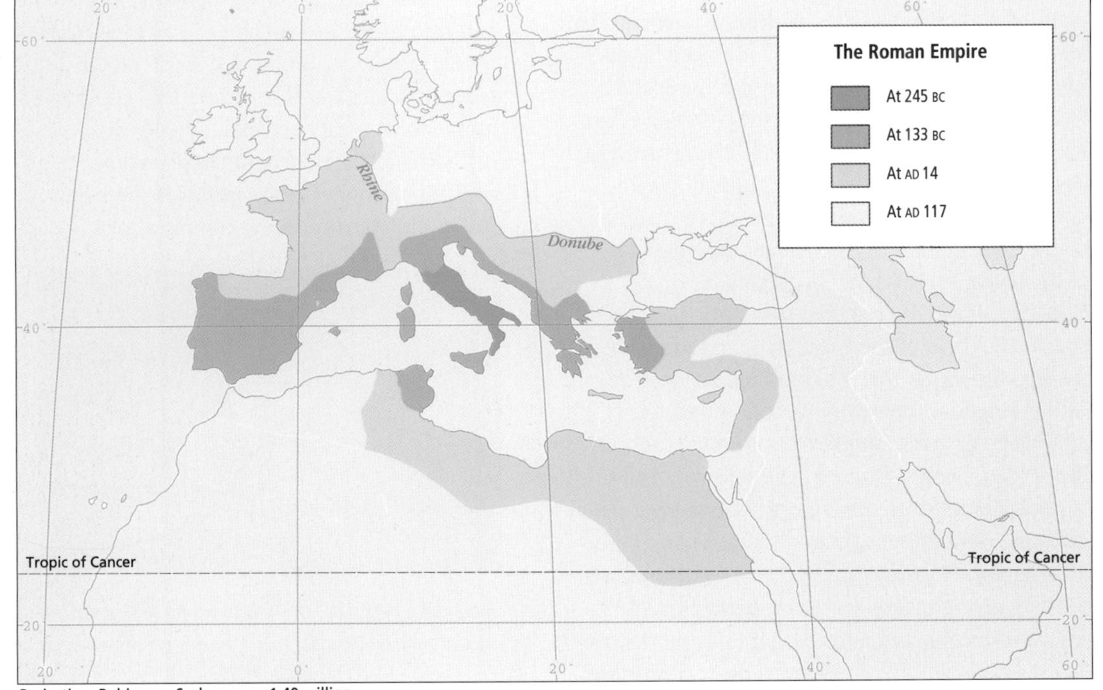

This map (left) shows the gradual expansion of the Roman Empire, which reached its greatest extent during the reign of Trajan (AD 98–117). Construction of the Great Wall of China (right) began during the Qin Empire (221–206 BC). Extensive sections of the wall were rebuilt during the 15th and 16th centuries.

influence of the North African city of Carthage. Over the next 100 years, the Romans fought three major wars—known as the Punic Wars—against Carthage to gain control of the western Mediterranean. By the end of the Third Punic War (146 BC), Carthage had been completely destroyed and Rome had emerged as by far the strongest force in the region. The empire subsequently extended eastward to Greece and the Middle East, where it benefited greatly from Greek advances in art, learning, and technology. Later still, the empire expanded to include large areas of present-day France, Germany, and England, spreading Hellenic culture and Roman political and social institutions across most of Europe.

During the first century BC, the Roman Empire expanded rapidly. Under Pompey, Roman armies seized parts of the Middle East, including Syria (above) in 64 BC; in the west, Julius Caesar (above right) led the conquest of Gaul in 58–50 BC. Both generals subsequently laid claim to the title of emperor. Victory in a short civil war allowed Caesar to begin his reign in 48 BC.

RELIGIONS OF THE WORLD

Religions are a feature of almost all of the world's cultures. They have been the inspiration for much of the world's great art, music, architecture, and literature, but also the source of longstanding disputes and local, regional, and international conflicts.

The tenets and forms of religious belief vary widely. While most religions involve the worship of a deity or deities, supreme beings play only a minor role in some faiths such as Theravada Buddhism. Nor do all religions have practices, core doctrines, and moral codes that are common to every follower. For example, while Hinduism retains a self-identity developed historically through confrontation with other religious traditions such as Buddhism, Islam, and Christianity, it remains extremely diverse internally.

The great majority of the world's religions evolved among particular peoples who had no interest in attracting converts. Few tribal peoples, for instance, would attempt to persuade their neighbors to adopt their religious beliefs and practices. Similarly, some prominent religions such as Hinduism and Judaism make no effort to seek converts. However, religion is frequently the cause of great social conflict, particularly where two or more proselytizing religions are in competition. Even within religions that have a core doctrine, comparatively minor differences of faith or practice can cause bitter divisions—past tensions between Christian denominations are a good example of this. Frequently, religious conflicts are aggravated by historical factors and by the extent to which religious divisions are overlaid by other divisions, such as language, ethnicity, and class.

Ethnic religions 4.0%
Sikhs 0.4%
Judaism 0.3%
Christianity 33.0%
Islam 4.0%
Other 4.7%
Buddhism 6.0%
Chinese folk religions 6.2%
Hinduism 12.8%
No religion 13.0%

World religions

One-third of the world's population identify themselves as Christians, with about half belonging to the Roman Catholic Church. The next largest religious group is Islam, which includes nearly one-fifth of the world's population. These two major faiths are monotheistic—that is, they are based on the belief that there is only one God—and both developed out of Judaism. Hinduism, a non-proselytizing religion followed by almost 13 percent of the world's population, is the third largest faith. Buddhism, which is the third largest proselytizing religion, has approximately 325 million adherents.

Judaism was originally the tribal religion of a people who traced themselves back to Abraham. Abraham is said to have migrated with his clan from the city of Ur in Mesopotamia to Canaan in the eastern Mediterranean. His descendants moved to Egypt, where they were later enslaved, and were then led back to Canaan by Moses around 1200 BC. Although Judaism has a comparatively small number of contemporary adherents (around 14 million), it is significant both for its role in the development of Christianity and Islam and for its continuing influence on cultural and historical events.

This pie chart shows the percentages of the world's population belonging to the major religions. Despite their small number, the Jews (above right) have had a major influence on history, culture, and other religions.

Christianity originated as a movement within Judaism. Fundamental to its doctrine is the belief that Jesus Christ was the Messiah prophesied in the Old Testament. After Christ's crucifixion, Christian doctrines were disseminated throughout the Mediterranean by the apostles and by missionaries, the most prominent of whom was Saint Paul (also known as Saul of Tarsus). Christianity then spread throughout the Roman Empire, first among Jewish communities and then into the general population.

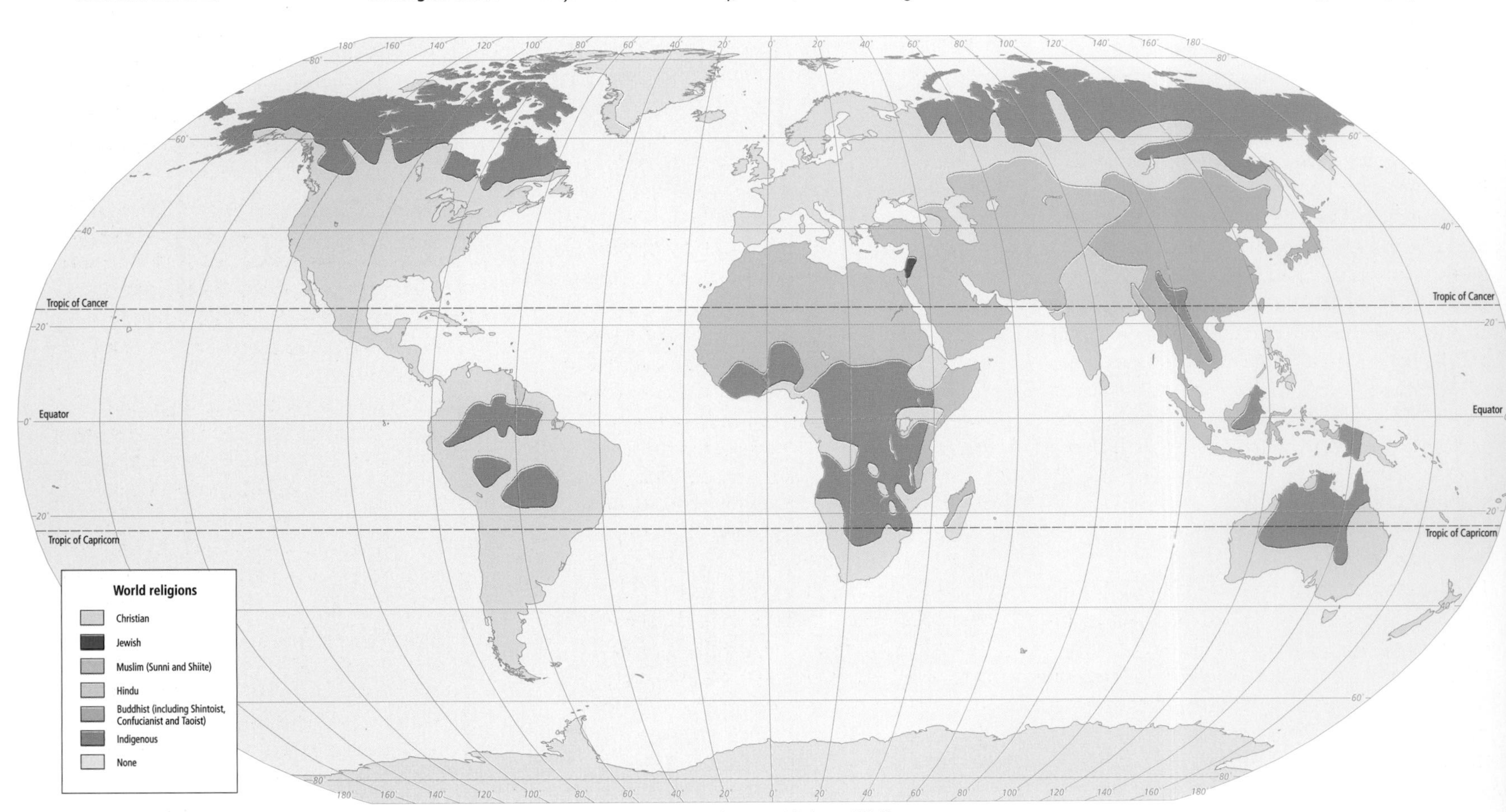

Christianity spread rapidly through Europe after the fall of the Roman Empire; churches can be found all over Britain (left). Tibetan Buddhism (below) is based on a tradition called Tantric Buddhism which emerged in India in the seventh century AD. Islam spread to Southeast Asia along trade routes, reaching Malaysia (below left) in the fourteenth century.

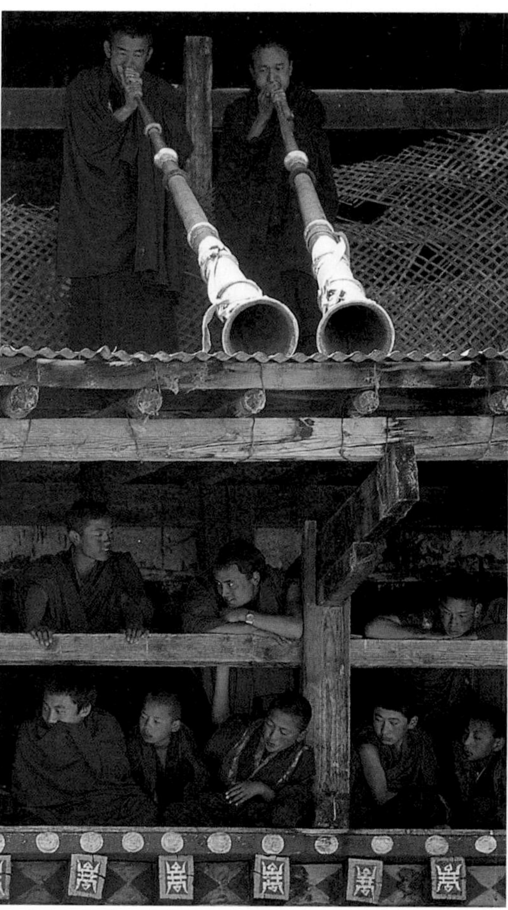

Early persecution of Christians by the Romans gave way to tolerance early in the fourth century AD when the emperor Constantine converted and Christianity became the official state religion. Christianity continued to spread after the fall of the empire in the fifth century, reaching most of Europe by the end of the first millennium. Later, particularly during the era of European expansion in the fifteenth and sixteenth centuries, missionary activity disseminated Christianity to other parts of the world. Over the centuries, theological disputes have resulted in major schisms, out of which have grown the Orthodox, Catholic, Protestant, and other traditions.

Islam was founded early in the seventh century AD by Muhammad, a merchant from the prosperous Arabian city of Mecca. Muhammad had contact with both Jewish and Christian communities, and he came to regard the Judaeo-Christian prophets, including Christ, as forerunners of Islam. After receiving revelations about the worship of one God (Allah), Muhammad began to preach against the polytheistic practices of his home city. Persecution then forced him and his followers to flee to Medina. This migration (Hegira), which took place in AD 622, marks the beginning of the Muslim calendar. By the time of his death in AD 632, Muhammad had become the political and spiritual leader of much of Arabia. After his death, Muslims expanded their territory beyond the Arabian peninsula. At its peak, the Arab Empire stretched from Spain and Morocco in the west to Afghanistan and central Asia in the east, but the Islamic religion was carried even farther into Asia and Africa by Muslim traders.

Eastern deities

Hinduism has its roots in Vedism, the religion of the Indo-European peoples who inhabited northern India during the second millennium BC. The religion's sacred texts are the Vedas which explore humankind's place in the cosmos and describe the roles played by various gods in the functioning of the universe. During the first millennium AD, cults associated with two of these deities, Vishnu and

Shiva, spread throughout the continent. Hinduism has a large and faithful following among the diverse peoples of the Indian subcontinent, but it has relatively few adherents elsewhere, except among the descendants of Indian emigrants. This is in part due to its non-proselytizing nature.

Like Christianity and Islam, Buddhism, the third major proselytizing religion, is also based on the religious enlightenment experienced by one man. However, it has much earlier origins. According to tradition, Siddhartha Gautama lived in northeastern India in the sixth century BC, and was reared in the royal household. In his adulthood, Siddhartha is said to have sought enlightenment, which he achieved through a night of meditation, thereby becoming the Buddha or Awakened One. For 45 years he traveled India as an itinerant teacher while formalizing his religious precepts. His teachings spread into southern Asia, where the first Buddhist tradition, the Theravada (meaning "doctrine of the elders"), still prevails in Sri Lanka, Myanmar, Cambodia, Laos, and Thailand. However, it retains few followers in India. Buddhism also spread to the east (Tibet, China, and Japan), where the second tradition, Mahayana (meaning "great vehicle") Buddhism, emerged in the second century BC. A more liberal tradition, Mahayana is said to express greater compassion and social concern than the more aloof Theravada Buddhism.

What is religion?

Scholars have found it extremely difficult to come up with a definition that will allow a clear-cut distinction between religious and non-religious phenomena. In broad terms, religion covers the beliefs and associated practices that focus on the relationship between humans and the supernatural, represented by a god or gods. These beliefs and practices address the ultimate questions of human existence, providing a sense of meaning and purpose to life. Frequently, they also create a feeling of fellowship and community with others who share the same beliefs and practices.

Approached in these terms, religions or religious activity can be found in all, or nearly all, eras and places, although the emphasis placed on religion by particular communities may vary greatly. Scholars have sometimes been surprised to discover that certain tribal or peasant peoples, who might have been assumed to be preoccupied with religion, are in fact relatively indifferent to it.

Religious practices may also have their origins in the need to regulate or control communities. Religion may enforce "taboo" or unacceptable behavior in order to preserve a peaceful and sustainable society.

TRADERS AND TRAVELERS

Humans moved from place to place either individually or in groups long before written records existed. The earliest records show they were impelled by a desire to occupy more fertile areas, by a desire for booty, by an urge to trade, by religious piety which took them on pilgrimages, by a thirst for knowledge, and sometimes by the fear of invasion.

Before the Christian era, Buddhism led monks from the East to travel to India to visit sites where Gautama had been. Nearly 2,000 years later, Ibn Battuta, an Islamic qadi (religious judge), after setting out in AD 1325 to go to Mecca, as all good Mohammedans sought to do, found that he could not rest until he had visited every Muslim state in Asia, Africa, and Europe. Although on his return to Fez, the sultan's court was incredulous at Battuta's stories, they were written down, and in such ways knowledge of the world was spread.

The spread and decline of empires

The growth of empires fostered trade and treaties, both with neighbors and with more distant powers. The Han Empire in China, for example, traded with Phoenicians, Carthaginians, Syrians, and the Roman Empire in silks, iron, furs, glass, and other exotic goods. Merchants also brought back knowledge—in the first century AD, a Greek navigator wrote of the Indian Ocean, where Hindu traders competed with merchants from the Red Sea and Arabs dealing in wax and ivory, rhinoceros horns, tortoiseshell, and palm oil.

However, nomads were always pressing at the frontiers of such empires, seeking to loot and ransack. Loose confederations of "barbarians"—as the civilized empires considered them—hungry for plunder, breached the defences. The Roman Empire bought their "barbarians" off for a time by settling some on the borders, as confederates, to keep out other tribes, but eventually pressures caused the empire's defences to tumble. In AD 410, Rome itself was overrun.

The influx of mixed Germanic tribes was precipitated by the driving force of the Huns, who, according to the Goths, were the offspring of witches and evil spirits. No one knows where they originated. From the Carpathian mountains, however, they moved into the Mediterranean region and, by AD 450, under Attila, were poised to crush and drive out the Goths. Then their alliances crumbled, and they disappeared from Europe as quickly as they had come.

Instead, waves of Ostrogoths, Visigoths, Franks, and Saxons arrived and settled in England, France, Spain, Italy, and parts of North Africa, mixing with the local inhabitants, quarrelling amongst themselves and moving on to settle in new areas.

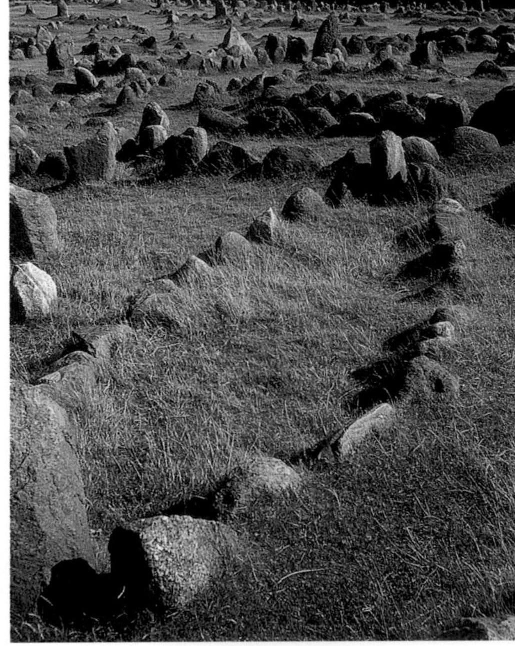

The Arab Empire

While Western Europe was fragmented and trade was declining, in the East, the Byzantine Empire remained the bulwark of Christianity against the rising Arab Empire. Mohammed's followers were spurred on by the idea of jihad, or holy war, which combined religion with military exploits. After taking Syria and Egypt, they swept along the North African coast, took the Maghrib, and crossed into Spain. They attacked Byzantium by sea and blockaded Constantinople between AD 673 and 678. In the eighth century, the caliphs of Damascus and Baghdad ruled an empire that stretched from Persia to Morocco.

The Arabs were also starting to dominate Africa by the eighth century. The peoples of the plateau between the Niger and the Benin had mined and used gold and copper, and later iron, long before Christ. Exotic archaeological finds and the presence of Asian food plants clearly show that trade began early in these areas. Tribal organization became more sophisticated, in order to control and tax trade and the trade routes. By the eighth century, empires such as Ghana had emerged. The Arabs had been pushing their way down the east coast of Africa well before Mohammed. They visited trading posts such as Sofala and dealt with the inland kingdoms, exchanging exotic goods for gold. After AD 700, they began colonizing the coast, establishing settlements such as Mogadishu and Mombasa. They also moved south across the Sahara, and established Arabic kingdoms.

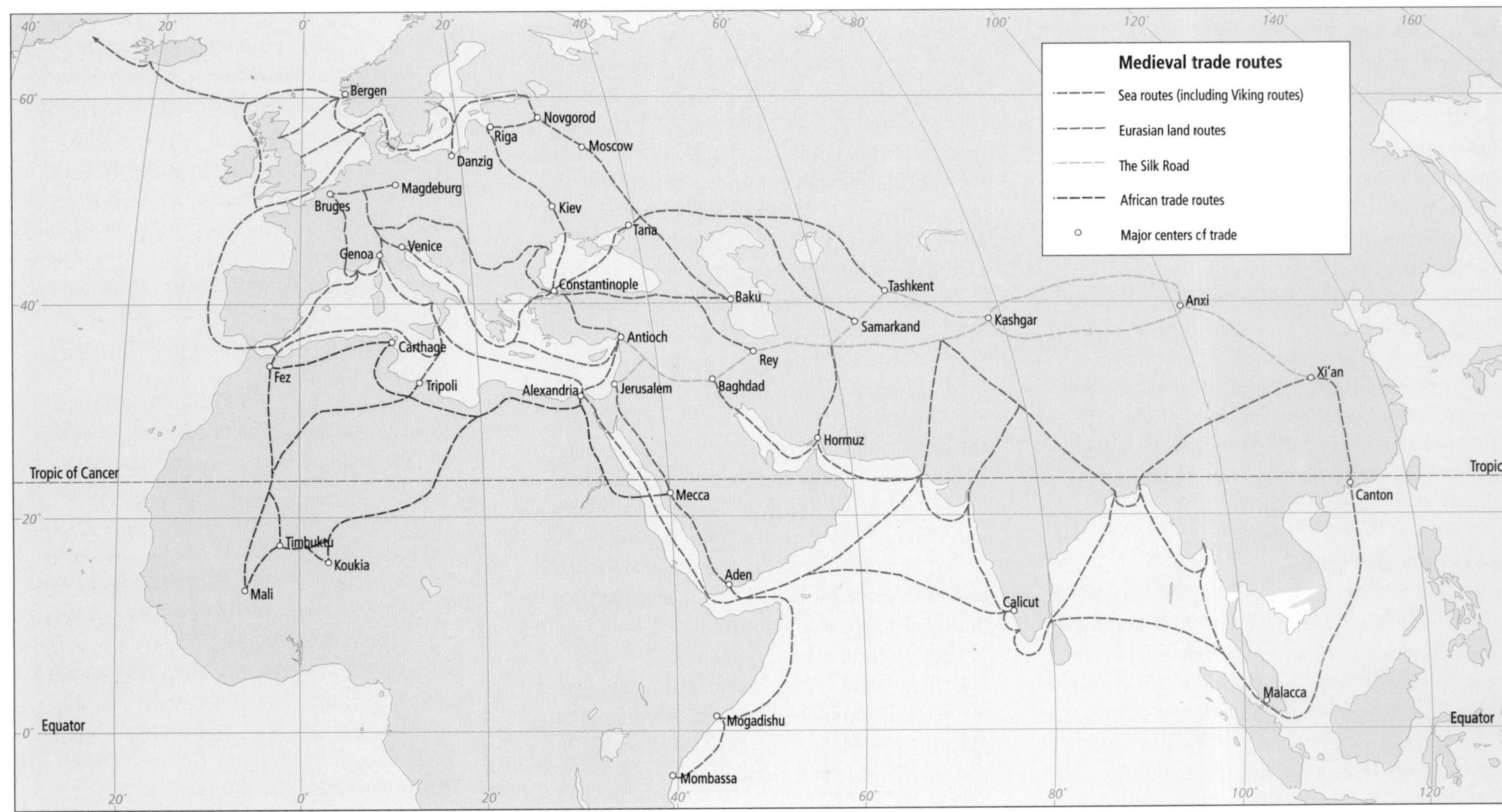

Projection: Robinson Scale approx 1:70 million

Viking graves in Denmark (far left) are a reminder of the early European territorial wars. Khiva (left) was a trading post on the trade route between East and West. Zanzibar (below), an island south of Mombasa, was for many years the center of the slave trade in Africa. Venice today (bottom) is not the major trading power it was in the thirteenth century.

The Arabs next pushed east across the Indian Ocean, carrying Islam to India and overwhelming the Hindu trading colonies of Sumatra, Java, and Borneo, and eventually acquiring a firm footing in Canton and other major Chinese cities.

The Chinese Empire

In the period after the Han, successive empires had been established in China, some ruled by nomad invaders. The Tang had subdued their neighbors and ruled from Korea to the frontiers of Persia. They had also established extensive links with the West. When Canton was sacked in 879, the slaughtered included large numbers of Nestorian Christians, Arabs, Jews, and Zoroastrians.

Western Europe

In the eighth century, driven by population pressure, Viking settlers from Scandinavia set out along the inland rivers to Constantinople to fight for the emperor, and by sea in longboats to prey upon the coasts of Northern Europe. Sturdy fighters and skilled sailors, the Vikings explored the western routes via Iceland and Greenland towards the American continent, perhaps even landing there. In time, they settled—in Scotland, Ireland, northern England, and Normandy—and turned to trading.

After the spread of the Arab Empire had been halted in the West by the battle of Poitiers in 732, a new and fragile balance of power saw trade reviving in Western Europe. In 1095, the West felt strong enough to challenge Islam for possession of Jerusalem, and two centuries of Crusades (religious wars) began. The Crusades, however, did not hinder the growing trade in the Mediterranean.

Merchants sought protection behind city walls and, by the twelfth century, fought for the right to govern themselves as independent communities. In Italy, luxury goods brought overland from the mythic Eastern lands of India and Cathay could now be imported from the Near Eastern ports. Genoa, Florence, and Venice became the starting point for travelers and pilgrims going to Jerusalem. In the north, cities along the great rivers and the Baltic coasts joined in a federation called the Hanse to strengthen their power and regulate trade in the fish and forest products they exported.

Even so, it was the Arabs who could move freely and upon whose knowledge the West relied—few Western merchants traveled to Asia.

The Mongols

Paradoxically, it was the Mongols who reopened the great land trade routes to the West and enabled Western merchants and missionaries to visit the East. The nomads who inhabited the great steppes were united by Genghis Khan in the first part of the thirteenth century into a powerful empire, with its capital at Korokaras. The Mongol hordes provided an extremely effective army, whose tactics left all who faced it outmatched—so much so that that it was seen as an instrument of divine will and punishment. They annexed Russia, ravaged Hungary, overwhelmed China, and set up the Mongol Empire. This empire was ruled in Marco Polo's time by Kublai Khan, whose ambitions stretched to conquering Java and Japan. In 1258, the Mongols defeated the Turks and took Iraq and Persia. They controlled communications between these centers and enticed or forced skilled workers and traders to live with them.

It was only when the Mongols were eventually converted to Islam and became more sedentary that the Ottoman Turks were able to retake the Arab Empire and once again cut off Western travelers from land routes to India and China.

Marco Polo

Marco Polo, a thirteenth-century Venetian, is possibly the most famous of early Western travelers. His journey to the Mongol Empire followed a long trading journey that his father and his uncle had made. He learnt Mongolian, and for many years served as an official for the emperor Kublai Khan. His account of his travels, which he dictated while in prison after having been captured by the Genoese, was the major source of Western knowledge of the Far East until the nineteenth century.

EXPLORERS AND SETTLERS

Carrying goods by water may have been cheap in the days of the great empires, but it was fraught with difficulties. Sailing out of sight of land required astronomical and mathematical skills, and sophisticated instruments. The combination of wind, tide, and current with a difficult and rocky shore could be a lethal one.

At the height of the era of world exploration, no one ruled the seas, and pirates were a constant threat. Many of the most honored explorers, such as Vasco da Gama, Alfonso de Albuquerque, and Francis Drake, were also pirates. Seaborne empires such as that of Sri Vijaya had existed before, but during this time, the European empires were unparalleled in their domination of the oceans.

Early explorers

The disruption of overland trade that occurred as a result of the Turks taking Constantinople in 1453 stimulated the search for sea routes to the East. Portugal had long been pushing down the western coast of Africa, albeit slowly, and had established a military hold on that coast which excluded traders from other countries. In 1488, Bartholomew Diaz reached the Cape of Good Hope.

Many had sailed west from Europe by this time, and all had been lost. But in 1492, Christopher Columbus found a route and, upon his return, brought the unexpected news of "unknown lands" which were not part of Asia. However, the eastward passage was still of more immediate promise, and in 1497, Vasco da Gama, with the help of an Arab pilot, penetrated the Arab-dominated Indian Ocean.

In an epic voyage that took from 1519 to 1522, Ferdinand Magellan, sailing westward, showed that the world was indeed round. French, Dutch, and English explorers and seafarers were soon blocking the Spanish and Portuguese attempts to monopolize these trading routes.

Southeast Asia

In Asia, trade was the primary objective of exploration. The existing highly developed, wealthy, sophisticated empires were largely invulnerable. However, Portuguese merchants, in well-armed ships, and protected by forts and royal fleets, did succeed in competing with the established Arab merchants.

In 1500, the Portuguese obtained trading rights on the west coast of India. In 1510, they settled in Malacca, the great emporium from which ships went to Borneo, Ternate, Tidore, and Amboina, and eventually to China and Japan. About 1565, the Spanish established an alternative route, with ships regularly crossing the Pacific to the Philippines. As the market for spices became saturated, trade in gold, ivory, silks, Indian cotton textiles, Chinese porcelain, tea, and coffee developed. By 1600, the Dutch and English East India companies had entered the competition, and eventually the Dutch controlled most of the spice trade from Batavia.

For more than two centuries, the costs of governing a distant state restricted colonization. In India, for instance, the British East India Company hesitated to assume direct rule until pushed by French competition. Only in the nineteenth century did direct rule become common.

South and Central America

The discovery of gold, silver, pearls, and industrial raw materials made the Americas attractive to the Europeans. The conquest of the Aztec and Inca empires enabled Spain to establish its rule

from the Caribbean to Mexico, Peru, and Chile, while the Portuguese colonized Brazil. A steady trickle of fortune hunters from Spanish dominions in Europe took over the land and its inhabitants, causing an economic and cultural transformation. Despite the humanitarian protests of missionaries, exploitation of local labor, plus epidemics and diseases brought by the Europeans resulted in up to 95 percent of the indigenous population dying.

African slaves were imported to work the mines whose silver had such profound effects on sixteenth-century Europe. Sugar, cotton, and tobacco production also required intensive labor, and so the slave trade grew. Hides, indigo, cochineal, forest products, dyes, and drugs also went east in return for manufactured metals, guns, and

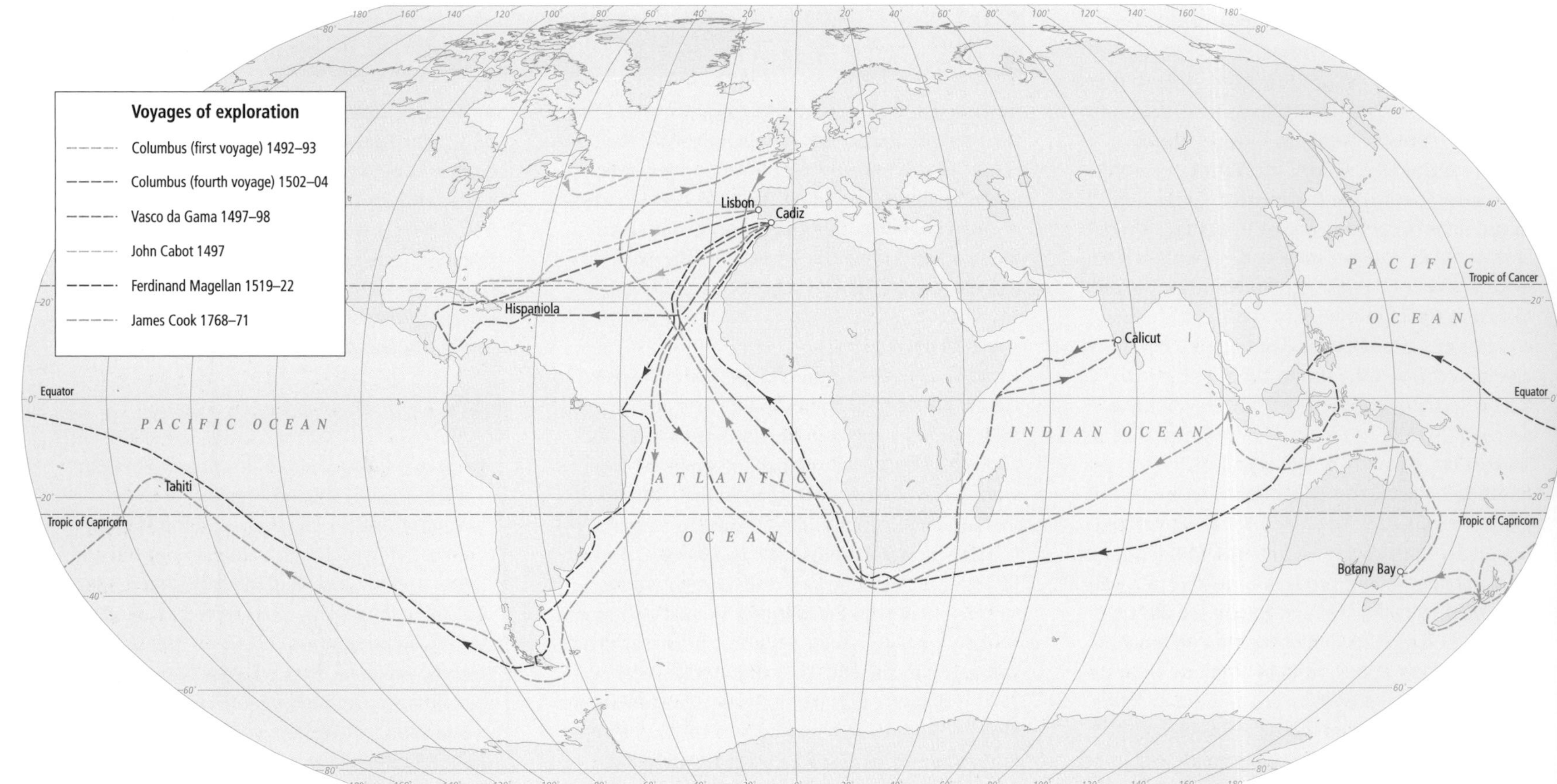

Projection: Robinson Equatorial Scale approx 1:110 million

Workers in Cochin, India (left) still deal in spices—here, turmeric. This Dutch map of the East Indies (below) is from the early colonial days. A replica of Captain Cook's Endeavour *(bottom) reminds us of the vessels sailed during the age of exploration. Machu Picchu, in Peru (bottom left), is a moving record of a long-dead civilization.*

textiles. By the seventeenth century, the Dutch, English and French were also involved.

North America

The temperate areas of North America, already inhabited by Native American Indians, were initially less interesting to the European states. Cod fishing off Newfoundland did not need shore settlements. The French, Dutch, and English, however, all eventually established east coast settlements, from the early seventeenth century. There was royal supervision, but no state financing of these colonies. Each of the colonies had its own government, constitution, and purpose. Many were established as a refuge from religious persecution, and sought self-sufficiency. Staple exports were hard to find, migrants hard to entice, and transportation of convicts was an unsatisfactory solution. So total populations remained low.

Southern colonies such as Virginia grew tobacco and, later, cotton, and increasingly used slave labor. The other colonies supplied basic foodstuffs to the Caribbean. In the eighteenth century, sugar, cotton, and tobacco still dominated as exports. Migration was becoming more attractive, though, as the economic revolution in Europe displaced laborers. The wars of independence opened the United States to migrants from all over Europe, and as the numbers of migrants grew, settlers moved west. In the nineteenth century, this trickle became a flood.

Growth of a world system

European exploration established a worldwide network—regular long-distance trading voyages took up to two years or more, so exploiting the new discoveries required some form of settlement. Europeans established trading posts wherever they went. They also soon required more capital, bigger ships, and new forms of organization. Shipyards alone required the kind of complex organization that was soon used in the factories of the Industrial Revolution. European merchants became global carriers, meeting local requirements

and introducing new commodities—horses and cotton to America; maize and turkeys to Europe.

Australasia was the last area to be drawn into this global network. In 1787, the British government chose Australia as a destination for convicts; the plan included the colonies being self-supporting. Initially, there was little but timber to offer world trade, and Europeans struggled to adapt the livestock and crops they brought with them to local conditions. Eventually, minerals were discovered as the interior of Australia was explored, wool became a staple, and convict transportation was replaced by free migration.

Ecologically, the world has been transformed by exploration and its consequences—and not always for the better. In many places, the indigenous population has been largely swept aside through disease, displacement, and massacre, and survives today only as a small minority.

As worldwide trading routes developed, so too did the movement of people attracted by the prospect of personal betterment. In the nineteenth and twentieth centuries, population pressure and sometimes persecution in the homeland pushed millions, mainly young males, to move to new countries. The Scots and Irish went to the United States and Australia; Jews left Eastern Europe for Israel, Britain, and America; Indian workers settled in South Africa, the South Pacific

islands, and East Africa; and Chinese laborers went to the goldfields in America, Australia, and elsewhere. Cultures have become mixed and modified as people intermarried and adapted to new conditions.

The world is round

On September 20, 1519, the *Trinidad*, *San Antonio*, *Victoria*, *Concepción*, and *Santiago*, under the command of Ferdinand Magellan, set out to travel west from Spain and return from the east. News of the terrors and dangers of the journey—the empty Pacific, the difficulties of finding water and victuals, the strange cultures of the natives—only served to increase Western fascination with new horizons.

Magellan himself died en route in 1521, and it was del Cano who brought the single surviving ship back to Spain in September 1522. The expedition members had suffered mutiny and desertion, disease and famine, attacks by natives, involvement in local wars, and the treachery of supposed allies. They had proven that the Spice Islands could be reached by sailing west, but concluded that the length of the voyage made it uneconomic.

THE INDUSTRIAL WORLD

Modern industrial societies were born in the eighteenth century, when an expanding workforce and rapid developments in technology resulted in the transformation of the social and economic structure of British society. Over the past 200 years, industrialization has spread to other parts of the globe, distributing the commercial benefits of technology and improving the lifestyles of many, but also creating social and political problems, particularly in urban areas.

Preindustrial Britain

The Industrial Revolution began in Great Britain in the second half of the eighteenth century. Several factors made Britain ripe for industrial development. Improvements in agricultural methods during the first half of the century had reduced the number of workers required to produce sufficient food for the population, making agricultural laborers available for industrial production. At the same time, wealth for investment had accumulated to a considerable degree, and much of it was concentrated in the hands of commercially minded individuals. A growing class of artisans and practical scientists possessed a high level of expertise in technologies, such as machinery, that could be readily applied to production processes. Continuing improvements in inland transportation, particularly river, canal, and road transport, allowed the rapid distribution of goods. Finally, Britain's growing empire provided it with access to vast overseas markets.

The Industrial Revolution

The first phase of the Industrial Revolution took place between the 1780s and 1830s, and was based on the early mechanization of production processes. The new industrial system focused on textiles (especially cotton) and textile machinery, and employed waterpower as its principal source of energy. It centered on the city of Manchester, in northern England. Here, in 1780, Richard Arkwright, inventor of the water-powered spinning frame, opened the largest factory yet built, employing 600 workers. Britain's position as head of the world's largest empire gave it a massive advantage in the textile trade; it could ensure a plentiful and cheap supply of cotton from the slave-labor-based plantations in the American South, and its powerful navy could protect its trade.

This first phase of industrial development was limited in two senses: it was narrowly focused (upon the textile industry), and it applied existing knowledge and skills rather than transforming the country's technological base. It was, however, revolutionary in that new economic relationships were forged between people, a new system of production was created, and a new society and historical epoch emerged.

The evolution and spread of industry

The second phase of the Industrial Revolution occurred between the 1840s and 1880s, and was revolutionary in technological terms. Iron and steel manufacture in factories powered by steam engines represented a major innovation. When this technology was used to develop railroads and steamships, the country entered a new phase of production and transport. Britain became "the workshop of the world", supplying the materials for a remarkable burst of railroad-building activity in Europe and in former colonies of European nations. Factories now employed thousands of

workers, rather than hundreds. The effects of this iron-and-steel-based Industrial Revolution on Britain were much more pronounced than were those of its predecessor. The employment generated was considerably greater, wages and living standards increased significantly, and British exports, which included foreign investments in railroads, rose phenomenally.

The revolution soon spread, with Germany and the USA among the first nations to industrialize on a large scale. Railroads helped achieve the integration of nation-states in Europe and opened up the Americas, as well as new colonies elsewhere. In the USA, the expansion and settlement of the frontier beyond the Mississippi River is closely associated with the penetration of the new railroads, the "Iron Horse".

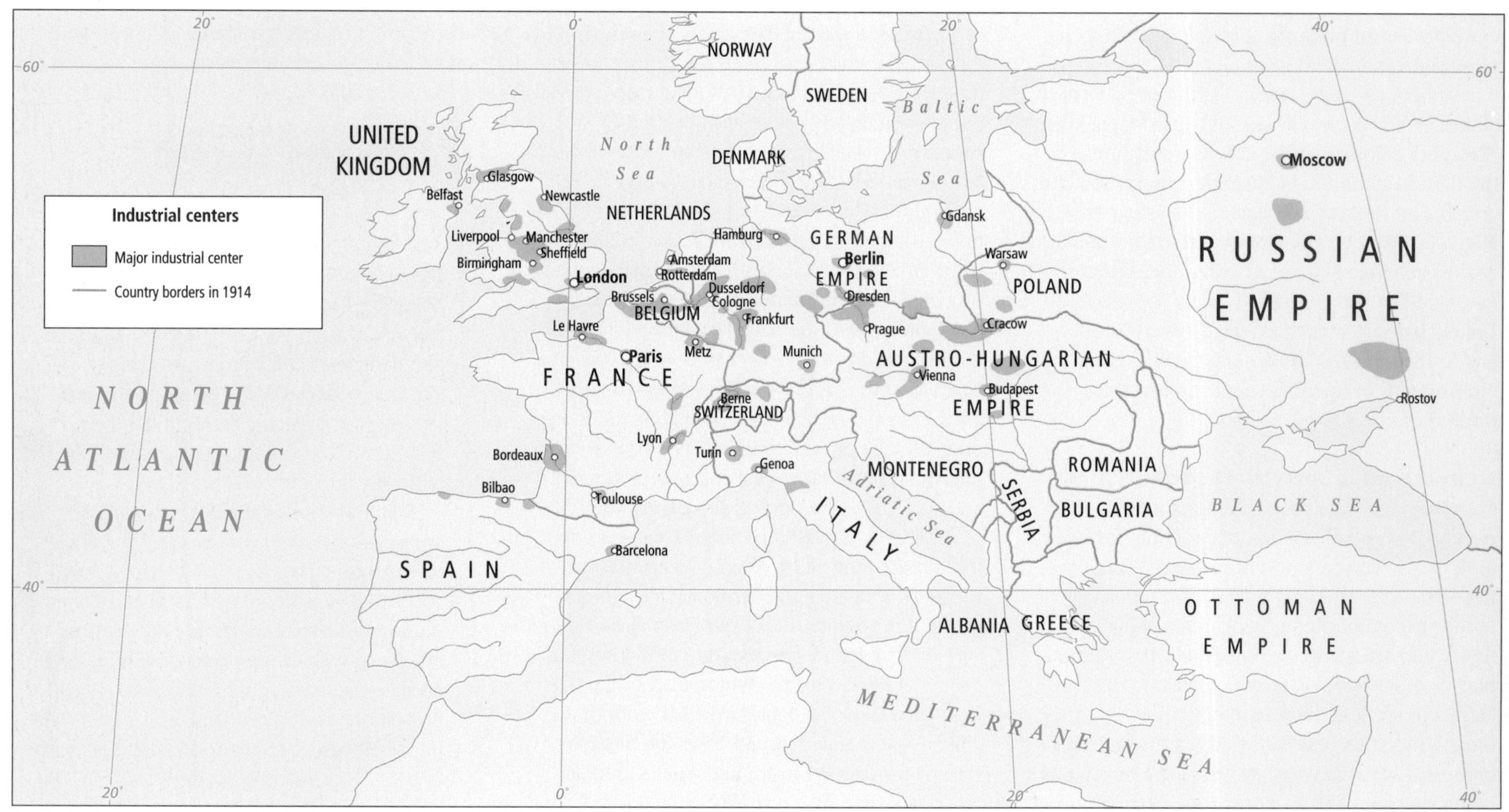

A steam train (above) and a textile mill (below) are potent symbols of early industrializaion. The Firth of Forth bridge (left) is more recent—a marvel of Victorian engineering. In countries such as India (bottom), modern technologies are replacing those of earlier times.

Modern industrialization

The third phase of the Industrial Revolution began in the last decades of the nineteenth century up to the First World War. Advances in electrical and heavy engineering and industry, and the exploitation of steel alloys and heavy chemicals allowed warfare on an unprecedented scale. New factory systems combined electricity with power tools, overhead cranes, and more durable materials. Giant firms, cartels, and monopolies became the leading commercial organizations, and the ownership of capital rapidly became concentrated. The map on the left shows major European industrial centers at the time of the war. Germany and the USA had already began to rival the United Kingdom for industrial supremacy. At the same time, other nations, including Switzerland and the Netherlands, industrialized. Soon, Europeans introduced industrial practices to other parts of the world.

The Industrial Revolution continues to this day with the industrialization in the last few decades of nations like Taiwan, Korea, Singapore, Mexico, Brazil, and Thailand. This process has created a somewhat artificial but widely adopted distinction between "developed" countries—those which are industrialized—and "developing" countries, which still depend largely on agriculture.

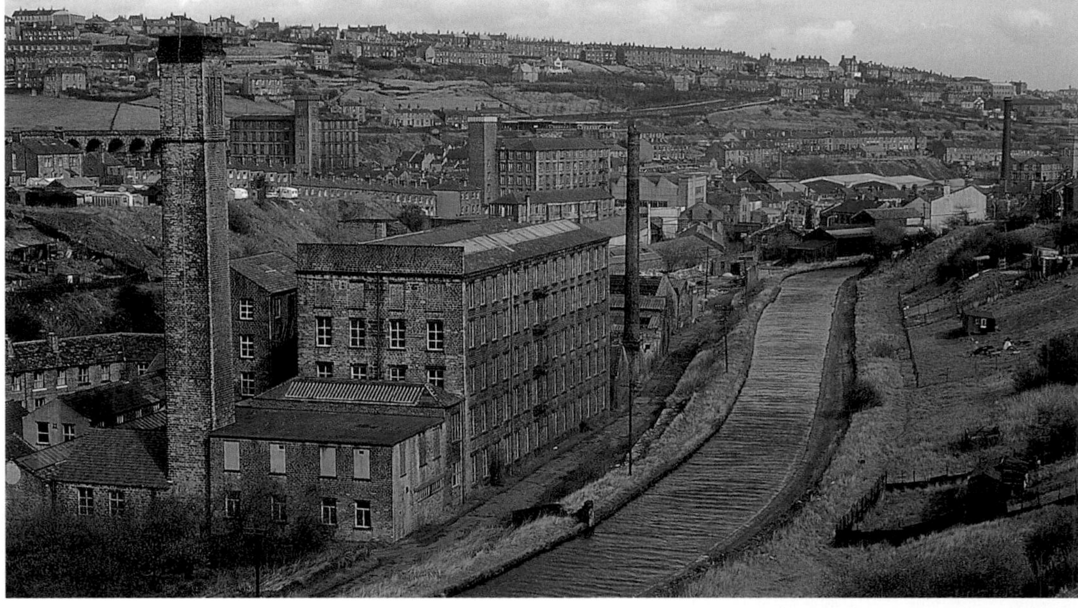

The consequences of industrialization

The application of industrial technology to an economy generally results in a population shift from rural to urban areas, as agricultural employment dwindles and people move to cities to work in industries and services. This process is known as urbanization. In the nineteenth century, the population of London, for example, rose from about 1 million in 1800 to almost 7 million in 1900.

While new industries raised living standards for many, the urban poor suffered overcrowding, poor sanitation, and pollution. There are many parallels between the social conditions in nineteenth-century United Kingdom cities and those in newly industrialized cities today. For example, the rapid expansion of an urban area such as Mexico City, which has grown from 3 million inhabitants in 1950 to about 18 million today, has resulted in acute social problems—water shortages, severe air pollution, and a chronic lack of adequate housing.

Recently, the industrialization of certain developing countries has had an interesting effect on the economies of the world's first industrial nations. Newly industrialized nations, particularly in Southeast Asia, have attracted manufacturing investment from the older developed countries; to such an extent that there has actually been a decline in manufacturing jobs—a deindustrialization process—in the countries where the first and second phases of the Industrial Revolution initially occurred. The United Kingdom, Germany, and the USA have all deindustrialized to some extent.

But today's era of industrialization differs significantly from its earlier phases. Owing to new forms of technology, particularly in transport and communications, the contemporary industrial system extends to all corners of the globe, and encompasses most commodities. The Industrial Revolution has now entered its worldwide phase, integrating selected localities as workshops of emerging global factories.

THE NATION-STATE

The world's nation-states, as represented today by the lines on a political map of the world, evolved over the past 500 years. Sixteenth-century Europe, for example, consisted of approximately 1,500 politically independent units. Yet by the start of the twentieth century, the continent was made up of only 20 nation-states. Since then, nation-states have flourished—today there are 192 nations and 65 territories on the political map of the world. New supranational groups emerging at the end of the twentieth century have led many commentators to question the ability of nation-states to solve problems within their own borders and deal with the powerful forces operating at a regional or worldwide level.

From city-state to nation-state

Before the appearance of the nation-state in Europe, city-states such as Venice, Antwerp, and Amsterdam occupied center stage in politics and economics. For much of the seventeenth and eighteenth centuries, Amsterdam was the control center for local, regional, and even worldwide affairs. The creation of the first nation-states, or more accurately, territorial nation-states, occurred during the 1770s and 1780s.

The catalyst was competitive rivalry between Amsterdam, England, and France. The incorporation of national territory was a new feature of the political landscape, and it gave nation-states major economic and military advantages over city states. In economic terms, for example, the nation-state could profit from its national market for goods. In military terms, it could more readily raise an army from its citizenry.

What do we mean by the term nation-state? It is useful to think of a nation-state as a combination of three elements: nation (ethnicity), state (the institutionalized regime of power), and territory (the spatially bounded area of state control).

A nation is a group of people who believe that they are an ethnic community with deep historical roots and the right to their own sovereign state. Nationalism is the cause through which such groups claim their right to be a sovereign power within a particular territory. Nationalism has its origins in the convergence of capitalism with print technology in the sixteenth century. The creation of separate vernacular print communities led to the decline of Latin as a lingua franca, and played a critical role in forming national identities.

Although ethnic identity was a significant factor in the formation of many nation-states, nations seldom consist of a single ethnic group. Indeed, such entities are extremely rare, Iceland being one of very few contemporary examples. A survey of 164 nations in 1984 counted 589 ethnic groups, an average of more than three ethnic groups per nation. A major role of mass education has been to integrate diverse ethnic groups and regional minorities into a single community, often called the "melting-pot approach" to nation-building.

The city-state of Venice (left) was an important trading center from the tenth century onward. Today it forms part of a modern nation-state, the republic of Italy. These Dutch-style buildings in Suriname (below) hint at the nation's past history when it was part of the Dutch colonial empire.

The second element of a nation-state, the state, refers to the institutions of political power within a country. These include its legislature, judiciary, political parties, and security forces. State power is organized into a wide variety of regimes, including constitutional monarchies, republics, theocracies, and totalitarian dictatorships. In the 1990s, three out of five states in the world were democracies—this is a historic high.

The third element that is used to define a nation is its territory, the physical area over which it has control. This area is normally marked out by geographical boundaries. Nation-state territories have typically been viewed as economic, political, social, and cultural containers that are largely sovereign and entitled to be free from outside interference. However, disputes over boundaries and national sovereignty have led to a number of major conflicts, particularly during the years of the twentieth century.

The rise of the nation-state

The process of dividing the world outside Europe into nation-states occurred largely in the context of the empires that the major colonizers—Spain, Portugal, The Netherlands, France, and the United Kingdom—had built during the previous four centuries. Most of the border lines on the contem-

Internal conflicts between groups who consider themselves to be of a separate nation can lead to a state fragmenting into smaller ones, as in the former Yugoslavia (right). Indian Sikhs on parade (below right): the world's largest democracy is home to a wide range of ethnic groups.

porary political map of the world have their origins in two major phases of decolonization.

The first phase unfolded over the half-century following the American War of Independence in 1776. About 100 colonies combined to form the current nation-states in the Americas. Little further decolonization occurred for more than a century, until around the time of the Second World War. Notable exceptions were the British settler colonies of Canada, Australia, and South Africa. The second major phase of decolonization began after the Second World War, when "the winds of change" blew through Africa, South and Southeast Asia, and islands in the Caribbean and the Pacific and Indian Oceans. This resulted in the formation of another approximately 110 nation-states.

Nation-states continued to be created in the 1990s—15 nations were created as a result of the break-up of the Soviet Union in 1991, for example. Eritrea, Slovenia, Croatia, and Macedonia became independent in 1991, as did the Czech Republic, Slovakia, and Namibia in 1994. The final outcome of the break-up of Yugoslavia is still uncertain. Internal ethnic tension in some areas has grown enormously, and ethnic-based nationalist movements continue to emerge. This kind of conflict is currently the most common—of the 89 armed conflicts that occurred between 1989 and 1992, only 3 were between nations.

At the same time, in Europe, where the nation-state first began, the European Union, a supra-national regional state, continues to transform the European political landscape. Most of Western Europe has now been combined within the European Union, while a number of other European states have applied for admission and await entry. Some commentators see the European Union as the beginning of the end of the territorial nation-state as we have known it; it has undoubtedly changed long-held ideas on what makes a nation.

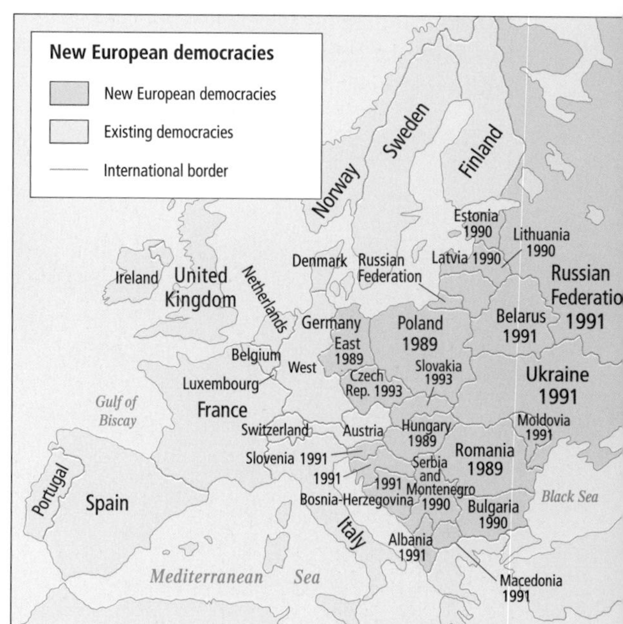

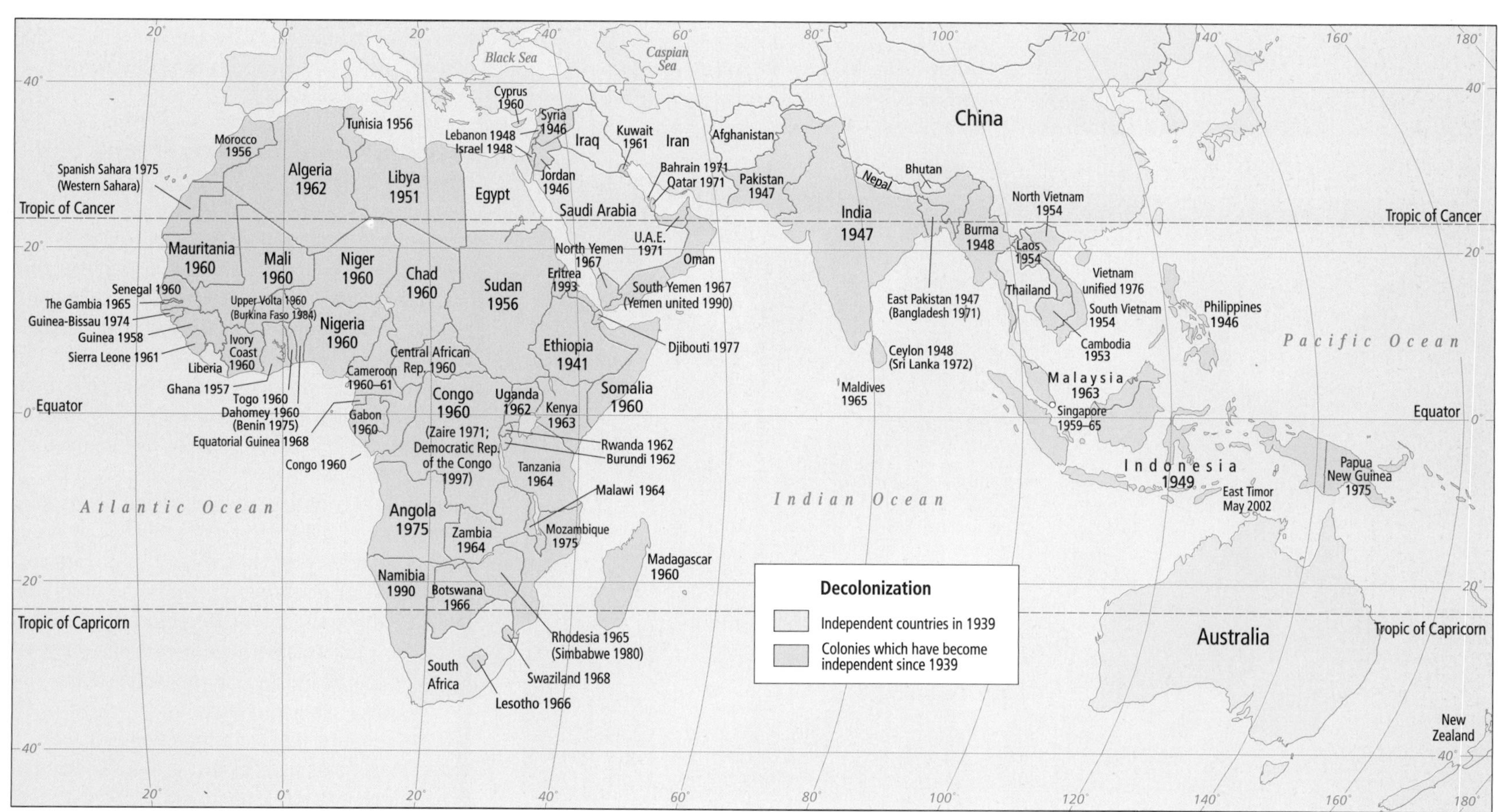

INTERNATIONAL ORGANIZATIONS

During the second half of the twentieth century, international organizations, including intergovernmental and nongovernmental bodies, have grown significantly in both number and stature. Today, there are about 500 intergovernmental organizations, such as the United Nations (UN) and the International Monetary Fund (IMF), and approximately 5,000 nongovernmental organizations (NGOs), including the Red Cross and Amnesty International. That represents roughly five times the number that were active at the end of the Second World War.

International organizations form an important part of the social glue that binds the nations and peoples of the world together. They create a set of rules, norms, and procedures—encapsulated in international law, particularly in the form of treaties and conventions signed by nation-states—that define the expected conduct of participants in the international community.

United Nations

The largest and most influential intergovernmental organization is the United Nations. Its predecessor was the League of Nations, which was founded at the end of the First World War, in an attempt to prevent further international conflict. Based in Geneva, the League gradually expanded its membership and became a focus for growing numbers of nongovernmental bodies. However, the refusal of the United States to ratify the League's covenant, and the League's inability to prevent expansion by Germany, Italy, and Japan in the 1930s led to its ceasing operations during the Second World War.

The United Nations (UN) was established in San Francisco in 1946, and now has its headquarters in New York. As with the League of Nations, the main motivation for the creation of the UN was collective security. Half a century later, the membership of the UN has grown to 191, and only one nation (Taiwan) and a small number of territories (including French Polynesia and the Channel Islands) are not formal member states.

On the world stage, the UN is critically important, but relatively weak and often controversial. At times it has appeared to be an impotent and ineffective institution that more resembles a debating society for the superpowers, their client states, and major power blocs than anything remotely like a "world government".

It is, of course, important to remember that the UN is not a world government, in that its member states remain independent and sovereign entities. Furthermore, most of the member states clearly have an ambivalent attitude towards the organization. For example, the Norwegians are strong supporters of the UN, but refuse to accept UN directives on whaling. The USA frequently seeks UN support for military intervention abroad, but constantly defers payment of its UN dues. Resulting financial difficulties hamper UN operations. Even after the Cold War, when it seemed to have grown enormously in importance and stature, the UN operated on about the same budget as the Tokyo fire department.

Refugees in the Sudan (below) and the young Somali girl (left) are likely to receive assistance from international organizations—via UN peacekeeping forces.

During the half-century following the establishment of the UN, other collective issues, including environmental, economic, and legal issues, have been placed under the umbrella of the intergovernmental system. For example, the World Bank and the International Monetary Fund (IMF) have become responsible for managing a wide variety of international economic issues: the IMF coordinates international currency exchange and the balance of international payments, and the World Bank borrows the savings of rich nations and lends them to poor nations under conditions not available on the private capital markets.

Nongovernmental organizations

Nongovernmental organizations (NGOs) are private organizations that are today regarded as legitimate players on the world stage alongside nation-states and intergovernmental organizations. Generally, however, NGOs have significantly less power and far fewer financial resources.

Most NGOs are primarily concerned with the empowerment of marginal and impoverished sectors of the world's population through increasing those people's participation in resolving their own problems. NGOs tend to focus upon specific issues. For example, Greenpeace raises awareness of environmental issues, Planned Parenthood campaigns for reproductive rights and family planning, groups such as the International Federation of the Red Cross and the Red Crescent Societies provide disaster relief, and Médecins Sans Frontières provides medical care.

International organizations and human rights

Human rights is one highly significant area where international organizations have created the emerging rules, norms, and legal instruments that link nations and their citizens together in an embryonic worldwide system. Human rights are the laws, customs, and practices that have evolved to protect people, minorities, groups, and races from oppressive rulers and governments.

Before the Second World War, international human rights issues were restricted to matters such as slavery or armed conflict, and discussions about human rights (and recognition of them) took place mainly within the borders of particular nation-states. A turning point in the history of human rights occurred on December 10, 1948, when the Universal Declaration of Human Rights was adopted by the General Assembly of the UN without a dissenting vote.

Over the next half-century, major advances were made. Most significantly, a series of international covenants was drafted and adopted by the

A land rights protest in Australia (above). International human rights organizations are increasingly exerting pressure on governments to recognize indigenous peoples' rights.

UN and subsequently ratified by individual nation-states. Once ratified by a nation-state, the human rights legislation was usually incorporated within the state's own legal system.

Although the UN has been prominent in human rights legislation, private individuals and nongovernmental organizations such as Amnesty International have frequently provided the political pressure that has persuaded intergovernmental and national agencies to act. Often, though, such action has been taken only reluctantly and retrospectively. The fact that countless millions of people have suffered (and many still do) terrible violations of their rights as human beings, even since the Declaration of Human Rights, is something of an indictment of the Declaration and of the UN's ability and will to enforce it. Most observers still regard the Declaration of Human Rights as inadequate and in need of enforcement. Its emergence, and the opportunity it created to bring such issues to world attention, are one positive result of the growth in importance of international organizations. While this has certainly produced a world that is better than it was, it is still by no means all that it could be.

Again, the ambivalent attitudes of nation-states to international organizations is a significant factor, affecting their ability to function effectively. For example, when concerns about human rights in Afghanistan were raised by the UN and NGO representatives in 1998, the ruling Taliban militia asked the organizations to leave the country. Yet, when it appeared that Iran may have been ready to invade Afghanistan to protect some of its own citizens, the Taliban sought support from the UN to keep Iran out. At the beginning of the twenty-first century, the idea of setting up global governance is still on the world's agenda, but only just.

THE UNITED NATIONS SYSTEM

International Court of Justice — **General Assembly** — **Security Council**

Secretariat | **General Assembly**

Committees

Trusteeship Council | **Security Council**

Peacekeeping Operations
International Tribunals
Military Staff Committees
Standing Committees

Economic and Social Council (ECOSOC)

UN Programs:

INSTRAW	UN International Research and Training Institute for the Advancement of Women
ITC	International Trade Center
UNCHS	UN Center for Human Habitats
UNCTAD	UN Conference on Trade and Development
UNDCP	UN Drug Control Program
UNDP	UN Development Program
UNEP	UN Environment Program
UNFPA	UN Fund for Population Activities
UNHCF	UN High Commission for Refugees
UNICEF	UN Children's Emergency Fund
UNIFEM	UN Development Fund for Women
UNITAR	UN Institute for Training and Research*
UNU	UN University
WFC	World Food Council
WFP	World Food Program

Functional Commissions
Regional Commissions
Standing Committees
Expert Bodies

Specialized Agencies:

FAO	Food and Agriculture Organization, Rome
ICAO	International Civil Aviation Organization, Montreal
IFAD	International Fund for Agricultural Development, Rome
ILO	International Labor Organization, Geneva
IMF	International Monetary Fund, Washington
IMO	International Maritime Organization, London
ITU	International Telecommunications Union, Geneva
UNESCO	UN Educational, Scientific, and Cultural Organization, Paris
UNIDO	UN Industrial Development Organization, Vienna
UPU	Universal Postal Union, Berne
WHO	World Health Organization, Geneva
WIPO	World Intellectual Property Organization, Geneva
WMO	World Meteorological Association, Geneva
WTO	World Trade Organization, Geneva*

World Bank Group, Washington

IBRD	International Bank for Reconstruction and Development
IDA	International Development Association
IFC	International Finance Corporation
MIGA	Multilateral Investment Guarantee Agency

** Does not report to ECOSOC*

GLOBALIZATION

Globalization refers to a change of scale in human processes and activities which has occurred during the last quarter of a century—one in which the nation-state is giving way, in many fields, to global organizations. Until recently, it was generally felt that human and environmental affairs could and should be conducted at a national level. Nation-states were, in principle at least, sovereign or independent units. Of course, nation-states had relations with one another, and these were referred to as international, as in the terms "international trade" and "international relations". In the 1990s, however, "international" and "internationalization" have been increasingly replaced by "global" and "globalization", as national boundaries have begun to seem less significant in economic, political, cultural, and environmental terms.

The global economy

Transnational corporations—companies that operate in a large number of countries—are the movers and shakers of the modern global economy. Among the firms with operations that are nearly worldwide are Exxon and Royal Dutch Shell in petroleum; McDonalds, Seagrams, Sara Lee, Nabisco and Nestlé in food and beverages; BMW, Ford, Volkswagen, and General Motors in automobiles; and Mitsubishi and Mitsui in banking, manufacturing, and trade.

Although few (if any) companies can be described as truly global at this time—most still focus on certain markets and report to shareholders in their home country—the term "global" is commonly used in business circles to identify a level of operations that many companies hope to attain in the not-too-distant future. This would involve a truly international workforce, shareholders in a number of nation-states, and products that are sold in all markets.

The flow of money from country to country is also encouraging the surge in economic globalization. National boundaries are no barrier to the movement of funds; thanks to modern telecommunications and computer technology, funds can now be rapidly transferred to any part of the globe. Such transactions have, it now appears, created a much more volatile and less secure world. In a matter of weeks in the middle of 1997, the Asian economic miracle became the Asian economic meltdown as a result of the massive and rapid withdrawal of global funds.

The phenomenal growth of the Internet has created opportunities for even small companies to operate at a global level. By selling goods via the World Wide Web, a firm can now compete in markets where it could not previously have established a presence, whether for geographical, political, or financial reasons. Governments are struggling to cope with the implications of this for the regulation of trade within their countries. How, for example, do they impose sales taxes on goods or services that are purchased in the virtual market of cyberspace?

Many commentators assert that globalization will transform the world economy in the twenty-first century, leaving no national products, no national corporations, no national industries, and no national economies. To succeed in the global marketplace, countries will have to depend entirely on the skills of their inhabitants, and will have to deal with powerful external forces that could create an ever-widening gulf between skilled, globally aware citizens and a growing unskilled, out-of-touch underclass.

World politics

The globalization of politics has resulted in the decline of the nation-state and the growth of international organizations. Although they remain the principal players on the world political stage, nation-states now appear less independent and less sovereign than they used to. One response to this has been to look to international organizations such as the United Nations to assume some of the roles previously played by nation-states.

Perhaps the most significant political event in the 1990s was the end of the Cold War. During the Cold War (1946–91), most nation-states belonged to one of three geopolitical worlds: the First World, consisting of developed capitalist nations, and dominated by the USA; the Second World, consisting of developed communist nations, and dominated by the Soviet Union; and the Third World, consisting of developing nations that were in theory not aligned with either of the superpowers. The demise of the Cold War brought an end to these divisions, and created a geopolitical situation no longer driven by the rivalry of two opposing superpowers.

Some commentators believe that this has created a vacuum, where no effectively organized power system exists. In the past, when major geopolitical shifts occurred, one dominant power was typically replaced by another: Great Britain (as the United Kingdom was known) replaced Amsterdam, and the USA later replaced the United Kingdom. Globalization has produced a world so complex and integrated that it no longer seems possible for a single nation-state to play the dominant role that these nations once played. The growing emphasis on and allocation of power to international organizations can be seen as an attempt to fill this power vacuum.

The global village

Discussions of the globalization of culture often begin with the expression "global village", a term coined in the 1960s by Marshall McLuhan, an American commentator. He believed that television would replace the printed word as the primary medium of wider social integration, eventually uniting the people of the world through their collective participation in media events. In the 1990s, events such as the Gulf War, the annual Academy Awards, the death of an English princess, and certain sporting competitions were watched on television by people in almost all the world's countries—an audience of between 1 and 2 billion people.

Dealings on the Tokyo Stock Exchange (right) can affect the economy of many other countries; financial centers such as Chicago (below) are experiencing the globalization of trade.

The fact that a rapidly growing number of people are involved in maintaining the global village raises a number of questions. For instance, will globalization mean an inevitable cultural homogenization? Opinion is sharply divided on this question. A great deal of evidence supports the view that a global culture is developing. On the other hand, powerful movements which actively resist this cultural homogenization have also emerged—militant Islamic, Hindu, and Zionist organizations, for example.

One issue that has played a major role in raising awareness of the ways in which we truly are a global community is the environment. The first Earth Day in 1970 marked the beginning of mass awareness of the global significance of environmental issues. Over the next three decades, evidence of the extent of degradation of Earth's natural environment caused by human activity has mounted. This has forced governments and individuals to examine their impact on the natural world, and has encouraged political cooperation at a global level to effect change.

A series of international environmental forums have been held, including Stockholm (1972), the Earth Summit at Rio de Janeiro (1992), and the Population Conference at Cairo (1994). All stressed the worldwide and interconnected nature of the growing environmental crisis. The Earth Summit was attended by an unprecedented 130 heads of state, 1,500 nongovernmental organizations, and 7,000 accredited journalists. However, despite the willingness of many nations to discuss these issues globally, the desire or ability to act locally may be absent.

The slogan "Think globally, act locally" has been widely employed to express the scale shift involved in this transformation of economics, politics, culture, and nature—from what used to be thought local or national concepts to what are now recognized as (or have become) international, global concerns.

Globalization may prove to be the key change in the twenty-first century.

Advertising signs in this village in Peru (below) are an example of the penetration of multi-national corporations into a developing country.

Oceania and Antarctica

Asia and the Middle East

1.8 MILLION BP Hominids of *Homo erectus* species living in Java, Indonesia

1.9 MILLION BP Modern hominids resembling *Homo habilis* living in caves in Sichuan Province, China

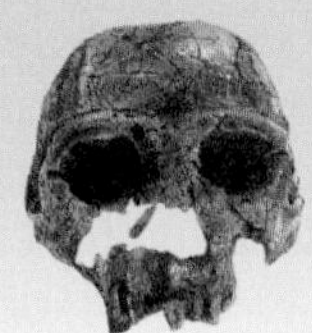

Skull of Homo erectus

800,000 BP *Homo erectus* using simple rafts on Indonesian island of Flores

460,000 BP Earliest known controlled use of fire at Zhoukoudian Cave, China

130,000 BP *Homo neanderthalensis* (Neanderthals) living in western Asia; they have social organization and hunt using strategy and cooperation

90,000 BP *Homo sapiens sapiens* present at several sites in Israel

Europe and the Russian Federation

1.5 MILLION BP Hominids arrive from Africa

780,000 BP Tool-using hominids living in northern Spain. Classified as *Homo heidelbergensis*, they may have been the ancestors of Neanderthals

500,000 BP Archaic *Homo sapiens* appears in Europe

130,000 BP Emergence of *Homo neanderthalensis* (Neanderthals); they have social organization and hunt using strategy and cooperation

100,000 BP Neanderthals burying their dead; possibly using burial rituals and decorating graves

Africa

5.0 MILLION BP The southern ape (Australopithecine) family splits into three branches, which will slowly evolve into gorillas, chimpanzees, and humans

4.0 MILLION BP Earliest recognizable hominid (form of human), *Australopithecus ramidus*, living in southern and eastern Africa

3.5 MILLION BP Footprints left at Laetoli, Tanzania, by *Australopithecus afarensis*, a hominid that walks upright

3.0 MILLION BP Hominids living in caves in southern Africa feeding on plants and animals

2.3 MILLION BP Emergence of *Homo habilis* in East Africa, a hominid associated with first use of crude stone tools

1.9 MILLION BP Hominids of more modern appearance, *Homo ergaster*, appear in Africa, probably evolving from *Homo habilis*

1.5 MILLION BP Hominids spread northward, crossing Sahara Desert region at time of abundant vegetation

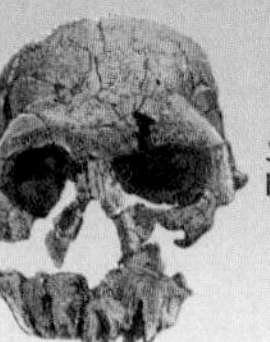

Skull of Homo ergaster

800,000 BP Archaic *Homo sapiens* evolves in Africa

200,000 BP Anatomically modern humans, distinguished by larger brain and use of more sophisticated tools, inhabit a number of cave sites in southern Africa

150,000–100,000 BP Modern humans, *Homo sapiens sapiens*, appear in various parts of Africa and begin to migrate northward

North and Central America

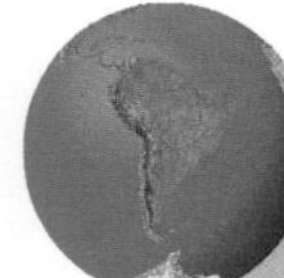

South America

60,000–40,000 BP *Homo sapiens sapiens* enters Australia and New Guinea from Southeast Asia, possibly by raft or canoe—the earliest known seaworthy vessels

40,000 BP Rock art appears in Australia; many early works consist of simple patterned engravings etched in rock

35,000 BP Humans hunting wallabies on grasslands of Tasmania, Australia

30,000 BP Earliest evidence of cremation at Lake Mungo, southeastern Australia

Seafaring groups inhabit the islands east of New Guinea

28,000 BP Buka Island in the Solomons group is colonized

25,000 BP Stone blades and hatchet tools in use in northern Australia and New Guinea

18,000 BP Rock paintings appear in Arnhem Land, northwestern Australia

Obsidian is traded in the Bismarck Archipelago, Melanesia

Sharpened kangaroo femur, 12,000 BP

9000 BP Crops including bananas, taro, and sugarcane cultivated in New Guinea

8000 BP Land bridge between New Guinea and Australia is submerged

---

68,000 BP *Homo sapiens sapiens* living in parts of China

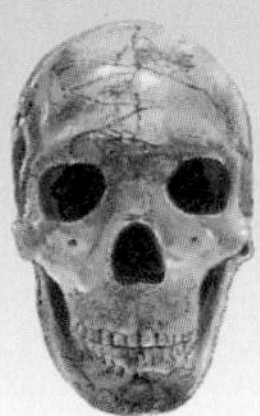

Neanderthal skull

40,000 BP Neanderthals disappear from the fossil record in western Asia

20,000 BP Modern humans (*Homo sapiens sapiens*) migrate across Eurasia as far as Siberia

Jomon pot, 12,500–9,500 BP

12,500 BP Jomon people of Japan produce the world's first clay vessels

12,000 BP Dogs domesticated in southwestern Asia

11,000 BP Cultivation of domesticated grains such as wheat and barley in the Fertile Crescent

10,000 BP Cattle domesticated in Anatolia, in present-day Turkey

9,500 BP Evidence of rice cultivation in central China

9,000 BP Crops including sesame and eggplant are cultivated in the Indus Valley

Pigs domesticated in Anatolia, Turkey

8,500 BP Smelting of copper, gold, and lead in southwestern Asia

7,500 BP Pottery is produced in China

'escraper tool m France, .000–35,000 BP

50,000 BP Simple engravings carved on cave walls in eastern Europe

40,000 BP *Homo sapiens sapiens* arrives from Africa, bringing more sophisticated tools and skills

35,000 BP Neanderthals disappear from the fossil record, perhaps displaced by *Homo sapiens sapiens*

Appearance of Cro-Magnon peoples, noted for their use of bone tools and sewn hides

32,000 BP First cave art appears in southwestern France and northern Spain

Austrian fertility figure, 20,000 BP

15,000 BP First evidence of use of watercraft in the Mediterranean

15,000–12,000 BP Magdalenian phase, during which most of the best-known cave art is produced, including the galleries of Lascaux, France, and Altamira, Spain

14,000 BP Elaborate huts of interlocked mammoth bones built to provide shelter during winter at Mezhirich, Ukraine

10,500 BP Beginning of colonization of Mediterranean islands, which takes 4,000 years

8,000 BP Permanent farming settlements established in southeastern Europe

---

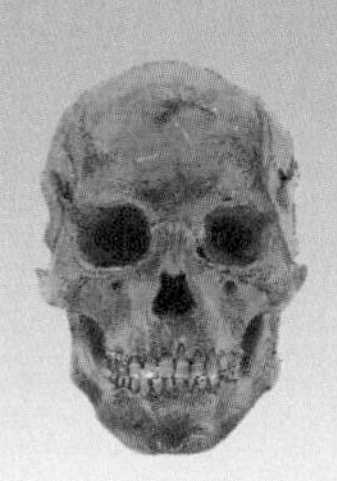

Skull of Homo sapiens sapiens

25,000 BP Paintings on rock slabs made by Stone Age hunter-gatherers in Namibia show animals such as elephants and giraffes

23,000 BP Rock paintings on inland shelters show ceremonial dancers and herds of game animals, including antelope

12,000 BP Rock carvings in the Sahara Desert, in present-day Algeria, depict North African aurochs

9000 BP Pottery containers in use in settled areas of the Nile Valley, Egypt

8000 BP Crops including figs and chufa are cultivated in the Nile Valley, Egypt

---

North American Clovis point tool, c. 11,500 BP

35,000–12,000 BP *Homo sapiens sapiens* enters North America across Bering Strait land bridge between Asia and present-day Alaska, and spreads southward

14,500 BP Disputed date for evidence of human habitation at Meadowcroft Shelter in southwestern Pennsylvania; site includes firepits, stone tools, and plaited basketry

12,000 BP Date of earliest reliable evidence of human habitation of North America, found at sites in Alaska

11 000 BP Numerous human settlements appear across present-day United States

Humans hunt mammoths at Clovis, New Mexico

Dogs domesticated

10,000 BP Hunters use trenches to trap and kill bison at Casper, Wyoming

9,000 BP Native peoples of Mesoamerica begin to collect plants more intensively, perhaps beginning domestication

---

Monte Verde hut, 12,500 BP

25,000 BP Disputed date for evidence of human habitation of eastern South America, including Pedra Furada in Brazil

12,500 BP Humans inhabiting Monte Verde in southern Chile; evidence includes stone tools, animal skins on poles, and plant remains

12,000 BP Well-organized hunter-gatherers living in the cold high-altitude puna grasslands of modern-day Peru, feeding on plants and vicuñas (a relative of the llama)

11,000 BP Humans inhabit Cueva Fell, Tierra del Fuego, southern Chile

10,000 BP Potatoes cultivated in the Andes of present-day Bolivia

8,500 BP Beans and chili peppers cultivated in central Andes

Oceania and Antarctica

4500–4000 BC People living on High Cliffy Island off Western Australia build stone structures as dwellings or for ceremonial purposes

4000 BC Pig husbandry and vegetable growing (mainly taro) in mainland New Guinea

Forest cleared on the Bismarck Archipelago to increase agricultural production

3600 BC Simple pottery is made on Vanimo coast of northern New Guinea

3500 BC Giant clam-shell adzes in use in Sepik-Ramu basin of New Guinea

2500 BC "Saltwater" people of the Kimberley Coast region of northwestern Australia use fire-hardened spears for fishing

Lapita pottery, c. 1100 BC

1600 BC Austronesian colonization of New Guinea and the Bismarck Archipelago followed by emergence of Lapita culture, named for its distinctive pottery bearing complex geometric designs

1500 BC Fiji is settled by Lapita people

1200 BC Lapita people colonize New Caledonia, Tonga, Samoa

Asia and the Middle East

5000 BC First settlements appear in Mesopotamia, the fertile area between the Tigris and Euphrates rivers

4200 BC Copper and bronze being worked in Mesopotamia

4000 BC Sailing ships in use in Mesopotamia

3500 BC Small cities based on earlier farming communities appear in Sumer, the southern part of Mesopotamia

3000 BC Sumerians develop a writing system consisting of pictograms pressed in clay tablets; they also develop the first wheeled vehicles

People from southern Asia (Austronesians) begin expansion south and east into the Philippines, eastern Indonesia, and New Guinea

2600 BC Writing system based on pictograms in use in China

2400 BC Harappa civilization merges diverse cultures in the Indus Valley; Harappan building methods involve use of bricks and architectural planning

2200 BC Semites migrate from Arabia to Mesopotamia and found Babylonian and Assyrian kingdoms

1800 BC Indo-Europeans spread to the Middle East and eastern Mediterranean

1595 BC The Hittites, a powerful Indo-European people from Hattusas in present-day Turkey, sack Babylon; by 1500 BC they control all of Asia Minor

1500 BC The Aryans, an Indo-European people, migrate from central Asia to northern India

1290 BC Tradition date for Moses le the Hebrews fron slavery in Egypt t to tribal lands in Canaan (Palestine

Europe and the Russian Federation

5000 BC Earliest evidence of burials in Scandinavia

Land bridge between Britain and Europe submerged by rising sea levels

Copper in use in southeastern Europe

4000 BC Farming reaches northern Europe

Horses domesticated in the Ukraine; they become the main means of transport throughout Europe and Asia and confer major advantages in battle

Poulnabrone tomb, Ireland, 3000 BC

2500 BC Rise of Minoan civilization—Europe's first—on the island of Crete and in surrounding Aegean region

Dolmen, large standing stones usually topped by a horizontal stone, are erected in Scandinavia

1800 BC Stone circle at Stonehenge, Wiltshire, England, completed; work may have started as early as 3500 BC

1650 BC Writing systems known as Linear A and Linear B in use in Crete and mainland Greece; Linear A is a Minoan script, whereas Linear B constitutes an early form of Mycenaean Greek

1600–1500 BC Minoan centers destroyed by invaders or earthquakes

Rise of Mycenaean civilization on Greek mainland

1250–1200 BC Mycenean centers destroyed by conflict or earthquakes

Africa

5000 BC Growth of Nubian settlement in the Nile Valley; agricultural methods begin to spread southward

4000 BC People living in central Sudan in loosely organized communities, tending cattle, sheep, and goats as well as continuing to hunt and fish

Copper smelting in Egypt

3000 BC Donkeys used for farming in the Nile Valley

First scientific astronomy observations in Egypt and Babylonia

Yams and palm oil domesticated in tropical West Africa

Beginning of Bantu expansion from West Africa into Congo Basin

2650 BC Nile Valley civilization flourishes; pyramids constructed during this period are the most elaborate burial tomb structures to date

2200 BC Ducks and geese domesticated in Egypt

2000 BC Kingdom of Kush established in middle Nile Valley

Invention of the water wheel in Egypt

1500 BC Trade routes between North Africa and the rest of Africa are disrupted by the spread of the Sahara Desert

Egyptians conquer Kush

1333–1323 BC Tutankhamun reigns as Pharaoh of Egypt, coming to the throne at age nine and ruling from Memphis near Cairo with the help of regent, Ay

1290 BC Rock temples of Abu Simbel built in Egypt by Ramese

North and Central America

5000 BC Caribbean islands colonized by people arriving in dugout canoes from the Yucatán Peninsula, present-day Mexico

Plants such as squash, amarinth, chili, and gourds cultivated in Tehuacán Valley, Mesoamerica

Gill-net fishing practiced in Pacific Northwest

3500 BC Bison hunted on the Great Plains

Beginning of classic period of Northwest Coast culture of Pacific Northwest, characterized by lavish ceremonies and ornate woodwork

Turkeys domesticated in Mesoamerica

2500 BC Squash cultivated in eastern North America, as well as sumpweed, goosefoot, and sunflowers, whose large seeds are stored as winter food

Simple pottery appears in North America

Olmec head

1300 BC People in southeastern North America, in the area known as the lower Mississippi, build major earthworks such as those found at Poverty Point in Louisiana

1200 BC Olmec civilization spreads throughout much of Mesoamerica; it lasts for 900 years

South America

5000 BC In the central Andes, beans are cultivated

4000 BC Llamas, alpacas, and guinea pigs domesticated in Peru

3500 BC Valdivia culture begins to develop in the Andes (in present-day Ecuador); it is characterized by a complex social culture and village life

Manioc (cassava) and potato cultivated in many parts of the Andes and Amazonia

3000 BC Cotton grown at Valdivia centers of Ancon and Huaca Prieta in coastal valleys of present-day Peru; mound architecture built at nearby sites such as El Paraiso

Valdivia culture produces incised ceramics at Puerto Horniga

Squash, capsicum, and peppers grown in Peruvian Andes

2500 BC Elaborate temples and mounds constructed in Peruvian highlands

1800 BC Huge ceremonial complexes built in coastal valleys of Peru at sites including Casma Valley

1200 BC Terracing used to increase agricultural output in Andes

1000 BC Settlement of southern Mariana islands of Micronesia

500 BC A distinctive Polynesian culture emerges in islands of southwestern Pacific

Bronze vessel from China

1020 BC Israelites establish a kingdom in Palestine

528 BC Buddhism begins under Siddhartha (Gautama Buddha) in Benares, India, and later spreads to Sri Lanka, Myanmar, Laos, Thailand, and other parts of southern Asia

400 BC Cast iron in use in China

331 BC Alexander the Great conquers the Persian Empire, winning a decisive battle at Gaugamela, Mesopotamia

221–211 BC Shih Huang orders construction of Great Wall of China to protect Qin Empire against nomadic tribes of northern steppes

112 BC Development of the Silk Road as a trading route between China and the West

c. 5 BC Birth of Jesus Christ in Bethlehem

800 BC Etruscans settle in central-western Italy between the Arno and Tiber rivers

Phoenician colonies established in Spain, Sardinia, and Sicily

776 BC The Olympic Games, a combination of religious festival and athletic contest, first held in Delphi and Olympia, Greece

750 BC Rise of Greek city-states including Athens, Corinth, Sparta, and Thebes

Etruscan alphabet in use

Work begins on the Acropolis, Athens

620 BC Roman alphabet, derived from Etruscan, in use

600–400 BC Growth of Celtic warrior societies; major centers include Hunsrück-Eifel region of Germany and Champagne district of France

336 BC Alexander the Great succeeds father Philip II as ruler of Macedonia; he soon tightens control of Greek city-states and expands Macedonian Empire into Asia

c. 350–322 BC Aristotle writes his major works, advancing the idea that Earth is the center of the universe around which other planets revolve

290 BC Romans take control of central Italy

264–241 BC First Punic War between Rome and Carthage initiates long battle for dominance of Mediterranean

218–201 BC Hannibal crosses the Alps to invade Italy from the north, beginning the Second Punic War

146 BC Rome emerges victorious from Third Punic War

51 BC Julius Caesar conquers Celtic tribes of Gaul as far as the Rhine; he reaches Britain in 55 BC, but Romans do not occupy the country until 43 AD

1000 BC Bantu expansion reaches Rift Valley

Kush becomes independent

750 BC Kingdom of Kush-Meroë conquers Egypt and rules until 670 BC

Phoenicians colonize coast of North Africa

Gold sheath from Kush-Meroë KIngdom

480 BC City of Carthage flourishes and holds sway over the western Mediterranean

300 BC African rice is grown in the Niger delta

275 BC The first lighthouse to use reflected light from a fire to warn sea traffic of danger is built at Alexandria in Eygpt

200 BC Paper made from papyrus in use in Egypt is used all over the western world

146 BC Carthage destroyed by Roman army at end of Third Punic War

1000 BC Agriculture, in the form of the cultivation of maize, established in southwestern North America

650 BC Appearance of Zapotec hieroglyphs, the earliest form of Mesoamerican writing

600 BC Team games played with a rubber ball on ball courts in San Lorenzo and La Venta in present-day Mexico; the games may have involved human sacrifices

500 BC Adena people of midwestern North America build mounds for ceremonial purposes

Monte Albán, in Mexico's southern highlands, becomes capital city of Zapotec culture; it thrives for about 1,200 years

300 BC The pyramids of the sun temple in Teotihuacan, Mexico, are completed

Hohokam, Mogollon, and Anasazi peoples inhabit southern North America; the Anasazi occupy villages built beneath overhanging cliffs in and around Chaco Canyon, New Mexico

200 BC In northeastern North America, Hopewell culture begins to take over from Adena; the Hopewell become the region's first farmers

1000 BC The Chavín culture begins to flourish in northern Andes

900 BC Carving of Tello Obelisk, an ornate granite monolith from Chavín de Huántar, one of the most remarkable artefacts of Chavín culture

750 BC Gold mining taking place in central Andes

Tello Obelisk, 900 BC

200 BC Rise of Nasca culture in Peru, noted for its immense geometric figures etched into the ground and only visible from the air; the patterns may mark the sun's passage at solstice

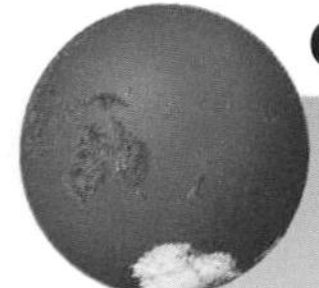

Oceania and Antarctica

AD 186 One of the world's most violent volcanic eruptions occurs at Mt Taupo, New Zealand, destroying surrounding forests over a radius of 75 km (47 miles)

Fishhook from Marquesas Islands

AD 0 Marquesas Islands colonized

AD 500 Polynesian settlers reach Hawaii and Easter Island

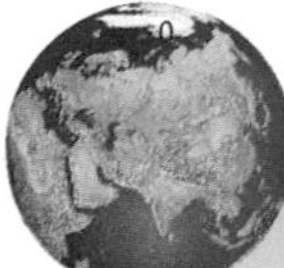

Asia and the Middle East

AD 220 Demise of Han Empire in China

Stone sculpture, Gupta dynasty

AD 527–565 Byzantine Empire (359–1453) reaches its zenith under Justinian I

c. AD 30 Crucifixion of Jesus Christ in Jerusalem

AD 319–450 Gupta dynasty flourishes in India

c. AD 500 Buddhism and Confucianism introduced to Japan from China

AD 622 Followers of Mohammed (570–632), founder of Islam, flee to Medina to escape persecution; this event denotes the start of the Muslim calendar

Europe and the Russian Federation

AD 117 Roman Empire reaches its greatest extent under Trajan; in Britain, the northern boundary is later marked by Hadrian's Wall (built AD 122)

AD 330 Roman Emperor Constantine I converts to Christianity, which subsequently becomes the Empire's official religion

AD 450 Germanic tribes from northern Europe, such as the Angles, Jutes, and Saxons, begin to settle in England

AD 476 Western Roman Empire comes to an end when Romulus Augustus is ousted by Goths

AD 79 The cities of Pompeii and Herculaneum, Italy, are destroyed by the eruption of Mt Vesuvius

AD 140 The Greek astronomer Ptolemy publishes his *Almagest*, an encyclopaedia of scientific information, including his theory that Earth is the center of the universe

AD 443 Attila leads Huns and other barbarian tribes into western Europe; he is turned back in 450 at Châlons by a coalition of Franks and Visigoths led by Aetius

AD 452 Venice founded by refugees from central Europe fleeing the attacks of Attila the Hun

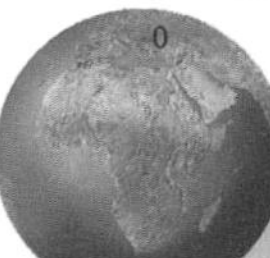

Africa

Pillar at Aksum

c. AD 350 Aksum converts to Christianity; the empire extends inland

c. AD 570 Nubian kingdom converts to Christianity

AD 0–100 Kingdom of Aksum in present-day Ethiopia becomes a major trading center; elaborate temples and palaces are constructed

AD 400–500 Bantu people migrate to southern Africa seeking land for grazing sheep and cattle and planting crops; they soon displace Khoisan hunter-gatherers

AD 634 Arabs begin to colonize North Africa

North and Central America

c. AD 200 Pyramid of the Sun is built at Teotihuacán in eastern Mexico

AD 426 Mayan dynasty of 16 kings founded at Copán in present-day Honduras

Jade ritual offering, Copán dynasty

AD 700 Start of the Pueblo period in southwestern North America; native peoples including Hopi and Zuni live in villages built mainly of adobe

AD 100 Mayan hieroglyphic writing comes into use

AD 250 Start of the Classic phase of Mayan civilization; growth of Mayan city-states on Yucatán Peninsula (Mexico) and in present-day Guatemala

AD 550–800 Mayan civilization reaches its zenith

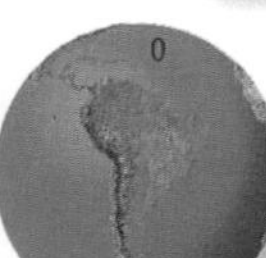

South America

AD 200–600 Moche civilization of Peru produces highly decorated ceramic pots and murals for public buildings; the Pyramid of the Sun in Moche Valley is the region's largest adobe structure

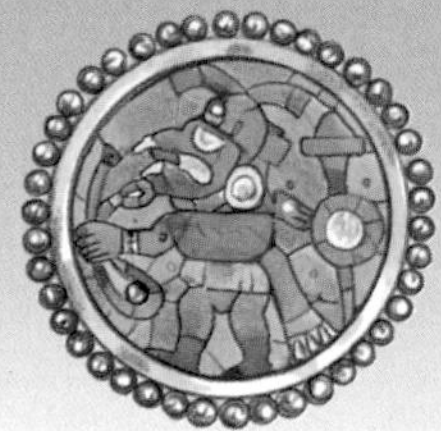

Moche ear ornament

AD 700 Sicán culture flourishes in the Batán Grande area of Peru's northern coast; the capital city includes 12 adobe pyramids and tombs for leaders

AD 100 Tiwanaku and Wari develop as principal urban centers of southern-central Andes

AD 500 Wari becomes major Andean city with strong administrative structures, large buildings, and highly developed crafts, including ceramics

AD 800 Fishhooks in use along the southeast coast of Australia, similar to those found in New Guinea

AD 900–1000 Polynesians first reach New Zealand islands and settle

Gigantic stone statues are erected on Easter Island

Pitcairn Islands are colonized by Polynesians

Easter Island statue

1300 Chatham Islands, 800 km (500 miles) east of New Zealand, become the last Pacific islands to be colonized by Polynesian settlers

AD 868 The first wood-block-printed book, *The Diamond Sutra,* appears in China

AD 960 Beginning of Song Dynasty in China, which will last until 1279; it adopts Neo-Confucianism as official philosophy

1000 Chinese scientists invent gunpowder

1038 Seljuk Turks start Turkish Muslim dynasty; by 1071, it controls Asia Minor

1048 First movable type in use in China, consisting of clay characters in an iron frame

1096–99 First Crusaders temporarily wrest Jerusalem from Arab control

1100 Chinese invent the magnetic compass

1147–49 Second Crusade ends in failure to recapture Holy Land

1189 Third Crusade led by Richard I of England and Philippe II of France leads to truce with Arabs

1192 Yoritomo becomes first Shogun (commander-in-chief) of Japan, initiating the so-called Kamakura period, which is dominated by Samurai and lasts until 1333

1275–92 Italian merchant Marco Polo resident at court of Mongol emperor Kublai Khan in China

1368 After a century of Mongol rule, the Ming dynasty takes power in China, initiating a 300-year period of isolation during which art and culture flourish

1369 Mongol leader Tamerlane assumes leadership of Samarkand; he later extends his empire into Persia and India

AD 711 Moors invade Spain, bringing Islamic influence to Europe

AD 771 Charlemagne becomes king of the Franks; he soon expands Frankish Empire in central Europe

AD 800 Charlemagne crowned Holy Roman Emperor in Rome by Pope Leo III

Viking people of Scandinavia begin to explore and plunder the European coastline; they eventually colonize Iceland and parts of Britain and set up trading posts in eastern Europe

1066 Norman king William I (Conqueror) invades England and commissions Domesday Book to assess the wealth of the country; population estimated at around 2 million

1232 Pope Gregory IX establishes the Inquisition, a special court set up at Toulouse, France, to investigate heresies against the Catholic Church

1280 Windmills in use in western Europe

1300 The Renaissance begins in Italy and spreads throughout Europe

1326 Gunpowder being used in cannons

1337 Start of the Hundred Years War between England and France

1346 Black Death (bubonic plague) spreads from Asia Minor to Italy and from there to the rest of Europe; 25 percent of the European population die within five years

AD 800 Rise of the Kingdom of Ghana in West Africa, which lasts until 1050

AD 900 Trading routes established between East and West Africa as well as across the Sahara

c. 1000 Growth of urban centers in southern Africa; craftworks are traded widely

Rise of kingdoms of Yoruba in present-day Nigeria

Rise of empire of Great Zimbabwe in East Africa, which flourishes until 1400

1050 Tokolor people of Senegal, West Africa, become the first group south of the Sahara to follow Islam

1062 Almoravid Muslim sect takes control of Morocco, establishing its capital at Marrakesh

1100 Different language groups begin to emerge, including the Xhosa and the Zulu

1130 Almohad Muslim sect rises up against corrupt Almoravids, taking control of North Africa and ruling until 1212

1150 Emergence of Hausa city-states in present-day Nigeria

1200 Mali Empire, in present-day Ghana, establishes Muslim rule in West Africa; it lasts 200 years

1300 Emergence of the Benin Empire of Nigeria, West Africa

Construction of royal court at Great Zimbabwe

1312–37 Mali Empire reaches its zenith

1340 Empire of Songhai, a strong trading state in present-day Mali, founded on Niger River

1350 Complex irrigation methods in use in East African Rift Valley

AD 800 Native Americans living in present-day Illinois start to abandon hunter-gatherer way of life in favor of agriculture; maize becomes a major crop

Mayan population of Copán Valley reaches 20,000

AD 980 Viking outlaw Erik the Red establishes settlement in Greenland; population of settlement may have reached 5,000, but it is eventually abandoned in 15th century when climate becomes colder

1000 Viking explorers land on various parts of American coast including Baffin Island, Labrador, and Newfoundland (possibly the place known as Vinland in Norse legends)

Toltecs of Tula (in present-day Hidalgo, Mexico) found an empire which flourishes for next 200 years

1150 Growth of communities in present-day Alabama, Georgia, and Oklahoma; they produce many decorated ceremonial objects

1200 Several tribes, including the Mexica, migrate to the Valley of Mexico,.leading to the foundation of Aztec civilization; they begin terracing mountain slopes for food cultivation

1250 Emerald Mound, a huge ceremonial site near Natchez Trace Parkway, Mississippi, in use

c. 1300 Drought in southwestern USA forces Anasazi and other native peoples to abandon homelands

1325 Aztecs establish their capital of Tenochtitlán, which grows into a major city with 250,000 inhabitants; it later becomes Mexico City

AD 725 Tiwanaku becomes a major Moche population center with up to 50,000 inhabitants

AD 800 Machu Picchu, a site of religious and symbolic importance for the Inca people, is built in the mountains above the Urubamba Valley in Peru

AD 850 Chimiú people found Chimor Empire and build capital of Chan Chan in the Moche valley; by 1100 it has a population of 8,000

Inca ceramic plate

1200 Cuzco becomes capital of Inca civilization; Inca cultivate mountainous areas with irrigation canals in order to feed a growing population

1250 Emergence of Killke style of ceramics in the Cuzco area; this will later become the distinctive style of the Inca civilization

Oceania and Antarctica

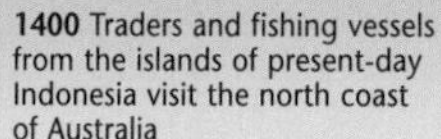

1400 Traders and fishing vessels from the islands of present-day Indonesia visit the north coast of Australia

Temple city of Nan Madol in use off the island of Temwen, Micronesia; built of stone on artificial islands, it is only accessible by boat

c. 1500 Moas hunted to extinction in New Zealand

Moa

Asia and the Middle East

1405 Death of Tamerlane

1453 Constantinople falls to the Ottoman Turks

Ottoman Constantinople

1498 Portuguese sailor Vasco da Gama reaches the Malabar coast in India after sailing round the Cape of Good Hope

1502 Founding of Safavid dynasty in Persia by Ismail, who proclaims himself shah; the dynasty lasts until 1736

1526 Mogul Empire founded when Babar invades Hindustan and conquers all of northern India; for 200 years the empire is well administered, centralized, and prosperous

1534 Ottoman Turks invade Mesopotamia taking Tabriz and Baghdad

1543 Shipwrecked Portuguese traders become the first Europeans to visit Japan; they introduce the first firearms to the country

Europe and the Russian Federation

1400 Leprosy eradicated in most parts of Europe due to improved diet and sanitation

1450 Beginning of Little Ice Age which brings harsh winters, wet summers, and food shortages to Europe for next 400 years

Johannes Gutenberg builds the first printing press

1453 End of the Hundred Years War between England and France

1455 Gutenberg prints the Mazarin Bible at Mainz, Germany

1478 Queen Isabella of Spain sets up Spanish Inquisition to investigate heretical activities

1492 Spanish expel Moors from Granada, their last stronghold in Spain

1517 Reformation begins when German priest Martin Luther nails 95 theses challenging the power of the Catholic Church to a church door in Wittenberg; the movement soon spreads throughout Europe

1538 Flemish geographer Gerardus Mercator uses the name "America" on maps for the first time

1543 Nicholas Copernicus proposes that Earth revolves around the Sun, challenging the traditional Ptolemaic view that the opposite was true

1546 Mercator declares that Earth has a magnetic pole

Africa

1400–1500 Rise of Nyoro kingdom in present-day Uganda

1415 Portuguese explore North and West African coast in caravels, a new kind of sturdy sailing vessel, capturing Ceuta under Henry the Navigator

1450 Rise of empires of Congo and Ndongo in central Africa (present-day Congo and Democratic Republic of the Congo)

State of Bono in West Africa becomes an important gold-mining center

1464 Songhai secedes from Mali; in 1468, it captures Timbuktu

1471 Portuguese establish forts on West African coast and begin trading in gold

1486 Portuguese reach Angola on the West African coast

1488 First Portuguese vessels arrive at the Cape of Good Hope

1500 Rise of the Bornu Empire in northern Nigeria following Kanem Empire's demise; it reaches its zenith at end of century

1517 Ottoman Turks take control of Egypt after defeating the Mamelukes (Muslim slave soldiers) and rule for the next 250 years

North and Central America

Aztec mask

1400 End of the early Aztec phase sees widespread use of chinampas, swamplands reclaimed for agricultural plantations

c. 1450 Pueblo farmers of southwestern North America trade with plains-hunters of the north, exchanging corn, cotton goods, and pottery for buffalo meat and hides

c. 1460 Mississippian Native American societies living along river valleys of eastern North America increasingly dependent on agriculture; they build large earthen mound structures for religious ceremonies

1492 Italian seafarer Christopher Columbus reaches the Caribbean and discovers Watling Island, Cuba, and Haiti

1494 Treaty of Tordesillas divides the New World between Spain and Portugal; the treaty is rejected by other European maritime powers

1497 John Cabot and son Sebastian explore the east coast of North America

1500 Aztec Empire at its height

1519 Spanish conquistador Hernán Cortéz meets Aztec ruler Montezuma II at Tenochtitlán, Mexico; two years later, he seizes the city and Montezuma

1524 Italian navigator Giovanni da Verrazzano explores northeast coast of North America

Spanish conquer Mayan lands

1539 Spanish explorer Hernando de Soto reaches Florida and travels up the Mississippi River

1540–42 Spanish explorer Francisco Coronado explores southwestern North America

South America

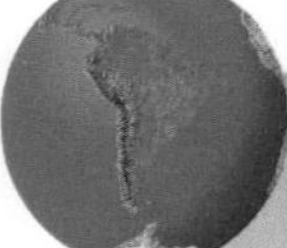

1400 Rise of Inca Empire known as Tawantinsuyu; Incas develop building techniques of great precision and begin to construct an extensive road system

1438 Pachacuti becomes Inca leader and begins expanding empire

1450 Incas conquer Chimú state in Peru

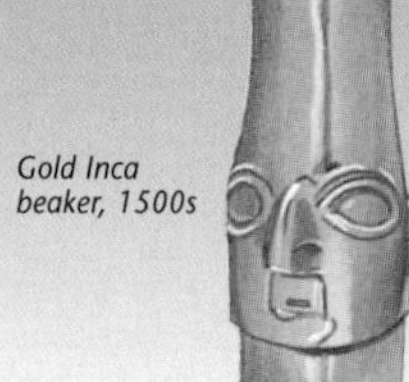

Gold Inca beaker, 1500s

1499 Amerigo Vespucci sails from Spain to South America

1500 Pedro Alvarez Cabral discovers Brazil and claims it for Portugal

1516 Spanish explorer Juan Díaz de Solís becomes the first European to land in present-day Argentina; he is killed by Querandi indians

1521 Spanish explore northern coast of South America and start a colony in what becomes Venezuela

1525 Civil war breaks out in Inca Empire between north led by Atahualpa and south led by his brother Huáscar

1532 Spanish conquistador Francisco Pizarro imprisons Inca emperor Atahualpa; despite an enormous ransom being paid, Atahualpa is executed

1545 Spanish discover silver at Potosí in central Andes, starting a rush to exploit this valuable resource

1568 Spanish sailors visit the Solomon Islands

1595 Spanish sailor Mendaña de Neyra discovers and names the Marquesas Islands, which now are part of French Polynesia

1606 Dutchman Willem Janszon lands on north coast of Australia

Spanish navigator Luis Vaez de Torres sails through the strait that subsequently bears his name without realizing that a continent lies to his south

1616 Dutch sea captain Dirck Hartog lands on the west coast of Australia

Dutch navigators Willem Schouten and Jakob le Maire visit Tonga

1642–43 Dutch navigator Abel Tasman lands on Van Diemen's Land (now Tasmania), claiming possession for the Netherlands; he then discovers the west coast of New Zealand and sights the eastern islands of Fiji and Tongatapu in the Tongan group

1644 Tasman charts part of the coastline of northern and western Australia

1688 English adventurer William Dampier spends two months on the west coast of Australia

1699 Dampier returns to explore the west coast of Australia; unimpressed, he sails north for New Guinea

1568 Akbar, greatest of the Moghuls and grandson of the empire's founder Babar, conquers Chitor in Rajasthan, quells the Rajput princes, and takes control of the region

1580 Unification of Japan under Oda Nobunaga

1597 Dutch establish trading post at Batavia (Jakarta) in Dutch East Indies

1600 British East India Company established to develop trade in Asia and challenge the trading empires of the Portuguese and Spanish; similar trading companies subsequently set up by Dutch (1602) and French (1604)

1603 Tokugawa Shogunate begins rule in Japan, continuing until 1867

1623 At trading center of Ambon, Dutch behead British traders accused of plotting to take over the Dutch fortress; incident creates friction between trading powers

1632–43 Taj Mahal, a white marble mausoleum, built at Agra, India, by Emperor Shah Jehan in memory of his wife Mumtaz Mahal

1639 English colonists settle at Madras in India

1643 First French missionaries arrive in Vietnam

1644 The Manchus, a people from Manchuria, invade China from northwest and establish Qing dynasty, bringing peace and prosperity

1674 Dutch traders help local Muslim leader, Amangkurat I, head of the kingdom of Maturam, Indonesia, to suppress rebellion; in return, Dutch gain possession of parts of central Java

1683 China seizes Formosa (Taiwan)

1569 Mercator produces *Cosmographia*, which includes the first navigational maps of the world

1571 Battle of Lepanto halts maritime expansion of Ottoman Empire

1572 In France, 10 years of religious conflict climax in St Bartholomew's Day Massacre of 3,000 Huguenots (Protestants) in Paris; many Huguenots seek refuge in England

1588 Spanish Armada, Philip II of Spain's invasion force against England, is defeated by Sir Francis Drake in the English Channel

1603 King James VI of Scotland becomes James I of England

1609 Mathematician-astronomer Galileo Galilei improves the recently invented telescope and describes Jupiter's satellites

Johannes Kepler announces his laws of planetary motion

1618 Start of Thirty Years War between Protestant powers—England, Holland, Scandinavia, and German states—and Spain and the Habsburg Empire

1642–48 English Civil War leads to execution of Charles I

1643 Barometer invented by Italian scientist Evangelista Torricelli

1661 Ottoman Turks invade Transylvania and Hungary

1665 The Great Plague of London takes 70,000 lives between July and October; the following year much of the city is destroyed by a fire lasting from February 2 to 9

1675 Greenwich Observatory established by English astronomer Edmond Halley

1682 Edmond Halley identifies a bright comet and correctly predicts that it will reappear in 1758 and approximately every 77 years thereafter

1699 Under Treaty of Carlowitz, defeated Turks forced to cede most of Balkans to Austrian Habsburgs

Yoruba sculpture

1591 Morocco defeats Songhai, bringing the empire to an end

1600 Oyo Empire becomes one of the most successful of the Yoruba states after the leader Orompoto uses proceeds of trade to build a large army

1613 Portuguese priest and explorer Pedro Paez discovers the source of the Blue Nile: Lake Tana in Tanzania

1619 First slaves from West Africa shipped to Virginia, North America, by Dutch traders

1626 French establish settlements on Madagascar but island does not become a colony until 1896

1637 French establish military base in Senegal, West Africa

1652 Dutch East India Company establishes garrison at site of modern-day Cape Town

1657 First Dutch settlers take up land grants at Liesbeeck River near Cape Town

First slaves brought to the Cape from India, Indonesia, and West Africa by Dutch

1660 Rise of Bambara kingdoms of Segu and Kaarta on the Niger River; by 1670 they have replaced the Mandingo Empire

1670 Rise of Ashanti Empire in West Africa in modern-day Ghana; by early eighteenth century its rulers are supplying slaves to Dutch and British traders

1583 The English found a colony at St Johns, Newfoundland

1584 Sir Walter Raleigh claims Virginia on east coast of North America for England; attempts to form a permanent settlement fail

1605 Port Royal in Nova Scotia becomes the first French settlement in North America

1607 Jamestown, Virginia, becomes first permanent English settlement in North America

1619 The first slaves from West Africa are sold in Virginia, North America, by Dutch traders

1620 The Pilgrim Fathers leave Plymouth, England, and cross the Atlantic to the New World in the *Mayflower*

1624 The Dutch establish a settlement at New Netherlands, North America

1642 The French establish site of Montréal on the St Lawrence seaway

1663 The North American French colonies form a Province by amalgamating as New France, with Québec as the capital

1670 Hudson's Bay Company founded in London by English and French merchants seeking to establish fur trade in the Hudson Bay region of northeastern Canada

1682 René La Salle explores the Mississippi River and claims Louisiana for France

1553 First settlements of Santiago del Estero and Tucumán in Argentina founded by Spanish arriving from Peru in search of gold and silver

1567 Two million South American Indians die from typhoid fever introduced by Spanish soldiers

1573 Córdoba and Mendoza grow as part of trade routes between Chile and Argentina

1580 Spanish colonists establish settlement at Buenos Aires on La Plata estuary

1616 Dutch navigator Willem Schouten sights Cape Horn, the tip of South America

1620 Expansion of silver mining at Potosí, Bolivia

1624 Dutch seize Brazilian territory of Bahia; they later take control of the rich sugar-producing area of Pernambuco (1630–54)

1630 Portuguese begin to import large numbers of slaves from Africa to work on sugar plantations of northeastern Brazil, displacing native populations

Ankle fetter used to secure slaves

1695 Large gold deposits discovered in central Brazil, in the area now known as Minas Gerais, triggering an influx of prospectors

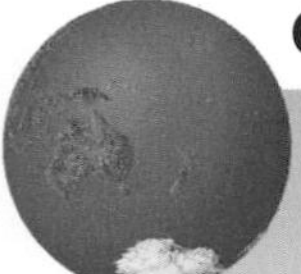

Oceania and Antarctica

1722 Dutch explorer Jacob Roggeveen explores the Pacific, visiting Samoa and Easter Island as well as Makatea, Bora-Bora, and Maupiti

Captain James Cook, 1728–79

1765 British explorer John Byron sails through the Pacific while searching for the "Great South Land," and visits numerous islands including the Gilbert Islands

1766–69 Comte Louis Antoine de Bougainville, scientist and navigator, travels widely throughout the Pacific, visiting Tahiti, the New Hebrides, New Britain, and New Guinea

1770 After visiting Tahiti and New Zealand, English navigator Captain James Cook charts the east coast of Australia and lands at Botany Bay

1788 First Fleet under Captain Arthur Phillip arrives at Botany Bay to found a British penal colony; disappointed with Botany Bay, Phillip establishes the colony at Port Jackson

1793 First free British settlers arrive in New South Wales, Australia

Asia and the Middle East

1707 Mt Fuji, Japan's biggest volcano, erupts

1715 Chinese conquer Mongolia and Turkestan

1730 An earthquake on the island of Hokkaido, Japan, causes the deaths of 137,000 people

1740 British East India Company takes over Mogul land

Dutch and British armies oust Portuguese spice traders and establish ports at Madras, Bombay, and Calcutta

1755 The Nawab of Bengal occupies Calcutta, taking many British prisoners, some of whom die in the "Black Hole," a small room used as a jail; British, led by Robert Clive, retake Calcutta

1761 British capture of Pondicherry marks the end of French colonial power in India

1769 Severe famines in Bengal lead to rural depopulation for more than 20 years

1771 Political crisis of the "Tay Son Rebellion" in Vietnam under which the old Confucian order is threatened by reforms inspired by Western ideas

British East India Company coat of arms

Europe and the Russian Federation

1701–14 War of Spanish Succession

1707 Act of Union unites Scotland and England as Great Britain

1713 Peace of Unsikaupunki ends the Great Northern War between Sweden and Russia; after more than 350 years of allegiance to Sweden, Finland comes under Russian control (until 1721)

1725 John Harrison, English clockmaker, invents a device for measuring longitude at sea and on land

1735 Swedish naturalist Carl Linnaeus publishes *Systema Naturae*, a system for classifying plants and animals; his basic hierarchy is still in use

1755 Lisbon is destroyed by a major earthquake; it is the first earthquake to be studied by scientists

1760 Rise of Amsterdam as world's major economic center

1769 After several years of development, Scotsman James Watt invents the double-acting rotary steam engine which is introduced to textile mills and other factories

1781 German-born English astronomer Sir William Herschel discovers the planet Uranus; Herschel's studies form the basis of modern astronomy

1789 The French Revolution begins with the storming of the Bastille and lasts for 10 years

Africa

1713 Native Khoikhoi pastoralists of South Africa replaced by "trekboer" settler farmers in search of grazing land; huge numbers of native Khoisan people die in smallpox epidemic

South African San or Bushman

1757 Sultan Muhammad ibn Abd Allah brings peace and stability to Morocco after a period of unrest and economic decline

1760 Slaves are traded in increasing numbers in what is now Gabon, West Africa, often in exchange for European goods such as guns, textiles, and rum

1779 Sporadic warfare breaks out in south between Dutch and British colonists and indigenous Xhosa people; the conflict lasts for the next 100 years

1787 British set up a colony at Sierra Leone, West Africa

1790 In present-day northern Nigeria, the Islamic Fulani people from Senegal wage a holy war (jihad) against the Hausa kings

1795 British occupy Cape Town, a vital supply post on Britain's expanding trade routes prior to opening of the Suez canal; British settlers arrive in increasing numbers

Scottish explorer Mungo Park reaches the Niger River

North and Central America

1720 Spanish soldiers invade Texas

1740–48 War between Britain and France over North America

1752 American scientist and diplomat Benjamin Franklin proves that lightning is an electrical discharge and invents the lightning conductor

1763 Peace of Paris treaty ending Seven Years War in Europe awards Canada to Britain

1770–72 British adventurer Samuel Hearne explores territories to the northwest of Hudson Bay in northern Canada

1775 Beginning of American War of Independence (to 1783); the following year the 13 American colonies adopt the Declaration of Independence, thereby founding the USA

1787 Delegates at a national constitutional convention—the "Founding Fathers"—create the US Constitution

1789–93 Alexander Mackenzie explores northwestern North America, crossing over the Rockies to reach the Pacific Ocean

1791 Canada is divided into French- and English-speaking territories by the Constitutions Act

1793 Eli Whitney invents the cotton gin, a mechanical threshing machine

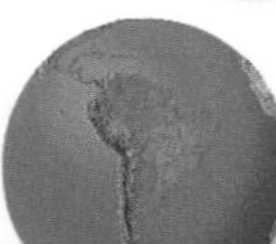

South America

1700 Bourbon Spain establishes the Viceroyalty of New Grenada in central and South America; Peru is forced to release control of Guayaquil in modern-day Ecuador

1743 Charles-Marie de la Condamine, a French scientist given the task of measuring a degree of longitude on the equator, takes measurements in Ecuador and then explores the Amazon, bringing back samples of the rubber tree and platinum

1770–80 Improved navigational methods strengthen links between Europe and Latin America, creating opportunities for economic growth

1780 Tupac Amaru II leads an unsuccessful revolt by native people against Spanish rule in Peru

1790 Native people and imported Africans used as slaves on plantations in Brazil; many die from European diseases

1799–1804 German scientist Alexander von Humboldt explores central and South America

1803 British penal settlements founded in Hobart and Port Arthur in Tasmania

1820 Russian naval officer Captain Fabian von Bellingshausen is possibly the first person to see Antarctica

1837 Frenchman Lieutenant Jules Dumont d'Urville discovers Joinville Island, off Antarctica

1839–43 British explorers Ross and Crozier map the coast of Antarctica in the *Erebus* and the *Terror*; two volcanoes are later named after the ships

1840 The Treaty of Waitangi gives Britain sovereignty over New Zealand but also gives Maori people sovereignty over their lands (as well as British citizenship), creating conflicting expectations

1851 Beginning of the Australian Gold Rush

1861 Thomas Mort builds the first refrigeration unit for the transportation of meat in Sydney, Australia

Gold Rush in New Zealand

1868 Transportation of convicted criminals from Britain to Australia ends with the arrival of the last convict ship in Western Australia

1893 New Zealand becomes the first country in the world to give the vote to women

1895 Norwegian whaler Henryk Johan Bull becomes the first person to land on the Antarctic continent at what is now Cape Adare

Beginning of severe droughts in Australia which last for the next seven years

---

1800 British East India Company trading in China; British smuggle opium into China to offset other exports and Opium War breaks out when Chinese object

1815 The largest volcanic eruption ever, at Tambora, Indonesia, kills at least 10,000 people; more than 80,000 later die of starvation and disease resulting from climatic effects of eruption

1842 Treaty of Nanjing ends first Opium War; China cedes Hong Kong to Britain

1850 Failure of monsoon rains in northern India causes famine lasting more than 30 years

1857 The Indian Revolt against heavy taxes results in considerable loss of British and Indian lives; it is ruthlessly suppressed

1876 Queen Victoria becomes Empress of India

1880s Indian Nationalist Movement, including Indian National Congress, campaigns for an end to British rule

1883 Krakatau, Indonesia, erupts, killing 36,000 people; the explosion is heard up to 3,650 km (1,400 miles) away

1887–88 Huang (Yellow) River in China floods, killing 1 million people

1891 A severe earthquake in Japan kills up to 10,000 people

1894–95 Sino-Japanese War breaks out over Korea—Japan emerges victorious and annexes Formosa (Taiwan)

1804 After conquering much of western Europe, including the Netherlands, Switzerland, and northern Italy, Napoleon crowns himself emperor of France

1815 Napoleon defeated by British army at Waterloo

1834 British mathematician Charles Babbage invents the "analytical machine," forerunner of the computer

1835 French mathematician Gaspard de Coriolis describes how winds and ocean currents are deflected clockwise around high-pressure systems in northern hemisphere and anti-clockwise in southern hemisphere

Halley's comet reappears, as he had predicted

1848 Revolutions occur in various parts of Europe, including Germany, France, Austria, and Italy

1850 Karl Marx, a German economist living in London, publishes *The Communist Manifesto*

French physician Louis Pasteur advances a theory that germs cause disease

1859 Publication of Charles Darwin's *The Origin of Species*, which expounds the theory of natural selection

1861 Italy becomes a single state under King Victor Emmanuel II of Sardinia after Giuseppe Garibaldi and his "red shirts" defeat Bourbon troops

1871 Unification of Germany under Emperor William I

Charles Darwin, 1809–82

1899 French meteorologist Teisserenc de Bort discovers that temperature stops decreasing at around 10 km (6 miles) above sea level; this leads to discovery of atmospheric layers

---

c.1800 Zulu nation founded in what is now Kwazulu-Natal, South Africa, forcing Shoshangane clan into Swaziland and Mzilikazi clan into Zimbabwe

1830–48 France conquers Algeria

1836–38 10,000 Boer (Dutch) settlers unhappy with British rule in the Cape set out on Great Trek to seek new territories in Natal and Orange River region

1853 Scottish explorer and missionary David Livingstone begins his exploration of central Africa

1858 English explorers John Speke and Richard Burton discover Lake Victoria; Speke later discovers the source of the Nile

1860 Laborers from India are imported by Natal farmers to work on farms and plantations

1861 British occupy Lagos in Nigeria

1869 The Suez Canal opens, allowing a much reduced voyage time between the Mediterranean Sea and the Indian Ocean

1870 Gold and diamonds discovered in South Africa

1871 US journalist Henry Morton Stanley locates Livingstone, who has mapped the river systems of central Africa and traced the source of the Zambeze

1880–81 British attempts to bring the Boer republics (of Orange Free State and Transvaal) into a federation fail when the Boers defeat the British in the First Boer War

1884–85 Conference held in Berlin divides up remaining African territories between Germany, France, and Britain

1899 Start of the Second Boer War between British and Afrikaners (Boers)

Gold-mining industry in South Africa employs 110,000 workers; almost 100,000 are African laborers

---

1803 Napoleon sells almost 3 million sq km (900,000 sq miles) of southern central North America to the USA in a deal known as the Louisiana Purchase

1804–05 US army officers Meriwether Lewis and William Clark explore the Missouri River, cross the Rocky Mountains, and reach the Pacific Ocean

1813 Mexico declares its independence

1824 The Erie Canal opens, creating a navigational route between the Great Lakes and the Atlantic Ocean

1837 Samuel Morse demonstrates the electric telegraph in New York

1848 As a result of victory over Mexico, the USA gains vast areas of western and southern North America

Discovery of gold in California causes an influx of prospectors in the first Gold Rush

1861–65 American Civil War between the North and the South caused by disputes over political and economic issues, including the abolition of slavery

Gold nugget

1867 USA purchases Alaska from Russia

1876 Scots-born American Alexander Graham Bell invents the telephone

1879 Thomas Edison invents electric lighting

1886 The transcontinental Canadian Pacific Railway is completed

1898 Spanish-American War ends with Cuba becoming independent and the USA gaining Puerto Rico, Guam, and the Philippines

---

1808 Prince John, royal ruler of Portugal, is forced to flee from Portugal and declares Rio de Janiero capital of the worldwide Portuguese Empire; he returns to Portugal in 1821

1816 Argentina declares independence from Spain

1822 Prince John's son Pedro declares Brazil's independence and is crowned Emperor

1824 Simón Bolívar wins a victory over Spanish troops at Ayacucho, Peru, ending Spanish control in South America

1830 Argentina lays claim to Islas Malvinas (the Falkland Islands); three years later, Britain occupies the islands

1866 San Roque Dam built on the Paraná River, Argentina, to supply hydroelectric power and water for irrigation

1870 Rubber production soars in the Amazon area of Brazil, attracting migrants from the eastern seaboard and from Europe

1879 Population of Gran Chaco region of Argentina grows rapidly as a result of the expansion of the beef industry, with large numbers of immigrants arriving from Europe

1879–83 Pacific War between Chile, Peru, and Bolivia over nitrate deposits results in Chile taking territory in southern Peru

1880 Japanese immigrants begin to settle in southeastern Brazil to profit from rapid growth of coffee plantations

1888 Brazil abolishes slavery: 750,000 people are freed

1889 Brazil becomes a republic

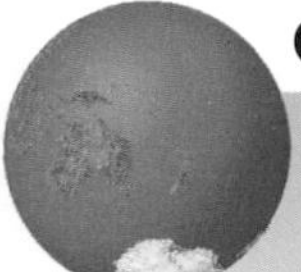

Oceania and Antarctica

1901–04 British navy captain Robert Scott undertakes the first inland exploration of Antarctica

1907 Englishman Ernest Shackleton, a member of Scott's earlier expedition, reaches the South Magnetic Pole in Antarctica

1914–18 330,000 Australians and 100,000 New Zealanders travel overseas to fight in the First World War

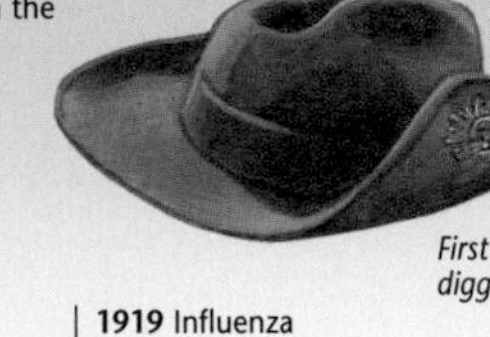

First World War digger's hat

1928 Australian aviator Bert Hinkler arrives at Darwin, Australia, after a 15-day flight from Croydon, England, via Rome, Egypt, India, Malaya, and Java

1939 Australia and New Zealand send troops to support Britain in the Second World War; hundreds of thousands fight in Europe and the Pacific

1947 New Zealand's parliament adopts the Statute of Westminster (1931) which gives it formal independence from the UK

1901 Federation of the six Australian colonies results in the formation of the Commonwealth of Australia

1911 Norwegian explorer Roald Amundsen and his team become the first to reach the South Pole on December 11; just over one month later a British expedition under Captain Scott accomplishes the same feat, but the team perishes on the return journey

1919 Influenza pandemic leaves thousands of Australians dead

1930 The Depression hits Australia and New Zealand

Amy Johnson arrives at Darwin, Australia, having flown solo from London, UK; she fails by only 4 days to beat Hinkler's record

1942 Japanese troops occupy New Guinea

Japanese submarines enter Sydney Harbour, Australia

Asia and the Middle East

1907 France seizes Lao territories east of the Mekong River; formerly under control of Thailand, they include much of present-day Cambodia, Laos, and Vietnam

1934 Mao Ze Dong leads the Long March of the Communist revolutionaries across China

1945 First atomic bombs dropped on Japanese cities of Hiroshima and Nagasaki by USA, bringing the war in the Pacific to an end

1946 Start of war in Indochina between French colonial powe[rs] and Vietnamese nationalists led by Ho Chi Minh (to 1954)

Mao Ze Dong, 1893–1976

1900 In Peking (Beijing), the Boxer Rebellion of Chinese nationalists against foreign interests is put down by British and Russian forces

1911 Rebels proclaim Chinese republic under Sun Yat-sen; last Chinese Emperor Pu Yi relinquishes throne in the following year

1927–28 Civil War in China between the Communist party and the Kuomintang (Nationalist Party) under Chiang Kai-Shek; Nationalists take Beijing

1948 State of Israel proclaimed following partition of Palestine

1947 India gains independence and is partitioned, with Pakistan becoming separate Muslim state

1949 Communi[st] party take[s] control of China

Europe and the Russian Federation

1914 Assassination of Archduke Francis-Ferdinand at Sarajevo in Bosnia triggers the First World War between Germany, Austria-Hungary, and the Ottoman Empire on one side, and Britain, France, and Russia on the other; more than 8 million soldiers die

1917 The second Russian Revolution takes place in March and Russian royal family killed; in October, the Bolsheviks seize power

1928 The world's first antibiotic, penicillin, is discovered by Scottish scientist Alexander Fleming

1936–39 Spanish Civil War between Nationalists and Republicans results in General Franco becoming Nationalist head of state of the Falangist (Fascist) government

1945 Second World War ends in Europe (8 May) and the Pacific (2 September); the death toll includes more than 14 million soldiers and about 27 million civilians

1905 Bloody suppression of riots in St Petersburg leads to the first Russian Revolution

1916 German-born physicist Albert Einstein publishes his General Theory of Relativity, which suggests that the universe is expanding

1918–19 Influenza pandemic leaves millions of Europeans dead and kills up to 40 million worldwide

1933 Adolf Hitler becomes Chancellor of Germany; his National Socialist Party ends democratic rule

1939 Germany invades Poland, starting the Second World War

Africa

1907 Mahatma Gandhi campaigns in South Africa for civil rights of ethnic Indian population

1931 South Africa granted independence by Britain as a member of the Commonwealth

1949–50 Racial apartheid becomes the official policy of the National Party government of South Africa

African National Congress flag

1902 Britain emerges victorious from Second Boer War

1912 The African National Congress (ANC) founded in South Africa by a small group of educated black Africans seeking political rights

1935 Seeking to expand its African territories, Italy invades Ethiopia, capturing Addis Ababa in 1936; Haile Selassie flees until British troops restore him to office during Second World War

North and Central America

1903 First successful flights in heavier-than-air machines made by brothers Orville and Wilbur Wright at Kitty Hawk, North Carolina

1917 United States enters First World War

1927 Charles Lindbergh makes the first nonstop solo flight across the Atlantic Ocean from Roosevelt Field, New York, to Le Bourget near Paris

1941 Japanese attack on US naval base at Pearl Harbor, Oahu Island, Hawaii, brings USA into the Second World War; during the war, the USA loses 292,000 troops, Canada 43,000

1948 Universal Declaration of Human Rights adopted by General Assembly of UN in New York; it sets out minimum standards of civil and political rights to which all people are entitled

Wright brothers' Flyer III, 1905

1902 Mt Pelée, Martinique, erupts, killing 20,000 and burying the town of St Pierre

1906 San Francisco is devastated by a major earthquake measuring 8.3 on the Richter scale

1918 Influenza pandemic begins in North America; it eventually kills up to 40 million worldwide

1929 The Wall Street Crash of October 24 causes widespread financial instability; it is followed by the Great Depression which spreads worldwide

1945 Founding charter of United Nations (UN) signed by 51 nations in San Francisco

South America

1930s Huge population growth and urbanization occurs, particularly in Argentina and Uruguay, chiefly as a result of large-scale immigration

1942 Brazil supports Allies in Second World War and sends 25,000 troops to fight in Italy

1946 Juan Perón becomes President of Argentina with backing of both arm[y] and labor unions

1914 First World War initially disrupts Latin American trade, but for some countries this is followed by an export-led boom which lasts until the Depression

1932–35 Paraguay defeats Bolivia in war over Chaco region; final settlement negotiated in 1938 awards Chaco territory to Paraguay

1944 A massive earthquake kills 5,000 people in the Andean San Juan province of Argentina

1951 Australia, New Zealand, and the USA sign the ANZUS defence treaty; the signatories agree to offer mutual support in the event of an attack on any of the other parties

1960 Swiss diver Jacques Piccard and the US navy's Donald Walsh explore the Mariana Trench in the Pacific Ocean to a depth of 11,000 m (36,089 feet)—the lowest known point on the ocean floor

1975 Papua New Guinea becomes independent

Thousands of refugees from Vietnam, Laos, and Cambodia, many of them ethnic Chinese, begin to flee to Australia by boat

1985 New Zealand's anti-nuclear policy sours relations with traditional allies France and the United States

Antarctic penguin

1959 Antarctic Treaty bans military activity in Antarctica; signatories also agree to suspend territorial claims

1974 Cyclone Tracy destroys Darwin in northern Australia

1979 Scientists discover a hole in the ozone layer above Antarctica

1996–97 Despite world-wide protests, France concludes a series of nuclear weapon tests on Muraroa Atoll in the South Pacific before agreeing to sign the UN Test Ban Treaty

1953 Mt Everest is climbed for the first time by New Zealand explorer Edmund Hillary and Sherpa Tenzing Norgay

1959 China suppresses revolt in Tibet; Tibet's spiritual leader, the Dalai Lama, flees to India

1975 Vietnam War ends with the fall of Saigon after the withdrawal of US troops

1995 A massive earthquake lasting less than a minute kills 5,000 people in Kobe, Japan, and causes massive disruption to transport and industry

1950 Korean War begins when North Korean communist troops invade South Korea; the war lasts until 1953, with US troops fighting on the South Korean side

Potala Palace, Tibet

1957 Vietnam War starts when North Vietnamese (Viet Cong) attack South Vietnamese

1965 US troops based in South Vietnam committed to aid South Vietnamese forces

1976 An earthquake in Tangshan near Beijing, China, kills more than 200,000 people and injures another 150,000

1991 Mt Pinatubo in the Philippines erupts killing 30 people and leaving 10,000 homeless

Following Iraq's occupation of the oil-rich state of Kuwait, US combines with the UK, France, and other allies to defeat Iraq in the Gulf War

2003 The United States and the UK are leading a coalition of 32 countries attack Iraq without sanction by the UN Security Council and topple the regime of Saddam Hussein. They hand nominal control over to a council in June 2004; first democratic elections are supposed to be held in early 2005

1961 Russian cosmonaut Yuri Gagarin becomes the first man in space and the first to orbit Earth

Berlin Wall erected by the East German government to stop citizens escaping to the West

1957 The space age starts with the launching by Russia of Sputnik I, a satellite capable of orbiting Earth

Sputnik 1, 1957

1967 A military junta seizes power in Greece overthrowing the government led by King Constantin II. Georgios Papadopoulos heads the junta and is elected president in 1973

1974 Turkish troops invade northern Cyprus following the overthrow of the island's president, Greek Archbishop Makarios; fighting between Greek and Turkish Cypriots results in the creation of a neutral corridor across the island

1984 HIV, the virus that causes AIDS and has already taken the lives of millions worldwide, is identified by Luc Montaigner at the Institut Pasteur, Paris

1989 Collapse of Communism in the Soviet Union and Eastern Europe: Russian leader Mikhail Gorbachev and US President George Bush declare the end of the Cold War, and the Berlin Wall is dismantled

1986 An accident at the Chernobyl nuclear power station in the Ukraine contaminates a huge area and spreads fallout across Europe

Russia launches Mir, an Earth-orbiting space station

1991 Civil War in former Yugoslavia between Croatia and Bosnia; UN sends peacekeeping forces

Collapse of the Soviet Union

1995 Talks at Dayton, Ohio, USA, aimed at ending conflict in Bosnia, lead to a peace agreement; hostilities are gradually halted

1956 Egypt closes Suez Canal; British, French, and Israeli troops invade to reopen it but UN intervenes to halt fighting

Independence of Morocco, Tunisia, and Sudan recognized by France

1953 Military coup in Egypt ends monarchy of King Farouk and imposes republic

1960 Massacre of 67 anti-apartheid demonstrators at Sharpeville, Johannesburg, South Africa

1961 South Africa becomes a republic; sanctions imposed by several countries in response to apartheid policies

1962 Nelson Mandela and other members of ANC imprisoned in South Africa

Algerian war of independence ends French rule

1964 Former British colony of Rhodesia (now Zimbabwe) declares independence

1967 Civil war in Nigeria; Biafra secedes until 1970

World's first heart transplant carried out in Cape Town by Dr Christiaan Barnard

1976 Young blacks protesting against compulsory Afrikaans language lessons are gunned down by police at Soweto, Johannesburg, South Africa

1977 Commencement of civil war and famine in Ethiopia, which lead to thousands of deaths

1993 Civil war in Rwanda between Hutu and Tutsi people results in the slaughter of hundreds of thousands of Tutsi

1990 ANC leader Nelson Mandela freed from prison in South Africa; the following year, apartheid is abolished

1994 Global population problems discussed at World Population Conference, Cairo, Egypt

Nelson Mandela elected President in first nonracial, democratic general election in South Africa

1961 US President John F. Kennedy backs an invasion of communist Cuba by exiled Cubans but fails to send US troops; Fidel Castro's forces easily repulse the attack at the Bay of Pigs

1963 Assassination of President John F. Kennedy

1968 Martin Luther King and Robert Kennedy assassinated

1969 US astronauts Neil Armstrong and Buzz Aldrin make first landing on the moon from the spaceship *Apollo 11*

1974 US Space probe Mariner 10 sends back the first close-up pictures of the rings surrounding the planets Mercury and Venus

1981 First flight of the space shuttle *Columbia*

First case of AIDS recognized

1980 Eruption of Mt St Helens, Washington State, USA—one of the largest in modern times

1982 A volcanic eruption at El Chichón, Mexico causes the deaths of 3,500 people and blackens the sky for almost two days

1989 US invades Panama

Space shuttle

2001 On 11 September terrorists of the El Qaida movement fly commercial airplanes into the Pentagon and the towers of the World Trade Center in New York, which collapse. Another hijacked plane crashes in Pennsylvania. Around 3000 people lose their life

1960 In Santiago, Chile, 5,000 people are killed by an earthquake

1955 General strike in Argentina; Perón and wife Eva sent into exile

1970 Salvador Allende of Chile becomes the world's first freely elected Marxist president

1973–76 Perón returns to Argentina and is re-elected, but dies in 1974; his third wife Isobel governs until Army chiefs arrest her; thousands subsequently killed by "security forces"

1973 Allende is deposed and killed in a military coup led by General Augusto Pinochet

1982–83 The century's most severe episode of the El Niño effect: Chile experiences record rainfall

1982 Argentina invades Falkland Islands; Britain uses military force to retake the islands by 14 June

1988 General Pinochet's rule in Chile rejected by large majority in plebiscite

1992 Global environmental problems debated at first Earth Summit in Rio de Janiero, Brazil

Alberto Fujimori, President of Peru, suspends parliament claiming corruption among government officials; a new constitution is approved in 1993

Part 3

Regions of the World

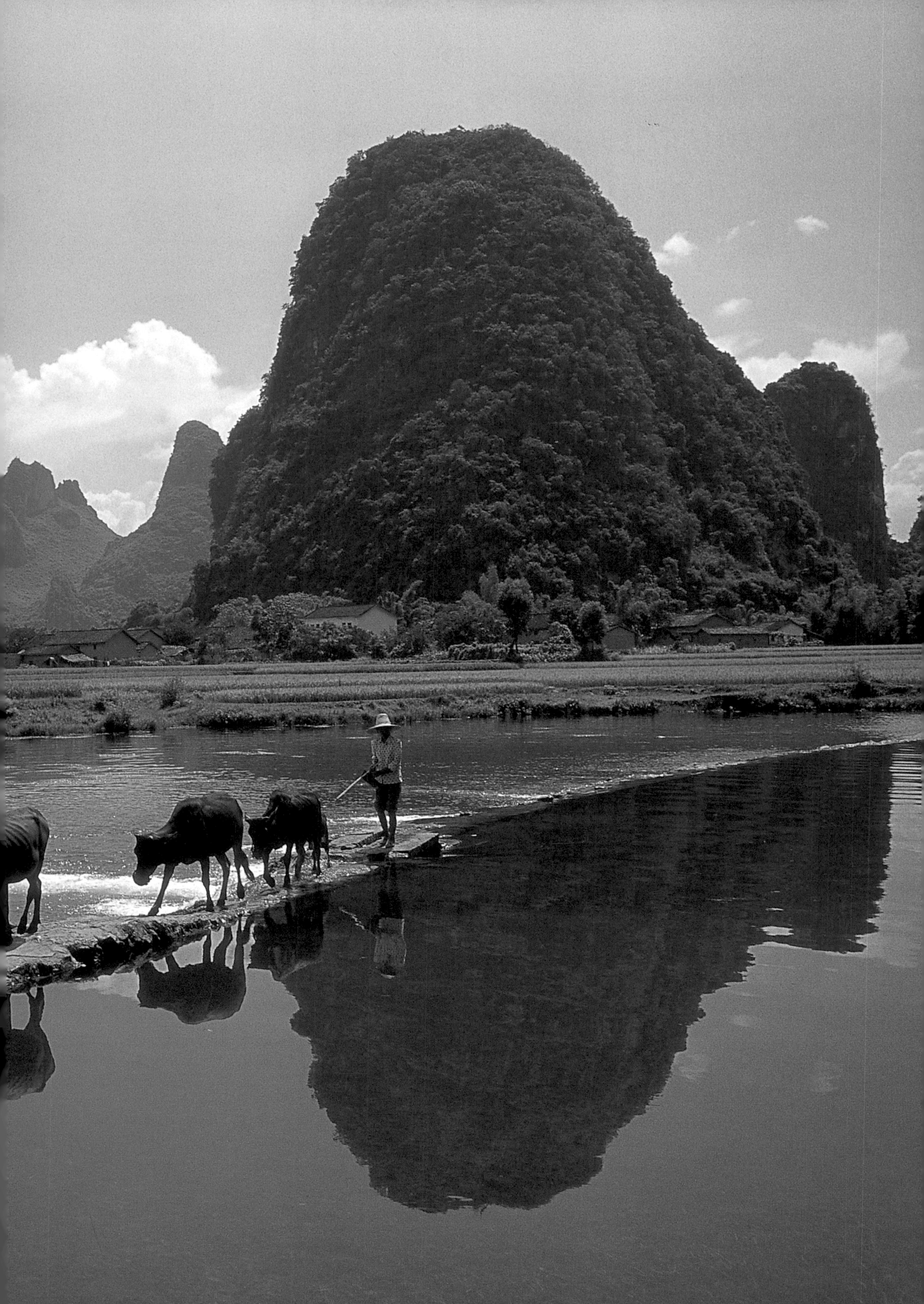

World regions: The Changing Scene

Culture is one way of defining world regions: the Middle East and Central Asia, for example, have a broadly Islamic culture in common (above). North America stretches from Canada (opposite) to Mexico and can be defined by its geographical, as well as its cultural, boundaries.

Geographers, in their attempt to subdivide Earth's land surface into coherent areas, developed the concept of regions. Regions can be delineated within continents or within countries, depending at what scale study is being conducted.

Regions are parts of the world that have some degree of similarity in one or more characteristics, such as physiography, climate, culture, or economy. For example, a Himalayan region can be based on physiography, a Saharan region determined by its desert climate, a Confucian East Asia region determined by a dominant culture, and a European Economic Community region defined by countries linked by economic cooperation. In this atlas, however, much larger regions have been identified.

Regions, under whatever criteria they are defined, must be geographically contiguous. Countries adjacent to each other often share a major characteristic. Thus, the countries of Southeast Asia have a tropical, humid climate which ensures the growing of tropical crops such as tropical fruits, tea, coffee, and rubber. In contrast, several Middle Eastern countries have arid climates which inhibit large scale agriculture. Southeast Asia and the Middle East can be considered as regions where climate is one of the distinguishing characteristics.

In other cases, culture may be an important criterion for defining a region. The Middle East, besides being climatically different from other parts of Asia, also differs culturally. North and Central America have considerable cultural and economic differences that justify their being differentiated. This is also true for Africa, North Africa differing in several aspects from the countries south of the Sahara.

Very often a number of small countries lying close to each other may share one or more characteristics. This is the case with the small island nations of the Pacific. They can then be said to lie within an identifiable region or sub-region. On the other hand, some large countries, such as the Russian Federation have sufficient climatic and cultural diversity within their borders for sub-regions to be identified.

The naming and defining of continents was the first attempt to mark out large regions on the map of the world. Because the continents were named and defined by Europeans, the perspectives used were European. For example, some names came from ancient Greece where the lands lying to its east were named Asia and the lands to its west were called Europe. Because of the European perspective, it became customary to refer to the eastern lands close to Europe as the Near East, the lands lying far to the east as the Far East, and the lands in between as the Middle East.

Europe and Asia are geographically contiguous, forming the Eurasian landmass, but there are sufficient differences between them for them to be identifiable as two separate continents. This traditional separation is largely based on cultural and historical factors, the lines dividing the two continents being accepted by convention.

Africa, the two American continents, Australia, and Antarctica are easily defined because of their separation from other landmasses. Australia, New Zealand, and several Pacific islands are customarily included in a large region known as Oceania that includes a variety of climates, economies, and cultures. The only factor that gives Oceania its coherence is that these lands form a large cluster in the Central and South Pacific Ocean.

Regions or sub-regions can be identified within most of the world's continents. For instance, the large continent of Asia contains areas with distinctive characteristics that allow them to be considered as regions. Asia has been customarily subdivided into East Asia, Southeast Asia, South Asia (the Indian subcontinent), West Asia (the Middle East), Central Asia, and North Asia (Siberia). Monsoon Asia (or Asia-Pacific), a larger region, defined on the basis of climate, stretches across East, Southeast, and South Asia. Monsoon Asia is humid, extremely populous, and has extensive agriculture. Central Asia and the Middle East, on the other hand, are more arid, less populated, and have limited scope for agriculture, except where irrigated water is available.

Europe was within the last half century politically divided into Eastern and Western Europe. This ideological divide resulted in contrasting economic systems, the residual effects of which can still be seen. On economic grounds, Eastern and Western Europe can be considered as sub-regions. Climate can be used to differentiate Mediterranean Europe from lands north of the Alps.

In this atlas, the world has been divided up in seven regions, which are identical to the continents and some of which are split up into subregions: Oceania; Asia and the Middle East, consisting of the subregions Southeast Asia, East Asia, Indian Subcontinent, and the Middle East; Europe with its subregions Northern, Central, Southwestern, Southeastern, and Eastern Europe, as well as the British Isles; Africa, divided into Northern, Western, Central, Eastern, and Southern Africa; North and Central America with the additional subregion of the Caribbean; South America; and the Polar Regions.

Information is provided on each region in a systematic way, recognizing that for some areas and countries data is relatively sparse and incomplete. The descriptions of each area have been organized into sections in order to show difference and similarities as well as highlight those factors responsible for natural, economic, and social conditions.

The World: Physical

ARCTIC OCEAN
Spitsbergen
Greenland (Kalaallit Nunaat)
GREENLAND SEA
NORWEGIAN SEA
Iceland
Nordkapp
BARENTS SEA
Novaya Zemlya
KARSKOYE MORE
Severnaya Zemlya
Poluostrov Taymyr
Ozero Taymyr
MORE LAPTEVYKH
Ostrov Kotel'nyy
Severo-Sibirskaya Nizmennost'
Scandinavia
Gulf of Bothnia
BALTIC SEA
Onezhskoye Ozero
Ladozhskoye Ozero
North European Plain
Volga
Ural'skiy Khrebet
Ob
Zapando Sibirskaya Ravnina
Yenisey
Yeniseyskiy Kryazh
Sredne-Sibirskoye Ploskogor'ye
Lena
Verkhoyanskiy Khrebet
Khrebet Cherskogo
Indigirka
Stanovoy Khrebet
OKHOTSKOYE MORE
Ostrov Sakhalin
British Isles
NORTH SEA
Dnyapro
Rhine
Carpathian Mts
SEA OF AZOV
ARAL SEA
Balqash Köli
Mongol Altayn Nuruu
Ozero Baykal
Da Hinggan Ling
Amur
Bay of Biscay
ALPS
Pyrenees
Appennines
Iberian Peninsula
Balkan Pen.
BLACK SEA
Gora El'brus 5641 m
CASPIAN SEA
Syrdar'ya
Amu Darya
Tian Shan
Gobi
SEA OF JAPAN
Hokkaidō
Honshū
Kyūshū
Strait of Gibraltar
MEDITERRANEAN SEA
ATLAS MTS
Euphrates
Tigris
Dasht-e Kavir
Dasht-e Lut
Hindu Kush
Indus
Kunlun Shan
HIMALAYA
Huang
YELLOW SEA
EAST CHINA SEA
Chang
Kuril Ost.
SAHARA
Libyan Des.
L. Nasser
Nile
RED SEA
An Nafūd Desert
Persian Gulf
Kuh-ha-ye Zagros
Arabian Peninsula
Ar Rub' al Khālī
Thar Desert
Ganga (Ganges)
Mt Everest 8848 m
Nansei - shotō
Taiwan
Tropic of Cancer
SAHEL
ARABIAN SEA
Western Ghats
Deccan
Eastern Ghats
Bay of Bengal
Phanlwin
Mekong
Hainan
Luzon
PHILIPPINE SEA
Lac Tchad (Lake Chad)
Gulf of Aden
Horn of Africa
Ethiopian Highlands
SOUTH CHINA SEA
Philippines
ANDAMAN SEA
Lake Volta
Niger
Cape Comorin
Sri Lanka
Mindanao
SULU SEA
Malay Peninsula
CELEBES SEA
MOLUCCA SEA
Gulf of Guinea
Equator
Congo Basin
Lake Victoria
Great Rift Valley
Kilimanjaro 5895 m
Borneo
Sumatera (Sumatra)
Sulawesi (Celebes)
Jazirah Doberai
Pk Jaya 5030 m
BISMARCK SEA
New Guinea
Congo
L. Tanganyika
JAVA SEA
BANDA SEA
ARAFURA SEA
TIMOR SEA
Arnhem Land
Cape York Pen.
Great Barrier Reef
CORAL SEA
St Helena
Zambezi
Mozambique Channel
Madagascar
INDIAN OCEAN
Mauritius
Lake Kariba
Limpopo
Kimberley Plateau
Barkly Tableland
Tropic of Capricorn
Namib Desert
Kalahari Dessert
Great Sandy Desert
Simpson Desert
GREAT DIVIDING RANGE
Great Victoria Desert
Drakensberg
Nullarbor Plain
Great Australian Bight
Eyre Pen.
Tasmania
SOUTH ATLANTIC OCEAN
Îles Crozet
Îles de Kerguélen
Arctic Circle
Antarctic Circle

ARCTIC OCEAN
Greenland (Kalaallit Nunaat)
Banks Island
Prince of Wales Island
Somerset Island
Baffin Bay
Point Barrow
Ostrov Vrangelya
BEAUFORT SEA
Victoria Island
Baffin Island
CHUKCHI SEA
Brooks Range
Bering Strait
Great Bear Lake
Davis Strait
Denmark Strait
Arctic Circle
Baker Lake
Southampton Island
Mt McKinley 6194 m
Hudson Strait
Iceland
Great Slave Lake
Hudson Bay
Nunap Isua
BERING SEA
Gulf of Alaska
Aleutian Islands
LABRADOR SEA
Labrador
Queen Charlotte Islands
ROCKY MTS
Lake Winnipeg
Lake Manitoba
Vancouver Island
Newfoundland
Lake Superior
Lake Huron
Great Plains
Lake Michigan
Missouri
Lake Ontario
Nova Scotia
Appalachian Mts
NORTH ATLANTIC OCEAN
Great Salt Lake
Lake Erie
Cape Cod
NORTH PACIFIC OCEAN
Mississippi
Cape Lookout
Bermuda
Rio Grande
Baja California
Gulf of Mexico
Bahamas
Hawaiian Islands
Cuba
Tropic of Cancer
Cabo San Lucas
Peninsula de Yucatán
Greater Antilles
Leeward Islands
Lesser Antilles
Windward Islands
Caribbean Sea
Trinidad
Marshall Islands
Llanos
Guiana Highlands
Polynesia
Islas Galápagos
Equator
Amazonas
Selvas
Amazon Basin
Îles Marquises
Îles Tuamotu
Archipel de la Société
Viti Levu
Lago Titicaca
Planalto do Mato Grosso
Brazilian Highlands
Nouvelle Calédonie
Tropic of Capricorn
Gran Chaco
Pitcairn Is
Paraná
Isla de Pascua (Easter Island)
Cerro Aconcagua 6960 m
Kermadec Is
SOUTH PACIFIC OCEAN
Pampas
North I.
SOUTH ATLANTIC OCEAN
New Zealand
Chatham Is
South I.
Patagonia
Archipiélago de los Chonos
Auckland Is
Archipiélago de la Reina Adelaida
Falkland Islands
South Georgia
Cabo de Hornos (Cape Horn)
Isla Grande de Tierra del Fuego
Antarctic Pen.
Antarctic Circle
Scale 1:87,500,000
Projection: Mercator
kilometers
miles

The World: Political

ARCTIC OCEAN
SVALBARD (Nor.)
Novaya Zemlya
Novosibirskiy Ostrova
JAN MAYEN (Nor.)
BARENTS SEA
Arctic Circle
ICELAND
SWEDEN
FINLAND
FAEROE IS (Den.)
NORWAY
Oslo
Helsinki
Stockholm
Tallinn
ESTONIA
Rīga
LATVIA
DENMARK
København
UNITED KINGDOM
LITHUANIA
Vilnius
Minsk
ISLE OF MAN (U.K.)
Dublin
IRELAND
Amsterdam
NETH.
Berlin
POLAND
BELARUS
London
BELG.
GERMANY
Warszawa
Bruxelles
LUX.
Praha
Luxembourg
CZECH REP.
SLOVAKIA
Kyyiv
CHANNEL ISLANDS (U.K.)
Paris
LIECH.
Wien
Bratislava
UKRAINE
Bern
AUST.
Budapest
MOLDOVA
SWITZ.
SLOV.
HUNG.
ROMANIA
Chişinău
FRANCE
Ljubljana
CROAT.
Beograd
Zagreb
B.-H.
Bucureşti
Sarajevo
YUG.
Sofiya
ANDORRA
Madrid
Roma
Tiranë
MACE.
BULGARIA
ALBANIA
Skopje
PORTUGAL
SPAIN
ITALY
GREECE
Lisboa
Tūnis
Athína
GIBRALTAR (U.K.)
MALTA
Valletta
Madeira (Port.)
Rabat
Alger
TUNISIA
Tarābulus
Islas Canarias (Sp.)
MOROCCO
ALGERIA
LIBYA
EGYPT
W. SAHARA
Tropic of Cancer
MAURITANIA
Nouakchott
MALI
NIGER
CHAD
SUDAN
SENEGAL
Dakar
GAMBIA
GUINEA-BISSAU
Bamako
Niamey
BURKINA FASO
Ouagadougou
NIGERIA
Conakry
GUINEA
SIERRA LEONE
CÔTE D'IVOIRE
GHANA
TOGO
BENIN
Porto-Novo
Abuja
Freetown
LIBERIA
Monrovia
Yamoussoukro
Accra
Lomé
Malalabo
CAMEROON
Yaoundé
EQ. GUINEA
Equator
SÃO TOMÉ & PRÍNCIPE
Libreville
GABON
Brazzaville
CONGO
Kinshasa
DEM. REP. OF THE CONGO
Ndjamena
C.A.R.
Bangui
Al Kharţūm
Asmara
ERITREA
ETHIOPIA
Ādīs Ābeba
Djibouti
DJIBOUTI
SOMALIA
Muqdisho
UGANDA
Kampala
KENYA
Nairobi
Kigali
RWANDA
Bujumbura
BURUNDI
TANZANIA
Dodoma
Luanda
ANGOLA
ZAMBIA
Lusaka
MALAWI
Lilongwe
Moroni
COMOROS
MAYOTTE (Fr.)
Harare
ZIMBABWE
MOZAMBIQUE
Antananarivo
MADAGASCAR
NAMIBIA
Windhoek
BOTSWANA
Gaborone
Pretoria
Maputo
Mbabane
SWAZILAND
Bloemfontein
Maseru
LESOTHO
SOUTH AFRICA
Cape Town
ASCENSION ISLAND (ST HELENA)
ST HELENA (U.K.)
Tropic of Capricorn
TRISTAN DA CUNHA (U.K.)
GEORGIA
T'bilisi
ARM.
AZER.
Bakı
Yerevan
Ankara
TURKEY
Lefkosia
CYPRUS
SYRIA
IRAQ
Dimashq
LEBANON
Bayrūt
JORDAN
Yerushalayim
ISRAEL
'Ammān
Baghdād
Tehrān
IRAN
Al Qāhirah
Al Kuwayt
KUWAIT
BAHRAIN
Al Manāmah
Ad Dawḩah
QATAR
Ar Riyāḑ
Abū Zaby
U.A.E.
Masqaţ
OMAN
SAUDI ARABIA
YEMEN
Şan'ā'
Suquţrá (Yemen)
ARABIAN SEA
RUSSIAN FEDERATION
Moskva
Astana
KAZAKHSTAN
UZBEKISTAN
TURKMENISTAN
Ashgabat
Bishkek
KYRGYZSTAN
Toshkent
Dushanbe
TAJIKISTAN
Kābol
AFGHANISTAN
Islāmābād
PAKISTAN
New Delhi
NEPAL
Kathmandu
BHUTAN
Thimphu
BANGLADESH
Dhaka
INDIA
MYANMAR
Bay of Bengal
Yangon
THAILAND
Krung Thep
LAOS
Viangchan
Hà Nôi
VIETNAM
CAMBODIA
Phnum Pénh
SRI LANKA
Colombo
MALDIVES
Male
Ulaanbaatar
MONGOLIA
Beijing
CHINA
P'yŏngyang
NORTH KOREA
Sŏul
SOUTH KOREA
JAPAN
Tōkyō
OKHOTSKOY MORE
Ostrov Sakhalin
Kuril'skiye
T'ai-pei
TAIWAN
Manila
PHILIPPINES
GUAM (U.S.A.)
NORTHERN MARIANAS (U.S.A.)
Bandar Seri Begawan
BRUNEI
MALAYSIA
Kuala Lumpur
SINGAPORE
Koror
PALAU
MICRONESIA
INDONESIA
Jakarta
CHRISTMAS ISLAND (Aust.)
EAST TIMOR
PAPUA NEW GUINEA
Port Moresby
Victoria
SEYCHELLES
Chagos Archipelago
BRITISH INDIAN OCEAN TERRITORY (U.K.)
COCOS (KEELING) ISLANDS (Aust.)
ASHMORE & CARTIER ISLANDS ISLANDS (Aust.)
CORAL SEA ISLANDS (Aust.)
MAURITIUS
Port Louis
RÉUNION (Fr.)
INDIAN OCEAN
AUSTRALIA
Canberra
Tasmania
Île Amsterdam (Fr.)
FRENCH SOUTHERN & ANTARCTIC ISLANDS (Fr.)
Prince Edward Is (S. Africa)
Îles Crozet (Fr.)
Îles de Kerguélen (Fr.)
HEARD & McDONALD ISLANDS (Aust.)
SOUTH ATLANTIC OCEAN
BOUVERT ISLAND (Nor.)
SOUTHERN OCEAN
ANTARCTICA
Antarctic Circle

GREENLAND (KALAALLIT NUNAAT) (Den.)
ICELAND
Reykjavík
CANADA
U.S.A.
UNITED STATES OF AMERICA
MEXICO
CUBA
BRAZIL
PERU
COLOMBIA
VENEZUELA
BOLIVIA
ARGENTINA
CHILE
ECUADOR
PARAGUAY
URUGUAY
NORTH ATLANTIC OCEAN
SOUTH ATLANTIC OCEAN
PACIFIC OCEAN
BEAUFORT SEA
CHUKCHI SEA
BERING SEA
Gulf of Alaska
Hudson Bay
Baffin Bay
Baffin Island
Davis Strait
Bering Strait
Banks Island
Victoria Island
Ostrov Vrangelya
Aleutian Islands
Newfoundland
ST PIERRE AND MIQUELON (Fr.)
Ottawa
Washington D.C.
Azores (Port.)
BERMUDA (U.K.)
BAHAMAS
Nassau
Gulf of Mexico
La Habana
México
Isla Guadalupe (Mex.)
Islas Revillagigedo (Mex.)
MIDWAY ISLANDS (U.S.A.)
Hawaiian Islands (U.S.A.)
WAKE ISLAND (U.S.A.)
JOHNSTON ATOLL (U.S.A.)
Dalap-Uliga-Darrit
KINGMAN REEF (U.S.A.)
PALMYRA ATOLL (U.S.A.)
Bairiki
BAKER AND HOWLAND ISLANDS (U.S.A.)
JARVIS ISLAND (U.S.A.)
KIRIBATI
Funafuti
TUVALU
TOKELAU (N.Z.)
WALLIS & FUTUNA (Fr.)
SAMOA
Apia
AMERICAN SAMOA (U.S.A.)
Port-Vila
FIJI
Suva
TONGA
NIUE (N.Z.)
COOK ISLANDS (N.Z.)
Nuku'alofa
Îles Marquises
Archipel de la Société
Îles Tuamotu
Tahiti
FRENCH POLYNESIA (Fr.)
PITCAIRN IS. (U.K.)
Isla de Pascua (Chile)
Sala y Gómez (Chile)
Archipiélago Juan Fernández (Chile)
Kermadec Is (N.Z.)
North I.
Wellington
Chatham Is (N.Z.)
Bounty Is (N.Z.)
Antipodes Is (N.Z.)
Campbell I. (N.Z.)
Islas Galápagos (Ecu.)
Kingston
JAMAICA
BELIZE
Belmopan
HAITI
DOMINICAN REPUBLIC
Santo Domingo
ST KITTS & NEVIS
ANTIGUA & BARBUDA
DOMINICA
ST VINCENT & THE GRENADINES
ST LUCIA
BARBADOS
GRENADA
TRINIDAD & TOBAGO
Port of Spain
Guatemala
GUATEMALA
EL SALVADOR
San Salvador
HONDURAS
Tegucigalpa
NICARAGUA
Managua
San José
COSTA RICA
PANAMA
Panamá
Caracas
Georgetown
GUYANA
SURINAME
Paramaribo
FRENCH GUIANA (Fr.)
Bogotá
Quito
Lima
La Paz
Sucre
Brasília
Asunción
Santiago
Buenos Aires
Montevideo
CAPE VERDE
Praia
Trindade (Brazil)
FALKLAND ISLANDS (U.K.)
SOUTH GEORGIA & SOUTH SANDWICH ISLANDS (U.K.)
Cabo de Hornos
South Shetland Islands (U.K.)
South Orkney Islands (U.K.)
BELLINGSHAUSEN SEA
Antarctic Peninsula
Arctic Circle
Tropic of Cancer
Equator
Tropic of Capricorn
Antarctic Circle
K L M N P Q R S T
180° 160° 140° 120° 100° 80° 60° 40°
70° 60° 50° 40° 30° 20° 10° 0° 10° 20° 30° 40° 50° 60°
1 2 3 4 5 6 7 8 9 10 11 12 13 14 15
0 1500 3000 4000 kilometers
0 1000 2000 miles
Scale 1:87,500,000
Projection: Mercator

Oceania

Oceania

Oceania is the name given to a group of islands spread over 8.5 million sq km (3.3 million sq miles) in the Pacific Ocean, the majority of which lie in the southern hemisphere. The islands range in size from the large island continent of Australia, through medium-sized nations such as Papua New Guinea and New Zealand, to much smaller countries, such as Vanuatu and Tonga.

On cultural grounds, the islands can be divided into four groups. The first, Micronesia, lies east of the Philippines and includes the Federated States of Micronesia, Palau, the Marshall Islands, Nauru, and the USA dependencies of Guam and the Northern Mariana Islands. Melanesia, the second group, lies east of Indonesia and Australia, and includes Papua New Guinea, the Solomon Islands, Vanuatu, Fiji, Tonga, Tuvalu, and Samoa and the dependencies of New Caledonia (France) and American Samoa. Polynesia, the third, lies in the center of the Pacific Ocean, and includes Kiribati, French Polynesia, and the dependencies of Niue, the Cook Islands (NZ), the Pitcairn Islands (UK), and Hawaii (part of the USA). The fourth group comprises Australia and New Zealand. Unlike the other groups, these islands have indigenous populations, but the majority of the population are people who have migrated from Europe over the last two centuries. Australian dependencies include Norfolk Island in the Pacific Ocean and the Cocos (Keeling) and Christmas Islands in the Indian Ocean.

Physical features

Physiographically, the islands of Oceania can be classed into four categories. First there is Australia, situated in the middle of the Indo-Australian Plate, where there was no mountain building during the Tertiary geological era. Australia's eastern high-lands, the eroded remnants of old mountains, are a series of elevated plateaus; the western half of the country is an ancient eroded plateau linked to the east by vast sedimentary basins.

In the second category are the islands lying along the collision boundaries between crustal plates. In the South Pacific, New Zealand, Papua New Guinea, the Solomon Islands, and Fiji are within the collision zone between the Indo-Australian and the Pacific plates. In the North Pacific, the Mariana Islands lie along the collision boundary of the Eurasian and Pacific plates. These collisions have produced folded mountain ranges. New Zealand and Papua New Guinea have young mountain ranges, some peaks exceeding 3,000 m (10,000 ft).

The third category includes volcanic islands such as Fiji, which rise from the floor of the Pacific Ocean basin. Much smaller than the countries in the second category, they are mostly made up of high mountains, with some low-lying fringes along the coastlines, including coral reefs.

Finally, there are coral islands and atolls, such as Tuvalu. Atolls form low-lying circular coral reefs which enclose lagoons. The atolls typically develop around submerged volcanic cones. In some places, such as in Guam, coral islands have been raised by crustal movements.

Climate and vegetation

Oceania can be divided into two climatic zones: temperate and tropical. A large part of Australia and all of New Zealand lie in the temperate zone, while most of the island countries of the Pacific are tropical. Persistent trade winds dominate much of Oceania, and tropical cyclones often cause considerable damage.

Large parts of Australia are arid or semiarid. Humid zones are found along most of the east coast and Tasmania, and in part of the northern coast during summer. Most of New Zealand, Papua New Guinea and most of the islands in the Pacific are humid. However, droughts associated with the El Niño phenomenon have been frequent in recent decades in northern Australia and Papua New Guinea.

Rainforests, both tropical and temperate, occur in all the humid regions of Oceania—Australia and the larger and high (mostly volcanic) islands. However, deforestation has taken place in several places, such as parts of eastern Australia, Tasmania, New Zealand, and the Solomon Islands.

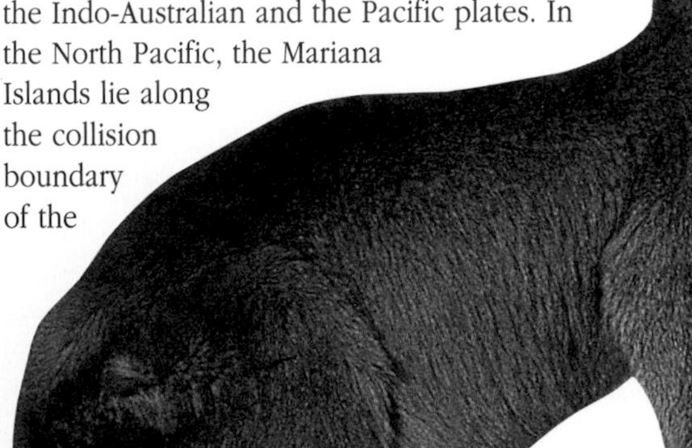

The kangaroo, probably Australia's most well known native animal. While some such animals are threatened with extinction, kangaroos are in fact regarded as pests by many.

Isolation has been a major factor in the development of unique species of animals, birds, and plants in the Pacific islands. The spread of human habitation and hunting has seriously affected native animals, especially in Australia—several species are extinct or endangered.

Population

In 2000 the population of Oceania totalled 31 million. Australia and New Zealand accounted for 22.4 million people and Papua New Guinea for 4.7 million people. The remaining 3.9 million inhabitants are scattered on many small islands over a large area. Life expectancy for the area as a whole is 71.8 years for males and 76.6 for females. The annual population growth rate averages 1.2 percent but this varies widely, with one percent for Australia and New Zealand, 2.4 percent for Papua New Guinea, and 2.1 percent for Melanesia. Rates of urbanization vary widely too, being 89 percent for Australia and New Zealand and 17.4 percent for Papua New Guinea.

Agriculture

Agriculture in Oceania can be divided into three kinds: labor-intensive subsistence agriculture, which occurs in most of the tropical islands of the Pacific; plantation crops, which are cultivated in the medium-sized tropical islands; and capital-intensive agriculture, which is found in Australia and New Zealand.

Subsistence agriculture in the Pacific islands consists of short-life items such as cassava, taro, yams, breadfruit, and sweet potatoes. Bananas and papayas are the most commonly grown fruits. Coconut palms grow on almost all the islands, and are a source of fresh food. Oil is extracted from the dried coconut meat (copra). Copra is exported from countries such as Vanuatu and Samoa. Cash crops, often a legacy of colonial times, are also important in some of the Pacific nations—sugar in Fiji and cocoa in Vanuatu.

Fishing is important for the majority of Pacific islands, as their economic zones extend to the 200 nautical mile limit—a large area compared to the size of many of the islands. Several islands have granted fishing licenses to Japanese, South Korean, and Taiwanese companies.

Palms in the Finke Valley, central Australia (left), and forests edging Lake Matheson in southern New Zealand (above). The New Ireland coast (right), and a young girl in traditional dress and face paint (above right), both in Papua New Guinea.

Industrialization

Australia and New Zealand both have modern diversified economies with well-established infrastructures. Australia is particularly well favored as it has rich mineral deposits and energy sources. Manufacturing, including food processing, makes an important contribution to the economy of these two Pacific nations.

In contrast, the other islands of the Pacific are not industrially developed. Papua New Guinea, is rich in minerals such as copper and gold, and has recently discovered natural gas fields. There are nickel deposits in New Caledonia and gold in Fiji, both of which are exported rather than used in local industries.

Many islands in the Pacific have few resources; some have insufficient land for their people and a number lack adequate supplies of drinking water. This shortage of natural resources, coupled with poor infrastructures, has impeded industrial development. Industry in most of the islands is limited to food processing.

Tourism has become an important source of revenue for much of Oceania. Australia and New Zealand offer tourists modern amenities and facilities, while the beautiful scenery of tropical Pacific Islands like Fiji, Tahiti, Vanuatu, and the Northern Mariana Islands attract visitors.

Languages

Culturally, Oceania can be divided into two major groups: the predominantly European settlements of Australia and New Zealand, and Melanesia, Polynesia, and Micronesia, which have been long settled by Oceanic peoples. New Caledonia is partially settled by Europeans.

During the colonial era, the entire region came under European influence. This resulted in English and French becoming important languages, depending on the colonial powers (Britain, America, and France). English is the official language of New Zealand, Australia, Papua New Guinea, the Solomon Islands, Vanuatu, and Fiji. French is spoken in New Caledonia and French Polynesia. On several of the Pacific islands, particularly Papua New Guinea and Vanuatu, pidgin is a common lingua franca.

In Australia, only remnants of the numerous Aboriginal languages that were spoken in the continent before European settlement still exist. Several of these languages are found in the Northern Territory and the northern part of Western Australia (the Kimberleys), where Walmadjeri is becoming a common language among several Aboriginal tribes. In New Zealand, which has a significant Maori population, the Maori language is widely spoken.

Numerous languages are found in Melanesia, Polynesia, and Micronesia. In Papua New Guinea, hundreds of languages are spoken, Austronesian languages being spoken along the coastline and Papuan languages in the highlands. Austronesian languages such as Fijian in Fiji and Tahitian, Tongan, and Samoan in Polynesia are widespread.

Boundary disputes and wars

The whole region was affected by the Japanese invasion during the Second World War, and was the site of many important battles. No significant boundary disputes exist in the region. In recent decades, boundaries have been drawn up for Oceanic economic zones. However, there have been civil disturbances in both Fiji and New Caledonia—the former related to the struggle for a less racially biased government in the years after Fiji became a republic in 1970, the latter related to the wish of some of the people to become independent from France.

Nations

Dependencies & territories

Oceania

New Zealand

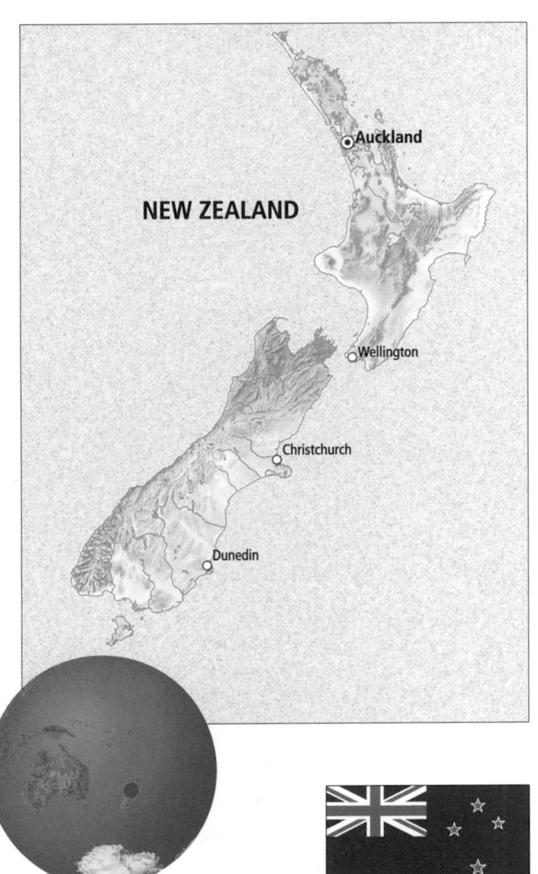

OVERSEAS TERRITORIES

Cook Islands
Niue
Tokelau

Fact File

Official name New Zealand

Form of government Monarchy with single legislative body (House of Representatives)

Capital Wellington

Area 268,680 sq km (103,737 sq miles)

Time zone GMT + 12 hours

Population 3,940,000

Projected population 2015 4,141,000

Population density 14.7 per sq km (38 per sq mile)

Life expectancy 78.2

Infant mortality (per 1,000) 6.2

Official language English

Other language Maori

Literacy rate 99 %

Religions Anglican 17.5 %, Roman Catholic 13 %, Presbyterian 13 %, other Christian 17 %, other 2.5 %, unaffiliated 37 %

Ethnic groups European 71.7 %, Maori 14.5 %, other (including Samoan, Tongan, Cook Islander, Asian) 13.8 %

Currency New Zealand dollar

Economy Services 70 %, industry 20 %, agriculture 10 %

GNP per capita US$19,500

Climate Temperate: warmer in north, colder in south and wetter in west

Highest point Mt Cook 3,764 m (12,349 ft)

Map reference Pages 132–33

Mountainous, partly volcanic, and situated approximately 1,600 km (1,000 miles) southeast of Australia, New Zealand is the biggest of the island groups that constitute Oceania. It consists of two main islands, which are separated by Cook Strait, as well as several smaller islands, and three small territories in the Pacific Ocean. The country's temperate climate has wide regional variations, the northern part of the North Island being subtropical while in the southern extremity of the South Island winter snow is common.

New Zealand has a liberal and progressive political history, pioneering votes for women in 1893, introducing a welfare state including a health service in 1938, and having a creditable record in ethnic relations.

The first people to arrive in the country were the Polynesian ancestors of the Maori around 750 to 1,000 years ago. In 1642 the Dutch explorer Abel Tasman was probably the first European to sight the islands, and in 1769 Captain James Cook was the first to land on them. The period that followed was characterized by settlement by whalers and sealers, and by Maori tribal warfare using modern firearms. This conflict came to an end when the Maori chiefs ceded sovereignty to the British Crown in the Treaty of Waitangi, which was signed on 6 February 1840. This day is still celebrated annually as the "Waitangi Day", New Zealand's national holiday.

After this date systematic and mostly peaceful colonization took place. By the 1860s, however, conflicts arose between settlers and Maori over land rights, especially in the North Island, eventually giving rise to outright war. When hostilities came to an end in 1872 the outcome in terms of landholding was decidedly in the settlers' favor. In recent years claims for compensation to Maori have become a major political issue. Aotearoa, which means "Land of the Long White Cloud", is the Maori name for New Zealand.

Geologically, New Zealand is a relatively young country. The Southern Alps in the South Island emerged from the sea in the course of the past 10 to 15 million years, while the volcanic action that shaped much of North Island occurred between 1 and 4 million years ago. The comparatively low ranges on North Island are formed from folded sedimentary rocks with higher volcanic peaks. Overlaying these rocks in the center of the North Island is a plateau of lava, pumice, and volcanic tuff. Minor earthquakes are common in New Zealand, and there are many areas of volcanic and geothermal activity on the North Island. Three volcanoes dominate the central plateau (Ruapehu being the most active of them) while Lake Taupo, the country's largest natural lake, occupies an ancient crater. In the South Island the Southern Alps form a northeast-southwest oriented ice-capped central massif with Mt Cook at its center. Glaciers descend the flanks of this massif and on the rainy western side forested slopes fall steeply to the sea. On the east, broad outwash fans lead to the much drier, treeless lowlands of the Canterbury Plains. The rugged, forested coastline of the South Island's far southwest, deeply indented with fiords, comprises Fiordland, the country's largest national park.

Few landscapes have been as extensively transformed by humans as that of New Zealand. From 1850 to 1950 vast areas of forest in the North Island were cleared, leaving steep, bare hills which were sown with grass for grazing herds of sheep. Erosion is now a serious problem in many of these areas. Rich pastures produced by year-round rain made agriculture the original foundation of the economy. The

Timeline

c. AD 900 Polynesians reach New Zealand islands and settle, founding *Aotearoa*—Land of the Long White Cloud

c. 1500–1600 Maori build many *pa*, earthwork forts, to protect communities, and settle Chatham Islands

c. 1500–1600 Moas, large flightless birds, hunted to extinction; Maori live off seals, fish, root fern, and cultivate kumera, taro

1642–43 Abel Tasman explores coasts of the islands for Dutch East India Co. Does not land and recommends no action be taken

1769 Captain James Cook sails around both islands and claims them for Britain; Maori population 100,000

1791 Traders from Sydney begin sealing and whaling, some settling in Bay of Islands

1835 Britain establishes a protectorate over New Zealand

1840 Treaty of Waitangi gives Britain sovereignty over New Zealand and Maori sovereignty over their lands

1852 European population 28,000, including 15,000 colonists brought in by New Zealand Co (founded 1838)

1853 New Zealand granted self-government; first provincial superintendents and councils are elected

1860 Gold rush in Otago brings European and Asian immigrants; another rush occurs in Canterbury in 1864

1860 Maori Wars between Maori and British over land; Maori resistance worn down after defeat at Te Ranga

1881 Refrigeration allows export of dairy produce and meat to European markets, helping to overcome economic depression

1900 Maori population down to 40,000 due to disease and warfare; European population about 1 million

1914 New Zealand troops join Australians in support of Allies; in 1915 they help establish ANZAC legend in landings at Gallipoli

1931 Country's worst earthquake hits Hawke Bay, killing more than 250 people and devastating cities of Napier and Hastings

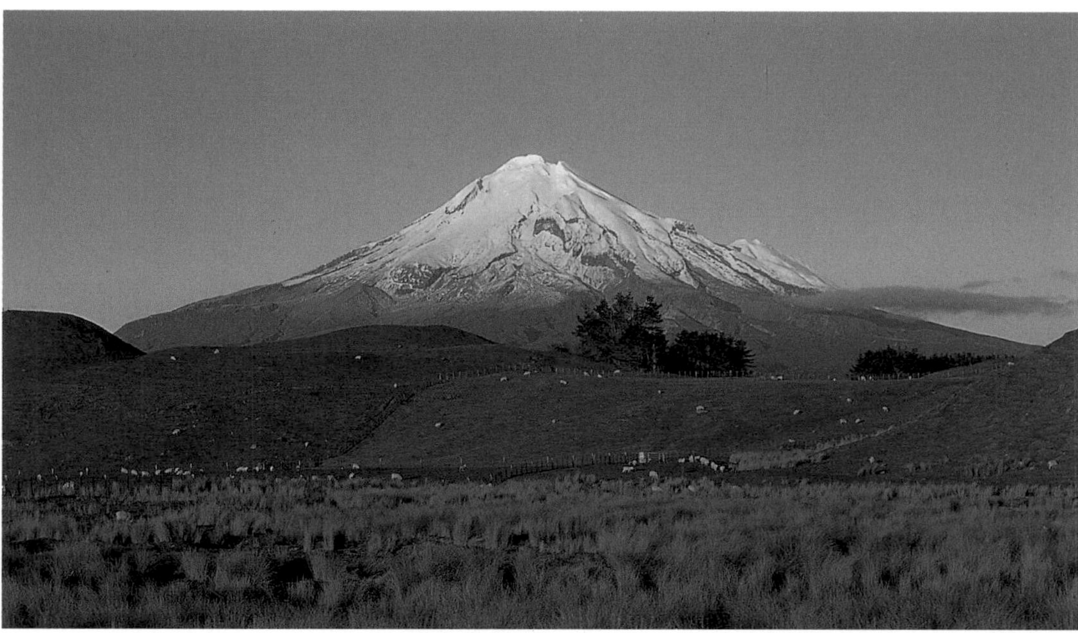

The kea, the world's only alpine parrot, is widespread on the South Island of New Zealand (above); Snowcapped Mt Taranaki on the North Island (right).

export of frozen mutton to Britain began as early as 1881, and New Zealand is still one of the world's main exporters of wool, cheese, butter, and meat. While in earlier years these product were distributed primarily to Great Britain, today they are exported to Australia, the USA, Japan, and other parts of Asia. Since 1984 successive governments have sought to reorient the largely agrarian economy towards a more industrialized, open economy that is better positioned to compete globally. This was part of a wider attempt at economic reform which aimed to reduce the role of the state and increase that played by private enterprise.

New Zealand has only limited petroleum resources, though it does produce natural gas—almost a third of which is used to make synthetic petrol. There are large reserves of coal. The most important source of domestic energy is hydroelectric power, easily generated because of the favorable rainfall and terrain. This has allowed the development of aluminum production using imported bauxite. In recent years, new products have been developed for new international markets. One of these is kiwifruit, the main fresh fruit export in 1996; new varieties of high-quality apples are currently a leading export. A minor feature of the rural scene only twenty years ago, vineyards are now widespread, Marlborough, Hawke Bay, and Gisborne are some of the outstanding main wine-producing regions. Forest products play a vital economic role. Radiata pine, the main commercial timber, is grown in vast state pine forests. Cutting rights to parts of these areas have been sold and the industry as a whole widely privatized.

New Zealand's varied natural scenery, combining quiet harbors and sunlit beaches, with volcanoes, lakes, alpine snowfields and fiords, draws more than 1.5 million visitors per year. As a dollar-earner tourism is second only to primary industry.

1939–45 New Zealand supports Allies in Europe, also raising a Third Division to aid US forces in the Pacific and defend their own country

1950s Postwar boom leads to migration from rural areas to the cities by Maori

1975 Maori protests culminate in a Land March from the far north to Wellington

1985 David Lange's Labour Government bans nuclear-powered and nuclear-missile carrying ships from New Zealand ports

Australia

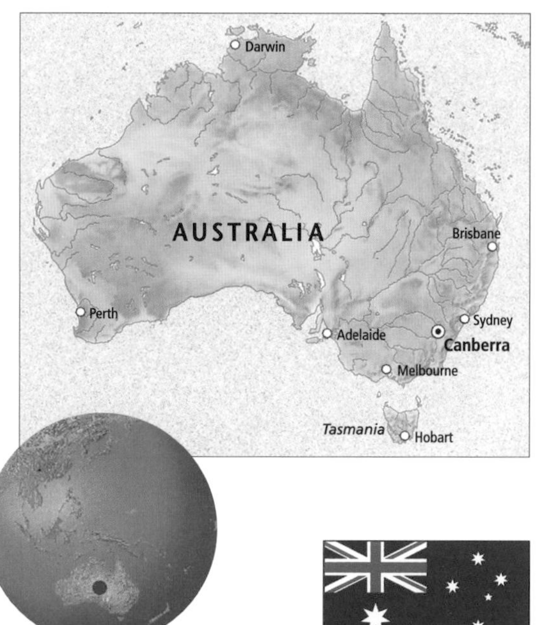

Fact File

Official name Commonwealth of Australia

Form of government Federal constitutional monarchy with two legislative bodies (Senate and House of Representatives)

Capital Canberra

Area 7,686,850 sq km (2,967,893 sq miles)

Time zone GMT + 8–10 hours

Population 19,547,000

Projected population 2015 21,910,000

Population density 2.54 per sq km (6.6 per sq mile)

Life expectancy 80

Infant mortality (per 1,000) 4.9

Official language English

Other languages Indigenous languages (e. g. Aranda, Warlpiri, Pitjantjatjara, Tiwi), Italian, Greek

Literacy rate 100 %

Religions Roman Catholic 27 %, Anglican 22 %, other Christian 22 %, other 12.4 %, none 16.6 %

Ethnic groups European 95 %, Asian 4 %, other (including Aboriginals) 1 %

Currency Australian dollar

Economy Services 78 %, industry 16 %, agriculture 6 %

GNP per capita US$ 27,000

Climate Hot and arid in center; tropical in north with one wet season (November to March); temperate in southeast and along southern coasts

Highest point Mt Kosciuszko 2,229 m (7,313 ft)

Map reference Pages 134–35

Australia is both the world's smallest continental landmass and the sixth-largest country. Most of it consists of low plateaus, and almost one-third is desert. First occupied about 40,000 to 50,000 years ago by peoples from Asia (the ancestors of today's Aboriginals), Australia was visited by Dutch explorers in the seventeenth century, including Abel Tasman in 1642 and 1644, and by the Englishman William Dampier in 1688 and 1699. After being claimed for Britain by Captain James Cook in 1770, a penal colony was established by the British in what is now Sydney in 1788. Some 160,000 convicts arrived before "transportation" from Britain was phased out in the nineteenth century. By then many free settlers had also arrived, and the gold rushes of the 1850s attracted still more people. With both wool and wheat exports providing economic security, the settler population sought greater independence from Britain, and a measure of self-government was granted in 1850. In 1901 the six states formed themselves into the Commonwealth of Australia, and in the 100 years since federation the country has become a successful, prosperous modern democracy. Current concerns include the consequences of economic dependence on Asian markets at a time of recession, demands for the frank acknowledgment of the history of Aboriginal displacement and dispossession, and whether there should be a republican government.

The Western Plateau constitutes the western half of the Australian continent. Made of ancient rocks, the plateau rises near the west coast—the iron-rich Hamersley Range representing its highest elevation in the northwest—and then falls eastward toward the center of the continent. The arid landscape alternates between worn-down ridges and plains, and depressions containing sandy deserts and salt lakes. There is

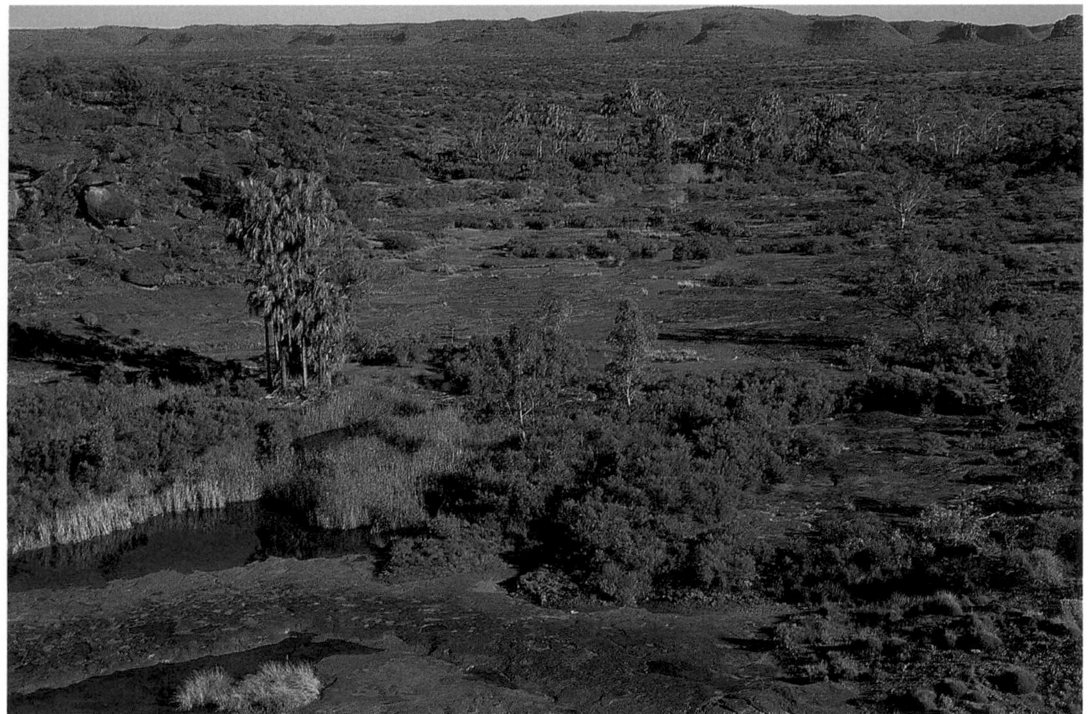

little surface water. The flatness of the plateau is interrupted by the MacDonnell and Musgrave mountain ranges in the center of the continent and the Kimberley and Arnhem Land plateaus in the north. Sheep and cattle are raised on large holdings in parts of this region.

The Central Lowlands forming the Great Artesian Basin, and river systems including the Carpentaria, Eyre, and Murray basins constitute a nearly continuous expanse of lowland that runs north to south. The river systems feed into Lake Eyre, the Bulloo system, or the Darling River. While the Murray Basin is the smallest of the three, its rivers—the Murray and its tributary the Darling—are Australia's longest and most important. Artesian bores make cattle and sheep raising possible through much of the semiarid Central Lowlands.

The Eastern Highlands (known as the Great Dividing Range) and the relatively narrow eastern coastal plain constitute Australia's third main geographic region. This has the greatest relief, the heaviest rainfall, the most abundant and varied vegetation, and accordingly the densest human settlement. A notable feature of the eastern marine environment is the Great Barrier Reef. The world's most expansive coral reef complex, it lies off the northeast coast, stretching some 2,500 km (1,550 miles) from the Tropic of Capricorn to Papua New Guinea. A major tourist attraction, with over 400 types of coral and 1,500 species of fish, it is today protected as the Great Barrier Reef Marine Park.

The island of Tasmania, to the southeast of mainland Australia, has spectacular mountain wilderness areas and more than thirty percent of the state is protected World Heritage areas, national parks, and reserves.

Australian plant and animal life is quite distinctive. The most common trees are the gums *(Eucalyptus)* and wattles *(Acacia)*. Highly adaptable, *Eucalyptus* varieties range from the tall flooded gum, found on the fringes of rainforests, to the mallee which grows on dry plains. Most native mammals are marsupials, and include kangaroos, koalas, wombats, and possums. Australia's monotremes—the platypus and the echidna—which both lay eggs and suckle their young, are unique in all the world. There are also about 400 species of reptile and some 700 species of bird. Australia's vulnerability to introduced plant and animal species was dramatically shown by the spread of prickly pear, which took over vast areas of rural New South Wales and Queensland in the 1920s, and the plagues of rabbits that devastated pastures for a century until the 1960s. Both scourges have been tamed by biological controls.

Once heavily dependent on the pastoral industry—nearly one-third of Australia is still used for grazing sheep—the nation's economy is now more diversified, with an important manufacturing sector. Australia is also rich in mineral resources, the leading export earners being iron ore from Western Australia and coking coal from Queensland and New South Wales. In addition bauxite is mined in the Northern Territory and Queensland.

In recent years Australia has produced more than one-third of the world's diamonds, fourteen percent of its lead, and eleven percent of its uranium and zinc. Because commodities account for more than eighty percent of exports, falling commodity prices have severe economic effects: an apparently irreversible decline in world demand for wool has cast a shadow over the pastoral industry. The government has been encouraging increased exports of manufactured goods—cars are being exported to the Gulf States, for example—but international competition is intense. The 1998 Asian economic downturn affected the tourist industry, which was the largest single foreign exchange earner, with 12.8 percent of the total.

STATES

New South Wales • Sydney
Queensland • Brisbane
South Australia • Adelaide
Tasmania • Hobart
Victoria • Melbourne
Western Australia • Perth

TERRITORIES

Australian Capital Territory • Canberra
Northern Territory • Darwin

OVERSEAS TERRITORIES

Ashmore and Cartier Islands
Christmas Island
Cocos (Keeling) Island
Coral Sea Islands
Heard and McDonald Islands
Norfolk Island

Finke Gorge National Park in the Northern Territory (above). The Apostles, Port Campbell National Park, Victoria (right). Women at Maketti Fou Market in Samoa (right page).

Timeline

c. 40,000 BP First Australians arrive in log canoes or sail boats from southeast Asia

c. 25,000 BP Earliest evidence of cremation, Lake Mungo, New South Wales

c. 15,000 BP Rock art paintings created in shelters and caves of northwest Australia

c. 13,000 BP People of robust appearance with thick skulls and large jaws living at Kow Swamp, Murray Valley, Victoria

c. 6000–5000 BC Dingoes brought to Australia, probably domesticated dogs belonging to people migrating from southeast Asia

1606 Dutch navigator Willem Jansz, first European to set foot in Australia, lands on Cape York Peninsula

1642 Dutch navigator Abel Tasman lands in Van Diemen's Land (now Tasmania), taking possession for Holland

1770 James Cook explores the east coast of Australia and the New Zealand islands, claiming both for Great Britain

1788 First Fleet under Captain Arthur Phillip arrives; penal colony set up in Port Jackson. Aboriginal population c. 750,000

1813 First European crossing of the Blue Mountains, west of Sydney, opens up inland plains to pastoralists

1829 Charles Sturt explores the Darling River system and later travels inland to disprove the myth of an inland sea

1851 Gold discoveries first in New South Wales and then Victoria; gold rushes generate wealth and population increase

1855–56 Augustus Charles Gregory makes first west-to-east land crossing of the continent

1868 Transportation of convicts abolished; last ship lands in Fremantle, WA

1914–18 Australia sends 417,000 troops to fight in First World War; 54,000 killed in battle and 155,000 wounded

1919 More than 6,000 people die in the worst 'flu epidemic in New South Wales history

1933 Aboriginal population reduced to 66,000 as a result of suppression and disease

Tuvalu

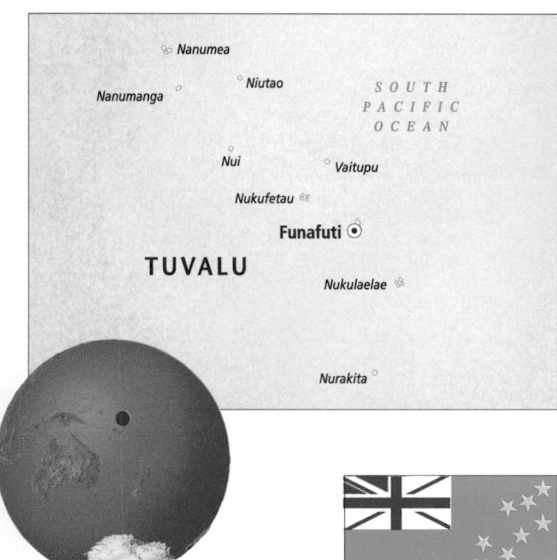

Fact File

Official name Tuvalu

Form of government Constitutional monarchy with single legislative body (Parliament)

Capital Funafuti

Area 26 sq km (10 sq miles)

Time zone GMT + 12 hours

Population 11,150

Projected population 2015 12,000

Population density 428.8 per sq km (1,115 per sq mile)

Life expectancy 67

Infant mortality (per 1,000) 22

Official languages Tuvaluan, English

Literacy rate 55 %

Religions Church of Tuvalu (Congregationalist) 97 %, Seventh-Day Adventist 1.4 %, Baha'i 1 %, other 0.6 %

Ethnic groups Polynesian 97 %, other 3 %

Currency Tuvaluan dollar, Australian dollar

Economy Agriculture and fishing 70 %, services 28 %, industry 2 %

GNP per capita US$ 1,100

Climate Tropical, moderated by trade winds

Highest point Unnamed location on Niulakita 4.6 m (15 ft)

Map reference Page 139

Tuvalu is a tiny Pacific island state which holds the distinction of having the world's smallest economy. It consists of five coral atolls and four reef islands, none of which is more than 5 m (15 ft) above sea level, about midway

between Hawaii and Australia. Formerly known as the Ellice Islands (and once part of the British colony of the Gilbert and Ellice Islands), they were first populated by Polynesian migrants from Samoa and Tonga some time in the fourteenth century—the language used today is a Polynesian-Samoan dialect. Though the islands were sighted by the Spanish in the sixteenth century, further European contact did not take place until the eighteenth century, and it was not until 1826 that the whole group was finally discovered and mapped. In the 1860s labor recruiters known as "blackbirders" became active, either inveigling or abducting islanders for work on Fijian and Australian sugar plantations (the population fell from 20,000 in 1850 to 3,000 in 1880).

The abuses of the labor trade led the British government to annex the islands as a protectorate in 1892. Though brought together as a single administrative unit, the Micronesian Gilbertese and the Polynesian Tuvaluans were not comfortable with this arrangement, and in 1978 Tuvalu became an independent state closely linked with Britain.

Tuvalu's chain of coral islands is 579 km (360 miles) long, consisting north to south of the islands of Nanumea, Niutao, Nanumanga, Nui, Vaitupu, Nukufetau, Funafuti (the capital), Nukulaelae, and Niulakita. There are no streams or rivers on any of the islands, and groundwater is not drinkable. All water needs must be met by catchment systems with storage facilities. Although the soil is of poor quality, subsistence farming supports about seventy percent of the population. The limited range of food crops that can be cultivated, such as taro. must be grown in special pits dug out of the coral. Although the islands support no export crop other than coconuts, the area of the maritime Exclusive Economic Zone is 1.2 million sq km (500,000 sq miles). The rich fishing grounds within this zone are a source of revenue from license fees paid by fishing fleets from Taiwan, Korea, and the USA. Too small, remote, and lacking in amenities to be able to establish a tourist industry, government revenues come mainly from the sale of stamps and coins and from remittances: large numbers of Tuvalu men live and work abroad, some as seamen and others mining phosphate on Nauru. The value of imports exceeds exports by 200 to 1. Substantial income is generated by an international trust fund established in 1987 by Australia, New Zealand, and the United Kingdom, which is also supported by Japan and South Korea.

1941 Australia's involvement in Second World War dominated by entry of Japanese after Pearl Harbor

1949 Construction of Snowy Mountain's hydroelectric scheme, Australia's largest (completed in 1972)

1967 Referendum accords citizenship to Aboriginal people for the first time by a vote of 90.8 percent of the population

1974 Cyclone Tracy destroys most of Darwin, Northern Territory

1991–92 Severe drought associated with El Niño climate pattern affects eastern Australia

1992 High Court ruling (Mabo) that Australia was not "empty" when Europeans arrived allows native title claims to proceed

Samoa

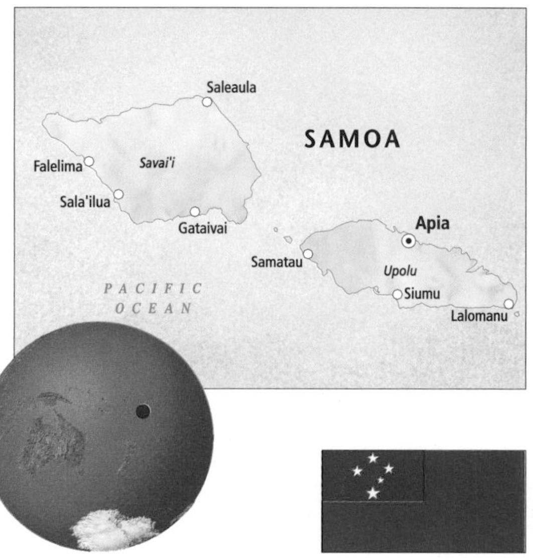

Fact File

Official name Independent State of Samoa

Form of government Constitutional monarchy with single legislative body (Legislative Assembly)

Capital Apia

Area 2,860 sq km (1,104 sq miles)

Time zone GMT – 11 hours

Population 174,800

Projected population 2015 179,000

Population density 61.2 per sq km (158.3 per sq mile)

Life expectancy 69.8

Infant mortality (per 1,000) 30.7

Official languages Samoan, English

Literacy rate 80 %

Religions Christian 99.7 % (50 % associated with London Missionary Society), other 0.3 %

Ethnic groups Samoan 92.6 %, mixed Polynesian-European 7 %, European 0.4 %

Currency Tala

Economy Agriculture 65 %, services and tourism 30 %, industry 5 %

GNP per capita US$ 3,500

Climate Tropical, wet season from December to April followed by a cooler dry season from May to November

Highest point Mauga Silisili 1,857 m (6,089 ft)

Map reference Pages 136, 141

The Samoan islands lie in the South Pacific about midway between Hawaii and New Zealand. Consisting of the two big islands of Savai'i and Upolu, plus seven small islands and a number of islets, Samoa is a larger island group with a much greater population than American Samoa, which lies further east, but has a more uncertain economic future.

Believed to have been originally settled by Tongans around 1000 BC, the islands of Samoa were first visited by Europeans when the French explorer Louis Antoine de Bougainville arrived in 1766. A mission was established in 1835 by the London Missionary Society. In the late nineteenth

century control of the islands was contested by three colonial powers—Britain, Germany, and the USA—Germany taking control for a short period from 1899. After the First World War the islands were administered by New Zealand. In 1962 Samoa regained full independence and signed a friendship treaty with New Zealand. Samoa is a society in which chiefly rank plays an important part, matai (men who head extended families) having a good deal more power, prestige, and authority than commoners. This system has delayed the introduction of full democracy. In 1991 the first direct elections under a universal franchise were held, but only matai were allowed to be candidates.

The larger islands of Samoa are volcanic, Savai'i experiencing major eruptions in 1902 and 1911. The interiors of Savai'i and Upolu are broadly similar; their mountainous central regions are densely forested and cut by a number of fast-flowing rivers. Major streams include the Sili and Faleata on Savai'i, and the Vaisigano on Upolu. Narrow coastal plains lie between the highlands and the sea; coral reefs lie offshore. Other than arable land (nineteen percent), the only natural resources are hardwood forests and fish. Yams, breadfruit, banana, and papaya are grown for food, and cocoa, taro, and coconuts (for oil, copra, and cream) are cultivated for export.

With assistance from the United Nations, fishing has also become a significant export industry. Reforestation programs have been introduced with the aim of keeping timber exports at a sustainable level. Power for industry—a Japanese automobile parts factory opened in 1991—is mainly provided by hydroelectricity.

The economy depends heavily on remittances from Samoans working overseas and on foreign aid to support a level of imports that significantly exceeds export earnings. Tourism has become the most important growth industry. Many of the more than 50,000 visitors per year come to see the house that was once lived in by the Scottish writer Robert Louis Stevenson. It is now the official residence of the Samoan Head of State.

Tonga

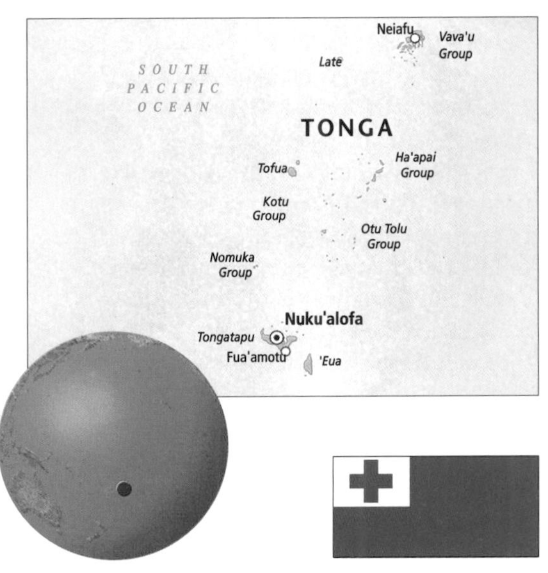

Fact File

Official name Kingdom of Tonga

Form of government Constitutional monarchy with single legislative body (Legislative Assembly)

Capital Nuku'alofa

Area 748 sq km (289 sq miles)

Time zone GMT + 12 hours

Population 106,140

Projected population 2015 110,000

Population density 141.9 per sq km (554.1 per sq mile)

Life expectancy 68.6

Infant mortality (per 1,000) 13.7

Official languages Tongan, English

Literacy rate 98.5 %

Religions Protestant 60 % (including Free Wesleyan 43 %, other 17 %), Roman Catholic 16 %, Mormon 12 %, other 12 %

Ethnic groups Polynesian 98 %, European 2 %

Currency Pa'anga

Economy Agriculture 70 %, industry and services 30 %

GNP per capita US$ 2,200

Climate Tropical, moderated by trade winds; wettest period December to March

Highest point Mt Kao 1,033 m (3,389 ft)

Map reference Pages 136, 141

The Polynesian kingdom of Tonga consists of an archipelago of 170 islands (36 of them inhabited) northeast of New Zealand in the South Pacific. Samoa lies to the north and Fiji to the west. Inhabited since about 1000 BC, they were named the "Friendly Isles" by Captain James Cook when he visited them in the 1770s. When Wesleyan missionaries arrived in the 1820s the people quickly began to adopt Christianity. In 1900, after Germany made colonial moves toward the islands, the King of Tonga signed a Treaty of Friendship and Protection with Britain.

Tonga was never fully colonized, and its people see themselves and their royal family as unique in the Pacific. A monarchy in which the king and a small group of hereditary nobles have a permanent majority in the Legislative Assembly, Tonga is now experiencing growing demands for a more democratic form of government. Although politicians of the newly established Pro-Democracy Movement have been harrassed for sedition and defamation there are signs the king may be ready for change: in 1995 he announced that it would only be a matter of time before a fully elected government was created.

North to south Tonga's three main groups of islands are Vava'u, Ha'apai, and Tongatapu, the archipelago dividing into two parallel belts of islands. In the east there are low, fertile coralline-limestone formations. In the west the terrain is higher and volcanic, the island of Kao, north of Tofua, rising to 1,033 m (3,389 ft). Mountainous landscapes of volcanic rock are found on the Vava'u group and one island in the Ha'apai group. In 1995 a new volcanic island which had emerged from the sea was discovered in the Ha'apai group. About 25 percent of Tonga's land area is arable, but surface water is rare on the coral islands.

Most of the people of Tonga live by subsistence farming, the main food crops being yams, taro, and cassava. Two-thirds of exports come from coconuts, bananas, and vanilla beans, other cash crops being pumpkin, fruits and vegetables, cocoa, coffee, ginger, and black pepper. Despite the high level of agricultural activity a good deal of food has to be imported, most of it coming from New Zealand. In the early 1990s the economy continued to grow, largely because of a rise in pumpkin exports, increased foreign aid, and a number of construction projects. Tourism is now the main source of hard currency earnings, but Tonga remains dependent on sizeable aid funds, plus remittances from its many citizens who live and work in New Zealand, Australia, and the USA.

Papua New Guinea

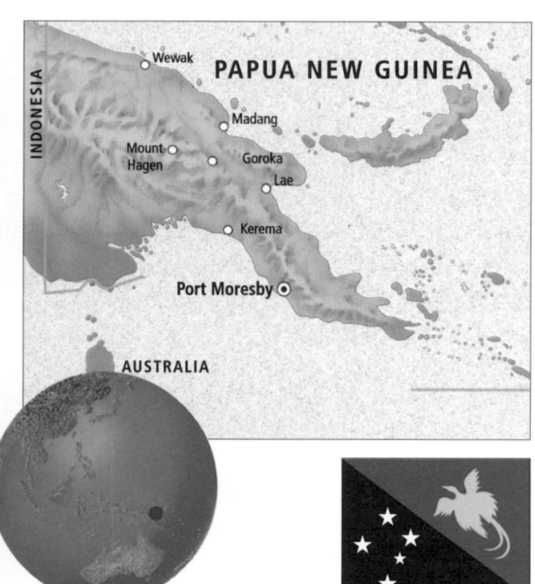

Fact File

OFFICIAL NAME Independent State of Papua New Guinea

FORM OF GOVERNMENT Constitutional monarchy with single legislative body (National Parliament or House of Assembly)

CAPITAL Port Moresby

AREA 461,690 sq km (178,258 sq miles)

TIME ZONE GMT + 10 hours

POPULATION 5,172,000

PROJECTED POPULATION 2015 6,642,000

POPULATION DENSITY 11.2 per sq km (29.0 per sq mile)

LIFE EXPECTANCY 63.8

INFANT MORTALITY (PER 1,000) 56.5

OFFICIAL LANGUAGES English, Pidgin, Motu

OTHER LANGUAGES Approximately 750 indigenous languages

LITERACY RATE 64.5 %

RELIGIONS Protestant 44 % (including Lutheran 16 %; Presbyterian, Methodist, London Missionary Society 8 %; Anglican 5 %; Evangelical Alliance 4 %; other sects 11 %), indigenous beliefs 34 %, Roman Catholic 22 %

ETHNIC GROUPS New Guinea Papuan 84 %; Polynesian, Chinese, European and other 16 %

CURRENCY Kina

ECONOMY Agriculture 64 %, services and industry 36 %

GNP PER CAPITA US$ 2,400

CLIMATE Tropical, with wet season December to March

HIGHEST POINT Mt Wilhelm 4,509 m (14,793 ft)

MAP REFERENCE Page 140

Papua New Guinea consists of the eastern half of the large island of New Guinea, the 600 or so smaller islands of the Bismarck Archipelago, and the island Bougainville in the west. It lies north of northeastern Australia, just south of the equator. The largely rural population of "mainland" Papua New Guinea is made up of hundreds of distinct tribal groups, speaking more than 750 different languages. They can be broadly divided into the lowlanders of the coast and the more isolated highlanders of the mountainous interior. The main island was named New Guinea in 1545 by a Spanish explorer who thought its people resembled those of the African Guinea coast. During the last two centuries the Netherlands, Germany, Japan, and Australia have controlled parts of it at different times. The western half—West Irian (Irian Jaya)—is now part of Indonesia; the eastern half, most recently administered by Australia, became fully independent as Papua New Guinea in 1975. Australia's relationship remains close, and it contributes twenty percent of the state budget.

A cordillera of rugged mountains runs down the main island. Covered with tropical forest, these mountains have an average elevation of between 2,500 m and 4,600 m (8,000 ft and 15,000 ft). In high and isolated valleys there are settlements where people live by cultivating traditional garden crops such as sweet potato, sugar cane, bananas, maize, and cassava. Pigs are raised, but are eaten mainly at ceremonies for status and ritual purposes. Taro is a staple food of the villagers in the lowlands, where yams and sago are also grown. Most of the soil is heavily leached, and fertile only in lowland areas and upland basins. On the southwestern coast the Fly River forms a vast swampy delta plain that is one of the world's biggest wetlands. The other major islands further east (New Ireland, New Britain, Manus, and Bougainville) are mainly of volcanic origin and are generally ringed by coral reefs. Nearly three-quarters of the land area of Papua New Guinea is covered with dense rainforest.

The country does have a variety of natural resources but rugged terrain and the high cost of infrastructure make their extraction difficult. Much travel and transport is only possible by air. While most people live by subsistence agriculture, copper and gold account for about sixty percent of export earnings. The main cash crops are coffee, cocoa, coconuts, palm kernels, tea, and rubber. Timber from the forests is also important. The government is looking to petroleum and mineral exports to drive its program of economic development, but there are social and political obstacles to be overcome. Corruption is endemic, tribal and criminal violence are high, and what was once the world's biggest copper mine—Panguna on Bougainville—has been closed for years. The Bougainville people are culturally kin to the people of the Solomons and strongly resent their domination by Papua New Guinea. Grievances over their share of the proceeds from the mine and compensation have become a demand for independence. After eruptions of violence in the 1990s, however, the government managed to consolidate the situation since 2001.

A Samoan church with a Mediterranean influence (left page). Mudmen at Mt Hagen, in the Papua New Guinea highlands (right).

Solomon Islands

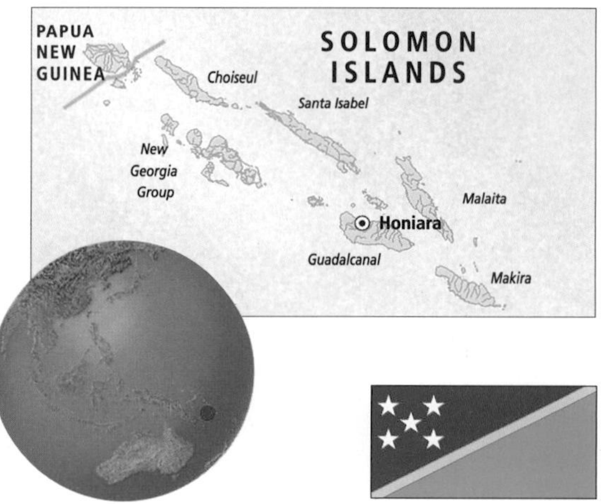

Fact File

OFFICIAL NAME Solomon Islands

FORM OF GOVERNMENT Constitutional monarchy with single legislative body (National Parliament)

CAPITAL Honiara

AREA 28,450 sq km (10,985 sq miles)

TIME ZONE GMT + 11 hours

POPULATION 495,000

PROJECTED POPULATION 2015 719,000

POPULATION DENSITY 17,4 per sq km (45.1 per sq mile)

LIFE EXPECTANCY 72.4

INFANT MORTALITY (PER 1,000) 22.1

OFFICIAL LANGUAGE English

OTHER LANGUAGES Pidgin, approximately 80 different indigenous languages

LITERACY RATE 62 %

RELIGIONS Protestant 77 % (including Anglican 34 %, Baptist 17 %, United 11 %, Seventh-Day Adventist 10 %), Roman Catholic 19 %, indigenous beliefs 4%

ETHNIC GROUPS Melanesian 93%, Polynesian 4%, Micronesian 1.5%, European 0.8%, other 0.7%

CURRENCY Soloman Islands dollar

ECONOMY Agriculture 85%, services 10%, industry 5%

GNP PER CAPITA US$ 1,700

CLIMATE Tropical, most rain falling November to April

HIGHEST POINT Mt Makarakomburu 2,447 m (8,126 ft)

MAP REFERENCE Pages 140, 141

The Solomon Islands lie in the western Pacific, northeast of Australia. Inhabited by Melanesian people since about 1000 BC, they consist of two chains of islands running southeast of Bougainville. They were named by the Spanish navigator Alvaro de Mendana, who visited them in 1568 and thought he had found "the riches of Solomon." Twenty years later he returned and established a small, short-lived colony on the Santa Cruz Islands. Outside contacts were few in the ensuing centuries. In the 1870s and 1880s labor recruiters called "blackbirders" were busy inveigling islanders into working on Australian sugar plantations and their unsavory activities led Britain to establish a protectorate over the Southern Solomons in 1893.

In the Second World War the Solomons were occupied by the Japanese. The battle for Guadalcanal saw fierce fighting between Japanese and US forces, the islands overall being the scene of several major Allied naval and military victories. In recent years relations with Papua New Guinea have been strained because of the Solomon Islands' support for secessionists on Bougainville and the rebels of the Bougainville Revolutionary Army. Although Bougainville is geographically and ethnically a part of the Solomon Islands group, it has been treated politically as a part of Papua New Guinea for more than one hundred years.

Geologically, the islands represent a part of the submerged outermost crustal fold of the ancient Australian continent. Their interiors are rugged and mountainous. The six main islands—Guadalcanal, Malaita, New Georgia, Makira (formerly San Cristobal), Santa Isabel, and Choiseul—are all of volcanic origin, and have densely forested ranges with steep-sided river valleys. Around the coasts are narrow plains where most of the population live as subsistence farmers growing beans, coconuts, palm kernels, rice, potatoes, and vegetables. Palm oil, cocoa and copra are leading agricultural exports, and tuna fish is the single biggest earner. Forestry is an important industry but the unsustainable level of timber extraction is an environmental concern. The islands are rich in undeveloped mineral resources such as lead, zinc, nickel, gold, bauxite, and phosphate—significant phosphate deposits are being mined on Bellona Island. The government is nearly insolvent and depends on foreign aid; another problem is the high population growth rate.

Vanuatu

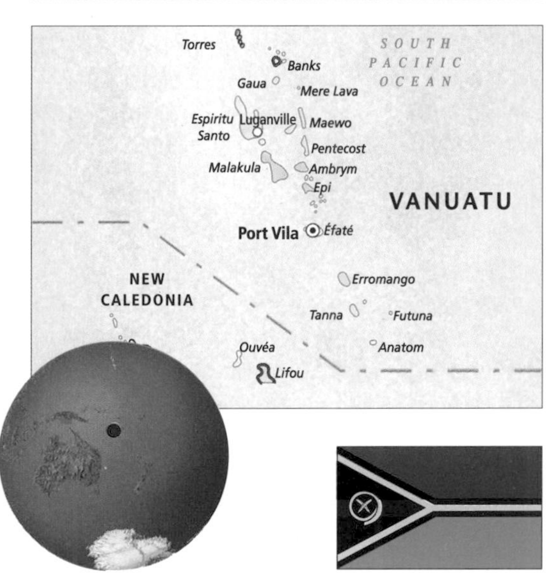

Fact File

OFFICIAL NAME Republic of Vanuatu

FORM OF GOVERNMENT Republic with single legislative body (Parliament)

CAPITAL Port Vila

AREA 14,760 sq km (5,699 sq miles)

TIME ZONE GMT + 11 hours

POPULATION 196,200

PROJECTED POPULATION 2015 282,000

POPULATION DENSITY 13.3 per sq km (34.4 per sq mile)

LIFE EXPECTANCY 61.3

INFANT MORTALITY (PER 1,000) 59.6

OFFICIAL LANGUAGES English, French

OTHER LANGUAGE Bislama (ni-Vanuatu-pidgin), about 110 Melanesian languages

LITERACY RATE 53%

RELIGIONS Presbyterian 36.7%, Anglican 15%, Catholic 15%, indigenous beliefs 7.6%, Seventh-Day Adventist 6.2%, Church of Christ 3.8%, other 15.7%

ETHNIC GROUPS Melanesian 94%, French 4%, other (including Vietnamese, Chinese, Pacific Islanders) 2%

CURRENCY Vatu

ECONOMY Agriculture 75%, services 22%, industry 3%

GNP PER CAPITA US$ 1,300

CLIMATE Tropical, moderated by trade winds

HIGHEST POINT Mt Tabwemasana 1,877 m (6,152 ft)

MAP REFERENCE Pages 136, 141

Vanuatu is an archipelago in the South Pacific consisting of thirteen large islands and seventy islets. Part of Melanesia, it lies northeast of New Caledonia and west of Fiji. Inhabited since 5000 BC, it was first visited by Europeans when the Portuguese arrived in 1606. After Captain Cook explored the islands in 1774 he named them the New Hebrides, and they were jointly administered by France and Britain from 1887. In the late 1800s labor recruiters inveigled and sometimes kidnapped islanders for work on sugar plantations in Australia and Fiji. Aside from this, the islands remained isolated until the Second World War, when Espíritu Santo and Port Vila became major US military bases in the Pacific. In 1980 the archipelago became independent under the name Vanuatu. Since then, after surviving a secession attempt by a francophone movement on the island of Espíritu Santo, the country has had a volatile but democratic political life. Vanuatu is populated almost entirely by ethnic Melanesians speaking 110 distinct languages—the world's highest per capita density of language forms. The lingua franca is a form of pidgin known as Bislama.

Most of the islands are mountainous and volcanic in origin, with coral beaches and offshore reefs. The interior is forested, with limited land for coastal cultivation. Some 75 percent of the people live by subsistence farming, growing taro, yams, sweet potatoes, bananas, and cassava for food, as well as cash crops such as coconuts, cocoa, and coffee. Fishing is also important. Unlike most South Pacific islands, beef raising is of economic significance, livestock numbering some 130,000 head of cattle. Meat canning is an industry. Frozen beef and fish are exported. Other exports include copra, shells, coffee, and cocoa. Mineral deposits are negligible. Recently the government has emphasized tourist development (tourism is now the second largest earner of foreign exchange after copra), offshore banking, and foreign investment, advertising Vanuatu's potential as a finance center and tax haven. There is a "flag of convenience" shipping registry of some sixty ships from twenty countries.

Fiji

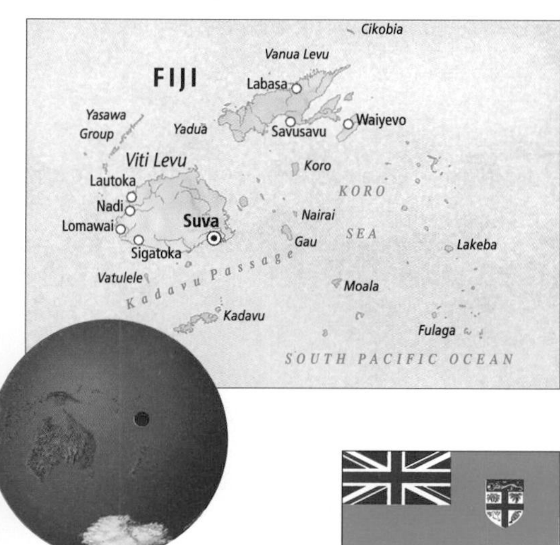

Fact File

Official name Republic of Fiji

Form of government Republic with two legislative bodies (Senate and House of Representatives)

Capital Suva

Area 18,270 sq km (7,054 sq miles)

Time zone GMT + 12 hours

Population 857,000

Projected population 2015 925,000

Population density 44.5 per sq km (121.5 per sq mile)

Life expectancy 68.6

Infant mortality (per 1,000) 13.7

Official language English

Other languages Fijian, Hindustani

Literacy rate 92.5 %

Religions Christian 52 % (Methodist 37 %, Roman Catholic 9 %), Hindu 38 %, Muslim 8 %, other 2 %

Ethnic groups Fijian 49 %, Indian 46 %, other (including European, other Pacific Islanders, Chinese) 5 %

Currency Fiji dollar

Economy Agriculture 67 %, services and industry 33 %

GNP per capita US$ 5,200

A coastal village in the Solomon Islands, with some Second World War pontoons (left page top). The Parliament House buildings in Suva, Fiji (above). Fruit and vegetables for sale at Port Vila Market, Vanuatu (below).

Climate Tropical, with wet season November to April

Highest point Mt Tomanivi 1,324 m (4,344 ft)

Map reference Pages 137, 141

Fiji consists of an archipelago of more than 800 islands and islets, 110 of them inhabited, located about two-thirds of the way from Hawaii to New Zealand. Lying on the air route from Australia to the west coast of the USA, Fiji is well served by flights, and is attracting an increasing number of tourists. Originally inhabited by Melanesian islanders organized into a number of tribes, the islands were visited by Dutch explorers in 1643, and from 1800 attracted growing numbers of traders, along with missionaries who converted the people to Christianity. A period of intense tribal warfare was brought to an end when the paramount chief ceded sovereignty to the British in 1874. Five years later, in 1879, the British began bringing in Indian laborers for the purpose of sugar production; by the time Fiji obtained its independence in 1970 their descendants outnumbered the country's ethnic Fijians.

Racial divisions have caused tension and instability, as for many years the Indian immigrants were treated as second-class citizens, despite their vital role in the sugar industry. A coup in 1987, led by a Fijian army officer against a democratically elected government in which Indians were the majority, led to a new constitution in 1990 which was racially weighted to ensure permanent indigenous Fijian rule. Many Indian-Fijians emigrated as a result. In May 1999, the Indian leader of the Fijian Labor Party, Mahandra Chaudrey, was democratically elected Prime Minister. In May 2000, coup plotters, led by indigenous Fijian George Speight, took Chaudrey and other parliamentarians hostage, resulting in a period of martial law until March 2001.

The main islands are of volcanic origin. About seventy percent of the population live on the two biggest—Viti Levu and Vanua Levu. These have a sharp and rugged relief, rising to Mt Tomanivi on Viti Levu. The islands lie in a cyclone path (Cyclone Kina caused much damage in 1993) and trade winds bring heavy rain to their eastern sides. Dense tropical forest covers the higher slopes. Sugarcane is grown on the fertile coastal plains, sugar exports and tourism with 250,000 visitors per year being Fiji's main sources of foreign exchange. Fiji has one of the most developed of the Pacific island economies, producing (as well as sugar) copra, gold, silver, clothing, and timber.

Palau

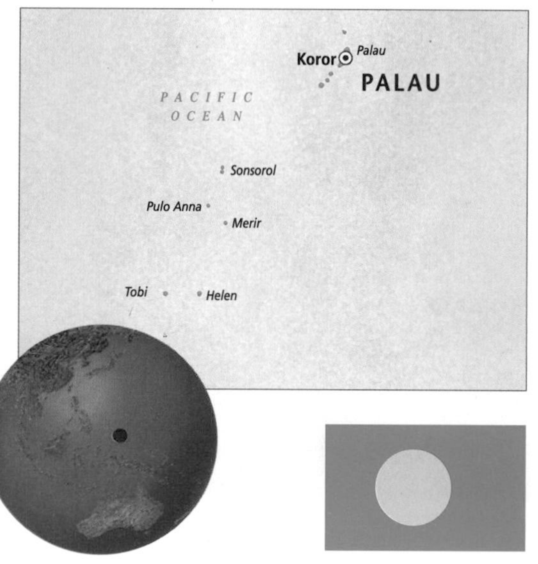

Fact File

Official name Republic of Palau

Form of government Republic in free association with the USA; two legislative bodies (Senate and House of Delegates)

Capital Koror

Area 458 sq km (177 sq miles)

Time zone GMT + 10 hours

Population 19,400

Projected population 2015 26,000

Population density 42.4 per sq km (109.6 per sq mile)

Life expectancy 69.2

Infant mortality (per 1,000) 16.2

Official languages Palauan, English

Other languages Sonsoral, Angaur, Japanese, Tobi

Literacy rate 92 %

Religions Roman Catholic 41 %, indigenous Modekngei religion 25 %, Protestant 25 %, other 9 %

Ethnic groups Palauan (mixed Polynesian, Melanesian, Malayan) 83 %, Filipino 10 %, other 7 %

Currency US dollar

Economy Government, agriculture, fishing, tourism

GNP per capita US$ 9,000

Climate Tropical, with wet season May to November

Highest point Mt Ngerchelchauus 242 m (794 ft)

Map reference Page 138

Palau consists of several groups of islands in the northwest Pacific, about 750 km (450 miles) east of the Philippine island of Mindanao. The westernmost of the Micronesian Caroline chain, and settled by Southeast Asian migrants from about 1000 BC, the islands have in the past 100 years been successively occupied and controlled by Spain, Germany, Japan, and the USA. After Spain's defeat in the 1898 Spanish-American War they were sold to

Germany. Japan seized and held the islands from the outbreak of the First World War until the Second World War, when Japanese and US forces fought for control over them. In 1978 Palau rejected incorporation into the neighboring Federated States of Micronesia (a union of the rest of the Caroline Islands); in 1981 it adopted a constitution banning nuclear weapons and military bases in the area; and in 1982 it entered into a Compact of Free Association with the USA which contained military provisions in conflict with its constitution. After a lengthy political stalemate, in 1993 voters finally approved the Compact, which provides US$ 500 million in aid over fifteen years in exchange for the right of the USA to maintain military facilities there. In 1994 Palau became the 185th member of the UN, and in 1995 it joined the South Pacific Forum.

Palau, an archipelago of six separate groups of islands, consists of 26 islands and over 300 islets. The terrain varies from the mountainous main island of Babelthuap to low coral islands usually fringed by reefs. Natural resources consist of forests, minerals (including gold), marine products, and deep-seabed minerals. The rural people live by subsistence agriculture, growing coconuts, cassava, and sweet potatoes (though the rugged terrain of the larger islands makes farming difficult), and by fishing. Industries include tourism, craft items made from shell, wood, and pearls, and some commercial fishing. Exports include trochus shell, tuna, copra, and handicrafts. The government is the main employer, and relies heavily on aid from the USA. As a result, the population has a per capita income twice that of the Philippines.

Micronesia

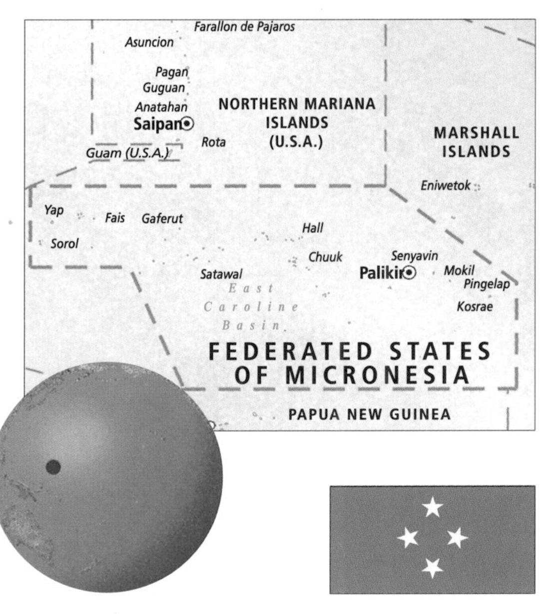

Fact File

OFFICIAL NAME Federated States of Micronesia

FORM OF GOVERNMENT Federal Republic in free association with the USA; single legislative body (Congress)

CAPITAL Palikir

AREA 702 sq km (271 sq miles)

TIME ZONE GMT + 9–10 hours

POPULATION 136,000

PROJECTED POPULATION 2015 172,000

POPULATION DENSITY 193.7 per sq km (501.8 per sq mile)

LIFE EXPECTANCY 68.5

INFANT MORTALITY (PER 1,000) 34.0

OFFICIAL LANGUAGE English

OTHER LANGUAGES Micronesian and Polynesian languages

LITERACY RATE 89 %

RELIGIONS Roman Catholic 50 %, Protestant 47 %, other and none 3 %

ETHNIC GROUPS Micronesian and Polynesian

CURRENCY US dollar

ECONOMY Agriculture, fishing, services, textiles

GNP PER CAPITA US$ 2,000

CLIMATE Tropical. Heavy rainfall year-round and occasional typhoons

HIGHEST POINT Totolom 791 m (2,595 ft)

MAP REFERENCE Page 138

The Federated States of Micronesia consist of four states—Yap, Chuuk (Truk), Pohnpei, and Kosrae—made up of four island groups spread out across 3,200 km (2,000 miles) of ocean. Formerly known as the Caroline Islands, they are located in the northern Pacific about halfway between Australia and Japan. They are populated by Micronesian and Polynesian peoples divided into nine separate ethnic groups.

First settled around 1000 BC, the islands were visited by Spanish seafarers in 1565 and were annexed by Spain in 1874. In 1899 Spain sold them to Germany, and at the beginning of the First World War Japan took posession of them. After Japan's defeat in the Second World War, the USA took over the administration of the islands. US control ended in 1986 when the Federated States of Micronesia and the USA signed a fifteen-year Compact of Free Association that is currently renegotiated. This granted internal self-government, with the USA retaining responsibility for the country's defense.

During the course of the Second World War Chuuk was one of Japan's most important bases in the Pacific Ocean. Tourists now come to the island to scuba dive among the numerous wartime wrecks in the lagoon.

The 607 widely scattered islands of Micronesia vary geologically from high and mountainous terrain to low coral atolls. Most of the islands are volcanic in origin, and the hot, rainy climate produces lush vegetation and tropical rainforest. Volcanic outcrops occur on Pohnpei, Kosrae, and Chuuk. Some of the atolls lack any surface water. Droughts occur frequently on Chuuk, often leading to water rationing. In 1992 emergency supplies of water had to be brought from Guam to Chuuk by the US Navy.

Subsistence fishing and farming occupies the majority of the population, with farmers growing tropical fruits and vegetables, coconuts, cassava (tapioca), sweet potatoes, and black pepper, and raising pigs and chickens. Fish, bananas, and black pepper are exported, and as a result of attempts at economic diversification a clothing industry has been developed.

Aside from deposits of high-grade phosphate the islands have few mineral resources. Imports exceed exports by a ratio of more than four to one, and the country as a whole depends heavily on financial aid from the USA. There is some potential for tourism—with their rich marine life the islands are a prime destination for scuba divers—but poor infrastructure and the country's remoteness hinder further development.

Some of the islands of Palau, seen from the air (top). Mangroves in Micronesia (above). An aerial view of some of the Marshall Islands (right).

Marshall Islands

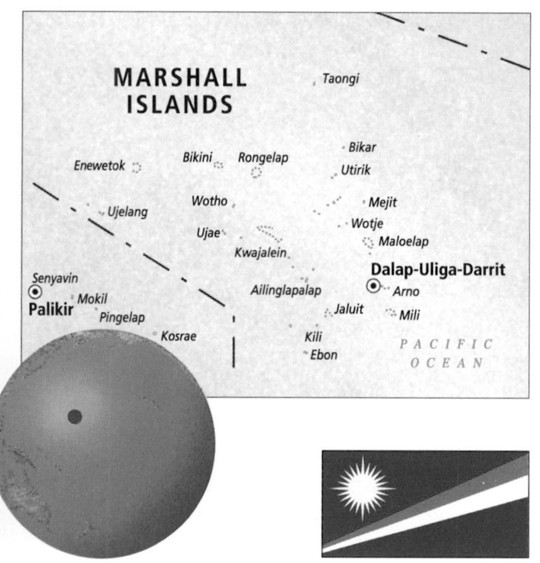

Fact File

OFFICIAL NAME Republic of the Marshall Islands

FORM OF GOVERNMENT Republic in free association with the USA; two legislative bodies (Parliament and Council of Chiefs)

CAPITAL Dalap-Uliga-Darrit

AREA 181 sq km (70 sq miles)

TIME ZONE GMT + 12 hours

POPULATION 73,600

PROJECTED POPULATION 2015 116,500

POPULATION DENSITY 406.8 per sq km (1051.4 per sq mile)

LIFE EXPECTANCY 66.2

INFANT MORTALITY (PER 1,000) 38.7

OFFICIAL LANGUAGE English

OTHER LANGUAGES Marshallese, Japanese

LITERACY RATE 93.7 %

RELIGIONS Protestant 90 %, Roman Catholic 8 %, other 2 %

ETHNIC GROUPS Micronesian 97 %, other 3 %

CURRENCY US dollar

ECONOMY Agriculture, fishing, tourism

GNP PER CAPITA US$ 1,600

CLIMATE Tropical, with wet season May to November

HIGHEST POINT Unnamed location on Likiep 10 m (33 ft)

MAP REFERENCE Pages 138–39

A group of 31 coral atolls, five islands, and 1,152 islets, the Republic of the Marshall Islands is situated in the northern Pacific about halfway between Hawaii and Papua New Guinea. Settled around 2000 BC, the islands were visited by Spanish seafarers in 1529, and since 1874 have been successively under Spanish, German, Japanese, and US control. In 1986 they entered into a Compact of Free Association with the US. During the years after the Second World War the Marshalls became known as the location where the USA carried out nucleur bomb tests (on Bikini and Enewetak Atolls between 1946 and 1958). Claims for compensation by those affected or displaced by the tests have been settled in recent years, an award of US$ 40 million to 1,150 Marshall Islanders being made by the Nuclear Claims Tribunal in 1995. Cleanup work to remove residual radiation from Bikini Lagoon continues.

The terrain consists of low coral limestone and sand islands. Two archipelagoes of islands run roughly parallel northeast to southwest, the easternmost chain being a continuation of the Gilbert Islands of western Kiribati. Originating as coral reefs formed upon the rims of submerged volcanoes, each of the main islands encloses a lagoon. Bordering the cyclone belt, and nowhere higher than 10 m (30 ft) above sea level, they are vulnerable to storms and tidal waves. In June 1994 a tidal wave swept over the capital on Majuro Atoll.

On the outlying atolls a typical Pacific island subsistence economy survives, centered on agriculture and fishing. Small farms produce commercial crops such as coconuts, tomatoes, melons, and breadfruit, and a handful of cattle ranches supplies the domestic meat market. Industry consists of handicrafts, fish processing, and copra production, and the main exports are tuna, copra, and coconut oil products. About ten percent of the population is employed in the tourist industry (visitors come from Japan and the USA), now the main source of foreign exchange. Imports are eleven times export rates, all fuel must be imported, and the country as a whole is heavily dependent on aid from the US plus income from the US leasing of Kwajalein Atoll for missile testing. With US grants scaled back since 2001, every economic activity helping the country is being explored.

Kiribati

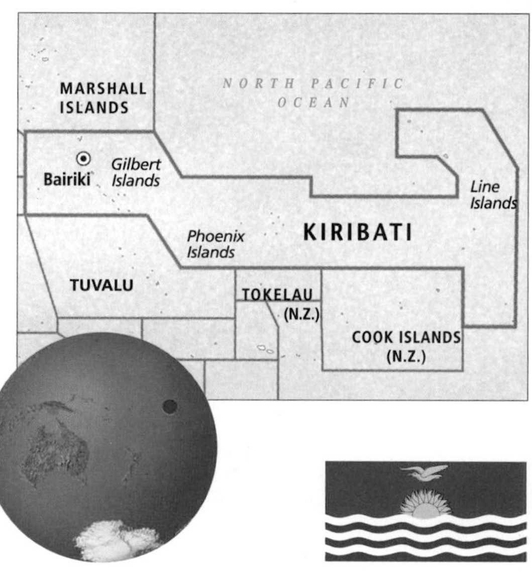

Fact File

OFFICIAL NAME Republic of Kiribati

FORM OF GOVERNMENT Republic with single legislative body (National Assembly)

CAPITAL Bairiki

AREA 717 sq km (277 sq miles)

TIME ZONE GMT +12/11 hours

POPULATION 96,400

PROJECTED POPULATION 2015 100,000

POPULATION DENSITY 134.4 per sq km (348.0 per sq mile)

LIFE EXPECTANCY 60.5

INFANT MORTALITY (PER 1,000) 52.6

OFFICIAL LANGUAGE English

OTHER LANGUAGE Gilbertese

LITERACY RATE 90 %

RELIGIONS Roman Catholic 52.6 %, Protestant (Congregational) 40.9 %, other (including Seventh-Day Adventist, Baha'i, Church of God, Mormon) 6.5 %

ETHNIC GROUPS Predominantly Micronesian with small Polynesian and non-Pacific minorities

CURRENCY Australian dollar

ECONOMY Agriculture, copra production, fishing

GNP PER CAPITA US$ 840

CLIMATE Tropical, moderated by trade winds

HIGHEST POINT Unnamed location on Banaba Island 81 m (266 ft)

MAP REFERENCE Page 139

The Republic of Kiribati (pronounced Kiribass) consists of 33 scattered coral atolls in three separate groups in the mid-Pacific, plus the volcanic island, Banaba. The three groups are the seventeen former Gilbert Islands in the west, the eight Phoenix Islands, and the eight Line Islands.

Banaba Island has provided the region with the most income. It is one of three great phosphate rock islands in the Pacific Ocean, the others being Nauru and Makatea. The people of Kiribati are Micronesian, though the Banabans pride themselves on being ethnically distinct.

Kiritimati Island (also known as Christmas Island), one of the Line Islands, was the site of

the first British nuclear tests in the Pacific in 1957, but is now a favored location for tourist development. For Kiribati as a whole, it is difficult to see what else besides tourism can be developed as a national source of income—it is classified by the United Nations as a Least Developed Country. The phosphate deposits on Banaba had been exhausted by the time of independence in 1979. Copra (68 percent), seaweed (sixteen percent) and fish (fifteen percent) are now the main exports. A basic subsistence economy still flourishes, with small farms and gardens producing taro, breadfruit, and sweet potatoes. Kiribati imports little food but it depends heavily on foreign aid, largely from the UK and Japan. Aid has been 25 to fifty percent of gross domestic product in recent years.

Though Kiribati is a democracy, the political parties continue to be strongly influenced by a traditional chief system and have little formal organization. A major difficulty for Kiribati today is the problem of environmental degradation from the overpopulation of Tarawa, the island capital to which many Kiribati have migrated because of the lack of job opportunities elsewhere.

Huts on a coconut plantation in Kiribati (above). Phosphate mine on Nauru (below). Pristine waters off the Cook Islands (right page).

Nauru

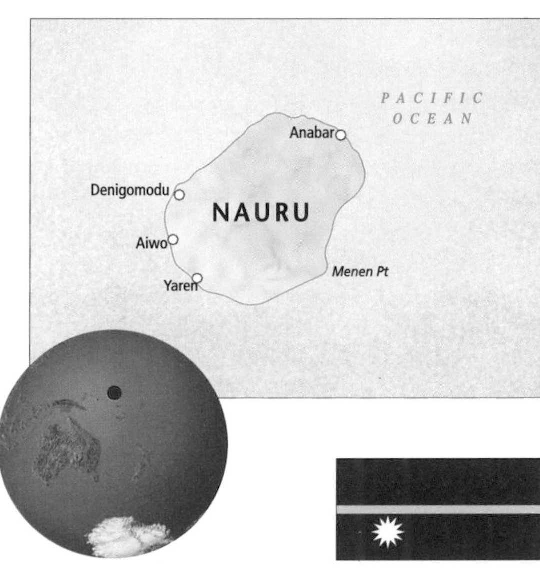

Fact File

OFFICIAL NAME Republic of Nauru

FORM OF GOVERNMENT Republic with single legislative body (Parliament)

CAPITAL None; government offices in Yaren

AREA 21 sq km (8.1 sq miles)

TIME ZONE GMT + 11.5 hours

POPULATION 12,400

PROJECTED POPULATION 2015 17,000

POPULATION DENSITY 590.5 per sq km (1,530.9 per sq mile)

LIFE EXPECTANCY 61.6

INFANT MORTALITY (PER 1,000) 10.5

OFFICIAL LANGUAGE Nauruan

OTHER LANGUAGE English

LITERACY RATE 99 %

RELIGIONS Protestant 66 %, Roman Catholic 33 %

ETHNIC GROUPS Nauruan 58 %, other Pacific Islander 26 %, Chinese 8 %, European 8 %

CURRENCY Australian dollar

ECONOMY Phosphate mining, financial services, coconut production

GNP PER CAPITA US$ 5,000

CLIMATE Tropical, with wet season November to February

HIGHEST POINT Unnamed location 61 m (200 ft)

MAP REFERENCE Pages 138–39

Nauru is a tiny island in the Pacific 3,000 km (2,000 miles) northeast of Australia. It is the world's smallest republic and, because of the wealth of its phosphate deposits, Nauruans enjoy one of the highest per capita incomes in the Third World. This situation is coming to an end, however. By the year 2006 the phosphate is expected to run out, and it is not clear what the people will do then.

Although little is known of the original Polynesian inhabitants of the island, it was first visited by Europeans when a British ship stopped there in 1798. Clan warfare among the Polynesians became widespread in the 1870s, leading the Germans (who then controlled the Marshall Islands, and whose traders were active on Nauru) to incorporate it into their administration in 1888. Phosphate mining by both a German and a British company began in 1906. After the First World War the administration of Nauru passed to Australia and independence was granted in 1968. In 1970 Australia, New Zealand, and Great Britain relinquished their joint control of the phosphate industry to a Nauruan governmental agency, the Nauru Phosphate Corporation.

The island is a 21 sq km (8.1 sq mile) raised coral reef with a central plateau. This plateau consists of phosphate beds created by seabird droppings over the course of many centuries. It is encircled by a fertile belt of semicultivated land where most of the people live. A ring road forms a continuous strip settlement around the coastal perimeter, where houses and other buildings occupy the only habitable land. After more than ninty years of continual phosphate mining, much of the rest of the island—in effect a largely worked-out quarry—has an aspect of lunar desolation. The climate is hot and humid, but because clouds sometimes miss the small island, years can pass without any rainfall at all. What little vegetation there is consists of coconut palms, breadfruit trees, and scrub.

Phosphate is the country's only resource. About eighty percent of the island is now uninhabitable and uncultivable, and as a result all food, fuel, manufactured goods, building materials, and machinery are imported. The high proportion of processed foods in the inhabitants' diet has led to widespread obesity, and approximately one-third of the people suffer from non-insulin-dependent diabetes. Although many Nauruans live in traditional houses, they tend to spend their considerable incomes on luxury cars and electrical goods. Much phosphate income has been invested in trust funds to serve the country's long-term needs, but not all the investments have been wise and since 1990 dividends have fallen sharply.

Dependencies and Territories

American Samoa

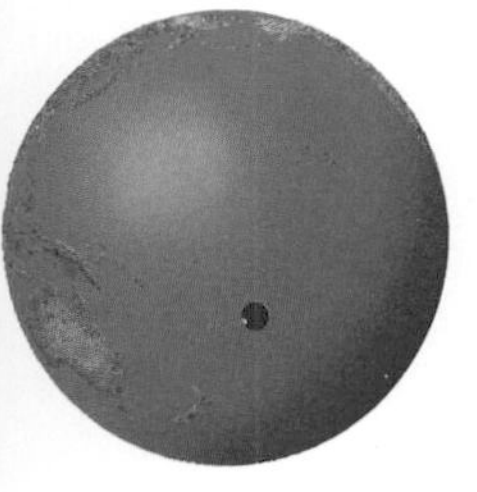

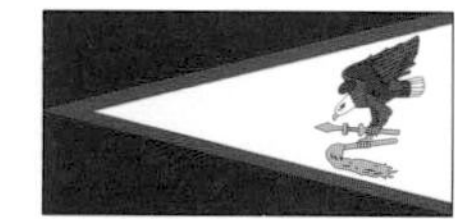

Fact File

OFFICIAL NAME Territory of American Samoa

FORM OF GOVERNMENT Unincorporated and unorganized territory of the USA

CAPITAL Pago Pago

AREA 199 sq km (77 sq miles)

TIME ZONE GMT – 11 hours

POPULATION 68,700

LIFE EXPECTANCY 75.5

INFANT MORTALITY (PER 1,000) 10.1

LITERACY RATE 97 %

CURRENCY US dollar

ECONOMY Fishing 34 %, government 33 %, other 33 %

CLIMATE Tropical; wet season November to April

MAP REFERENCE Pages 136, 141

Consisting of aroup of five volcanic islands and two atolls in the South Pacific located about midway between Hawaii and New Zealand, American Samoa has been settled by Polynesian peoples since about 800 BC. The first European contact was made by the Dutch in 1722. British missionaries were active in the region from 1830 onwards. In 1872 the USA won exclusive rights from the High Chief to use Pago Pago as a strategic base for the American fleet. Pago Pago has one of the best natural deepwater harbors in the region, sheltered by surrounding mountains from rough seas and high winds. About ninety percent of trade is with the USA, which heavily subsidizes the economy. Tuna fishing, processing, and export are the foundation of private sector economic activity.

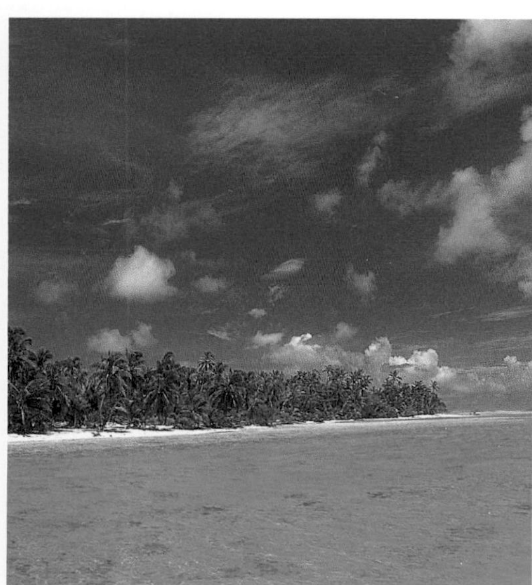

Ashmore and Cartier Islands

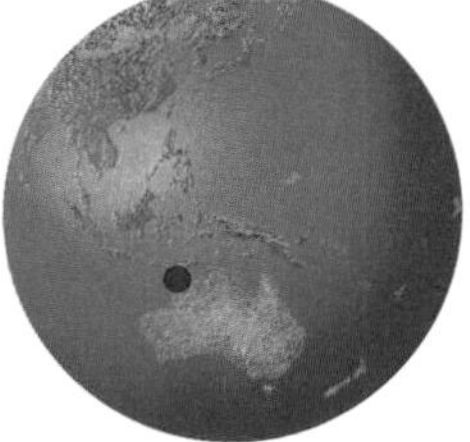

Fact File

OFFICIAL NAME Territory of Ashmore and Cartier Islands

FORM OF GOVERNMENT External territory of Australia

CAPITAL None; administered from Canberra

AREA 5 sq km (2 sq miles)

TIME ZONE GMT + 8 hours

POPULATION No permanent population

CLIMATE Tropical

MAP REFERENCE Page 134

Uninhabited islands in the Indian Ocean northwest of Australia, Ashmore and Cartier Islands are at no point higher than 3 m (10 ft) above sea level. The terrain consists of sand and coral. The islands are surrounded by reefs and shoals that can pose a maritime hazard. The Australian government monitors the state of the Ashmore Reef National Nature Reserve by regularly sending experts. The defense of the islands is also in the hands of the Australian government and the Royal Australian Navy and Air Force make visits from time to time.

Baker and Howland Islands

Fact File

OFFICIAL NAME Baker and Howland Islands

FORM OF GOVERNMENT Unincorporated territory of the USA

CAPITAL None; administered from Washington DC

AREA 3 sq km (1.2 sq miles)

TIME ZONE GMT – 10 hours

POPULATION No permanent population

CLIMATE Hot, dry, and windy

MAP REFERENCE Page 139

Baker Island is an uninhabited atoll in the North Pacific, midway between Hawaii and Australia. The terrain consists of a low coral island surrounded by a narrow reef. The island's climate is equatorial with little rainfall, constant wind, and burning sun. Used by the US military during the Second World War, it is now primarily a nesting habitat for seabirds and marine wildlife. Howland Island is an uninhabited atoll nearby. Another low coral island surrounded by a narrow reef, it has no supply of fresh water. Entry to Baker and Howland Islands, a National Wildlife Refuge run by the US Department of the Interior, is prohibited except by special-use permit.

Cook Islands

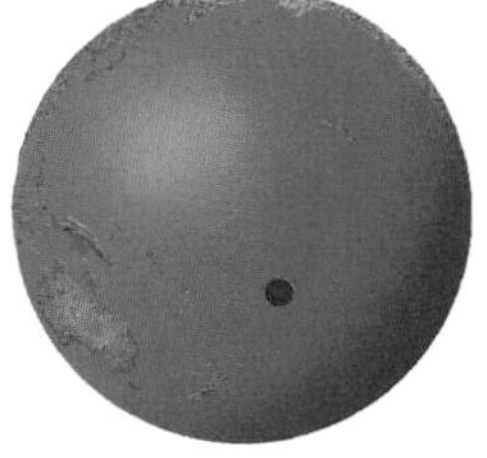

Fact File

OFFICIAL NAME Cook Islands

FORM OF GOVERNMENT Self-governing territory of New Zealand

CAPITAL Avarua

AREA 240 sq km (93 sq miles)

TIME ZONE GMT – 10 hours

POPULATION 20,800

LIFE EXPECTANCY 71.1

INFANT MORTALITY (PER 1,000) 24.7

LITERACY RATE 95 %

CURRENCY New Zealand dollar

ECONOMY Agriculture, services, some industry

CLIMATE Tropical, moderated by trade winds

MAP REFERENCE Pages 136–37, 139

About 3,500 km (2,175 miles) northeast of New Zealand, the Cook Islands consist of 24 widely separated coral atolls in the north, and hilly, volcanic islands in the south. The Polynesian inhabitants are believed to have settled the islands around AD 500 to 800. They were visited by the Spanish in 1595; explored by Captain James Cook in 1773 and 1777; Christianized by British missionaries after 1821; and annexed to New Zealand in 1901. Since independence in 1965 the islands have been self-governing in free association with New Zealand. They have a fully responsible government, with elections every five years to a 25-member parliament, based on full adult suffrage. The climate is tropical with plentiful rainfall. Agriculture provides the economic base, and the main export earners are fruit, copra, and clothing. Marine culture has recently led to the production of black pearls and trochus shell. Financial services are available. New Zealand is both the main trading partner (taking 96 percent of exports) and the source of substantial aid. In the course of recent years, tourism has been expanding.

French Polynesia

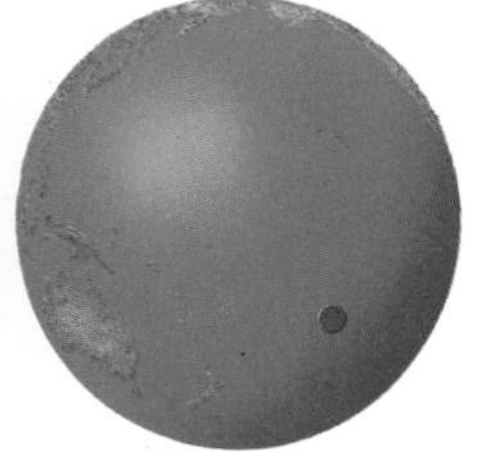

Fact File

OFFICIAL NAME Territory of French Polynesia

FORM OF GOVERNMENT Overseas territory of France

CAPITAL Papeete

AREA 4,167 sq km (1,609 sq miles)

TIME ZONE GMT – 10 hours

POPULATION 258,000

LIFE EXPECTANCY 75.2

INFANT MORTALITY (PER 1,000) 9

LITERACY RATE 98 %

CURRENCY CFP (Comptoirs Français du Pacifique) franc

ECONOMY Services 68 %, industry 19 %, agriculture 13 %

CLIMATE Tropical

MAP REFERENCE Page 137

French Polynesia comprises five archipelagoes in the South Pacific, midway between Australia and South America, scattered over an area of ocean as large as Europe. They include the Society Islands (Archipel de la Société), the Marquesas (Îles Marquises), the Tubuai Islands, and the Tuamotus (Archipel des Tuamotu). The Polynesian inhabitants first settled the islands about 2,000 years ago. European contact dates from 1767. The conversion of the islanders to Christianity began in 1797 and after three years of armed resistance the chiefs of Tahiti accepted French colonial control in 1843. The islands send two deputies and a senator to the French Assembly in Paris, and since 1984 have had a local territorial assembly as well. Famous for providing the artist Gauguin with his best-known subjects, French Polynesia has been in the news more recently as a site for French nuclear testing on the atoll of Mururoa. This ceased in 1995. Large military expenditures over the preceding thirty years have provided the islands with employment, high wages, and improved infrastructure, and resulted in seventy percent of the population moving to live on Tahiti. Tourism now accounts for twenty percent of the gross domestic product, and cultured pearls are the main export.

Uninhabited Clipperton Island, a coral atoll in the Pacific Ocean west of Mexico, is administered by France from French Polynesia.

Guam

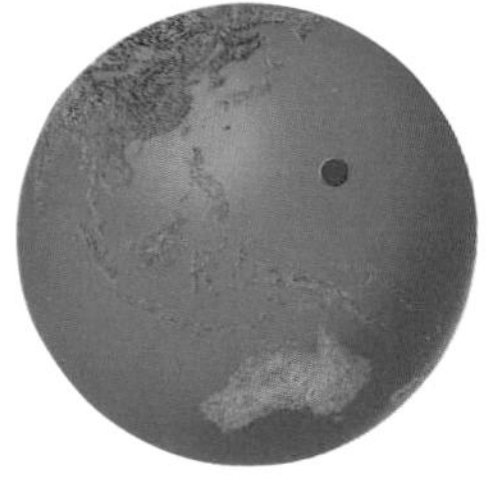

Fact File

OFFICIAL NAME Territory of Guam

FORM OF GOVERNMENT Organized, unincorporated territory of the USA

CAPITAL Agana

AREA 541 sq km (209 sq miles)

TIME ZONE GMT + 10 hours

POPULATION 161,000

LIFE EXPECTANCY 78.1

INFANT MORTALITY (PER 1,000) 6.6

LITERACY RATE 99 %

CURRENCY US dollar

ECONOMY Services and tourism 54 %, government 40 %, other 6 %

CLIMATE Tropical, moderated by trade winds; wet season July to October

MAP REFERENCE Page 138

The largest and most southerly of the Mariana Islands in the northwest Pacific, Guam lies about 2,000 km (1,200 miles) due east of Manila in the Philippines. Originally settled by Malay-Filipino peoples around 1500 BC, Guam was mapped by Ferdinand Magellan in 1521, claimed by Spain from 1565, and since Spain's defeat in the Spanish-American War in 1899 has been administered by the USA. Of volcanic origin, Guam consists of a relatively flat coralline limestone plateau (which is the source of most fresh water for the island), with steep coastal cliffs and narrow coastal plains in the north, low-rising hills in the center, and mountains in the south. About half its population are Chamorro, of mixed Indonesian, Spanish, and Filipino descent. The island is of great strategic importance to the USA and about one-third of its land is occupied by American naval and airforce facilities. This has resulted in a high standard of living, and there are concerns about the unemployment that is likely to follow the planned closing of four naval installations. As a Pacific tourist destination Guam is second only to Hawaii.

Jarvis Island

Fact File

OFFICIAL NAME Jarvis Island

FORM OF GOVERNMENT Unincorporated territory of the USA

CAPITAL None; administered from Washington DC

AREA 4.5 sq km (1.7 sq miles)

TIME ZONE GMT – 10 hours

POPULATION No permanent population

CLIMATE Hot, dry, and windy

MAP REFERENCE Page 139

An uninhabited island in the South Pacific, Jarvis Island lies about midway between Hawaii and the Cook Islands. A sandy coral islet with a fringing reef, it has a tropical climate with little rain and no fresh water. Guano deposits were worked until late in the nineteenth century, and Millersville settlement on the west of the island was used as a weather station from 1935 until the Second World War. Ground cover consists of sparse bunch grass, prostrate vines, and low-growing shrubs. The island is mainly a nesting place for seabirds and marine wildlife. Entry is by special-use permit only.

Johnston Atoll

Fact File

OFFICIAL NAME Johnston Atoll

FORM OF GOVERNMENT Unincorporated territory of the USA

CAPITAL None; administered from Washington DC

AREA 2.8 sq km (1.1 sq miles)

TIME ZONE GMT – 10 hours

POPULATION No permanent population

ECONOMY US military base

CLIMATE Hot, dry, and windy

MAP REFERENCE Page 139

This remote coral atoll consisting of two islets, Johnston Island and Sand Island, lies in the North Pacific about one-third of the way between Hawaii and the Marshall Islands. The atoll is 5 m (16 ft) above sea level at its highest point and has a dry tropical climate, northeast trade winds ensuring little seasonal temperature variation. Mined during the nineteenth century for its extensive guano deposits, the atoll is now home to approximately 1,200 US military personnel. It was formerly used as a nuclear weapons testing site. The territory is administered by the US Defense Nuclear Agency and managed cooperatively by the DNA and the Fish and Wildlife Service of the US Department of the Interior as part of the National Wildlife Refuge system.

Kingman Reef

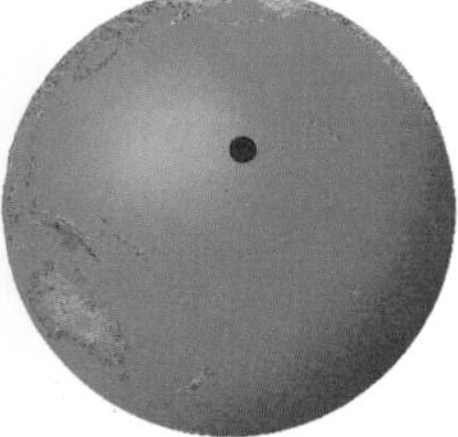

Fact File

OFFICIAL NAME Kingman Reef

FORM OF GOVERNMENT Unincorporated territory of the USA

CAPITAL None; administered from Washington DC

AREA 1 sq km (0.4 sq miles)

TIME ZONE GMT – 10 hours

POPULATION No permanent population

CLIMATE Tropical, moderated by sea breezes

MAP REFERENCE Page 139

A barren triangular-shaped reef in the North Pacific, Kingman Reef is about halfway between Hawaii and American Samoa. No more than 1 m (3 ft) above sea level, and awash most of the time, the reef is a maritime hazard. Although no economic activity takes place and the reef is uninhabited, the deep interior lagoon was used as a halfway station between Hawaii and American Samoa when Pan American Airways used flying boats in the Pacific in 1937 and 1938. While there is no land flora, the reef is rich in marine life. It is administered by the US Navy.

Cocos (Keeling) Islands

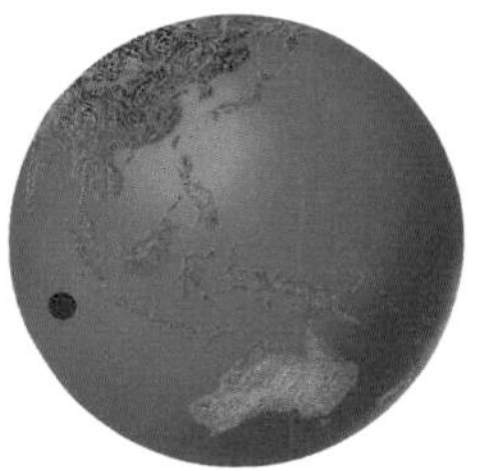

Fact File

OFFICIAL NAME Territory of Cocos (Keeling) Islands

FORM OF GOVERNMENT External territory of Australia

CAPITAL West Island

AREA 14 sq km (5.4 sq miles)

TIME ZONE GMT + 7 hours

POPULATION 630

LIFE EXPECTANCY Not available

INFANT MORTALITY (PER 1,000) Not available

LITERACY RATE Not available

CURRENCY Australian dollar

ECONOMY Coconut and copra production

CLIMATE Tropical, moderated by trade winds

MAP REFERENCE Page 134

The Cocos (Keeling) Islands are a group of 27 coral atolls in the Indian Ocean midway between Australia and Sri Lanka. When discovered in 1609 by the East India Company's Captain William Keeling they were uninhabited. In 1827 the Scot John Clunies-Ross brought some Malays with him and established a settlement. The inhabited islands today are Home Island, where the Cocos Malays live, and West Island, with a small European community. The group has been administered

The peaks of Anau and Nunue Bora Bora, French Polynesia (left page bottom). Bora Bora resort and lagoon on the Society Islands (above center). Looking out over the city and bay, Guam (below).

directly by the Australian government since a referendum in 1984. Coconuts are the sole cash crop, copra and fresh coconuts the major export earners. Though local gardens and fishing make a contribution, additional food and other necessities must come from Australia.

Coral Sea Islands

Fact File

OFFICIAL NAME Coral Sea Islands Territory

FORM OF GOVERNMENT External territory of Australia

CAPITAL None; administered from Canberra

AREA 3 sq km (1.2 sq miles)

TIME ZONE GMT + 10 hours

POPULATION No permanent population

CLIMATE Tropical

MAP REFERENCE Page 135

These uninhabited sandy islands and coral reefs are located in the Coral Sea northeast of Australia's Great Barrier Reef. The numerous small islands and reefs are scattered over a sea area of about 1 million sq km (386,000 sq miles), with Willis Islets the most important. Nowhere more than 6 m (20 ft) above sea level, the area is an important nesting area for seabirds and turtles. There are no permanent freshwater resources and the islands are occasionally subject to cyclones. Although there are no indigenous inhabitants, three meteorologists are stationed there. Defense is the responsibility of Australia, the islets being regularly visited by the Royal Australian Navy. Australia controls the activities of visitors.

Midway Islands

Fact File

OFFICIAL NAME Midway Islands

FORM OF GOVERNMENT Unincorporated territory of the USA

CAPITAL None; administered from Washington DC

AREA 5.2 sq km (1.9 sq miles)

TIME ZONE GMT – 10 hours

POPULATION No permanent population

ECONOMY US military base

CLIMATE Tropical, moderated by sea breezes

MAP REFERENCE Page 139

The two Midway Islands constitute part of an atoll in the northern Pacific at the extreme western end of the Hawaiian chain, 1,931 km (1,200 miles) northwest of Hawaii. Their name derives from their position midway along the old shipping route from California to Japan.

The atoll is almost completely flat, and none of the land is higher than 4 m (13 ft) above sea level. During the Second World War it was the scene of a major battle between Japan and the USA, and afterward it was used as a naval airbase, which was closed down in 1993. Today, it is a wildlife refuge. From 1996 until 2001 the refuge was open to the public, but it is currently temporarily closed. When people lived on the island, they were serviced by the port of Sand Island, Johnston Atoll.

New Caledonia

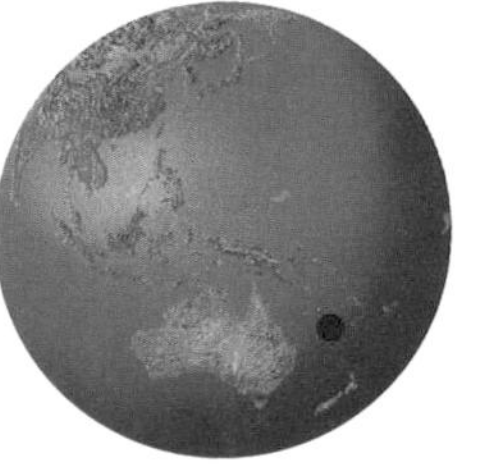

Fact File

OFFICIAL NAME Territory of New Caledonia and Dependencies

FORM OF GOVERNMENT Overseas territory of France

CAPITAL Nouméa

AREA 19,060 sq km (7,359 sq miles)

TIME ZONE GMT + 11 hours

POPULATION 208,000

LIFE EXPECTANCY 73.3

INFANT MORTALITY (PER 1,000) 8.2

LITERACY RATE 91 %

CURRENCY CFP (Comptoirs Français du Pacifique) franc

ECONOMY Services 40 %, agriculture 32 %, industry 28 %

CLIMATE Tropical, moderated by trade winds

MAP REFERENCE Pages 136, 141

New Caledonia is a group of islands 1,500 km (900 miles) off the northeast coast of Australia. Rich in minerals, and with more than fourty percent of the world's known nickel resources, it is France's largest overseas territory. First populated by indigenous Kanaks (who call the land Kanaky) around 4000 BC, the islands were visited by the Spanish in the sixteenth and seventeenth centuries, were named by Captain James Cook in 1774, and were used as a penal settlement by France between 1853 and 1897. By the end of the nineteenth century French settlers owned more than ninety percent of the land. Dissatisfaction with their situation led to violent resistance from the Kanaks during the 1970s and 1980s, but more recently they have come to accept French rule. The Kanaks now represent only 43 percent of the population, while 37 percent are of European descent. The main island, Grand Terre, consists of coastal plains with a mountainous interior. Only a small amount of land is suitable for cultivation. New Caledonia's prosperity is almost entirely dependent on nickel production, so the economy is at the mercy of varying world demand. Tourism from France, Japan, and Australia is also important.

Niue

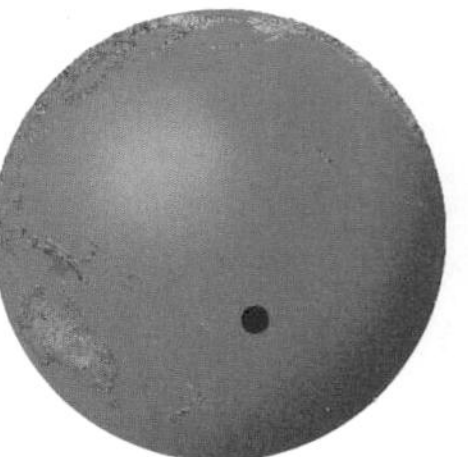

Fact File

OFFICIAL NAME Niue

FORM OF GOVERNMENT Self-governing territory in free association with New Zealand

CAPITAL Alofi

AREA 260 sq km (100 sq miles)

TIME ZONE GMT – 11 hours

POPULATION 2,100

LIFE EXPECTANCY Not available

INFANT MORTALITY (PER 1,000) Not available

LITERACY RATE 95 %

CURRENCY New Zealand dollar

ECONOMY Agriculture, industry (food processing, coconuts), services

CLIMATE Tropical, moderated by trade winds

MAP REFERENCE Pages 132, 136

Niue is one of the world's biggest coral atolls, lying about 700 km (400 miles) east of Tonga in the South Pacific. The terrain consists of a central limestone plateau with steep cliffs around the coast; the highest point is 68 m (223 ft). The economy is heavily dependent on aid from the New Zealand government. Most of the inhabitants live by subsistence farming. Light industry consists of processing passionfruit, lime oil, honey, and coconut cream. The sale of postage stamps and tourism are also a source of foreign currency. Remittances from family members living overseas supplement domestic income: lack of employment opportunities on the island means that five out of six of the people of Niue live and work in New Zealand.

Northern Mariana Islands

Fact File

OFFICIAL NAME Commonwealth of the Northern Mariana Islands

FORM OF GOVERNMENT Territory of the USA; commonwealth in political union with the USA

CAPITAL Saipan

AREA 477 sq km (184 sq miles)

TIME ZONE GMT + 10 hours

POPULATION 77,300

LIFE EXPECTANCY 76

INFANT MORTALITY (PER 1,000) 5.6

LITERACY RATE 97 %

CURRENCY US dollar

ECONOMY Tourism, industry, agriculture

CLIMATE Tropical, moderated by trade winds

MAP REFERENCE Page 138

These islands are located in the North Pacific about three-quarters of the way between Hawaii and the Philippines. Unlike the nearby Caroline Islands, the Northern Marianas chose not to seek independence in 1987, preferring to remain part of the USA. There are fourteen main islands including Saipan, Rota, and Tinian. The southern islands are limestone with level terraces and fringing coral reefs; the northern islands are volcanic, with active volcanoes on Pagan and Agrihan. There is little seasonal variation in the tropical marine climate, as the temperature is moderated by northeast trade winds. The people of the islands belong to a variety of ethnic groups and include Chamorros (mixed Indonesian, Spanish, and Filipino), Micronesians, Japanese, Chinese, and Koreans. The economy is substantially supported by the USA. Tourism is a fast-growing source of income, employing increasing numbers of the workforce and bringing in most revenue. Cattle ranches produce beef, and small farms produce coconuts, breadfruit, tomatoes, and melons. Industry consists of handicrafts, light manufacturing, and garment production.

Norfolk Island

Fact File

OFFICIAL NAME Territory of Norfolk Island

FORM OF GOVERNMENT External territory of Australia

An aerial view of Amadee Island, New Caledonia (left page). Clear blue waters form an inlet on the South Pacific island of Niue (top). Historic colonial buildings and ruins on Norfolk Island (above).

CAPITAL Kingston

AREA 35 sq km (14 sq miles)

TIME ZONE GMT + 11.5 hours

POPULATION 1,860

LIFE EXPECTANCY Not available

INFANT MORTALITY (PER 1,000) Not available

LITERACY RATE Not available

CURRENCY Australian dollar

ECONOMY Tourism, agriculture

CLIMATE Subtropical

MAP REFERENCE Pages 133, 136

Some 1,400 km (850 miles) east of Australia, Norfolk Island is inhabited by descendants of the famous mutineers from HMS *Bounty*. Of volcanic origin, the island was uninhabited when discovered by Captain James Cook in 1774. After serving as a penal settlement in Australia's early history it became a refuge for the entire population of the Pitcairn Islands' *Bounty* mutiny survivors, who were resettled there in 1856. (Some later returned to live on Pitcairn Island.) The present inhabitants speak a mixture of nineteenth century English, Gaelic, and Old Tahitian. They enjoy a degree of autonomy and have rejected proposals to become a part of the Australian state. While there is no income tax, the government raises revenue from customs duty, liquor sales, a public works levy, financial institutions levy, and departure fees. Tourism is the main activity, the island receiving around 30,000 visitors each year.

Palmyra Atoll

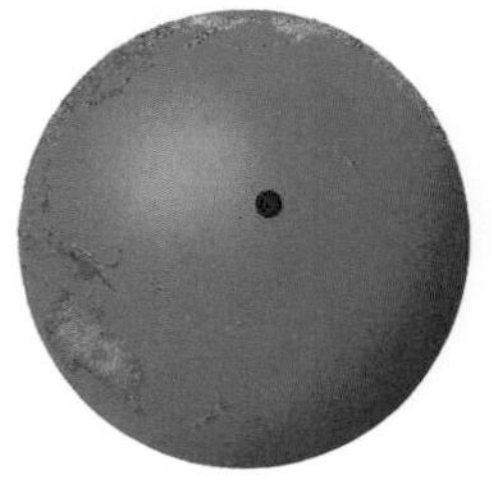

Fact File

OFFICIAL NAME Palmyra Atoll

FORM OF GOVERNMENT Incorporated territory of the USA

CAPITAL None; administered from Washington DC

AREA 12 sq km (4.6 sq miles)

TIME ZONE GMT – 10 hours

POPULATION No permanent population

CLIMATE Tropical

MAP REFERENCE Page 139

A privately owned uninhabited atoll in the northern Pacific, Palmyra Atoll lies about halfway between Hawaii and Samoa. At no point more than 2 m (6 ft) above sea level, the atoll consists of about fifty islets covered with dense vegetation, coconut palms, and balsa-like trees that grow up to 30 m (100 ft) tall. A number of roads and causeways were built during the Second World War, but they are now overgrown and unserviceable, as is the airstrip. In 1990 a Hawaiian property developer took out a 75-year lease from its owners, the Fullard-Leo brothers. There are plans to turn the atoll into a "get away from it all" tourist complex.

Pitcairn Islands

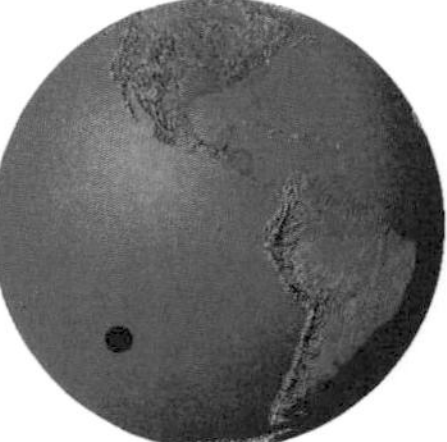

Fact File

OFFICIAL NAME Pitcairn, Henderson, Ducie, and Oeno Islands

FORM OF GOVERNMENT Dependent territory of the United Kingdom

CAPITAL Adamstown

AREA 47 sq km (18 sq miles)

TIME ZONE GMT – 8.5 hours

POPULATION 47

LIFE EXPECTANCY Not available

INFANT MORTALITY (PER 1,000) Not available

LITERACY RATE Not available

CURRENCY New Zealand dollar

ECONOMY Fishing, agriculture, services

CLIMATE Tropical, with rainy season from November to March

MAP REFERENCE Page 137

The Pitcairn Islands are located in the South Pacific about midway between Peru and New Zealand. They have a rugged volcanic formation, cliffs along a rocky coast, and a tropical, hot, and humid climate. The islands are the United Kingdom's most isolated dependency. Uninhabited when they were discovered by Europeans, they were used as a refuge by the mutineers from HMS *Bounty* in 1790, some of whose descendants still live there speaking a part-Tahitian, part-English dialect. They exist by fishing and subsistence farming. The fertile valley soils produce fruits and vegetables including citrus, sugarcane, watermelons, bananas, yams, and beans. Barter is an important economic activity. The main source of revenue is the sale of postage stamps and handicrafts to passing ships.

Tokelau

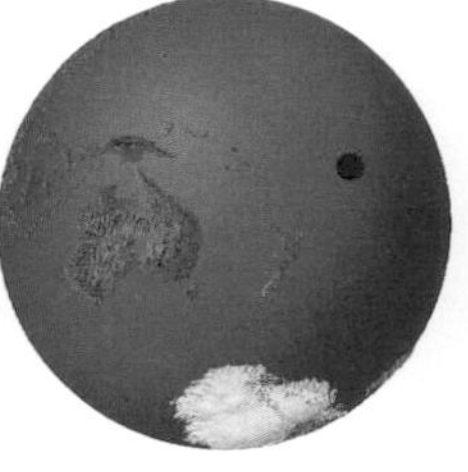

Fact File

OFFICIAL NAME Tokelau

FORM OF GOVERNMENT Territory of New Zealand

CAPITAL None; administrative center on each atoll

AREA 10 sq km (3.9 sq miles)

TIME ZONE GMT – 11 hours

POPULATION 1,430

LIFE EXPECTANCY Not available

INFANT MORTALITY (PER 1,000) Not available

LITERACY RATE Not available

CURRENCY New Zealand dollar

ECONOMY Agriculture, industry

CLIMATE Tropical, moderated by trade winds April to November

MAP REFERENCE Page 139

Tokelau is a small group of islands in the southern Pacific about midway between Hawaii and New Zealand. The islands consist of low coral atolls, none of the atolls rises higher than 5 m (16 ft) above sea level enclosing large lagoons. Situated in the Pacific typhoon belt (a cyclone in 1990 destroyed a great deal of Tokelau's infrastructure), they have a tropical climate moderated by trade winds. There are limited natural resources, and subsistence farmers grow coconuts, breadfruit, papaya, and bananas. Small-scale industry produces copra, woodwork, plaited craft goods, stamps, and coins. An anticipated tuna cannery is expected to help sustain the economy, and it is hoped that a catamaran link between the various atolls will boost tourism. Aid from New Zealand is the main source of revenue and money remitted by relatives who live and work in New Zealand is a vital source of domestic income.

Wake Island

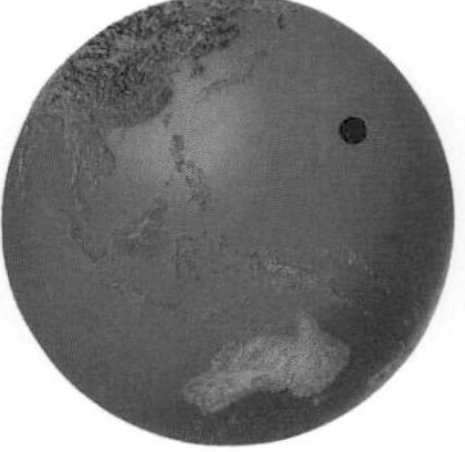

Fact File

OFFICIAL NAME Wake Island

FORM OF GOVERNMENT Unincorporated territory of the USA

CAPITAL None; administered from Washington DC

AREA 6.5 sq km (2.5 sq miles)

TIME ZONE GMT + 12 hours

POPULATION No permanent population

ECONOMY US military base

CLIMATE Tropical

MAP REFERENCE Page 138

Wake Island is located in the North Pacific about two-thirds of the way between Hawaii and the Northern Mariana Islands. It consists of three tiny coral islets linked by causeways around a lagoon. The islets are built on fragments of the rim of an extinct underwater volcano, the lagoon being the former crater. With no indigenous inhabitants or economic activity, the 300 or so US military personnel stationed on Wake Island provide help in the case of emergency landings by aircraft on transpacific flights.

Wallis and Futuna Islands

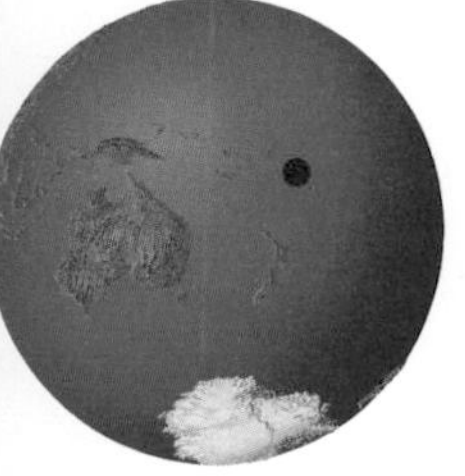

Fact File

OFFICIAL NAME Territory of the Wallis and Futuna Islands

FORM OF GOVERNMENT Overseas territory of France

CAPITAL Mata Utu

AREA 274 sq km (106 sq miles)

TIME ZONE GMT + 12 hours

POPULATION 15,600

LIFE EXPECTANCY Not available

INFANT MORTALITY (PER 1,000) Not available

LITERACY RATE Not available

CURRENCY CFP (Comptoirs Français du Pacifique) franc

ECONOMY Agriculture, fishing

CLIMATE Tropical, with wet season November to April

MAP REFERENCE Page 139

This group comprises three main islands—Futuna, Alofi and Wallis (Uvea)—and twenty islets, located west of Samoa and north-east of Fiji. They are of volcanic origin, with low hills rising to 765 m (2,510 ft) at Mt Singavi. All the main islands have fringing reefs. In the hot wet season from November to April 2,500–3,000 mm (100–120 in) of rain may fall. This rain, combined with deforestation (timber is used locally for fuel), has eroded the terrain of Futuna. The people live by subsistence farming. Exports are negligible and French aid is essential to the islands. First settled perhaps 2,000 years ago, and visited by the Dutch in 1616, the islands became a French protectorate in 1886. In a referendum on independence in 1959 they chose to become a French Overseas Territory. There is no independence movement.

The problem of coral bleaching

Coral reefs constitute one of the Earth's great diverse ecosystems. They are made of limestone formed by millions of tiny marine animals and can only live in tropical seas within a narrow range of physical and chemical conditions. Coral reefs generally form only when winter water temperatures exceed 18 °C (64 °F) and when light levels are high. Coral is found in the rock record in the form of fossils dating back to the Paleozoic Era. However, although coral has survived this long, it is not immune to the impact of human activities.

In recent years scientists have become interested in the apparent link between the death of large tracts of coral in the Pacific and Caribbean regions and global warming. The greenhouse effect—a result of changes in the amounts of carbon dioxide and other gases in the atmosphere since the industrial revolution—is the cause of this global warming. Satellite data from the US National Oceanographic and Atmospheric Administration show a warming trend in sea-surface temperatures since 1982. In some areas, such as along the Great Barrier Reef in Australia, a combination of higher than usual summer temperatures and the run-off from floods (which reduces salinity) appears to be damaging the coral. As the essential conditions required for the maintenance of a healthy reef system are disrupted, the coral formations turn white.

What will happen to coral reefs in the future? Are the bleaching episodes observed in recent years in so many tropical areas really due to global warming or are there other causes? Predictions that ocean surface temperatures in the tropics may rise by up to 5 °C (41 °F) in the 21st century are no longer considered fantasy. If this happens, it could greatly disturb even resilient ecosystems, such as coral reefs, and reduce the Earth's biodiversity as well as the ability of societies to live and work in these areas.

Christmas Island

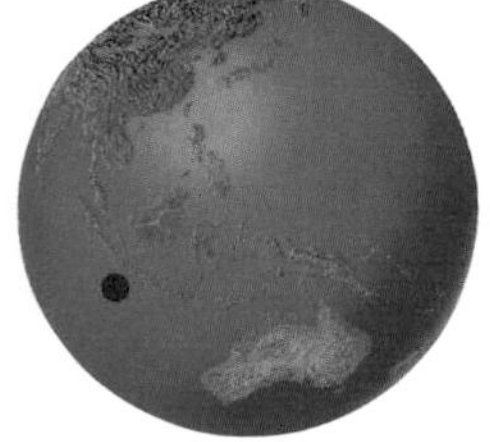

Fact File

OFFICIAL NAME Territory of Christmas Island

FORM OF GOVERNMENT External territory of Australia

CAPITAL The Settlement

AREA 135 sq km (52 sq miles)

TIME ZONE GMT + 7 hours

POPULATION 470

LIFE EXPECTANCY Not available

INFANT MORTALITY (PER 1,000) Not available

LITERACY RATE Not available

CURRENCY Australian dollar

ECONOMY Mining, tourism

CLIMATE Tropical, moderated by trade winds

MAP REFERENCE Page 134

A small island in the Indian Ocean, Christmas Island is about 300 km (200 miles) south of Java. Coastal cliffs rise steeply to a central plateau. Formerly uninhabited, Chinese and Malayan labor was brought in to mine the island's rich phosphate deposits in the 1890s, and from 1900 the people enjoyed an economic boom. The mine now operates under strict environmental controls to preserve remaining rainforest. After heavy Australian government investment in infrastructure, a hotel complex was opened in 1993.

Bananas are grown on Tokelau (left page bottom). Coconuts are piled on a beach in the Pacific Islands (below).

Oceania: Physical

A 120° B 130° C 140° D 150° E 160°

Sonsorol
Pulo Anna
Merir
Tobi
Helen
Namoluk
Mortlock Is
Lukunor
Ngatik
Caroline Islands
Nukuoro
CELEBES SEA
Borneo
Halmahera
Waigeo
Kapingamarangi Atoll
Melanesia
Kep. Togian
MOLUCCA SEA
Biak
Yapen
Ninego Group
Kaniet Is
St Matthias Group
Manus
Admiralty Islands
New Hanover
Solomon Islands
Sulawesi (Celebes)
CERAM SEA
Seram
BISMARCK SEA
New Ireland
Nuguria Is
Green Is
Buka
Tauu Is
Laut
Buru
JAVA SEA
Buton
BANDA SEA
Kai Besar
Kep. Aru
New Guinea
Mt Wilhelm 4509 m
New Britain
Bougainville
Ontong Java
Choiseul
Kep. Kangean
Selayar
Jawa (Java)
FLORES SEA
Kep. Babar
Kep. Tanimbar
Dolak
Lake Murray
Mt Victoria 4038 m
Owen Stanley Range
SOLOMON SEA
Santa Isabel
Bali
Lombok
Sumbawa
Flores
Kep. Sermata
Gulf of Papua
Trobriand Is
Woodlark
New Georgia Group
Timor
ARAFURA SEA
Louisiade Arch.
Guadalcanal
Sumba
Sawu
Roti
Melville I.
Wessel Is
Torres Strait
Prince of Wales I.
C. York
Tagula
Rossel
Bellona
Rennell
Cape Londonderry
Joseph Bonaparte Gulf
Daly
Arnhem Land
Groote Eylandt
Gulf of Carpentaria
Cape York Peninsula
Cape Melville
TIMOR SEA
Kimberley Plateau
Lake Argyle
Victoria
Great Barrier Reef
CORAL SEA
Coral Sea Islands
Hinchinbrook Island
Tanami Desert
Barkly Tableland
Great Dividing Range
Great Sandy Desert
Whitsunday Group
Îles Chesterfield
Barrow I.
North West Cape
Pilbara
Hamersley Range
Lake Mackay
Lake Disappointment
Torilla Pen.
Tropic of Capricorn
Ashburton
Diamantina
Hervey Bay
Shark Bay
Mt Augustus 1105 m
Gibson Desert
MacDonnell Ranges
Australia
Great Artesian Basin
Sandy Cape
Fraser I.
Murchison
863 m Uluru (Ayers Rock)
Simpson Desert
Cooper
Lake Carnegie
Moreton I.
North Stradbroke I.
Lake Eyre North
Strzelecki Desert
Great Victoria Desert
Grey Range
Paroo
Lake Barlee
Lake Eyre South
Darling Range
Lake Moore
Lake Torrens
Lake Frome
Nullarbor Plain
Darling
Lord Howe I.
Lake Gairdner
Lake Macfarlane
Great Australian Bight
Lachlan
Cape Hawke
Eyre Pen.
Murray
Murrumbidgee
Botany Bay
Cape Leeuwin
Point d'Entrecasteaux
Cape Pasley
Spencer Gulf
Jervis Bay
Kangaroo I.
Mt Kosciuszko 2229 m
Encounter Bay
Cape Jaffa
Glenelg
TASMAN SEA
Cape Howe
Cape Otway
Bass Strait
Furneaux Group
King I.
Flinders I.
Cape Grim
Tasmania
Macquarie Harbour
Mt Ossa 1617 m
Great Oyster Bay
South Bruny I.
South East Cape
SOUTHERN OCEAN

1 2 3 4 5 6 7
0° 10° 20° 30° 40° 50°

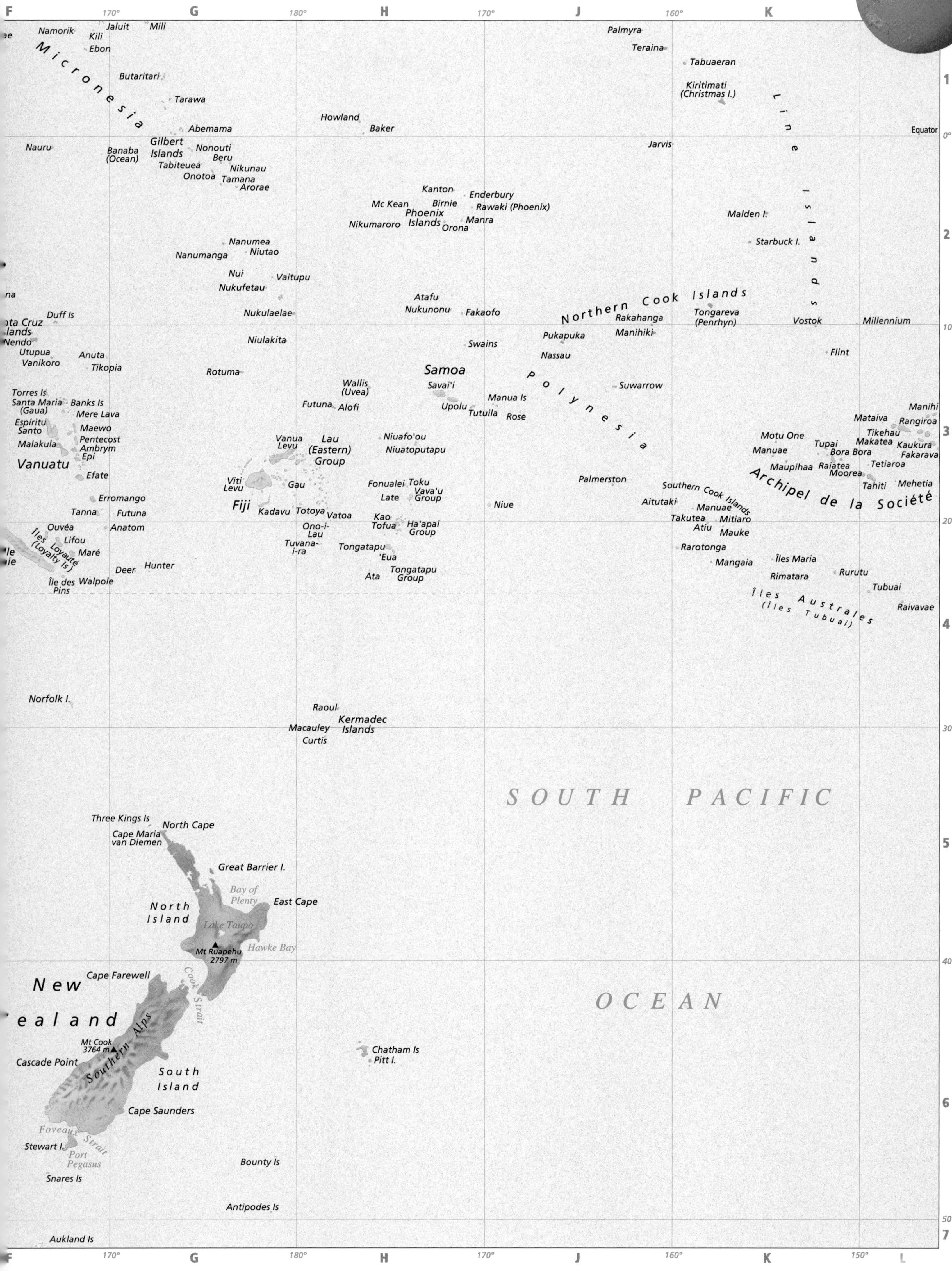

F 170° G 180° H 170° J 160° K

Namorik Jaluit Mili Kili Ebon
Micronesia
Butaritari
Tarawa
Abemama
Gilbert Islands
Nauru
Banaba (Ocean)
Nonouti
Beru
Tabiteuea
Nikunau
Onotoa
Tamana
Arorae
Palmyra
Teraina
Tabuaeran
Kiritimati (Christmas I.)
Line Islands
Howland
Baker
Jarvis
Equator 0°
Kanton
Enderbury
Mc Kean
Birnie
Rawaki (Phoenix)
Phoenix Islands
Manra
Nikumaroro
Orona
Malden I.
Starbuck I.
Nanumea
Niutao
Nanumanga
Nui
Vaitupu
Nukufetau
Nukulaelae
Atafu
Nukunonu
Fakaofo
Northern Cook Islands
Rakahanga
Tongareva (Penrhyn)
Manihiki
Pukapuka
Nassau
Vostok
Millennium
Flint
Duff Is
Santa Cruz Islands
Nendo
Utupua
Vanikoro
Anuta
Tikopia
Niulakita
Rotuma
Swains
Samoa
Savai'i
Upolu
Tutuila
Manua Is
Rose
Polynesia
Suwarrow
Wallis (Uvea)
Futuna
Alofi
Torres Is
Santa Maria (Gaua)
Banks Is
Mere Lava
Espiritu Santo
Maewo
Pentecost
Malakula
Ambrym
Epi
Vanuatu
Efate
Erromango
Tanna
Futuna
Anatom
Vanua Levu
Lau (Eastern) Group
Niuafo'ou
Niuatoputapu
Viti Levu
Gau
Fiji
Kadavu
Totoya
Vatoa
Fonualei
Toku
Late
Vava'u Group
Kao
Tofua
Ha'apai Group
Ono-i-Lau
Tuvana-i-ra
Tongatapu
'Eua
Ata
Tongatapu Group
Niue
Palmerston
Southern Cook Islands
Aitutaki
Manuae
Takutea
Mitiaro
Atiu
Mauke
Rarotonga
Mangaia
Manihi
Mataiva
Rangiroa
Tikehau
Motu One
Tupai
Makatea
Kaukura
Fakarava
Manuae
Bora Bora
Maupihaa
Raiatea
Tetiaroa
Moorea
Tahiti
Mehetia
Archipel de la Société
Ouvéa
Lifou
Îles Loyauté (Loyalty Is)
Maré
Deer
Hunter
Île des Pins
Walpole
Îles Maria
Rimatara
Rurutu
Tubuai
Îles Australes (Îles Tubuai)
Raivavae
Norfolk I.
Raoul
Kermadec Islands
Macauley
Curtis
SOUTH PACIFIC OCEAN
Three Kings Is
North Cape
Cape Maria van Diemen
Great Barrier I.
Bay of Plenty
East Cape
North Island
Lake Taupo
Mt Ruapehu 2797 m
Hawke Bay
Cape Farewell
New Zealand
Cook Strait
Mt Cook 3764 m
Southern Alps
Cascade Point
South Island
Cape Saunders
Chatham Is
Pitt I.
Foveaux Strait
Stewart I.
Port Pegasus
Snares Is
Bounty Is
Antipodes Is
Aukland Is

1 2 3 4 5 6 7
0° 10° 20° 30° 40° 50°

F 170° G 180° H 170° J 160° K 150° L

0 200 400 600 800 1000 kilometers
0 200 400 600 miles
Scale 1:25,000,000 Projection: Mercator

Oceania: Political

BRUNEI
PHILIPPINES
MALAYSIA
CELEBES SEA
PALAU
MICRONESIA
Borneo
Sulawesi (Celebes)
MOLUCCA SEA
INDONESIA
BANDA SEA
JAVA SEA
FLORES SEA
EAST TIMOR
ARAFURA SEA
TIMOR SEA
PAPUA NEW GUINEA
BISMARCK SEA
SOLOMON SEA
CORAL SEA
CORAL SEA ISLANDS (Aust.)
ASHMORE AND CARTIER ISLANDS (Aust.)
AUSTRALIA
WESTERN AUSTRALIA
NORTHERN TERRITORY
QUEENSLAND
SOUTH AUSTRALIA
NEW SOUTH WALES
VICTORIA
A.C.T.
TASMANIA
Great Australian Bight
Bass Strait
Torres Strait
Gulf of Carpentaria
Joseph Bonaparte Gulf
Tropic of Capricorn
Darwin
Katherine
Wyndham
Derby
Broome
Halls Creek
Port Hedland
Karratha
Tennant Creek
Mount Isa
Cairns
Townsville
Whitsunday Group
Mackay
Rockhampton
Gladstone
Barcaldine
Alice Springs
Newman
Carnarvon
Meekatharra
Maryborough
Fraser I.
Noosa Heads
Charleville
Toowoomba
Brisbane
Geraldton
Coober Pedy
Ballina
Grafton
Coffs Harbour
Bourke
Kalgoorlie-Boulder
Tamworth
Port Macquarie
Lord Howe I. (Aust.)
Perth
Broken Hill
Ceduna
Dubbo
Port Augusta
Whyalla
Port Pirie
Newcastle
Orange
Bathurst
Sydney
Wollongong
Bunbury
Busselton
Esperance
Albany
Port Lincoln
Gawler
Adelaide
Murray Bridge
Wagga Wagga
Canberra
Queanbeyan
Albury
Kangaroo I.
Mount Gambier
Ballarat
Geelong
Melbourne
Warrnambool
King I.
Furneaux Group
Flinders I.
Burnie
Devonport
Launceston
Hobart
South Bruny I.
TASMAN SEA
SOUTHERN OCEAN
Sonsorol
Tobi
Helen
Kot
Halmahera
Waigeo
Yapen
Buru
Kep. Aru
Kep. Babar
Kep. Tanimbar
Dolak
Jawa (Java)
Bali
Flores
Sumba
Timor
Roti
Melville I.
Wessel Is
New Guinea
Ninego Group
Admiralty Islands
New Hanover
New Ireland
Nuguria Is
Wewak
Madang
Mount Hagen
Goroka
Lae
Kerema
Port Moresby
New Britain
Bougainville
Green Is
Buka
Trobriand Is
Woodlark
Louisiade Arch.
Tagula
Rossel
Namoluk
Ngatik
Mortlock Is
Lukunor
Caroline Islands
Nukuoro
Kapingamarangi Atoll
Tauu Is
Choiseul
New Georgia Group
Santa Is
Honiara
Guadalcanal
Bellona
Rennell
Îles Chesterfield

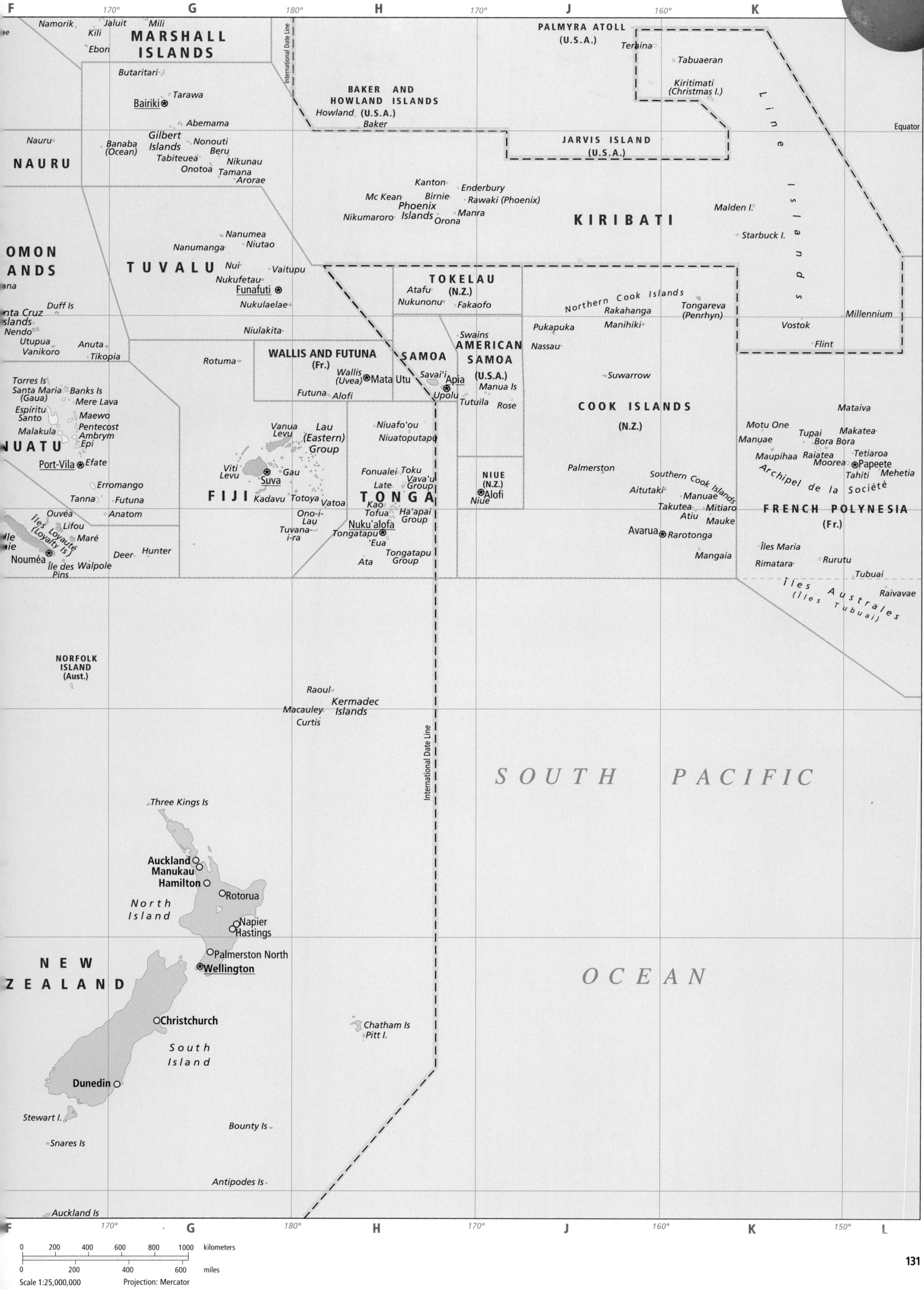

F 170° G 180° H 170° J 160° K

MARSHALL ISLANDS
Namorik
Jaluit
Mili
Kili
Ebon
Butaritari
Tarawa
Bairiki
Abemama
Gilbert Islands
Nonouti
Beru
Nikunau
Tabiteuea
Onotoa
Tamana
Arorae
Banaba (Ocean)
Nauru
NAURU
International Date Line
BAKER AND HOWLAND ISLANDS
Howland (U.S.A.)
Baker
PALMYRA ATOLL (U.S.A.)
Teraina
Tabuaeran
Kiritimati (Christmas I.)
Line Islands
JARVIS ISLAND (U.S.A.)
Equator
0°
Kanton
Enderbury
Mc Kean
Birnie
Rawaki (Phoenix)
Phoenix Islands
Nikumaroro
Manra
Orona
KIRIBATI
Malden I.
Starbuck I.
Nanumea
Nanumanga
Niutao
SOLOMON ISLANDS
TUVALU
Nui
Vaitupu
Nukufetau
Funafuti
Nukulaelae
Niulakita
Santa Cruz Islands
Duff Is
Nendo
Utupua
Vanikoro
Anuta
Tikopia
TOKELAU (N.Z.)
Atafu
Nukunonu
Fakaofo
Northern Cook Islands
Rakahanga
Tongareva (Penrhyn)
Manihiki
Pukapuka
Nassau
Vostok
Millennium
Flint
10°
Swains
AMERICAN SAMOA (U.S.A.)
SAMOA
WALLIS AND FUTUNA (Fr.)
Wallis (Uvea)
Mata Utu
Futuna
Alofi
Savai'i
Apia
Upolu
Manua Is
Tutuila
Rose
Rotuma
Suwarrow
COOK ISLANDS (N.Z.)
Mataiva
Torres Is
Santa Maria (Gaua)
Banks Is
Mere Lava
Espiritu Santo
Maewo
Pentecost
Ambrym
Malakula
Epi
VANUATU
Port-Vila
Efate
Erromango
Tanna
Futuna
Anatom
Vanua Levu
Lau (Eastern) Group
Niuafo'ou
Niuatoputapu
Motu One
Manuae
Tupai
Bora Bora
Makatea
Maupihaa
Raiatea
Moorea
Tetiaroa
Papeete
Tahiti
Mehetia
Archipel de la Société
Viti Levu
Suva
Gau
FIJI
Kadavu
Totoya
Vatoa
Fonualei
Toku
Late
Vava'u Group
TONGA
Kao
Tofua
Ha'apai Group
Ono-i-Lau
Tuvana-i-ra
Nuku'alofa
Tongatapu
'Eua
Tongatapu Group
Ata
NIUE (N.Z.)
Alofi
Niue
Palmerston
Southern Cook Islands
Aitutaki
Manuae
Takutea
Mitiaro
Atiu
Mauke
Avarua
Rarotonga
Mangaia
FRENCH POLYNESIA (Fr.)
20°
Îles Maria
Rimatara
Rurutu
Tubuai
Raivavae
Îles Australes (Îles Tubuai)
Ouvéa
Îles Loyauté (Loyalty Is)
Lifou
Maré
Nouméa
Île des Pins
Walpole
Deer
Hunter
NORFOLK ISLAND (Aust.)
Raoul
Kermadec Islands
Macauley
Curtis
30°
SOUTH PACIFIC OCEAN
Three Kings Is
Auckland
Manukau
Hamilton
Rotorua
North Island
Napier
Hastings
Palmerston North
Wellington
NEW ZEALAND
40°
Christchurch
South Island
Chatham Is
Pitt I.
Dunedin
Stewart I.
Bounty Is
Snares Is
Antipodes Is
Auckland Is
50°

1 2 3 4 5 6 7

F 170° G 180° H 170° J 160° K 150° L

0 200 400 600 800 1000 kilometers
0 200 400 600 miles
Scale 1:25,000,000
Projection: Mercator

Oceania

New Zealand

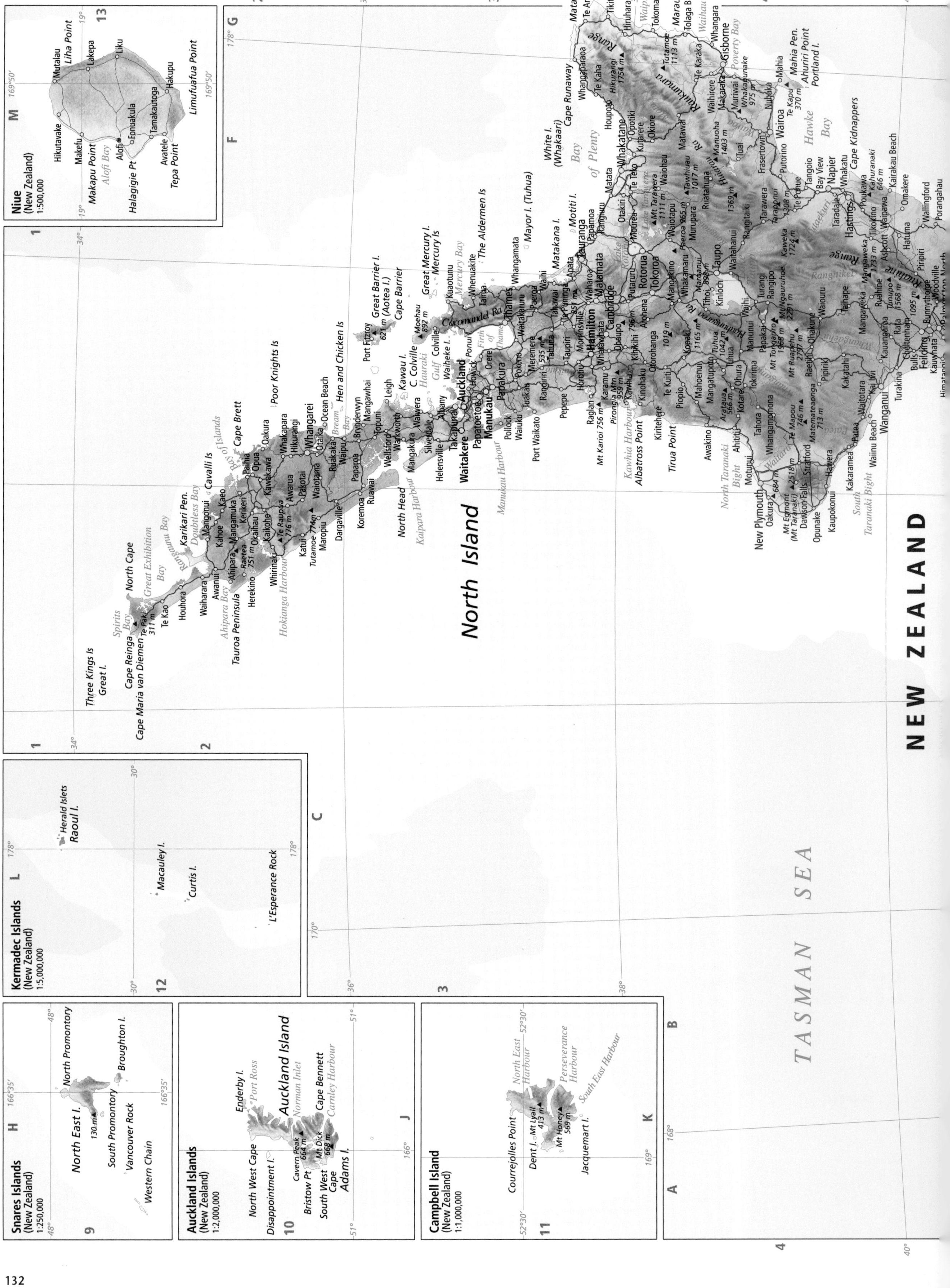
NEW ZEALAND
North Island
TASMAN SEA
Auckland
Manukau
Waitakere
Hamilton
Tauranga
Rotorua
Taupo
Gisborne
Napier
Hastings
New Plymouth
Wanganui
Whangarei
Whakatane
Bay of Plenty
Hawke Bay
Poverty Bay
North Cape
Cape Reinga
Three Kings Is
Great Barrier I.
Kaipara Harbour
Manukau Harbour
Firth of Thames
Lake Taupo
East Cape
Cape Kidnappers
Mt Ruapehu 2797 m
Mt Egmont (Mt Taranaki) 2518 m
North Taranaki Bight
South Taranaki Bight
Niue (New Zealand) 1:500,000
Alofi
Kermadec Islands (New Zealand) 1:5,000,000
Raoul I.
Macauley I.
Curtis I.
L'Esperance Rock
Snares Islands (New Zealand) 1:250,000
North East I.
Broughton I.
Auckland Islands (New Zealand) 1:2,000,000
Auckland Island
Adams I.
Enderby I.
Campbell Island (New Zealand) 1:1,000,000
Perseverance Harbour
Jacquemart I.
Dent I.

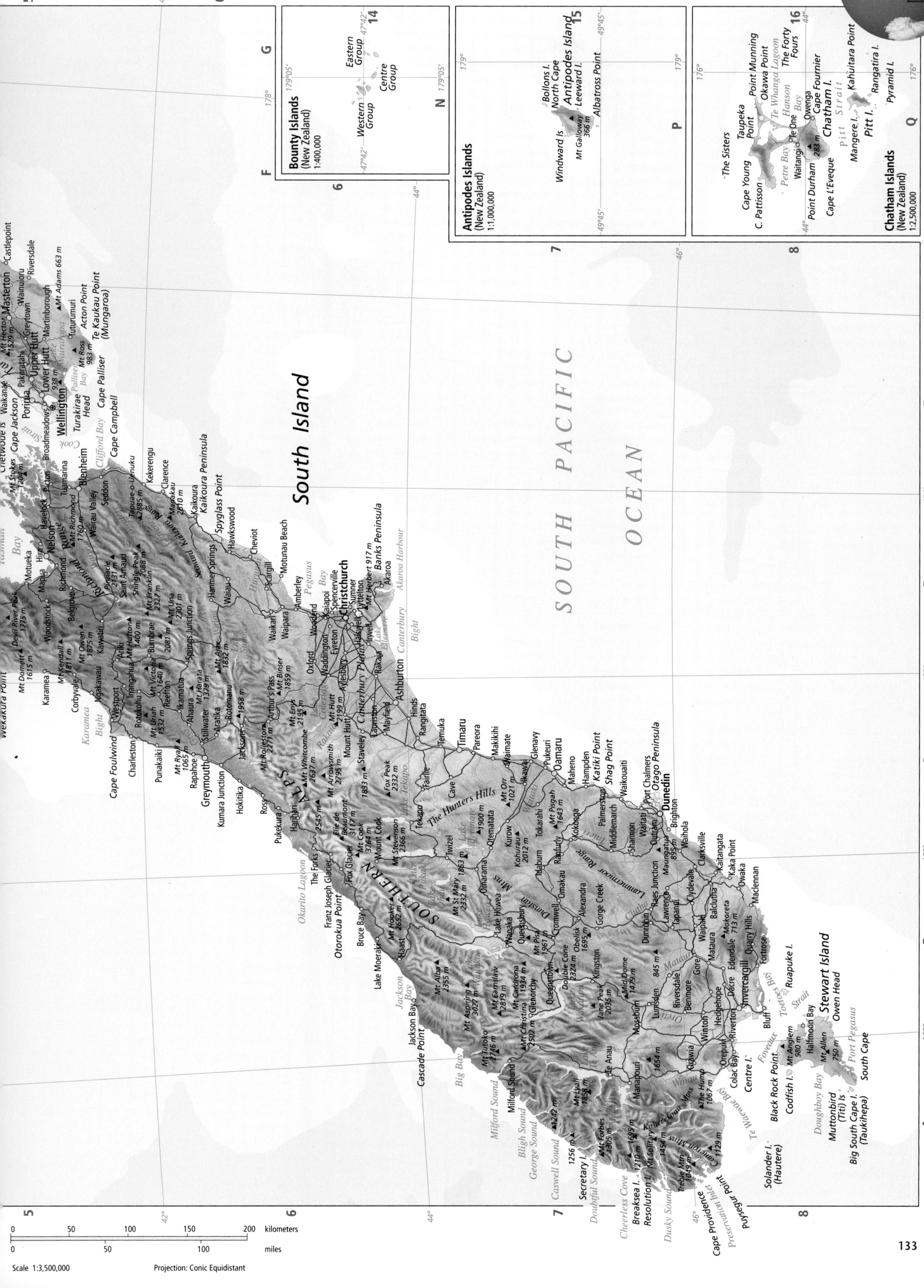

South Island

SOUTH PACIFIC OCEAN

Tasman Bay
Karamea Bight
Cape Foulwind
Charleston
Punakaiki
Greymouth
Kumara Junction
Hokitika
Ross
Pukekura
Harihari
Okarito Lagoon
The Forks
Franz Joseph Glacier
Otorokua Point
Fox Glacier
Bruce Bay
Lake Moeraki
Haast
Jackson Bay
Cascade Point
Big Bay
Milford Sound
Bligh Sound
George Sound
Caswell Sound
Secretary I.
Doubtful Sound
Cheerless Cove
Breaksea I.
Resolution I.
Dusky Sound
Cape Providence
Preservation Inlet
Puysegur Point
Te Waewae Bay
Solander I. (Hautere)
Black Rock Point
Codfish I.
Doughboy Bay
Muttonbird (Titi) Is
Big South Cape I. (Taukihepa)
South Cape
Port Pegasus
Stewart Island
Owen Head
Halfmoon Bay
Mt Anglem 980 m
Mt Allen 750 m
Foveaux Strait
Toetoes Bay
Ruapuke I.
Bluff
Invercargill
Fortrose
Centre I.
Colac Bay
Riverton
Orepuki
Wekakura Point
Mt Domett 1615 m
Devil River Peak 1775 m
Karamea
Motueka
Mapua
Hira
Nelson
Richmond
Woodstock
Mt Kendall 1811 m
Corbyvale
Mt Owen 1875 m
Belgrove
Ngakawau
Kawatiri
Westport
Ariki
Rotokohu
Inangahua
Mt Hutton 1400 m
Mt Uriah 1532 m
Mt Victoria 1640 m
Reefton
Burnbrae 2081 m
Mt Ryall 1065 m
Rapahoe
Ikamatua
Ahaura
Mt Harata 1379 m
Springs Junction
Stillwater
Aratika
Rotomanu
Mt Ajax 1832 m
Jacksons
1958 m
Mt Rolleston 2271 m
Arthur's Pass
Mt Binser 1859 m
Mt Enys 2195 m
Mt Whitcombe 2637 m
2545 m
Mt Arrowsmith 2795 m
Mt Hutt 2199 m
Elie de Beaumont 3117 m
Mt Cook 3764 m
Mount Cook
Mt Hooker 2652 m
Mt Stevenson 2366 m
Fox Peak 2332 m
1833 m
SOUTHERN ALPS
Richmond Range
Mt Richmond 1760 m
Pinnacle 2131 m
Saint Arnaud
Shingle Peak 2088 m
Mt Franklin 2327 m
Mt Una 2301 m
Tapuae-o-Uenuku 2885 m
Manakau 2610 m
Seaward Kaikoura Range
Mt Stokes 1204 m
Chetwode Is
Cape Jackson
Havelock
Picton
Tuamarina
Blenheim
Wairau Valley
Seddon
Clifford Bay
Cape Campbell
Kekerengu
Clarence
Kaikoura
Kaikoura Peninsula
Spyglass Point
Hawkswood
Hanmer Springs
Waiau
Cheviot
Scargill
Motunau Beach
Waikari
Waipara
Amberley
Pegasus Bay
Oxford
Woodend
Waddington
Eyreton
Kaiapoi
Spencerville
Christchurch
Sumner
Lyttelton
Halswell
Irwell
Mt Herbert 917 m
Banks Peninsula
Akaroa
Akaroa Harbour
Aylesbury
Mount Hutt
Staveley
Canterbury Plains
Lauriston
Mayfield
Rakaia
Lake Ellesmere
Lake Coleridge
Lake Sumner
Ashburton
Canterbury Bight
Hinds
Rangitata
Tekapo
Lake Tekapo
Lake Pukaki
Lake Ohau
Fairlie
Temuka
Cave
Timaru
Pareora
Twizel
1863 m
Lake Benmore
1900 m
The Hunters Hills
Mt St Mary 2332 m
Mt Alba 2355 m
Mt Aspiring 3027 m
Lake Wanaka
Lake Hawea
Omarama
Otematata
Makikihi
Waimate
Mt Orr 1021 m
Kurow
Kohurau 2012 m
Ikawai
Glenavy
Mt Tutoko 2746 m
Mt Earnslaw 2819 m
Mt Cardrona 1934 m
Mt Christina 2502 m
Wanaka
Queensbury
Dunstan Mtns
Mt Pisa 1961 m
Glenorchy
Queenstown
Cromwell
Idaburn
Tokarahi
Mt Pisgah 1643 m
Pukeuri
Oamaru
Ranfurly
Omakau
Maheno
Hampden
Katiki Point
Shag Point
Kokonga
Double Cone 2324 m
Obelisk 1695 m
Alexandra
Lake Wakatipu
Jane Peak 2035 m
Kingston
Gorge Creek
Lammermoor Range
Palmerston
Middlemarch
Waikouaiti
Shannon
Waitati
Port Chalmers
Otago Peninsula
Outram
Dunedin
Brighton
Mid Dome 1479 m
Mossburn
1242 m
1256 m
Mt Lyall 1858 m
Lake Te Anau
Te Anau
Mt Forbes 1305 m
Manapouri
Lake Manapouri
1210 m
1695 m
Mt Solitary
Kaherekoau Mtns
1454 m
Treble Mtn 1049 m
Hauroko
Cameron Mtns
1129 m
The Hump 1067 m
1654 m
Lumsden
845 m
Dunrobin
Raes Junction
Lawrence
Tapanui
Maungatua 895 m
Waihola
Clutha
Riversdale
Benmore
Gore
Clydevale
Oreti
Mataura
Waiau
Orawia
Winton
Hedgehope
Dacre
Edendale
Waipahi
Balclutha
Mokoreta 713 m
Clarksville
Kaitangata
Kaka Point
Owaka
Quarry Hills
Maclennan
Cook Strait
Broadmeadows
Porirua
Wellington
Pauatahanui
Upper Hutt
Lower Hutt
938 m
Turakirae Head
Palliser Bay
Cape Palliser
Lake Wairarapa
Mt Ross 983 m
Waikanae
Mt Hector 1529 m
Masterton
Castlepoint
Greytown
Wainuioru
Riversdale
Martinborough
Mt Adams 663 m
Tuturumuri
Acton Point
Te Kaukau Point (Mungaroa)

Bounty Islands
(New Zealand)
1:400,000

Western Group
Centre Group
Eastern Group
47°42′
179°05′

Antipodes Islands
(New Zealand)
1:1,000,000

Bollons I.
North Cape
Windward Is
Antipodes Island
Mt Galloway 366 m
Leeward I.
Albatross Point
49°45′
179°

Chatham Islands
(New Zealand)
1:2,500,000

The Sisters
Cape Young
Taupeka Point
Point Munning
C. Pattisson
Okawa Point
Te Whanga Lagoon
Petre Bay
Te One
Hanson Bay
The Forty Fours
Waitangi
Point Durham
283 m
Owenga
Cape Fournier
Chatham I.
Cape L'Eveque
Pitt Strait
Mangere I.
Kahuitara Point
Pitt I.
Rangatira I.
Pyramid I.
44°
176°

0 50 100 150 200 kilometers
0 50 100 miles
Scale 1:3,500,000
Projection: Conic Equidistant

Australia

Christmas Island
(Australia)
1:1,000,000
8
105° 30′
N
Flying Fish Cove
North East Pt
North West Pt
Murray Hill
359 m
Ross Hill
321 m
10° 30′
Egeria Pt
Smithson Bight
South Pt
Medwin Pt

Cocos (Keeling) Islands
(Australia)
1:1,000,000
10
96° 50′
Q
Wreck Pt
North Keeling I.
INDIAN
OCEAN
12°
South Keeling
Islands
Horsburgh I.
(Luar)
Direction I.
Home I.
Ujong Tanjong
Pulo Pandang
West I.
(Panjang)
South I.
(Atas)

Ashmore Reef and
Cartier Islet
(Australia)
1:2,000,000
9
123° 30′
P
Hibernia Reef
West
Islet
Ashmore
Reef
Middle
Islet
East Islet
Cartier Islet

Macquarie Island
(Australia)
1:1,000,000
11
159°
R
Hasselborough Bay
North Head
Buckles Bay
Anare Station
54° 30′
Langdon Pt
Bauer Bay
Mt Elder
371 m
Sandy Bay
Prion Lake
Mt Waite
422 m
Mt Eitel 341 m
Sandell Bay
Victoria Pt
Major Lake
Mt Hamilton
433 m
Mt Fletcher
428 m
Caroline Cove
Mt Jeffryes 399 m
South West Pt
Hurd Pt

Heard Island and
McDonald Islands
(Australia)
1:2,500,000
12
73° 30′
S
Anzac Peak
715 m
Corinthian Head
Laurens Pen.
Morgan I.
53°
McDonald
Islands
West Bay
Spit Pt
Heard I.
Mawson Peak
2745 m
Lambeth
Bluff

INDONESIA
Sawu
Roti
198
TIMOR SEA
ASHMORE AND
CARTIER ISLANDS
(Aust.)
Ashmore Reef
Cartier I.
Melville I.
Croker I.
Bathurst I.
Van
Diemen
Gulf
Cobourg
Pen.
Beagle Gulf
Darwin
Palmerston
Berry Springs
Jabiru
Annaburroo
Adelaide River
Pine
Creek
Cape Ford
Joseph
Bonaparte
Gulf
Napier Broome Bay
Cape Londonderry
Admiralty Gulf
Kalumburu
Bigge I.
Bonaparte
Archipelago
Katherine
Mataranka
Daly
Wyndham
Kununurra
Timber
Creek
Victoria River
Wayside Inn
Larrimah
Lake Argyle Village
Lake Argyle
Top Springs
Daly Waters
Collier Bay
KIMBERLEY
Kupingarri
Cape Leveque
Lombadina
King Sound
King Leopold Ranges
Kalkarindji
Derby
Mt Broome
935 m
Fitzroy
Ord
Broome
Roebuck Bay
Fitzroy Crossing
Halls Creek
NORTHERN
TERRITORY
Lagrange
Sandy
Lake
Sturt
Tanami
Tennant Creek
Eighty Mile
Beach
Sandfire Roadhouse
Lake Gregory
Desert
Port Hedland
Pardoo Roadhouse
GREAT SANDY
Lake
White
Nickol Bay
Dampier
Karratha
Roebourne
Marble Bar
Percival
Lakes
AUST
Barrow I.
PILBARA
Oakover
DESERT
Lake Mackay
Yuendumu
Onslow
Pannawonica
Nullagine
Lake
Dora
Lake Auld
Exmouth Gulf
Fortescue
North West Cape
Exmouth
Nanutarra
Roadhouse
Wittenoom
Hamersley Range
Lake
MacDonald
Lake Lewis
Mt Tom Price
1073 m
Tom Price
Alice Springs
MacDonnell
Lake
Disappointment
Coral Bay
Paraburdoo
Mt Meharry
1253 m
Newman
Lake Hopkins
Lake Neale
Lake Amadeus
Ashburton
Gibson Desert
Minilya
Roadhouse
Tropic of Capricorn
Lake MacLeod
Mt Augustus
1105 m
Yulara
Erldunda
Katatjuta (Mt Olga)
1066 m
Uluru (Ayers Rock)
863 m
Kulgera
Gascoyne
Bernier I.
Carnarvon
Lake
Carnegie
Boyd Lagoon
Mt Woodroffe
1435 m
Dorre I.
Musgrave Ranges
Shark Bay
Wiluna
Dirk Hartog I.
Denham
Lake Wells
Marla
Steep Point
Overlander
Roadhouse
Meekatharra
GREAT VICTORIA
SOUTH
Murchison
WESTERN AUSTRALIA
Lake
Austin
DESERT
AUSTRALIA
Mount Magnet
Lake Noondie
Laverton
Kalbarri
Leonora
Lake Carey
Jubilee Lake
Lake Maurice
INDIAN
Northampton
Lake
Barlee
Lake
Marmion
Lake Minigwal
Houtman Abrolhos
Mullewa
Geraldton
Lake
Ballard
Menzies
Lake Rebecca
Dongara
Lake Moore
OCEAN
Wubin
Kalgoorlie-Boulder
Nullarbor Plain
Moora
Coolgardie
Kambalda
Lake Lefroy
Madura
Eucla
Fowlers Bay
Penong
Wongan Hills
Lake Cowan
Goomalling
Southern Cross
Merredin
Balladonia
Twilight
Cove
Great
Fowlers Bay
Streaky
Muchea
Northam
Lake Hope
York
Norseman
Lake Dundas
Australian Bight
Anxious
Perth
Rockingham
Kwinana
Hyden
Mandurah
Corrigin
Pinjarra
Narrogin
Lake King
Ravensthorpe
Esperance
Bunbury
Geographe Bay
Collie
Wagin
Katanning
Cape Arid
Busselton
Kojonup
Jerramungup
Archipelago of
the Recherche
Margaret River
Bridgetown
Manjimup
Cape Leeuwin
Augusta
Mount Barker
Walpole
Albany
Denmark
Flinders Bay
SOUTHERN OCEAN

A B C D E F G
1 2 3 4 5 6 7
105° 110° 115° 120° 125° 130°
15° 20° 25° 30° 35° 40°

PAPUA NEW GUINEA
CORAL SEA
SOLOMON SEA
CORAL SEA ISLANDS (Aust.)
GREAT BARRIER REEF
QUEENSLAND
NEW SOUTH WALES
VICTORIA
TASMANIA
AUST. CAPITAL TERRITORY
JERVIS BAY TERRITORY
GREAT DIVIDING RANGE
SOUTH PACIFIC OCEAN
TASMAN SEA
Gulf of Carpentaria
Cape York Peninsula
Simpson Desert
Strzelecki Desert
Barkly Tableland
Bass Strait
Tropic of Capricorn
Brisbane
Sydney
Melbourne
Canberra
Adelaide
Hobart
Cairns
Townsville
Rockhampton
Newcastle
Wollongong
Gold Coast
Îles Chesterfield (New Caledonia)
Lord Howe I. (Aust.)
Norfolk Island (Australia) 1:1,000,000
Lord Howe Island (Australia) 1:1,000,000
Scale 1:12,500,000
Projection: Azimuthal Equal Area
kilometers
miles

South Pacific

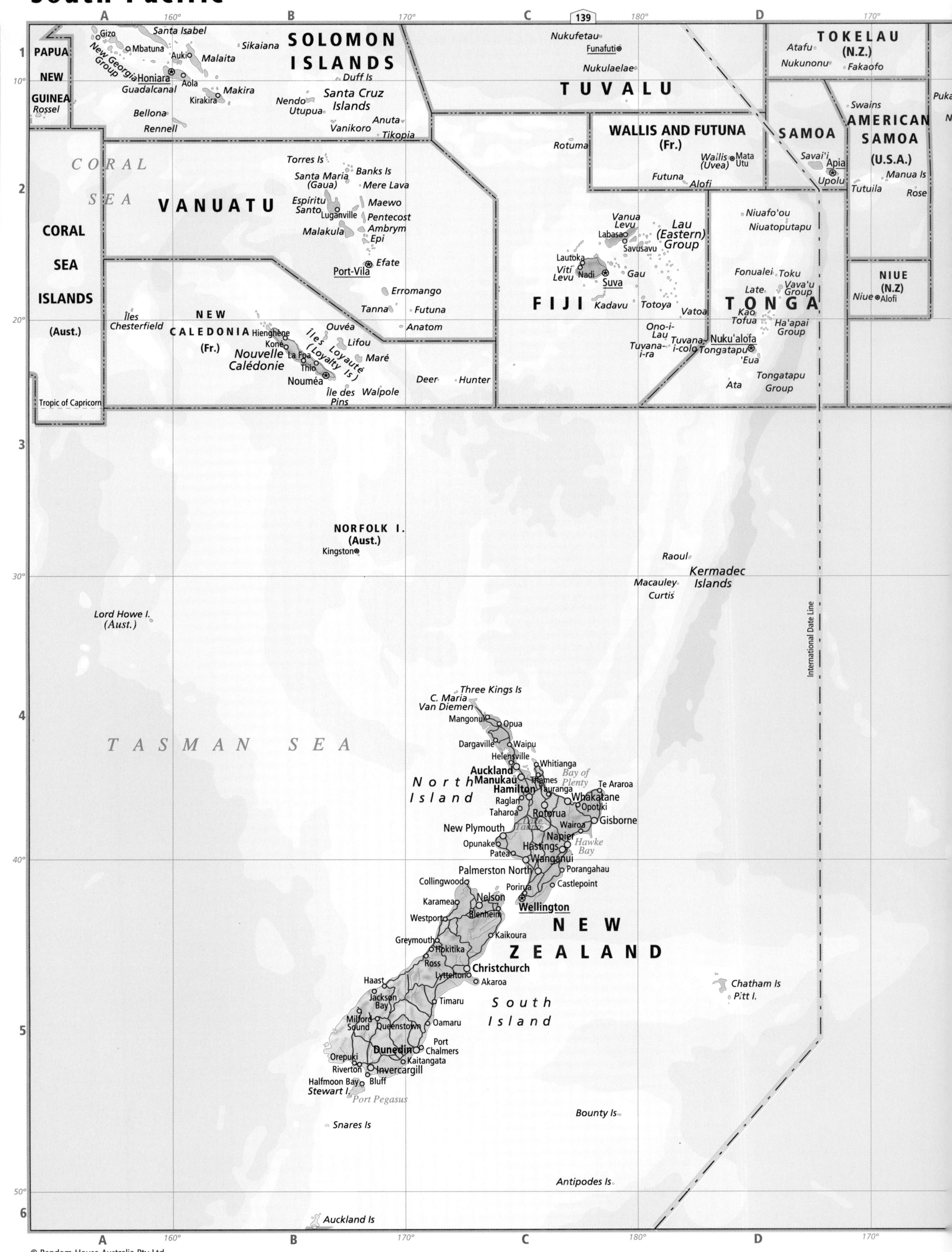
SOLOMON ISLANDS
PAPUA NEW GUINEA
Rossel
Gizo
Santa Isabel
Mbatuna
New Georgia Group
Auki
Malaita
Sikaiana
Honiara
Guadalcanal
Aola
Makira
Kirakira
Bellona
Rennell
Duff Is
Santa Cruz Islands
Nendo
Utupua
Anuta
Vanikoro
Tikopia
TUVALU
Nukufetau
Funafuti
Nukulaelae
TOKELAU (N.Z.)
Atafu
Nukunonu
Fakaofo
Swains
SAMOA
AMERICAN SAMOA (U.S.A.)
Savai'i
Apia
Upolu
Tutuila
Manua Is
Rose
WALLIS AND FUTUNA (Fr.)
Rotuma
Wallis (Uvea)
Mata Utu
Futuna
Alofi
CORAL SEA
VANUATU
Torres Is
Banks Is
Santa Maria (Gaua)
Mere Lava
Espíritu Santo
Luganville
Maewo
Pentecost
Malakula
Ambrym
Epi
Efate
Port-Vila
Erromango
Tanna
Futuna
Anatom
CORAL SEA ISLANDS (Aust.)
NEW CALEDONIA (Fr.)
Îles Chesterfield
Hienghène
Koné
Nouvelle Calédonie
La Foa
Thio
Nouméa
Ouvéa
Lifou
Îles Loyauté (Loyalty Is)
Maré
Île des Pins
Walpole
Deer
Hunter
Tropic of Capricorn
FIJI
Vanua Levu
Labasa
Savusavu
Lau (Eastern) Group
Lautoka
Viti Levu
Nadi
Suva
Gau
Kadavu
Totoya
Vatoa
Ono-i-Lau
Tuvana-i-ra
Tuvana-i-colo
TONGA
Niuafo'ou
Niuatoputapu
Fonualei
Toku
Late
Vava'u Group
Kao
Tofua
Ha'apai Group
Nuku'alofa
Tongatapu
'Eua
Tongatapu Group
Ata
NIUE (N.Z)
Niue
Alofi
NORFOLK I. (Aust.)
Kingston
Raoul
Kermadec Islands
Macauley
Curtis
Lord Howe I. (Aust.)
International Date Line
TASMAN SEA
Three Kings Is
C. Maria Van Diemen
Mangonui
Opua
Dargaville
Waipu
Helensville
Whitianga
Auckland
Manukau
Thames
Bay of Plenty
Te Araroa
Hamilton
Tauranga
Whakatane
Opotiki
Raglan
Taharoa
Rotorua
Lake Taupo
Gisborne
New Plymouth
Wairoa
Napier
Opunake
Hastings
Hawke Bay
Patea
Wanganui
Porangahau
Palmerston North
North Island
Collingwood
Castlepoint
Porirua
Karamea
Nelson
Blenheim
Wellington
Westport
NEW ZEALAND
Kaikoura
Greymouth
Hokitika
Ross
Christchurch
Lyttelton
Akaroa
Haast
Jackson Bay
Timaru
Milford Sound
Queenstown
Oamaru
South Island
Port Chalmers
Dunedin
Orepuki
Kaitangata
Riverton
Invercargill
Halfmoon Bay
Bluff
Stewart I.
Port Pegasus
Snares Is
Chatham Is
Pitt I.
Bounty Is
Antipodes Is
Auckland Is
139
A
B
C
D
1
2
3
4
5
6
160°
170°
180°
10°
20°
30°
40°
50°

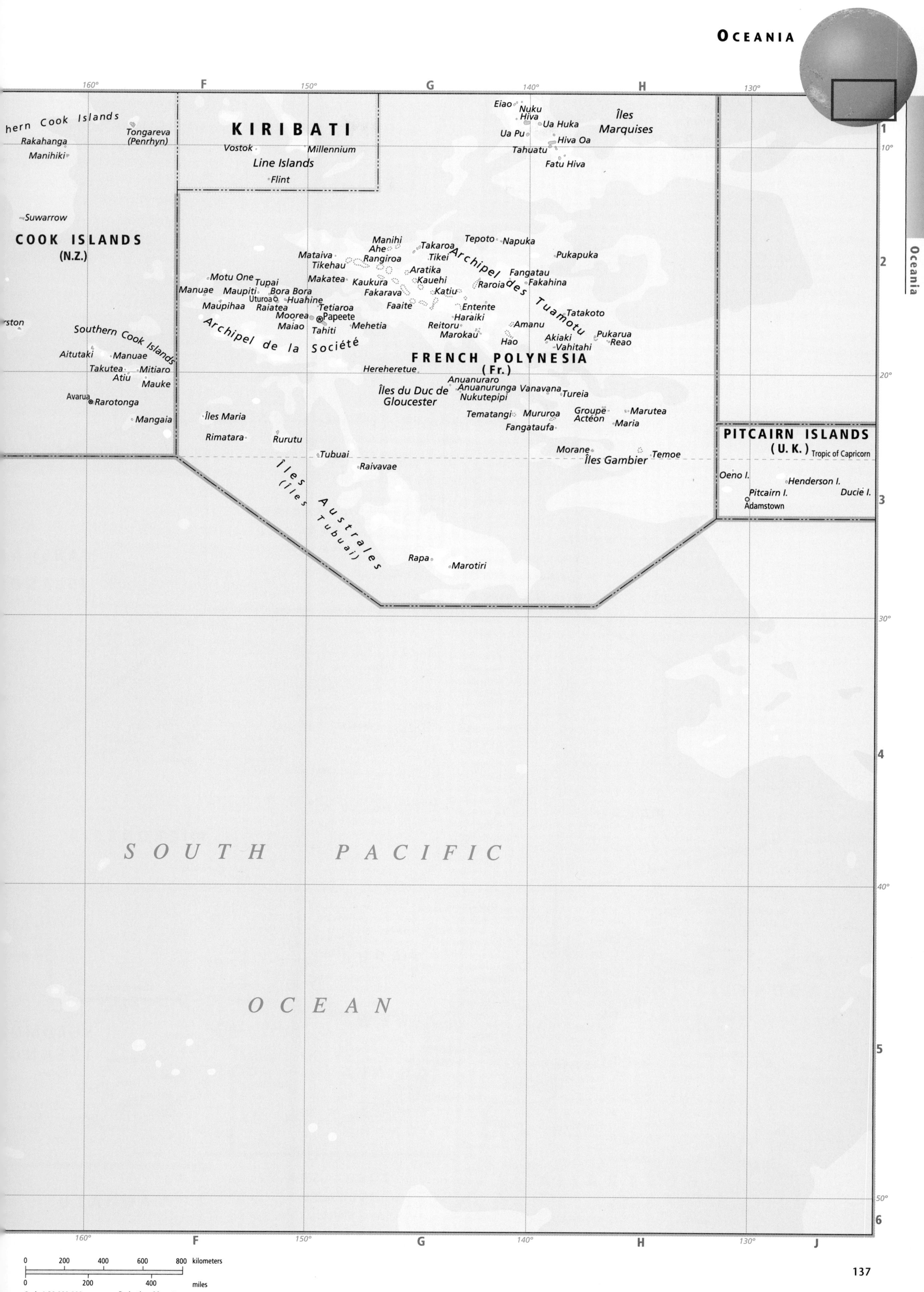
KIRIBATI
Vostok
Millennium
Line Islands
Flint
Tongareva
(Penrhyn)
Rakahanga
Manihiki
Suwarrow
COOK ISLANDS
(N.Z.)
Southern Cook Islands
Aitutaki
Manuae
Takutea
Mitiaro
Atiu
Mauke
Avarua
Rarotonga
Mangaia
Eiao
Nuku Hiva
Ua Huka
Ua Pu
Hiva Oa
Tahuatu
Fatu Hiva
Îles Marquises
Manihi
Ahe
Rangiroa
Mataiva
Tikehau
Takaroa
Tikei
Tepoto
Napuka
Pukapuka
Archipel des Tuamotu
Aratika
Kauehi
Makatea
Kaukura
Fakarava
Katiu
Raroia
Fangatau
Fakahina
Motu One
Tupai
Manuae
Maupiti
Bora Bora
Uturoa
Huahine
Maupihaa
Raiatea
Tetiaroa
Faaite
Entente
Haraiki
Moorea
Papeete
Maiao
Tahiti
Mehetia
Reitoru
Marokau
Amanu
Hao
Tatakoto
Akiaki
Vahitahi
Pukarua
Reao
Archipel de la Société
FRENCH POLYNESIA
(Fr.)
Hereheretue
Anuanuraro
Anuanurunga
Vanavana
Tureia
Nukutepipi
Îles du Duc de Gloucester
Tematangi
Mururoa
Fangataufa
Groupe Actéon
Marutea
Maria
Îles Maria
Rimatara
Rurutu
Tubuai
Raivavae
Morane
Îles Gambier
Temoe
Îles Australes
(Îles Tubuai)
Rapa
Marotiri
PITCAIRN ISLANDS
(U. K.)
Tropic of Capricorn
Oeno I.
Henderson I.
Pitcairn I.
Ducie I.
Adamstown
SOUTH PACIFIC OCEAN
160°
150°
140°
130°
10°
20°
30°
40°
50°
F
G
H
J
1
2
3
4
5
6
0 200 400 600 800 kilometers
0 200 400 miles
Scale 1:20,000,000
Projection: Mercator

North Pacific

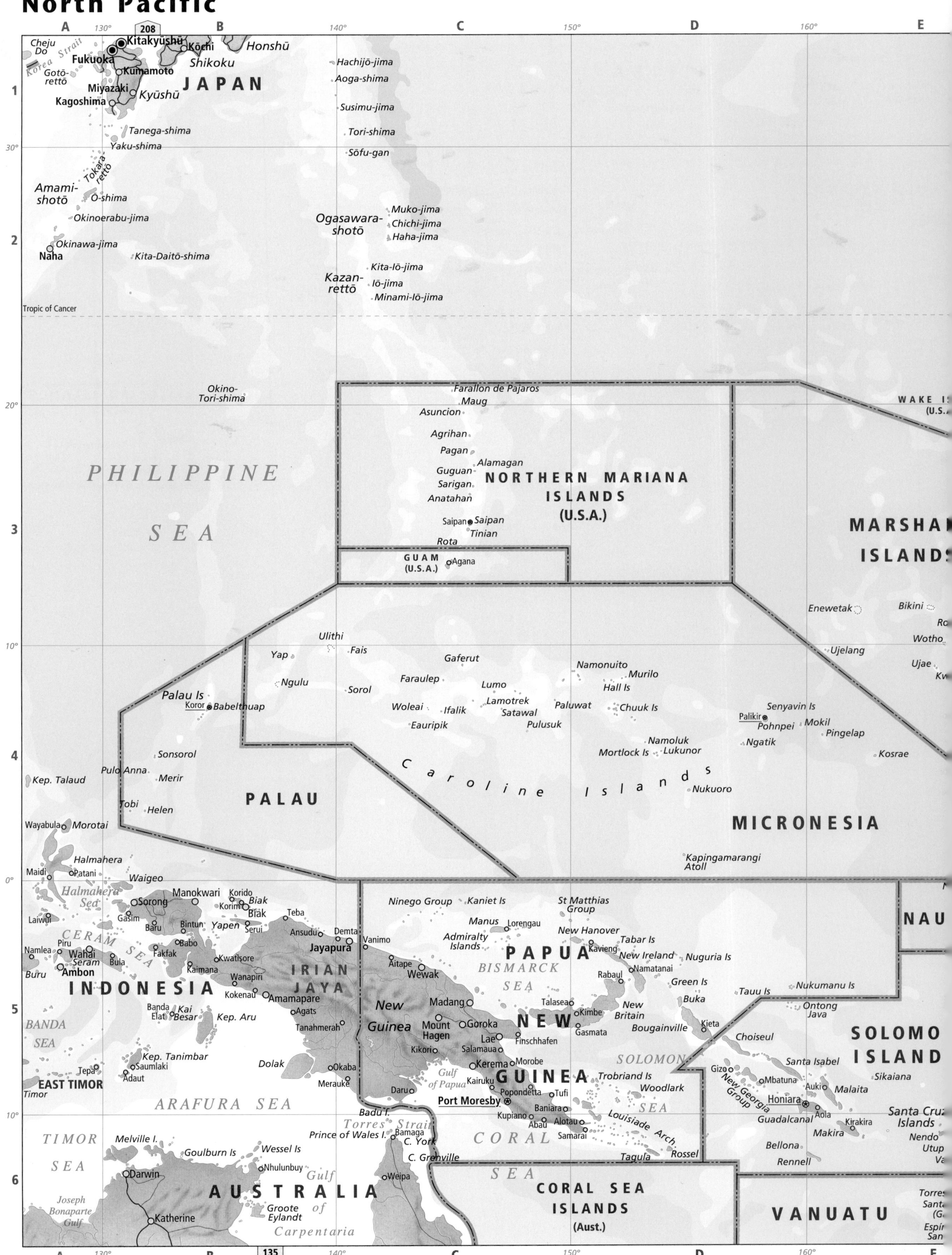

JAPAN
Honshū
Shikoku
Kyūshū
Kitakyūshū
Fukuoka
Kumamoto
Miyazaki
Kagoshima
Kōchi
Cheju Do
Korea Strait
Gotō-rettō
Tanega-shima
Yaku-shima
Tokara-rettō
Amami-shotō
O-shima
Okinoerabu-jima
Okinawa-jima
Naha
Kita-Daitō-shima
Hachijō-jima
Aoga-shima
Susimu-jima
Tori-shima
Sōfu-gan
Ogasawara-shotō
Muko-jima
Chichi-jima
Haha-jima
Kazan-rettō
Kita-Iō-jima
Iō-jima
Minami-Iō-jima
Tropic of Cancer
Okino-Tori-shima
PHILIPPINE SEA
NORTHERN MARIANA ISLANDS (U.S.A.)
Farallon de Pajaros
Maug
Asuncion
Agrihan
Pagan
Alamagan
Guguan
Sarigan
Anatahan
Saipan
Tinian
Rota
GUAM (U.S.A.)
Agana
WAKE I (U.S.
MARSHALL ISLANDS
Enewetak
Bikini
Wotho
Ujelang
Ujae
Ulithi
Fais
Yap
Ngulu
Sorol
Gaferut
Faraulep
Woleai
Ifalik
Eauripik
Lumo
Lamotrek
Satawal
Pulusuk
Namonuito
Murilo
Hall Is
Paluwat
Chuuk Is
Palikir
Senyavin Is
Pohnpei
Mokil
Pingelap
Ngatik
Namoluk
Mortlock Is
Lukunor
Kosrae
Nukuoro
Caroline Islands
MICRONESIA
Kapingamarangi Atoll
Palau Is
Koror
Babelthuap
PALAU
Sonsorol
Pulo Anna
Merir
Tobi
Helen
Kep. Talaud
Wayabula
Morotai
Halmahera
Maidi
Patani
Waigeo
Halmahera Sea
Sorong
Manokwari
Korido
Korim
Biak
Laiwui
Gasim
Baru
Bintuni
Yapen
Serui
Teba
CERAM SEA
Namlea
Piru
Wahai
Seram
Bula
Buru
Ambon
Babo
Fakfak
Kwatisore
Kaimana
Wanapiri
INDONESIA
Kokenau
Amamapare
Agats
Tanahmerah
IRIAN JAYA
Ansudu
Demta
Jayapura
Vanimo
Banda Elat
Kai Besar
Kep. Aru
BANDA SEA
Kep. Tanimbar
Saumlaki
Adaut
Tepa
EAST TIMOR
Timor
Dolak
Okaba
Merauke
ARAFURA SEA
TIMOR SEA
Melville I.
Goulburn Is
Wessel Is
Nhulunbuy
Darwin
Katherine
Joseph Bonaparte Gulf
AUSTRALIA
Groote Eylandt
Gulf of Carpentaria
Weipa
Badu I.
Torres Strait
Prince of Wales I.
Bamaga
C. York
C. Grenville
Ninego Group
Kaniet Is
St Matthias Group
Manus
Lorengau
Admiralty Islands
New Hanover
Kavieng
Tabar Is
New Ireland
Namatanai
Nuguria Is
PAPUA
BISMARCK SEA
Aitape
Wewak
Rabaul
Green Is
Buka
Madang
Talasea
Kimbe
New Britain
Gasmata
Bougainville
Kieta
New Guinea
Mount Hagen
Goroka
Lae
Finschhafen
NEW GUINEA
Kikori
Salamaua
Kerema
Morobe
SOLOMON SEA
Gulf of Papua
Kairuku
Popondetta
Tufi
Daru
Port Moresby
Kupiano
Baniara
Abau
Alotau
Samarai
Trobriand Is
Woodlark
Louisiade Arch.
Rossel
Tagula
CORAL SEA
CORAL SEA ISLANDS (Aust.)
NAURU
Tauu Is
Nukumanu Is
Ontong Java
Choiseul
Santa Isabel
Gizo
New Georgia Group
Mbatuna
Auki
Malaita
Honiara
Aola
Guadalcanal
Makira
Kirakira
Bellona
Rennell
SOLOMON ISLANDS
Sikaiana
Santa Cruz Islands
Nendo
Utup
VANUATU
208
135

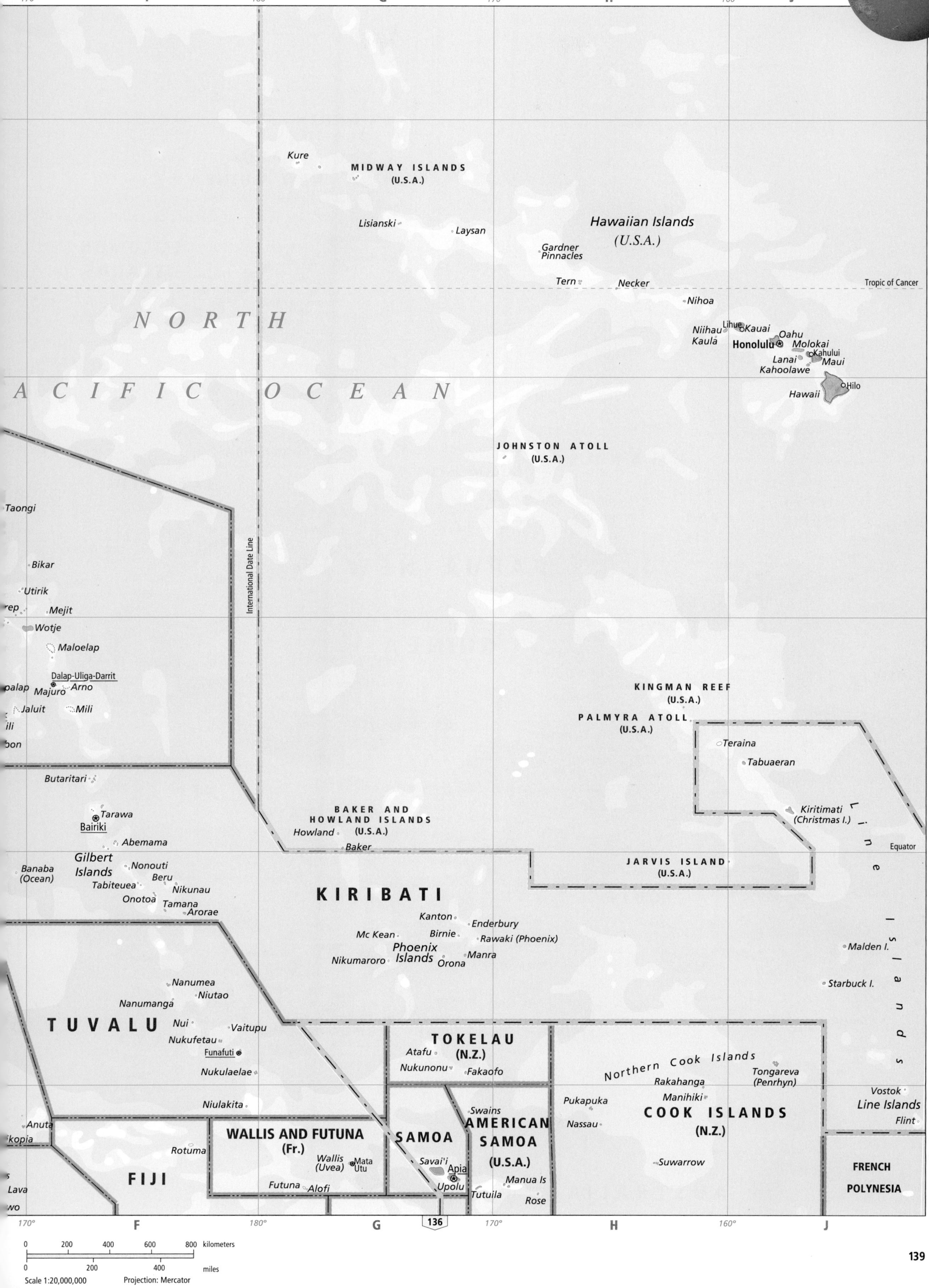

170° F 180° G 170° H 160° J

1

30°

Kure

MIDWAY ISLANDS
(U.S.A.)

Lisianski

Laysan

Hawaiian Islands
(U.S.A.)

Gardner
Pinnacles

2

Tern

Necker

Tropic of Cancer

Nihoa

N O R T H

Niihau

Lihue

Kauai

Kaula

Honolulu

Oahu

Molokai

Kahului

Lanai

Maui

Kahoolawe

20°

A C I F I C O C E A N

Hilo

Hawaii

JOHNSTON ATOLL
(U.S.A.)

Taongi

3

International Date Line

Bikar

Utirik

rep

Mejit

Wotje

10°

Maloelap

Dalap-Uliga-Darrit

palap

Majuro

Arno

KINGMAN REEF
(U.S.A.)

Jaluit

Mili

PALMYRA ATOLL
(U.S.A.)

ili

bon

Teraina

4

Tabuaeran

Butaritari

Tarawa

Bairiki

BAKER AND
HOWLAND ISLANDS
(U.S.A.)

Howland

Kiritimati
(Christmas I.)

Abemama

Baker

Equator

0°

Banaba
(Ocean)

Gilbert
Islands

Nonouti

Beru

JARVIS ISLAND
(U.S.A.)

Tabiteuea

Nikunau

Onotoa

Tamana

KIRIBATI

Arorae

Kanton

Enderbury

Mc Kean

Birnie

Rawaki (Phoenix)

Phoenix
Islands

Malden I.

Nikumaroro

Orona

Manra

5

Line Islands

Nanumea

Starbuck I.

Niutao

Nanumanga

TUVALU

Nui

Vaitupu

TOKELAU
(N.Z.)

Nukufetau

Atafu

Funafuti

Nukunonu

Fakaofo

Northern Cook Islands

Nukulaelae

Tongareva
(Penrhyn)

Rakahanga

10°

Vostok

Manihiki

Niulakita

Pukapuka

Line Islands

Swains

Anuta

AMERICAN
SAMOA
(U.S.A.)

COOK ISLANDS
(N.Z.)

Flint

Nassau

ikopia

WALLIS AND FUTUNA
(Fr.)

SAMOA

Rotuma

6

Wallis
(Uvea)

Mata
Utu

Savai'i

Apia

Suwarrow

FRENCH
POLYNESIA

FIJI

Lava

Futuna

Alofi

Upolu

Manua Is

Tutuila

Rose

wo

170° F 180° G 136 170° H 160° J

0 200 400 600 800 kilometers

0 200 400 miles

Scale 1:20,000,000 Projection: Mercator

Papua New Guinea

A B 144° 148° E 156° F

PACIFIC OCEAN

Green Is
Nissan I.
NORTH SOLOMONS
C. Hanpan
Hanahan
Buka I.
Sohano
PAPUA NEW GUINEA
Bougainville I.
Kunua
Mt Balbi 2715 m
Wakunai
Torokina
Arawa
Kieta
Panguna
Aropa
Mt Taraka 2219 m
Motupena Point
Boku
Buin
Nukiki
Choiseul
Sasamungga
SOLOMON ISLANDS
Shortland I. (Alu)
Treasury Is
Mono I.
Vella Lavella
Kia
Santa Isabel
160°

PACIFIC OCEAN

Equator

Ninigo Group
Kaniet Is
MANUS
Manus I.
Lorengau
Admiralty Is
Southwest Point
Mt Dremsel 702 m
C. Siemens
Mussau I.
St Matthias Group
NEW IRELAND
New Hanover
Umbukul
Taskul
Kavieng
Meteran
Mangai
Tabar Is
Lakuramau
Lihir Group
Lihir Is
Dyaul I.
Konos
BISMARCK ARCHIPELAGO
New Ireland
Tanga Is
Namatanai
PAPUA NEW GUINEA

WEST SEPIK
EAST SEPIK
Vanimo
Leitre
Ossima
Sissano
Aitape
Imonda
Paup
Yakamul
Dagua
Kairiru I.
Mushu
Schouten Is
Torricelli Mts 1238 m
Dreikikir
Mt Ulbanep
Amanab
Nuku
Maprik
Wewak
Mendam
Kaup
C. Girgir
Green River
Angoram
Watam
Manam I.
Bunapas
Bogia
C. Gourdon
Sepik
Kubkain
Hunstein Range
Tangu
Karkar I.
Yuat
Keram
Josephstaal
MADANG
New Guinea
Central Range
Mt Schrader 2052 m
Alexishafen
Ok Tedi
Telefomin
ENGA
Ramu
Simbai
Madang
Long I.
Tabubil
Porgera
Wabag
Tabibuga
Bismark Range
Astrolabe Bay
Kopiago
Laiagam
Usino
Ningerum
Tari
WESTERN HIGHLANDS
Saidor
Mt The Sugarloaf 3962 m
4509 m
Malalamai
Rumginae
Banz
Mt Wilhelm
Goroka
Kiunga
Mt Sisa 2678 m
Nipa
Mendi
Mount Hagen
Kundiawa
Henganofi
Kaiapit
SOUTHERN HIGHLANDS
Mt Giluwe 4368 m
Mt Michael 3647 m
Kainantu
4121 m
Lake Murray
SIMBU
EASTERN HIGHLANDS
Mt Bangeta
Mt Bosavi 2507 m
Erave
MOROBE
Finschhafen
C. Cretin
Strickland
2254 m
Mt Tabletop 3686 m
Lae
East Bay
Fly
Kikori
Mt Duau 1830 m
Mumeng
Salamaua
Turama
Purari
Bulolo
Sapanda
Wau
Lasanga I.
Aiambak
Kubeai
Kikori
Mt Eruki 2232 m
WESTERN
Misiki
Baimuru
Morobe
Emeti
Aramia
Garaina
C. Blackwood
Kerema
Duru
Goe
Balimo
GULF
Tauri
Wasua
Serki
Buk
Kiwai I.
Gulf of Papua
Morehead
Malam
Oriomo
Bula
Daru
Mari
Boigu I.
Saibai
Saibai I.
Torres Strait
Badu I.
Moa I.
Thursday I.
Prince of Wales I.
C. York
Bamaga

Manga
Feni Is
Takis
Rabaul
BISMARCK SEA
C. Pomas
Kokopo
Witu Is
Garove I.
Open Bay
Mt Sinewit 2438 m
Bakop
C. St George
Unea I.
Lolobau I.
Magma Point
2334 m
Mt Ulawun
Talasea
Crater Point
Sampun
Gloucester
Hoskins
Pomio
Siassi
Sag Sag
Aria
Kimbe
Malmal
Umboi I.
New Britain
Fulleborn
Uvol
Gasmata
Kandrian
EAST NEW BRITAIN
WEST NEW BRITAIN
SOLOMON SEA

Mt Strong 3587 m
C. Ward Hunt
Mt Albert Edward 3990 m
Ioma
Kumusi Point
Trobriand Is
Losuia
Popondetta
Bereina
Mt Victoria 4038 m
NORTHERN (ORO)
Woodlark I.
Kairuku
Kulumadau
Tufi
C. Nelson
Owen Stanley Range
Goodenough I.
Port Moresby
Mt Victory 1908 m
Vivigani
Bolubolu
Fergusson I.
NATIONAL CAPITAL DISTRICT
Salamo
C. Vogel
D'Entrecasteaux Is
Baniara
Mt Simpson 2883 m
Esa'ala
Sehulea
MILNE BAY
Kwikila
Kupiano
Wedau
Abau
Normanby I.
CENTRAL
Alotau
Orangerie Bay
Misima I.
Samarai
Louisiade Archipelago
Rossel I.
Tagula
Tagula I.
C. Siri

CORAL SEA
Shelburne Bay
Bramwell
C. Grenville
QUEENSLAND
Duyfken Point
Andoom
Portland Roads
Weipa
Albatross Bay
AUSTRALIA

199
135

A 144° B 148° C 152° D

kilometers 0 100 200 300 400
miles 0 100 200
Scale 1:7,000,000
Projection: Mercator

Islands of the Pacific

A B

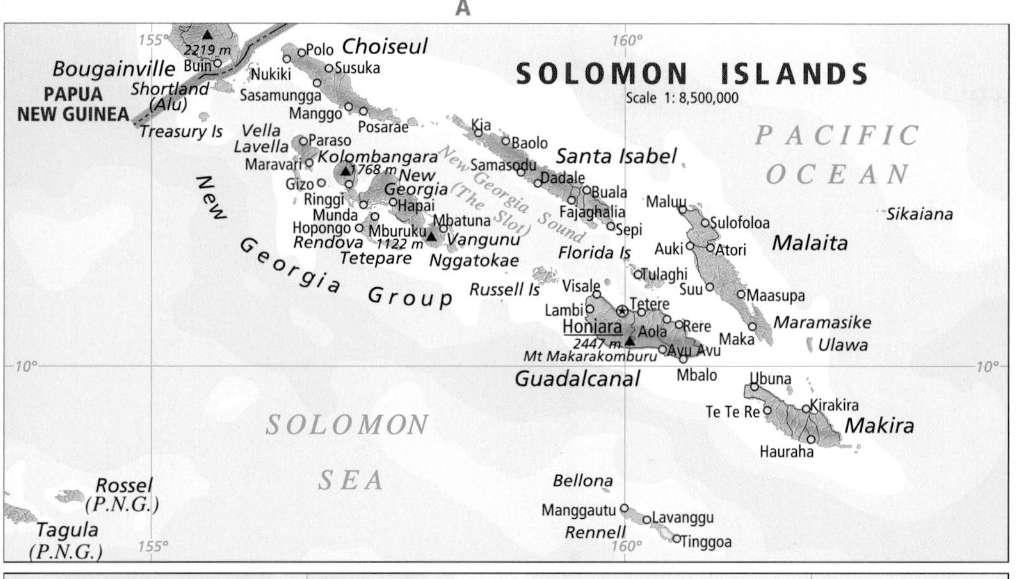
SOLOMON ISLANDS
Scale 1: 8,500,000
Bougainville
Buin
2219 m
PAPUA NEW GUINEA
Shortland (Alu)
Treasury Is
Choiseul
Polo
Susuka
Nukiki
Sasamungga
Manggo
Posarae
Vella Lavella
Paraso
Kolombangara
Maravari
Gizo
Ringgi
Munda
Hopongo
Mburuku
Rendova
Tetepare
1768 m
New Georgia
Hapai
Mbatuna
Vangunu
1122 m
Nggatokae
New Georgia Group
New Georgia Sound (The Slot)
Kia
Baolo
Samasodu
Santa Isabel
Dadale
Buala
Fajaghalia
Sepi
Maluu
Sulofoloa
Malaita
Auki
Atori
Florida Is
Tulaghi
Russell Is
Visale
Suu
Maasupa
Lambi
Tetere
Honiara
Aola
Rere
Maramasike
Maka
Ulawa
2447 m
Mt Makarakomburu
Avu Avu
Guadalcanal
Mbalo
Ubuna
Kirakira
Te Te Re
Makira
Hauraha
Sikaiana
PACIFIC OCEAN
SOLOMON SEA
Rossel (P.N.G.)
Tagula (P.N.G.)
Bellona
Manggautu
Lavanggu
Rennell
Tinggoa
155°
160°
10°

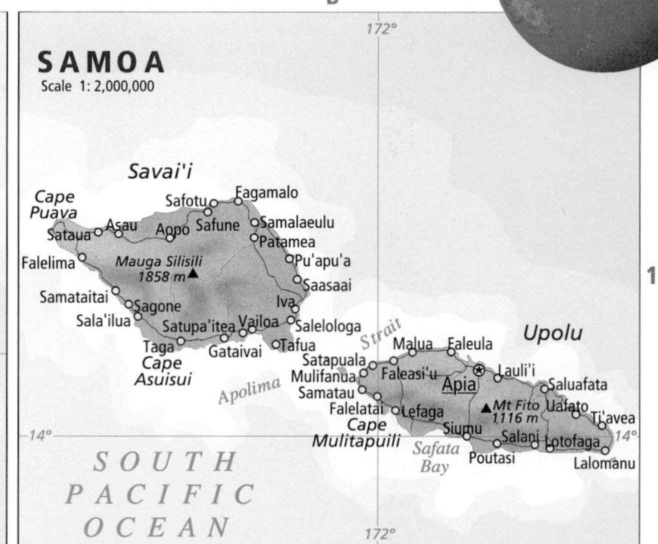
SAMOA
Scale 1: 2,000,000
Savai'i
Cape Puava
Safotu
Fagamalo
Sataua
Asau
Aopo
Safune
Samalaeulu
Patamea
Falelima
Mauga Silisili
1858 m
Pu'apu'a
Saasaai
Samataitai
Sagone
Sala'ilua
Satupa'itea
Vailoa
Iva
Salelologa
Taga
Gataivai
Tafua
Cape Asuisui
Apolima
Strait
Malua
Faleula
Upolu
Satapuala
Faleasi'u
Apia
Lauli'i
Mulifanua
Saluafata
Samatau
Falelatai
Lefaga
Mt Fito
1116 m
Uafato
Ti'avea
Cape Mulitapuili
Siumu
Salani
Lotofaga
Safata Bay
Poutasi
Lalomanu
SOUTH PACIFIC OCEAN
172°
14°

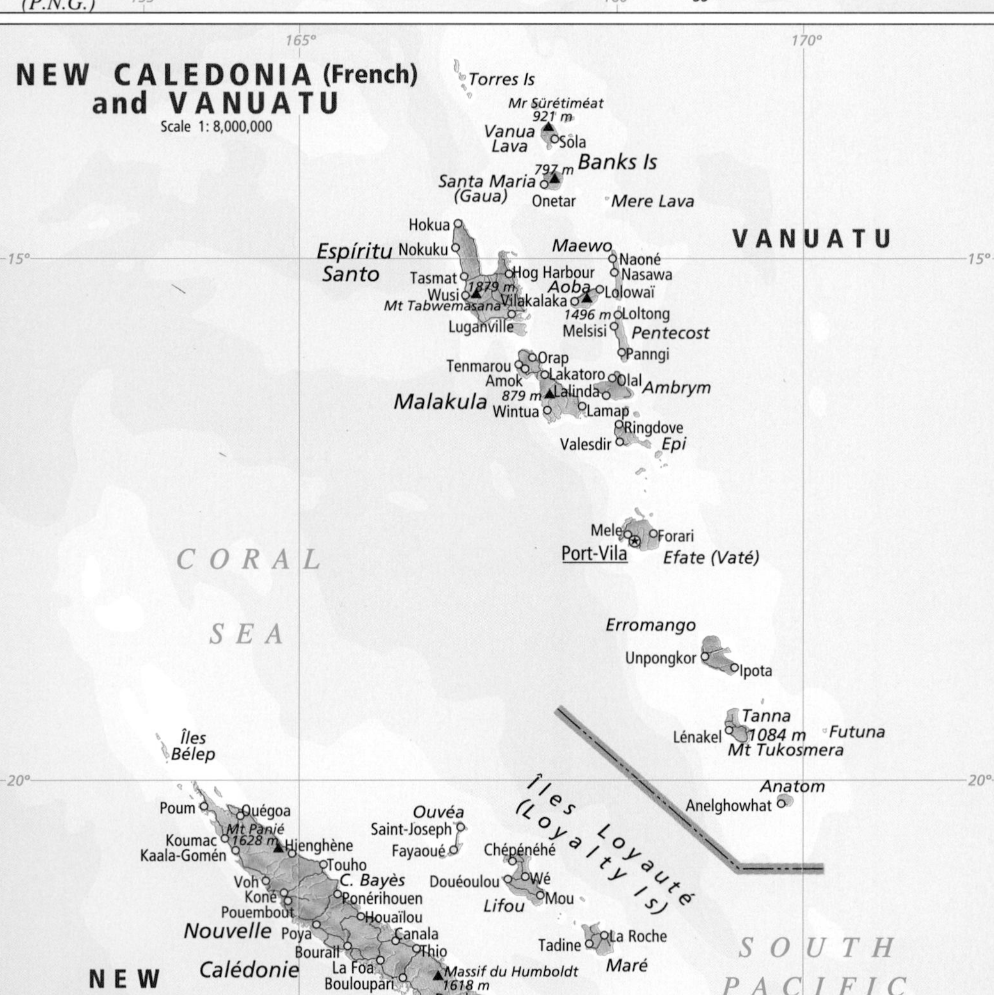
NEW CALEDONIA (French) and VANUATU
Scale 1: 8,000,000
Torres Is
Mr Sürétiméat
921 m
Vanua Lava
Sola
797 m
Banks Is
Santa Maria (Gaua)
Onetar
Mere Lava
Hokua
VANUATU
Espíritu Santo
Nokuku
Maewo
Naoné
Nasawa
Tasmat
Hog Harbour
Aoba
1879 m
Wusi
Mt Tabwemasana
Vilakalaka
Lolowaï
1496 m
Loltong
Luganville
Melsisi
Pentecost
Panngi
Tenmarou
Orap
Amok
Lakatoro
Olal
879 m
Lalinda
Ambrym
Malakula
Wintua
Lamap
Ringdove
Valesdir
Epi
Mele
Forari
Port-Vila
Efate (Vaté)
CORAL SEA
Erromango
Unpongkor
Ipota
Tanna
Lénakel
1084 m
Futuna
Mt Tukosmera
Anatom
Anelghowhat
Îles Bélep
Poum
Ouégoa
Mt Panié
1628 m
Koumac
Hienghène
Kaala-Gomén
Touho
Voh
C. Bayès
Koné
Ponérihouen
Pouembout
Houaïlou
Nouvelle Calédonie
Poya
Canala
Bourail
Thio
La Foa
Boulouparis
Massif du Humboldt
1618 m
Dumbea
Yaté
NEW CALEDONIA
Nouméa
Mont-Dore
Ouvéa
Saint-Joseph
Fayaoué
Chépénéhé
Douéoulou
Wé
Mou
Lifou
Îles Loyauté (Loyalty Is)
Tadine
La Roche
Maré
Vao
Île des Pins (Isle of Pines)
Walpole
SOUTH PACIFIC OCEAN
165°
170°
15°
20°

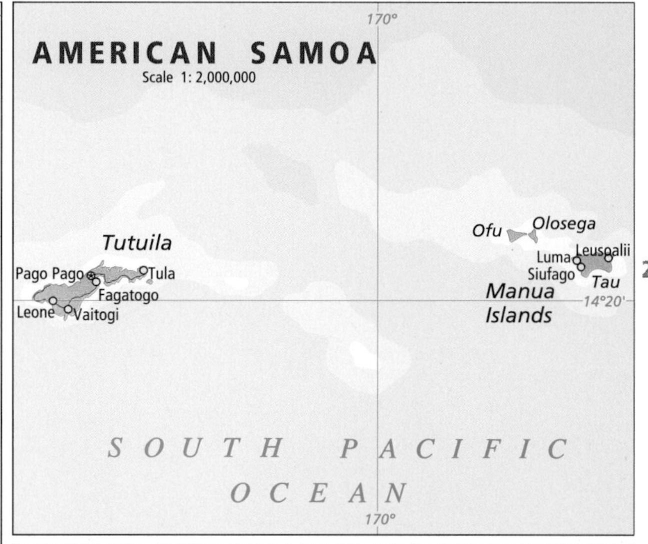
AMERICAN SAMOA
Scale 1: 2,000,000
Tutuila
Pago Pago
Tula
Fagatogo
Leone
Vaitogi
Ofu
Olosega
Luma
Leusoalii
Siufago
Tau
Manua Islands
SOUTH PACIFIC OCEAN
170°
14°20'

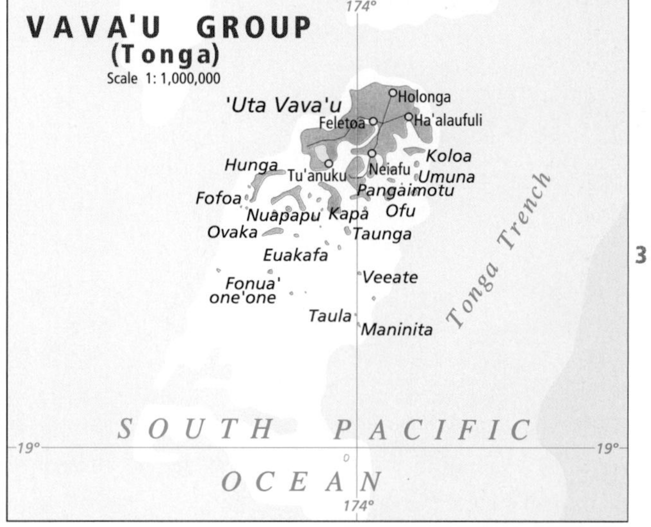
VAVA'U GROUP (Tonga)
Scale 1: 1,000,000
'Uta Vava'u
Holonga
Feletoa
Ha'alaufuli
Hunga
Tu'anuku
Neiafu
Koloa
Umuna
Pangaimotu
Fofoa
Nuapapu
Kapa
Ofu
Ovaka
Taunga
Euakafa
Fonua' one'one
Veeate
Taula
Maninita
Tonga Trench
SOUTH PACIFIC OCEAN
174°
19°

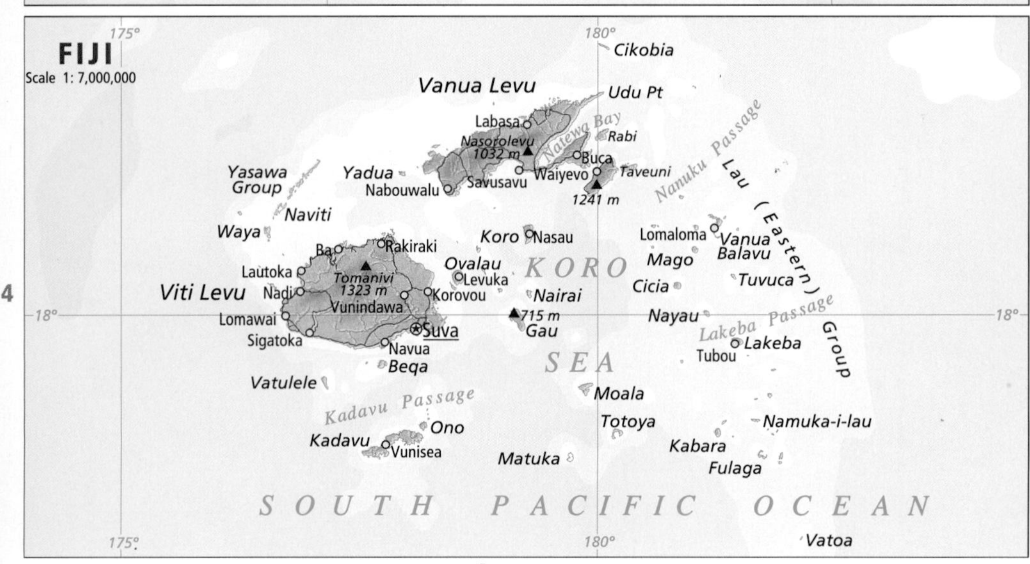
FIJI
Scale 1: 7,000,000
Cikobia
Vanua Levu
Udu Pt
Labasa
Natewa Bay
Nasorolevu
1032 m
Rabi
Buca
Yasawa Group
Yadua
Nabouwalu
Savusavu
Waiyevo
Taveuni
1241 m
Nanuku Passage
Naviti
Waya
Koro
Nasau
Lomaloma
Vanua Balavu
Ba
Rakiraki
Lautoka
Tomanivi
1323 m
Ovalau
Levuka
KORO SEA
Mago
Viti Levu
Nadi
Korovou
Nairai
Cicia
Tuvuca
Lau (Eastern) Group
Lomawai
Vunindawa
715 m
Gau
Nayau
Sigatoka
Suva
Navua
Beqa
Lakeba Passage
Lakeba
Tubou
Vatulele
Kadavu Passage
Moala
Ono
Totoya
Kadavu
Vunisea
Namuka-i-lau
Kabara
Matuka
Fulaga
SOUTH PACIFIC OCEAN
Vatoa
175°
180°
18°

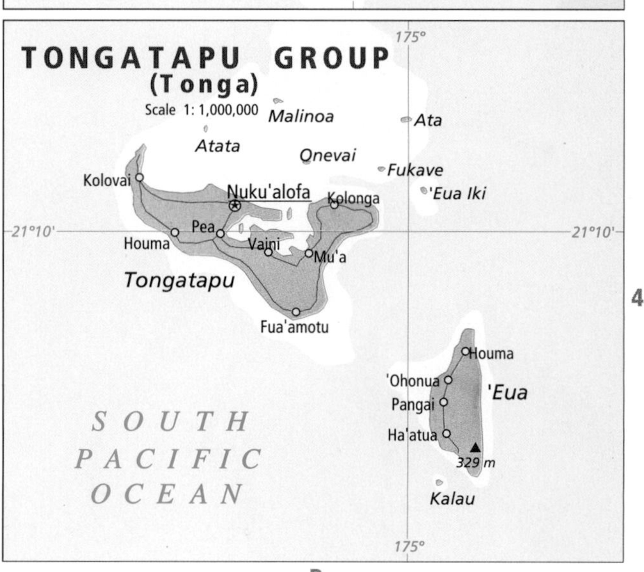
TONGATAPU GROUP (Tonga)
Scale 1: 1,000,000
Malinoa
Ata
Atata
Onevai
Kolovai
Fukave
Nuku'alofa
Kolonga
'Eua Iki
Pea
Houma
Vaini
Mu'a
Tongatapu
Fua'amotu
Houma
'Ohonua
Pangai
'Eua
Ha'atua
329 m
Kalau
SOUTH PACIFIC OCEAN
175°
21°10'

A B

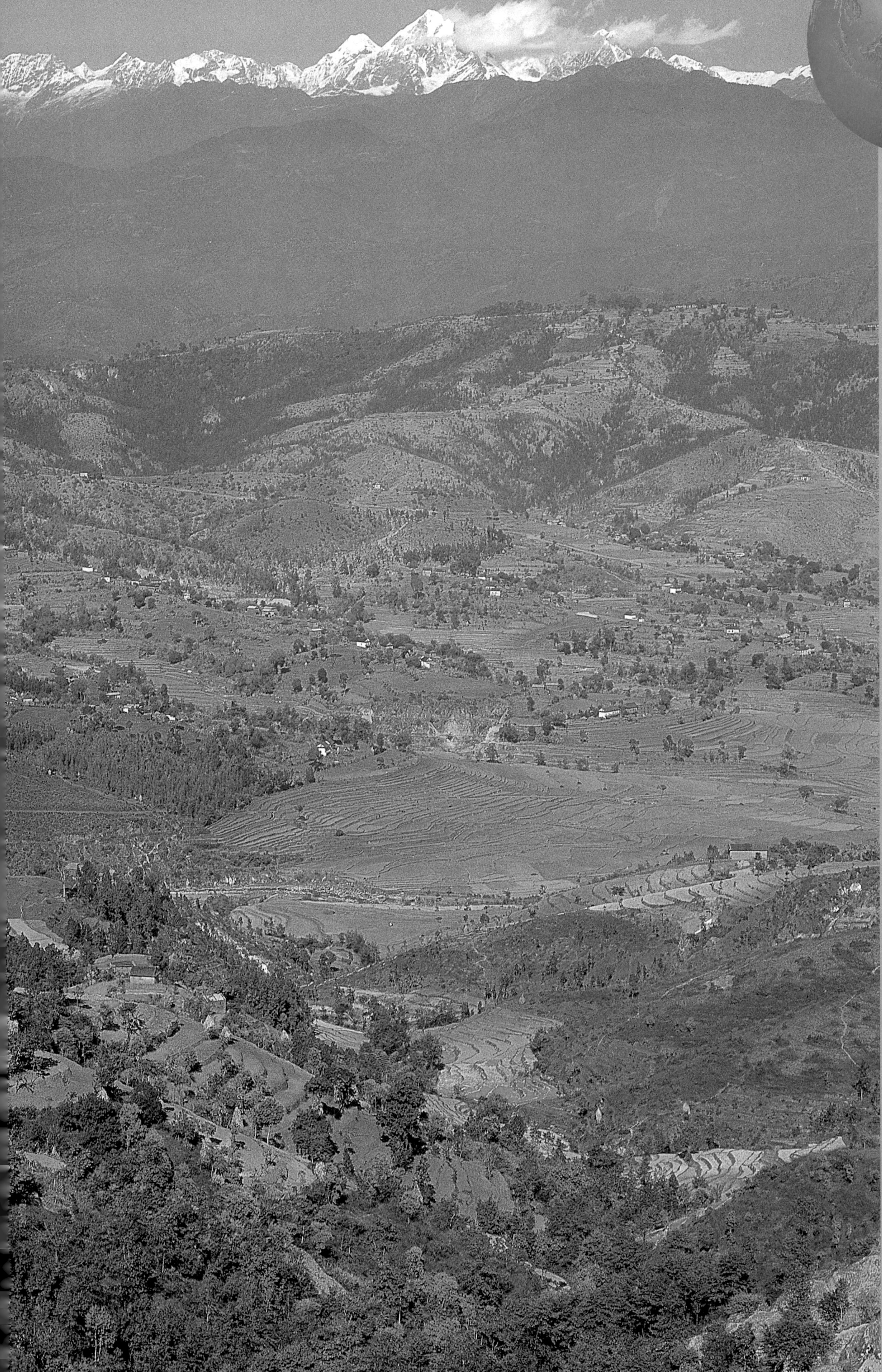
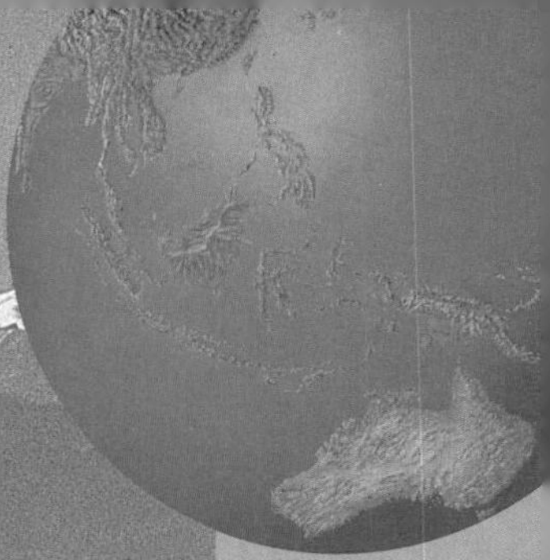

Asia and th Middle East

Asia

Asia, the largest continent, covers 43.6 million sq km (16.8 million sq miles), about one-third of the world's land surface. Its western boundaries are the Ural Mountains, the Ural River, the Caspian and Black seas and the Dardanelles Straits, which separate Europe from Asia. The Red Sea and the Suez Canal separate Asia from Africa. Indonesia is the southeasternmost country of Asia.

Asia is traditionally divided into East, Southeast, South, the Indian subcontinent, Central, and North Asia (Siberia, which is part of the Russian Federation, is included with Europe). The Middle East is discussed on the following pages.

Southeast Asia contains the three archipelagic nations of Indonesia, Malaysia and the Philippines; Singapore and Brunei; and the Indochinese nations of Laos, Vietnam, Cambodia, Thailand, and Myanmar (Burma). East Asia includes China, Japan, North and South Korea, and Taiwan. The Indian subcontinent includes India, Pakistan, Bangladesh and Sri Lanka; Nepal and Bhutan in the Himalayas; and the coral island archipelago of the Maldives. Central and West Asia include the former Soviet republics of Kazakhstan, Uzbekistan, Kyrgyzistan, Tajikistan, Turkmenistan, Azerbaijan, and Armenia as well as Mongolia and mountainous Afghanistan.

Physical features

Asia is a very geologically active continent. Large areas are covered by mountain and volcanic chains—the world's highest mountain range (the Himalayas), the Indonesian volcanic arc, and the volcanic chains of Japan and the Philippines. Asia also contains some parts of the world's most ancient (Pre-Cambrian) formations, in the Indian and Arabian Peninsulas and in Siberia.

Mountain ranges, plateaus, and basins lie within Asia's heartland. The world's highest plateau is in Tibet, averaging 4,000 m (13,000 ft) in altitude, and is bounded to the south by the Himalayas, to the north by the Kunlun Range, and to the west by the Karakoram Range. Further north, the Tarim and Dzungarian basins lie close to sea level, while the Turfan Depression is 142 m (470 ft) below it.

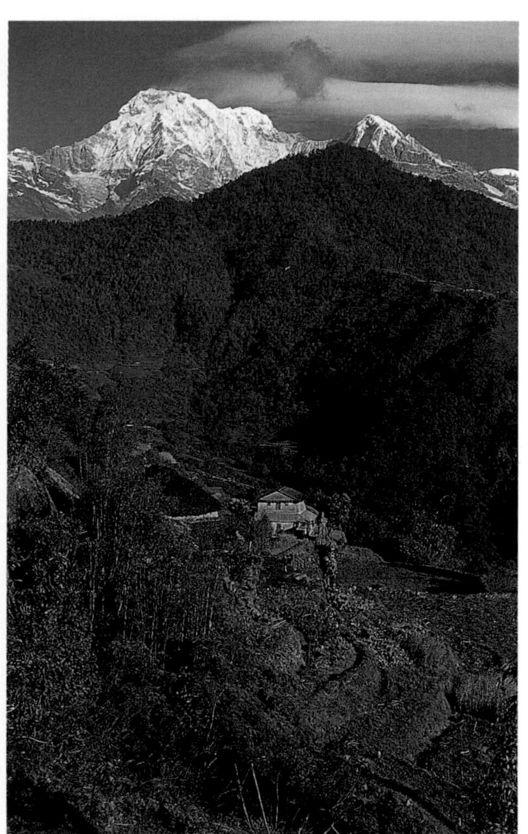

Numerous streams and nineteen major rivers, ranging from 2,500 to 5,500 km (1,500 and 3,400 miles) in length, flow in Asia. These include the Yangtze and Huang Rivers in China, the Indus and Ganges Rivers of the Indian subcontinent and the Mekong River on the Indochinese Peninsula.

Climate and vegetation

Asia can be broadly divided into a humid monsoon belt in South, Southeast, and East Asia and an arid to semiarid zone, in Central Asia.

During summer, the monsoons blow north, toward the continental margins, while in winter they reverse direction and blow toward the south. Some East Asian areas receive rainfall from both monsoons. The Himalayan Range and adjacent mountain ranges concentrate summer rainfall in parts of South and Southeast Asia. Hot, humid climates prevail in South and Southeast Asia while cold climates, with snowfall during winter, are found in more northern parts (the Himalayas and the mountain ranges in Central Asia). The Plateau of Tibet has an extremely cold climate.

Tropical rainforests once covered large parts of South and Southeast Asia, but are now being cleared for agriculture and logging, especially of hardwoods. This threatens the plant and animal diversity of these forests, which is very high.

Broad-leaf evergreen forests cover parts of subtropical East Asia. There are deciduous forests further north in cool, temperate climates, and boreal forests where the winters are cold. The Plateau of Tibet is an almost treeless tundra, with mosses, grasses, lichens, and a few small shrubs.

Grasslands cover areas in the rainshadow belts where rainfall is limited: tropical grasslands in the Deccan Plateau in India and the Khorat Plateau in Thailand, and temperate grasslands (steppes) in the semiarid parts of Central Asia.

Central Asia is predominantly arid to semiarid, with warm summers and winters where the temperature can fall below freezing. The Gobi Desert, the coldest dry desert, lies in this region.

Terraced fields in India (left), a carved entrance in Bali (top), and a curious monkey in Indonesia (above) demonstrate the variety of landform zones and land uses in Asia.

Population

Asia's vast population (3,680 million inhabitants, as of 2000, representing some 60.6 percent of the world's people) is predominantly found in the monsoon belt. The population explosion within the last fifty years (some countries experienced a three-fold increase during this period) is the result of advances in agriculture and improved medical facilities. During this period, life expectancies improved throughout Asia. Life expectancy is currently highest in East Asia (71.9 years for males and 77.1 years for females) and lowest in South Asia (61.2 years for males and 63 years for females). The high population growth rate has subsided, being currently 2.5 percent in East Asia to 4.4 on the Indian subcontinent.

Population indicators for the most developed Asian countries are similar to those for many Western countries: low population growth rates and high life expectancies characterize the more industrialized nations such as Japan and Singapore. High growth rates and much lower life expectancies, however, are found in the least developed countries, such as Bangladesh and Nepal. These characteristics reflect the enormous differences in standards of living between the most and least developed countries in Asia. Urbanization is highest in the most developed areas, but despite having a number of large cities and growing urbanization, Asia still has a low urban population—35 percent.

Industrialization in most Asian countries has, as elsewhere, centered on major urban areas. Labor from rural areas has drifted to urban centers in search of employment. The ensuing urban population explosion has put pressure on infrastructure, and given rise to problems such as the growth of slum dwellings, traffic congestion, and air and water pollution.

The Flaming Cliffs in Mongolia's arid Gobi Desert, Central Asia (above). This Vietnamese woman (below) is carrying wood from her home in the hills to sell.

Agriculture

A high proportion of Asia's population lives on the alluvial plains of rivers (and their deltas) of the monsoon belt, and is engaged in agriculture.

The monsoon belt is noted for its intensive rice and wheat farming. The population explosion created enormous demand for food. The area under cultivation was expanded through deforestation and by farming marginal areas, such as the borders of deserts, but the Green Revolution was more successful: high-yielding seeds, fertilizers and pesticides often tripled grain yields. However, environmental problems, caused by the chemicals used and by invasions of insects, have raised a number of concerns. In semiarid Central Asia, wheat farming and animal rearing are the main forms of agriculture. With irrigation, cotton is now successfully grown in several places.

Industrialization

By the 1980s, several East Asian countries had developed industrialized economies, largely dependent on imported raw materials, particularly minerals and energy supplies. Manufacturing in Asia ranges from labor-intensive industries such as clothing in the less developed economies to electronics, computers, and motor vehicles in the more developed ones. Japan, the world's second-largest economy, manufactures electronic goods, steel, motor vehicles and ships. Japan's approach has been imitated by South Korea, Taiwan, Hong Kong and Singapore, which have all rapidly industrialized. Thailand, Malaysia, the Philippines, and Indonesia have followed suit.

China and India initially aimed at agricultural and industrial self-sufficiency to support their enormous populations. They possess huge agricultural sectors, but their exports have shifted progressively to industrial products. They have considerable scientific expertise—in nuclear and space technology and satellite launching services (China), and computer programming (India).

The Central Asian nations, following the break-up of the former Soviet Union, are making a slow and painful transition from a state-controlled to a free market economy. There is, as yet, limited industrialization in the countries of Central Asia. Kazakhstan produces metals and chemicals and Azerbaijan, which is rich in petroleum deposits and may establish petroleum-based industries, currently manufactures mining equipment.

Languages

Many languages, belonging to several language families, are spoken in Asia. Chinese Mandarin, Cantonese, and Wu are the most widely spoken in East Asia. Japanese is increasingly important. In Southeast Asia, Indonesian and Malaysian predominate, while languages of the Chinese-Tibetan family, such as Burmese and Thai, are spoken in the mainland belt. South Asia has two major language families: Indo-Aryan in the north, of which Hindi and Urdu are the most widespread, and Dravidian, which includes Tamil, in the southern areas. In Central Asia, Ural-Altaic languages, several of which are related to Turkish, are mainly used.

Russian is widely spoken in the former Soviet republics, and of the colonial languages, only English is still important, and continues to spread.

Boundary disputes and wars

Armed conflicts continued after the Second World War in Asia, especially during the decolonization phase. The communist revolution in China resulted in the separation of Taiwan, which China does not accept. Wars resulted in the division of both Korea and Vietnam into two nations: communist North and democratic South. The Vietnam war ended in 1975, when the country reunified. North and South Korea remain technically at war.

Following the division of British India into India and Pakistan in 1947, there was armed conflict over the divided Himalayan state of Jammu and Kashmir; this issue is still unresolved. War between India and Pakistan resulted in 1971 in the creation of the Bangladesh. Armed conflicts along the disputed boundaries of China have taken place between China and India along the Himalayas, between China and Russia along the Amur River, and between China and Vietnam along their common border. Indonesia incorporated the former Portuguese colony of now independent East Timor. The ownership of the Spratly Islands in the South China Sea is causing tension between China, Malaysia, Philippines, Vietnam, and Taiwan. The "War on Terror" in Afghanistan and Iraq has dominated affairs throughout the region since late 2001.

Nations

Dependencies & territories

The Middle East

The term "Middle East" applies to the belt of countries in Southwest Asia that lies between Afghanistan and Turkey. It stretches southward to include the Arabian Peninsula. The Middle East is characterized by its arid climate, its petroleum riches, and the prevalence of Islam as its predominant religion. The Middle East forms a strategic belt between the dynamic developing industrial countries of Asia and the long-developed countries of Europe.

The countries of Iran, Iraq, Syria, Turkey, and Cyprus form the northern belt, while toward their south lie Lebanon, Israel, Jordan and the states of the Arabian Peninsula. Saudi Arabia occupies a large part of the peninsula; Oman and Yemen share the southern part of the peninsula and the United Arab Emirates, Bahrain, Qatar, and Kuwait lie along the Arabian (also known as Persian) Gulf.

Afghanistan lies in the area where the Middle East, South Asia, and Central Asia meet. The North African nations of Egypt, Sudan, and Libya are also sometimes considered part of the Middle East, for linguistic and cultural reasons.

Physical features

The collision of the Iranian and Arabian tectonic plates with the Eurasian Plate resulted in the mountain ranges that run from Turkey to Iran. The belt between Turkey and Iran is characterized by elongated mountain ranges such as the Zagros and Alborz ranges in Iran and the Pontic and Taurus Mountains in Turkey. These ranges form part of the extensive Alpine-Himalayan Mountain Range system that was formed during the Tertiary geological period. This area is prone to earthquakes, of which there have been several in recent decades. There are plateaus in both Turkey (Anatolian Plateau) and Iran.

In contrast to the geologically active Tertiary mountain belt, the Arabian Plateau is part of an ancient and geologically stable shield.

Jumeura Mosque, Dubai, in the United Arab Emirates (below left). Shiraz-style grapevines with clay supports in Iran (right). These ancient ruins at Buşrá ash Shām, in Syria (right page, bottom), remind us how long human civilization has existed in this area.

Climate and vegetation

The Middle East is predominantly arid to semi-arid, except for the areas that adjoin the Mediterranean, Aegean, Black and Caspian Seas. The region is characterized by high temperatures, especially in the Arabian, Syrian and Iranian deserts. In contrast, winter temperatures close to freezing point occur in the highlands and snow falls in some of the higher mountainous areas. There are great seasonal temperature differences on the plateaus, as shown by Tehrān and Ankara, which reach temperatures of about 30 °C (85 °F) in summer and fall as low as freezing point in winter.

The region receives little annual rainfall, except for winter rain in the areas bordering the Mediterranean, and there is a serious shortage of fresh water in the Gulf area. Vegetation in this region is dominated by thorny scrubland.

The Euphrates and Tigris are the largest rivers in the Middle East. Several short rivers flow into the Mediterranean, Black, and Caspian Seas.

Population

The population of the region is about 297.4 million (1998). Life expectancies have improved in recent years and now stand at 65.9 years for males and 70.3 years for females. The population growth rate is moderate, at 2.2 percent. Urbanization has been increasing steadily during recent decades and now stands at 66 percent; this reflects the decreasing importance of agriculture and pastoralism in the economies of these countries. In several countries, particularly in the Gulf States, petroleum has indirectly assisted the growth of urbanization as oil-generated revenues have been invested in urban areas and projects.

Agriculture

Because of the arid climate, only a small part of the region can support agriculture.

The Euphrates and Tigris Rivers, with their alluvial plains and extensive irrigation, are significant agricultural areas, but their rising salinity levels constitute a major problem. The region has a great need for irrigation—Syria, for example, has built the Euphrates Dam to irrigate the northeastern part of the country. Israel has also developed areas of intensive irrigation-based agriculture.

Wheat, barley, and rice are the major cereals. Important cash crops include tobacco, sugarcane, cotton, fruits and tea. Dates are a common fruit and are cultivated in oasis areas. Livestock mostly consists of camels, sheep, and goats; herds of goats have been blamed for stripping the ground bare of vegetation, which has resulted in soil erosion and the acceleration of desertification in some areas.

Agriculture based on growing olives, grapes, citrus fruits and apples is found in the Mediterranean coastal areas.

Fishing is important in several places, including the Black and Caspian seas.

Industrialization

Petroleum reserves are the region's most abundant resource. Oil-rich Saudi Arabia, Iran, Iraq, Kuwait, and the United Arab Emirates have economies predominantly based on petroleum exports, which makes them vulnerable to fluctuations in the price of petroleum. Petroleum prices escalated during the mid to late 1970s, but since then prices have fallen considerably. Oil wealth has facilitated the import of foodstuffs, manufactured goods, and luxury items, and has been also used for military purchases and development.

The hot, arid areas of the region are largely unsuited to the establishment of industries. The lack of fresh water is so severe in the Gulf region that desalinization plants have been set up to produce potable water. Oil-based electricity is generated in the oil-rich countries, and coal-based electricity is widely used in Turkey. Hydroelectric power is produced in Syria and Turkey.

Industries that use local materials, such as food processing, petroleum refining, and petrochemical industries, have been developed in some places. Some light consumer-based industries, including textiles, footwear, cigarettes, and paper, have also been established. The countries of the eastern Mediterranean are comparatively more industrialized than the rest of the region, but frequent conflicts with neighboring countries in the area have hampered their ability to maintain production.

Languages

Three language families—the Indo-European, Turkic, and Semitic—are found in the Middle East. The Indo-European languages represented include Persian, Pashto, Kurdish, Armenian, and Baluchi. Turkish and Azerbaijani are Turkic languages, and Arabic and Hebrew are Semitic.

Boundary disputes and wars

The region has experienced several conflicts and wars within the last fifty years. The Israeli-Arab conflict has been the most prominent and is yet to be resolved. Lebanon was drawn into the conflict, which adversely affected its economy.

Iraq's attempt to conquer the Arab-speaking region of southwestern Iran lasted for years, and drained both Iraq and Iran of resources. Iraq's conquest of Kuwait, the subsequent Gulf War, the ousting of Saddam Hussein and the attempt to install a democratic regime in 2003/04 mainly by a coalition of the United States and Great Britain have seriously affected Iraq's economy.

The Kurdish-speaking area, shared by Turkey, Iraq, and Iran, has also been involved in armed conflict, in its attempt to secure independence.

The Turkish conquest of the northern, Turkish-speaking part of Cyprus has strained relations between Greece and Turkey.

The birthplace of Aphrodite in Cyprus (far left). Traditional trading dhows in Doha, Qatar (left). Women in the Gaza Strip demonstrate for the release of Palestinian prisoners (below). International fast food in Dubai (above)

Nations

Autonomous regions

Southeast Asia

Indonesia

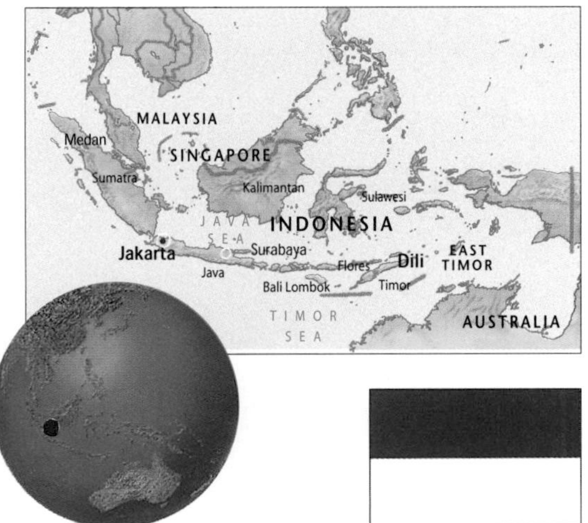

Fact File

Official name Republic of Indonesia

Form of government Republic with single legislative body (House of Representatives)

Capital Jakarta

Area 1,919,440 sq km (741,096 sq miles)

Time zone GMT +7–9 hours

Population 231,328,000

Projected population 2015 250,068,000

Population density 120.5 per sq km (312.1 per sq mile)

Life expectancy 68.3

Infant mortality (per 1,000) 39.4

Official language Bahasa Indonesia

Other languages English, Dutch, indigenous languages

Literacy rate 83.8%

Religions Muslim 88%, Protestant 6%, Roman Catholic 2%, Hindu 2%, Buddhist 1%, other 1%

Ethnic groups Javanese 45%, Sundanese 14%, Madurese 7.5%, coastal Malays 7.5%, other 26%

Currency Rupiah

Economy Agriculture 54%, services 38%, industry 8%

GNP per capita US$ 3,000

Climate Tropical, with wet season December to March (except in Moluccas where wet season is June to September)

Highest point Puncak Jaya 5,030 m (16,502 ft)

Map reference Pages 198–99, 200–01

After 30 years of economic progress, the collapse of the economy in 1998 triggered an outbreak of violent protest against the government. A change of leadership followed in 1999, and promises of new and more open elections. Nevertheless, long-suppressed class, ethnic, and religious conflicts have been unleashed. Guerrilla groups have fought for a long time against the national unity imposed on the numerous Indonesian islands by Jakarta's urban elite. Islamic fundamentalism also seems to have gained ground since 11 September 2001.

The 13,677 islands of the world's largest archipelago (6,000 of them inhabited) rest on the platform of two continental shelves. The southern chain of islands, from Sumatra to Timor, including Borneo, form part of the Sunda shelf, a largely submerged extension of the Asian continent. The northern Moluccas and New Guinea rest on the Sahul shelf, a northern extension of the Australian continent. Between the shelves, Sulawesi and the southern Moluccas form the island summits of suboceanic mountain ranges flanked by sea trenches 4,500 m (14,800 ft) deep. All Indonesia's main islands are mountainous: Sumatra, Java, and the Lesser Sunda Islands (Nusa Tengara) form an arc containing 200 volcanoes, many of which are active—Krakatoa (Pulau Rakata) among them.

In Sumatra, along with 10 active volcanoes there are a number of crater lakes, such as Lake Toba, at an altitude of 900 m (2,953 ft). Much of the island was once forested but over-cutting of timber in the lowlands means that native forest is now restricted to reserves and national parks. Isolated mountain forests remain in remote areas. The heavily populated island of Java has a long range containing 50 active volcanoes and 17 that are only recently dormant.

Throughout the archipelago many coasts are lined with mangrove swamps, notably in eastern Sumatra and southern Kalimantan. Several of the islands are of great beauty: tourism, not only to Bali, has been a major activity in recent years.

Indonesia's complex and varied population, and its four major religions—Islam, Hinduism, Christianity, and Buddhism—reflect the country's varied history. Hinduism was the first major religious influence 2,000 years ago, followed by Buddhism in the seventh century AD. Hindu-Buddhist religious authority began to decline with the collapse of the Majapahit Empire in the fourteenth century, and the arrival of Arab traders from the west gradually established Islam as the dominant religion.

Under Dutch colonial rule from 1608, the islands were from 1830 subject to a severe regime known as the Culture System. This involved the forced cultivation of commercial crops for export and resulted in a distortion of the traditional economy. Indonesia fell to the Japanese in the Second World War. After 1945 Indonesia became independent.

About 18 percent of Indonesia's land area is permanently cultivated. Most people live by agriculture, growing rice, maize, cassava, and sweet potato. There are also extensive plantations producing rubber, palm oil, sugarcane, coffee, and tea. The last 30 years have seen an intensive state-directed drive toward industrialization, based on abundant natural resources: oil, natural gas, timber, metals, and coal. Prosperity was initially tied to oil exports, but now the economy's growth depends on the continuing expansion of non-oil exports.

East Timor

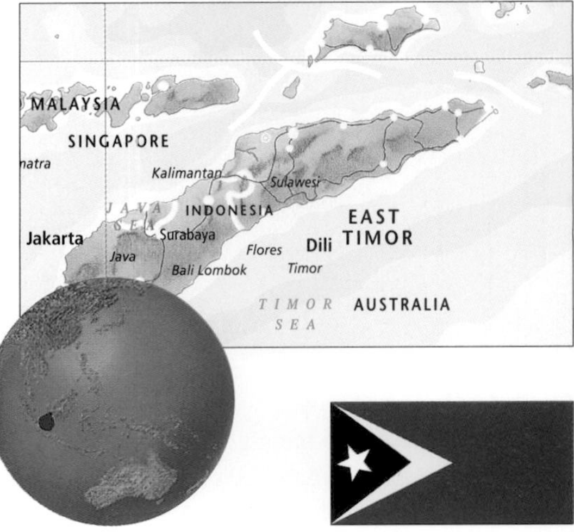

Fact File

Official name Democratic Republic of Timor-Leste

Form of government Republic with one legislative body

Capital Dili

Area 15,007 sq km (5,794 sq miles)

Time zone GMT +9 hours

Population 998,000

Projected population 2015 1,060,000

Population density 66.5 per sq km (172.2 per sq mile)

Life expectancy 65.2

Infant mortality (per 1,000) 50.5

Official languages Portuguese, Tetum

Other languages English, Bahasa Indonesia, Galole, Mambae, Kemak, and 12 other indigenous languages

Literacy rate 48 %

Religions Roman Catholic 90 %, small minorities of Muslims, Protestants, and Buddhists

Ethnic groups Timoran 78 %, Indonesian 20 %, Chinese 2 %

Currency U.S. Dollar

Economy Agriculture 25.4 %, services 57.4 %, industry 17.2 %

GNP per capita US$ 475

Climate Tropical, with wet season December to March

Highest point Tata Mailau 2,963 m (9,717 ft)

Map reference 198

First settled by the Portuguese in 1520, the eastern part of the island of Timor was annexed by Indonesia in 1976. In 1999, the UN intervened and formed a transitional administration providing the country with its governance that communicates directly with the East Timorese to ensure their participation in the administration. The economy of the mountainous country is based on agricultural produce, pearls, and fishing.

Philippines

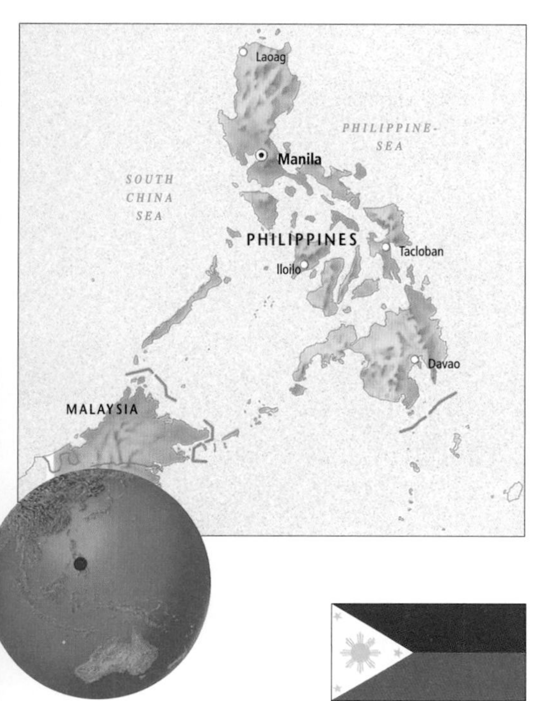

Fact File

OFFICIAL NAME Republic of the Philippines

FORM OF GOVERNMENT Republic with two legislative bodies (Senate and House of Representatives)

CAPITAL Manila

AREA 300,000 sq km (115,830 sq miles)

TIME ZONE GMT +8 hours

POPULATION 84,526,000

PROJECTED POPULATION 2015 95,881,000

POPULATION DENSITY 281.8 per sq km (729.7 per sq mile)

LIFE EXPECTANCY 68.1

INFANT MORTALITY (PER 1,000) 27.9

OFFICIAL LANGUAGES Filipino (Tagalog)

OTHER LANGUAGES English, more than 80 indigenous languages

LITERACY RATE 94.6 %

RELIGIONS Roman Catholic 83 %, Protestant 9 %, Muslim 5 %, Buddhist and other 3 %

ETHNIC GROUPS Malay 95.5 %, Chinese 1.5 %, other 3 %

CURRENCY Philippine peso

ECONOMY Services 48 %, agriculture 42 %, industry 10 %

GNP PER CAPITA US$ 900

CLIMATE Tropical, with wet season June to November

HIGHEST POINT Mt Apo 2,954 m (9,692 ft)

MAP REFERENCE Page 204

The Philippines present a combination that is unique in Asia. The people are Malayo-Polynesian; the majority of the population is Roman Catholic; English is the only common language in a country that has 87 native tongues; nearly four centuries of Spanish colonialism have left a flavor of Latin America; and 100 years of US influence (following the Spanish-American War in 1898) mean that the Philippines is also somewhat Americanized.

Long ago, and before the Spaniard explorer Ferdinand Magellan arrived from across the Pacific on his round-the-world voyage in 1521, Islam had reached the southern island of Mindanao. It is still the religion of a substantial minority in that part of the country. The Spanish then imposed whatever unity the archipelago can be said to have (there are 7,107 islands), building haciendas and sugar plantations on its main islands. Administered by the USA from 1898, the Philippines was occupied by the Japanese during the Second World War, was governed by the corrupt Marcos regime from 1965 to 1986—when a widespread popular rebellion finally forced him into exile—and faced a wide range of insurgencies over more than 40 years. The first insurgents were communist; more recently they have often been members of the Islamic Moro Liberation Front.

There are three main island groupings within the archipelago: the Luzon group, the Visayan group, and the Mindanao and Sulu Islands. Luzon to the north and Mindanao to the south are the two biggest islands and together they constitute two-thirds of the country's total land area.

All the main islands have a rugged mountainous and volcanic topography with narrow coastal belts, a north–south alignment of upland ridges, and rivers that drain northwards. North of Manila Bay, and stretching to the shores of the Lingayan Gulf, is Luzon's heavily populated central plain. This is an important rice-producing area. Beyond hills to the northeast lies the fertile valley of the Cagayan River. Irrigated rice terraces, constructed by the Igorot people, rise up the mountain slopes of northern Luzon. The peninsulas of southeastern Luzon contain a number of volcanoes. The highest peak in the Philippines, Mt Apo (2,954 m, 9,693 ft), is on Mindanao.

Government investment and a range of tax concessions have been tried to encourage industrial development. Mixing agriculture and light industry, the Philippine economy has been growing at a steady rate in recent years, without approaching the dynamic performance of other countries in the region.

While rice is the Philippines' main food crop, maize is the staple on the islands of Cebu, Leyte, and Negros, reflecting the country's old connection with Spanish America.

The country is well supplied with mineral resources and nickel, tin, copper, zinc and lead are processed in smelting and refining works. The Philippines is also the world's biggest supplier of refractory chrome, and the second biggest user of geothermal power after the USA. Foreign invest-ment turned sluggish as a consequence of the 1998 regional economic slowdown. Persistent weaknesses include rudimentary infrastructure, power failures due to inadequate generating capacity, low savings rates, and a foreign debt of US$ 45 billion.

Borobudur, the world's largest Buddhist monument, was built in the ninth century BC on the island of Java (left page, top). A coral reef in the Philippines (bottom left). The so-called "Chocolate Hills" in Bohol in the Philippines (top right).

Brunei

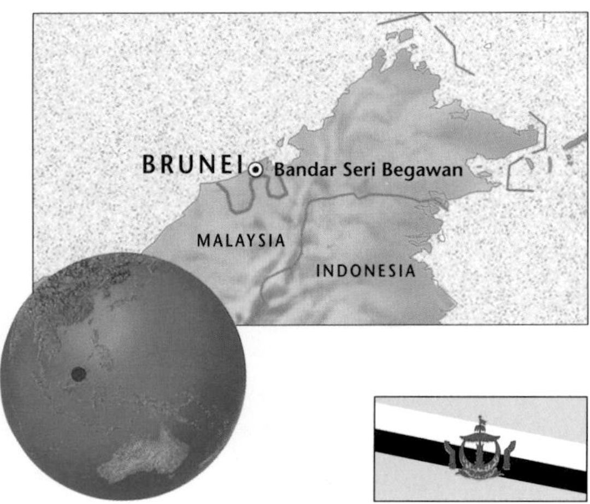

Fact File

Official name State of Brunei

Form of government Sultanate with advisory council of Cabinet Ministers

Capital Bandar Seri Begawan

Area 5,770 sq km (2,228 sq miles)

Time zone GMT +8 hours

Population 351,000

Projected population 2015 417,000

Population density 60.8 per sq km (157,5 per sq mile)

Life expectancy 74.1

Infant mortality (per 1,000) 14

Official languages English, Malay

Other language Chinese, Iban

Literacy rate 88.2 %

Religions Muslim 63 %, Buddhism 14 %, Christian 8 %, indigenous beliefs and other 15 %

Ethnic groups Malay 64 %, Chinese 20 %, other 16 %

Currency Bruneian dollar

Economy Services 87 %, industry 9 %, agriculture 4 %

GNP per capita US$ 18,000

Climate Tropical

Highest point Gunong Pagon 1,850 m (6,070 ft)

Map reference Page 201

Oil was discovered in the sultanate of Brunei in 1929. By the time it became independent on 1 January 1984 this small country on the north coast of Borneo was already prosperous. Today its oil revenues have made Brunei's sultan perhaps the richest man in the world, and given its people one of the highest per capita incomes in Asia. There is no income tax, the government subsidizes food and housing, and provides free medical care. The downside is that all government employees (two-thirds of the workforce) are banned from political activity, and the Sultan of Brunei rules by decree. Some nongovernmental political groupings have been allowed but the sultan remains firmly in control. There is disquiet among Bruneians over the rising number of resident foreigners, as demand for both skilled and unskilled labor brings contract workers in from outside.

Brunei consists of two semi-enclaves on the northwest coast of Borneo which are bordered by the Malaysian state of Sarawak. They are separated by a few kilometers of coastline where the Limbang River enters Brunei Bay. The topography in both areas consists of hills bordering a narrow, swampy coastal plain. More than two-thirds of the country is tropical forest.

Brunei is almost entirely supported by exports of oil and natural gas. Petroleum revenues account for more than 40 percent of gross domestic product. Production is carried out by Brunei Shell Petroleum in which the government holds a 50 percent stake. Most crude oil is exported to Japan, South Korea, Taiwan, and the USA. Liquefied natural gas is produced in one of the world's biggest plants, at Lumut in Malaysia, and is sold to power and gas companies in Tokyo and Osaka. About 80 percent of Brunei's food is imported, but there has been a push to achieve agricultural self-sufficiency. Small farms grow rice, fruit, and vegetables. The government Forestry Department, which controls all forest reserves, is expanding into value-added activities such as furniture production.

Fair in Bandar Seri Begawan, Brunei (above). A view of Singapore's central business district (below). Street vendor with customers in Malaysia (right page bottom).

Singapore

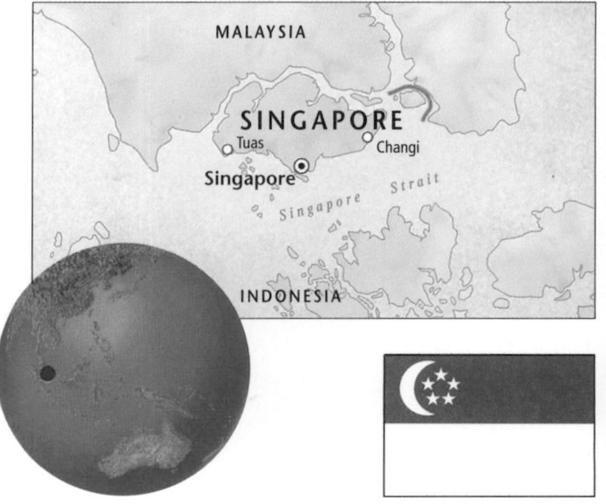

Fact File

Official name Republic of Singapore

Form of government Republic with single legislative body (Parliament)

Capital Singapore

Area 633 sq km (244 sq miles)

Time zone GMT +8 hours

Population 4,453,000

Projected population 2015 4,756,000

Population density 7,034.8 per sq km (18,262.3 per sq mile)

Life expectancy 80.3

Infant mortality (per 1,000) 3.6

Official languages Malay, Chinese, Tamil, English

Literacy rate 93.5 %

Religions Buddhist and Taoist 56 %, Muslim 19 %, Christian 15 %, Hindu 5 %, other 5 %

Ethnic groups Chinese 76.4 %, Malay 14.9 %, Indian 6.4 %, other 2.3 %

Currency Singapore dollar

Economy Services 70 %, industry 29 %, agriculture 1 %

GNP per capita US$ 24,700

Climate Tropical

Highest point Bukit Timah 162 m (531 ft)

Map reference Page 200

A muddy, mangrove-swampy islet nobody wanted in 1819, Singapore is now a leading Asian city-state with one of the highest standards of living in the world. This was achieved without any resources beyond the skills and commitment of its citizens and the economic vision of its leadership. Standing at the southern extremity of the Malay Peninsula, Singapore was established as a free-trading port and settlement early in the nineteenth century by the English colonial administrator Sir Stamford Raffles. Without customs tariffs or other restrictions it drew numbers of Chinese immigrants, and after the opening of the Suez Canal played a leading role in the growing trade in Malaysian rubber and tin.

After the Second World War, during which it was occupied by the Japanese, it reverted to its former status as a British crown colony. In 1963 it became part of Malaysia, but, after two years, tensions between Chinese Singapore and the Malay leadership in Kuala Lumpur led Malaysia to force the island to go it alone. Under Lee Kuan Yew, prime minister for 31 years until 1990, a strategy of high-tech industrialization enabled the economy to grow at a rate of 7 percent a year. However, freedom of speech is constrained, political debate limited, and both public behavior and private life are watched closely (chewing gum is forbidden, and vandalism punished by caning).

Singapore Island is largely low-lying, with a hilly center. With limited natural freshwater resources, water is brought from the Malaysian mainland nearby. Reservoirs on high ground hold water for the city's use. Urban development has accelerated deforestation and swamp and land reclamation: 5 percent of the land is forested, and 4 percent is arable. In addition to the main island of Singapore there are 57 smaller islands lying within its territorial waters, many of them in the Strait of Singapore, which opens from the busy seaway of the Strait of Malacca. Between the main island and the Malaysian mainland is the narrow channel of the Johore Strait. A causeway across this strait links Malaysia to Singapore.

While the foundation of its economic growth was the export of manufactured goods, the government has in recent years promoted Singapore as a financial services and banking center, using the latest information technology. In 1995 this sector led economic growth. Singapore is a world leader in biotechnology. Rising labor costs threaten the country's competitiveness today, but its government hopes to offset this by increasing productivity and improving infrastructure. Despite the reduced growth rate accompanying the Asian economic downturn in 1998 there are plans for major infrastructural development: an additional section for Changi International Airport, extensions to the mass rapid transit system, and a deep-tunnel sewerage project to dispose of wastes. In applied technology, per capita output, investment, and industrial harmony, Singapore possesses many of the attributes of a large modern country.

Malaysia

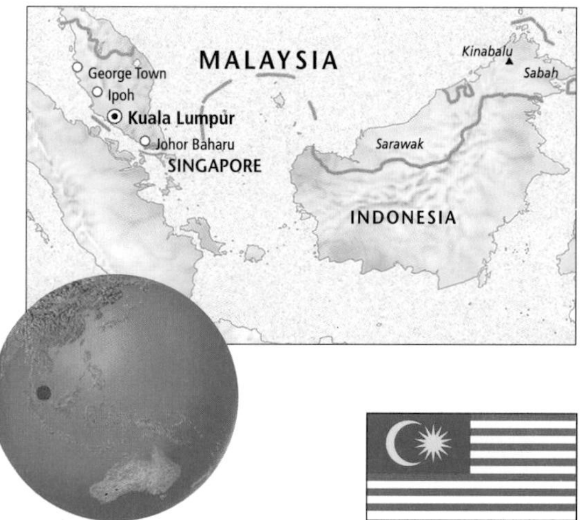

Fact File

Official name Malaysia

Form of government Federal constitutional monarchy with two legislative bodies (Senate and House of Representatives)

Capital Kuala Lumpur

Area 329,750 sq km (127,316 sq miles)

Time zone GMT +8 hours

Population 22,663,000

Projected population 2015 27,911,000

Population density 68.7 per sq km (178.0 per sq mile)

Life expectancy 71.4

Infant mortality (per 1,000) 19.7

Official language Malay (Bahasa Malaysia)

Other languages Austronesian languages, Aslian, Chinese languages, Tamil, English

Literacy rate 83 %

Religions Muslim 53 %, Buddhist 17.3 %, Confucian and Taoist 11.6 %, Christian 8.6 %, Hindu 7 %, other 2.5 %

Ethnic groups Malay 59 %, Chinese 32 %, Indian 9 %

Currency Ringgit (Malaysian dollar)

Economy Agriculture 42 %, services 39 %, industry 19 %

GNP per capita US$ 9,000

Climate Tropical, with northeast monsoon October to February and southwest monsoon May to September

Highest point Gunung Kinabalu 4,100 m (13,450 ft)

Map reference Pages 200–01

Malaysia consists of the southern part of the Malay Peninsula, with Thailand to its north, plus the regions of Sarawak and Sabah in northern Borneo. Like Singapore, which lies at the southern tip of the Malay Peninsula, Malaysia has enjoyed an impressive record of economic growth in recent times that was, however, severely hit by the 1998 economic crisis.

In the fifteenth century a part of Malaysia was famous as the Kingdom of Malacca (now Melaka), a state that became powerful through its control of local sea routes and shipping. In 1414 the ruler of Malacca adopted Islam, which is still the religion of Malaysia today. Seized by the Portuguese to serve as a base for the lucrative spice trade in 1511, and held by the Dutch from 1641, Malacca was captured by the British in 1795.

In 1819, the British took control of Singapore, as well, and in 1867 they established the Straits Settlements, which consisted of Penang Island (Pinang) in the northeast, Malacca, and Singapore, as a crown colony.

During the Second World War Malaysia was occupied by the Japanese. In 1945, Great Britain resumed control over what was then called Malaya, but an alliance led by Tunku Abdul Rahman finally gained Malaysia's independence from the British. A guerrilla war then broke out, led by communists who were sympathetic to the Chinese Revolution. This insurgency was defeated after a four-year military campaign, after which the country evolved into the modern state it is today.

Ethnic tensions continue to exist, principally between the Malays, who are the most

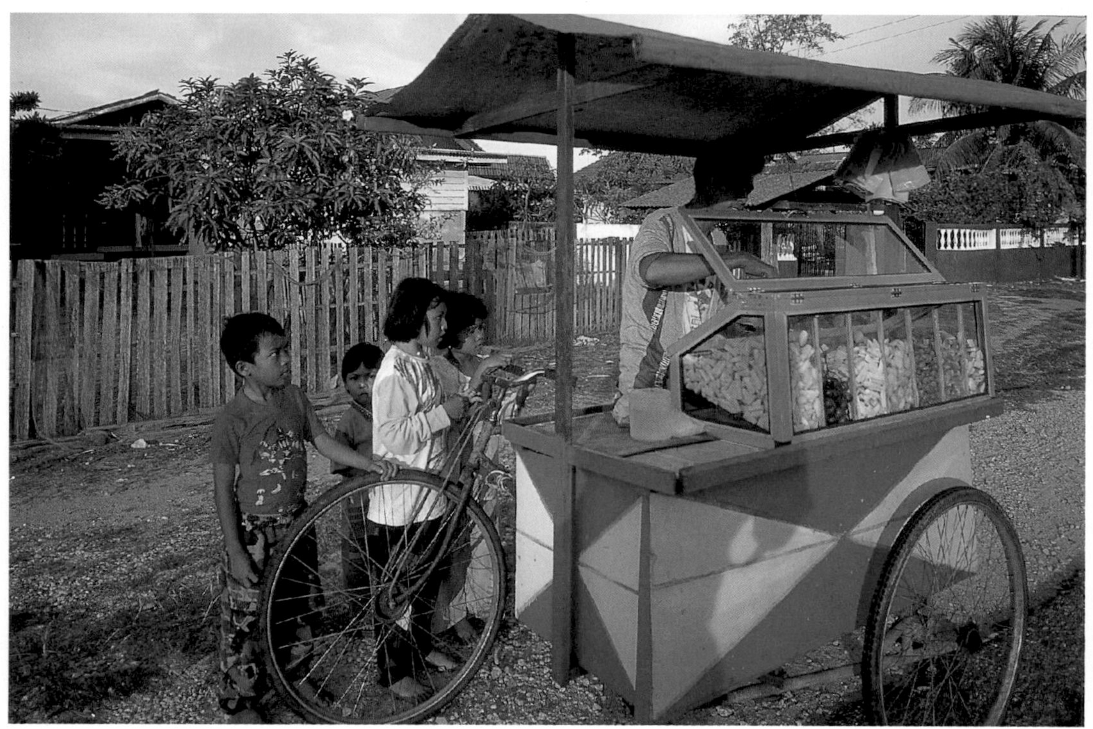

numerous group, and the Chinese, who are smaller in number but considerably more prosperous. There were riots between the Malays and Chinese in 1969 with heavy loss of life. The many "affirmative action" provisions that are now in place to open opportunities for Malays at the expense of Chinese and Indians are strongly resented by the latter groups. There are also a number of unresolved territorial disputes with neighboring states—Sabah in Borneo, for example, being claimed by the Philippines.

Fold mountains aligned on a north-south axis dominate the Malay Peninsula. There are seven or eight distinct chains of mountains, many of which have exposed granite cores. Climbing to 2,189 m (7,181 ft) at Gunung Tahan, the main range divides the narrow coastal belt to the east from the fertile alluvial plains in the west. To the south lies poorly drained lowland, marked by isolated hills, some of which rise to over 1,060 m (3,500 ft). Several smaller rivers have also contributed to the margin of lowland around the peninsular coasts.

About 2,000 km (1,250 miles) east of the Malay Peninsula, northern Borneo has a mangrove-fringed coastal plain about 65 km (40 miles) wide, rising behind to hill country averaging 300 m (1,000 ft) in height. This ascends through various secondary ranges to the mountainous main interior range. The granite peak of Gunung Kinabalu, the highest mountain in Southeast Asia, rises from the northern end of this range in Sabah, towering above Kinabalu National Park. Dense rainforest in Sarawak and Sabah support a great diversity of plants and animals.

With a mixture of private enterprise and public management, the Malaysian economy averaged a healthy rate of nine percent annual growth from 1988 to 1995. Substantial inroads are being made towards the reduction of poverty and real wages are rising. New light industries including electronics are playing an important role in this development: Malaysia is the world's biggest producer of disk drives. Heavy industry has also grown: Malaysia's "national car", the Proton, is now being exported.

The traditional mainstays of the economy, however, remain rice, rubber, palm oil, and tin—Malaysia being the world's foremost producer of palm oil and tin. Rice, however, is becoming a problem. Subsistence farming has regularly failed to ensure self-sufficiency in food, and rice production does not meet demand. The main industries on the peninsula are rubber and palm oil processing and manufacturing, light industry, electronics, tin mining, smelting, logging, and timber processing. The main activities on Sabah and Sarawak are logging, petroleum production, and the processing of agricultural products. Malaysia exports more tropical timber than any other country, and the tribal people of Sarawak have been campaigning against the scale of logging on their land. The Asian economic downturn in 1997 and 1998 saw a depreciation of the Malaysian currency and a marked slowing of the growth of their economy.

Cambodia

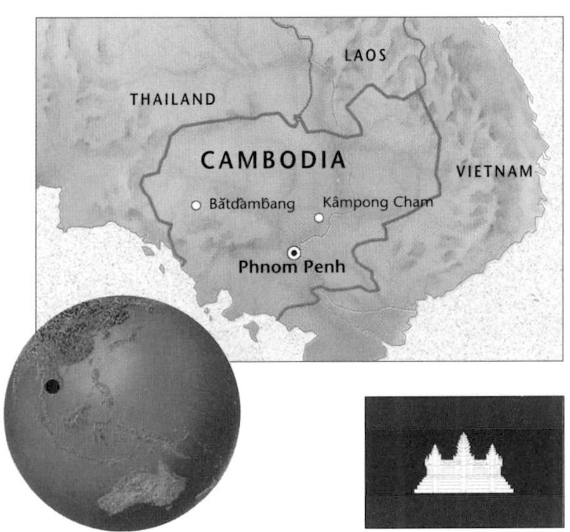

Fact File

OFFICIAL NAME Kingdom of Cambodia

FORM OF GOVERNMENT Constitutional monarchy with single legislative body (National Assembly)

CAPITAL Phnom Penh

AREA 181,040 sq km (69,900 sq miles)

TIME ZONE GMT +7 hours

POPULATION 12,776,000

PROJECTED POPULATION 2015 18,585,000

POPULATION DENSITY 70.6 per sq km (182.8 per sq mile)

LIFE EXPECTANCY 57.1

INFANT MORTALITY (PER 1,000) 64

OFFICIAL LANGUAGE Khmer

OTHER LANGUAGE French, Vietnamese, Chinese

LITERACY RATE 35 %

RELIGIONS Theravada Buddhism 95 %, other 5 %

ETHNIC GROUPS Khmer 90 %, Vietnamese 5 %, Chinese 1 %, other 4 %

CURRENCY Riel

ECONOMY Agriculture 80 %, services and industry 20 %

GNP PER CAPITA US$ 1,500

CLIMATE Tropical, with wet season May to November

HIGHEST POINT Phnum Aôral 1,810 m (5,938 ft)

MAP REFERENCE Page 203

The Southeast Asian country of Cambodia is famous both culturally and politically. At Angkor Wat and Angkor Thom it has the world's largest group of religious buildings, a priceless relic of the Hindu Khmer Empire (AD 802 to 1432). It also saw an outbreak of communist fanaticism in the 1970s in which over 2 million people died. Under French rule for almost a century from 1863, Cambodia won independence in 1954. In the late 1950s and during the 1960s there was a short period of relative stability in which the country developed its agricultural resources and rubber plantations and managed to achieve self-sufficiency in food.

Years of internal political struggles, in combination with Cambodia's involvement in the Vietnam War, led to a takeover by the Communist Khmer Rouge under the leadership of Pol Pot in 1975. With the aim of creating a classless agrarian society, money and private property were abolished, the professional classes were murdered (anyone with glasses was considered intellectual, and therefore at risk), and townspeople were brutally moved into the countryside and left to fend for themselves. Half a million refugees fled to Thailand, and between one eighth and one quarter of the entire population died. The regime fell in 1978 and Pol Pot went into hiding, but civil war continued for some years; Pol Pot died in 1998 without ever having to face trial for the atrocities that were committed under his direction. A devastated and desperately poor nation,

stripped of what little economic infrastructure and trained personnel it once had, Cambodia is still in the process of putting itself together again.

The country's heartland consists of a wide basin drained by the Mekong River. In the center of this lies the Tonlé Sap (Great Lake), surrounded by a broad plain. When the rain is meager and the Mekong is low—from November to June—the lake drains south toward the sea. But during the rainy season when the Mekong is high—from July to October—the flow reverses, and the lake doubles its area to become the largest freshwater lake in Southeast Asia. The wealth of the fabled "gentle kingdom" of Cambodia consists of fish from the lake and rice from the flooded lowlands, a year-round water supply being provided by an extensive system of irrigation channels and reservoirs. Directly south of the lake, the Cardamom (Chuŏr Phnum Kravan) and Elephant (Chuŏr Phnum Dămrek) Mountains look out over a narrow coastal plain.

Reconstructing the Cambodian economy is bringing almost as many costs as benefits. Tropical rainforest timber, especially teak and rosewood, is Cambodia's most important resource. For twenty years it was sold in huge quantities by all the various factions in order to finance their war efforts. Now indiscriminate tree-felling is a major environmental problem. A 1992 moratorium on logging is largely being ignored, and gems are another resource but strip mining is causing habitat loss, and the destruction of mangrove swamps is threatening the sustainability of fisheries. Starting from a very low base, growth was strong in the early 1990s, but a lack of skills at all levels of administration and management, as well as the rampaging corruption, is slowing progress.

Angkor Wat is the largest of the many temples built by the Khmer people in Cambodia about 1,000 years ago (above). Rice paddies in east Malaysia (left page).

Regional conflicts

1946 Vietnam: Return of French after Second World War. Outbreak of First Indochina War.
1954 Vietnam: Defeat of French at Dien Bien Phu. Division of Vietnam into North supported by USSR and South supported by USA.
1960 Vietnam: Communists in South initiate guerrilla war as Viet Cong.
1961 Vietnam: USA sends "military advisers" to South Vietnam to fight Viet Cong.
1964 US Congress approves war with Vietnam. US bombs Vietnamese sanctuaries in Laos, plus Ho Chi Minh Trail—north-south supply route.
1965 Vietnam: Arrival of first US combat troops. Start of intense US bombing of North Vietnam which continues until 1968.
1970 Right-wing coup in Cambodia deposes Prince Sihanouk. In exile Sihanouk forms movement backed by communist Khmer Rouge.
1974 Cambodia: Sihanouk and Khmer Rouge capture Phnom Penh. Thousands die as revolutionary programs are enforced (1975).
1975 Vietnam: Fall of Saigon. North Vietnamese and Viet Cong take power in South. Laos: Communist Pathet Lao seize power.
1976 Cambodia: Sihanouk resigns—all power held by Pol Pot, leader of the Khmer Rouge.
1978 Vietnam invades Cambodia.
1979 Vietnam captures Phnom Penh. Pol Pot flees, and is held responsible for more than 2 million deaths.
1989 Vietnamese troops leave Cambodia.
1991 Cambodia: Sihanouk again head of state. Flight of Khmer Rouge officials.
1992 Vietnam: Foreign investment permitted; Communist Party monopoly unchanged.
1993 Cambodia: UN-supervized elections. Departure of UN peace mission.
1995 Normalization of US-Vietnam diplomatic relations.
1997 Cambodia: Violent coup restores power to communists under Hun Sen.
1998 Cambodia: Pol Pot dies.
2002 East Timor gains independence.

Vietnam

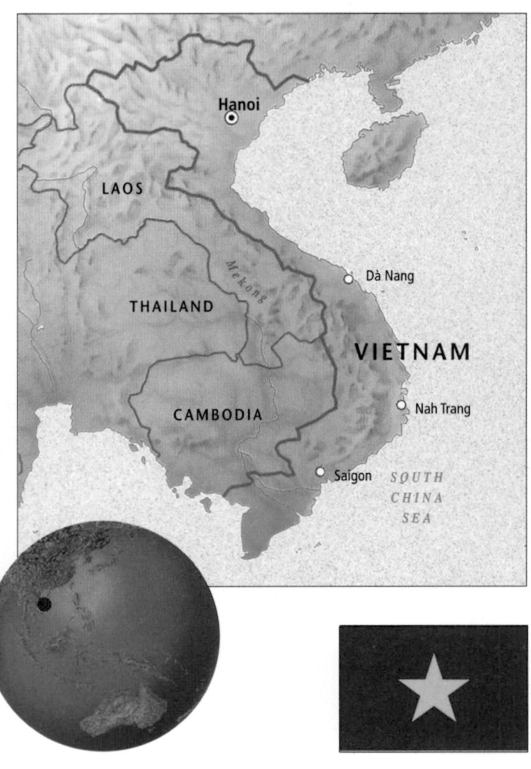

Fact File

Official name Socialist Republic of Vietnam
Form of government Communist state with single legislative body (National Assembly)
Capital Hanoi
Area 329,560 sq km (127,243 sq miles)
Time zone GMT +7 hours
Population 81,099,000
Projected population 2015 94,413,000
Population density 246.1 per sq km (637.4 per sq mile)
Life expectancy 69.9
Infant mortality (per 1,000) 29.3
Official language Vietnamese
Other languages Chinese, French, English, Khmer, indigenous languages
Literacy rate 93.7 %
Religions Buddhist 55 %, Roman Catholic 7%, Taoist, Islam and indigenous beliefs 38 %
Ethnic groups Vietnamese 85 %–90 %, Chinese 3 %, other 7 %–12 %
Currency Dong
Economy Agriculture 65 %, industry and services 35 %
GNP per capita US$ 2100
Climate Tropical in south, subtropical in north; wet season May to October
Highest point Fan Si Pan 3,143 m (10,312 ft)
Map reference Page 203

Vietnam is located on the eastern side of the Indochinese Peninsula. A long, narrow strip of country lying between two major river systems, Vietnam bears the scars of one of the longest and most devastating wars of the second half of the twentieth century. Historically, it was for more than a thousand years under Chinese

domination, achieving a degree of independence in AD 939. Christian missionary activity began in the seventeenth century and it was a French colony from 1883. During the Second World War a communist-led resistance movement fought the Japanese, and later fought the returning French, defeating them decisively in 1954. The country was divided into two mutually hostile regimes, with a communist government in the North and a French- and later US-backed government in the South. The North initiated twenty years of insurgency and then full-scale war (the North backed by the USSR, the South by the USA with at one stage 500,000 troops), eventually winning in 1975 and establishing the Socialist Republic of Vietnam.

About 66 percent of Vietnam's land area is dominated by the heavily forested terrain of the Annam Highlands (or Chaîne Annamitique). The crest of this range mostly follows the western border with Laos in the north and Cambodia to the south. At either end of the country are intensively cultivated and densely populated river deltas—the Red River Delta in the north, which is also fed by waters from the valley of the Da, and the Mekong Delta in the south. Both are major rice-growing areas. Rice is the main staple and export crop, Vietnam being the world's third-largest exporter. Other food crops include sweet potato and cassava. On the mountain slopes of the Annam Highlands tea, coffee, and rubber plantations have been established.

Most mineral resources are located in the north and include anthracite and lignite. Coal is the main export item and is the principal energy source.

After 10 years during which a typical communist command economy was imposed, along with collectivized agriculture, the government changed direction. In 1986 the more liberal *doi moi* ("renovation") policy was introduced. Investment was welcomed from outside, and during the period 1990 to 1995 real growth averaged more than 8 percent annually.

Foreign capital contributed to a boom in commercial construction, and there was strong growth in services and industrial output. Crude oil remains the country's largest single export, now amounting to a quarter of exports overall, slightly more than manufactures. But progress is handicapped by a continuing strong commitment to state direction and bureaucratic controls. Banking reform is needed and administrative and legal barriers delay investment. A new constitution of 1992 somewhat limits the influence of the Communist Party and liberalizes economy and politics. The human rights situation has since improved but censure and the still powerful CPV continue to curtail civil rights substantially.

Laos

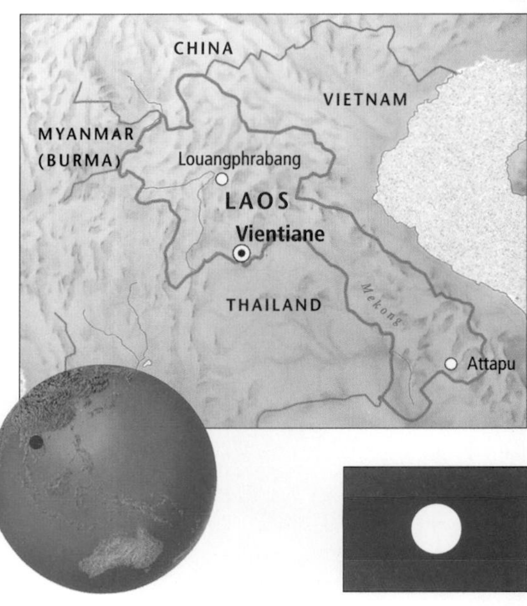

Fact File

Official name Lao People's Democratic Republic

Form of government Communist state with single legislative body (National Assembly)

Capital Vientiane

Area 236,800 sq km (91,428 sq miles)

Time zone GMT +7 hours

Population 5,778,000

Projected population 2015 7,334,000

Population density 24.4 per sq km (63.2 per sq mile)

Life expectancy 59.9

Infant mortality (per 1,000) 91

Official language Lao

Other languages French, Chinese, Vietnamese

Literacy rate 57 %

Religions Buddhist 60 %, animist and other 40 %

Ethnic groups Lao Loum (lowland) 68 %, Lao Theung (upland) 22 %, Lao Soung (highland) 9 %,

ethnic Vietnamese and Chinese 1 %

Currency Kip

Economy Agriculture 80 %, services and industry 20 %

GNP per capita US$ 1,630

Climate Tropical monsoonal, with wet season May to October

Highest point Phou Bia 2,817 m (9,242 ft)

Map reference Pages 202–03

Laos is the only landlocked country in Southeast Asia. It also has one of the last official communist regimes, and is the poorest state in the region. Once the home of the fourteenth century kingdom of Lan Xang (the Million Elephant Kingdom), Laos became a French protectorate in 1893. Independent in 1953, it was fought over by royalists, communists, and conservatives from 1964 onward. It was used as a military supply route by the North Vietnamese during the Vietnam War and was heavily bombed with defoliants by the USA in the late 1960s. In 1975 it fell into the hands of the communist Pathet Lao who established a one-party state. Although the leadership has for economic reasons relaxed its doctrinal grip—the 1978 collectivization of agriculture was reversed in 1990—many hill-tribe people, such as the Hmong, remain alienated from the regime. Some continue guerrilla resistance, while others live in exile in Thailand. A new constitution in 1991 confirmed the monopoly of the communist Lao People's Revolutionary Party.

From the mountains in the northwest and the Plateau de Xiangkhoang, the country extends southeast, following the line of the Anamitique Range. A number of rivers cross the country westward from this range to the Mekong River which forms the western border, among them the Banghiang, the Noi, and the Theun. The fertile Mekong floodplains in the west provide the only generally cultivable lowland. Despite deforestation and erosion, forest still covers 55 percent of the country.

Most of the Laotian people are engaged in subsistence agriculture. In addition to the staple, rice, other crops which are grown include maize, vegetables, tobacco, coffee, and cotton. Opium poppies and cannabis are grown illegally: Laos is the world's third-largest opium producer.

The policy of privatization and decentralization that was adopted in 1986 has produced growth averaging 7.5 percent annually since 1988. Textile and garment manufacture was established, as well as motorcycle assembly. The country's primitive infrastructure is a major handicap to continued growth. Laos has no railroads, its roads are inadequate, and its telecommunications severely limited. For the foreseeable future the economy will depend heavily on overseas aid.

A fisherman casting his net from a basket boat in Vietnam (left page top). Women at a market in Hanoi (left page above). Vietnamese farmers working in the rice fields (left page below). View of the Mekong plain (above right).

Indochina

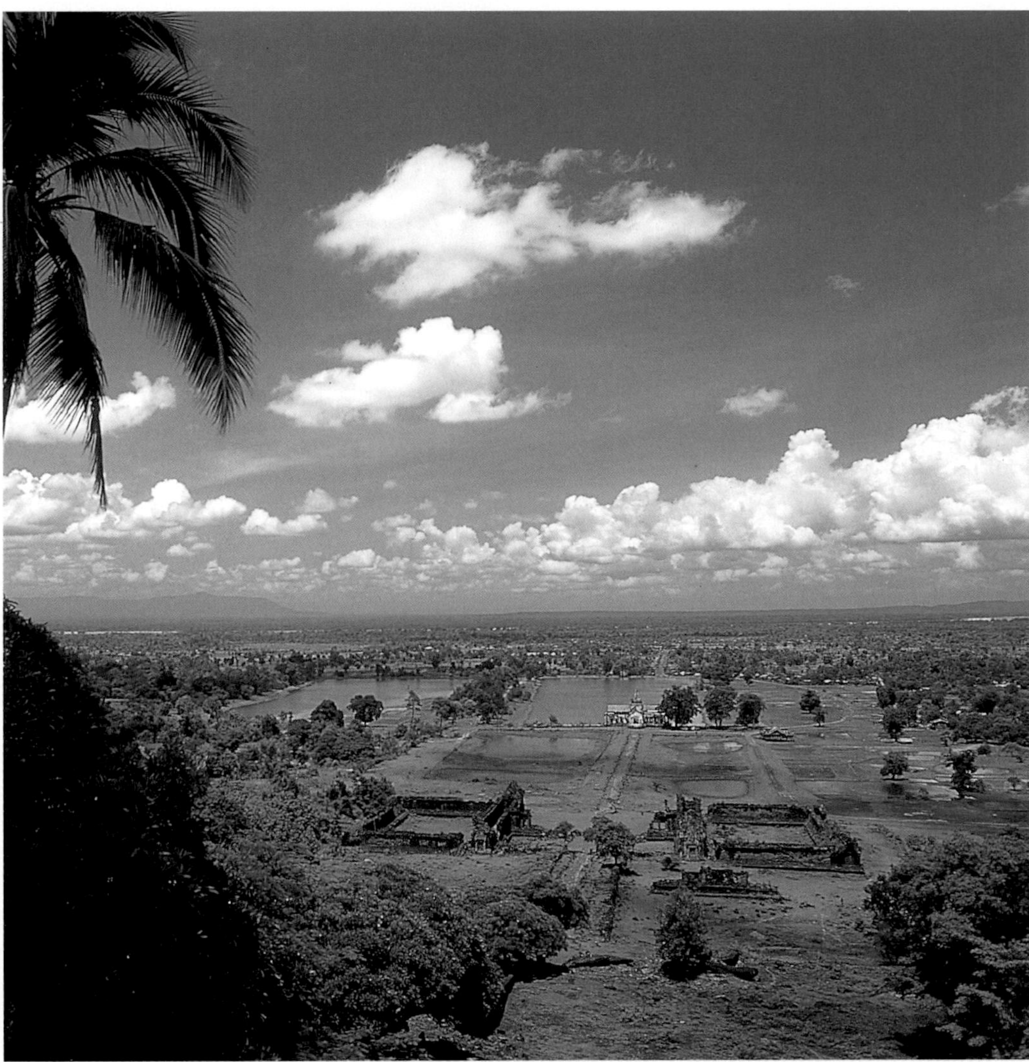

The term Indochina indicates that cultural influences from India and China are intermingled throughout this region. Also once known as French Indochina, it consists of the three states of Vietnam, Laos, and Cambodia, all of which were formerly associated with France in a political group known as the French Union. Despite the fact that the French exercised political control over their countries from the late nineteenth century, the Vietnamese, Cambodian, and Laotian royal houses continued to exercise wide authority. The Japanese occupied Indochina during the Second World War, but interfered little in the existing colonial arrangements; only after 1945 did the military turmoil begin which was to convulse the region.

In 1945, following the withdrawal of the Japanese, the Vietnamese communist nationalist leader Ho Chi Minh proclaimed the Democratic Republic of Vietnam. The returning French attempted to hold their colonial possession together, but soon the protracted guerrilla struggle that became known as the First Indochina War broke out. The forces in the North received support from the Chinese. In 1954 after the siege of Dien Bien Phu, both France and China agreed to a ceasefire. North Vietnam and South Vietnam were divided along the 17th parallel, and France had to withdraw from the region and recognize the independence of its former colonies Vietnam, Laos, and Cambodia.

During the 1960s North Vietnamese attempts to infiltrate and subvert the southern area led to the Second Indochina War, also know as the Vietnam War. This period saw increasing United States military involvement in the defense of South Vietnam. The US gave strong support to the South Vietnamese government and in 1961 the US commenced sending military advisers. The US actively entered the Vietnam War in 1964. Fighting continued until the Paris ceasefire of 1973, and Saigon was ultimately captured by the North Vietnmese in 1975.

Between 1954 and 1975 about 1,000,000 North Vietnamese soliders, 200,000 South Vietnamese soldiers and 500,000 civilians were killed. Between 1961 and 1975 about 56,500 US soldiers were killed. In 1976 the Socialist Republic of Vietnam was established.This period also saw the rise and fall of the Khmer Rouge regime in Cambodia, and was followed by a Vietnamese invasion of Cambodia in 1978. Before withdrawing from Cambodia Vietnam installed in power the Communist Khmer People's Revolutionary Party (now the Cambodian People's Party) whose domination of the political system, reinforced by a violent coup in 1997, is a source of international concern.

Today several boundary disputes exist between the three countries of Indochina. In addition to Vietnam's claims to various islands in the South China Sea, sections of the boundary between Cambodia and Vietnam are in dispute, and the maritime boundary between these countries is not defined. Similar boundary disputes also exist between Laos and Thailand.

Thailand

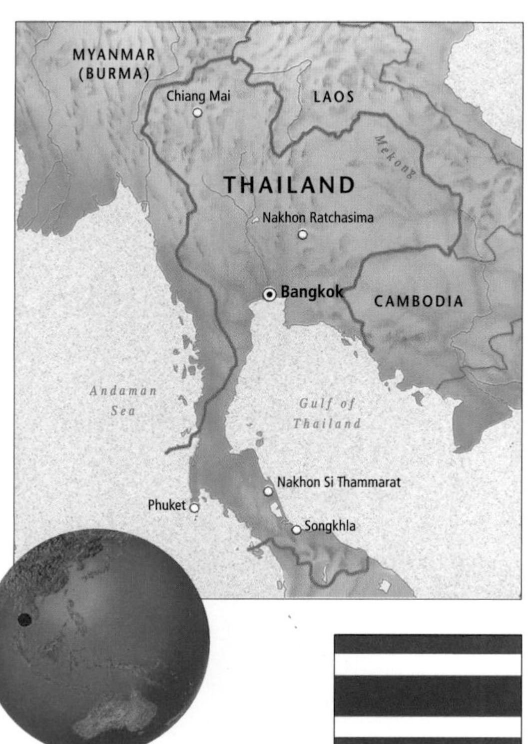

Fact File

OFFICIAL NAME Kingdom of Thailand

FORM OF GOVERNMENT Constitutional monarchy with two legislative bodies (Senate and House of Representatives)

CAPITAL Bangkok

AREA 514,000 sq km (198,455 sq miles)

TIME ZONE GMT +7 hours

POPULATION 62,355,000

PROJECTED POPULATION 2015 72,490,000

POPULATION DENSITY 121.3 per sq km (314.2 per sq mile)

LIFE EXPECTANCY 69.2

INFANT MORTALITY (PER 1,000) 29.5

OFFICIAL LANGUAGE Thai

OTHER LANGUAGES Chinese, Malay, English

LITERACY RATE 93.8 %

RELIGIONS Buddhist 95 %, Muslim 3.8 %, Christian 0.5 %, Hindu 0.1 %, other 0.6 %

ETHNIC GROUPS Thai (Siamese, Shan, Lao) 75 %, Chinese 14 %, other 11 %

CURRENCY Baht

ECONOMY Agriculture 70 %, services 24 %, industry 6 %

GNP PER CAPITA US$ 6,600

CLIMATE Tropical, with wet season June to October, cool season November to February, hot season March to May

HIGHEST POINT Doi Inthanon 2,576 m (8,451 ft)

MAP REFERENCE Pages 202–03

Lying between Burma, Laos, and Cambodia, Thailand has a system of "semi-democracy" that has somehow preserved it from the misfortunes of its neighbors. Known as Siam until 1939, it was the home of the Buddhist kingdom of Ayutthaya from the fourteenth to the eighteenth centuries, during which time the monarch came to be regarded as a sort of god-king, and a bureaucratic administration system was developed. The Chakkri Dynasty was founded in 1782 at Bangkok, and in the late nineteenth century its representatives ushered Siam into the modern age: treaties with the West were signed, slavery abolished, and study abroad encouraged. The king acquiesced in a bloodless coup which set up a constitutional monarchy in 1932. Since then civilian and military governments have alternated, climaxing in the events of 1992, when violent demonstrations against another military general taking over the government led the king to intervene, and the constitution was amended. The prime minister now has to be an elected member of parliament. The military continues to play an important, though decreasing, part in both political and industrial life.

Thailand can be divided into four regions. To the north there are forested mountain ranges which are the southernmost extension of the Himalayas. The rich intermontane valleys of the Rivers Ping, Yom, Wang, and Nan support intensive agriculture and the forests produce teak and other valuable timbers. The forests provide a home for many hill tribes who live by the alternating cultivation of dry rice and opium poppies. In the northeast lies the Khorat Plateau, a region of poor soils sparsely vegetated with savanna woodlands where crops of rice and cassava are grown. The third region is the central plains—Thailand's rice bowl—with vistas of rice fields, canals, rivers, and villages on stilts. The mountainous southern provinces on the Malay Peninsula are dominated by tropical rainforest. The hills produce tin ore and plantation rubber and the picturesque islands off the west coast draw tourists.

Agriculture is still the main employer, although its economic importance is declining. Rice is the principal crop and Thailand is still one of the world's leading exporters. Other crops include sugar, maize, rubber, manioc, pineapples, and seafoods. Mineral resources include tin ore, lead, tungsten, lignite, gypsum, tantalum, fluorite, and gemstones. Thailand is the world's second largest producer of tungsten, and the third largest tin producer. Tourism is the largest single source of foreign exchange, the development of resorts on the coast along the Andaman Sea having been a major success.

The development of urban manufacturing industry, involving the export of high-technology goods, has been the most significant feature of the economy in recent years. This and the development of the service sector have fueled a growth rate of 9 percent since 1989. Thailand's domestic savings rate of 35 percent is a leading source of capital, but the country has also received substantial investment from overseas. Beginning in 1997, Thailand was the first country in the region to be affected by a range of problems associated with the Asian economic downturn—a falling currency, rising inflation, and unemployment heading toward 2 million.

Myanmar (Burma)

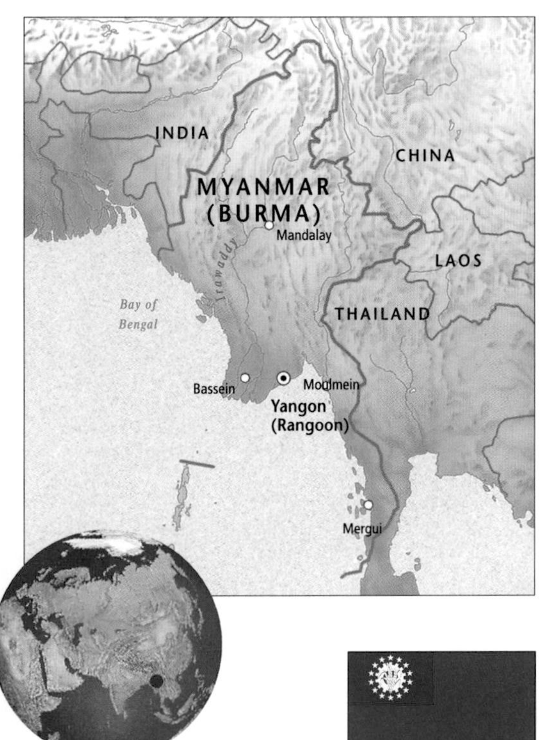

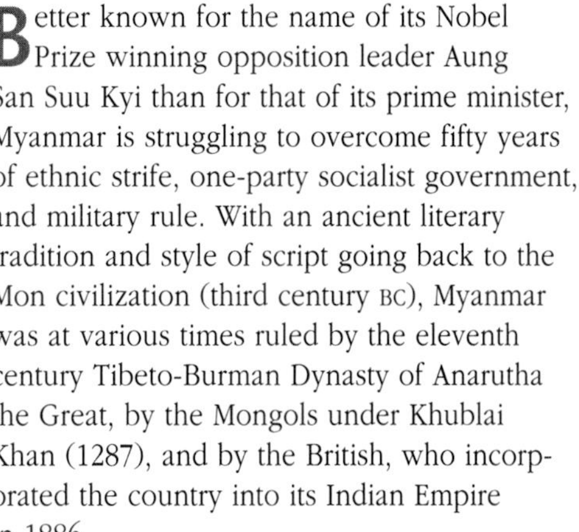

Fact File

OFFICIAL NAME Union of Myanmar (Burma)

FORM OF GOVERNMENT Military regime; legislative body (People's Assembly) has never convened since military takeover in 1988

CAPITAL Yangon (Rangoon)

AREA 678,500 sq km (261,969 sq miles)

TIME ZONE GMT + 6.5 hours

POPULATION 42,239,000

PROJECTED POPULATION 2015 46,322,000

POPULATION DENSITY 62.3 per sq km (161.2 per sq mile)

LIFE EXPECTANCY 55.4

INFANT MORTALITY (PER 1,000) 72.1

OFFICIAL LANGUAGE Burmese

OTHER LANGUAGES Indigenous languages (Shan, Kachin, Karen), English

LITERACY RATE 83.1 %

RELIGIONS Buddhist 89 %, Christian 4 % (Baptist 3 %, Roman Catholic 1 %), Muslim 4 %, other 3 %

ETHNIC GROUPS Burman 68 %, Shan 9 %, Karen 7 %, Rakhine 4 %, Chinese 3 %, Mon 2 %, other 7 %

CURRENCY Kyat

ECONOMY Agriculture 64 %, services 27 %, industry 9 %

GNP PER CAPITA US$ 1,500

CLIMATE Tropical monsoon; dry zone around Mandalay; moderate temperature on Shan Plateau

HIGHEST POINT Hkakabo Razi 5,881 m (19,294 ft)

MAP REFERENCE Pages 202, 205

Ruins of a Thai Buddhist temple (left page bottom). Landscape near Chiang Mai, in Thailand (top center). Two hill tribe women from the mountains of northern Thailand (above). Buddhist temple ruins at Pagan in Myanmar (bottom).

Better known for the name of its Nobel Prize winning opposition leader Aung San Suu Kyi than for that of its prime minister, Myanmar is struggling to overcome fifty years of ethnic strife, one-party socialist government, and military rule. With an ancient literary tradition and style of script going back to the Mon civilization (third century BC), Myanmar was at various times ruled by the eleventh century Tibeto-Burman Dynasty of Anarutha the Great, by the Mongols under Khublai Khan (1287), and by the British, who incorporated the country into its Indian Empire in 1886.

After the country gained independence from Great Britain in 1948, General Ne Win's Burmese Socialist Program Party swiftly abolished all private enterprise and private trade, nationalized industry, and placed the country under military control. Within a short time, one of the region's richest countries had become an impoverished backwater. For decades, a substantial portion of the government's energy and 35 percent of its budget has been directed towards efforts to suppress ethnic insurgent movements led by Karens, Shans, Kachins, Mons, and others. In order to fund their resistance, these groups grew opium poppies, a traditional crop, which has led to the country becoming the world's largest opium producer.

Situated on the Bay of Bengal between Bangladesh and Thailand, Myanmar consists of central lowlands, where 75 percent of the population lives, enclosed by mountains to the north, bordering China, and west, bordering India, and the Shan Plateau to the east forming a frontier with Laos. The western mountains run southwest along the Indian border and form a series of forested ridges, ending in the Arakan Yoma Range (Pegu Yoma). From the mountains in the north the Irawaddy River flows south 2,100 km (1,300 miles), passing the ancient city of Mandalay and the capital of Yangon (Rangoon) on its way to the Andaman Sea. While the coast has a wet climate, the inner region, sheltered from the seasonal monsoon, has an annual rainfall of less than 100 cm (40 in). Here, in narrow valleys, small-scale irrigation supports such crops as rice, sugarcane, cotton, and jute.

Myanmar is quite rich in natural resources, having fertile soils and good fisheries, along with teak, gems, and natural gas and oil. Recently there has been some liberalization of the economy, most notably of small scale enterprise. Twenty-five percent, however, remains under state control, and the key industries—in energy, heavy industry, and foreign trade—consist of twenty military-run enterprises. A recent boom in trade with China has filled the north with Chinese goods and foreign visitors. Economic weaknesses include a shortage of both skilled labor, and trained managers and technicians. Price controls have led to an economy that is permeated by the black market. Published estimates of Myanmar's foreign trade are therefore greatly understated.

East Asia

China

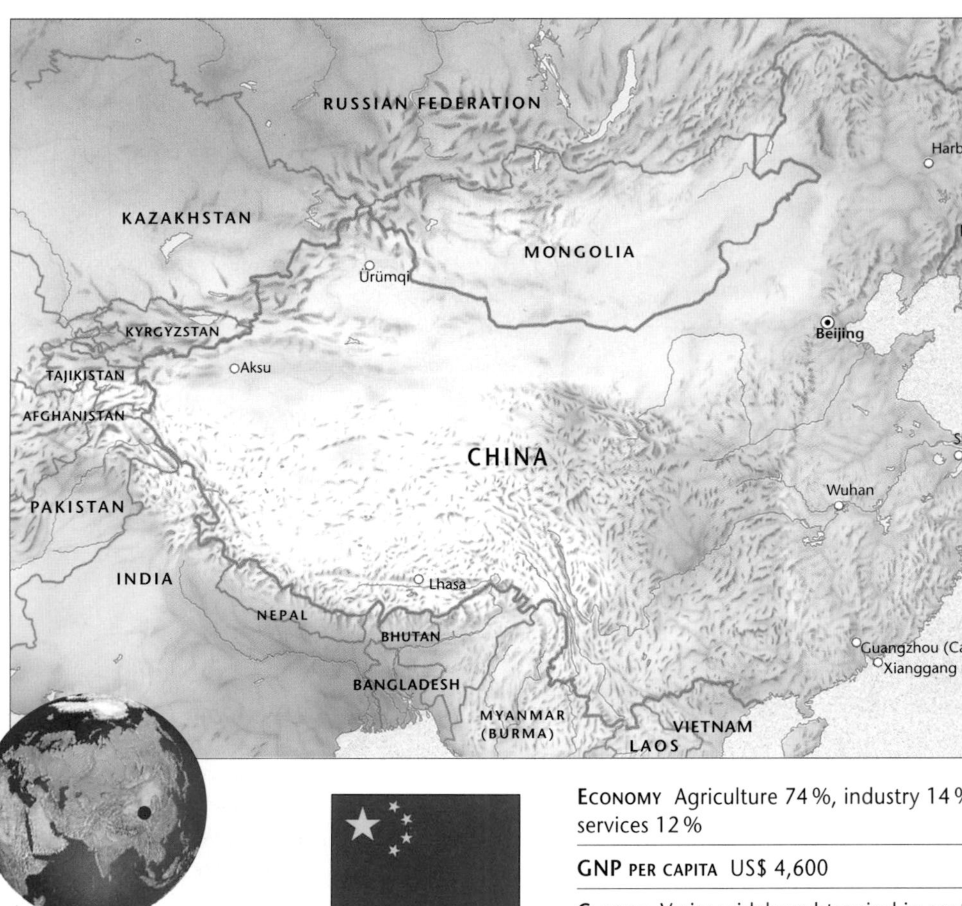

Fact File

OFFICIAL NAME People's Republic of China

FORM OF GOVERNMENT Communist republic with single legislative body (National People's Congress)

CAPITAL Beijing

AREA 9,596,960 sq km (3,705,386 sq miles)

TIME ZONE GMT +8 hours

POPULATION 1,284,304,000

PROJECTED POPULATION 2015 1,410,287,000

POPULATION DENSITY 133.8 per sq km (346.6 per sq mile)

LIFE EXPECTANCY 71.9

INFANT MORTALITY (PER 1,000) 27.3

OFFICIAL LANGUAGE Mandarin Chinese

OTHER LANGUAGES Yue (Cantonese), Wu (Shanghaiese), Minbei (Fuzhou), Minnan (Hokkien-Taiwanese), other minority languages (Tibetan, Uyguran, Mongolian)

LITERACY RATE 89.9 %

RELIGIONS Officially atheist; traditionally Confucian, Taoist, Buddhist; small Muslim and Christian minorities

ETHNIC GROUPS Han Chinese 92 %, other (including Zhuang, Uygur, Hui, Yi, Tibetan, Miao, Manchu, Mongol, Buyi, Korean) 8 %

CURRENCY Yuan

ECONOMY Agriculture 74 %, industry 14 %, services 12 %

GNP PER CAPITA US$ 4,600

CLIMATE Varies widely: subtropical in southeast; temperate in east; cold and arid on southwestern Tibetan plateau; arid in northern deserts; cold temperate in northeast

HIGHEST POINT Mt Everest 8,848 m (29,028 ft)

MAP REFERENCE Pages 205, 206, 210–11, 212–13, 214–15

Although it is the third largest country in the world, and the most populous, China today remains something of an enigma to much of the rest of the world: it has an increasingly capitalistic economy, but political control remains solidly in the hands of an old-style Communist Party leadership. There is a great deal riding on how successfully this "socialist market economy" works. With a civilization extending back more than 5,000 years, China's history has tended to combine long periods of dynastic stability with shorter periods of sudden and dramatic change. Approximately in the last hundred years China has once again gone through a series of convulsive social, political, and economic transformations. Once isolated, agrarian, and indifferent to other societies and cultures, China's future is now that of a modern industrial nation trading with much of the world. Politically it remains a one-party state. The political reforms that would be necessary to bring about greater democracy are widely discussed in western media, as are civil liberties and human rights issues, but they are not yet on the agenda of China itself.

Physical features and land use

China can be divided into three major geographic regions: the mountains to the west, including the vast Plateau of Tibet; the series of deserts and desert basins starting in the northwest with the Tarim Basin and the Taklimakan Desert, reaching across the Nei Mongol Plateau (Nei Mongol Gaoyuan) to Manchuria (Taklimakan Shamo) in the northeast; and the largely low-lying eastern region consisting of the valleys and floodplains of the Chang Jiang (Yangtze) and Huang (Yellow) Rivers, extending to the coastal plains including the Pearl River in the south.

The melting snows of the Plateau of Tibet feed several major rivers—the Brahmaputra, flowing south to India, the Salween (Nu) of Myanmar (Burma), and the Mekong which skirts Laos and Thailand before passing through Cambodia and reaching the sea in Vietnam. In addition, the plateau is the source of both the Huang (Yellow), and the mighty Chang Jiang (Yangtze), China's two main rivers, both of which drain into the East China Sea. The Plateau of Tibet, some parts of which are permanently covered in snow, is the highest region in the world, averaging about 4,900 m (16,000 ft), with ranges rising from 6,100 to 7,300 m (20,000 to 24,000 ft). It is bounded to the north by the Kunlun Shan Range, and to the south along the borders of India, Nepal, and Bhutan by the mountain system of the Himalayas. The plateau is a harsh environment, hostile to human settlement, and most of the plateau's 2 million inhabitants live in the southern region. The Himalayan ranges also have great political significance. They form a massive rampart along China's southwestern frontier, and for centuries they have provided a natural defensive barrier against the west. This is one of the reasons China is unwilling to allow the pressure for Tibetan independence to take it beyond the status of an "autonomous region".

The second geagraphic region of China stretches from the Tarim Basin and Dzungarian Basin (Junggar Pendi) in the northwest, past the southern fringes of the Gobi Desert to Northern Manchuria. For the most part it is too arid and cold for agriculture. Here, pastoralists such as the Uighurs of Xinjiang keep sheep, goats, and herds of horses. However, some oasis crops are grown around the rim of the Taklimakan Desert, and there are small farming settlements in the Gansu corridor to the north of the Qilian Mountains. The Turfan Depression (Turpan Pendi) (both the lowest and the hottest place in China at 154 m [505 ft] below sea level) lies northeast of the Tarim Basin. East of the Gobi Desert lies the agricultural area of the Manchurian Plain, where coarse grains and soy beans are cultivated. In Northern Manchuria the growing season is extremely short: only ninety days a year are frost free.

The eastern region of central China is where two-thirds of the country's people live. This was the cradle of Chinese civilization. On the region's fertile alluvial plains the most distinctive features of China's economic and social life developed—intensive irrigated agriculture and the Chinese peasant family. Known as "China's Sorrow," the Huang (Yellow) River makes its way across the North China Plain. For hundreds of years it caused repeated, serious flooding, with enormous loss of life, but today modern flood-control schemes have reduced this danger.

Further south, near the Chang Jiang (Yangtze) delta, the plain changes into a landscape characterized by large lakes and intricate networks of canals, many of them centuries old. The Chang Jiang is China's largest and most important river, and much of it is navigable, providing an essential transportation route. When the river level is high, vessels of 10,000 tonnes may reach Wuhan, and 1,000-tonne barges can reach Chongqing in Sichuan. What is called the "Red Basin" of Sichuan is a fertile and highly productive area far up the Chang Jiang, separated from the lower valley by steep-sided gorges. It is intensively cultivated, and the landscape is dominated by rice fields arranged in terraces extending up the hillsides. Summer weather in the central valley of the Chang Jiang is hot and humid, with temperatures at Nanjing reaching 44 °C (111 °F).

A distinctive landscape in southern China (famous for centuries as an inspiration for Chinese landscape painters) is found in northeastern Guizhou Province, where limestone spires and pinnacles rise above small, intensively cultivated plains. This heavily eroded area is marked by sinkholes, caverns, and underground streams. In the coastal lowlands of Guangdong Province, in the far south, the climate is tropical and farmers enjoy a year-round growing season. On Hainan Island, flanking the Gulf of Tongking, it is possible to cultivate three crops of rice per year. Other crops grown in the south include sugar, bananas, and tropical fruits. During the summer, cyclones and typhoons frequently strike the southeast coast.

Early history

Civilization arose along the borders of the North China Plain. Here, about 1700 BC, the Shang Dynasty originated in the Huang Valley. Noted for their craftsmanship in bronze, along with important achievements as the use of the wheel, the calendar, and a form of writing, the Shang Dynasty lasted until 1122 BC. The next dynasty, the Zhou, lasted several centuries. It was in this time that the teachings of the philosopher-teacher Confucius (551–479 BC) originated, which provided a pattern for Chinese society for centuries to come. Iron casting, metal coinage, and silk were also introduced at this time. During the short-lived Qin Dynasty (221–206 BC) a ruler arose named Qin Shihuang. He unified the nation, began the fortification of China's northern boundary with the Great Wall, and established the civil service. He was buried at Lintong with an army of 6,000 terracotta warriors which are still standing and continue to be a major tourist attraction.

In 206 BC the Han Dynasty was begun. During the four centuries of the Han, the Chinese invented paper and the seismograph, steel was first made, Buddhism was introduced from India, and the boundaries of China were extended nearly to their present limits. Under the Sui (AD 581–618) a large part of the Grand Canal linking the north with the Chang Valley was built. During the 300 years of the Tang Dynasty which followed, China became the world's most extensive empire. Paper money was adopted, block printing was invented, and priceless ceramic vases were produced. In these centuries and those of the Song Dynasty (AD 960–1269), China's population, threatened by incursions of nomads from the north, began to concentrate in the warmer, more productive south. By the thirteenth century most people lived in the south, including the Chang Valley. The Song Dynasty is sometimes regarded as China's Golden Age. Trade with other nations expanded, and Chinese shipping took porcelain and silk to the East Indies, India, and Africa.

Northern invaders ended the Song Dynasty. By 1223 Ghengis Khan's Mongols held control over much of the north, and in 1260 Kublai Khan proclaimed himself emperor, with Beijing as his capital. Unified by the conquests of the

Threshing rice after harvesting (below). Buddhist prayer flags in the Potala Palace, in Lhasa, Tibet (above right). The countryside near Yangshuo in Guangxi Zhuangzu Zizhiqu Province (below right).

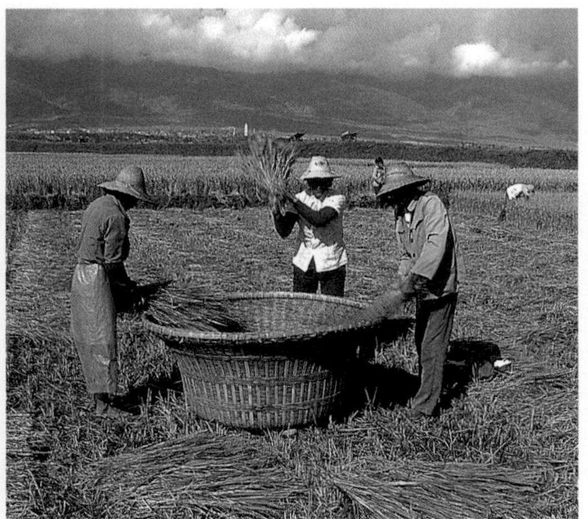

Mongol tribes, by 1300 the empire reached from Kiev to the Persian Gulf, and from Burma to Korea. Muslims, Christians, and Armenians all came to China at this time—among them possibly the Italian Marco Polo, who claimed in his writings that he served under Kublai Khan.

After the Mongols were overthrown, Chinese rule was re-established under the Ming Dynasty in 1368, and the Great Wall was restored and extended to its present length of 6,400 km (4,000 miles). During the three centuries of Ming rule numerous palaces were built, including the Imperial Palace at Beijing, and Chinese ships explored as far afield as the Red Sea. It was during this period that the first Christian missions began to appear in China: the Jesuits established themselves with the Portuguese at Macao in the sixteenth century.

Chinese civilization's main features, however, had been laid down in the time of the Han, Tang, and Song. During the rule of those dynasties Confucianism became the pervasive social ethic, which placed great value on the subordination of the individual to both family and state. In addition, porcelain manufacture and silk production reached a rare perfection; and various inventions were made which found their way to the West, most notably that of gunpowder and of paper. Despite the development of large cities and the growth of an educated bureaucratic elite, Chinese society remained largely agricultural, and its economic base depended on the productivity of the rural peasantry.

The Qing Dynasty (1683–1912) represented a return to power of northern people, the Manchus, descendants of the Mongols. Aggressive at first, seizing Taiwan and garrisoning Tibet, by the nineteenth century the Qing government had become weak and corrupt. Famine and unrest had made the country vulnerable to external forces, and by the century's end China had been divided into spheres of influence among the major Western powers, a disintegration hastened by peasant uprisings (the Taiping Rebellion of 1850–64) and military defeats (the Sino-Japanese War of 1894–95). In 1912 the last of China's emperors abdicated and a republic was proclaimed.

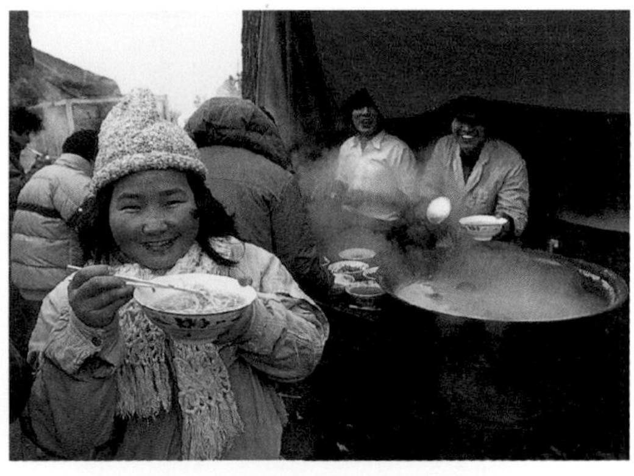

Modern history

Political and military disorder prevailed during the next forty years. At first the country was fought over by rival warlords. Two hostile competing political movements offered solutions to this chaos—the Kuomintang (or Chinese National Party), and the Communist Party (founded in 1921)—but neither was able to assert overall control. Then in 1931 Japan seized Manchuria, and in 1937 war broke out between China and Japan. During this time the communists sharpened their military and political skills. Mao Zedong gained the support of the peasantry and demonstrated that it was possible to succeed at guerrilla warfare. Hostilities between the Kuomintang and the communists were temporarily suspended in order to defeat Japan. But once this was achieved, in 1945, a civil war broke out, that eventually claimed more than 12 million lives. Victory went to the communists, and the People's Republic of China was proclaimed in October 1949.

Mass starvation, malnutrition, and disease were all brought under control in the inital years of communist rule and land reform was begun. As part of a planned economy the rural population was organized into 50,000 communes—units which farmed the land collectively. Communes also had responsibility for running rural industries, schools, and clinics. During these years morale and dedication were high. Many of the former middle classes suffered grave privations in "re-education camps", but living standards improved for the majority of the people, and corruption and bureaucratic sloth were not a major problem.

Mao Zedong, however, was determined to push ahead with radical programs of industrialization and political change. In 1958 the "Great Leap Forward" initiative tried to industrialize the country using the organization of the communes, and to increase steel production by using backyard furnaces. It was a disaster of colossal proportions. Between 1959 and 1961 failed economic policies led to far-spread famine, disease, and attempted rebellion. As many as 20 million people died.

Mao increasingly suspected his associates of disloyalty, believing some wanted to take "the capitalist road". In 1966 he launched the Great Proletarian Cultural Revolution to extirpate "old thought, old culture, old customs and old habits". China's local authorities were, in effect, put on trial, many community members were abused and tormented, and the Red Guards rampaged through numerous cities destroying property and wrecking ancient works of art.

In 1967 the army was called in to restore order. Mao's death in 1976 brought change. There was even, in 1978, a brief flirtation with free speech. Deng Xiaoping, a new leader with a different vision of Chinese communism, but no less determined to assert his power, began the process of economic liberalization which has led to today's state-managed capitalism and rigid political regime.

Timeline

1.9 MYA Appearance of early hominids who closely resemble *Homo habilis* (Longgupo Cave, Sichuan Province)

800,000 BP Hominid *Homo erectus*, now considered to have evolved in Asia; present in China possibly 1.8 MYA

460,000 BP Earliest claimed evidence of controlled use of fire (Zhoukoudian Cave) by *Homo erectus*, called "Peking Man"

68,000 BP *Homo sapiens sapiens* present in China

7500 BC Farmers of central and southern China domesticate foxtail millet and rice

5500 BC First thick clay pottery used in fishing villages along southern coastline

2600 BC Writing system based on pictograms in use—many characters similar to those still used today

800 BC Population more than 13 million under the Chou Dynasty

214 BC First part of Great Wall of China completed under Qin Dynasty to protect against Turkish and Mongol invasions

206 BC Shi Huangdi (First Emperor) is buried with 6,000 life-size terracotta warriors at Chang-an near Xi'an

c. 100 AD Paper made from hemp and rags in use with solid inks in north-west China

618 Tang Dynasty sees great economic development; Grand Canal links Huang and Chang rivers (completed 1283)

1213 Genghis Khan leads Mongolian invasion—up to 30 million Chinese are slaughtered

1279 The Mongols under Kublai Khan (grandson of Genghis Khan) take control of all China; Beijing now the capital

Taiwan and Tibet complicate China's relations with the West. China insists that Taiwan (the Republic of China) must rejoin the mainland as a province. In the case of Tibet, it may be that the exiled, but highly popular religious leader, the Dalai Lama, has awakened unrealistic hopes for political independence. Tibet itself, however, has severely suffered under the regime, and thousands of its people have been killed. China's historic use of the region as a defensive bulwark in the west means that independence is unlikely. Civil rights do not exist in other parts of China, either. Law is arbitrary, and the courts are usually conducted by army personnel without legal training. Students demonstrating in Beijing for greater democracy in 1989 were met with tanks and hundreds were killed and injured in the well-known Tiananmen Square massacre. In 1998 an attempt to organize an independent political party was crushed and its leaders jailed.

The economy

China is a country with plentiful and diverse natural resources. Coal deposits exist in most of its 22 provinces, and there are seventy major production centers, of which Hebei, Shanxi, Shandong, Jilin, and Anhui are the most important. China also has deposits of iron ore, and is a major producer of tungsten. Industries produce iron, steel, coal, machinery, armaments, textiles, and petroleum. Of these, the main exports are textiles, chemicals, light industrial goods, armaments, oil, and oil products. This will soon change, however, as the rapid increase in the use of automobiles in China in the early years of the twenty-first century have already led to a drastic increase in fuel comsumption. China is on the verge of becoming a net importer of oil, which is having a notable effect on the world oil prices that are rising due to the increased demand. Questions about the Chinese economy are not centered on resources, skills or capacity. Instead, they concern the ideological clash between a market-oriented economy and the rigid controls of the Communist Party.

In 1978 the leadership began moving away from Soviet-style central planning. In agriculture, household responsibility replaced collectivization and brought an immediate rise in productivity. In industry, the decision-making power of plant managers and local officials was increased, small-scale private enterprise was allowed, and foreign investment and trade were encouraged. As a result, agricultural output doubled in the 1980s and industry made major gains. Gross domestic product has tripled since 1978.

The present system, however, combines some of the worst features of communism (bureaucracy, inertia, and corruption) and of capitalism (windfall gains and high inflation). Additional difficulties arise from revenue collection of every kind; from extortion and other economic malpractices; and from inefficient state enterprises. Up to 100 million rural workers are adrift between country and city. The amount of arable land continues to decine. Serious environmental problems exist—air pollution from the use of coal, and water pollution from industrial effluents; falling water tables and nation-wide water shortages; and the fact that less than ten percent of sewage is treated.

Part of the Great Wall of China (left page top). Girl eating noodles (left page bottom). Downtown Hong Kong, seen from the air (right). A government building in Shanhaiguan (below).

PROVINCES AND CAPITALS

Anhui • Hefei
Fujian • Fuzhou
Gansu • Lanzhou
Guangdong • Guangzhou
Guizhou • Guiyang
Hainan • Haikou
Hebei • Shijiazhuang
Heilongjiang • Harbin
Henan • Zhengzhou
Hubei • Wuhan
Hunan • Changsha
Jiangsu • Nanjing
Jiangxi • Nanchang
Jilin • Changchun
Liaoning • Shenyang
Qinghai • Xining
Shaanxi • Xi'an
Shandong • Jinan
Shanxi • Taiyuan
Sichuan • Chengdu
Yunnan • Kunming
Zhejiang • Hangzhou

AUTONOMOUS REGIONS

Guangxi Zhuangzu • Nanning
Nei Monggol • Hohhot
Ningxia Huizu • Yinchuan
Tibet (Xizang) • Lhasa
Xinjiang Uygur • Ürümqi

SPECIAL ADMINISTRATIVE REGIONS

Xianggang (Hong Kong) • Xianggang (Hong Kong)
Macao • Macao

MUNICIPALITIES

Beijing, Shanghai, and Tianjin

275 Marco Polo, a enetian, supposedly isits China (until 292) to establish trade nks with the country e calls "Cathay"

1644 The Manchus establish Qing Dynasty, bringing peace and prosperity; the population rises to 200 million by 1700

1800 British smuggle in opium; war breaks out in 1839 when Chinese object. Treaty in 1842 ends war; China cedes Hong Kong to Britain

1887–88 Huang River floods killing as many as 2.5 million people. It has flooded 1,500 times in the last 3,500 years

1900 Chinese "Boxer" rebellion in Peking (Beijing) against foreign interests put down by British and Russian forces

1911 Rebels proclaim republic—Emperor Pu Yi abdicates in 1912. In 1913 Sun Yat-sen founds Kuomintang (Nationalist Party)

1927–28 Civil War between Communist party and Kuomintang under Chiang Kai-Shek; Nationalists take Beijing

1934 Mao Zedong leads Long March of the Communists across China

1949 Mao Zedong proclaims People's Republic of China after a four-year civil war costing 12 million lives

1950 China invades Tibet; the Dalai Lama, Tibet's spiritual leader, flees to India

1958 "Great Leap Forward" to foster development damages economy and leads to severe food shortages; 20 million die by 1962

1979 "One-child families" policy introduced to curb population growth

1989 Pro-democracy demonstrations crushed by the use of tanks in Tiananmen Square, Beijing, with hundreds killed

1990 Census shows that China's population exceeds 1.1 billion people

1997 China regains control of Hong Kong, imposes 'One China, two systems' policy

1998 Chang Jiang River floods kill 3,000 with 250,000 homeless

1999 New constitution introduces "rule of law"

Taiwan

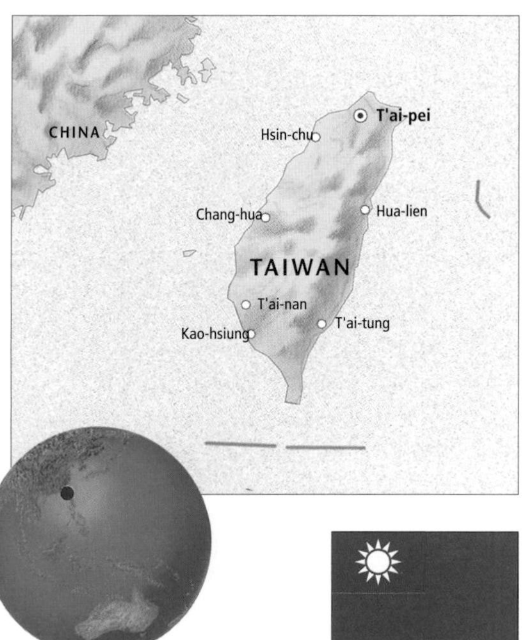

Fact File

Official name Republic of China

Form of government Republic with two legislative bodies (National Assembly and Legislative Yuan)

Capital T'ai-pei (Taipei)

Area 35,980 sq km (13,892 sq miles)

Time zone GMT +8 hours

Population 22,548,000

Projected population 2015 24,945,000

Population density 626.7 per sq km (1,623.1 per sq mile)

Life expectancy 76.7

Infant mortality (per 1,000) 6.8

Official language Mandarin Chinese

Other languages Taiwanese, Min, Hakka, Malayo-Polynesian languages

Literacy rate 94 %

Religions Buddhist, Confucian, and Taoist 93 %; Christian 5 %; other 2 %

Ethnic groups Taiwanese 84 %, mainland Chinese 14 %, indigenous 2 %

Currency New Taiwain dollar

Economy Services 49 %, industry 30 %, agriculture 21 %

GNP per capita US$ 17,200

Climate Tropical, with wet season May to September

Highest point Yu Shan 3,997 m (13,113 ft)

Map reference Page 206

Taiwan is a large island off the coast of China which, with support from the USA, has acted as a de facto independent country for the past 50 years. This is strongly opposed by China, which from the seventeenth century controlled the island and made it a Chinese province in the 1880s. However, Beijing has not had effective control of Taiwan for 100 years. It was ceded to Japan in 1895 (after Japanese victory in the Sino-Japanese War). From 1949 until the present it has been under the Nationalist Kuomintang (KMT), who after being driven from mainland China by the communists in 1949 used Taiwan as their last refuge. Ruling dictatorially over the Taiwanese until 1987, the KMT turned the country into a political, military, and economic fortress.

Seated in the UN as the official representative of China for two decades, Taiwan was displaced in 1971, and still has a marginal status in the international community. Today, after democratic elections, multiple parties are represented in the National Assembly, and both the president and the prime minister are native-born Taiwanese.

High mountains extending the length of the island occupy the central and eastern parts of Taiwan. The mountains of the Central Range, or Taiwan Shan, are the top of a submerged mountain chain, and rise steeply up from the east coast. Lush vegetation is found through much of the interior—the poor commercial quality of most of the timber has preserved it as forest cover. Rising to altitudes of more than 3,000 m (10,000 ft), the lower slopes support evergreens such as camphor and Chinese cork oak, while further up pine, larch, and cedar dominate. Rice is grown on the well-watered lowlands of the western coastal plain. Other crops include sugarcane, sweet potatoes, tea, bananas, pineapples, and peanuts.

Economically, agriculture is now of less importance than Taiwan's thriving industrial sector. The country as a whole demonstrated an almost unprecedented growth rate of 9 percent annually for three decades until 1996. During this period it was successively the world's biggest producer of television sets, watches, personal computers, and track shoes. Among Taiwan's strengths are its highly educated workforce, many US-trained, with an inside knowledge of the US market. Today the leading exports are electrical machinery, electronic products, textiles, footwear, foodstuffs, and plywood and wood products. With huge dollar reserves, Taiwan has become a major investor in China, Malaysia, and Vietnam. The Asian economic downturn in 1998 has had a steadying effect, but Taiwan is better situated than most to weather the storm. Political relations with China remain cool.

North Korea

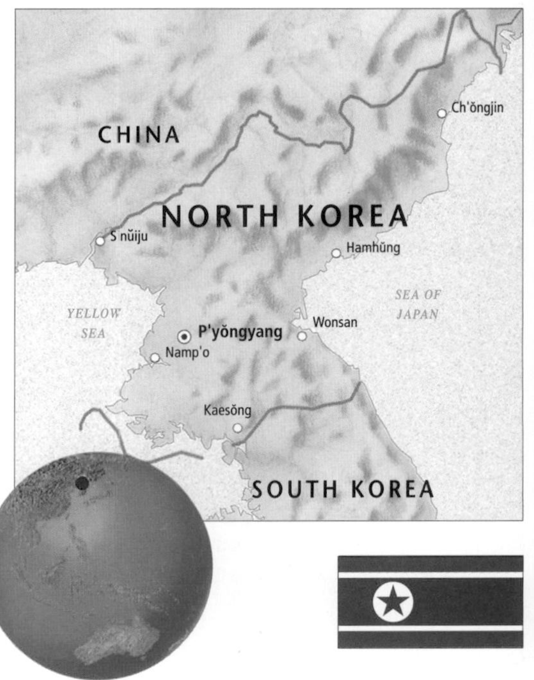

The Korean War, 1950–53

Occupied by Japan from 1910 until the Second World War, in 1945 Korea found itself divided between a Soviet-controlled north and an American-controlled south, with a frontier along the 38th parallel. This de facto division of the peninsula was formalized in 1948. In June 1950 heavily armed troops and tanks from the communist People's Republic of North Korea invaded the south, precipitating three years of bitter conflict.

Authorised by a UN resolution, American and South Korean troops, supported by contingents from Britain, Canada, France, and other allies, then fought to reclaim southern territory under the UN flag. Their success soon had the North Koreans in retreat, and American seaborne landings put allied troops far behind the North Korean lines. A crisis then arose when the allied commander, General Douglas MacArthur, neared

Fact File

Official name Democratic People's Republic of Korea

Form of government Communist state with single legislative body (Supreme People's Assembly)

Capital P'yongyang

Area 120,540 sq km (46,540 sq miles)

Time zone GMT +9 hours

Population 22,224,000

Projected population 2015 24,396,000

Population density 184.4 per sq km (477.5 per sq mile)

Life expectancy 71.3

Infant mortality (per 1,000) 22.8

Official language Korean

Literacy rate 99 %

Religions Buddhist and Confucian 51 %, traditional beliefs 25 %, Christian 4 %, other 20 %

Ethnic groups Korean 100 %

Currency Won

Economy Services and industry 64 %, agriculture 36 %

GNP per capita US$ 1,000

Climate Temperate, with cold, snowy winters and warm, wet summers

Highest point Mt Paektu 2,744 m (9,003 ft)

Map reference Page 208

the border of China. Hundreds of thousands of Chinese "volunteers" poured across the Yalu River into North Korea, and drove the allies far into the south once more. A counter-offensive in 1951 pushed the North Koreans and Chinese troops back to the vicinity of the 38th parallel, where an armistice took place in 1953.

After almost 40 years of tension and a series of minor military clashes a non-aggression pact was negotiated between North and South Korea in 1991. While the war resulted in North Korea becoming a rigid Stalinist state, it also ensured decades of US economic and military protection for South Korea.

For some the war is still not over: in October 1998 a 72-year-old South Korean soldier, who escaped from the north after 45 years as a prisoner-of-war, reported that 30 others like him were still being held in North Korean camps.

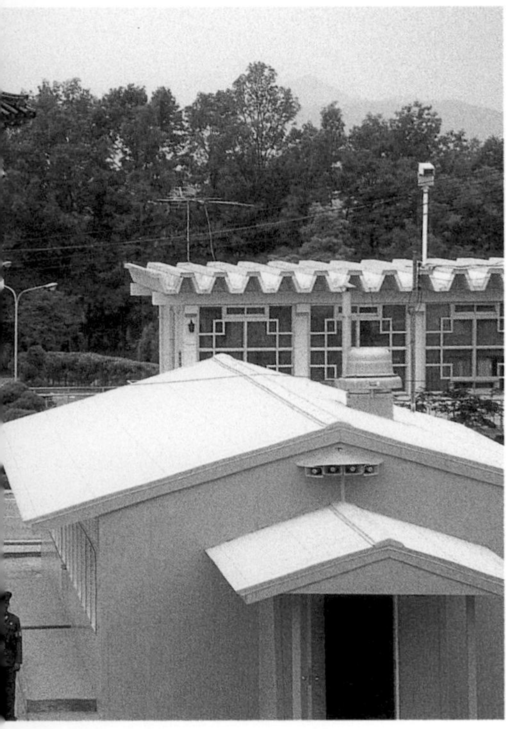

North Korea occupies the northern half of the Korean Peninsula. It is separated from South Korea along the ceasefire line that was established at the end of the Korean War (1950–53), roughly along the 38th parallel. After a period as an independent kingdom in the tenth century AD, control of Korea was disputed for hundreds of years between China and Japan, the latter seizing it as a colony in 1910. Following the Second World War it became a separate communist state and after the Korean War it developed into a rigidly closed totalitarian state system. The 50-year-long personal rule of Kim Il Sung ("Great Leader") passed by hereditary succession to his son Kim Jong Il ("Dear Leader") in 1994. The people of North Korea are classed by the state into three quasi-castes: loyal, wavering, and hostile. Membership of a caste determines whether an individual receives either education or employment. Citizens are subject to arbitrary arrest and execution for criticizing the Korean leaders or listening to foreign broadcasts. Unceasing political indoctrination takes place through the media, the workplace, the military, mass spectacles, and cultural events.

Mountains and rugged hills occupy most of the Korean Peninsula, and dominate its northern half. In the northeast the volcanic peak of Mt Paektu is surrounded by the Kaema Plateau. High forested mountains, cut by river gorges, lie along the border with Manchuria, northeast China. Other mountain chains extend north to south along the east coast. The Yalu River valley in the northwest marks the Korean-Chinese border, while to the southwest the fertile Chaeryŏng and Pyongyang plains are the main areas for agricultural activity. The principal crop is rice, followed by millet and other grains. Fruit and vegetables are grown, as well as oilseed rape, flax, and cotton.

The North Korean economy is run according to the Stalinist model. More than 90 percent of operations are controlled by the state, agriculture is totally collectivized, and state-owned industry produces 95 percent of all manufactured goods. Despite over 50 years of complete control by the state, the country is still not self-sufficient in food. The industrial sector produces military weapons, chemicals, minerals (including coal, magnesite, iron ore, graphite, copper, zinc, lead, and precious metals), along with a number of food products and textiles.

During the late 1990s the economy was in crisis: power supplies were unreliable and food shortages were causing famine in the countryside. Flooding in 1995 damaged harvests and led North Korea to seek foreign aid for the first time in decades; aid donors were muted in their response, demanding proof that aid had been properly distributed. North Korea continues to fall farther behind South Korean development and living standards.

Business street in Taipei, Taiwan (left page bottom).
Korean border posts on the 38th parallel (below center).

South Korea

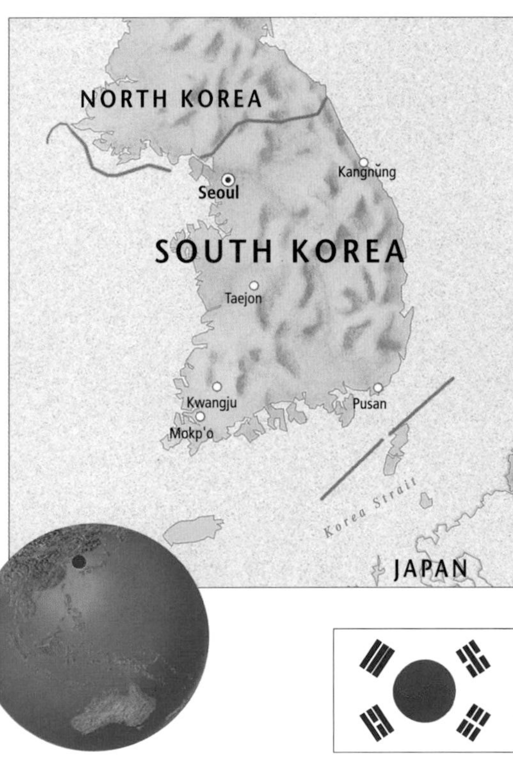

Fact File

Official name Republic of Korea

Form of government Republic with single legislative body (National Assembly)

Capital Seoul

Area 98,480 sq km (38,023 sq miles)

Time zone GMT +9 hours

Population 48,324,000

Projected population 2015 50,631,000

Population density 490.7 per sq km (1,270.9 per sq mile)

Life expectancy 74.9

Infant mortality (per 1,000) 7.6

Official language Korean

Other language English, Japanese

Literacy rate 98 %

Religions Christianity 21 %, Buddhism 24 %, Confucianism 1.5 %, other 1 %, no religion 52.5 %

Ethnic groups Korean 99.9 %, Chinese 0.1 %

Currency Won

Economy Services 55 %, industry 27 %, agriculture 18 %

GNP per capita US$ 19,400

Climate Temperate, with cold winters and hot, wet summers

Highest point Halla-san 1,950 m (6,398 ft)

Map reference Page 208

South Korea occupies the southern half of the Korean Peninsula. The border between South and North Korea consists of the ceasefire line established at the end of the Korean War (1950–53), roughly corresponding to the original pre-1950 border at the 38th parallel. The kingdom of Korea was dominated by either China or Japan for many centuries and finally annexed by Japan in 1910. After Japan's defeat at the

end of the Second World War, Korea was divided between a northern Soviet zone of influence, and a southern zone under US control. These zones soon became separate political entities. In 1950 communist North Korea invaded South Korea, and though the war ended in a stalemate in 1953, bitter hostility between north and south endures to the present day, with covert operations continuing.

In the 40-year period following 1953, both Koreas diverged socially, politically, and economically. South Korea, after a few years under the authoritarian rule of its first president, established constitutional liberalism in the Second Republic of 1960. From then until his assassination in 1979 it was under the elected presidency of General Park Chung Hee, who laid the basis for the economic success of the modern South Korean state with a combination of state planning and free-market incentives.

While questionable practices flourished at the top (two former presidents have been jailed) the country achieved a remarkable record of growth. Only 30 years ago its standard of living was much the same as the poorer countries of Africa. Today its gross domestic product per capita is nine times India's, fourteen times North Korea's, and on a par with some economies of the European Union. Regionally, its technological and scientific prowess is second only to Japan's.

More than 80 percent of South Korea's terrain is mountainous. Along the eastern side of the country the Tabaek-Sanmaek Mountains descend north to southwest. The Han and Naktong Rivers drain from these mountains through low-lying plains—the Han to the northwest, the Naktong to the south. Densely populated and intensively farmed, these plains cover 15 percent of South Korea's total land area. Rice, a staple crop in which the country is almost self-sufficient, is grown on family-owned farms. Other food crops include barley and fruit such as apples, grapes, peaches, nectarines, and plums. Silk and tobacco are produced for the export market.

About two-thirds of South Korea is forested. As many as 3,000 small islands lie off the west and south coasts, including Cheju which has South Korea's highest peak, the extinct volcano Halla-san at 1,950 m (6,398 ft).

There is little at the high-tech end of modern industry that South Korea does not manufacture and sell. It produces electronic equipment, machinery, ships, and automobiles. Textiles, an early item in its drive for export success, remain significant, along with clothing, food processing, chemicals, and steel. Real gross domestic product grew by an average of ten percent from 1986 to 1991, then tapered off. With the downturn in the Asian economies in 1998 the economy shrank for the first time in years, but the country won praise from the IMF (International Monetary Fund) for acting promptly in order to wipe out billions in bad bank loans and purge companies that were unviable.

A broad avenue in Seoul, South Korea (above). Rural scenery in South Korea (below). A traditional house in rural Japan (right page top). The Ginza district in Tokyo, Japan (left).

Japan

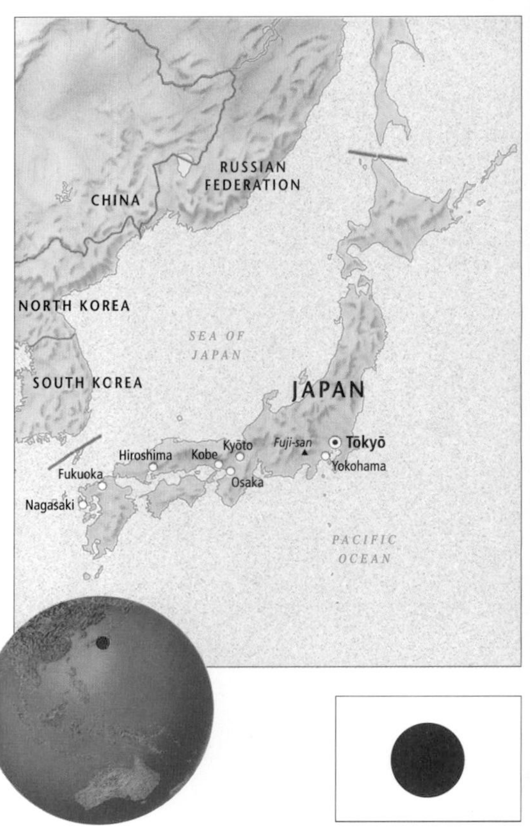

Fact File

Official name Japan

Form of government Constitutional monarchy with two legislative bodies (House of Councillors and House of Representatives)

Capital Tokyo

Area 377,835 sq km (145,882 sq miles)

Time zone GMT +9 hours

Population 126,975,000

Projected population 2015 127,522,000

Population density 336.1 per sq km (823.3 per sq mile)

Life expectancy 80.9

Infant mortality (per 1,000) 3.8

Official language Japanese

Literacy rate 99 %

Religions Shinto and Buddhist 84 %, other (including Christian 0.7 %) 16 %

Ethnic groups Japanese 99.4 %, other (mainly Korean) 0.6 %

Currency Yen

Economy Services 69 %, industry 24 %, agriculture 7 %

GNP per capita US$ 28,000

Climate Ranges from cold temperate in north to

Timeline

4500 BC Islands of Japan inhabited by peoples from Asia. They are later known as Jomon after their pottery

c. 1500 BC Rice is introduced from China and cultivated in the islands for the first time

660 BC Legendary leader Jimmu Tenno is Japan's first emperor and founds imperial dynasty which still holds office today

400 BC Wet rice farming introduce from Korean penir intensive agricultu enables larger pop ulation to survive

AD 200 In the Yayoi pe (until c. AD 700) ric grown in irrigated fi and people live in villa protected by moats wooden palisa subtropical in south; wet season June to July

Highest point Fuji-san (Mt Fuji) 3,776 m (12,388 ft)

Map reference Pages 208–09

Mainly mountainous, with intensively cultivated coastal plains, the archipelago of Japan lies off the east Asian coast close to Korea and China. By the early 1990s it had become an industrial and trading colossus second only to the USA. But cracks in the country's apparently impregnable economic facade began to appear in 1998 as the yen slid steadily against the dollar. The nation's vast scientific and technological resources, its highly educated personnel, and its substantial trade surpluses mean that it is better placed than most countries to cope with this and other problems.

History

First populated by migrants from mainland Asia, by the fifth century AD Japan was controlled by a number of clans. During the next 300 years several features of Chinese civilization were introduced, including Buddhism, Chinese script, and methods of administration, while cities modeled on those of the Tang Dynasty were built at Nara (AD 710) and Kyoto (AD 794). Centralized government, however, failed to eventuate and the clan basis of society prevailed. From the twelfth century until the rise of the Tokugawas, power was held by rival groups of feudal lords, or shoguns, and the emperor was a largely symbolic figure. Lasting from 1192 to 1867, the shogun era fostered an ethical code known as bushido (the path of the warrior, or samurai) that stressed loyalty, frugality, and courage.

Until 1945 Japan remained unconquered. Two Mongol fleets sent to invade the country were destroyed by typhoons in 1274 and 1281, founding the legend of a kamikaze or "divine wind" sent to protect "the land of the Gods". From 1603 a form of semi-centralized feudal rule was imposed by the ruling shogunate, the Tokugawas. Under this family, some 250 daimyo (or "great names") ran their own estates watched by state inspectors and a network of spies. Western influence appeared briefly in 1542, when missionaries arrived from Macao bringing clocks, carpets, guns, and Christianity. The reaction of the Tokugawas was to close the door: from 1639 Japan's citizens were not allowed to travel abroad, and trading contacts were limited to a single Dutch settlement at Nagasaki.

This ended in 1853 when Commodore Perry of the US Navy brought a squadron of warships into Yokohama Harbor, demanding that the country's ports be opened to Western trade. The now weak Tokugawa shogunate collapsed, imperial rule was resumed under the Meiji Restoration, and within 50 years Japan had become westernized and a rising industrial force. Victories in wars with China (1894–95) and Russia (1904–05) led to the seizure of Taiwan and Korea. Expanding imperial ambitions led later to the invasion of China, and eventually, in 1941, to an attack on Hawaii and Japan's entry into the Second World War. Allied victory in 1945 was followed by the introduction of a liberal, US-imposed democratic constitution which has since guided the nation's development.

Physical features and land use

Four large islands, so closely grouped that bridges and a tunnel now connect them, make up 98 percent of Japan's territory. They occupy a highly unstable zone on the earth's crust, and earthquakes and volcanic eruptions are frequent: 140,000 died in the 1923 earthquake which hit Yokohama and part of Tokyo; 6,000 died in the Kobe earthquake of January 1995. Folding and faulting has produced a mosaic of landforms throughout Japan, mountains and hills alternating with small basins and coastal plains. Inland there are several calderas and volcanic cones, the most famous being Fuji-san (3,776 m; 12,388 ft), the highest mountain in Japan, which last erupted in 1707.

Hokkaido, the northernmost of the main islands, is the most rural and traditional. Japan's biggest and most productive farming region, it has a climate similar to the US midwest—which may be why American advisors established wheat farming there in the 1860s. Hokkaido now produces more than half of Japan's grains. Southwest of Hokkaido lies the island of Honshu, where the Japanese Alps provide spectacular scenery. The Kanto Plain where Tokyo stands is the largest of various small alluvial plains, their soils enriched by centuries of careful cultivation. Today the conurbation this plain supports is Japan's most heavily industrialized and densely populated region. From southwestern Honshu across the two southern islands of Shikoku and Kyushu a complex of mountain peaks and undulating uplands stretches down to the Ryukyu

Islands (Nansei-Shotō), which includes Okinawa, before extending south toward Taiwan.

Economy

Japan's economy is notable for government-industry cooperation, a motivated population with a strong work ethic, high educational levels, and a mastery of high technology. These factors combined with a small defense allocation (1 percent of gross domestic product) have made it the second most powerful economy in the industrialized world. Japan is one of the world's largest and most advanced producers of steel and non-ferrous metallurgy, heavy electrical equipment, construction and mining equipment, motor vehicles and parts, communications and electronic equipment, machine tools, automated production systems, railroad rolling stock, ships, chemicals, textiles, and processed foods. Industry depends heavily on imported raw materials and fuel. The small agricultural sector is highly protected and subsidized; its crop yields are among the world's highest. Self-sufficient in rice, Japan imports about fifty percent of its other grain needs. After decades of spectacular growth, the late 1990s saw a marked contraction. The need for reconstruction remains evident, amid mounting fears of a banking crisis due to bad debts.

300 Large-scale immigration from the Asian continent until around 750 leads to a big increase in the population

550 Buddhism introduced from China

794 Japanese capital moves from Nara, the eastern end of the Tang Silk Road trade route, to Heian (called later Kyoto) until 1185

1281 Mongol conqueror Kublai Khan's invasion plans fail when his fleet is destroyed by a typhoon

1543 Portuguese sailors visit islands of southern Kyushu, making Europe aware of the wealth of the Japanese islands

1600 Honshu, Shikoku, and Kyushu united under the Tokugawa shogunate which rules for more than 250 years

1707 Mt Fuji, Japan's biggest volcano, erupts

1730 An earthquake on the island of Hokkaido causes the deaths of 137,000 people

1875 Population reaches more than 35 million; Tokyo 1 million by end of the century

1883 Tsunami kills 30,000 people. Three years later a tsunami occurs off Honshu and kills 28,000 people

1923 The Great Kanto earthquake, fires, and tsunamis destroy much of Tokyo-Yokohama and kill more than 140,000 people

1945 USA drops atomic bombs, destroying Hiroshima and Nagasaki. Second World War ends

1964 Shinkansen high-speed "bullet train" links Tokyo and Kyoto traveling at speeds of 210 km (130 miles) an hour

1994 Population of Tokyo-Yokohama exceeds 8 million

1995 Earthquake destroys much of Kobe city and kills 6,000 people

Indian subcontinent

Sri Lanka

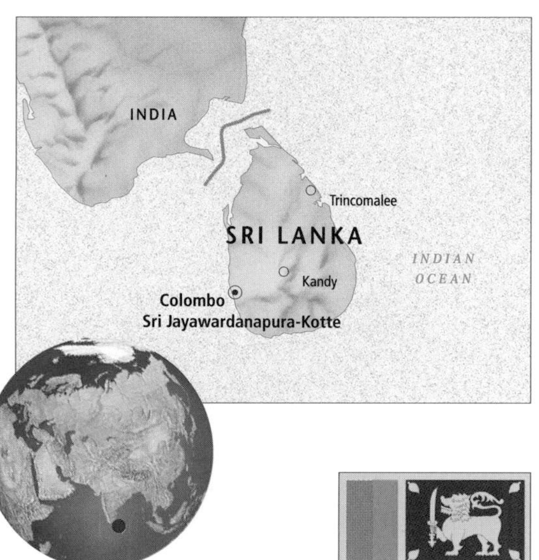

Fact File

Official name Democratic Socialist Republic of Sri Lanka

Form of government Republic with single legislative body (Parliament)

Capital Colombo (Sri Jayawardanapura-Kotte)

Area 65,610 sq km (25,332 sq miles)

Time zone GMT + 5.5 hours

Population 19,577,000

Projected population 2015 21,451,000

Population density 298.4 per sq km (772.8 per sq mile)

Life expectancy 72.4

Infant mortality (per 1,000) 15.7

Official language Sinhala, Tamil

Other languages Malayan, English

Literacy rate 90.2 %

Religions Buddhist 69 %, Hindu 15 %, Christian 8 %, Muslim 8 %

Ethnic groups Sinhalese 74 %, Tamil 18 %, Sri Lankan Moor 7 %, other 1 %

Currency Sri Lankan rupee

Economy Services 45 %, agriculture 43 %, industry 12 %

GNP per capita US$ 3,250

Climate Tropical; southwest wetter with most rain falling April to June and October to November; northeast drier with most rain falling December to February

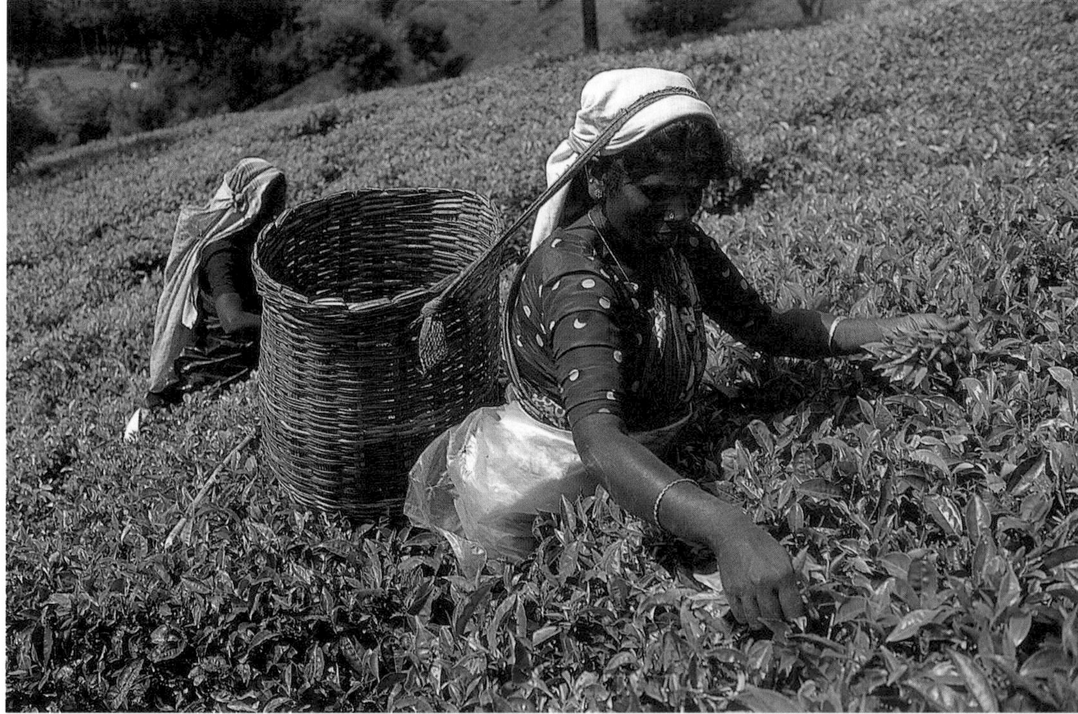

Highest point Mt Pidurutalagala 2,524 m (8,281 ft)

Map reference Page 216–17

Sri Lanka is a large, scenically dramatic island off India's southeast coast, and was known as Ceylon until 1972. It has a mountainous center, and a string of coral islets called "Adam's Bridge" link it to India in the northwest. Over the last 50 years the country has suffered intermittent strife. For over 1,000 years a minority of Hindu Tamils in the north and a majority of Sinhalese elsewhere have lived side by side. From the sixteenth century successive European nations—the Portuguese, the Dutch, and the British—visited and left their ethnic mark. Britain controlled the whole island from 1815, and brought in large numbers of additional Tamil plantation workers from south India later that century.

When Sri Lanka gained its independence in 1948 the majority Sinhalese stripped 800,000 Tamils of citizenship and the right to vote, and made Sinhala the country's sole official language. From that point onwards there has been civil unrest and from 1983 there has been civil war. The Tamil demand for an autonomous northern state has been complicated by separate leftist insurrections by radical Sinhalese seeking to overthrow the government. Sri Lanka has a large number of political parties and movements on the left (including one which is officially Trotskyist) which have added intransigence to its political life. Civil war and insurgencies have taken at least 50,000 lives.

With high mountains, intermontane plateaus, and steep river gorges, the rugged terrain of the central uplands dominates the island. Much of this higher ground is devoted to growing tea on large plantations. Falling away to the southwest, the terrain declines towards the sandy coastal lowlands where coconuts are grown (Sri Lanka is the world's fifth-largest producer). Rubber is the third important plantation crop. Overall, 37 percent of the country supports tropical vegetation and open woodland. Though it has been reduced by deforestation, rainforest still covers the wettest areas. The fertile, rice-growing northern plains are bordered to the southeast by the Mahaweli River.

Among Sri Lanka's mineral resources are a variety of precious and semi-precious stones including sapphire, ruby, tourmaline, and topaz. Also mined are graphite, mineral sands, and phosphates. About 43 percent of the workforce is engaged in agriculture, the main subsistence crop being rice—although production falls considerably short of the country's requirements. Fruit, vegetables, and spices are grown as staples as well as for export and Sri Lanka is one of the world's main exporters of tea. But today industry, dominated by the manufacture of clothing and expanding in special Export Processing Zones, has overtaken agriculture as the principal source of export earnings. The uncertain economic climate created by civil strife continues to cloud the nation's prospects, deterring tourists and discouraging foreign investment.

Maldives

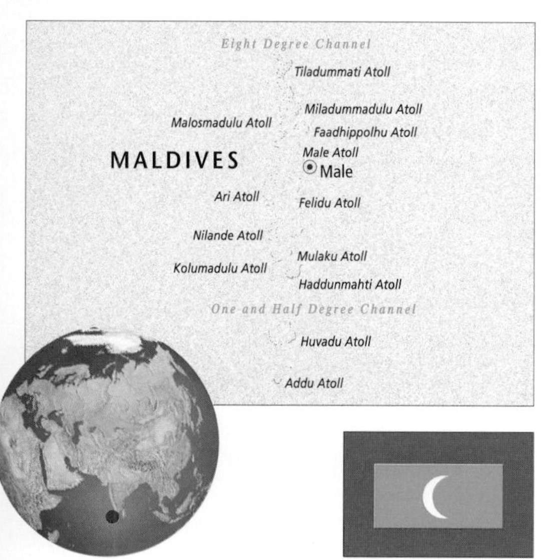

Fact File

Official name Republic of the Maldives

Form of government Republic with single legislative body (Citizens Council)

Capital Male

Area 300 sq km (116 sq miles)

Time zone GMT + 5 hours

Population 320,000

Projected population 2015 453,000

Population density 1,066.7 per sq km (2,758.6 per sq mile)

Life expectancy 62.9

Infant mortality (per 1,000) 61.9

Official language Divehi

Other languages Arabic, English, Hindi

Literacy rate 93.2 %

Religions Predominantly Sunni Muslim

Ethnic groups Sinhalese, Dravidian, Arab, African

Currency Rufiyaa

Economy Tourism, fishing, manufacturing

GNP per capita US$ 3,870

Climate Tropical, with wet season May to August

Highest point Unnamed location on Wilingili 24 m (79 ft)

Map reference Page 216

The Maldive Archipelago consists of an 800 km (500 mile) string of nearly 2,000 islands and atolls (202 of them inhabited) southwest of India's southern tip, Cape Comorin. Made up of tiny islets ringed by white sands and clear blue lagoons, they have recently been developed as tourist resorts and receive up to 300,000 visitors each year. Long ago, their first visitors were probably Dravidians from southern India, in around 400 BC. Centuries later, the islands seem to have been taken over by people from Sri Lanka—Divehi, the national language, is a form of Sinhalese, one of the official languages on Sri Lanka. In 1153 the king of the Maldives ordered his subjects to adopt Islam in place of Buddhism: today the people are mainly Sunni Muslims and there are 689 mosques. For the next 800 years the islands were ruled as a Muslim sultanate, though there was a brief period, between 1558 and 1573, of Portuguese control from Goa. The British established a protectorate in 1887, the islands achieved independence in 1965, and the sultan was deposed in 1968. Since then government has been in the hands of a small group of influential families, and by 1995 the president then in office, a wealthy businessman, had survived three attempted coups. Younger political contenders who have tasted democracy abroad are pressing for a more open regime.

The atolls of the Maldives are coral reefs which have grown up around the peaks of a submerged volcanic mountain range. None of them rise more than 1.8 m (6 ft) above sea level. There is concern that if the greenhouse effect causes a rise in sea levels, some may be submerged. Apart from that, the islands lose their natural protection due to the depletion of the reef—coral lime is often used as building material. Adequate rainfall supports a variety of tropical vegetation, and palm and breadfruit trees occur naturally.

Food crops include coconuts, bananas, mangoes, sweet potatoes, and spices. Agriculture plays a role in the economy, though constrained by the small amount of cultivable land, and most staple foods must be imported. In the lagoons and the open sea fish are plentiful. Bonito and tuna are leading exports, fishing being the second leading growth sector of the economy. Manufacturing, consisting mainly of garment production, boat building, and handicrafts, accounts for 15 percent of gross domestic product. Since the 1980s tourism has been the leading growth sector, and now accounts for more than 60 percent of foreign exchange receipts. At present more than 90 percent of tax revenue comes from import duties and tourism-related taxes.

India

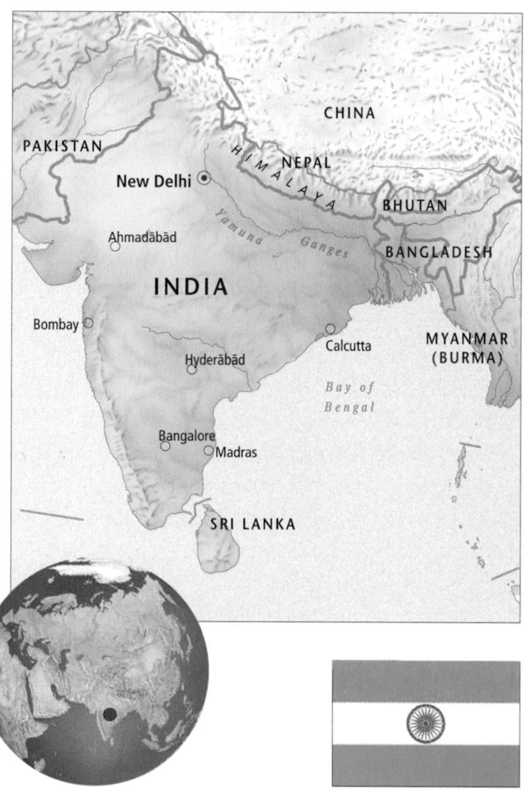

Fact File

Official name Republic of India

Form of government Federal republic with two legislative bodies (Council of States and People's Assembly)

Capital New Delhi

Area 3,287,590 sq km (1,269,338 sq miles)

Time zone GMT + 5.5 hours

Population 1,045,826,000

Projected population 2015 1,230,484,000

Population density 318.1 per sq km (823.9 per sq mile)

Life expectancy 63.2

Infant mortality (per 1,000) 61.5

Official languages Hindi, Bengali, Telugu, Marathi, Tamil, Urdu, Gujarati, Malayalam, Kannada, Oriya, Punjabi, Assamese, Kashmiri, Sindhi, Sanskrit, English

Other languages Hindustani, about 700 indigenous languages

Literacy rate 92 %

Religions Hindu 80 %, Muslim 14 %, Christian 2.4 %, Sikh 2 %, Buddhist 0.7 %, Jain 0.5 %, other 0.4 %

Ethnic groups Indo-Aryan 72 %, Dravidian 25 %, Mongoloid and other 3 %

Currency Indian rupee

Economy Agriculture 63 %, services 26 %, industry 11 %

GNP per capita US$ 2,540

Tea pickers on a tea estate in the highlands of Sri Lanka (left page top). The facade of a Hindu temple in Sri Lanka (left page bottom). One of the many palm-fringed beaches in the Maldives (below).

CLIMATE Tropical in south, temperate in north; monsoons June to September

HIGHEST POINT Kanchenjunga 8,598 m (28,208 ft)

MAP REFERENCE Pages 216–17, 218–19

India is the world's largest democracy, and one of the oldest and most successful in Asia. It is also the world's second most populous country, encompassing a great variety of peoples, several major religious groupings, and more than 700 languages. In the fifty plus years since it gained independence from Britain in 1947, India has on the whole managed humanely and responsibly where other countries in the region have become totalitarian, or succumbed to military rule.

There are, however, major conflicts—there have been three wars with neighboring Pakistan alone. The dispute with Pakistan over the territory of Kashmir remains unresolved. The caste system produces endemic injustice. Millions of its citizens live in desperate poverty. But Indians can change their government democratically by going to the polls, and the lot of most people has slowly but steadily improved. After a long period of state regulation of industry, significant barriers that hinder outside investment, and a maze of protectionist controls, the country is beginning to open its economy to the outside world. Population growth, however, at a rate of 1.44 percent on a base of more than a billion people, tends to cancel out much of the potential benefit from the nation's gains.

Physical features and land use

North to south, India can be divided into three main regions: the Himalayas and their foothills; the Indo-Gangetic Plain; and the Deccan Plateau. From the northernmost border, the heavily glaciated terrain of the Himalayas—the world's highest mountains—cover 15 percent of the total surface area. The name itself comes from the Nepalese *him* ("snows") and *alya* ("home of"), the mountains being revered as the home of the gods. They rise to elevations of over 7,000 m (23,000 ft) in the Ladakh and Karakoram ranges. The western highlands towards the Karakorams are harsh, dry, and inhabited only by small communities of herdspeople. At lower altitudes alpine meadows are grazed by the sheep of migratory pastoralists who arrive in the summer with their flocks. Lower still, rice terraces and orchards are found in the Vale of Kashmir.

The eastern highlands of northern Assam are markedly different. They are much wetter—this is where rhododendrons and magnolias grow wild and where terraced hills support buckwheat, barley, and rice. The climate of the high plateau of Meghalaya, separated from the Himalayas by the valley of the Brahmaputra River, is damp and cool. On its southern flanks Cherrapunji has one of the world's highest rainfalls, averaging 10,798 mm (421.1 in) per year.

South of the northern mountains lie the terai or foothill plains; still further south the main plains region of India stretches from the western coastal lowlands, in a northern arc past the Thar

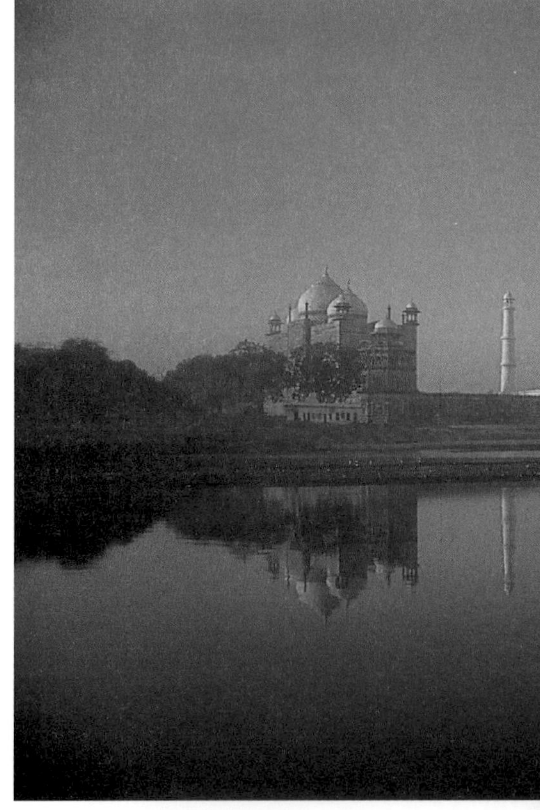

Desert and down the Gangetic Plain to the mouth of the Hooghly River on the Bay of Bengal. In the northwest—the Punjab and Haryana—farmers grow winter wheat, summer rice, cotton, and sugarcane, with sorghum in the drier areas. On the lowlands of the central part of Uttar Pradesh millet and sorghum are preferred to wheat and rice. Jute is cultivated where the Ganges enters the distribu-

Timeline

c. 3500 BC First civilizations in Indus Valley (now Pakistan)—planting crops and domesticating sheep, cattle, and goats

2600 BC Dravidian peoples develop cities of Harappa and Mohenjo Daro in Indus Valley

1500 BC Aryan tribes from central Asia force Dravidians southward. Aryans plant wheat and barley, and introduce caste system

530 BC First invasion by Persians (Iranians) who sieze Gandhara (now Afghanistan) and parts of Punjab

c. 500 BC Buddhism becomes widely accepted over the next 300 years but Hinduism eventually predominates

326 BC Alexander the Great invades India near the Indus River (now Pakistan) but is unable to sustain the colony when attacked

320 BC Maurya Dynasty (until c. 185 BC) rules an empire covering almost all India from a base at Patna

300 AD Gupta Dynasty begins. Separate kingdoms allowed to prosper within the Gupta Empire for 200 years

1200 Delhi Sultanate brings Muslim rule to India, destroying many Hindu temples and building great mosques in their place

1497 Vasco da Gama reaches trading port of Calicut; Portuguese later establish trading supremacy in Indian Ocean

1526 Babar conquers northern India, establishing Mogul Empire. Empire prospers for 200 years

1555 Emperor Akbar the Great, regarded as the greatest of the Moguls, subdues Rajput princes to control India

1632 Taj Mahal bui at Agra by Emperor Shah Jehan in memory of his wife Mumtaz Mahal (completed 1643)

Women washing clothes beside the Ganges in Varanasi (left page bottom left). Drying chilis in Rajasthan (left page bottom right). The Taj Mahal near Agra (top center). The severe poverty of innumerable people such as those here in the streets of Varanasi is one of the major problems in India (above).

tary system of the delta, while mangrove swamps line the marine margins of the delta itself.

The Thar Desert in the northwest contains a broad area of dunes in Rajasthan; southwest of this lie the cotton-growing lands of Gujarat, which includes the low peninsular plateau of Kathiawar between the Gulf of Khambhat and the Gulf of Khachchh, not far from the Pakistan border. The Vindya Range east of the Gulf of Khambhat separates the Indo-Gangetic Plain from peninsular India and the Deccan Plateau. This plateau contains some of the world's oldest rocks, large tracts being covered with later basalt flows. The western edge of the plateau is defined by the mountain chain of the Western Ghats. At the foot of these mountains lies a coastal plain with coconut groves, fishing villages, rice fields, and tapioca plantations. On the plateau itself the main crops are millet and pulses.

History

Of India's various civilizations, the earliest developed in the Indus Valley (c. 2600 BC) and in the Ganges Valley (c. 1500 BC). At this time the subcontinent was mainly peopled by ethnic Dravidians. It is thought that the Indus civilization succumbed to an invasion of Sanskrit-speaking Aryan peoples who introduced the caste system, a scheme of social division that is fundamental in Indian life. Another important early civilization was the Maurya, which under Ashoka, who reigned from 273 to 232 BC, came to dominate the subcontinent. Later, a succession of Arab, Turkish, and Mongol influences led to the founding of the Mogul Empire in 1526, which under Akbar (1542–1605) was extended throughout most of northern India and part of the Deccan. It was during the time of Mogul rule that the Taj Mahal was built by Shah Jahan.

The British effectively controlled India from 1805, introducing a civil service and a code of law during the nineteenth century which have profoundly shaped the nation since that time. With the advent of independence in 1947, the division between Hindus and Muslims resulted in the violent and tumultuous partition of the country into India and Pakistan. This first major division to split the country indicates that the most serious rifts within Indian society tend to be religious. In recent years the Sikhs of the Punjab have also been agitating for independence.

Economy

Once essentially rural, India's economy is now a mix of village farming, modern agriculture, handicrafts, a variety of modern industries, and innumerable support services. During the 1980s economic growth allowed a marked increase in real per capita private consumption. Since 1991 production, trade, and investment reforms have provided new opportunities for Indian business and some 200 million middle-class consumers. Among the nation's strengths is a home market of some 900 million, along with a workforce that includes many who are highly skilled, including those trained in high-tech areas such as computer programming.

The textile sector is highly efficient. There has been a massive rise in foreign investment as the country has been opened up to foreign competition. The downside of this situation includes a sizeable budget deficit along with high defense spending (including that for nuclear weapons) because of the continuing conflict with Pakistan. Other negative features include an absence of even elementary social services, poor roads, inadequate port facilities, and an antiquated telecommunications system.

STATES AND CAPITALS

Andhra Pradesh • Hyderabad
Arunachal Pradesh • Itanagar
Assam • Dispur
Bihar • Patna
Goa • Panaji
Gujarat • Gandhinagar
Haryana • Chandigarh
Himachal Pradesh • Simla
Jammu and Kashmir • Srinagar (summer) Jammu (winter)
Karnataka • Bangalore
Kerala • Trivandrum
Madhya Pradesh • Bhopal
Maharashtra • Mumbai (Bombay)
Manipur • Imphal
Meghalaya • Shillong
Mizoram • Aizawi
Nagaland • Kohima
Orissa • Bhubaneswar
Punjab • Chandigarh
Rajastan • Jaipur
Sikkim • Gangtok
Tamil Nadu • Madras
Tripura • Agartala
Uttar Pradesh • Lucknow
West Bengal • Calcutta

UNION TERRITORIES

Andaman and Nicobar Islands • Port Blair
Chandigarh • Chandigarh
Dadra and Nagar Haveli • Silvassa
Daman and Diu • Daman
Delhi • Delhi
Lakshadweep • Kavaratti
Pondicherry • Pondicherry

1740 East India Co (founded 1600) takes over Mogul land. Dutch, British establish ports at Madras, Bombay, Calcutta

1769 Severe famines in Bengal lead to rural depopulation for more than 20 years

1800 East India Co trades between Britain, Europe, China. India produces raw materials for British factories

1850 Failure of monsoon rains causes famines in northern India for more than 30 years

1857 Indian Revolt against heavy taxes results in considerable loss of British and Indian lives. It is ruthlessly suppressed

1876 Queen Victoria becomes Empress of India

1880s Indian Nationalist Movement begins pressure for an end to British rule; violent attacks by extremists

1883 Commission on famine recommends building irrigation canals to supply water from Himalayas to grain-producing areas

1921 After more than 12 million deaths in flu epidemic of 1918–19 India's population surges; by 1921 it passes 250 million

1943 Severe food shortages in Bengal made worse by the army using scarce supplies results in loss of many lives

1947 India gains independence. Pakistan becomes a separate Muslim state (East and West). India takes over Kashmir

1965 Border war with Pakistan over Kashmir

1971 East Pakistan becomes independent country of Bangladesh; India's population reaches 500 million

1998 India tests nuclear weapons, followed by Pakistan; tension over Kashmir issue continues

2001, 2002 Severe terrorist attacks are blamed on Pakistan and lead India and Pakistan to the brink of a nuclear war

Bangladesh

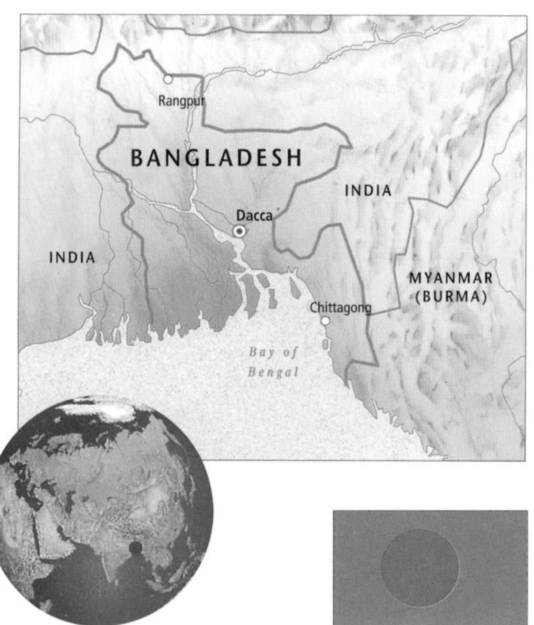

Bangladesh: women doing agricultural work (top). Bus station in Dacca, Bangladesh (above). The Taksang monastery in Bhutan (right page bottom).

Fact File

Official name People's Republic of Bangladesh

Form of government Republic with single legislative body (National Parliament)

Capital Dacca

Area 144,000 sq km (55,598 sq miles)

Time zone GMT + 6 hours

Population 133,377,000

Projected population 2015 183,159,000

Population density 926.2 per sq km (2,399.0 per sq mile)

Life expectancy 60.9

Infant mortality (per 1,000) 68.1

Official language Bangla

Other language Other Indo-Aryan as well as Tibeto-Burmese languages, Munda, Mon-Khmer-languages, English

Literacy rate 56 %

Religions Muslim 83 %, Hindu 16 %, other (mainly Buddhist, Christian) 1 %

Ethnic groups Bengali 98 %, Biharis and tribal peoples 2 %

Currency Taka

Economy Agriculture 57 %, services 33 %, industry 10%

GNP per capita US$ 1,750

Climate Tropical, with three seasons: cool, dry winter (October to March); hot, humid summer (March to June); and cool, wet monsoon (June to October)

Highest point Mt Keokradong 1,230 m (4,035 ft)

Map reference Page 219

Known for tropical cyclones and endemic poverty, the small and densely populated country of Bangladesh lies north of the Bay of Bengal. Most of its frontier is with India and it has a short border with Myanmar (Burma) in the southeast. The name Bangladesh means "the land of the Bengalis", a people who have contributed a great deal to Indian history. Once a part of the Mauryan Empire of the fourth century BC, Bengal has been mainly Muslim since the thirteenth century, though during its more recent history its Muslim people have often been ruled by Hindu overlords. At the time of the partition of India in 1947, this situation led to the founding of East Pakistan, the oriental wing of the Muslim state that was set up following independence from Britain. In 1971 resentment of the power and privileges accorded to West Pakistan resulted in East Pakistan breaking away and forming the independent state of Bangladesh. Since then its history has been one of political coups, dissolved parliaments and civil unrest, compounded by recurring natural disasters. In 1991 the worst cyclone in memory killed over 140,000 people.

Bangladesh is low and flat, its physiography determined by three navigable rivers—the Ganges (Padma), Brahmaputra (Jamuna) and the smaller Meghna. At their confluence they form the biggest delta in the world. The western part of this delta, which is over the border in India, is somewhat higher, and is less subject to flooding. What is called the "active delta" lies in Bangladesh and this region is frequently flooded. During monsoons the water rises as much as 6 m (18 ft) above sea level, submerging two-thirds of the country, and the delta's changing channels are also hazardous to life, health, and property. However, the floods are also beneficial in that they renew soil fertility with silt, some of it washed down from as far away as Tibet. Whole new islands are formed by alluvial deposition, and the highly fertile silt can yield as many as three rice crops a year. The far southeastern region of Chittagong has the only high country in Bangladesh, with forested ridges and rubber plantations.

Bangladesh is a major recipient of international aid. Disbursements of aid are currently running at more than 1,000 times the annual value of foreign investment. Despite the efforts of the international community, however, it remains one of the world's poorest and least developed nations. Rice is the main crop in the country's basically agrarian economy, followed by jute, tea, and sugarcane. Bangladesh is the world's largest supplier of high quality jute. About half the crop is exported in its raw form and the rest is processed for export as hessian, sacking, and carpet backing. A modern paper industry utilizes bamboo from the hills. Other industries include textiles, fertilizer, glass, iron and steel, sugar, cement, and aluminum. Fishing, in the wide net of freshwater rivers and lakes as well as in the Bay of Bengal, is also economically important. An important source of foreign currencies are the money transfers of the many Bangladeshis working abroad. They send substantial amounts to support their families at home. However, there are a number of serious impediments to further progress. They include frequent cyclones and floods, inefficient state-owned enterprises, a labor force growing (as a consequence of a steady population growth) faster than it can be absorbed by agriculture alone, the desolate infrastructure and delays in developing energy resources such as natural gas, which is the only fuel that is gained in any amount worth mentioning. A program intended to achieve a higher liberalization of the economy has been introduced; however, corruption and the meddling and interfering of the military as well as the inertia of political forces have made it hard to bring the program to fruition.

Issues in Bangladesh

After 15 years of military rule multi-party politics returned to Bangladesh in 1990, and the country's first woman prime minister, Begum Khaleda Zia, leader of the Bangladesh Nationalist Party (BNP), was elected in 1991. However, in the same year the authority of the president was severely curtailed and political factionalism divides the nation. Bangladesh remains politically unstable.

There are few major differences in the national policies of the political parties and the antagonism between them appears to be fuelled largely by the dislike of the country's prominent female politicians for each other (the opposition Awami League is also led by a woman). Despite the fact that women are heading the political system, women in Bangladesh face discrimination in health care, education, and employment. In addition, dowry related violence against women does occur.

Religious divides exist, as elsewhere in the region. Tension between Bangladesh's Hindus and the Muslim majority is a problem, and Buddhist tribes in the southeast are agitating for autonomous rule. Relations with neighboring India are also strained, although in 1996 the countries signed a treaty agreeing to share resources after an Indian dam on the Ganges River reduced water available for irrigation in Bangladesh.

An exodus of refugees from Myanmar (Burma)—as many as 200,000 by early 1992—also stretches Bangladesh's scarce resources.

International aid finances 90 percent of state capital spending and an economic liberalization program has been introduced.

Bhutan

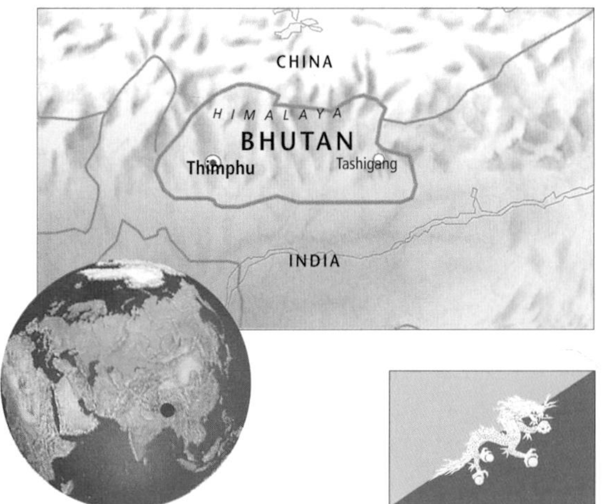

Fact File

Official name Kingdom of Bhutan

Form of government Monarchy with single legislative body (National Assembly)

Capital Thimphu

Area 47,000 sq km (18,147 sq miles)

Time zone GMT + 5.5 hours

Population 2,094,000

Projected population 2015 3,070,000

Population density 44.6 per sq km (115.4 per sq mile)

Life expectancy 53.2

Infant mortality (per 1,000) 106.8

Official language Dzongkha

Other languages Tibeto-Burmanese (among them Bumthangkha, Sarchopkha, Tsangla) and Indo-Aryan languages (including Nepalese)

Literacy rate 42.2 %

Religions Lamaistic Buddhism 75 %, Hinduism 25 %

Ethnic groups Bhote (Tibetan) 50 %, ethnic Nepalese 35 %, indigenous or migrant tribes 15 %

Currency Ngultrum

Economy Agriculture 93 %, services 5 %, industry and commerce 2 %

GNP per capita US$ 1,200

Climate Tropical on southern plains; cool winters and hot summers in central valleys; cold winters and cool summers in mountains

Highest point Kula Kangri 7,553 m (24,780 ft)

Map reference Page 219

A tiny landlocked kingdom nestling in the Himalayas between India and Tibet, Bhutan is difficult to visit, and remains largely closed to the outside world. It is the world's most "rural" country, with less than six percent of its population living in towns and over ninety percent dependent on agriculture to make their living. Despite its isolation and apparent tranquillity, the country is torn by fierce, long-standing ethnic tensions which its absolute monarch does little to mitigate. Bhutan's longest-resident ethnic group consists of the Tibetans who probably migrated there 1,000 years ago. Early in the twentieth century, in order to end continual fighting between rival warlords in the area, the British administration in neighboring India established a hereditary monarch in Bhutan, the "Dragon King", in 1907.

The monarch is head of both the state and the government. Though the current king is a modernizer, intent on changing Bhutan's feudal ways, his emphasis on a sense of national identity founded on the language, laws, and dress of his own Drukpa group has stirred up bitter opposition among the resident Hindu Nepalese in southern Bhutan. Many have been deported, and others have fled to

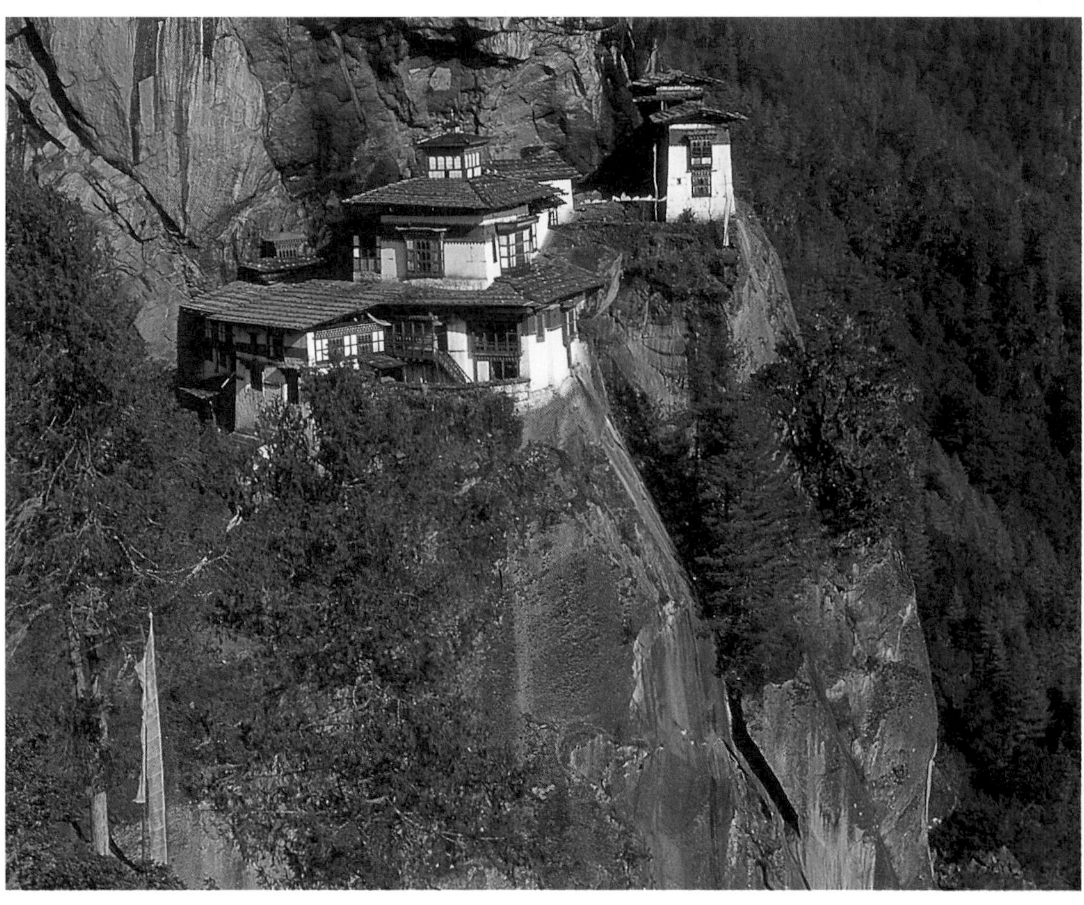

refugee camps in southeast Nepal. Dzongkha, which has been proclaimed the official language of the country, is the natural language of only sixteen percent of Bhutan citizens. In 1998 the king announced that in the future Bhutan's rulers would have to step down if they received a no-confidence vote from the National Assembly.

There are three main regions distinguished largely by altitude—the Great Himalayas, crowned by enormous peaks along the border with Tibet; the slopes and fertile valleys of the Lesser Himalayas, which are divided by the Wong, Sankosh, Tongsa and Manas Rivers; and the Duars Plain which opens out towards India from the foothills of the mountains. The central uplands and foothills are cultivated with food staples including maize, wheat, barley, and potatoes. This area supports the greatest portion of the population. Below this the Duars Plain falls away into broad tracts of semitropical forest, savanna, and bamboo jungle. Forests still cover nearly 75 percent of Bhutan's land area, and timber is both exported to India and used in Bhutan itself as fuel.

Almost all trade is with India. As an export, timber is outweighed in importance by cement. Other revenue-earning activities include a closely supervised and limited tourist industry (visitors are restricted to 4,000 per year), as well as the sale of stamps. Bhutan has tremendous hydropower potential, but most manufacturing is of the cottage-industry type. Development projects such as road construction rely to a alrge extent on Indian migrant labor. Though stabilized at a low level (the economy is one of the world's smallest and poorest) the country's balance of payments is strong, with comfortable reserves.

Mt Everest and surrounding peaks in Nepal (below). Villagers on a suspension bridge in northern Pakistan (right page top). The road between Quetta in Pakistan and the border with Iran (right page bottom).

Nepal

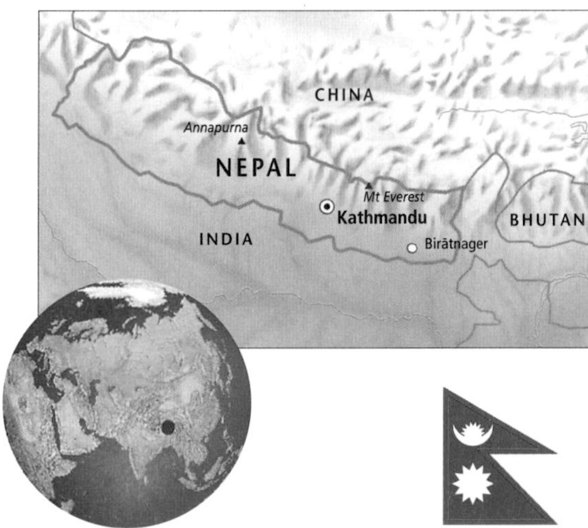

Fact File

Official name Kingdom of Nepal

Form of government Constitutional monarchy with two legislative bodies (National Council and House of Representatives)

Capital Kathmandu

Area 140,800 sq km (54,363 sq miles)

Time zone GMT + 5.5 hours

Population 25,874,000

Projected population 2015 32,138,000

Population density 183.8 per sq km (475.9 per sq mile)

Life expectancy 58.6

Infant mortality (per 1,000) 72.4

Official language Nepali

Other languages Indo-Aryan languages (among them Maithili and Bihari), Tibeto-Burmese languages (including Tamang, Newari)

Literacy rate 27.5 %

Religions Hindu 90 %, Buddhist 5 %, Muslim 3 %, other 2 %

Ethnic groups Nepalese 52 %, Maithili 11 %, Bhojpuri 8 %, Tamang 4 %, Newari 3 %, others 22 %

Currency Nepalese rupee

Economy Agriculture 93 %, services 6 %, industry 1 %

GNP per capita US$ 1,400

Climate Subtropical in south, with wet season July to October; cold and snowy in north, wetter in east

Highest point Mt Everest 8,848 m (29,028 ft)

Map reference Pages 218–19

The birthplace of the Buddha in c. 568 BC, Nepal is a small landlocked kingdom on the southern slopes of the Himalayas. It is surrounded by India to the west, south, and east, and has a border with China (Tibet) to the north. Tourists coming to trek in the mountains and climb the peaks contribute to national income, but Nepal remains one of the world's poorest countries. Historically, it was influenced both by the Buddhist/Mongol culture of Tibet and by the Hindu/Indian culture of the subcontinent. The present royal family established its rule in 1769. During British colonial rule in India a British resident was installed to provide "guidance" in foreign affairs. In 1959 the country's first elections were held (the Nepali Congress party winning), but in 1960 the king suspended the constitution, and no further elections were held until 1992. In the late 1990s a parliamentary impasse existed: neither the Nepali Congress nor the United Marxist-Leninist (UML) parties had clear majorities enabling them to govern in their own right. On June 1, 2002, the king and nine of his family members were killed in a massacre. His brother and successor is trying to introduce a more liberal system in the country.

The mountainous heart of Nepal, consisting of the towering Himalayas (including the highest and third-highest peaks in the world, Mt Everest and Kanchenjunga) and the lower Siwalik Range to the south, covers three-quarters of the country. Three main river systems cut the Himalayas, the Karnali (feeding the Ganges), the Gandak, and the Kosi. Kathmandu stands among fruit trees and rice fields typical of Nepal's densely populated uplands. Further south, on the Terai/Ganges Plain, farming settlements grow rice, wheat, maize, sugarcane, and jute which are the country's economic maintstay.

Some ninety percent of Nepalis live by subsistence farming, and many do not live well: more than forty percent of Nepal's citizens are undernourished. Most industry is concerned with the processing of jute, sugarcane, tobacco, and grain. Recently textile and carpet production has expanded and now provides 85 percent of foreign exchange earnings. The country has limitless hydropower resources. Electricity could be sold to Indian industry south of the border, and various schemes have been proposed, but environmental considerations weigh against them. Restructuring is needed. International aid funds 62 percent of Nepal's development budget and 34 percent of total budgetary expenditure.

Pakistan

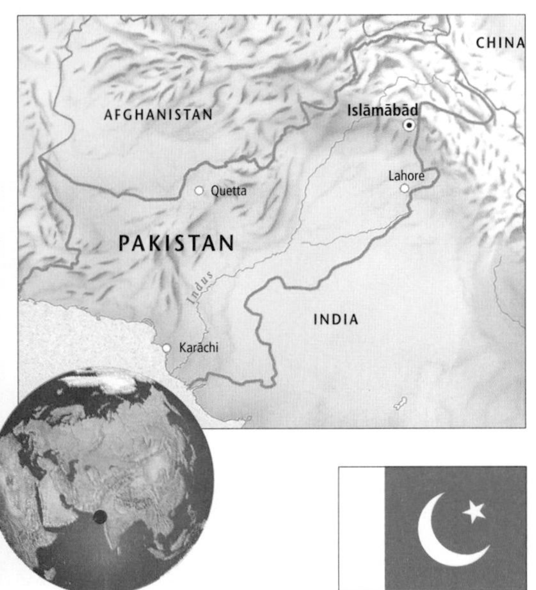

Fact File

OFFICIAL NAME Islamic Republic of Pakistan

FORM OF GOVERNMENT Republic with two legislative bodies (Senate and National Assembly)

CAPITAL Islāmābād

AREA 803,940 sq km (310,401 sq miles)

TIME ZONE GMT + 5 hours

POPULATION 147,664,000

PROJECTED POPULATION 2015 204,267,000

POPULATION DENSITY 183.7 per sq km (475.7 per sq mile)

LIFE EXPECTANCY 61.8

INFANT MORTALITY (PER 1,000) 78.5

OFFICIAL LANGUAGES Urdu

OTHER LANGUAGES Punjabi, Sindhi, Urdu, Pashto, Baluchi, Brahvi, English

LITERACY RATE 42.7 %

RELIGIONS Muslim 97 % (Sunni 77 %, Shi'a 20 %), other (Christian, Hindu) 3 %

ETHNIC GROUPS Punjabi 50 %, Sindhi 15 %, Pashtun (Pathan) 15 %, Mohajir (Indian immigrants and their descendants) 8 %, Baloch 5 %, other 7 %

CURRENCY Pakistani rupee

ECONOMY Agriculture 50 %, services 38 %, industry 12 %

GNP PER CAPITA US$ 2,100

CLIMATE Mainly arid; temperate in northwest, cold and snowy in mountains

HIGHEST POINT K2 8,611 m (28,251 ft)

MAP REFERENCE Page 221

Pakistan occupies the valley of the Indus and its tributaries in the northwest of the Indian subcontinent. Its most sensitive political frontiers are with India to the east and Afghanistan to the west. It has shorter borders with Iran and China.

A part of India until 1947, Pakistan shares with it a history of early civilizations, migrations, and invasions—farmers in the Indus Valley were already using elaborate irrigation works by the second millennium BC. At the time of partition in

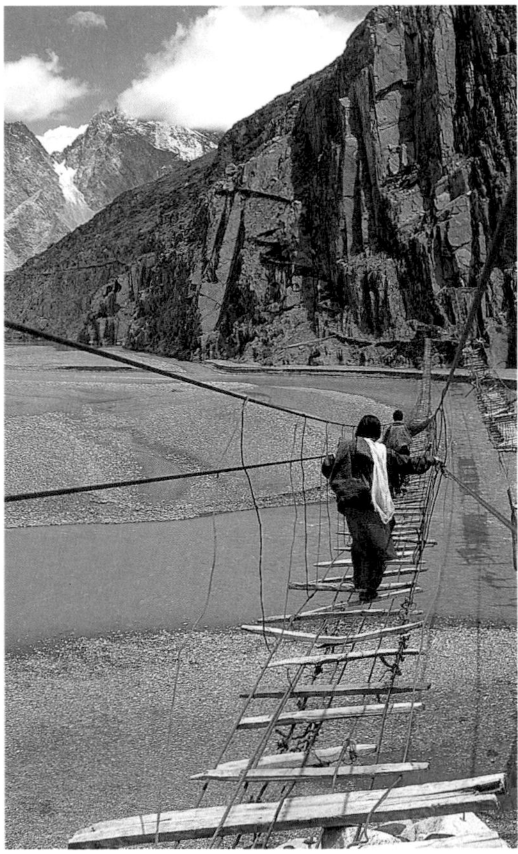

1947, Pakistan was two widely separated territories (West and East Pakistan). A dispute over Kashmir has poisoned relations with India since that time. In 1971 East Pakistan achieved independence as Bangladesh. In that year the populist leader Ali Bhutto assumed power in Pakistan, and in 1973 announced a program of "Islamic socialism" under which banks, insurance companies, heavy industry, and even education were nationalized. Since 1977, when he was overthrown by General Zia ul-Haq (and subsequently executed), military and civilian rule have alternated, accompanied by varying degrees of violence and disorder.

Although 97 percent of Pakistan's population is Muslim, there is a wide range of ethnic groupings, languages, and conflicts. The main linguistic separation is between Iranian languages such as Baluchi and Pashto on one hand, and the Indo-Aryan languages of Punjabi, Sindhi, and Urdu on the other. Each of Pakistan's minorities has its own particular concerns. In the northwest of the country the Pathans want to join their kinsmen over the Afghan frontier. The Urdu-speaking Mohajirs migrated by the millions from India at the time of partition and make up the majority of the population in Karachi and Hyderabad. They resent Punjabi domination and the rule of the old land-owning elite.

The whole of Pakistan is drained by the Indus River. Rising in the Great Highlands of the north it flows southwest, joined by tributaries such as the Jhelum, Chenab, Beas, Ravi, and Sutlej, and forms a fertile and densely populated floodplain in the east of the country before spilling into the Arabian Sea. The waters of this basin feed into one of the largest irrigation systems in the world, the total area being 13 million hectares (32 million acres). Two constructions, one at Tarbela on the Indus, and the other at Mangla on the Jhelum, are among the world's biggest earth- and rock-filled dams. West of the Indus delta is an ascending landscape of alternating ridges and arid basins, some containing salt marshes like the Hamun-i-Mashkel. In the extreme northwest are the Great Highlands, with the Khyber Pass on the frontier with Afghanistan to the west and the spectacular peaks of the Karakoram and Pamirs to the east. Along with Nanga Parbat, these include the second highest mountain in the world—K2, Mt Godwin Austen (8,611 m; 28,251 ft) on the border of Tibet.

Irrigation agriculture combined with the new plant varieties that were introduced as part of the "green revolution" during the 1970s produces abundant cotton, wheat, rice, and sugarcane. Fruit and vegetables are also grown widely, while opium poppies and cannabis are illegally cultivated to supply the international drug trade. Despite the fact that approximately half the population work on the land, agriculture now accounts for less than a quarter of the national income.

Karachi is a considerable manufacturing center for the production of textiles, as is Lahore. Other industries produce a wide variety of petroleum products, construction materials, foodstuffs, and paper products. The country has large reserves of unused minerals: copper, bauxite, phosphates, and manganese. However, Pakistan also faces a range of problems. The country's economy is dependent on the highly competitive textile sector, there is a chronic trade deficit and debt burden, and much of the nation's revenue goes into funding massive defense spending on items such as nuclear weaponry and the army.

Saudi Arabia

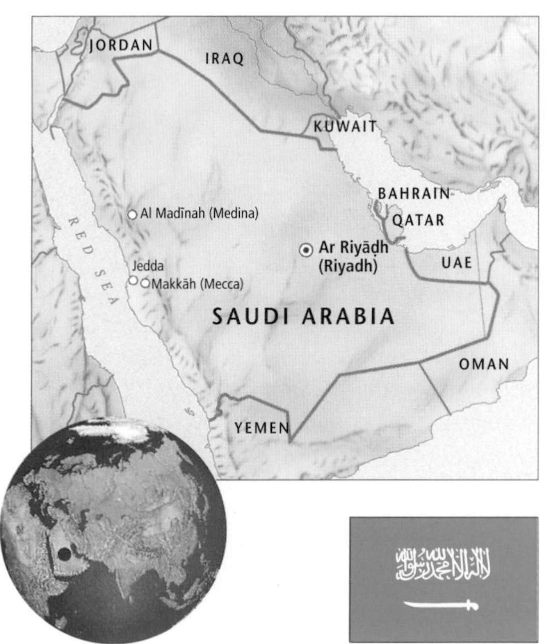

Fact File

OFFICIAL NAME Kingdom of Saudi Arabia

FORM OF GOVERNMENT Monarchy with advisory Consultative Council

CAPITAL Ar Riyadh (Riyadh)

AREA 1,960,582 sq km (756,981 sq miles)

TIME ZONE GMT + 3 hours

POPULATION 23,514,000

PROJECTED POPULATION 2015 31,748,000

POPULATION DENSITY 12 per sq km (31.1 per sq mile)

LIFE EXPECTANCY 68.4

INFANT MORTALITY (PER 1,000) 49.6

OFFICIAL LANGUAGE Arabic

OTHER LANGUAGE English

LITERACY RATE 78 %

RELIGIONS Sunni Muslim 85 %, Shi'a Muslim 15 %

ETHNIC GROUPS Arab 90 %, mixed African-Asian 10 %

CURRENCY Saudi riyal

ECONOMY Agriculture 49 %, services 37 %, industry 14 %

GNP PER CAPITA US$ 10,600

CLIMATE Mainly hot and arid; some areas rainless for years

HIGHEST POINT Jabal Sawdā' 3,133 m (10,279 ft)

MAP REFERENCE Pages 220–21

Saudi Arabia occupies the majority of the Arabian Peninsula and covers an area about the size of western Europe. With one-quarter of the world's petroleum reserves, it supplies several major industrial nations with oil. Its role as the custodian of Islam's most holy places, Mecca (Makkah) and Medina (Al Madīnah), is an equally important feature of this country. Aloof from international affairs for many years, Saudis steeled themselves to fight Iraq (which they had earlier supported) in 1990–91. The 500,000 Western troops who entered the country (considered by many to be a profanation of Muslim land) were seen by Saudis as both necessary and unwelcome. The war highlighted tensions in a society which remains largely feudal in terms of politics (192 people were beheaded in 1995), yet because of its oil cannot entirely escape the influence of the modern world.

Mecca was Muhammad's birth-place (c. 570) and Medina (al Madīnah) the place where Islam was born. In the eighteenth century the Sa'ud Bedouins adopted a severe branch of Islam—the Wahhabi Movement. With its austere criminal code, this was established by the Saudis throughout their country early in the twentieth century. During the 1930s most Saudis were still living traditional desert lives, but this changed dramatically when oil was found near Riyadh in 1937. The lavish spending for which the royal family was known in the 1960s and 1970s ended with the sharp drop in oil prices of the 1980s. This is now starting to have effects on society as a whole. People who were content to live under absolute monarchic rule with prodigious benefits may now increasingly be questioning the balance of power. Per capita income fell from $17,000 in 1981 to $10,600 in 2002.

A range of mountains extends northwest to southeast, parallel to the Red Sea, arising to 3,133 m (10,279 ft) at Jabal Sawdā in the southwest, which is Saudi Arabia's highest peak. The Asir Highlands in this southwestern corner is the only region that receives reliable rainfall. Benefiting from the monsoon, the slopes are terraced to grow grain and fruit trees. Further east, separated from the mountains by a wide stretch of basaltic lava, is the high central desert plateau of Najd. The eastern border of this region is a vast arc of sandy desert, broadening into the two dune-wastes of Arabia: An Nafūd in the north, and Ar Rub' al Khāli, or "Empty Quarter", to the south—the latter being the world's largest expanse of sand. Some Bedouin nomads still live here as traders and herdsmen. Over 95 percent of Saudi Arabia is arid or semiarid desert.

Petroleum accounts for 75 percent of budget revenue, 35 percent of gross domestic product, and ninety percent of export earnings. Saudi Arabia has the largest known reserves of petroleum in the world (26 percent of the proven total), is the single largest exporter of petroleum, and has taken full advantage of this by developing world-class associated industries. For more than a decade, however, expenditures have outstripped income. The government plans to restrain public spending and encourage more non-oil exports. As many as 4 million foreign workers are employed in Saudi Arabia, and the 2 million pilgrims who come to make the traditional pilgrimage to Mecca each year also contribute largely to national income.

Pilgrims in Mecca (left). Saudis at a market wearing traditional dress (above). A Yemeni desert town (right page).

Yemen

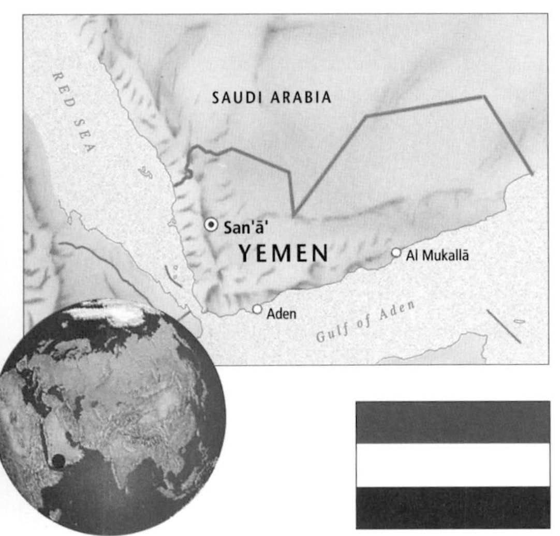

Fact File

OFFICIAL NAME Republic of Yemen

FORM OF GOVERNMENT Republic with single legislative body (House of Representatives)

CAPITAL San'ā'

AREA 527,970 sq km (203,849 sq miles)

TIME ZONE GMT + 3 hours

POPULATION 18,702,000

PROJECTED POPULATION 2015 33,118,000

POPULATION DENSITY 35.4 per sq km (91.7 per sq mile)

LIFE EXPECTANCY 60.6

INFANT MORTALITY (PER 1,000) 66.8

OFFICIAL LANGUAGE Arabic

OTHER LANGUAGE South Arab languages (e. g. Soqutri)

LITERACY RATE 38 %

RELIGIONS Muslim: predominantly Sunni in the south, Shi'ite majority in the north

ETHNIC GROUPS Predominantly Arab; small mixed African-Arab and Indian minorities

CURRENCY Yemeni rial

ECONOMY Agriculture 63 %, services 26 %, industry 11 %

GNP PER CAPITA US$ 820

CLIMATE Mainly arid; humid in southwest and cooler in western highlands; drier in east

HIGHEST POINT Jabal an-Nabi Shu'ayb 3,760 m (12,336 ft)

MAP REFERENCE Page 220

Yemen occupies the southwestern corner of the Arabian Peninsula. Although its people have been Muslim for centuries it has deeply divided political allegiances and was two separate countries until 1990. North Yemen became independent of the Ottoman Empire in 1918, and in 1962 the Yemen Arab Republic (YAR) was proclaimed. The politics of the YAR tended to be conservative and Islamic. South Yemen came under British influence in 1839 and Aden became a vital port on the sea route to India. In 1967 the British withdrew from the region, and in 1969 the People's Democratic Republic of Yemen was proclaimed—the only Marxist state in the Arab world.

The north and south had been mutually hostile since independence, but a turning point came with the Soviet collapse in 1989. Having lost USSR support, South Yemen sought political union with the YAR. In 1990 the two countries became the Republic of Yemen. In 1994 an assassination attempt on a northern politician led to civil war and the south's attempted secession. An uneasy peace prevails.

The narrow Red Sea coastal plain of Tihāma, extending south from Saudi Arabia, is generally barren: here, cotton-growing predominates. From the coast the land rises steeply to a comparatively fertile and well-cultivated interior. Around San'ā' vines are cultivated and a variety of fruit crops are grown. The mountains overlooking San'ā' rise to Jabal an-Nabi Shu'ayb, the highest point on the Arabian Peninsula. From these heights a number of rivers drain east toward the Ar Rub' al Khālī (Empty Quarter) where they disappear into the sands. Along the coast of the Gulf of Aden a sandy plain rises inland to the rugged Yemen Plateau, which to the north slopes down to the uninhabited wastes of the Rub al-Khali. In this region ten percent of the mainly rural population are nomadic.

Despite oil and gas reserves, Yemen is weak economically. In the Gulf War of 1990–91 Yemen supported Iraq. As punishment, Saudi Arabia and Kuwait expelled hundreds of thousands of Yemeni workers. Their remittances ceased and they became a huge burden on the economy. The government then abandoned agricultural subsidies and farmers stopped growing food and export crops. Instead they planted a shrub called qat—a stimulant used by Yemenis that has no export value. High inflation and political conflicts make it difficult to implement long-range economic policies and reforms.

Oman

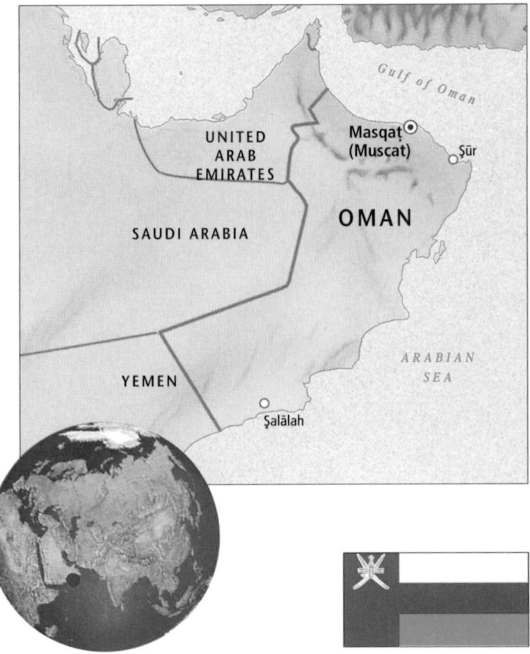

Fact File

OFFICIAL NAME Sultanate of Oman

FORM OF GOVERNMENT Monarchy with advisory Consultative Council

CAPITAL Masqaṭ (Muscat)

AREA 212,460 sq km (82,031 sq miles)

TIME ZONE GMT + 4 hours

POPULATION 2,714,000

PROJECTED POPULATION 2015 4,110,000

POPULATION DENSITY 12.8 per sq km (33.1 per sq mile)

LIFE EXPECTANCY 72.3

INFANT MORTALITY (PER 1,000) 21.8

OFFICIAL LANGUAGE Arabic

OTHER LANGUAGES Baluchu, Farsi (Persian), Urdu, English

LITERACY RATE 80 %

RELIGIONS Ibadhi Muslim 75 %, Sunni Muslim, Shi'a Muslim and Hindu 25 %

ETHNIC GROUPS Mainly Arab with Baluchi, Indian, Pakistani, Sri Lankan, Bangladeshi, African minorities

CURRENCY Omani rial

ECONOMY Agriculture 50 %, services 28 %, industry 22 %

GNP PER CAPITA US$ 8,200

CLIMATE Mainly hot and arid; light rains in south June to September

HIGHEST POINT Jabal Ash Shām 2,980 m (9,777 ft)

MAP REFERENCE Pages 220–21

Oman is the third-largest country in the Arabian Peninsula. Situated on the peninsula's eastern corner, it looks across the Arabian Sea toward Baluchistan and India—in fact Baluchis form a small but significant part of the population. A small, separate, and highly strategic piece of Oman's territory is the tip of the Musandam Peninsula, com-

manding the entrance to the Strait of Hormuz. The Omani capital of Masqaṭ (Muscat) was a trading center for hundreds of years, dhows sailing to India in one direction and down the African coast to Zanzibar in the other. Zanzibar itself was an Omani conquest, and in the 1960s, when it became part of Tanzania, many Arab Zanzibaris came to Oman. From 1798 Oman had strong ties with the British, and it became a British protectorate. Full independence came in 1971.

Sultan Qabus Ibn Sa'id rules his country as an absolute monarch, advised by a majlis ash shura ("consultative council"), but in the late 1990s the country was moving towards a constitutional government. In the late 1960s Oman faced a leftist rebellion in the western province of Dhofur, encouraged and supported by the People's Republic of Yemen across the border. This was defeated in 1975. Since then, with the country enjoying the prosperity of its oil and natural gas (huge additional reserves were discovered in 1991), peace has reigned.

In the north the limestone Hajar Mountains overlook the fertile coastal plain of al-Batinah. Most of Oman's population lives along the alluvial al-Batinah strip, where date gardens stretch for more than 250 km (155 miles). The Jabal Akhdar ridge is the highest part of the Hajar Range, rising to 3,107 m (10,193 ft). Soils in the upland region are poor: herders use the area for running camels, sheep, and goats. Wadis cutting the Jabal Akhdar ridge, underground canals, and wells provide a certain amount of irrigation. North of the Ẓufār (Dhofar) uplands in the southwest the desert meets the sandy wastes of the Saudi Arabian Ar Rub' al Khāli (or "Empty Quarter").

Rural Omanis live by subsistence agriculture, growing dates, limes, bananas, alfalfa, and vegetables. Pastoralists keep camels, cattle, sheep, and goats. The smaller urban population, however, including a considerable number of guest workers, depends on imported food. The national economy as a whole is dominated by the oil industry: petroleum accounts for nearly ninety percent of export earnings, about 75 percent of government revenues, and roughly forty percent of gross domestic product. Oman has proved oil reserves of 4 billion barrels, which are equal to twenty year's supply at the present rate of extraction.

United Arab Emirates

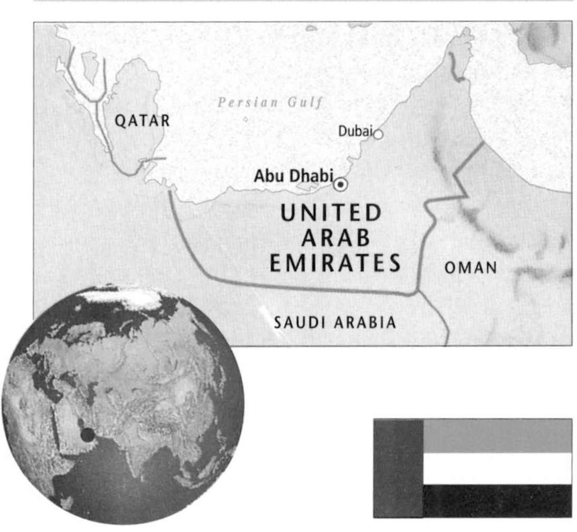

Fact File

Official name United Arab Emirates

Form of government Federation of Emirates with one advisory body (Federal National Council)

Capital Abu Dhabi

Area 75,581 sq km (29,182 sq miles)

Time zone GMT + 4 hours

Population 2,446,000

Projected population 2015 3,230,000

Population density 32.4 per sq km (83.8 per sq mile)

Life expectancy 74.5

Infant mortality (per 1,000) 16.1

Official language Arabic

Other languages Hindi, Urdu, Farsi (Persian), English

Literacy rate 79.2 %

Religions Muslim 96 % (Shi'a 16 %); Christian, Hindu, other 4 %

Ethnic groups Emiri 19 %, other Arab and Iranian 23 %, South Asian 50 %, other expatriates 8 % (only 20 % of population are citizens)

Currency Emirian dirham

Economy Services 57 %, industry 38 %, agriculture 5 %

GNP per capita US$ 21,100

Climate Mainly arid; cooler in eastern mountains

Highest point Jabal Yibir 1,527 m (5,010 ft)

Map reference Pages 220–21

People in the seven small principalities that form the United Arab Emirates lived for centuries as seagoing traders on the shores of the Persian Gulf. When piracy became a nuisance in 1820, Britain entered into truces with the local emirs to end attacks on shipping, and established a protectorate in the region. Soon the principalities were known as the Trucial States. In 1971 they became independent and formed the federation of sheikdoms now known as the United Arab Emirates (UAE). They are situated along the southern coast of the Persian Gulf between the Qatar Peninsula to the west and the Straits of Hormuz, and share borders with Qatar, Saudi Arabia, and Oman.

Abū Zaby (Abu Dhabi) is more than six times the size of all the other states put together, has the biggest population, and is the main oil producer. In the form of federal funds, it contributes to development projects in the poorer states. The port in Dubayy (Dubai) is one of the world's largest maritime facilities, and has attracted companies from 58 countries active in the petroleum industry, trading, and financial services. A major economic contribution has been made by expatriates who flocked to the country during the 1970s' oil boom—only twenty percent of UAE citizens are native born. Whether this workforce can now be 'Emiratized' is a concern, as is the growth of Islamic fundamentalism among the young. In world affairs the UAE is a force for moderation in the Arab world. It maintains close links with the UK and USA.

The Gulf coast features saline marshes merging inland with barren desert plains. In the east there is a range of steep mountains. These are an extension of Oman's Hajar Mountains, running northward along the Musandam Peninsula. The sheikhdom of Al Fujayrah looks out from this peninsula onto the Gulf of Oman, and contains the only highland expanse. Less than 1.2 percent of UAE land is arable, and most vegetation is sparse and scrubby. Virtually all agricultural activity is found in the emirates of Sharjah, Ras al Khaimana, Ajman, and Fujairah, where oasis date palms grow. Government incentives, however, plus irrigation works, have increased the number of farmers fourfold in recent years. While much food is imported, self-sufficiency in wheat is still a target.

Once an impoverished region of small desert sheikhdoms, the UAE has since 1973 been transformed into a modern state with a high standard of living. Oil and gas production is the largest economic sector, accounting for 89 percent of export revenue. Though in the short term the fortunes of the economy fluctuate with the price of gas and oil, at the present level of production oil reserves should last more than 100 years. Increased privatization is being encouraged by the government, and service industries are being developed. Although the UAE is much stronger economically than most of the Gulf States, a number of weaknesses remain. While the largest solar-powered water-production plant in the Gulf region is at Taweela, industrial development is likely to be limited by the fact that water will always be in short supply. There is a lack of skilled labor. Most raw materials and foodstuffs have to be imported.

Kuwait

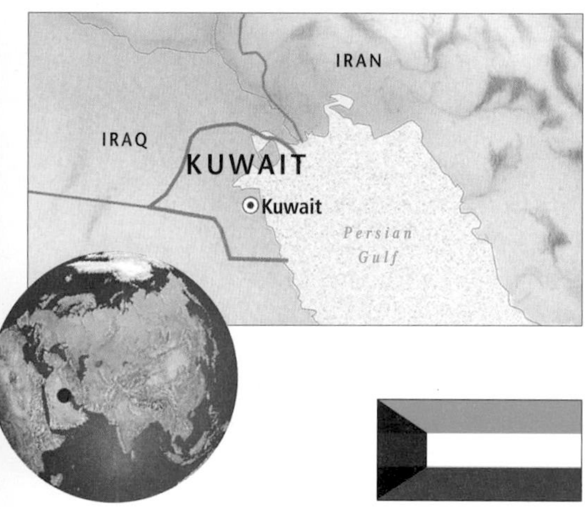

Fact File

Official name State of Kuwait

Form of government Constitutional monarchy with single legislative body (National Assembly)

Capital Al Kuwayt (Kuwait)

Area 17,820 sq km (6,880 sq miles)

Time zone GMT + 3 hours

Population 2,112,000

Projected population 2015 2,766,000

Population density 118.5 per sq km (307.0 per sq mile)

Life expectancy 76.5

Infant mortality (per 1,000) 10.9

Official language Arabic

Other language English

Literacy rate 78.6 %

Religions Muslim 85 % (Sunni 45 %, Shi'a 30 %, other 10 %), other (including Christian, Hindu, Parsi) 15 %

Ethnic groups Kuwaiti 45 %, other Arab 35 %, South Asian 9 %, Iranian 4 %, other 7 %

Currency Kuwaiti dinar

Economy Services 90 %, industry 9 %, agriculture 1 %

GNP per capita US$ 15,100

Climate Arid, with cool winters and hot, humid summers

Highest point Ash Shakayah 290 m (951 ft)

Map reference Page 220

The Arab emirate of Kuwait lies in the northwest corner of the Persian Gulf, dwarfed by its neighbors Iraq, Iran, and Saudi Arabia. Beneath its surface lie huge oil reserves. It was settled by wandering Arab peoples in the eighteenth century. When Germany and Turkey were eyeing Kuwait possessively in the nineteenth century it formed a defensive alliance with Great Britain, becoming a British protectorate in 1914. In 1961, when it gained independence, Kuwait was claimed by Iraq.

A constitution was inaugurated by the as Sabah ruling family in 1962. Whenever the National Assembly has been critical, however, it has been suspended. In 1990, Iraq invaded. The Kuwaitis endured six months of brutality and the destruction of the city of Kuwait before a US-led international coalition expelled the Iraqis in 1991. During the occupation 400,000 residents fled the country; 200,000 Palestinian migrant workers were not allowed to return, as the Palestinian Liberation Organization had supported Iraq. The destruction of Kuwaiti oil wells by Iraq and deliberate oil-spills in the Gulf have caused environmental costs still difficult to assess. The damage done in the Third Gulf War in 2003 was much less severe.

Kuwait consists of an undulating sandy plateau which rises westward to an elevation of about 300 m (1,000 ft) on the Iraq-Saudi Arabia border. Along the border the plateau is cut to a depth of 45 m (150 ft) by the Wādī al Bāṭin. In the northeast there are a few salt marshes and in the northwest is the Jal az-Zawr escarpment. Vegetation is mostly limited to salt-tolerant plants along the coast, though in modern urban areas green spaces have been produced by irrigating imported soil. The territory of Kuwait also includes nine islands, of which Bubiyan is the largest.

Kuwait owns ten percent of the world's proven crude oil reserves. Its petroleum sector currently accounts for nearly half of gross domestic product, ninety percent of export revenues, and seventy percent of government income. With the exception of fish, Kuwait depends almost wholly on food imports, though hothouses and hydroponics produce some fruit and vegetables. About 75 percent of potable water must be distilled or imported. The shortage of water constrains industrial activities, which at present include petrochemical production, food processing, desalination, construction materials, and salt. The World Bank has urged the government to push ahead with privatization, including in the oil industry.

Qatar

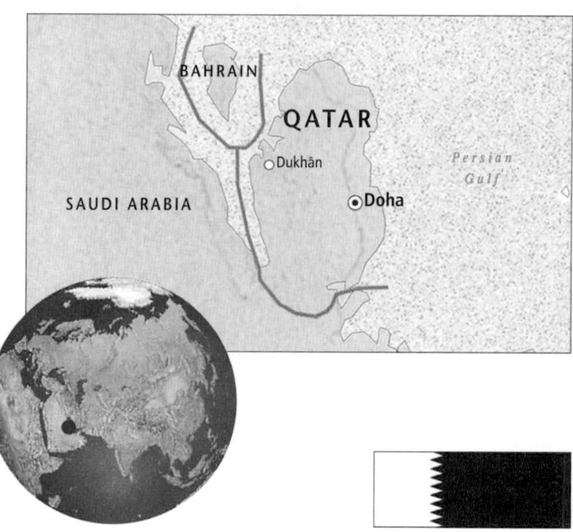

Fact File

Official name State of Qatar

Form of government Monarchy with Advisory Consultative Council

Capital Ad Dawḥah (Doha)

Area 11,000 sq km (4,247 sq miles)

Time zone GMT + 3 hours

Population 794,000

Projected population 2015 1,135,000

Population density 72.2 per sq km (187.0 per sq mile)

Life expectancy 72.9

Infant mortality (per 1,000) 20.7

Official language Arabic

Other language Urdu, Farsi (Persian), English

Literacy rate 79 %

Religions Muslim (Sunni and Wahhabi) 95 %, other (among them Hindu, Christian, Baha'i) 5 %

Ethnic groups Arab 40 %, Pakistani 18 %, Indian 18 %, Iranian 10%, other 14 %

Currency Qatari rial

Economy Services 50 %, industry (particularly oil production and refining) 48 %, agriculture 2 %

GNP per capita US$ 21,200

Climate Hot and arid; humid in summer

Highest point Qurayn Aba al Bawl 103 m (338 ft)

Map reference Page 220

Qatar is a small, wealthy emirate in the Persian Gulf. In 1971 it chose not to join the neighboring United Arab Emirates as a member state, but to go it alone. Recently it has continued to act with independence, signing a security pact with the USA in 1995 involving the stationing of 2,000 US troops, while simultaneously challenging the Gulf Cooperation Council's policy on Iraq. During the 2003 war againt Iraq led by the United States, the United Kingdom and their allies, the military headquarter was located in Doha. The peninsula it occupies, projecting north from the southern shore of the Persian Gulf near Bahrain,

A village in the Oman mountains, surrounded by terraced cultivation (left page above). Kuwait City, the capital of Kuwait (below).

consists of flat and semiarid desert. Most of its population are guest workers from the Indian subcontinent, Iran, and North Africa.

Qatar was ruled for centuries by the Khalifah dynasty. A rift in dynastic affairs opened in 1783, war with Bahrain followed in 1867, and then the British intervened to set up a separate emirate under the ath Thani family. Qatar became a full British protectorate in 1916. At this time it was occupied by nomadic Bedouin wandering the peninsula with their herds of goats and camels. Oil production, which commenced in 1949, changed everything and now almost ninety percent of the people live in the capital city of Ad Dawḥah (Doha) or its suburbs. The northern parts of Qatar are dotted with abandoned villages.

A bloodless palace coup in 1995 saw the present emir displace his father, a move that was accepted without fuss. The emir of Qatar rules as an absolute monarch. He occupies the office of prime minister and he appoints his own cabinet. He is advised by a partially elected thirty-member majlis ash shura (consultative council). From time to time there are calls for democratic reforms from prominent citizens.

The Qatar Peninsula is mainly low-lying except for a few hills in the west of the country at Jabal Dukhān (the Dukhan Heights) and some low cliffs in the northeast. Sandy desert, salt flats, and barren plains cut by shallow wadis (creek beds) occupy 95 percent of its land area. There is little rainfall aside from occasional winter showers. As a result of the shortage of fresh water Qatar is dependent on large-scale desalinization facilities. Summers are usually hot and humid; winter nights can be cool and chilly. Drought-resistant plant life is mainly found in the south. However, by tapping groundwater supplies, Qatar is now able to cultivate most of its own vegetables.

Crude oil production and refining is by far the most important industry. Oil accounts for more than thirty percent of gross domestic product, about 75 percent of export earnings, and seventy percent of government revenues. Reserves of 3.3 billion barrels should ensure continued output at present levels for at least another 25 years. Oil has given Qatar a per capita gross domestic product that is comparable to some of the leading western European industrial economies. Long-term goals include the development of offshore wells and economic diversification.

Bahrain

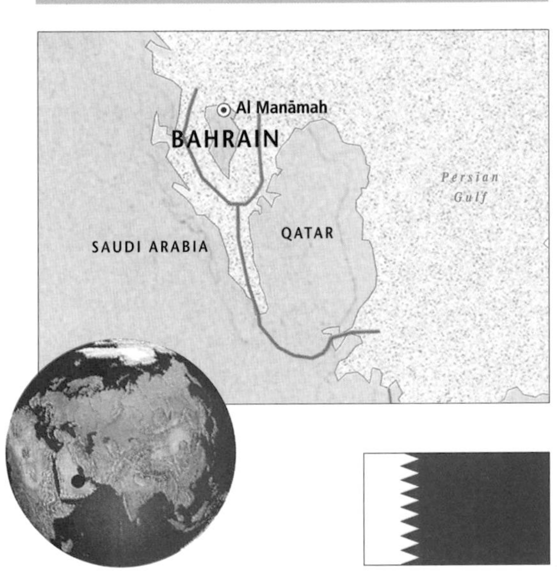

Fact File

OFFICIAL NAME State of Bahrain

FORM OF GOVERNMENT Traditional monarchy

CAPITAL Al Manāmah (Manama)

AREA 620 sq km (239 sq miles)

TIME ZONE GMT + 3 hours

POPULATION 657,000

PROJECTED POPULATION 2015 793,000

POPULATION DENSITY 1,059.7 per sq km (2,749.0 per sq mile)

LIFE EXPECTANCY 73.5

INFANT MORTALITY (PER 1,000) 19.2

OFFICIAL LANGUAGE Arabic

OTHER LANGUAGES English, Farsi (Persian), Urdu

LITERACY RATE 88.5 %

RELIGIONS Shi'a Muslim 75 %, Sunni Muslim 25 %

ETHNIC GROUPS Bahraini 63 %, Asian 13 %, other Arab 10 %, Iranian 8 %, other 6 %

CURRENCY Bahraini dinar

ECONOMY Industry and commerce 85 %, agriculture 5 %, services 7 %, government 3 %

GNP PER CAPITA US$ 13,000

CLIMATE Mainly arid, with mild winters and hot, humid summers

HIGHEST POINT Jabal ad Dukhān 122 m (400 ft)

MAP REFERENCE Page 220

The State of Bahrain is a cluster of 35 small, low-lying islands located in the Persian Gulf, just 28 km (17 miles) from the west coast of the Qatar Peninsula. The islands were once the heart of the ancient Dilmun civilization and have been a trading center for more than 4,000 years. Bahrain was the first of the Gulf States to export oil, soon after reserves were discovered in 1932. A 25 km (16 mile) causeway links the main island to Saudi Arabia.

After the collapse of Beirut in Lebanon in the 1970s, which previously had been the region's main commercial center, Bahrain began to provide banking and financial services, at the same time increasing its transport and communication facilities. When the elected assembly was dissolved in 1975 and the country reverted to traditional authoritarian rule, there was growing unrest among the fundamentalist Shi'ite Muslim majority. Encouraged in their resistance by Iran, the Shi'ites resent their low status under Bahrain's Sunni Muslim ruling family. In the opinion of Shi'ite fundamentalists this family is unacceptable for a number of reasons: It belongs to a branch of Islam they regard as oppressive, it is liberal and modernizing in its economic policies, and it is a supporter of US policy. US military air bases on Bahrain were essential strategic assets during the 1990–91 Gulf War.

Consisting of barren rock, sandy plains, and salt marshes, the landscape of Bahrain is low-lying desert for the most part, rising to a low central escarpment. Winters are dry and mild, summers hot and humid. There are no natural freshwater resources. All the country's water needs must be met by groundwater from springs and from desalinated sea water. Imported soil has been used to create several small fertile areas, and domestic agricultural production is actually capable of meeting local demand for fruit and vegetables. However, the degradation of the existing arable land is an environmental concern, along with damage to coastlines, coral reefs, and sea life resulting from spills of oil and oil-tanker discharges.

Waning oil production since the 1970s has forced Bahrain to diversify its economy. Since the opening of the causeway linking the country to Saudi Arabia in 1986 there has been a boom in weekend tourism, with visitors pouring in from the Gulf States. Bahrain is now the Arab world's most important banking center, and numerous multinational firms with business in the Gulf have offices in the country. Ship repairs are also undertaken in Bahrain. Petroleum production and processing account for approximately eighty percent of export receipts. Natural gas has assumed greater importance, and is used to supply local industries, including an aluminum smelting plant. However, unemployment among the young, especially among the Shi'ite majority, is a cause of social unrest and continuing economic concern.

Israel

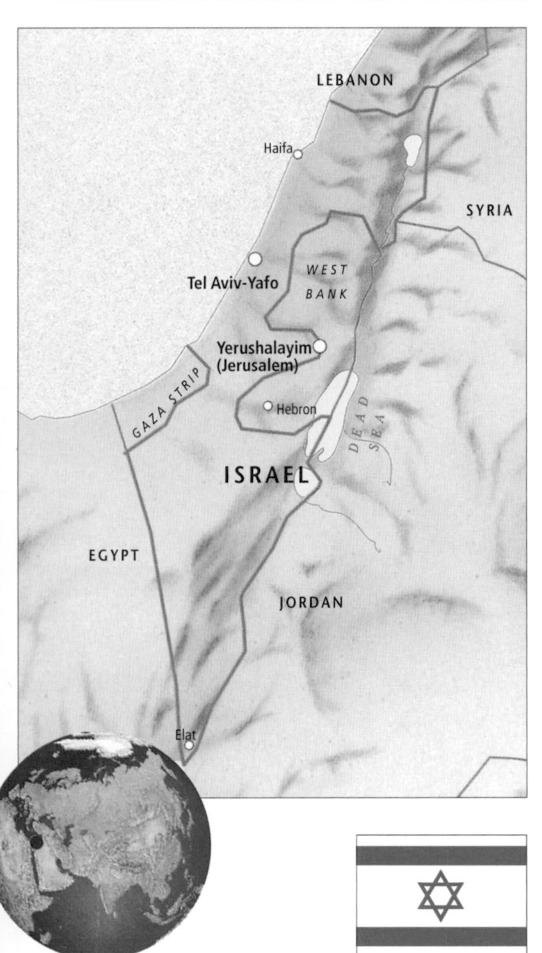

Fact File

Official name State of Israel

Form of government Republic with single legislative body (Knesset)

Capital Jerusalem

Area 20,770 sq km (8,019 sq miles)

Time zone GMT + 2 hours

Population 6,030,000

Projected population 2015 7,714,000

Population density 290.3 per sq km (752.0 per sq mile)

Life expectancy 78.9

Infant mortality (per 1,000) 7.6

Official languages Hebrew, Arabic

Other languages Yiddish, English, French, German, Hungarian, Romanian, Russian, Spanish

Literacy rate 95 %

Religions Jewish 82 %, Muslim 14 %, Druze 2 %, Christian 2 %

Ethnic groups Jewish 82 %, Arab 17 %, other 1 %

Currency Shekel

Economy Services 75 %, industry 21 %, agriculture 4 %

GNP per capita US$ 19,000

Climate Temperate along coast, hot and dry in south and east

Highest point Har Meron 1,208 m (3,963 ft)

Map reference Page 225

Created as a Jewish homeland in 1948, Israel is a small country with an illustrious past that involves three of the world's great religions, and an uncertain future. For fifty years, through a succession of wars with hostile Arab neighbors, a secular, democratic political system has managed to constrain strong religious tendencies deeply rooted in the past. Key events in the Jewish history of the region are: first, the occupation of the land by the twelve tribes of Israelites 4,000 years ago; second, the scattering (or "diaspora") of the one surviving tribe, the Jews, following a failed revolt against Rome in AD 138; third, the rise of Zionism in the nineteenth century advocating a Jewish homeland in Palestine as a solution to centuries of exile and persecution; fourth, the Holocaust, which reinforced arguments for territorial independence; and fifth, the proclamation of the State of Israel in May 1948, leading to the emigration of many Palestinian Arabs. Since then there has been continual strife between the new state and its neighbors. Israel's subsequent seizure and occupation of additional territories (see entries for Gaza Strip and West Bank) has been bitterly resisted by their Arab inhabitants. This conflict has intensified as Jewish religious fundamentalists continue to expand their settlements in contested areas. After the country signed a peace treaty with Egypt in 1979 and especially while Prime Minister Yitzhak Rabin conducted a policy of appeasement with Jordan and the Palestinians until he was murdered in 1995 by a Jewish extremist, the peace process made quite some progress and the foundation of an independent Palestinian state is also the declared goal of the international community. However, ongoing acts of terrorism by Arab fanatics as well as the very harsh politic of the State of Israel in its pursuit of domestic security continue to pose a severe threat to the peace process.

Geographically, Israel consists of four main regions: the Mediterranean coastal plain of Sharon, irrigated by the Qishon, Soreq, and Sarida Rivers; the rolling hills extending from Galilee in the north to Judea in the center; the Jordan-Red Sea section of the Rift Valley running north to south the full length of the eastern frontier from the Golan Heights to the Gulf of Aqaba; and the great southern wedge of desert plateau called the Negev (Ha Negev), which makes up about half of Israel's total land area. With irrigation, the Mediterranean coastal plain is fertile fruit-growing country. In the drier southern stretches its dunes have been stabilized with grass and tamarisk and reclaimed for pasture. The northern hill country around Galilee has good rainfall and a rich black soil weathered from basalt. Here and around Judea, pine and eucalyptus trees have been planted to anchor the soil and retain water. The Valley of Jezreel ('Emeq Yizre'el), lying between Galilee and Samaria to the south, has deep alluvial soils which are intensively tilled for market gardening. The Jordan-Western Negev Scheme—the most ambitious of Israel's various irrigation projects—diverts water from the upper Jordan and other sources through a series of culverts and canals south to the Negev. The desert is widely covered with blown sand and loess, but tomatoes and grapes grow well when supplied with water.

Israel has the most industrialized economy in the region. Iron is smelted at Haifa and there are steel foundries at Acre. Chemical manufacturing takes place at Haifa and in plants by the Dead Sea. A national electricity grid provides power to widely dispersed towns where factories produce textiles, ceramics, and other products. In the Negev south of Beersheba new settlements mine oil, copper, and phosphates, the factories using potash and salt from the Dead Sea. Israel is largely self-sufficient in food production except for grains. Diamonds, high-technology equipment, and agricultural products are leading exports. About half the government's external debt is owed to the USA, its main source of aid. To earn foreign exchange the government has been targeting high-tech international market niches such as medical scanning equipment. Matters of continuing economic concern include the high level of unemployment following large-scale immigration from the former USSR, and the need to import strategically important raw materials.

A spice seller in a Bahrain market (left page top). The Old City of Yerushalayim (Jerusalem) from the Mount of Olives, with the golden dome of the al Aqsa Mosque (below).

Jordan

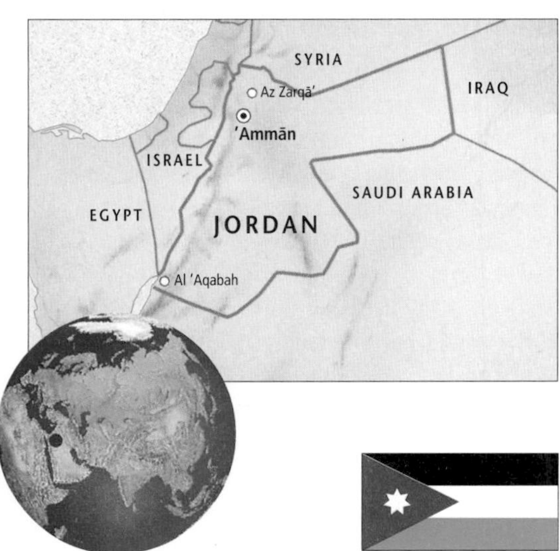

Fact File

Official name Hashemite Kingdom of Jordan

Form of government Constitutional monarchy with two legislative bodies (House of Notables and House of Representatives)

Capital 'Ammān

Area 89,213 sq km (34,445 sq miles)

Time zone GMT + 2 hours

Population 5,308,000

Projected population 2015 7,191,000

Population density 59.5 per sq km (154.1 per sq mile)

Life expectancy 77.7

Infant mortality (per 1,000) 19.6

Official language Arabic

Other language English

Literacy rate 86.6 %

Religions Sunni Muslim 92 %, Christian 8 %

Ethnic groups Arab 98 %, Circassian 1 %, Armenian 1 %

Currency Jordanian dinar

Economy Services 64 %, industry 26 %, agriculture 10 %

GNP per capita US$ 4,300

Climate Mainly arid, but northwest temperate with cool, wet winters and hot, dry summers

Highest point Jabal Ramm 1,754 m (5,755 ft)

Map reference Page 225

The small Arab kingdom of Jordan, rich in historic associations and sites, lies between Saudi Arabia, Israel, and Syria, and also shares a border with Iraq. It has to deal with Israel on the one hand and with Israel's various Arab antagonists on the other, while accommodating huge numbers of refugees. After the Ottoman Turks were driven out during the First World War the British installed the Hashemite monarchy in 1921. In 1946 Jordan became independent, and King Hussein reigned from 1952 until his death in 1999.

Governing Jordan has not been easy, many problems being connected with what is known as the West Bank. As a result of the Six Day War in 1967, the territory west of the Jordan River, and formerly part of Jordan, came under Israeli control. This area, containing both Jerusalem and much of Jordan's most fruitful land, remains a trouble spot. With emigré Palestinians using Jordan as a base for guerrilla activities (they were expelled in 1970–71), through two Gulf Wars in which Jordan was sympathetic to Iraq (its major supplier of oil), and with the recent expansion of Israeli settlements in the area, the West Bank became impossible to regain or to administer. In 1988 Jordan ceded it to the PLO.

The Red Sea-Jordan section of the Rift Valley forms the country's western border. It contains the Jordan River valley, the Dead Sea (the lowest point on the earth's surface, at 400 m/1,312 ft below sea level), the Sea of Galilee, and Wadī al Arabah. Parts of the Jordan Valley and the highlands east of the Rift Valley are irrigated, making arable farming possible. Crops include vegetables, olives, and fruit. Eighty percent of Jordan's land area is desert. In the north it merges with the Syrian Desert and in the south with the deserts of Saudi Arabia. Less than 0.5 percent of the country is forested, mainly in the east. Vegetation ranges from Mediterranean plants in the mountains to grass, sagebrush and shrubs in the steppe country.

Jordan has poor water, oil, and coal supplies. In the late 1970s and early 1980s it received substantial Arab aid and the economy grew at more than ten percent a year. In the late 1980s reductions in aid and in worker remittances slowed and imports outstripped exports. In 1991 the Second Gulf War overwhelmed the country. Worker remittances came to a halt, trade contracted, and additional refugees arrived, further straining resources. Recovery since that time has been uneven. Poverty, debt, and unemployment are continuing problems.

One of the many rock-cut facades in the ancient city of Petra in Jordan (below). Byblos Harbor in Lebanon (right page bottom). Krac des Chevaliers in Syria, a French Crusader castle built in the twelfth century (right page top).

Lebanon

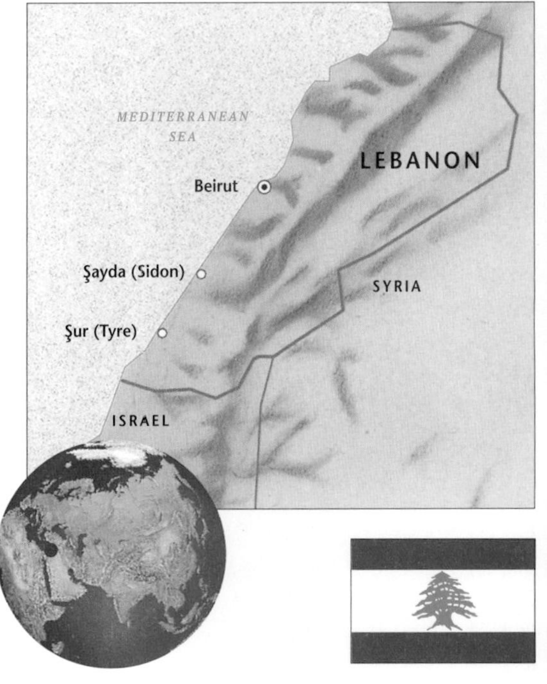

Fact File

Official name Republic of Lebanon

Form of government Republic with single legislative body (National Assembly)

Capital Beirut

Area 10,400 sq km (4,015 sq miles)

Time zone GMT + 2 hours

Population 3,678,000

Projected population 2015 4,219,000

Population density 353.7 per sq km (916.1 per sq mile)

Life expectancy 71.8

Infant mortality (per 1,000) 27.4

Official languages Arabic

Other languages Armenian, Kurdish, French, English

Literacy rate 86.4 %

Religions Muslim 70 %, Christian 30 %

Ethnic groups Arab 95 %, Armenian 4 %, other 1 %

Currency Lebanese pound

Economy Services 60 %, industry 28 %, agriculture 12 %

GNP per capita US$ 5,200

Climate Temperate, with short mild, wet winters and long, hot, dry summers. In winter rainfall in mountains often turns to snow

Highest point Qurnat as Sawdā' 3,088 m (10,131 ft)

Map reference Page 225

Lebanon, a small country on the eastern shore of the Mediterranean Sea, consists of the region that was once known as the Levant. It has a history that goes back at least 5,000 years. First settled by the Phoenicians around 3000 BC, it saw Alexander the Great (356–323 BC) conquer the Phoenician city of Tyre, and it later became part of the Roman Empire. Early in the seventh century AD Maronite Christians (named after Maro, a Syrian monk who was the sect's founder) settled in northern Lebanon; later, Druze Arabs, who are aligned with Shi'ite Islam, settled in the south of the country, and Sunni Muslims came to the coastal towns. From the eleventh to the thirteenth century the region was a center of confrontation between Western Christians and Muslims during the Crusades. It then became part of the Muslim Mameluke Empire. In 1516 the Ottoman Turks took control of the country, their rule finally ending with conquest by the British and French during the First World War.

From 1920, following the withdrawal of Turkish forces, a French administration sought to balance the interests of the country's various religious groups. During this period Beirut, which already had a cosmopolitan air, took on a distinctly French flavor. The city became both a center of international commerce and a playground of the rich. The country gained independence in 1946. Deep and persistent tensions between Muslim and various non-Muslim sections of the population led to an outbreak of guerrilla war in 1975. For the next fifteen years much of the country was devasted by civil war, and much of its urban infrastructure was destroyed.

From the narrow coastal plain along the Mediterranean, where crops are grown with the aid of irrigation, the land rises eastward to form the Lebanon Mountains (Jabal Lubnān). Running from north to south, these cover about thirty percent of Lebanon's land area. Between the harsh slopes of this range and the Anti-Lebanon Chain (Jabal ash Sharqī) that borders Syria lies the fertile el Beqaa Valley which is another agricultural area. This is traversed by the River Litani on its journey south, before emptying into the Mediterranean Sea above Şūr (the ancient city of Tyre).

Decades of fighting have left the Lebanese economy in ruins and there is a severe housing shortage. Tourism, which was once an important source of revenue, is beginning to revive with the rebuilding of the once-popular Corniche seafront area at Beirut. Since the decline of industry as a result of the war, agriculture has come to play a more important role: crops include apples, citrus fruits, bananas, carrots, grapes, tomatoes, and olives. Opium poppies and cannabis are illegally produced for export. Traditional areas of activity in the past were banking, food processing, textiles, cement, oil refining, and chemicals. The country now depends heavily on foreign aid.

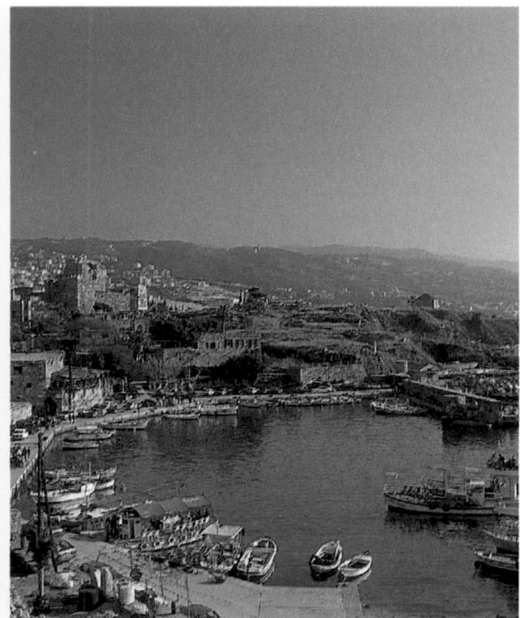

Syria

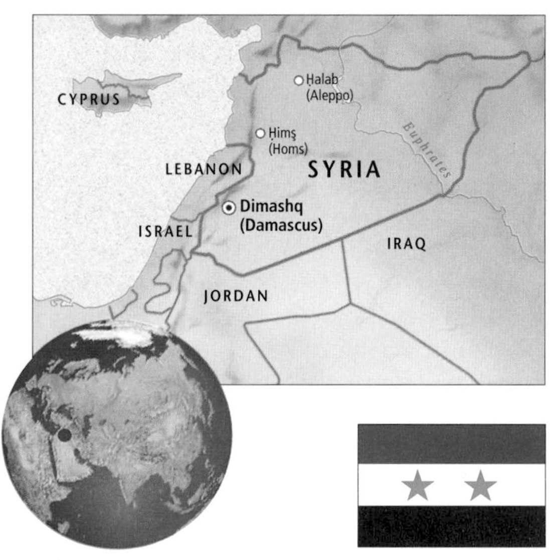

Fact File

OFFICIAL NAME Syrian Arab Republic

FORM OF GOVERNMENT Republic with single legislative body (People's Council)

CAPITAL Dimashq (Damascus)

AREA 185,180 sq km (71,498 sq miles)

TIME ZONE GMT + 2 hours

POPULATION 17,156,000

PROJECTED POPULATION 2015 23,206,000

POPULATION DENSITY 92.6 per sq km (240.0 per sq mile)

LIFE EXPECTANCY 69.1

INFANT MORTALITY (PER 1,000) 32.7

OFFICIAL LANGUAGE Arabic

OTHER LANGUAGES Kurdish, Armenian

LITERACY RATE 70.8 %

RELIGIONS Sunni Muslim 74 %, other Muslim sects 16 %, Christian 10 %; tiny Jewish communities

ETHNIC GROUPS Arab 90 %; Kurdish, Armenian and other 10 %

CURRENCY Syrian pound

ECONOMY Services 63 %, agriculture 22 %, industry 15 %

GNP PER CAPITA US$ 3,200

CLIMATE Temperate, with mild, wet winters and dry, hot summers; arid in interior

HIGHEST POINT Jabal ash Shaykh 2,814 m (9,232 ft)

MAP REFERENCE Pages 200, 225

Syria is in the eastern Mediterranean, with Iraq and Turkey to the east and north and Lebanon, Israel and Jordan to the west and south. Throughout history it has played a key role in the region. Over the years Egyptians, Hittites, Persians, Greeks, and Romans came and went. Converted to Islam when overrun by the Arabs in 634, the Syrians' capital Damascus became a major center during the Umayyad Dynasty. Crusaders seized much of Syria in the twelfth century, but were ousted by the Kurdish general Saladin. Under French control from 1920, Syria became independent in 1946. After various military coups and counter-coups the Ba'ath Party seized power in 1963, and from 1971 until his death in 2000 party leader Hafez al-Assad has ruled Syria with an iron fist. A member of the minority Alawite religious sect, he has faced resistance from other Muslims, notably the Sunni majority. But when the Sunni Muslim Brotherhood rose against Damascus in 1992 their revolt was crushed, with up to 20,000 deaths. Following the Second Gulf War in 1991 Syria received huge amounts of aid as a result of its unexpected support for the coalition against Iraq. As a member of the Security Council, however, it sternly opposed the Third Gulf War in 2003.

Syria's Mediterranean coast, well-watered from subterranean sources, is one of the country's most fertile, intensively farmed, and densely populated regions. Inland is the Ghab Depression, a rift valley flanked by two mountain ranges. Here the Orontes ('Āşī) River flows through gorges and wide valleys. To the south, the Heights of Hermon rise above the eastern slopes of the Anti-Lebanon Range (Jabal ash Sharqī). Snowmelt from the range provides water for Damascus. Inland lies the Syrian Desert (Bādiyat ash Shām), crossed by the Euphrates River (Firat Nehri). Oil was discovered along the Euphrates in the 1980s. Power from the Euphrates barrage produces seventy percent of Syria's electricity.

Under the socialist Ba'ath Party most industry is government controlled. The main industries are textiles, food processing, beverages, tobacco, phosphate rock mining, petroleum, and cement. Oil, textiles, cotton, and agricultural produce are the main exports. The country has many weak government-owned firms and low productivity. Oil production has begun to ebb and unemployment is expected to rise as the more than sixty percent of the population that is under twenty years old enters the labor force. Syria's Gulf War aid windfall of $5 billion has been spent.

Iraq

Fact File

Official name Republic of Iraq

Form of government Republic in transition with interim government

Capital Baghdād

Area 437,072 sq km (168,753 sq miles)

Time zone GMT + 3 hours

Population 24,002,000

Projected population 2015 33,550,000

Population density 54.9 per sq km (142.2 per sq mile)

Life expectancy 67.4

Infant mortality (per 1,000) 57.6

Official languages Arabic

Other languages Kurdish, Assyrian, Armenian

Literacy rate 58 %

Religions Muslim 97 % (Shi'a 60 %–65 %, Sunni 32 %–37 %), Christian or other 3 %

Ethnic groups Arab 75 %–80 %, Kurdish 15 %–20 %, other (including Turkoman, Assyrian) 5 %

Currency Iraqi dinar

Economy Services 48 %, agriculture 30 %, industry 22 %

GNP per capita Est. US$ 2,500

Climate Mainly arid, with cold winters and hot summers; winter snows in northern mountains

Highest point Kūh-e Hājī Ebrāhīm 3,600 m (11,811 ft)

Map reference Page 220

If any country has the right to call itself the cradle of Western civilization it is Iraq. The first city-states in the region date from nearly 3500 BC. The land "between the waters" of the Tigris and the Euphrates Rivers (the meaning of the old name Mesopotamia) has seen many empires come and go. Babylon defeated its old rival Assyria here in 612 BC, and in the seventh century BC the territory was seized by the Persians; Baghdad became the greatest commercial and cultural center of the Muslim world. The Persians held Iraq until they were conquered by Alexander the Great in 334 BC.

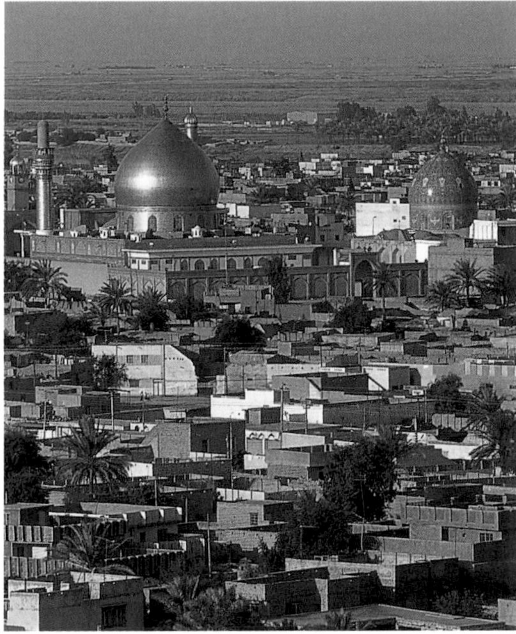

Part of the Ottoman Empire from 1534 to 1918, Iraq became independent in 1932.

Modern Iraq has been involved in three major conflicts in the space of twenty years: the First Gulf War between Iraq and Iran, 1980–88, the Second Gulf War in which it invaded Kuwait, 1990–91, and finally the Third Gulf War in 2003 that ended in the downfall of Saddam Hussein's regime and the attempt to install a democratic form of government.

After the days of the early Mesopotamian empires, the Arab peoples brought Islam to Iraq in the seventh century AD. Like Iran, Iraq has a majority of Shi'ite Muslims. Unlike Iran, the ruling elite in Iraq are Sunni Muslims who fear their own Shi'ites are secretly loyal to Iran. This underlies the tension within Iraqi society and was the reason for the very restrictive politics of Saddam Hussein. The situation of the Kurds relates to an ethnic rather than a religious division. Distrusted and persecuted in every land in which they live (Turkey, Iran, Iraq, Syria, and Armenia) Iraq's Kurds were assaulted by Baghdad with chemical weapons in the 1980s.

In the far northeast Iraq shares part of the Zagros Mountains (Kūhhā-ye Zāgròs) with Iran. In the west its territory includes a piece of the Syrian Desert. The rest of the country falls into two broad physiographic categories—the lowland desert to the west which makes up nearly forty percent of the total land area; and the Tigris-Euphrates basin known formerly as Mesopotamia. Here the two rivers flow southeast roughly parallel, before meeting in a vast swamp on their way to the Persian Gulf. In this swamp live communities of Marsh Arabs, Shi'ite Muslims targeted by the leadership in Baghdad after an attempted rebellion following the Second Gulf War. Most Iraqi agricultural activity takes place in the alluvial Tigris-Euphrates plain, where one-third of the farms are irrigated. Vegetables and cereals are the most important crops. In addition to the rice grown in warmer lowland areas, wheat and barley are cultivated in the temperate country near the Zagros Mountains. Exports have fallen sharply, but in better times Iraq's date crop met eighty percent of world demand.

View across the rooftops of Sāmarrā', Iraq, to the River Tigris (left). A portion of the facade of the Imam Mosque in Eşfahan, Iran (right page bottom).

Three wars, the second followed by international embargoes designed to force acceptance of UN inspection of weapons of mass destruction, have severely damaged the Iraqi economy. It was formerly dominated by the oil sector, but today oil exports are probably no more than ten percent of their former level. Agricultural development has been hampered by labor shortages, salinization, and the dislocation caused by earlier land reform and collectivization programs. Living standards continue to deteriorate. Shortages were exacerbated by the government's spending of huge sums on both its army and internal security. Presently it remains to be seen whether the efforts of the newly installed interim government, which works closely with the US- and UK-led forces, will manage to establish peace and promote economic development.

Middle East conflicts

1964 Iran: Ayatollah Khomeini exiled for criticism of Shah's secular state.
1967 Israel: Six Day War with Arab states; seizes the Gaza Strip, Sinai, the Golan Heights, and the West Bank of the Jordan River.
1972 Iraq: Nationalization of western-owned Iraq Petroleum Company.
1973 Egypt and Syria join in attack on Israel and fight 18-day war.
1979 Israel: Peace Treaty signed with Egypt. Iraq: Saddam Hussein takes over. Iran: Fall of the Shah. Ayatollah Khomeini returns from exile. Iran declared an Islamic Republic.
1980 Iraqi invasion starts Iran–Iraq War.
1986 UN Security Council blames Iraq for war with Iran.
1988 Iran: US naval ship shoots down Iranian airliner, 290 killed. End of Iran-Iraq Gulf War. Iraqi troops use chemical weapons on Kurds.
1990 Iran and Iraq resume diplomatic relations. Iraq invades and annexes Kuwait.
1991 Western allies with UN mandate liberate Kuwait. UN requires Iraq to accept weapons monitoring and to destroy weapons of mass destruction.
1993 Israel: PLO recognizes Israel in return for Palestinian autonomy in Gaza Strip and Jericho.
1994 Iraq recognizes Kuwaiti sovereignty.
1995 Israel: Palestinian autonomy extended to much of West Bank. Prime Minister Rabin assassinated.
1997 UN charges Iraqi officials with blocking weapons inspections. Iran: Mohammed Khatami, more liberal than his predecessors, becomes president.
1998 Iraq: Obstruction of UN weapons inspectors and fear of Iraq's biological weapons program leads to heavy bombing by US and UK.
2003 Iraq: Saddam Hussein's regime is overthrown by US and UK forces and a small coalition; severe international criticism.
2004 Iraq: Administration handed over to an interim governing council in June

Iran

Fact File

OFFICIAL NAME Islamic Republic of Iran

FORM OF GOVERNMENT Theocratic republic with single legislative body (Islamic Consultative Assembly)

Capital Tehrān

AREA 1,648,000 sq km (636,293 sq miles)

TIME ZONE GMT + 3.5 hours

POPULATION 66,623,000

PROJECTED POPULATION 2015 87,103,000

POPULATION DENSITY 40.4 per sq km (104.7 per sq mile)

LIFE EXPECTANCY 70.3

INFANT MORTALITY (PER 1,000) 28.1

OFFICIAL LANGUAGE Farsi (Persian)

OTHER LANGUAGES Turkic, Kurdish, Luri, Baloch, Azerbaijanian, Arabic, Armenian

LITERACY RATE 68.6%

RELIGIONS Shi'a Muslim 89 %, Sunni Muslim 10 %, other (including Zoroastrian, Jewish, Christian, and Baha'i) 1 %

ETHNIC GROUPS Persian 51 %, Azerbaijani 24 %, Gilaki and Mazandarani 8 %, Kurd 7 %, Arab 3 %, Lur 2 %, Baloch 2 %, Turkmen 2 %, other 1 %

CURRENCY Rial

ECONOMY Services 46 %, agriculture 33 %, industry 21 %

GNP PER CAPITA US$ 7,000

CLIMATE Mainly arid, temperate in far north; cold winters and hot summers

HIGHEST POINT Qolleh-ye Damāvand 5,671 m (18,605 ft)

MAP REFERENCE Pages 220–21, 222

Iran is one of the largest of the Persian Gulf States. It has borders with ten other countries in the region including Afghanistan, Pakistan, and Turkey. Now the home of the world's largest theocracy, and the main center for militant Shi'a Islam, Persia (as it was formerly known) has seen the rise and fall of a number of civilizations, including those of the Medes, Persians, Greeks, and Parthians. In the seventh century it was overrun by an invasion of Arabs who introduced Islam, a religion which under the Safavids in 1502 became the Shi'ite form of the faith that prevails today. Oil was discovered in Iran in 1908. From that time on Persia (retitled in the 1920s by a Shah who adopted the name Iran because it meant "Aryan") became of growing interest to the great powers, and the requirements of international oil companies began to figure in Iranian life.

After the Second World War the Iranians found the corrupt and despotic rule of Shah Reza Pahlavi intolerable, and in 1979 he was overthrown in the first national revolution to be led by Islamic fundamentalists. This event has had profound effects and repercussions throughout the Muslim world. Iran's subsequent support for Islamic radicalism abroad soon led to strained relations with Central Asian, Middle Eastern, and North African nations, as well as the USA. More recently, Iran's economic difficulties and isolation have caused a general relaxation both in the domestic regime and in its external affairs.

The entire central region of Iran is dominated by a high, arid plateau (average elevation 1,200 m; 3,937 ft), most of it salt desert, containing the Dasht-e Lūt (Great Sand Desert) and the Dasht-e-Kavīr (Great Salt Desert). Mountain ranges surround the plateau: the volcanic Elburz Range (Reshteh-ye Kūhhā-ye Alborz) along the Caspian Sea; the Khorasan and Baluchestan Ranges in the east and southeast; and the Zagros Mountains (Kūhhā-ye Zāgros) inland from the Persian Gulf.

The most productive parts of Iran, and the most heavily populated, lie on its periphery. In the north are the fisheries, tea gardens, and rice fields of the Caspian shore. In Khuzestan to the south there are sugar plantations and oilfields—a prime target of the Iraqis when they invaded in 1980 at the start of the eight-year Iran-Iraq War. Westward lie the wheatfields of Azarbaijan, while to the east are the fruit groves of the oases of Kavir in Kavir (Dasht-e Kavīr) and Lut in Lut Desert (Dasht-e Lūt).

Approximately eight percent of Iran's land is arable, and eleven percent of it is forested, mostly in the provinces of Gilan and Mazandaran which border the Caspian Sea. The province of Tehrān, which includes the country's capital of the same name in the north, is by far the most densely populated region supporting about eighteen percent of the population.

In the years after 1945 Iran's economy became almost totally dependent on oil, and earnings from oil exports still provide 85 percent of its export revenue. But by the end of the war with Iraq (1980–88) production had fallen to just half the level of 1979. This, combined with the general fall in oil prices, and a surge in imports that began in 1989, has left Iran in severe financial difficulties, and there has been a marked decline in the general standard of living. Ideological considerations hamper effective reforms: there is a continuing struggle between the powerful religious leadership on the one hand, and reformist politicians on the other, over how to run a modern economy. The mullahs (the Islamic clergy) object to the government using borrowed money and are firmly opposed to the importation of "corrupt" Western technology.

Overall, the Iranian economy is a mix of centrally planned large-scale state enterprise; village-based agriculture producing wheat, barley, rice, sugar beet, tobacco, and pistachio nuts; and small-scale private trading and service ventures.

Central and West Asia

Afghanistan

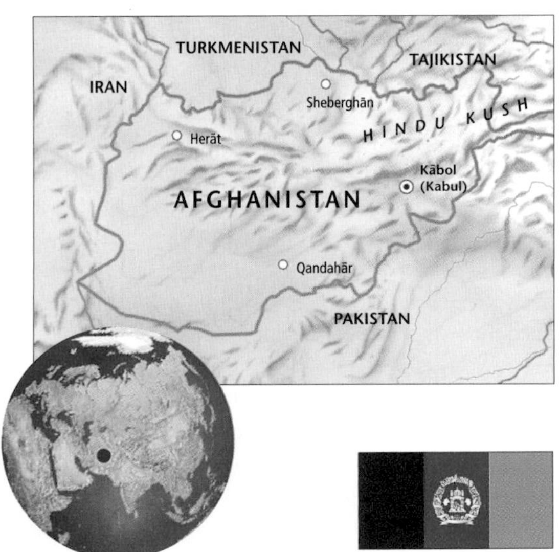

Fact File

Official name Islamic State of Afghanistan

Form of government Transitional government

Capital Kābol (Kabul)

Area 647,500 sq km (250,000 sq miles)

Time zone GMT + 4.5 hours

Population 27,756,000

Projected population 2015 35,577,000

Population density 42.9 per sq km (111 per sq mile)

Life expectancy 46.6

Infant mortality (per 1,000) 144.8

Official languages Dari (Afghan Persian), Pashto

Other languages Uzbek, Turkmen, Indi and Pamiri languages, Dravidian

Literacy rate 36 %

Religions Sunni Muslim 84 %, Shi'a Muslim 15 %, other 1 %

Ethnic groups Pashtun 38 %, Tajik 25 %, Hazara 19 %, Uzbek 6 %, other 12%

Currency Afghani

Economy Agriculture 61 %, services 25 %, industry 14 %

GNP per capita US$ 800

Climate Mainly semiarid, but arid in southwest and cold in mountains; hot summers and cold winters

Highest point Nowshak 7,485 m (24,557 ft)

Map reference Page 221

Afghanistan is a landlocked country in the central part of South Asia with nearly three-quarters of its territory mountainous. It shares a western frontier with Iran, while Pakistan is across the southeastern border. Once a part of the ancient Persian Empire, Afghanistan was conquered by Alexander the Great in 328 BC. In the seventh century AD it adopted Islam. From 1953 it was closely allied with the former Soviet Union. In 1979 the Soviet government intervened to install a communist faction, and though constantly beseiged by mujahideen guerrilla fighters, maintained its military occupation until 1989. After the overthrow of the communist government in 1992 the mujahideen began fighting among themselves along ethnic lines. In 1996–2001, the Sunni Muslim Taliban militia, associated with the majority Pashtun, was in control of the country and imposed a strict Islamic rule, but was overthrown in late 2001 by an international alliance.

Geographically, the country's largest area is the thinly populated central highlands. This comprises most of the Hindu Kush, the second highest range in the world, with several peaks over 6,400 m (21,000 ft). The northeast is seismically active. Much of the rest is desert or semidesert, except for a few fertile and heavily populated valleys, among them Herāt in the northwest. Most agriculture takes place on the northern plains, near the frontiers of Turkmenistan, Uzbekistan, and Tajikistan. The country's main river basins are those of the Amu Darya, Helmand, and Kābol.

Afghanistan is very poor: a list of 192 countries ranked for calorie intake in 1995 placed Afghanistan 191. It depends largely on wheat farming and the raising of sheep and goats. During the Soviet occupation and the subsequent internecine conflict, one-third of the population left the country, 6 million refugees fleeing to Pakistan and Iran. Many have now gone home to an economically devastated land. Millions of people lack food, clothing, housing, and medical care. Though data are shaky, it is likely that the country's most profitable crop is opium, Afghanistan reputedly being the world's second largest producer after Myanmar (Burma), and a major source of hashish.

Kazakhstan

Fact File

Official name Republic of Kazakhstan

Form of government Republic with two legislative bodies (Senate and Majilis)

Capital Aqmola (Astana)

Area 2,717,300 sq km (1,049,150 sq miles)

Time zone GMT + 6 hours

Population 16,742,000

Projected population 2015 15,957,000

Population density 6.2 per sq km (16 per sq mile)

Life expectancy 63.4

Infant mortality (per 1,000) 59

Official language Kazakh

Other language Russian

Literacy rate 98.4 %

Religions Muslim 47 %, Russian Orthodox 44 %, Protestant 2 %, other 7 %

Ethnic groups Kazak 41.9 %, Russian 37 %, Ukrainian 5.2 %, German 4.7 %, Uzbek 2.1 %, Tatar 2 %, other 7.1 %

Currency Tenge

Economy Services 43 %, industry 31 %, agriculture 26 %

GNP per capita US$ 5,900

Climate Mainly arid; cold winters and hot summers; cooler in north

Highest point Khan Tängiri Shyngy 6,995 m (22,949 ft)

Map reference Pages 222–23

With a land area nearly as large as India, Kazakhstan is an important member of the newly formed Commonwealth of Independent States (CIS). In earlier times, when it was a Soviet Republic, authorities used the region for testing nuclear weapons and for exiling ethnic minorities.

In the 1950s and 1960s when the Soviet "virgin lands" project was underway, vast tracts of pasture were sown with wheat or given over to livestock production, and waters from rivers running into the Aral Sea were used in irrigation schemes. As a result, the sea shrank by seventy percent.

During the years of Soviet domination, high levels of immigration from Russia resulted in the Kazakhs being outnumbered. Outmigration of Russians since 1991 and the return of many expatriates has resulted in a Kazak majority once more, but ethnic tensions remain high.

Much of the country is tablelands—the eroded tableland of the east featuring shallow uplands, depressions, and lakes—and there are also several mountains ranges in the east including the Altai Range (Mongol Altayn Nuruu). Running from north to south, steppe country gives way to desert or semidesert, though irrigation schemes have made large areas productive between the Aral Sea and Lake Balkhash (Balqash Köli).

With a climate marked by intense winter cold and extreme summer heat, rainfall is generally low. The lakes in the center of the country are saline, as are the marshes in the west, and in the central region there are few permanent rivers. The grassy steppes of the north are the most naturally fertile part of the country. Though the region has traditionally been associated with livestock rearing (Kazakhstan still supports up to 200,000 nomadic shepherds and herdsmen) the agricultural policies of the Soviet period converted much pasture to grain cultivation. By 1989 the country accounted for twenty percent of the entire cultivated area of the Soviet Union and twelve percent of its grain output.

Other crops grown include fruits, potatoes, vegetables, sugar beet, and cotton. High quality wool is produced, and Kazakhstan supplies meat to surrounding countries. Industry is based mainly on processing raw materials: fuel, metals, textiles, chemicals, and food. Products include rolled metals, agricultural machinery, plastics, clothing, footwear, paper, and cement. Well endowed with oil and gas reserves, the country also has deposits of coal, iron ore, bauxite, copper, nickel, tungsten, zinc, and silver. In addition, it holds seventy percent of CIS gold reserves. The government has been pursuing a moderate program of reform and privatization—investment incentives have been established, state controls have been lifted, and assets privatized. But government control of key industries remains extensive. Lack of pipeline transportation for oil export hinders a likely source of economic growth.

Environmental problems are extensive and severe. Radioactive or toxic chemical sites associated with weapons development are widespread. The drying up of the Aral Sea has left a crust of chemical pesticides which is periodically blown about in noxious dust storms.

Uzbekistan

Fact File

Official name Republic of Uzbekistan

Form of government Republic with single legislative body (Supreme Assembly)

Capital Toshkent (Tashkent)

Area 447,400 sq km (172,741 sq miles)

Time zone GMT + 6 hours

Population 25,564,000

Projected population 2015 30,554,000

Population density 57.1 per sq km (148 per sq mile)

Life expectancy 63.9

Infant mortality (per 1,000) 71.1

Official language Uzbek

Other languages Russian, Tajik

Literacy rate 99 %

Religions Muslim 88 % (mostly Sunnis), Eastern Orthodox 9 %, other 3 %

Ethnic groups Uzbek 71.4 %, Russian 8.3 %, Tajik 4.7 %, Kazak 4.1 %, Tatar 2.4 %, other 9.1 %

Currency Som

Economy Agriculture 43 %, services 35 %, industry 22 %

GNP per capita US$ 2,500

Climate Mainly arid, with cold winters and long, hot summers

Highest point Adelunga Toghi 4,301 m (14,111 ft)

Map reference Pages 222–23

Uzbekistan stretches from the shrinking Aral Sea to the heights of the western Pamirs. Its main frontiers are with Kazakhstan to the north and Turkmenistan to the south. The Uzbek people are of Turkic origin and seem to have taken their name from the Mongol Öz Beg Khan (AD 1313–40), who may also have converted them to Islam. In the fifteenth century they moved south into their present land. The Muslim cities of Samarqand and Bukhoro are in Uzbekistan, Bukhoro being a major religious center. Muslims unable to visit Mecca can become hajis by visiting Bukhoro seven times instead. In the former USSR the territory was the Uzbek Soviet Socialist Republic, and Uzbek leaders suffered much during Stalin's purges. In 1991 Uzbekistan became independent and is today ruled by the old communist elite as a de facto one-party state. The most populous of the Central Asian republics, Uzbekistan also has the greatest variety of ethnic groups. This is often a source of conflict. The Turkish-speaking Uzbeks clash with the Farsi-speaking Tajiks, and the Meskhetian Turks (deported from Georgia to Central Asia by Stalin) clash with the Uzbeks in the Fergana Valley. In 1999/2000, the Islamic Movement tried in vain to erect an Islamic Caliphate there.

The city of Kābol in Afghanistan, devastated by years of warfare (left page bottom). The Tila Kara Marasa, in Registan Square, Samarqand, Uzbekistan, built in the seventeenth century (above).

The middle region of Uzbekistan consists of the desert plains of the Kyzyl Kum (Peski Kyzylkum). While some of this area supports herders with cattle and sheep, today it is more important for its oil and gas reserves. To the west is the river delta formed where the Syrdar'ya (Oxus) enters the Aral Sea, while the Ustyurt Plateau lies in the extreme northwest. East of the Kyzyl Kum, beyond the capital of Toshkent and the Chatkal Mountains, is a spur jutting into Kyrgyzstan. This contains a large part of the fertile Fergana Basin. Uzbekistan is the world's fourth-largest cotton producer, and the Fergana Valley bears the environmental scars of the fertilizers and pesticides which helped to bring this about.

Although it grows large quantities of cotton, Uzbekistan is unable to produce enough grain for its own needs, importing it from Russia, Kazakhstan, and the USA. A rethinking of the Soviet-style economy has yet to take place.

As well as one of the world's largest goldmines, at Murantau, Uzbekistan has large deposits of natural gas, petroleum, coal, and uranium. Gas is currently used domestically, but it could become a major export. After 1991 the government tried to strengthen the economy with subsidies and tight price controls. Inflation rose to 1,500 percent at one point and in 1995 food rationing had to be introduced. At present, efforts are being made to tighten monetary policies, expand privatization, and to reduce the state's role in the economy, but so far there have been few serious structural changes.

Mongolia

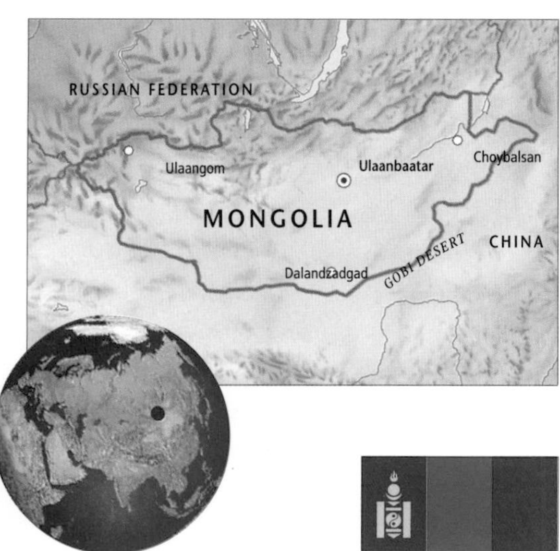

Fact File

Official name Mongolia

Form of government Republic with single legislative body (State Great Hural)

Capital Ulaanbaatar

Area 1,565,000 sq km (604,247 sq miles)

Time zone GMT + 8 hours

Population 2,695,000

Projected population 2015 3,085,000

Population density 1.7 per sq km (4.5 per sq mile)

Life expectancy 64.6

Infant mortality (per 1,000) 52

Official language Khalka Mongol

Other languages Turkic, Russian, Chinese, Kazakh

Literacy rate 97.8 %

Religions Tibetan Buddhist 90 %, Shamanist, with small Muslim minority

Ethnic groups Mongol 90 %, Kazakh 4 %, Chinese 2 %, Russian 2 %, other 2 %

Currency Tugrik

Economy Mainly agriculture with some industry

GNP per capita US$ 1,770

Climate Cold and arid

Highest point Tavan Bogd Uul 4,374 m (14,350 ft)

Map reference Pages 300–01

The world's largest and most thinly populated landlocked country, Mongolia has a reputation for isolation. Its deserts, severe climate, and widely scattered population of nomadic pastoralists have tended to keep it isolated from modern life. Historically, however, Mongolia enjoyed its hour of glory. In the thirteenth century the Mongol tribes were united under the leadership of Ghengis Khan (1162–1227), who then established the largest empire yet known, at its peak extending from eastern Europe to the Pacific Ocean and into northern India. The Mongol Empire collapsed in 1368, after which Mongolia (also known as Outer Mongolia to distinguish it from Inner Mongolia, one of China's Autonomous Regions) fell under Chinese control. Following the Russian Civil War (1918–22) the Chinese were expelled. Today, after seventy years within the Soviet system, the country is trying to remake itself in a more democratic mold.

Mongolia can be divided into two regions. In the northwest lie the Mongolian Altai Mountains (Mongol Altayn Nuruu), along with the Hangayn (Hangayn Nuruu) and Hentiyn Ranges (Govĭ Altayn Nuruu). Here, high mountains alternate with river valleys and lakes. Pastures support large herds of cattle and sheep, and wheat is cultivated. At the highest levels of the Altai in the northwest boreal forests cover the slopes. The second region is the southern half of the country. This is semidesert steppe changing further south to salt-pans, shallow depressions, and the arid stony wastes of the Gobi Desert.

While today more people live in towns than in the country, Mongolia nontheless remains a land of nomadic pastoralists. Herds of goats, sheep, yaks, camels, and horses still provide the base of the traditional economy, and Mongolia has the highest number of livestock per capita in the world. Cattle raising accounts for more than two-thirds of all production. Under the Soviets textiles and food processing were developed, and with aid from the USSR and Comecon (Council for Mutual Economic Assistance) mineral deposits such as copper, molybdenum, and coking coal were developed. Mongolia is the world's third biggest producer of fluorspar.

Recently, new laws have been passed regulating mining, banking, foreign investment, tourism, and economic planning. Mongolia continues to attract foreign aid, but suffers from the loss of Russian financial support. So far, foreign funds have not been found for the development of Mongolia's considerable oil and gas reserves.

Kyrgysztan

Fact File

Official name Kyrgyz Republic

Form of government Republic with two legislative bodies (Assembly of People's Representatives and Legislative Assembly)

Capital Bishkek

Area 198,500 sq km (76,641 sq miles)

Time zone GMT + 6 hours

Population 4,823,000

Projected population 2015 5,836,000

Population density 24.3 per sq km (62.9 per sq mile)

Life expectancy 63.6

Infant mortality (per 1,000) 75.9

Official language Kyrghiz

Other language Russian

Literacy rate 97 %

Religions Sunni Muslim 70 %, Christian (predominantly Russian Orthodox) 30 %

Ethnic groups Kyrghiz 52.5 %, Russian 21.5 %, Uzbek 13 %, Ukrainian 2.5 %, German 2.5 %, other 8 %

Currency Som

Economy Services 41 %, agriculture 38 %, industry 21 %

GNP per capita US$ 2,800

Climate Subtropical in southwest, temperate in valleys, cold and snowy in mountains

Highest point Pik Pobedy 7,439 m (24,406 ft)

Map reference Page 223

Kyrgyzstan is a small, mountainous, landlocked country in Central Asia. China lies over the massive peaks of the Tian Shan Range along its southeast border, Kazakhstan is to the north, and Uzbekistan and Tajikistan are to the southwest. Not only is Kyrgyzstan the least urbanized of all the ex-Soviet republics, its population is growing faster in rural areas than in the towns. Native Kyrgyz are barely a majority and ethnic tension

A Mongolian musician playing a horsehair fiddle (left). Women at the market in the town of Osh, Kyrgyzstan (right page top). Melon sellers at a market in Turkmenistan (right page bottom).

with Uzbeks and other nationals from nearby countries is a feature of everyday life. Fierce clashes between Kyrgyz and Uzbeks took place in the border city of Osh in 1990. Historically, the once nomadic Muslim Kyrgyz pastoralists are descended from refugees of Mongolian and Turkic origin who entered the region in the thirteenth century, escaping from Mongol invaders. For a while in the eighteenth century the region came under Manchu domination, then during the nineteenth century Russia began to colonize the country. Russian immigrants took the best land, settling in the low-lying, fertile areas. For years after the country's incorporation into the Soviet Union in the 1920s, resistance was carried out by local guerrilla groups called *basmachi*. Since independence in 1991, Kyrgyzstan has pursued liberal political and economic policies.

Geographically, Kyrgyzstan is dominated by the western end of the Tian Shan Range, which rises to Pik Pobedy (7,439 m; 24,406 ft) on the Chinese border. A large part of this mountain range is permanently snow-capped. The rest of the country is made up of a series of mountainous parallel ridges, separated by deep valleys and basins. The deep waters of Lake Ysyk-Köl are surrounded by snowy mountains in the northeast. The Fergana Valley, which is the main lowland region, lies in the southwest.

Much of the lower land is pasture for sheep, pigs, cattle, goats, horses, and yaks. Irrigated land is used to produce crops ranging from sugar beet and vegetables to rice, cotton, tobacco, grapes, and mulberry trees (for feeding silkworms). There are major salination problems caused mainly by the excessive irrigation of cotton.

Cotton, wool, and meat are the main agricultural products and exports: one of Kyrgyzstan's strengths is agricultural self-sufficiency. It has small quantities of coal, oil, gas, and the extensive snow-covered ranges ensure great hydropower potential. Energy policy aims at developing these resources in order to make the country less dependent on Russia. After the introduction of market reforms, and a program to control inflation, attention has turned to stimulating growth. This will not be easy: the economy is still dominated by the state and by the mentality of collective farming. Foreign aid plays a major role in the country's budget.

Turkmenistan

Fact File

Official name Republic of Turkmenistan

Form of government Republic with single legislative body (Parliament)

Capital Ashgabat

Area 488,100 sq km (188,455 sq miles)

Time zone GMT + 5 hours

Population 4,689,000

Projected population 2015 6,059,000

Population density 9.6 per sq km (24.9 per sq mile)

Life expectancy 61.1

Infant mortality (per 1,000) 73.2

Official language Turkmen

Other languages Russian, Uzbek

Literacy rate 98 %

Religions Muslim 87 %, Eastern Orthodox 11 %, other 2 %

Ethnic groups Turkmen 73.3 %, Russian 9.8 %, Uzbek 9 %, Kazak 2 %, other 5.9 %

Currency Manat

Economy Agriculture 44 %, services 36 %, industry 20 %

GNP per capita US$ 4,700

Climate Mainly arid, with cold winters and hot summers

Highest point Ayrybaba 3,139 m (10,298 ft)

Map reference Page 222

Turkmenistan is in southern Central Asia. From the Caspian Sea it stretches east to Afghanistan, and borders Iran to the south. Kazakhstan and Uzbekistan lie to the north. The Turkmen are probably descended from the same tribes as the Seljuk and Ottoman Turks who conquered what is now Turkey in the eleventh century. Russia annexed Turkmenistan in 1884 and began colonizing it in 1906. In 1924 it became the Turkmen Soviet Socialist Republic. Fierce local resistance to Sovietization continued into the 1930s and there were mass arrests of cultural and religious leaders. Turkmenistan declared its independence in 1991 but little has changed politically. It remains a one-party state and the first secretary of the former Communist Party is now the president, elected with a 99.5 percent share of the vote. The chief difference is that the government can now seek outside capital to develop the country's vast natural gas reserves, and looks to Muslim countries rather than Russia for support.

More than ninety percent of the country is arid, the greater part of it being the Kara Kum Desert. Most of the Kara Kum is made up of the plains of the Krasnovodskoye Plato, but ten percent consists of huge sand dunes. In the east the Amu Darya River forms part of the Afghanistan border. This river once fed the Aral Sea but from the 1950s much of its water was diverted into the Kara Kum Canal which crosses two-thirds of the country westward to Kizyl-Arvat (Gyzlarbat). This provided irrigation for cotton, but also helped dry up the Aral Sea. To the west of the plateau the land falls to the Caspian shore.

Turkmenistan is poor, despite its natural gas and oil reserves. Half its irrigated land is planted in cotton but industrial development has been limited. Apart from Astrakhan rugs and food processing, industry is largely confined to mining sulfur and salt, and natural gas production. Through 1995 inflation soared, and falling production saw the budget shift from a surplus to a deficit. Since independence in 1991 there have been few changes in economic policy, leading to growing poverty and a shortage of basic foods. Cotton and grain harvests were disastrous in 1996 and desertification remains a serious problem.

Tajikistan

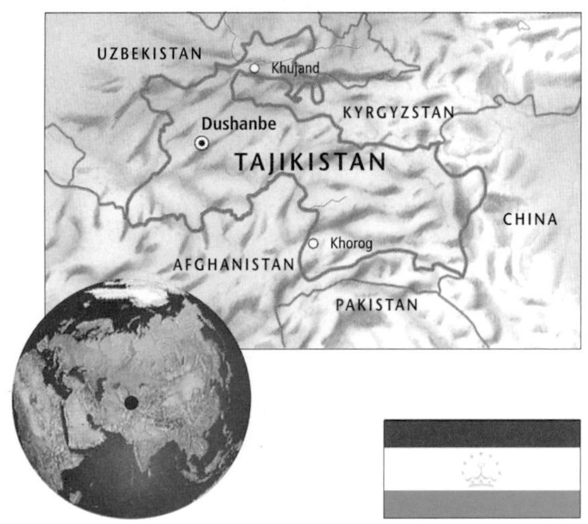

Fact File

Official name Republic of Tajikistan

Form of government Republic with single legislative body (Supreme Assembly)

Capital Dushanbe

Area 143,100 sq km (55,251 sq miles)

Time zone GMT + 6 hours

Population 6,720,000

Projected population 2015 7,097,000

Population density 47 per sq km (121.6 per sq mile)

Life expectancy 64.3

Infant mortality (per 1,000) 114.8

Official language Tajik

Other language Russian, Uzbek

Literacy rate 98 %

Religions Sunni Muslim 80 %, Shi'a Muslim 5 %, other (including Russian Orthodox) 15 %

Ethnic groups Tajik 65 %, Uzbek 25 %, Russian 3.5 %, other 6.5 %

Currency Tajik ruble

Economy Agriculture 43 %, services 35 %, industry 22 %

GNP per capita US$ 1,140

Climate Mild winters and hot summers in valleys and on plains, drier and much colder in mountains

Highest point Pik imeni Ismail Samani 7,495 m (24,590 ft)

Map reference Page 223

Tajikistan lies between Uzbekistan, Afghanistan, and China on the western slope of the Pamirs. It also shares a border with Kyrgyzstan to the north. The country is an irregular shape because it was carved out of the Soviet Republic of Uzbekistan on Stalin's orders in 1929. This was intended to deal with Tajik resistance to the Soviet regime, but as it left the two Tajik centers of Samarqand and Bukhoro in Uzbekistan, it merely added another grievance. The Tajiks are Persian-Iranian culturally and linguistically, not Turkic-Mongol like many other peoples of Central Asia. Immigration of both Uzbeks and Russians during the Soviet era caused further resentment. Since independence in 1991 ethnic hostility has resulted in a state of near civil war. Tens of thousands were killed and thousands more have fled to Afghanistan and Kyrgyzstan. Only in 1997 was a peace achieved. It remains a major objective to overcome the destructions of the war.

A long finger of territory in the north contains the only fertile agricultural region. This is the western end of the Fergana Valley through which the Syrdar'ya drains northwest toward the Aral Sea. Cotton is the chief crop, though cereals and fruit are also grown. The region has seen the overuse of pesticides on cotton, and the drying up of the distant Aral Sea has been aggravated by water taken for irrigation. Between this valley and one to the south drained by the Vakhsh stand the Turkestan and Gissar Ranges. This substantial physical divide also corresponds to the political divide between the Uzbek communists in the north and the Islamic secularists in the south. Most of eastern Tajikistan consists of the Pamirs, a part of the Tien Shan Range of western China.

Tajikistan has the second-lowest per capita gross domestic product of any former USSR republic, the fastest growing population, and a low standard of living. Agriculture is the most important sector and cotton the main crop. The country has limited mineral resources, including silver, gold, uranium, and tungsten. Hydropower provides energy for the manufacture of aluminum, cotton textiles and clothing, and for food processing. The economy is weak from years of conflict. Subsidies once provided by the USSR are gone, along with markets—Russia once bought Tajik uranium for its weapons program. Basic subsistence for many people depends on foreign aid. Social instability, plus the continuation of Soviet-era politicians and officials in power, has prevented economic reforms.

Armenia

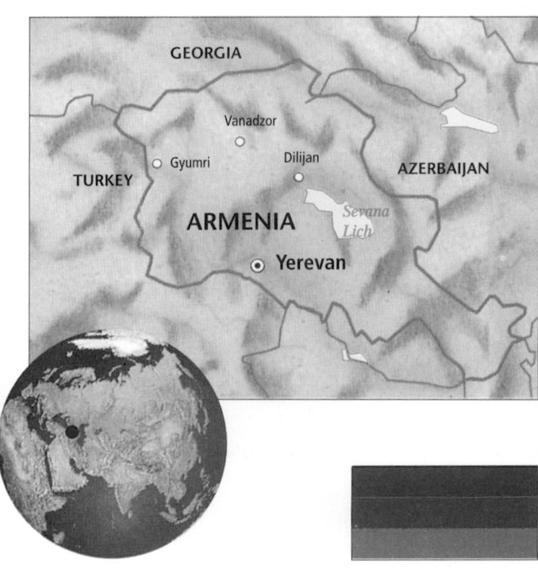

Fact File

Official name Republic of Armenia

Form of government Republic with single legislative body (National Assembly)

Capital Yerevan

Area 29,800 sq km (11,506 sq miles)

Time zone GMT + 4 hours

Population 3,330,000

Projected population 2015 3,808,000

Population density 111.7 per sq km (289.4 per sq mile)

Life expectancy 66.6

Infant mortality (per 1,000) 41.1

Official language Armenian

Other language Russian

Literacy rate 99 %

Religions Armenian Orthodox 94 %, other (Russian Orthodox, Muslim, Protestant) 6 %

Ethnic groups Armenian 93 %, Azeri 3 %, Russian 2 %, other (mainly Kurdish) 2 %

Currency Dram

Economy Industry 28 %, agriculture 27 %, services 26 %, other 19 %

GNP per capita US$ 3,350

Climate Mainly dry, with cold winters and warm summers; cooler in mountains

Highest point Aragats Lerr 4,090 m (13,419 ft)

Map reference Page 222

Armenia is a small, mountainous, Christian country, landlocked between hostile Muslim neighbors. To the east is Azerbaijan, and to the west is Turkey, which inflicted genocidal massacres on the Armenian people between 1894 and 1915. The legendary resting place of Noah's Ark after the Flood (its capital supposedly founded by Noah himself), Armenia had already existed as a distinct country for 1,000 years when in the fourth century AD it became the first in the world to make Christianity its state religion. The country has been fought over at various times by Romans, Persians, and Mongols. It became a Soviet Socialist Republic in 1922 and gained its independence from the Soviet Union in 1991. In 1988 there was a devastating earthquake which killed 25,000 people and destroyed power stations and other infrastructure, and in the same year conflict began over Nagorno-Karabakh, an internal Azerbaijani area largely populated by Christian Armenians which is claimed by Armenia.

The mountains of the Lesser Caucasus (Malyy Kavkaz) cover most of the country. The landscape is rugged, and includes extinct volcanoes and high lava plateaus cut with ravines. An active seismic area, the frequency of earthquakes in Armenia indicates that mountain-building is still taking place. Although the city of Ararat is in Armenia, Mt Ararat itself is across the border in Turkey. The centrally located Lake Sevan (Sevana Lich) lies nearly 2,000 m (6,000 ft) above sea level, but its use for hydropower has drained it to a point where drinking water supplies are threatened. Steppe vegetation is the main cover and drought-resistant grasses and sagebrush grow on the lower mountain slopes, where jackals, wildcats, and the occasional leopard are found.

As a Soviet Republic, Armenia developed an industrial sector, supplying machine building tools, textiles, and other manufactured goods to other republics in return for raw materials and energy. It has few natural resources, although formerly lead, copper, and zinc were mined, and there are deposits of gold and bauxite. Agriculture is an important source of income. In irrigated areas around Yerevan, crops include grapes, almonds, figs, and olives, while apples, pears, and cereals are grown on higher ground. Armenia is also known for its quality brandies and wines. Economic decline in the period from 1991 to 1994 was a direct result of the ongoing conflict over Nagorno-Karabakh. In retaliation for Armenia's military activities in the region, Turkey and Azerbaijan blockaded pipeline and railroad traffic into the country, causing chronic energy shortages. There have been improvements, but full economic recovery is unlikely before Armenia's conflict with its neighbors is settled.

A yurt in the Pamir region of Tajikistan (left page top). View over the city of Yerevan in Armenia, with Mt Ararat in the background (below).

Azerbaijan

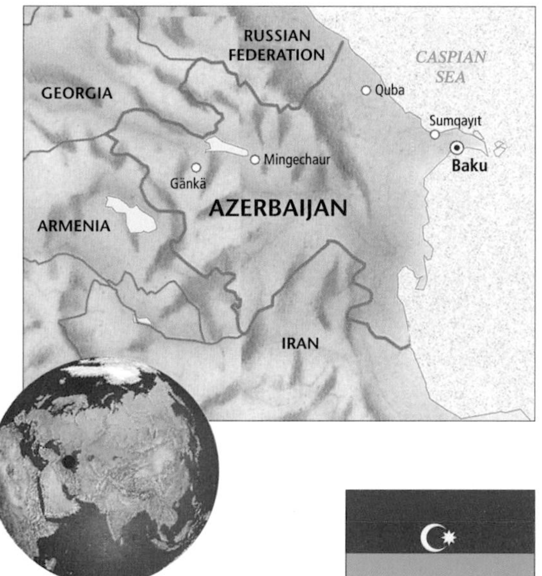

Fact File

Official name Azerbaijani Republic

Form of government Federal republic with single legislative body (National Assembly)

Capital Baki (Baku)

Area 86,600 sq km (33,436 sq miles)

Time zone GMT + 4 hours

Population 7,799,000

Projected population 2015 8,725,000

Population density 90.1 per sq km (233.3 per sq mile)

Life expectancy 63.1

Infant mortality (per 1,000) 82.7

Official language Azerbaijani

Other languages Russian, Armenian

Literacy rate 97 %

Religions Muslim 93.4 %, Russian Orthodox 2.3 %, Armenian Orthodox 2.3 %, other 2 %

Ethnic groups Azeri 90 %, Dagestani peoples 3.2 %, Russian 2.5 %, Armenian 2.3 %, other 2 %

Currency Manat

Economy Services 42 %, agriculture 32 %, industry 26 %

GNP per capita US$ 3,300

Climate Mainly semiarid

Highest point Bazardüzü Dağ 4,466 m (14,652 ft)

Map reference Page 222

Oil was being collected from the Caspian Sea near Baku at least 1,000 years ago, when the area was known as "land of eternal fire" because of burning natural gas flaming out of the ground. Today oil from Baku continues to be the mainstay of the Azerbaijani economy. The home of an independent Azeri state as early as the fourth century BC, the region later fell under the influence of Persia, then in the eleventh century Turkic-speaking people moved in and assumed control. A period of affiliation with the Soviets following the Russian Revolution led to Azerbaijan becoming a member of the Soviet Union in 1936. In 1990 it was one of the first Soviet Republics to declare independence.

Since 1988 there have been troubles with Armenia over the region of Nagorno-Karabakh in southwestern Azerbaijan. This territorial dispute (Armenia now holds twenty percent of the region, most of the people in Nagorno-Karabakh being Christian Armenians) remains a major political problem for the newly independent state.

A range of the Great Caucasus (Bol'shoy Kavkas) running at an angle toward the Caspian Sea separates Russia from Azerbaijan, and reaches almost as far as Baku. South of this range, draining out of the foothills of the Caucasus in Georgia, the Kura (Kür) River reaches a broad floodplain, some of which lies below sea level. The mountains of the Lesser Caucasus (Malyy Kavkaz) form much of Nagorno-Karabakh in the southwest and also stand between Azerbaijan and its isolated enclave-territory Naxçivan. Although a Naxçivan independence movement exists, this territory, which is surrounded by Iran and Armenia, is regarded by the government as part of the Azerbaijan state. Dry and subtropical, the lowlands experience mild winters and long, hot summers, and are frequently affected by drought. Plant cover consists of steppe grassland in the drier lowland regions, woods in the mountains, and swamps in the southeast.

Early this century Baku supplied as much as half the world's oil, but production declined steadily during the final years under Soviet control as plants became antiquated and maintenance was neglected. The 1994 ratification of a $7.5 billion deal with a consortium of Western oil companies marked a turning point, and a revival in this sector can be expected. Baku was the fifth biggest city in Soviet Russia and had a well diversified industrial sector. It is hoped the oil deal will stimulate new production of chemicals, textiles, and electrical goods.

Though Azerbaijan has only a small amount of arable land, it is a major producer of cotton, tobacco, grapes, and other fruit. Sturgeon from the Caspian was an important source of caviar but this industry is threatened by serious water pollution. One hundred years of intensive oil production, plus overuse of toxic defoliants in cotton growing, have taken a severe environmental toll. Azerbaijani scientists consider the Abseron Peninsula, where Baku stands, to be one of the most ecologically devastated areas in the world.

Georgia

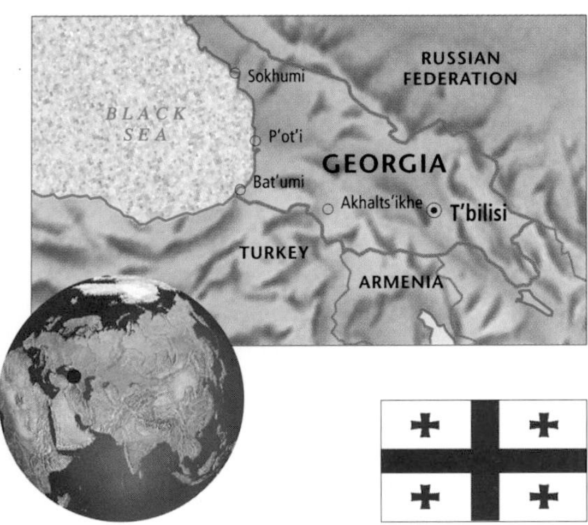

Fact File

Official name Republic of Georgia

Form of government Republic with single legislative body (Parliament)

Capital T'bilisi

Area 69,700 sq km (26,911 sq miles)

Time zone GMT + 4 hours

Population 4,961,000

Projected population 2015 4,775,000

Population density 71.2 per sq km (184.3 per sq mile)

Life expectancy 64.7

Infant mortality (per 1,000) 51.8

Official language Georgian

Other languages Russian, Armenian, Azeri, Abkhasian, Ossetian

Literacy rate 99 %

Religions Christian Orthodox 75 % (Georgian Orthodox 65 %, Russian Orthodox 10 %), Muslim 11 %, Armenian Apostolic 8 %, unknown 6 %

Ethnic groups Georgian 70 %, Armenian 8 %, Russian 6.5 %, Azeri 5.5 %, Ossetian 3 %, Abkhaz 2 %, other 5 %

Currency Lari

Economy Services 44 %, industry 31 %, agriculture 25 %

GNP per capita US$ 3,100

Climate Temperate, with cool winters and hot, dry summers; subtropical on Black Sea coast

Highest point Gora Kazbek 5,047 m (16,558 ft)

Map reference Page 222

A mountainous country in the shadow of the Great Caucasus (Bol'shoy Kavkas), Georgia lies on the shore of the Black Sea between the Russian Federation and Turkey, and has borders with Armenia and Azerbaijan in the southeast. It has a long national history. The land of the Golden Fleece in Greek mythology (Colchis was today's Plain of Kolkhida) Georgia was conquered by Romans, Persians, Arabs, Tartars, and Turks before falling to the Russians around 1800. Nevertheless, it has a strong culture, with a literary tradition based on a distinctive language and alphabet.

In 1991 Georgia rushed to proclaim its independence from the crumbling Soviet Union. Since then it has been chronically unstable, fighting off internal secessionist demands from both Abkhazia and—until 1994—South Ossetia. The town of Gori is the birthplace of Georgia's most famous son, Josef Stalin.

Georgia has four main areas: the Great Caucasus Range (Bol'shoy Kavkas) to the north which provides a natural boundary with Russia; the Black Sea Plain in the west, including the subtropical Kholkida lowlands; the eastern end of the Lesser Caucasus (Malyy Kavkaz) to the south, whose peaks and plateaus extend into Turkey and Armenia; and a central plateau called the Kartalinian Plain, where the capital of T'bilisi stands, and which divides the northern and southern ranges. Further east, the Kura (Kür) River and its tributaries drain through a number of upland valleys toward Azerbaijan and the Caspian Sea. The mountains contain extensive woodlands (nearly forty percent of the country is forested) with broadleaf beech, oak, and chestnut at lower levels, and a sparse cover of birch on the higher slopes.

Georgia is an agricultural country, and the main industries are food processing and wine production. Collectivization had less impact on Georgia than elsewhere in the Soviet Union, so the recovery of its rural sector post-1991 has been fairly painless. Privately owned plots flourish, agriculture as a whole producing citrus fruits, tea (the main crop), grapes, tobacco, wheat, barley and vegetables, while perfumes are made from flowers and herbs. The Imeretia district has a flourishing silk industry. Other products from a small industrial sector include machinery, chemicals, and textiles. Manganese, copper, cobalt, and vanadium are mined. Tourism was once important, but has been damaged by civil strife. There are severe energy shortages. In the long term, hopes for Georgian economic progress hinge on re-establishing trade ties with Russia, and on international transportation (such as handling oil from Azerbaijan) through its Black Sea ports.

Turkey

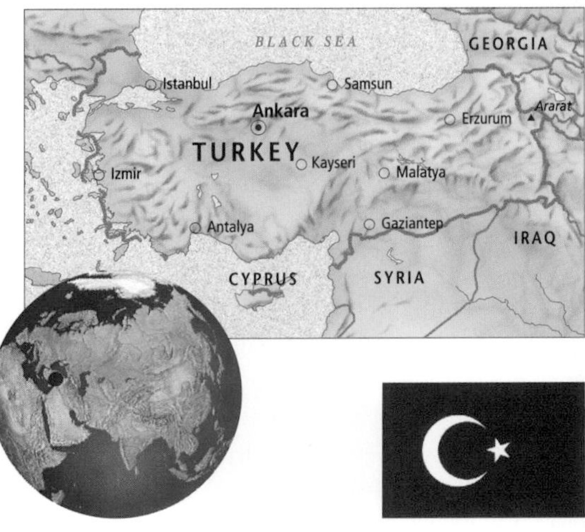

Fact File

Official name Republic of Turkey

Form of government Republic with single legislative body (Grand National Assembly of Turkey)

Capital Ankara

Area 780,580 sq km (301,382 sq miles)

Time zone GMT + 2 hours

Population 67,309,000

Projected population 2015 79,004,000

Population density 86.2 per sq km (223.3 per sq mile)

Life expectancy 71.5

Infant mortality (per 1,000) 45.8

Official language Turkish

Other languages Kurdish, Arabic

Literacy rate 85 %

Religions Muslim 99.8 % (mostly Sunni), other 0.2 %

Ethnic groups Turkish 80 %, Kurdish 20 %

Currency Turkish lira

Economy Agriculture 50 %, services 35 %, industry 15 %

GNP per capita US$ 7,000

Climate Temperate, with mild, wet winters and hot, dry summers; arid in the interior

Highest point Ağrı Dağı (Mt Ararat) 5,166 m (16,949 ft)

Map reference Page 224

Asia Minor, a large mountainous plateau lying between the Black Sea and the Mediterranean, forms the main part of Turkey. A much smaller part, European Turkey or Thrace, lies across the narrow straits of the Bosphorus and the Dardanelles. Early in the twentieth century Turkey's leader Kemal Ataturk (1881–1938) attempted to create a modern Islamic state that was willing and able to be a part of Europe. At the end of the twentieth century, with Islamic fundamentalism a growing internal force and no end in sight to the repression of the Kurds, his legacy is uncertain. Full integration with Europe may become an object of concrete negotiations if the inspection due at the end of 2004 demonstrate that Turkey is fulfilling all preconditions. Apart from economic and human rights questions this includes the solution of the situation of the Turkish Kurds as well as the status of the island of Cyprus. Turkey has occupied the Muslim north of Cyprus since 1974, but their claim is not recognized internationally. The Kurds in southeastern Turkey are demanding an independent homeland. Opposed by the state, this conflict has resulted in an estimated 19,000 deaths so far.

Historically, Asia Minor or Anatolia was the stage on which some famous scenes have been enacted. The legendary city of Troy stood on the shore of the Aegean. Ephesus and its ruins can still be visited today. Astride the Bosphorus, Constantinople (now Istanbul) was the capital of the Byzantine Empire from the fourth century AD until it fell to the Seljuk Turks in 1453. Later, during the height of its expansion in the sixteenth century, the empire of the Ottoman Turks spread throughout the Middle East and North Africa, carrying Islam through the Balkans to Vienna. From this time the Ottoman Empire steadily declined (becoming known as "the sick man of Europe") until it was finally dismantled at the end of the First World War. The boundaries of the present Turkish state were set in 1923.

European Turkey has fertile rolling plains surrounded by low mountains. The main feature of the Asian provinces is the largely semiarid Central Anatolian Plateau (1,000 to 2,000 m; 3,300 to 6,600 ft) much of which is used for grazing sheep. On its southern flank the three main ranges of the Taurus Mountains lie inland from the Mediterranean coast. In addition to timber, the uplands provide summer grazing for the flocks of the plateau. The Pontic Mountains stretching west to east along the Black Sea boundary of the plateau are more densely wooded, and have fertile plains. A number of other ranges further east culminate in the volcanic cone of Ağrı Dağı (Mt Ararat) (5,166 m; 16,949 ft). Important minerals found in the thinly populated eastern regions include chrome, copper, oil, and gold. Tobacco and figs are grown in two fertile valleys that lead westward down from the plateau to the Aegean Sea. Cotton is produced on the plain near the southern city of Adana.

The Turkish economy combines modern industry and commerce with village agriculture and crafts. Though still of importance, agriculture has been overtaken by manufacturing. A busy industrial sector produces textiles, processed foods, steel, petroleum, construction materials, lumber, and paper, while coal, chromite, and copper are mined. Energy for industry comes in part from oil that is imported, but also from domestic coal and from the country's abundant hydroelectric power.

During the 1980s growth averaged more than seven percent a year. In 1994 an outbreak of triple-digit inflation led to a period during which public debt, money supply, and the current account deficit were simultaneously out of control. Severe austerity measures and structural reforms were required in order to correct the situation. Shifting political coalitions and economic instability present a challenge for Turkey today.

Cyprus

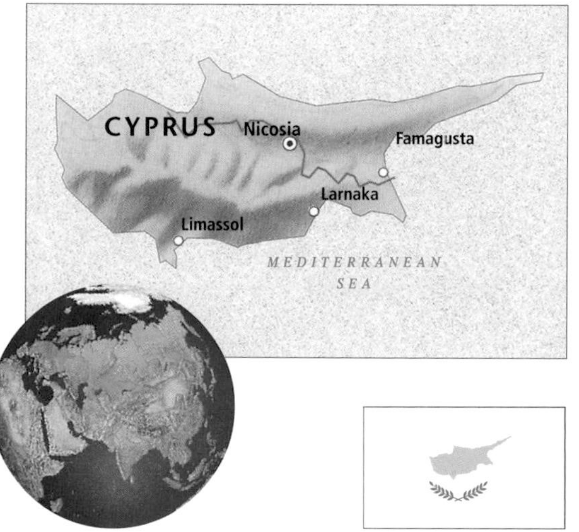

Fact File

Official name (Greek/Turkish) Republic of Cyprus

Form of government Two de facto republics each with single legislative body: House of Representatives in Greek area, Assembly of the Republic in Turkish area

Capital Lefkosia (Nicosia)

Area 9,250 sq km (3,571 sq miles)

Time zone GMT + 2 hours

Population 768,000

Projected population 2015 864,000

Population density 83 per sq km (215.1 per sq mile)

Life expectancy 77.1

Infant mortality (per 1,000) 7.7

Official languages Greek, Turkish

Other language English

Literacy rate 97 %

Religions Greek Orthodox 78 %, Muslim 18 %, other 4 %

Ethnic groups Greek 78 %, Turkish 18 %, other 4 %

Currency Cypriot pound, Turkish lira

Economy Services 67 %, industry 19 %, agriculture 14 %

GNP per capita US$ 15,000 (Greek part of the island), US$ 7,000 (Turkish part of the island)

Climate Temperate, with cool, wet winters and warm, dry summers

Highest point Olympos 1,951 m (6,404 ft)

Map reference Page 224

Cyprus takes its name from "kypros," the Greek word for copper. It was an important metal 3,000 years ago, in classical times, and is still exported today. Occupied by a succession of Phoenicians, Greeks, and Romans, held from 1571 by the Turks and by the British from 1878, Cyprus today is a deeply divided island. The southern part forms the Republic of Cyprus proper, where most of the population lives. Since 1982 the northern part has consisted of an autonomous region calling itself the Turkish Republic of Northern Cyprus (see box). The Greek part of the island became part of the EU in 2004 after voting down reunification with the Turkish north.

Along the north coast runs the long limestone range of the Kyrenia Mountains. Just south of this range is the fertile Mesaoria Plain between Morphou and Ammochostos (Famagusta) where grapes, potatoes, citrus fruits, and cereals are grown, and the steeper land supports sheep, goats, and cattle. In the south is the broad, mineral-rich massif of Troödos, which contains the copper. This constitutes fifty percent of the country's total land area and is a good geological example of an ophiolite, a dome of mineral-rich sub-oceanic rocks. Both major rivers flow from this massif—the Pedieas to Ammochostos Bay (Famagusta Bay), the Karyoti to Morphou Bay. Nearly half the total area of Cyprus is arable and twenty percent of this is irrigated.

The gap between the economic fortunes of the two parts of Cyprus continues to grow wider. The agriculturally based Turkish north, severely disrupted by the events of 1974, has not recovered well, and has suffered considerably from inflation. It continues to produce some cereals, meat, fruits, and olives. The Greek Cypriot southern half of the island has prospered from a greater diversity of activities, including tourism, manufacturing, and the income from military installations, such as the British air base of Akrotiri near Limassol. Manufactured products include cigarettes, wine, clothing, footwear, and cement.

Walls like those of a fortress surround this church in Georgia (left page top). Buildings carved from rock in Cappadocia, Turkey (below).

The Cyprus question

The Cypriots were among the first Christians. Between 644 and 975 the island was attacked and invaded multiple times in the course of the expansion of Islam. In 1195, after the Thrid Crusade, the island was awarded to the family of Guy de Lusignan as recompensation for his loss of the crown of Jerusalem. In 1487 the island came under the tutelage of the Venetians.

In 1571 the Ottomans conquered the island and slew many of its Greek inhabitants before they settled their own countrymen there. With the decline of the Ottoman Empire in the nineteenth century, a treaty was concluded with the United Kingdom that handed control of the islands over to the British crown (in 1925 Cyprus became an official colony). Soon the Greek Cypriots started to advocate the unification of the island with Greece. This was supported by the leaders of the Greek Orthodox church who argued that eighty percent of the population wanted to become part of the "mother country". In 1931 fighting broke out in Nicosia. After the Second World War the claim for unification was renewed. The political situation became even more explosive when another Greek group appeared who opted for the independence of the island.

In 1960 Cyprus became independent but soon new fights broke out. For ten years Greeks and Turks contested for suppremacy. In 1974 Turkish troups invaded the north of the island and occupied forty percent of the island, expelling approximately 200,000 Greeks to the south. Nine years later Northern Cyprus declared its independence. It was only recognized by Turkey and is ruled by a government headed by a president. A great opportunity to reunite the two halves was voted down by the population of the Greek part of the island shortly before Greek Cyprus joined the EU in 2004; whether this will change in the near future remains doubtful.

Dependencies and

Gaza Strip

Fact File

Official name Gaza Strip (preferred Palestinian term, Gaza District)

Form of government Disputed by Israel and Palestinian National Authority; interim self-government administered by Palestinian Legislative Council

Capital Gaza

Area 360 sq km (139 sq miles)

Time zone GMT + 2 hours

Population 1,226,000

Life expectancy 71.2

Infant mortality (per 1,000) 74.8

Literacy rate Not available

Currency Israeli shekel

Economy Industry 44 %, services 36 %, agriculture 20 %

Climate Temperate. Mild winters; warm, dry summers

Map reference Page 225

The Gaza Strip is a disputed territory on the Mediterranean with a large permanent exile population of Palestinians, most of whom are descended from those who fled Israel in 1948. Egypt lies to the south and Israel surrounds it to the east and north. Like the West Bank, the Gaza Strip has been in Israeli hands since the Six Day War of 1967. Formally incorporated into Israel in 1973, eight Israeli settlements have been built since 1967. From the time Israel assumed control, the Gaza Strip has been the scene of unrest and violence, the town of Gaza witnessing the Palestinian intifada ("uprising") in 1987–89. The accord reached between the Palestine Liberation Organization (PLO) and Israel in May 1994 gave self-rule to the Gaza Strip pending "final status" talks to take place in the future. The cycle of violence, involving Palestinian bombings in Israel and Israeli reprisals, makes a resolution of the territory's status difficult to achieve. A declaration of independence for Palestine that had been planned for May 1999 was postponed until some later date still to be defined. Since any Middle East peace plan vitally depends on the solution of the Palestinian-Israeli conflict, the USA started a new attempt at solving the crisis with the "Road Map" in 2003.

A frontier point with UN supervision in Nicosia, Cyprus (top). A flourishing olive tree in Cyprus that is about 1,000 years old (bottom). A semi-permanent home on the West Bank, an area still in dispute (right page top).

Territories in Asia

West Bank

Fact File

OFFICIAL NAME West Bank

FORM OF GOVERNMENT Disputed by Israel and Palestinian National Authority; interim self-government administered by Palestinian Legislative Council

CAPITAL Jerusalem

AREA 5,860 sq km (2,263 sq miles)

TIME ZONE GMT + 2 hours

POPULATION 2,164,000

LIFE EXPECTANCY 72.5

INFANCY MORTALITY (PER 1,000) 21.2

LITERACY RATE Not available

CURRENCY Israeli shekel, Jordanian dinar

ECONOMY Industry 45 %, services 34 %, agriculture 21 %

CLIMATE Temperate, with cool to mild winters and warm to hot summers

MAP REFERENCE Page 225

Under a 1947 UN agreement this area on the west bank of the Jordan River was to become Palestinian when the State of Israel was formed. After the 1967 Six Day War Israel had control of a larger area than originally proposed. The building of Israeli settlements since then has been bitterly resented by the more than ninty-five percent Palestinian Arab population. The area depends on remittances from workers in Israel. Lack of jobs has also led to many working in the Gulf States. But the *intifada* in 1987–89 reduced the numbers working in Israel, and many West Bank workers were sent home following Palestinian support for Iraq in the Gulf War. Unemployment presently is about twenty-six percent. Under a 1993–95 Israeli-PLO declaration certain powers were to be transferred to a Palestinian Legislative Council, but ongoing Palestinian bombings in Israel, Israeli reprisals, and persistent Israeli settlement construction make a speedy end to strife unlikely. Whether the resumption of talks that came about as a consequence of heightened US pressure in 2003 will indeed lead to the resolution of the remaining problems—one of them being the status of Jerusalem, claimed as capital by the Palestinians as well as by the Israelis—and the foundation of an independent Palestinian state in 2005 is highly doubtful. Corruption and scandals in the Palestinian leadership and their inability to keep fundamentalist terrorists at bay as well as Israel's policy of targeting and assassinating people they deem dangerous seem to make peace almost impossible.

British Indian Ocean Territory

Fact File

OFFICIAL NAME British Indian Ocean Territory

FORM OF GOVERNMENT Dependent territory of the United Kingdom

CAPITAL None

AREA 60 sq km (23 sq miles)

TIME ZONE GMT + 5 hours

POPULATION No permanent population

ECONOMY Air Force base

CLIMATE Tropical, moderated by trade winds

MAP REFERENCE Page 104

Otherwise known as the Chagos Islands, and the location of the US-UK military base of Diego Garcia, the British Indian Ocean Territory is a group of 2,300 islets located about 1,600 km (1,000 miles) from southern India and 600 km (400 miles) south of the Maldives. The islets are coral atolls and once supported a few people who produced copra for export. The islets were bought for $3 million by Britain from Mauritius but have been uninhabited since the plantations were closed and the population relocated to Mauritius in 1973.

Paracel Islands

Fact File

OFFICIAL NAME Paracel Islands

FORM OF GOVERNMENT Disputed territory occupied by China, but claimed by Taiwan and Vietnam

CAPITAL None

AREA Not available

TIME ZONE GMT + 8 hours

POPULATION No permanent population; Chinese garrisons

CLIMATE Tropical. Prone to typhoons

MAP REFERENCE Page 203

Situated in the South China Sea, the Paracel Islands consist of two groups of coral atolls: the Crescent Group in the west and the Amphitrite Group in the East. They are a collection of coral atolls about one-third of the way from central Vietnam to the northern Philippines. The Chinese have garrisoned the islands and have built port facilities and an airport on Woody Island. The Paracel Islands are often hit by tropical storms and are the center of a regional dispute because oil and natural gas are thought to exist within their territorial waters. Not only China, but also Vietnam and Taiwan claim their possession.

Spratly Islands

Fact File

OFFICIAL NAME Spratly Islands

FORM OF GOVERNMENT Disputed territory claimed by China, Taiwan, Vietnam, Malaysia, and the Philippines

CAPITAL None

AREA 5 sq km (1.9 sq miles)

TIME ZONE GMT + 8 hours

POPULATION No permanent population

CLIMATE Tropical. Prone to typhoons

MAP REFERENCE Page 203

The Spratly Islands consist of a collection of reefs, islands, and atolls scattered across a large area of the South China Sea, about two-thirds of the way from southern Vietnam to the southern Philippines. Brunei has made Louisa Reef an exclusive economic zone, but has not publicly claimed the island. The islands are subject to territorial disputes because of their proximity to oil- and gas-producing sedimentary basins.

Asia and the Middle East: Physical

30° 6 40° 5 50° 4 60° 3 70° 2 80° 1

ATLANTIC OCEAN
British Isles
Ireland
NORWEGIAN SEA
GREENLAND SEA
ARCTIC OCEA
Arctic Circle
Svalbard
Zemlya Frantsa-Iosifa
Bay of Biscay
English Channel
Strait of Gibraltar
Tejo
Guadalquivir
Iberian Peninsula
Pyrenees
Massif Central
Loire
Rhein (Rhine)
Skagerrak
Galdhøpiggen 2469 m
Scandinavia
Norakapp
BARENTS SEA
Novaya Zemlya
Jebel Toubkal 4165 m
Atlas Mountains
Grand Erg Occidental
Islas Baleares
Mont Blanc 4807 m
TYRRHENIAN SEA
MEDITERRANEAN SEA
Corse
Sardegna
Gulf of Bothnia
BALTIC SEA
Gulf of Finland
Elbe
Kol'skiy Poluostrov
Beloye More
Ostrov Kolguyev
KARSKOYE MORE
Ostrov Vaygach
Poluostrov
Appennino
ADRIATIC SEA
Dinara
Wisla
North European Plain
Daugava
Ladozhskoye Ozero
Onezhskoye Ozero
Gydanskiy Poluostrov
Grand Erg Oriental
Sicilia
Hora Hoverla 2061 m
Carpathian Mts
Dnyapro
Sredne-Russkaya Vozvyshennost'
Rybinskoye Vodokhranilishche
Pechora
Ural'skiy Khrebet (Ural Mountains)
Ob'
SAHARA
IONIAN SEA
Dunarea
Stara Planina
Volga
Yenisey
Zapadno Sibirskaya Ravnina
Tropic of Cancer
MEDITERRANEAN SEA
Dnipro
Krymsʹkyy Pivostriv (Crimean Peninsula)
BLACK SEA
Irtysh
Khalīj Surt
AEGEAN SEA
Sea of Azov
Kriti
Anatolia
Bol'shoy Kavkaz
Caspian Depression
Toros Dağları
Anadolu Dağları
Gora El'brus 5641 m
Ertis
Mongol Altayn Nuruu
Libyan Desert
Mughalzhar Tauy
Aral Sea
Cyprus
Tavan Bogd Uul 4374 m
Tibesti
Western Desert
CASPIAN SEA
Ağrı Dağı (Mt Ararat) 5137 m
Plato Ustyurt
Jabal ash Shaykh 2814 m
Peski Kyzylkum
Sīnā'
Euphrates
Balqash Köli
Nile
Eastern Desert
Bādiyat ash Shām (Syrian Desert)
Tigris
Reshteh-ye Kūhhā-ye Alborz (Elburz Mts)
Amu Darya
Pic Pobedy 7439 m
Tian Shan
Al Ḥijāz
An Nafūd
Dasht-e Kavīr
Pik Imeni Ismail Samani 7495 m
Lake Nasser
Kūhhā-ye Zāgros (Zagros Mountains)
Iranian Plateau
Dasht-e Lūt
Tarim Pendi
RED SEA
Persian Gulf
Helmand
Hindu Kush
Kunlun Sha
Arabian Peninsula
K2 8611 m
Sulaiman Range
Indus
Qingzang Gaoyu (Plateau of Tibe
Sutlej
Nyainqên Sh
HIMALAY
Gulf of Oman
Indo-Gangetic Plain
Ar Rub'al Khālī
Thar Desert
Mt Everest 8848 m
755
Ganga
(Ganges)
Bra
Rann of Kachchh
Vindhya Range
Sātpura Range
Ethiopian Highlands
Gulf of Aden
Deccan
Mouths of the Ganges
Equator
Lake Albert
Lake Turkana
Godavari
Suquṭrá
ARABIAN SEA
Bay of Bengal
Great Rift Valley
Lake Victoria
Western Ghats
Eastern Ghats
Kirinyaga (Mt Kenya) 5199 m
Lake Tanganyika
Andam Islan
Kilimanjaro 5895 m
Palk Strait
Cape Comorin
Sri Lanka
Nic Isla
INDIAN OCEAN
Maldives
Seychelles
Comoros
Madagascar

E 40° F 50° G 60° H 70° J 80° K 90°

BERING SEA
Aleutian Islands
Poluostrov Kamchatka
OKHOTSKOYE MORE
Ostrov Sakhalin
Kuril'skiye Ostrova
PACIFIC OCEAN
Hokkaidō
Honshū
Fuji-san 3776m
SEA OF JAPAN
Shikoku
Kyūshū
YELLOW SEA
EAST CHINA SEA
Nansei-shotō
Taiwan
Luzon Strait
PHILIPPINE SEA
Luzon
Philippines
Samar
Mindoro
Panay
Palawan
Negros
Mindanao
SULU SEA
SOUTH CHINA SEA
CELEBES SEA
Halmahera
Palau
New Guinea
Pk Jaya 5030 m
Jazirah Doberai
Admiralty Islands
BISMARCK SEA
New Ireland
New Britain
Solomon Islands
Bougainville Island
SOLOMON SEA
Gulf of Papua
Kepulauan Aru
Dolak
Torres Strait
Cape York Peninsula
CORAL SEA
Great Barrier Reef
ARAFURA SEA
Gulf of Carpentaria
Seram
Buru
BANDA SEA
Kepulauan Tanimbar
Maluku (Moluccas)
Molucca Sea
Sulawesi (Celebes)
Buton
Selat Makasar
Borneo
G. Kinabalu 4101 m
Natuna Besar
Malay Peninsula
Strait of Malacca
Sumatera (Sumatra)
G. Kerinci 3800 m
Bangka
Selat Karimata
JAVA SEA
Jawa (Java)
Bali
BALI SEA
Sumbawa
Sumba
SAVU SEA
FLORES SEA
Flores
Timor
TIMOR SEA
Gulf of Thailand
Tônlé Sab
Mekong
Indo-China Peninsula
Hainan
Gulf of Tonkin
Ostrov Vrangelya
CHUKCHI SEA
Chukotskoye Nagor'ye
VOSTOCHNO-SIBIRSKOYE MORE
Ostrov Kotel'nyy
Kolymskoye Nagor'ye
Sredinnyy Khrebet
Khrebet Cherskogo
Verkhoyanskiy Khrebet
Siber' (Siberia)
Vilyuyskoye Vodokhranilishche
Stanovoy Khrebet
Stanovoye Nagor'ye
Zeyskoye Vodokhranilishche
Ozero Baykal (Lake Baikal)
Yablonovyy Khrebet
Xiao Hinggan Ling
Da Hinggan Ling
Sikhote-Alin
Ozero Khanka
Amur
Plateau of Mongolia
Gobi
Changbai Shan
Korea Bay
Bo Hai
Korea Strait
Huangtu Gaoyuan
Great Plain of China
Qin Ling
Sichuan Pendi
Tai Hu
Poyang Hu
Dongting Hu
Wuyi Shan
Hengduan Shan
Tropic of Cancer
Equator
Tropic of Capricorn

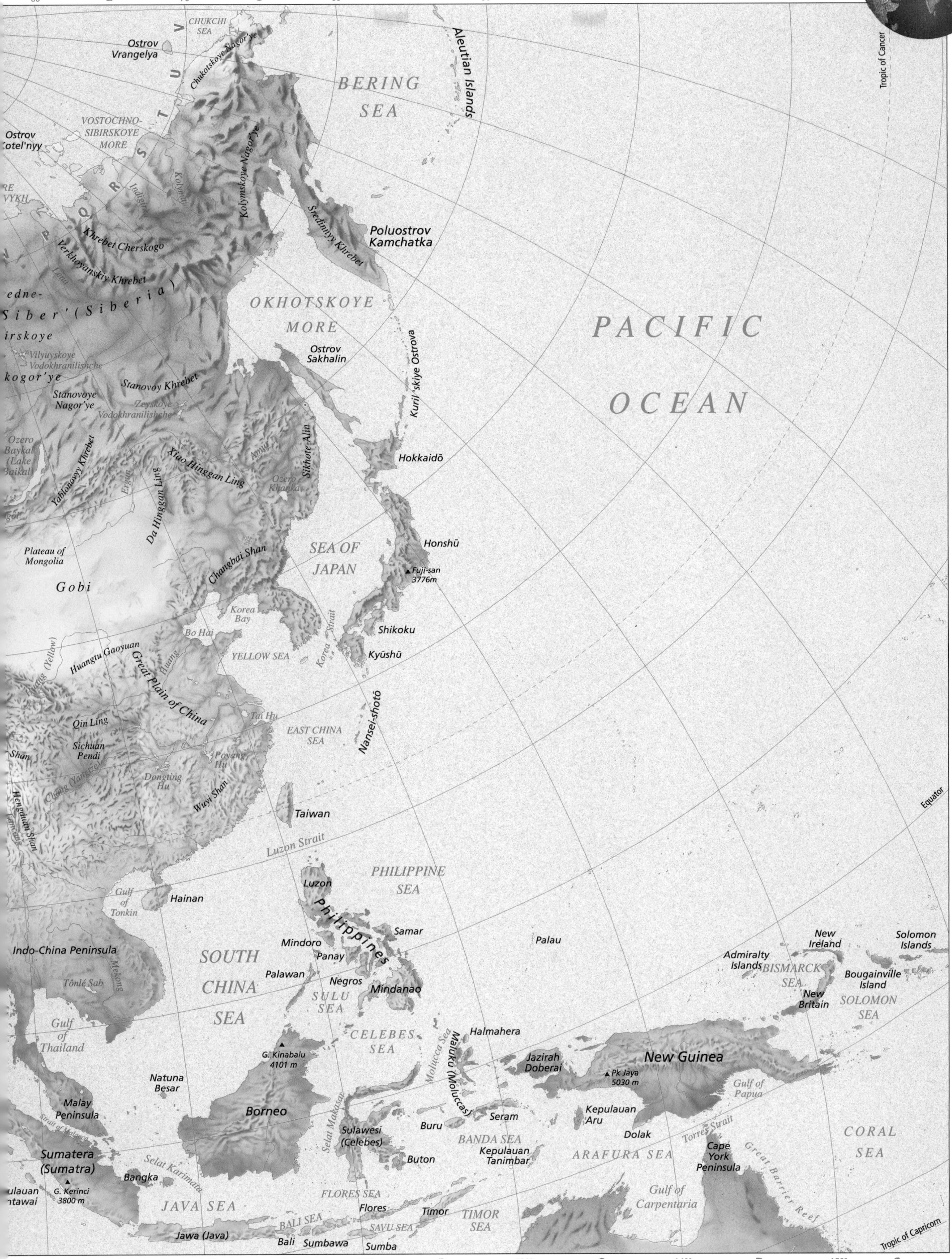

kilometers 500 1000 1500 2000

miles 250 500 750 1000 1250

Scale 1:35,000,000

Projection: Two Point Equidistant

Asia and the Middle East: Political

30° 6 40° 5 50° 4 60° 3 70° 2 80° 1

ATLANTIC OCEAN

ARCTIC OC

IRELAND

SVALBARD (Nor.)

Zemlya Frantsa-Iosifa

PORTUGAL

UNITED KINGDOM

NORWAY

Arctic Circle

Nordkapp

Novaya Zemlya

SPAIN

FRANCE BELGIUM NETH.

DENMARK

SWEDEN

FINLAND

Murmansk

MOROCCO

ANDORRA LUX.

GERMANY

Novaya Zemlya

SWITZ. LIECH.

RUSSIAN FED.

ESTONIA

Severodvinsk

Vorkuta

Noril'sk

MONACO

AUSTRIA CZECH REPUBLIC POLAND

LITHUANIA

LATVIA

Arkhangel'sk

SAN MARINO

SLOVENIA

Sankt-Peterburg

Cherepovets

Syktyvkar

RUSSIAN

ALGERIA

VATICAN CITY

CROATIA

ITALY

BOSNIA & HERZEGOVINA

HUNGARY

SLOVAKIA

BELARUS

Rybinsk Vologda

Moskva

Berezniki

Serov

Surgut

TUNISIA

SERBIA & MONTENEGRO

ROMANIA

UKRAINE

Tula Vladimir

Nizhniy Novgorod

Perm'

Nizhnevartovsk

MALTA

ALBANIA MACEDONIA

MOLDOVA

Lipetsk

Saransk Kazan'

Nizhniy Tagil

Yekaterinburg

BULGARIA

Tambov

Penza Ul'yanovsk

Ufa

Kurgan

Omsk

Tomsk Krasno

GREECE

İstanbul

Rostov-na-Donu

Kamyshin

Samara

Chelyabinsk

Novosibirsk

Novokuz

İzmir Bursa

Volgograd

Aqtöbe Orsk

Kökshetaū

Sterlitamak

Pavlodar Barnaul

LIBYA

NIGER

Konya

Ankara

GEORGIA Groznyy

Sochi

Atyraū

KAZAKHSTAN

Astana Semey

Tropic of Cancer

Lefkosia

TURKEY

T'bilisi

ARMENIA

Adana

Yerevan

Bakı

Qyzylorda

Balqash Köli

Qaraghandy

Öskemen

20°

CYPRUS

Halab

AZERBAIJAN

Tabrīz

UZBEKISTAN

Taraz

Almaty

Kuytun

CHAD

Bayrūt

LEBANON

SYRIA

Yerushalayim Dimashq

ISRAEL

'Ammān

IRAQ

Arāk

TURKMENISTAN

Ashgabat

Shymkent

Bishkek

Toshkent

KYRGYZSTAN

Ürümqi

EGYPT

JORDAN

Baghdād

Tehrān

Qom

Samarqand

TAJIKISTAN

Dushanbe

Aksu

Korla

An Najaf

Mashhad

Mazār-e Sharīf

Hotan

Al Başrah

Eşfahān

Herāt

Kābol

Peshāwar

Srīnagar

KUWAIT

Abādān

IRAN

Kermān

AFGHANISTAN

Islāmābād

Al Kuwayt

Shīrāz

Qandahār

Gujrānwāla

SUDAN

Jiddah

Ar Riyād

BAHRAIN

Al Manāmah

Zāhedān

Quetta

Faisalābād Lahore

Makkah

QATAR Ad Dawhah

Bandar-e 'Abbās

Multān Ludhiāna

SAUDI ARABIA

UNITED ARAB EMIRATES

Dubayy

Abū Zaby

Masqat

PAKISTAN

Abohar

Dehra Dūn

Lhasa

ERITREA

Sukkur

New Delhi Delhi

NEPAL

Thimphu

San'a'

OMAN

Hyderābād

Jodhpur

Jaipur

Āgra

Kathmandu

BHU

YEMEN

DJIBOUTI

'Adan

Karāchi

Ajmer

Gwalior

Lucknow

Gorakhpur

Jhānsi

Kanpur

Patna

BANGLADE

DEM. REP. OF THE CONGO

Suquṭrá (Yemen)

Ahmadābād

Indore

Allahābād

Vārānasi

Dh

ETHIOPIA

Lake Albert

UGANDA

Lake Turkana

Rājkot

Vadodara

Bhopāl

Jabalpur

Bokāro

Jamshedpur

Equator

Surat

Nāgpur

BANGLADE

Calcutta

Chitt

Lake Victoria

ARABIAN SEA

Mumbai

Pune

INDIA

Bhubaneshwar

Sitt

RWANDA

Kolhāpur

Solāpur

Warangal

Vishākhapatnam

Bay of Ben

BURUNDI

Lake Tanganyika

KENYA

SOMALIA

Belgaum

Hyderābād

Dhārwād

Vijayawāda

Guntur

Hubli

Bangalore

Andamar (India)

TANZANIA

Mysore

Chennai

Kozhikode

Coimbatore

Salem

Tiruchchirāppalli

Lake Malawi

Kochi

Madurai

Tirunelveli

Nico (In

Colombo SRI LANKA

MALAWI

Amirante Isles (Seychelles)

SEYCHELLES

Male MALDIVES

MOZAMBIQUE

COMOROS

Aldabra Is (Seychelles)

INDIAN OCEAN

Farquhar Group (Seychelles)

BRITISH INDIAN OCEAN TERRITORY (U.K.)

MAYOTTE (Fr.)

Chagos Archipelago

MADAGASCAR

E 40° F 50° G 60° H 70° J 80° K 90°

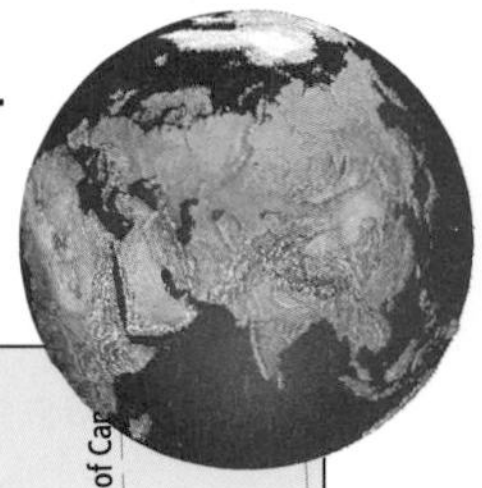

80° 2 70° 3 60° 4 50° 5 40° 6 30°
St Lawrence I. (U.S.A.)
Ostrov Vrangelya
Anacyr
BERING SEA
Aleutian Islands
MIDWAY ISLANDS (U.S.A.)
Tropic of Cancer
Novosibirskiye Ostrova
Magadan
Petropavlovsk-Kamchatskiy
OKHOTSKOYE MORE
Yakutsk
RATION
Ostrov Sakhalin
Kuril'skiye Ostrova
PACIFIC OCEAN
Komsomol'sk-na-Amure
Yuzhno-Sakhalinsk
Khabarovsk
Ozero Baykal
Blagoveshchensk
Chita
Ulan-Ude
Asahikawa
Hokkaidō
Sapporo
Hakodate
Aomori
Akita
Jiamusi
Qiqihar
Harbin
Jixi
Vladivostok
Mudanjiang
Changchun
Jilin
Ch'ŏngjin
Yamagata
Fukushima
Honshū
WAKE ISLAND (U.S.A.)
Ulaanbaatar
Siping
Liaoyuan
Sea of Japan
Tōkyō
Yokohama
NGOLIA
Shenyang
Fushun
NORTH KOREA
Anshan
P'yŏngyang
Kyōto
Ōsaka
Kōbe
Shikoku
MARSHALL ISLANDS
Zhangjiakou
Dalian
Sŏul
Inch'ŏn
Beijing
Tangshan
Pusan
Hiroshima
JAPAN
Taegu
Kitakyūshū
Shijiazhuang
Tianjin
SOUTH KOREA
Fukuoka
Kumamoto
Kyūshū
Kagoshima
Shizuishan
Taiyuan
Jinan
Qingdao
Yuci
Xinxiang
Xintai
Zhengzhou
Kaifeng
Lanzhou
Luoyang
Nanjing
Nantong
Shanghai
Xi'an
Xuchang
Hefei
Ningbo
Nansei-shotō (Japan)
NORTHERN MARIANA ISLANDS (U.S.A.)
Wuhu
Wuhan
Huangshi
Hangzhou
Wenzhou
Nanchong
Chengdu
Nanchang
Chongqing
Changsha
Fuzhou
T'ai-pei
Neijiang
Luzhou
Hengyang
T'ai-chung
GUAM (U.S.A.)
Zunyi
Huaihua
Zixing
Chia-i
TAIWAN
Guilin
Xiamen
Kao-hsiung
Equator
Dali
Guangzhou
Shaoguan
Liuzhou
Foshan
Dongguan
Nanning
Zhuhai
Juilong
MICRONESIA
Xianggang (Hong Kong)
Zhanjiang
Luzon
PHILIPPINES
Hà Nôi
Hải Phòng
Hainan Dao
Baguio
LAOS
Angeles
Quezon City
Lucena
Viangchan
Manila
Mindoro
Tacloban
Đà Nang
SOUTH CHINA SEA
THAILAND
Bago
Cebu
Bougainville
Moulmein
Negros
New Ireland
VIETNAM
PALAU
Cagayan de Oro
New Britain
SOLOMON ISLANDS
Krung Thep
CAMBODIA
Palawan
Mindanao
Davao
Phnum Pénh
Zamboanga
PAPUA NEW GUINEA
Thanh Phố Hồ Chí Minh
Gulf of Thailand
Kota Kinabalu
CELEBES SEA
Jayapura
Halmahera
Bandar Seri Begawan
BRUNEI
Manado
New Guinea
Kota Baharu
Kuala Terengganu
MALAYSIA
Ipoh
Kuala Lumpur
Seremban
Singapore
SINGAPORE
Kalimantan
Samarinda
Balikpapan
Sulawesi
Ambon
Seram
Pekanbaru
Pontianak
CORAL SEA ISLANDS (Aust.)
Padang
Banjarmasin
INDONESIA
ARAFURA SEA
Jambi
Sumatera
Palembang
Ujungpandang
EAST TIMOR
Flores
Melville I.
Gulf of Carpentaria
Bandarlampung
Semarang
Madura
Sumbawa
Timor
Jakarta
Jawa
Surabaya
Bali
Lombok
AUSTRALIA
Bandung
Yogyakarta
Malang
Sumba
8 9 10 11 12
100° M 110° N 120° P 130° Q 140° R 150° S
0 500 1000 1500 2000 kilometers
0 250 500 750 1000 1250 miles
Scale 1:35,000,000
Projection: Two Point Equidistant

East Indonesia

A
B
C
D
116°
120°
124°
204
201
1
2
3
4
5
6
4°
0°
4°
8°
12°
LABUAN
Victoria
BRUNEI
Bandar Seri Begawan
Muara
Brunei Bay
Kuala Penyu
Beaufort
Telupid
G. Trus Madi 2649 m
Kinabatangan
Lokan
SABAH
Sukau
Lamag
Lahad Datu
Pinangah
Tawitawi I.
Tapul Group
PHILIPPINES
Batulaki
Sarangani Is
Tg Baram
Lutong
Miri
Sapulut
Kunak
Tel. Darvel
P. Timbun Mata
Semporna
Tawau
Kalabakan
Sibutu I.
Sibutu Group
P. Sebatik
G. Mulu 2371 m
G. Harun 2160 m
MALAYSIA
Long Teru
Batu Niah
Baram
Tinjar
G. Murud 2438 m
Longbawan
G. Basakan 1372 m
P. Mandul
Sesayap
Tarakan
Tangung
Mantadau
SARAWAK
Long Murum
Peg. Iran
G. Bakayan 1599 m
Nyurang
Tanjungselor
KALIMANTAN
Tanjungredeb
Tg Batu
P. Maratua
Rumah Kulit
Kayan
BORNEO
G. Guguang 2467 m
G. Kemal 2053 m
Longnawan
Barung
Tintang
Peg. Sambaliung
Pulai
G. Liangpran 2240 m
TIMUR
Pelawanbesar
G. Menyapa 2000 m
Peg. Muller
Mahakam
Menyapa
Sepasu
Equator
Kembangjanggut
Bontang
Longiram
Danau Melintang
Danau Semayang
Danau Jempang
Purukcahu
Samarinda
KALIMANTAN
Kualakurun
Benangin
Muarapayang
G. Lumut 1233 m
Balikpapan
Kahayan
Pendang
TENGAH
G. Serempaka 1380 m
Tel. Adang
Kupangnunding
Tanahgrogot
Palangkaraya
Amuntai
Barito
Kapuas
Peg. Meratus
Jangeru
G. Besar 1892 m
Tel. Pamukan
Pulangpisau
KALIMANTAN
Rantau
SELATAN
Banjarmasin
Kotabaru
P. Sebuku
Martapura
Pagatan
Semaras
Kintap
P. Laut
Batakan
Tg Selatan
Selat Laut
Tg Layar
JAVA SEA
Kep. Masalembu
Selat Makasar
Tg Arus
G. Dako 2304 m
Tolitoli
Bukaan
Tg Kandi
SULAWESI
Tel. Amurang
Manado
Tondano
Tg Mangkalihat
Tg Samia
UTARA
Peg. Paleleh
G. Tentolomatinan 2207 m
Tinabogan
G. Ogoamas 2565 m
Tembito
Boroko
Kotamobagu
D. Limboto
Gorontalo
Marisa
Bilungala
G. Bulawa 1970 m
Onggunoi
Tinombo
Tg Dampelas
Sigenti
Tg Manimbaya
Kasimbar
Tel. Tomini
Kep. Togian
Selat Walea
Donggala
Tawaeli
Toboli
Parigi
Tg Api
Tg Batuhitam
Bunta
Luwuk
Teku
Tg Santigi
Palu
SULAWESI
Tel. Poso
G. Katopasa 2835 m
2400 m
G. Tumpu
Pakuli
Sedoa
Batui
Selat Peleng
P. Peleng
SULAWESI (CELEBES)
Poso
Uekuli
2565 m
TENGAH
G. Tenamatua
Taripa
Danau Poso
Kep. Banggai
Teluk Tolo
Danau Matana
G. Kambuno 2950 m
Peg. Quarles
G. Gandadiwata 3074 m
Mamuju
Tg Kai
Wotu
Tg Bulupulu
Rantepao
Palopo
Danau Towuti
Tg Lasoni
Makale
Peg. Mekongga
3455 m
G. Rantekombola
Tg Tapaulama
Tel. Matarape
Majene
Polewali
Tel. Mandar
G. Mekongga 2790 m
P. Manui
SULAWESI
Siwa
Tel. Bone
Kendari
Parepare
Danau Tempe
Singkang
Watunea
Walanae
P. Padamarang
Kolaka
Kolono
P. Wowoni
Watampone
SULAWESI
Tampo
Dauleo
Raha
SELATAN
TENGGARA
Tg Goram
Ujungpandang (Makassar)
Maros
Sinjai
Pising
P. Muna
P. Buton
2876 m
G. Lompobatang
P. Kabaena
Mawasangka
Kep. Tukangbesi
Bira
Tg Pemali
Selat Selayar
P. Selayar
Benteng
Kep. Talaud
Geme
Beo
Mangaran
Tahuna
P. Sangihe
Ngalipaeng
CELEBES SEA
P. Siau
Ulu
P. Tahulandang
P. Biaro
P. Bangka
P. Halmahera
Ternate
MOLUCCA SEA
Menanga
P. Mangole
P. Taliabu
Auponhia
P. Sanana
Tg Waka
P. Buru
Tg Palpetu
Bara
Namlea
G. Kapalatmada 2729 m
Tifu
BANDA SEA
P. Madura
Kep. Kangean
INDONESIA
P. Tanahjampea
P. Kalao
Asambi
P. Kalaotoa
P. Bonerate
Situbondo
Bondowoso
BALI SEA
FLORES SEA
Jawa (Java)
G. Raung 3332 m
Bali
Singaraja
G. Rinjani 3726 m
G. Tambora 2821 m
Tg Besi
Reo
P. Adonara
Kep. Alor
Laliki
Arwala
Airpanas
Hatpaas
P. Wetar
Banyuwangi
Negara
G. Agung 3142 m
BALI
Mataram
Sumbawa Besar
Dompu
Bima
P. Komodo
Labuhanbajo
Larantuka
Nebe
Lamakera
Kalabahi
Alor
Selat Wetar
Lautem
Tutuala
Denpasar
Selong
Sumbawa
Raba
G. Ranakah 2382 m
Ruteng
G. Kelimutu 1200 m
Maumere
Kep. Solor
P. Pantar
Dili
Manatuto
Baukau
Los Palos
Lore
JAWA TIMUR
P. Nusa Penida
Praya
Lombok
Plampang
P. Rinca
Flores
Ende
Paga
Aileu
2963 m
G. Tata Mailau
EAST TIMOR
Vikeke
NUSA TENGGARA BARAT
Tg Sasar
NUSA TENGGARA TIMUR
Pantemakassar
Atambua
Suai
Timor
Waingapu
SAVU SEA
G. Mutis 2427 m
Kefamenanu
Waikabubak
Sumba
G. Wanggamet 1225 m
Barate
Soe
Baing
P. Sawu
Kupang
Tg Ela
TIMOR SEA
Tg Pukuatu
Selat Roti
Nembrala
Roti
INDIAN OCEAN

PACIFIC OCEAN
HALMAHERA SEA
CERAM SEA
ARAFURA SEA
IRIAN JAYA
MALUKU
WEST SEPIK
EAST SEPIK
WESTERN
New Guinea
AUSTRALIA
PEG. VAN REES
Peg. Maoke
Peg. Jayawijaya
P. Waigeo
Rabia
Warmandi
Koor
Mega
G. Kwoka 3000 m
Ambuaki
Kaironi
Manokwari
Tg Manundi
P. Supiori
Korido
Korim
P. Biak
Biak
Tg Wararisbari
Sorong
Mubrani
Sajam
Tg Memori
Namber
Tg Dadi
P. Salawati
Gasim
Germakolo
Rawas
G. Mebo 2940 m
Oransbari
P. Numfor
Seget
Ransiki
P. Num
Selat Yapen
P. Yapen
Atkri
Tamulol
Baru
Robooksibia
P. Rumberpon
P. Misool
Inanwatan
Tg Sabra
Tomu
P. Waar
Tg Ranbausawa
Serui
Tel. Waropen
Pamdai
Tg D'Urville
Teba
Danau Rombebai
Sarmi
Maffin
Betaf
Ansudu
Kaptiau
Demta
Depapre
Jayapura
Danau Sentani
Tel. Berau
Tel. Bintuni
Babo
Tel. Cenderawasih
Kokas
Tanisapata
Rufrufua
Fakfak
Siembra
G. Dom 1430 m
Vanimo
Leitre
Sissano
Ossima
Aitape
Imonda
Krau
Torricelli Mts
Amanab
Green River
Wahai
Bula
Amahai
Haya
Bemu
P. Seram
Kilwo
Urung
Tg Marsimang
P. Karas
Tel. Sebakor
Tg Tongerai
Mirobia
Kaimana
Kwatisore
Nabire
Danau Yamur
Tel. Kamrau
P. Adi
Tg Papisoi
Wandai
Danau Paniai
Enarotali
G. Ubia 4234 m
Pk Jaya 5030 m
Tembagapura
G. Angemuk 3962 m
Wamena
Pk Trikora 4730 m
Pk Yamin 4595 m
Pk Mandala 4700 m
Kubkain
Kep. Gorong
Kep. Watubela
Wanapiri
Aiduna
Uta
Kokenau
Amamapare
Telefomin
Tabubil
Kep. Kai
Tg Borang
P. Kai Besar
P. Kai Kecil
Banda Elat
Dobo
Dosi
Kep. Aru
Tg Weduar
Tg Ngoni
Agats
Ningerum
Rumginae
Kiunga
Tanahmerah
Lake Murray
Tg Laru Mat
Tg Waarlangier
Tafermaar
Tg Ngabordamlu
Tg De Jongs
Mapi
Kep. Tanimbar
Watmuri
P. Yamdena
Batkes
Saumlaki
Latdalam
Adaut
Tepa
Kep. Babar
Eliase
Sermata
P. Dolak
Pembre
Kimaan
Okaba
Kladar
Tg Vals
Wamal
P. Komoran
Kumbe
Merauke
Aiambak
Duru
Goe
Serki
Buk
Morehead
Bula
Mari
Boigu I.
Torres Strait
Badu I.
Moa I.
Thursday I.
Prince of Wales I.
Bamaga
Dundas Strait
C. Van Diemen
Cobourg Pen.
C. Cockburn
Bathurst I.
Melville I.
C. Keith
Goulburn Is
Van Diemen Gulf
C. Hotham
Beagle Gulf
Darwin
Wessel Is
Cape Wessel
Howard Island
Melville Bay
Nhulunbuy
Equator
E F G H
132° 136° 140°
4° 0° 4° 8° 12°
1 2 3 4 5 6
134
140
0 100 200 300 400 kilometers
0 100 200 miles
Scale 1:7,000,000
Projection: Mercator

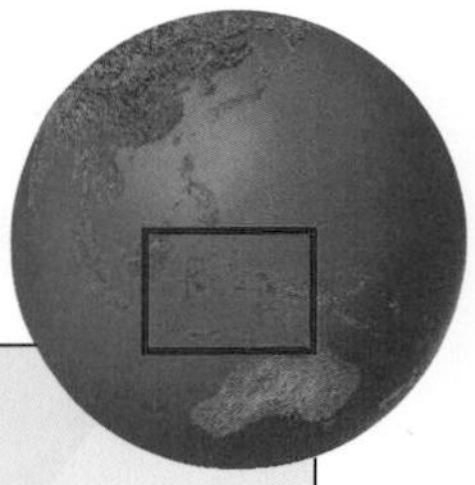

Asia and the Middle East

West Indonesia • Malaysia • Singapore

Nicobar Islands (India)
Little Nicobar
Great Nicobar
Bananga

P. We • Sabang
P. Breueh
⊛ Banda Aceh
Sigli Bireuen
Lhokkruet
Calang
Takengon
G. Geureudong 2855 m
Lhokseumawe
Lhoksukon
Peureulak
Langsa
U. Tamiang
Tg Jambuair
G. Abongabong 2985 m
ACEH
G. Lembu 3077 m
Pangkalanbrandan
Tg Raya
Blangkejeren
G. Leuser 3404 m
G. Bandahara 3012 m
Binjai
Belawan
⊛ Medan
Labuhanhaji
Tapaktuan
Kabanjahe
Tebingtinggi
G. Sibayak 2094 m
Tanjungbalai
Tg Dewa
Sidikalang
P. Semosir
Pematangsiantar
Prapat
Tg Pertandangan
P. Simeulue
Sinabang
Danau Toba
Balige
Labuhanbilik

Siborongborong
Barus
Tarutung
Kotapinang
SUMATERA UTARA
Langgapayung
P. Bangkaru
P. Tuangku
Sibolga
Tel. Tapanuli
P. Musala
Bagansiapiapi
Tg Dowi
Padangsidempuan
Lahewa
Gunungsitoli
P. Nias
Sirombu
Pasirpengarayan
Buatan
Telukdalam
Natal
Kotanopan
Duri
Airbangis
G. Ophir 2912 m
Bangkinang
Pekanbaru
RIAU
P. Pini
Sasak
Kep. Batu
Danau Maninjau
Payakumbuh
Tembilahan
P. Tanahmasa
Bukittinggi
G. Marapi 2891 m
Japura
P. Tanahbala
Danau Singkarak
Taluk
Rengat
Seberida
Tg Sigep
Padang
Solok
Kagologolo
SUMATERA BARAT
Sungaidareh
Dusunmudo
P. Siberut
Painan
G. Kerinci 3800 m
Muarabungo
⊛ Jambi
Muarasiberut
Danau Kerinci
JAMBI
Siberimanua
Tapan
Bangko
Bayunglincir
P. Sipura
Katiet
Surulangun
Pasapuat
Sekayu
P. Pagai Utara
Mukomuko
G. Masurai 2935 m
SUMATERA SELATAN
Palembang
P. Pagai Selatan
Kayuagung
Tg Beritarikap
Ketaun
Lais
Muaraaman
Muarabeliti
P. Sanding
Kepahiang
G. Daun 2467 m
Perabumulih
Umbulan
Gayohpecoh
Bengkulu
Muaraenim
Baturaja
Tais
Lahat
G. Dempo 3159 m
Pagaralam
BENGKULU
Manna
G. Patah 2817 m
Martapura
Muaradua
Menggala
Bintuhan
G. Pesagi 2231 m
Kotabumi
Metro
Labuhanm
Krui
LAMPUNG
Bandarlam
P. Enggano
Kayaapu
Kotaagung
Tg Batuberagam

INDIAN

OCEAN

Equator

THAILAND
Ko Lanta
Kantang
Songkhla
Hat Yai
Satun
Pattani
P. Langkawi
Kangar
Yala
Narathiwat
Rangae
PERLIS
Jitra
Kota Baharu
Alor Setar
Pasir Puteh
KEDAH
Jeli
Macang
P. Redang
Sungai Petani
G. Noring 1862 m
Kuala Kerai
PINANG
Bintang
George Town ⊛
Butterworth
G. Camah 2171 m
Kuala Terengganu
P. Pinang (Penang)
KELANTAN
G. Lawit 1519 m
PERAK
G. Gagau 1376 m
TERENGGANU
Taiping
Kuala Kangsar
⊛ Ipoh
G. Tahan 2187 m
G. Mandi Angin 1459 m
Kampar
Kuala Dungun
G. Batu Puteh 2131 m
Kuala Lipis
Cukai
Bidor
G. Benom 2107 m
G. Liang Eas 1933 m
G. Tapis 1512 m
Tg Gelang
Kuantan
PAHANG
Raub
Gambang
Karak
Maran
Pekan
SELANGOR
Temerloh
Kuala Selangor
Shah Alam
Kelang
⊛⊛ **Kuala Lumpur**
KUALA LUMPUR
Seremban
P. Tioman
NEGERI SEMBILAN
Port Dickson
Segamat
Tg Resang
Kep. Anam
Tg Tuan
Labuhanbilik
G. Ledang 1276 m
Labis
Jemaluang
Tg Senebui
MELAKA
Melaka
Muar
G. Belumut 1010 m
JOHOR
Batu Pahat
Ayer Hitam
Dumai
Kota Tinggi
P. Rupat
Pontian Kecil
Johor Baharu
P. Bengkalis
⊛ **Singapore**
P. Padang
SINGAPORE
P. Rangsang
P. Bintan
Kep. Ria
P. Tebingtinggi
Rempang
Tandjungpinang
P. Mendol
P. Kundur
P. Galang
P. Sebangka
Tg Datuk
P. Lingga
Kep. Lingga
Kelume
Sambau
P. Singkep
Selat Berhala
P. Singkep
Labu
Tg Jabung
Tel. Kampa
Muntok
P. B
P. B
Pangkalpinang
Be
Tg Rata
Balimbing
P. Tabuan
P. Sertun
Krakatau
P. Panaitan
Tg Guhakolak
Pelabu
Tel. Pelabu

MALAYSIA
Sembawang
Selat Johor
P. Seletar
Woodlands
Yishun
Tg Punggol
Kranji Res.
Sarimbun Res.
Murai Res.
Selatar Res.
P. Ubin
Choa Chu Kang
Bukit Panjang
Ang Mo Kio
Upper Peirce Res.
P. Serangoon
Punggol
Poyan Res.
Sungei Seletar Res.
Serangoon Harbour
Jurong West
Lower Peirce Res.
Bishan
Pasir Ris
Changi
Bukit Batok
Hougang
Tengeh Res.
Jurong Town
Bukit Timah
Serangoon
Tampines
Changi Airport
Jurong East
SINGAPORE
Toa Payoh
Bedok Res.
Tuas
Bukit Timah 162 m
Paya Lebar
Jurong Industrial Estate
Clementi
Bedok
Pandan Res.
MacRitchie Res.
Katong
Pasir Panjang
Geylang
P. Pesek
P. Merlimau
Tiong Bahru
P. Pesek Kechil
Pasir Panjang
Telok Blangah
P. Ayer Chawan
P. Seraya
P. Ayer Merbau
P. Sakra
Tg Berlayar
P. Brani
Straits of Singapore
Sentosa

0 5 10 kilometers
0 5 miles
Scale 1:297,000

CHRISTMAS ISLAND (Aust.)

Asia and the Middle East

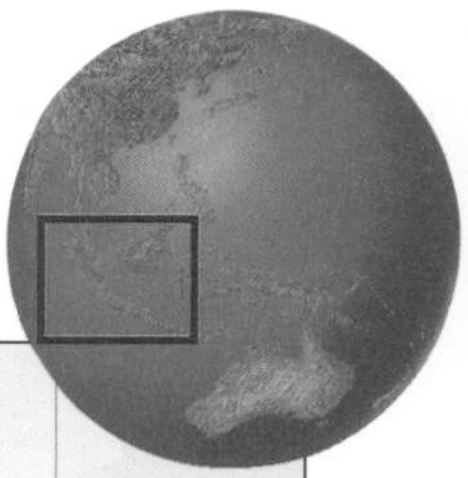

204

108° E 112° F 116° G 120° H

SOUTH CHINA SEA

P. Balambangan
P. Banggi
P. Malawali
Kudat
Tel. Paitan
P. Jambongan
Langkon
Kanibongan
Tuaran
G. Kinabalu 4101 m
Tel. Labuk
Kota Kinabalu
Lingkabau
SABAH
Sandakan
Kuala Penyu
Telupid
Sukau
Tapul Group
Tawitawi I.
LABUAN
Victoria
Lokan
Beaufort
G. Trus Madi 2649 m
Kinabatangan
Lamag
BRUNEI
Muara
Brunei Bay
Bandar Seri Begawan
Pinangah
Lahad Datu
Tel. Darvel
Kunak
Sibutu I.
Tg Baram
Lutong
Sapulut
Kalabakan
P. Timbun Mata
Sibutu Group
Tawau
Semporna
Miri
G. Pagon 1850 m
G. Mulu 2371 m
G. Harun 2160 m
P. Sebatik
P. Natuna Besar
Long Teru
Batu Niah
Tinjar
Longbawan
G. Basakan 1372 m
Tg Payong
Baram
G. Murud 2438 m
P. Mandul
P. Lagong
Sesayap
Tangung
Tarakan
Tg Kidurong
SARAWAK
Bintulu
Mantadau
P. Subi
P. Midai
P. Subi Besar
Tatau
P. Panjang
P. Serasan
Mukah
Long Murum
Nyurang
Tanjungselor
Tg Sirik
P. Bruit
Selat Serasan
MALAYSIA
Kejaman
Peg. Iran
G. Bakayan 1599 m
Sibu
Mukah
Tg Batu
P. Maratua
Tg Datu
Tel. Datu
Sarikei
Julau
Rajang
Baleh
Rumah Kulit
Kayan
G. Kemal 2053 m
Tanjungredeb
Tg Munggguresak
Sematan
Tg Sipang
Tg Po
Saratok
Song
Kapit
Peg. Hose
Longnawan
G. Guguang 2467 m
Paloh
Kuching
Debak
BORNEO
Tintang
Barung
Sambas
Bau
Bandar Sri Aman (Simanggang)
Embaluh
KALIMANTAN TIMUR
Peg. Sambaliung
Tg Arus
Tg Gunung
Pemangkat
G. Niut 1701 m
G. Lawit 1767 m
G. Kerihun 1980 m
G. Liangpran 2240 m
G. Menyapa 2000 m
Pelawanbesar
Pulai
Tg Mangkalihat
G. Dako 2304 m
Tolitoli
Singkawang
Danau Luar
Danau Sentarum
Putussibau
Peg. Muller
Menyapa
Sepasu
Tinabogan
G. Ogoamas 2565 m
Sai
Mahakam
Ngabang
Tg Dampelas
Tinombo
Tg Bangkai
Mempawah
Sanggau
Kapuas
Sintang
Kembangjanggut
Tg Manimbaya
Sigenti
Equator
Pontianak
Bontang
0°
KALIMANTAN BARAT
Longiram
Danau Melintang
Danau Semayang
Kasimbar
Tg Putus
Nangapinoh
Danau Jempang
SULAWESI TENGAH
Teluk Tomini
Kertamulia
G. Saran 1758 m
Kuwalan
G. Raya 2278 m
Purukcahu
Samarinda
Selat Makasar
Donggala
Tawaeli
Toboli
P. Padangtikar
Telukbatang
Kahayan
Peg. Schwaner
Kualakurun
Benangin
Parigi
Sukadana
G. Sebayan 1377 m
Palu
Tel. Poso
P. Maya
Sandai
KALIMANTAN TENGAH
Muarapayang
G. Lumut 1233 m
Balikpapan
Pakuli
Sedoa
Kep. Karimata
Tel. Sukadana
Pawan
Tumbangsamba
Pendang
Poso
Tentena
Taripa
Nangatayap
Memala
Mendawai
SULAWESI (CELEBES)
Tg Bawang
Ketapang
Arut
Sampit
Katingan
G. Serempaka 1380 m
Tel. Adang
Kupangnunding
Tanahgrogot
Selat Karimata
Seruyan
Barito
Danau Poso
P. Belitung
Sukaraja
Palangkaraya
Amuntai
Jangeru
G. Kambuno 2950 m
Kendawangan
Pangkalanbuun
Sampit
Mamuju
G. Gandadiwata 3074 m
Wotu
Tanjungpandan
P. Bawal
P. Gelam
Kumai
Danau Sembulu
G. Besar 1892 m
Tel. Pamukan
Peg. Quarles
Tg Bulupulu
Manggar
Dendang
Tg Sambar
Pulangpisau
Rantepao
Tg Kai
Tg Keluang
Tel. Kumai
Semuda
Rantau
Peg. Meratus
KALIMANTAN SELATAN
Makale
G. Rantekombola 3455 m
Tel. Sampit
Banjarmasin
Kotabaru
Masupu
Polewali
Tg Puting
Tg Malatayur
Martapura
P. Sebuku
Majene
Tel. Mandar
Siwa
Pagatan
Kintap
Semaras
Selat Laut
P. Laut
SULAWESI SELATAN
Tel. Bone
Batakan
Parepare
Singkang
Tg Selatan
Selat Laut
Tg Layar
Danau Tempe
Walanae
INDONESIA
Watampone
Maros
JAVA SEA
Ujungpandang (Makassar)
G. Lompobatang 2876 m
Sinjai
Bira
Kep. Masalembu
Selat Selayar
JAKARTA RAYA
Jakarta
Kep. Karimunjawa
P. Bawean
Benteng
P. Selayar
Pamanukan
Indramayu
JAWA TENGAH
Tg Bugel
Subang
Keling
G. Muria 1602 m
Tg Benda
Purwakarta
Cirebon
Jepara
Bandung
Pekalongan
Kudus
Rembang
Tuban
Ketapang
P. Madura
Kep. Kangean
G. Careme 3078 m
Tegal
Semarang
Blora
Bangkalan
G. Slamet 3418 m
Salatiga
Solo
Gresik
Garut
Wonosobo
Surabaya
Pamekasan
P. Tanahjampea
Tasikmalaya
Ciamis
Purwokerto
Magelang
Surakarta (Solo)
Selat Madura
Situbondo
BALI SEA
P. Kalao
Garut
Cilacap
G. Lawu 3265 m
Madiun
Pasuruan
FLORES SEA
JAWA BARAT
Tel. Penanjung
Yogyakarta
Ponorogo
G. Liman 2561 m
Probolinggo
3088 m
Bondowoso
Bali
G. Rinjani 3726 m
G. Tambora 2821 m
Parangtritis
Pacitan
Kediri
Malang
G. Semeru 3676 m
G. Argopuro
G. Raung 3332 m
Singaraja
Tg Besi
Reo
JAWA (JAVA)
YOGYAKARTA
Blitar
Kepanjen
Jember
Negara
3142 m
G. Agung
Mataram
Sumbawa Besar
Dompu
Bima
P. Komodo
Labuhanbajo
Banyuwangi
BALI
Raba
JAWA TIMUR
P. Nusa Barung
Denpasar
Praya
Selong
Plampang
G. Ranakah 2382 m
Ruteng
P. Nusa Penida
Lombok
Sumbawa
P. Rinca
Flores
NUSA TENGGARA BARAT
Tg Sasar
Waingapu
Waikabubak
G. Wanggamet 1225 m
Sumba
NUSA TENGGARA TIMUR
Baing

198

1 2 3 4 5

Asia and the Middle East

108° E 112° F 116° G 120° H

0 100 200 300 400 kilometers
0 100 200 miles
Scale 1:7,000,000
Projection: Mercator

Thailand • Laos • Cambodia • Vietnam

CHINA
GUANGXI ZHUANGZU ZIZHIQU
GUANGDONG
XIANGGANG (HONG KONG)
Guangzhou (Canton)
Nanning
Jiulong (Kowloon)
Xianggang (Hong Kong)
Macao
Zhuhai
Shenzhen
Haikou
HAINAN
Hainan Dao
Gulf of Tonkin
LAOS
CAMBODIA
VIETNAM
Hà Nôi (Hanoi)
Hải Phòng
Huế
Đà Nẵng
Phnum Pénh (Phnom Penh)
Thanh Phố Hồ Chí Minh (Saigon)
SOUTH CHINA SEA
XISHA QUNDAO (Paracel Island) (Sovereignty disputed)
SPRATLY ISLANDS (Sovereignty disputed)
MALAYSIA
Kota Kinabalu
Scale 1:7,000,000
Projection: Mercator
kilometers
miles

206

Asia and the Middle East

Philippines

A 116° B 120° C 124° D

Batan Is
Basco
Babuyan Is
Babuyan Channel
Mayraira Pt
Bangui
Palaui I.
C. Engaño
Abulog
Aparri
Bacarra
Laoag
Agbulu
Gonzaga
Batac
Mt Sicapoo 2048 m
Badoc
Alcala
Cabugao
Tuao
Vigan
Bangued
Tuguegarao
Narvacan
Tabuk
Lubuagan
Candon
Bontoc
Ilagan
Palanan Pt
Cervantes
Cauayan
Banaue
San Fernando
Santiago
Luzon
Mt Pulog 2934 m
Bauang
Bagabag
Bolinao
Lingayen Gulf
Baguio
Sierra Madre
Tarigtig Pt
Cabauyan I.
Agno
Dagupan
C. San Ildefonso
Lingayen
Villasis
Baler Bay
San Carlos
San Jose
Baler
High Peak 2037 m
Tarlac
Cabanatuan
Iba
Capas
Botolan
Angeles
Gapan
Dingalan Bay
Mt Pinatubo 1759 m
San Fernando
Malolos
Polillo Is
Olongapo
Quezon City
Infanta
Balanga
Manila
Lamon Bay
Bagac
Manila Bay
Calagua Is
Mariveles
Labo
Muntinglupa
Santa Cruz
Calamba
Mt Labo 1544 m
Daet
Yog Pt
Nasugbu
San Pablo
San Miguel Bay
Calatagan
Lipa
Lucena
Calauag
Tinambac
Viga
Lubang Is
Batangas
Sipocot
Lagonoy
Catanduanes I.
Golo I.
Lobo
Tayabas Bay
Naga
Pili
Lagonoy Gulf
Virac
C. Calavite
Calapan
Boac
Santa Cruz
Nabua
Paluan
Mt Halcon 2587 m
Marinduque I.
San Andres
Batan I.
Mamburao
San Francisco
Tabaco
Rapu Rapu I.
Pinamalayan
Naujan
Legaspi
Mindoro
Donsol
Sorsogon
Sablayan
Bongabong
Burias I.
Bulan
Matnog
Mt Baco 2488 m
Romblon
Sibuyan I.
Ticao I.
Calintaan
Tablas I.
Catarman
San Jose
Mt Guiting-guitin 2050 m
Masbate
Allen
Mt Capotcan 850 m
Busuanga
Busuanga I.
Bulalacao (San Pedro)
Mandaon
Masbate I.
Calbayog
Coron
Ilin I.
Balud
Asid Gulf
Placer
Catbalogan
Taft
Culion I.
Coron I.
Semirara Is
Pulanduta Pt
Biliran I.
Samar
Nelyan Pt
Nabas
Pucio Pt
Kalibo
VISAYAN SEA
Naval
Borongan
Linapacan I.
Roxas
Llorente
Iloc I.
Culasi
Carigara
El Nido
Batas I.
Tibiao
Sara
Daanbantayan
Tacloban
Maytiguid I.
Cuyo Is
Bugasong
Passi
Bantayan
San Remigio
Guiuan
Panay
Ormoc
Taytay
San Jose
Iloilo
Silay
Cadiz
Leyte
Imuruan Bay
Bacolod
Camotes Is
Homonhon I.
Boayan I.
Dumaran I.
Miagao
Baybay
Leyte Gulf
Bacao
Anini-y
Bago
San Carlos
Toledo
Danao
Desolation Pt
Caruray
Panay Gulf
Negros
Mandaue
Sogod
Ulugan Bay
Roxas
Lapu-Lapu
Hilongos
Loreto
Cleopatra Needle 1593 m
Cebu
Maasin
Dinagat I.
Honda Bay
Kabankalan
Pintuyan
Bacungan
Cauayan
Bohol
Siargao I.
Anepahan
Puerto Princesa
Sipalay
Dalaguete
Guindulman
Surigao
Dapa
Long Pt
Panagtaran Pt
Tagbilaran
Bucas Grande I.
Victoria Peak 1709 m
Palawan
Hinoba-an
Santander
L. Mainit
Quezon
Aborlan
Santa Catalina
Dumaguete
Camiguin I.
Cantilan
Rasa I.
Tolong Bay
Siquijor I.
Diuta Pt
Mt Hilonghilong 2012 m
Tandag
Island Bay
Siaton
Balingoan
Mt Mantalingajan 2073 m
Brooke's Point
Balingasag
Butuan
Dapitan
Bayugan
Rio Tuba
San Antonio Bay
Dipolog
Gingoog
Salvacion
El Salvador
Lianga
C. Buliluyan
Oroquieta
Iligan Bay
Cagayan de Oro
Hinatuan
Pandanan I.
Bugsuk I.
SULU SEA
Mt Malindang 2425 m
Jimenez
Lugait
Sindangan
Ozamiz
Iligan
Malaybalay
Sanco Pt
Bislig
Mindanao
Panganuran
Liloy
Marawi
Valencia
Balabac
Pagadian
Kalatungan Mts 2865 m
Balabac I.
Ipil
Kabasalan
Lake Lanao
Monkayo
Cateel
Siocon
Malabang
Kibawe
Baganga
Agusan
Tungawan
Margosatubig
Parang
Tagum
Caraga
P. Banggi
P. Balambangan
Sibuco
Olutlanga I.
Cotabato
Midsayap
Mabini
P. Malawali
Bolong
Pikit
Mt Apo 2954 m
Samal I.
Kudat
Tel. Paitan
Zamboanga
Sacol I.
Moro Gulf
Kidapawan
Davao
Mati
P. Jambongan
Isabela
Lamitan
Linao Pt
Tacurong
Digos
Lamigan Pt
Langkon
Basilan I.
Lake Buluan
Davao Gulf
Kanibongan
Maluso
1011 m
Lebak
Norala
Koronadal
Surallah
C. San Augustin
Tuaran
G. Kinabalu 4101 m
Tel. Labuk
Mt Matutum 2295 m
Malita
Patikul
Jolo I.
General Santos (Dadiangas)
Kota Kinabalu
Lingkabau
Jolo
Sandakan
Kiamba
SABAH
Tapul I.
Kuala Penyu
Telupid
Lokan
Sukau
Tapul Group
Glan
Victoria
Beaufort
G. Trus Madi 2649 m
Kinabatangan
Lamag
Tawitawi I.
Siasi
Sulu Archipelago
Batulaki
Brunei Bay
Sarangani Is
Muara
MALAYSIA
Lahad Datu
Pinangah
Bandar Seri Begawan
Tel. Darvel
Sibutu I.
CELEBES
BRUNEI
Kunak
P. Timbun Mata
Sibutu Group
Geme
Kalabakan
Semporna
Tawau
SEA
Kep. Talaud
Beo
G. Harun 2160 m
P. Sebatik
G. Murud 2438 m
Longbawan
G. Basakan 1372 m
Mangaran
Sesayap
P. Mandul
INDONESIA
Tahuna
P. Sangihe
SOUTH CHINA SEA
PHILIPPINE SEA
PHILIPPINES

201
198

A 116° B 120° C 124° D 128°

kilometers 0 100 200 300 400
miles 0 100 200
Scale 1:7,000,000
Projection: Mercator

Myanmar (Burma) • Bangladesh • Bhutan

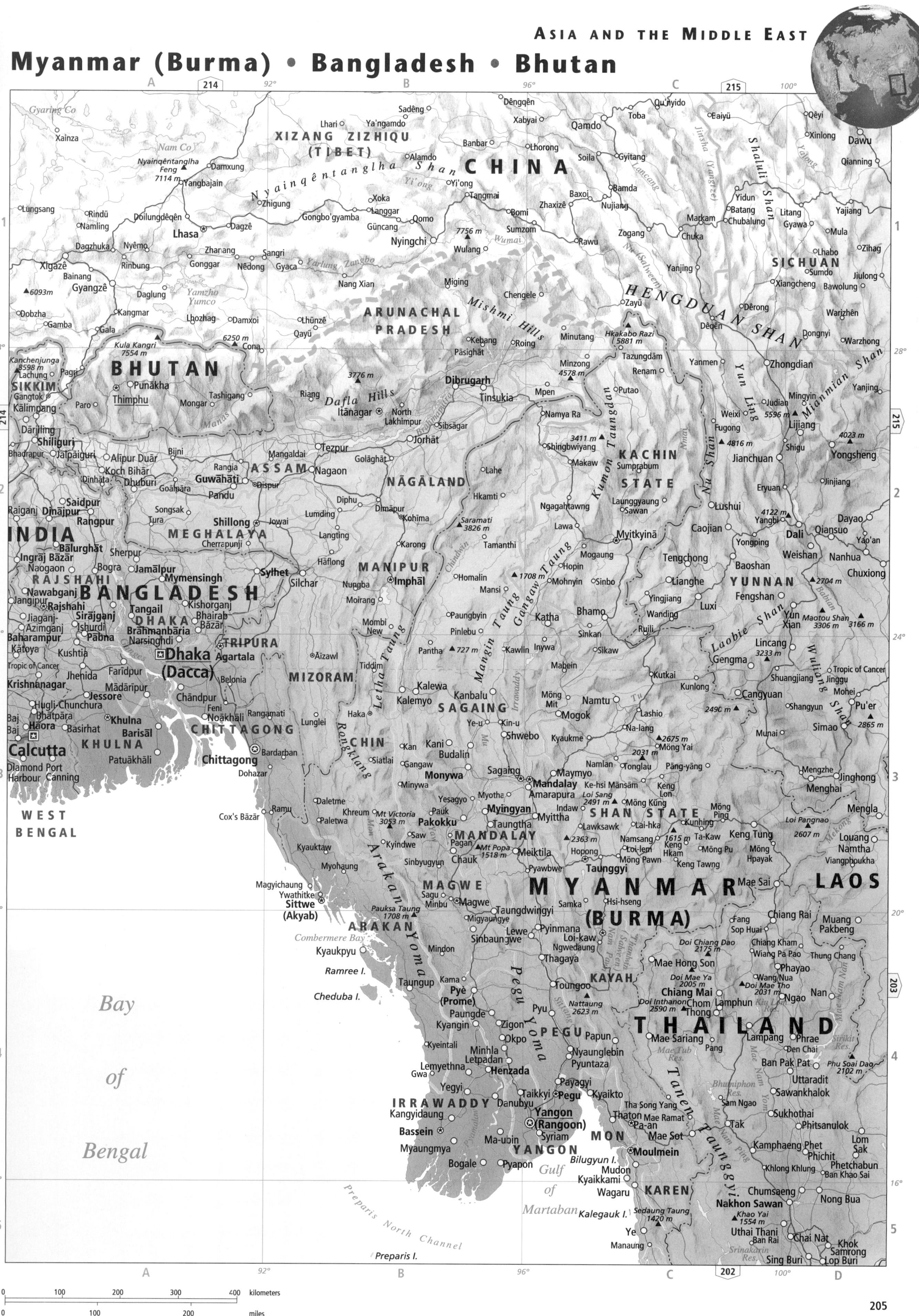
XIZANG ZIZHIQU
(TIBET)
CHINA
Nyainqêntanglha Shan
Lhasa
ARUNACHAL
PRADESH
BHUTAN
Thimphu
SIKKIM
Mishmi Hills
HENGDUAN SHAN
SICHUAN
ASSAM
NĀGĀLAND
MEGHALAYA
MANIPUR
INDIA
BANGLADESH
RAJSHAHI
DHAKA
Dhaka
(Dacca)
TRIPURA
MIZORAM
KHULNA
CHITTAGONG
Chittagong
Calcutta
WEST
BENGAL
KACHIN
STATE
YUNNAN
SAGAING
CHIN
MANDALAY
Mandalay
SHAN STATE
MAGWE
MYANMAR
(BURMA)
LAOS
ARAKAN
Arakan Yoma
KAYAH
THAILAND
PEGU
Pegu Yoma
IRRAWADDY
YANGON
Yangon
(Rangoon)
MON
KAREN
Bay
of
Bengal
Gulf
of
Martaban
Preparis North Channel
Combermere Bay
Ramree I.
Cheduba I.
Preparis I.
Tropic of Cancer
Hkakabo Razi
5881 m
Kula Kangri
7554 m
Kanchenjunga
8598 m
Nyainqêntanglha Feng
7114 m
0 100 200 300 400 kilometers
0 100 200 miles
Scale 1:7,000,000
Projection: Mercator

Southeast China

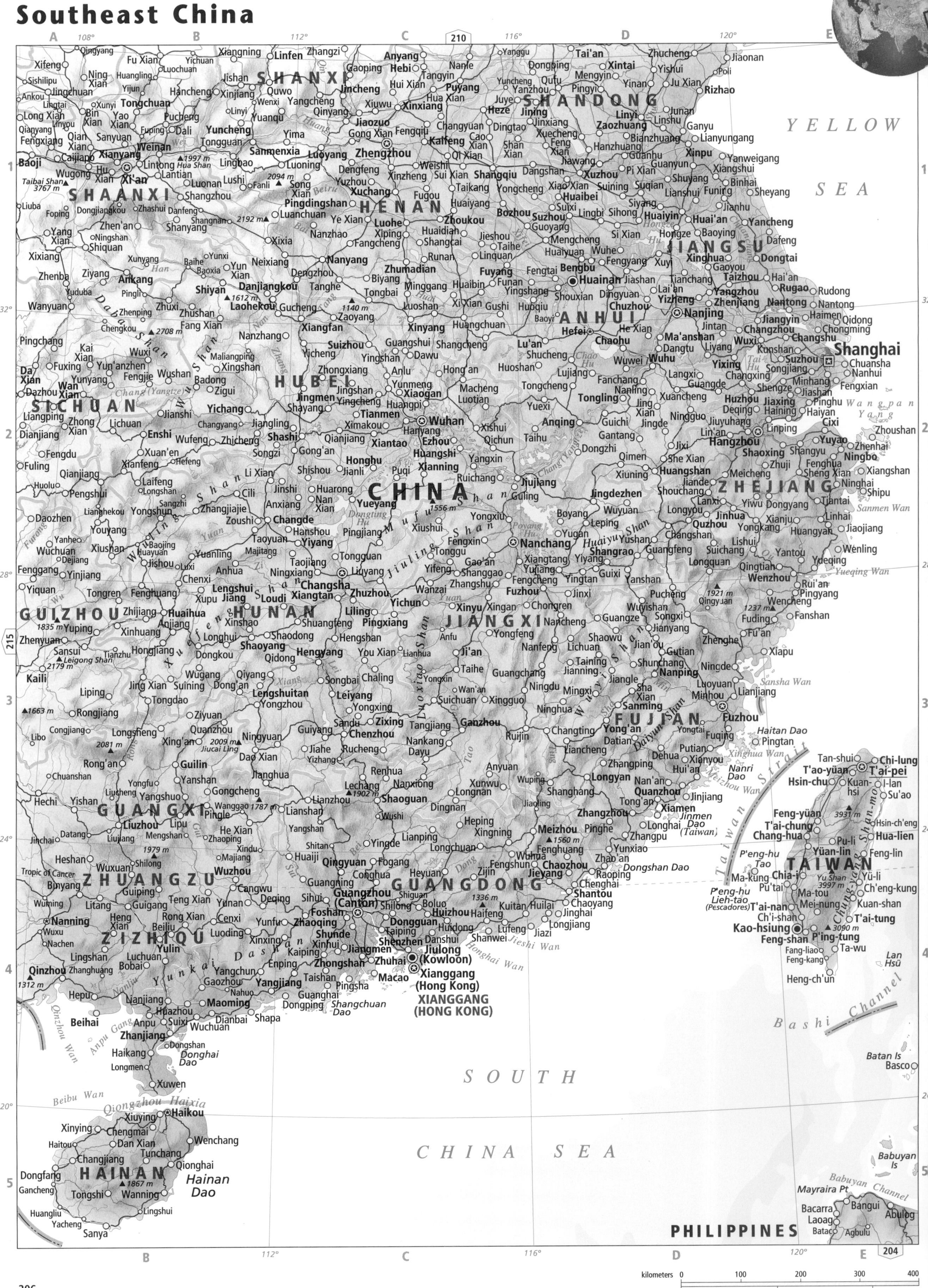

kilometers 0 100 200 300 400

miles 0 100 200

Scale 1:7 000,000

Projection: Equidistant Conic

Xianggang (Hong Kong) and Guangdong, China

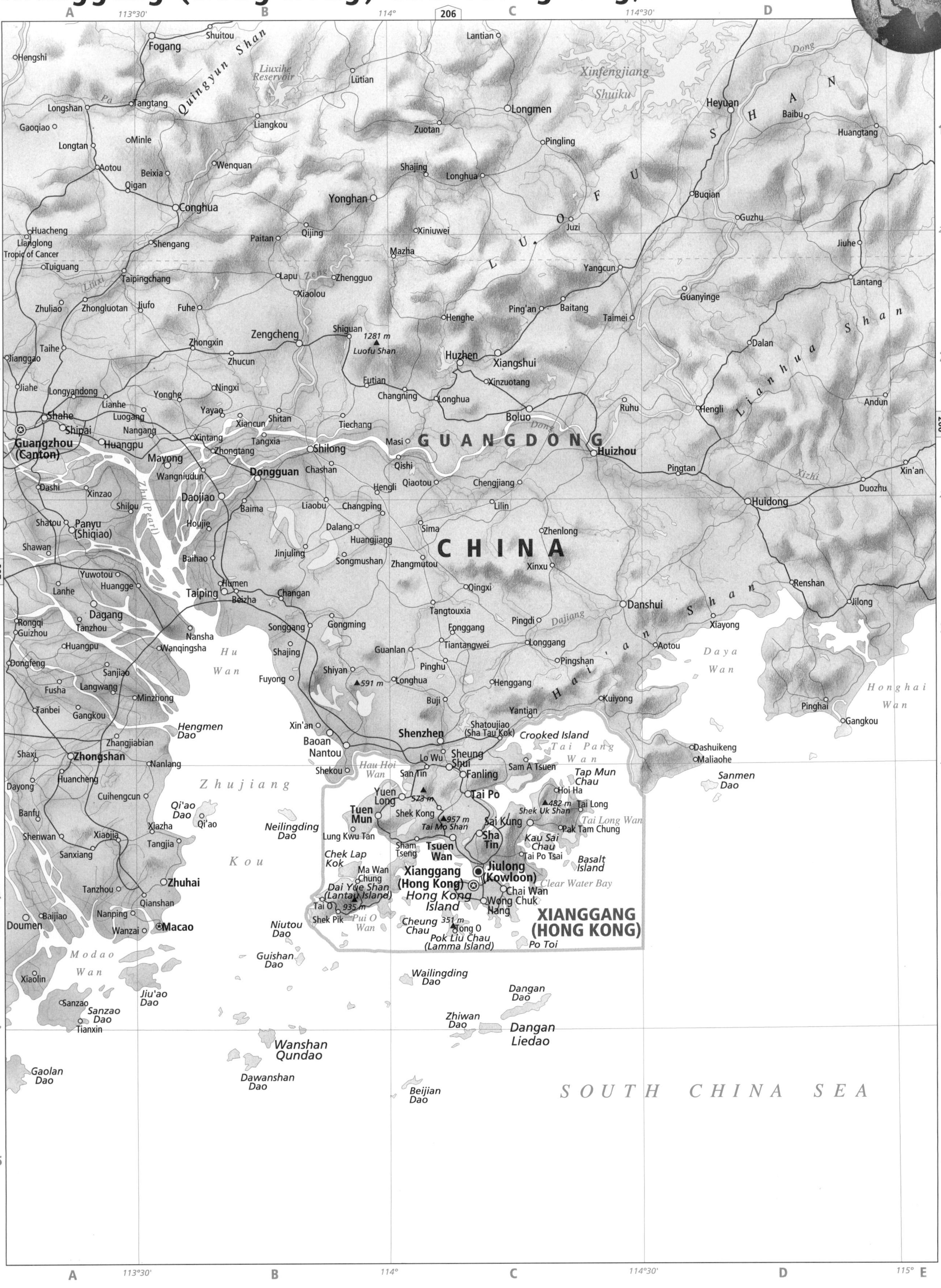

A
113°30'
B
114°
206
C
114°30'
D

Hengshi
Fogang
Shuitou
Qingyun Shan
Liuxihe Reservoir
Lütian
Lantian
Dong
Xinfengjiang Shuiku
Pa
Tangtang
Longshan
Gaoqiao
Liangkou
Longmen
Heyuan
Baibu
Huangtang
Zuotan
Pingling
Longtan
Minle
Aotou
Wenquan
Beixia
Qigan
Shajing
Longhua
Buqian
Conghua
Yonghan
Luofu Shan
Juzi
Guzhu
Huacheng
Lianglong
Tropic of Cancer
Shengang
Paitan
Qijing
Xiniuwei
Mazha
Jiuhe
Tuiguang
Liuxi
Taipingchang
Lapu
Zeng
Zhengguo
Xiaolou
Yangcun
Lantang
Guanyinge
Zhuliao
Zhongluotan
Jiufo
Fuhe
Henghe
Ping'an
Baitang
Taimei
Taihe
Zhongxin
Zengcheng
Shiguan
1281 m
Luofu Shan
Huzhen
Xiangshui
Dalan
Lianhua Shan
Jianggao
Zhucun
Jiahe
Longyandong
Lianhe
Yonghe
Ningxi
Futian
Changning
Longhua
Xinzuotang
Andun
Shahe
Shipai
Luogang
Nangang
Yayao
Shitan
Xiancun
Tiechang
Boluo
Dong
Ruhu
Hengli
Guangzhou (Canton)
Huangpu
Xintang
Tangxia
Zhongtang
Shilong
Masi
GUANGDONG
Huizhou
Mayong
Wangniudun
Dongguan
Chashan
Qishi
Pingtan
Xizhi
Xin'an
Dashi
Xinzao
Zhu (Pearl)
Daojiao
Hengli
Qiaotou
Chengjiang
Duozhu
Shilou
Baima
Liaobu
Changping
Lilin
Huidong
Shatou
Panyu (Shiqiao)
Houjie
Dalang
Sima
Zhenlong
Shawan
Huangjiang
CHINA
Baihao
Jinjuling
Songmushan
Zhangmutou
Xinxu
Yuwotou
Lanhe
Huangge
Humen
Taiping
Beizha
Changan
Qingxi
Renshan
Jilong
Dagang
Tangtouxia
Rongqi
Guizhou
Tanzhou
Nansha
Songgang
Gongming
Fenggang
Pingdi
Dajiang
Danshui
Xiayong
Huangpu
Wanqingsha
Hu Wan
Shajing
Guanlan
Tiantangwei
Longgang
Aotou
Daya Wan
Dongfeng
Sanjiao
Fuyong
Shiyan
Pinghu
Pingshan
Fusha
Langwang
591 m
Longhua
Henggang
Haifeng Shan
Honghai Wan
Minzhong
Tanbei
Gangkou
Buji
Kuiyong
Yantian
Pinghai
Gangkou
Hengmen Dao
Xin'an
Shenzhen
Shatoujiao (Sha Tau Kok)
Crooked Island
Zhangjiabian
Baoan
Nantou
Tai Pang Wan
Dashuikeng
Shaxi
Zhongshan
Nanlang
Lo Wu
Sheung Shui
Maliaohe
Zhujiang
Shekou
Hau Hoi Wan
San Tin
Fanling
Sam A Tsuen
Tap Mun Chau
Sanmen Dao
Dayong
Huancheng
Cuihengcun
Yuen Long
523 m
Tai Po
Hoi Ha
Banfu
Qi'ao Dao
Qi'ao
Tuen Mun
Shek Kong
957 m
Tai Mo Shan
482 m
Shek Uk Shan
Tai Long
Tai Long Wan
Sai Kung
Pak Tam Chung
Shenwan
Xiaojia
Xiazha
Neilingding Dao
Lung Kwu Tan
Sha Tin
Kau Sai Chau
Sanxiang
Tangjia
Kou
Chek Lap Kok
Sham Tseng
Tsuen Wan
Tai Po Tsai
Basalt Island
Ma Wan
Chung
Jiulong (Kowloon)
Tanzhou
Zhuhai
Dai Yue Shan (Lantau Island)
Xianggang (Hong Kong)
Hong Kong Island
Chai Wan
Clear Water Bay
Qianshan
Tai O
935 m
Wong Chuk Hang
Doumen
Baijiao
Nanping
Shek Pik
Pui O Wan
XIANGGANG (HONG KONG)
Wanzai
Macao
Niutou Dao
Cheung Chau
351 m
Tong O
Pok Liu Chau (Lamma Island)
Po Toi
Modao Wan
Guishan Dao
Xiaolin
Wailingding Dao
Jiu'ao Dao
Dangan Dao
Sanzao
Sanzao Dao
Tianxin
Zhiwan Dao
Dangan Liedao
Wanshan Qundao
Gaolan Dao
Dawanshan Dao
Beijian Dao
SOUTH CHINA SEA

1
2
3
4
5
23°30'
23°
22°30'
22°

A
113°30'
B
114°
C
114°30'
D
115°
E

0 25 50 kilometers
0 20 miles
Scale 1:900,000
Projection: Equidistant Conic

Japan • Korea

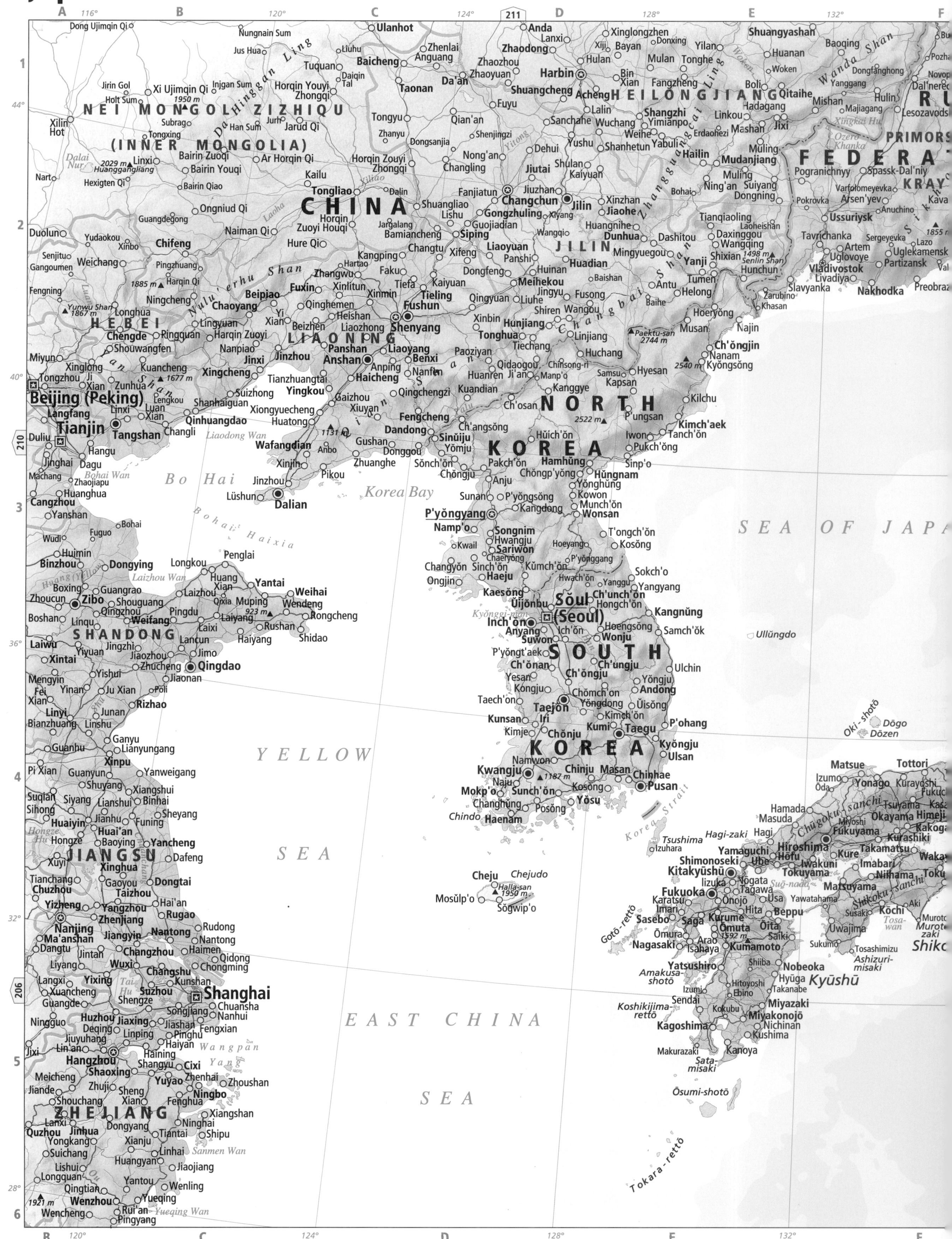
CHINA
NEI MONGOL ZIZHIQU
(INNER MONGOLIA)
HEILONGJIANG
JILIN
LIAONING
HEBEI
SHANDONG
JIANGSU
ZHEJIANG
NORTH KOREA
SOUTH KOREA
RUSSIAN FEDERATION
PRIMORSKIY KRAY
Beijing (Peking)
Tianjin
Shanghai
Harbin
Changchun
Jilin
Shenyang
Anshan
Dalian
Qingdao
Nanjing
Hangzhou
Ningbo
Vladivostok
P'yŏngyang
Sŏul (Seoul)
Inch'ŏn
Taejŏn
Taegu
Pusan
Kwangju
Ulsan
Hamhŭng
Ch'ŏngjin
Wŏnsan
Kaesŏng
Cheju
Chejudo
Halla-san 1950 m
Paektu-san 2744 m
Fukuoka
Kitakyūshū
Shimonoseki
Hiroshima
Nagasaki
Kumamoto
Kagoshima
Miyazaki
Matsuyama
Okayama
Kyūshū
Shikoku
Tsushima
Korea Strait
Gotō-rettō
Ōsumi-shotō
Tokara-rettō
Oki-shotō
Ullŭngdo
Bo Hai
Bohai Wan
Liaodong Wan
Laizhou Wan
Korea Bay
Bohai Haixia
YELLOW SEA
EAST CHINA SEA
SEA OF JAPAN
Da Hinggan Ling
Zhangguangcai Ling
Changbai Shan
Hangzhou Wan
116°
120°
124°
128°
132°
44°
40°
36°
32°
28°
211
210
206

JAPAN

PACIFIC OCEAN

Hokkaidō

Honshū

Kuril'skiye Ostrova (Kuril Islands)

Administered by Russian Federation, claimed by Japan.

La Perouse Strait

Proliv Friza

Urup

Iturup

Kunashir

Shikotan

Sado-shima

Izu-shotō

Rebun-tō

Rishiri-tō

Okushiri-tō

Wakkanai

Sapporo

Asahikawa

Kushiro

Hakodate

Aomori

Akita

Morioka

Sendai

Niigata

Tōkyō

Yokohama

Kawasaki

Nagoya

Fuji-san 3776 m

EAST CHINA SEA

Nansei-shotō (Ryukyu Islands)

Okinawa-shotō

Sakishima-shotō

Amami-shotō

Okinawa

Naha

Nago

Tropic of Cancer

PACIFIC OCEAN

0 100 200 300 400 kilometers

0 100 200 miles

Scale 1:7,000,000

Projection: Equidistant Conic

Northeast China • Mongolia

RUSSIAN FEDERATION
MONGOLIA
NEI MONGOL ZIZHIQU
(INNER MONGOLIA)
CHINA
RESPUBLIKA TYVA
RESPUBLIKA BURYATIYA
IRKUTSKAYA OBLAST'
UST'-ORDYNSKIY BURYATSKIY A.O.
AGINSKIY BURYATSKIY A.O.
HÖVSGÖL
DZAVHAN
ARHANGAY
BULGAN
SELENGE
TÖV
HENTIY
DORNOD
BAYANHONGOR
DUNDGOVĬ
DORNOGOVĬ
ÖMNÖGOVĬ
SÜHBAATAR
GANSU
NINGXIA HUIZU ZIZHIQU
QINGHAI
SHAANXI
SHANXI
HEBEI
Ulaanbaatar
(Ulan Bator)
Irkutsk
Ulan-Ude
Chita
Beijing
(Peking)
Tianjin
Hohhot
Baotou
Yinchuan
Lanzhou
Xining
Taiyuan
Shijiazhuang
Zhangjiakou
Datong
Jining
Wuhai
Linhe
Erenhot
Saynshand
Dalandzadgad
Mandalgovĭ
Choybalsan
Baruun-Urt
Öndörhaan
Darhan
Erdenet
Mörön
Uliastay
Bayanhongor
Arvayheer
Tsetserleg
Kyakhta
Sühbaatar
Ozero Baykal
(Lake Baikal)
Hangayn Nuruu
Govĭ Altayn Nuruu
Gurvan Sayhan Uul
Hentiyn Nuruu
Khrebet Khamar-Daban
Yablonovyy Khrebet
Malkhanskiy Khrebet
Badain Jaran Shamo
Yabrai Shan
Lang Shan
Heli Shan
Lüliang Shan
Taihang Shan
Gobi
Huang (Yellow)
Selenge
Orhon
Kerulen (Herlen)
Onon
Tuul
A B C D E F
2 3 4 5 6
96° 100° 104° 108° 112° 116°
52° 48° 44° 40° 36°
301
213
215
206

Northwest China • East Kazakhstan • Mongolia

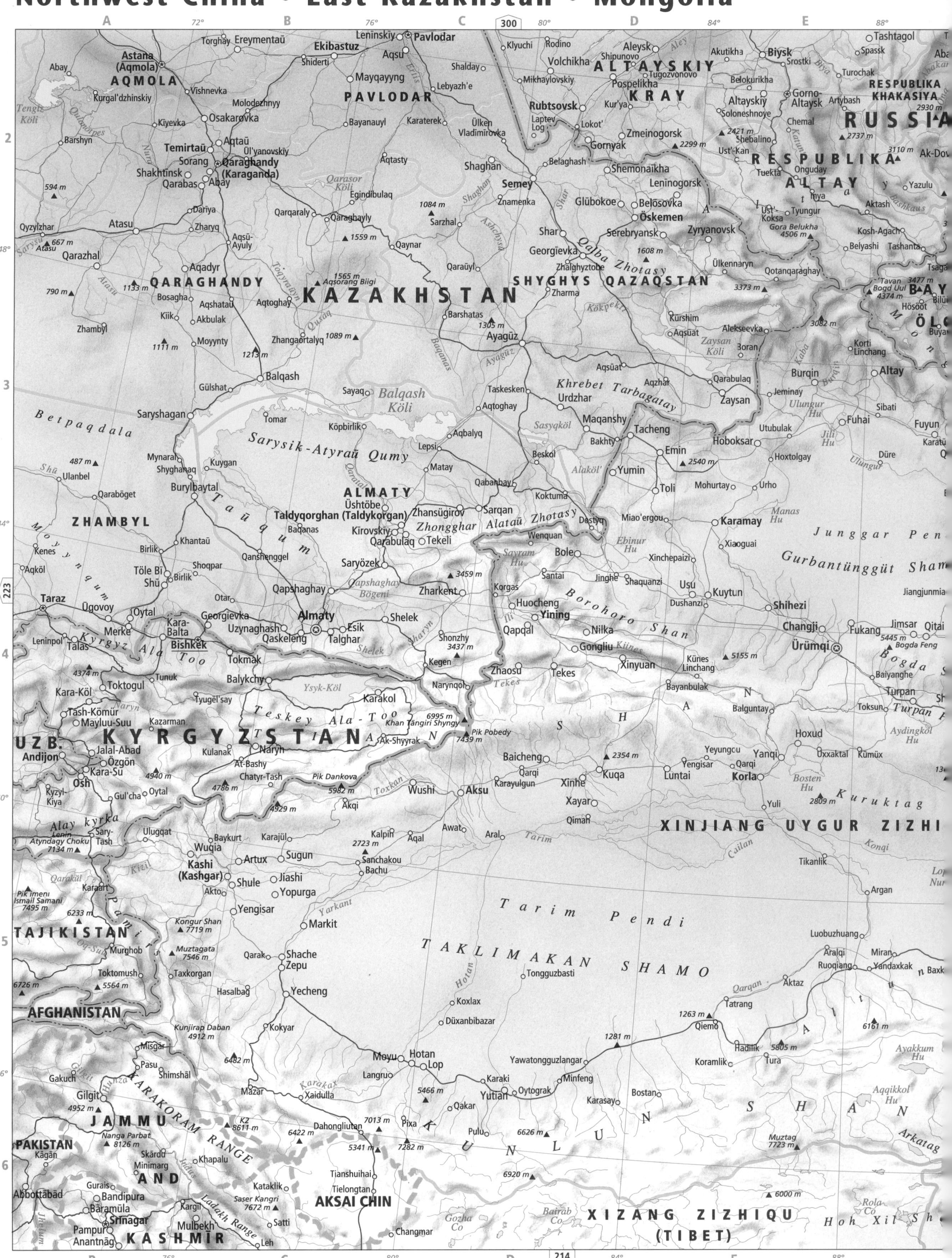

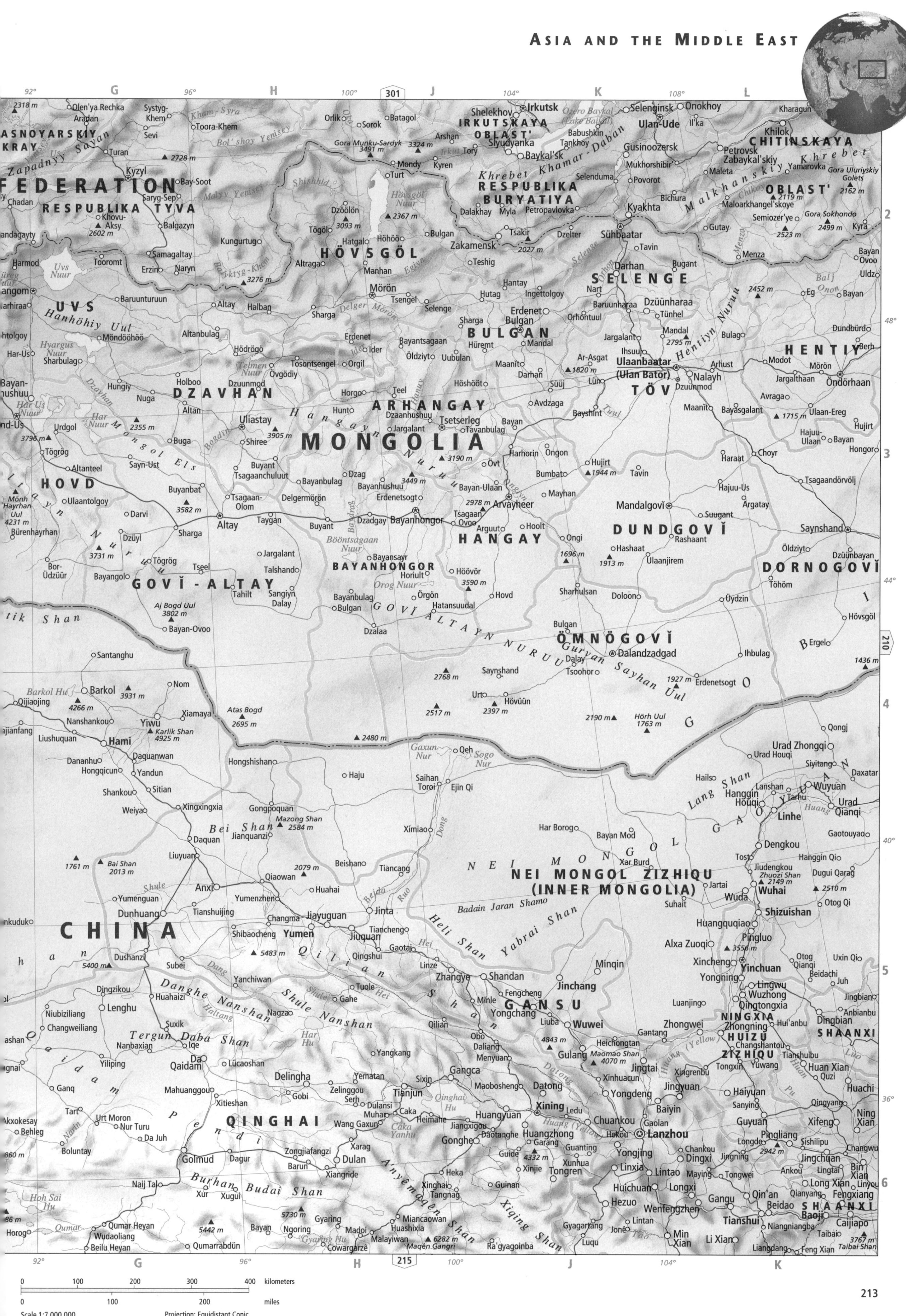

FEDERATION
RESPUBLIKA TYVA
IRKUTSKAYA OBLAST'
RESPUBLIKA BURYATIYA
CHITINSKAYA OBLAST'
MONGOLIA
HÖVSGÖL
UVS
HOVD
DZAVHAN
ARHANGAY
BULGAN
SELENGE
TÖV
HENTIY
GOVĬ-ALTAY
BAYANHONGOR
HANGAY
DUNDGOVĬ
DORNOGOVĬ
ÖMNÖGOVĬ
CHINA
NEI MONGOL ZIZHIQU
(INNER MONGOLIA)
GANSU
QINGHAI
NINGXIA HUIZU ZIZHIQU
SHAANXI
Irkutsk
Ulan-Ude
Ulaanbaatar
(Ulan Bator)
Kyzyl
Uliastay
Altay
Mörön
Erdenet
Darhan
Sühbaatar
Kyakhta
Tsetserleg
Arvayheer
Bayanhongor
Mandalgovĭ
Saynshand
Dalandzadgad
Öndörhaan
Hami
Barkol
Yumen
Jiayuguan
Jiuquan
Zhangye
Jinchang
Wuwei
Xining
Lanzhou
Yinchuan
Wuhai
Shizuishan
Linhe
Golmud
Dunhuang
Tianshui
Baoji
Gobi
Hangay Nuruu
Govĭ Altayn Nuruu
Gurvan Sayhan Uul
Qilian Shan
Bei Shan
Qaidam Pendi
Burhan Budai Shan
A'nyêmaqên Shan
Xiqing Shan
Heli Shan
Yabrai Shan
Badain Jaran Shamo
Lang Shan
Hentiyn Nuruu
Khrebet Khamar-Daban
Zapadnyy Sayan
Malkhanskiy Khrebet
Huang (Yellow)
Uvs Nuur
Hövsgöl Nuur
Ozero Baykal (Lake Baikal)
92°
96°
100°
104°
108°
48°
44°
40°
36°
G
H
J
K
L
2
3
4
5
6
301
210
215
0
100
200
300
400
kilometers
0
100
200
miles
Scale 1:7,000,000
Projection: Equidistant Conic

Southwest China

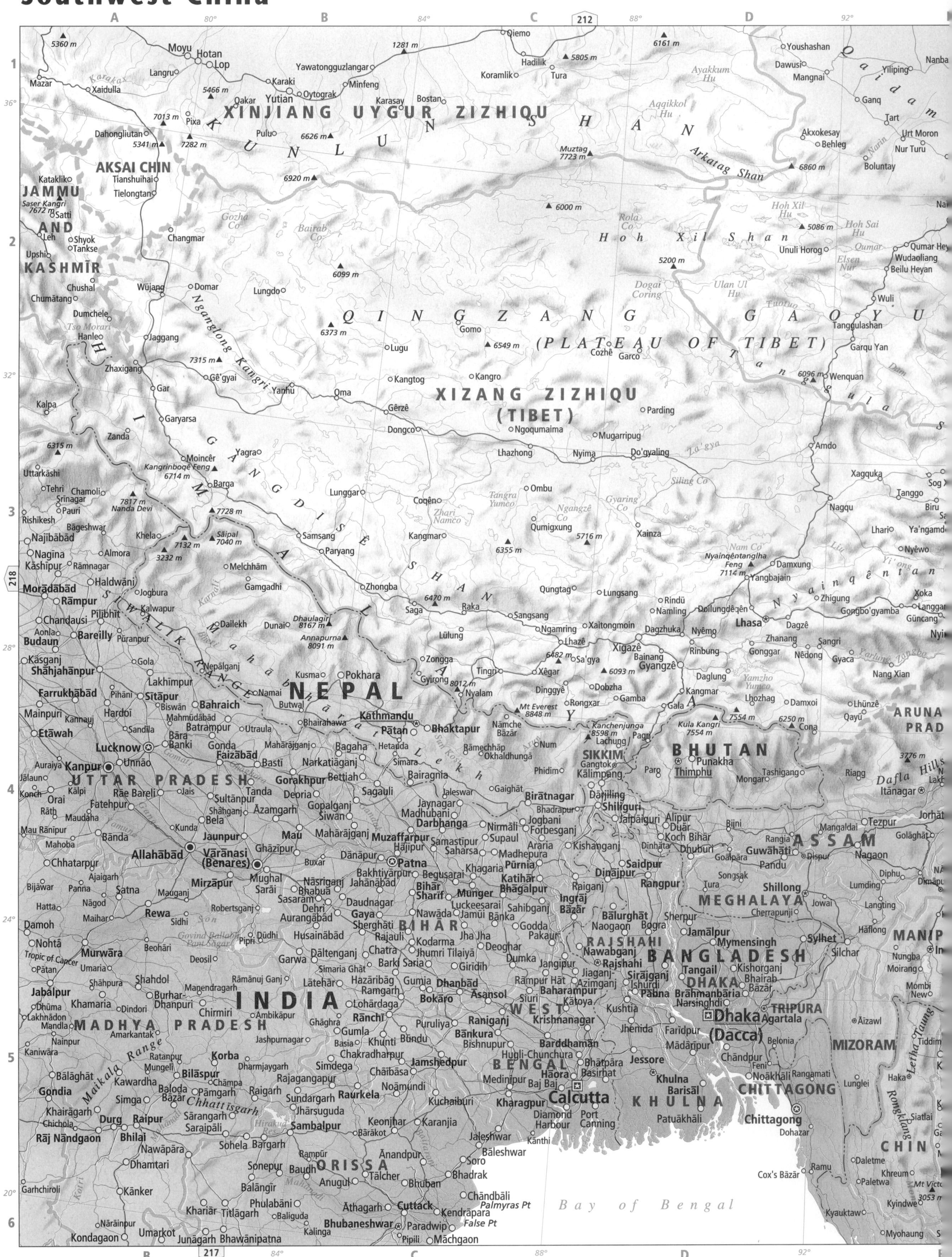

XINJIANG UYGUR ZIZHIQU
KUNLUN SHAN
AKSAI CHIN
JAMMU AND KASHMĪR
QINGZANG GAOYUAN
(PLATEAU OF TIBET)
XIZANG ZIZHIQU
(TIBET)
Hoh Xil Shan
Arkatag Shan
Tanggula Shan
GANGDISĒ SHAN
Nyainqêntanglha Shan
NEPAL
BHUTAN
SIKKIM
ARUNACHAL PRADESH
ASSAM
MEGHALAYA
BANGLADESH
RAJSHAHI
DHAKA
KHULNA
CHITTAGONG
TRIPURA
MIZORAM
MANIPUR
CHIN
INDIA
UTTAR PRADESH
BIHĀR
MADHYA PRADESH
WEST BENGAL
ORISSA
Bay of Bengal
Lhasa
Kathmandu
Thimphu
Dhaka (Dacca)
Calcutta
Patna
Lucknow
Kanpur
Allahābād
Vārānasi (Benares)
Chittagong
Mt Everest 8848 m
Kanchenjunga 8598 m
Annapurna 8091 m
Dhaulagiri 8167 m
Nanda Devi 7817 m
Kangrinboqê Feng 6714 m
Muztag 7723 m
Tropic of Cancer
Maikala Range
Mahābhārat Lekh
Siwalik Range

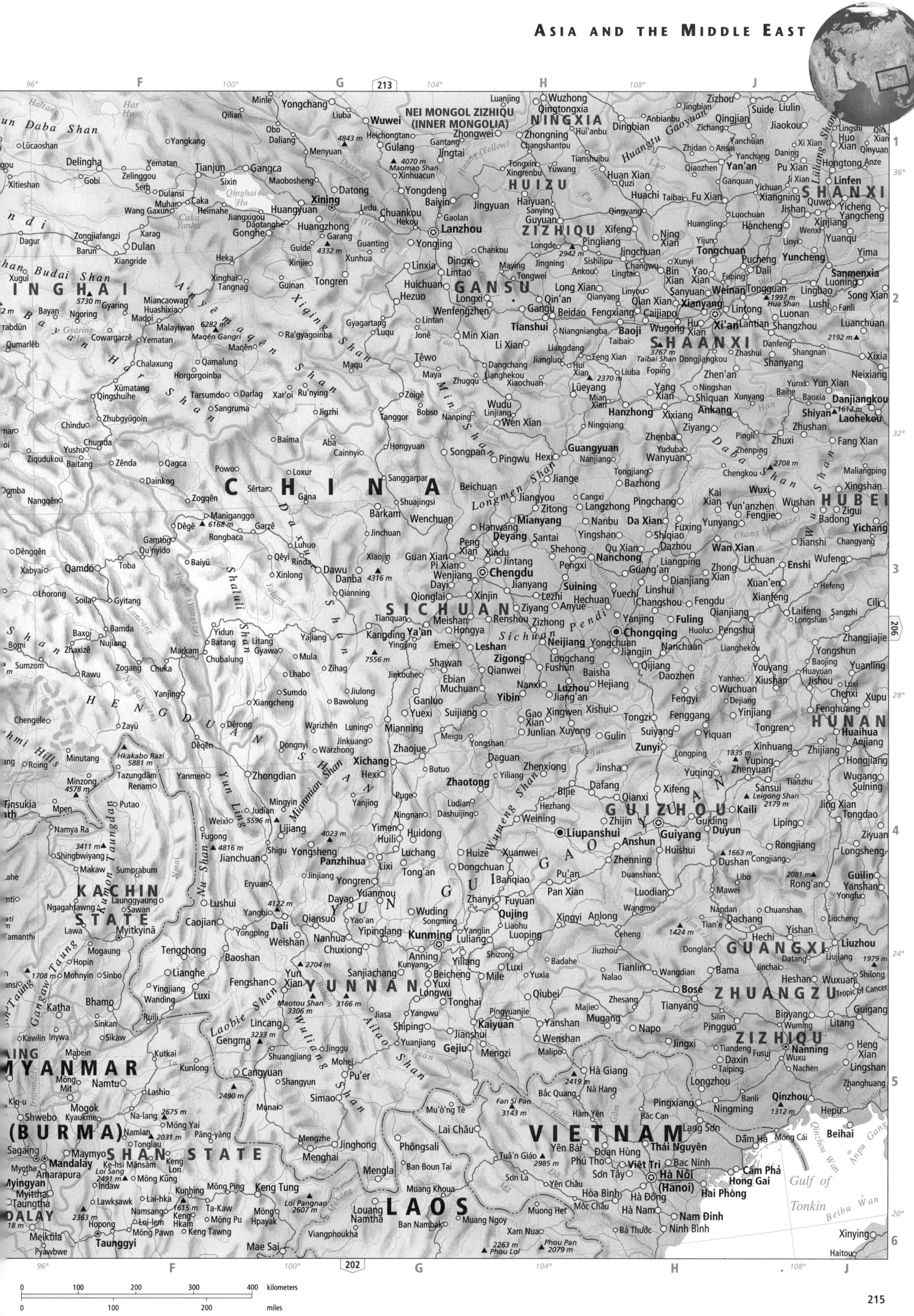

F
G
213
H
J
96°
100°
104°
108°
NEI MONGOL ZIZHIQU (INNER MONGOLIA)
NINGXIA
HUIZU
ZIZHIQU
GANSU
SHAANXI
SHANXI
QINGHAI
CHINA
SICHUAN
HUBEI
HUNAN
GUIZHOU
GUANGXI
ZHUANGZU
ZIZHIQU
YUNNAN
KACHIN STATE
MYANMAR (BURMA)
SHAN STATE
LAOS
VIETNAM
Daba Shan
Bayan Har Shan
A'nyêmaqên Shan
Xiqing Shan
Min Shan
Longmen Shan
Daxue Shan
Shaluli Shan
Hengduan Shan
Yun Ling
Nu Shan
Kumon Taungdan
Wumeng Shan
Yungui Gaoyuan
Sichuan Pendi
Dalou Shan
Wuliang Shan
Ailao Shan
Laobie Shan
Miǒnmian Shan
Huangtu Gaoyuan
Lüliang Shan
Qinghai Hu
Gulf of Tonkin
Beibu Wan
Qinzhou Wan
Xining
Lanzhou
Yinchuan
Xi'an
Chengdu
Chongqing
Guiyang
Kunming
Nanning
Hà Nội (Hanoi)
Mandalay
Taunggyi
Wuwei
Delingha
Golmud
Tianshui
Baoji
Hanzhong
Mianyang
Nanchong
Zigong
Yibin
Luzhou
Leshan
Ya'an
Kangding
Xichang
Panzhihua
Dali
Lijiang
Zhaotong
Liupanshui
Qujing
Gejiu
Kaiyuan
Baise
Liuzhou
Guilin
Haiphong
Beihai
Qinzhou
Zunyi
Yichang
Enshi
Shiyan
Ankang
Yan'an
Tongchuan
Weinan
Xianyang
Guangyuan
Dazhou
Suining
Neijiang
Fuling
Wanxian
Kaili
Duyun
Anshun
Hà Giang
Lao Cai
Lai Châu
Yên Bái
Việt Trì
Thái Nguyên
Nam Định
Ninh Bình
Lạng Sơn
Hòn Gai
Cẩm Phả
Luang Namtha
Phôngsali
Mengla
Jinghong
Simao
Myitkyinā
Bhamo
Lashio
Maymyo
Hkakabo Razi 5881 m
Fan Si Pan 3143 m
Gongga Shan 7556 m
Maqên Gangri 6282 m
Taibai Shan 3767 m
Hua Shan 1997 m
Scale 1:7,000,000
Projection: Equidistant Conic
0 100 200 300 400 kilometers
0 100 200 miles
202
206

South India • Sri Lanka

Bay of Bengal
OCEAN
ORISSA
GHATS
MYANMAR (BURMA)
ARAKAN
MAGWE
PEGU
IRRAWADDY
PONDICHERRY
ANDAMAN AND NICOBAR ISLANDS
Andaman and Nicobar Islands (India)
Andaman Is
Nicobar Is (India)
Bāleshwar
Bhadrak
Chāndbāli
Palmyras Pt
Kendrāpara
False Pt
Paradwip
Cuttack
Bhubaneshwar
Māchgaon
Konārak
Puri
Chilka Lake
Brahmapur
Chatrapur
Sompeta
Parlākimidi
Narasannapeta
Srīkākulam
Vizianagaram
Waltair
Vishākhapatnam
Anakāpalle
Tuni
Rājahmundry
Kākināda
Yanam
Pālakollu
Narasapur
Chirāla
Jhārsuguda
Sambalpur
Bargarh
Keonjhar
Ānandpur
Soro
Tālcher
Anugul
Jājapur
Āthagarh
Sonepur
Baudh
Balāngir
Phulabāni
Titlāgarh
Kalinga
Baliguda
Khariār
Bhawānipatna
Junāgarh
Umarkot
Khallikot
Asika
1076 m
Gunupur
Jaypur
Jagdalpur
Pāppadāhāndi
Palkonda
Mālkāngiri
Nawāpāra
Dhamtari
Kānker
Pāmgarh
Sārangarh
Baloda
Saraipāli
Sohela
Hirakud Res.
Krishnadevipeta
Trincomalee
Mutur
Batticaloa
Amparai
Pottuvil
Wellawaya
Hambantota
Sittwe (Akyab)
Kyauktaw
Myohaung
Magyichaung
Ywathitke
Oyster I.
Combermere Bay
Kyaukpyu
Ramree I.
Cheduba I.
Taungup
Sinbyugyun
Sagu
Magwe
Minbu
Migyaungye
Taungdwingyi
Pauksa Taung 1708 m
Mindon
Kama
Pyè (Prome)
Paungde
Zigon
Kyangin
Okpo
Minhla
Letpadan
Henzada
Kyeintali
Gwa
Lemyethna
Yegyi
Danubyu
Kangyidaung
Ma-ubin
Bassein
Myaungmya
Bogale
Preparis North Channel
Preparis I.
Preparis South Channel
Great Coco I.
Little Coco I.
Coco Channel
Landfall I.
C. Price
North Andaman
Saddle Peak 738 m
Pahlāgaon
Middle Andaman
South Andaman
Port Blair
Rutland I.
Duncan Passage
Nachuge
Little Andaman
Ten Degree Channel
Car Nicobar I.
Kakana
Tarasa Dwip I.
Camorta I.
Misha
Sombrero Channel
Little Nicobar
Bananga
Great Nicobar
84°
88°
92°
20°
16°
12°
8°
4°
Scale 1:7,000,000
Projection: Equidistant Conic
kilometers
miles

219
214

Asia and the Middle East

North India • Pakistan • Nepal

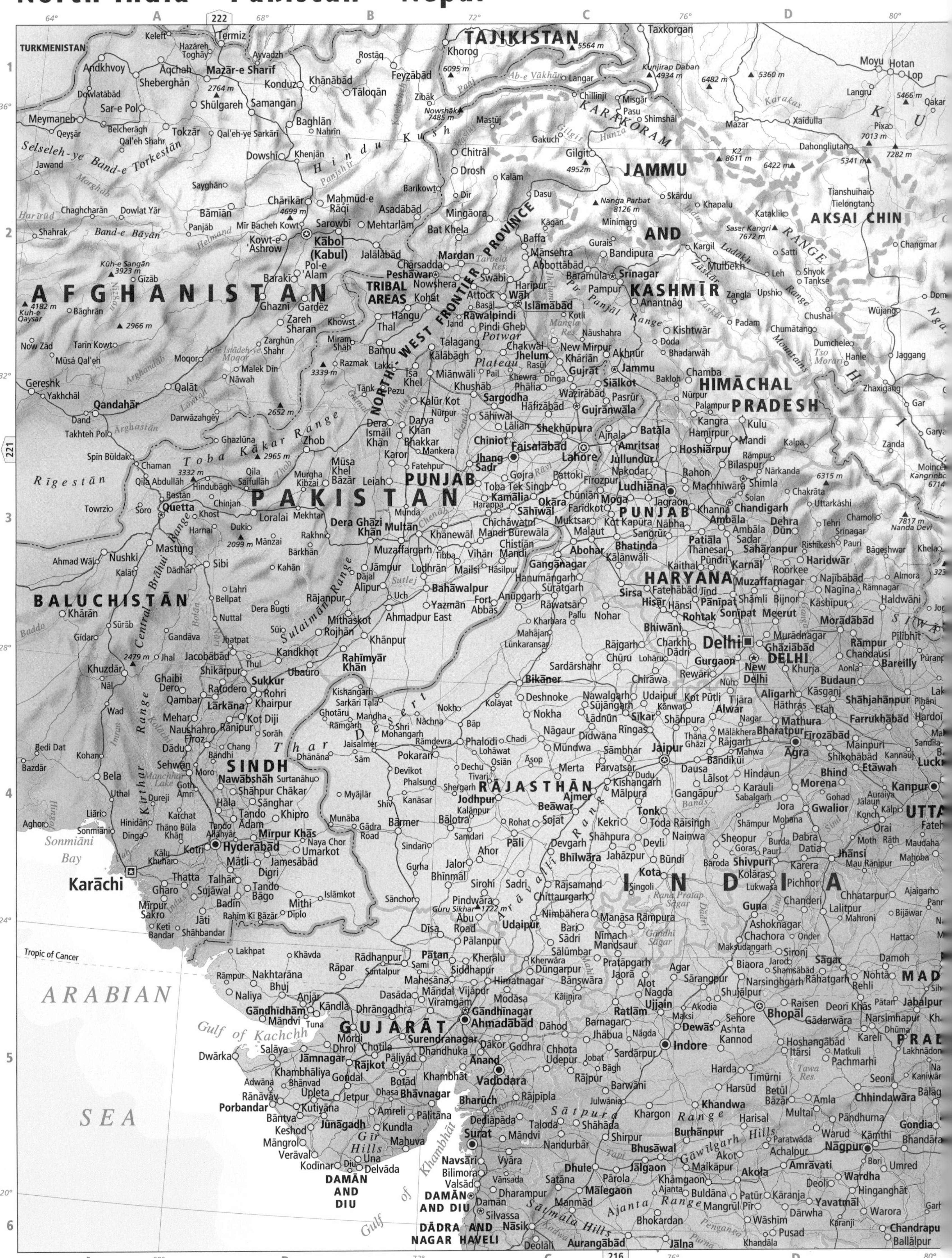

TURKMENISTAN
TAJIKISTAN
AFGHANISTAN
PAKISTAN
INDIA
BALUCHISTĀN
SINDH
PUNJAB
NORTH-WEST FRONTIER PROVINCE
TRIBAL AREAS
JAMMU AND KASHMĪR
AKSAI CHIN
HIMĀCHAL PRADESH
HARYANA
DELHI
RĀJASTHĀN
GUJARĀT
DAMĀN AND DIU
DĀDRA AND NAGAR HAVELI
ARABIAN SEA
Gulf of Kachchh
Gulf of Khambhāt
Sonmiāni Bay
Tropic of Cancer
Hindu Kush
KARAKORAM
Toba Kākar Range
Sulaimān Range
Central Brāhui Range
Kīrthar Range
Thar Desert
Aravalli Range
Sātpura Range
Gir Hills
Potwar Plateau
Pīr Panjāl Range
Zāskār Range
Ladākh Range
Rīgestān
Kābol (Kabul)
Islāmābād
Rāwalpindi
Peshāwar
Lahore
Faisalābād
Multān
Quetta
Qandahār
Hyderābād
Karāchi
Srinagar
Amritsar
Ludhiāna
Chandīgarh
Delhi
New Delhi
Jaipur
Āgra
Ahmadābād
Vadodara
Surat
Rājkot
Indore
Bhopāl
Nāgpur
Kanpur
K2 8611 m
Nanga Parbat 8126 m

222
221
216

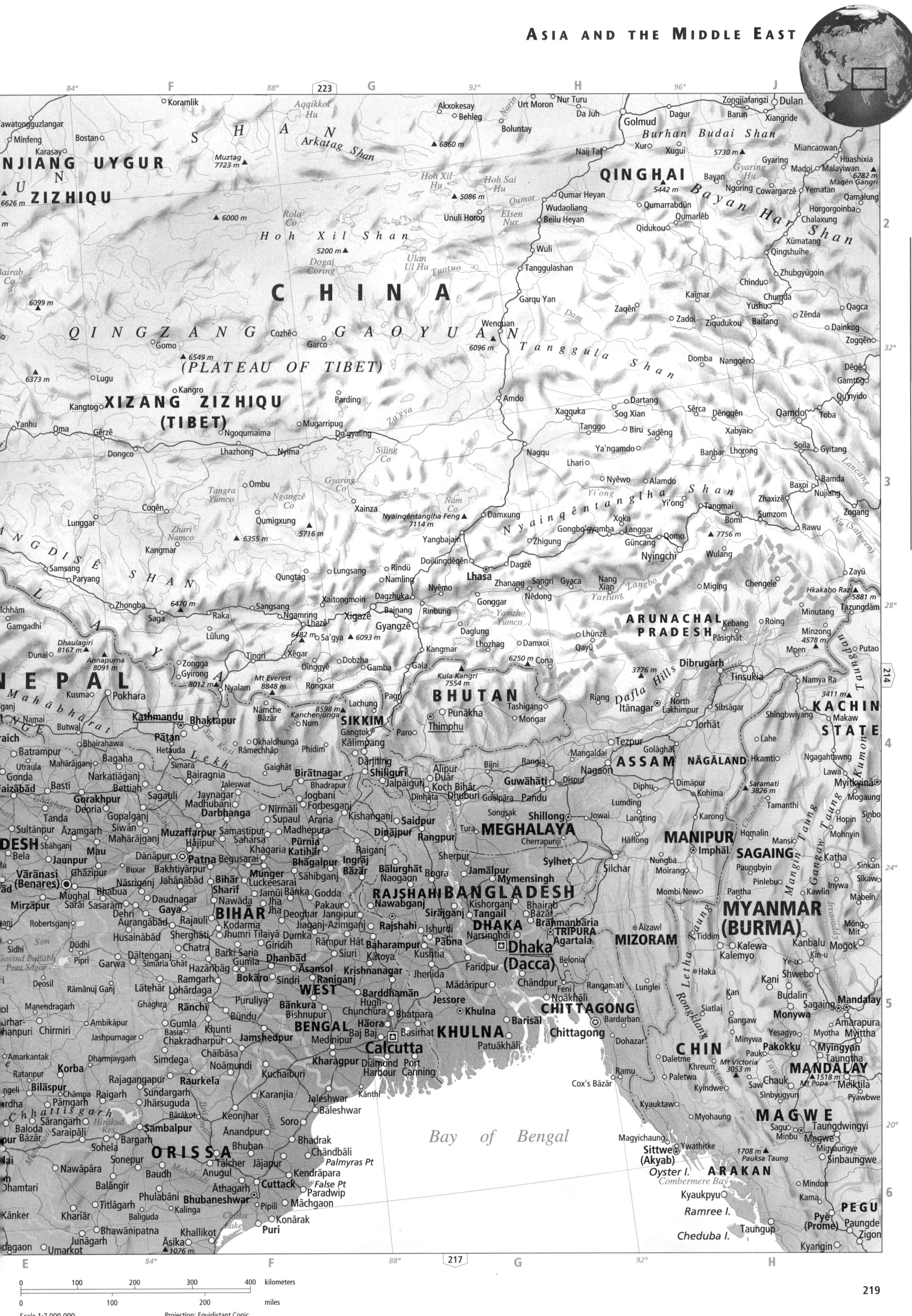

0 100 200 300 400 kilometers
0 100 200 miles
Scale 1:7,000,000
Projection: Equidistant Conic

Middle East

224 222 362 367

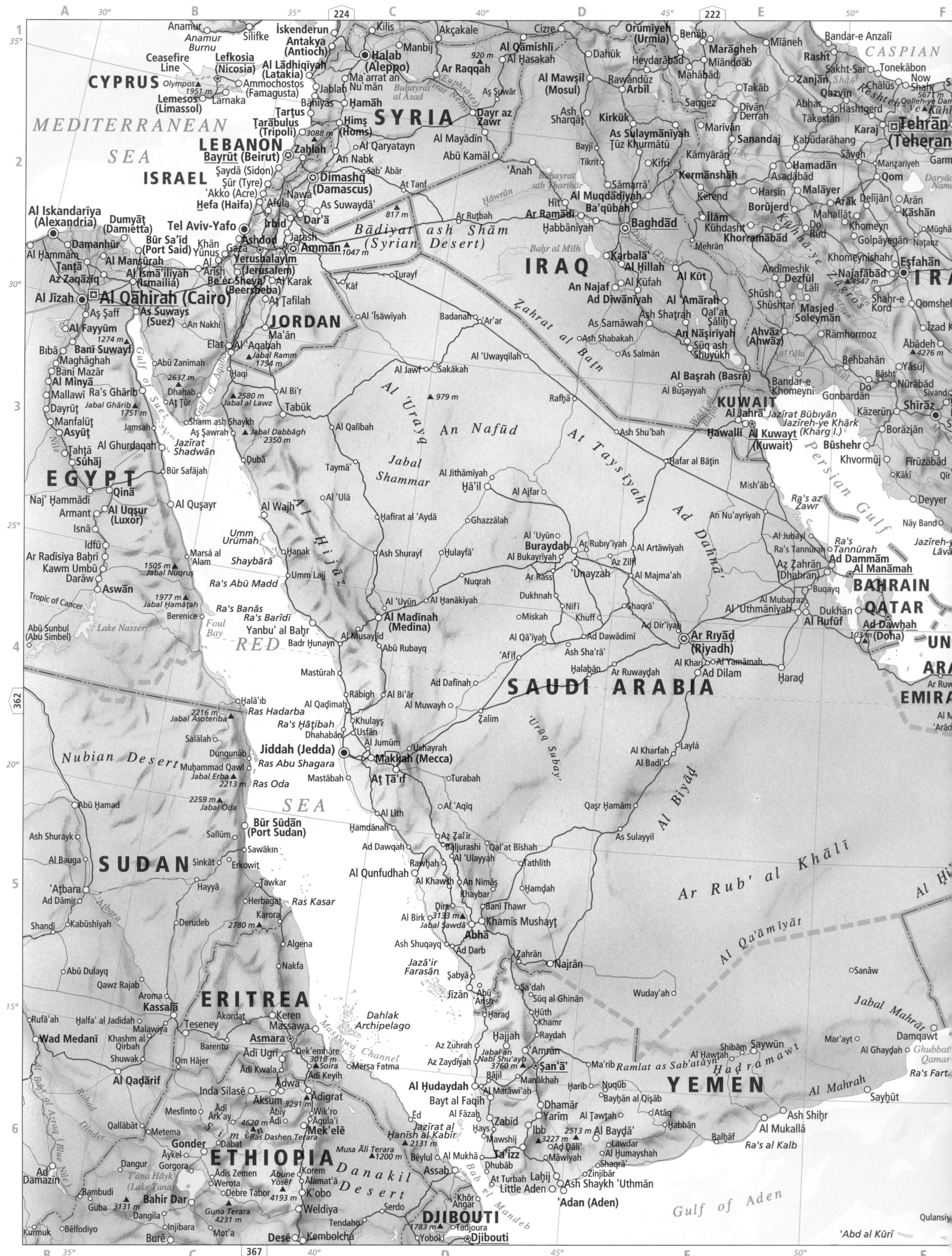

CYPRUS
Lefkosia (Nicosia)
Lemesos (Limassol)
Larnaka
Ammochostos (Famagusta)
Ceasefire Line
Anamur
Silifke
İskenderun
Antakya (Antioch)
Kilis
Halab (Aleppo)
Al Lādhiqīyah (Latakia)
Manbij
Akçakale
Ar Raqqah
Cizre
Al Qāmishlī
Al Ḩasakah
Dahūk
Orūmīyeh (Urmia)
Al Mawşil (Mosul)
Arbīl
Ḩamāh
Ḩimş (Homs)
Ţarţūs
Ţarābulus (Tripoli)
SYRIA
Dayr az Zawr
MEDITERRANEAN SEA
LEBANON
Zaḩlah
Bayrūt (Beirut)
Şaydā (Sidon)
Şūr (Tyre)
'Akko (Acre)
Hefa (Haifa)
ISRAEL
Dimashq (Damascus)
As Suwaydā'
Tel Aviv-Yafo
Ashdod
Yerushalayim (Jerusalem)
Ammān
Irbid
Be'er Sheva' (Beersheba)
Al Karak
JORDAN
Ma'ān
Al 'Aqabah
Elat
Al Iskandarīya (Alexandria)
Dumyāţ (Damietta)
Būr Sa'īd (Port Said)
Al Manşūrah
Ţanţā
Az Zaqāzīq
Al Ismā'īlīyah (Ismailia)
Al Jīzah
Al Qāhirah (Cairo)
As Suways (Suez)
Al Fayyūm
Banī Suwayf
Al Minyā
Asyūţ
Sūhāj
Qinā
Al Uqşur (Luxor)
Aswān
EGYPT
Lake Nasser
Tropic of Cancer
Bādiyat ash Shām (Syrian Desert)
IRAQ
Baghdād
Karbalā'
Al Ḩillah
An Najaf
Al Kūt
Al Başrah (Basra)
KUWAIT
Al Kuwayt (Kuwait)
Tabūk
Al Jawf
Ḩā'il
Buraydah
An Nafūd
Al Madīnah (Medina)
Yanbu' al Baḩr
Jiddah (Jedda)
Makkah (Mecca)
Aţ Ţā'if
Ar Riyāḑ (Riyadh)
SAUDI ARABIA
Ad Dammām
Al Manāmah
BAHRAIN
QATAR
Ad Dawḩah (Doha)
Ar Rub' al Khālī
Persian Gulf
CASPIAN
Tehrān (Teheran)
Qom
Eşfahān
Ahvāz (Ahwāz)
Shīrāz
Būshehr
Kermānshāh
Hamadān
Tabrīz
RED SEA
Nubian Desert
Būr Sūdān (Port Sudan)
SUDAN
Kassalā
ERITREA
Asmara
Massawa
Dahlak Archipelago
ETHIOPIA
Gonder
Bahir Dar
Mek'elē
Danakil Desert
DJIBOUTI
Djibouti
Abhā
Khamīs Mushayţ
Jīzān
Najrān
Şan'ā'
Al Ḩudaydah
Ta'izz
'Adan (Aden)
Al Mukallā
YEMEN
Gulf of Aden
Bab el Mandeb

TURKMENISTAN
AFGHANISTAN
PAKISTAN
INDIA
OMAN
JAMMU AND KASHMIR
ARABIAN SEA
Gulf of Oman
Gulf of Kachchh
Gulf of Khambhat
Strait of Hormuz
Dasht-e Lūt
Dasht-e Kavīr
Dasht-e Mārgow
Rīgestān
Thar Desert
Hindu Kush
Karakoram Range
Ladakh Range
Zaskar Mountains
Pīr Panjāl Range
Toba Kakar Range
Sulaiman Range
Kirthar Range
Siāhān Range
Central Makrān Range
Sātmala Hills
Western Ghats
Gir Hills
Al Hajar
Jazīrat Maşīrah
Laccadive Is
Mashhad
Herāt
Kābol (Kabul)
Kandahār
Quetta
Zāhedān
Kermān
Bandar-e 'Abbās
Masqaţ (Muscat)
Karāchi
Hyderābād
Multān
Lahore
Islāmābād
Rāwalpindi
Peshāwar
Faisalābād
Delhi
New Delhi
Jaipur
Ahmadābād
Vadodara
Surat
Mumbai (Bombay)
Pune
Indore
Srinagar
K2 8611 m
Nanga Parbat 8126 m
Kūh-e Taftān 4042 m
Kūh-e Hazār 4420 m
Kūh-e Bazmān 3489 m
Kūh-e Sangān 3923 m
Ra's al Ḩadd
Ra's al Madrakah
Scale 1:10,000,000
Projection: Equidistant Conic
0 100 200 300 400 kilometers
0 100 200 miles

Kazakhstan • Central Asian Republics

Asia and the Middle East

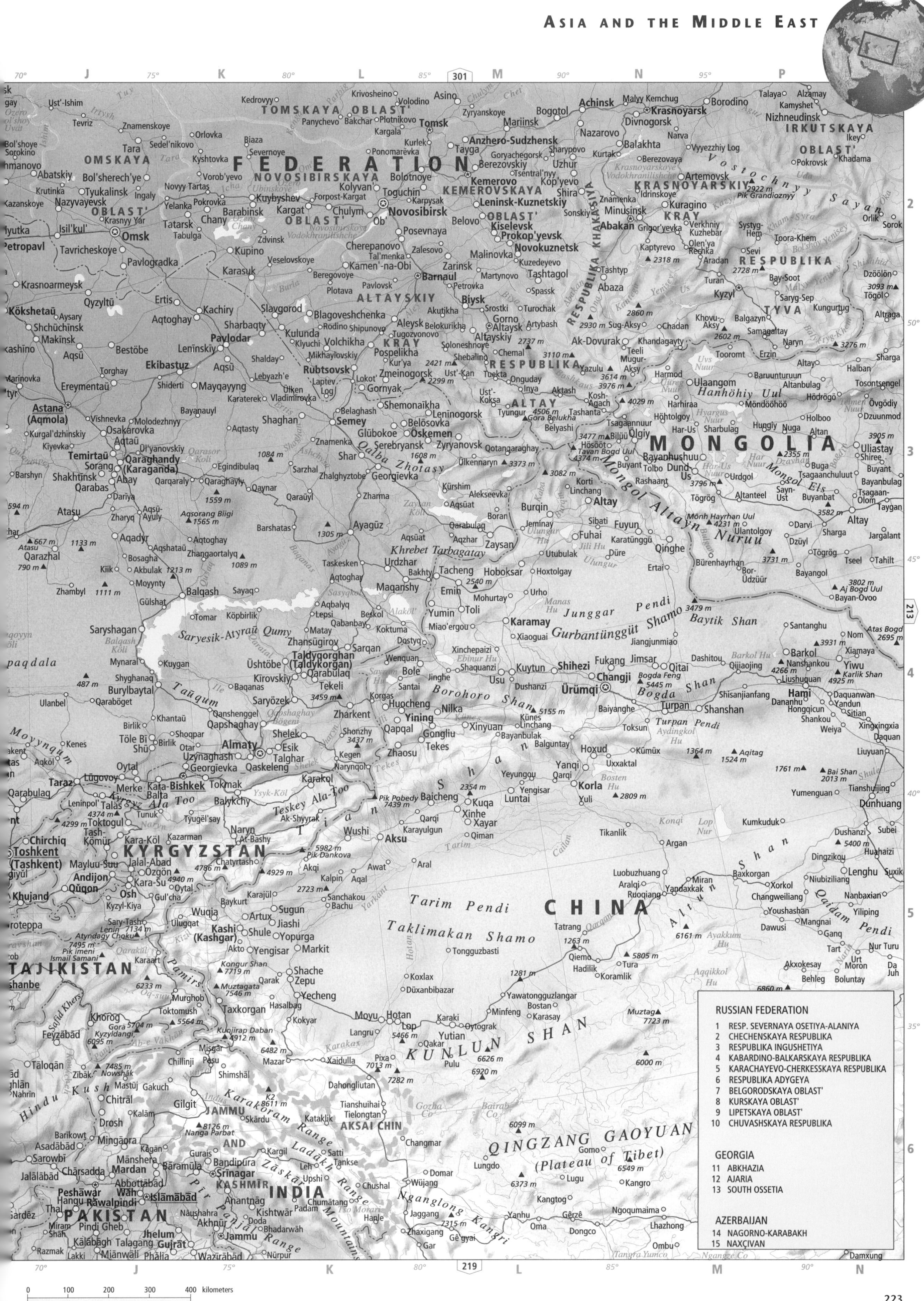

Asia and the Middle East
301
219
213
FEDERATION
MONGOLIA
CHINA
KYRGYZSTAN
TAJIKISTAN
PAKISTAN
INDIA
JAMMU AND KASHMIR
AKSAI CHIN
TOMSKAYA OBLAST'
OMSKAYA OBLAST'
NOVOSIBIRSKAYA OBLAST'
KEMEROVSKAYA OBLAST'
ALTAYSKIY KRAY
KRASNOYARSKIY KRAY
IRKUTSKAYA OBLAST'
RESPUBLIKA TYVA
RESPUBLIKA ALTAY
RESPUBLIKA KHAKASIYA
Junggar Pendi
Gurbantünggüt Shamo
Tarim Pendi
Taklimakan Shamo
Tian Shan
Kunlun Shan
Altun Shan
Qaidam Pendi
Qingzang Gaoyuan (Plateau of Tibet)
Karakoram Range
Hindu Kush
Mongol Altayn Nuruu
Turpan Pendi
Saryesik-Atyraū Qumy
Astana (Aqmola)
Novosibirsk
Omsk
Krasnoyarsk
Barnaul
Almaty
Bishkek
Ürümqi
Toshkent (Tashkent)
Islāmābād
Rawalpindi
Srinagar
Kashi (Kashgar)
Hotan
Hami
RUSSIAN FEDERATION
1 RESP. SEVERNAYA OSETIYA-ALANIYA
2 CHECHENSKAYA RESPUBLIKA
3 RESPUBLIKA INGUSHETIYA
4 KABARDINO-BALKARSKAYA RESPUBLIKA
5 KARACHAYEVO-CHERKESSKAYA RESPUBLIKA
6 RESPUBLIKA ADYGEYA
7 BELGORODSKAYA OBLAST'
8 KURSKAYA OBLAST'
9 LIPETSKAYA OBLAST'
10 CHUVASHSKAYA RESPUBLIKA
GEORGIA
11 ABKHAZIA
12 AJARIA
13 SOUTH OSSETIA
AZERBAIJAN
14 NAGORNO-KARABAKH
15 NAXÇIVAN
0 100 200 300 400 kilometers
0 100 200 miles
Scale 1:10,000,000
Projection: Equidistant Conic

Turkey • East Europe

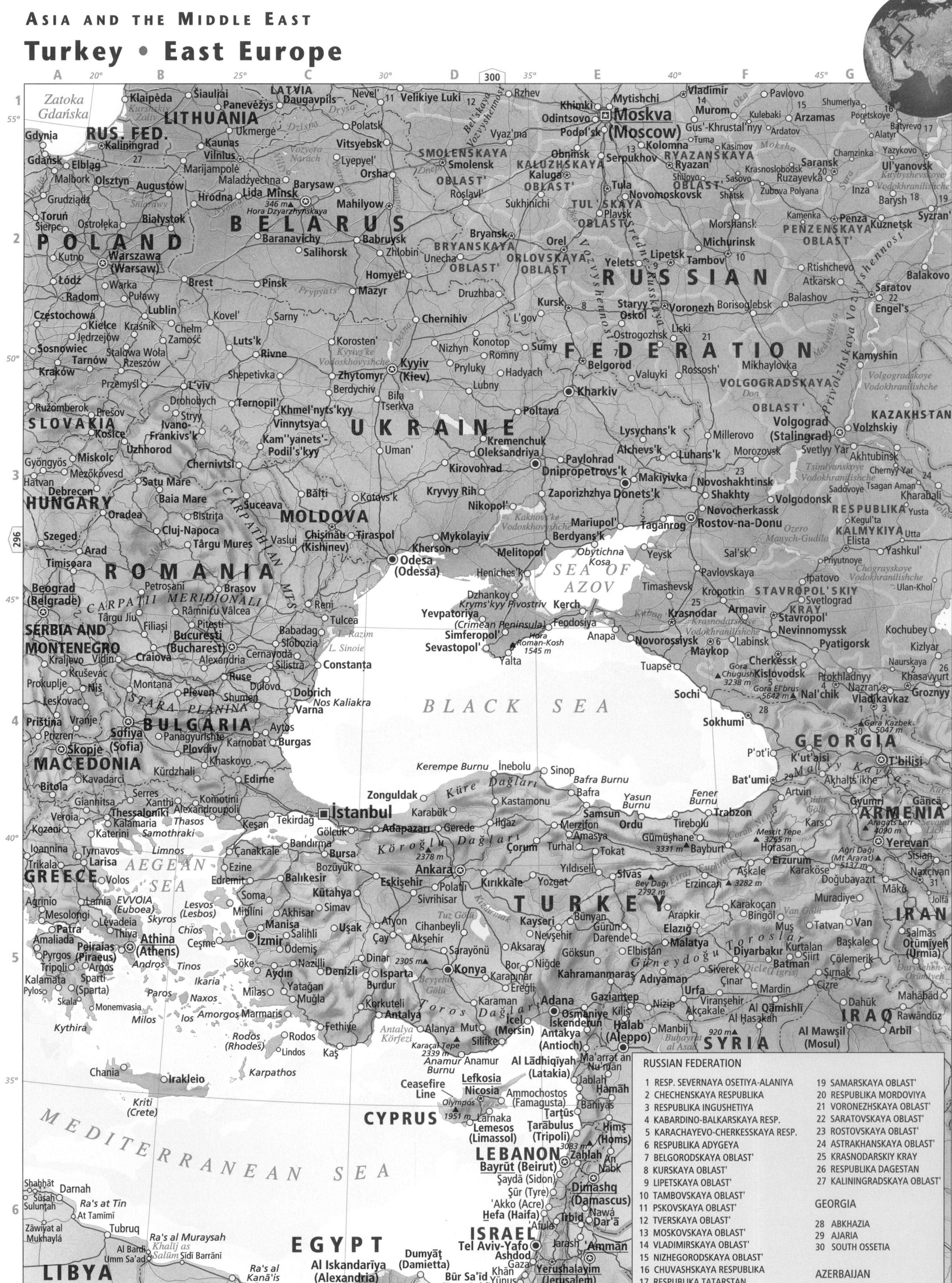

RUSSIAN FEDERATION
1 RESP. SEVERNAYA OSETIYA-ALANIYA
2 CHECHENSKAYA RESPUBLIKA
3 RESPUBLIKA INGUSHETIYA
4 KABARDINO-BALKARSKAYA RESP.
5 KARACHAYEVO-CHERKESSKAYA RESP.
6 RESPUBLIKA ADYGEYA
7 BELGORODSKAYA OBLAST'
8 KURSKAYA OBLAST'
9 LIPETSKAYA OBLAST'
10 TAMBOVSKAYA OBLAST'
11 PSKOVSKAYA OBLAST'
12 TVERSKAYA OBLAST'
13 MOSKOVSKAYA OBLAST'
14 VLADIMIRSKAYA OBLAST'
15 NIZHEGORODSKAYA OBLAST'
16 CHUVASHSKAYA RESPUBLIKA
17 RESPUBLIKA TATARSTAN
18 UL'YANOVSKAYA OBLAST'
19 SAMARSKAYA OBLAST'
20 RESPUBLIKA MORDOVIYA
21 VORONEZHSKAYA OBLAST'
22 SARATOVSKAYA OBLAST'
23 ROSTOVSKAYA OBLAST'
24 ASTRAKHANSKAYA OBLAST'
25 KRASNODARSKIY KRAY
26 RESPUBLIKA DAGESTAN
27 KALININGRADSKAYA OBLAST'
GEORGIA
28 ABKHAZIA
29 AJARIA
30 SOUTH OSSETIA
AZERBAIJAN
31 NAXÇIVAN
BLACK SEA
SEA OF AZOV
MEDITERRANEAN SEA
AEGEAN SEA
POLAND
BELARUS
LITHUANIA
RUS. FED.
RUSSIAN FEDERATION
UKRAINE
MOLDOVA
ROMANIA
SLOVAKIA
HUNGARY
SERBIA AND MONTENEGRO
BULGARIA
MACEDONIA
GREECE
TURKEY
GEORGIA
ARMENIA
KAZAKHSTAN
IRAN
IRAQ
SYRIA
LEBANON
ISRAEL
CYPRUS
EGYPT
LIBYA
SMOLENSKAYA OBLAST'
KALUZHSKAYA OBLAST'
RYAZANSKAYA OBLAST'
TUL'SKAYA OBLAST'
BRYANSKAYA OBLAST'
ORLOVSKAYA OBLAST
PENZENSKAYA OBLAST'
VOLGOGRADSKAYA OBLAST'
STAVROPOL'SKIY KRAY
RESPUBLIKA KALMYKIYA
CARPATHIAN MTS
kilometers 0 100 200 300 400
miles 0 100 200
Scale 1:10,000,000
Projection: Equidistant Cor

East Mediterranean

Scale 1:3,500,000 Projection: Equidistant Conic

0 100 200 kilometers

0 50 100 miles

Europe and the Russian Federation

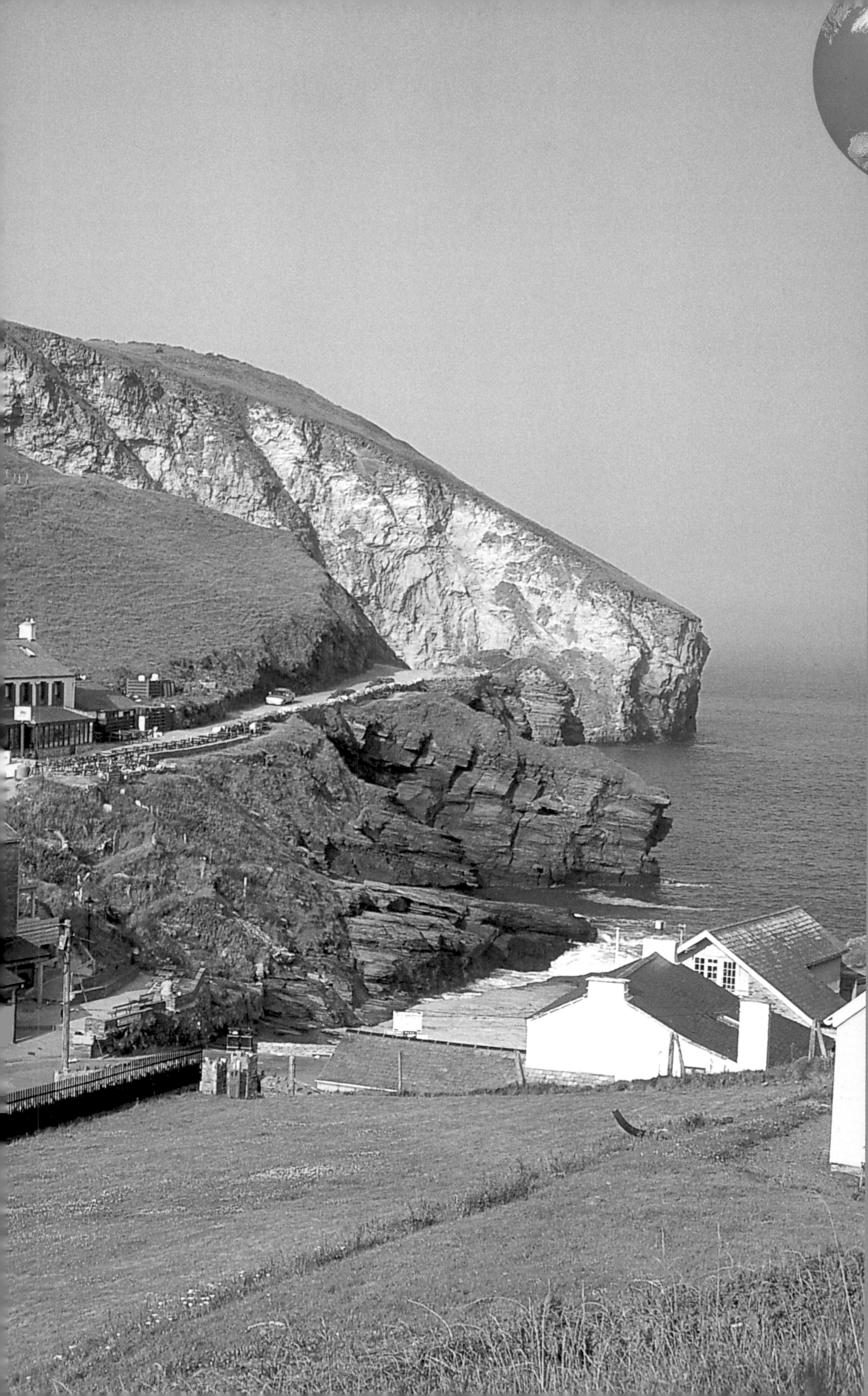

Europe and the Russian Federation

Covering 10.5 million sq km (4 million sq miles), Europe is the second smallest continent in the world. It is part of the Eurasian landmass and its conventional separation from Asia is therefore more cultural than physical. The Ural Mountains and Ural River, the Caspian and Red Seas, and the Dardanelles Straits separate Europe from Asia and, to the south, the Mediterranean Sea separates it from Africa.

The countries of Europe can be divided into three groups: Western Europe, Eastern Europe (most countries of which came under the influence of the former Soviet Union), and the countries that emerged from the break-up of the former Soviet Union. Each of these groups can be distinguished by the history of its political systems.

Western Europe includes Andorra, Austria, Belgium, Denmark, Finland, France, Germany, Greece, Iceland, Ireland, Italy, Liechtenstein, Luxembourg, Malta, Monaco, the Netherlands, Norway, Portugal, San Marino, Spain, Sweden, Switzerland, the United Kingdom and Vatican City. There are also several dependencies: Guernsey, Jersey, the Isle of Man, and Gibraltar are dependencies of the United Kingdom, the Faeroe Islands of Denmark and Svalbard of Norway.

The nations of Eastern Europe are Poland, Hungary, the Czech Republic, Slovakia, Bulgaria, Romania, Slovenia, Croatia, Bosnia and Herzegovina, Macedonia, Serbia and Montenegro (formerly Yugoslavia) and Albania.

When the former Soviet Union broke up, several new nations emerged in Europe and Asia; the European nations consist of the Russian Federation, Ukraine, Belarus, Latvia, Lithuania, Estonia, and Moldova.

During the last 500 years, Europe has exerted a strong influence on the rest of the world through colonialism. Several Western European countries were colonial powers and their languages have become international; European sciences, laws, and arts have spread around the globe. European companies developed commercial agriculture, mining, and manufacturing in their colonies. The colonial powers promoted European migration to the Americas, Australia, and New Zealand—Europeans are now the dominant people there. Many Europeans also migrated to South Africa.

Physical features

The elongated Tertiary Period mountain chain that stretches between the Alps in France and the Carpathians in Romania, rising 3,000 to 4,500 m (10,000 to 15,000 ft), is a prominent feature in Europe. In contrast, there are geologically old and worn-down mountains in Scandinavia and northern Britain. Glacial carving, including sharp-peaked mountains (such as the Matterhorn) and flat-bottomed, steep-sided glacial valleys as in Switzerland, is found in most European mountainous areas. Along the Scandinavian coasts there are fiords, which are glacial valleys drowned by the sea. There are extensive plains in Central and Eastern Europe and France. Europe is well watered by a large number of rivers—the Volga, the Danube, the Rhône, and the Rhine. Many of these rivers are navigable far inland and are interconnected in places by canals.

Climate and vegetation

Although much of Europe can be described as humid temperate, significant climatic differences exist within its borders. The climates of Western Europe are moderated by the Atlantic Ocean, which is warmed by the waters of the Gulf Stream. In contrast, the winter temperatures in continental Russia are below freezing.

The northernmost parts of Europe are treeless, with very cold winters and mild summers. Further south is the taiga, with broad-leaf deciduous and needle-leaf coniferous trees covering large tracts of land, particularly in Russia.

Cool, humid temperate climates stretch along the coast of the Atlantic Ocean between northern Spain and Norway, including Iceland. This area is characterized by mixed forests, but most of the original trees have been cleared. Some forests, like the Black Forest, have been harmed by acid rain.

Further inland, Central and Eastern Europe experience more extreme temperature ranges. There is a semiarid belt in the south, and forests are found in the wetter and higher areas. The drier regions with less reliable rainfall, such as the Ukraine and southwestern Russia, are characterized by extensive steppes of short grasses.

The southern Mediterranean belt experiences hot, dry summers and cool, wet winters. Forests and scrub cover large areas.

A valley (with vineyards) in Switzerland (below), and a beech forest in Germany (right), both in Western Europe.

Population

The population of Europe at present (excluding the Russian Federation) totals 728 million. The relatively high standards of living in most European nations are reflected in life expectancies of 70.1 years for males and 78.2 years for females. Population numbers are stable, with a near zero growth rate. The Russian Federation has 145 million people; its life expectancies are 62.3 years for males and 73 years for females.

There has been significant urbanization in Europe since the nineteenth century, and this accelerated following the Second World War. Currently 74 percent of the population lives in cities and towns (84 percent in northern Europe and 65 percent in southern Europe); the figure for the Russian Federation is 73 percent.

Agriculture

Europe has a well-developed agricultural economy based on a wide range of food and animal products. Farming is more advanced in Western Europe, in terms of technology and organization, than in the former communist countries of Eastern Europe, which experimented with collectivized agriculture for several decades. Farm size varies considerably, but pressure to create larger farm units is changing the agricultural landscape.

Within Europe's cool, humid zone, mixed farming (grain growing and livestock rearing) is widespread. Wheat, barley, and rye are the main grains, and sheep and cattle the main livestock. Dairy farming is important in some of the cool countries such as the Netherlands and Denmark. Apples and pears are significant fruits.

Southern Europe, with its warm, dry summers and mild winters, is suited to growing grapes, citrus fruits, and olives. Irrigation is extensively used in parts of the Mediterranean areas for growing rice, for example.

There is extensive fishing in the Atlantic Ocean and in both the Mediterranean and Black Seas.

Industrialization

Europe was the first part of the world to become industrialized, and through scientific innovation and extensive use of technology, remains one of the world's most developed regions. British and French industries, in particular, benefited from raw materials supplied by their colonies; the colonies in turn provided markets for manufactured goods.

Manufacturing in Europe ranges from the processing of agricultural raw materials, as in the production of wine and olive oil, and the manufacturing of basic industrial items such as steel, petroleum refining, chemicals, fertilizers and cement, to the production of highly sophisticated items like cars, ships, aircraft, and electronic goods.

While European industries largely import the minerals they require, there are some significant mineral deposits in the region: coal (in several places), petroleum (in the North Sea and Eastern Europe), and iron ore (in Ukraine and Russia). The Russian Federation exports natural gas by pipeline to several European countries, and it is also a major producer of gold.

Considerable damage was done to industry and infrastructure during both world wars, particularly the second, but Europe rebuilt. Western Europe prospered, with large-scale restructuring and industrialization, while communist-controlled Eastern Europe lagged behind. These nations are now joining the market economy, but it will take time for them to catch up. Currently some East European nations are economically stagnant, and the Russian Federation, facing economic collapse, needs foreign aid to restructure its economy.

Industrialization and urbanization have taken their toll on the environment. Air pollution, acid rain, and river-water pollution are common. Sulfur dioxide levels have been reduced, thanks to international cooperation, but emission of nitrogen oxides remains high. The Mediterranean, Black and Baltic Seas have been badly affected by the discharge of waste products.

Languages

Europe has a large number of languages, most of them belonging to the three major Indo-European language family groups: the Latin-based or Romance languages, the Germanic, and the Slavic.

The Latin-based languages include Spanish, Italian, French, Portuguese, and Romanian. The Germanic languages comprise English, German, Dutch, Danish, Swedish, and Norwegian. Latvian and Lithuanian are distinct Baltic languages. Celtic languages (Irish and Scottish Gaelic and Welsh) are spoken by minorities in the British Isles and also in France (Breton). The main Slavic languages are Russian, Ukrainian, Belarusian, Polish, Czech, Slovak, and Bulgarian, while another group (Serbo-Croatian, Slovene, and Macedonian) is found in the Balkans.

Other languages include Greek, Albanian, and Turkish, which are spoken in parts of the Balkans; Finnish in Scandinavia; and Basque and Catalan in Spain and France.

While most European nations have a dominant language, there are some exceptions. Switzerland has French, German, and Italian-speaking zones, and Belgium is divided into Flemish and French-speaking areas. There are German-speaking areas in Hungary, the Czech Republic, Poland, and France, and there are Russian-speaking minorities in all the former Soviet Union nations.

Boundary disputes and wars

The First and Second World Wars both began as boundary disputes between European countries before engulfing most of the continent. The domination of Eastern Europe by the powerful former Soviet Union resulted in a political, ideological, and military "iron curtain" dividing the continent until the early 1990s. Currently most of Europe's national boundaries are accepted, with some exceptions. The break-up of Yugoslavia resulted in ethnic wars which sought to redraw the existing boundaries; this was notable in the division of Bosnia and Herzegovina. The current division of Cyprus into Greek and Turkish areas is a source of friction between those countries. Spain's claim to British-held Gibraltar is another contested issue, though otherwise these countries remain friendly.

Several language-based separatist movements exist in Europe, some involving armed conflict—in the Basque and Catalan regions of Spain, Corsica (in France), and Kosovo (in Serbia).

Nations

Dependencies

St Basil's Church, in Moscow, Russia (below), is an example of art that has been so often created in the name of religion. Nikaia, in the Aegean Islands (above left), has been inhabited by humans for thousands of years.

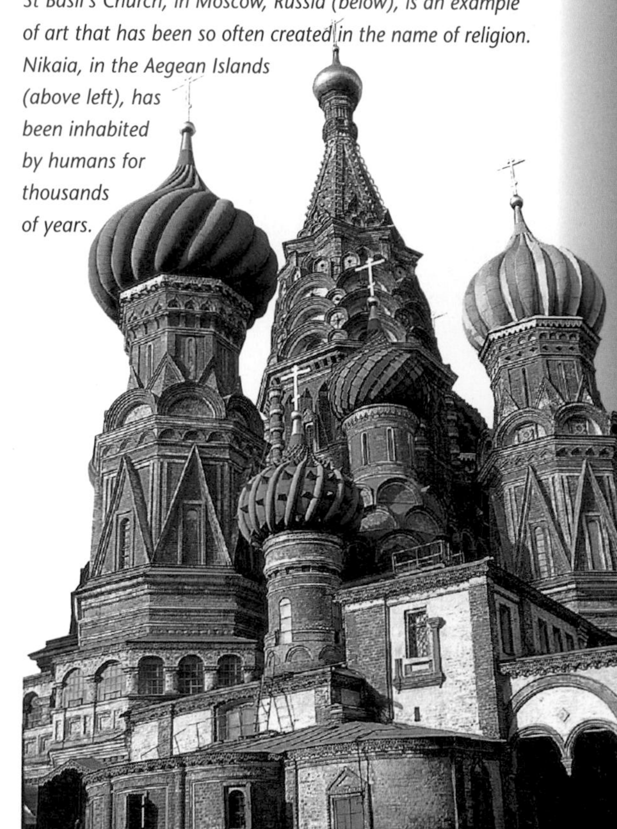

Northern Europe

Iceland

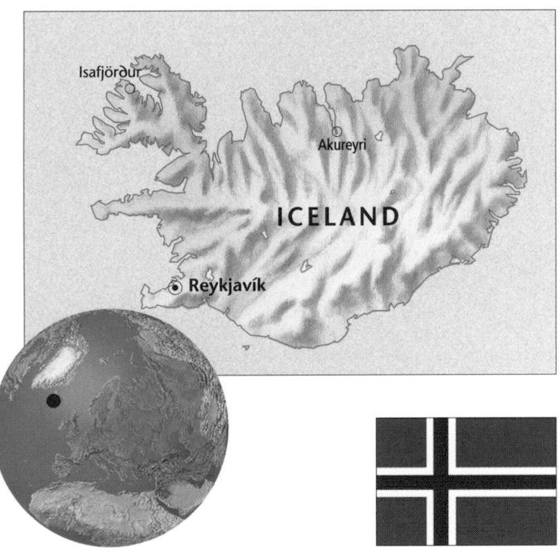

Fact File

OFFICIAL NAME Republic of Iceland

FORM OF GOVERNMENT Republic with single legislative body (Parliament)

CAPITAL Reykjavík

AREA 103,000 sq km (39,768 sq miles)

TIME ZONE GMT

POPULATION 280,000

PROJECTED POPULATION 2015 305,000

POPULATION DENSITY 2.7 per sq km (6.9 per sq mile)

LIFE EXPECTANCY 79.7

INFANT MORTALITY (PER 1,000) 3.5

OFFICIAL LANGUAGE Icelandic

LITERACY RATE 99.9 %

RELIGIONS Lutheran 96 %; other Protestant and Roman Catholic 3 %; none 1 %

ETHNIC GROUPS Icelandic 97 %; others including Danish, American, British, Norwegian, German 3 %

CURRENCY Króna

ECONOMY Services 61 %, industry 35 %, agriculture 4 %

GNP PER CAPITA US$ 27,100

CLIMATE Cool temperate, with cool, windy winters and mild, wet summers

HIGHEST POINT Hvannadalshnukur 2,119 m (6,952 ft)

MAP REFERENCE Page 284

True to its name, one-tenth of the total area of the island of Iceland, in the north Atlantic Ocean, is covered in icefields and glaciers. The human occupation of this island, which lies just south of the Arctic Circle, dates back to the late ninth century AD when Norwegian Vikings settled there. In the thirteenth century the Icelanders submitted to Norwegian rule and a century and a half later, when the Norwegian and Danish monarchies were combined, they came under Danish control. In 1918 Iceland was granted its independence, but still owed allegiance to the Danish monarch. In 1944, as the result of a referendum, Iceland chose to become a republic.

In 1972, because of its economic dependence on the surrounding seas, Iceland, without consultation with other nations, more than quadrupled the extent of its territorial waters from twelve to fifty nautical miles. Three years later it extended them to 200 nautical miles, a provocative move that brought condemnation, particularly from Britain, and gave rise to serious aggression at sea between Icelandic and British fishing vessels. After long and tense negotiations Britain was later granted some degree of access to the disputed waters.

In addition to icefields and glaciers, Iceland's spectacularly rugged and volcanic landscape includes hot springs, sulphur beds, geysers, lava fields, deep rocky canyons, and plummeting waterfalls. There are numerous small freshwater lakes and 200 volcanoes, many of which are active. Earth tremors, and occasionally larger quakes, are a frequent feature.

The interior of the island consists mainly of an elevated plateau of basalt, interspersed with occasional high peaks. There are small areas of forest and very little arable land. In the north, however, there are extensive grasslands where a small number of sheep, cattle, and horses can graze. More than ninety percent of the population lives in towns and cities around the coast, mainly in the southwest corner near Reykjavík.

Deep-sea fishing is the backbone of Iceland's economy, with fish and associated products constituting more than two-thirds of the country's exports. Apart from fish processing, aluminum smelting from imported bauxite and cement manufacture are growing industries. All of Iceland's domestic and industrial electricity needs are met by locally generated power from hydroelectric or geothermal plants. About one in four Icelanders is employed in manufacturing and processing industries. Iceland attracts about 150,000 tourists a year, more than half its permanent population, making tourism an important income-earner.

The people of Iceland enjoy a very high standard of living. Their economy is robust but is susceptible to variations in international fish prices. The country's free healthcare system has contributed to a life expectancy that is among the highest in the world.

Feda on Feda Fiord, Kvinestal, Norway (right page top). High plateau country, dotted with tiny lakes, in Norway (bottom center).

Norway

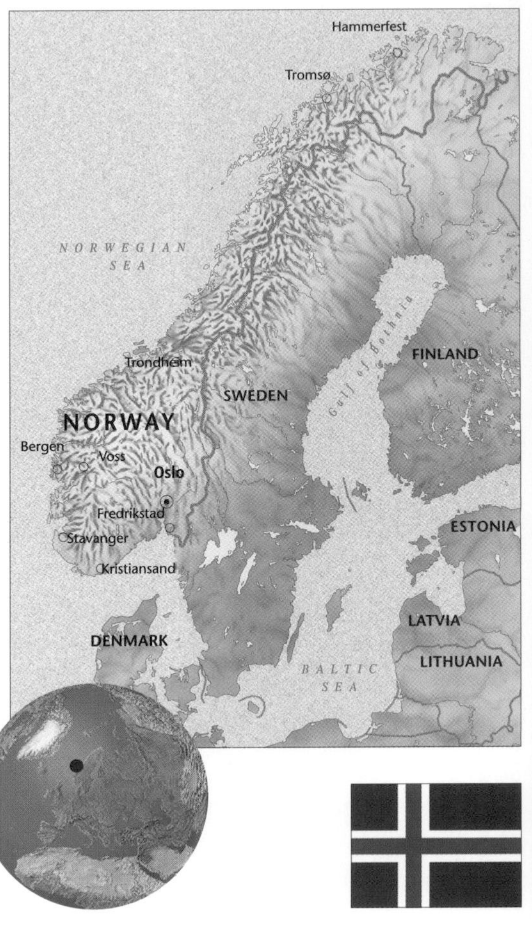

Fact File

OFFICIAL NAME Kingdom of Norway

FORM OF GOVERNMENT Constitutional monarchy with single legislative body (Parliament)

CAPITAL Oslo

AREA 324,220 sq km (125,181 sq miles)

TIME ZONE GMT + 1 hour

POPULATION 4,525,000

PROJECTED POPULATION 2015 4,670,000

POPULATION DENSITY 14 per sq km (36.1 per sq mile)

LIFE EXPECTANCY 78.9

INFANT MORTALITY (PER 1,000) 3.9

OFFICIAL LANGUAGE Norwegian

OTHER LANGUAGES Lapp, Finnish

Literacy rate 100 %

Religions Lutheran 94 %; Baptist, Pentecostalist, Methodist and Roman Catholic 6 %

Ethnic groups Germanic (Nordic, Alpine, Baltic) 97 %, others include Lapp minority 3 %

Currency Norwegian krone

Economy Services 61 %, industry 36 %, agriculture 3 %

GNP per capita US$ 31,800

Climate Cold in north and inland, temperate and wet on coast

Highest point Glittertind 2,469 m (8,101 ft)

Map reference Pages 284–85, 286

Norway's long, narrow landmass wraps around the western part of Sweden and the north of Finland and shares a land border with the northwest tip of the Russian Federation. Its rugged western coastline is washed by the North Sea in the south and the Norwegian Sea further north. Its northern tip juts into the Arctic Ocean, making it the northernmost part of Europe. To the south the Skagerrak Strait separates it from the northern tip of Denmark. Like the Swedes and Danes, modern Norwegians are descendents of the Vikings, Teutonic peoples who settled the area and, from the ninth to the eleventh centuries AD, raided and conquered lands to the north, east, and west. In the fourteenth century Denmark, Sweden, and Norway came under Danish rule. Although Sweden became independent in the sixteenth century, Norwegians remained subject to the Danes. In 1815, at the end of the Napoleonic Wars, in which Denmark sided with France, control of Norway was transferred to the Swedish crown. The modern Norwegian state dates from 1905, when the country declared its independence. Norway remained neutral in the First World War and was not attacked. However, Nazi forces invaded in 1940 and, despite spirited resistance, subdued the country. Norway joined the NATO alliance in 1949, and in 1994, as already in 1972, attempted to join the European Union, a move that was thwarted when the option was defeated at a referendum. Norway is a parliamentary democracy with a monarch as the titular head of state.

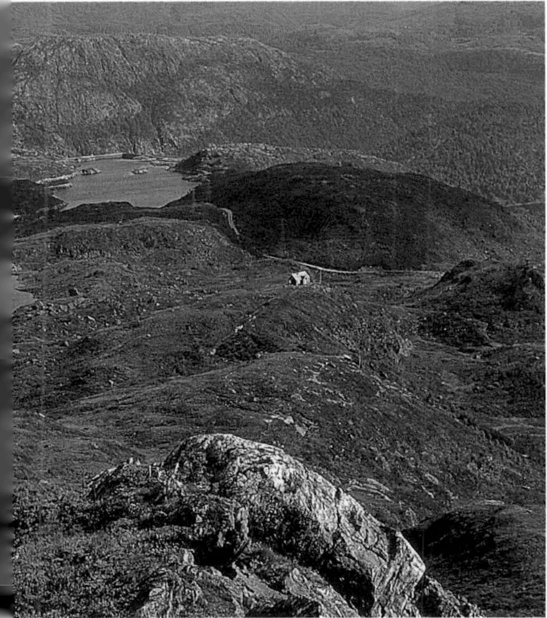

Norway's more than 21,000 km (13,000 miles) of coast is punctuated by deep fiords. Most of the country consists of mountains with deep valleys formed by ancient glaciers. There are also vast areas of high plateaus. More than one-quarter of the land surface is forested, mainly with conifers, and there are many lakes. The population is centered in the lowlands on the southern coasts and in the southeast. Only a tiny proportion of the land area is suitable for cultivation and agriculture is limited mainly to areas around lakes.

Norway has large oil and gas reserves in the North Sea and produces more oil and gas than any other European country. Its electricity, produced mainly from hydroelectric plants, is used largely to power industry. Key industries include pulp and paper manufacture, shipbuilding, and aluminum production. Fishing and fish farming are also major industries and farmed salmon is a main export.

Overseas Territories

Bouvet Island
Jan Mayen
Peter Island
Svalbard

Sweden

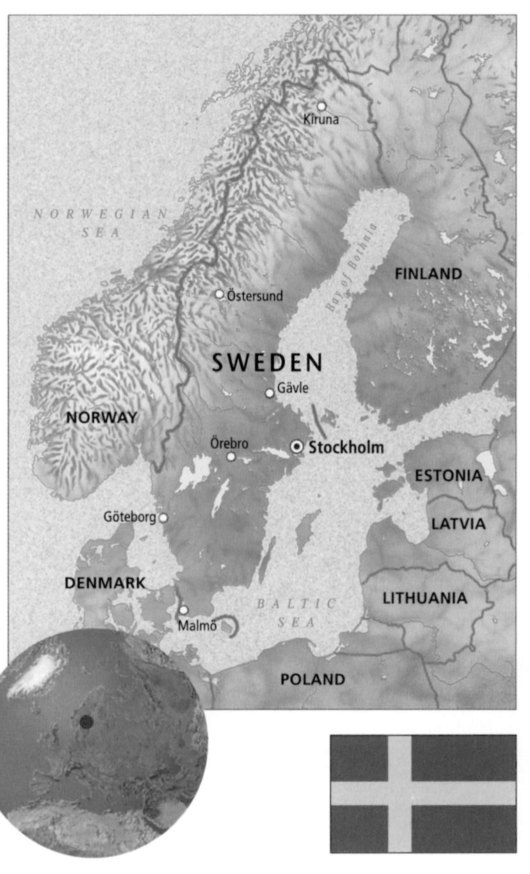

Fact File

Official name Kingdom of Sweden

Form of government Constitutional monarchy with single legislative body (Parliament = Riksdag)

Capital Stockholm

Area 449,964 sq km (173,731 sq miles)

Time zone GMT + 1 hour

Population 8,877,000

Projected population 2015 8,625,000

Population density 19.7 per sq km (51.1 per sq mile)

Life expectancy 79.8

Infant mortality (per 1,000) 3.4

Official language Swedish

Other languages Lapp, Finnish

Literacy rate 99 %

Religions Lutheran 94 %, Roman Catholic 1.5 %, Pentecostal 1 %, other 3.5 %

Ethnic groups Swedish 91 %, others include Lapp, Finnish, Yugoslav, Danish, Norwegian, Greek, Turkish 9 %

Currency Swedish krona

Economy Services 68.6 %, industry 28.2 %, agriculture 3.2 %

GNP per capita US$ 25,400

Climate Temperate in the south, with cold winters and mild summers; subpolar in the north, with severe winters

Highest point Kebnekaise 2,111 m (6,926 ft)

Map reference Pages 284–85

The fourth largest country in Europe, Sweden shares the Scandinavian Peninsula with Norway, which sits between it and the North

PROVINCES

**Älvsborg • Blekinge • Gävleborg
Göteborg and Bohus • Gotland
Halland • Jämtland • Jönköping
Kalmar • Kopparberg • Kristianstad
Kronoberg • Malmöhus • Norrbotten
Örebro • Östergötland • Skaraborg
Södermanland • Stockholm • Uppsala
Värmland • Västerbotten
Västernorrland • Västmanland**

Atlantic Ocean. To the northeast Sweden shares a border with Finland, and its eastern coastline is separated from the west coast of Finland by the Gulf of Bothnia. Its southern shores are washed by the Baltic Sea, and south of the land border with Norway the Kattegat Strait divides it from the northern tip of Denmark. Close to Sweden's southeast tip are Gotland and Öland, the largest of many islands dotted around the Swedish coastline.

By the seventh century AD, Teutonic tribes from the south had occupied much of central Sweden, and between the ninth and the eleventh centuries Swedes took part in Viking raids deep into Russia and south to the Black Sea. Over the following five centuries Sweden and Denmark vied for Scandinavian supremacy. Both Sweden and Norway came under the Danish crown in 1397, but fifty years later the Swedes rebelled and elected their own king. The accession to the Swedish throne in 1523 of Gustav I ended Danish claims to all but the south of Sweden. During the next 200 years Sweden became one of the most powerful states in Europe, annexing parts of Estonia, Finland, and Poland, driving the Danes out of southern Sweden, and playing a crucial role in curbing Habsburg expansion in northern Europe. At the beginning of the eighteenth century, however, a coalition of Russia, Poland, and Denmark forced Sweden to relinquish its Baltic possessions.

At the end of the Napoleonic wars, in 1815, Norway was ceded to Sweden, a union that lasted until 1905. In the mid-nineteenth century the beginnings of parliamentary democracy were introduced in Sweden with the establishment of a two-chamber parliament, although suffrage was limited largely to landowners and industrialists. Universal adult suffrage was introduced in 1919.

Sweden remained neutral in both the First and the Second World Wars. Following the Second World War it tried unsuccessfully to form a military alliance with Denmark and Norway. When these nations joined NATO Sweden did not follow, fearing closer ties with the West might damage its relations with the Soviet Union, and give it an excuse to absorb Finland into the Soviet bloc. Since then, although maintaining a high level of defence preparedness, it has kept its distance from NATO and maintained its reputation for neutrality, for playing an active role in international affairs, and as a negotiator in international disputes.

During the 1960s and early 1970s the Social Democrats, who had laid the foundations of a welfare state since 1932, held the majority of seats in the Riksdag and were able to govern alone. They then inaugurated the more radical socialist policies which came to define modern Swedish politics. Welfare services were extended, and "the Swedish Way" was seen by socialists as a model for the rest of Europe. After 1982 Olof Palme's government introduced what it called a middle way between capitalism and communism, with annual levies on profits and wages which went into "wage-earner funds" used to buy stock in private firms for the benefit of labor. Palme was assassinated in mysterious circumstances in Stockholm in 1986. By then the economic costs of the welfare state were becoming evident. The country had almost zero economic growth, and was becoming less competitive in world markets.

From the late 1970s domestic policy discussion has been less along socialist/capitalist lines and more concerned with ecological issues. Sweden has taken the lead in a number of environmental debates, and has been the venue of influential conferences devoted to such matters as global warming and greenhouse gases. An application for EC (now EU) membership was lodged in 1992. In 1995 it was admitted to the European Union. Sweden is a constitutional monarchy with a single-chamber parliament that is elected every three years.

Physical features and land use

Northeastern Sweden is a region of low plateaus that drop away to a coastal plain along the Gulf of Bothnia, but rise to the Kjólen Mountains along the Norwegian border. Most of the country's more than 95,000 lakes are in this mountainous region. Shaped by ancient glaciers, many of the lakes are in the upper valleys of the numerous rivers that flow east to the Gulf of Bothnia. They are the source of most of Sweden's hydroelectricity, which is gradually replacing nuclear energy as the main means of power generation. The mountains are heavily forested. Despite extensive land clearing for agriculture in the south, well over half the country remains forested, with spruce, pine and birch among the most prominent trees.

Central Sweden is a lowland area that stretches between Stockholm in the east and the country's

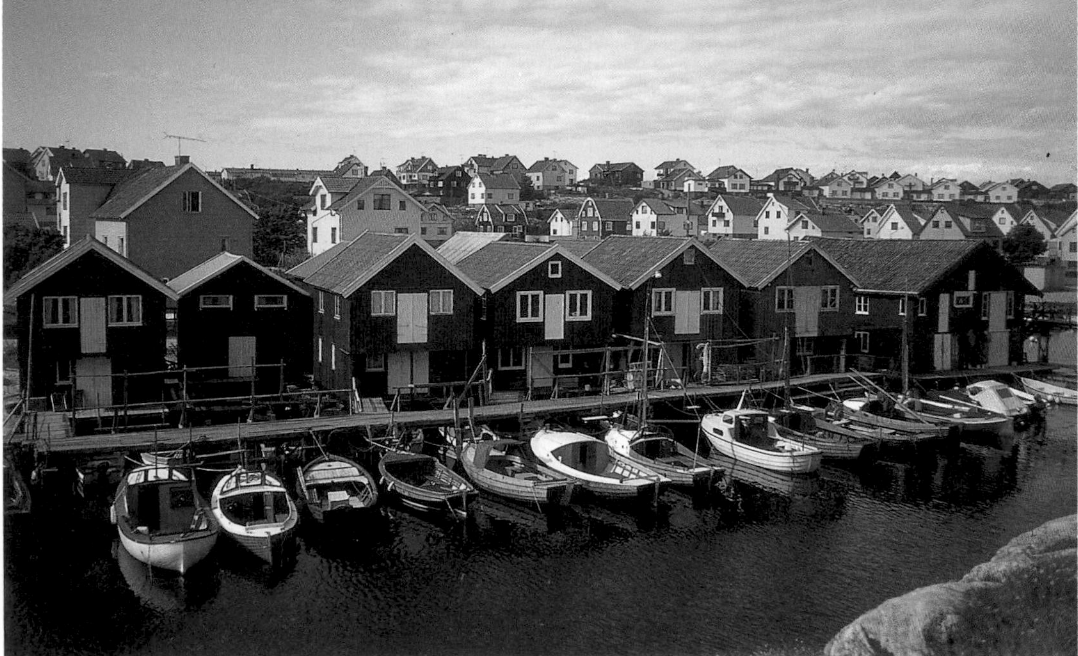

Stadshuset in Stockholm, Sweden (above). Rows of holiday chalets and small boats in Smøgen, Sweden (left). Early summer foliage in a birch forest (below). Cafés along the harbor in Copenhagen, Denmark (right page).

second largest city, Göteborg, in the southwest. Four large lakes—the only remnants of a strait that once joined the Baltic to the Kattegat Strait—cover much of this region, the most heavily populated part of the country. The rich soils around these lakes support much of Sweden's agricultural produce, which includes cereals and vegetables and fodder crops for large herds of cattle. Dairy farming is the main form of agriculture, and Sweden is self-sufficient in dairy products.

South of the lakes is a low, largely infertile plateau and further south, stretching to the tip of the peninsula and across to the island of Gotland, is a rich plain—the most intensively cultivated part of the country. Significant areas of woodland still survive here, dotted between stretches of farming and grazing land.

Although it lacks oil and coal reserves, Sweden is rich in mineral resources, most of which are concentrated in the northeast. These include iron ore, zinc, lead, copper, and silver, and almost one-sixth of the world's known reserves of uranium.

Industry, commerce, and culture

Sweden's vast forests are the basis for timber and paper manufacturing industries that form almost one-fifth of the country's exports. Machines, cars, trucks, aircraft, chemical and electrical goods, and communication equipment are among the chief manufacturing industries, based in the central region and Malmö in the southwest.

Apart from the Saami people (Lapps) in the far north of the country, Sweden is ethnically and culturally quite homogeneous. Despite there being a relatively high rate of unemployment, its citizens enjoy one of the highest standards of living in Europe and an extensive range of government-provided social services. Sweden also boasts one of Europe's highest rates of female participation throughout its workforce.

Denmark

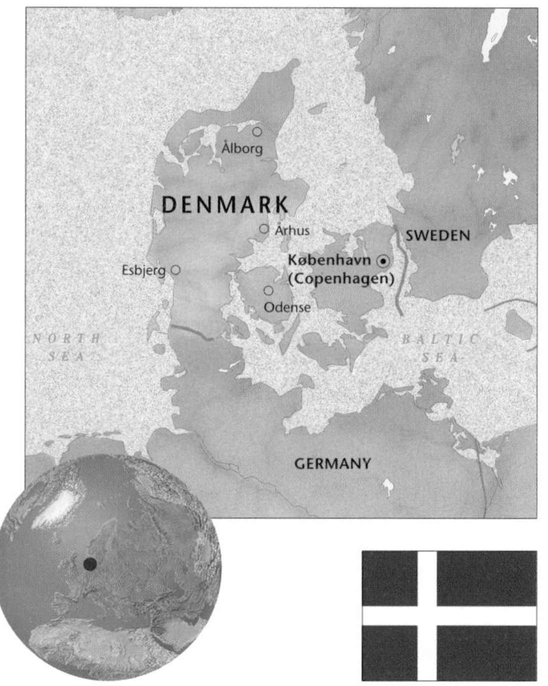

Fact File

Official name Kingdom of Denmark

Form of government Constitutional monarchy with one legislative body (Parliament)

Capital Copenhagen (København)

Area 43,070 sq km (16,629 sq miles)

Time zone GMT + 1 hour

Population 5,369,000

Projected population 2015 5,372,000

Population density 124.7 per sq km (322.9 per sq mile)

Life expectancy 76.9

Infant mortality (per 1,000) 5.0

Official language Danish

Other languages Faroese, Greenlandic, German

Literacy rate 100 %

Religions Lutheran 91 %, other Protestant and Roman Catholic 2 %, other 7 %

Ethnic groups Danish 97.1 %, German 1.6 %, Turkish 0.5 %, Swedish 0.4 %, British 0.2 %, other 0.2 %

Currency Danish krone

Economy Services 75 %, industry 20 %, agriculture 5 %

GNP per capita US$ 29,000

Climate Temperate, with cold, wet winters and mild summers

Highest point Yding Skovhoj 173 m (568 ft)

Map reference Page 286

Denmark is both the smallest and the southernmost of the Scandinavian countries. Most of its land area consists of the Jutland Peninsula, which pushes northward from the northwestern tip of Germany. The North Sea washes Denmark's western coast, the Skagerrak Strait lies to the north separating it from the southern coast of Norway, and the Kattegat Strait separates it from the southwestern tip of Sweden. The Baltic Sea is to the east and here, stretching almost as far as the southwestern tip of Sweden, is an archipelago of more than 400 islands. The largest of these islands is Sjaelland, on which is situated the Danish capital, Copenhagen.

Like the inhabitants of Sweden and Norway, modern Danes are descended from Viking invaders who from the fifth century AD moved northward into Scandinavia and then outward to other parts of western and eastern Europe. For much of its history, Denmark was the dominant country in Scandinavia. At the end of the fourteenth century, Norway and Sweden, as well as Iceland, were united under the Danish crown. The Swedes elected their own monarch fifty years later, but Norway continued to be part of Denmark for more than 400 years—until 1815, when the Congress of Vienna awarded it to Sweden in retaliation for Denmark having supported Napoleon Bonaparte. Despite its neutrality, Denmark was

Scandinavia

Today the term Scandinavia is often understood to refer only to Norway and Sweden, which both occupy the Scandinavian Peninsula, and the more southerly peninsula and islands that make up Denmark. Many people, however, would also include Finland, Iceland, and the Faeroe Islands, which are possessions of Denmark. These countries are also collectively referred to as the Nordic countries, or Norden.

Culturally, geographically, and geologically, the countries of Scandinavia have much in common and the whole region forms a distinctive part of Europe. All of them lie close to the Arctic Circle and share a cold, moist, and often harsh climate, which is mitigated in parts of Scandinavia by the effect of the Gulf Stream. All five countries have a high degree of ethnic and religious homogeneity. Lutheran is the overwhelmingly predominant religion in every part of Scandinavia. The languages of four of the countries are closely related, but Finnish is entirely different and is more closely related to the Estonian language. Historical links are also very strong and during the fifteenth century the countries were united under Danish rule. For five centuries, until 1809, Finland was under Swedish control and Swedish was the language of its ruling classes. For almost a century, until 1905, Norway was ruled by Sweden, and Iceland only gained its independence as late as 1944, after almost five and a half centuries of Danish rule and domination.

Greenland has been part of Denmark since the early eighteenth century. Situated to the west of Iceland, it is ethnically distinct and geographically closer to North America. Although it was granted home rule in 1979 its inhabitants are still Danish citizens and Denmark still controls Greenland's foreign affairs.

Despite climatic difficulties, Scandinavian economies have traditionally depended heavily on agriculture and fishing. The improvements in agricultural techniques and technologies that flowed from the Industrial Revolution were slow to be implemented in Scandinavia and until late in the nineteenth century the region remained economically stagnant. In recent years, however, there have been significant technological innovations and increasing industrialization and Scandinavians now enjoy some of the highest standards of living in Europe.

invaded by Germany during 1940. Liberated by British forces in 1945, Denmark joined the NATO alliance following the war, and in 1973 became a member of the European Union. Denmark is a constitutional monarchy, with a hereditary monarch. Its single-house parliament, which is headed by a prime minister, is elected every four years.

Almost the whole of Denmark is low-lying and its surface is covered in many places by rocky glacial debris, most prominently in the undulating mass of moraine that runs down the center of the Jutland Peninsula. This divides the peninsula into two distinct regions. To the west is a sandy landscape with extensive dunes and lagoons along the North Sea coast. To the east lies a loam plain, which extends across the islands of the archipelago, as far as the Baltic coast. This fertile region supports significant crops of barley, wheat, and sugar beet and a thriving livestock and dairying industry. Fishing, which is still a leading Danish industry, is based for the most part on the extensive, shallow lagoons that lie along the western coastline of Jutland.

As well as constituting a significant proportion of the country's exports, Denmark's agricultural and fishing produce also provide the raw materials for food processsing industries, which are a major source of employment. Other significant industries, for which Denmark imports most of the raw materials, are iron and metal working, machinery manufacturing, and furniture making. Despite having a relatively high unemployment rate during much of the 1990s, Denmark is a prosperous country and Danes generally enjoy a high standard of living. An extensive social security system means that serious poverty is comparatively rare throughout the country.

OVERSEAS TERRITORIES

Faeroe Islands
Greenland

Finland

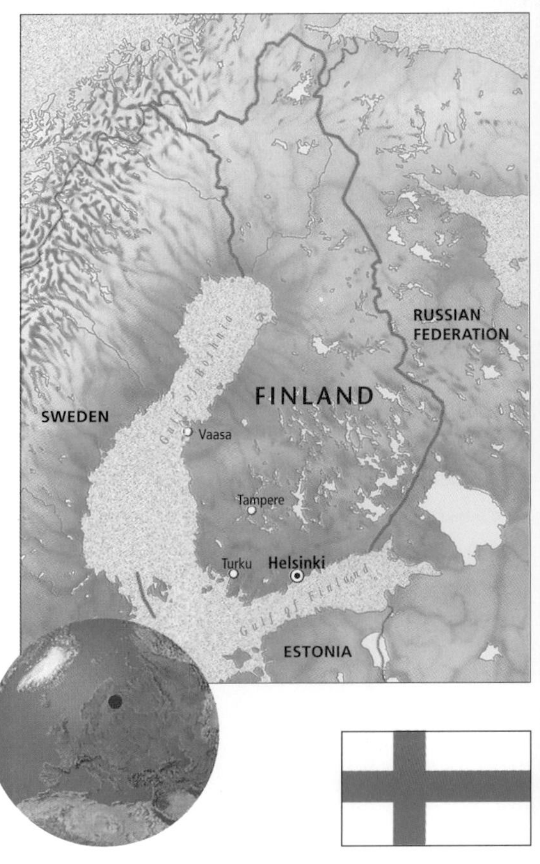

Fact File

OFFICIAL NAME Republic of Finland

FORM OF GOVERNMENT Republic with single legislative body (Parliament)

CAPITAL Helsinki

AREA 338,145 sq km (130,558 sq miles)

TIME ZONE GMT + 2 hours

POPULATION 5,184,000

PROJECTED POPULATION 2015 5,180,000

POPULATION DENSITY 15.3 per sq km (39.7 per sq mile)

LIFE EXPECTANCY 77.8

INFANT MORTALITY (PER 1,000) 3.8

OFFICIAL LANGUAGES Finnish, Swedish

OTHER LANGUAGES Russian, Lapp

LITERACY RATE 100 %

RELIGIONS Lutheran 89 %, Greek Orthodox 1 %, none 9 %, other 1 %

ETHNIC GROUPS Finnish 93.6 %, Swedish 6.2 %, others (including Lapp, Gypsy, Tatar) 0.2 %

CURRENCY Euro

ECONOMY Services 60 %, industry 34 %, agriculture 6 %

GNP PER CAPITA US$ 26,200

CLIMATE Mainly cold temperate, but polar in arctic regions

HIGHEST POINT Haltiatunturi 1,328 m (4,357 ft)

MAP REFERENCE Pages 284–85, 287

Except for a small section of Norway which cuts it off from the Arctic Ocean, Finland is the most northerly country in continental Europe. As well as its northern boundary with Norway, Finland borders northern Sweden to the west and the Russian Federation in the east. In the south, the Gulf of Finland, the easternmost part of the Baltic Sea, separates it from Estonia, and on the west the Gulf of Bothnia, a northern inlet of the Baltic, sits between it and southern Sweden.

Modern Finland has its roots in a seventh century AD invasion by tribes from the Volga. They displaced the Lapps, Asiatic people who had lived in the area for centuries, and drove them north. Only about 2,500 Lapps, or Sami, who have their own culture and language, now survive in the north, tending reindeer herds. Viking incursions followed and in the twelfth century Swedes invaded Finland, bringing Christianity. Finland remained under Swedish control for the next 650 years, until 1809, when the Russians took over. Swedish influence is still evident in the country's significant Swedish-speaking minority, and the fact that some towns have both Finnish and Swedish names. A relatively benign Russian rule allowed considerable freedoms and encouraged a resurgence of the Finnish language, which had largely fallen into disuse. A more oppressive regime towards the end of the century fanned Finnish nationalism, and at the time of the Russian Revolution in 1917 the country seized its independence.

Finland's harsh climate and the ruggedness of its northern regions means that most of its people live in the more moderate south. Much of the land consists of flat expanses of granite rock, the legacy of extensive glaciation. Remnants of an ancient mountain range, rising in places to more than 1,000 m (3,300 ft), exist in Lapland, the northern part of the country. There are more than 60,000 substantial lakes throughout Finland, mainly in the south, and tens of thousands of smaller ones. Forests, mainly of pine, birch, and spruce cover more than half the land area, contributing to the country's heavy reliance on timber-related industries, including wood processing, pulp, and papermaking.

Less than one-tenth of Finland's land is arable and agricultural production, which includes cereals, potatoes and sugar beet, is confined to the summer months, when the country is not snowbound.

In the 1980s living standards in Finland rose markedly, rivaling those of Sweden, although they fell back in the recession of the early 1990s. The country has an effective government-sponsored health system and the population is one of the most literate and highly educated in the world.

Estonia

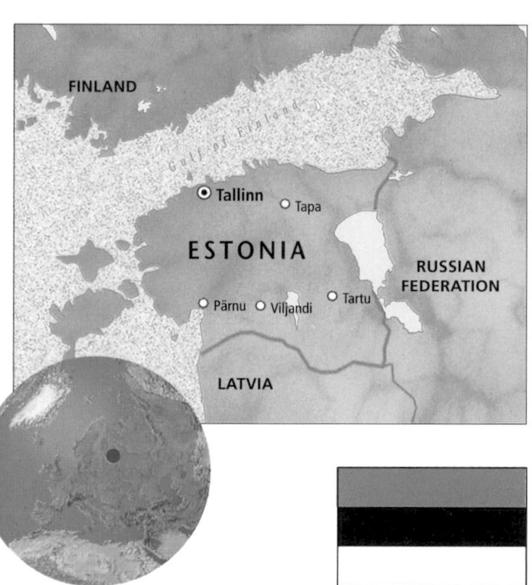

Fact File

Official name Republic of Estonia

Form of government Republic with single legislative body (Parliament)

Capital Tallinn

Area 45,100 sq km (17,413 sq miles)

Time zone GMT + 3 hours

Population 1,416,000

Projected population 2015 1,190,000

Population density 31.4 per sq km (81.3 per sq mile)

Life expectancy 70.0

Infant mortality (per 1,000) 12.3

Official language Estonian

Other languages Latvian, Lithuanian, Russian

Literacy rate 100 %

Religions Lutheran 96 %; Eastern Orthodox and Baptist 4 %

Ethnic groups Estonian 61.5 %, Russian 30.3 %, Ukrainian 3.2 %, Belarusian 1.8 %, Finnish 1.1 %, other 2.1 %

Currency Kroon

Economy Industry 65 %, services 28 %, agriculture 7 %

GNP per capita US$ 10,900

Climate Cool temperate; cold winters and mild summers

Highest point Mt Munamagi 318 m (1,043 ft)

Map reference Page 287

It has been claimed that Estonia's flag, consisting of a blue, a black, and a white horizontal bar, represents the country's blue skies, black soils, and snowy winters. This, the smallest and least populous of the three Baltic countries, contains more than 1,500 lakes within its borders and its land area includes more than 800 islands in the Baltic Sea and the Gulf of Finland. The largest of the lakes, Lake Peipus, is in the far east of the country and forms most of its border with Russia.

Russia has been the dominant power in Estonia's recent history and the large ethnic Russian minority bears witness to this. From the thirteenth until the eighteenth century the Estonians were ruled by outsiders, first the Germans and then the Swedes. In 1721 Russia assumed control and ruled the country for almost 200 years. Occupied by Germany during the First World War, Estonia declared its independence in 1918. This was achieved in 1920 when, after an armed struggle, Russia

The medieval rooftops of Tallinn, the capital of Estonia (above). Savonlinna, a city on the Finnish Seenplatte, in the foreground the fortress Olavinlinna (below). The harbor of Stockholm, Sweden (left page).

formally recognized the small country. It was a short-lived victory, however. During the Second World War Estonia was overrun first by the Russians and then by the Germans. In 1944 it was returned to the Soviets and remained part of the USSR until it once again declared itself independent in August 1991, following Lithuania's example of the previous year. Since 2004 Estonia has been a member of the EU.

Most of Estonia is low-lying and flat or gently undulating. Large areas of land are barren and stony, a legacy of the glaciers that once covered much of the landscape. There are extensive woodlands which supply the raw materials for the country's important timber and woodworking industries. Engineering and textile manufacture are also significant. Despite its black soils, little of the land is arable and the main agricultural industries are dairying and livestock raising, especially pig farming. Mineral resources are meager, though extensive deposits of shale are used in the production of gas and chemical products.

Compared with other former Soviet republics, the people of Estonia enjoy a high standard of living. The economy, after declining for some years following independence, has improved steadily as increasing trade with Western countries has shielded Estonia from some of the effects of the declining Russian economy.

Strollers in Tallinn, the capital of Estonia, which is the country's main port (below center). The Latvian capital Riga (right page bottom). More than 60 % of the Latvian population lives in cities. The rooftops of a town in Latvia (right). The picturesque castle of Trakai in Lithuania (right page top).

The Baltic States

The nations of Estonia, Latvia, and Lithuania, on the eastern edge of the Baltic Sea, are collectively known as the Baltic States. Similar in their physical environments and sharing a common history of almost uninterrupted Russian domination from the eighteenth century until they achieved independence in 1991, the three countries have quite distinct ethnic and linguistic identities, as well as diverse earlier histories.

The ethnic composition of Estonia and Latvia reflects the long period of Russian rule, with native Estonians and Latvians comprising under two-thirds of their respective populations, the rest being made up mainly of ethnic Russians and immigrants from other former Soviet countries. Lithuania is more ethnically homogeneous. In all three countries, however, more than nine out of ten people claim the native language as their own. Latvian and Lithuanian are both Indo-European languages, but Estonian is more closely related to Finnish. The strong German influence on both Estonian and Latvian culture is manifested in the dominance of the Lutheran religion in those countries, while the predominance of Catholics in Lithuania stems from that country's past links with Poland. In the fifteenth century Lithuania was a major European power, whose territories took in parts of Belarus and Ukraine and stretched from the Baltic to the Black Seas. In the sixteenth century it merged with Poland and the countries remained united for more than 200 years. Estonia and Latvia, on the other hand, were never great powers, enduring about 1,000 years of foreign domination before gaining their independence.

Near the end of the First World War in 1918 the Baltic States became independent, but in 1940 they were incorporated into the Soviet Union and occupied by Soviet troops, a move that was sanctioned by the Germans but never recognized by the United States, even following the war. A deliberate policy of Russification took place during the 1950s. This resulted in massive immigration, often of manual workers, from Russia and the forced emigration of many highly qualified native Baltic peoples to other parts of the Soviet Union. Despite this, nationalistic aspirations in the region remained undiminished and after an attempted coup against Soviet leader Mikhail Gorbachev in 1991, the Baltic States declared and were granted their independence. Soon after, they became members of the United Nations, and in 2004 they joined the EU.

Latvia

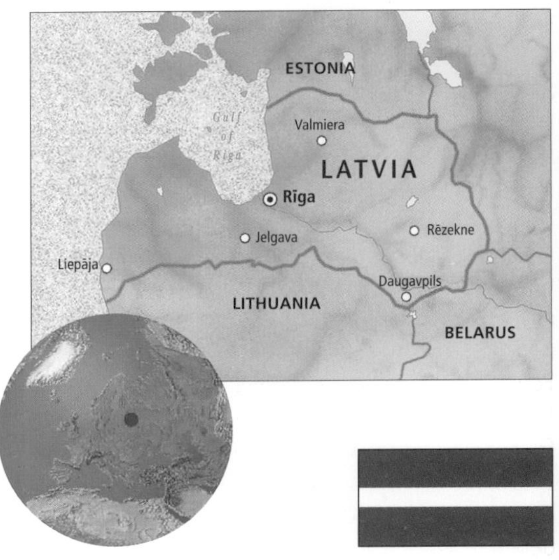

Fact File

OFFICIAL NAME Republic of Latvia

FORM OF GOVERNMENT Republic with single legislative body (Parliament)

CAPITAL Riga

AREA 64,100 sq km (24,749 sq miles)

TIME ZONE GMT + 2 hours

POPULATION 2,367,000

PROJECTED POPULATION 2015 2,225,000

POPULATION DENSITY 36.9 per sq km (95.6 per sq mile)

LIFE EXPECTANCY 69.0

INFANT MORTALITY (PER 1,000) 15.0

OFFICIAL LANGUAGE Latvian

OTHER LANGUAGES Russian

LITERACY RATE 99.8 %

RELIGIONS Mainly Lutheran with Russian Orthodox and Roman Catholic minorities

ETHNIC GROUPS Latvian 51.8 %, Russian 33.8 %, Belarusian 4.5 %, Ukrainian 3.4 %, Polish 2.3 %, other 4.2 %

CURRENCY Lats

ECONOMY Services 43 %, industry 41 %, agriculture 16 %

GNP per capita US$ 8,300

Climate Temperate; cold, wet winters, mild summers

Highest point Gaizinkalns 312 m (1,024 ft)

Map reference Page 287

Latvia lies between its sister Baltic republics of Estonia to the north and Lithuania to the south, its coastline along the Baltic Sea indented by the Gulf of Riga. To the east and southeast respectively it shares borders with the Russian Federation and Belarus. Like Estonia and Lithuania, Latvia has been controlled by foreign powers for most of its history. For more than 1,000 years its inhabitants, the Letts, have been ruled successively by Germans, Poles, Swedes, and finally Russians. In 1991 Latvia declared its independence from the Soviet Union. It is now a multi-party parliamentary democracy with an elected president as its head of state. Since independence, the Communist Party of Latvia has been banned.

The country is mostly flat with hillier land in the east. There are large areas of bogs and swamps and about forty percent of the land is woodland or forest, in which oak and pine predominate. Small farms account for most agriculture, which is mainly dairy farming and cattle raising. Some grain and vegetable crops are also grown. Forestry and fishing, which were important in earlier times, have enjoyed a resurgence in recent years.

Latvia is the most heavily industrialized of the Baltic States. It has few mineral resources and imports the raw materials needed for its industries—the manufacture of electrical goods, shipbuilding, and train and vehicle making. It relies on its former ruler for energy supplies and much of the Russian Federation's oil and gas exports pass through the Latvian port of Venspils. Air and water pollution from industrial wastes is a matter of concern.

Latvia's economy was severely affected in 1995 by bank failures and financial scandals, and its dependence on Russia limits its development. Latvians have a reasonable standard of living, although discrepancies in wealth are marked.

Lithuania

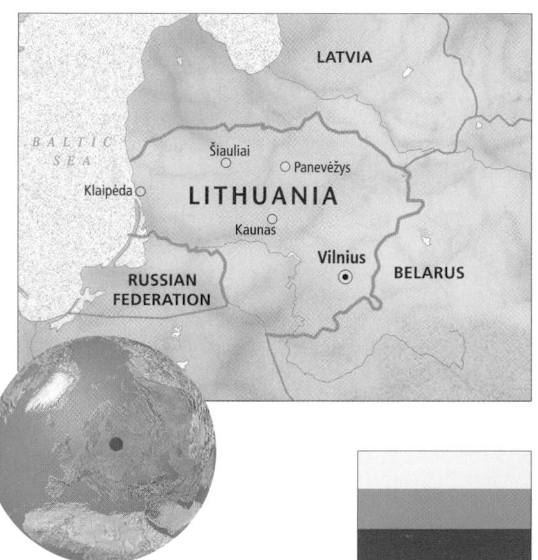

Fact File

Official name Republic of Lithuania

Form of government Republic with single legislative body (Parliament)

Capital Vilnius

Area 65,200 sq km (25,174 sq miles)

Time zone GMT + 2 hours

Population 3,601,000

Projected population 2015 3,538,000

Population density 55.2 per sq km (143.0 per sq mile)

Life expectancy 69.4

Infant mortality (per 1,000) 14.3

Official language Lithuanian

Other languages Russian, Polish, Belarusian

Literacy rate 98 %

Religions Roman Catholic 90 %; Russian Orthodox, Muslim and Protestant minorities 10 %

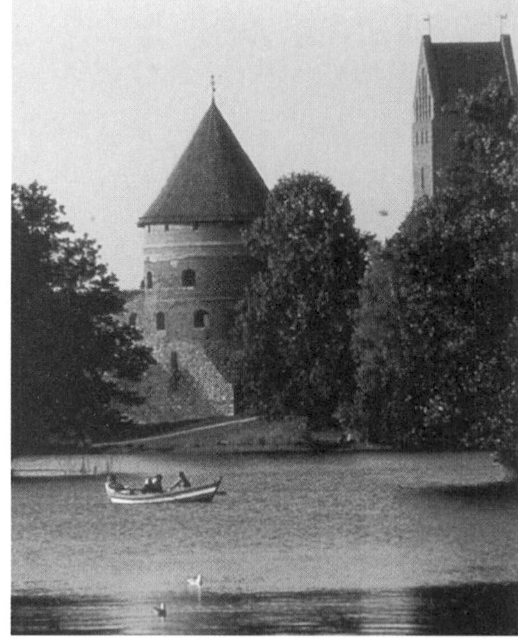

Ethnic groups Lithuanian 80.1 %, Russian 8.6 %, Polish 7.7 %, Belarusian 1.5 %, other 2.1 %

Currency Litas

Economy Services 53 %, industry 36 %, agriculture 11 %

GNP per capita US$ 8,400

Climate Temperate; cold winters and mild summers

Highest point Mt Juozapine 292 m (958 ft)

Map reference Pages 287, 289

The largest of the Baltic states, Lithuania has borders with Latvia to the north, Belarus to the east and southeast, Poland to the south, and the Russian Federation—the enclave Kaliningrad—to the southwest. The Baltic Sea lies to its west. In the thirteenth century, Lithuania was united under a Christian king, in the sixteenth century it merged with Poland, then in 1795 it came under Russian control. Occupied by Germany in the First World War, Lithuania became independent in 1918. It became part of the Soviet Union in 1940 and was then invaded by Germany. When Soviet armies arrived in 1944, over 200,000 people, more than three-quarters of them Jews, had perished. In 1991 the country declared its independence from the Soviet Union. It is now a multi-party democracy with a president as head of state and a prime minister as head of government. Like the other Baltic states it is also a member of the UN and the EU.

Most of Lithuania consists of a relatively fertile plain with extensive marshlands and forests. Many marshes have been reclaimed for growing cereal and vegetable crops. Sand dunes predominate along the Baltic coast and there is a range of hills dotted with more than 3,000 lakes in the southeast. Numerous rivers traverse the landscape.

Machine manufacturing, petroleum refining, shipbuilding, and food processing are some of Lithuania's key industries, but they have resulted in soil and groundwater contamination. The country has few natural resources and depends on Russia for oil and most of the raw materials needed for its industries. The main forms of agriculture are dairy farming and pig and cattle raising. Continuing dependence on Russia and a high rate of inflation are among factors that make Lithuania the least prosperous of the Baltic states.

Central Europe

Germany

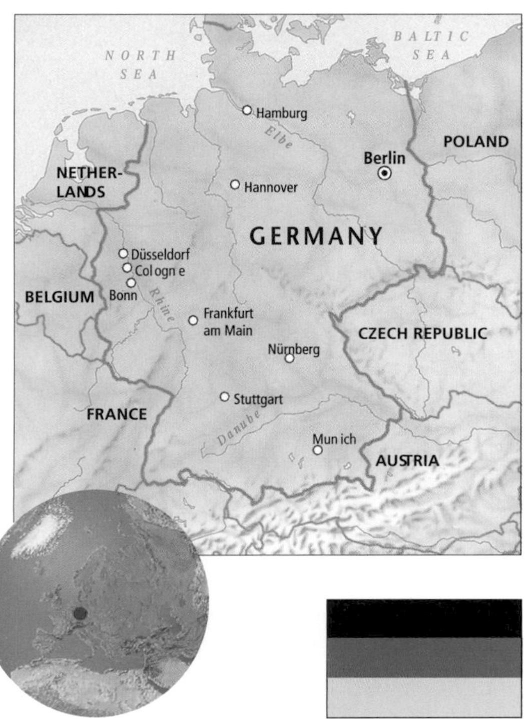

STATES

Baden-Württemberg • Bavaria • Berlin Brandenburg • Bremen • Hamburg Hesse • Lower Saxony • Mecklenburg-West Pomerania • North Rhine-Westphalia Rhineland-Palatinate • Saarland • Saxony Saxony-Anhalt • Schleswig-Holstein Thuringia (Thüringen)

Norman Foster's new dome of the Reichstag, Berlin (below left). The gable of the Hamlin Leisthaus (below right). View from Philosophenweg onto Heidelberg with Alte Brücke and castle (above center). Neuschwanstein in Bavaria, built by Ludwig II, late-nineteenth century (right page bottom).

Fact File

OFFICIAL NAME Federal Republic of Germany

FORM OF GOVERNMENT Federal republic with two legislative bodies (Federal Council and Federal Assembly)

CAPITAL Berlin

AREA 357,021 sq km (137,846 sq miles)

TIME ZONE GMT + 1 hour

POPULATION 83,252,000

PROJECTED POPULATION 2015 80,673,000

POPULATION DENSITY 233.2 per sq km (603.9 per sq mile)

LIFE EXPECTANCY 77.8

INFANT MORTALITY (PER 1,000) 4.7

OFFICIAL LANGUAGE German

OTHER LANGUAGES Turkish, Italian, Greek, Dutch, Spanish, Danish, Frisian, Sorbian

LITERACY RATE 99 %

RELIGIONS Protestant 34.1 %, Roman Catholic 33.4 %, unaffiliated or other 32.5 %

ETHNIC GROUPS German 91.0 %, Turkish 2.5 %, Croatian, Bosnian and Serb 1.6 %, Italian 0.7 %, Greek 0.4 %, Polish 0.3 %, other 3.5 %

CURRENCY Euro

ECONOMY Services 64 %, industry 34.5 %, agriculture 1.5 %

GNP PER CAPITA US$ 26,600

CLIMATE Temperate, with cool, wet winters (colder in east and south) and mild summers

HIGHEST POINT Zugspitze 2,962 m (9,718 ft)

MAP REFERENCE Pages 288–89

Landlocked except for two stretches of coast along the North and Baltic Seas, Germany shares land borders with nine countries. Poland is located to the east; the Czech Republic to the southeast; Austria and Switzerland to the south; France to the southwest; and Luxembourg, Belgium and the Netherlands to the west. Germany's coastlines are separated by the Jutland Peninsula, at the southern end of which Germany borders Denmark.

History

The area currently occupied by Germany was roughly defined in the tenth century AD when Duke Conrad became king of the German-speaking eastern part of the Frankish Empire, which had been established several centuries earlier by Charlemagne and had dissolved into several parts after his death. Several kings

brought about substantial changes in the territory of the German Empire. Especially during the reign of the Saxon Emperor Otto I (AD 936–973), Germany's territory was extended eastward. In 1273, however, the accession of the Austrian Rudolf of Habsburg to the throne ushered in a long period of Austrian domination. The rise of Protestantism under Martin Luther during the sixteenth and seventeenth centuries as well as the Counter-Reformation of the Catholic Church flamed nationalist as well as religious passions and fueled several insurgencies, unrests and wars, such as the peasants' revolt in 1524, which were savagely suppressed. At the same time the territorial princes used the unrests to lead campaigns to enlarge their spheres of influence and their territories. The climax of this century of wars was the Thirty Years War of 1618–48 in which, amid wholesale devastation, German states achieved the right to religious, if not political, autonomy and the emperor lost his de facto dominance over the empire.

Austria, home of the Habsburg dynasty of emperors and up until that time the leading power, was substantially weakened by the long years of war and this encouraged individual German states such as Saxony, Hanover, Bavaria, and Brandenburg/Prussia to increase their power. During the eighteenth century, under the leadership of Frederick II the Great, Prussia developed into a major European power, gaining control of much of present-day Poland, formerly ruled by Austria. At the end of the eighteenth century, Napoleon's armies overran both Austria and Prussia, which effectively brought the German Empire to an end in 1806. After Napoleon's defeat in 1815 Prussia became the dominant force in a German Confederation, a loose union of German princedoms. This confederation, however, was still nominally under Austrian—the emperor's—control. In 1866, under the leadership of Otto von Bismarck, the Prussians defeated the Austrian Habsburgs, driving them out of Germany. Bismarck was also instrumental in bringing about the Franco-Prussian War of 1870–71. The Prussian victory, which culminated in the coronation of Wilhelm I of

Prussia as German emperor in Versailles, consolidated Prussia as the leading European power and brought northern and southern Germany together to form a unified German Empire (Reich). Now the king of Prussia was emperor of Germany as well.

Germany's expansionist ambitions and its aggressive arms build-up during the last years of the nineteenth century in combination with the manifold rivalries between the various European powers led to international tensions that finally erupted in the First World War. At the end of the war, in 1918, Germany found itself along with its allies Austria and Turkey, defeated and its emperor, Wilhelm II, in exile. All other German kings and princes were forced to abdicate as well. In 1919, the Weimar Republic, with a president and legislature elected by universal suffrage, ruling a German territory that was substantially smaller than the pre-war state had been. However, popular resentment was fanned by the loss of German territory and the harsh regime of reparations that were imposed by the Treaty of Versailles. This resentment was exacerbated by a high rate of unemployment, soaring inflation in the 1920s and the onset of serious economic depression at the end of the decade. Extremist groupings to the left and right of the political spectrum thrived and battled over their ideological differences in bloody street fights. In 1933 Adolf Hitler was elected chancellor as head of the National Socialist (Nazi) Party (NSDAP), promising to return the country to its former level of influence and power. The "Führer" soon eliminated all democratic organs, ruthlessly pursued his goals and cruelly suppressed any opposition. Eventually, Hitler plunged Europe into the Second World War when he invaded Poland in September 1939. Especially the Jews suffered from his reign of terror: More than six million Jewish people troughout Europe were murdered and maltreated in concentration and labor camps before the war ended in 1945.

At the end of the war a defeated and devastated Germany was divided into two principal zones, the western half administered by Britain, France, and the United States, and the eastern part under Soviet control (Poland and the Soviet Union had first incorporated large parts of eastern Prussia into their territories). In 1949 this resulted in the creation of two separate states: the Federal Republic of Germany in the west, under a democratically elected government and firmly embedded in the western alliances; and the Democratic Republic of Germany under a central, Soviet-dominated communist government in the east. Thus divided, the two Germanies became a focal point for Cold War tensions in Europe over the next 40 years. Control of the city of Berlin, in East German territory, was divided between the two countries. East Berlin was sealed off when communist authorities constructed a wall between the two parts of the city in 1961.

As the Soviet Union faltered in the late 1980s, waves of unrest in East Germany led to the collapse of its government and the reunification of the whole country in October 1990, with Berlin as its capital. In December, elections including the entire country were held. Germany's political system is based on the 1949 West German constitution, which stipulates a parliament elected by universal suffrage for a four-year term with a president, elected by both houses of the parliament for a five-year term, as titular head of state.

Physical features and land use

Germany is divided into many different landforms. The southern part of the country is generally mountainous and heavily forested. In the southwestern region east of the Rhine River which forms the border with France, is the vast expanse of rugged wooded peaks that constitute the Black Forest, an extension of Switzerland's Jura Mountains. Further east the thickly wooded Bavarian Plateau rises out of the Danube Valley, leading to the spectacular peaks of the Alps along the border between Austria and Germany in the far southeast.

The central part of Germany is also a highland area, part of a chain of mountains and hills that extends from France as far east as the Carpathians. These, too, are heavily wooded, particularly in the more mountainous regions. The valleys are often fertile and undulating and extensively planted with crops and vines. The highest and most rugged peaks are found in the Harz Mountains in the north of these central uplands. In the northern part of the central uplands, where the country slopes toward the northern plain, there are areas of fertile soil that support crops such as wheat, barley, and sugar beet.

Northern Germany is an extensive lowland plain that covers about one-third of the country's area. Part of the North European Plain that stretches eastward into Russia, it is a region of fertile pasture and croplands, sandy heaths and stretches of marshland. A network of northward-flowing rivers, most notably the Elbe and its tributaries, drains this northern plain.

About one-third of German land is cultivated. Cereal crops are widely grown, as well as beets and potatoes. Large areas are used as pastures. Especially in the Hallertau region hops is grown for the German beers that are famous throughout the world. Vineyards are most widespread in the valleys of the Rhine and Mosel Rivers. Especially in the south, along the shores of the Bodensee (or Lake of Constance) which lies between Germany, Switzerland and Austria, fruit is cultivated wherever the climate will allow it. Cattle and pigs are the principal livestock and are concentrated mainly on the northern plain and in the foothills of the Alps.

Industry, commerce, and culture

Manufacturing industry, centered largely in the Ruhr Valley but also in such cities as Frankfurt, Stuttgart, Munich, Hannover, Hamburg, and Berlin among many others, is the main strength of the German economy. Coal is the only mineral resource of which Germany has large reserves, although its importance has declined in recent decades as oil has replaced it as the primary industrial fuel. Iron and steel production support well-developed machine manufacturing and other metal industries. Cement, chemical, automobile, and electronic industries are also significant.

Unification has resulted in the juxtaposition of one of the world's most developed and efficient industrial economies with one that was mostly uncompetitive and outmoded in its methods and equipment. As a result, Germany has suffered considerable economic and social disruption as the more affluent western part of the country has had to subsidize attempts to improve conditions in the east. There is still a noticeable discrepancy between standards of living in east and west, and wages in the east are considerably lower. The move to a market economy in the former East Germany, with its emphasis on greater efficiency, has created high levels of unemployment. Under the former communist regime unemployment was virtually non-existent.

Netherlands

Fact File

OFFICIAL NAME Kingdom of the Netherlands

FORM OF GOVERNMENT Constitutional monarchy with two legislative bodies (First Chamber and Second Chamber)

CAPITAL Amsterdam; The Hague is the seat of government

AREA 41,865 sq km (16,164 sq miles)

TIME ZONE GMT + 1 hour

POPULATION 16,068,000

PROJECTED POPULATION 2015 16,420,000

POPULATION DENSITY 383.8 per sq km (994.1 per sq mile)

LIFE EXPECTANCY 78.6

INFANT MORTALITY (PER 1,000) 4.3

OFFICIAL LANGUAGE Dutch

OTHER LANGUAGES Frisian

LITERACY RATE 99 %

RELIGIONS Protestant 35 %, Roman Catholic 34 %, Muslim 3%, other 2 %, unaffiliated 26 %

ETHNIC GROUPS Dutch 95.8 %, Turkish 1.2 %, Moroccan 0.9 %, other 2.1 %

CURRENCY Euro

ECONOMY Services 71 %, industry 26 %, agriculture 3 %

GNP PER CAPITA US$ 26,900

CLIMATE Temperate, with cool winters and mild summers

HIGHEST POINT Mt Vaalserberg 321 m (1,053 ft)

MAP REFERENCE Page 288

Situated in northwestern Europe, with a western and northern coastline on the North Sea, the Netherlands is bordered by Germany to its east and Belgium to its south. About half the area of this low-lying nation is below sea level and the country is saved from inundation only by a series of coastal dikes and sand dunes, heavily planted with marram grass to prevent erosion, and a complex network of canals and waterways, into which excess water is pumped from low-lying areas and then carried to the rivers that flow to the coast. For centuries the Dutch have been engaged in battle with the sea, and have gradually reclaimed huge amounts of land from it. In the last century more than 3,000 sq km (1,160 sq miles) of land were added. The most spectacular reclamation was the Zuiderzee project that began in 1920 and was completed almost 50 years later. Several polders were created in the former bay, the largest of them being Flevoland and the Noordoostpolder. The newly gained areas are important for settling and economy. They substantially relieve the agglomerations in the south of the country.

In the first century BC the Germanic peoples of the Low Countries, which include present-day Belgium and Luxembourg, were colonized by Roman armies. From the fifth century AD the region came under the successive control of Frankish, Burgundian, Austrian, and finally, in the fifteenth century, Spanish rulers. In 1568, William of Orange, outraged by Spain's suppression of a spreading Protestant movement, led a revolt. In 1581 the seven northern provinces of the Low Countries declared their independence as the United Provinces of the Netherlands.

This set the scene for the consolidation and expansion of Dutch power throughout the seventeenth century. Trading posts and colonies were established in the East Indies (now Indonesia), the Caribbean (the Antilles), Africa, and South and North America. This period also saw the emergence of the Netherlands as a great maritime nation and a blossoming of Dutch art, literature, and scientific achievements.

The French, under Napoleon, invaded in 1794. After the defeat of France, the Congress of Vienna united the Netherlands, Belgium, and Luxembourg under a Dutch monarch in 1814. Belgium declared itself independent in 1831 and Luxembourg was granted autonomy in 1848. In 1848 a new constitution was introduced reducing the power of the monarch and investing greater authority in the Estates-General, as the parliament is still called. This laid the groundwork for the later emergence of a parliamentary democracy under a monarch with strictly formalized and limited powers.

The Netherlands remained neutral in the First World War and its neutrality was respected by both sides. In the Second World War it was overrun by Nazi forces in 1940, in blatant breach of interntional law. Its East Indies colonies were invaded by Japan. At the end of the war, the Netherlands began an armed conflict with rebel forces in its East Indies colony. It finally granted them independence, as the Republic of Indonesia, in 1949. Suriname, in South America, became independent in 1975, leaving the Antilles and Aruba as the Netherlands' only overseas territories.

After the Second World War the Netherlands joined the NATO alliance and became one of the founder members of the European Economic Community, later the European Community and then the European Union. In 1992

the Treaty on European Union, the Maastricht Treaty, was signed in the southern Dutch city of Maastricht.

Physical features and land use

Almost all of the Netherlands is flat and much of the landscape is covered by small farming plots, intensively cultivated and surrounded by ditches or canals. Dotting the landscape are windmills which for centuries have been used to drain the land. These are now largely picturesque as they have been supplanted by motor pumps. Much of this land is dedicated to horticulture, especially the growing of tulips and other bulb plants, often in tandem with vegetable produce.

Cattle farming and dairying, the country's main forms of agriculture, are strongest in the northwest, in the provinces of North Holland and Friesland, on either side of the Ijsselmeer, the area of the Zuiderzee project. The Ijsselmeer is an expanse of fresh water, separated from the salt water of the Waddenzee by a dike that is 32 km (20 miles) long. This lies between the northwest coast and a succession of accumulations of sand which are known as the West Frisian Islands. On the land side, streets are built on the dike.

Further south, near the coast, is a succession of densely populated urban areas that include Amsterdam and the other major Dutch cities, including Rotterdam, one of the world's largest ports. Together with other important cities such as Haarlem, The Hague, Utrecht, Delft, and Leyden, the main centers Amsterdam and Rotterdam form an extended agglomeration, called the Randstad Holland. Just south of this urban conglomeration, the major rivers that flow into the Netherlands—among them the Rhine from Germany and the Schelde and the Meuse from Belgium—share a common delta area. The only relief from flat land is in the far southeast, where a range of hills rises in places to about 100 m (300 ft).

Industry and commerce

Concentrated in the heavily populated urban southwest, manufacturing industry employs about one in five members of the workforce. Food processing, chemical and electrical machinery manufacture, metal, engineering, electronic products, and petroleum refining are major industries. Natural gas is the country's principal natural resource, and there are extensive reserves in the north.

Most Dutch people enjoy an affluent lifestyle, although some groups of immigrants on the fringes of the cities live in conspicuous poverty. Social services are well developed and the country has one of the best state-funded healthcare systems in the world.

OVERSEAS TERRITORIES

Aruba
Netherlands Antilles

Houses and houseboats along one of Amsterdam's canals (left page top). Spreading fields of bulbs in the Netherlands (bottom). Renaissance buildings in Antwerp, Belgium (below).

Belgium

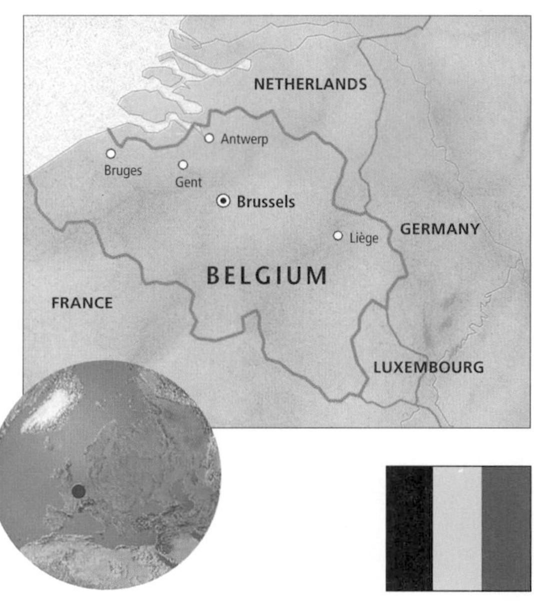

Fact File

Official name Kingdom of Belgium

Form of government Federal constitutional monarchy with two legislative bodies (Senate and Chamber of Deputies)

Capital Brussels

Area 30,510 sq km (11,780 sq miles)

Time zone GMT + 1 hour

Population 10,275,000

Projected population 2015 10,272,000

Population density 336.8 per sq km (872.2 per sq mile)

Life expectancy 78.1

Infant mortality (per 1,000) 4.6

Official languages French, Dutch, German

Literacy rate 98 %

Religions Roman Catholic 75 %, Protestant or other 25 %

Ethnic groups Fleming 55 %, Walloon 33 %, other 12 %

Currency Euro

Economy Services 77 %, industry 20 %, agriculture 3 %

GNP per capita US$ 29,000

Climate Temperate, with mild, wet winters and cool summers

Highest point Mt Botrange 694 m (2,277 ft)

Map reference Pages 288, 291

This small, densely populated country has a 60 km (40 mile) coastline on the North Sea and is bounded by France to the west and south, Luxembourg at its southeastern corner, Germany to the east, and the Netherlands to the north. Its name derives from the Belgae, the Gallic race that occupied the area when invading Roman armies arrived in the first century BC. Over more than 2,000 years the region has been dominated by a succession of foreign powers, which explains Belgium's linguistic diversity. From the eighteenth century, Belgium was ruled by Austria, France,

contribution to the economy is not significant. Sugar beet, potatoes, wheat, and barley are the main crops and livestock consists largely of pigs and cattle.

Belgium is a heavily industrialized country and its population is highly urbanized. Except for coal, it is poor in natural resources and relies heavily on imported raw materials to fuel its industries. Almost all the industrial centers are in the Flemish area in the north of the country. Antwerp, Europe's third-largest port and the most populous city in Belgium handles the largest part of the country's imports and exports, and it is the center of numerous heavy industries including petroleum refining, plastics, petrochemicals, and heavy machinery manufacture. The manufacture of textiles is particularly associated with the cities of Ghent and Bruges. Iron and steel making, food processing, and glass manufacture are some of the other important industries.

Many of the major industrial centers are connected by a network of canals, along which barges transport cargo. One of the most celebrated of these is the Albert Canal, which links Liège with Antwerp.

While heavy industry has contributed significantly to Belgium's export earnings, it has had a decidedly negative impact on the environment. The Meuse River, which is a major source of drinking water, has been severely polluted by industrial wastes and fertilizers. The acid rain that falls on Belgium and its neighboring countries has been attributed largely to the air pollution that is caused by Belgian industry.

Approximately seventy-five percent of the population are Roman Catholic. There also are Protestant congregations as well as quite a number of Jews. The social security system in Belgium is exemplary. As a consequence, the average life expectancy is one of the highest in Europe.

The historic city of Bruges in Belgium (above left). Cows grazing in the Belgian countryside (below left). La Roque Gageac, a picturesque town on the slopes of the Dordogne Valley in France (below).

then the Netherlands. In 1830 the Belgians declared their independence and installed Leopold I, a relative of the future English Queen Victoria, as their king. Today the country is a parliamentary democracy with a monarch as head of state.

Belgium's population is divided into two main groups. The larger group, the Flemings, lives mostly in the north of the country and speaks Flemish, which is closely related to Dutch. The south is inhabited by the French-speaking Walloons. There is also a German-speaking community to the east of the city of Liège. Brussels, the capital, is officially bilingual. It is the headquarters of the European Union and the North Atlantic Treaty Organization, NATO. Due to the large variety of organizations headquartered here, Brussels is occasionally called the secret capital of Europe. It is one of the most important service centers of Western Europe and is also the home of many banking and insurance firms.

Inland of the beaches and sand dunes along the North Sea lies a narrow strip of drained, reclaimed marshland, intespersed with dikes and traversed by canals. This region gives way to a central, fertile low-lying plain that rises to a low plateau north of the Meuse-Sambre river system. South of these rivers lie Belgium's uplands. In this rugged, sparsely populated area there are a number of mountain ranges, the most extensive of which is the Ardennes. This heavily wooded high plateau of sandstone and shale is punctuated by flat-topped peaks and cut by deep chasms and valleys. Forestry is the main industry in this southern region, where oak and beech trees predominate. Coal mining, once important around the city of Charleroi in the south of Belgium, is now declining.

Belgium's agriculture is centered on its rich northern plain, where crops are secondary to livestock rearing. Although about half the land area has been cleared for agriculture, its

Luxembourg

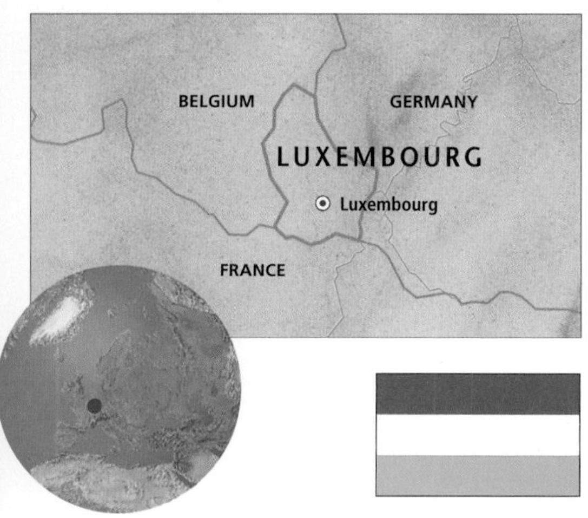

Fact File

Official name Grand Duchy of Luxembourg

Form of government Constitutional monarchy with single legislative body (Chamber of Deputies)

Capital Luxembourg

Area 2,586 sq km (998 sq miles)

Time zone GMT + 1 hour

Population 449,000

Projected population 2015 518,000

Population density 173.6 per sq km (449.9 per sq mile)

Life expectancy 77.5

Infant mortality (per 1,000) 4.7

Official language Luxembourgish

Other languages French, German

Literacy rate 100 %

Religions Roman Catholic 97 %, Protestant and Jewish 3 %

Ethnic groups Luxembourger 70 %, other 30 % (mainly French, Portuguese, Belgian, German, Italian, Duch, Spanish and others)

Currency Euro

Economy Services 77 %, industry 19 %, agriculture 4 %

GNP per capita US$ 44,000

Climate Temperate, with cool winters and mild summers

Highest point Burgplatz 559 m (1,834 ft)

Map reference Page 291

The Grand Duchy of Luxembourg is one of the smallest countries in Europe. Situated in northern Europe, it shares borders with Belgium to the west and France to the south. Three connecting rivers—the Our, Sûre, and the Moselle—separate it from Germany to the east. Part of the Holy Roman Empire from the tenth century AD, Luxembourg became an independent duchy in 1354, one of hundreds of such states in medieval Europe. It is the only one to survive today as an independent nation. Throughout the intervening centuries, Luxembourg has come under Austrian, Spanish, French, and Dutch rule. In 1830 part of the duchy was taken over by Belgium when that country split from the Netherlands. Luxembourg separated from the Netherlands in 1890. Germany occupied Luxembourg during both world wars and annexed it in 1942. After the Second World War it became a founding member of NATO and in 1957 joined the European Economic Community. It has been a keen advocate of European cooperation and was the first country, in 1991, to ratify the Maastricht Treaty. Luxembourg is a constitutional monarchy, with the Grand Duke as head of state, and a prime minister as head of an elected 21-member Council of State. The country's official language, Luxembourgish, is a dialect of the German language and strongly influenced by French. In schools, both German and French are taught, the latter being the main language in the higher grades.

The northern part of Luxembourg is called the Oesling. Covering about one-third of the country's total area, it is part of the densely forested Ardennes mountain range. Numerous river valleys dissect this northern region and deer and wild boar abound. It is a rugged, picturesque area but has poor soils. In contrast, the southern two-thirds, known as the Gutland or Bon Pays (meaning good land), consists of plains and undulating hills covered with rich soils and extensive pastureland. The Gutland area is still strongly agricultural. Wheat, barley, potatoes, and grapes are the principal crops and more than 5 million cattle and 6 million pigs are raised.

Iron ore deposits in the south of the country contributed to the development of a thriving iron and steel industry. These deposits are now less abundant and industries such as food processing, chemical manufacturing and tire making now rival steel in importance. A growing service sector, especially in banking, has become increasingly central to the country's prosperity.

The people of Luxembourg are among the most affluent in Europe. Unemployment is low and salaries, especially among urban workers, are high.

France

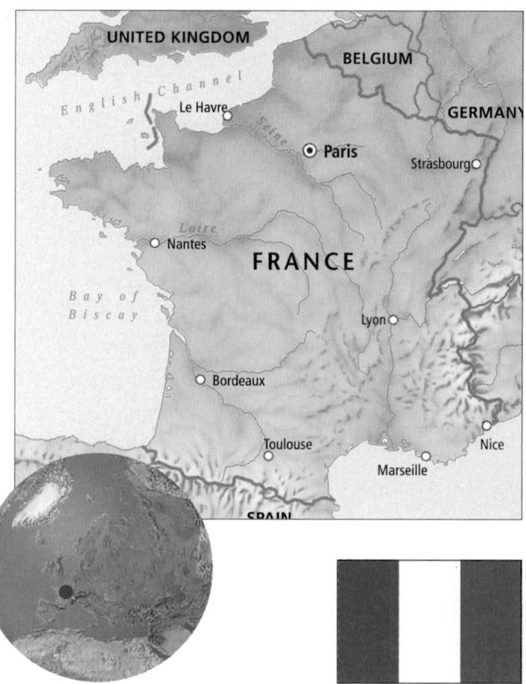

Fact File

Official name French Republic

Form of government Republic with two legislative bodies (Senate and National Assembly)

Capital Paris

Area 547,030 sq km (211,208 sq miles)

Time zone GMT + 1 hour

Population 59,766,000

Projected population 2015 61,852,000

Population density 109.3 per sq km (283.0 per sq mile)

Life expectancy 79.1

Infant mortality (per 1,000) 4.4

Official language French

Other languages Provençal, Breton, Alsatian, Corsican, Catalan, Basque, Flemish, German, Arabic

Literacy rate 99 %

Religions Roman Catholic 90 %, Protestant 2 %, Jewish 1 %, Muslim 1 %, unaffiliated 6 %

Ethnic groups French 95 %; others, including Algerian, Portuguese, Moroccan, Italian, and Spanish 5 %

Currency Euro

Economy Services 70 %, industry 28 %, agriculture 2 %

GNP per capita US$ 25,700

Climate Temperate, with cool winters and mild summers; warmer on the Mediterranean coast

Highest point Mont Blanc 4,807 m (15,771 ft)

Map reference Pages 290–91

Situated at the west of continental Europe, France roughly resembles a hexagon and has three long stretches of coastline. To the north the English Channel separates it from the southern coast of England (the Channel

Tunnel now links the two), to the west it faces the Bay of Biscay, and its southern shores are on the Mediterranean Sea. To the northeast and east, it shares borders with Belgium, Luxembourg, Germany, Switzerland, and Italy, and in the far southwest the Pyrenees Mountains separate it from Spain. Southeast of the mainland, in the Mediterranean, is the French island of Corsica.

History

A political entity roughly equivalent to the area of present-day France was first established in AD 843, when the Treaty of Verdun divided the enormous Frankish Empire, which had reached its high point under Charlemagne, between Charlemagne's three grandsons. These divisions corresponded approximately to what are now France, Germany, and Italy. Charles the Bald thus became king of Francia Occidentalis. His Carolingian Dynasty lasted only until 987, when territorial fighting between feudal lords led to the election of Hugh Capet, who controlled the region around Paris, as king. The Capetian Dynasty lasted for almost 350 years, during which time it consolidated its power and extended its territory. When the crown passed to Philip VI, the first of the Valois rulers, in 1328, France was a great European power, although much of its present territory was in the hands of the English, who also laid claim to sovereignty over all of France. In 1338 there began a series of wars which later became known as the Hundred Years War. Despite a major French defeat at Agincourt in 1415, these conflicts eventually led to the expulsion of the English from nearly all of France by the middle of the fifteenth century.

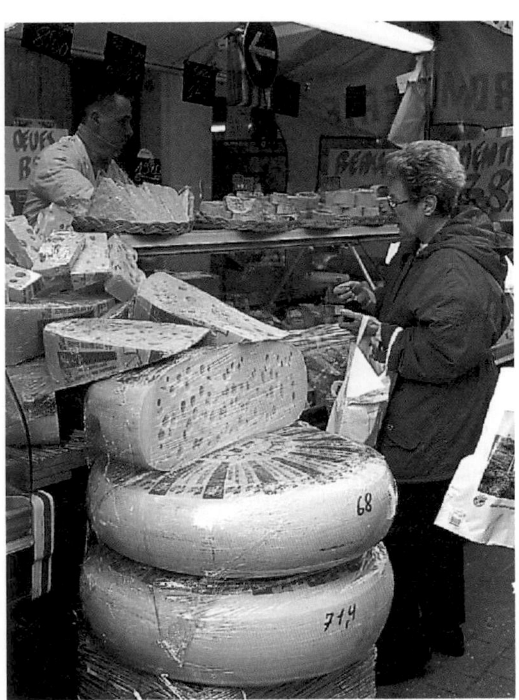

In the second half of the sixteenth century, France was wracked by religious wars between Catholics and Protestants (Huguenots). These finally ended in 1598 with the accession of the first Bourbon king, the Protestant-turned-Catholic Henry of Navarre. Under the Bourbons, and especially under the 72-year reign of Louis XIV that ended in 1715, the monarchy reigned supreme and France acquired colonies in places as far afield as India, North America, and the Caribbean. Under royal patronage, French literature, art, and music flourished, and the royal court in Versailles was the most opulent in Europe and became a role model for basically every European prince. Such immense luxury, however was only possible due to ruthless exploitation of the Sun King's subjects. After his death, weak leadership, extremely high taxation and a series of debilitating wars during the eighteenth century led to the popular unrest that culminated in the French Revolution of 1789, which overthrew the monarchy and deposed the nobility but soon collapsed into a period of anarchy and savagery. The rise of Napoleon Bonaparte restored some stability and he conquered large parts of Europe between 1799 and 1814, only to lose it again. He was ultimately defeated in 1815 at the Battle of Waterloo, in Belgium, and sentenced to exile on St Helena Island where he died in 1821.

Napoleon's defeat ushered in a period of political instability that saw first the restoration of the monarchy, which was twice overthrown in revolutions (1830 and 1848), then the installation of Napoleon's nephew, Louis-Napoleon, first as president of a republic and then as the Emperor Napoleon III. The defeat of France in the Franco-Prussian War of 1870–71 led to a new republic and a period of relative stability in which France acquired new colonies in Africa and Indochina.

During the twentieth century France suffered grievously in both world wars. In the trench warfare of the First World War, almost a million and a half French lives were lost and the northwest of the country was devastated. In the Second World War northern France was occupied by German forces and the south was administered from Vichy by a pro-Nazi collaborationist government led by Maréchal Pétain.

Political instability continued after the Second World War, as France unsuccessfully waged a war against insurgents in Indochina and as unrest in French-controlled Algeria threatened to bring down the government. In 1957 France's Second World War hero,

A cheese shop in Paris (left). The Arc de Triomphe, built by Emperor Napoleon I, is one of the landmarks of the French capital Paris (above center).

Charles de Gaulle, was invited to assume power, under a constitution that greatly increased the powers of the president. This constitution has since undergone a number of revisions, the latest being in 2000. The French president, who controls defense and finance, is elected by universal suffrage for a five-year term. There are two houses of parliament, the National Assembly and the Senate. The representatives in the National Assembly, who hold legislative authority, are elected every five years, while one-third of the Senate, with an advisory role, are chosen at three-year intervals.

Physical features and land use

Much of France is low-lying with almost two-thirds of its land at an elevation of less than 250 m (800 ft). These lowland regions, interspersed with a number of hilly areas, stretch from the Belgian and German borders across the north to the rugged Breton Peninsula in the west, and inland to the Pyrenees in the southwest. Further east, along the Mediterranean coast and hemmed in by mountains, is the low-lying region of western Provence in the Rhône Delta. Except for the far northeast, which forms part of the Flanders Plain, most of these lowland areas comprise the basins of France's four main rivers and their tributaries. In the north, the Seine flows northwest through Paris and the surrounding Île-de-France to the English Channel. France's longest river, the Loire, flows north through the central region, then westward to the Atlantic Ocean. Further south the Garonne, which rises in the Pyrenees, drains much of southwest France on its way to the Atlantic near Bordeaux; and in the east the Rhône, rising in Switzerland, flows west to

Timeline

- **35,000 BP** Neanderthal people lived in caves, sometimes burying dead using decorated tombstones
- **30,000–20,000 BP** Cro-Magnon population in the southwest spreads out to northern and eastern regions
- **15,000–10,000 BP** Cave paintings at sites such as Lascaux and Pech Merle depicting bulls, mammoths, horses, and humans
- **600 BC** Greek merchants establish Massilia (later Marseilles) as a port on the Mediterranean coast
- **400 BC** Franks and Visigoths move east into Gaul, defeating the Romans
- **59–50 BC** Roman legions led by Julius Caesar occupy the entire area of Gaul (France)
- **AD 987** Hugh Capet becomes the first of the Capetian kings to rule all France
- **1309–77** The papacy moves from Rome to Avignon in southern France
- **1337–1453** France and England fight the Hundred Years war; despite English victories at Crécy and Agincourt the French triumph
- **1562–98** Wars of religion between Catholics and Huguenots (Protestants)
- **1643** Religious persecution causes 200,000 Huguenots to flee, resulting in economic decline
- **1789** The storming of the Bastille by the Paris mob marks the start of the French Revolution
- **1792** First French Republic established; Louis XVI executed (1793)
- **1799** Napoleon Bonaparte seizes power; first as consul and later as Emperor of France
- **1814–15** Napoleon exiled to St Helena after losing Battle of Waterloo; monarchy restored under Louis XVIII

Lyon where, fed by the Saône from the north, it courses due south to the Mediterranean.

In the center and south of the country a vast central plateau, the Massif Central, covers almost a sixth of the total land area. Much of its landscape is rugged, characterized by granite outcrops, extinct volcanic peaks, and deep gorges. At its highest point, it reaches almost 1,900 m (6,000 ft). East of the Massif Central, separated from it by the Rhône Valley, are the Alps, which form the border with Italy and extend to the coast in the southeast corner of the country. North of the Alps, the Jura, characterized by high limestone cliffs, separate France from Switzerland and further north, the heavily forested Vosges Mountains fringe the Rhine Valley near the German border. In the far southwest the Pyrenees, which rival the Alps in rugged splendor but are less accessible, stand between France and Spain.

Industry, commerce, and agriculture

Second only to the USA as an exporter of agricultural produce, France produces a wide range of food, although most farms are relatively small and thus specialized on a smaller range of products. Over half the land area is cultivated, mainly in the low-lying regions, the most abundant crops being wheat, maize, barley, and sugar beet. Vast areas, especially in the Burgundy and Champagne regions in the central north, around Bordeaux in the southwest and the Rhône Valley in the south, are devoted to viticulture. France is Europe's second largest wine producer. Along the Mediterranean coast mainly fruit, olives and flowers are cultivated. Extensive fields devoted to perfume and healing plants such as the lavender grown in many parts of Provence constitute one of the specialties of the region. The Atlantic coast with its mild climate is used to cultivate special crops.

After Germany, France is the largest industrial power in Europe, and until recently many of its industries were state-owned. Paris, Lille, Nantes, and Strasbourg in the north, Lyon and Grenoble in the center, and Marseilles and Toulouse in the south are among the major manufacturing centers. The main industries include steelmaking, car, aircraft, and weapons manufacture, oil refining, machine making, textiles, and chemicals. The large woods are used for lumbering, the production of paper and furniture, as well as cork and diverse resins. The production of food and stimulants such as spirits is another important area. Mineral resources are not abundant, though there are reserves of iron ore, zinc, and uranium. Most of France's electricity, almost eighty percent, is generated by state-owned nuclear plants.

On average, the French enjoy one of the highest standards of living in the world, but there are considerable disparities between rich and poor, with considerable wealth concentrated in an area around Paris and parts of southern France. The state heavily subsidizes health services, which are particularly stressed by a high level of smoking and alcohol-related disease.

REGIONS

Alsace • Aquitaine • Auvergne • Basse-Normandie • Bourgogne • Bretagne • Centre • Champagne-Ardenne • Corse • Franche-Comté • Haute-Normandie • Île-de-France • Languedoc-Roussillon • Limousin • Lorraine • Midi-Pyrénées • Nord-Pas-de-Calais • Pays de la Loire • Picardie • Poitou-Charentes • Provence-Alpes-Côte d'Azur • Rhônes-Alpes

OVERSEAS TERRITORIES

French Guiana • French Polynesia • French Southern and Arctic Lands • Guadeloupe • Martinique • Mayotte • New Caledonia • Réunion • St Pierre and Miquelon • Wallis and Futuna Islands

The European Union

On 1 January 1999 eleven European countries adopted a new and common currency—the Euro. This momentous step marked the climax of a movement for closer European integration which had begun in 1957. In March of that year Belgium, France, the Federal Republic of Germany, Italy, Luxembourg, and the Netherlands signed a treaty which proposed the gradual integration of their economies in the European Economic Community (EEC, later called the European Community or EC). They planned to gradually eliminate restrictive quotas and import duties between member nations in order to allow the free movement of persons and capital within their common boundaries. It was hoped that the larger market that resulted would promote greater productivity, higher standards of living for all and, most of all, eliminate European wars.

The success of the Community led to a number of additional countries seeking membership. Others, however, objected to the surrender of sovereignty that was entailed: at first Britain, along with the Scandinavian nations, Switzerland, Austria, and Portugal, formed their own—though not very successful—free-trade area (known as the outer seven or EFTA) instead. Nor were the policies of the EEC uniformly successful: the Common Agricultural Policy, for example, led to the overproduction of butter, wine, and sugar in member countries. However, although national referenda on membership and treaty ratification have not been without a degree of controversy, most of the countries in Europe have now decided that the benefits of being a member of the EC outweigh the costs, and by 1997 all of the following states belonged: Austria, Belgium, Denmark, Finland, France, Germany, Greece, Ireland, Italy, Luxembourg, the Netherlands, Portugal, Spain, Sweden, and the UK. In 2004 ten more countries have joined the Union: Estonia, Latvia, Lithuania, Poland, the Czech Republic, Slowakia, Slovenia, Hungary, Malta and Cyprus (the Greek aprt of the island), and Bulgaria and Romania plan to follow suit in 2007.

With the ratification of the Maastricht Treaty in 1992 which prepared the way for monetary union and the Euro, the EEC and its associated bodies became formally known as the European Union (EU). An important feature of monetary union has been the establishment of an independent European Central Bank (ECB). This bank has as its main goal "price stability", a term meaning inflation of less than two percent per year. At present, since 2001, twelve EU-countries have introduced the new currency. The UK, Denmark, and Sweden decided not to adopt the Euro, while Greece has not yet been able to satisfy the economic criteria for monetary union.

1848 Riots in Paris, with street fighting between the army and mobs of hungry, unemployed workers

1870–71 France loses Franco-Prussian War; Alsace and Lorraine ceded to Germany

1889 The Eiffel Tower, an iron structure designed by Gustave Alexandre Eiffel for the Exhibition of the same year, built in Paris

1914 First World War starts: Allies create the Western Front in north France to stop German advance; deadlock lasts three and a half years—1,357,800 French casualties

1918 First World War ends with Treaty of Versailles under which Alsace and Lorraine are returned to France by Germany

1939 Start of Second World War and subsequent German invasion of France leads to occupation of Paris (1940)

1944 Allied troops reach Paris; General de Gaulle returns from exile in England to form a provisional government

1957 France joins other European nations in forming the European Common Market by signing the Treaty of Rome

1960 Rapid rise in immigration from ex-colonial territories in North Africa and the Caribbean brings concern over jobs; also first nuclear tests

1968 Student protests lead to a general strike over educational policies and political dissatisfaction; General de Gaulle resigns

1978 The disaster of the tanker ship *Amoco Cadiz* on the French Atlantic coast causes an environmental catastrophe

1994 Railway tunnel under English Channel connects France and the United Kingdom; idea first proposed in 1802 by Mathieu to Napoleon

2003 First purely EU peace corps led by French soldiers is sent by the EU to the civil war regions of the Democratic Republic of Congo

Monaco

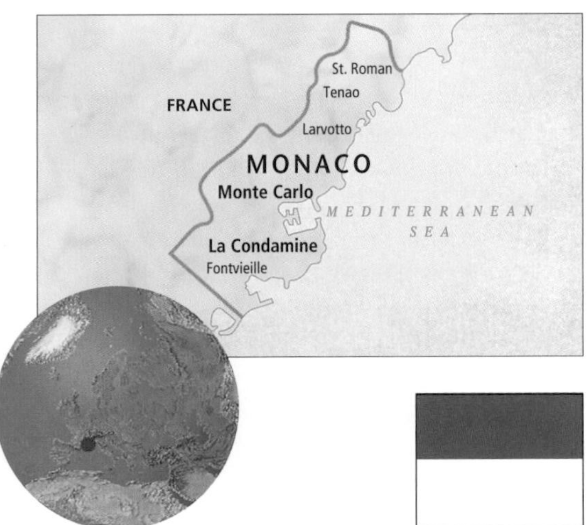

Fact File

OFFICIAL NAME Principality of Monaco

FORM OF GOVERNMENT Constitutional monarchy with single legislative body (National Council)

CAPITAL Monaco

AREA 1.9 sq km (0.7 sq miles)

TIME ZONE GMT + 1 hour

POPULATION 32,000

PROJECTED POPULATION 2015 37,000

POPULATION DENSITY 16,920.5 per sq km (45,714.3 per sq mile)

LIFE EXPECTANCY 79.1

INFANT MORTALITY (PER 1,000) 5.7

OFFICIAL LANGUAGE French

OTHER LANGUAGES Italian, English, Monégasque

LITERACY RATE 99 %

RELIGIONS Roman Catholic 95 %, other 5 %

ETHNIC GROUPS French 47 %, Monégasque 16 %, Italian 16 %, other 21 %

CURRENCY Euro

ECONOMY Tourism and services 90 %, industry 10 %

GNP PER CAPITA US$ 27,000

CLIMATE Temperate, with mild, wet winters and hot, dry summers

HIGHEST POINT Mt Agel 140 m (459 ft)

MAP REFERENCE Page 291

Monaco, the world's smallest independent nation after the Vatican City, sits on the Mediterranean coast in the far southeast corner of France. Except for its coastline, it is completely surrounded by French territory. In the thirteenth century the Genoese built a fortress there and in 1297 members of the Grimaldi family of Genoa established themselves as rulers. Grimaldi princes retained control for almost 500 years, until 1792, when an uprising deposed the reigning prince and declared the state a republic. France annexed Monaco the following year but in 1815, after the Congress of Vienna, it was placed under the protection of Sardinia. France annexed most of Monaco, including Menton, in 1848. In 1861, the Grimaldis were restored as rulers of less than half their former territory, governing under French protection. In 1911 democratic government was introduced by Prince Albert of Monaco. An 18-member National Council is elected every five years, but the head of government is selected by the monarch from a list drawn up by the French government. The present monarch, Prince Rainier III, is a descendant of the Grimaldis. He achieved fame in 1956 for his much-publicized marriage to the American film actress Grace Kelly.

Occupying the lower slopes of the Maritime Alps, Monaco is hilly and rugged. It is densely populated, mainly by foreign nationals. In the southwest is the industrial district of Fontvieille, which consists partly of land reclaimed from the sea. Further east is the old town of Monaco-Ville, where the royal palace is situated. La Condamine, the banking, commercial, and fashionable residential center, overlooks a sheltered harbor. Northeast of La Condamine is Monte Carlo, with its casino, luxury hotels, and apartment blocks.

Apart from pharmaceutical, food processing, and other light industries in Fontvieille, Monaco thrives on its attractions as a tourist haven. The major drawing card is the state-run casino, from which the citizens of Monaco are banned. Until 1962, Monaco's status as a tax haven attracted many wealthy French businesses. The people of Monaco still pay no income tax, but foreigners now do, though at quite favorable rates.

View of Monte Carlo, Monaco (below). An alpine vegetable farm in Switzerland (above center). View of Zürich, Switzerland (right page below). The Wetterhorn Mountain near Grindelwald in the Bernese Oberland, Switzerland (right page bottom).

Switzerland

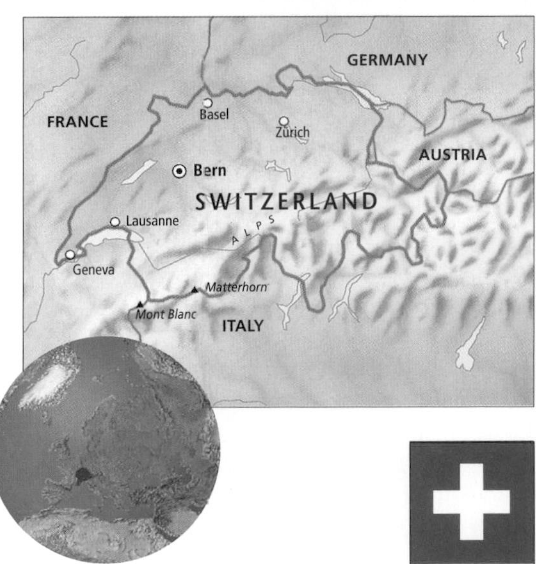

Fact File

OFFICIAL NAME Swiss Confederation

FORM OF GOVERNMENT Federal republic with two legislative bodies (Council of States and National Council)

CAPITAL Bern

AREA 41,290 sq km (15,942 sq miles)

TIME ZONE GMT + 1 hour

POPULATION 7,302,000

PROJECTED POPULATION 2015 7,863,000

POPULATION DENSITY 176.8 per sq km (458.0 per sq mile)

LIFE EXPECTANCY 79.9

INFANT MORTALITY (PER 1,000) 4.4

OFFICIAL LANGUAGES German, French, Italian, Romansch

OTHER LANGUAGES Spanish

LITERACY RATE 99 %

RELIGIONS Roman Catholic 46.1 %, Protestant 40 %, Muslim 2.2 %, Jewish 0.3 % other 11.4 %

ETHNIC GROUPS German-speaking Swiss 65 %, French-speaking Swiss 18 %, Italian-speaking Swiss 10 %, Romansch 1 %, other 6 %

CURRENCY Swiss franc

ECONOMY Services 62 %, industry 34 %, agriculture 4 %

GNP PER CAPITA US$ 31,700

CLIMATE Temperate, varying with altitude; generally cold winters and warm, wet summers

HIGHEST POINT Dufourspitze 4,634 m (15,203 ft)

MAP REFERENCE Pages 288, 291, 294

A landlocked country in central Europe, Switzerland shares borders with Italy to its south and southeast, France to its west, Germany to its north, and Austria and Liechtenstein to its east. This small nation has enjoyed a generally peaceful independence for more than 450 years, despite the conflicts that have often raged around it. Modern Switzerland dates back to the late thirteenth century when three German districts, or cantons, combined to form a federation. A century later other cantons had joined the federation, which survived as a unit despite linguistic differences and often intense and violent conflicts between Catholics and emerging Protestant groups. Although part of the Holy Roman Empire, and effectively under Habsburg domination, the Swiss cantons remained neutral during the Thirty Years War of 1618–48, at the end of which they were formally granted independence. In 1798 French revolutionary armies invaded Switzerland and declared it to be a centralized Helvetic Republic, named after Helvetia, the Roman province that had existed there in Roman times. In 1815, after the defeat of Napoleon, the Congress of Vienna declared Switzerland to be independent once more, as well as permanently neutral, and added two more cantons—Valais and the previously separate republic of Geneva.

The country has maintained this military neutrality ever since and its stance has been respected by its neighbors throughout numerous conflicts, including the First and Second World Wars. Religious tensions flared briefly in 1847, when the Catholic cantons seceded. The following year, however, a new constitution, inspired by that of the United States, re-established the former federation and defined Switzerland as a republic with a strong central government but with considerable powers still vested in individual cantons. In 1874 a new constitution was adopted which essentially confirmed this division of power. Switzerland's central government, which controls foreign policy, railway and postal services, and the mint, consists of an elected bicameral parliament, with a president and vice president elected by the Federal Assembly from among the members of the Federal Council for a one-year term. Women were granted the vote only in 1971, and in some regions of the Appenzell canton they still don't have suffrage.

Physical features and land use

Mountains dominate the Swiss landscape making it Europe's most mountainous country. They cover seven-tenths of the land area. The rest of the country consists of an elevated central plateau on which the majority of the population lives and which is the center of the country's agricultural, industrial, and economic activity. This area is bordered by a number of large lakes and drained by the River Aare, which rises in Lake Neuchâtel and flows northward into the Rhine, which constitutes Switzerland's border with Germany and part of Austria. Lake Neuchâtel is overlooked by the lightly wooded Jura Mountains, which separate Switzerland from France. More than half of Switzerland is covered by the peaks and glaciers of the Alps, which sweep across the south of the country. The most spectacular sections are in the Pennine Alps along the southwestern frontier with Italy. Both the Rhône and the Rhine Rivers originate in this alpine region and drain it in opposite directions, flowing respectively through the two largest lakes in the country, which are Lake Geneva in the far southwest, and Lake Constance in the far northeast.

About one-quarter of Switzerland consists of forests, which are found mainly in the valleys and on the lower slopes. Cypresses and figs are prominent among the tree species. About one-tenth of the land is arable. Crop cultivation is concentrated in the area immediately to the east and southeast of the Jura and in the valleys of the Rhône and Rhine Rivers. Wheat, potatoes, and sugar beet are the main crops. The principal agricultural activity, however, is dairy farming, although pig raising is also significant. Switzerland produces less than half its food needs.

Switzerland is not well endowed with mineral resources. Most of the country's electricity is generated by hydropower, but a significant amount is provided by the country's five nuclear power plants. A sixth nuclear plant was planned but was cancelled in the aftermath of the Chernobyl disaster in Ukraine in 1986.

Industry, commerce, and culture

Switzerland has for centuries been a world leader in the production of precision instruments such as clocks and watches. Other industries which are vital to the country's prosperity include heavy engineering, textile manufacture, clothing, chemicals and food processing. Swiss chocolate, sought after the world over because of its high quality, is also a major contributor to the national economy. Tourism, centered mainly on the Alps, attracts more than 12 million visitors annually.

Banking is highly developed and is one of the country's key industries. Switzerland attracts almost half the world's foreign investment capital and is the base of numerous multinational companies.

Although the country is divided geographically among its predominantly German-, Italian- and French-speaking populations, Switzerland is now a unified nation and its people have a strong sense of common purpose. This is attributable in large measure to Switzerland's status as one of the world's most stable and prosperous countries, with a very high per capita income.

Liechtenstein

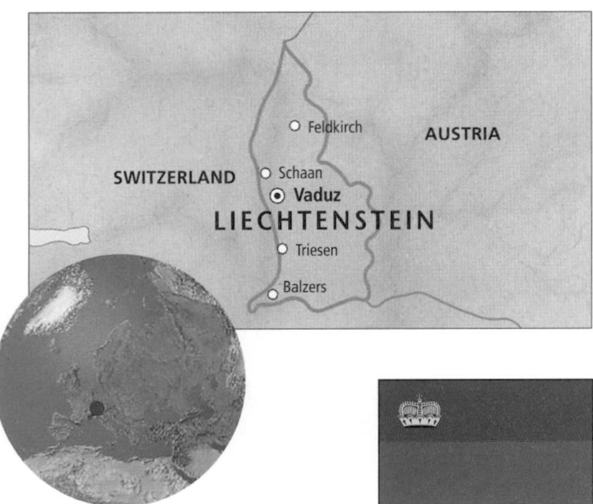

Fact File

OFFICIAL NAME Principality of Liechtenstein

FORM OF GOVERNMENT Constitutional monarchy with single legislative house (Parliament)

CAPITAL Vaduz

AREA 160 sq km (62 sq miles)

TIME ZONE GMT + 1 hour

POPULATION 32,800

PROJECTED POPULATION 2015 37,000

POPULATION DENSITY 205.0 per sq km (529.0 per sq mile)

LIFE EXPECTANCY 79.1

INFANT MORTALITY (PER 1,000) 4.9

OFFICIAL LANGUAGE German

LITERACY RATE 100 %

RELIGIONS Roman Catholic 87.3 %, Protestant 8.3 %, other 4.4 %

ETHNIC GROUPS Alemannic 95 %, Italian and other 5 %

CURRENCY Swiss franc

ECONOMY Services 50.2 %; industry, trade and building 48.1 %; agriculture, fishing and forestry 1.7 %

GNP PER CAPITA US$ 23,000

CLIMATE Temperate, with cold, wet winters and mild, humid summers

HIGHEST POINT Grauspitz 2,599 m (8,527 ft)

MAP REFERENCE Page 288

This small Central European country sits high in the Alps. To the west the Rhine River forms a border with Switzerland, with which Liechtenstein has political ties and whose currency it shares. Austria lies to the east and south. The country takes its name from the Austrian Liechtenstein family which, in 1699 and 1713, acquired two fiefdoms and formed them into the principality. It later came under French and then German influence. In 1866 it achieved independence, and two years later declared itself permanently neutral, a position it has since maintained. In all subsequent European wars, Liechtenstein has remained unmolested. Its head of state is an hereditary monarch who appoints a government on the recommendation of an elected parliament. Elections are held every four years and there is universal adult suffrage, although women have had the vote only since 1984.

The Rhine is the source of Liechtenstein's agricultural strength. Its floodplain, once marshy, has been drained and reclaimed for agricultural and pastoral use. The capital sits on a plateau overlooking the undulating expanses of the Rhine Valley. The slopes of the Rhatikon alpine range rise to impressive peaks in the south. From the southern highlands, the Samina River flows northward through the center of the country. Thick forests—of beech, maple, and ash—cover much of the mountain region.

The main agricultural industries are cattle, sheep, and pig raising, and some vegetables and cereal crops are grown. There is little heavy industry but prominent among light industries are textile and ceramic goods and the manufacture of electronic equipment. There are no mineral resources, and Liechtenstein imports all its fuel and raw materials. A major source of revenue is the sale of postage stamps. More than half the country's residents are foreign nationals, largely attracted by the country's low rates of taxation and its banking laws, which ensure great secrecy. The population's living standard is very high and the unemployment rate around 1.3 percent. The organization of health care is closely linked to the adjacent Swiss cantons.

Austria

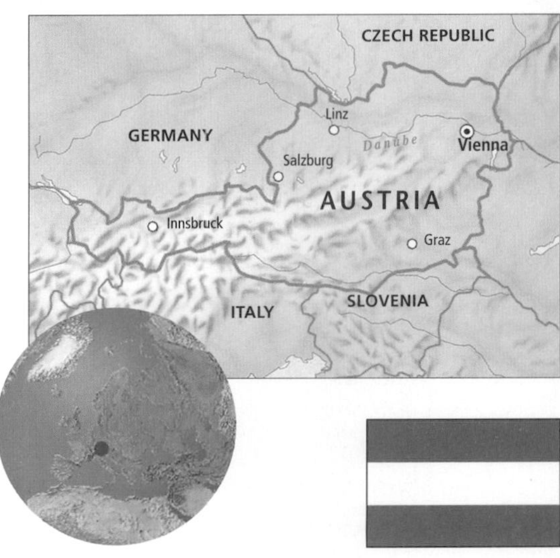

Fact File

OFFICIAL NAME Republic of Austria

FORM OF GOVERNMENT Federal republic with two legislative bodies (Federal Council and National Council)

CAPITAL Vienna (Wien)

AREA 83,850 sq km (32,374 sq miles)

TIME ZONE GMT + 1 hour

POPULATION 8,170,000

PROJECTED POPULATION 2015 8,368,000

POPULATION DENSITY 97.4 per sq km (272.4 per sq mile)

LIFE EXPECTANCY 78.0

INFANT MORTALITY (PER 1,000) 4.4

OFFICIAL LANGUAGE German

LITERACY RATE 98 %

RELIGIONS Roman Catholic 85 %, Protestant 6 %, other 9 %

ETHNIC GROUPS Austrian 90.9 %, Croatian, Slovene, Bosnian, Serb 4.2 %, Turkish 1.7 %, other 3.2 %

CURRENCY Euro

ECONOMY Services 64 %, industry 34 %, agriculture 2 %

GNP PER CAPITA US$ 27,700

CLIMATE Temperate with cold winters and mild to warm summers; colder in mountains

HIGHEST POINT Grossglockner 3,797 m (12,457 ft)

MAP REFERENCE Page 294

The present borders of this landlocked Central European country date back to the Treaty of Versailles of 1919, which presided over the dismantling of the Austro-Hungarian Empire. Germany lies directly to the north of Austria's narrow western boundary, Switzerland and Liechtenstein to its west, and Italy to its south. At its wider eastern end Slovenia lies to the south, Hungary and Slovakia to the east, and the Czech Republic to the north.

Austria's history for most of the last seven hundred years is bound up with the fortunes of the archdukes and later emperors of the Habsburg family who ruled it, and at times

much of the rest of Europe, from 1278 until the First World War. Roman conquest of most of present-day Austria was followed in the fourth and fifth centuries AD by invasions by Germanic and Celtic tribes and by the Franks under Charlemagne during the eighth century. The land fell to the King of Bohemia in 1252, only to be wrested from him by Rudolf of Habsburg just 26 years later. Rudolf called himself archduke and declared the title hereditary.

From then until the sixteenth century the Habsburg Empire expanded until it dominated much of Europe, including Spain (as well as its American colonies), part of Italy, the Netherlands, and Burgundy. Charles V, 1520–58, proudly stated that he ruled an empire in which the sun never set. During the sixteenth century Hungary and Bohemia came under Habsburg rule, and a Turkish siege of Vienna was repulsed.

Catholic Austria's forced capitulation to German Protestantism at the end of the Thirty Years War saw Austria take second place to France as the leading European power. However, it remained a significant force with dominion over much of Europe, despite its loss of control over Spain in the early eighteenth century, a debilitating War of Succession between 1740 and 1748, and defeat by Prussian forces in 1763.

Napoleon's victory at the Battle of Austerlitz was a low point for Austria, but upon Napoleon's defeat in 1814 Austria emerged as leader of a new German Confederation. Following the Austro-Prussian War of 1866, Austria and Hungary were combined under Habsburg rule to form the Austro-Hungarian Empire. However, it also meant that Austria lost its dominance in Germany to Prussia and ended up not being part of the German Empire that was created in 1871. The Austrian annexation of Bosnia and Herzegovina in 1908 created the circumstances which culminated in the assassination of the heir to the Austro-Hungarian throne in Sarajevo in 1914 and the outbreak of the First World War. When the empire ended after the war, the Habsburgs were expelled and Austria became a republic bounded by its present borders.

Annexed by Nazi Germany in 1938 under the Austrian-born Adolf Hitler, Austria was part of the Third Reich until occupied by Allied forces in 1945. The Allies did not withdraw until 1955, when Austria was recognized internationally as an independent, democratic, and permanently neutral state. Today Austria is governed by a bicameral parliament elected for four-year terms. The president, whose role is essentially ceremonial, is directly elected for a six-year term.

Physical features and land use

Almost two-thirds of Austria consists of the Alps, which sweep west to east across the country in a succession of ranges almost as far as Vienna. Much of the alpine area is characterized by snowfields, glaciers, and snowy peaks. About one-third of the country's population lives in the valleys between the ranges. Many passes such as the Brenner or Timmelsjoch have allowed people to traverse the mountain ranges of the Alps since antiquity. To the north of the Alps, the lower, heavily forested mountains of the Bohemian Massif, which cover about one-tenth of the land area, extend across the borders of the Czech Republic and Slovakia. Lowland areas lie along the eastern end of the Alps extending into Hungary, and in the Danube Valley in the north. Most of Austria's main transport routes traverse this northern "corridor," which links Germany with Vienna and countries farther east.

Almost all the arable land is in the northeast, and is divided between pasture and croplands. Root crops, such as potatoes and cereals, are the principal crops. There are also extensive vineyards which supply a significant wine industry. The main livestock are cattle and pigs.

Industry, commerce, and culture

Austria is not rich in mineral resources, although it has some reserves of oil, iron ore, brown coal, and magnesite—a major resource in chemical industries. It imports most of the raw materials it needs for the manufacturing industries that form the backbone of its economy. More than 70 percent of electricity is generated hydroelectrically. Iron and steelmaking are the principal heavy industries and are large export earners. Aluminum, chemicals, and food processing are also significant. Tourism, based largely on the many alpine ski resorts, but also on the cultural attractions of such cities as Vienna and Salzburg, contributes greatly to the country's economic well-being. There are about 18 million visitors each year.

Austrians are generally conservative in their social attitudes and financial habits. They are savers rather than spenders or investors and the country has a high proportion of its wealth in savings deposits. Much of the country's industry, including iron and steel, and energy production is nationalized and there is a well-developed system of state social services. Most Austrians enjoy a comfortable lifestyle, exceptions being the many refugees from the former Yugoslav republics who have entered the country during the 1990s.

Landscape Liechtenstein, in the background Vaduz Palace (left page bottom). Belvedere Palace in Vienna, one of the political and cultural metropolises in Europe (above). Winter in Zell am See, Austria (right).

Southwestern Europe

Portugal

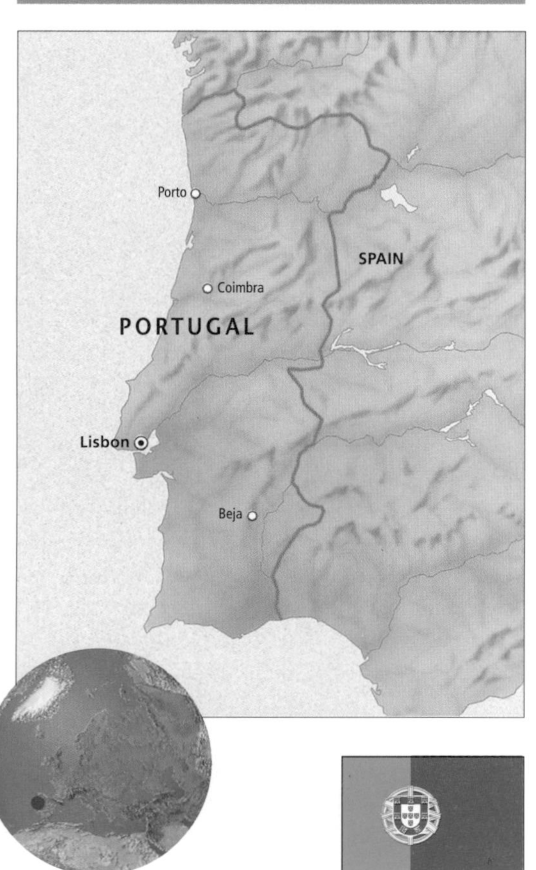

Fact File

OFFICIAL NAME Portuguese Republic

FORM OF GOVERNMENT Republic with single legislative body (Assembly of the Republic)

CAPITAL Lisbon

AREA 92,080 sq km (35,552 sq miles)

TIME ZONE GMT

POPULATION 10,084,000

PROJECTED POPULATION 2015 10,323,000

POPULATION DENSITY 109.5 per sq km (283.6 per sq mile)

LIFE EXPECTANCY 76.1

INFANT MORTALITY (PER 1,000) 5.8

OFFICIAL LANGUAGE Portuguese

LITERACY RATE 87.4 %

RELIGIONS Roman Catholic 97 %, Protestant 1 %, other 2 %

ETHNIC GROUPS Portuguese 98 %, African immigrants from former colonies 2 %

CURRENCY Euro

ECONOMY Services 56 %, industry 39 %, agriculture 5 %

GNP PER CAPITA US$ 18,000

CLIMATE Temperate; cool and rainy in north, warm and dry in south

HIGHEST POINT Ponta de Pico in the Azores 2,351 m (7,713 ft); Serra de Estrela on the mainland, 1,993 m (6,539 ft)

MAP REFERENCE Page 292

Situated at the western edge of the Iberian Peninsula, Portugal is shaped somewhat like a long, narrow rectangle. It has a long Atlantic coastline bordering its western edge, and a much shorter one at its southern extremity. Spain surrounds it on the other two sides.

From the second century BC until the fifth century AD, Portugal was part of the Roman Empire. As the empire collapsed the territory suffered a series of invasions—by Germanic tribes, Visigoths, and in the eighth century by Muslim Moors from northern Africa. The Moors were finally expelled by Christian invaders from Burgundy during the twelfth century and a Burgundian line of monarchs was established. An abortive Castilian attempt to seize the crown in the fourteenth century saw a new dynasty installed under John of Aviz, who reigned as John I. His son, Prince Henry the Navigator, encouraged widespread exploration and the establishment of a vast empire, with colonies in Africa, South America, India, and Southeast Asia. The invasion of Portugal by the Spanish in 1581, even though they were expelled 60 years later, heralded the decline in Portugal's influence. A French invasion in 1807 was reversed three years later when the British expelled the invaders in 1811.

During the nineteenth century widespread poverty and growing resentment at the power of the monarchy culminated in the 1910 revolution, in which the monarchy was overthrown. An army coup in 1926 installed Olivier Salazar as a right-wing dictator. He remained in power until 1968, but his successor, Marcello Caetano, was overthrown by a left-wing army coup in 1974, which eventually led to democratic elections in 1976. Portugal is now a democratic republic with a popularly elected president as head of state, and became a member of the European Union in 1985.

Portugal is divided fairly evenly into its wetter northern and more arid southern regions by the River Tagus. This river flows west into the country from Spain and then takes a southwesterly course toward the Atlantic, entering it at Lisbon (Lisboa). Highland forested areas dominate the north. The highest mountains are in the far north, especially in the east. Here the landscape is characterized by high plateaus punctuated by deep gorges and river valleys, which gradually descend to the western coastal plain. In these mountains are thick forests of both conifers and deciduous trees. South of the Douro River the landscape becomes less rugged and the slopes more gentle until they reach the plain around the Tagus. South of the Tagus, the country is mainly flat or undulating. In the Tagus Valley and further south are forests of cork oaks, the bark of which is used to produce cork for wine or for flooring. In the Algarve, in the far south, a range of hills runs across the country from the Spanish border to its southwestern tip.

Portugal has two self-governing regions in the Atlantic: the nine volcanic islands that constitute the Azores and the volcanic archipelago of two inhabited and two groups of

Farm buildings at the foot of Mt Giestoso in Minho Province, Portugal (left). The village of Ponte da Lima surrounded by terraced fields in Andrao, Portugal (right page bottom). The church S. Martín de la Cortinada in the Ordino Valley, Andorra (right page top).

Portuguese products

Portugal is famous for two products, cork and port. Before modern plastics were invented cork had no equal as a strong, lightweight, buoyant, impermeable, and elastic material. It is the bark of the cork oak, found in Portugal, Spain and the Mediterranean region. Cork was formerly used for lifebelts and floats on fishing nets, and is only slowly being replaced as a stopper for wine bottles by plastics. Its impermeability makes it also an increasingly sought-after raw material for the production of shoe soles. Portugal produces more cork than the rest of the world combined.

The bark is first harvested when a tree is about twenty years old, supplies being taken at subsequent ten-year intervals. The cork is removed by making cuts in the bark using a curved knife. The pieces are soaked in water, scraped, washed, and dried.

Port is a dark red, full-bodied fortified wine named after the town of Porto, from which it has been exported for many years. No one variety of grape is used. The wine's distinctiveness comes from the climate and soil of the mountainous Alto Douro region of north Portugal, and from the methods of cultivation and wine-making used in its production. Especially British capital contributed to the port industry, and the UK was for many years the main destination for the finished product.

uninhabited islets that make up Madeira. In 1987, Portugal signed a treaty to return its last territory, Macau, to China in 1999.

By Western European standards Portugal is still a highly rural society, with agriculture and fishing still employing a significant number of the country's workforce. Many farms, especially the smaller ones that predominate in the north, continue to use traditional methods. Cereals and vegetables are widely cultivated, and wine production, especially port wine from the Douro Valley, is the major agricultural activity. Manufacturing is growing in importance, much of it concerned with processing the country's agricultural products. Paper—based in recent years on fast-growing eucalyptis trees—and cork manufacture, and texiles and footwear, are among the significant industries. Tourism, especially in the warm, southern Algarve region, has greatly expanded, leading to rapid building development and considerable attendant environmental degradation.

Andorra

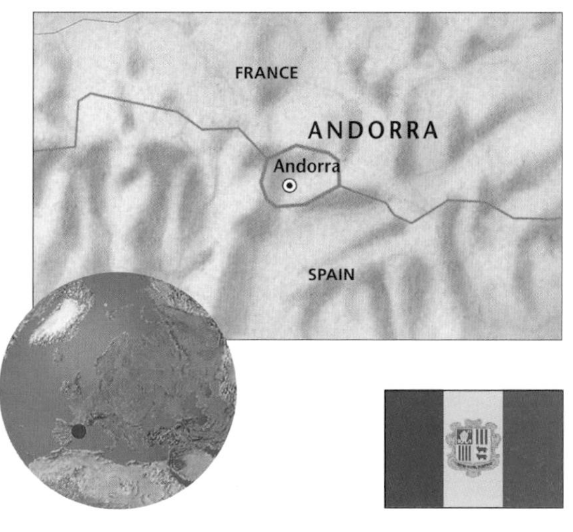

Fact File

OFFICIAL NAME Principality of Andorra

FORM OF GOVERNMENT Co-principality with single legislative body (General Council of the Valleys)

CAPITAL Andorra la Vella

AREA 450 sq km (174 sq miles)

TIME ZONE GMT + 1 hour

POPULATION 68,400

PROJECTED POPULATION 2015 80,000

POPULATION DENSITY 152.0 per sq km (393.1 per sq mile)

LIFE EXPECTANCY 83.5

INFANT MORTALITY (PER 1,000) 4.1

OFFICIAL LANGUAGE Catalan

OTHER LANGUAGES French, Spanish

LITERACY RATE 100 %

RELIGIONS Roman Catholic

ETHNIC GROUPS Spanish 61 %, Andorran 30 %, French 6 %, other 3 %

CURRENCY Euro

ECONOMY Tourism, tobacco production, financial services

GNP PER CAPITA US$ 19,000

CLIMATE Temperate; snowy winter, warm summers

HIGHEST POINT Coma Pedrosa 2,946 m (9,665 ft)

MAP REFERENCE Page 293

The tiny landlocked principality of Andorra sits high in the Pyrenees, between France and Spain. From 1278 Andorra's government was shared between France and Spain. For 300 years it was jointly administered by the Bishop of Urgel in Spain and the Count of Foix in France. In the sixteenth century sovereignty passed to the French king and, after the French Revolution of 1789, to the French head of state. Today the Bishop of Urgel and the French president are official chiefs of state. Since 1993, however, when the first democratic elections were held, authority has been vested in a 28-member General Council of the Valleys. France and Spain are responsible for its defence, and both have a representative on the General Council.

Andorra is mountainous with spectacular peaks. The country is snow-covered for six months in winter, but summers are warm and dry. Two south-flowing branches of the River Valira—the Valira del Nord and the Valira d'Orient—flow through a series of valleys and gorges between ranges. They join in the center of the country and flow as one stream into Spain. The Valira is a major source of hydroelectric power.

About one third of the population are citizens of Andorra: the rest are foreign residents, mainly French and Spanish. Almost two-thirds of the population live in the capital and the cities of Les Escaldes and Encamp. Tourism is the mainstay of the economy, and every year there are more than 12 million visitors, mainly skiers. Goods are duty-free in Andorra. This acts as a magnet to tourists and is vital to the economy, as is the sale of hydroelectricity to neighboring Catalonia. Banking services are significant, but there is little secondary industry, apart from cigarette and cigar making. As well as tobacco, some fruit, vegetables, and other crops are grown on the tiny amount of land that can be cultivated. Many of the village-dwellers are small farmers. Their sheep, cattle, and goats graze in the upland meadows during summer.

Spain

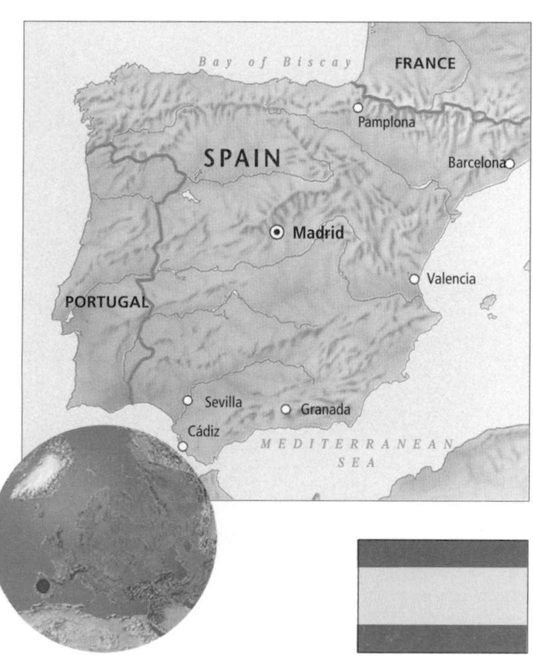

Fact File

OFFICIAL NAME Kingdom of Spain

FORM OF GOVERNMENT Constitutional monarchy with two legislative bodies (Senate and Congress of Deputies)

CAPITAL Madrid

AREA 504,750 sq km (194,884 sq miles)

TIME ZONE GMT + 1 hour

POPULATION 40,077,000

PROJECTED POPULATION 2015 39,018,000

POPULATION DENSITY 79.4 per sq km (205.6 per sq mile)

LIFE EXPECTANCY 79.1

INFANT MORTALITY (PER 1,000) 4.9

OFFICIAL LANGUAGE Spanish (Castilian)

OTHER LANGUAGES Catalan, Galician, Basque

LITERACY RATE 97 %

RELIGIONS Roman Catholic 99 %, other 1 %

ETHNIC GROUPS Ethnically homogenous, but divided into the following cultural/linguistic groups: Spanish 72.3 %, Catalan 16.3 %, Galician 8.1 %, Basque 2.3 %, Gypsy 1 %

CURRENCY Euro

ECONOMY Services 68 %, industry 21 %, agriculture 11 %

GNP PER CAPITA US$ 20,700

CLIMATE Temperate, with mild, wet winters and hot, dry summers; cooler and wetter in northwest

HIGHEST POINT Mulhacén 3,478 m (11,411 ft)

MAP REFERENCE Pages 292–93

Spain occupies the bulk of the Iberian Peninsula at the southwestern tip of Europe. It shares land borders with Portugal to the west, France to the north, and the tiny principality of Andorra, perched high in the Pyrenees on the border with France. To the west and south Spain has short stretches of coastline along the Atlantic Ocean, and to the north a long coast on the Bay of Biscay. Its southern tip is separated from Morocco by the narrow Strait of Gibraltar and its southeastern and eastern coastlines are on the western edge of the Mediterranean Sea.

The Iberian Peninsula had already experienced a long history of human habitation at the end of the third century BC, when the Romans subdued the Celts, Iberians, and Basques who lived there. The region remained a Roman colony until the Visigoths invaded early in the fifth century AD. Over the next three centuries the region became Christianized, but in AD 711 an invasion from Morocco in the south established what would become a flourishing Islamic civilization that lasted for six centuries. In the ninth century Christian invaders from the north gained control of Catalonia in the northeast, thus beginning a slow process of reconquest. By the early thirteenth century, the Moors only retained control of Granada in the south.

The marriage of Ferdinand II of Aragon and Isabella I of Castile in 1469 brought together the two most powerful states on the peninsula, and in 1492, when the Moors were finally expelled from Granada, Spain became a unified country under Catholic rule. Thus began a century of Spanish exploration and conquest in which Spain acquired colonies in Central and South America, as well as the Philippines in Southeast Asia. The Spanish also ruled a large part of Western Europe, including Portugal, the Netherlands, Austria, and parts of Italy.

The beginning of Spain's decline from being a dominant power in the world to a state of secondary importance can be traced to 1588, when Philip II sent his mighty armada of 130 ships in an abortive attempt to invade Protestant England. This defeat by the English spelled the end of Spain's maritime dominance. By 1714 Spain had lost all its European possessions and by 1826 it had been forced to surrender all its American colonies except Cuba and Puerto Rico.

A small farm in the province of Navarra (below). Fertile countryside in Catalonia (right).

Timeline

780,000 BP Stone tools used by hominids in northern Spain; classified as *Homo heidelbergensis*

280,000 BP Caves inhabited by *Homo Sapiens* at Atapuerca, Burgos, northern Spain, as well as Torralba and Ambrona

10,000 BC Images of bison painted on the walls of a deep cave at Altamira, northern Spain, probably used for ceremonies

5500 BC Sheep and wheat grown by early farmers along the western Mediterranean

3200 BC Larger communities develop around southern and southwestern Spain and Portugal, such as Los Millares, Almeria

3000 BC Iberian people, including Gauls and Basques, move in from the north to found towns on Iberian Peninsula

1000 BC Phoenician traders from eastern Mediterranean begin to colonize southern and eastern coasts of Spain

400 BC Carthaginians of North Africa take over much of Spain

218 BC After defeat of Carthaginians in the Second Punic War, Spain slowly becomes part of the Roman Empire

AD 476 Romans rename peninsula Hispania; lose control to Germanic tribes who occupy whole territory by 573

AD 711 Moors invade from North Africa bringing Islam and building palaces and mosques

962–1212 Christians push back Moors; Moors confined to Granada

1469 Marriage of Ferdinand of Aragon and Isabella of Castile brings together both kingdoms—almost all of modern Spain

1492 Columbus sails on first voyage in the service of Ferdinand and Isabella; Spanish take last Moorish stronghold, Granada

French revolutionary forces invaded Spain in 1794. They were defeated in 1814 and the Spanish Bourbon monarchy was restored. During the nineteenth and much of the twentieth century Spain has been destabilized by political turmoil and a series of military revolts and wars. Quarrels about the succession to the crown led to the removal of Isabella II from the throne in 1868, the declaration of a republic in 1873, and a military uprising in 1874 that restored the monarchy. In 1898 Spain and the United States fought a war at the end of which a defeated Spain was forced to cede its colonies of Cuba, Puerto Rico, and the Philippines to its adversary.

Spain remained neutral in both world wars, but was wracked by a bitter civil war from 1936 to 1939. Universal adult suffrage was introduced in 1931 and in 1936 the election of a Republican government with socialist leanings prompted an army officer, Francisco Franco, to lead a revolt against the government. With the support of right-wing Spanish forces and of Fascist Italy and Nazi Germany, and after the loss of 750,000 Spanish lives, Franco's forces were eventually victorious and Franco was installed as head of state. His dictatorial regime lasted until his death in 1975. Almost immediately the monarchy was restored and in June 1977 the first parliamentary elections since 1936 were held. In December 1978 a referendum approved a new constitution in which Spain was declared a parliamentary democracy with a monarch as head of state. There are two houses of parliament, both elected by universal adult suffrage for maximum terms of four years.

Physical features and land use

More than half Spain's land area is occupied by a central plateau, the Meseta, which has an average elevation of 700 m (2,300 ft). Much of the Meseta is harsh and barren. It is surrounded by mountain ranges to the north, northeast, south, and southwest, and is traversed by a low mountain range, the Sistema Central. The plateau is drained by three rivers—the Douro to the north of the Sistema Central, and the Tagus and Guadiana to its south—all of these rivers flow westward to the Atlantic.

In the far northeast of the country, between the Sistema Ibérico (a range that fringes the Meseta on the northeast and the Pyrenees to the north) is an extensive lowland area through which the Ebro River, which rises in the Basque country, flows south to the Mediterranean. In the southwest of Spain, beyond the Sierra Morena Range at the Meseta's southwestern edge, the Guadalquivir River drains another extensive lowlying region. In the far southeast is a coastal range, the Sistema Pinibético, which contains the snow-covered peaks of the Sierra Nevada, including the country's highest mountain, Mulhacén.

The Ramblas in Barcelona (above). Storks are among the many bird species found in southern Spain (right).

About one-tenth of Spain is heavily forested. Most of the forests are in the north and northwest, where the weather is wetter and more humid than in the center and south. Beech and oak predominate. Despite the fact that much of the country is arid and covered with low-growing scrub and water is a scarce resource, crops are widely grown. The most productive areas are in the north of the country, especially in the valley of the Ebro. There are significant crops of cereals, vegetables, fruits, and olives.

Spain is one of Europe's main producers of wine and there are 1.5 million hectares (3.7 million acres) of vineyards, mainly in the south and east. About one-fifth of Spain is pastureland, though cattle and dairying are largely confined to the north and pig farming to the southwest. Sheep are widespread on the Meseta, while goats graze in many of the more barren regions.

Industry and commerce

Although Spain has a wide range of mineral resources, it is not rich in any of them and imports the oil and gas needed to fuel its industries. These industries are concentrated towards the north, mainly around the major cities of Madrid and Barcelona. Spain is a major manufacturer of motor vehicles and a number of multinational companies have car manufacturing plants in parts of northern and central Spain. Steelmaking and shipbuilding are among the most significant heavy industries. There are important shipyards at Barcelona, on the Mediterranean coast, La Coruña in the far northwest, and Cádiz in the southwest. Chemical manufacture and fishing are also major industries. Spain has one of the world's largest fishing fleets, although its activities have been curtailed in recent years by European Union restrictions in response to serious fish stock depletions. About one in ten of Spain's workers are employed in the tourist industry.

While Spain is still a predominantly Catholic country, the influence of the Church has waned in recent years. This is reflected in the fact that Spain has one of the lowest birth rates in Europe, even though divorce is still relatively rare. Although most Spaniards enjoy a reasonably high standard of living, unemployment has been alarmingly high in recent years.

REGIONS

Baleares • Basque Country
Canary Islands • Cantabria
Castilla-La Mancha • Castilla y León
Catalonia • Ceuta and Melilla
Extremadura • Galicia • La Rioja
Madrid • Murcia • Navarra • Valencia

1516 King Charles I, grandson of Ferdinand and Isabella, is first Habsburg to rule Spain; becomes Holy Roman Emperor in 1519

1556 Charles's son becomes King Philip II; height of Spanish Empire in Americas, Europe, and Africa

1808 French invade Spain; Spanish resistance grows, French expelled in Peninsular War with the help of Great Britain (1814)

1820 Spanish troops refuse to sail to reconquer American colonies; revolt spreads, crushed with help of French troops

1860 Population begins to decline for almost a century due to emigration

1931 King Alfonso XIII flees after elections show preference for a republic; Spain briefly a democracy—deep political divisions

1936–38 Spanish Civil War; victorious Nationalists under General Franco enter Madrid in 1939

1960s Rapid industrialization, expansion of economy and growth in tourist resort development along Mediterranean

1970 Population grows following industrialization. More than 1 million immigrants in 10 years, almost half illegal

1973 Basque separatists (ETA) assassinate Prime Minister Carrero Blanco in Madrid

1975 On the death of Franco, Spain adopts political reform agenda despite accession of Juan Carlos (grandson of Alfonso XIII) as king

1976 Government under Prime Minister Suarez liberalizes politics, permits new parties to participate in elections (1977)

1980 The 2.5 million Basque people of northern Spain are granted limited autonomy

1986 Prime Minister González embarks on more economic development; Spain joins European Community (EC)

1995 Population more than 39 million; Spain lifts passport controls with EC nations

Italy

Fact file

OFFICIAL NAME Italian Republic

FORM OF GOVERNMENT Republic with two legislative bodies (Senate and Chamber of Deputies)

CAPITAL Rome

AREA 301,230 sq km (116,305 sq miles)

TIME ZONE GMT + 1 hour

POPULATION 57,715,000

PROJECTED POPULATION 2015 55,239,000

POPULATION DENSITY 191.6 per sq km (496.2 per sq mile)

LIFE EXPECTANCY 79.3

INFANT MORTALITY (PER 1,000) 5.8

OFFICIAL LANGUAGE Italian

OTHER LANGUAGES German, French, Greek, Albanian

LITERACY RATE 98 %

RELIGIONS Roman Catholic 98 %, other 2 %

ETHNIC GROUPS Italian, 94 %; German-, French-, Slovene- and Albanian-Italian communities 6 %

CURRENCY Euro

ECONOMY Services 71 %, industry 20 %, agriculture 9 %

GNP PER CAPITA US$ 25,000

CLIMATE Temperate; north has cool, wet winters and warm, dry summers; south has mild winters and hot, dry summers

HIGHEST POINT Mont Blanc 4,807 m (15,771 ft)

MAP REFERENCE Pages 294–95

Situated in southern central Europe, the Italian mainland consists of a long peninsula that juts out into the Mediterranean Sea. Shaped roughly like a long, high-heeled boot, this land mass is bordered to the north by Switzerland and Austria, to the west by France, and to the east by Slovenia. At the southwestern tip of the peninsula, the narrow Strait of Messina separates the toe of the boot from the large Italian island of Sicily, while further west in the Mediterranean, separated from the mainland by the Tyrrhenian Sea and sitting just south of the French island of Corsica, is the island of Sardinia, also part of Italy. About 70 other small islands, scattered mainly around the coasts of Sicily and Sardinia and off the western coast of the mainland, make up the rest of present-day Italy. The peninsula's eastern coastline is washed by the waters of the Adriatic Sea, across which lies the coast of Croatia.

History

Italy's capital, Rome, situated in central western Italy, was for 800 years, from about 400 BC, the hub of the mighty Roman Empire. At the height of their powers in the first and second centuries AD the Romans controlled the whole of the Italian Peninsula and vast swathes of Europe. Their empire stretched as far as Britain in the north, the Iberian Peninsula in the west, into Egypt in North Africa and eastward as far as the Persian Gulf. Italy became Christianized after the conversion of the Roman Emperor Constantine in AD 313. The sacking of Rome by the Visigoths in AD 410 precipitated a series of subsequent invasions which resulted, over the centuries, in the fragmentation of Italy into a number of states ruled by different powers. For some time all of Italy came under the control of the eastern Roman Empire, based in Constantinople. The Franks, under Charlemagne, gained control of much of northern Italy at the end of the eighth century AD, and in the eleventh century the Normans invaded Sicily, which led to the creation of a kingdom based around the southern city of Naples.

In the later Middle Ages a number of powerful city-states emerged in central and northern Italy, the most notable being Florence, Pisa, Venice, and Genoa. From the fourteenth century, these states, especially Florence, promoted a great cultural revival which involved a blossoming of artistic, musical, literary, and scientific activity. This revival, which gradually spread through most of Europe, is now known as the Renaissance.

France, Spain, and Austria vied for domination of different parts of Italy between the fifteenth and the eighteenth centuries. Most of Italy fell to Napoleon's armies in 1796–97, but after his downfall in 1815 Italy was again fragmented, with Austria the dominant power in the north. A series of uprisings during the 1820s and 1830s gave rise to the movement known as the Risorgimento (resurrection), which eventually led to the total unification of Italy and the installation of Victor Emmanuel II, the King of Sardinia, as King of Italy in 1861. During the next half-century Italy acquired a number of overseas territories including Eritrea, part of Somalia, and some Greek islands.

Although officially allied to Germany, Italy at first remained neutral in the First World War and later joined the Allied side. In 1919 Benito Mussolini, a former socialist, founded the Fascist Party as a bulwark against communism. In 1922 he seized power, setting up a dictatorship. Embarking on a policy of foreign conquest, Italy invaded Ethiopia in 1935. Fascist Italy joined the side of Nazi Germany in the Second World War but in 1943 it was invaded by Allied troops and subsequently declared war on its former German ally. Dismissed from the Italian government, Mussolini was installed by Germany as head of a puppet government in northern Italy but he was captured and executed by partisans in 1945.

After the war, Italy was stripped of its foreign territories. A referendum in 1946 resulted in the abolition of the monarchy and the establishment of a democratic republic. Since then, government in Italy has been wracked by instability as changing allegiances and coalitions have created a succession of short-lived governments. In 1993 a referendum approved a plan to simplify Italy's complex electoral system. Since 1994 three-quarters of the members of Italy's two houses of parliament have been elected by a simple majority of votes, while the rest are elected by proportional representation. The president, whose duties are largely ceremonial, is elected for a seven-year term. Both houses are elected for a maximum of five years.

Timeline

900 BC Etruscan civilization founded between Arno and Tiber Rivers by people arriving from the east; lasts till c. 200 BC

568 BC Langobardi (Lombards) seize much of northern Italy from Roman Empire

6th century BC Under rule of Etruscan kings Rome grows from village to wealthy city

AD 79 Mt Vesuvius near Naples erupts, buries city of Pompeii in lava and ash, and Herculaneum under mud

476 Germanic leader Odoacer defeats last Roman Emperor; ends dominance of western sector of Roman Empire

800 Pope Leo III crowns Charlemagne Emperor of the Romans

962 Otto the Great crowned Emperor of the Holy Roman Empire

1000 Rise of city-states such as Florence, Venice, Genoa, and Pisa which have strong commercial and cultural identities

c. 1300 Renaissance begins. Interest flourishes in arts, sciences, and literature as well as philosophy, politics, and religion

1345 Black Death, bubonic plague, kills more than one-quarter of the population

1519 King Charles I of Spain becomes Holy Roman Emperor. Seizes much of Italy including Rome and Milan from France

1663 Volcano Mt Etna erupts destroying much of the town of Catania, northeast Sicily

1796 Napole[...] Bonaparte invac[...] north Italy, setting independent repu[...] lics. Interest in Ital[...] independence gro[...]

Physical features and land use

Most of Italy is mountainous, with a central range, the Appenines, sweeping down the length of the peninsula and extending into Sicily, where the still-active volcanic peak of Mount Etna soars to a height of 3,323 m (10,902 ft) above sea level. Further north, near Naples, the active Mount Vesuvius offers evidence of the volcanic origins of Italy's mountains. The Appenines, which are rich in limestone, reach heights of almost 3,000 m (10,000 ft) in the Gran Sasso Range, east of Rome. The slopes of the Appenines are covered with thin soils, which in some places provide reasonable pasture. In the valleys there are some extensive stretches of arable land. At the far northwestern tip of the Italian Peninsula the Appenines merge with the Alps, which are generally higher than the Appenines and which arch right across the north of Italy, forming natural boundaries with the countries of Switzerland, Austria, and France. In the southern extremities of the Alps are a series of large, spectacular lakes which include the much visited Lago Maggiore, Lago di Como, and Lago di Garda. These lakes and the rivers that feed into them are the source of the hydroelectricity which supplies about half the electricity needs of industrialized northern Italy.

In the northeast of the country, enclosed by the Alps to the north and the west and the Appenines to the south, and stretching eastwards as far as the Adriatic coast, is the country's largest lowland region, known as the Plain of Lombardy. Drained by the River Po, which flows from west to east across the widest part of the country, this area is the most fertile as well as the most heavily industrialized and populous part of Italy. About two-fifths of Italy's crops are grown here. Agriculture is also extensive on the coastal plains on each side of the Appenines. Farms are mainly small. Crops include potatoes, wheat, maize, olives, and other vegetables as well as a wide range of citrus and stone fruits. Italy produces more wine than any other country and there are extensive vineyards, most particularly in the Chianti region in Tuscany. Sheep, pigs, and cattle are the principal livestock.

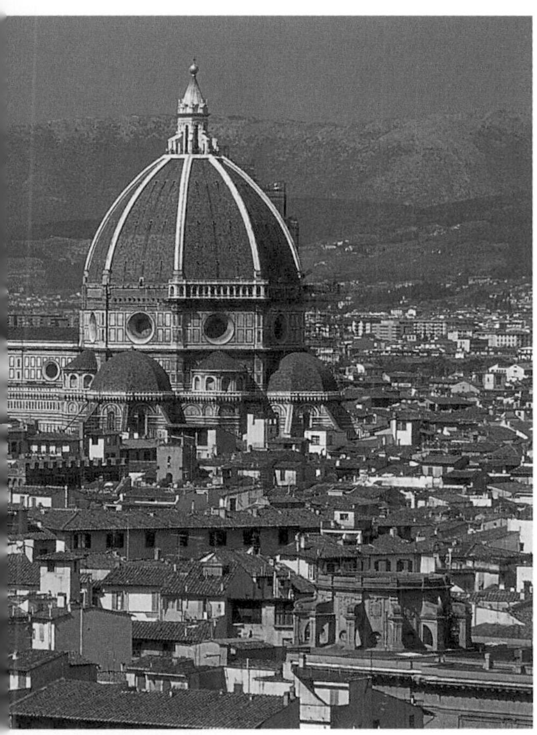

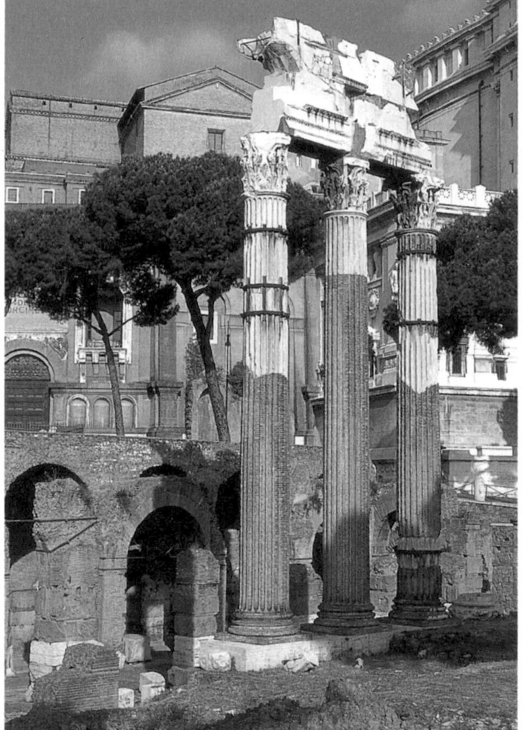

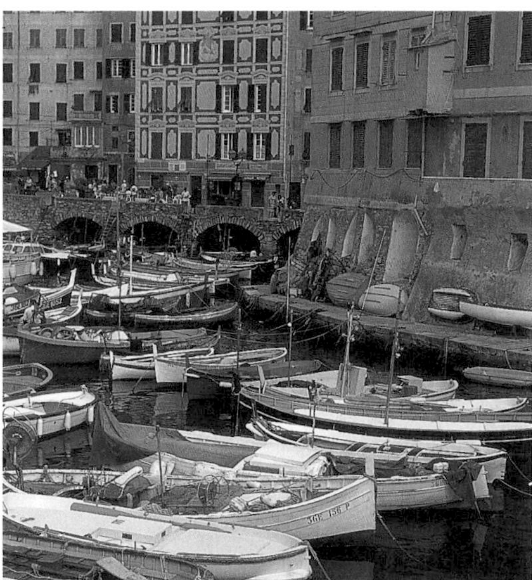

The Forum Romanum, once the centerpiece of the Roman Empire, Rome (above left). Fishing boats in the harbor of Camogli in Liguria, northern Italy (above right). The Tower of Pisa (below right). The rooftops of Florence, including the cathedral, seen from Piazzale Michelangelo (below left).

Industry, commerce, and culture

Apart from marble in the south, for which it is famous, and some oil deposits in Sicily, Italy is not well endowed with mineral resources and imports most of the energy needed by its highly developed industrial sector. This is concentrated overwhelmingly in the north of the country—although Naples, Bari, and Taranto in the south and Rome in the center have a certain amount of heavy industry—and is based around such cities as Milan, Turin, and Genoa. The building of cars, aircraft, and other transport equipment are major industries, as are tool, textile, clothing, and chemical manufacture.

Italy's manufacturing sector, which was heavily subsidized by the state, developed largely in the half-century since the Second World War, before which the economy was based predominantly on agriculture. It now employs about a fifth of the country's workforce. Tourism is an important source of income, with about 30 million people visiting Italy every year.

There is a great divide in Italy between the high living standards of the industrialized, affluent north and the much lower living standards of the largely undeveloped south, especially in Calabria in the far south. In the south unemployment is chronically high, investment is hard to attract, poverty is widespread, and for many people crime offers the best means of survival.

REGIONS

Abruzzi • Basilicata • Calabria
Campania • Emilia-Romagna
Friuli-Venezia Giulia • Lazio • Liguria
Lombardy • Marche • Molise
Piedmont • Puglia • Sardinia
Sicily • Trentino-Alto Adige • Tuscany
Umbria • Valle d'Aosta • Veneto

1814 Napoleon defeated by European powers; under Congress of Vienna most of Italy returns to Austrian rule

1858 French troops help Kingdom of Sardinia to push back Austrian troops, regaining most of northern Italy

1860 Garibaldi's redshirts regain control of Sicily; eventually they take all southern Italy, including Naples

1861 King Victor Emmanuel announces Kingdom of Italy to include entire peninsula except Rome, Venice, and San Marino

1908 Earthquake in Messina, Sicily, kills 120,000 people

1915 Italy joins Allies in First World War

1922 Mussolini becomes leader and the Fascist movement grows

1939 Start of Second World War; Italy enters on Germany's side nine months later, soon after the fall of France, in June 1940

1940 Italy's forces defeated in Eritrea, Ethiopia, and Greece; Mussolini overthrown, but reinstalled by Germans

1943 Allies invade Italy; Italian prime minister signs armistice with Allies; Italy declares war on Germany

1960s Rapid postwar industrialization brings prosperity to northern cities but the south remains largely agricultural and poor

1980 Earthquake in southern Italy kills more than 4,500 and leaves 400,000 homeless

1997 Earthquake in central Italy causes severe damage in St Francis' Dome in Assisi with its famous Giotto frescoes. Already in **2002** restoration of the paintings is completed

San Marino

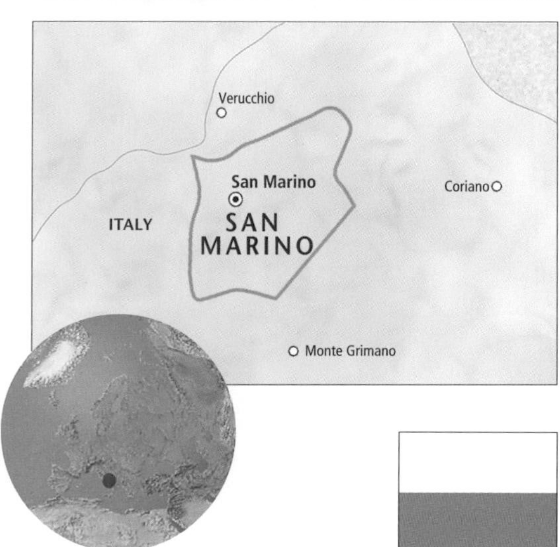

Fact File

Official name Republic of San Marino

Form of government Republic with single legislative body (Great and General Council)

Capital San Marino

Area 60 sq km (23 sq miles)

Time zone GMT + 1 hour

Population 27,700

Projected population 2015 31,000

Population density 461.7 per sq km (1,204.35 per sq mile)

Life expectancy 81.3

Infant mortality (per 1,000) 6.1

Official language Italian

Literacy rate 96 %

Religions Roman Catholic 95 %, other 5 %

Ethnic groups Sanmarinesi 87.1 %, Italian 12.4 %, other 0.5 %

Currency Euro

Economy Services 58 %, industry 40 %, agriculture 2 %

GNP per capita US$ 34,600

Climate Temperate, with mild winters and warm summers

Highest point Monte Titano 739 m (2,425 ft)

Map reference Page 294

Completely surrounded by Italian territory, most of the tiny state of San Marino sits on the slopes of Mount Titano in the Appenine Mountains, 20 km (12 miles) inland from the city of Rimini on the Adriatic coast of northern Italy. The republic takes its name from St Marinus who, so legend has it, arrived there with a group of followers in the fourth century AD and established a settlement. This makes it arguably the world's oldest surviving republic. Records of its existence can be traced back to the twelfth century. It became one of the many mini-states on the Italian Peninsula and was accorded papal recognition in 1631. The Sanmarinesi, as its inhabitants are known, offered refuge to Giuseppe Garibaldi when he passed through in 1849, pursued by his enemies. However, when the newly unified state of Italy was declared in 1861 the Sanmarinesi declined to join. San Marino fought with Italy in the First World War. In the Second World War it began by supporting Fascist Italy but later changed sides and was invaded by Germany. San Marino is a democratic republic with elections held every five years. Two Capitani regenti who are elected by the parliament and are in office for six months serve as heads of state. There is a single legislative body that consists of sixty members.

Square in San Marino with the old governmental building (above). St Peter's Square in Vatican City, seen from the roof of the basilica (below). One of Malta's megalithic temples, built more than 5,000 years ago (right page bottom).

This picturesque little country is centered on the fortified medieval town of San Marino, where most of the population lives. On the lower slopes, beneath the rugged limestone peak, are thick forests, expanses of pastureland and a string of ancient villages. Almost one-fifth of the land is used for agriculture. Cereals, olives, and vines are cultivated and sheep and goats are raised. Cheeses and wine are its principal agricultural products.

Since 1862 San Marino has had a friendship and cooperation treaty with Italy. It also shares its currency—since 2001 the Euro according to the Maastricht Treaty—and enjoys a standard of living roughly equivalent to that of its neighbor. About one in five Sanmarinesi workers are in the tourism industry, which caters to more than 2 million visitors each year, although many do not stay overnight but rather stay on the Adriatic Sea and take excursions into the ancient republic. Winemaking, textiles, and ceramics are significant industries. Even more important is the sale of the country's distinctive postage stamps, which are sought by collectors and account for up to ten percent of the country's revenues.

Vatican City

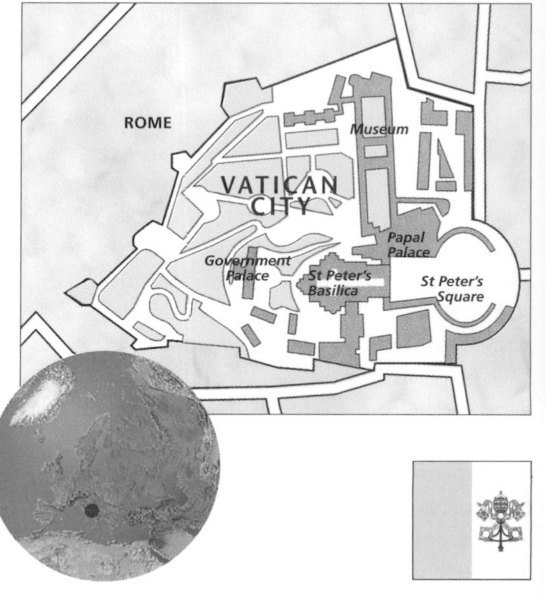

Fact File

Official name Vatican City State (Holy See)

Form of government Monarchical-sacerdotal state with single legislative body (Pontifical Commission)

Capital Vatican City

Area 0.44 sq km (0.16 sq miles)

Time zone GMT + 1 hour

Population 900

Projected population 2015 1,000

Population density 2,045.5 per sq km (5,625 per sq mile)

Life expectancy Not available

Infant mortality (per 1,000) Not available

Official languages Italian, Latin

Literacy rate 100 %

Religion Roman Catholic 100 %

Ethnic groups International

Currency Euro

Economy Services 100 %

GNP per capita Not available

Climate Temperate, with mild winters and hot summers

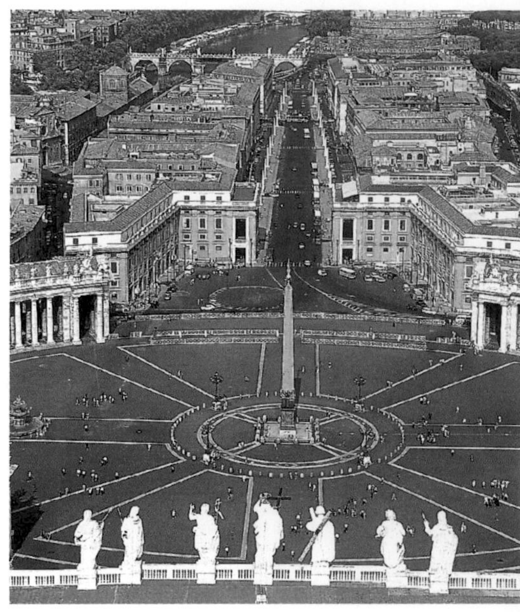

HIGHEST POINT Unnamed location 75 m (246 ft)

MAP REFERENCE Page 295

Occupying a hill in the city of Rome on the western bank of the Tiber, and including the pope's summer residence at Castel Gandolfo southeast of Rome, and ten churches throughout Rome as well, Vatican City is the world's smallest state, and probably its most homogeneous. Its population is 100 percent Catholic, and it is the home of the pope, the spiritual head of the Roman Catholic Church, and several hundred clergy and Catholic lay people, all employees of the Vatican.

Vatican City is all that remains of the former Papal States, which from the fourteenth to the nineteenth centuries expanded from a palace on the present site to cover an area—with changing borders—of almost 45,000 sq km (17,000 sq miles) which was a large part of mainland Italy. During the Risorgimento ("resurrection"), which resulted in the unification of Italy in the 1860s, most of this area was absorbed into the new Italian state headed by King Victor Emmanuael II. From 1870 until 1929, neither the Church nor successive Italian governments recognized each other's sovereignty over the area, which the Church refused to relinquish to the state. In 1929, however, Pope Leo XI and Mussolini concluded an agreement—the Lateran Treaty—under which the independence of the Vatican City State, and the pope's temporal sovereignty over it, was recognized in return for the Church's recognition of the kingdom of Italy. Under this treaty, Catholicism was also recognized as the state religion of Italy.

This provision, along with a number of other privileges enjoyed by the Church in Italy, was removed under a subsequent Church-state agreement, known as a "concordat", signed in 1984. Vatican City now has diplomatic relations with more than 100 countries, although it is the only remaining independent country not represented in the United Nations. It has the pope as its head of state, while responsibility for administration of the area is vested in a Commission of Cardinals. The roles of secretary of state, chief of staff, and foreign minister are filled by senior members of the clergy.

Surrounded by medieval walls, Vatican City contains the huge St Peter's Basilica, built between 1506 and 1626 by a number of architects, including Michelangelo and Bernini. Pilgrims come to visit the basilica in vast numbers throughout the year, but particularly to celebrate Christmas and Easter. Visitors also come to see the richly endowed Vatican Museums, which include the renowned Sistine Chapel (the personal chapel of the popes) in the Vatican Palace. Parklands cover most of Vatican City.

Vatican City has its own radio station, publishes a daily newspaper, and issues its own stamps and coins. It also has an army—the 100-strong Swiss Guard—which is responsible for maintaining security. Vatican state finances depend on voluntary contributions, interest on extensive investments, and on the income derived from millions of tourists.

Malta

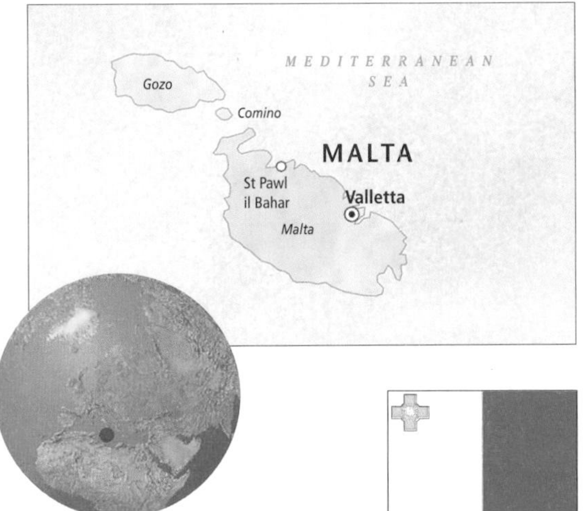

Fact File

OFFICIAL NAME Republic of Malta

FORM OF GOVERNMENT Republic with single legislative body (House of Representatives)

CAPITAL Valletta

AREA 320 sq km (124 sq miles)

TIME ZONE GMT + 1 hour

POPULATION 398,000

PROJECTED POPULATION 2015 411,000

POPULATION DENSITY 1,243.8 per sq km (3,209.7 per sq mile)

LIFE EXPECTANCY 78.3

INFANT MORTALITY (PER 1,000) 5.7

OFFICIAL LANGUAGES Maltese, English

LITERACY RATE 88.8 %

RELIGIONS Roman Catholic 98 %, other 2 %

ETHNIC GROUPS Mixed Arab, Sicilian, French, Spanish, Italian and English

CURRENCY Maltese lira

ECONOMY Government 37 %, services 26 %, manufacturing 22 %, teaching programs 9 %, construction 4 %, agriculture 2 %

GNP PER CAPITA US$ 17,000

CLIMATE Temperate, with mild, wet winters and hot, dry summers

HIGHEST POINT Dingli Cliffs 245 m (804 ft)

MAP REFERENCE Pages 361, 362

The Republic of Malta consists of an archipelago of three inhabited islands—Malta, Gozo, and Comino—and three tiny uninhabited islands, which are little more than rocky outcrops. They are situated in the center of the Mediterranean Sea 93 km (58 miles) south of Sicily. Malta is the largest and most populous of the islands. It contains the capital, Valletta, the country's fifth largest city, picturesquely situated on a promontory between two harbors, and the four larger cities of Birkirkara, Qormi, Hamrun, and Sliema. Successive civilizations have recognized the importance of Malta's position and the advantages of its many harbors. It was occupied successively by the Phoenicians, the Greeks, and the Romans. In the ninth century AD, when it was part of the Byzantine Empire, it was conquered by Arabs but fell two centuries later to Sicily and then in 1282 to Spain. In 1530 the Spanish king gave Malta to the Knights of St John, a religious order, which built and fortified the town of Valletta and occupied the island of Malta until it was seized by Napoleon in 1798. Britain took the island in 1800 and held it until 1947, when the country was granted self-government as a parliamentary democracy. In 1964 Malta gained full independence. In 1987 Malta created a new constitution that declared its political neutrality, a feature not affected by its entry into the EU in 2004.

The three inhabited islands are mostly flat—although the island of Malta is undulating in places—with spectacular rocky coastlines. There is little natural vegetation and there are no forests or major rivers. Low rainfall, poor drainage, a limestone base and a hot climate all contribute to the paucity of the islands' shallow soils, which, however, support a range of cereal and vegetable crops as well as substantial vineyards.

Apart from limestone for building, Malta has virtually no mineral resources and is heavily dependent on imported materials. It has no natural sources of energy and produces only one-fifth of its population's food needs. Tourism is the mainstay of the economy. Every year about a million visitors, mainly from the United Kingdom, arrive to enjoy its beaches, its historic towns, and its rugged scenery. Ship repairs and clothing and textile manufacture are other significant industries. The average income is low by Western standards and Maltese residents are among the least affluent of Western Europeans.

Southeastern Europe

Slovenia

Fact File

OFFICIAL NAME Republic of Slovenia

FORM OF GOVERNMENT Republic with two legislative bodies (National Assembly and National Council)

CAPITAL Ljubljana

AREA 20,256 sq km (7,821 sq miles)

TIME ZONE GMT + 1 hour

POPULATION 1,933,000

PROJECTED POPULATION 2015 1,926,000

POPULATION DENSITY 95.4 per sq km (247.2 per sq mile)

LIFE EXPECTANCY 75.3

INFANT MORTALITY (PER 1,000) 4.5

OFFICIAL LANGUAGE Slovenian

OTHER LANGUAGES Serbian, Croatian, Hungarian, Italian

LITERACY RATE 99 %

RELIGIONS Roman Catholic 96 %, Muslim 1 %, other 3 %

ETHNIC GROUPS Slovene 91 %, Croatian 3 %, Serbian 2 %, Muslim 1 %, other 3 %

CURRENCY Tolar

ECONOMY Services 52 %, industry 46 %, agriculture 2 %

GNP PER CAPITA US$ 18,000

CLIMATE Temperate, with colder winters and hotter summers inland

HIGHEST POINT Mt Triglav 2,864 m (9,396 ft)

MAP REFERENCE Page 294

This former Yugoslav republic shares borders with Italy to the west, Austria to the north, Hungary to the east, and Croatia to the south. The port of Koper on Slovenia's short coastline on the Gulf of Venice is an important transit point for products from Austria and much of Central Europe. First settled by Slavic peoples in the sixth century AD, Slovenia became a Hungarian province in the eleventh century. Austria gained control of the region in the sixteenth century, and Slovenia was later absorbed into the Austro-Hungarian Empire. At the end of the First World War it became part of the Kingdom of the Croats, Serbs, and Slovenes, which in 1929 became Yugoslavia. Like the rest of Yugoslavia, it was occupied by Axis powers during the Second World War. In 1991 it became the first Yugoslav republic to declare its independence. This prompted a military response from the Yugoslav army, which, however, withdrew its forces after a ten-day conflict. According to its constitution of 1991, Slovenia is a democratic republic with a directly elected president and a prime minister as head of the government. Since 2004 it has been a member of the EU.

Slovenia is mountainous, with the highest and most spectacular regions in the Slovenian Alps near the border with Austria in the northwest. Almost half the land is densely forested. There are areas of lowland in the west near the coast and much of the center and east of the country consists of undulating plains. The most fertile region is in the east, where the Drava River flows southward across the Pannonian Plain into Croatia.

Slovenia's tourist industry, based on its alpine scenery and its coastal beaches, remains important, although it has been adversely affected by conflicts in the region. Almost half the workforce is employed in mining and manufacturing industries. Metallurgy and heavy machine manufacture, including trucks and cars, are prominent among these. Textile manufacture is also widespread. The main mineral resource is coal and there are large mercury deposits in the northwest. Dairy farming and pig raising are the main agricultural activities. Slovenia's nuclear power plant, which supplies one-third of the country's electricity, is a cause of some international tension, especially with Austria.

Croatia

Fact File

OFFICIAL NAME Republic of Croatia

FORM OF GOVERNMENT Republic with two legislative bodies (House of Districts and House of Assembly)

CAPITAL Zagreb

AREA 56,538 sq km (21,829 sq miles)

TIME ZONE GMT + 1 hour

POPULATION 4,391,000

PROJECTED POPULATION 2015 4,622,000

POPULATION DENSITY 77.7 per sq km (201.2 per sq mile)

LIFE EXPECTANCY 74.1

INFANT MORTALITY (PER 1,000) 7.1

OFFICIAL LANGUAGE Croatian

OTHER LANGUAGES Serbian, languages of the minorities

LITERACY RATE 97 %

RELIGIONS Catholic 76.5 %, Orthodox 11.1 %, Slavic Muslim 1.2 %, Protestant 0.4 %, others 10.8 %

ETHNIC GROUPS Croat 78 %, Serb 12 %, Muslim 0.9 %, Hungarian 0.5 %, Slovene 0.5 %, others 8.1 %

Lake Bled in Slovenia (left page). Dubrovnik old town in Croatia that was heavily damaged during the Serbian-Croat War (right).

Currency Kuna

Economy Services 64.6 %, industry 31.1 %, agriculture 4.3 %

GNP per capita US$ 8,800

Climate Temperate; cold winters and warm summers inland, cooler and more temperate along coast

Highest point Dinara 1,830 m (6,004 ft)

Map reference Pages 294, 296

Croatia wraps around the northern and western extremities of Bosnia and Herzegovina, allowing its neighbor a tiny 20 km (12 mile) toehold south of its almost 600 km (375 mile) stretch of coastline on the Adriatic Sea. It also shares borders with Slovenia to the northwest, Hungary to the northeast, and Serbia and Montenegro to the east. The state of Croatia emerged in the ninth century AD, peopled by Slavic immigrants from present-day Ukraine. In 1091 it was invaded by Hungary with which it remained united until 1526 when most of the country came under the rule of the Ottoman Turks. In 1699 the Turks were driven out by the Austrian Habsburgs. Once again Croatia came under Hungarian rule, but with its own monarch. In 1867 Croatia became part of the Austro-Hungarian Empire. In 1918 it declared its independence and joined with its neighboring states to form the Kingdom of Serbs, Croats, and Slovenes—the precursor of the state of Yugoslavia. Serbian domination of the new country provoked agitation by Croation separatists, and in 1939 this led to Croatia's being declared a self-governing region within Yugoslavia. During the Second World War, the invading Axis powers proclaimed Croatia an independent state and installed a Fascist government intent on eliminating Serbs, Jews, and all political oppostion. At the war's end, Croatia once again became a republic in the reformed state of Yugoslavia. In 1991, after a referendum, Croatia declared its independence and was then plunged into civil war as Croatian Serbs, supported by the Yugoslav army, sought to incorporate Croatia into a "Greater Serbia." The war ended officially in 1992, but hostilities between Serbs and Croats continued until 1995.

Along Croatia's spectacular Dalmatian coast are scattered about 600 small rocky islands, many of them former alpine peaks, isolated by rises in sea level. Further inland in the north, the Pannonian Plain, traversed by the Drava, Danube, and Sava Rivers, is a fertile region centered around Zagreb, which is the hub of the country's agricultural production. A little more than one-fifth of the land is devoted to agriculture and about one-fifth of the population is directly involved in agricultural production. Cereal crops, fruit, and tobacco are widely grown and sheep are raised. Timber is a significant resource, and reserves of minerals, coal and iron are mined. Civil and other regional wars in the 1990s have seriously impeded Croatia's transition to a market economy and cut industrial production. The tourist industry, once of great economic significance, had largely ceased to exist in the early 1990s. However, following huge efforts to eliminate the destructions of war it is on the rise again.

Bosnia and Herzegovina

Fact File

Official name Republic of Bosnia and Herzegovina

Form of government Federal republic with two legislative bodies (Chamber of Municipalities and Chamber of Citizens)

Capital Sarajevo

Area 51,233 sq km (19,781 sq miles)

Time zone GMT + 1 hour

Population 3,965,000

Projected population 2015 4,279,000

Population density 77.4 per sq km (200.4 per sq mile)

Life expectancy 72.0

Infant mortality (per 1,000) 23.5

Official languages Serbian, Croatian

Literacy rate 82 %

Religions Muslim 40 %, Orthodox 31 %, Roman Catholic 15 %, Protestant 4 %, other 10 %

Ethnic groups Serb 40 %, Bosnian Muslim 38 %, Croat 22 %

Currency Dinar

Economy Not available; war disrupted employment

GNP per capita US$ 1,800

Climate Cold winters and warm summers; cooler in the north and southern mountains

Highest point Mt Maglic 2,386 m (7,828 ft)

Map reference Pages 294, 296

The federation of Bosnia and Herzegovina has a mere 20 km (12 miles) of coast at its southern tip on the Adriatic. It borders Croatia to the north and west and to the east it shares a border with what remains of the former Yugoslavia, today called Serbia and Montenegro. Serbs first settled in Bosnia in the seventh century AD. In the twelfth century the country came under Hungarian control, and Ottoman Turks conquered it two centuries later. It was ceded to the Austro-Hungarian Empire in 1908, and in 1918 became part of the Kingdom of Serbs, Croats, and Slovenes, which was later renamed Yugoslavia.

The republic was formed in 1994 when, after several years of fighting sparked by the breaking up of Yugoslavia in 1991, Bosnian Croats and Muslims agreed to joint control of the region. Fighting went on for a further 18 months as Bosnian Serbs, backed by Serbia, sought to have a portion of the country incorporated into Serbia. The war came to an uneasy end in 1995 when Serbia abandoned its claims on Bosnian territory. Now named Bosnia and Herzegovina, the country is divided for purposes of administration almost equally between the Muslim-Croat Federation and the Bosnian Serbs.

Much of the land is mountainous and the south consists largely of a harsh limestone plateau. About a quarter of the land, especially in the mountains, is covered in forests of pine and beech. Before the economy collapsed, forestry products were a major source of earnings. Most agriculture is centered in the fertile valley of the Sava River, which forms the border with Croatia. Crops include grapes, other fruit, and cereals. Sheep raising is also significant. Most farms are small and, with the disruption caused by warfare, tend to be inefficient.

Bosnia-Herzegovina imports food and relies heavily on United Nations aid. Years of warfare have brought industry virtually to a standstill. Health and education services have also been severely disrupted.

Macedonia

Fact File

OFFICIAL NAME Former Yugoslav Republic of Macedonia

FORM OF GOVERNMENT Republic with single legislative body (Assembly)

CAPITAL Skopje

AREA 25,333 sq km (9,781 sq miles)

TIME ZONE GMT + 1 hour

POPULATION 2,055,000

PROJECTED POPULATION 2015 2,075,000

POPULATION DENSITY 81.1 per sq km (210.1 per sq mile)

LIFE EXPECTANCY 74.3

INFANT MORTALITY (PER 1,000) 12.5

OFFICIAL LANGUAGE Macedonian

OTHER LANGUAGES Albanian, Turkish, Serbian, Croatian

LITERACY RATE 94 %

RELIGIONS Eastern Orthodox 67 %, Muslim 30 %, other 3 %

ETHNIC GROUPS Macedonian 65 %, Albanian 22 %, Turkish 4 %, Serb 2 %, Gypsy 3 %, other 4 %

CURRENCY Denar

ECONOMY Services 58 %, industry 38 %, agriculture 14 %

GNP PER CAPITA US$ 5,000

CLIMATE Temperate, with cold winters and hot summers

HIGHEST POINT Mt Korab 2,753 m (9,032 ft)

MAP REFERENCE Pages 296–97, 298

This small, landlocked Balkan country in southeastern Europe is bordered by Serbia and Montenegro to the north, Bulgaria to the east, Greece to the south, and Albania to the west. During the third century BC Macedonia was the heart of the Greek Empire. It later became a Roman province, but from the fourth century AD it was invaded numerous times. In the fourteenth century it came under Ottoman control. As the Ottoman Empire declined in the nineteenth century, Bulgaria, Greece, and Serbia contended for control of Macedonia and by the First World War it had been divided between them. Present-day Macedonia is essentially the region that was in Serbian hands at the end of the First World War. Macedonia was then incorporated into the Kingdom of Serbs, Croats, and Slovenes, which in 1929 became the Republic of Yugoslavia. In 1946 it became an autonomous republic within Yugoslavia. In 1991 Macedonia withdrew from Yugoslavia and it is now a multi-party democracy, governed by a legislative body with 120 elected members and a directly elected president. Tensions with neighbors remain high. Macedonia is also the name of a Greek province. This is why the official name of the country is "Former Yugoslav Republic of Macedonia".

Macedonia is largely isolated from its neighbors by mountains. Mountain ranges separate it from Greece in the south and the Korab Mountains in the west lie along the Albanian and Serbian borders. Much of the country is a plateau more than 2,000 m (6,500 ft) above sea level. The River Vadar rises in the northwest. It flows north, almost to the Yugoslavian border, then continues on a southeasterly course through the center of the country and into Greece.

One-quarter of the land is used for agriculture. Crops include cereals, fruits, vegetables, and cotton, and sheep and cattle are raised extensively. The country is self-sufficient in food and, thanks to its coal resources, in energy. Manufacturing industries have suffered since independence, partly because of trade embargoes imposed by Greece. Macedonia is the least developed of the former Yugoslav republics and is suffering a declining standard of living.

The town of Ohrid on the shore of Lake Ohrid in southwestern Macedonia (below). An old stone bridge spans a river in Montenegro, Serbia and Montenegro (right page top).

Serbia and Montenegro

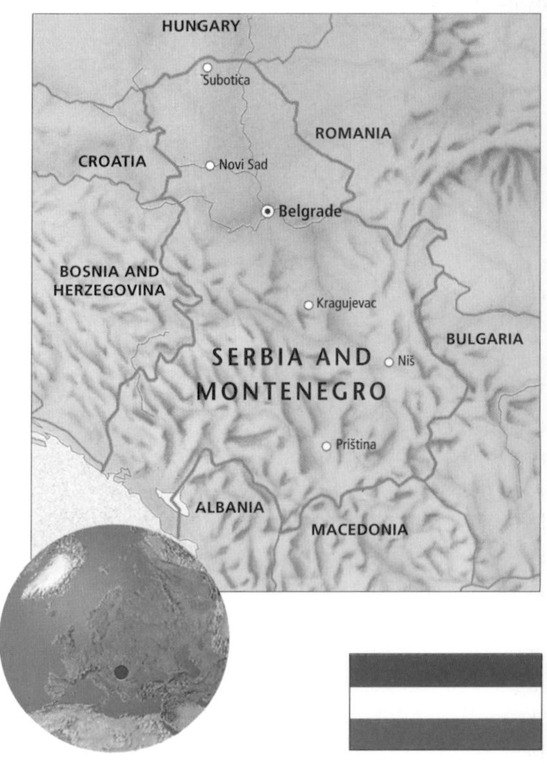

Fact File

OFFICIAL NAME Serbia and Montenegro

FORM OF GOVERNMENT Federal republic with two legislative bodies (Chamber of Republics and Chamber of Citizens)

CAPITAL Belgrade

AREA 102,350 sq km (39,517 sq miles)

TIME ZONE GMT + 1 hour

POPULATION 10,657,000

PROJECTED POPULATION 2015 10,309,000

POPULATION DENSITY 104.1 per sq km (269.7 per sq mile)

LIFE EXPECTANCY 73.7

INFANT MORTALITY (PER 1,000) 17.4

OFFICIAL LANGUAGE Serbian

OTHER LANGUAGES Albanian, Hungarian

LITERACY RATE 93 %

RELIGIONS Eastern Orthodox 65 %, Muslim 19 %, Roman Catholic 4 %, Protestant 1 %, other 11 %

ETHNIC GROUPS Serbian 63 %, Albanian 14 %, Montenegrin 6 %, Hungarian 4 %, other 13 %

CURRENCY Dinar

ECONOMY Not available; war disrupted employment

GNP PER CAPITA US$ 2,370

CLIMATE Temperate, with cold winters and hot summers

HIGHEST POINT Daravica 2,656 m (8,714 ft)

MAP REFERENCE Page 296

At its southwestern edge, Serbia and Montenegro, the "rump" republic of Yugoslavia, has a toehold on the Adriatic Sea. Otherwise it is landlocked, sharing borders with seven countries. Moving from the west around to south clockwise, these are Bosnia and Herzegovina, Croatia, Hungary, Romania, Bulgaria, Macedonia, and Albania. Serbia and Montenegro now comprises the republics of Serbia and Montenegro—all that remains of the former federation of Yugoslavia after four of its six constituent republics, Slovenia, Croatia, Bosnia and Herzegovina, and Macedonia—seceded in the early 1990s.

Yugoslavia came into existence in December 1918 as a combination of formerly separate Balkan states, most of which had been under Austro-Hungarian control. Serbia had become independent in 1878, bringing to an end five centuries of almost continuous Ottoman rule. The new country was originally called the Kingdom of Serbs, Croats, and Slovenes, but in 1929 the name Yugoslavia was adopted. During the Second World War Yugoslavia was invaded by Germany and the country was further devastated by civil war. More than a million Yugoslavs perished during this time. At the end of the war a communist government led by a Croat, Josip Broz, better known as Marshal Tito, came to power, but remained independent of the Soviet Union. After Tito died in 1980 ethnic tensions began to assert themselves, and in 1991 Croatia and Slovenia seceded, leading to four years of bitter ethnic-based conflict between Serbia and its neighbors. In the Kosovo province, mainly inhabited by muslim Albanians, the ethnic conflicts persisted. In 1999, after initial opposition of the Russian government, an international alliance and NATO reacted to massive actions of the Serbian army by bombing Yugoslavia. An international peace-keeping force led by Russia and the US has been installed in Kosovo since 2000. In the fall of 2000 elections brought reformers into power and in March 2003 a new constitution replaced the federal republic by the union of two states, Serbia and Montenegro. Each has their own president and parliament, but there is also one president heading the entire country as chief of state and leader of the government. A referendum in 2006 is planned to decide whether the union will persist.

Serbia and Montenegro are largely mountainous. The rocky peaks of the heavily forested Balkan Mountains separate Serbia from Bulgaria and Romania and stretch across much of southern and central Serbia and into Bosnia and Herzegovina. Much of Montenegro, in the southwest, is covered by the bare limestone ridges of the Dinaric Alps, which run from Slovenia south into Albania. In the north of the country and covering most of the province of Vojvodina, is the fertile Pannonian Plain. A number of rivers including the Sava, the Tisza and the Danube traverse this plain, which extends northwest into Croatia and Hungary.

Agricultural produce is centered on the northern plain, which supports substantial crops of wheat, maize, and vegetables as well as livestock and poultry. Agriculture in Montenegro is based mainly on the raising of sheep and goats. Serbia and Montenegro has considerable reserves of coal and petroleum and is largely self-sufficient in fuel. Most of these resources are in the northern province of Vojvodina and the troubled southern region of Kosovo. Mining and heavy machine manufacture are major contributors to the country's economy which, however, especially in Serbia remains seriously destabilized by years of warfare and the consequent disruption of trade links.

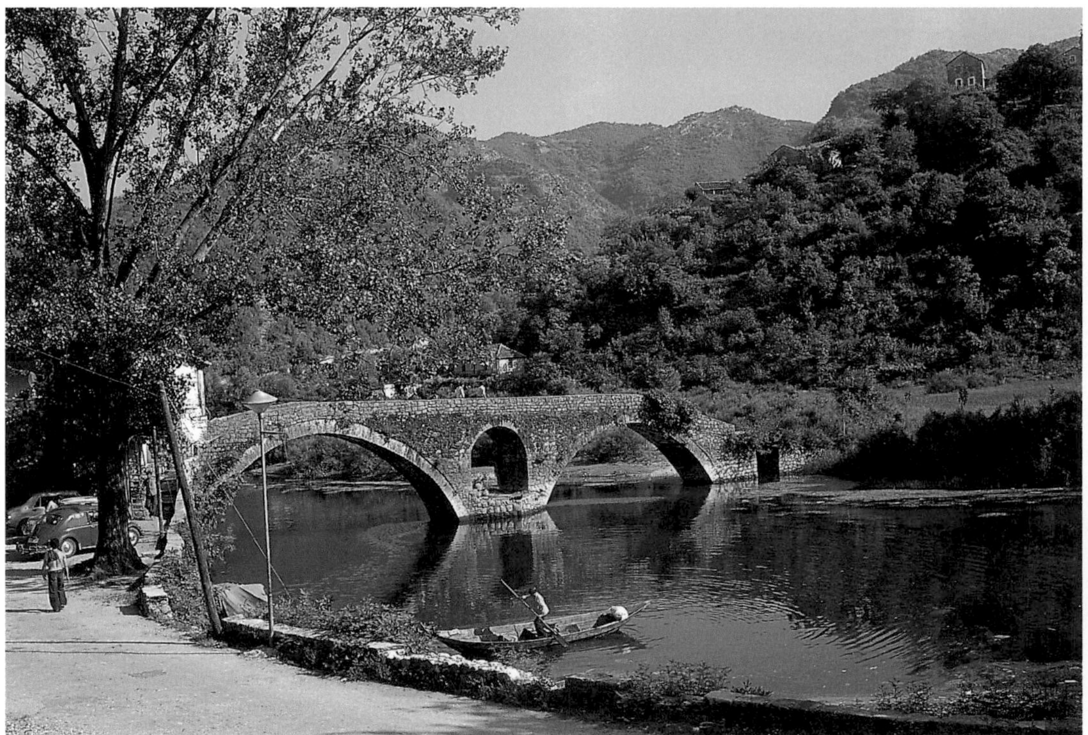

The Balkans

The Balkans is the collective name for the countries that occupy the Balkan Peninsula, the easternmost of the three peninsulas that jut southward into the Mediterranean Sea. It comprises the countries of Greece, Bulgaria, Romania, Moldova, Albania, Macedonia, Serbia and Montenegro, Bosnia and Herzegovina, Croatia, and Slovenia. The word Balkan emerged in the nineteenth century. It was the Turkish name for a mountain range in Bulgaria and at first was applied to the land that lay to the south of this range. At various times since, it has had different meanings. Since the First World War, which was sparked by the assassination of the heir to the Austro-Hungarian Empire in Sarajevo, Bosnia, the region has often been referred to as "the powder keg of Europe", and has had strong connotations of violence and ethnic conflict. In more recent times that phrase has acquired new significance and the term Balkan is increasingly used to refer specifically to those countries that formerly constituted the state of Yugoslavia.

The present troubles in the Balkans can be traced back to the reawakening of long-dormant nationalist sentiments as the formerly powerful Turkish Empire declined during the nineteenth century. This led to the formation of a number of nation states, some of which were under Austro-Hungarian domination until the end of the First World War. Many of these states were formed with scant regard to the ethnic, religious, or linguistic homogeneity of their populations. Thus significant populations of Muslim Albanians were incorporated into predominantly Christian Serbia and Macedonia and large numbers of Serbs, the most widely dispersed of the Balkan peoples, lived in Croatia and Bosnia, which is now called Bosnia and Herzegovina.

The explosive potential of this situation was largely contained after the formation of the federated state of Yugoslavia, in which Serbians were dominant, and during the Second World War, in which all Balkan countries suffered grievously.

Ethnic tensions remained suppressed during the regime of Marshal Tito after the Second World War. During this period, cold war politics dominated Europe, and Yugoslavia adopted relatively liberal socialist policies independently of the Soviet Union. Albania and Romania also pursued their own, albeit more oppressive, socialist agendas, but like Yugoslavia refused to bow to Soviet domination. Greece remained non-communist, but only after a bitter civil war, which saw the communists finally defeated in 1949.

The death of Tito in 1980 and the later disintegration of communist regimes in Eastern Europe set the scene for the breakdown of Yugoslavia into its component republics. A series of civil wars followed, as Serb minorities in Croatia and Bosnia and Herzegovina fought, with Serbian support, for the extension of Serbian territories. An uneasy truce was brokered in 1995, only after the deployment of United Nations forces. In 1998, simmering resentment by ethnic Albanians in the southern Yugoslav province of Kosovo erupted again into bloody warfare and led to brutal massacres by Yugoslav forces.

Hungary

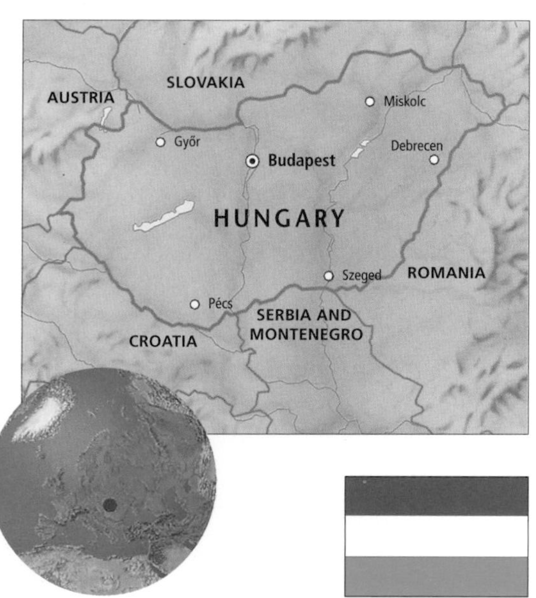

Fact File

OFFICIAL NAME Republic of Hungary

FORM OF GOVERNMENT Republic with single legislative body (National Assembly)

CAPITAL Budapest

AREA 93,030 sq km (35,919 sq miles)

TIME ZONE GMT + 1 hour

POPULATION 10,075,000

PROJECTED POPULATION 2015 9,254,000

POPULATION DENSITY 108.3 per sq km (280.5 per sq mile)

LIFE EXPECTANCY 71.9

INFANT MORTALITY (PER 1,000) 8.8

OFFICIAL LANGUAGE Hungarian

OTHER LANGUAGE Romany, German, Croatian, Slovakian, Romanian

LITERACY RATE 99 %

RELIGIONS Roman Catholic 67.5 %, Calvinist 20 %, Lutheran 5 %, other 7.5 %

ETHNIC GROUPS Hungarian 89.9 %, Gypsy 4 %, German 2.6 %, Serb 2 %, Slovak 0.8 %, Romanian 0.7 %

CURRENCY Forint

ECONOMY Services 59 %, industry 33 %, agriculture 8 %

GNP PER CAPITA US$ 13,300

CLIMATE Temperate; cold, wet winters and warm summers

HIGHEST POINT Mt Kékes 1,014 m (3,327 ft)

MAP REFERENCE Pages 289, 294, 296

A landlocked Central European country, Hungary shares borders with Serbia and Montenegro to the south, Croatia and Slovenia to the southwest, Austria to the west, Slovakia to the north, Ukraine to the northeast and Romania to the southeast. Modern Hungary had its beginnings in the eighth century AD, when the area was settled by the Magyars, nomadic tribes from the central Volga. Their kingdom thrived and expanded. In the sixteenth century the Turks seized the central part of Hungary and the northern and western sections of the country accepted Austrian Habsburg rule rather than submit to Turkish domination. In 1699 the Turks were driven out and the entire country came under Habsburg rule. Continuing unrest and the defeat of Austria by the Prussians in 1866 culminated in the establishment of Austria-Hungary as a dual monarchy in 1867. The defeat of Austria-Hungary in 1918 was followed by the establishment of the Hungarian nation, but with two-thirds of its former territory and almost 60 percent of its former population ceded to surrounding states. In the Second World War Hungary sided with Germany against the Soviet Union and was finally occupied by Soviet forces as they pushed southward in 1945. In 1948 communists again seized control with Soviet support, beginning 42 years of Soviet domination. A popular anti-communist uprising in 1956 was brutally suppressed by the Soviet Union. As the Soviet Union began to collapse a new constitution in 1989 set the scene for Hungary's first multi-party elections in 1990.

Hungary is drained by two southward-flowing rivers, the Danube and the Tisza. These two rivers traverse the Great Hungarian Plain, which occupies most of the eastern part of the country and more than half the total land area. West of the Danube a line of hills and mountains runs northeast from Lake Balaton, which covers an area of 370 sq km (140 sq miles), to the Slovakian border, where it joins the Carpathian Mountains. Northwest of these hills the Little Hungarian Plain extends to the westward-flowing Danube, which here separates Hungary from Slovakia. While most of the low-lying areas have long been cleared of trees, some of the forested areas still survive in the hills and mountains.

Most of the two plains areas are fertile agricultural country, although there are dry sandy expanses, as well as marshlands that are home to a rich variety of waterbirds. More than seventy percent of Hungary's agricultural land is devoted to crops, the most important of which are maize, wheat, sugar beet, and sunflowers. Of the rest, more than four-fifths are meadows and pasturelands and the rest are orchards and vineyards. Pigs and poultry are the most extensively farmed livestock.

Except for natural gas, bauxite, and lignite—a low quality coal that provides much of the country's energy—Hungary is poorly endowed with mineral resources. It imports most of the raw materials for its now largely privatized industries, among which iron and steel production and the manufacture of fertilizers, pharmaceuticals, and cement are prominent. Most of these industries are located in the north and are centered mainly around the capital, Budapest, and Miskolc, which is the second-largest city and is situated in the far northeast. Aluminum, using local bauxite, is manufactured north of Lake Balaton.

Hungarians enjoy a reasonable standard of living by the standards of former communist countries, though it still compares unfavorably with that in most Western countries. Pollution of air, soil, and water is a major problem and almost half the population lives in seriously affected areas.

Albania

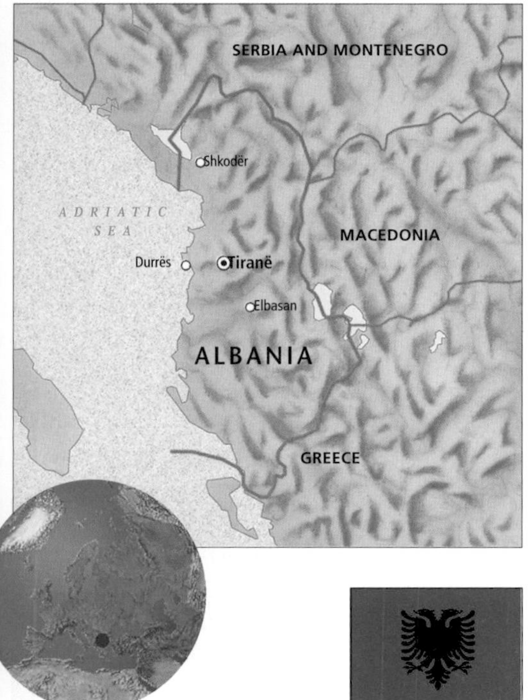

Fact File

Official name Republic of Albania

Form of government Republic with single legislative body (National Assembly)

Capital Tiranë

Area 28,750 sq km (11,100 sq miles)

Time zone GMT + 1 hour

Population 3,545,000

Projected population 2015 3,439,000

Population density 123.3 per sq km (319.4 per sq mile)

Life expectancy 72.1

Infant mortality (per 1,000) 38.6

Official language Albanian

Other languages Greek, Macedonian

Literacy rate 93 %

Religions Muslim 70 %, Albanian Orthodox 20 %, Roman Catholic 10 %

Ethnic groups Albanian 95 %, Greek 3 %, other 2 %

Currency Lek

Economy Agriculture 56 %, industry 21 %, services 23 %

GNP per capita US$ 4,500

Climate Mild temperate with cold, wet winters and warm, dry summers; colder in mountains

Highest point Maja e Korabit 2,753 m (9,032 ft)

Map reference Pages 296–97

Looking across the Danube in Budapest, Hungary (left page). The fourteenth-century citadel of Gjirokastër in Albania (above).

Albania shares borders with Greece to the southeast and Macedonia to the east. Serbia and Montenegro wraps around the northern part of the country. At its western edge it has a coastline 362 km (225 miles) long along the Adriatic Sea. For 500 years until 1912, when it became independent, Albania was part of the Ottoman Empire, and a large majority of the population is Muslim. In 1912 it declared its independence and in 1939 Albania was invaded by Italy. After the Second World War the country came into the Soviet sphere of influence. From 1946 until 1992 Albania was part of the Soviet bloc, although it often adopted policies independent of, and sometimes at odds with, the Moscow line. When the European communist system unraveled in the early 1990s Albania, in 1992, was the last country in Europe to abandon a communist regime.

Except for a narrow strip of plains along its coastline, Albania is hilly and mountainous. Most Albanian people eke out an existence through farming on the plains, which contain the only cultivable land. Even here, much of the country is marshy and difficult to access. Corn, wheat, barley, and fruits are among the main crops. Little is exported because transport methods are primitive. In most areas people use horse- or mule-drawn vehicles. Mountains cover seven-tenths of the country. In the north are the Albanian Alps, and there are highlands in the center and south. Numerous rivers, notably the Drin in the north, and the Vijose in the south, flow to the coast from the highlands. Albania has significant reserves of natural resources such as petroleum, iron, and other mineral ores, plus natural gas, but most remain undeveloped.

The mountainous landscape makes land access difficult, and marshes restrict access to much of the coast. Rail links are few and there are no railway lines to neighboring countries. This has contributed to Albania's relative cultural and linguistic distinctness. Despite its conversion to free market ideals, Albania has failed to emerge from the cycle of poverty, continuing food shortages, and violence, fed to a large extent by the flood of refugees from the troubles in former Yugoslavia.

Romania

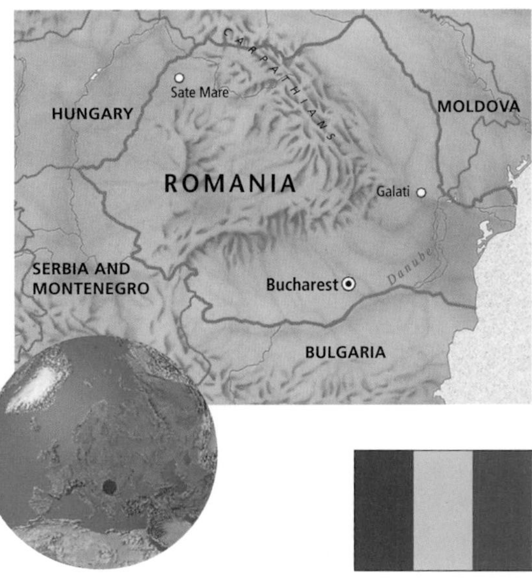

Fact File

Official name Romania

Form of government Republic with two legislative bodies (Senate and House of Deputies)

Capital Bucharest

Area 237,500 sq km (91,699 sq miles)

Time zone GMT + 2 hours

Population 22,318,000

Projected population 2015 21,437,000

Population density 94 per sq km (243.4 per sq mile)

Life expectancy 70.4

Infant mortality (per 1,000) 18.9

Official language Romanian

Other languages Hungarian, German, Romany

Literacy rate 97 %

Religions Romanian Orthodox 87 %, Roman Catholic 5 %, Protestant 5 %, other 3 %

Ethnic groups Romanian 89.1 %, Hungarian 8.9 %, other 2 %

Currency Leu

Economy Industry 38 %, services 34 %, agriculture 28 %

GNP per capita US$ 6,800

Climate Temperate; cold winters and warm, wet summers; cooler in Carpathian Mountains

Highest point Moldoveanu 2,544 m (8,346 ft)

Map reference Page 296

Except for its Black Sea coast, Romania is landlocked—by Ukraine to the north, Moldova to the northeast, Hungary to the west, Serbia and Montenegro to the southwest, and Bulgaria to the south. From the sixth century AD the country was often invaded. From the ninth to the eleventh centuries Magyars occupied part of Transylvania and between the fourteenth and sixteenth centuries Walachia, Moldova, and Transylvania formed part of the Ottoman Empire. At the end of the First World War, Bessarabia—most of present-day Moldova—Transylvania and Bukovina were restored to Romania. Much of this land was lost during the Second World War when Romania, which sided with Nazi Germany, came under Soviet control.

During Nicolai Ceausescu's oppressive regime, beginning in 1967, Romania distanced itself from the Soviets. In 1989 a popular uprising saw Ceausescu arrested and executed. Romania is now ruled by an elected parliament headed by a president.

The Carpathian Mountains curve through the center of the country, dividing the timbered uplands of Transylvania from the Danube Plain. The southern part of the range, the Transylvanian Alps, contains the highest peaks and the most rugged scenery. The fertile eastern plain is crossed by many tributaries of the Danube. To the east, around the Danube Delta, the land is marshy and dotted with numerous lakes and lagoons.

There has been a shift towards heavy industries since the 1970s but agriculture is still economically important. Maize, wheat, vegetables, and grapes for wine are the main crops and sheep and pigs the main livestock. Romania is rich in coal, natural gas, iron ore, and petroleum. Most of the raw materials for the country's industries are imported. Prominent industries include chemical and metal processing and machine manufacturing. Lumbering has depleted much of the country's forest and industry has caused widespread pollution. Moves to a market economy have been slow and Romania's standard of living remains relatively low.

Bulgaria

Fact File

OFFICIAL NAME Republic of Bulgaria

FORM OF GOVERNMENT Republic with single legislative body (National Assembly)

CAPITAL Sofia

AREA 110,910 sq km (42,822 sq miles)

TIME ZONE GMT + 2 hours

POPULATION 7,621,000

PROJECTED POPULATION 2015 6,816,000

POPULATION DENSITY 68.7 per sq km (178 per sq mile)

LIFE EXPECTANCY 71.5

INFANT MORTALITY (PER 1,000) 14.2

OFFICIAL LANGUAGE Bulgarian

OTHER LANGUAGES Turkish, Romany

LITERACY RATE 98 %

RELIGIONS Bulgarian Orthodox 85 %, Muslim 13 %, Jewish 0.8 %, Roman Catholic 0.5 %, Uniate Catholic 0.2 %; Protestant, Gregorian-Armenian and other 0.5 %

ETHNIC GROUPS Bulgarian 85.3 %, Turkish 8.5 %, Gypsy 2.6 %, Macedonian 2.5 %, Armenian 0.3 %, Russian 0.2 %, other 0.6 %

CURRENCY Lev

ECONOMY Services 45 %, industry 38 %, agriculture 17 %

GNP PER CAPITA US$ 6,600

CLIMATE Temperate, with cold, wet winters and hot, dry summers

HIGHEST POINT Mt Musala 2,925 m (9,596 ft)

MAP REFERENCE Pages 296–97

Bulgaria is situated on the east of the Balkan Peninsula with a coastline along the Black Sea. To the west it shares borders with Serbia and Montenegro as well as Macedonia. Turkey lies to its southeast, and Greece to its southwest. In the north the River Danube forms most of the border between Bulgaria and Romania.

Modern Bulgarians are descendants of the Bulgars, who arrived from north of the Danube in the late seventh century AD and established dominance over the Slavic races that had settled the area over the previous two centuries. The Christian religion, which is still dominant in the country, was established in the ninth century. A century of Byzantine domination in the eleventh and twelfth centuries was followed by a period of independence. In 1396 Turkish armies invaded and Bulgaria was then dominated for five centuries by the Turks until Russian intervention ended Ottoman rule in 1878. Full independence, however, did not come until 1908, when Prince Ferdinand of Saxe-Coburg, the elected ruler of Bulgaria, assumed the title of Tsar.

Bulgaria sided with the losing sides in both the First and Second World Wars, and as a result its boundaries changed several times as territories were ceded to it or confiscated. Its present boundaries were established by a 1947 treaty. From then until the fall of the Soviet Union in the early 1990s, Bulgaria remained one of the most loyal of Soviet satellites. A new constitution came into force in 1991 and the following year the first free elections were held.

The country's landscape is defined by three ranges of mountains and two extensive expanses of lowland. The Danube Valley is the country's richest agricultural area, producing significant yields of wheat, maize, and other cereal crops. The Balkan Mountains, running east-west across much of central Bulgaria, reach heights of up to 2,000 m (6,500 ft). They divide the Danube Valley from the southern lowlands, where tobacco and grapes are among the principal crops in the fertile valleys around the Maritsa River. The vineyards in this region produce some of southern Europe's finest wines. In the southwest the Rhodopi Massif, which contains the country's loftiest peak, forms the mountainous border with Greece.

More than ten million tourists, attracted to its Black Sea coastline, come to Bulgaria each year and contribute significantly to its economy. Most of the country's export earnings stem from its machinery and other manufacturing industries. While there have been tentative moves towards the establishment of a free market economy, high inflation, foreign debt, and worker unrest have contributed to a far from robust short-term economic outlook.

The Transylvanian Alps in Romania (above left). Alexander Nevsky Cathedral in Sofia, Bulgaria (below left). The city of Athens, the capital of Greece (right page).

Greece

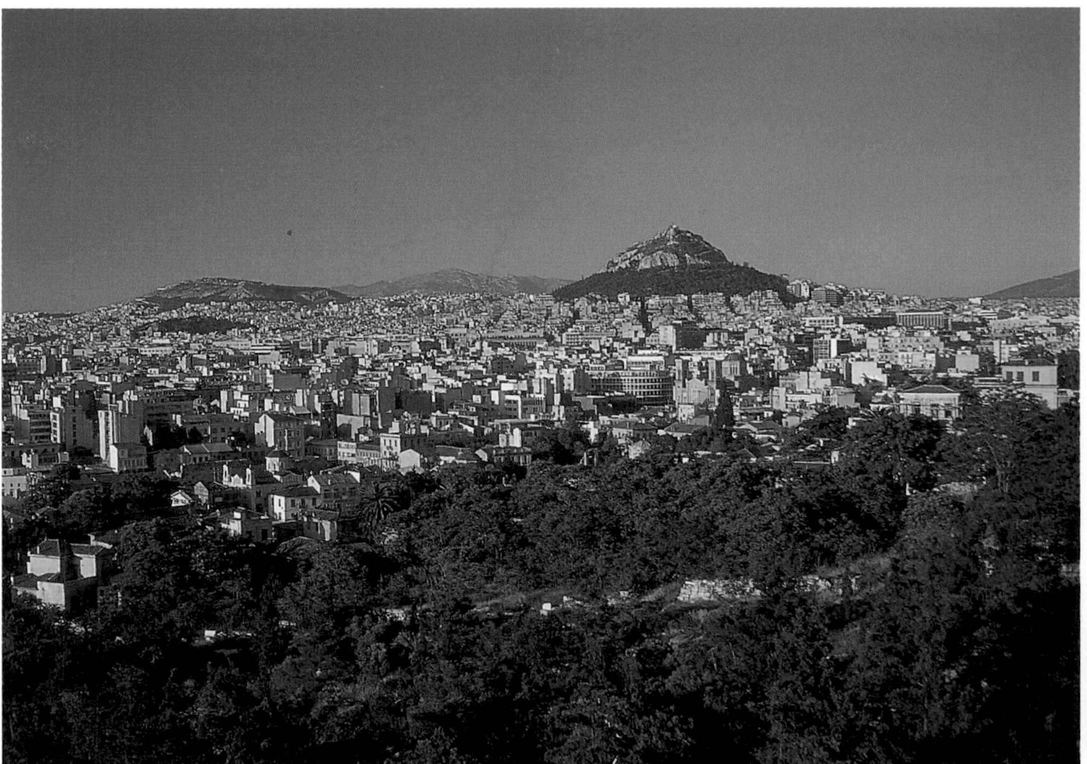

Fact File

Official name Hellenic Republic

Form of government Republic with single legislative body (Chamber of Deputies)

Capital Athens

Area 131,940 sq km (50,942 sq miles)

Time zone GMT + 2 hours

Population 10,645,000

Projected population 2015 10,472,000

Population density 80.7 per sq km (209 per sq mile)

Life expectancy 78.7

Infant mortality (per 1,000) 6.3

Official language Greek

Other languages Albanian, Macedonian, Turkish, Romanian

Literacy rate 97 %

Religions Greek Orthodox 98 %, Muslim 1.3 %, other 0.7 %

Ethnic groups Greek 98 %, other 2 %

Currency Euro

Economy Services 62 %, industry 24 %, agriculture 14 %

GNP per capita US$ 19,000

Climate Temperate, with mild, wet winters and hot, dry summers

Highest point Mt Olympus 2,917 m (9,570 ft)

Map reference Page 297

Mainland Greece occupies the southernmost part of the Balkan Peninsula. The western shores of this peninsula are washed by the Ionian Sea, while on the east the Aegean Sea lies between it and Turkey. In the north, Greece shares borders with Albania, and to the northeast with Macedonia and Bulgaria. In its far northeast corner there is a short border with Turkey. Dotted all over the Aegean Sea and also in the Ionian Sea are more than 1,500 Greek islands, only about ten percent of which are inhabited. South of the mainland, in the Mediterranean Sea, is the large island of Crete.

It was in Crete that the seeds of Greek civilization were sown. For more than 2,000 years, from about 3500 BC, the Minoan civilization grew and flourished here. In about the sixteenth century BC it spread to Mycenae, in the Peloponnese Peninsula. In the fifth century BC Athens emerged as the center of Greek culture. It developed rich traditions in literature, theater, philosophy and politics which established the values on which most modern Western civilizations are based. In the fourth century BC, under Alexander the Great, a vast Greek Empire spread across Asia as far as India and southward as far as Alexandria in Egypt. Subsumed into the Roman Empire by the beginning of the second century BC, Greece eventually came under Byzantine rule, where it remained until the fall of Constantinople in AD 1204. After a quick succession of foreign rulers, the Ottoman Turks conquered Greece towards the end of the fourteenth century. Modern Greece dates back to 1832, when the country emerged from almost 400 years of Turkish domination and established a monarchy.

In 1941 Greece was overrun, in the face of fierce resistance, by German and Italian troops. It was liberated during 1944 by British and Greek forces, but almost immediately the country was plunged into civil war as monarchists and communists fought for supremacy. This destructive and debilitating struggle finally ended in 1949 with a victory by the monarchists. However, a military coup in 1967 resulted in the monarchy being expelled and a republic being established under an oppressive dictatorship. This regime fell in 1974 after an abortive attempt to invade Cyprus. In 1975, civilian government was restored and Greece became a democratic republic with a president elected for a five-year term, and a single-chamber parliament headed by a prime minister elected every four years. Its political system soon proved stable enough that Greece was admitted as the tenth member of the EC in 1981.

Most of mainland Greece is mountainous, being dominated by the Pindos Mountains, an extension of the Dinaric Alps that extend southeastward throughout the peninsula from the Albanian border. The mountains that form Crete and the island of Rhodes, near the southwestern tip of Turkey, were once part of the same range. In the northeast the Rhodope Mountains form a natural border with Bulgaria. The only extensive low-lying areas are the northern plain, which extends from the Maritsa River on the Turkish border across the northern Aegean region to the Greek province of Macedonia, and the plain of Thessaly in the central eastern mainland. Much of the Greek landscape, including that of many of the islands, is sparsely vegetated and has a rugged, rocky grandeur that, together with its warm climate, its beaches, and its rich historic heritage, attracts more than ten million foreign visitors every year.

Despite its generally poor soils, Greece is heavily dependent on agriculture, which still employs about one-quarter of the workforce, largely on relatively small and inefficient farms. Wheat, olives, tobacco, and citrus and other fruits are among the main crops, and olives, particularly, are a major export item. Sheep and pigs are the principal livestock and are widely raised on the mainland and on Crete. Greece is almost self-sufficient in food production.

Not well endowed with mineral resources, Greece needs to import most of the raw materials for its industries, the majority of which are centered on Athens, though the area around Salonica in the northeast is also heavily industrialized. Food processing based on local agricultural production is important, as are textile manufacture and chemical processing. The tourist industry has helped the development of many local small-scale enterprises in such areas as ceramics, crafts, and textiles.

Eastern Europe

Czech Republic

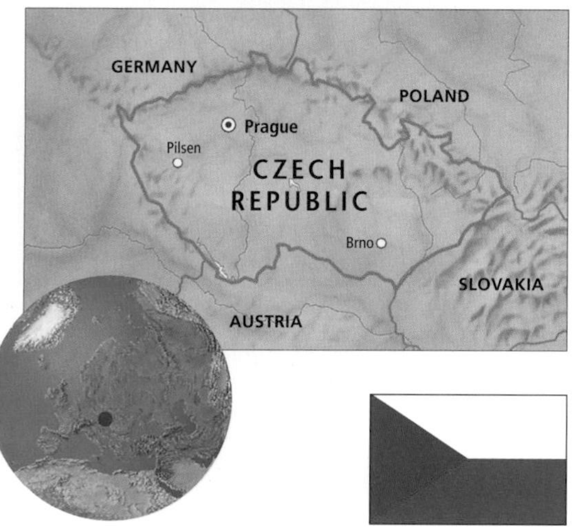

Fact File

OFFICIAL NAME Czech Republic

FORM OF GOVERNMENT Republic with two legislative bodies (Senate and Chamber of Deputies)

CAPITAL Prague

AREA 78,703 sq km (30,387 sq miles)

TIME ZONE GMT + 1 hour

POPULATION 10,257,000

PROJECTED POPULATION 2015 10,028,000

POPULATION DENSITY 130.3 per sq km (337.5 per sq mile)

LIFE EXPECTANCY 75.0

INFANT MORTALITY (PER 1,000) 5.5

OFFICIAL LANGUAGE Czech

OTHER LANGUAGE Slovak, German, Polish

LITERACY RATE 99.9 %

RELIGIONS Roman Catholic 39.2 %, Protestant 4.6 %, Orthodox 3 %, non-denominational 39.1 %, other 13.4 %

ETHNIC GROUPS Czech 94.4 %, Slovak 3 %, Polish 0.6 %, German 0.5 %, Gypsy 0.3 %, Hungarian 0.2 %, other 1 %

CURRENCY Koruna

ECONOMY Industry 47 %, services 45 %, agriculture 8 %

GNP PER CAPITA US$ 15,300

CLIMATE Temperate, with cold winters and mild, wet summers

HIGHEST POINT Mt Snezka 1,602 m (5,256 ft)

MAP REFERENCE Pages 288–89

The Bohemian city of Český Krumlov in the Czech Republic (right). The city of Trenčín in Slovakia (right page top).

A landlocked country in Central Europe, until 1993 the Czech Republic was linked to Slovakia, its neighbor to the southeast, from which it is separated by the Carpathian Mountains. The Czech Republic consists mainly of the ancient provinces of Bohemia in the west and Moravia in the east as well as part of the province of Silesia, but most of it now forms a portion of Poland.

Czechoslovakia came into existence in 1918 with the collapse of the Austro-Hungarian Empire at the close of the First World War. The Czechs and the Slovaks had been under one rule since 1471, and since 1526 had been under Austrian domination. Germany occupied Czech territory in 1939, establishing a protectorate of Bohemia-Moravia and setting up a separate state in Slovakia. In 1948 the communists came to power and the country, once again united, came under Soviet influence. Nationalist fervor was never far below the surface and in 1968 caused a movement for democracy. The "Prague Spring," led by Alexander Dubcek, was put down by an invasion of Soviet forces. In 1989 a popular movement led to a transition to a democratic state. Tensions between Czechs and the minority Slovaks led to a peaceful separation of the two states on 1 January 1993.

Bohemia consists largely of gentle hills and plateaus. Low ranges of mountains surround the province to the north, west, and south and the central plateau is traversed by the Elbe and Vltava Rivers, which merge and flow into Germany. Most of the country's agriculture is centered on this river system and much of its produce, including wheat, barley, and potatoes, is transported along these waterways. Bohemia and Moravia are separated by a plateau known as the Moravian Heights. While Moravia is hillier than Bohemia, the center of the province, around Brno, consists of an extensive low plain. Winters are colder and rainfall is heavier in Moravia than in Bohemia. Although not richly endowed with natural resources, reserves of black coal and iron ore have aided the development of iron and steelmaking as the country's major industries. Other important industries include clothing and car manufacture. Bohemian glass is famous worldwide. Industrial production, however, has fallen in the 1990s as the country moves toward a free market economy. Tourism has made up for some of this fall-off.

Czech conflict

The country formerly known as Czechoslovakia was at the center of successive conflicts in the twentieth century. It contains a volatile mixture of ethnic and political differences, and in the past fell victim to German and Soviet totalitarian regimes. Hitler used the disaffection of the German minority in the Sudetenland as an excuse for invading Czechoslovakia in 1938. An insecure period of democracy after 1945 (marred by the expulsion of the still-resident German population) was followed by a communist takeover under Soviet auspices in 1948. In 1968 an effort to democratize the system led by Alexander Dubcek was crushed by Soviet tanks. Along with other parts of Eastern Europe it won independence from communist control in 1989, and since 2004 has been a member of the EU—but these developments have been accompanied by the rise of ethnic separatism, and claims by former German citizens for restitution of property seized at the time of their expulsion after the Second World War. On 1 January 1993 the Czechs separated from the Slovaks in the "velvet divorce", and two republics—the Czech "western" and the Slovak "eastern"—came into existence. Under the presidency of the internationally renowned playwright Vaclav Havel (1993–2003), a wholesale dismantling of state economic controls and structures then took place. However, the government which undertook these extensive reforms collapsed amid scandal and economic chaos at the end of 1997.

Slovakia

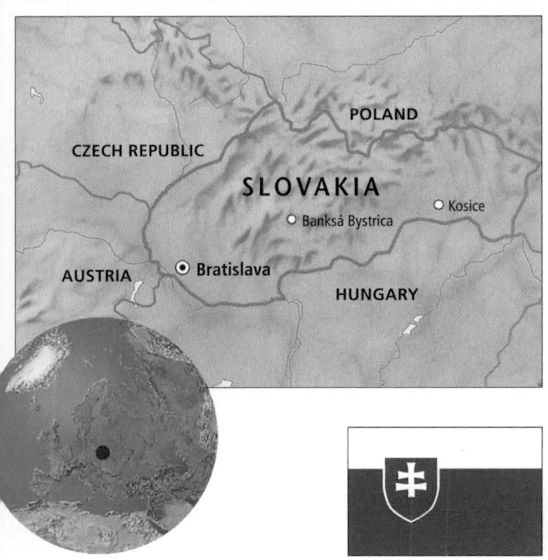

Fact File

Official name Slovak Republic

Form of government Republic with single legislative body (National Parliament)

Capital Bratislava

Area 48,845 sq km (18,859 sq miles)

Time zone GMT + 1 hour

Population 5,423,000

Projected population 2015 5,420,000

Population density 111 per sq km (287.6 per sq mile)

Life expectancy 74.2

Infant mortality (per 1,000) 8.8

Official language Slovak

Other language Hungarian, Czech

Literacy rate 99 %

Religions Roman Catholic 60.3 %, Protestant 8.4 %, Orthodox 4.1 %, other 27.2 %

Ethnic groups Slovak 85.7 %, Hungarian 10.7 %, others include Gypsy, Czech 3.6 %

Currency Koruna

Economy Services 44.3 %, industry 43.5 %, agriculture 12.2 %

GNP per capita US$ 12,200

Climate Temperate, with cold winters and warm, wet summers

Highest point Gerlachovka 2,655 m (8,711 ft)

Map reference Page 289

This small Central European country is bordered by Poland to the north, the Czech Republic to the northwest, Austria to the west, Hungary to the south, and Ukraine to the east. It is the smaller, less populous, and less industrially developed part of the former state of Czechoslovakia, which split peacefully in 1993 to form the two separate nations of Slovakia and the Czech Republic.

Ethnically distinct from their former compatriots, the Slovaks had lived for ten centuries under continuous Hungarian domination when in 1918 they merged with the Czechs to form a new, independent nation. At the beginning of the Second World War, Czechoslovakia was

invaded by Germany and the Germans installed a pro-Fascist government in Slovakia. Soviet troops restored the pre-war status quo in 1945 and communists seized power in 1948, making the country effectively a Soviet satellite. In 1968 Soviet forces invaded to put down an attempt to establish democracy under the leadership of Czechoslovakia's First Secretary, Alexander Dubcek, a Slovak. Twenty-one years later a revival of nationalism and a weakened Soviet Union led to a successful declaration of independence and the establishment of democratic government. Since its separation from the Czech Republic, Slovakia has been governed by a single-chamber parliament whose 150 members, or deputies, are elected for a four-year term.

Except for lowland areas in the south and southeast, most of the country is ruggedly mountainous, with extensive forests and tracts of pastureland. In the north of the country the high Carpathian Mountains extend along the Polish border, and further south the Tatra Mountains, an offshoot of the Carpathians and the Slovakian Ore Mountains, run parallel across the center of the country. Ski resorts in the Tatra Mountains attract large numbers of tourists. The Danube, which forms part of the border with Hungary, flows through an extensive fertile plain. Most of Slovakia's agriculture, which employs more than one-tenth of the workforce, is centered here and in the lowland area further to the east. Wheat and potatoes are the principal crops, and sheep, cattle, and pigs are widely raised.

Slovakia is poorly endowed with mineral resources. There are significant deposits of lignite, but most of it is poor in quality. Industries, which employ about one in three workers, are centered mainly around the cities of Bratislava in the southwest and Kosice in the southeast. Significant industries are iron and steelmaking, and car and clothing manufacture. The move from a centrally controlled to a privatized market economy has proceeded fitfully, and the country has suffered economically from the loss of subsidies that it used to receive from the Czech Republic.

Poland

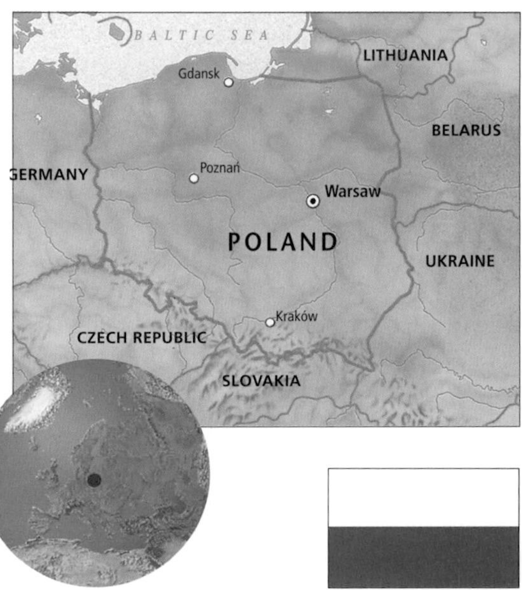

Fact File

Official name Republic of Poland

Form of government Republic with two legislative bodies (Senate and Parliament or Sejm)

Capital Warsaw

Area 312,685 sq km (120,727 sq miles)

Time zone GMT + 1 hour

Population 38,626,000

Projected population 2015 38,035,000

Population density 123.5 per sq km (319.9 per sq mile)

Life expectancy 73.7

Infant mortality (per 1,000) 9.2

Official language Polish

Literacy rate 99 %

Religions Roman Catholic 95 %; others include Eastern Orthodox, Protestant 5 %

Ethnic groups Polish 97.6 %, German 1.3 %, Ukrainian 0.6 %, Belarusian 0.5 %

Currency Zloty

Economy Services 55 %, industry 38 %, agriculture 7 %

GNP per capita US$ 9,500

Climate Temperate, with cold winters and warm, wet summers

Highest point Rysy 2,499 m (8,199 ft)

Map reference Page 289

Situated in northern Central Europe, Poland has a northern coastline on the Baltic Sea and shares land borders with seven countries. To the west the Oder River forms part of the border with Germany, while to the southwest the Sudeten Mountains separate it from the Czech Republic. The Carpathian Mountains form a natural boundary with Slovakia in the south. Ukraine and Belarus lie to the east, Lithuania is to the northeast, and a part of the Russian Federation is adjacent to Poland's northern coastline.

In the seventh and eighth centuries AD, Slavic peoples originally from the south of Europe—known as Polanie, or plain-dwellers—occupied most of Poland. In the tenth century their king was converted to Christianity, beginning a strong tradition of Catholicism that has survived to the present, despite attempts by post-war communist governments to suppress it. During the course of the next two centuries, invaders from Prussia divided up the country, which was reunited in the fourteenth century.

Poland retained its independence and at times even extended its power during the following two centuries, but again came under Prussian and Austrian control in the late eighteenth century. The nation regained its independence in 1918 with the defeat of Austria and Germany in the First World War. Early in the Second World War, Poland was attacked and overrun by Germany and then Russia, which divided the country between them until June 1941, when the Germans took full control. After the war Poland's borders shifted to the west, as portions of what was formerly Germany was ceded to Poland, and as the Soviets were granted control of substantial territories in the east. Under these arrangements Poland suffered a net loss of both territory and population. From that point on until 1989 Poland was effectively a vassal state of its much larger neighbor, the Soviet Union.

Growing civil unrest during the 1980s culminated in a series of strikes in a range of industries, organized by the trade union Solidarity. In 1989 the besieged government capitulated and allowed Solidarity to contest the government elections, which Solidarity won decisively. The first entirely free elections were held in 1991 and Lech Walesa, the leader of Solidarity, became Poland's first president. It is now a democratic republic with a directly elected president and a multi-party system. In 2004 it became a member of the EU.

Except for the mountain ranges in the south and southwest, most of Poland is low-lying, forming part of the North European Plain. The landscape is drained by numerous rivers, the most significant of which is the Vistula, which originates in the Carpathian Mountains and flows through the center of the country, through Warsaw, and on to the Baltic Sea near the industrial city of Gdansk. Most of this plain is fertile land covered with rich loess soil which supports a range of cereal and vegetable crops, in which Poland is almost self-sufficient, and livestock, the most important of which are cattle and pigs. In the northeast the country is more undulating, and much of northern Poland is dotted with extensive lakes. Towards the Baltic coast a range of hills known as the Baltic Heights slope down to a sandy coastal plain.

Agriculture, which once employed more than half of Poland's workforce, still accounts for just over a quarter of it. The post-war years saw a rapid expansion of heavy industries, which now include shipbuilding, based in Gdansk, and steel and cement manufacture based around the mining centers in the south. Many industrial activities are associated with Poland's rich coal reserves, and coal is used to generate more than half the country's electricity. Reliance on this form of fuel has resulted in serious air pollution and acid rain. Other mineral resources include natural gas, iron ore, and salt, on which important chemical industries are based.

Poland has been more successful than many former communist states in converting to a privatized economy. While many Poles have prospered from a growing number of entrepreneurial opportunities, however, others have seen their incomes substantially lowered. Unemployment remains comparatively high.

The rooftops of Gdansk in northern Poland, a major port and birthplace of the trade union Solidarity (below). An oil well in a village in Belarus (right page top). Yalta and the crowded promenade on the Sea of Azov, Ukraine (right page bottom).

Belarus

Fact File

OFFICIAL NAME Republic of Belarus

FORM OF GOVERNMENT Republic with single legislative body (Supreme Soviet)

CAPITAL Minsk

AREA 207,600 sq km (80,154 sq miles)

TIME ZONE GMT + 2 hours

POPULATION 10,335,000

PROJECTED POPULATION 2015 9,664,000

POPULATION DENSITY 49.8 per sq km (128.9 per sq mile)

LIFE EXPECTANCY 68.3

INFANT MORTALITY (PER 1,000) 14.1

OFFICIAL LANGUAGE Belarusian

OTHER LANGUAGE Russian, languages of the minorities

LITERACY RATE 98 %

RELIGIONS Eastern Orthodox 60 %, other (including Roman Catholic and small Muslim and Jewish communities) 40 %

ETHNIC GROUPS Belarusian 78 %, Russian 13 %, Polish 4 %, Ukrainian 3 %, other 2 %

CURRENCY Belarusian ruble

ECONOMY Industry 40 %, services 39 %, agriculture 21 %

GNP PER CAPITA US$ 8,200

CLIMATE Temperate, with cold winters and mild, wet summers

HIGHEST POINT Mt Dzyarzhynskaya 346 m (1,135 ft)

MAP REFERENCE Pages 287, 299, 300

Until 1991, when it declared its independence of the disintegrating Soviet Union, Belarus was known as the Byelorussian (which means "White Russian") Soviet Socialist Republic. Throughout its extensive and troubled history, Belarus has been dominated, invaded, and sometimes devastated by a succession of foreign powers. Initally settled by Slavic tribes in the sixth century AD, the country came under the control of Kiev in the ninth century. Three centuries later it was conquered by invading armies from neighboring Lithuania and in the sixteenth century, with the merging of Lithuania and Poland, Polish

influences were also dominant. During the course of the eighteenth century the region came under Russian control and even today Belarus is economically dependent on its huge and powerful eastern neighbor.

Belarus was ravaged in the First and Second World Wars. The German invasion of 1941 saw the deaths of 1.3 million people and the virtual annihilation of the country's Jewish population. Many of Belarus's buildings were reduced to rubble and its capital, Minsk, was razed. Further devastation, in the form of nuclear contamination, occurred in 1986 after the Chernobyl disaster in Ukraine, its neighbor to the south. Much of the farming land in the southern part of Belarus remains contaminated by fallout from the accident and is unsafe for cultivation.

The country is generally low-lying, the landscape varying from sandy hills in the north to swampy areas in the south, many of which have been drained and their rich soils cultivated. There are about 11,000 lakes and the country is traversed by numerous rivers, which complement the extensive road and railway networks as a major means of transportation. Forests and woodland cover about thirty percent of the country and almost half the land area is devoted to agriculture, the main crops being barley, rye, potatoes, sugar beet, and flax. There are large numbers of livestock, and dairy and pig farming are important industries.

Belarus is relatively poor in natural resources although it has significant reserves of peat and rock salt and small reserves of coal. It is deeply in debt to the Russian Federation and relies on Russia for the electricity needed to power its industries, which include vast petrochemical plants and truck manufacturing.

Strikes and industrial and political unrest have been a significant feature of Belarusian life during its short period as an independent nation, sometimes aggravated by the inability of the government to pay many of its workers. A controversial treaty signed with Russia in 1996 resulted in a substantial merging of aspects of the economy with that of its large neighbor. This was seen by many as a sign of a progressive whittling away of the country's independence.

Ukraine

Fact File

OFFICIAL NAME Ukraine

FORM OF GOVERNMENT Republic with single legislative body (Supreme Council)

CAPITAL Kiev

AREA 603,700 sq km (233,089 sq miles)

TIME ZONE GMT + 2 hours

POPULATION 48,396,000

PROJECTED POPULATION 2015 43,335,000

POPULATION DENSITY 80.2 per sq km (207.6 per sq mile)

LIFE EXPECTANCY 66.3

INFANT MORTALITY (PER 1,000) 21.1

OFFICIAL LANGUAGE Ukrainian

OTHER LANGUAGES Russian, Romanian, Hungarian, Polish

LITERACY RATE 98 %

RELIGIONS Predominantly Christian (Ukrainian Orthodox, Ukrainian Autocephalus Orthodox, Roman Catholic); small Protestant, Jewish and Muslim minorities

ETHNIC GROUPS Ukrainian 73 %, Russian 22 %, other 5 %

CURRENCY Hryvna

ECONOMY Services 46 %, industry 33 %, agriculture 21 %

GNP PER CAPITA US$ 4,200

CLIMATE Temperate, with cold winters and mild summers; warmer on Black Sea coast

HIGHEST POINT Hora Hoverla 2,061 m (6,762 ft)

MAP REFERENCE Pages 289, 298

Ukraine, formerly part of the USSR, has a southern coastline on the Black Sea and on the almost landlocked Sea of Azov. Surrounding it are seven other countries. From southeast across its northern border to southwest, they are the Russian Federation, Belarus, Poland, Slovakia, Hungary, Romania, and Moldova. The Ukrainian capital, Kiev, has existed since the ninth century AD, when a Viking tribe established a center there. A century later it was a powerful force in Eastern Europe. It was overrun by Mongols in the thirteenth century and then came under Polish control. In the seventeenth century the eastern part of Ukraine fell to the Russians, who eventually absorbed the whole of the country into their empire. Despite attempts to establish a separate state after the 1917 Revolution, invading Soviet armies subdued Ukraine in 1920. During the 1930s more than 3 million Ukrainians perished in a famine and another 6 million died in the Nazi occupation during the Second World War. After the war, part of western Ukraine that was under Polish occupation was returned, as was the Crimea, and Ukraine assumed its present boundaries under Soviet domination. Ukraine declared its independence in 1991 as the Soviet Union began to break up, although it still retains close ties with Russia. It is now a democratic republic, with a directly elected president as head of state.

Formerly referred to as "the granary of the Soviet Union", most of Ukraine consists of fertile black-soil plains that produce an abundance of wheat and other cereal grains as well as vegetables, fruits, and fodder crops. Much of the country's agricultural output remains affected by the widespread contamination caused by the nuclear accident at Chernobyl, near the Belarus border, in 1986.

There are mountainous areas in the southwest, where the Carpathian Mountains sweep down from Poland, and in the Crimean Peninsula in the far south. The Dnieper River flows through the heart of the country and empties into the Black Sea. In its northern plain there are large stretches of marshland and many forest-rimmed lakes. In the south, bordering the Black Sea, much of the landscape is a semiarid, treeless plain.

Coal is Ukraine's most abundant and heavily exploited mineral resource. There are also significant reserves of natural gas, uranium, and oil, though the latter remains largely unexploited. Steel production, machine building, engineering, and chemical processing are the main industries. These industries are centered around the large cities and coalfields in the east of the country. In the post-Soviet era, the Ukrainian economy has suffered periods of extremely high inflation and growth has been hampered by a largely conservative legislature that has resisted many attempts at reform. There is widespread poverty, exacerbated by a declining healthcare system.

Moldova

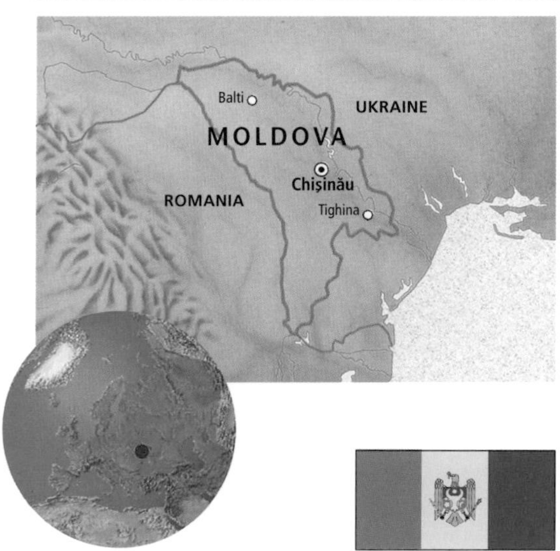

Fact File

OFFICIAL NAME Republic of Moldova

FORM OF GOVERNMENT Republic with single legislative body (Parliament)

CAPITAL Chisinau

AREA 33,700 sq km (13,012 sq miles)

TIME ZONE GMT + 2 hours

POPULATION 4,435,000

PROJECTED POPULATION 2015 4,152,000

POPULATION DENSITY 131.6 per sq km (340.8 per sq mile)

LIFE EXPECTANCY 64.7

INFANT MORTALITY (PER 1,000) 42.2

OFFICIAL LANGUAGE Moldovan

OTHER LANGUAGES Russian, Ukrainian, Gagauz (Turkish dialect)

LITERACY RATE 96 %

RELIGIONS Eastern Orthodox 98.5 %, Jewish 1.5 %

ETHNIC GROUPS Moldovan/Romanian 64.5 %, Ukrainian 13.8 %, Russian 13 %, Gagauz 3.5 %, Bulgarian 2 %, Jewish 1.5 %, other 1.7 %

CURRENCY Leu

ECONOMY Services 45.5 %, agriculture 34.4 %, industry 20.1 %

GNP PER CAPITA US$ 3,000

CLIMATE Temperate, with mild winters and warm summers

HIGHEST POINT Mt Balaneshty 430 m (1,411 ft)

MAP REFERENCE Page 296

Moldova is a small, landlocked country in southeastern Europe near the northern shores of the Black Sea. To the west the Prut River separates Moldova from Romania. Otherwise, it is completely enclosed by Ukrainian territory. Bessarabia—the section between the Prut and Dniester Rivers—which comprises almost all of present-day Moldova, was under Ottoman rule until 1812, when it passed to Russian control. With the collapse of the Russian Empire after the First World War, Bessarabia merged in 1918 with Romania, with which it is ethnically and linguistically almost identical.

The part of Moldova east of the Dniester remained under Russian control. As a result of the Nazi-Soviet Pact of 1940 Romania was forced to cede Bessarabia. Most of it was combined with a narrow strip of the Ukraine east of the Dniester to form the new state of Moldova. The remaining parts were incorporated into Ukraine.

After the Second World War, Moldova became a Soviet republic and systematic attempts were made to suppress all links with Romania. Large numbers of ethnic Romanians were forcibly removed to other countries in the Soviet Union, and Russian and Ukrainian immigration was fostered. Independence came in 1991 as the Soviet Union crumbled, but tensions between the predominantly Russian population in the region lying to the east of the Dniester, who wished to declare a separate republic, and the ethnic Romanians, who sought closer ties or even reunification, with Romania, resulted in violent clashes. In 1992, a joint Russian-Moldovan peacekeeping force was instituted to help restore order, although ethnic tensions persist. In 1994 a constitution was adopted that defined the country as a democratic republic. Moldova is the poorest nation in Europe and was the first former Soviet state to elect a communist president in 2001.

Most of the countryside of Moldova is lowlying but hilly steppe country. It is eroded by rivers and the landscape is cut by numerous deep valleys and gorges. Thick forests grow on many of the hillsides and most of the country is covered with thick, black, fertile soils. This fertile land, combined with a temperate climate, short winters and high summer rainfall, made Moldova one of the foremost producers of food in the former Soviet Union.

Agriculture remains the main element in the Moldovan economy. Vegetables, sunflower seeds, tobacco, wheat, and maize are the principal crops, as well as grapes, which contribute to a thriving winemaking and exporting industry. Cattle and pig raising are also widespread.

The country has minimal reserves of mineral resources and depends upon Russian imports for all its oil, gas, and coal supplies. Electricity, too, is mainly imported and due to the outdated electrical grid power shortages occur quite frequently. Industries include machine manufacturing and food processing.

The Commonwealth of Independent States

The Commonwealth of Independent States (CIS) is a loose confederation of twelve former Soviet republics that was formed after the breakdown of the Soviet Union in 1991. The idea for the formation of the commonwealth was agreed to at a meeting of Russian president Boris Yeltsin and the presidents of Belarus and Ukraine in Minsk, capital of Belarus, in early December 1991 and was ratified at Alma-Ata in Kazakhstan by eleven of the former Soviet republics on 21 December. Georgia and the three Baltic states of Estonia, Latvia, and Lithuania declined to join, although Georgia has since become a member. Not surprisingly, Russia assumed the status of dominant member of the group, taking control of all former Soviet embassies and consulates and occupying the former Soviet Union's seat on the United Nations Security Council. Minsk was designated as the administrative center of the new commonwealth, which was much more an alliance than a state entity. According to the agreement, the political independence of each state was guaranteed in return for a commitment to certain forms of economic and defence cooperation.

The commonwealth remains a tenuous confederation and there are many areas of dispute between its constituent members. There is a natural suspicion that the Russian Federation seeks to impose its political will on the other members, and this was in no way diminished in 1996 when the Russian parliament, or Duma, passed a non-binding resolution in favor of reinstating the former Soviet Union. Difficult economic conditions throughout the former Soviet Union have led to increasing support, especially in Belarus, for a return to the previous status quo.

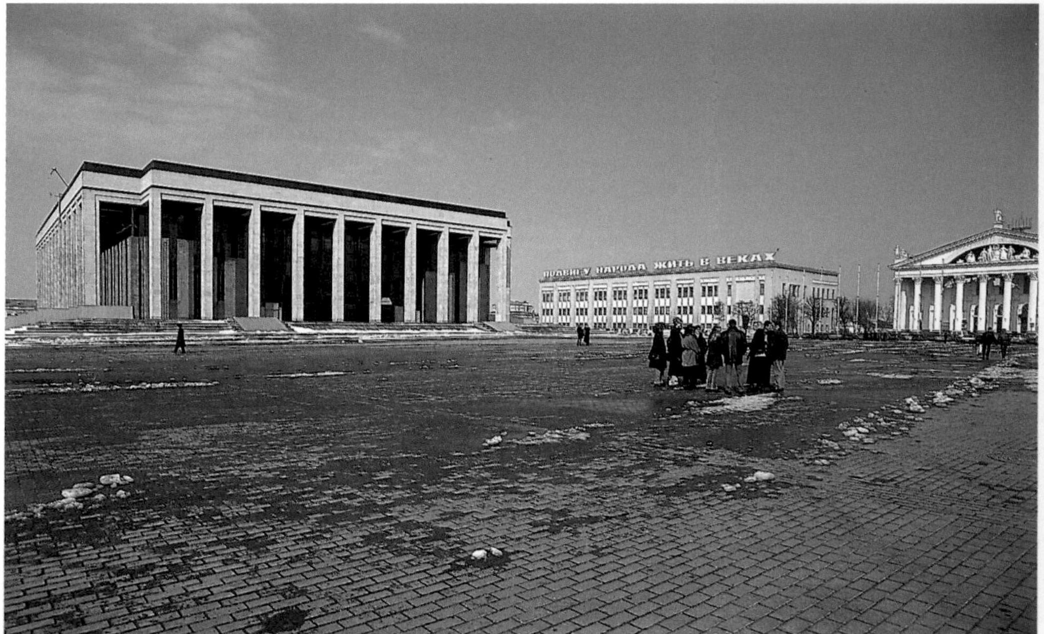

Russian Federation

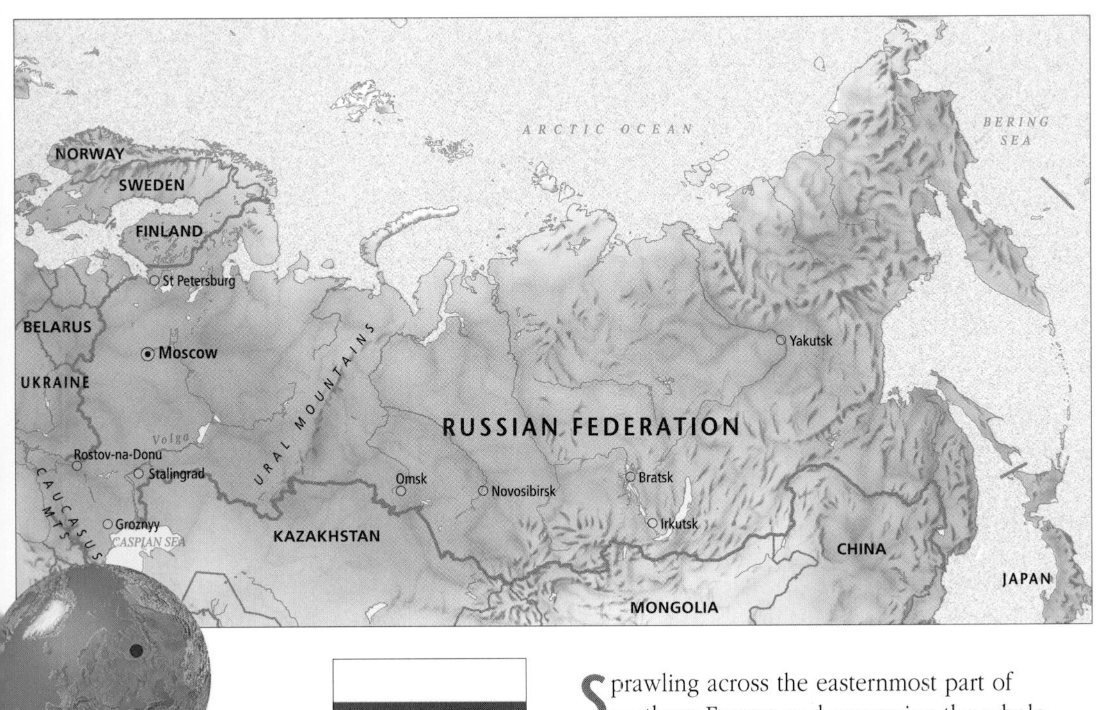

Fact file

Official name Russian Federation

Form of government Federal republic with two legislative bodies (Federation Council and State Duma)

Capital Moscow

Area 17,075,200 sq km (6,592,735 sq miles)

Time zone GMT + 3–12 hours

Population 146,979,000

Projected population 2015 133,314,000

Population density 8.6 per sq km (22.3 per sq mile)

Life expectancy 67.5

Infant mortality (per 1,000) 19.8

Official language Russian

Other languages More than 100 minority languages

Literacy rate 98 %

Religions Russian Orthodox 27 %; Muslim, Jewish, Roman Catholic and other minorities 73 %

Ethnic groups Russian 81.5 %, Tatar 3.8 %, Ukrainian 3 %, Chuvash 1.2 %, Bashkir 0.9 %, Belarusian 0.8 %, Moldovan 0.7 %, other 8.1 %

Currency Ruble

Economy Industry 27.1 %, agriculture 15.4 %, education and culture 10.8 %, other 46.7 %

GNP per capita US$ 8,800

Climate Warm and dry in far south; cold temperate (long, cold winters and short, mild summers) in most inland areas; polar in far north

Highest point Mt Elbrus 5,633 m (18,481 ft)

Map reference Pages 299, 300–01

Oktober Square with the Palace of the Republic in Minsk, capital of Belarus (left page). The gilded domes and turrets of Pushkin Palace in Moscow (above right). A river winding through fertile farming country in Russia (below right).

Sprawling across the easternmost part of northern Europe and occupying the whole of northern Asia, the Russian Federation, often called simply Russia, is the largest country in the world—it is almost twice the size of the United States—and it has the sixth largest population. Its 21 republics cover three-quarters of the area of what was for almost 70 years (until it collapsed in 1991) the Union of Soviet Socialist Republics (USSR).

The Russian Federation has long coastlines along the Arctic Ocean in the north and along the Pacific Ocean in the east. Its southeastern coastline is on the Sea of Japan and north of this the Kamchatka Peninsula encloses the Sea of Okhotsk. In its far southwestern corner there is a short stretch of coast along the Caspian Sea; a little further north, it briefly borders the Black Sea; and in the northwest, near St Petersburg, it touches on the eastern tip of the Gulf of Finland. Its mainland has borders with twelve other countries. In the far southeast it borders the northeast tip of North Korea. In the south it borders China in two places: to the east and the west of its long border with Mongolia. The western half of its southern border is with the former Soviet republic of Kazakhstan. To the west of the Caspian Sea are Azerbaijan and Georgia, and north of the Black Sea are Ukraine, Belarus, Latvia, and Estonia. Northeast of the Gulf of Finland is a border with Finland and at its very northwest tip the Russian Federation borders on a tiny part of Norway. Further west, tucked in between Lithuania and Poland, and with a coast on the Baltic Sea, is another small area of Russian territory, centered on the coastal city of Kaliningrad.

History

Until the sixth century AD, almost all of what is now Russia was inhabited only by nomadic tribes of Finnic and Slavic origin. In the sixth century peoples from what are now Iran and Turkey settled the part of southwestern Russia between the Carpathian Mountains and the Volga River, establishing a capital on the Caspian Sea. They in turn were overrun by Viking invaders and traders who spread southward along river routes from the Baltic Sea. One tradition has it that modern Russia dates back to the establishment of a dynasty by the Viking Rurik at Novgorod in AD 862. Soon after, however, the center of power moved farther southwest, to Kiev in present-day Ukraine, and a unified confederation known as Kievan Rus emerged. In the tenth century the leader

Vladimir was converted to Christianity. Over the next two centuries a Russian culture based on the traditions of Orthodox Christianity developed, but in the thirteenth century Kievan Rus fell to invaders from Mongolia and the confederation broke down into a number of dukedoms, under Mongol domination. The Muscovite dukes emerged as the most powerful, mainly through their role as tribute collectors for the Mongols. Opposition to Mongol rule gathered strength during the fourteenth century and in the fifteenth century the Muscovite Duke Ivan III finally expelled the Mongols. His grandson, Ivan IV, known as "The Terrible," was the first to declare himself "Tsar of all the Russians". Under his oppressive rule, which lasted from 1533 to 1584, the power of princes and landowners (known as "boyars") was broken and the Muscovite state spread eastward across the Urals and into what is now Siberia.

After Ivan's death, a series of internal disputes culminated in Polish invasion in 1609 and, after the ousting of the Poles in 1612, the emergence of the first Romanov tsar, Mikhail, in 1613. Under his grandson, Peter I (known as "The Great"), who ruled from 1696 to 1725, the country was renamed "Russia", and a new capital was established at St Petersburg. Territories along the Baltic were acquired from Sweden, and Western European ideas, technology, and styles of dress and other fashions were embraced. During the eighteenth and nineteenth centuries Russia extended its borders south and east into Asia.

The defeat of Napoleon's invading armies in 1812 confirmed Russia's status as a great power, but the country remained socially and industrially backward in comparison with Western Europe. A feudal system, under which peasants were bonded to landlords, remained until 1861, when Tsar Alexander II abolished serfdom. Alexander's political and social reforms earned him powerful enemies and led to his assassination in 1881. The oppressive rule of his successor, Alexander III, spawned the formation of the Marxist Russian Social Democratic Party in 1898, under the leadership of Vladimir Ilich Ulyanov, who called himself Lenin. Civil unrest intensified following Russia's defeat in its war with Japan in 1904–05, forcing Tsar Nicholas II to establish a parliament, known as the Duma, elected by a very limited suffrage, and to institute some civil liberty reforms.

These reforms, however, failed to stem the revolutionary tide, which was further strengthened by the reverses and heavy loss of life in the First World War. In February 1917 rioting and strikes broke out in the capital, St Petersburg. There was a massive defection of Russian troops, and Tsar Nicholas II abdicated, leading to the decisive revolution of October 1917, in which the All-Russian Communist Party emerged as the ruling force with Lenin as dictatorial leader. Four years of civil war ensued until the communists fully took control. In December 1922, Russia, with Moscow as its capital, became the dominant power in the newly formed Union of Soviet Socialist Republics, having seized Georgia, Armenia, and Azerbaijan and established its ascendancy in Ukraine and central Asia.

Following Lenin's death in 1924, there was a bitter factional struggle for power. By 1929 Joseph Vissarionovich Dzhugashvili, who called himself Stalin, "Man of Steel", was the undisputed leader and remained in power until he died in 1953. Under his regime, agriculture was collectivized, industry expanded, and brutal labor camps were established in Siberia for those suspected of espousing dissident ideas. Political rivals and enemies, whether real or imagined, were routinely eliminated in a series of ruthless purges. In one purge in 1929–30, hundreds of thousands of peasants who opposed farm collectivization were either murdered or sent away to remote, desolate parts of the country. Farm collectivization led to immense agricultural disruption and resulted in famine in the early 1930s in which many thousands of people died.

Russia and the rest of the Soviet Union suffered terribly during the Second World War. At first allied with Germany in 1939 and 1940 the Soviet Union seized territory in Poland and Romania, and annexed the Baltic republics of Estonia, Latvia, and Lithuania. In 1941, Hitler's troops suddenly invaded the Soviet Union, and in the occupation and struggles that ensued in the following four years an estimated 20 million Soviet citizens were killed.

At the end of the war, the regions that were occupied by Soviet forces—most of Eastern Europe—came under Soviet domination. This gave rise to a forty-year period of international tension as the Soviet Union and the United States assumed the mantles of mutually distrustful, competing superpowers, each building up an arsenal of ever more potentially destructive nuclear weapons. During the premiership of Stalin's successor, Nikita Khrushchev, the Soviet Union and its satellites entered into a defense treaty, the Warsaw Pact, to oppose the Western NATO alliance. Nuclear war seemed a real danger in 1962, when a Soviet attempt to place nuclear weapons on Cuba was met by a United States blockade. Khrushchev's humiliating backdown in this crisis, as well as a serious rift between Russia and communist China, led to his removal from office the next year and his replacement by Leonid Brezhnev.

The Brezhnev era lasted until 1982, and during this time Soviet-Western relations fluctuated. Periods of relaxation, which became known as "détente", alternated with times of renewed suspicion and hostility. Despite this, and despite the USSR's invasions of Czechoslovakia in 1968 and Afghanistan in December 1979, genuine agreements about arms reduction were achieved. During the brief premierships of Brezhnev's two immediate successors, East-West relations soured again. However, in 1985, the accession to the leadership of Mikhail Gorbachev led to an era of greater trust as well as to a less dictatorial and more open style of political leadership, and the first tentative moves toward a loosening of government controls over the economy. The terms *glasnost,* meaning "openness", and *perestroika*, meaning "restructuring", were used widely at this time in reference to Gorbachev's reforms.

Growing social unrest, deteriorating economic conditions, and a resurgence of nationalism in a number of Soviet republics created immense strains in the Soviet Union. An attempted coup by communist conservatives took place in 1991 but was put down, largely through the heroic opposition of Boris Yeltsin, who emerged as the de facto leader of the country, enjoying widespread popular support.

Against Gorbachev's wishes, the Soviet Union was officially dissolved in December 1991 and replaced by the Commonwealth of Independent States (CIS; see box on page 270). Gorbachev then resigned as president and Yeltsin assumed control. Yeltsin's leadership was confirmed in a national referendum that was held in 1993 and, despite a poor economic situation and widespread hardship as well as serious misgivings about his health, Yeltsin was reelected president in 1996. In the parliamentary, or Duma, elec-

Timeline

20,000 BP Huts made from mammoth bones covered in animal skins at Mezhirich in Ukraine region

4000 BC Horses domesticated on the steppes, first mainly as draft animals but later (2000 BC) as fast transport in warfare

AD 300 Spread of peoples including Huns, Goths, and Magyars into forests west of the Ural Mountains

AD 770 Germanic traders and soldiers from Baltic move into Volga region previously occupied by Finnic and Slavic groups

AD 830 Scandinavian merchants establish new base in the Volga region, close to present-day Ryazan

AD 882 Scandinavian groups capture Kiev; Russia takes its name from Kievan Rus, term given by Slavic groups to the Black Sea area

1237 Russia becomes part of Mongol Empire until late 1400s, extending the empire's boundaries to Arctic, Baltic and Pacific

1318 Mongols appoint Yuri of Moscow Crown Prince; he makes Moscow an important center and later the capital of Russia

1547 Ivan IV, known as "the Terrible", is crowned tsar and takes the title for all Russia

1613 Mikhail IV is the first Romanov tsar; his family rules until the murder of Nicholas II in 1918

1697 First recorded eruption of Klyuchevskaya Volcano in Kamchatka, Siberia

1703 Peter the Great opens Russia to Western ideas. Builds St Petersburg on the Baltic Sea, making it the capital in 1712

1725 Catherine the Great becomes Empress. Encourages Western ideas in arts and education. Most Russians impoverishe tions, however, conservative nationalists, some of them stridently anti-Western, received widespread support.

A new constitution adopted in 1993 established a two-chambered Federal Assembly, headed by a prime minister, who is appointed by the president. The president is popularly elected for a five-year term and has considerable independent powers, including the right to dissolve parliament.

Physical features and land use

Stretching all the way from the Arctic Ocean in the north to the border with Kazakhstan in the south, the Ural Mountains separate European Russia in the west from the vast Siberian Plain to the east. European Russia, where most of the population lives and where the bulk of Russian industry and agriculture is located, consists mainly of a huge fertile plain, the East Europe Plain, which has an average elevation of 170 m (550 ft) but rises to a maximum of 400 m (1,300 ft). In the far southwest, the Caucasus Mountains form a natural boundary with Georgia and Azerbaijan, and there are upland areas in the far north near the border with Finland. In the western part of the plain are the Valdai Hills, in which the Volga and Dnieper Rivers have their source.

Most of Russia's agriculture is concentrated in the south of the plain, as the harsh climates further north are not conducive to growing crops or raising livestock. Less than one-tenth of Russia's land area is under cultivation. Cereals are the main crops, although in most years the country produces only about half the grain it requires. The rest has to be imported. Livestock raising, most commonly poultry, cattle and dairy farming, is also based mainly in the west.

To the east of the Ural Mountains, the Siberian Plain is largely desolate, treeless, and flat. Central Siberia, to the east of the Yenisey River, is a region of plateaus that range from between 450 and 900 m (1,500 and 3,000 ft) in height and rise in the south to a series of mountain ranges that border Mongolia and China. Lowlands flank these plateaus to the north and east. East of the Lena River the country rises again toward the rugged and mountainous east coast. South of the Bering Sea, the Kamchatka Peninsula and the Kuril Islands form part of the Pacific "Ring of Fire". This is an area of considerable geothermal activity and there are about thirty active volcanoes.

The landscape of northern Russia is mainly arctic tundra—a treeless expanse which remains frozen throughout the year. Tundra vegetation consists of sedges, grasses, mosses, lichens, and ground-hugging plants. Further south, and in the southwest, the landscape varies between tracts of semidesert and expanses of forest, largely conifers, known as the taiga.

Industry, commerce, and culture

Russia, and especially Siberia, has abundant mineral resources. These contributed greatly to the country's rapid transformation during the Soviet period from a predominantly agricultural economy to one that was heavily industrialized. These mineral resources underpin the federation's present reliance on heavy industry and provide important mining exports. They include coal, petroleum, natural gas, iron ore, bauxite, copper, lead, zinc, and gold and other precious metals. Steelmaking, the manufacture of agricultural machinery, chemicals, textiles, and food processing are among the principal industries, centered on such large cities to the west of the Ural Mountains as Moscow, St Petersburg, Novgorod, and Volgograd, but also in a number of cities in Siberia such as Yekaterinburg and Novosibirsk.

The country's move toward a market economy has been fraught with difficulties and has been accompanied by a marked increase in social and financial inequalities as a new class of rich entrepreneurs has emerged. The majority of Russians live in relative poverty, victims of steeply rising prices and severe shortages of food and other basic consumer items. Corruption and crime have also increased significantly and a number of the leaders of organized crime are among the richest citizens in the nation. These conditions were aggravated by a virtual collapse of the Russian economy in 1998 and continuing political uncertainty based on serious doubts, unallayed by official reassurances, about the capacity of the president, Boris Yeltsin, who suffers chronic ill health. There are strong movements within the country for a return to centralized control of the economy and for a more aggressive nationalistic approach to relations with the West.

Shoppers in Arbat Street, a prosperous part of Moscow (left page top). Fishing through a hole in the ice, using large nets, in Siberia (above). St Petersburg, once the capital of Russia, seen from across the misty Neva River (below).

Russia has contributed much to literature, music, and the performing arts, especially in the nineteenth century. Writers such as Ivan Sergeevich Turgenev prepared the way for other giants of literature like Leo Tolstoy and Fyodor Mikhailovich Dostoyevsky. Among composers, Pyotr Ilyich Tchaikovsky and Igor Stravinsky established Russia's place in musical history. The Imperial Russian Ballet was founded in 1735, and Russian ballet has become internationally renowned for its choreography and dancers like Anna Pavlova and Rudolf Nureyev.

773–74 The easants Revolt weeps across Russia om the Urals to ne Volga but is put own by troops

1812 Napoleon's invasion of Russia defeated. Most of the 500,000 French forces die or are captured

1890 Migration of large numbers of people from eastern Russia to Siberia and Asia lasts for around 10 years

1891 Construction of the Trans-Siberian Railroad from Moscow to Vladivostok begins. Not completed until 1916

1914 Germany declares war on Russia and for three years Russia sides with Allies

1917 Revolution puts Bolsheviks in power after storming of the Winter Palace, at St Petersburg

1918 Tsar Nicholas II and family are shot, allegedly at the hands of the Bolsheviks; Moscow again capital of Russia

1918–20 Communists victorious in a civil war with the anti-communist White Russians

1928 First Five-Year Plan introduced to further centralize the economy and increase industrial and agricultural production

1929 Stalin becomes undisputed leader and rules USSR for more than 20 years until his death in 1953

1935 Great Purge by Stalin's secret police takes many lives; millions starve in a famine partly caused by farm collectivization

1941 Russia sides with Allies in Second World War after Germany invades USSR and is defeated in the Battle of Stalingrad (1943)

1956 Bezymianny Volcano in Kamchatka, Siberia, erupts leaving ash 50 cm (20 in) deep 10 km (6 miles) from volcano

1985 Gorbachev heads Communist Party; pursues policies of *perestroika* ("economic restructuring") and *glasnost* ("openness")

1986 Chernobyl nuclear reactor in Ukraine explodes; cancers from radiation kill up to 40,000 worldwide

2002 In the Rome Declaration Russia becomes a partner with equal rights in the NATO

United Kingdom

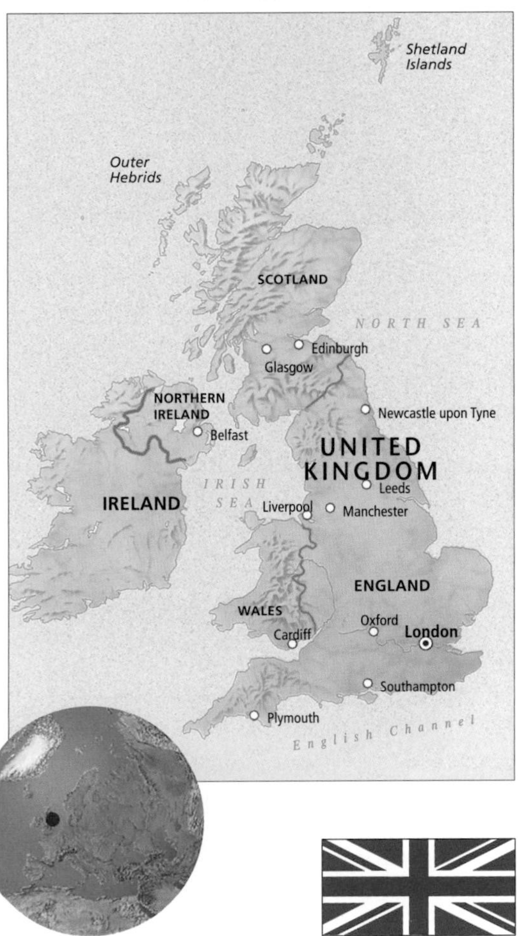

Fact File

OFFICIAL NAME United Kingdom of Great Britain and Northern Ireland

FORM OF GOVERNMENT Constitutional monarchy with two legislative houses (House of Lords and House of Commons)

CAPITAL London

AREA 244,820 sq km (94,525 sq miles)

TIME ZONE GMT

POPULATION 59,778,000

PROJECTED POPULATION 2015 60,566,000

POPULATION DENSITY 244.2 per sq km (632.4 per sq mile)

LIFE EXPECTANCY 78.0

INFANT MORTALITY (PER 1,000) 5.5

OFFICIAL LANGUAGE English

OTHER LANGUAGES Welsh, Scots Gaelic, Manx, Cornish

LITERACY RATE 99 %

RELIGIONS Anglican 63 %, Roman Catholic 14 %, Presbyterian 4 %, Methodist 3 %, Muslim 3 %, other 13 %

ETHNIC GROUPS English 81.5 %, Scottish 9.6 %, Irish 2.4 %, Welsh 1.9 %, Northern Irish 1.8 %, other 2.8 %

CURRENCY Pound sterling

ECONOMY Services 78 %, industry 20 %, agriculture 2 %

GNP PER CAPITA US$ 25,300

CLIMATE Temperate, with cool winters and mild summers; generally wetter and warmer in the west, and cooler in the north

HIGHEST POINT Ben Nevis 1,343 m (4,406 ft)

MAP REFERENCE Pages 302–03

Lying just north of the westernmost edge of continental Europe, the United Kingdom consists of the large island of Great Britain, the far northeast corner of the island of Ireland, which sits across the Irish Sea to the west, and several hundred small islands scattered around the British coast. The United Kingdom is separated by the English Channel from the north coast of France which, at its nearest point, is no more than 32 km (20 miles) away, and a rail tunnel under the Channel now links England and France. England, in the south and southwest, occupies the greatest part of the island. Scotland is to the north, and Wales in the west juts out into the Irish Sea. The long eastern coast of Great Britain faces the North Sea; its western coastline is on the Atlantic Ocean and the Irish Sea.

History

Thanks partly to the natural protection offered by surrounding waters, but also to its maritime supremacy in certain periods of history and to a degree of good fortune in others, Britain is unique among major European nations in that it has escaped foreign invasion for almost 1,000 years. When William, Duke of Normandy led his successful invasion in 1066, it was the culmination of a long series of incursions that the island kingdom had suffered since the first invasion by the Romans in the first century AD.

Within 60 years of their arrival in Britain in AD 55, the Romans had established control over England and Wales and later introduced Christianity. When they finally withdrew at the beginning of the fifth century, the Britons eventually fell prey to Germanic tribes from

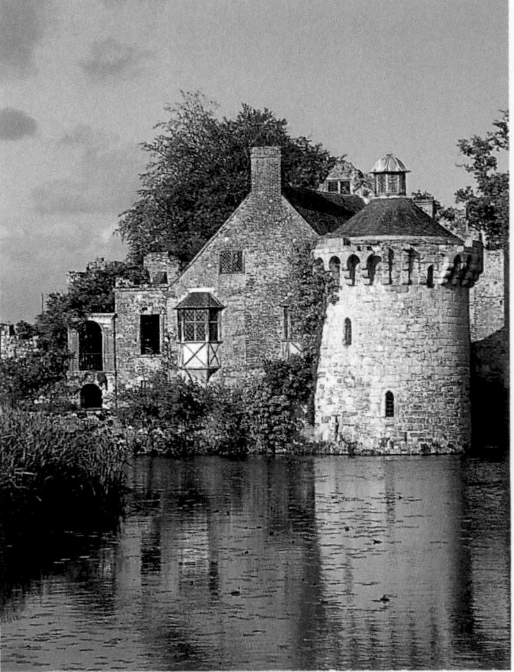

Scandinavia and the Low Countries. By the eighth century most of Britain, except the far west and the north, had succumbed and the country was divided into a number of Anglo-Saxon kingdoms.

Viking attacks from Norway and Denmark occurred during the course of the eighth and ninth centuries, with Danish invaders controlling much of north and northeast England by the late ninth century. United under the kings of Wessex by the middle of the tenth century, England again fell to Danish control early in the eleventh century. When Edward the Confessor came to the throne in 1042, he presided over a unified, but fractious, kingdom. On his death in 1066 both his brother-in-law, Harold, and his cousin, William of Normandy, claimed the throne. William was victorious at the Battle of Hastings and was crowned on Christmas Day 1066.

The feudal system of government developed by William the Conqueror gave significant power to the nobles. Under Henry II, the first Plantagenet king, power became more centralized in the crown. This and increasing civil unrest during the reign of John, led to a revolt by nobles, who in 1215 forced the king to sign the Magna Carta, a document limiting royal power and enshrining basic civil rights. This in turn gave rise to the development of a more consultative style of government, and, by the late thirteenth century, to the establishment of a House of Commons with powers to raise taxes.

Under Edward I (1272–1307) Wales was brought under English control, much of Ireland was subjugated, and a portion of Scotland was conquered. In 1314, however, at the Battle of

Timeline

200,000 BC Hominids living in southeastern Britain use stone tools and hunt animals

12,000 BC Paleolithic hunters carve mammal bones at Cresswell Crags, Derbyshire; one shows a dancing man, others, animal heads

4000 BC Tribes from various parts of Europe arrive; they farm and live in villages, burying their dead in earth mounds

3300 BC Construction of a large stone circle begins: Stonehenge completed 1800 BC

43 BC–AD 446 Roman occupation of Britain brings wealth, military skills, and Christianity; Hadrian's Wall built AD 120

AD 410 Anglo-Saxons settle in south England destroying remains of Roman culture; later, Danish Vikings settle in north and east

1066 Norman invasion. William I's *Domesday Book* assesses Britain's wealth and estimates population about 2 million

1300 Population reaches 5 million after expanding rapidly as a result of more efficient farming methods

1489 Enclosure of common land forces many people off the land, causing rebellions and rural depopulation

1500 Little ice age of cold winters and wet summers (which continues until 1700) causes crop failures across the country

1536 Parliament formally makes Wales part of English territory

1664–66 Great Plague kills more than 75,000 of London's population of around 450,000, then spreads to other parts of the country

1707 Act of Union between England and Scotland creates United Kingdom of Great Britain

1750 Use of iron grows rapidly; machines for spinning and weaving invented in late 1700s, accelerating Industrial Revolution

1801 Act c[...] Unio[...] extended t[...] join Irelan[...] to Unite[...] Kingdom

Bannockburn, the English were driven out of Scotland. Between 1338 and 1453, in a series of devastating wars known as the Hundred Years War, England lost all its French territories. This led to a further 30 years of civil war, known as the Wars of the Roses, which culminated in the accession to the throne of Henry VII, the first of the Tudor monarchs, in 1485.

The Tudor dynasty lasted until 1603, and during this time, especially during the reign of Elizabeth I (1558–1603), England became a leading power in the world, enjoying a golden age in which colonies were established in North America, British navigators sailed to remote corners of the globe, and there was a notable flowering of English theater, first and foremost thanks to William Shakespeare. During the reign of Elizabeth's father, King Henry VIII, Protestantism, in the form of the Church of England, had been established in England.

When Elizabeth died without an heir, James VI of Scotland, the first Stuart king, succeeded her, combining the two kingdoms and reigning as James I of England. Attempts by his son, Charles I, to curb the powers of parliament led to the outbreak of civil war in 1642. With the victory of the parliamentary armies, led by Oliver Cromwell, in 1646, the monarchy was abolished and a commonwealth, virtually a military dictatorship, set up under Cromwell. The Commonwealth did not long survive the death of Cromwell and in 1660 Charles II was installed as king. When his brother, the Catholic James II, attempted to restore Catholic domination, however, he was ousted and his Protestant daughter, Mary, and her Dutch husband, William of Orange, accepted the crown in 1689. In the same year, parliament enacted legislation barring Catholics from the throne. In 1690, at the Battle of the Boyne, their armies defeated a Catholic uprising in Ireland. In 1707 an Act of Union between the Scottish and English parliaments formally joined the two countries. Scottish rebellions against British rule were finally put down in 1746, when Charles Edward Stuart (Bonnie Prince Charlie) was defeated in the Battle of Culloden.

Under the Hanoverian monarchs, the first of whom, George I, accepted the throne in 1814 as King of Great Britain and Ireland, greater power devolved to the parliament. In 1721, Sir Hugh Walpole became the first prime minister to head a ministry that exercised executive power with the sanction of parliament. The eighteenth century, too, was a period of great expansion of British power that saw the acquisitions of British colonies in India and Canada and the exploration and colonization of Australia. A major setback was the loss of the American colonies in 1776. The military defeat of Irish rebels in 1798 led to an Act of Union that formally joined the two countries, the UK and Ireland, in 1801. Defeat of Bonaparte at Waterloo in 1815 confirmed Britain as the world's leading power.

The nineteenth century was a time of further expansion and consolidation of Britain's influence and power. By the end of Queen Victoria's 64-year reign in 1901, Britain's colonies extended throughout much of the world, including large parts of Africa, although by then Australia, New Zealand, and Canada had gained their independence and demands for Irish independence were growing. During the century a number of Reform Bills brought in significant democratic reforms and the Industrial Revolution resulted in increasing industrialization, urban growth, and a slowly rising standard of living.

Three-quarters of a million British soldiers were killed during the First World War, which also left the country considerably weakened economically. This situation was exacerbated by the Great Depression. After a protracted and bitter struggle, Ireland, with the exception of the provinces of Northern Ireland, became independent in 1922 and British troops faced growing unrest in India and in parts of the Middle East. Following the Second World War, in which British cities, especially London, were subjected to sustained German bombardment from the air, Britain endured almost a decade of austerity.

India gained its independence in 1947, and in 1956 Britain suffered a humiliating defeat in its armed attempt to prevent Egypt's nationalization of the Suez Canal. In 1982 Britain was again at war, this time against Argentina, which attempted to seize the Falkland Islands. In a two-week conflict, Britain repulsed the Argentines with the loss of 255 British lives. In recent years bitter violence between Catholics and Protestants in Northern Ireland has been a major preoccupation of British governments. Since 1995, however, there have been developments, including the intervention of the United States and the Belfast Treaty of 1998 that established partial autonomy for Northern Ireland, that augur well for a peaceful resolution of this conflict.

Britain, as a member of the European Union and a signatory of the Maastricht Treaty, is a significant force in Europe as it moves closer to political and economic integration. It is one of the world's most stable multi-party democracies in spite of ongoing debate about the role and viability of the monarchy and of its unelected, and largely hereditary, upper house of parliament, the House of Lords, which is in the process of reform. Power resides in the House of Commons, which is elected by universal adult suffrage for terms of five years.

Physical features and land use

The United Kingdom has a considerable variety of landscapes, ranging from craggy mountain ranges and tranquil upland lakes in the north, to gently rolling hills and green plains that are characteristic of the south and southeast. The majority of the mountain ranges are very old, geologically speaking.

Scotland is the most mountainous part of the country. Mainland Scotland has three main regions: the Highlands in the north, the Southern Uplands near the border with England, and in between the flatter, though often hilly, Central

Scotney Castle in Kent, southeastern England (left page). A tile-hung house in a village in southern England (right). Ebbw Valley British Steel tinplate mill in the town of Ebbw Vale, south Wales (far right).

1825 World's first public railway opens between Stockton and Darlington, starting a worldwide boom in railway construction

1837 Queen Victoria crowned. Rule lasts until 1901, coincides with period of great wealth and growth of British Empire

1845–46 Potato crop failure causes Great Famine in Ireland; millions die or emigrate to England, USA, Canada, Australia

1901 The population of Britain reaches 42 million after rapid population growth in the second half of the nineteenth century

1914–18 First World War against Germany causes the loss of more than 900,000 British Empire lives

1920 Northern Ireland separates from the rest of Ireland and remains part of the United Kingdom; the Irish Free State (southern Ireland) is set up in 1921

1930s Unemployment rises to 3 million; some relief provided by economic progress in manufacturing industries

1939–45 Cities across Britain bombed during Second World War—widespread damage and the loss of thousands of lives

1945 Churchill loses election to Labour Party's Attlee who begins a program of reconstruction, reform, and nationalization

1957 Extensive postwar migration from Commonwealth regions such as Pakistan, India, and West Indies

1967 Britain fails to join the EC; membership not achieved until 1973; sterling devalued

1975 Offshore North Sea oilfields begin operation, boosting the UK economy; Britain becomes self-sufficient in oil

1994 Passenger train services through the fixed-link railway tunnel under the English Channel link France and the UK

1999 Scotland and Wales elect regional parliaments as part of the devolution program

CONSTITUENT COUNTRIES

England • London
Scotland • Edinburgh
Northern Ireland • Belfast
Wales • Cardiff

OVERSEAS TERRITORIES

Anguilla
Bermuda
British Indian Ocean Territory
British Virgin Islands
Cayman Islands
Falkland Islands
Gibraltar
Guernsey
Isle of Man
Jersey
Montserrat
Pitcairn Islands
St Helena
South Georgia and the South Sandwich islands
Turks and Caicos islands

Lowlands. It also has several groups of offshore islands: the Shetlands in the far north, the Orkneys off the northeastern tip of the mainland, and the Inner and Outer Hebrides off the northwestern coast. The most rugged country is in the north, where two granite ranges, the North West Highlands and the Grampians, dominate the scene. In the northwest the mountains are cut by deep glaciated valleys and the coastline is rocky and deeply indented. South and east of the Great Glen, which contains the famous Loch Ness, are the Grampians, where Britain's highest peaks are found. Here, the country is generally less harsh, and there are stretches of sheep-grazing land and forested slopes where there are herds of deer. East of the Grampians is a rich agricultural lowland area that stretches in an arc from near Inverness around to Aberdeen.

Scotland's two largest cities, Glasgow and Edinburgh, lie in the Central Lowlands, the most populous region and Scotland's industrial heart. The Central Lowlands contain several ranges of undulating hills and are drained by the eastward-flowing Tay and Forth Rivers and the westward-flowing Clyde. The area east of Edinburgh is prime country, both for stock raising and crop cultivation. The Southern Uplands, gentler and less lofty than their northern counterparts, are characterized by hills, moorlands, and picturesque valleys, and in the valley of the Tweed and its tributaries are large areas of sheltered farmland. The Cheviot Hills in the south form a natural border with England.

Beginning just south of the Cheviot Hills and running southward as far as north Derbyshire are the Pennine Mountains, a predominantly limestone range of hills, plateaus, expanses of moorlands, and soft, green valleys, which are often referred to as the Dales. West of the Pennines, and separated from it by the valley of the Eden River, are the Cumbrian Mountains, a region of craggy peaks with many lakes. This is England's famous Lake District. To the east of the Pennines are the elevated expanses of the North York Moors.

South of the Pennines, beginning around the fertile valleys of the Trent and Avon Rivers, the countryside becomes flatter and gently undulating, reaching its lowest point in the marshy fen country north of Cambridge. Numerous ranges of hills provide relief from the generally rolling countryside. The most notable hills are the Cotswolds in the central southwest, where England's longest river, the Thames, begins its course eastward across the country, passing through London and out to the North Sea.

Wales, which juts out into the Irish Sea to the west of England, is more mountainous, its center dominated by the Cambrian Mountains, in which the Severn, Britain's second longest river, arises. Mount Snowdon, in Snowdonia, a large national park in northern Wales, rises to 1,085 m (3,559 ft) and is the highest peak in England and Wales.

Northern Ireland is flat for the most part, but to the north of Belfast is the Antrim Plateau, whose basalt cliffs provide some of the country's most arresting coastal scenery.

Industry, commerce, agriculture, and culture

Crop cultivation in Britain is concentrated mainly in the east and southeast of the country. Wheat is the principal crop, though potatoes and fruits are widely cultivated. Pasturelands are more common in the west and southwest, where sheep and cattle raising and dairy farming predominate. Although the United Kingdom exports much of its produce, it still imports about one-third of its food needs.

The United Kingdom has traditionally relied on coal for its energy resources, and there are still adequate reserves. However, the replacement of most coal-fired power stations with gas-powered facilities in recent years has resulted in the near closure of the coal-mining industry. The country also has a number of nuclear power stations which are a continuing subject of controversy. Oil and gas reserves in the North Sea are a major source of revenue, and have helped to make the country self-sufficient in energy.

Manufacturing was once the mainstay of the British economy, with a large proportion of heavy industry centered on industrial cities in the Midlands such as Birmingham, Manchester, and Liverpool. Food processing, machinery, and textile manufacture are still among the principal manufacturing industries. Motor vehicle and aircraft manufacture are long-established core industries, although much of the motor vehicle industry is now owned by foreign companies. Most of the raw materials needed to supply Britain's industries have to be imported from other countries.

Apart from the ethnic and cultural minorities found in Wales and Scotland, Britain's population is relatively homogeneous. Since the 1950s, however, large numbers of immigrants from former British colonies in the Caribbean, Asia (especially India and Pakistan), and Africa have changed the racial composition, most notably in inner-city areas, where the majority of ethnic minorities have congregated. Despite certain tensions, these immigrants are now generally accepted as an integral, if still relatively disadvantaged, part of British society.

Britain's economy is one of the most developed in Western Europe and its people enjoy a high standard of living, although there are considerable variations in levels of affluence. Universal free education and health systems are maintained by the state, although some social services and the value of pensions, including those for the elderly, have been sharply cut back in recent years.

A unionist mural in Belfast, Northern Ireland (above).
A cobbled shopping street in Dublin, Ireland (below).

Ireland

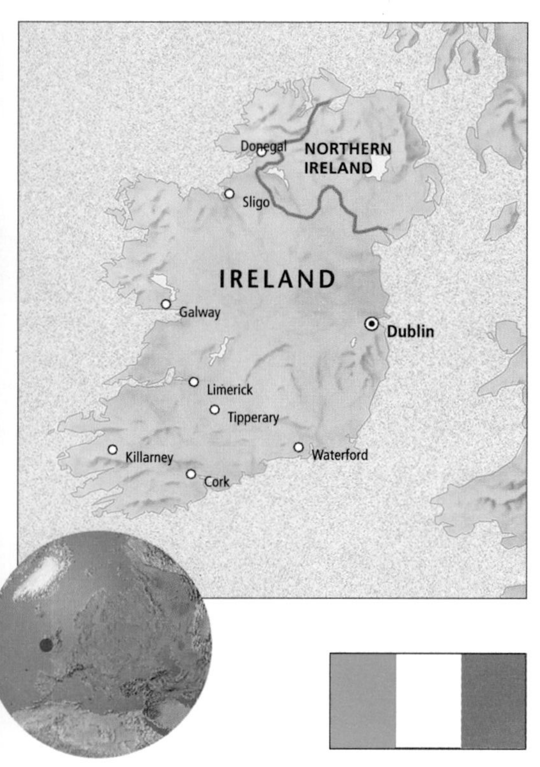

Fact File

Official name Ireland, Eire

Form of government Republic with two legislative bodies (Senate and House of Representatives)

Capital Dublin

Area 70,280 sq km (27,135 sq miles)

Time zone GMT

Population 3,883,000

Projected population 2015 4,410,000

Population density 55.3 per sq km (143.1 per sq mile)

Life expectancy 77.2

Infant mortality (per 1,000) 5.4

Official languages Irish Gaelic, English

Literacy rate 98 %

Religions Roman Catholic 93 %, Anglican 3 %, other 4 %

Ethnic groups Celtic 94 %, English minority

Currency Euro

Economy Services 69 %, industry 18 %, agriculture 13 %

GNP per capita US$ 28,500

Climate Temperate, with cool, wet winters and mild summers; wetter in the west

Highest point Carrauntoohil 1,041 m (3,415 ft)

Map reference Pages 303, 309

Situated in the northern Atlantic Ocean and separated from the British mainland to the east by the Irish Sea, the republic of Ireland covers more than three-quarters of the island of Ireland. The northeast corner comprises the six counties that form Northern Ireland, which is part of the United Kingdom.

In the fourth century BC, Gaelic-speaking invaders conquered the island and established a Celtic civilization. Tradition has it that St Patrick brought Christianity to Ireland in AD 432, and to this day Catholicism remains the dominant religion. From the eighth century AD Viking raiders attacked the coasts and settled some coastal regions, but they were finally repulsed in 1014. During the twelfth century, the pope, Adrian IV, ceded the entire island to the English crown, but another five centuries were to pass before local opposition was finally subjugated. From 1846 to 1851 disease destroyed the Irish staple crop, potatoes, leading to famine and more than a million deaths. Roughly half the population emigrated at this time, mainly to the USA.

Although the Irish were granted a degree of autonomy in the eighteenth century, opposition to British rule festered throughout the nineteenth century, leading to the unsuccessful Easter Rebellion of 1916 and the eventual granting of home rule to most of the island, as the Irish Free State, in 1921. In 1949 the Republic of Ireland was declared and formal ties with the British crown were severed. Today Ireland is a parliamentary democracy, with a popularly elected president as head of state and two houses of parliament.

Most of the landscape consists of a low-lying limestone plain, with undulating hills and areas of fertile soils. Small lakes and peat bogs abound throughout the countryside. Mountain ranges run along much of the coast, creating some of Europe's most spectacular coastal scenery, especially in the southwest. The most significant ranges are the Wicklow Mountains in the southeast and Macgillicuddy's Reeks in the far southwest. The Shannon, the country's longest river, rises in the Iron Mountains not far from the Northern Ireland border. It drains the central plain and flows through a number of Ireland's largest lakes.

Traditionally an agricultural country, Ireland now relies mainly on manufacturing and processing industries for its present, relatively healthy, economic strength. The country joined the European Community in 1973. Four in ten members of the population live in urban areas. Clothing, pharmaceuticals, and the manufacture of heavy machinery contribute largely to Ireland's export earnings and tourism is also significant. More than 3 million people visit Ireland every year. About one in eight workers is still involved in agriculture, mainly in livestock raising and dairying, but also in cultivating crops such as potatoes, barley, and wheat. The country has reserves of natural gas, oil and peat.

The Troubles in Northern Ireland

Ever since Britain's granting of independence to the Irish Free State in 1921, Northern Ireland has been a troubled province, a place where terrorism and sectarian strife have been the norm. The arrangements for the government of Northern Ireland created bitter resentment among its minority Catholic population. Northern Ireland was granted self-government, with its own parliament in Belfast, but maintaining strong links with the British government in London. The government ruled blatantly in favor of the Protestant majority, excluding Catholics from positions of authority or influence. Catholics moved in great numbers from the country to Belfast and other cities in order to find work, almost invariably in menial jobs in shipbuilding, textile, and other industries.

The Irish Republican Army (IRA), which had used guerrilla tactics against the British during Ireland's struggle for independence, became a threat to the stability of Northern Ireland, carrying out sporadic attacks on Protestant targets. When in 1948 the Irish Free State, as Ireland was then called, left the British Commonwealth and became the Republic of Ireland, battle lines became marked. The IRA began to campaign aggressively for Northern Ireland to be absorbed into the republic and for a breaking of ties with Britain, but for the next two decades it made little progress in the face of Northern Ireland's largely apathetic Catholic population.

However, as discrimination, especially in housing and employment, continued in Northern Ireland, Catholics grew increasingly militant, and in the late 1960s waged a widespread campaign for increased civil rights. Their demonstrations provoked counter-demonstrations by militant Protestants and a 30-year period of violent sectarian clashes was launched. The situation was aggravated by the arrival of British troops, ostensibly to maintain the peace. They were soon perceived by Catholics to be acting in the interests of the Protestants, especially after 1972, when they opened fire on Catholic demonstrators in Londonderry, killing 13 of them. In March 1972, in the wake of this incident, the British government suspended the parliament in Belfast and instituted direct rule for the province from London, a move that antagonized people on both sides of the struggle.

The desire of one section of the IRA to abandon violence led to a split in 1969. A wing of the IRA—the Provisionals, or Provos—consisting mainly of younger members, remained committed to terrorism and during the 1970s and 1980s carried out repeated bombings, murders, and kidnappings of both civilians and British army personnel, not only in Ireland, but also on the British mainland. Protestants in Northern Ireland responded in kind. From the early 1970s until the mid-1990s more than 3,000 people died in the conflict, and many more were wounded. The most prominent victim was Earl Mountbatten, who was assassinated in the Irish Republic in 1979. Northern Ireland towns and cities were divided into Catholic and Protestant zones, and an atmosphere of fear and distrust prevailed.

Any possibility of a negotiated peace was thwarted by the determination of successive British governments not to recognize or to have discussions with the IRA. This situation changed in 1994, when the Provisional IRA suspended its terrorist campaign and talks, at first in secret, but later open, were held in London. The talks broke down in 1996 when the Provisional IRA revoked its cease-fire and continued its attacks. The Belfast or Good Friday Agreement of 1998 sets out a plan for devolved government in Northern Ireland and could, in spite of a flare of violence in 2000, lead to a stable solution.

Dependencies in Europe

Faeroe Islands

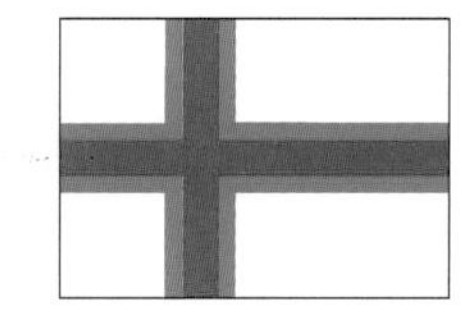

Fact file

OFFICIAL NAME Faeroe Islands

FORM OF GOVERNMENT Self-governing overseas administrative division of Denmark

CAPITAL Torshavn

AREA 1,400 sq km (541 sq miles)

TIME ZONE GMT

POPULATION 46,000

LIFE EXPECTANCY 78.7

INFANT MORTALITY (PER 1,000) 6.7

LITERACY RATE Not available

CURRENCY Danish krone

ECONOMY Mainly fishing; some agriculture, light industry, and services

CLIMATE Mild winters, cool summers; foggy and windy

MAP REFERENCE Page 302

The Faeroes are an archipelago of 22 islands in the north Atlantic Ocean between Scotland and Iceland, eighteen of which are inhabited. Though part of Danish territory, the Faeroes have enjoyed a high degree of autonomy since 1948. They have their own parliament, elected for four-year terms. In the eleventh century these islands came under Norwegian control, but when the crowns of Norway and Denmark combined in the fourteenth century, Denmark became the dominant power. Since 1709 the islands have been administered by Denmark. The Faeroes, formed from volcanic lava, are rocky, with spectacular cliffs along the coasts. Sheep raising has been the economic mainstay, though recently fishing has supplanted it in importance. Despite international criticism, the Faeroese continue whaling.

Gibraltar

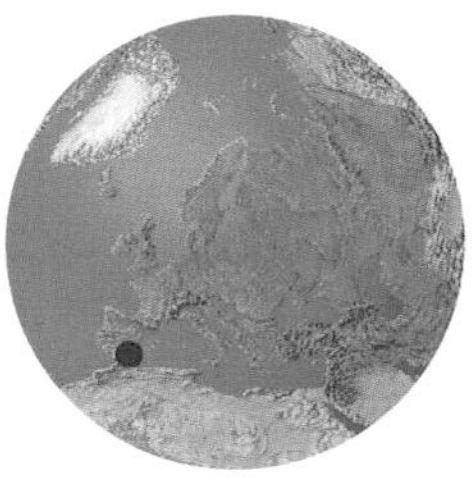

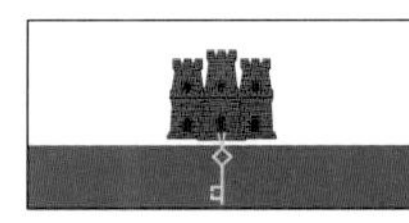

Fact file

OFFICIAL NAME Gibraltar

FORM OF GOVERNMENT Self-governing dependent territory of the United Kingdom

CAPITAL Gibraltar

AREA 6.5 sq km (2.5 sq miles)

TIME ZONE GMT + 1 hour

POPULATION 28,000

LIFE EXPECTANCY 77.2

INFANT MORTALITY (PER 1,000) 5.4

LITERACY RATE Not available

CURRENCY Gibraltar pound

ECONOMY Financial services, tourism, manufacturing, horticulture

CLIMATE Temperate; mild winters and warm summers

MAP REFERENCE Page 292

Jutting into the Strait of Gibraltar at the southwest tip of Spain, Gibraltar sits at the entrance to the Mediterranean Sea. Spain's capture of Gibraltar in 1462 ended seven centuries of Moorish rule. Seized by the British and Dutch in 1704, it was ceded to Britain in 1713 and, despite subsequent Spanish attempts to take it back, it has remained in British hands ever since. Spain and Britain still dispute possession of "The Rock". In two referendums in 1967 and 2002 an overwhelming majority of the inhabitants voted for staying with the UK. Gibraltar has its own elected parliament and is virtually autonomous. Britain maintained a military garrison until 1991, then handed over control to the local regiment. Gibraltar consists of a high rocky mountain, joined to the Spanish mainland by a sandy plain. Tourism is highly important for its economy.

Guernsey

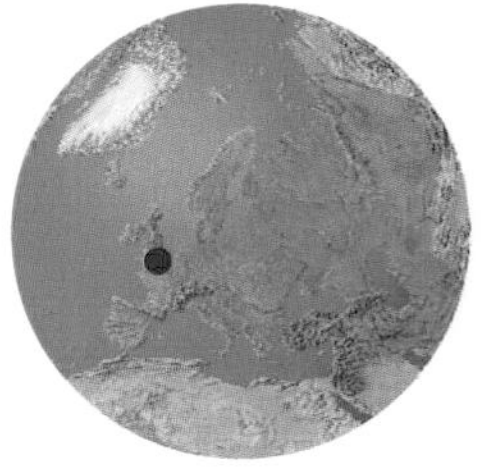

Fact File

OFFICIAL NAME Bailiwick of Guernsey

FORM OF GOVERNMENT British crown dependency

CAPITAL St Peter Port

AREA 63 sq km (24 sq miles)

TIME ZONE GMT

POPULATION 65,000

LIFE EXPECTANCY 79.9

INFANT MORTALITY (PER 1,000) 4.9

LITERACY RATE Not available

CURRENCY Guernsey pound

ECONOMY Financial services, tourism, manufacturing, horticulture

CLIMATE Temperate; mild winters and cool summers

MAP REFERENCE Page 304

Guernsey, the second largest of the Channel Islands, lies in the English Channel 50 km (30 miles) to the west of France. Though it is a British dependency, it is effectively self-governing, and administers all the other Channel Islands bar Jersey. During the Second World War they were the only region of Britain to be occupied by German troops. Picturesque scenery, a gentle climate, and the relaxed lifestyle of its inhabitants make tourism an economic mainstay. Market gardening is also important and the island is famed for its distinctive cattle. Immigration is strictly controlled.

The Isle of Man

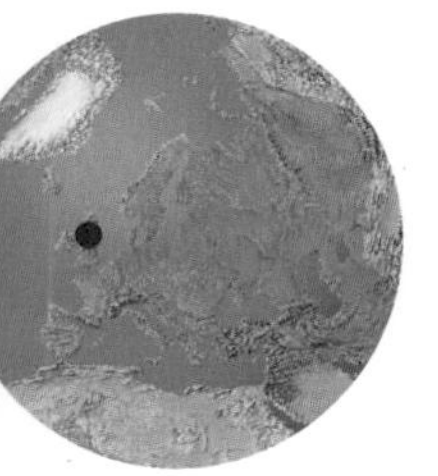

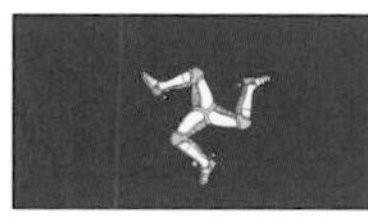

Fact File

Official name The Isle of Man

Form of government British crown dependency

Capital Douglas

Area 588 sq km (227 sq miles)

Time zone GMT

Population 74,000

Life expectancy 77.8

Infant mortality (per 1,000) 6.3

Literacy rate Not available

Currency Manx pound

Economy Services 72 %, industry 22 %, transport and communication 6 %

Climate Temperate; cool, wet winters and mild summers

Map reference Page 306

The Isle of Man is situated in the Irish Sea between the west coast of England and Northern Ireland, and just south of Galloway in Scotland. At its southern tip is a tiny uninhabited island, the Calf of Man, which is a nature reserve. Two regions of uplands in the center of the main island are divided by a valley extending from Douglas, on the east coast, to Peel, on the west.

The Isle of Man is a dependency of the British crown, but has its own legislature, legal system, and taxation system. Traditionally agriculture and fishing have been the main sources of income, but it now depends mainly on tourism and financial and business services. Although English is the main language, the local Gaelic language—known as Manx—was almost defunct, but serious efforts are being made to reestablish it as a widely spoken language that is taught in schools.

St Peter Port, in Guernsey (left page left). A seaside town on the Isle of Man (left page right). A skidoo and sleds on Svalbard (top). The castle of Montorgueil on Jersey (right).

Jersey

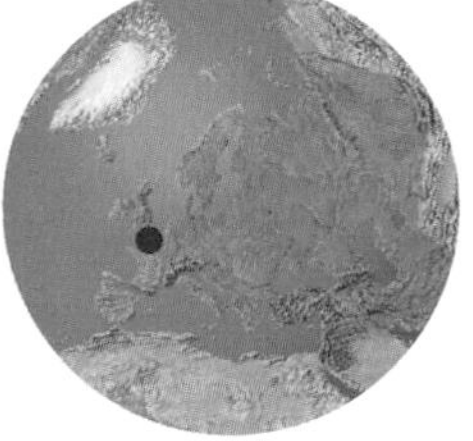

Fact File

Official name Bailiwick of Jersey

Form of government British crown dependency

Capital St Helier

Area 117 sq km (45 sq miles)

Time zone GMT

Population 90,000

Life expectancy 78.8

Infant mortality (per 1,000) 5.5

Literacy rate Not available

Currency Jersey pound

Economy Financial services, agriculture, tourism

Climate Temperate; mild winters and cool summers

Map reference Page 290

Jersey, the largest and most populous of the Channel Islands, lies in the English Channel, 20 km (12 miles) from the west coast of the Cherbourg Peninsula in northern France. Said to be the sunniest part of the British Isles, it is noted for its superb beaches. These account for the booming tourist industry which, along with financial services, has in recent years supplanted agriculture as the mainstay of the economy.

Jersey is a dependency of the British crown, but it has its own legislature and a tax regime that is entirely independent and whose low rates attract many foreign businesses. Jersey cattle are among the most important exports, and flower cultivation is also a significant source of income.

Svalbard

Fact File

Official name Svalbard

Form of government Territory of Norway

Capital Longyearbyen

Area 62,049 sq km (23,957 sq miles)

Time zone GMT + 1 hour

Population 2,900

Life expectancy Not available

Infant mortality (per 1,000) Not available

Literacy rate Not available

Currency Norwegian krone

Economy Mainly coal mining, some tourism

Climate Polar, moderated by Gulf Stream ocean current; cold winters and cool summers

Map reference Page 300

Situated in the Arctic Ocean about 650 km (400 miles) north of Norway, Svalbard consists of nine bleak, rocky, and icy islands. From Viking times until the sixteenth century, these islands remained unknown. Recently they have served as a base for Arctic explorers. Svalbard's coal reserves have been mined by a number of nations under Norway's supervision. Now, only Norway and Russia mine the much depleted deposits. Vegetation on the islands is restricted to mosses, lichens, and a few hardy, low-growing plants. Visitors are attracted by the many migratory birds.

The Channel Islands

The Channel Islands lie in the English Channel between 15 and 50 km (10 and 30 miles) off the coast of Normandy in northern France. As well as the two largest islands of Jersey and Guernsey, there are the smaller islands of Sark and Alderney and a number of even smaller islands. In all, the Channel Islands cover an area of only 200 sq km (80 sq miles).

Since the Norman invasion of England in 1066, these islands have been dependencies of the British crown and are the only part of the Duchy of Normandy to have been retained by Britain after 1204.

Both Jersey and Guernsey have separate legislatures and their own taxation systems, independent of Britain. While English is the most widely spoken language, French is also common and it is the official language of the Jersey legislature. The majority of the place names on Jersey are French.

Especially during the summer, both English and French tourists flock to these islands, and tourism, along with financial services, is now the mainstay of the islands' economies. The residents of the islands enjoy a high standard of living, maintained by strictly enforced residential controls.

Europe: Physical

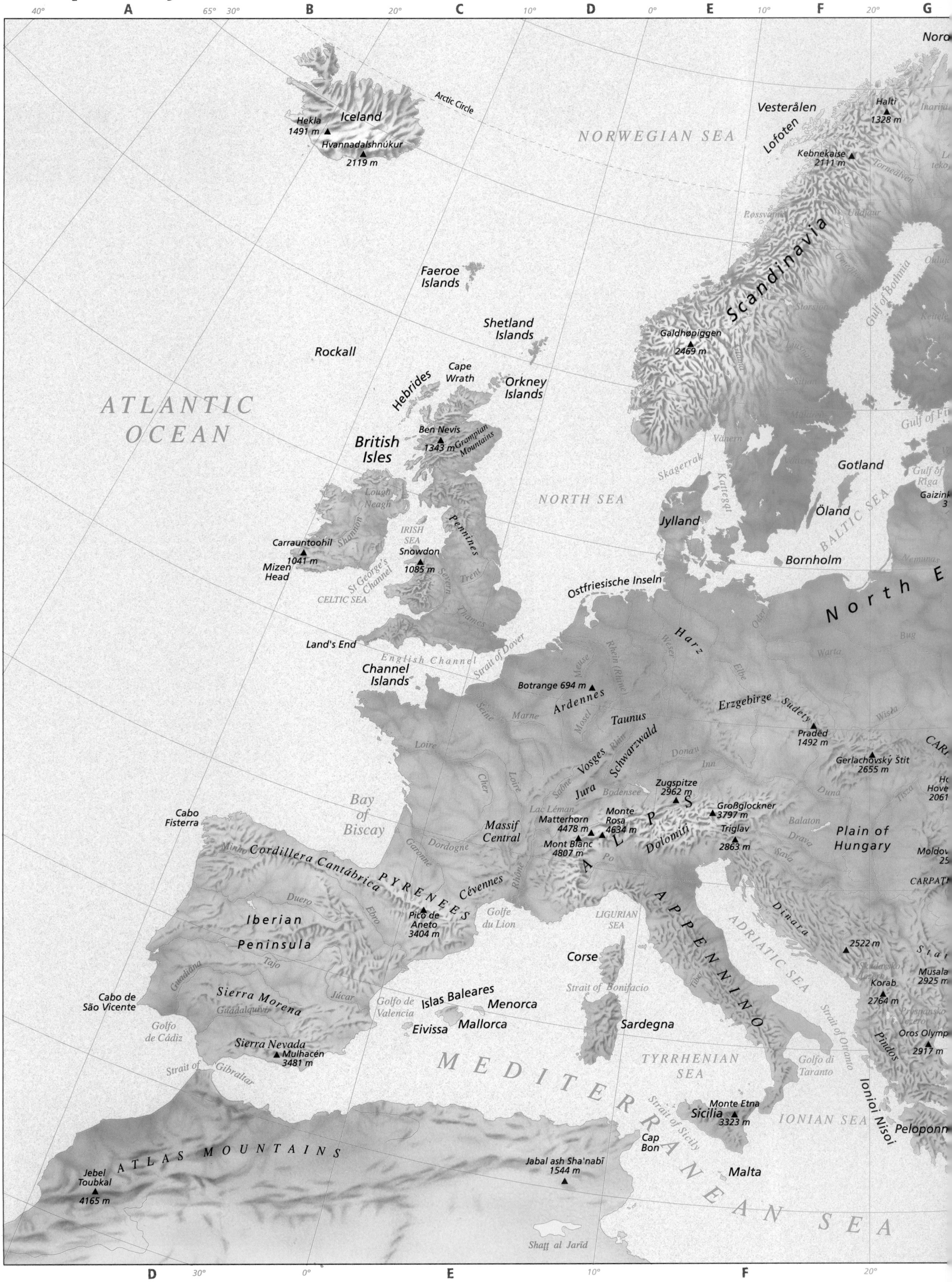

Iceland
Hekla 1491 m
Hvannadalshnúkur 2119 m
Arctic Circle
NORWEGIAN SEA
Vesterålen
Lofoten
Halti 1328 m
Kebnekaise 2111 m
Faeroe Islands
Shetland Islands
Scandinavia
Galdhøpiggen 2469 m
Rockall
Cape Wrath
Orkney Islands
Hebrides
ATLANTIC OCEAN
Ben Nevis 1343 m
Grampian Mountains
British Isles
Gotland
Öland
BALTIC SEA
Skagerrak
Kattegat
Vänern
NORTH SEA
Jylland
Lough Neagh
IRISH SEA
Pennines
Carrauntoohil 1041 m
Snowdon 1085 m
Mizen Head
Shannon
St George's Channel
CELTIC SEA
Severn
Trent
Thames
Bornholm
Ostfriesische Inseln
North E
Land's End
English Channel
Strait of Dover
Channel Islands
Harz
Botrange 694 m
Ardennes
Rhein (Rhine)
Weser
Elbe
Oder
Erzgebirge
Sudety
Praděd 1492 m
Taunus
Seine
Marne
Mosel
Loire
Vosges
Schwarzwald
Donau
Inn
Gerlachovský Štit 2655 m
Jura
Saône
Bodensee
Zugspitze 2962 m
Lac Léman
Matterhorn 4478 m
Monte Rosa 4634 m
Mont Blanc 4807 m
ALPS
Großglockner 3797 m
Triglav 2863 m
Dolomiti
Bay of Biscay
Cabo Fisterra
Massif Central
Dordogne
Garonne
Rhône
Po
Balaton
Drava
Sava
Plain of Hungary
Cordillera Cantábrica
Miño
PYRENEES
Cévennes
Pico de Aneto 3404 m
Golfe du Lion
LIGURIAN SEA
APPENNINO
ADRIATIC SEA
Dinara
Iberian Peninsula
Duero
Ebro
Tajo
Corse
Strait of Bonifacio
Guadiana
Sierra Morena
Guadalquivir
Júcar
Golfo de Valencia
Islas Baleares
Menorca
Mallorca
Eivissa
Cabo de São Vicente
Golfo de Cádiz
Sierra Nevada
Mulhacén 3481 m
Sardegna
TYRRHENIAN SEA
Strait of Otranto
Golfo di Taranto
Pindos
Oros Olympos 2917 m
Korab 2764 m
Musala 2925 m
2522 m
Strait of Gibraltar
MEDITERRANEAN SEA
Strait of Sicily
Monte Etna 3323 m
Sicilia
IONIAN SEA
Ionioi Nisoi
Cap Bon
Malta
ATLAS MOUNTAINS
Jebel Toubkal 4165 m
Jabal ash Sha'nabī 1544 m
Shaṭṭ al Jarīd

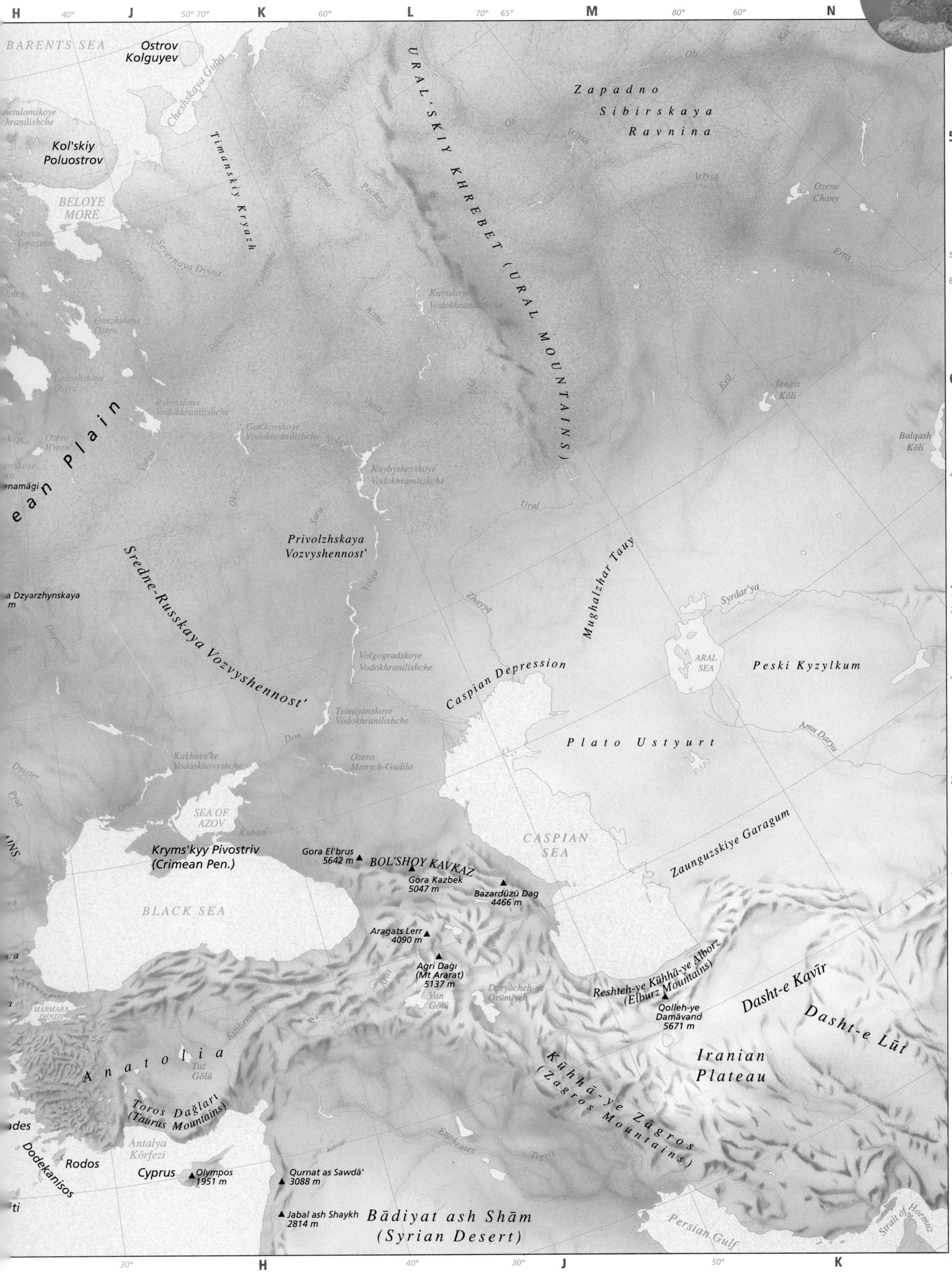

H 40° J 50° 70° K 60° L 70° 65° M 80° 60° N

BARENTS SEA
Ostrov Kolguyev
Cheshskaya Guba
Kol'skiy Poluostrov
BELOYE MORE
Timanskiy Kryazh
URAL'SKIY KHREBET (URAL MOUNTAINS)
Zapadno Sibirskaya Ravnina
Ob'
Irtysh
Ozero Chany
Pechora
Izhma
Usa
Severnaya Dvina
Vychegda
Onega
Onezhskoye Ozero
Ladozhskoye Ozero
Rybinskoye Vodokhranilishche
Gor'kovskoye Vodokhranilishche
Kamskoye Vodokhranilishche
Kama
Sukhona
Vyatka
Volga
Ozero Il'men
Kuybyshevskoye Vodokhranilishche
Ertis
Esil
Tengiz Köli
Balqash Köli
Ural
Oka
Sura
Privolzhskaya Vozvyshennost'
Sredne-Russkaya Vozvyshennost'
Mughalzhar Tauy
Zhayyq
Syrdar'ya
ARAL SEA
Peski Kyzylkum
Volgogradskoye Vodokhranilishche
Caspian Depression
Tsimlyanskoye Vodokhranilishche
Plato Ustyurt
Amu Darya
Don
Kakhovs'ke Vodoskhovyshche
Ozero Manych-Gudilo
Dnister
Prut
Dnipro
SEA OF AZOV
Kuban'
Krymskyy Pivostriv (Crimean Pen.)
Gora El'brus 5642 m
BOL'SHOY KAVKAZ
Gora Kazbek 5047 m
Bazardüzü Dag 4466 m
CASPIAN SEA
Zaunguzskiye Garagum
BLACK SEA
Aragats Lerr 4090 m
Ağri Daği (Mt Ararat) 5137 m
Aras
Van Gölü
Daryācheh-ye Orūmīyeh
Reshteh-ye Kūhhā-ye Alborz (Elburz Mountains)
Qolleh-ye Damāvand 5671 m
Dasht-e Kavīr
Dasht-e Lūt
Iranian Plateau
MARMARA DENIZI
Kizilirmak
Anatolia
Tuz Gölü
Toros Dağları (Taurus Mountains)
Kūhhā-ye Zāgros (Zagros Mountains)
Antalya Körfezi
Dodekanisos
Rodos
Cyprus
Olympos 1951 m
Qurnat as Sawdā' 3088 m
Jabal ash Shaykh 2814 m
Euphrates
Tigris
Bādiyat ash Shām (Syrian Desert)
Persian Gulf
Strait of Hormuz

5 6 7 8 9 10

30° H 40° 30° J 50° K

0 150 300 450 600 750 kilometers
0 150 300 450 miles
Scale 1:15,000,000
Projection: Conic Equidistant

Europe and the Russian Federation

Europe: Political

A
B
C
D
E
F
G
3
4
5
6
7
8
9
10
ARCTIC OCEAN
Arctic Circle
Hammerfest
Alta
Tromsø
Akureyri
Hafnarfjörður
Reykjavík
ICELAND
Seyðisfjörður
Höfn
Narvik
Kiruna
Bodø
Mo i Rana
Luleå
Skellefteå
Steinkjer
SWEDEN
Trondheim
Umeå
Kristiansund
Örnsköldsvik
Kokko
Molde
Östersund
Vaasa
Härnösand
Tórshavn
FAEROE ISLANDS (Den.)
Lillehammer
Sundsvall
Shetland Islands
NORWAY
Tampere
Hämeenlinna
Rockall (U.K)
Bergen
Hamar
Gävle
Ahvenanmaa (Åland)
Turku
Orkney Islands
Oslo
Falun
Maarianhamina
Drammen
Karlstad
Västerås
Uppsala
UNITED KINGDOM
Inverness
Stavanger
Skien
Moss
SCOTLAND
Aberdeen
Arendal
Örebro
Stockholm
Kristiansand
Mariestad
Norrköping
Linköping
Pärnu
ATLANTIC OCEAN
Dundee
Glasgow
Edinburgh
Göteborg
Jönköping
N. IRELAND
Ålborg
Gotland
Belfast
Newcastle upon Tyne
NORTH SEA
DENMARK
Kalmar
Galway
IRELAND
ISLE OF MAN (U.K.)
ENGLAND
Århus
Karlskrona
Liepāja
Riga
Dublin
Öland
Limerick
Bradford
Leeds
København
Helsingborg
Šiauliai
Waterford
Manchester
Kingston upon Hull
Esbjerg
Malmö
Klaipėda
LITHUA
Cork
Liverpool
Sheffield
Odense
Bornholm
Kaliningrad
RUSSIAN FED.
Birmingham
Nottingham
Kiel
Gdańsk
WALES
Leicester
Bremerhaven
Lübeck
Rostock
Koszalin
Elbląg
Swansea
Coventry
Groningen
Schwerin
Cardiff
Bristol
London
NETHERLANDS
Hamburg
Szczecin
Amsterdam
Bremen
Bydgoszcz
Toruń
Białystok
's-Gravenhage
Hannover
Berlin
Plymouth
Portsmouth
Rotterdam
Poznań
POLAND
Brighton
Antwerpen
Essen
Münster
Magdeburg
Bruxelles
Dortmund
Kalisz
Warszawa
CHANNEL IS (U.K.)
Lille
Düsseldorf
Leipzig
Łódź
Radom
Le Havre
Amiens
BELGIUM
Köln
Dresden
Głogów
Brest
Bonn
GERMANY
Wrocław
Kielce
Lublin
Caen
Rouen
LUXEMBOURG
Wiesbaden
Chemnitz
Luxembourg
Frankfurt am Main
Praha
Katowice
Rennes
Paris
Reims
Le Mans
Mannheim
Nürnberg
CZECH REPUBLIC
Ostrava
Kraków
Angers
Orléans
Nancy
Karlsruhe
Brno
Nantes
Tours
Strasbourg
Stuttgart
Regensburg
SLOVAKIA
Košice
Freiburg im Breisgau
Augsburg
FRANCE
Dijon
Basel
Linz
Wien
Bratislava
Zürich
München
Salzburg
Miskolc
Poitiers
Besançon
Bern
Vaduz
LIECHTENSTEIN
AUSTRIA
Limoges
Innsbruck
Budapest
Debrecen
Genève
SWITZERLAND
A Coruña
Lyon
Graz
HUNGARY
Cluj-N
Gijón
Bordeaux
Clermont-Ferrand
Bolzano
SLOVENIA
Maribor
Vigo
Oviedo
Saint-Étienne
Trento
Ljubljana
Szeged
Arad
Ourense
Santander
Bilbao
Donostia-San Sebastián
Milano
Venezia
Pécs
Braga
León
Vitoria-Gasteiz
Grenoble
Trieste
Zagreb
Novi Sad
Timişoara
Porto
Toulouse
Torino
Verona
Padova
Rijeka
CROATIA
Bragança
Burgos
Pamplona
Nîmes
Genova
La Spezia
Bologna
Beograd
Coimbra
Viseu
Valladolid
Logroño
Montpellier
Nice
Monaco
MONACO
Rimini
Zadar
BOSNIA AND HERZEGOVINA
SERBIA AND MONTENEGRO
PORTUGAL
Salamanca
ANDORRA
Perpignan
Andorra la Vella
Marseille
Pisa
Firenze
San Marino
SAN MARINO
Sarajevo
Santarém
Madrid
Alcalá de Henares
Zaragoza
Corse
Split
Mostar
Niš
Lisboa
Toledo
Barcelona
Perugia
Dubrovnik
Priština
Setúbal
Badajoz
Cuenca
Ajaccio
VATICAN CITY
Roma
Pescara
Podgorica
Beja
Évora
SPAIN
Tarragona
Castelló de la Plana
Kukës
Skopje
MACEDONIA
Faro
Córdoba
Albacete
Valencia
Palma de Mallorca
Sassari
ITALY
Foggia
Tiranë
Huelva
Sevilla
Jaén
Bari
ALBANIA
Jeréz de la Frontera
Alicante
Islas Baleares
Sardegna
Napoli
Salerno
Vlorë
Thessaloniki
Cádiz
Málaga
Granada
Murcia
Taranto
Lecce
GIBRALTAR (U.K.)
Almería
Cartagena
Cagliari
Cosenza
Ioannina
Ceuta (Sp.)
MEDITERRANEAN SEA
Catanzaro
GREE
Palermo
Messina
Marsala
Reggio di Calabria
Patra
Melilla (Sp.)
Catania
Tripoli
Siracusa
MOROCCO
Valletta
MALTA
ALGERIA
TUNISIA

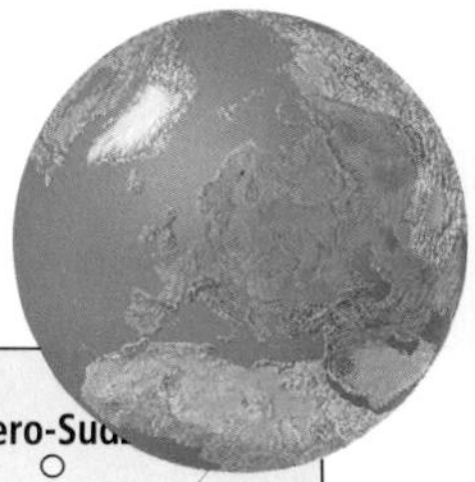

RUSSIAN FEDERATION

KAZAKHSTAN

UZBEKISTAN

TURKMENISTAN

IRAN

TURKEY

SYRIA

IRAQ

UKRAINE

GEORGIA

AZERBAIJAN

ARMENIA

AFGHANISTAN

CYPRUS

ISRAEL

JORDAN

SAUDI ARABIA

KUWAIT

OMAN

U.A.E.

MOLDOVA

CASPIAN SEA

BLACK SEA

Arctic Circle

Murmansk, Monchegorsk, Apatity, Kandalaksha, Severodvinsk, Arkhangel'sk, Kem', Mezen', Nar'yan Mar, Inta, Pechora, Ukhta, Syktyvkar, Kotlas, Medvezh'yegorsk, Petrozavodsk, Sankt-Peterburg, Kolpino, Cherepovets, Vologda, Novgorod, Rybinsk, Kostroma, Yaroslavl', Ivanovo, Tver', Sergiyev Posad, Moskva, Murom, Velikiye Luki, Kolomna, Obninsk, Ryazan', Smolensk, Kaluga, Tula, Novomoskovsk, Bryansk, Orel, Lipetsk, Tambov, Voronezh, Kursk, Belgorod, Chernihiv, Sumy, Kyyiv, Zhytomyr, Kharkiv, Poltava, Kremenchuk, Luhans'k, Dniprodzerzhyns'k, Donets'k, Makiyivka, Kirovohrad, Taganrog, Rostov-na-Donu, Kryvyy Rih, Zaporizhzhya, Mariupol', Bălți, Mykolayiv, Melitopol', Chișinău, Kherson, Odesa, Simferopol', Sevastopol', Novorossiysk, Krasnodar, Maykop, Armavir, Stavropol', Cherkessk, Nal'chik, Groznyy, Vladikavkaz, Makhachkala, Sochi, Astrakhan', Volzhskiy, Volograd, Saratov, Engel's, Balakovo, Penza, Saransk, Syzran', Tol'yatti, Samara, Novokuybyshevsk, Ul'yanovsk, Dimitrovgrad, Arzamas, Nizhniy Novgorod, Cheboksary, Kazan', Naberezhnyye Chelny, Al'met'yevsk, Ufa, Sterlitamak, Salavat, Orsk, Orenburg, Sol'-Iletsk, Magnitogorsk, Chelyabinsk, Zlatoust, Izhevsk, Sarapul, Votkinsk, Vyatka, Perm', Solikamsk, Berezniki, Nizhniy Tagil, Yekaterinburg, Pervoural'sk, Kamensk-Ural'skiy, Kurgan, Serov, Tyumen', Ishim, Nazyvayevsk, Omsk, Tatarsk, Rubtsovsk, Barnaul, Biysk, Novosibirsk, Leninsk-Kuznetskiy, Kemerovo, Tomsk, Anzhero-Sud..., Kolpashevo, Nizhnevartovsk, Surgut, Igrim, Nyagan'

Homyel', Mazyr, Brăila, Galați, București, Constanța, Varna, Burgas, Stara Zagora, Rodos

Scale 1:15,000,000

0 150 300 450 600 750 kilometers

0 150 300 450 miles

Projection: Conic Equidistant

Europe and the Russian Federation

North Scandinavia • Iceland

GREENLAND SEA
Arctic Circle
ICELAND
Reykjavík
Akureyri
Hafnarfjörður
Vatnajökull
Hofsjökull
Langjökull
Mýrdalsjökull
Ódáðahraun
Faxaflói
Breiðafjörður
Húnaflói
Bakkaflói
Hvannadalshnúkur 2119 m
Bárðarbunga 2000 m
Herðubreið 1682 m
Hekla 1491 m
Ísafjörður
Húsavík
Egilsstaðir
Höfn
Vík
ATLANTIC OCEAN
NORWEGIAN SEA
NORWAY
SWEDEN
NORDLAND
TROMS
NORRBOTTEN
NORD-TRØNDELAG
SØR-TRØNDELAG
MØRE OG ROMSDAL
OPPLAND
HEDMARK
JÄMTLAND
VÄSTERBOTTEN
VÄSTERNORRLAND
Vesterålen
Lofoten
Vestfjorden
Tromsø
Narvik
Bodø
Mo i Rana
Mosjøen
Namsos
Steinkjer
Trondheim
Kristiansund
Molde
Kiruna
Gällivare
Jokkmokk
Arjeplog
Sorsele
Storuman
Lycksele
Vilhelmina
Umeå
Örnsköldsvik
Härnösand
Östersund
Kebnekaise 2111 m
Snøhetta 2286 m
286

South Scandinavia • Baltic States

284

NORWEGIAN SEA
NORTH SEA
Skagerrak
Kattegat
NORWAY
SWEDEN
DENMARK
GERMANY
MØRE OG ROMSDAL
TRØNDELAG
SOGN OG FJORDANE
OPPLAND
HEDMARK
HORDALAND
BUSKERUD
TELEMARK
ROGALAND
AUST-AGDER
VEST-AGDER
VESTFOLD
ØSTFOLD
AKERSHUS
OSLO
JÄMTLAND
GÄVLEBORG
KOPPARBERG
VÄRMLAND
ÖREBRO
GÖTEBORG OCH BOHUS
SKARABORG
ÄLVSBORG
JÖNKÖPING
ÖSTERGÖTLAND
HALLAND
KRONOBERG
KRISTIANSTAD
BLEKINGE
MALMÖHUS
SCHLESWIG-HOLSTEIN
Oslo
Bergen
Stavanger
Kristiansand
Göteborg (Gothenburg)
København (Copenhagen)
Malmö
Helsingborg
Ålborg
Århus
Odense
Kiel
Jotunheimen
Jostedalsbreen
Jylland
Fyn
Sjælland
Lolland
Falster
Bornholm
Vänern
Vättern
Hanöbukten
Deutsche Bucht
Kieler Bucht
Mecklenburger Bucht
Jammerbugten
Oslofjorden

288

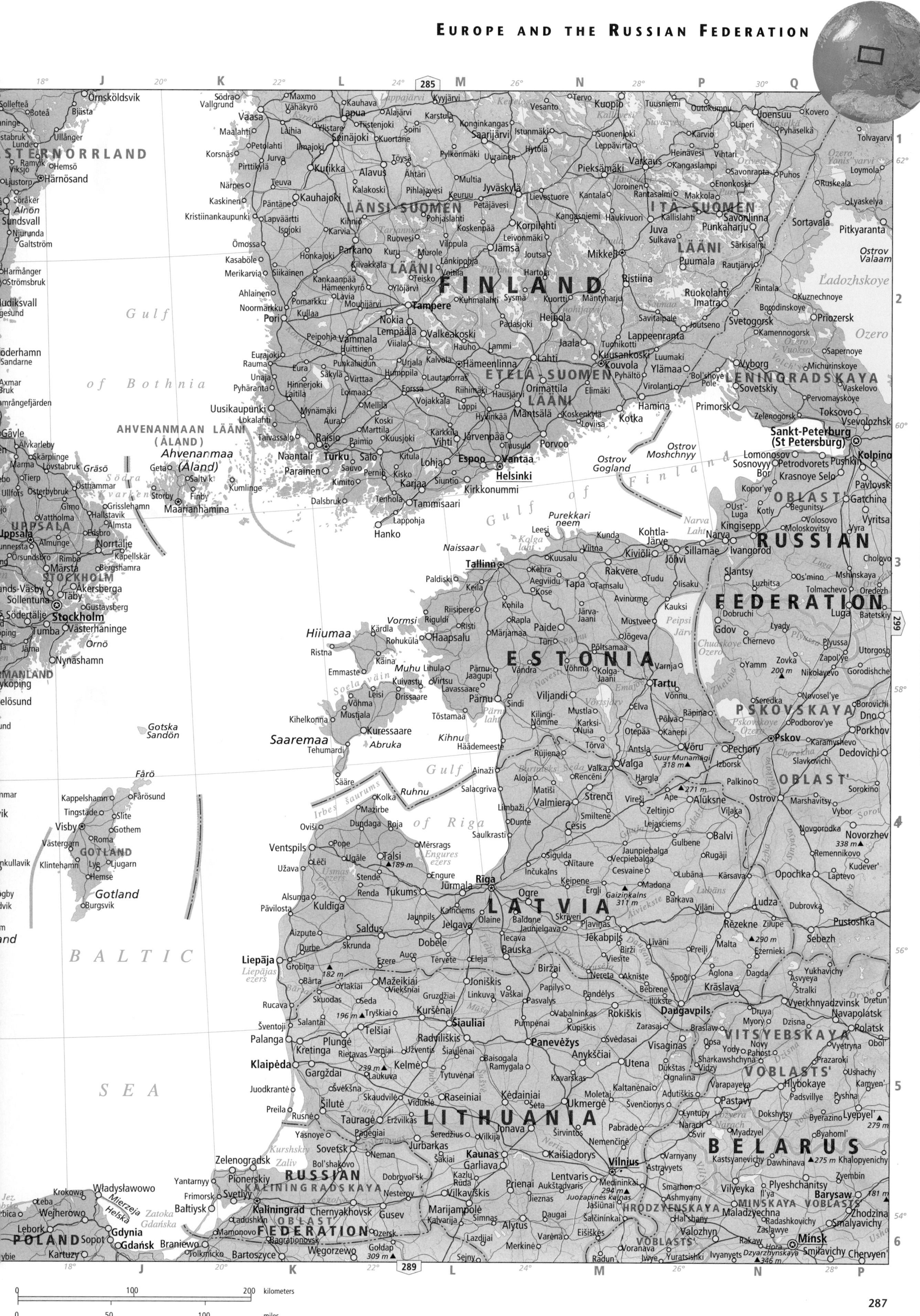

0 100 200 kilometers

0 50 100 miles

Scale 1:3,500,000

Projection: Equidistant Conic

Europe and the Russian Federation

Central Europe

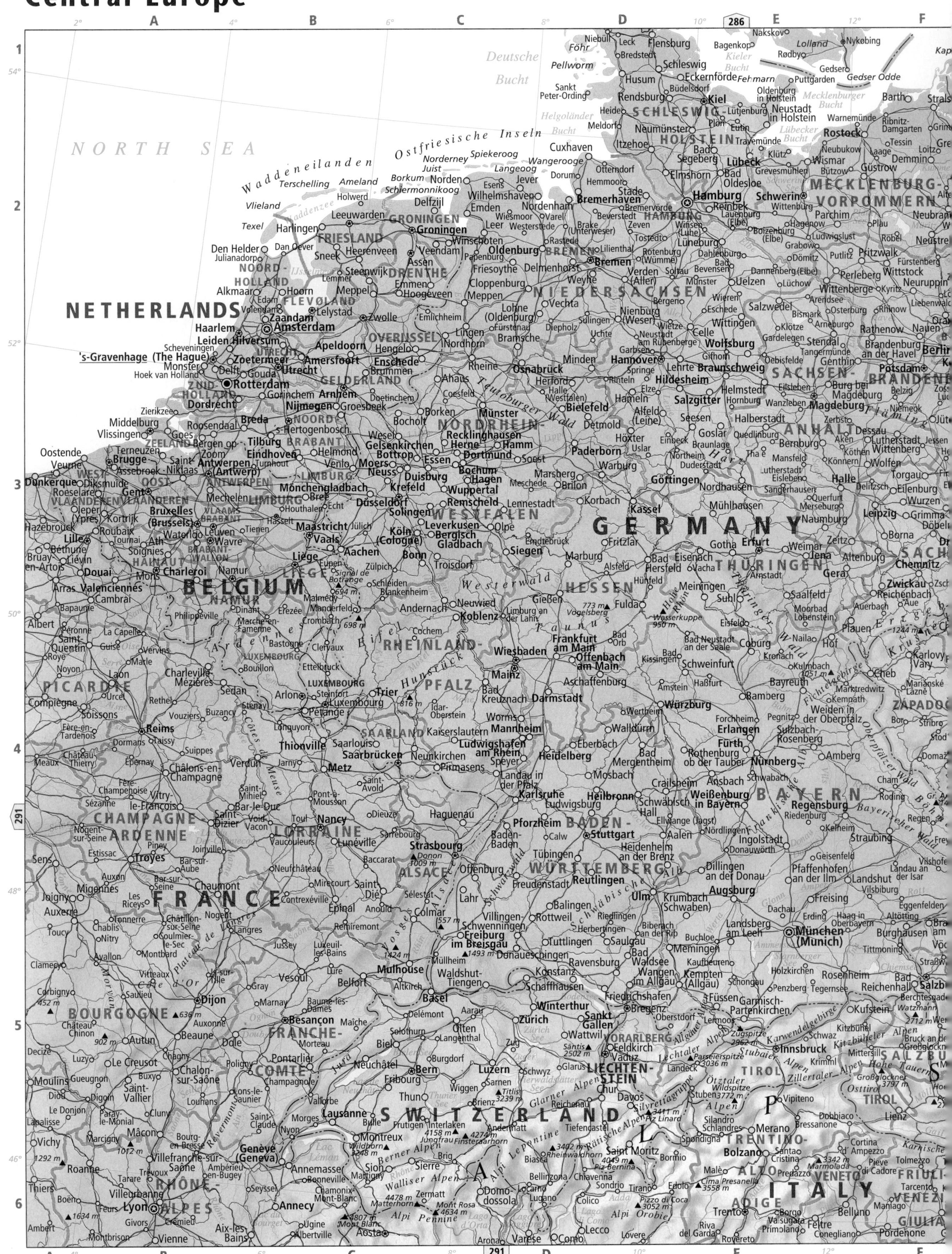
A
B
C
D
E
F
1
2
3
4
5
6
286
291
NORTH SEA
Deutsche Bucht
Waddeneilanden
Ostfriesische Inseln
NETHERLANDS
BELGIUM
GERMANY
FRANCE
SWITZERLAND
LIECHTENSTEIN
ITALY
LUXEMBOURG
GRONINGEN
FRIESLAND
DRENTHE
NOORD-HOLLAND
FLEVOLAND
OVERIJSSEL
GELDERLAND
UTRECHT
ZUID-HOLLAND
ZEELAND
NOORD-BRABANT
LIMBURG
ANTWERPEN
WEST-VLAANDEREN
OOST-VLAANDEREN
HAINAUT
NAMUR
LIÈGE
SCHLESWIG-HOLSTEIN
MECKLENBURG-VORPOMMERN
HAMBURG
BREMEN
NIEDERSACHSEN
SACHSEN-ANHALT
NORDRHEIN-WESTFALEN
HESSEN
THÜRINGEN
RHEINLAND-PFALZ
SAARLAND
BADEN-WÜRTTEMBERG
BAYERN
PICARDIE
CHAMPAGNE-ARDENNE
LORRAINE
ALSACE
BOURGOGNE
FRANCHE-COMTÉ
RHÔNE-ALPES
VORARLBERG
TIROL
TRENTINO-ALTO ADIGE
Amsterdam
's-Gravenhage (The Hague)
Rotterdam
Utrecht
Bruxelles (Brussels)
Antwerpen (Antwerp)
Luxembourg
Hamburg
Bremen
Hannover
Köln (Cologne)
Düsseldorf
Frankfurt am Main
Stuttgart
München (Munich)
Nürnberg
Strasbourg
Zürich
Bern
Genève (Geneva)
Lyon
Dijon
Reims
Lille

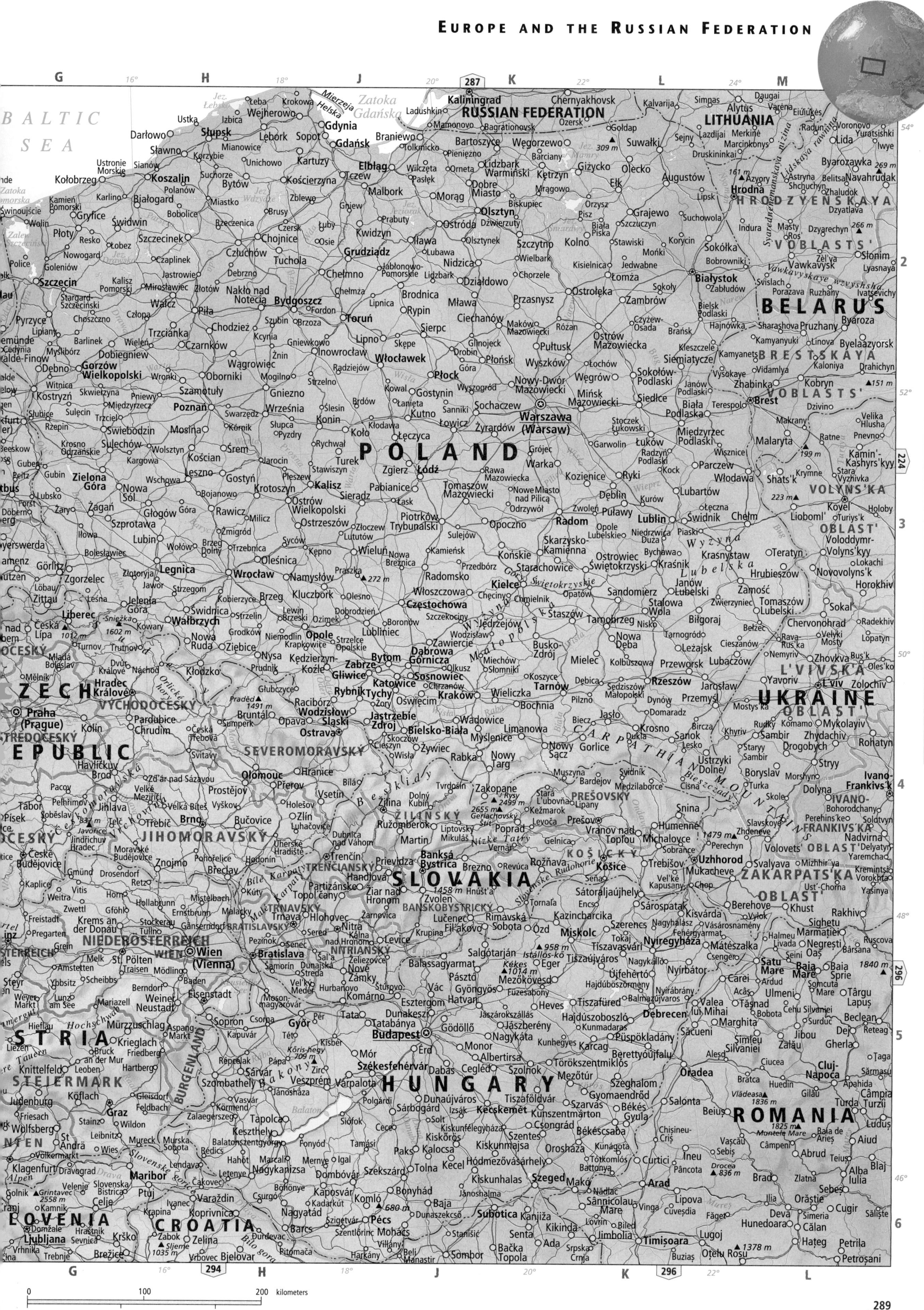

0 100 200 kilometers
0 50 100 miles
Scale 1:3,500,000
Projection: Equidistant Conic

France • Switzerland

CELTIC SEA
ENGLISH CHANNEL
BAY OF BISCAY
Golfe de Gascogne
ENGLAND
CHANNEL ISLANDS (U.K.)
FRANCE
SPAIN
BRETAGNE
BASSE-NORMANDIE
HAUTE-NORMANDIE
PAYS DE LA LOIRE
CENTRE
POITOU-CHARENTES
LIMOUSIN
AQUITAINE
MIDI-PYRÉNÉES
ASTURIAS
CANTABRIA
PAÍS VASCO
NAVARRA
CASTILLA Y LEÓN
LA RIOJA
ARAGÓN
CATALUÑA
ANDORRA
Cordillera Cantábrica
PYRENEES
Southampton
Portsmouth
Brighton
Plymouth
Exeter
Cherbourg
Le Havre
Rouen
Caen
Rennes
Brest
Lorient
Nantes
Angers
Tours
Le Mans
Orléans
Poitiers
La Rochelle
Limoges
Angoulême
Bordeaux
Toulouse
Bayonne
Pau
Donostia-San Sebastián
Bilbao
Santander
Oviedo
Gijón
León
Burgos
Vitoria-Gasteiz
Pamplona
Logroño
Andorra la Vella
304
305
292
293

BELGIUM
GERMANY
SWITZERLAND
AUSTRIA
ITALY
LIECHTENSTEIN
MONACO
LUXEMBOURG
SAN MARINO
LIGURIAN SEA
Golfe du Lion
Golfo di Genova
Corse (Corsica) (Fr.)
Europe and the Russian Federation
0 100 200 kilometers
0 50 100 miles
Scale 1:3,500,000
Projection: Equidistant Conic

Spain • Portugal

ATLANTIC
OCEAN
PORTUGAL
GALICIA
ASTURIAS
CASTILLA Y LEÓN
EXTREMADURA
VIANA DO CASTELO
BRAGA
VILA REAL
BRAGANÇA
PORTO
AVEIRO
VISEU
GUARDA
COIMBRA
CASTELO BRANCO
LEIRIA
SANTARÉM
PORTALEGRE
LISBOA
SETÚBAL
ÉVORA
BEJA
FARO
GIBRALTAR (U.K.)
MOROCCO
Cordillera Cantábrica
Costa Verde
Sierra de Gredos
Sierra de Aracena
Golfo de Cádiz
Costa de la Luz
Strait of Gibraltar
A Coruña
Ferrol
Santiago de Compostela
Lugo
Ourense
Vigo
Pontevedra
Oviedo
Gijón
León
Porto
Braga
Coimbra
Lisboa (Lisbon)
Setúbal
Évora
Faro
Lagos
Salamanca
Zamora
Cáceres
Badajoz
Mérida
Sevilla
Huelva
Córdoba
Cádiz
Jeréz de la Frontera
Algeciras
Gibraltar
Ceuta (Sp.)
Tanger (Tangier)
Tetouan (Tetuán)
Cabo Ortegal
Cabo Fisterra
Cabo Carvoeiro
Cabo Espichel
Cabo de São Vicente
Cabo de Santa Maria
A
B
C
D
E
1
2
3
4
5
12°
10°
8°
6°
42°
40°
38°
36°

FRANCE
MIDI-PYRÉNÉES
AQUITAINE
LANGUEDOC-ROUSSILLON
PROVENCE-ALPES-CÔTE-D'AZUR
ANDORRA
CATALUÑA
ARAGÓN
NAVARRA
LA RIOJA
PAÍS VASCO
VALENCIA
CASTILLA-LA MANCHA
MURCIA
SPAIN
ISLAS BALEARES
Islas Baleares (Balearic Islands)
Mallorca
Menorca
Eivissa (Ibiza)
Formentera
Cabrera
Golfe du Lion
Golfo de Valencia
MEDITERRANEAN SEA
Costa Brava
Costa Daurada
Costa del Azahar
Costa Blanca
Costa Vasca
ALGERIA
Alger (Algiers)
Barcelona
Valencia
Zaragoza
Toulouse
Marseille
Montpellier
Andorra la Vella
Palma de Mallorca
Alicante
Murcia
Cartagena
Almería
Granada
Pamplona
Bilbao
Donostia-San Sebastián
Vitoria-Gasteiz
Logroño
Lleida
Tarragona
Castelló de la Plana
Albacete
Teruel
Cuenca
Huesca
Perpignan
Oran
Mostaganem
Chlef
Blida

F G H J K
1 2 3 4 5

0 100 200 kilometers
0 50 100 miles
Scale 1:3,500,000
Projection: Equidistant Conic

Europe and the Russian Federation

Italy • Austria

288
289
291
296
GERMANY
CZECH REPUBLIC
SLOVAKIA
HUNGARY
AUSTRIA
SWITZERLAND
SLOVENIA
CROATIA
BOSNIA AND HERZEGOVINA
FRANCE
SAN MARINO
LIECHTENSTEIN
MONACO
ADRIATIC SEA
LIGURIAN SEA

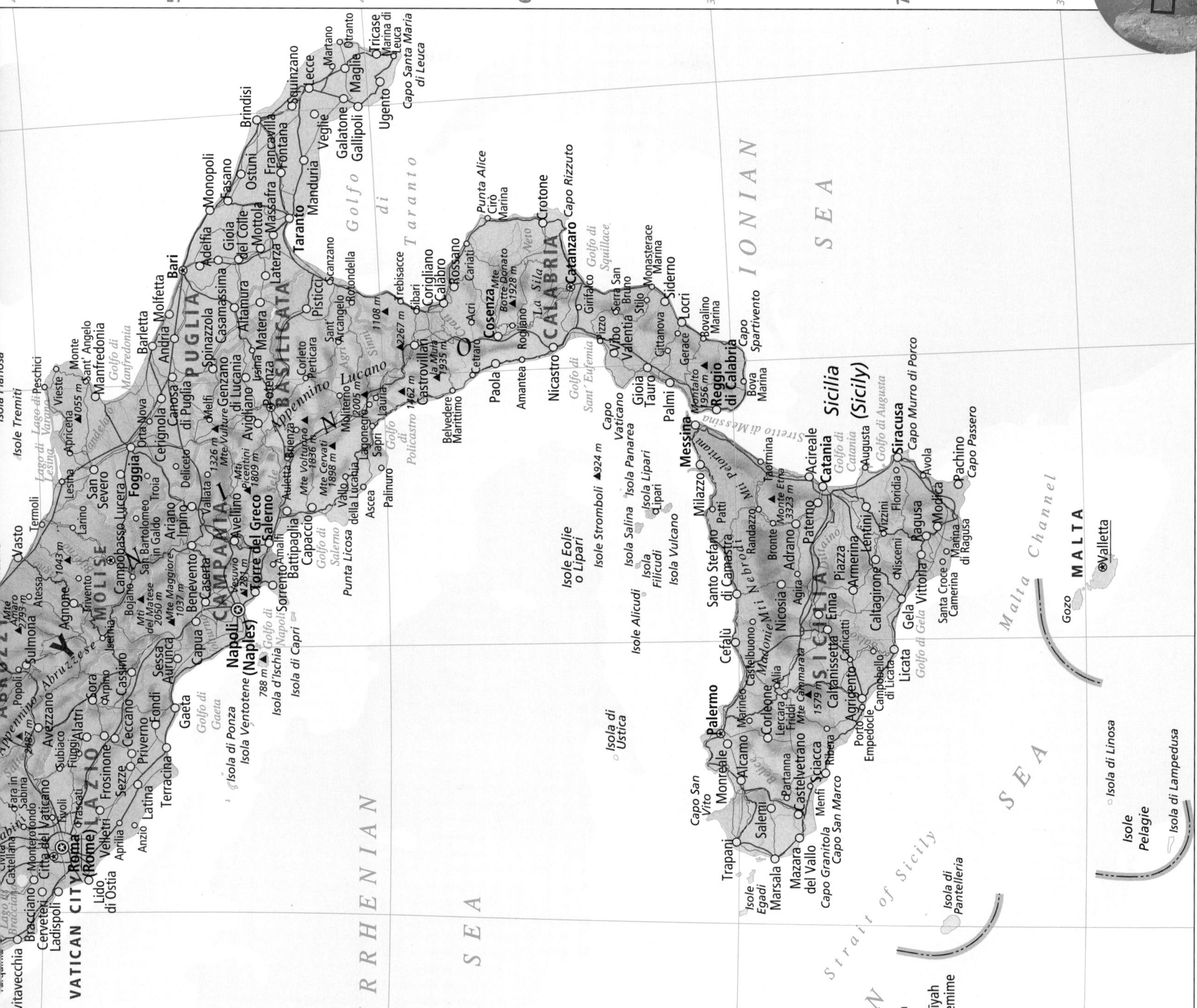

0 100 200 kilometers

0 50 100 miles

Scale 1:3,500,000

Projection: Equidistant Conic

Southeast Europe

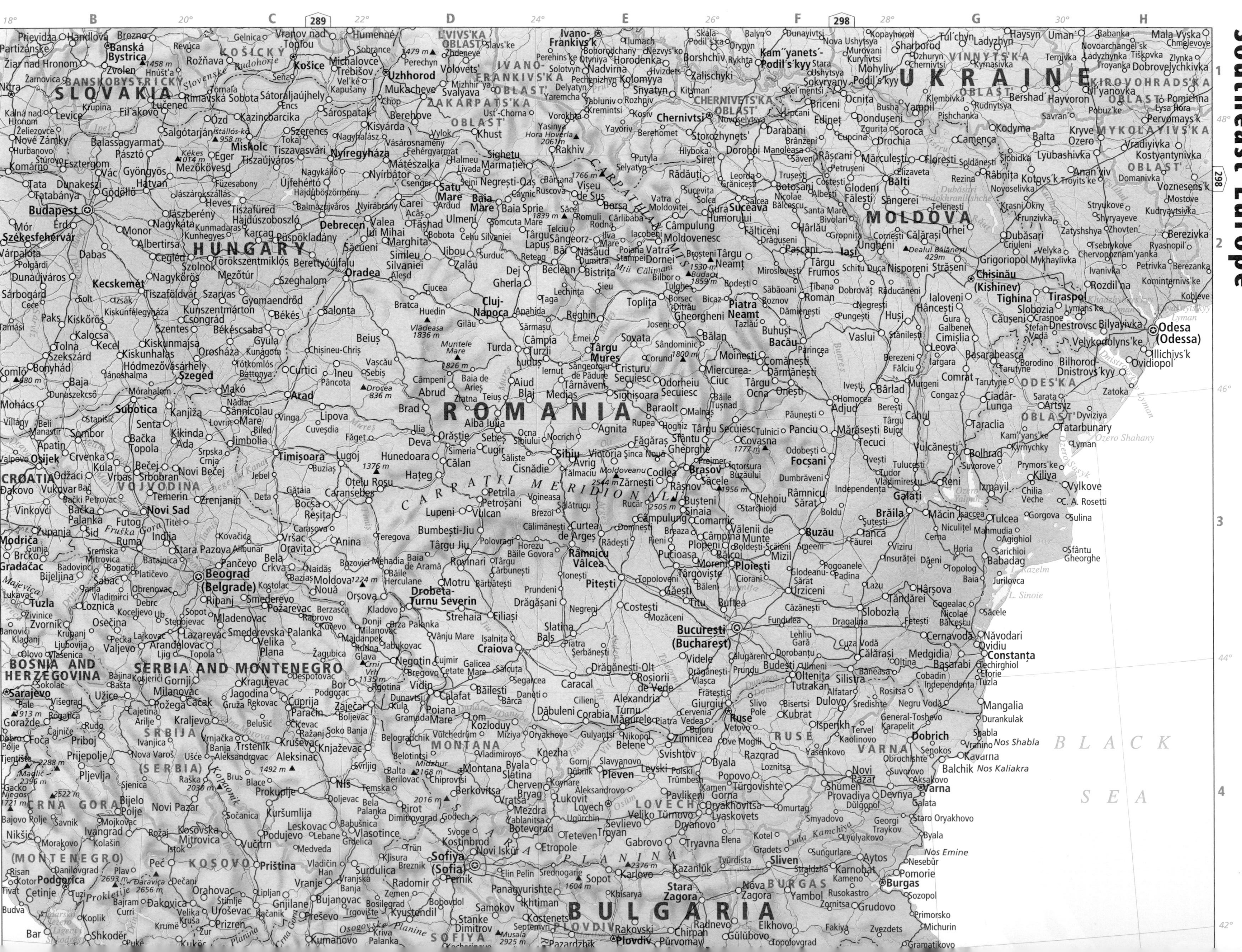
UKRAINE
MOLDOVA
ROMANIA
BULGARIA
HUNGARY
SLOVAKIA
SERBIA AND MONTENEGRO
BOSNIA AND HERZEGOVINA
CROATIA
BLACK SEA
Budapest
Beograd (Belgrade)
Bucureşti (Bucharest)
Chişinău (Kishinev)
Odesa (Odessa)
Sofiya (Sofia)
Sarajevo

298

0 100 200 kilometers

0 50 100 miles

Scale 1:3,500,000

Projection: Equidistant Conic

East Europe • Turkey

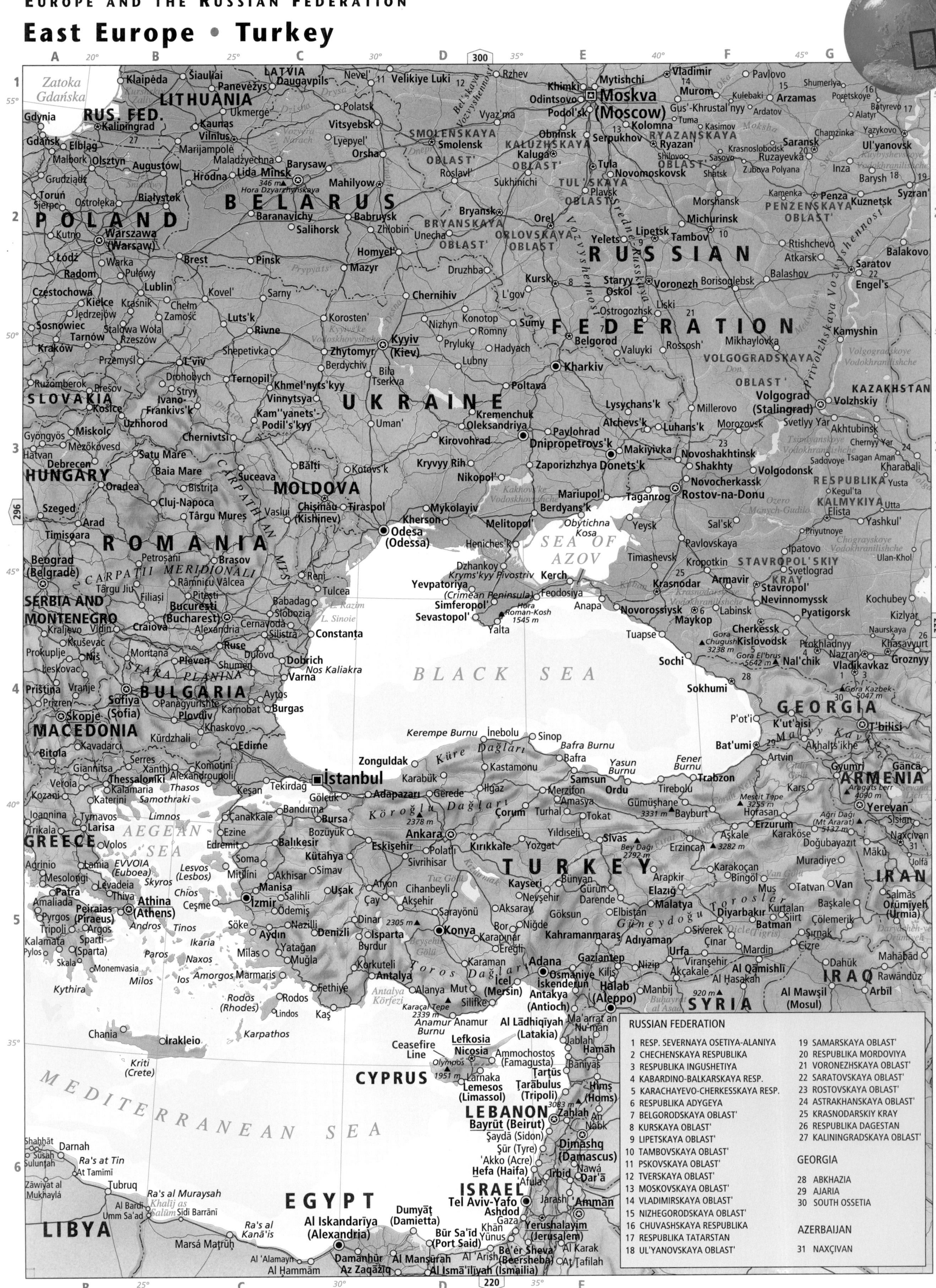

RUSSIAN FEDERATION
1 RESP. SEVERNAYA OSETIYA-ALANIYA
2 CHECHENSKAYA RESPUBLIKA
3 RESPUBLIKA INGUSHETIYA
4 KABARDINO-BALKARSKAYA RESP.
5 KARACHAYEVO-CHERKESSKAYA RESP.
6 RESPUBLIKA ADYGEYA
7 BELGORODSKAYA OBLAST'
8 KURSKAYA OBLAST'
9 LIPETSKAYA OBLAST'
10 TAMBOVSKAYA OBLAST'
11 PSKOVSKAYA OBLAST'
12 TVERSKAYA OBLAST'
13 MOSKOVSKAYA OBLAST'
14 VLADIMIRSKAYA OBLAST'
15 NIZHEGORODSKAYA OBLAST'
16 CHUVASHSKAYA RESPUBLIKA
17 RESPUBLIKA TATARSTAN
18 UL'YANOVSKAYA OBLAST'
19 SAMARSKAYA OBLAST'
20 RESPUBLIKA MORDOVIYA
21 VORONEZHSKAYA OBLAST'
22 SARATOVSKAYA OBLAST'
23 ROSTOVSKAYA OBLAST'
24 ASTRAKHANSKAYA OBLAST'
25 KRASNODARSKIY KRAY
26 RESPUBLIKA DAGESTAN
27 KALININGRADSKAYA OBLAST'
GEORGIA
28 ABKHAZIA
29 AJARIA
30 SOUTH OSSETIA
AZERBAIJAN
31 NAXÇIVAN
LITHUANIA
RUS. FED.
BELARUS
POLAND
RUSSIAN FEDERATION
UKRAINE
SLOVAKIA
HUNGARY
MOLDOVA
ROMANIA
SERBIA AND MONTENEGRO
BULGARIA
MACEDONIA
GREECE
TURKEY
GEORGIA
ARMENIA
IRAN
IRAQ
SYRIA
CYPRUS
LEBANON
ISRAEL
EGYPT
LIBYA
KAZAKHSTAN
BLACK SEA
SEA OF AZOV
AEGEAN SEA
MEDITERRANEAN SEA
Moskva (Moscow)
Kyyiv (Kiev)
Minsk
Warszawa (Warsaw)
Bucureşti (Bucharest)
Chişinău (Kishinev)
Sofiya (Sofia)
İstanbul
Ankara
Athina (Athens)
T'bilisi
Yerevan
Nicosia
Dimashq (Damascus)
Bayrūt (Beirut)
Tel Aviv-Yafo
Yerushalayim (Jerusalem)
'Ammān
Al Iskandarīya (Alexandria)

Europe and the Russian Federation

kilometers 0 100 200 300 400

miles 0 100 200

Scale 1:10,000,000

Projection: Equidistant Con

West Russian Federation

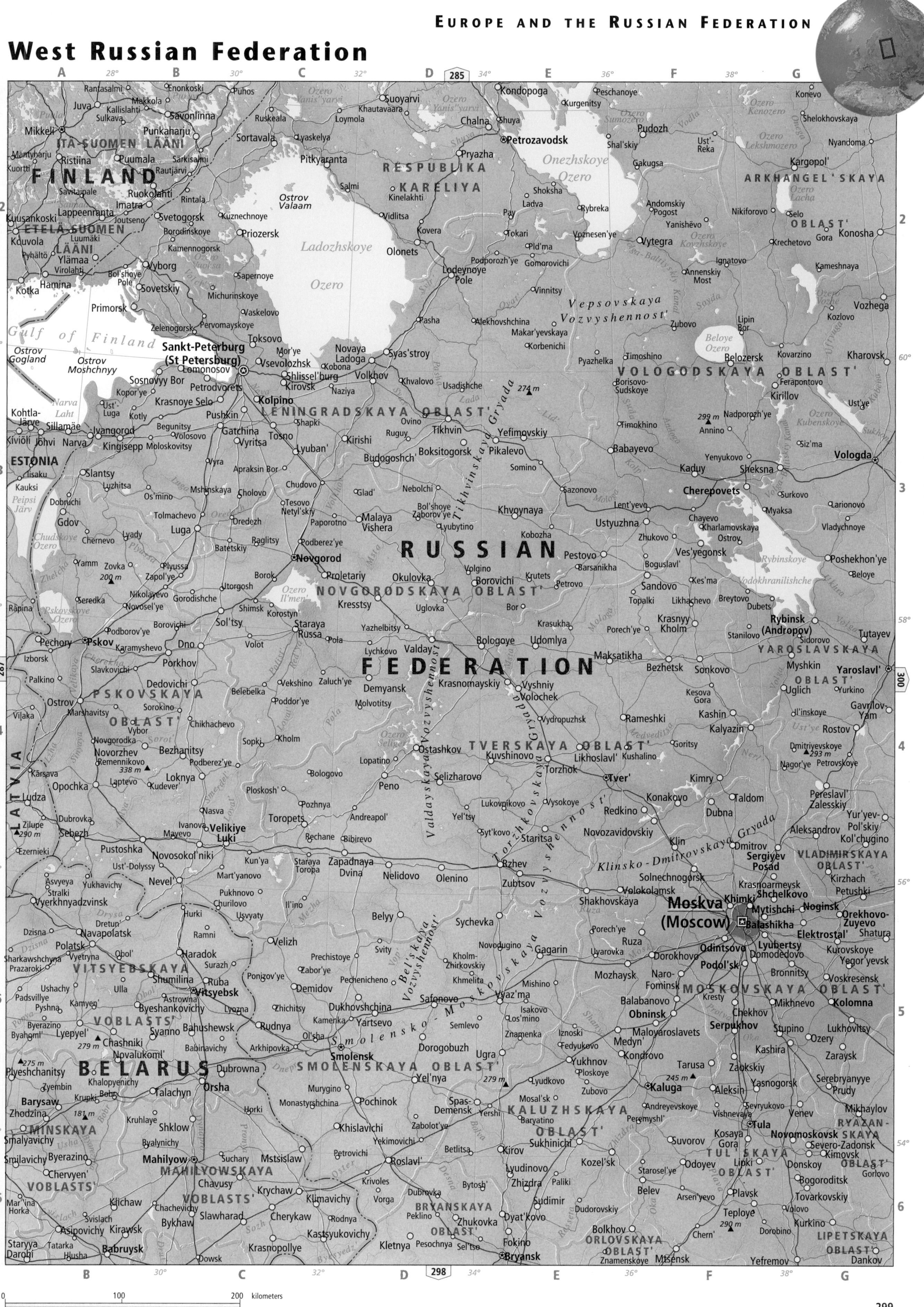

Europe and the Russian Federation

0 100 200 kilometers
0 50 100 miles
Scale 1:3,500,000
Projection: Equidistant Conic

Russian Federation and Surrounding Countries

306
291
296
220
212
ARCTIC
BARENTS SEA
KARSKOYE MORE
BELOYE MORE
NORTH SEA
BALTIC SEA
BLACK SEA
SEA OF AZOV
CASPIAN SEA
ARAL SEA
Gulf of Bothnia
Gulf of Finland
Arctic Circle
SVALBARD (Nor.)
Spitsbergen
Nordaustlandet
Barentsøya
Edgeøya
Kong Karl's Land
Zemlya Aleksandry
Zemlya Georga
Zemlya Frantsa-Iosifa
Ostrov Greem-Bell
Ostrov Komsomolets
Ostrov Pioner
Ostrov Oktyabr'skoy Revolyutsii
Novaya Zemlya
Mys Zhelaniya
Ostrov Mezhdusharskiy
Ostrov Kolguyev
Mys Kanin Nos
Poluostrov Rybachiy
Nordkapp
Cheshskaya Guba
Ostrov Vaygach
Ostrov Belyy
Poluostrov Yamal
Gydanskiy Poluostrov
Pyasinskiy Zaliv
Obskaya Guba
UNITED KINGDOM
Orkney Islands
Shetland Islands
Glasgow
Edinburgh
Elgin
Aberdeen
Sunderland
York
NORWAY
Stavanger
Kristiansand
Bergen
Drammen
Lillehammer
Oslo
Ålesund
Trondheim
Bodø
Narvik
Harstad
Tromsø
SWEDEN
Göteborg (Gothenburg)
Örebro
Västerås
Linköping
Jönköping
Uppsala
Gävle
Stockholm
Gotland
Östersund
Sundsvall
Umeå
Skellefteå
Luleå
Kiruna
Malmö
Helsingborg
DENMARK
København (Copenhagen)
Ålborg
Odense
FINLAND
Turku
Pori
Tampere
Vaasa
Jyväskylä
Kuopio
Oulu
Kemi
Rovaniemi
Inari
Lakselv
Helsinki
GERMANY
Hannover
Hamburg
Kiel
Rostock
Berlin
Groningen
POLAND
Poznań
Szczecin
Gdynia
Olsztyn
Łódź
Warszawa (Warsaw)
Wrocław
Kielce
Radom
Kraków
Białystok
Kaliningrad
R.F.
ESTONIA
Tallinn
Tartu
LATVIA
Rīga
Ventspils
Liepāja
Valmiera
Daugavpils
LITHUANIA
Šiauliai
Vilnius
BELARUS
Minsk
Brest
Pinsk
Baranavichy
Homyel'
Orsha
Vitsyebsk
UKRAINE
Kyyiv (Kiev)
Lutsk
Rivne
Zhytomyr
L'viv
Ivano-Frankivs'k
Chernivtsi
Chernihiv
Sumy
Kharkiv
Dnipropetrovs'k
Donets'k
Luhans'k
Kryvyy Rih
Mykolayiv
Odesa (Odessa)
Yevpatoriya
Simferopol'
Kerch
Mariupol'
Chişinău
Bălţi
MOLDOVA
Kazan'
RUSSIAN FEDERATION
Sankt-Peterburg (St. Petersburg)
Pskov
Novgorod
Velikiye Luki
Smolensk
Tver'
Rzhev
Moskva (Moscow)
Mytishchi
Podol'sk
Kaluga
Tula
Bryansk
Orel
Kursk
Belgorod
Staryy Oskol
Voronezh
Lipetsk
Tambov
Michurinsk
Ryazan'
Vladimir
Ivanovo
Yaroslavl'
Kostroma
Rybinsk
Cherepovets
Vologda
Bologoye
Petrozavodsk
Murmansk
Zapolyarnyy
Kandalaksha
Polyarnyye Zori
Kovdor
Kola
Kem'
Belomorsk
Segezha
RESPUBLIKA KARELIYA
Medvezh'yegorsk
Severodvinsk
Arkhangel'sk
Onega
Mezen'
Kamenka
Kargopol'
Kotlas
Vel'sk
Nyandoma
Konosha
Shenkursk
Rochegda
Vendinga
Usogorsk
Syktyvkar
Ukhta
Vuktyl
Pechora
Usinsk
Inta
Vorkuta
Nar'yan Mar
RESPUBLIKA KOMI
Labytnangi
Salekhard
Yar-Sale
Novyy Port
Yamburg
Nadym
Urengoy
Noyabr'sk
Tambey
Gyda
Antipayuta
Dudinka
Noril'sk
Kayyerkan
Igarka
Nizhniy Novgorod
Kineshma
Murom
Arzamas
Dzerzhinsk
Saransk
Penza
Cheboksary
Yoshkar-Ola
Kotel'nich
Vyatka
Glazov
Izhevsk
Votkinsk
Perm'
Solikamsk
Berezniki
Kazan'
Naberezhnyye Chelny
Al'met'yevsk
Ul'yanovsk
Tol'yatti
Samara
Syzran'
Saratov
Engel's
Balakovo
Kamyshin
Volgograd (Stalingrad)
Rostov-na-Donu
Shakhty
Taganrog
Novocherkassk
Krasnodar
Novorossiysk
Tuapse
Sochi
Maykop
Armavir
Stavropol'
Nevinnomyssk
Pyatigorsk
Nal'chik
Vladikavkaz
Groznyy
Makhachkala
Derbent
Kizlyar
Astrakhan'
Elista
Ufa
Sterlitamak
Salavat
Orenburg
Orsk
Oktyabr'skiy
Zlatoust
Miass
Chelyabinsk
Yekaterinburg
Kamensk-Ural'skiy
Pervoural'sk
Nizhniy Tagil
Serov
Ivdel'
Tyumen'
Tobol'sk
Kurgan
Ishim
Omsk
Tara
Nazyvayevsk
Tatarsk
Novosibirsk
Kuybyshev
Karasuk
Barnaul
Biysk
Rubtsovsk
Aleysk
Gorno-Altaysk
Tomsk
Asino
Kolpashevo
Kargasok
Strezhevoy
Nizhnevartovsk
Surgut
Langepas
Kogalym
Sovetskiy
Nyagan'
Igrim
Beloyarskiy
Kemerovo
Anzhero-Sudzhensk
Leninsk-Kuznetskiy
Belovo
Mezhdurechensk
Novokuznetsk
Achinsk
Krasnoyarsk
Kansk
Abakan
Kuragino
Lesosibirsk
Kyzyl
RESPUBLIKA ALTAY
RESPUBLIKA KHAKASIYA
RESPUBLIKA TYVA
Severo-Yeniseyskiy
Severnyye Uvaly
Zapadno-Sibirskaya Ravnina
KAZAKHSTAN
Atyraū
Oral
Aqtöbe (Aktyubinsk)
Qostanay (Kustanay)
Rūdnyy
Petropavl
Kökshetaū
Astana (Aqmola)
Temirtaū
Qaraghandy
Pavlodar
Ekibastuz
Semey
Öskemen
Zhezqazghan
Balqash
Aqtaū (Aktau)
Beyneu
Emba
Shalqar
Qyzylorda (Kzyl-Orda)
Shymkent
Taraz
Almaty
Taldyqorghan
Ayagöz
Zaysan
Mughalzhar Tauy
Betpaqdala
Moyynqum
Balqash Köli
Aqsorang Biigi 1565 m
UZBEKISTAN
QORAQALPOGHISTON RESPUBLIKASI
Nukus
Urganch
Qunghirot
Toshkent (Tashkent)
Samarqand
Bukhoro
Qarshi
Nawoiy
Plato Ustyurt
TURKMENISTAN
Türkmenbashi
Dashhowuz
Ashgabat
Mary
Chärjew
Bayramaly
Tejen
Turanskaya Nizmennost'
KYRGYZSTAN
Bishkek
Osh
Talas
TAJIKISTAN
Dushanbe
Khorog
Pamirs
AFGHANISTAN
Herāt
Mazār-e Sharīf
Feyzābād
Hindu Kush
PAKISTAN
IRAN
Tehrān (Teheran)
Tabrīz
Rasht
Qom
Hamadān
Eşfahān
Yazd
Kāshān
Mashhad
Sabzevār
Gorgān
Birjand
Kermān
Dasht-e Kavīr
Dasht-e Lūt
GEORGIA
T'bilisi
Bat'umi
Sokhumi
ARMENIA
Yerevan
AZERBAIJAN
Bakı (Baku)
Sumqayıt
Gäncä
TURKEY
CHINA
Ürümqi
Shihezi
Yining
Karamay
Altay
Kashi (Kashgar)
Aksu
Kuqa
Korla
Hami
Barkol
Qinghe
Yecheng
Shache
Dunhuang
Anxi
Junggar Pendi
Tarim Pendi
Tian Shan
Kongur Shan 7719 m
1524 m
Ulaangom
Ölgiy
Ak-Dovurak
B
C
D
E
F
G
H
J
K
L
1
2
3
4
5
6
7

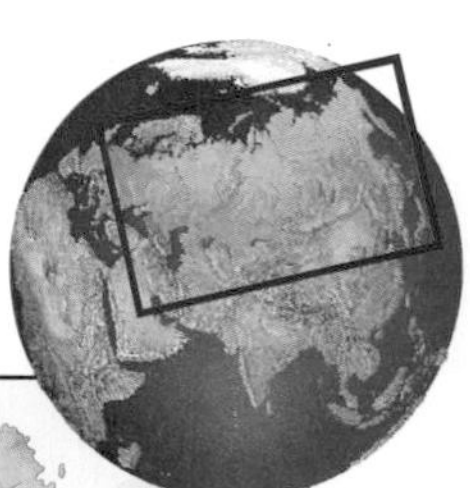

RUSSIAN FEDERATION

1 RESPUBLIKA DAGESTAN
2 RESPUBLIKA INGUSHETIYA
3 CHECHENSKAYA RESPUBLIKA
4 RESP. SEVERNAYA OSETIYA-ALANIYA
5 KABARDINO-BALKARSKAYA RESPUBLIKA
6 KARACHAYEVO-CHERKESSKAYA RESPUBLIKA
7 RESPUBLIKA ADYGEYA
8 RESPUBLIKA KALMYKIYA
9 RESPUBLIKA MORDOVIYA
10 CHUVASHSKAYA RESPUBLIKA
11 RESPUBLIKA TATARSTAN
12 RESPUBLIKA MARIY EL
13 UDMURTSKAYA RESPUBLIKA
14 RESPUBLIKA BASHKORTOSTAN

GEORGIA

15 ABKHAZIA
16 AJARIA
17 SOUTH OSSETIA

AZERBAIJAN

18 NAGORNO-KARABAKH
19 NAXÇIVAN

0 200 400 600 800 kilometers
0 200 400 miles
Scale 1:20,000,000 Projection: Equidistant Conic

The British Isles

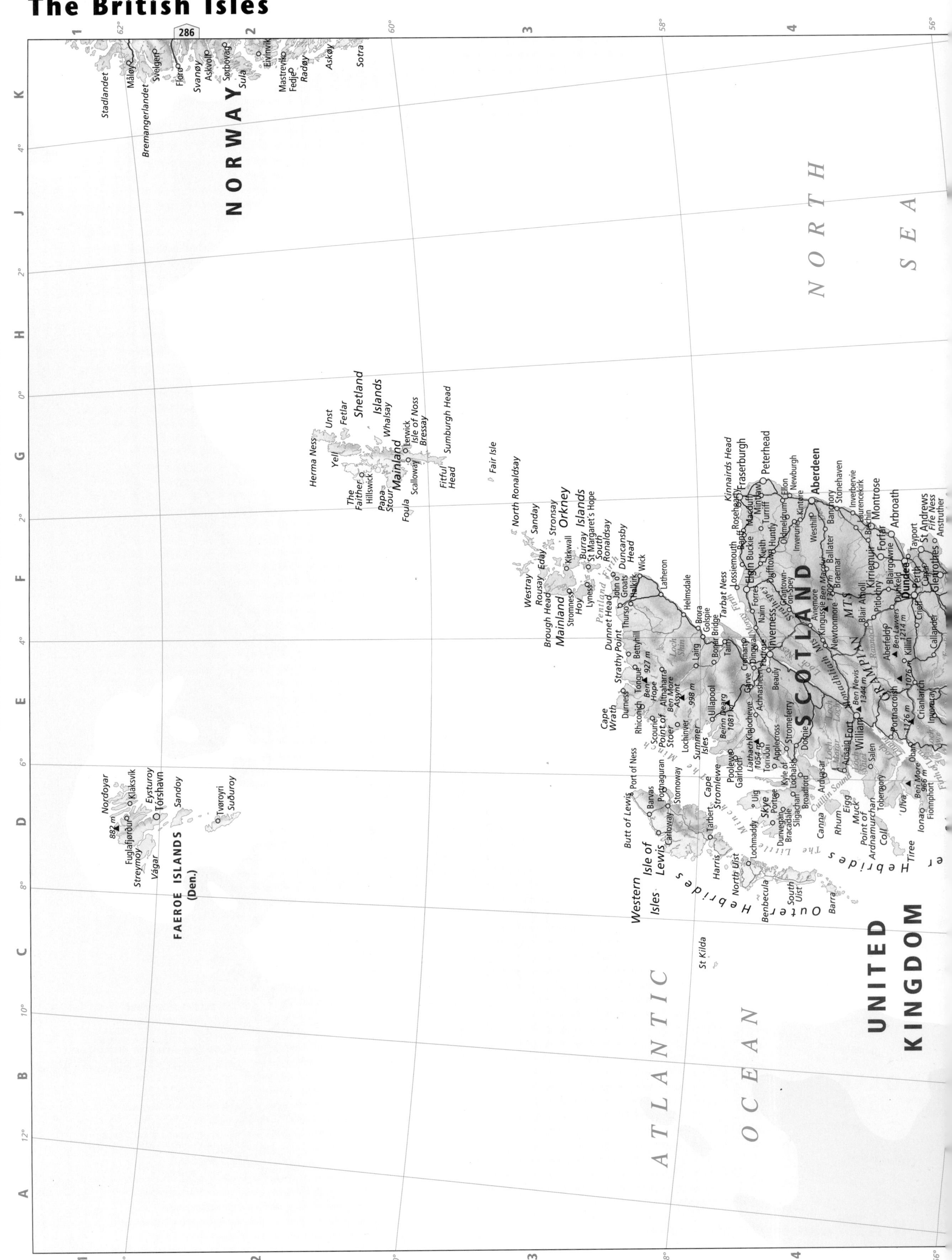
286
NORWAY
FAEROE ISLANDS
(Den.)
Shetland
Islands
Orkney
Islands
SCOTLAND
UNITED
KINGDOM
NORTH
SEA
ATLANTIC
OCEAN
Outer
Hebrides
Western
Isles
Isle of
Lewis
Skye
Aberdeen
Inverness
Peterhead
Fraserburgh
Dundee
Fair Isle
St Kilda
Tórshavn
Sandoy
Suðuroy
Eysturoy
Streymoy
Vágar
Nordoyar
Sotra
Stadlandet
Bremangerlandet

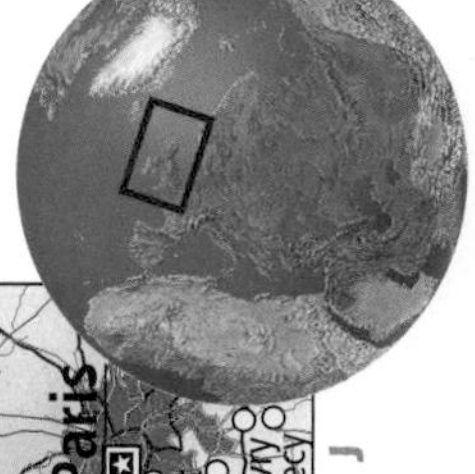

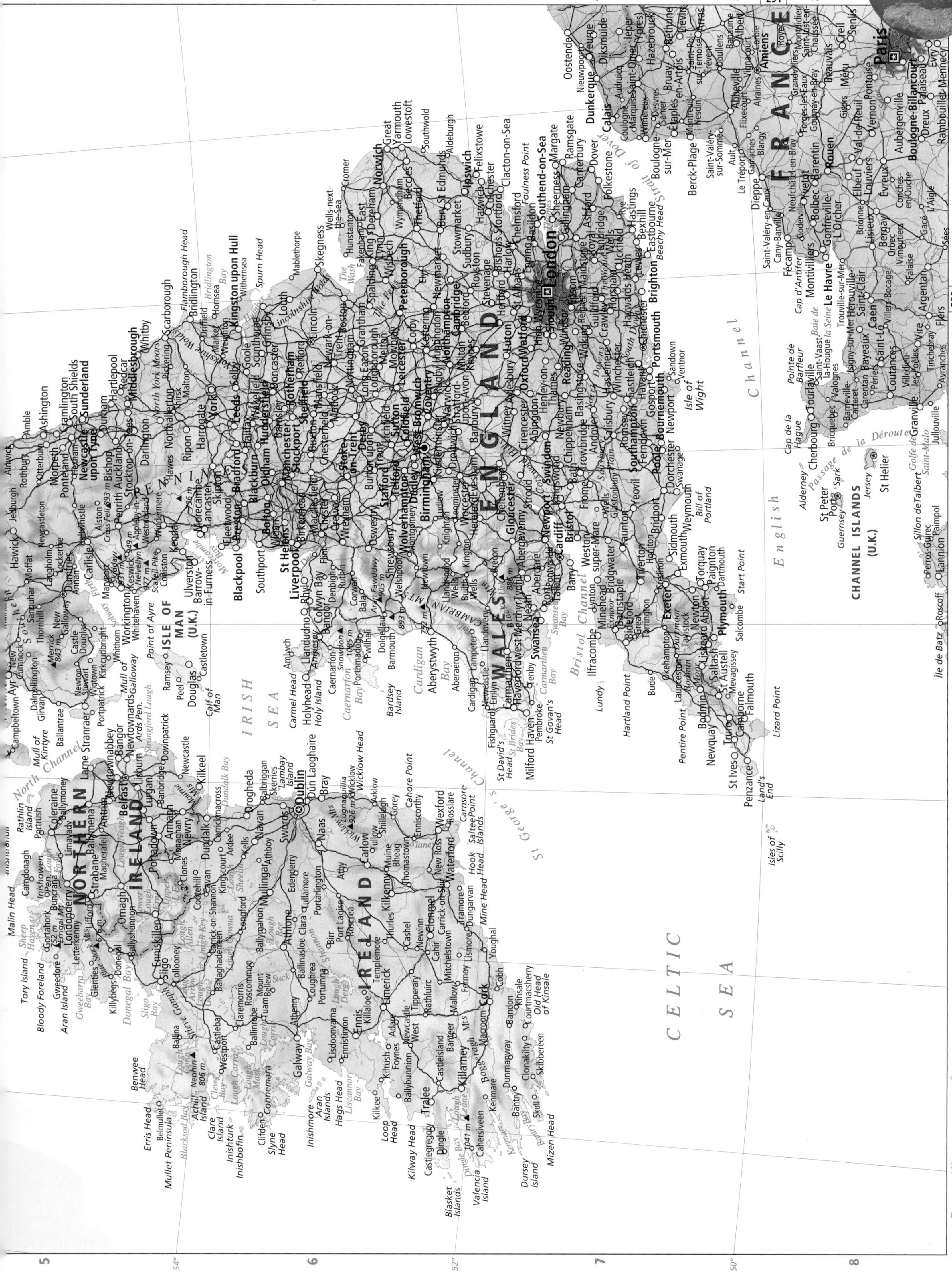

0 100 200 kilometers

0 50 100 miles

Scale 1:3,500,000

Projection: Equidistant Conic

South England • Wales

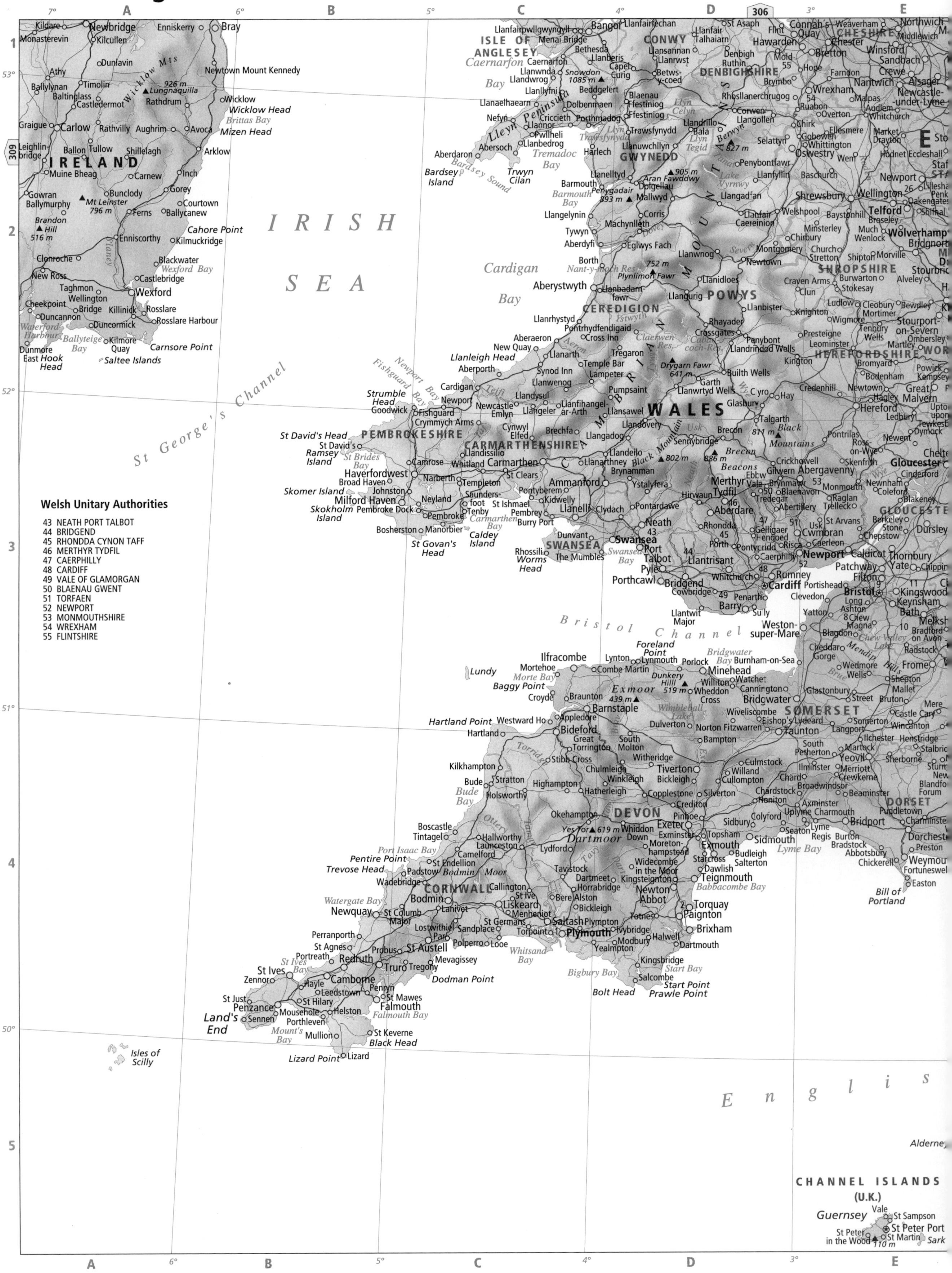

Welsh Unitary Authorities

43 NEATH PORT TALBOT
44 BRIDGEND
45 RHONDDA CYNON TAFF
46 MERTHYR TYDFIL
47 CAERPHILLY
48 CARDIFF
49 VALE OF GLAMORGAN
50 BLAENAU GWENT
51 TORFAEN
52 NEWPORT
53 MONMOUTHSHIRE
54 WREXHAM
55 FLINTSHIRE

CHANNEL ISLANDS (U.K.)

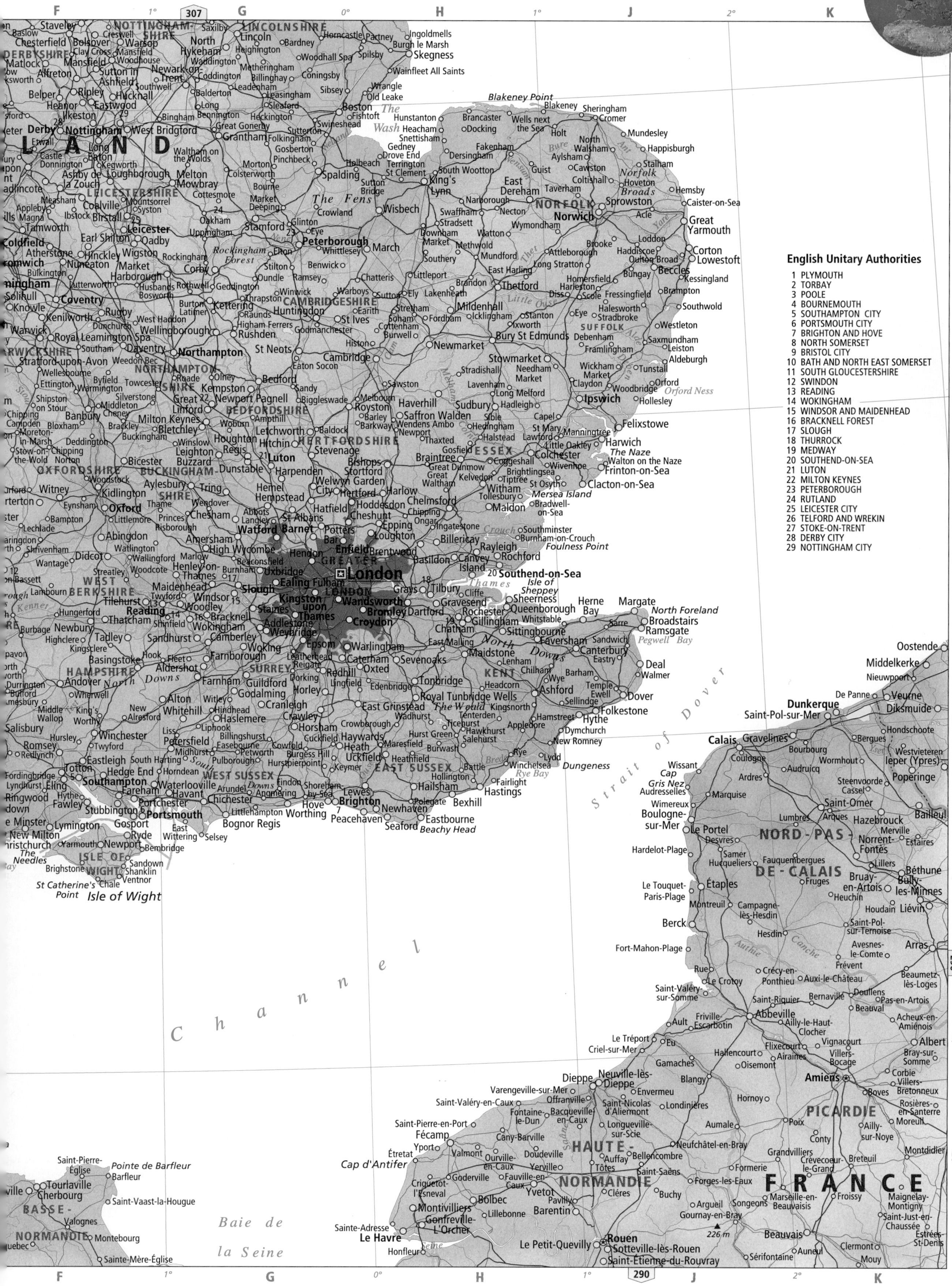

English Unitary Authorities

1 PLYMOUTH
2 TORBAY
3 POOLE
4 BOURNEMOUTH
5 SOUTHAMPTON CITY
6 PORTSMOUTH CITY
7 BRIGHTON AND HOVE
8 NORTH SOMERSET
9 BRISTOL CITY
10 BATH AND NORTH EAST SOMERSET
11 SOUTH GLOUCESTERSHIRE
12 SWINDON
13 READING
14 WOKINGHAM
15 WINDSOR AND MAIDENHEAD
16 BRACKNELL FOREST
17 SLOUGH
18 THURROCK
19 MEDWAY
20 SOUTHEND-ON-SEA
21 LUTON
22 MILTON KEYNES
23 PETERBOROUGH
24 RUTLAND
25 LEICESTER CITY
26 TELFORD AND WREKIN
27 STOKE-ON-TRENT
28 DERBY CITY
29 NOTTINGHAM CITY

0 50 100 kilometers
0 25 50 miles

Scale 1:1,500,000

Projection: Equidistant Conic

North England

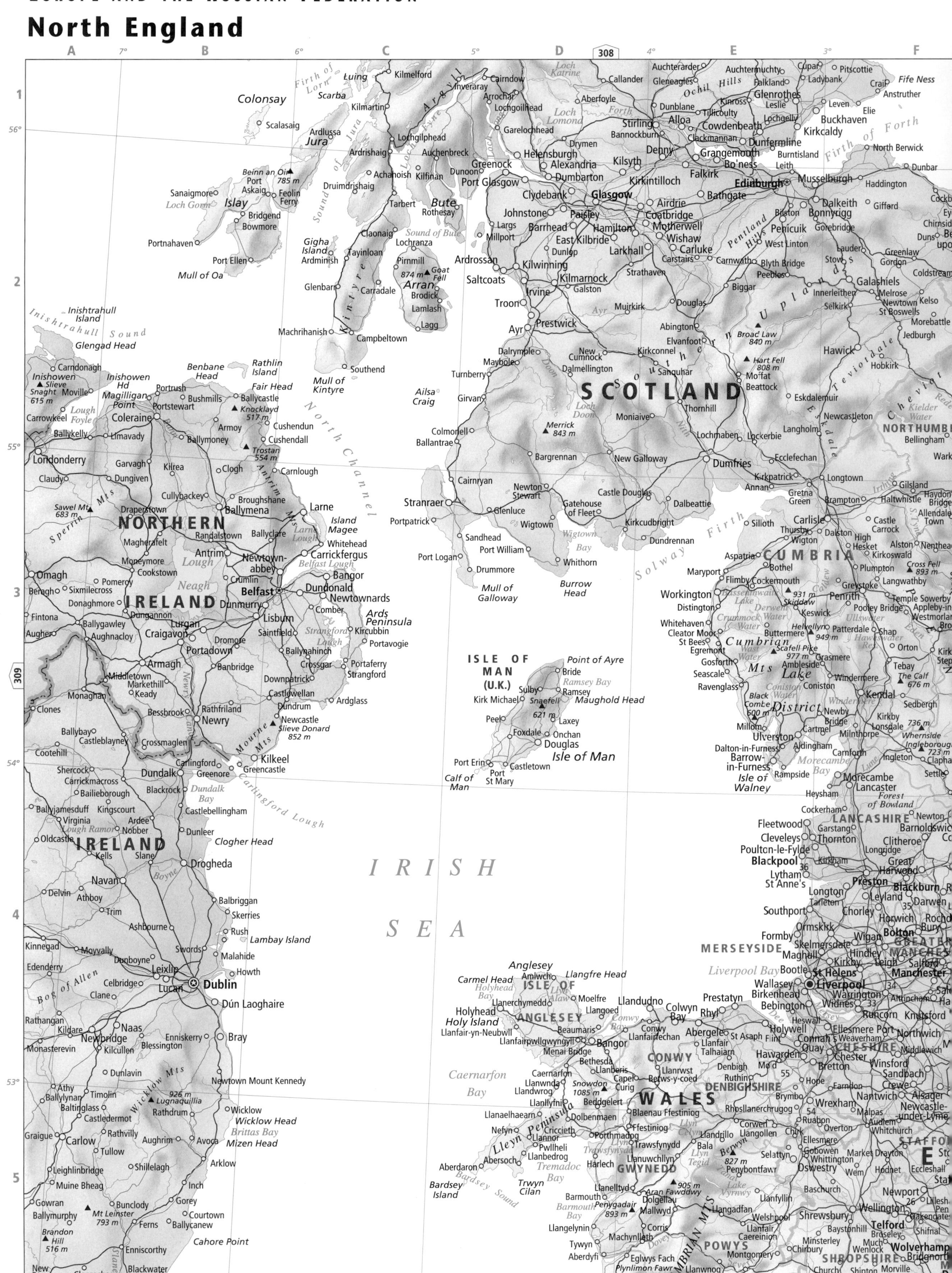

A
B
C
D
E
F
308
309
304
7°
6°
5°
4°
3°
56°
55°
54°
53°
1
2
3
4
5
SCOTLAND
NORTHERN
IRELAND
IRELAND
WALES
ISLE OF MAN (U.K.)
Isle of Man
CUMBRIA
LANCASHIRE
MERSEYSIDE
NORTHUMBE
CONWY
DENBIGHSHIRE
GWYNEDD
POWYS
SHROPSHIRE
CHESHIRE
ISLE OF ANGLESEY
IRISH
SEA
North Channel
Solway Firth
Firth of Forth
Firth of Lorn
Sound of Jura
Sound of Bute
Inishtrahull Sound
Liverpool Bay
Caernarfon Bay
Tremadoc Bay
Cardigan Bay
Dundalk Bay
Carlingford Lough
Wexford Bay
Morecambe Bay
Wigtown Bay
Belfast Lough
Strangford Lough
Lough Neagh
Lough Foyle
Loch Lomond
Loch Katrine
Colonsay
Jura
Islay
Arran
Bute
Gigha Island
Mull of Kintyre
Mull of Oa
Mull of Galloway
Ailsa Craig
Rathlin Island
Island Magee
Ards Peninsula
Lleyn Peninsula
Bardsey Island
Holy Island
Anglesey
Lambay Island
Isle of Walney
Southern Uplands
Cumbrian Mts
Lake District
Cambrian Mts
Mourne Mts
Wicklow Mts
Sperrin Mts
Antrim Mts
Ochil Hills
Pentland Hills
Cheviot Hills
Forest of Bowland
Bog of Allen
Edinburgh
Glasgow
Paisley
Greenock
Dumbarton
Stirling
Falkirk
Dunfermline
Kirkcaldy
Motherwell
Hamilton
Kilmarnock
Ayr
Prestwick
Troon
Irvine
Ardrossan
Saltcoats
Girvan
Stranraer
Dumfries
Lockerbie
Moffat
Hawick
Jedburgh
Galashiels
Peebles
Carlisle
Workington
Whitehaven
Maryport
Penrith
Keswick
Kendal
Barrow-in-Furness
Lancaster
Morecambe
Fleetwood
Blackpool
Preston
Blackburn
Southport
Liverpool
Birkenhead
Bootle
St Helens
Wigan
Bolton
Manchester
Warrington
Runcorn
Chester
Crewe
Wrexham
Shrewsbury
Telford
Wolverhampton
Oswestry
Douglas
Ramsey
Peel
Castletown
Point of Ayre
Snaefell
Belfast
Newtownabbey
Bangor
Carrickfergus
Larne
Ballymena
Antrim
Lisburn
Craigavon
Lurgan
Portadown
Armagh
Newry
Coleraine
Londonderry
Omagh
Dungannon
Newcastle
Slieve Donard
Kilkeel
Dundalk
Drogheda
Navan
Dublin
Dún Laoghaire
Bray
Wicklow
Arklow
Carlow
Naas
Lugnaquillia
Holyhead
Bangor
Llandudno
Colwyn Bay
Rhyl
Prestatyn
Caernarfon
Snowdon
Pwllheli
Harlech
Dolgellau
Aberdyfi
Machynlleth
Welshpool
Newtown

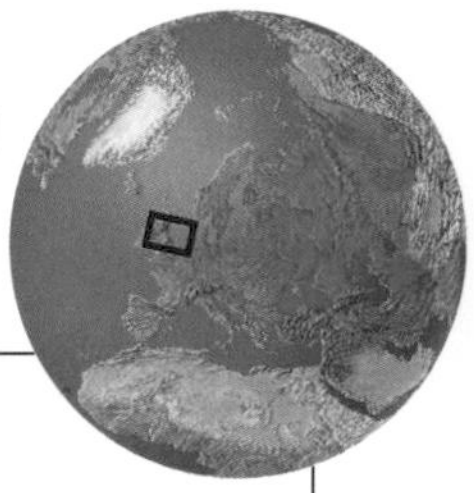

English Unitary Authorities

23 PETERBOROUGH
24 RUTLAND
25 LEICESTER CITY
26 TELFORD AND WREKIN
27 STOKE-ON-TRENT
28 DERBY CITY
29 NOTTINGHAM CITY
30 NORTH EAST LINCOLNSHIRE
31 KINGSTON UPON HULL
32 NORTH LINCOLNSHIRE
33 HALTON
34 WARRINGTON
35 BLACKBURN WITH DARWEN
36 BLACKPOOL
37 YORK CITY
38 DARLINGTON
39 HARTLEPOOL
40 STOCKTON-ON-TEES
41 MIDDLESBROUGH
42 REDCAR AND CLEVELAND

Welsh Unitary Authorities

54 WREXHAM
55 FLINTSHIRE

NORTH SEA

TYNE & WEAR
NORTH YORKSHIRE
EAST RIDING OF YORKSHIRE
SOUTH YORKSHIRE
LINCOLNSHIRE
NOTTINGHAMSHIRE
DERBYSHIRE
LEICESTERSHIRE
CAMBRIDGESHIRE
NORFOLK
ENGLAND

305

0 50 100 kilometers
0 25 50 miles
Scale 1:1,500,000
Projection: Equidistant Conic

Scotland

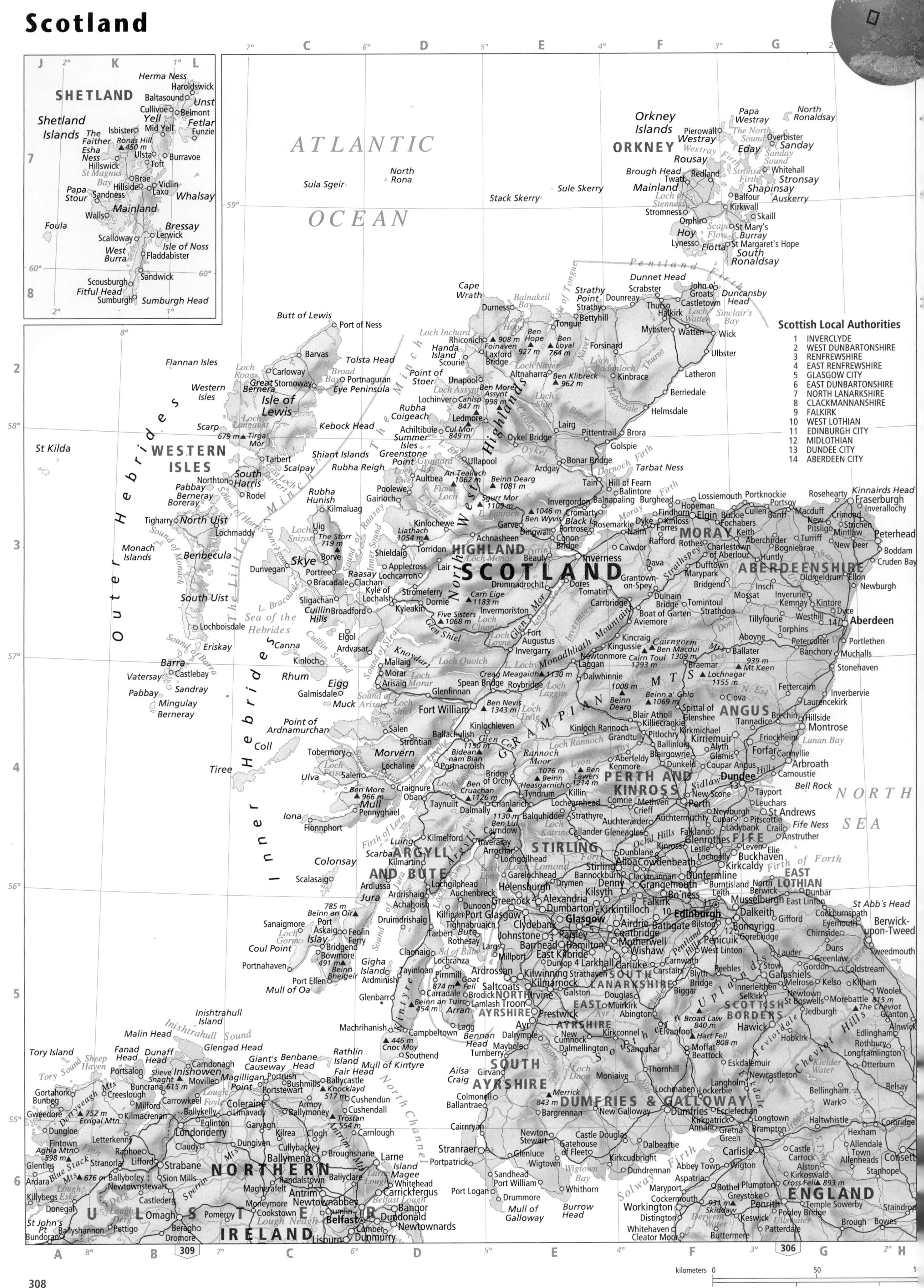
SHETLAND
Shetland Islands
ORKNEY
Orkney Islands
ATLANTIC
OCEAN
NORTH
SEA
WESTERN ISLES
Outer Hebrides
Inner Hebrides
Sea of the Hebrides
The Minch
The Little Minch
North West Highlands
GRAMPIAN MTS
Monadhliath Mountains
Southern Uplands
Cheviot Hills
North Channel
Pentland Firth
Moray Firth
Firth of Forth
Solway Firth
Firth of Lorn
Firth of Clyde
SCOTLAND
HIGHLAND
MORAY
ABERDEENSHIRE
ANGUS
PERTH AND KINROSS
FIFE
STIRLING
ARGYLL AND BUTE
EAST LOTHIAN
SCOTTISH BORDERS
SOUTH LANARKSHIRE
NORTH AYRSHIRE
EAST AYRSHIRE
SOUTH AYRSHIRE
DUMFRIES & GALLOWAY
NORTHERN IRELAND
ULSTER
IRELAND
ENGLAND
Isle of Lewis
Skye
Mull
Islay
Jura
Arran
Ben Nevis 1343 m
Ben Macdui 1309 m
Inverness
Aberdeen
Dundee
Perth
Edinburgh
Glasgow
Stirling
Fort William
Oban
Lerwick
Kirkwall
Stornoway
Belfast
Londonderry
Carlisle
Scottish Local Authorities
1 INVERCLYDE
2 WEST DUNBARTONSHIRE
3 RENFREWSHIRE
4 EAST RENFREWSHIRE
5 GLASGOW CITY
6 EAST DUNBARTONSHIRE
7 NORTH LANARKSHIRE
8 CLACKMANNANSHIRE
9 FALKIRK
10 WEST LOTHIAN
11 EDINBURGH CITY
12 MIDLOTHIAN
13 DUNDEE CITY
14 ABERDEEN CITY
309
306
kilometers 0 50
miles 0 25 50
Scale 1:2,000,000
Projection: Equidistant Conic

Ireland

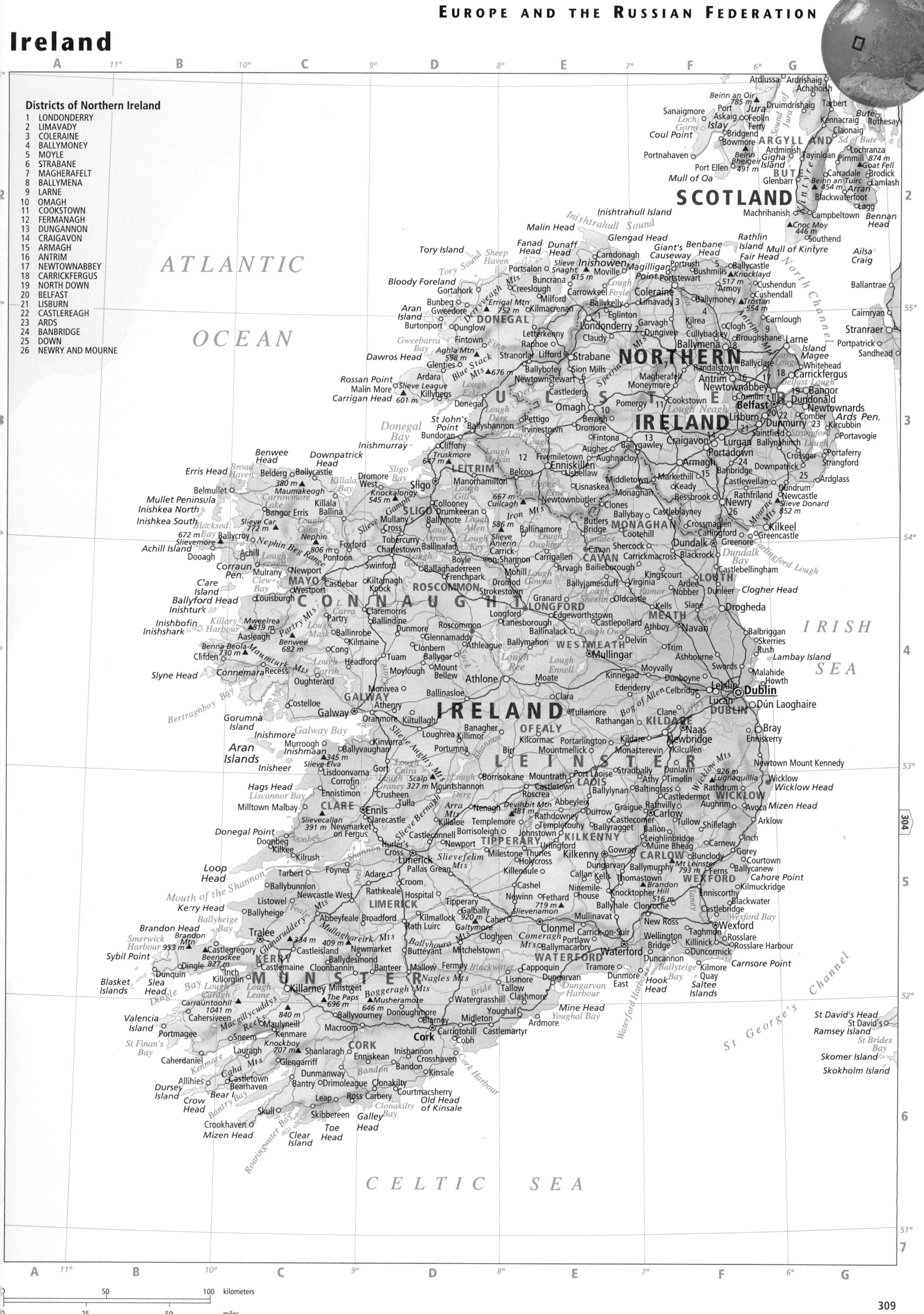
Districts of Northern Ireland
1 LONDONDERRY
2 LIMAVADY
3 COLERAINE
4 BALLYMONEY
5 MOYLE
6 STRABANE
7 MAGHERAFELT
8 BALLYMENA
9 LARNE
10 OMAGH
11 COOKSTOWN
12 FERMANAGH
13 DUNGANNON
14 CRAIGAVON
15 ARMAGH
16 ANTRIM
17 NEWTOWNABBEY
18 CARRICKFERGUS
19 NORTH DOWN
20 BELFAST
21 LISBURN
22 CASTLEREAGH
23 ARDS
24 BANBRIDGE
25 DOWN
26 NEWRY AND MOURNE
ATLANTIC OCEAN
IRISH SEA
CELTIC SEA
St George's Channel
North Channel
SCOTLAND
NORTHERN IRELAND
IRELAND
ULSTER
CONNAUGHT
LEINSTER
MUNSTER
DONEGAL
LEITRIM
SLIGO
MAYO
ROSCOMMON
GALWAY
CLARE
LIMERICK
KERRY
CORK
TIPPERARY
WATERFORD
WEXFORD
KILKENNY
CARLOW
WICKLOW
LAOIS
OFFALY
KILDARE
DUBLIN
MEATH
WESTMEATH
LONGFORD
CAVAN
MONAGHAN
LOUTH
ARGYLL AND BUTE
Dublin
Belfast
Cork
Limerick
Galway
Londonderry
Waterford
Athlone
Sligo
Wexford
Drogheda
Dundalk
Kilkenny
Killarney
Tralee
Ennis
Mullingar
Newry
Armagh
Omagh
Enniskillen
Strabane
Coleraine
Ballymena
Larne
Bangor
Lisburn
Dún Laoghaire
Bray
Lough Neagh
Lough Derg
Lough Ree
Lough Corrib
Lough Mask
Donegal Bay
Galway Bay
Dingle Bay
Bantry Bay
Mouth of the Shannon
Aran Islands
Achill Island
Inishowen
Malin Head
Mizen Head
Carrauntoohil 1041 m
Lugnaquillia 926 m
Slieve Donard 852 m
Errigal Mtn 752 m
Stranraer
Campbeltown
Islay
Jura
Arran
St David's Head
Skomer Island
Skokholm Island
Ramsey Island
Scale 1:2,000,000
Projection: Equidistant Conic
kilometers
miles
0 50 100
0 25 50
Europe and the Russian Federation
304

Africa

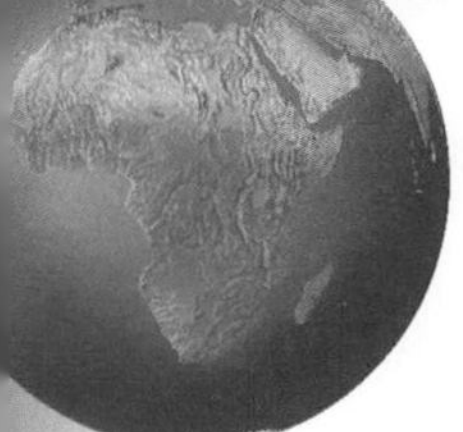

Africa

Africa, the world's second-largest continent, covers 30.3 million sq km (11.6 million sq miles). It is separated from Europe by the Mediterranean Sea and from Asia by the Red Sea and the Suez Canal. It is bounded by the Atlantic Ocean to the west and the Indian Ocean to the east.

Africa can be broadly divided in two based on culture and to some extent climate: North Africa, and Africa south of the Sahara. Arid North Africa includes Morocco, Western Sahara, Algeria, Tunisia, Libya, and Egypt, all of which are climatically and culturally akin to the Middle East.

South of them a semiarid zone stretches across Mauritania, Mali, Niger, Chad, Sudan, Ethiopia, and Somalia. Humid tropical Africa includes Guinea, Guinea-Bissau, Sierra Leone, Liberia, Côte d'Ivoire, Ghana, Togo, Benin, Nigeria, Cameroon, the Central African Republic, Gabon, Congo, the Democratic Republic of the Congo (formerly Zaire), Uganda, Kenya, Tanzania, Angola, Zambia, Malawi, Zimbabwe, and Mozambique. Southern Africa includes large regions of semiarid and arid land. Namibia is largely desert and there are extensive arid areas in Botswana and South Africa.

Physical features

Africa consists of a number of plateaus, dissected in the east by the Rift Valley. Volcanic eruptions and elongated lakes and valleys are found along this rift. The Atlas Mountains in the northwest of the continent are the only geologically recent mountains in Africa.

Africa has several long rivers. The Nile, around 6,693 km (4,160 miles) long, arises in the Kenyan highlands, flows north and disgorges in the Mediterranean. The basins of the Congo (around 4,630 km [2,880 miles] long), the Zambeze (around 2,735 km [1,700 miles] long) and the Niger (around 4,100 km [2,150 miles]) cover vast areas.

Climate and vegetation

Africa is a continent of climatic contrasts. Arid North Africa contains the world's largest hot desert, the Sahara. Drought- and fire-resistant shrubs and grasses are found there. To its north lie narrow zones along the Mediterranean coast with cool, wet winters and hot, dry summers.

On the southern border of the Sahara lies the Sahel, consisting of thorny woodlands and grasslands with scattered trees. Rainfall is generally low and variable. The area is prone to severe droughts, such as those in the 1980s in Ethiopia and in the 1990s in Somalia. Injudicious cattle herding and grain farming contributed to desertification.

In central and west Africa, equatorial and tropical conditions prevail, with annual rainfall exceeding 1,270 mm (50 in). Forests and woodlands cover large areas. The forests are layered—shrubs and mosses at lower layers and large tree canopies at higher layers. Each layer possesses abundant and distinct wildlife. East Africa has a monsoon climate, and its forests are less dense. In areas of lesser rainfall (less than 380 mm [15 in]), thorny woodlands and grasslands occur. The forests of Africa harbor chimpanzees and gorillas, and their bird life is profuse.

The vegetation of the semiarid lands of the southernmost part of Africa, notably around the borders of the Kalahari Desert, consists of thorny scrub and grasslands. A greater variety of plants occurs in the wetter coastal and upland areas of the southeast parts of South Africa.

Africa's savannas possess among the richest and most diverse animal populations of the world. Zebras, antelopes, giraffes, elephants, rhinoceros, and wildebeest roam in herds, preyed upon by carnivores such as lions, tigers, leopards, hyenas, jackals, and foxes. Bird life includes ostriches and raptors such as eagles and hawks.

Large-scale hunting of wildlife, begun during the colonial era, has had a major impact on Africa's animals. The most notable example has been the quest for ivory—world bans on the trading of ivory have reduced the threat to elephant populations. Other threatened species are white and black rhinoceros, the pygmy hippopotamus, the black wildebeest and some types of zebra.

Islands off the African coast also have their distinct (and distinctive) plant and animal species, notably the lemurs in Madagascar, and the seas are also rich in animal life, including whales, seals, dugongs, and manatees.

Zebras (left) and elephants (top) are among the most beloved of African animals. These Sudanese people (center) are migrating to Egypt in search of work.

Population

From being the apparent origin of the human species, Africa's population has grown to 795.7 million people (2000). The high rate of population increase between 1985 and 1990 of three percent per annum put pressure on resources and food supplies; currently the growth rate has fallen to 2.2 percent. Life expectancies are low in comparison with other continents: 47.9 years for males and 50 years for females.

In arid North Africa, populations are concentrated along the Mediterranean. In Egypt, ninety percent of the country's people live along the banks of the Nile River and on its delta. In humid tropical Africa, populations are more dispersed.

A lack of employment in rural areas during the twentieth century has caused a drift to the cities, resulting in fringe urban settlements with poor facilities. In 2000, an estimated 37.2 percent of Africa's people lived in urban areas.

Agriculture

More than sixty percent of Africa's people depend upon agriculture for their livelihood. Farming is mostly of the subsistence variety—the Hausa people in the west African savannas grow grains and herd animals, and the Tuareg people in the Sahara practice pastoralism, for example.

Rice, maize, and wheat are grown in several parts of Africa, either where rainfall is adequate or through the use of irrigation (in Egypt and Nigeria). Fruits and vegetables are also grown: bananas and mangoes in humid tropical areas, date palms in arid areas, and citrus fruits, grapes, and olives in areas with a Mediterranean climate.

Plantation agriculture and large-scale farming were established by Europeans in tropical humid

Africa and southern Africa. The plantations provide some countries with their main export earnings—tea and coffee in Burundi and Rwanda, peanuts in Senegal, and tobacco in Malawi.

Prolonged droughts in several parts of Africa, especially in the semiarid Sahel, have severely affected food production. Agricultural production has also been disrupted by civil wars and wars between neighboring countries.

In the countries of the Gulf of Guinea, tropical forests are logged for valuable timbers including mahogany, but forest depletion destroys animal habitats and may affect the global climate.

Industrialization

Mineral-rich Africa exports most of the minerals it extracts. Algeria, Libya, and Nigeria are major petroleum producers, and oil is also found in Angola, Benin, Guinea-Bissau, and Egypt; natural gas occurs in Algeria, Libya, and Egypt. A rich metallic ore belt extending from central to southern Africa contains copper, zinc, and lead in the Democratic Republic of the Congo and Zambia, iron ore in South Africa and Zimbabwe, nickel in Botswana and South Africa, and manganese in South Africa. South Africa is a major gold and platinum producer. Diamonds are mined in Namibia, South Africa, the Democratic Republic of the Congo, and Angola. Uranium is found in the Central African Republic.

Several African countries obtain more than half their export earnings from a single commodity: Libya, Nigeria, Gabon, Angola, and Egypt from petroleum; Guinea from bauxite. Even South Africa, with its diversified economy, depends on gold for forty percent of its export earnings.

Despite the continent's natural resources, there are no developed countries in Africa. A large proportion of African countries have low indicators for nutrition, education, health, and life expectancy. The United Nations designates these as the world's least developed nations. Several countries, such as Somalia and the Sudan, are not self-sufficient in food production and have during drought and war desperately needed food and aid.

Relatively few African countries have developed significant manufacturing industries. The major exception is South Africa, which now exports machinery and other equipment. During the years of apartheid, however, their racially-based separate development policy created a wide gulf in living standards between the majority black and minority white populations, which will take considerable time to bridge. Egypt and Kenya produce textiles, processed foods, and cement.

Languages

A large number of languages are spoken in Africa, but many, such as Tigre and Chadic in northeast Africa and Berber in North Africa, are restricted to small tribal groups. Zulu is spoken by a large group in South Africa. Arabic is the main language of North Africa and the adjoining countries just south of the Sahara. Some languages are widely used, such as Swahili in east Africa and Hausa in west Africa. Malagasy, spoken in Madagascar, is related to Southeast Asian languages.

During the colonial period, several European languages became official languages in various parts of Africa, and French, Portuguese, and English are still spoken over large areas. These languages allow communication between tribal groups which speak different languages.

Boundary disputes and wars

From the sixteenth century onward, Africa was overrun by colonial powers including France, Britain, Portugal, Spain, and Germany. The colonists had great impact in the areas of language, law, and education. The current borders of the nations of Africa were determined during colonial times, too, and often cut across tribal areas, separating members of the same ethnic groups while bringing together traditionally antagonistic tribes: The Somalis for instance found themselves in Somalia, Kenya, and Ethiopia.

Following decolonization, several tribal conflicts have erupted, such as the genocide of Tutsis by the Hutus in Rwanda in 1994. Nigeria had a lengthy period of insurrection when its southern part seceded to form the short-lived Republic of Biafra. A similar conflict currently rages in southern Sudan. These internal conflicts and military coups have inhibited development in large areas of Africa—the civil war in the Democratic Republic of the Congo between 1999 and 2003 killed approximately 2.5 million people; war-torn Somalia has, at present, no effective central government; and Zulu demands for greater autonomy are causing tension in South Africa.

This traditionally costumed dancer from Malawi (above right) entertains at both funerals and more cheerful festivities.

Dependencies & territories

Autonomous communities

Nations

North Africa

Morocco

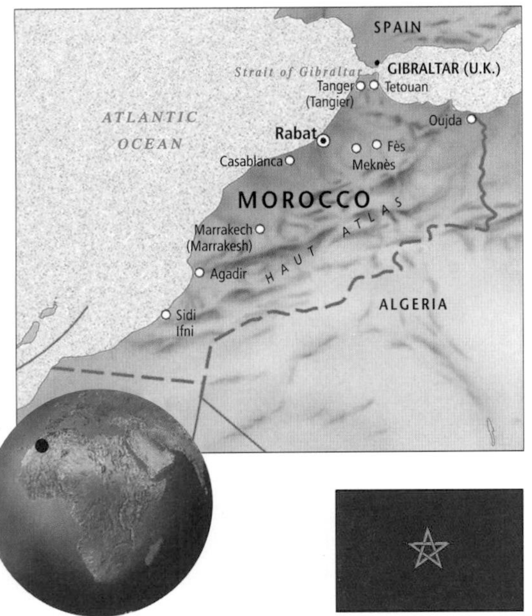

Fact File

Official name Kingdom of Morocco

Form of government Constitutional monarchy with single legislative body (Chamber of Representatives)

Capital Rabat

Area 446,550 sq km (172,413 sq miles)

Time zone GMT

Population 31,168,000

Projected population 2015 37,680,000

Population density 69.8 per sq km (180.8 per sq mile)

Life expectancy 69.7

Infant mortality (per 1,000) 46.5

Official language Arabic

Other languages Berber languages, French, Spanish

Literacy rate 43.7 %

Religions Muslim 98.7 %, Christian 1.1 %, Jewish 0.2%

Ethnic groups Arab-Berber 99.1 %, Jewish 0.2 %, other 0.7 %

Currency Moroccan dirham

Economy Agriculture 46 %, services 29 %, industry 25 %

GNP per capita US$ 3,700

Climate Temperate along northern coast, arid in south, cooler in mountains

Highest point Jebel Toubkal 4,165 m (13,665 ft)

Map reference Pages 360–61

Morocco's earliest inhabitants were the Berbers, who still live in the country today. At one time under Carthaginian rule, and then a part of the Roman Empire, the Berbers were overrun by Arabs in the seventh century AD and converted to Islam. The country's name derives from the Arabic Maghrib al-aqsa ("the farthest west"), and because of the protective barrier of the Atlas Mountains, Morocco has always been less a part of the Arab world than the other North African states. Under political pressure from Spain and France during the nineteenth century, Morocco became a French protectorate in 1912. About 35 percent of the people live in the highlands and are Berber-speaking, while the Arab majority live in the lowlands.

Under the rule of King Hassan II (1961–99) and since of his son Mohammed VI, Morocco has followed generally pro-Western policies. Hassan's popularity at home owed a good deal to Morocco's disputed territorial claim to the phosphate-rich resources of Western Sahara across the southern border. A costly armed struggle with the Polisario Front guerrilla movement of Western Sahara led to a ceasefire in 1992, by which time 170,000 of the native-born Sahrawis of the region had become refugees in Algeria. Sovereignty is still unresolved and a UN-organized referendum on its final status has been repeatedly postponed .

More than one-third of Morocco is mountainous. Three parallel ranges of the Atlas Mountains run southwest to northeast, where a plateau stretches toward the Algerian border. Most of the people living in the mountains are peasant cultivators and nomadic herders. Modern economic development is found mainly on the Atlantic plains and the plateaus—the fertile Moulouyan, Rharb, Sous, and High (Haut) Atlas plains constituting virtually all of Morocco's cultivable land. In the Rharb and Rif regions extensive areas are covered with cork oak, while on the northern slopes there are forests of evergreen oak and cedar. Wildlife includes Cuvier's gazelle, the Barbary macaque, and the mouflon (a wild sheep), while desert animals such as the fennec fox live in the south.

In 1995 Morocco suffered its worst drought in 30 years. This seriously affected agriculture, which produces about one-third of Morocco's exports and employs about half the workforce. Irrigation is essential over most of the country, the chief crops being barley and wheat along with citrus fruit, potatoes, and other vegetables. Dates are grown in desert oases. Along the Atlantic coast fishing plays a major role. The country's natural resources are still largely undeveloped. It has coal, iron ore, and zinc, along with the world's largest reserves of phosphates. Debt servicing, unemployment, the high rate of population increase, as well as the unresolved territorial claim to Western Sahara are all long-term problems.

Algeria

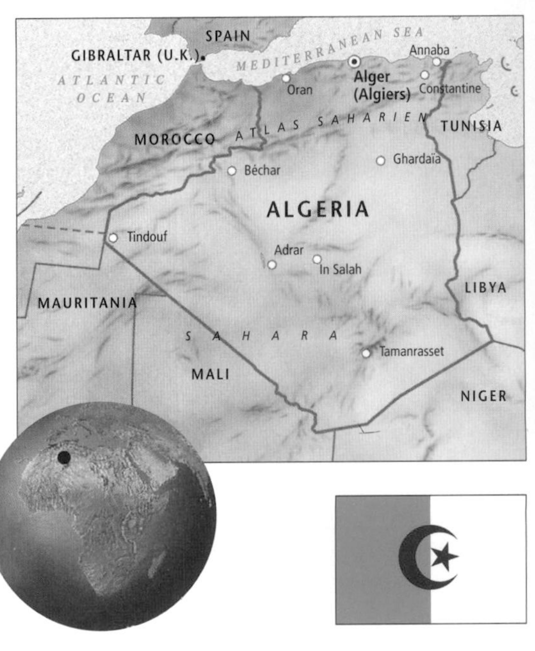

Fact File

Official name Democratic and Popular Republic of Algeria

Form of government Republic with single legislative body (National People's Assembly), but currently governed by military-backed council

Capital Alger (Algiers)

Area 2,381,740 sq km (919,590 sq miles)

Time zone GMT

Population 32,278,000

Projected population 2015 38,022,000

Population density 13.6 per sq km (35.1 per sq mile)

Life expectancy 70.2

Infant mortality (per 1,000) 39.1

Official language Arabic

Other languages French, Berber languages

Literacy rate 61.6 %

Religions Sunni Muslim 99 %, Christian and Jewish 1 %

Ethnic groups Arab-Berber 99 %, European 1 %

Currency Algerian dinar

Economy Services 75 %, agriculture 14 %, industry 11 %

GNP per capita US$ 5,600

Climate Mild temperate in north, with cool, wet winters and hot, dry summers; arid in south

Highest point Mt Tahat 2,918 m (9,573 ft)

Map reference Pages 360–61

The largest state in the north of Africa, Algeria was once a province of the Roman Empire known as Numidia, and since early times it has been the home of nomadic Berber peoples. Arabs came to the region during the seventh century, bringing Islam, and in the sixteenth century Algeria was incorporated into the Ottoman Empire. From the sixteenth to the nineteenth centuries Algeria posed a significant threat to all who used the nearby regions of the Mediterranean Sea. The pirates of what was at that time called the Barbary

A gold seller in Morocco (left page). The Algerian town of Ghardaïa lies at the eastern end of the Grand Erg Occidental, on the fringe of the Sahara Desert (above). Workmen renovating a building in Tunisia (below).

Coast made a lucrative living by trading in slaves and by attacking passing shipping. A French colony from 1848, Algeria won its independence in 1962 after eight years of bitter war. Thirty years of peace followed, but since 1992 the country has been torn by violence once more. In a ruthless civil conflict between the government and an outlawed fundamentalist party, the Islamic Salvation Front (FIS), tens of thousands have died.

More than ninety percent of Algeria's people live on the narrow, fertile, discontinuous coastal strip on the Mediterranean. One-third of the population lives by farming, and it is here that most of the country's arable land is found—only three percent of the whole country. Inland, and to the south, are the Maritime Atlas Mountains. Their northern slopes have a relatively reliable rainfall and support a shrinking forest of pines, cedars, evergreens, and cork oaks. A high plateau about 250 km (150 miles) wide lies between the coastal range and the Atlas Saharien Mountains. Beyond these, all the way to the boundaries of Mali and Niger, stretches the sandy, rocky waste of the Sahara Desert, dotted here and there with small oasis settlements.

As much as 85 percent of Algeria's land area is desert. In many parts of the country rain almost never falls and the summer heat is intense. Along the Mediterranean coast, however, while the summers are hot and dry the winters are wet. Wildlife on the inland plateaus includes wild boar and gazelle; in the desert there are small mammals such as the jerboa and the Saharan hare.

Oil and natural gas are the foundation of Algeria's economy and over the years revenue from these sources has encouraged a wide range of industrial development. From the late 1960s, the country's economy was run as a centrally controlled state system along Soviet lines. This began to change following 1989 with the introduction of market mechanisms. The farming region along the northern coast produces wheat, barley, oats, grapes, and olives, and supplies a wide variety of early fruit and vegetables to markets in Europe.

Tunisia

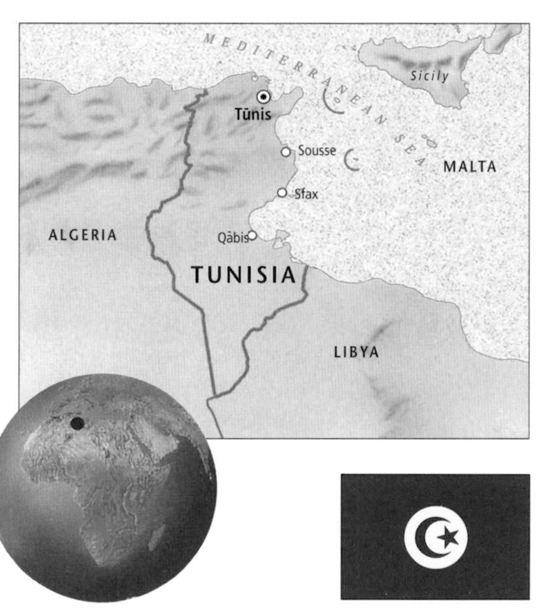

Fact File

OFFICIAL NAME Republic of Tunisia

FORM OF GOVERNMENT Republic with single legislative body (Chamber of Deputies)

CAPITAL Tūnis

AREA 163,610 sq km (63,170 sq miles)

TIME ZONE GMT + 1 hour

POPULATION 9,816,000

PROJECTED POPULATION 2015 11,257,000

POPULATION DENSITY 60 per sq km (155.4 per sq mile)

LIFE EXPECTANCY 74.2

INFANT MORTALITY (PER 1,000) 28.0

OFFICIAL LANGUAGE Arabic

OTHER LANGUAGE French, Berber languages

LITERACY RATE 66.7 %

RELIGIONS Muslim 98 %, Christian 1 %, Jewish 1 %

ETHNIC GROUPS Arab-Berber 98 %, European 1 %, Jewish 1 %

CURRENCY Dinar

ECONOMY Services 62 %, agriculture 22 %, industry 16 %

GNP PER CAPITA US$ 6,600

CLIMATE Temperate in north, with mild, rainy winters and hot, dry summers; desert in south

HIGHEST POINT Jabal ash Sha'nabī 1,544 m (5,065 ft)

MAP REFERENCE Page 361

Tunisia has a long history. Located in North Africa, across from Sicily, it was founded by Phoenician sailors 3,000 years ago, became famous as the Carthage of Queen Dido, and fell to the Romans in 146 BC. Arab conquest brought Islam to the region in the seventh century AD.

In modern times control of Tunisia was disputed by Italy, England, and France before it became a French protectorate in 1883. Ruled since independence in 1956 as a de facto one-party state, Tunisia held its first multi-party elections in 1994 (the government claiming 99.9 percent of the vote). Tunisia is a relatively prosperous country, strongly influenced by French and European culture, with a record of modest but steady economic growth. While Islamic fundamentalism is on the rise, women are treated with greater equality in Tunisia than elsewhere in the Arab world.

The eastern end of the Atlas Mountains juts across the border from Algeria in the north. A mountainous plateau called the Dorsale extends northeast sloping down to the coastal plains. Parallel to the Mediterranean Sea in the extreme northwest, the Kroumirie Mountains, covered with cork oaks, shelter the fertile valley of the Majardah River as it flows down from the Dorsale. Harnessed for hydroelectric power, this enters the sea near Tūnis across broad alluvial lowlands used for growing a wide variety of crops, some extensively irrigated, including wheat and barley, olives, sugar beet, citrus fruits, grapes, and vegetables. South of the mountains a dry expanse of plateau-steppe gives way to a series of salt lakes, the largest, Shaṭṭ al Jarīd, extending halfway across the country. The large remaining area to the south is desert.

Tunisia has a diverse economy. Agriculture is the main employer, but in recent years it has declined in importance as a revenue earner relative to mineral and petroleum exports. Most industrial production is based on agricultural and mining products. Real growth averaged 4.2 percent from 1991 to 1995, with moderate inflation. Growth in tourism has been a key factor. Since the 1960s Tunisia has been a popular destination for European tourists, drawn by winter sunshine, beaches, and Roman remains. In recent times there have been almost 2 million visitors per year, with tourism employing 200,000 people, but the activities of Islamic militants have had a dampening effect.

Libya

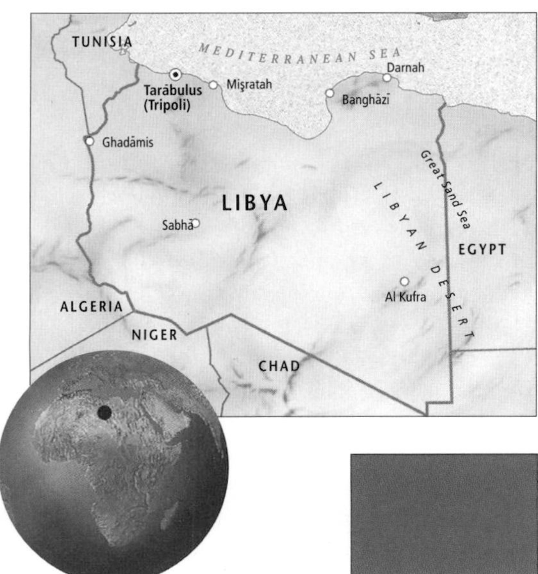

Fact File

OFFICIAL NAME Socialist People's Libyan Arab Jamahiriya

FORM OF GOVERNMENT Republic with single legislative body (General People's Congress)

CAPITAL Tarābulus (Tripoli)

AREA 1,759,540 sq km (679,358 sq miles)

TIME ZONE GMT + 2 hours

POPULATION 5,369,000

PROJECTED POPULATION 2015 7,058,000

POPULATION DENSITY 3.1 per sq km (7.9 per sq mile)

LIFE EXPECTANCY 75.9

INFANT MORTALITY (PER 1,000) 27.9

OFFICIAL LANGUAGE Arabic

OTHER LANGUAGES Berber languages, Italian, English

LITERACY RATE 76.2 %

RELIGIONS Sunni Muslim 97 %, other 3 %

ETHNIC GROUPS Berber and Arab 97 %; other (including Greek, Maltese, Italian, Egyptian, Pakistani, Turkish, Indian, Tunisian) 3 %

CURRENCY Libyan dinar

ECONOMY Services 51 %, industry 31 %, agriculture 18 %

GNP PER CAPITA US$ 7,600

CLIMATE Mainly arid; temperate along coast

HIGHEST POINT Bikubiti 2,285 m (7,497 ft)

MAP REFERENCE Page 362

First settled by the Greeks, and once part of the empire of Alexander the Great, Libya was ruled by the Romans for 500 years. Later, in AD 642, the region was conquered by the Arabs, and later still became part of the Ottoman Empire. It was occupied by Italy in 1911, and the years 1938 to 1939 saw Mussolini bring in 30,000 Italians to farm the Jefra Plain. Libya became independent in 1951. Since 1969, when he seized power, it has been a one-party socialist state ruled dictatorially by Colonel Muammar al Gaddafi. In 1992–99 the country suffered UN sanctions due to his support of terrorist cells.

The arid Saharan Plateau takes up a vast 93 percent of Libya's land area. The great expanse of the Sahara gives way to a fertile coastal strip along the Mediterranean coast, where the majority of the population lives, though only one percent of the total land area is arable. Tripoli stands on the Jefra Plain, Libya's most productive farming area. Cereals, particularly barley, are the most important crop. Sorghum is grown in the Fezzan to the south; wheat, tobacco, and olives are produced in the north; and dates and figs are cultivated at a few scattered oases in the desert. Predominantly low-lying, the desert terrain rises southward to Bikubiti in the Tibesti Range on the border with Chad. The country is without lakes or perennial rivers, and artesian wells supply nearly two-thirds of its water.

Oil provides almost all export earnings and about one-third of the gross domestic product. Though Libya's per capita gross domestic product is usually Africa's highest, the people suffer from periodic shortages of basic goods and foodstuffs caused by import restrictions. The largely state-controlled industrial sector (almost all the oil companies were nationalized in 1973) suffers from overstaffing and other constraints. However, oil revenues have enabled important state initiatives to be undertaken: the Great Manmade River Project being built to bring water from large aquifers under the Sahara to the coastal cities is one of the world's largest water development projects.

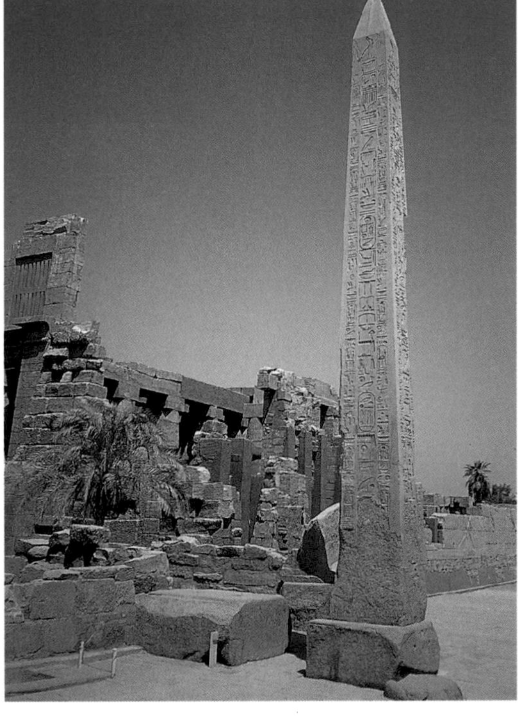

Egypt

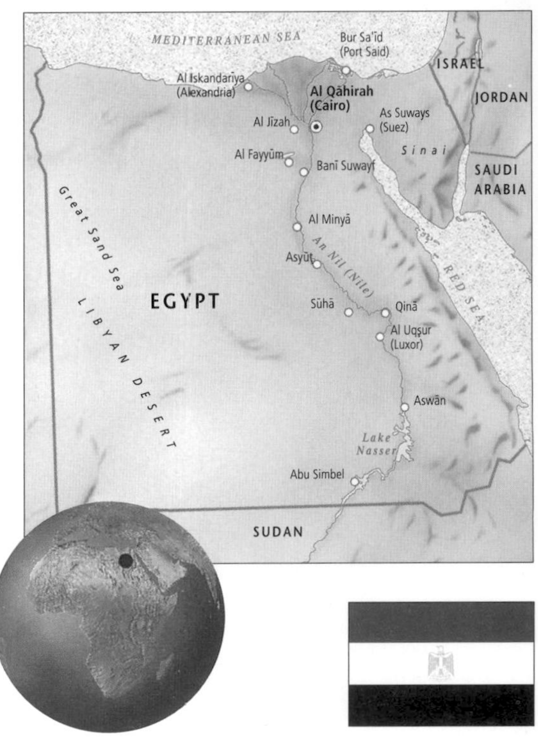

Fact File

OFFICIAL NAME Arab Republic of Egypt

FORM OF GOVERNMENT Republic with two legislative bodies (Advisory Council and People's Assembly)

CAPITAL Al Qāhirah (Cairo)

AREA 1,001,450 sq km (386,660 sq miles)

TIME ZONE GMT + 2 hours

POPULATION 70,713,000

PROJECTED POPULATION 2015 84,425,000

POPULATION DENSITY 70.6 per sq km (182.9 per sq mile)

LIFE EXPECTANCY 64.1

INFANT MORTALITY (PER 1,000) 58.6

OFFICIAL LANGUAGE Arabic

OTHER LANGUAGES English, French, ethnic languages

LITERACY RATE 51.4 %

RELIGIONS Muslim (mostly Sunni) 90 %, other (including Coptic Christian) 10 %

ETHNIC GROUPS Eastern Hamitic (Egyptian, Bedouin, and Berber) 99 %; other (including Greek, Nubian, Armenian, Italian, and French) 1 %

CURRENCY Egyptian pound

ECONOMY Services 54 %, agriculture 34 %, industry 12 %

GDP PER CAPITA US$ 3,700

CLIMATE Mainly arid, with mild winters and hot, dry summers

HIGHEST POINT Jabal Kātrīna 2,629 m (8,625 ft)

MAP REFERENCE Pages 362–63

Timeline

c. 3600 BC Agriculture begins in alluvial soils deposited in the Nile Valley; irrigation used for growing fruit and vegetables

c. 3100 BC King Menes founds first dynasty to rule nation; civilization begins with uniting of Upper and Lower regions in Nile Valley

c. 2650 BC The first pyramids are built during a 500-year period of peace and prosperity under the Old Kingdom

1991 BC Egypt's power expands—King Amenemhet I and his successors conquer Nubia and trade with Syria and Palestine

1497–26 BC King Thutmose III's reign marks height of Empire; buildings include Temple of Amon at Karnak

1153 BC Assassination of Ramses III; Egyptian power declines as a result of corruption and feuding between priests and kings

332 BC Egypt becomes part of Alexander the Great's empire; he builds the city of Alexandria on the Mediterranean coast

31 BC Rome takes control of Egypt when Mark Antony and Cleopatra's navy is defeated by Octavian's fleet at Battle of Actium

AD 642 Egypt comes under the control of Muslim Arabs from the regions to the east

1517 Ottoman Turks defeat the Mamelukes (Turks, Mongols, and Circassians) and rule for the next 250 years

1798 Napoleon conquers Egypt and leaves French troops in control of the country

1801 British and Ottoman troops expel French occupation forces from Egypt

Egypt is sometimes known as "the gift of the Nile" (An Nīl) because the waters of this famous river have always been the lifeblood of the country. Every year until the Aswan High Dam was built, the Nile would flood, spreading fertile silt across the floor of the valley. It was in the Nile Valley that Egyptian civilization began, 6,000 years ago, and the country was the first to have a society organized along political lines. The Great Pyramid itself, still one of the largest structures in the world, was built 5,000 years ago. Since then innumerable rulers and conquerors have come and gone—Persians, Greeks, and Romans being followed by the seventh-century conquests of Mohammed's followers and the conversion of the region to Islam. During the nineteenth century, after the construction of the Suez Canal in 1869, Egypt came increasingly under the influence of the French and the British. Britain made it a protectorate from 1914 to 1922. It was not until 1952 that Egypt became an independent republic.

Physical features and land use

Egypt is defined by the valley of the Nile and the spreading deserts on either side. The Nile rises at Lake Victoria, further south, and enters the country across the southern border, from Sudan. It first fills huge Lake Nasser, formed by the Aswan High Dam, which was completed in 1965. It then makes an eastward bend near Luxor before flowing steadily north. At Cairo the river fans out into a broad delta before entering the Mediterranean. The area north of Cairo is often known as Lower Egypt and the area south of Cairo as Upper Egypt.

Although the lands of the valley and the delta constitute only three percent of Egypt's total land area, this is where 99 percent of the people live and where nearly all agricultural activity takes place. West of the Nile, extending to the Libyan border, lies the Western (or Libyan) Desert. This arid limestone region consists of low valleys and scarps, and in the north contains a large area below sea level called the Qattara Depression. Scattered across the desert are isolated fertile oases where date palms grow. It is hoped to increase the agricultural production of these oases by using deep artesian bores.

Between the Nile and the Red Sea is the Eastern (or Arabian) Desert. Here, grasses, tamarisks, and mimosas grow, providing desert nomads with feed for their sheep, camels, and goats. Between the Gulf of Suez and the border with Israel is the almost uninhabited triangular limestone plateau of the Sinai Peninsula. Egypt's highest peak, Jabal Kātrīnā, is found in Sinai's mountainous south.

People and culture

While there are significant cultural differences between the ninety percent of the population who are Hamitic and the Afro-Nubian peoples of the Upper Nile near Sudan, Egypt has a long tradition of ethnic and religious tolerance. In Cairo and Alexandria there have always been sizeable colonies of Greeks and Armenians, and although most Jews have now left for Israel, there is still a small Jewish community in Cairo. The small number of desert Bedouin divide into two main groups. In the southern part of the Eastern Desert live the Arabdah and Bisharin (Hamitic Beja), while Saadi and Murabatin (of Arab and Berber ancestry) are found throughout the Western Desert.

Ancient Egypt's art, architecture, pyramids and tombs are among the treasures of civilization. Evidence from tombs shows that even at the time of the first recorded dynasty, about 4400 BC, furniture inlaid with ivory and ebony was being made, along with alabaster vessels and fine work in copper and gold. In the pyramid-building period between 3700 BC and 2500 BC the Great Pyramid of Cheops was erected, a project thought to have occupied 100,000 men for twenty years. The pyramids were themselves immense tombs, containing chambers in which dead kings were buried, supplied with all they might need—food, clothing, and furniture—in the afterlife. It is not known when exactly Christianity began in Egypt, but it was very early, around AD 40. The new faith was readily accepted since the hope of a future life coincided with the views of the Egyptians themselves.

Today about eight to ten percent of the people are Coptic Christians. The Copts claim to have received the gospel directly from St Mark, the first bishop of Alexandria. Their community has always valued education highly, and has contributed many figures to Egyptian public life. About ninety percent of the population are Muslim, mainly Sunni.

With the rise of Islamic fundamentalism, the most bitter conflict within Egypt is between the modernizing political elite and the fundamentalist Moslem Brotherhood. The latter is held responsible for terrorist activities, but today seems to be under control. Arabic is the official language, but several other languages are used by ethnic minorities, from Hamito-Sudanic among the Nubians to the Berber-related language of the Siwah tribe east of the Qattara Depression.

Economy and resources

Food crops have been grown in the fertile soils of the Nile floodplain and delta for many thousands of years. But a population of around 71 million, increasing by over one million per year, is placing considerable pressure on Egypt's agricultural resources. In addition, salination of land below the High Aswan Dam, land lost to growing urbanization, and desertification as a result of wind-blown sand, are all reducing the amount of arable land. Today much of Egypt's food is imported.

In manufacturing, textiles are by far the largest industry, and include spinning, weaving, and the dyeing and printing of cotton, wool, silk, and synthetic-fiber materials. Along with finished textiles, raw cotton remains one of the main exports, only exceeded in value by petroleum. There are plans to restore the Suez Canal's earning capacity by deepening and widening it for modern shipping. Most large-scale industrial plants in Egypt remain state-owned, overstaffed, and over-regulated, in need of both technical improvements and investment. This hampers the country's economic performance and is a challenge to governmental efforts at reform.

An obelisk, covered with hieroglyphs, among the ruins at Luxor (left page). The Red Sea and the Sinai Desert (below left). Cairo and the Nile at dusk (below right).

1869 Suez Canal completed, allowing quicker access to India and the Pacific

1882 British troops occupy Egypt

1914 Egypt made a protectorate of the United Kingdom

1922 Britain grants nominal independence

1940–42 German and Italian troops fight battles against Allied forces along the north coast of Egypt and in the Western Desert

1948–49 Egypt part of Arab League invasion of Israel after Palestine is partitioned into Arab and Jewish nations; Israel repels invasion

1953 Egypt becomes a republic, King Farouk is exiled

1956 President Nasser first nationalizes Suez Canal then closes it. Britain, France, and Israel invade to reopen canal—UN intervenes

1960 Construction of the Aswan High Dam on the River Nile begins; it creates Lake Nasser, flooding several ancient sites

1967 Egypt and other Arab nations attack Israel but are defeated in "Six Day War"; Israel occupies the Gaza Strip and Sinai

1979 President Sadat ends hostilities with Israel and signs an agreement under which Sinai is returned to Egyptian control

1981 President Sadat assassinated and succeeded by Hosni Mubarak

1990 Egypt opposes Iraq's invasion of oil-rich Kuwait and sides with US and European allies in the Gulf War

1992 Cairo damaged in an earthquake which kills more than 500 people

1997 In Upper Egypt Muslim fundamentalists attack tourists and kill 58 people

Western Africa

Mauritania

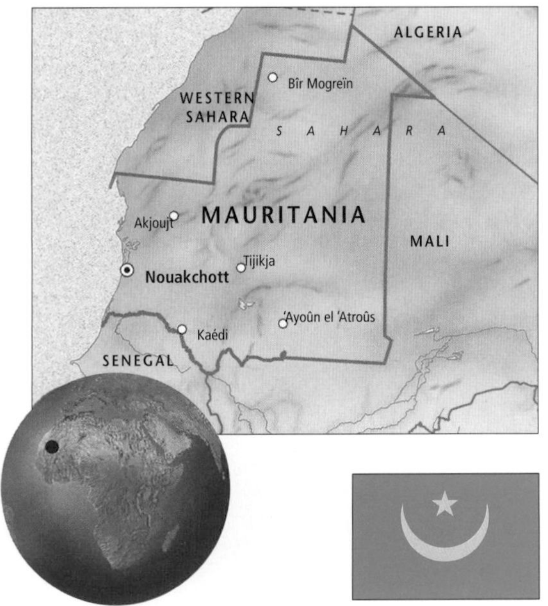

Fact File

Official name Islamic Republic of Mauritania

Form of government Republic with two legislative bodies (Senate and National Assembly)

Capital Nouakchott

Area 1,030,700 sq km (397,953 sq miles)

Time zone GMT

Population 2,829,000

Projected population 2015 4,105,000

Population density 2.7 per sq km (7.1 per sq mile)

Life expectancy 51.5

Infant mortality (per 1,000) 73.5

Official languages French, Hasaniya Arabic

Other languages Indigenous languages, Arabic

Literacy rate 41.2 %

Religions Muslim 99 %, other 1 %

Ethnic groups Arab-Berber Moor 81 %, Wolof 7 %, Toucouleur 5 %, Soninke 3 %, other (including Fulbe, Bambara, Sarakolé) 4 %

Currency Ouguiya

Economy Agriculture 69 %, services 22 %, industry 9 %

GNP per capita US$ 1,800

Climate Mainly arid, with wet season in far south (May to September)

Highest point Kediet Ijill 910 m (2,987 ft)

Map reference Pages 360, 364

Most of Mauritania consists of the wastes of the western Sahara Desert. Islam in the region dates from the Almoravid Empire of the twelfth century. Later, it was conquered by Arab bidan or "white" Moors (*Maure* in French, meaning Moor), nomads who subjugated and enslaved the black Africans of the south, producing a people of mixed Arab and African descent known as *harratin* or "black" Moors. Deep social tensions between the dominant "white" Moors, the "black" Moors, and the subordinate thirty percent of black African farmers in the south lie at the heart of Mauritanian politics. Slavery in Mauritania was not officially abolished until 1970, and it is estimated that tens of thousands of *harratin* still live as slaves. France entered the region early in the nineteenth century and established a protectorate in 1903. Independence finally came in 1960.

Inland from the low-lying coastal plains of the Atlantic seaboard there are low plateaus—a tableland broken by occasional hills and scarps. The Sahara Desert to the north, which forms 47 percent of Mauritania's total land area, rises to the isolated peak of Kediet Ijill. In the southern third of the country there is just enough rain to support Sahelian thornbush and grasses. After rain, cattle herders drive their herds from the Senegal River through these grasslands and in good years the livestock outnumber the general population five to one. During the 1980s the whole area suffered severely from drought and the nomadic population, which had numbered three-quarters of the national population, fell to less than one-third, many nomads abandoning rural life entirely for the towns.

Farmers near the Senegal River grow millet, sorghum, beans, peanuts, and rice, using the late-summer river floods for irrigation. A hydroelectric project on the river is intended to provide water for the irrigated cultivation of rice, cotton, and sugarcane, but drought has also driven many subsistence farmers from the land. Off the coast, cooled by the Canaries current, lie some of the richest fishing grounds in the world. Although about 100,000 tonnes of fish are landed annually, the potential catch is estimated at about 600,000 tonnes. Exploitation by foreign fishing boats threatens this source of revenue.

Cape Verde

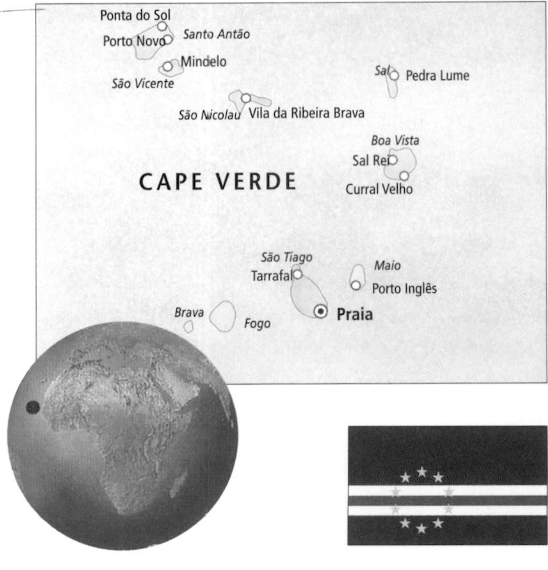

Fact File

Official name Republic of Cape Verde

Form of government Republic with single legislative body (People's National Assembly)

Capital Praia

Area 4,030 sq km (1,556 sq miles)

Time zone GMT – 1 hour

Population 409,000

Projected population 2015 567,000

Population density 101.5 per sq km (262.9 per sq mile)

Life expectancy 69.5

Infant mortality (per 1,000) 61.9

Official language Portuguese

Other languages Crioulo (blend of Portuguese and West African languages)

Literacy rate 71.6 %

Religions Roman Catholic and indigenous beliefs, often in combination 98 %; Protestant 2 %

Ethnic groups Mixed African-European 71 %, African 28 %, European 1 %

Currency Cape Verdean escudo

Economy Agriculture 52 %, services 25 %, industry 23 %

GNP per capita US$ 1,400

Climate Arid, with warm, dry summers

Highest point Pico do Cano (Mt Cano) 2,829 m (9,281 ft)

Map reference Page 360

Cape Verde consists of two small groups of islands 560 km (350 miles) off Dakar, Senegal, on the westernmost part of west Africa. These islands were discovered, uninhabited, by Portuguese navigators in 1456. For several centuries, until 1876, the islands were used by slave traders as a depot for assembling slaves and provisioning ships. As with other places involved in the slave trade, this activity influenced the composition of the population, with 71 percent being today of Afro-Portuguese background. Portuguese colonial administration came to an end with independence in 1975, but

View of the city of Mindelo and its harbor towards volcanic mountain peaks protruding from the sea, São Vicente, Cape Verde (below). Women removing small fish from a fishing net in Senegal (right).

because of limited opportunities on the islands more Cape Verdeans now live abroad than at home. Remittances are an important source of domestic income.

The northern group of islands is called the Barlavento or windward group; the southern is called the Sotavento or leeward group. Volcanic, with slopes weathered into unusual shapes by the wind, the land leads steeply up from the sea to mountainous heights. The active volcano of Mt Cano on the island of Fogo in the southern group is the highest point. The most densely populated areas are the coastal plain of São Tiago in the southern group, and Santa Antão and São Vicente in the northern group. A chronic lack of water makes agriculture difficult, and most of the productive farming is done in a small number of irrigated inland valleys. Droughts regularly devastate the crops of maize, beans, and sweet potatoes on which the majority of Cape Verdeans live. The effects of the drought that lasted from 1968 to 1982 were so severe that some 40,000 people emigrated to Portugal.

On the economic front Cape Verde faces a number of severe problems. The natural resource base is limited. The only minerals of any significance are salt and pozzolana, a volcanic rock that is used for making cement. Only two food products are exported—fish and bananas, each representing one-third of total exports. Although almost seventy percent of the population lives in the countryside, the gross national product share of agriculture is only thirteen percent, the tuna catch accounting for four percent of that figure. About ninety percent of food is imported and Cape Verde is heavily dependent on foreign aid.

Senegal

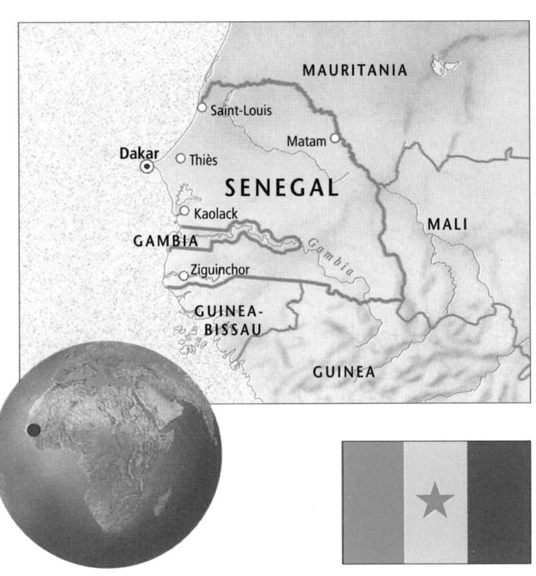

Fact File

Official name Republic of Senegal

Form of government Republic with single legislative body (National Assembly)

Capital Dakar

Area 196,190 sq km (75,749 sq miles)

Time zone GMT

Population 10,590,000

Projected population 2015 13,516,000

Population density 54 per sq km (139.8 per sq mile)

Life expectancy 62.9

Infant mortality (per 1,000) 55.4

Official language French

Other languages Wolof, Pulaar, Diola, Mandingo

Literacy rate 39.1 %

Religions Muslim 92 %, indigenous beliefs 6 %, Christian 2 % (mainly Roman Catholic)

Ethnic groups Wolof 36 %, Fulani 17 %, Serer 17 %, Toucouleur 9 %, Diola 9 %, Mandingo 9 %, European and Lebanese 1 %, other 2 %

Currency CFA (Communauté Financière Africaine) franc

Economy Agriculture 81 %, services 13 %, industry 6 %

GNP per capita US$ 1,580

Climate Tropical, with wet season June to October

Highest point Unnamed location in southeast 581 m (1,906 ft)

Map reference Page 364

Dakar, the capital of Senegal, lies on the westernmost point of west Africa and in the seventeenth and eighteenth centuries it was a major slave-trading base. French colonial control of Senegal was established during the suppression of the slave trade in the nineteenth century. As the administrative center of the huge region of French West

Africa, an effective road network was established in Dakar, plus extensive port facilities and a large civil service.

Independence from France came in 1960. Despite being a de facto one-party state for the next ten years, Senegal avoided military and dictatorial rule, and has recently liberalized its economic and political life. In 1982, Senegal joined with Gambia to form the nominal confederation of Senegambia. However, the envisaged integration of the two countries was never carried out, and the union was dissolved in 1989. Senegal's most serious problem is continuing armed revolt in the oil-rich southern province of Casamance, south of Gambia, a region that differs ethnically, economically, and geographically from the north.

Senegal is split by the near-enclave of Gambia and the Gambia River. To the north the land is drier, with sand dunes along the coast. Inland there are plains, savanna, and semidesert, where Fulani cattle-herders eke out an existence. South of Dakar and Cape Vert it is wetter and more fertile, with coastal mangrove swamps and forest inland. Sorghum is grown in the rainier areas of savanna bushland, while south of Gambia rice is cultivated on the floodplain of the Casamance River—the most fertile part of the country.

Peanuts have long been the foundation of Senegal's economy and are grown on half the cultivated land. Efforts are being made to diversify, and sugarcane, millet, cotton, and rice are now cultivated. Other than the recently developed oil fields in Casamance, with the promise of more offshore, natural resources are few. Though its arrangements are democratic, Senegal's ruling party has been in power since the 1950s, creating a network of patronage through the civil service, the judiciary, and the state-owned industries. Long-overdue reforms are therefore not likely to happen in the foreseeable future. Senegal receives a considerable amount of foreign aid.

Fishermen at a beach in Gambia fix their boats (below). Market street in Serekunda, Gambia (center).

Gambia

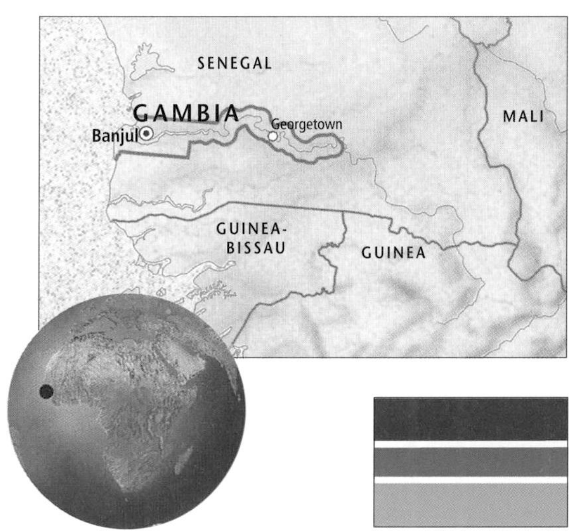

Fact File

OFFICIAL NAME Republic of the Gambia

FORM OF GOVERNMENT Republic with single legislative body (House of Representatives)

CAPITAL Banjul

AREA 11,300 sq km (4,363 sq miles)

TIME ZONE GMT

POPULATION 1,456,000

PROJECTED POPULATION 2015 1,781,000

POPULATION DENSITY 128.8 per sq km (333.7 per sq mile)

LIFE EXPECTANCY 54.0

INFANT MORTALITY (PER 1,000) 76.4

OFFICIAL LANGUAGE English

OTHER LANGUAGES Indigenous languages (including Madinka, Wolof, Fula), Arabic

LITERACY RATE 47.5 %

RELIGIONS Muslim 90 %, Christian 9 %, indigenous beliefs 1 %

ETHNIC GROUPS Indigenous 99 % (including Mandinka 42 %, Fula 18 %, Wolof 16 %, Jola 10 %, Serahuli 9 %), non-Gambian 1 %

CURRENCY Dalasi

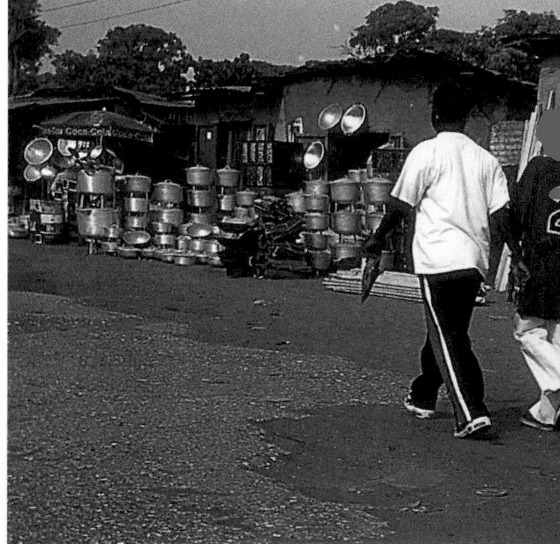

ECONOMY Agriculture 75 %; industry, commerce, and services 19 %; government 6 %

GNP PER CAPITA US$ 1,770

CLIMATE Tropical, with wet season June to November

HIGHEST POINT Unnamed location 53 m (174 ft)

MAP REFERENCE Page 364

Surrounded on nearly all sides by Senegal, Gambia is Africa's smallest independent state. Once a part of the Mali Empire, it became a British colony in 1816 and has been independent since 1965. Following independence it was governed for almost thirty years by Sir Dawda Jawara and the People's Progressive Party. A military coup displaced him in 1994. In 1996 a new constitution was adopted and the country returned to civil government. The country has been notably stable since, though resentment of the dominant Mandinka exists among minority tribal groups such as the Fula and Wolof.

A subtropical climate and a sunny dry season has enabled Gambia to expand tourism in recent years but the conflict between tourist life and the main religion, Islam, has made this controversial. In 1982 Gambia joined its neighbor, Senegal, in a union named the Senegambian Federation. This proved unsuccessful and was dissolved in 1989.

The Gambia River and its estuary are navigable for some 200 km (125 miles), allowing ships of up to 3,000 tonnes to reach Georgetown. Consisting of a riverine plain running inland 275 km (170 miles) from the estuary, Gambia's countryside is low and undulating, the land beside the river varying from swamp to savanna. Although rice is grown in the swamps and on the river floodplain, not enough is produced to meet domestic needs. Millet, sorghum, and cassava are grown on higher ground. On the upper river, a dam provides irrigation.

Gambia has unmined deposits of minerals such as ilmenite, rutile, and zircon. The economy has a limited agricultural base, with three-quarters of the population growing crops and raising livestock. Peanuts are the main cash crop, providing more than 75 percent of export earnings, and peanut processing is important industrially. Palm kernels are also exported. Because Banjul is the best harbor on the west African coast, much Senegalese produce passes through Gambia, and re-export forms one-third of economic activity.

Guinea-Bissau

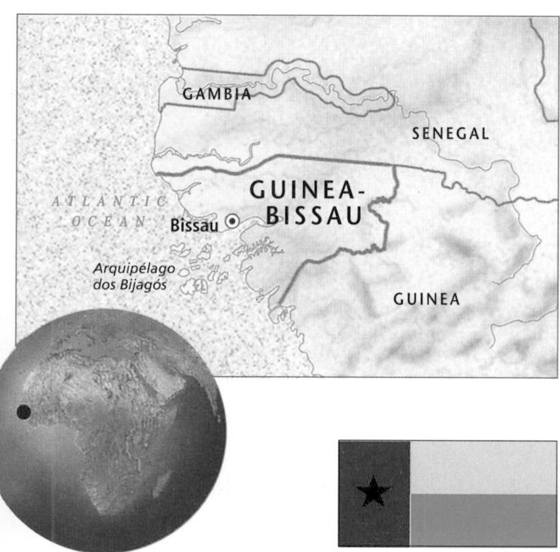

Fact File

OFFICIAL NAME Republic of Guinea-Bissau

FORM OF GOVERNMENT Republic with single legislative body (National People's Assembly)

CAPITAL Bissau

AREA 36,120 sq km (13,946 sq miles)

TIME ZONE GMT

POPULATION 1,346,000

PROJECTED POPULATION 2015 1,727,000

POPULATION DENSITY 37.3 per sq km (96.5 per sq mile)

LIFE EXPECTANCY 49.8

INFANT MORTALITY (PER 1,000) 109.5

OFFICIAL LANGUAGE Portuguese

OTHER LANGUAGES Crioulo (blend of Portuguese and West African languages), Fulbe, and other indigenous languages

LITERACY RATE 34 %

RELIGIONS Indigenous beliefs 65 %, Muslim 30 %, Christian 5 %

ETHNIC GROUPS Indigenous 99 % (including Balanta 30 %, Fula 20 %, Manjaca 14 %, Mandinga 13 %, Papel 7 %), European and mixed 1 %

CURRENCY CFA (Communauté Financière Africaine) franc

ECONOMY Agriculture 90 %, industry and services 10 %

GNP PER CAPITA US$ 900

CLIMATE Tropical, with wet season June to November

HIGHEST POINT Unnamed location in northeast 300 m (984 ft)

MAP REFERENCE Page 364

Guinea-Bissau is a small west African state between Guinea and Senegal. A large part of the country consists of mangrove swamps, estuaries, and islands, and it is both poor and underdeveloped. After the French and British used the area as a slave-trading station in the seventeenth and eighteenth centuries, Portugal named it Portuguese Guinea and claimed it as a colony in 1879. Independence, achieved in 1974, came following twelve years of guerrilla war.

One-party rule plus attempted coups and assassinations marked the next seventeen years. Moves towards multi-party democracy, designed to allow for ethnic divisons and inequalities, began in 1990. The contrast between the limited opportunities available to the 99 percent of the population which is African and the privileges of the tiny Afro-Portuguese elite is a major cause of tension. The existence of the opposition Democratic Front was made legal in 1991. Women face significant disadvantages and female genital mutilation is widespread.

Three main waterways—the Geba, Corubal, and Cacheu Rivers—mark the landscape. These wander across the plains toward broad estuaries and mangrove swamps on the coast. Here, the seasonal rainfall is especially heavy. Rice, the staple food, is grown on the floodplains and in the swamps, as well as on the offshore islands of the Arquipélago dos Bijagós, but not enough is produced to make the country self-sufficient. An area of upland savanna lies toward the border with Guinea in the southeast.

Mineral resources include phosphates, bauxite, and offshore oil but their development has been hampered by political instability, state controls, and (in the case of oil) disputes with Guinea and Senegal. Agriculture and fishing employ ninety percent of the workforce. Cashew nuts, peanuts, and palm kernels are the main exports. Economic reforms featuring monetary stability and private sector growth have been undertaken but progress is being hampered by the burden of high foreign debt and the many cultural and institutional constraints.

Guinea

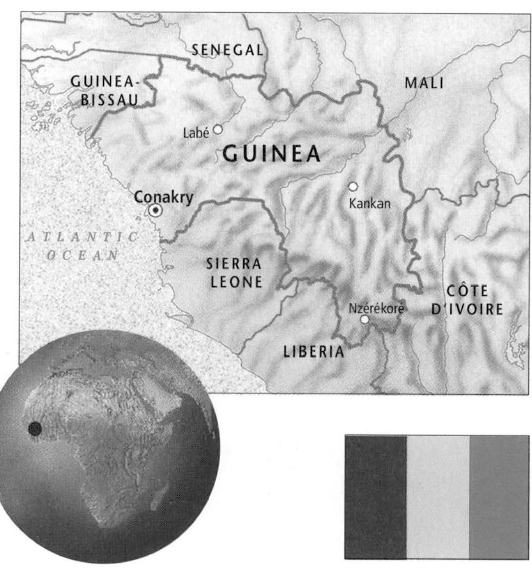

Fact File

OFFICIAL NAME Republic of Guinea

FORM OF GOVERNMENT Republic with single legislative body (People's National Assembly)

CAPITAL Conakry

AREA 245,860 sq km (94,926 sq miles)

TIME ZONE GMT

POPULATION 7,776,000

PROJECTED POPULATION 2015 11,300,000

POPULATION DENSITY 31.6 per sq km (81.9 per sq mile)

LIFE EXPECTANCY 46.3

INFANT MORTALITY (PER 1,000) 127.1

OFFICIAL LANGUAGE French

OTHER LANGUAGES Malinke languages, Fulbe and others

LITERACY RATE 35.9 %

RELIGIONS Muslim 85 %, Christian 8 %, indigenous beliefs 7 %

ETHNIC GROUPS Fulbe 40 %, Malinke 30 %, Soussou 20 %, smaller tribes 10 %

CURRENCY Guinean franc

ECONOMY Agriculture 80 %, industry and commerce 11 %, services 9 %

GNP PER CAPITA US$ 1,970

CLIMATE Tropical, with wet season May to November

HIGHEST POINT Mt Nimba 1,752 m (5,748 ft)

MAP REFERENCE Page 364

Guinea is on the African Atlantic coast to the north of Sierra Leone and Liberia. A slave-trading center from the fifteenth century, it became the colony of French Guinea in 1890. After achieving independence in 1958 it was for 25 years a one-party Marxist dictatorship under Ahmed Sékou Touré. A member of the Malinke tribe, he centralized and nationalized, attempted to enforce the use of local languages in place of French, and paid large numbers of state informers to monitor village and family life. Guinea now ranks last or near last on most international social development scales. Women

Children from rural Guinea (above). A mother with her child in front of her house in Sierra Leone (right). A traditional village of mud huts with thatched roofs in the Côte d'Ivoire (right page bottom).

face many disadvantages, including the practice of genital mutilation, which is widespread.

In the past twenty years governmental efforts at reform have led to a number of improvements, and in 1995 Guinea's first multi-party elections took place. The country has had to bear the additional burden of several hundred thousand refugees who have fled from the civil wars in Liberia and Sierra Leone. Many of these people are now returning home.

From mangrove swamps and lagoons along the coast, the land rises through densely forested foothills to the Fouta Djalon Highlands in the east. These highlands—from which the Gambia, Senegal, and Niger Rivers flow north and northeast—form a barrier between the coast and the grassland and savanna woodland of the Upper Niger Plains. Typical wildlife on the savanna includes lion and leopard, while crocodile and hippopotamus are found in the rivers.

The eighty percent of the workforce who live from agriculture are spread fairly evenly through the countryside. Those who live on the wet Atlantic coastal plain, much of which has been cleared for farming, cultivate bananas, palm oil, pineapples, and rice. Cattle are raised by nomadic herders in the interior.

Guinea possesses more than 25 percent of the world's reserves of high-grade bauxite, and three large bauxite mines contribute about eighty percent of the country's export revenue. Since it opened in 1984, the Aredor diamond mine has also been extremely profitable. Good soil and high yields give the country a prospect of self-sufficiency in food but the years of stifling state controls that were imposed by Touré have made market reforms difficult to implement, and what little infrastructure exists is greatly in need of modernizing. Corruption and harassment obstruct business growth. Aside from the bauxite industry, there is little foreign investment.

Sierra Leone

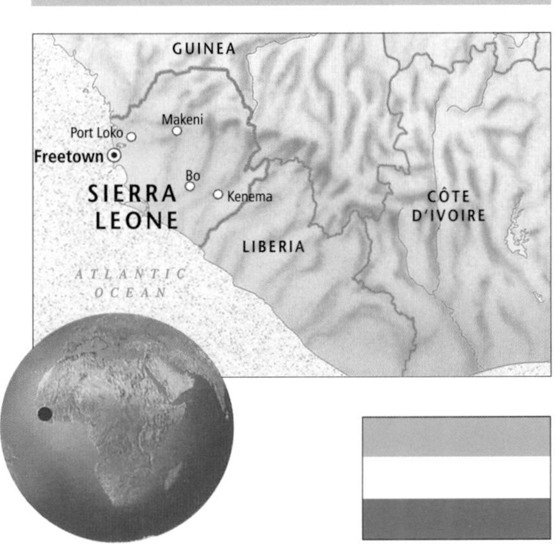

Fact File

OFFICIAL NAME Republic of Sierra Leone

FORM OF GOVERNMENT Republic with single legislative body (House of Representatives)

CAPITAL Freetown

AREA 71,740 sq km (27,699 sq miles)

TIME ZONE GMT

POPULATION 5,615,000

PROJECTED POPULATION 2015 7,115,000

POPULATION DENSITY 78.3 per sq km (202.7 per sq mile)

LIFE EXPECTANCY 46.0

INFANT MORTALITY (PER 1,000) 144.4

OFFICIAL LANGUAGE English

OTHER LANGUAGES Mande languages (including Malinké, Mende), Temne, Limba, Krio (Creole)

LITERACY RATE 31.4 %

RELIGIONS Muslim 60 %, indigenous beliefs 30 %, Christian 10 %

ETHNIC GROUPS 13 indigenous tribes 99 %, other 1 %

CURRENCY Leone

ECONOMY Agriculture 70 %, services 16 %, industry 14 %

GNP PER CAPITA US$ 500

CLIMATE Tropical, with wet season April to November

HIGHEST POINT Loma Mansa 1,948 m (6,391 ft)

MAP REFERENCE Page 364

Sierra Leone's capital, Freetown, was so named when the British government settled freed slaves there in 1787. Once the freed-slave settlers became a ruling class over the Africans already living in the country, deep social divisions opened. Many settlers, and foreign missionaries, were killed in a war with the indigenous Mende in 1898.

Once a British crown colony, and independent since 1961, Sierra Leone's recent history has been marked by military coups, ethnic factionalism, and violence. Since 1992, civil war has raged in the east and the south, thousands of lives have been lost and thousands of farms in the country's main grain growing areas abandoned. Liberian troops have been involved, and Libyan weapons. Child soldiers have been used by both sides. Following democratic elections in 2002 the government has slowly established its authority. However, the withdrawal of most UN peacekeepers in 2004 and the tenuous security situation in neighboring Liberia may present challenges to the continuation of Sierra Leone's stability.

Unlike most of west Africa, Sierra Leone is mountainous near the sea. These mountains are volcanic, and run southeast of Freetown on the Atlantic forming a thickly wooded peninsula (the Sierra Leone, or Lion Range). The peninsula interrupts a swampy coastal plain stretching north and south and dominated by mangrove forests. Rolling savanna uplands to the north, known as the Bolilands, were once the scene of government efforts to introduce large-scale mechanized rice cultivation. Rice is also grown in the seasonally flooded riverine grasslands of the southeast and in the swamps near Port Loco. Inland, to the northeast, the land rises to the Loma Mountains and the Tingi Hills. Rainfall on the coast is extremely high. The soils are heavily leached and weathered.

Subsistence farming dominates the agricultural sector, which employs about two-thirds of the population. Rice is the staple food crop and along with palm oil it is produced throughout Sierra Leone, except in the drier north. There, in the savanna, peanuts and cattle herding predominate. The country has substantial mineral resources, and the mining of diamonds, bauxite, and rutile or titanium ore provides essential hard currency. The economy is currently almost at a standstill because infrastructure has collapsed through neglect, and both the mining and agricultural sectors have been disrupted by civil war.

Liberia

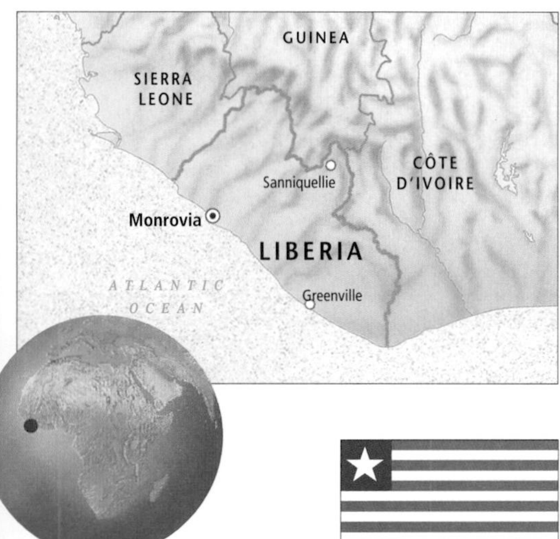

Fact File

OFFICIAL NAME Republic of Liberia

FORM OF GOVERNMENT Republic with single transitional legislative body (Transitional Legislative Assembly)

CAPITAL Monrovia

AREA 111,370 sq km (43,000 sq miles)

TIME ZONE GMT

POPULATION 3,289,000

PROJECTED POPULATION 2015 5,550,000

POPULATION DENSITY 29.5 per sq km (76.5 per sq mile)

LIFE EXPECTANCY 51.8

INFANT MORTALITY (PER 1,000) 130.2

OFFICIAL LANGUAGE English

OTHER LANGUAGES Indigenous languages

LITERACY RATE 38.3 %

RELIGIONS Indigenous beliefs 70 %, Muslim 20 %, Christian 10 %

ETHNIC GROUPS Indigenous tribes 95 % (including Kpelle, Bassa, Gio, Kru, Grebo, Mano, Krahn, Gola, Gbandi, Loma, Kissi, Vai, Bella), Americo-Liberian (descendants of repatriated slaves) 5 %

CURRENCY Liberian dollar

ECONOMY Agriculture 70 %, services 25 %, industry 5 %

GNP PER CAPITA US$ 1,100

CLIMATE Tropical, with wet season May to September

HIGHEST POINT Mt Wuteve 1,380 m (4,528 ft)

MAP REFERENCE Page 364

Settled by freed slaves after 1822, and a republic since 1847, the west African state of Liberia has always been a socially divided country. The coastal settlements of ex-slaves from the United States formed an élite with a Christian faith and an American colonial lifestyle. They had little in common with the long-established tribal peoples of the interior. During the long rule of the coastal Americo-Liberian élite the country was politically stable. It also made economic progress, the activities of the Firestone Rubber Company turning Liberia into a major rubber producer.

This ended in 1980 with a coup led by Master Sergeant Samuel Doe (a Krahn). When Doe was ousted by forces led by members of the Gio tribe in 1990, civil war began. Massacres and atrocities have marked succeeding years: famine threatens several regions, some 750,000 refugees have fled the country, organized economic life is at a standstill, and the rule of law has ended. In 1997 Charles Taylor was elected president but did not manage to control the rebel factions. Finally, in 2003, he was forced to abdicate. A transitional government of rebel, government, and civil society groups assumed control in October 2003. Chairman Gyude Bryant has a two-year mandate to oversee efforts to rebuild Liberia.

Liberia has three major geographic regions. Like its neighbors, it has a narrow sandy coastal strip of lagoons and mangrove swamps. Inland from the Atlantic Ocean are rolling hills covered in tropical rainforest, which rise to a plateau. This ascends to form a mountainous belt along the Guinean border. Most of the plateau region is grassland or forest—forests cover 39 percent of the land area. Only one percent of the country is arable.

Until the outbreak of civil war Liberia had been a producer and exporter of iron ore, rubber, timber, and coffee. Industries included rubber processing, food processing, construction materials, furniture making, palm oil processing, and diamond mining. Rice was the main staple, but some food was imported. The catch from coastal fisheries was supplemented by inland fish farms.

By the end of the 1990s war had destroyed much of the Liberian economy, especially the infrastructure in and around Monrovia. The business classes fled, taking with them their capital and expertise. With the collapse of the urban commercial part of the economy, many people have reverted to subsistence farming.

Côte d'Ivoire

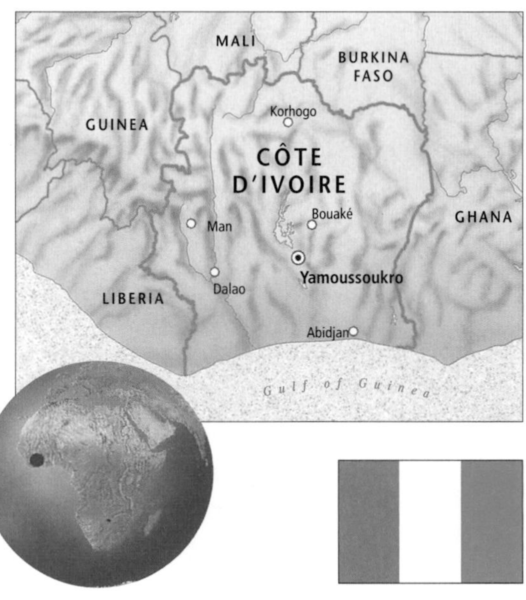

Fact File

OFFICIAL NAME Republic of Côte d'Ivoire

FORM OF GOVERNMENT Republic with single legislative body (National Assembly)

CAPITAL Yamoussoukro

AREA 322,460 sq km (124,502 sq miles)

TIME ZONE GMT

POPULATION 16,805,000

PROJECTED POPULATION 2015 21,529,000

POPULATION DENSITY 52.1 per sq km (135.0 per sq mile)

LIFE EXPECTANCY 44.7

INFANT MORTALITY (PER 1,000) 92.2

OFFICIAL LANGUAGE French

OTHER LANGUAGES Baule, Bete, Dioula, Senufo, Gur languages, Mande languages

LITERACY RATE 48.5 %

RELIGIONS Indigenous beliefs 63 %, Muslim 25 %, Christian 12 %

ETHNIC GROUPS About sixty different indigenous groups: Baule 23 %, Bete 18 %, Senoufou 15 %, other 44 %

CURRENCY CFA (Communauté Financière Africaine) franc

ECONOMY Agriculture 65 %, services 27 %, industry 8 %

GNP PER CAPITA US$ 1,550

CLIMATE Tropical, but drier in the north

HIGHEST POINT Mt Nimba 1,752 m (5,748 ft)

MAP REFERENCE Page 364

Côte d'Ivoire (Ivory Coast) is a west African country on the Gulf of Guinea. In the eighteenth century it was conquered by Baule people from Ghana. In 1893 it became a French colony, achieving independence in 1960. Since then, while retaining a close association with France, Côte d'Ivoire has been a more liberal and commercially oriented society than the socialist states established elsewhere in Africa in the 1960s. This, combined with political stability, has made it relatively prosperous. Under the thirty-year

leadership of Félix Houphouet-Boigny (who died in 1993) investment was secure, and most of this period saw sustained economic growth. In 1999 the first military coup in the country's history overthrew the government. The junta held elections in late 2000, excluding the opposition and rigging the results. Popular protest brought runner-up Laurent Gbagbo into power. Civil unrest continued until early 2003 when rebels were granted ministerial positions in a unity government. Implementation of the peace accord was resumed but issues such as land reform remain unresolved. Several thousand French and West African troops remain in Côte d'Ivoire to maintain peace.

A sandy strip of land some 64 km (40 miles) wide runs along the shore of the Atlantic, broken by sandbars and lagoons around Abidjan. Coastal shipping has always had trouble on the west African coast where there is heavy surf and there are no natural harbors. French construction of the Vridi Canal, giving access between Abidjan and the sea through the sandbars, created a valuable deep-water port. From the coast the land rises gently, and two rainy seasons and an equatorial climate provide a covering of rainforest further inland. There are three major national parks, with wildlife including elephant and pygmy hippopotamus.

Deforestation is a concern as hardwoods such as mahogany and ebony are felled. Growing in the place of native forest is plantation teak. Farther north the landscape changes to savanna grassland. Highlands are found in the northwest.

Côte d'Ivoire has varied mineral resources—petroleum, diamonds, manganese, bauxite, and copper—and is one of the world's main producers of coffee, cocoa beans, and palm oil. A large percentage of the population is engaged in farming, forestry, and livestock raising. Difficulties arise because of fluctuating coffee and cocoa prices but during the 1990s Côte d'Ivoire prospered, due mainly to the growth of new exports such as pineapples and rubber, trade and banking liberalization, and offshore oil and gas discoveries.

Mali

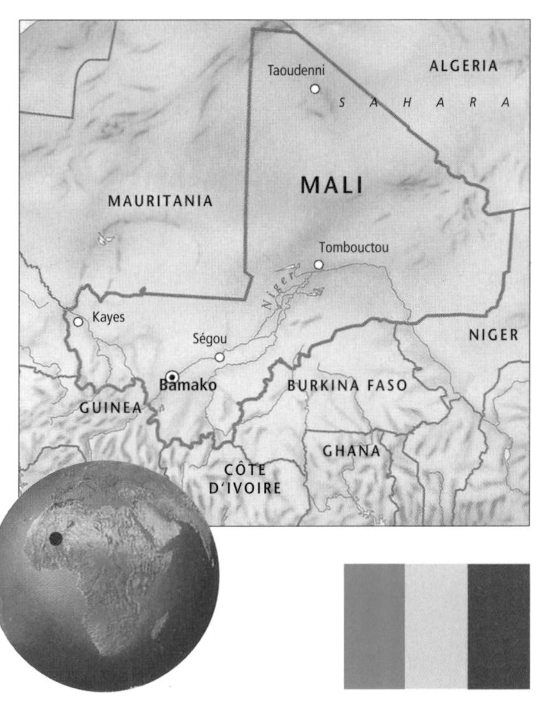

Fact File

OFFICIAL NAME Republic of Mali

FORM OF GOVERNMENT Republic with single legislative body (National Assembly)

CAPITAL Bamako

AREA 1,240,000 sq km (478,764 sq miles)

TIME ZONE GMT

POPULATION 10,341,000

PROJECTED POPULATION 2015 17,657,000

POPULATION DENSITY 8.3 per sq km (21.6 per sq mile)

LIFE EXPECTANCY 47.4

INFANT MORTALITY (PER 1,000) 119.6

OFFICIAL LANGUAGE French

OTHER LANGUAGES Bambara and other indigenous languages

LITERACY RATE 38 %

RELIGIONS Muslim 90 %, indigenous beliefs 9 %, Christian 1 %

ETHNIC GROUPS Mande 50 %, Peul 17 %, Voltaic 12 %, Songhai 6 %, Tuareg and Moor 10 %, other 5 %

CURRENCY CFA (Communauté Financière Africaine) franc

ECONOMY Agriculture 85 %, services 13 %, industry 2 %

GNP PER CAPITA US$ 840

CLIMATE Subtropical in south and southwest; arid in north

HIGHEST POINT Hombori Tondo 1,155 m (3,789 ft)

MAP REFERENCE Pages 361, 364–65

Mali is a landlocked west African country, watered by the River Niger in the south and with vast stretches of the Sahara Desert lying to the north. It derives its name from the Malinke or Mandingo people whose empire flourished between the eighth and fourteenth centuries. Later it was a center of trade and Islamic scholarship, based on the city of Timbuktu (now Tombouctou). At the end of the nineteenth century it became a colony of French West Africa, achieving independence in 1960. For the next thirty years the country was ruled by either civilian or military dictators. Demonstrations in 1991 in which about 100 people died were followed by the overthrow of the regime, and free elections were held for the first time in 1992.

There is a major ethnic division between the black African majority in the south and the minority of Arab Tuareg nomads in the north. Violent Tuareg guerrilla activity in northern Mali ended with a peace pact in 1995.

Mali's flat landscape consists mainly of plains and sandstone plateaus. The need for water is the main concern. The northern and virtually rainless Saharan plains are inhabited almost entirely by Tuareg nomads. The semiarid center—the Sahel—has in recent years suffered from devastating droughts. Such arable land as exists is found in the south, along the Senegal and Niger Rivers, the latter spreading out to form an inland delta before turning southward on its way to the border of Niger. These rivers provide water for stock and for irrigation. Rice is grown on irrigated land; millet, cotton, and peanuts grow elsewhere. Away from the rivers southern Mali is mostly savanna country where mahogany, kapok, and baobab trees grow, these being replaced further north by palms and scrub. Animal life includes lion, antelope, jackal, and hyena.

Some eighty percent of the labor force works in agriculture and fishing—dried fish is exported to Burkina Faso, Côte d'Ivoire, and Ghana. With 65 percent of its land either desert or semidesert, however, and industry limited mainly to a single gold mine, salt production, and small-scale textiles and shoes, Mali is extremely poor. As well as gold there are phosphates, uranium, bauxite, manganese, and copper but development is hampered by poor transport facilities and the fact that the country is landlocked. With expenditures almost double its revenues, Mali is a major recipient of foreign aid.

Burkina Faso

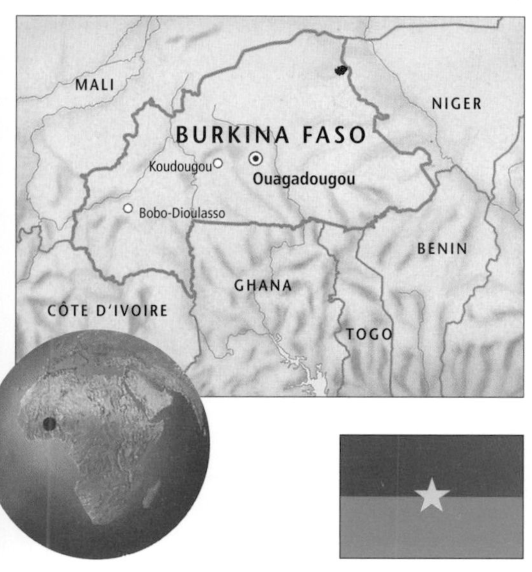

Fact File

OFFICIAL NAME Burkina Faso

FORM OF GOVERNMENT Republic with single legislative body (Assembly of People's Deputies)

CAPITAL Ouagadougou

AREA 274,200 sq km (105,869 sq miles)

TIME ZONE GMT

POPULATION 12,304,000

PROJECTED POPULATION 2015 18,509,000

POPULATION DENSITY 44.9 per sq km (116.2 per sq mile)

LIFE EXPECTANCY 46.1

INFANT MORTALITY (PER 1,000) 105.3

OFFICIAL LANGUAGE French

OTHER LANGUAGES Indigenous languages, Arabic, English

LITERACY RATE 36 %

RELIGIONS Muslim 50 %, indigenous beliefs 40 %, Roman Catholic 8 %, Protestant 2 %

ETHNIC GROUPS More than fifty indigenous tribes: the largest Mossi 48 %, Fulani 10 %, Mande 9 %; other including Gurunsi, Senufo, Lobi, Bobo 33 %

CURRENCY CFA (Communauté Financière Africaine) franc

ECONOMY Agriculture 87 %, services 9 %, industry 4 %

GNP PER CAPITA US$ 1,040

CLIMATE Tropical, with warm, dry winters and hot, wet summers

HIGHEST POINT Tena Kourou 749 m (2,457 ft)

MAP REFERENCE Page 364

Burkina Faso is a landlocked African country on the southern edge of the Sahara Desert. It is the size of Italy but has difficulty supporting its people. The desertification of the Sahel—the fringe of the Sahara running from Senegal to Chad—has severely affected large areas, though the parched savanna of the north and east still supports a nomadic population of cattle-herding Fulani. French colonial control was established between 1895 and 1897 and independence came in 1960. There were many military coups until 1992, accompanied by waves of executions, mostly the result of tribal power struggles. However, in 1992 Mali's first democratic election was held and Alpha Konare became president. After his reelection in 1997, he continued his political and economic reforms. In keeping with Mali's two-term constitutional limit, he stepped down in 2002 and was succeeded by Amadou Toure.

Near the capital city of Ouagadougou live the Mossi, the traditional rulers and the dominant tribal group, who have been in the region since the twelfth century. They grow sorghum and millet for food, and cultivate cash crops such as peanuts, cotton, and sesame seeds.

In the west and south is a sandstone plateau, while in the southwest are the spectacular Banfora Cliffs. The plateau is cut by the watercourses of the Red, White, and Black Volta Rivers (Volta Rouge, Blanche, and Noir), draining towards Ghana. Although these valleys have more farming potential than the arid north, they cannot yet be developed because of the tsetse and simulium flies that flourish near their rivers. At present the diseases carried by these insects prevent settlement.

Burkina Faso has few natural resources. There is manganese in the far northeast, but to develop it a 350 km (220 mile) extension of the Côte d'Ivoire railway from Abidjan is needed. Industries consist of unprofitable state corporations, a legacy of the country's years as a one-party socialist state. About ten percent of the land area is arable and more than eighty percent of the people work on the land. Drought has caused acute agricultural difficulties and the country depends heavily on foreign aid. Many people have emigrated, their wages, sent back from places such as the Côte d'Ivoire, providing much-needed income for their families. Tourists visit the Parcs Nationaux du W. du Niger, in the east—a reserve shared with Niger and Benin. Gazelles, antilopes, elephants, cape buffalo, and hippopotamus live there.

The city of Tombouctou, in Mali, following a dust storm (left page). The large covered market in Kumasi, central Ghana (right).

Ghana

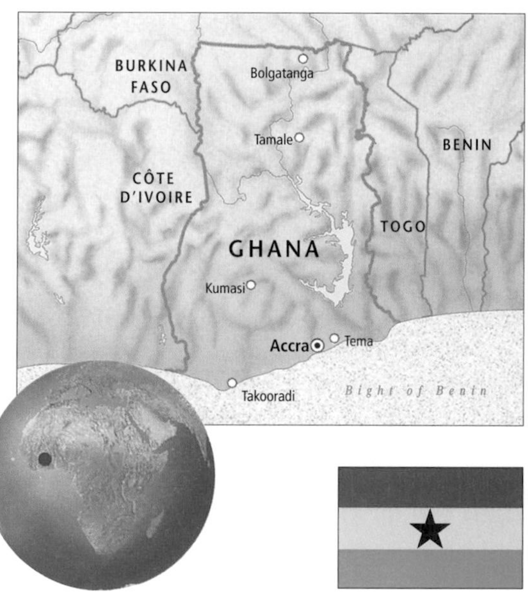

Fact File

OFFICIAL NAME Republic of Ghana

FORM OF GOVERNMENT Republic with single legislative body (Parliament)

CAPITAL Accra

AREA 238,540 sq km (92,100 sq miles)

TIME ZONE GMT

POPULATION 20,245,000

PROJECTED POPULATION 2015 26,378,000

POPULATION DENSITY 84.9 per sq km (219.8 per sq mile)

LIFE EXPECTANCY 56.3

INFANT MORTALITY (PER 1,000) 52.2

OFFICIAL LANGUAGE English

OTHER LANGUAGES Indigenous languages, including Akan, Mole-Dagbani, Ewe

LITERACY RATE 64.5 %

RELIGIONS Indigenous beliefs 38 %, Muslim 30 %, Christian 24 %, other 8 %

ETHNIC GROUPS Indigenous 99.8 % (including Akan 44 %, Moshi-Dagomba 16 %, Ewe 13 %, Ga 8 %), European and other 0.2 %

CURRENCY Cedi

ECONOMY Agriculture 59 %, services 30 %, industry 11 %

GNP PER CAPITA US$ 1,980

CLIMATE Tropical: warm and arid on southeast coast; hot and humid in southwest; hot and arid in north

HIGHEST POINT Mt Afadjato 880 m (2,887 ft)

MAP REFERENCE Page 364

Ghana was once known as the Gold Coast. A well-known source of gold in west Africa for a thousand years, the nation's modern name comes from the Ghana Empire of the eighth to the twelfth centuries. The Ashanti people established themselves in the seventeenth century, selling slaves to Portuguese, British, Dutch and Danish traders. Under British control from 1874, Ghana became the first tropical African colony to win independence in 1956. Soon after this it became a Soviet-style one-party state.

After 1966, Ghana was wracked by military coups for fifteen years before Flight-Lieutenant Jerry Rawlings took control in 1981. An election in 1996 returned Rawlings to power once more. In 2000 he could not run again since the constitution only allows for two terms. Although government pressure is often brought to bear, vigorous political debate takes place in a relatively free media, and despite economic troubles Ghana still has twice the per capita output of the poorer countries in west Africa.

Geographically, the country is formed by the basin of the Volta Rivers. A large area flooded by the Akosombo Dam is now Lake Volta. This provides hydroelectric power for smelting alumina into aluminum, and for use in the towns, mines, and industries of the Takoradi-Kumasi-Tema triangle. In the north there is savanna country. In earlier days the southern part of the country was covered by dense tropical forest. Much of this has been cleared for agriculture, especially for growing cocoa, which from 1924 until the present day has usually been the leading export.

Like other west African countries, Ghana has few natural harbors. Its coast consists mainly of mangrove swamps, with lagoons toward the mouth of the River Volta. The rivers are home to crocodile, manatee, and hippopotamus. The wildlife of the northern savanna includes lion, leopard, hyena, and antelope.

Ghana is well endowed with natural resources: gold, timber, industrial diamonds, bauxite, manganese, fish, and rubber. In 1995, largely as a result of increased gold, timber, and cocoa production, overall economic growth was about five percent. Although the economy is based on subsistence agriculture, Ghana is not self-sufficient in food. The government's efforts to reverse the statist policies of decades past continue, but face a number of obstacles. Public sector wage increases, and various peace-keeping missions, both internal and external, have strained the budget and led to inflationary deficit financing. Corruption is a continuing obstacle to growth.

Traditional houses in Togo (above). A public voodoo ritual in eastern Ghana (below). Children in a canoe paddle through a village of stilt houses, situated on a river in Benin (right page).

Togo

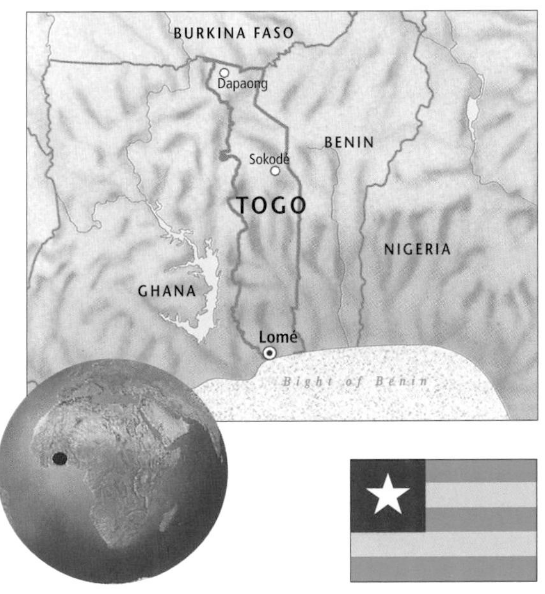

Fact File

Official name	Republic of Togo
Form of government	Republic with single legislative body (National Assembly)
Capital	Lomé
Area	56,790 sq km (21,927 sq miles)
Time zone	GMT
Population	5,286,000
Projected population 2015	6,576,000
Population density	93.1 per sq km (241.1 per sq mile)
Life expectancy	54.0
Infant mortality (per 1,000)	69.3
Official language	French
Other languages	Ewe, Mina, Dagomba, Kabye
Literacy rate	51.7 %
Religions	Indigenous beliefs 70 %, Christian 20 %, Muslim 10 %
Ethnic groups	Indigenous (Ewe, Mina, and Kabye are the largest of 37 tribes) 99 %, European and Syrian-Lebanese 1 %
Currency	CFA (Communauté Financière Africaine) franc
Economy	Agriculture 64 %, services 30 %, industry 6 %
GNP per capita	US$ 1,500
Climate	Tropical, with wet seasons March to July and October to November; semiarid in north, with wet season April to July
Highest point	Pic Baumann 986 m (3,235 ft)
Map reference	Page 364

Togo is a small west African country squeezed between Ghana and Benin. It was colonized by Germany in 1884, later becoming French Togoland. It became independent in 1960. A deep social division exists between the Kabye people in the north and the majority Ewe of the south. The Ewe are generally better educated, and live in the more developed part of the country, but have no say in government. This is run by Africa's longest serving president, General Eyadema, a Kabye who has held this position since his coup in 1967. The first multi-party elections took place in 1993.

Most people live on the coast and the adjacent plains. Inland a mountain chain crosses the country north to south. The far northwest is mainly granite tableland. Roads connect the northern savanna with the railhead of Blitta, and the phosphate mining area with its port of Kpeme. The River Oti crosses in the northwest between Burkina Faso and Ghana, and the River Mono drains south into the Gulf of Guinea. About a quarter of the land is arable. The most fertile land—28 percent of the country—is forested; here slash-and-burn cultivation occurs.

Togo depends on subsistence agriculture. Food crops include yams, cassava, maize, beans, rice, and sorghum. The main export crops are coffee, cocoa, and cotton, which together generate about thrity percent of earnings. Cattle, sheep, and pigs are raised in the north. The annual fish catch is about 14,000 tonnes. Togo is normally self-sufficient in food, though drought has recently cut productivity, and the deforestation caused by slash-and-burn agriculture is causing concern. Phosphate mining is the most important industrial activity.

Benin

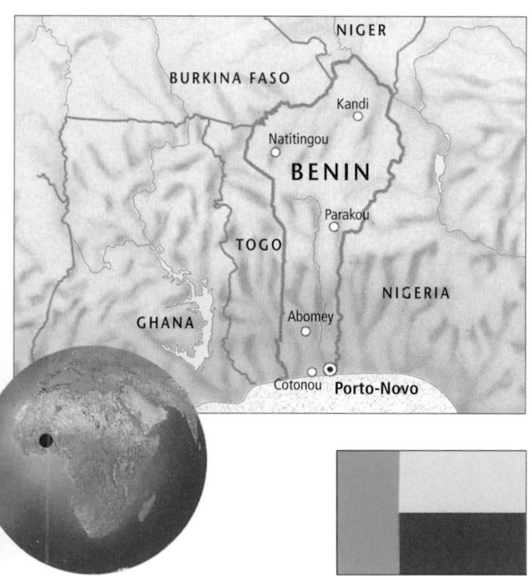

Fact File

Official name Republic of Benin

Form of government Republic with single legislative body (National Assembly)

Capital Porto-Novo

Area 112,620 sq km (43,483 sq miles)

Time zone GMT + 1 hour

Population 6,788,000

Projected population 2015 9,448,000

Population density 60.3 per sq km (156.1 per sq mile)

Life expectancy 49.7

Infant mortality (per 1,000) 88.5

Official language French

Other languages 60 indigenous languages

Literacy rate 37.5 %

Religions Indigenous beliefs 70 %, Muslim 15 %, Christian 15 %

Ethnic groups Indigenous 99 %, European and other 1 %

Currency CFA (Communauté Financière Africaine) franc

Economy Agriculture 70 %, services 23 %, industry 7 %

GNP per capita US$ 1,040

Climate Tropical; hot and humid in south, drier in north

Highest point Mt Tanekas 641 m (2,103 ft)

Map reference Page 365

Benin is a small west African country facing the Gulf of Guinea. It was once part of the Kingdom of Benin, famous for the brass portrait heads made for the Oba and his court in the fifteenth century. By 1625 it was known as Abomey (later Dahomey). Slavery and slave-raiding were endemic, and grew when firearms and external slave markets became available. The town of Ouidah became the shipping point for several million slaves, mostly prisoners captured in raids by the Dahomeyans against their enemies. The captives were sent mainly to Brazil, and most Afro-Brazilian religious cults derive from this area. Under French control from 1850, the country became independent in 1960, eventually falling under the control of General Mathieu Kerekou, who changed its name to Benin. In the 1990s the country slowly moved towards multi-party rule.

The Atakora Range (Chaine de l'Akatora) lies in northwestern Benin. To the northeast are the plains of the Niger, part of the boundary with the state of Niger being formed by the Niger River itself. Further south there are plateaus, and then a fertile plain where the Fon and Yoruba people live as subsistence farmers. Still further south, toward the Bight of Benin, lies a sandy strip with many lagoons. In the country's far north small numbers of Fulani people continue to live as nomads. Also in the north are two wildlife parks—the Parc National de la Pendjan and the Parcs Nationaux du W. du Niger—shared with Burkina Faso and Niger.

Subsistence agriculture, cotton production, and regional trade remain fundamental to Benin's economy. Offshore oilfields promised much when they began producing in 1982, but were soon affected by a fall in petroleum prices. As well as crude oil Benin sells cotton, palm-oil products, cocoa, and peanuts. Goods in transit through the port of Cotonou to Niger are charged a fee, and this is an additional source of revenue. Although a World Bank reform program was adopted in 1992, inefficient state enterprises and an overstaffed civil service are inhibiting economic progress.

Niger

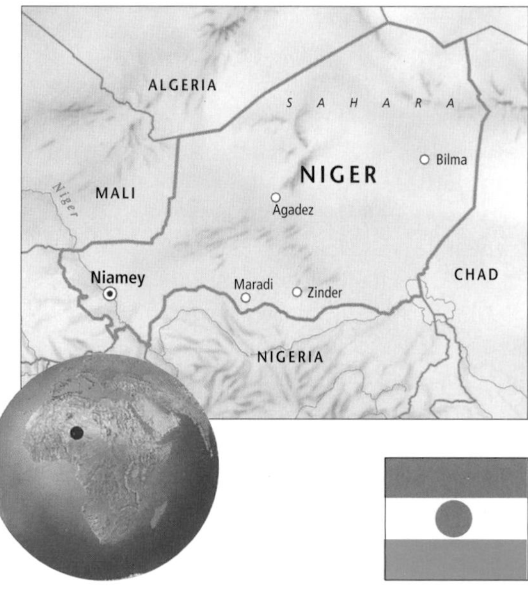

Fact File

Official name Republic of Niger

Form of government Republic with single legislative body (National Assembly)

Capital Niamey

Area 1,267,000 sq km (489,189 sq miles)

Time zone GMT + 1 hour

Population 10,640,000

Projected population 2015 18,482,000

Population density 8.4 per sq km (21.8 per sq mile)

Life expectancy 41.2

Infant mortality (per 1,000) 122.2

Official language French

Other languages Hausa, Djerma, Fulani and others

Literacy rate 15.3 %

Religions Muslim 80 %, Christian and indigenous beliefs 20 %

Ethnic groups Hausa 56 %, Djerma 22 %, Fula 8.5 %, Tuareg 8 %, Beri Beri 4.3 %, other (including 4,000 French expatriates) 1.2 %

Currency CFA (Communauté Financière Africaine) franc

Economy Agriculture 85 %, services 12 %, industry 3 %

GNP per capita US$ 820

Climate Mainly arid; tropical in south, with wet season June to October

Highest point Mont Bagzane 2,022 m (6,634 ft)

Map reference Pages 361, 362, 365

Niger is two-thirds desert, which may seem strange for a country that is named after a great river (the name "Niger" comes from the Tuareg word *n'eghirren*, for flowing water), but the River Niger only cuts across the extreme southwest of this large, landlocked country. Elsewhere, there is an arid landscape of stony basins, drifting sands, and a northern highland that forms part of the mountain chain stretching from Algeria to Chad.

The home of the Sokoto Empire of the Fulani in the nineteenth century, the region became part of French West Africa in 1922, and received independence in 1960. Then followed three decades of dictatorial civilian and military rule. Despite the multi-party elections held in 1993, continuing unrest caused by Tuareg rebels in the north and power struggles within the government led to the reimposition of military rule in 1996. With elections in 1999 the country returned to democracy in the so-called Fifth Republic.

Niger's central geographic feature is the Massif de l'Aïr. In these mountains, which rise out of the Saharan plains to jagged peaks up to 1,900 m (6,230 ft) high, there is sometimes sufficient rain for thorny scrub to grow. Formerly nomads grazed their camels, horses, cattle, and goats in this area, but devastating droughts in 1973 and 1983 destroyed their livelihood. To the east and west of the Massif de l'Aïr are the Saharan Desert plains of Ténéré du Tafassasset and the Western Talk. Sand and sandy soil cover most of the desert plains to the north and east, an area which is virtually rainless and, aside from small numbers of people living at the occasional palm-fringed oasis, uninhabited. Plant life includes kapok and baobab trees. Buffalo, antelope, lion, hippopotamus, and crocodiles are found in Niger but their survival today is more a matter of chance than good management.

With its gross domestic product growth barely matching the growth of its population, Niger is one of the most impoverished countries in Africa. More than 95 percent of its people earn a living from farming and trading. Where the Niger River crosses the country in the far southwest there are fertile arable soils: crops include yams, cassava, and maize, and rice in areas where the river floods. On the drier land toward Lake Chad (Lac Tchad) millet and sorghum are grown. The drought that has affected extensive areas of the Sahel has reduced Niger from self-sufficiency to being an importer of food. Tin and tungsten are mined, and there are reserves of iron ore, manganese, and molybdenum. During the 1970s, when prices were high, uranium became the main source of revenue, and it continues to be the country's most valuable export. Between 1983 and 1990, however, revenues fell by fifty percent. At present the government of Niger relies on aid for both operating expenses and for public investment.

Chad

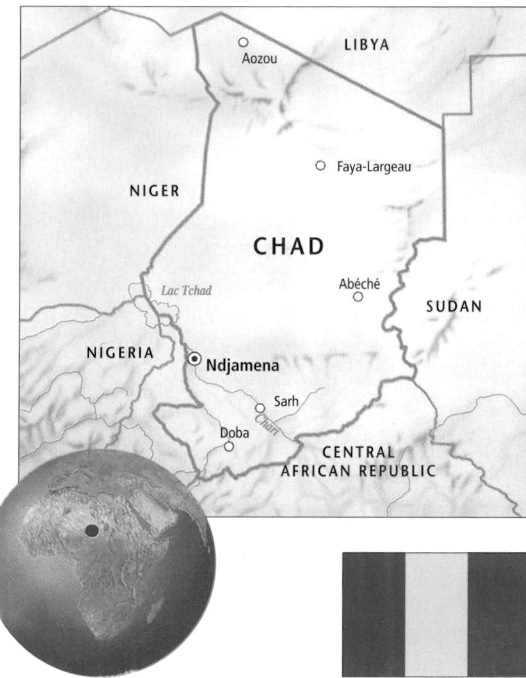

Fact File

Official name Republic of Chad

Form of government Republic with single legislative body (Higher Transitional Council)

Capital Ndjamena

Area 1,284,000 sq km (495,752 sq miles)

Time zone GMT + 1 hour

Population 8,998,000

Projected population 2015 12,376,000

Population density 7.0 per sq km (18.2 per sq mile)

Life expectancy 51.3

Infant mortality (per 1,000) 93.5

Official languages French, Arabic

Other languages More than 100 indigenous languages

Literacy rate 40 %

Religions Muslim 50 %, Christian 25 %, indigenous beliefs 25 %

Ethnic groups More than 200 indigenous groups: north mainly Arabic, south mainly African

Currency CFA (Communauté Financière Africaine) franc

Economy Agriculture 85 %, services and industry 15 %

GNP per capita US$ 1,030

Climate Tropical in south, arid in north

Highest point Emi Koussi 3,415 m (11,204 ft)

Map reference Pages 362, 365, 366

Chad is a landlocked North African country twice the size of France. Much of it is semidesert and thinly populated, and it is one of the poorest and least developed countries in the world. Chad was conquered by the Sudanese warlord Rabah Zobeir late in the nineteenth century, but with 200 distinct ethnic groups in the population a sense of national unity has been slow to emerge. After France established control of the region in 1911 it became part of French Equatorial Africa for fifty years, achieving independence in 1960. Since then there has been almost constant civil war, aggravated by the main ethnic divide—that between the desert-dwelling Muslim Arabs in the north and the non-Muslim African farmers in the south. Whether the peace treaties of 2002 and 2003 will prove successful remains to be seen.

The country can be loosely divided into four regions. In the center are broad, arid savanna plains. To the north are deserts with large areas of mobile sand dunes along the southern Sahara. In the northwest are the volcanic mountains of the Tibesti, rising to the 3,415 m (11,204 ft) peak of Emi Koussi. Though surrounded by desert these mountains attract rain, and some farming takes place in the valleys. In the south the valleys of the Chari and Logone Rivers support most of Chad's agriculture, including cotton-growing. Both these rivers drain into Lake Chad (Lac Tchad). But a series of droughts has reduced them to little more than streams, while the shallow Lake Chad itself is steadily shrinking as the desert advances.

Chad's economic difficulties have both political and climatic causes. Civil war in the 1980s disrupted agriculture and spread lasting division, while continuing government corruption and its inability to pay its employees have led to resentment in the civil service. Desertification has had an impoverishing effect, especially among pastoral peoples like the Fulbe in the Sahel. While oil production from a field discovered at Doba might provide a significant long-term source of revenue, eighty percent of the population is likely to depend on subsistence farming for some time and the country will continue to rely on foreign aid.

Nigeria

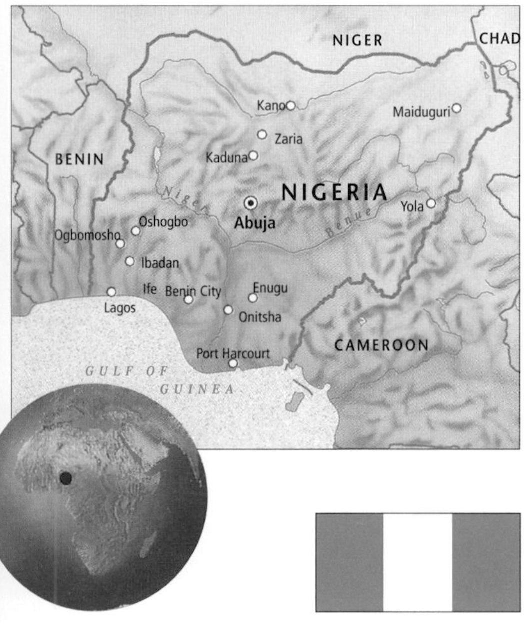

Fact File

OFFICIAL NAME Federal Republic of Nigeria

FORM OF GOVERNMENT Republic transitioning from military to civilian rule

CAPITAL Abuja

AREA 923,770 sq km (356,668 sq miles)

TIME ZONE GMT + 1 hour

POPULATION 129,935,000

PROJECTED POPULATION 2015 165,313,000

POPULATION DENSITY 140.7 per sq km (364.3 per sq mile)

LIFE EXPECTANCY 50.6

INFANT MORTALITY (PER 1,000) 72.5

OFFICIAL LANGUAGES English

OTHER LANGUAGES French, Hausa, Yoruba, Ibo, Fulani

LITERACY RATE 57.1 %

RELIGIONS Muslim 50 %, Christian 40 %, indigenous beliefs 10 %

ETHNIC GROUPS About 250 indigenous groups the largest of which are Hausa, Fulani, Yoruba, Ibo 68 %; Kanuri, Edo, Tiv, Ibidio, Nupe 25 %; other 7 %

CURRENCY Naira

ECONOMY Services 51 %, agriculture 45 %, industry 4 %

GNP PER CAPITA US$ 840

CLIMATE Tropical in south, with wet season April to October; arid in north

HIGHEST POINT Chappal Waddi 2,419 m (7,936 ft)

MAP REFERENCE Page 365

With the continent's largest population, huge oil revenues, and a territory that is four times the size of the United Kingdom, Nigeria is one of Africa's most important nations. It also ranks as one of the most corrupt countries in the world, and a place where tensions between the main tribal groups are close to breaking point.

Such tensions are not new to the area: regional and ethnic conflict go back to the days of Nigeria's ancient city-states. The life of the Yoruba people centered on the city of Ife, while the Hausa kingdom was in the north. The kingdom of Benin, well known for its portrait bronzes of past rulers, was in the west, and a number of communities of Ibo lived in the southeast. Bringing all these peoples together to form a single nation has proven difficult: since independence, in 1960, there has been a series of military dictatorships, and only ten years of elected government. An unsuccessful attempt to secede by the Ibo in 1967 (who set up an independent state named Biafra) failed in 1970, following a bitter civil war in which thousands of people died. A new constitution was adopted in 1999, and a peaceful transition to civilian government was completed.

Physical features and land use

Nigeria's coast on the west African Gulf of Guinea consists of long, sandy beaches and mangrove swamps where its rivers flow into the sea. The mouth of the Niger forms an immense delta, threaded with thousands of creeks and lagoons, with Port Harcourt on one of the main channels. Upstream it divides, the Benue (Bénoué) River leading east into Cameroon and the Niger heading northwest toward Benin. These two large rivers provide transport, by boat, for cargo and people. High rainfall on the coast and in the river valleys enables yams, cassava, maize, and vegetables to be grown and on floodland alongside the rivers rice is cultivated.

In the rainy forested belt to the north the hills gradually rise to the semiarid central savanna plateau, and then to the Jos Plateau, reaching 1,780 m (5,840 ft) at Share Hill. Up the Benue (Bénoué) River to the east the land rises to the wooded slopes of the Adamaoua Massif and the Cameroon highlands. From these hill-slope areas come such products as cocoa, rubber, hardwoods, and palm oil. North of the Jos Plateau the savanna becomes dry, in many places degenerating into arid Sahelian scrub, where both herds and herders have difficulty surviving. Around Lake Chad (Lac Tchad) the typical vegetation is hardy acacia and doum palms.

Together, the river systems of the Niger and the Benue (Bénoué) drain sixty percent of Nigeria's total land area. Though much reduced by clearing for cultivation, the Nigerian rainforests still produce mahogany and iriko. Wildlife includes elephant, chimpanzee, and the red river hog.

A nomadic family in Chad outside their home (left page bottom). An antelope in Chad (left page top). Donkeys are used to transport produce in a village in Nigeria (above).

People and culture

In addition to the Yoruba, Fulani, Hausa, and Ibo, Nigeria has 245 much smaller ethnic groups. Not only are they divided along lines of ethnicity, language, and regional dialect, there is also a major religious division. The north of the country is largely Islamic (the religion of the Hausa and Fulani) while the south is for the most part Christian, combined with indigenous African beliefs. Outbreaks of communal violence in the north sometimes occur as a result of clashes between Islamic fundamentalists and missionary Christians. Despite widespread Christian proselytizing there is evidence that Islamic influence is gradually growing in the south.

Although seventy percent of the labor force works in agriculture, and many rural people are subsistence farmers, Nigerians have also lived in cities for centuries. This contrasts with many other parts of Africa. Long before European commercial expansion into the region, places such as Benin City, Kano, Ibadan, and Ife were administrative and trading centers with sizeable populations. As in other parts of west Africa, women in the non-Islamic Nigerian cultures play a prominent role in commercial life.

Economy and resources

Nigeria is rich in natural resources and these are the basis of its economy. They include tin, columbite, iron ore, coal, limestone, lead, zinc, and natural gas. By far the most important, however, is oil: Nigeria is OPEC's fourth largest producer, with oil providing eighty percent of government revenue and ninety percent of export earnings overall. This has led to what many consider over-dependence on a single commodity. In addition it has provided a limitless source of independent wealth for the political elite.

Agricultural production has failed to keep pace with population growth, and Nigeria is now a food importer. There are fundamental imbalances in the economy that result in chronic inflation and a steadily depreciating currency. Investors are wary because of political instability and corruption at the highest levels of government. Domestic and international debts prevent an agreement with the IMF on debt relief.

Central Africa

Cameroon

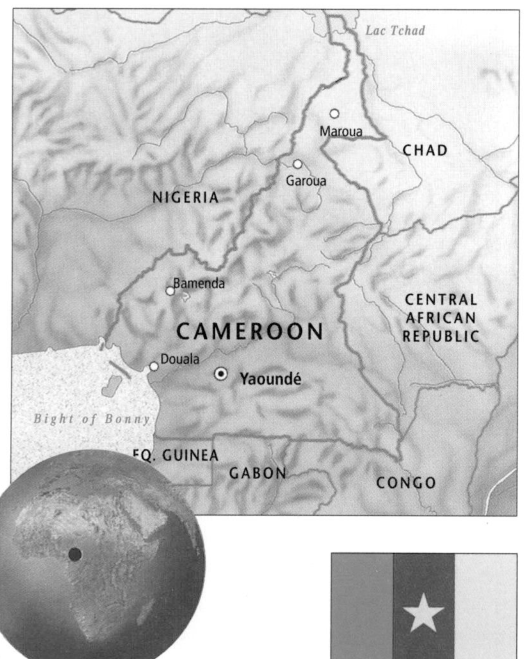

Fact File

OFFICIAL NAME Republic of Cameroon

FORM OF GOVERNMENT Republic with single legislative body (National Assembly)

CAPITAL Yaoundé

AREA 475,440 sq km (183,567 sq miles)

TIME ZONE GMT + 1 hour

POPULATION 16,185,000

PROJECTED POPULATION 2015 20,226,000

POPULATION DENSITY 34 per sq km (88.2 per sq mile)

LIFE EXPECTANCY 54.4

INFANT MORTALITY (PER 1,000) 68.8

OFFICIAL LANGUAGES French, English

OTHER LANGUAGES 24 African languages

LITERACY RATE 63.4 %

RELIGIONS Indigenous beliefs 51 %, Christian 33 %, Muslim 16 %

ETHNIC GROUPS Cameroon Highlanders 31 %, Equatorial Bantu 19 %, Kirdi 11 %, Fulani 10 %, Northwestern Bantu 8 %, Eastern Nigritic 7 %; other African 13 %; non-African 1 %

CURRENCY CFA (Communauté Financière Africaine) franc

ECONOMY Agriculture 74.4 %, industry and transport 11.4 %, services 14.2 %

GNP PER CAPITA US$ 1,700

CLIMATE Tropical in south and along coast, semiarid in north

HIGHEST POINT Mt Cameroon 4,095 m (13,435 ft)

MAP REFERENCE Page 365

The African state of Cameroon is on the Gulf of Guinea, with Nigeria to the west and Equatorial Guinea, Gabon, and Congo to the south. The Portuguese arrived in 1472, and Cameroon is named after the prawns, *camarãos*, they found here. A German colony from 1884, and later ruled by both British and French, Cameroon became independent in 1960. Although it was a one-party state for thirty years, opposition parties have been allowed since 1991. One of the more prosperous African countries, Cameroon is home to more than 200 distinct tribes and peoples. There is also a broad distinction between the English- and French-speaking parts of the population. In response to the demands of the former, and the protests and demonstrations they made in 1996, Cameroon applied for entry and was admitted to the British Commonwealth.

The country can be divided into four regions. First, an area of tropical forest, plateau, and coastal plain extends from the southern frontier to the Sanaga River. Most of the population is concentrated in this southern part. Second, north of this river and Lake Mbakaou (M'Bakaou Reservoir), the land rises to the highlands of the Adamaoua Massif. Third is the mountainous western extension of the Adamaoua Massif which includes Mt Cameroon. Occasionally active, this 4,095 m (13,435 ft) volcanic cone is the highest mountain in west Africa. Fourth is the arid savanna north of the Benue

(Bénoué River) and towards Lake Chad (Lac Tchad). This region of savanna supports elephant, lion, and leopard, and a national park—the Parc National de la Bénoué—has been established there.

Cameroon's prosperity was helped by the oil boom between 1970 and 1985. Since then conditions have been more difficult, with prices for coffee, cocoa, and petroleum, the country's major exports, falling. Three-quarters of the population are farmers who, in addition to coffee and cocoa, grow bananas, oilseed, grains, and manioc. Camercon is self-sufficient in food, but a range of other economic difficulties exists. Serious inflation occurred in 1994. The dismantling of unproductive state industries has been slow to show results, and the swollen ranks of the civil service remain a fiscal burden.

A small village on Cameroon's arid savanna (left page bottom). Falls on the Kotto River in the Central African Republic (left).

Central African Republic

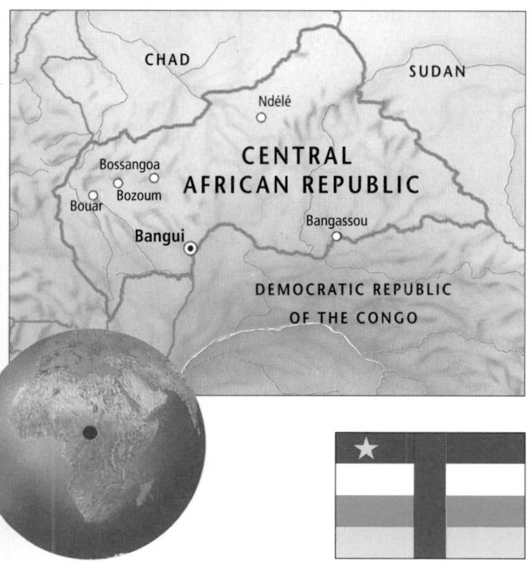

Fact File

OFFICIAL NAME Central African Republic

FORM OF GOVERNMENT Republic with single legislative body (National Assembly)

CAPITAL Bangui

AREA 622,980 sq km (240,533 sq miles)

TIME ZONE GMT + 1 hour

POPULATION 3,643,000

PROJECTED POPULATION 2015 4,877,000

POPULATION DENSITY 5.8 per sq km (15.1 per sq mile)

LIFE EXPECTANCY 43.6

INFANT MORTALITY (PER 1,000) 92.2

OFFICIAL LANGUAGE French

OTHER LANGUAGES Sangho, Arabic, Hunsa, Swahili

LITERACY RATE 60 %

RELIGIONS Protestant 25 %, Roman Catholic 25 %, indigenous beliefs 24 %, Muslim 15 %, other 11 %

ETHNIC GROUPS Baya 34 %, Banda 27 %, Mandjia 21 %, Sara 10 %, Mboum 4 %, M'Baka 4 %

CURRENCY CFA (Communauté Financière Africaine) franc

ECONOMY Agriculture 84 %, services 13 %, industry 3 %

GNP PER CAPITA US$ 1,300

CLIMATE Tropical, with hot, dry winters and hot, wet summers

HIGHEST POINT Mt Kayagangir 1,420 m (4,659 ft)

MAP REFERENCE Pages 365, 366

The Central African Republic (CAR) is a landlocked plateau just north of the equator. It is bordered on the west and north by Cameroon and Chad, and on the east and south by Sudan, the Democratic Republic of Congo, and Congo. By the time of European exploration the population of forest-dwelling Pygmies was much reduced, having been largely replaced by Bantu and Azande people. The region was for centuries used as a slave source by African slave-traders from the Sudan. When France took control in 1911 it ended slave-trading. The CAR was run as part of French Equatorial Africa until independence in 1958. After thirty years of political instability and military governments civilian rule was established in 1993. In March 2003 a military coup deposed the civilian government. Even though civil society groups and the main parties support the transitional government there is doubt whether the elections scheduled for 2004 or 2005 will be democratic. The government still does not fully control the countryside, where pockets of lawlessness persist.

The average elevation of the CAR plateau is between 2,000 and 2,500 m (6,500 and 8,000 ft). These uplands form a watershed dividing the Congo and Nile river basins. North of the high ground of the Massif des Bongos the land drains towards the interior along water courses into swamps in southern Chad. South of this massif numerous rivers feed into the Ubangi. To the west the Massif du Yadé forms a boundary with Cameroon.

In the south and southeast are forests containing hardwoods such as mahogany and ebony. Dense rainforest in this area provides one of the last homes of the lowland gorilla. Much of the rest of the land is savanna. Plantation forestry undertaken by foreign timber interests has in some places added significantly to natural soil erosion.

The CAR economy is based on subsistence agriculture combined with forestry. Food crops include manioc, yams, millet, maize, and bananas. Cotton, coffee, and tobacco are grown for cash. Industries include sawmills, textiles, footwear, and bicycle assembly. About eighty percent of export revenue comes from diamond mining.

The country's economic prospects are constrained by its position, its limited resources, its unskilled workforce, and its poor infrastructure. In addition, tuberculosis, leprosy, and sleeping sickness are widespread. These factors are likely to keep the CAR dependent on foreign aid for some time.

Equatorial Guinea

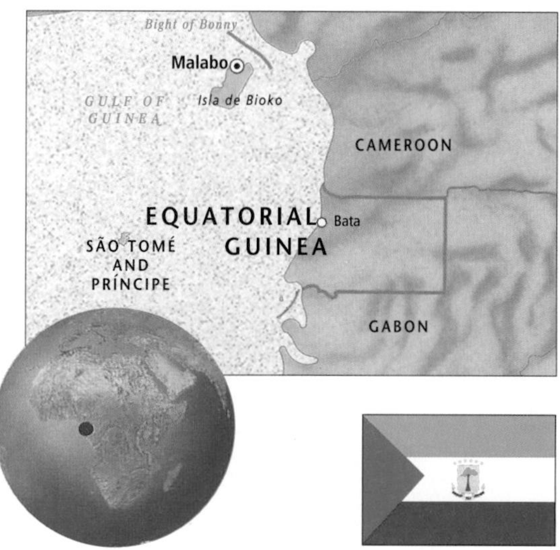

Fact File

OFFICIAL NAME Republic of Equatorial Guinea

FORM OF GOVERNMENT Republic with single legislative body (House of People's Representatives)

CAPITAL Malabo

AREA 28,050 sq km (10,830 sq miles)

TIME ZONE GMT + 1 hour

POPULATION 499,000

PROJECTED POPULATION 2015 692,000

POPULATION DENSITY 17.8 per sq km (46.1 per sq mile)

LIFE EXPECTANCY 54.4

INFANT MORTALITY (PER 1,000) 91.0

OFFICIAL LANGUAGE Spanish

OTHER LANGUAGES Indigenous languages, including Fang, Bubi, Ibo; pidgin English

LITERACY RATE 78.5 %

RELIGIONS Roman Catholic 85 %, indigenous beliefs 15 %

ETHNIC GROUPS Fang 80 %, Bubi 15 %, other 5 %

CURRENCY CFA (Communauté Financière Africaine) franc

ECONOMY Agriculture 66 %, services 23 %, industry 11 %

GNP PER CAPITA US$ 2,100

CLIMATE Tropical; wetter on coast

HIGHEST POINT Pico Basile 3,011 m (9,879 ft)

MAP REFERENCE Page 365

Equatorial Guinea consists of five islands in the Gulf of Guinea, plus the small mainland area of Río Muni that lies between Cameroon and Gabon. The largest of the islands, Bioco, was originally Portuguese, and was known for centuries as the slave depot and trans-shipment base of Fernando Po. The Spanish took over in 1778.

After gaining independence from Spain in 1968 Equatorial Guinea fell into the hands of Francisco Macias Nguema. A member of the Mongomo clan of the Fang tribe, his bloody and despotic rule lasted eleven years, after which he was overthrown and later executed. His nephew, also a Fang, continued to govern in much the same way, observers describing the presidential elections of 1996 and 2002 as a political farce.

Street scene in a provincial town in Equatorial Guinea (left top). This house in São Tomé built in Portuguese colonial style has seen better days (left bottom). Cocoa is dried in Mekome Nkodje, Gabon (right page bottom).

Equatorial Guinea illustrates the problems faced by tribal groups trying to adapt to democratic political arrangements.

The island of Bioco is mountainous and volcanic, with fertile soils. It has long supported cocoa on the lowland, and there are coffee plantations on the higher slopes which rise to Pico Basile. Rugged terrain and waterfalls are found in the southern half of the island. On the thinly populated area of mainland, mangrove swamps along the coast lead inland to dense tropical forests. Here, foreign companies have timber concessions, felling okoume and mahogany.

In addition to timber, the country exports cocoa and coffee. In the years before independence, cocoa plantations on Bioco and the mainland provided Equatorial Guinea with the highest per capita income in west Africa. By the end of the Macias era, however, the state was in political and economic ruins and some 100,000 of the population had fled as refugees to neighboring countries. Most of those who remain in the country today are subsistence farmers growing yams, cassava, and bananas.

Equatorial Guinea has a variety of undeveloped mineral resources: titanium, iron ore, manganese, uranium, and alluvial gold. Recently oil exploration has been successful, and increased production of oil and natural gas is anticipated. Aid programs are currently in limbo, having been cut off because of gross governmental corruption and mismanagement.

São Tomé and Príncipe

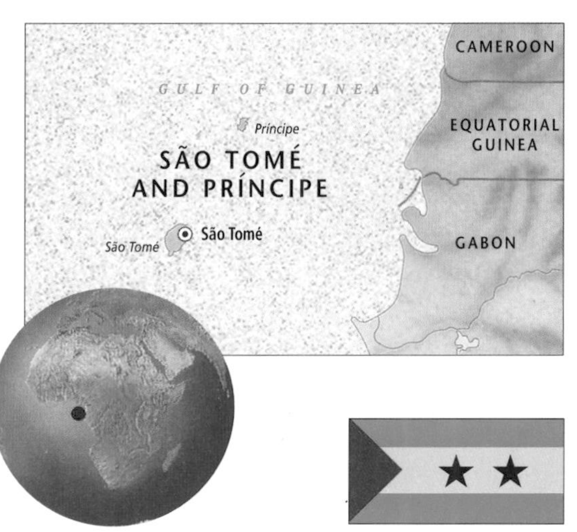

Fact File

OFFICIAL NAME Democratic Republic of São Tomé and Príncipe

FORM OF GOVERNMENT Republic with single legislative body (National People's Assembly)

CAPITAL São Tomé

AREA 960 sq km (371 sq miles)

TIME ZONE GMT

POPULATION 171,000

PROJECTED POPULATION 2015 178,000

POPULATION DENSITY 178.1 per sq km (460.9 per sq mile)

LIFE EXPECTANCY 65.9

INFANT MORTALITY (PER 1,000) 47.5

OFFICIAL LANGUAGE Portuguese

OTHER LANGUAGES Crioulo (blend of Portuguese and West African languages)

LITERACY RATE 79.3 %

RELIGIONS Roman Catholic 80 %, Protestant and other 20 %

ETHNIC GROUPS Predominantly mixed African-Portuguese, with various African minorities

CURRENCY Dobra

ECONOMY Mainly agriculture and fishing

GNP PER CAPITA US$ 1,200

CLIMATE Tropical, with wet season October to May

HIGHEST POINT Pico de São Tomé 2,024 m (6,640 ft)

MAP REFERENCE Pages 365, 373

São Tomé and Prïncipe are two islands lying off the coast of Gabon in the Gulf of Guinea. They were occupied in the 1520s by the Portuguese, who used slaves as laborers on the sugar plantations. The population now consists mainly of the Afro-Portuguese descendants of these first immigrants, plus contract laborers brought from Mozambique and Cape Verde to work on cocoa plantations in the nineteenth century. Following independence in 1975, a one-party Marxist regime was imposed. For a time the islands were allied to the Soviet bloc and Russian and Cuban military advisors were brought in. At a referendum in 1990, however, 72 percent of the people voted in favor of democratic government. Now the main concern of the government is to rebuild the country's relationship with Portugal and to secure beneficial working relationships with the EU and the USA. Nevertheless, the situation has not been stable. The leadership has changed frequently and there were two unsuccessful coup attempts in 1995 and 2003.

An extinct volcano, São Tomé is the largest and most populous of the two main islands, some 440 km (273 miles) off the coast of Gabon. Low lying in the northeast and the southwest, it rises to Pico de São Tomé in the volcanic highlands. The island of Príncipe lies about 150 km (100 miles) to the northeast. As well as the two main islands there are also a number of rocky islets—Caroco, Pedras, Tinhosas, and Rôlas. On both São Tomé and Príncipe, streams drain to the sea from mountainous interiors, up to seventy percent of which are densely forested. The climate is hot and humid, moderated to a certain extent by the cold Benguela current that flows up Africa's western shore.

Following independence in 1975 the cocoa plantations which formed the foundation of the country's economy deteriorated as a result of mismanagement aggravated by drought. By 1987 the production of cocoa had fallen to 3,500 tonnes from an annual output of 9,000 tonnes prior to 1975. While there has been some economic recovery in recent years, São Tomé and Príncipe have had serious balance of payments problems. During the 1980s agriculture diversified into palm oil, pepper, and coffee but since then production has faltered. Deforestation and soil erosion are increasing causes for concern. Today, São Tomé imports ninety percent of its food, all its fuel and most manufactured goods. The recent discovery of oil in the Gulf of Guinea, however, may very well have a significant impact on the country's economy.

Gabon

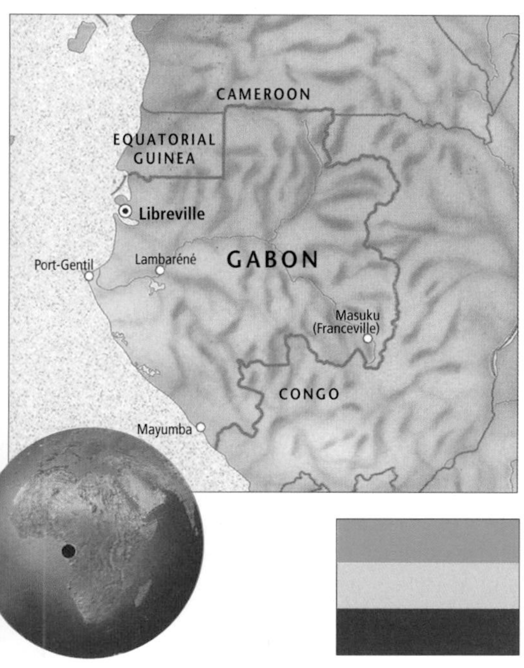

Fact File

Official name Gabonese Republic

Form of government Republic with single legislative body (National Assembly)

Capital Libreville

Area 267,670 sq km (103,347 sq miles)

Time zone GMT + 1 hour

Population 1,234,000

Projected population 2015 1,757,000

Population density 4.6 per sq km (11.9 per sq mile)

Life expectancy 49.1

Infant mortality (per 1,000) 93.5

Official language French

Other languages Indigenous languages (including Fang, Myene, Bateke, Bapounou/ Eschira, Bandjabi)

Literacy rate 63.2 %

Religions Christian 55 %–75 %, Muslim less than 1 %, indigenous beliefs 3 %

Ethnic groups Mainly Bantu tribes (including Fang, Eshira, Bapounou, Bateke) 92 %, foreign Africans and Europeans 8 %

Currency CFA (Communauté Financière Africaine) franc

Economy Agriculture 65 %, industry and commerce 30 %, services 5 %

GNP per capita US$ 5,500

Climate Tropical, with dry season mid-May to mid-September

Highest point Mt Iboundji 1,575 m (5,167 ft)

Map reference Page 368

A slave station for the Portuguese after their arrival in 1483, Gabon was administered by France from 1842. After the French navy suppressed the still-continuing local slave trade, it released captives at a place on the coast which it named Libreville (Libertyville). Since Gabon achieved independence in 1966 France has continued to play a role in the country's politics and in its relatively prosperous oil-based economy.

The original inhabitants of this heavily forested equatorial country were probably Pygmies; today the main tribal group is the Fang. However, the thirty-year rule of President El Hadj Omar Bongo (a Bateke who converted to Islam under Libyan influence in 1973) depended on a coalition that was designed to exclude the Fang from power. Widespread dissatisfaction with this state of affairs led to the introduction of a multi-party system in 1991. Whether this has allowed other ethnic groups a real voice in Gabonese politics is not yet clear. However, the country has in the meantime developed into an island of stability in the region and since 1994 there have not been any complaints concerning human rights questions.

Geographically, a coastal plain marked by sandbars and lagoons is interrupted by the estuary of the Ogooué River. The wooded basin of this large watercourse dominates Gabon, sixty percent of the country's land area being drained by its tributaries. These flow down from the African central plateau and the borders of Equatorial Guinea and Cameroon to the north, and from Congo to the east and south.

Before the development of oil and manganese in the early 1970s, valuable timbers were one of the country's main exports. These included Gabon mahogany, ebony, and walnut. Even today as much as two-thirds of Gabon's total land area consists of untouched rainforest, but the completion in 1986 of the Trans-Gabon Railway from the port of Owendo to the interior town of Massoukou is likely to lead to further exploitation of timber resources.

Gabon has considerable mineral resources. It has about one-quarter of the world's known reserves of manganese, and is the world's fourth biggest manganese producer. France imports most of its uranium from Gabon. Oil currently accounts for fifty percent of gross domestic product. This figure, when combined with Gabon's small population, gives a distorted picture of the country's per capita earnings, disguising the fact that more than half the country's people still make their living by subsistence farming. A wide gap separates rural people from the urban élite and the country faces economic problems.

Congo

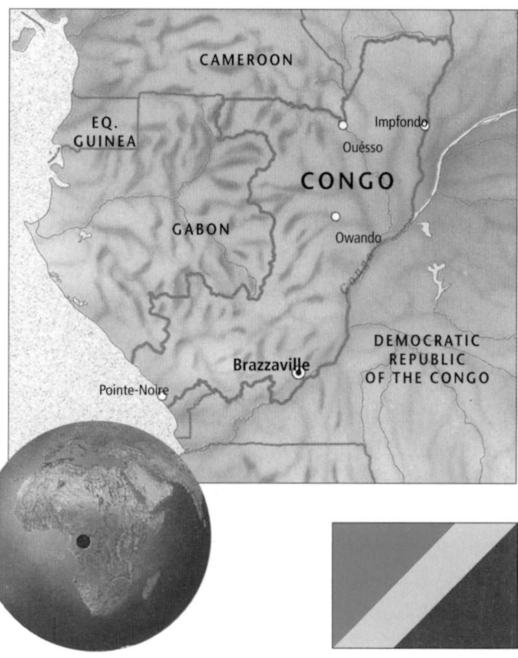

Fact File

Official name People's Republic of the Congo

Form of government Republic with two legislative bodies (Senate and National Assembly)

Capital Brazzaville

Area 342,000 sq km (132,046 sq miles)

Time zone GMT + 1 hour

Population 2,959,000

Projected population 2015 4,730,000

Population density 7.9 per sq km (22.4 per sq mile)

Life expectancy 47.7

Infant mortality (per 1,000) 97.9

Official language French

Other languages African languages (particularly Lingala, Kikongo and Monokutuba)

Literacy rate 74.9 %

Religions Christian 50 %, indigenous 48 %, Muslim 2 %

Ethnic groups About 75 different tribes: Kongo 48 %, Sangha 20 %, Teke 17 %; other 15 %

Currency CFA (Communauté Financière Africaine) franc

Economy Agriculture 75 %, industry and services 25 %

GNP per capita US$ 900

Climate Tropical, with wet season March to June

Highest point Mt Berongou 903 m (2,963 ft)

Map reference Page 368

From the Atlantic coast, Congo extends 1,000 km (600 miles) inland to the border of the Central African Republic. Its history is obscure, although the first inhabitants may have been Pygmies. Later it was home to the Kongo peoples who supplied slaves for Portuguese traders. In the nineteenth century it was explored by the French-Italian Pierre Savorgnan de Brazza, who gave his name to the capital city, and whose activities led to the region becoming part of French Equatorial Africa in 1891. Congo has been independent since 1960. Ten years after independence, Congo declared itself a People's Republic and Africa's first communist state. Since 1991, however, there have been attempts to introduce the principles of legal opposition and multi-party democracy. In 1997 a brief civil war restored former Marxist President Sassou-Nguesso, but also started a five-year period of ethnic unrest. Finally, in March 2003 southern-based rebel groups agreed to a peace accord.

Road transport within Congo is hampered by tropical rains that make the unpaved roads unuseable but water transport to the interior and the northeast is comparatively easy. Two mighty rivers, the Congo and the Ubangi, provide a commercially navigable highway along virtually the entire eastern frontier.

From a coastal strip on the Atlantic seaboard, the Rivers Kouilou and Niari lead up to the heights of the Massif du Mayombé. This range is crossed by a spectacular French-built railway joining Brazzaville with the port of Pointe-Noire. The Congo below Brazzaville has many cataracts, and the railway was built to carry freight around them. Beyond the massif the land falls away northward to the central plateau, where numerous rivers drain east into the Ubangi and the Congo itself.

Though more than half the Congolese live in towns, subsistence agriculture engages one-third of the workforce, and most of the food produced and consumed is cassava. Rice, maize, and vegetables are also grown, and coffee and cocoa are exported. Some sixty percent of the country is still covered in tropical forest. Timber was once a leading export, but today ninety percent of exports consists of oil. Apart from that, Congo allows other countries such as Gabon or the Central African Republic to use its port and other transport facilities. Manufacture, for example the processing of agricultural products or the production of textiles and shoes in the larger cities, is also an economic enterprises of some importance. Despite its comparative wealth, the government has mortgaged a large part of its oil earnings for expensive development projects.

Democratic Republic of Congo

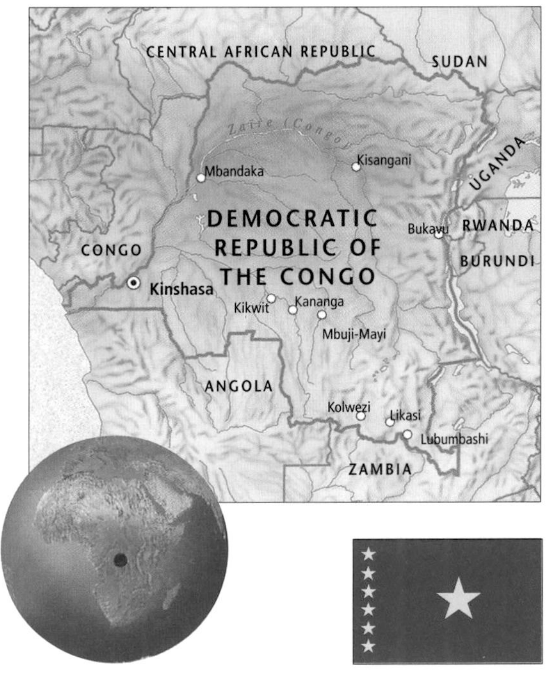

Fact File

OFFICIAL NAME Democratic Republic of the Congo

FORM OF GOVERNMENT Presidential rule

CAPITAL Kinshasa

AREA 2,345,410 sq km (905,563 sq miles)

TIME ZONE GMT + 1/2 hour

POPULATION 55,226,000

PROJECTED POPULATION 2015 84,045,000

POPULATION DENSITY 23.5 per sq km (61.0 per sq mile)

LIFE EXPECTANCY 49.1

INFANT MORTALITY (PER 1,000) 98.1

OFFICIAL LANGUAGE French

OTHER LANGUAGES Lingala, Kingwana, Kikongo, Tshiluba

LITERACY RATE 77.3 %

RELIGIONS Roman Catholic 50 %, Protestant 20 %, Kimbanguist 10 %, Muslim 10 %, other indigenous beliefs 10 %

ETHNIC GROUPS More than 200 indigenous groups, mostly of Bantu origin: Kongo, Luba, Mongo, Mangbetu-Azande 51%; other 48%

CURRENCY New zaire

ECONOMY Agriculture 72 %, services 15 %, industry 13 %

GNP PER CAPITA US$ 590

CLIMATE Tropical; wet season north of equator from April to October, wet season south of equator from November to March

HIGHEST POINT Mt Stanley 5,110 m (16,765 ft)

MAP REFERENCE Pages 368–69

The Democratic Republic of the Congo (DRC), formerly called Zaire, is the centerpiece of central Africa. It is the third-largest country on the continent after Algeria and Sudan and has one of the largest navigable rivers in the world. Historically occupied by the Kongo, Luba, Lunda, and Azande peoples, this enormous region fell into the hands of King Leopold of Belgium in 1885, who exploited it as a private domain. After international condemnation of his brutal rule, in 1908 it became a colony of Belgium. The country won its independence in 1960.

Since that time, 35 years of dictatorial mismanagement and corruption as a one-party state under the control of President Mobutu Sese Seko (who died in 1997) have brought the DRC to the point of collapse. The troubles of its neighbors have added to its own. War and disorder in Sudan, Rwanda, Burundi, and Angola have driven hundreds of thousands of refugees across the borders into the DRC. A military occupation of Kinshasa was successful in bringing the Mobutu regime to an end in 1997. His successor, President Laurent Kabila was assassinated in 2001 and succeeded by his son Joseph. In 2003 the EU dispatched troups to the country to help. Whether the current government of national unity will be successful remains to be seen.

Geographically the DRC is dominated by a single feature—the immense basin of the Congo River. The eastern rim of this basin is formed by the Mitumba Mountains (Monts Mitumbe) along the Rift Valley, and the volcanic Ruwenzori Range. In the far southeast Lake Mweru feeds into the Congo's main northward-flowing tributary, the Lualaba. Looping north and west in a great horseshoe, the Congo is joined on the borders of the Central African Republic by the Ubangi. After several cascades below Kinshasa as it descends from the central plateau, the Congo empties into the Atlantic Ocean. The equatorial climate of the main river basin supports one of the world's most extensive rainforests, home to rare animals such as okapi and gorilla. The savanna grasslands of the east and south are home to giraffe, lion, antelope and rhinoceros.

Potentially one of Africa's richest countries, the DRC is currently one of its poorest. Most of its people try to survive the breakdown of civil society by subsistence farming and petty trade. Cash crops such as coffee, sugar, and palm oil continue to be produced, but a severe lack of infrastructure hampers trade. Meanwhile, hyperinflation, large government deficits, and falling mineral production mean that no end to the nation's economic difficulties is yet in sight.

A village in the Congo highlands (left page bottom). Dusk on the Congo River in the Democratic Republic of the Congo (left). Angolan women pounding millet in the traditional way (below).

Angola

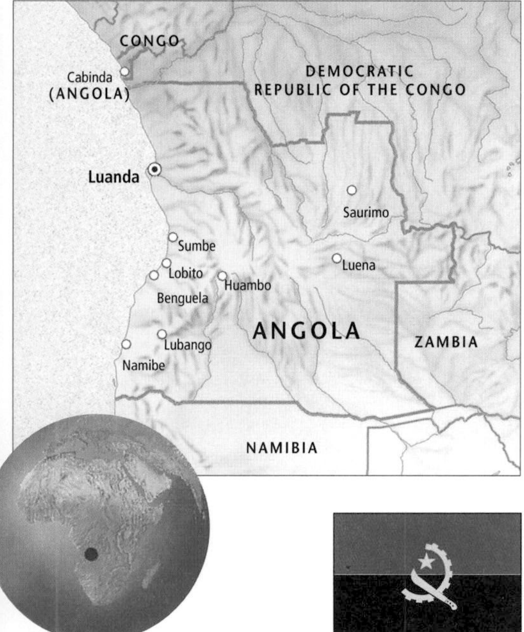

Fact File

OFFICIAL NAME Republic of Angola

FORM OF GOVERNMENT Republic with single legislative body (National Assembly)

CAPITAL Luanda

AREA 1,246,700 sq km (481,351 sq miles)

TIME ZONE GMT + 1 hour

POPULATION 10,979,000

PROJECTED POPULATION 2015 13,548,000

POPULATION DENSITY 8.8 per sq km (22.8 per sq mile)

LIFE EXPECTANCY 38.9

INFANT MORTALITY (PER 1,000) 131.7

OFFICIAL LANGUAGE Portuguese

OTHER LANGUAGES Bantu, other African languages

LITERACY RATE 42 %

RELIGIONS Indigenous beliefs 47 %, Roman Catholic 38 %, Protestant 15 %

ETHNIC GROUPS Mainly indigenous, including Ovimbundu 37 %, Kimbundu 25 %, Bakongo 13 %; mixed European-African 2 %, European 1 %, other 22 %

CURRENCY Kwanza

ECONOMY Industry 67 %, services 25 %, agriculture 8 %

GNP PER CAPITA US$ 1,900

CLIMATE Mainly tropical with wet season November to April; semiarid in south and along coast

HIGHEST POINT Mt Môco 2,620 m (8,596 ft)

MAP REFERENCE Pages 368, 370

A large country on Africa's southwest coast, Angola is bordered by the states of the Democratic Republic of the Congo to the north, Zambia to the east, and Namibia to the south. The small but resource-rich province of Cabinda lies separated from the rest of Angola to the north of the Congo River, wholly surrounded by Congo.

A Portuguese colony since the sixteenth century, Angola was the source of an estimated three million slaves who were sent to Brazil and other places across the Atlantic, largely to work on sugar plantations. The country received its independence in 1975 and for the next twenty years was wracked by civil war. The government, having established a Marxist one-party state supported by the USSR and especially Cuba, was then challenged by the forces of Jonas Savimbi, who was backed by the USA. The truce mediated between the two parties by the United Nations, which came into force in 1994, did not last for long. A national unity government was installed in 1997, but serious fighting resumed in late 1998, rendering hundreds of thousands of people homeless. After the death of Jonas Savimbi in 2002 both parties stopped fighting after an estimated 1.5 million people had lost their lives in fighting over the past quarter of a century. The reconstruction of the devastated country and the reconciliation of the different groups are the most pressing issues for the current government, but there is hope that the country finally may come to rest.

Angola can be divided into two main regions. There are the relatively narrow coastal plains, and an extensive tableland that rises from them and dominates the rest of the country. Divided roughly east to west across the center, this tableland drains into the Congo Basin to the north, and into the rivers of the Zambeze Basin to the south and east. While the tableland is fairly level in the south, the highlands become mountainous in central and southwestern Angola. In the province of Cabinda there are dense tropical rainforests, and heavy rains can be expected for seven months of the year. Savanna woodland is found on much of the tableland, becoming mainly grassy plains to the south, dotted with acacia and baobab trees. The cold Benguela current that flows north from the southern Atlantic Ocean has a moderating effect on the heat of the coastal region. Toward Namibia on the southern border the coastal strip becomes desert.

Angola is rich in petroleum, gold, and diamonds, and has reserves of iron ore, phosphates, feldspar, bauxite, and uranium. It has large areas of forest, productive fisheries off the Atlantic coast, and extensive areas of arable land. While the country is capable of producing coffee, sisal, and cotton, the years of civil war have resulted in economic disarray and the country's output per capita for many years was one of the lowest in the world. Subsistence agriculture supported up to ninety percent of the people and much of the nation's food still has to be imported.

Eastern Africa

Sudan

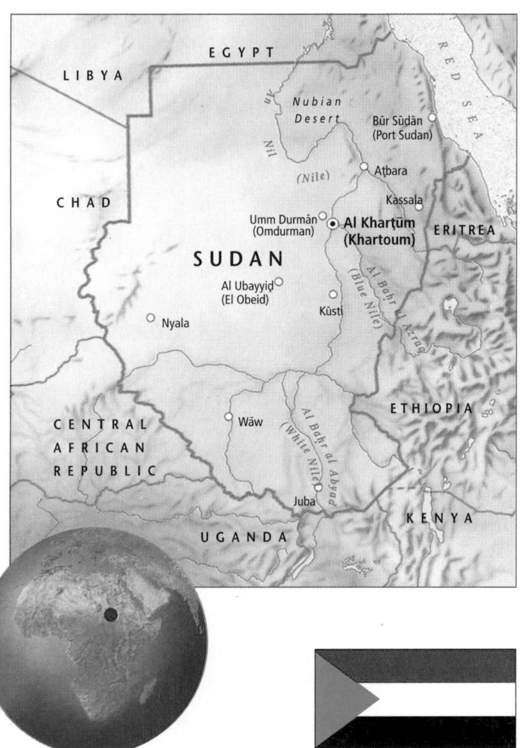

Fact File

Official name Republic of the Sudan

Form of government Military regime with single transitional legislative body (Provisional National Assembly)

Capital Al Kharṭūm (Khartoum)

Area 2,505,810 sq km (967,493 sq miles)

Time zone GMT + 2 hours

Population 38,091,000

Projected population 2015 42,433,000

Population density 15.2 per sq km (39.4 per sq mile)

Life expectancy 57.3

Infant mortality (per 1,000) 67.1

Official language Arabic

Other languages Nubian, Ta Bedawie, English, indigenous languages

Literacy rate 46.1 %

Religions Sunni Muslim 70 %, indigenous beliefs 25 %, Christian 5 %

Ethnic groups African 52 %, Arab 39 %, Beja 6 %, other 3 %

Currency Sudanese pound

Economy Agriculture 63 %, services 33 %, industry 4 %

GNP per capita US$ 1,360

Climate North mainly arid; south tropical, with wet season April to October

Highest point Mt Kinyeti 3,187 m (10,456 ft)

Map reference Pages 362–63, 366–67

South of Egypt, Sudan is Africa's largest country, and the pathway to the headwaters of the Nile (An Nil). It is also one of Africa's most divided countries. Known in Ancient Egypt as Nubia, its northern region came under Islamic Arab control in the fourteenth century, and Egyptian and British rule in the nineteenth. With some 570 distinct ethnic groups and over 100 languages, it has been difficult for Sudan to form a modern state.

Since achieving independence from Egypt and Britain in 1956 Sudan has seen military rule, coups, and civil conflict for all but ten of the next forty years. The main cause is the determination of the Muslim north to impose Arab and Islamic values on the varied African, animist, and Christian peoples of the south. Strict sharia (Muslim) law has been proclaimed but is widely ignored. After the government's "war of annihilation" against the 1.5 million Nuba people, supported by opposition groups, it has now also turned against the Muslim, but black, population of the Darfur province. Over half a million people have died in the past twelve years, the miseries of the ethnic Africans being compounded by famine, displacement, rape, and the enslavement of women and children. One task of relief workers has been to purchase the freedom of slaves.

In northern Sudan the rocky Sahara Desert stretches westward to become a waste of sand dunes, the land rising to 3,071 m (10,075 ft) at the Darfur Massif toward the border with Chad. In the east the Red Sea Mountains rise 2,000 m (6,500 ft) above a narrow coastal plain. Most people live near the south-north flowing Nile (An Nil), a river that divides into two streams at Khartoum. From here the source of the Blue Nile (Al Bahr al Azraq) can be traced southeast to the Ethiopian border and Lake Tana. The White Nile (Al Bahr al Abyad) runs southwards into the vast marshland of the Sudd (where dense, floating vegetation makes navigation difficult), then further upstream to Uganda and its headwaters in Lake Albert.

About 80 percent of Sudan's workforce are farmers. There is a heavy emphasis on growing cotton, at the expense of food crops, as it accounts for 24 percent of export revenue. Food crops include sorghum (the staple) along with millet, wheat, barley, and peanuts. Declining rainfall and huge displacements of the rural population as a result of war have played havoc with production in recent years. The socialist government is resisting reform: in 1990 the IMF declared Sudan noncooperative because of nonpayment of debts. At present aid comes mainly from Iran. Natural resources include copper, chromium ore, zinc, tungsten, mica, silver, and gold. Some gold is mined.

Crumbling pyramids in the desert at Merouë in the Sudan witness its long common history with Egypt (right).

Eritrea

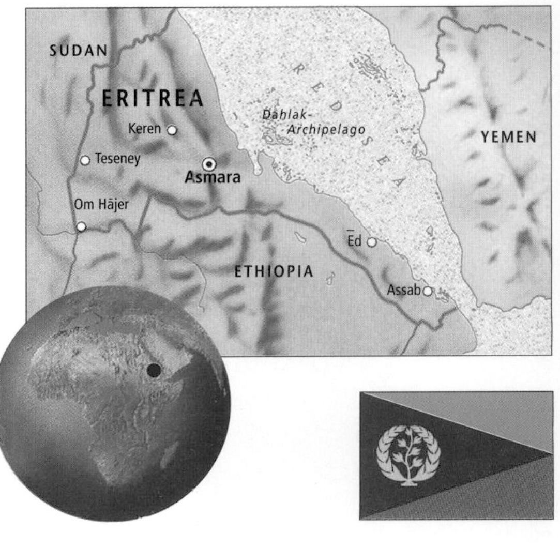

Fact File

Official name State of Eritrea

Form of government Transitional government with single legislative body (Legislative Assembly)

Capital Asmara

Area 121,320 sq km (46,842 sq miles)

Time zone GMT + 3 hours

Population 4,466,000

Projected population 2015 5,720,000

Population density 36.8 per sq km (95.3 per sq mile)

Life expectancy 56.6

Infant mortality (per 1,000) 73.6

Official languages Tigrinya, Arabic

Other languages Tigré, other indigenous languages, English

Literacy rate 25 %

Religions Muslim 50 %, Christian (Coptic Christian, Roman Catholic, Protestant) 50 %

Ethnic groups Tigrinya 50 %, Tigré and Kunama 40 %, Afar 4 %, Saho (Red Sea coast dwellers) 3 %, other 3 %

Currency Nakfa

Economy Services 54 %, industry 29 %, agriculture 17 %

GNP per capita US$ 740

Climate Hot and arid along coast, cooler and wetter in highlands; wet season June to September

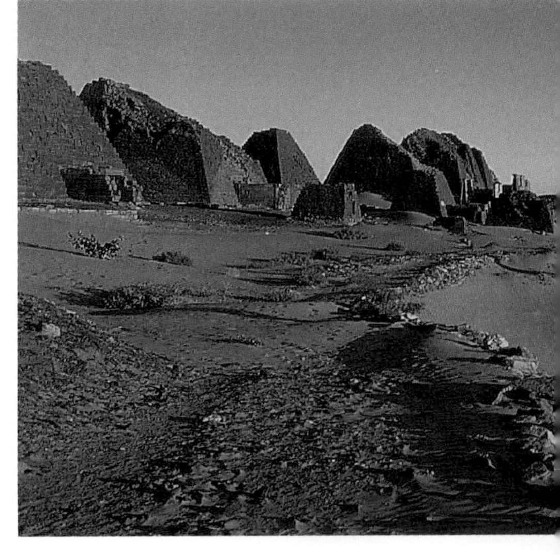

HIGHEST POINT Soira 3,018 m (9,899 ft)

MAP REFERENCE Page 367

Eritrea was part of the Aksum Kingdom 2,000 years ago. In the fourth century AD Coptic Christianity was brought to the country, and a member of the Coptic Christian community, Issaias Ifawerki, is now its president. Italian influence in the region began in 1882, and despite the depredations of Mussolini between 1935 and 1941, Eritrea's modernization dates from those years. Italy introduced Western education and industry.

Forced to join Ethiopia in 1962, Eritrea began a thirty-year war of independence, first against the emperor and then against Ethiopia's Soviet-armed and financed Mengistu regime. Fighting from trenches dug from rock in the mountains, and in spite of inferior weapons, the Eritrean troops hung on. Victory and separate nationhood were won in 1993. In 1998 war broke out again for two and a half years and since 2000 a UN peacekeeping operation has monitored a 25 km- (15.5 mile-)wide temporary security zone on the border with Ethiopia. An international commission, organized to resolve the border dispute, posted its findings in 2002 but final demarcation is on hold due to Ethiopian objections.

Consisting of a hot dry desert strip along the Red Sea shore, Eritrea is dominated by rugged mountains in the north, and in the southeast by the arid coastal plain of the Danakil Desert. In and around this desert live the Afar, camel-keeping nomads. The country is bordered on the north by the Sudan, with whom it has uneasy relations, and on the south by Djibouti. Before independence, Eritrea provided Ethiopia's only access to the sea other than through Djibouti. The prospect of being landlocked as a result of Eritrean secession—which is what happened—strengthened Ethiopian resolve during the war.

Poor and war-torn, with its roads and railways destroyed, since 1993 Eritrea has faced the task of reconstruction. Obligatory military service provides labor for public works. During the war trees were cut down by the enemy to deprive Eritrean soldiers of hiding places: these are being replanted by the thousand. In the long term offshore oil deposits may prove important, but the population currently survives by subsistence farming, growing sorghum, lentils, vegetables, and maize. This is supplemented by food aid on which 75 percent of the people rely.

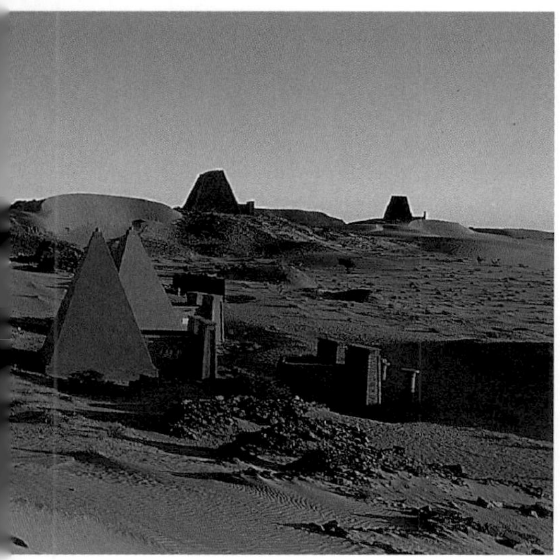

Causes of famine in Africa

Famine has been a serious problem on the African continent since very early times—there are records of famines in Egypt 6,000 years ago. A good corn harvest in Egypt was essential to the well-being of the region as a whole. A bad harvest affected not only Egypt but also the neighbors with whom it traded. Famine usually occurred because of annual variations in the extent of the flooding of the River Nile, and therefore in the yield of grain for food. Such famines were related to inherent difficulties in the kind of intensive floodplain agriculture that has been practiced over the centuries in the Nile Valley.

Prolonged drought and the spread of deserts in marginal areas are other common causes of famine. Hungry people allow their goats to graze on the sparse vegetation that grows on desert fringes, which frequently results in the plants dying and the desert spreading. This can be seen in the vast sub-Saharan region of the Sahel. A third type of famine is largely the result of human actions. Chronic warfare of the kind that has recently plagued the southern Sudan seriously disrupts agricultural production, displacing such large numbers of people that crops are neither planted nor harvested.

Finally, there is the kind of famine that affected Ethiopia under the Marxist Dergue during 1984–85, which was a direct result of government policies. Huge collectivization programs were initiated in the midst of war and cultivators were forcibly taken from their own land to work on state farms—many of those removed were "resettled" as punishment for their suspected hostility to the regime. This seriously affected the morale of the population and food production throughout the country decreased dramatically. A report prepared by the organization Cultural Survival concluded that the principal reasons for food shortages in Ethiopia at that time were the forcible redistribution of land to people unable or unwilling to work it; the confiscation of grain and livestock; and forced labor programs and military recruitment, which resulted in a sharp decline in the labor force available for agricultural work.

In Africa as elsewhere, the United Nations World Food Programme (WFP) is the main agency that is active in famine relief. Helping as many as 53 million people worldwide, it operates in virtually all the sub-Saharan African countries. The WFP's Food for Life Program helps people affected by humanitarian crises, such as that in Rwanda and Burundi in 1994. In April 1994 WFP workers provided food for what amounted to a huge city of refugees on the border of Rwanda and Tanzania, where 250,000 people were gathered without food, water, or shelter.

The WFP Food for Growth Program targets needy schoolchildren, mothers who are breast-feeding, and the elderly. In Ethiopia the WFP Food for Work Program, which pays workers with food for their service on development projects, has contributed to the planting of large numbers of trees; in Somalia the same program has been involved in repairing irrigation canals.

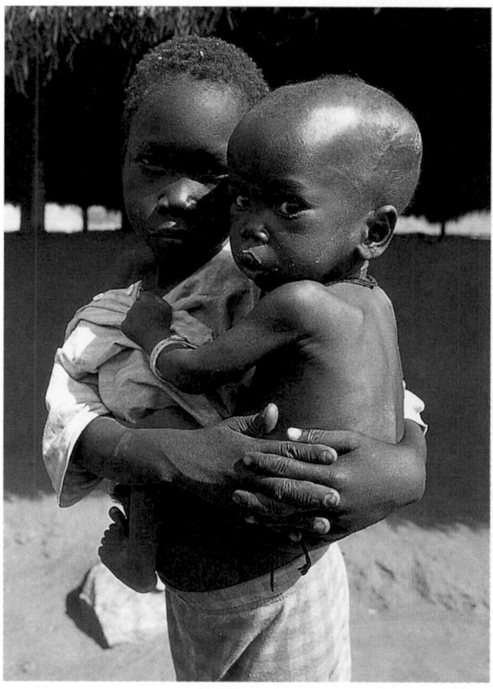

Desert encroaching on an African town (below). Children affected by famine (right).

Ethiopia

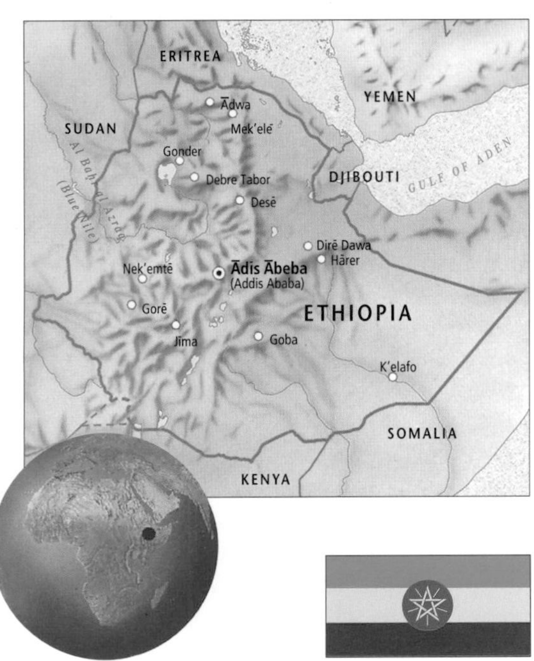

Fact File

OFFICIAL NAME Federal Democratic Republic of Ethiopia

FORM OF GOVERNMENT Federal republic with two legislative bodies (Federal Council and Council of People's Representatives)

CAPITAL Ādīs Ābeba (Addis Ababa)

AREA 1,127,127 sq km (435,184 sq miles)

TIME ZONE GMT + 3 hours

POPULATION 67,673,000

PROJECTED POPULATION 2015 89,765,000

POPULATION DENSITY 60.0 per sq km (155.5 per sq mile)

LIFE EXPECTANCY 44.2

INFANT MORTALITY (PER 1,000) 98.6

OFFICIAL LANGUAGE Amharic

OTHER LANGUAGES More than 100 indigenous languages, Arabic, English

LITERACY RATE 35.5 %

RELIGIONS Muslim 45 %–50 %, Ethiopian Orthodox 35 %–40 %, animist 12 %, other 3 %–8 %

ETHNIC GROUPS Oromo 40 %, Amhara and Tigrean 32 %, Sidamo 9 %, Shankella 6 %, Somali 6 %, Afar 4 %, Gurage 2 %, other 1 %

CURRENCY Birr

ECONOMY Agriculture 80 %, services 12 %, industry 8 %

GNP PER CAPITA US$ 700

CLIMATE Tropical on lowlands, uplands more temperate; wet season April to September

HIGHEST POINT Ras Dashen Terara 4,620 m (15,157 ft)

MAP REFERENCE Pages 366–67

Ethiopia was known as the land of Punt by the Ancient Egyptians. In the fourth century AD it adopted Coptic Christianity, and despite strong Islamic influences since that time, including a Muslim invasion in 1523, many people remain Christian today. Although Mussolini's Italy occupied the country between 1935 and 1941, Ethiopia was never a colony—in fact under Emperor Haile Selassie it had imperial ambitions, and attempted to subjugate both the Somalis and the people of Eritrea. Haile Selassie was deposed in 1974 by a military coup; this triggered a civil war that exacerbated the effects of the famine in 1984. Always poor, Ethiopia is currently destitute—thirty years of war and resulting famine are the legacy of the Marxist dictatorship of Mengistu Haile Mariam. His regime ended in 1991, when he was deposed.

The landscape is dominated by a mountainous volcanic plateau divided in two by the Rift Valley. The western highlands, with an average height of 2,700 m (8,800 ft), are the source of the Blue Nile, which spills out in a cataract from Lake Tana to flow south and west, before finally flowing north into Sudan. East of the western highlands is the Danakil Desert, where a depression falls to 116 m (380 ft) below sea level. This is one of the hottest places on earth. In the highlands, however, the climate is moderate to warm, with frosts at night and occasional falls of snow on the mountains. The eastern highlands below the Rift Valley fall away to the border with Somalia. In the aftermath of Ethiopia's war with its Somali neighbor the southern section of this border is only provisional, and there is an ongoing dispute regarding the Ogadēn region.

More than ninety percent of the country's industry, concerned with food processing, the manufacture of textiles, and chemical and metal production, is owned and managed by the state. Inefficiencies and overstaffing are widespread. This is the result of the Mengistu regime's effort to establish a centrally controlled Soviet-model economy. Various reform measures have been proposed and the government intends to sell off some state-owned plants, but progress is slow.

Drought in the years 1981 to 1985, combined with an unsuccessful attempt to collectivize agriculture, resulted in a famine in which an estimated 1 million people died. Today, rural production accounts for half of gross domestic product and eighty percent of employment. Repair of war-damaged roads and railways continues. Although Ethiopia still needs food aid there is a growing emphasis on aid in the form of credit for infrastructure development.

Djibouti

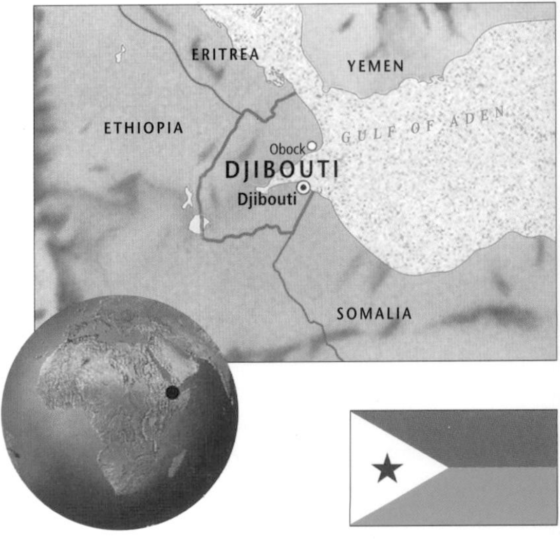

Fact File

OFFICIAL NAME Republic of Djibouti

FORM OF GOVERNMENT Republic with single legislative body (Chamber of Deputies)

CAPITAL Djibouti

AREA 22,000 sq km (8,494 sq miles)

TIME ZONE GMT + 3 hours

POPULATION 467,000

PROJECTED POPULATION 2015 703,000

POPULATION DENSITY 21.5 per sq km (55.0 per sq mile)

LIFE EXPECTANCY 51.6

INFANT MORTALITY (PER 1,000) 99.7

OFFICIAL LANGUAGES Arabic, French

OTHER LANGUAGES Somali, Afar

LITERACY RATE 46.2 %

RELIGIONS Muslim 94 %, Christian 6 %

ETHNIC GROUPS Somali 60 %, Afar 35 %, other (including French, Arab, Ethiopian, and Italian) 5 %

CURRENCY Djiboutian franc

ECONOMY Services 75 %, agriculture 14 %, industry 11 %

GNP PER CAPITA US$ 1,400

Climate Semiarid; particularly hot on coast

Highest point Mousa Alli (Musa Ālī Terara) 2,028 m (6,654 ft)

Map reference Page 367

One of the smallest African countries, Djibouti stands at the entrance to the Red Sea from the Gulf of Aden. This strategic location near the world's busiest shipping lanes has resulted in it being used as a base by European nations for a hundred years. After the construction of the Suez Canal, the British and French took an interest in Djibouti as a way of protecting their investment in the canal route to Europe, the town of Djibouti becoming the capital of French Somaliland in 1892. Although Djibouti won independence in 1977, France continues to play a role in its affairs and maintains a significant military presence in the country.

Since 1977 there has been a continuous political struggle between the majority Issa (who are Somali) and the minority Afar (also known as Danakil). Somalia, across the southeastern border, supports the Issa. Eritrea, to the north, supports the Afar, as does Ethiopia. Thus, both Issa and Afar have numerous external allies watching over their interests and inclined to interfere. The port of Djibouti is also the terminus of rail traffic for the vast landlocked hinterland of Ethiopia, a crucial matter for that state. Unrest among the Afars minority during the 1990s led to multi-party elections in 1999. A peace accord in 2001 ended the final phases of a ten-year uprising by Afar rebels.

Djibouti is one of the hottest places on earth, little rain falls, and water is in high demand. A subterranean river named the Ambouli is one essential source. Two-thirds of the population live in the capital city itself. Those who live elsewhere mostly inhabit the relatively fertile coastal strip along the Gulf of Tadjoura (Golfe de Tadjoura), avoiding the burning interior plateau and its volcanic wastes. Almost ninety percent of the interior terrain is desert, with a vegetation of scrub and desert thorns. Here, nomadic goat and camel herders eke out a living.

Djibouti's economy is that of a free trade zone providing essential services for the region. It has few natural resources (though geothermal energy is being developed, and natural gas has been found), little industry, and agricultural production mainly provides fruit and vegetables for domestic consumption. The services it renders are those of a transit port, of great value to Ethiopia and Somalia, and of an international depot and refueling center. Originally established by the French in the nineteenth century, the port is now being developed as a container facility.

Somalia

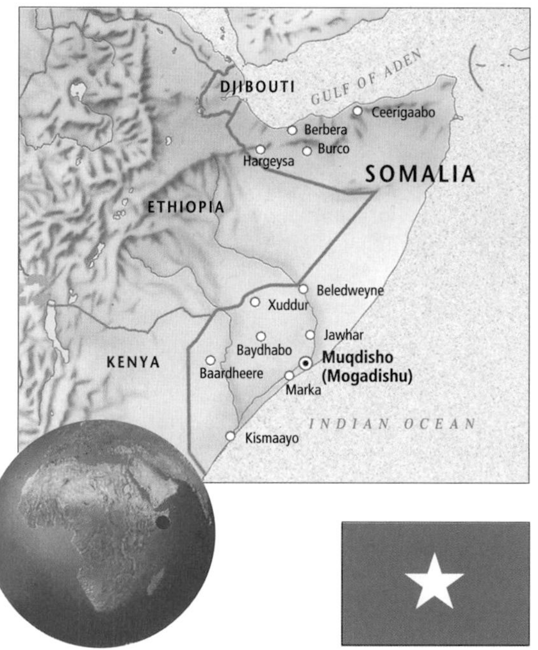

Fact File

Official name Somali Democratic Republic

Form of government Republic; no effective central government exists at the present time

Capital Muqdisho (Mogadishu)

Area 637,660 sq km (246,200 sq miles)

Time zone GMT + 3 hours

Population 7,754,000

Projected population 2015 15,405,000

Population density 12.2 per sq km (31.5 per sq mile)

Life expectancy 47

Infant mortality (per 1,000) 122.2

Official language Somali

Other languages Arabic, Italian, English

Literacy rate 37.8 %

Religions Sunni Muslim with tiny Christian minority

Ethnic groups Somali 85 %, remainder mainly Bantu with small Arab, Asian, and European minorities 15 %

Currency Somali shilling

Economy Agriculture 76 %, services 16 %, industry 8 %

GNP per capita US$ 550

Climate Mainly hot and arid, with higher rainfall in the south

Highest point Mt Shimbiris 2,416 m (7,927 ft)

Map reference Page 367

Somalia, a coastal state on the Horn of Africa, is in one respect unlike any other African country. It is the only place where the whole population feels that they are "one people"—Somali—and because of this ethnic homogeneity it has the makings of a nation state. Briefly under the control of Egypt from 1875, the region became a British protectorate in 1885. In 1889 Italy took control of the eastern coast, and from then on the country was divided into British Somaliland in the north and Italian Somaliland in the south and east. It has been independent since 1960.

Traders at the goat and donkey market in Lalibela, in northern Ethiopia (left page). An aerial view of the city of Djibouti, on the Gulf of Aden (below). A group of Somali villagers (above).

The history of the people of Somalia since independence has been one of repression (under the Soviet-aligned Siyad Barre), military adventure (the invasion of the Ethiopian Ogaden), and civil war. When in 1992 an estimated 2,000 people were dying from war and starvation each day, the United Nations intervened, but its troops were unable to stop the military and civil unrest and withdrew. Anarchy and banditry now prevail and Somalia is riddled by corruption. The power of the interim government ruling since 2000 is only recognized in Muqdisho. Warlords rule the rest of the country. In the absence of any central authority, and without a functioning government in Muqdisho, the northern area once known as British Somaliland seceded and proclaimed itself an independent state. Centered on the city of Hargeysa, it calls itself the Somaliland Republic. It has not been recognised internationally but has proven politically stable since 1998.

Along the northern shore facing the Gulf of Aden lies the semiarid Guban coastal plain. Behind this is a range of mountains, the Ogo Highlands, running eastward from Ethiopia to the point of the Horn itself. South of the highlands is the Haud Plateau, and beyond this the land slopes down toward the Indian Ocean. Much of Somalia has semidesert thornbush and dry savanna cover. Only in the better watered south is there enough rainfall to support meager forests and grassland. Arable farming takes place between the Rivers Jubba and Shabeelle in the south. The Shabeelle, blocked by dunes, provides water for irrigation. Bananas from this area are a major export, mainly to Italy. Rival clans fight over this important resource; some plantation work is done by women and children in slave-labor conditions guarded by armed militia.

Nomadic pastoralists form much of the population in the north. Searching for grass and water, they wander with their herds across the state boundaries between southern Djibouti, the Ogaden, and northeast Kenya. Livestock accounts for forty percent of gross domestic product and 65 percent of export earnings. In the south, in addition to the export crop of bananas, food crops of sugar, sorghum, and maize are grown. A small industrial sector is based on the processing of food products, but the prevailing disorder has caused many facilities to be shut down.

Uganda

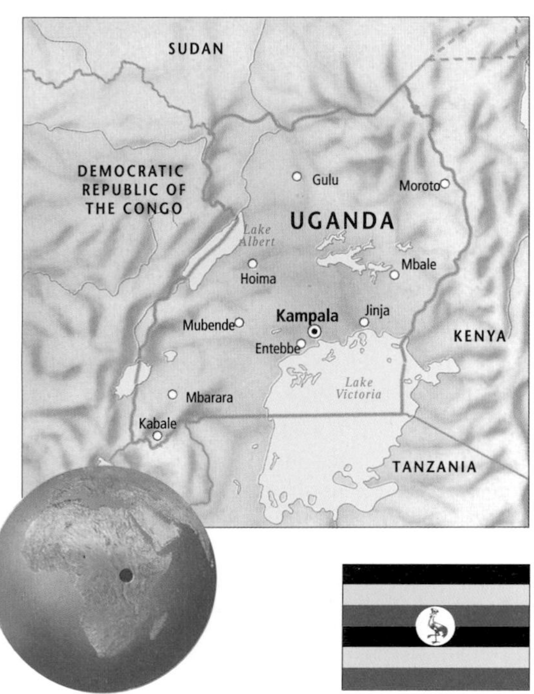

Fact File

OFFICIAL NAME Republic of Uganda

FORM OF GOVERNMENT Republic with single legislative body (National Assembly)

CAPITAL Kampala

AREA 236,040 sq km (91,135 sq miles)

TIME ZONE GMT + 3 hours

POPULATION 24,700,000

PROJECTED POPULATION 2015 38,739,000

POPULATION DENSITY 104.6 per sq km (271.0 per sq mile)

LIFE EXPECTANCY 43.8

INFANT MORTALITY (PER 1,000) 89.4

OFFICIAL LANGUAGE English

OTHER LANGUAGES Luganda, Swahili, Bantu and Nilotic languages

LITERACY RATE 62.7 %

RELIGIONS Roman Catholic 33 %, Protestant 33 %, indigenous beliefs 18 %, Muslim 16 %

ETHNIC GROUPS Indigenous tribal groups 99 % (mainly Ganda, Teso, Nkole, Nyoro, Soga), other 1 %

CURRENCY Ugandan shilling

ECONOMY Agriculture 86 %, services 10 %, industry 4 %

GNP PER CAPITA US$ 1,200

CLIMATE Tropical, with two wet seasons March to May and September to November; semiarid in northeast

HIGHEST POINT Mt Stanley 5,110 m (16,765 ft)

MAP REFERENCE Page 366

Extending north from Africa's largest body of water, Lake Victoria, the east African state of Uganda is a country of lakes and marshland. With a mild climate and varied resources—from fertile soil to freshwater fish to copper—it was once called "the pearl of Africa". After independence in 1962, however, its people suffered two decades of civil war, military coups, atrocities, and massacres, the worst period being the ten years under Idi Amin. It is estimated that between 1966 and Yoweri Museveni's takeover in 1986 more than half a million Ugandan inhabitants were killed.

The Museveni regime has overseen a return to peace and prosperity. Because the tribal basis of the old political parties was a cause of conflict, the government banned overt political activity, while inviting participation in a "one-party/no-party" policy of national unity. Multi-party elections in 1994, 1996, and 2001 returned and confirmed Museveni to power, but this taste of democracy created expectations of greater local autonomy. Some people are demanding the restoration of the region's traditional kingdoms.

Uganda's lake system is the source of the Nile. The pattern of lakes originates in the tilting and faulting of the Rift Valley, with the Ruwenzori Range on the western side of the country and the extinct volcano of Mt Elgon to the east. North of the lakes lies a savanna of trees and grassland, where farmers grow millet and sorghum for food, with cotton and tobacco as cash crops. Certain areas where cattle herding is impossible because of tsetse flies have been designated wildlife parks. Desert nomads live in arid Karamoja still further north. Coffee, tea, and sugarcane are grown in the south, which is the most fertile region and has the highest rainfall. This is the most densely settled part of the country, and is where the industrial center of Jinja is located, not far from Kampala, near the large Owen Falls hydroelectric plant.

Agriculture is the basis of the economy, with coffee the main export. Since 1986 the government has been engaged in raising producer prices for export crops, increasing prices for petroleum products (all oil must be imported), and raising civil service wages. Railways are being rebuilt. With the return of prosperity and public order, Indo-Ugandan entrepreneurs (expelled by the Obote and Amin regimes) are beginning to return from exile. The mining of gold and cobalt in the Ruwenzori region is also expected to resume.

Kenya

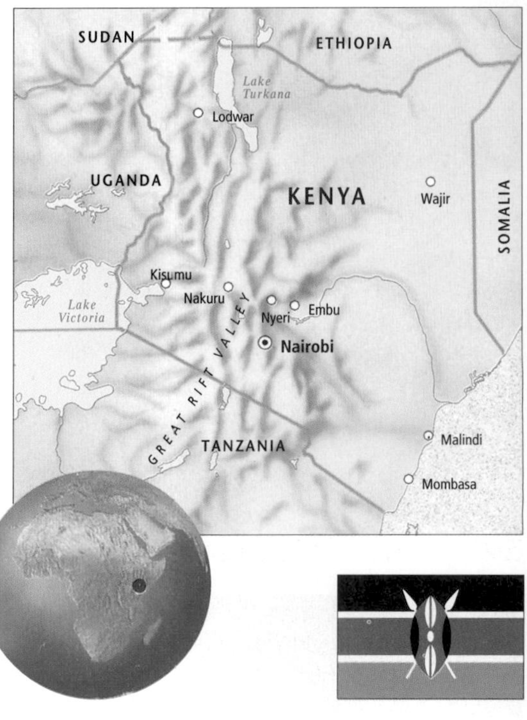

Fact File

OFFICIAL NAME Republic of Kenya

FORM OF GOVERNMENT Republic with single legislative body (National Assembly)

CAPITAL Nairobi

AREA 582,650 sq km (224,961 sq miles)

TIME ZONE GMT + 3 hours

POPULATION 31,139,000

PROJECTED POPULATION 2015 40,001,000

POPULATION DENSITY 53.4 per sq km (138.4 per sq mile)

LIFE EXPECTANCY 44.9

INFANT MORTALITY (PER 1,000) 67.2

OFFICIAL LANGUAGES English, Swahili

OTHER LANGUAGES Indigenous languages

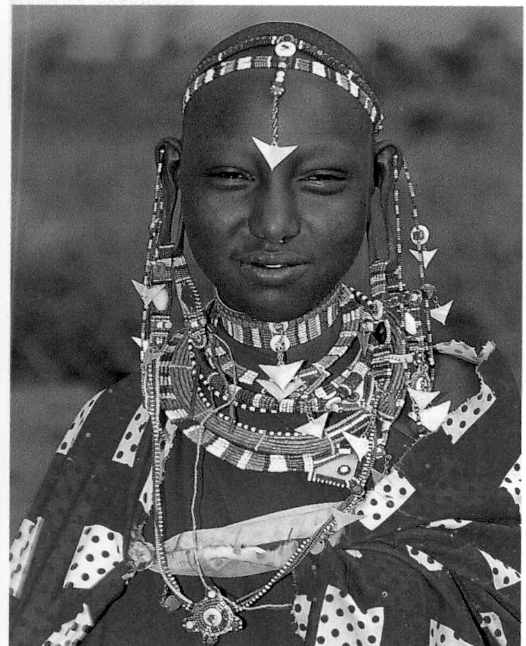

The Ruwenzoris in western Uganda, Africa's highest range of mountains (left page). Zebras in the Masai Mara National Reserve in Kenya (top). A Masai woman in traditional dress (above).

LITERACY RATE 78.1 %

RELIGIONS Protestant 38 %, Roman Catholic 28 %, indigenous beliefs 26 %, other 8 %

ETHNIC GROUPS Kikuyu 22 %, Luhya 14 %, Luo 13 %, Kalenjin 12 %, Kamba 11 %, Kisii 6 %, Meru 6 %, other 16 % (including Asian, European, Arab 1 %)

CURRENCY Kenya shilling

ECONOMY Agriculture 81 %, services 12 %, industry 7 %

GNP PER CAPITA US$ 1,000

CLIMATE Coastal regions tropical, with wet seasons April to May and October to November; inland plateau cooler and drier

HIGHEST POINT Mt Kenya 5,199 m (17,057 ft)

MAP REFERENCE Pages 368–69

Kenya, in east Africa, is where humankind may have originated: remains of humans and pre-humans found in the Olduvai Gorge on the border to Tanzania go back several million years. By the tenth century AD Arabs had settled along the coast, and in the nineteenth century both Britain and Germany became interested in the region. In 1920 Kenya became a British colony, the pleasant climate in the highlands attracting English immigrants who displaced Kikuyu farmers and took their land.

After the Second World War, widespread resentment at this expropriation erupted in the violent Mau Mau rebellion which lasted eight years. Independence came in 1963. Since then, control of the state and its resources has been contested by political parties allied with particular tribes, the domination of the Kikuyu yielding to a trial of multi-party democracy in 1991. The current government's main issue is the fight against corruption.

The Kenya Highlands consist of a fertile plateau formed by volcanoes and lava flows. The highlands are divided in two by the Rift Valley, the Eastern Highlands falling away toward the densely populated plain near Lake Victoria, and the Western Highlands descending to the valleys of the Tana and Galana Rivers as they cross the Nyika Plain to the north of Mombasa. The populous and fertile coastal belt is fringed by mangrove swamps, coral reefs, and groups of small islands. In the sparsely populated north toward Lake Turkana desert conditions prevail. Kenya's wildlife, consisting of the full range of African fauna, can be seen in the country's several large national parks, and has made it a leading destination for tourists for many years.

By African standards, Kenya has a stable and productive economy. It has a broad and highly successful agricultural base, with cash crops such as coffee and tea. It also has east Africa's largest and most diversified manufacturing sector, producing small-scale consumer goods such as plastics, furniture, batteries, textiles, and soap. But the country also has one of the world's highest rates of population growth: between 1988 and 2000 it experienced an 82 percent increase in population, a figure exceeded only by Haiti.

This continuous increase in the number of its citizens is accompanied by deforestation, lack of drinking water, and infrastructural breakdown. Floods have destroyed roads, bridges, and telecommunications. Crime, including the murder of visitors and ethnic massacres, has caused a steep decline in the number of tourists.

Tanzania

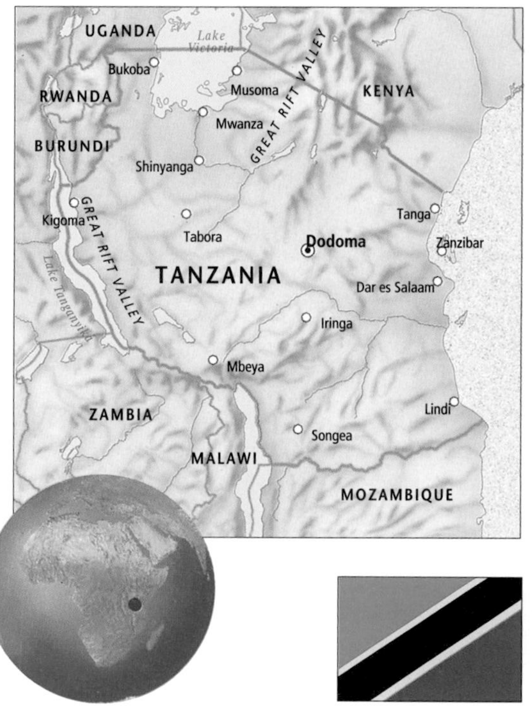

Fact File

OFFICIAL NAME United Republic of Tanzania

FORM OF GOVERNMENT Republic with single legislative body (National Assembly)

CAPITAL Dodoma

AREA 945,090 sq km (364,899 sq miles)

TIME ZONE GMT + 3 hours

POPULATION 37,188,000

PROJECTED POPULATION 2015 49,343,000

POPULATION DENSITY 39.3 per sq km (101.9 per sq mile)

LIFE EXPECTANCY 51.7

INFANT MORTALITY (PER 1,000) 77.9

OFFICIAL LANGUAGES Swahili, English

OTHER LANGUAGES Indigenous languages

LITERACY RATE 78.2 %

RELIGIONS Mainland: Christian 45 %, Muslim 35 %, indigenous beliefs 20 %; Zanzibar: Muslim 99 %, other 1 %

ETHNIC GROUPS Indigenous 99 %, other 1 %

CURRENCY Tanzanian shilling

ECONOMY Agriculture 86 %, services 9 %, industry 5 %

GNP PER CAPITA US$ 610

CLIMATE Mainly tropical; hot and humid along coast, drier inland, cooler in mountains

HIGHEST POINT Mt Kilimanjaro 5,895 m (19,340 ft)

MAP REFERENCE Page 369

With Africa's highest mountain (Kilimanjaro) and Serengeti National Park, Tanzania is well known to the outside world. It also the home of some of East Africa's most ancient human remains, those found at Olduvai Gorge on the Kenyan border dating back 2 million years. From the eighth century AD onward, the country's coastal region was subject to Islamic influence from Arab traders who dealt in slaves and ivory. In the nineteenth century British and German settlers arrived.

Tanzania won independence from England in 1961, becoming a de facto one-party state under Julius Nyerere, whose version of African socialism prevailed until he retired in 1985. Opposition parties were allowed in 1992. An uprising by pro-Tanzanian forces violently incorporated the Muslim island of Zanzibar in 1964: unreconciled Islamic interests on the island represent a potential flashpoint. In 1995 the first democratic elections held in the country since the 1970s put an end to the one-party rule. Since then, two more elections have been held and won by the ruling party. They were brought about because of Zanzibar's semi-autonomous status and popular opposition and were highly contentious. International observers claimed voting irregularities.

From the coast, Tanzania stretches across a plateau averaging about 1,000 m (3,000 ft) to the Rift Valley lakes of Malawi (Lake Nyasa) and Tanganyika. The eastern Rift Valley, with the alkaline Lake Natron, and Lakes Eyasi and Manyara, divides the Northern Highlands. These are dominated by Mt Kilimanjaro near the Kenyan border. The Southern Highlands overlook Lake Malawi (Lake Nyasa). Semiarid conditions in the north and tsetse flies in the west-central areas mean that people mainly live on the country's margins. Attempts to farm the savanna woodland have failed.

Though repressive, Nyerere's government achieved relatively high levels of education and welfare, but the economy languished as a result of falling commodity prices abroad and inefficient and corrupt state corporations at home. Over eighty percent of the workforce live off the land, producing cash crops such as coffee, tea, sisal, cotton, and pyrethrum, along with food crops of maize, wheat, cassava, and bananas. Since 1985 there has been some liberalization of the market, along with an effort to boost tourism and a substantial increase in gold production. Reforms have increased private sector growth and investment.

A crater lake in Volcanoes National Park, Rwanda (above). Mt Kilimanjaro, the highest mountain in Africa, is in Tanzania (below).

Rwanda

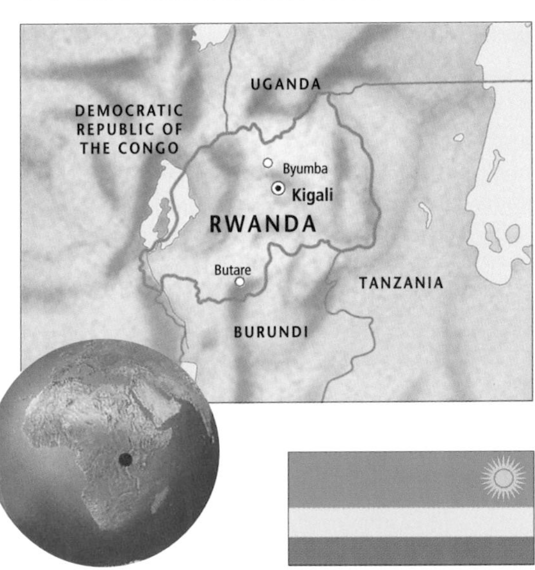

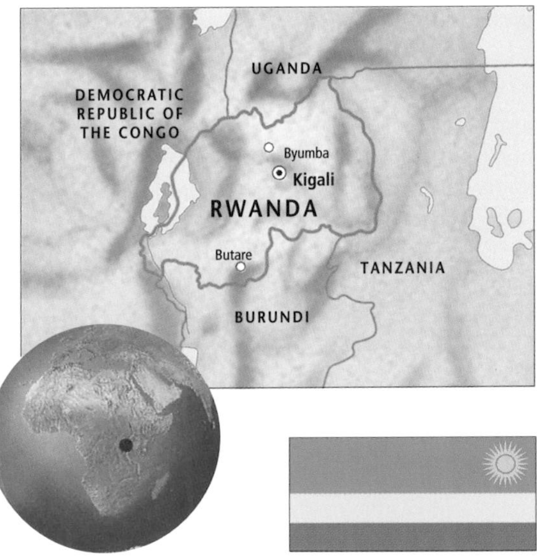

Fact File

Official name Republic of Rwanda

Form of government Republic with transitional legislative body (National Assembly)

Capital Kigali

Area 26,340 sq km (10,170 sq miles)

Time zone GMT + 2 hours

Population 7,398,000

Projected population 2015 10,504,000

Population density 280.9 per sq km (727.4 per sq mile)

Life expectancy 38.7

Infant mortality (per 1,000) 117.8

Official languages French, Kinyarwanda

Other language Swahili, English

Literacy rate 48.0 %

Religions Roman Catholic 65 %, Protestant 9 %, Muslim 1 %, indigenous beliefs and other 25 %

Ethnic groups Hutu 80 %, Tutsi 19 %, Twa (Pygmy) 1 %

Currency Rwandan franc

Economy Agriculture 93 %, services 5 %, industry 2 %

GNP per capita US$ 1,000

Climate Tropical, with two wet seasons (October to December and March to May)

Highest point Karisimbi 4,519 m (14,826 ft)

Map reference Page 369

A small landlocked country in central Africa, Rwanda shares much of its social history with Burundi, across its southern border. In the fifteenth and sixteenth centuries a tall cattle-herding people called Tutsi, probably from Sudan, came to the region and formed a small feudal aristocracy that dominated the more numerous Hutu farmers who had settled in the area some time before them. Since then, the Hutu people have endured the situation with

The endangered mountain gorilla still survives in the highlands of Rwanda (above). At the cloth market in Bujumbura, the capital of Burundi (below).

resentment. In recent times, beginning with a Hutu revolt in 1959 (independence from Belgium came in 1962), there have been decades of ethnic strife and intermittent violence, with hundreds of thousands of deaths occurring on both sides. This culminated in the massacre of approcimately 800,000 Tutsi (and also some moderate Hutu) by Hutu in 1994, waves of refugees spilling out into the Democratic Republic of Congo, Burundi, Tanzania, and Uganda. It took substantial international assistance and political reforms—including the first local elections in 1999 and the first post-genocide presidential and legislative elections in 2003—for the country to boost investment and agricultural output and to foster reconciliation. Massive population displacements, a Hutu extremist insurgency, and involvement in two wars in the neighboring Democratic Republic of the Congo continue to hinder Rwanda's efforts.

Rwanda is the most densely populated country in Africa. Almost thirty percent of the land is arable, steep slopes are intensively cultivated, and terracing and contour plowing are used in order to keep erosion to a minimum. Lake Kivu and a part of the southward-flowing Ruzizi River form the western boundary of the country. From here the land rises steeply to the mountains, part of the Rift Valley, which constitute the Nile-Congo divide. To the north are the mountains, and several volcanoes, of the Mufumbiro Range. These include one of the last refuges of the mountain gorilla. From the heights of the eastern rim of the Rift Valley a plateau slopes eastward toward the Tanzanian border, the River Kagera marshes, and a number of lakes.

During peacetime, Rwanda's production of coffee and tea constituted eighty to ninety percent of total exports. Pyrethrum and sugarcane are other cash crops, cassava, maize, bananas, sorghum, and vegetables being crops grown for food. In keeping with their history as former nomadic herders, the Tutsi people keep cattle. The Hutu generally keep sheep and goats. Arable land is overused and deforestation and soil erosion are widespread. Natural resources include gold, tin, tungsten, and natural gas, but they are undeveloped because of infrastructure and transport difficulties. Political and ethnic disorder have affected the economy which suffers from infrastructural damage, lack of maintenance, looting, and the widespread destruction of property and crops. Recovery of production to earlier levels will take time.

Burundi

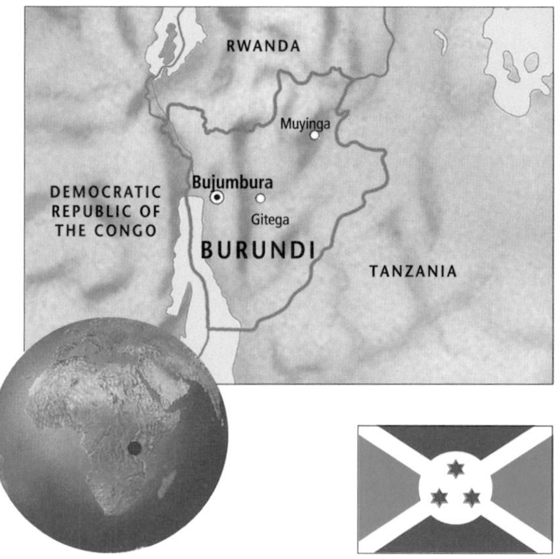

Fact File

Official name Republic of Burundi

Form of government Republic with single legislative body (National Assembly)

Capital Bujumbura

Area 27,830 sq km (10,745 sq miles)

Time zone GMT + 2 hours

Population 6,374,000

Projected population 2015 9,835,000

Population density 229.0 per sq km (593.2 per sq mile)

Life expectancy 45.9

Infant mortality (per 1,000) 70.0

Official languages Kirundi, French

Other languages Swahili

Literacy rate 35.3 %

Religions Roman Catholic 62 %, indigenous beliefs 32 %, Protestant 5 %, Muslim 1 %

Ethnic groups Hutu 85 %, Tutsi 14 %, Twa (Pygmy) 1%

Currency Burundi franc

Economy Agriculture 93 %, services 5.5 %, industry 1.5 %

GNP per capita US$ 600

Climate Tropical, with wet seasons March to May and September to December

Highest point Mt Heha 2,760 m (9,055 ft)

Map reference Page 369

Burundi is a small, landlocked country in central Africa. Some time in the past a tall cattle-herding people known as the Tutsi (or Watussi) moved into Burundi from the north. Originating on the Upper Nile, the Tutsi established themselves as a ruling class over the much more numerous and physically shorter Bantu farmers called Hutu. This deeply divided social order has been the source of periodic outbreaks of violence, hundreds of thousands of people having been massacred by both sides. The region's original inhabitants were the forest-dwelling Twa (or Pygmy), but few remain. A new transitional government, inaugurated in 2001, was to be the first step toward holding national elections in 2004.

Burundi's topography resembles other lands along the Rift Valley. A narrow strip along the northeastern shore of Lake Tanganyika forms one boundary, which then extends up the valley of the River Ruzizi in the direction of Lake Kivu. From this lowland area an escarpment rises steeply up to the highlands which make up the rest of the country. The mountainous ridge east of Lake Tanganyika forms a watershed between the river systems of the Congo and the Nile. On its eastern slopes the land then falls away into the valley of the Ruvuvu River as it makes its way toward Tanzania and Lake Victoria. Malaria in the lowlands is endemic, a situation the continuing civil disorder makes difficult to change.

About ninety percent of Burundi's people depend on subsistence agriculture, growing corn, sorghum, sweet potatoes, bananas, and manioc. The Tutsi herders produce meat and milk. Export earnings come mainly from coffee, which contributes 81 percent, along with tea, cotton grown in the Ruzizi Valley, and hides. Three factors affect foreign exchange earnings and government revenue: the vagaries of the climate, international coffee prices, and civil unrest. Even when the first two are favorable, the struggle between Tutsi and Hutu which has been a continuing feature of Burundi life since 1993 as well as the fact that approximately 670,000 refugees from the neighboring Rwanda and Democratic Republic of the Congo live here has virtually brought cash cropping to a halt. Under the direction of the International Monetary Fund the government has tried to diversify exports but continuing discord makes it difficult to implement reforms.

Southern Africa

Zambia

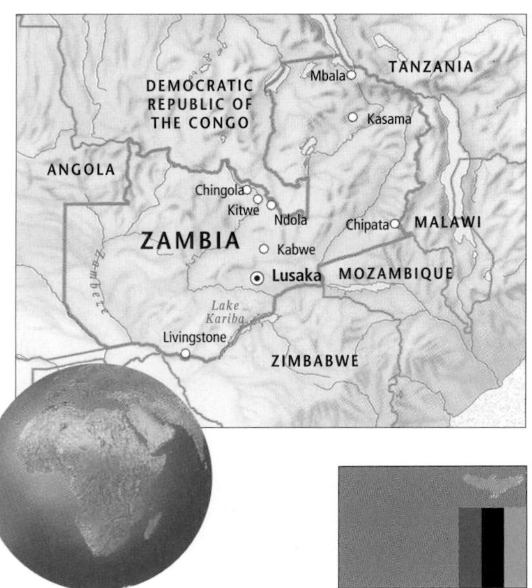

Fact File

OFFICIAL NAME Republic of Zambia

FORM OF GOVERNMENT Republic with single legislative body (National Assembly)

CAPITAL Lusaka

AREA 752,610 sq km (290,583 sq miles)

TIME ZONE GMT + 2 hours

POPULATION 9,960,000

PROJECTED POPULATION 2015 14,796,000

POPULATION DENSITY 13.2 per sq km (34.3 per sq mile)

LIFE EXPECTANCY 37.3

INFANT MORTALITY (PER 1,000) 89.4

OFFICIAL LANGUAGE English

OTHER LANGUAGES About seventy indigenous languages including Bemba, Kaonda, Lozi, Lunda, Luvale, Nyanja, Tonga

LITERACY RATE 78.9 %

RELIGIONS Protestant 84 %, Hindu 35 %, Roman Catholic 26 %, other including Muslim as well as indigenous beliefs 5 %

ETHNIC GROUPS Indigenous 98.7 %, European 1.1 %, other 0.2 %

CURRENCY Kwacha

ECONOMY Agriculture 85 %, services 9 %, industry 6 %

GNP PER CAPITA US$ 870

CLIMATE Tropical, with three seasons: cool and dry May to August, hot and dry August to November, wet December to April

HIGHEST POINT Mafinga Hills 2,301 m (7,549 ft)

MAP REFERENCE Pages 368–69, 370–71

Zambia is a landlocked country in south-central Africa. It stretches from Victoria Falls in the south to Lake Tanganyika in the north, and is one of the world's major copper producers. Ancestral branches of the Zambian Tonga first entered the area in the eighth century AD, but other African groups now living there are more recent arrivals—the Ngoni and Kololo came as fugitives from Zulu aggression in 1835. Formerly a British colony, and once known as Northern Rhodesia, Zambia became independent in 1964. From that year it was ruled for more than a quarter of a century by President Kaunda, who nationalized commerce and industry and built a one-party socialist state. In 1991, economic decline and political agitation led to Zambia's first free elections. Kaunda was defeated, but even though international observers criticized irregularities in the elections of 1996 and 2001 it looks like democracy prevails. Currently opposition groups hold a majority of the seats in the National Assembly. Since 2002 a large-scale anti-corruption campaign has been in place.

A wide expanse of high plateau broken by scattered mountains and valleys, Zambia is drained by the Zambeze in the west and south, where the river forms a boundary with Zimbabwe and Namibia. Below Victoria Falls the Zambeze is dammed at the Kariba Gorge to form one of the largest artificial lakes in the world, Lake Kariba. Power from the Lake Kariba hydroelectric station is shared with Zimbabwe. Another major river, the Luangwa, runs southwest from the Malawi border down a broad rift valley to join the Zambeze at the frontier of Mozambique.

Compared with its neighbors, Zambia has a high ratio of urban dwellers who are dependent on the rural sector for food. Commercial farming of maize in the central districts, and other food crops such as sorghum and rice, is proving insufficient to meet their needs. This situation has been aggravated both by drought and the phasing out of agricultural subsidies.

Zambia is dependent on copper production, which accounts for over eighty percent of export earnings. Production is down, however, and so are world copper prices, which is intensifying the difficulties caused by high inflation and shrinking internal food supplies. In the post-Kaunda years there has been some attempt at privatization and budgetary reform, but this has produced little improvement. In 1995 four of Zambia's twenty banks failed. Most export earnings go towards paying off the 7 billion dollar external debt—itself to some extent a product of bureaucratic misuse of funds.

Malawi

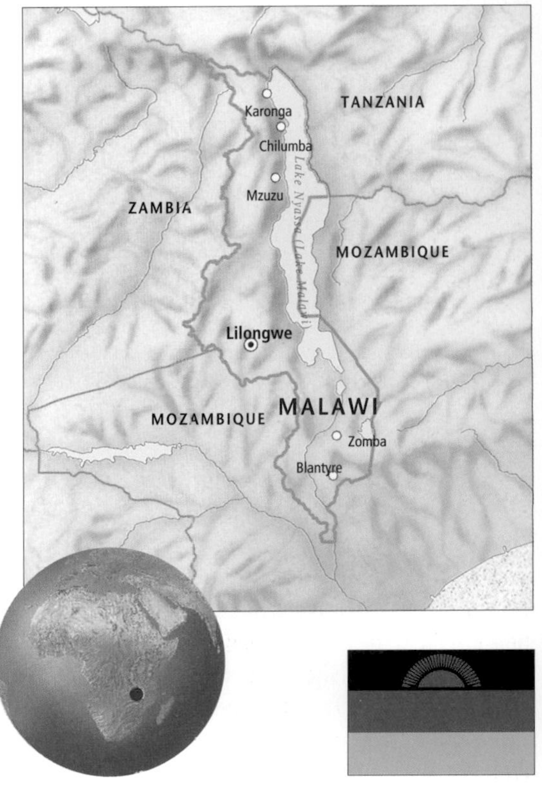

Fact File

OFFICIAL NAME Republic of Malawi

FORM OF GOVERNMENT Republic with single legislative body (National Assembly)

CAPITAL Lilongwe

AREA 118,480 sq km (45,745 sq miles)

TIME ZONE GMT + 2 hours

POPULATION 10,702,000

PROJECTED POPULATION 2015 15,656,000

POPULATION DENSITY 90.3 per sq km (233.9 per sq mile)

LIFE EXPECTANCY 36.6

INFANT MORTALITY (PER 1,000) 120.0

OFFICIAL LANGUAGES Chichewa, English

OTHER LANGUAGES Indigenous languages

LITERACY RATE 58 %

RELIGIONS Protestant 55 %, Roman Catholic 20 %, Muslim 20 %, indigenous beliefs 5 %

ETHNIC GROUPS Indigenous tribes: Malavi (including Chewa, Nyanja, Tumbuke, Tonga) 58 %, Lomwe 18 %, Yao 13 %, Ngoni 7 %; Asian and European 4 %

CURRENCY Kwacha

ECONOMY Agriculture 82 %, services 15 %, industry 3 %

GNP PER CAPITA US$ 660

CLIMATE Tropical, with wet season November to April

HIGHEST POINT Mt Mulanje 3,002 m (9,849 ft)

MAP REFERENCE Page 369

Malawi is a hilly and in places mountainous country at the southern end of Africa's Rift Valley, one-fifth of it consisting of Lake Malawi (Lake Nyasa). The lake contains 500 fish species which support a sizeable fishing industry. Most of the country's people are descended from the

Bantu who settled the area centuries ago. Arab slave-trading was suppressed by the incoming British in 1887–89, and in 1907 the country became the British Protectorate of Nyasaland. Independence in 1964 put Dr Hastings Banda in charge and he ruled dictatorially for thirty years. Cumulative difficulties, including drought and crop failures, some 800,000 refugees from Mozambique, and resentment at the apparent assassination of political opponents, led to Dr Banda's removal and Malawi's first multi-party elections in 1994.

At the southern end of Lake Malawi (Lake Nyasa) the Shire River runs through a deep, swampy valley flanked by mountains to the east. Most of the population lives in this southern region, growing maize as the main food crop and cultivating cash crops such as peanuts and sugarcane. The western central plateau rises northward to the Nyika Uplands, where rainfall is highest. In the Shire Highlands to the south, tea and tobacco are grown on large estates. Savanna grassland in the valleys gives way to open woodland, much of which has been cleared for cultivation. Wildlife is largely confined to reserves.

Agriculture provides more than ninety percent of exports. Reserves of bauxite and uranium exist, but not in commercially usable quantities. Hydroelectricity supplies only about three percent of total energy use—most needs are met from fuelwood, which is resulting in continued deforestation. The economy depends heavily on foreign aid.

Mozambique

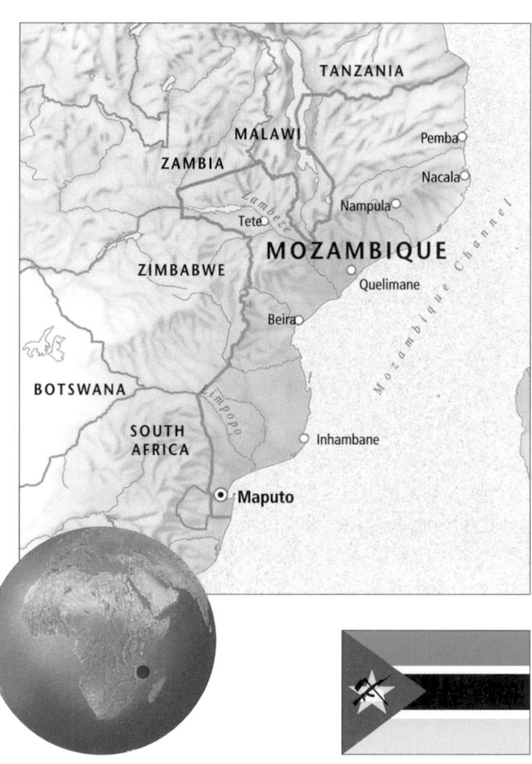

Fact File

OFFICIAL NAME Republic of Mozambique

FORM OF GOVERNMENT Republic with single legislative body (Assembly of the Republic)

CAPITAL Maputo

AREA 801,590 sq km (309,494 sq miles)

TIME ZONE GMT + 2 hours

POPULATION 19,608,000

PROJECTED POPULATION 2015 23,526,000

POPULATION DENSITY 24.5 per sq km (63.4 per sq mile)

LIFE EXPECTANCY 35.5

INFANT MORTALITY (PER 1,000) 138.6

OFFICIAL LANGUAGE Portuguese

OTHER LANGUAGES Indigenous languages

LITERACY RATE 42.3 %

RELIGIONS Indigenous beliefs 50 %, Christian 30 %, Muslim 20 %

ETHNIC GROUPS Indigenous tribes (including Shangaan, Chokwe, Manyika, Sena, Makua) 99.7 %, other 0.3 %

CURRENCY Metical

ECONOMY Agriculture 85 %, services 8 %, industry 7 %

GNP PER CAPITA US$ 900

CLIMATE Mainly tropical: wet season December to March

HIGHEST POINT Monte Binga 2,436 m (7,992 ft)

MAP REFERENCE Pages 369, 371

Lying on the southeast coast of Africa facing Madagascar, Mozambique is divided in two by the Zambeze River. This division is also found in its social and political life: people in the north support the Renamo party, while south of the river they support Frelimo. Visited by Vasco da Gama in 1498 and colonized by the Portuguese in search of gold, Mozambique remained a slave-trading center until the 1850s.

A long war of liberation against Portugal led to independence in 1975 and brought the Marxist Frelimo (Mozambique liberation front) to power. Frelimo's one-party regime was then challenged by a guerilla movement, Renamo, supported by South Africa. The ensuing civil war, aggravated by famine, led to nearly 1 million deaths. By 1989 Mozambique was world's poorest country. That year Frelimo renounced Marxism. At multi-party elections in 1994 it won by a narrow majority.

A considerable amount of rain falls in the north; south of the Zambeze conditions are much drier. North of Maputo, the only natural harbor, is a wide coastal plain where there are coconut, sugar, and sisal plantations, and small landholders grow maize and peanuts. Inland, the terrain rises to the high veld.

Economically, Mozambique faces a huge task of reconstruction and the government is trying to redistribute large areas of land that were seized by the state to peasants. Agricultural output is only 75 percent of its 1981 level and grain is imported. Industry is operating at less than half capacity. There are substantial agricultural, hydropower and petroleum resources as well as deposits of coal, copper and bauxite but these are largely undeveloped.

Lake Malawi (Lake Nyasa), near Chilumba, looking toward Mozambique (above). The massive Victoria Falls on the Zambeze River in Zimbabwe (below).

Zimbabwe

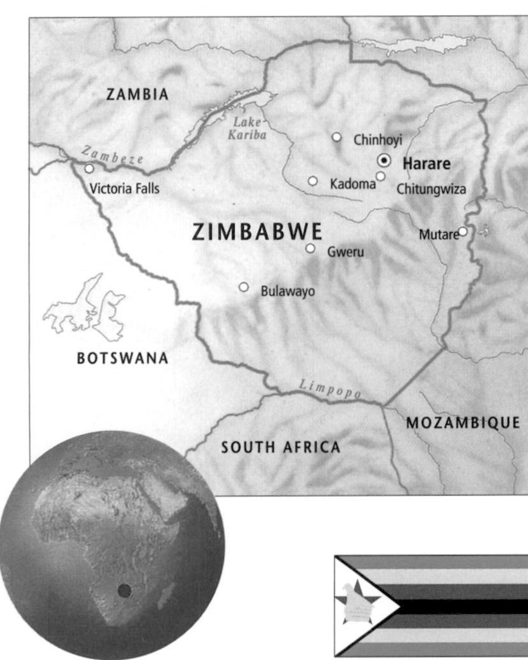

Zimbabwe is a landlocked country south of Zambia. Zimbabwe means "house of the chief" in the Shona language and refers to what are known as the Great Ruins, built by Bantu peoples in the country's south and thought to date from the ninth century AD. The country's two main tribes today, the minority Ndebele (popularly known as Matabele) and the majority Shona, arrived as nineteenth-century fugitives from the warlike expansion of the Zulus under King Shaka.

British settlement began in the 1890s, and there were 280,000 whites in the country in 1965 when their leader, Ian Smith, declared independence from the UK. African guerrilla action to overthrow Smith led to black majority rule in 1980. Since then the government has been led by Robert Mugabe, a Shona. Though he renounced Marxism-Leninism in 1991, and market reforms are on the agenda, during the 1990s Zimbabwe has edged closer to being a de facto one-party state. After the introduction of more democratic measures Mugabe returned to a more and more dictatorial style of government. In order to strengthen his position in 2000 he forced white farmers from their land and redistributed it to his followers. The elections for parliament in 2001 as well as the presidential elections of 2002 were rigged, ignoring international protest. Opposition and labor groups launched general strikes in 2003 to pressure Mugabe to retire but security forces continued their brutal repression of opponents.

Some 25 percent of the country consists of a broad mountainous ridge known as the High Veld, which crosses the country southwest to northeast. On the northeastern Mozambique border it climbs to the peak of Inyangani. The rolling plateaus of the middle veld fall gently away north and south of this central upland, reaching the riverine low veld regions near the Limpopo River in the south and the Zambeze in the north. On the northern border the Zambeze plunges over Victoria Falls into a number of gorges. The falls, with Lake Kariba further downriver, along with several national parks, are among Zimbabwe's principal tourist attractions. Almost forty percent of electricity needs are met by hydroelectric power, much of it from the Kariba Dam facility shared with Zambia.

Zimbabwe's near self-sufficiency in food is a by-product of the trade boycotts and economic isolation imposed on the white minority regime of Ian Smith after 1965. This forced both agriculture and manufacturing to diversify. African farms are still mainly small-scale subsistence operations, growing maize, cassava, and wheat. Large-scale enterprises produce most of the cash crops such as tobacco, cotton, and sugarcane, and earn much of agriculture's 35 percent share of national export revenue. Zimbabwe's mineral resources include coal, chromium, asbestos, gold, nickel, copper, iron, vanadium, lithium, tin, and platinum. Mining employs only five percent of the workforce, but minerals and metals account for about forty percent of exports.

Fact File

Official name Republic of Zimbabwe

Form of government Republic with single legislative body (Parliament)

Capital Harare

Area 390,580 sq km (150,803 sq miles)

Time zone GMT + 2 hours

Population 11,377,000

Projected population 2015 16,338,000

Population density 29.1 per sq km (75.4 per sq mile)

Life expectancy 36.5

Infant mortality (per 1,000) 63.0

Official language English

Other languages Shona, Ndebele

Literacy rate 85 %

Religions Mixed Christian-indigenous beliefs 50 %, Christian 25 %, indigenous beliefs 24 %, Muslim and other 1 %

Ethnic groups Indigenous 98 % (Shona 71 %, Ndebele 16 %, other 11 %), European 1 %, other 1 %

Currency Zimbabwean dollar

Economy Agriculture 65 %, services 29 %, industry 6 %

GNP per capita US$ 2,450

Climate Tropical, moderated by altitude; wet season November to March

Highest point Inyangani 2,592 m (8,504 ft)

Map reference Page 371

Botswana

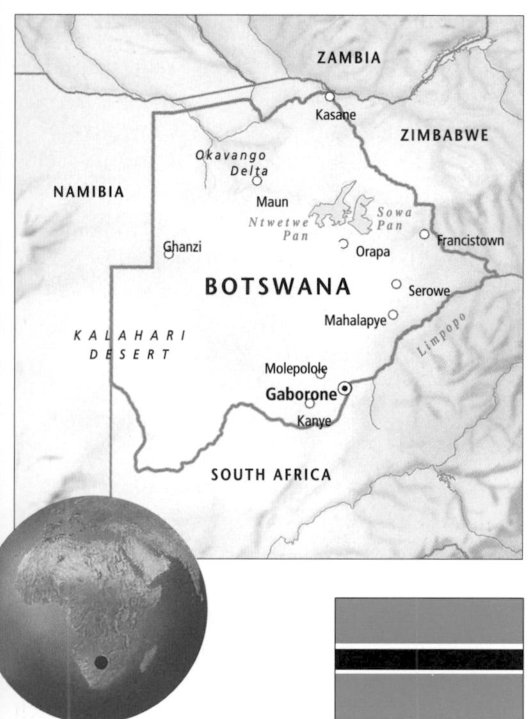

Fact File

Official name Republic of Botswana

Form of government Republic with two legislative bodies (House of Chiefs and National Assembly)

Capital Gaborone

Area 600,370 sq km (231,803 sq miles)

Time zone GMT + 2 hours

Population 1,592,000

Projected population 2015 1,694,000

Population density 2.7 per sq km (6.9 per sq mile)

Life expectancy 35.3

Infant mortality (per 1,000) 64.7

Official language English

Other languages Setswana and other indigenous languages

Literacy rate 69.8 %

Religions Indigenous beliefs 50 %, Christian 50 %

The Round House, one of the Great Ruins in Zimbabwe built by Bantu peoples (left). Zimbabwean dancers in masks and traditional dress (left page bottom left). Lions and vultures around a kill in Chobe National Park in northern Botswana (left page bottom right).

Ethnic groups Tswana 94 %, Khoikhoin 2.5 %, Ndebele 1.3 %, other 2.2 %

Currency Pula

Economy Services 51 %, mining and agriculture 49 %

GNP per capita US$ 7,800

Climate Semiarid to arid, with warm winters and hot summers

Highest point Tsodilo Hill 1,489 m (4,885 ft)

Map reference Pages 370–71

A large, dry, landlocked tableland, Botswana is bordered on the south by South Africa, a country with which it has strong historical and economic links. To the west is Namibia (the border touches on Zambia in the north near Victoria Falls) and to the northeast lies a 600 km (370 mile) frontier with Zimbabwe. Originally peopled by the nomadic San, also known as Bushmen, Botswana's more fertile eastern parts later became settled by Bantu Tswana. In the nineteenth century, after gold had been discovered near the Tati River, the area became the focus of a colonial dispute between the British and the Boers of neighboring Transvaal (now Gauteng) in South Africa. Britain established the British Bechuanaland Protectorate in 1885. This name and status within the British Empire was retained until independence in 1966, when Bechuanaland became Botswana.

Geographically a part of the Southern African Plateau, more than half of Botswana consists of the Kalahari Desert. Substantial parts of the remainder of the country consist of saltpans and swamps. There is little surface water except in the north and east, in the basins of the Okavango, Chobe, and Limpopo Rivers. Variations in climate and a limited rainfall enable a certain amount of scrub and thornbush to grow in the Kalahari. The dominant vegetation in Botswana

African wildlife

Nowhere on earth is there anything to equal the variety of African wildlife, much of which can still be seen in a natural setting. There are ninety species of hoofed mammal alone, including a tremendous variety of antelope, from the giant eland to the swift impala. Africa is home to the world's fastest animal, the cheetah, and also the world's largest land animal, the African elephant. In the giraffe it has the tallest animal in the world, while Africa's chimpanzees and gorillas represent families of primates closer to *Homo sapiens* than any others.

The future welfare of African wildlife is a matter of major international concern. Today, many animals only survive in the many national parks throughout the continent, the oldest and best-known being Kruger National Park in South Africa. Kenya's parks include the 20,000 sq km (8,000 sq mile) expanse of Tsavo, one of the biggest. Tanzania's Serengeti National Park has unrivaled herds of antelope, and the migratory movements of wildebeest amid lions, leopards and other predators—not to mention crocodiles in the rivers—provide a glimpse of life on the grasslands of east Africa as it has been for thousands of years.

Only one large African mammal is known to have become extinct in historical times: this is an antelope called the blaubok. However, there were so few white rhinoceros at the end of the nineteenth century that they were thought to be extinct. Then a few were discovered in the South African province of Natal, and as a result of careful protection in South African national parks their numbers had grown to 6,375 by 1994. Outside South Africa very few white rhinoceros have survived: there may be no more than eighty in Kenya. A number of other animals are endangered, including the critically endangered mountain gorillas found only in small regions in the Democratic Republic of the Congo, Uganda, and Rwanda.

In the early twentieth century professional hunters from Europe and America depleted great numbers of animals such as lion, rhinoceros, and buffalo. Today, the main threat comes from Africans themselves. Pastoral people kill wildlife because antelope compete for grassland with their cattle. Many mountain gorillas died during the civil wars in Rwanda in the 1990s. Most killing in Kenya and Tanzania is done by poachers seeking decorative skins, ivory, and rhino horn. Although the killings are illegal, there is a great demand for these items on the international market and they fetch very high prices, especially when one considers the poverty that reigns in these countries. A 2 kg (4 lb) rhino horn sells for up to US$ 122,000 in Asia, where in powdered form it is valued as an aphrodisiac. It is estimated that in the last two decades 40,000 rhinos have been killed for their horns.

The management of wild animal populations is not easy. After policies designed to ensure the survival of elephants were followed in Tsavo National Park, herds grew until there are now too many elephants for the land to support. This is damaging the habitat of other native species.

A typical kraal (village) in Swaziland (left). A traditional dugout boat on the shore of the Okavango River in Botswana (below). A village in the Maluti Mountains foothills in Lesotho (right page).

is savanna grassland, which provides sufficient grazing for about 100,000 widely scattered Bantu cattle herders to make a living.

At the time of independence, cattle were almost the country's only export, and Botswana was one of the poorest countries in the world. Since that time the economy has been transformed by the development of mining. Both copper and nickel are exported but the main earner has been diamonds, providing as much as eighty percent of export revenue. Tourism is also important as the seventeen percent of Botswana's land area that is given over to national parks and game reserves attracts numerous visitors. A large proportion of the population still live as subsistence farmers raising cattle and growing crops such as maize, sorghum, vegetables, and fruit. Difficulties include an unemployment rate of twenty percent, overgrazing, and desertification. Botswana also suffers from having the world's highest rate of AIDS/HIV infections: forty percent of the population. The disease, however, is fought with the most progressive and comprehensive programs.

Swaziland

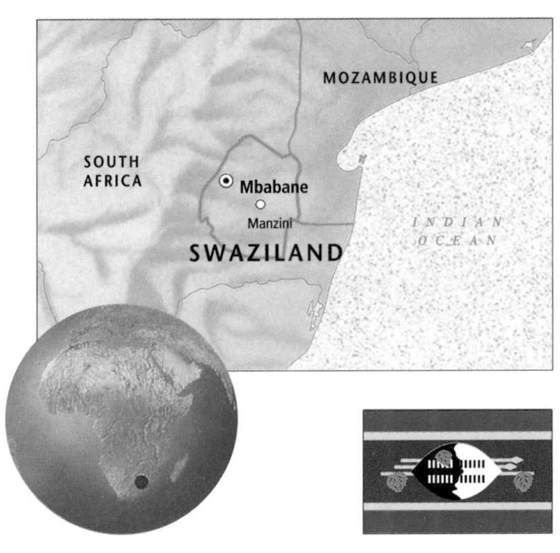

Fact File

OFFICIAL NAME Kingdom of Swaziland

FORM OF GOVERNMENT Monarchy with two legislative bodies (Senate and House of Assembly)

CAPITAL Mbabane

AREA 17,360 sq km (6,703 sq miles)

TIME ZONE GMT + 2 hours

POPULATION 1,124,000

PROJECTED POPULATION 2015 1,363,000

POPULATION DENSITY 64.7 per sq km (167.7 per sq mile)

LIFE EXPECTANCY 37

INFANT MORTALITY (PER 1,000) 109.4

OFFICIAL LANGUAGES English, Swazi

OTHER LANGUAGES Minority languages

LITERACY RATE 78.3 %

RELIGIONS Christian 60 %, indigenous beliefs 40 %

ETHNIC GROUPS Indigenous 97 %, European 3 %

CURRENCY Lilangeni

ECONOMY Agriculture 60 %, industry and services 40 %

GNP PER CAPITA US$ 4,200

CLIMATE Temperate, with wet season November to March

HIGHEST POINT Emlembe Peak 1,862 m (6,109 ft)

MAP REFERENCE Page 371

Swaziland is a tiny landlocked kingdom almost surrounded by South Africa. Across its eastern border it is about 130 km (80 miles) from the Indian Ocean and the Mozambique port of Maputo. Enjoying relative stability and prosperity, popular among South African tourists for its wildlife reserves, mountain scenery, and casinos, the kingdom's hereditary Bantu monarchy—one of the oldest on the African continent—is now being pressed to modernize and accept constitutional reforms. In 1977 King Sobhuza II dissolved the parliament and assumed absolute power. His son, King Mswati III since 1986, showed little interest in accepting the reforms demanded by widespread student protests during the 1990s. In 1998 he allowed general elections for 55 representatives who, together with ten members appointed by the king, form the parliament. However, he continues to rule autocratically and only grudgingly admits any democratic reforms.

The country owes its autonomy to events in the mid-nineteenth century. The Swazi were then facing Zulu expansion, as well as pressure from Boer farmers. They sought and received British protection, and from 1906 Swaziland became a British protectorate and was administered by the high commissioner for Basutoland (now Lesotho), Bechuanaland (now Botswana), and Swaziland. Full independence came in 1968.

The landscape descends in three steps from west to east. The high veld in the west is mountainous with a temperate climate, and supports grasslands and plantations of pine and eucalyptus. Mixed farming takes place in the middle veld, the most populous area, where black Swazi subsistence farmers grow maize, sorghum, and peanuts. Cash crops such as sugarcane, citrus fruits, and tobacco are produced by often white-run agribusinesses and by Swazi on resettlement schemes. Livestock are raised on the low veld.

Swaziland's economy is relatively diversified and buoyant: during the 1980s it grew at a rate of 4.5 percent a year. Relaxed investment rules have ensured a supply of development capital, and project aid has been forthcoming from a number of donors. Sugar and forestry products are the main earners of hard currency, and are produced by white residents on large plantations. The country has small deposits of gold and diamonds. Mining was once important, but is now in decline. The high-grade iron ore deposits were depleted by 1978 and health concerns have cut the demand for asbestos. Remittances from workers living in South Africa provide up to twenty percent of household income. The main threat to the Swazi way of life comes from land pressure due to high population growth. Family planning is being promoted.

Lesotho

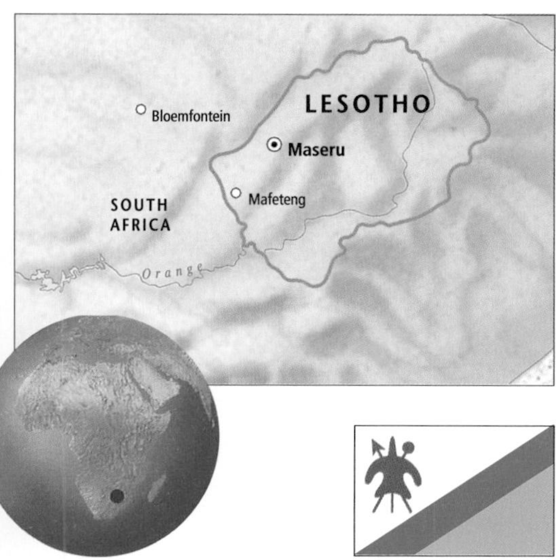

Fact File

OFFICIAL NAME Kingdom of Lesotho

FORM OF GOVERNMENT Constitutional monarchy with two legislative houses (Senate and National Assembly)

CAPITAL Maseru

AREA 30,350 sq km (11,718 sq miles)

TIME ZONE GMT + 2 hours

POPULATION 2,208,000

PROJECTED POPULATION 2015 2,621,000

POPULATION DENSITY 72.8 per sq km (188.4 per sq mile)

LIFE EXPECTANCY 47

INFANT MORTALITY (PER 1,000) 82.6

OFFICIAL LANGUAGES Sesotho, English

OTHER LANGUAGES Zulu, Afrikaans, French, Xhosa

LITERACY RATE 83 %

RELIGIONS Christian 80 %, indigenous beliefs 20 %

ETHNIC GROUPS Sotho 99.7 %, European and Asian 0.3 %

CURRENCY Loti

ECONOMY Agriculture 73 %, services and industry 27 %

GNP PER CAPITA US$ 2,450

CLIMATE Temperate, with cool, dry winters and hot, wet summers

HIGHEST POINT Thabana-Ntlenyana 3,482 m (11,424 ft)

MAP REFERENCE Page 371

Lesotho is a small landlocked country entirely surrounded by South Africa. Formerly the British Protectorate of Basutoland, it is the only country in the world where all the land is higher than 1,000 m (3,300 ft). About two-thirds of the terrain is mountainous, and at higher altitudes it often snows throughout the winter. As the head of a fragile constitutional monarchy, the king of Lesotho has no executive or legislative powers: traditionally, he could be elected or deposed by a majority vote of the College of Chiefs. Proposals to unite Lesotho with post-apartheid South Africa have been resisted by members of the population who feel an independent state will better defend their cultural heritage. In 1998, violent protests and a military mutiny following a contentious election prompted a brief but bloody South African military intervention. Constitutional reforms have since restored political stability; peaceful parliamentary elections were held in 2002.

A high mountainous plateau declining from east to west, Lesotho's highest ridges were formed on basaltic lavas. Treeless, with steep valleys, the wet highlands are soft and boggy in summer and frozen in winter. Numerous river valleys and gorges dissect the plateau, among them the River Orange. To the northwest the border of the country is defined by the Caledon River. This is flanked by a 30 to 65 km (18 to 40 mile) strip of fertile land which supports most of Lesotho's farmers and provides the bulk of its agriculturally useful land. Subsistence crops include maize, sorghum, wheat, and beans. Sheep and goats are kept for wool and mohair on the high plateau.

Lesotho is without important natural resources other than water. Hopes are held for the future of a major hydroelectric facility, the Highlands Water Scheme, which will sell water to South Africa and become a major employer and revenue earner. The scheme will supply all of Lesotho's energy requirements. In scattered hamlets, cottage industry produces woven mohair rugs. Manufacturing based on farm products consists of milling, canning, and the preparation of leather and jute. Roughly sixty percent of Lesotho's male wage earners work across the border in South Africa, mostly as laborers in mines. The wages they send back provide some 45 percent of domestic income.

Namibia

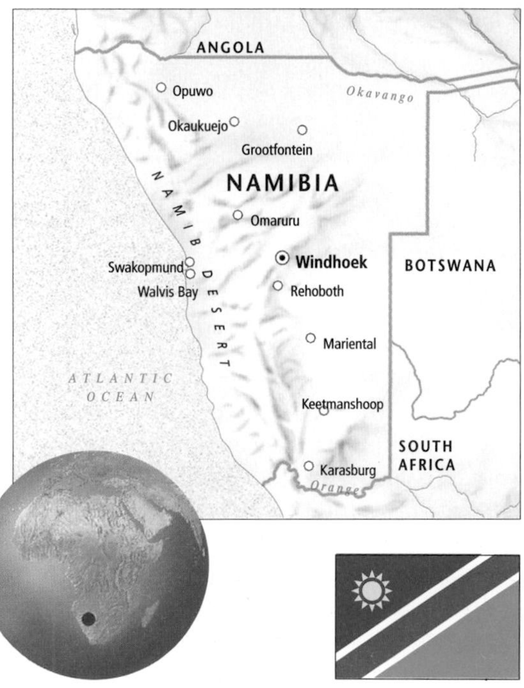

Fact File

OFFICIAL NAME Republic of Namibia

FORM OF GOVERNMENT Republic with two legislative bodies (National Council and National Assembly)

CAPITAL Windhoek

AREA 825,418 sq km (318,694 sq miles)

TIME ZONE GMT + 2 hours

POPULATION 1,821,000

PROJECTED POPULATION 2015 2,313,000

POPULATION DENSITY 2.2 per sq km (5.7 per sq mile)

LIFE EXPECTANCY 39

INFANT MORTALITY (PER 1,000) 72.4

OFFICIAL LANGUAGE English

OTHER LANGUAGES Afrikaans, German, indigenous languages

LITERACY RATE 38.0 %

RELIGIONS Christian 85 % (Lutheran at least 50 %, other Christian denominations 35 %), indigenous beliefs 15 %

ETHNIC GROUPS Indigenous tribes 86 % (including Ovambo 50 %, Kavangos 9 %, Herero 7 %, Damara 7 %), mixed indigenous-European 7.4 %, European 6.6 %

CURRENCY Namibian dollar

ECONOMY Agriculture 60 %, industry and commerce 19 %, services 8 %, government 7 %, mining 6 %

GNP PER CAPITA US$ 4,500

CLIMATE Mainly arid, with higher rainfall inland

HIGHEST POINT Konigstein 2,606 m (8,550 ft)

MAP REFERENCE Page 370

A large, arid country in southwest Africa, Namibia was born of the European scramble for colonies in the nineteenth century. The German connection with the area (formerly South West Africa) began with the arrival of missionaries in the 1840s. Namibia was a German protectorate from 1884; the scene of a brutal German punitive action in 1904 in which the Herero were decimated—approximately 60,000 were killed—and scattered; under South African control for many years; and endured 23 years of a bitter anti-colonial war that began in 1966. In 1989 an election gave the guerrilla movement SWAPO (the South West African People's Organization) victory at the polls, and in 1990 came independence.

The virtually uninhabited sand dunes of the Namib Desert fringe the country's south Atlantic coastline. A major escarpment inland separates the desert from a north-south range of mountains that includes the Tsaris Mountains, Aûas Mountains, and Mt Erongo. The interior plateau, which occupies the eastern part of the country, has an average elevation of 1,500 m (5,000 ft) and is covered with the dry scrub grassland typical of the Kalahari Desert. Largely rainless, the coast is often shrouded in fog. Here, welwitschia plants, some of them up to 2,000 years old, live by absorbing moisture from the fog that rolls in from the sea. Namibia's wildlife is typical of southern Africa, with Etosha National Park providing sanctuary for baboon, antelope, elephant, giraffe, zebra, and lion.

Namibia's natural resources include diamonds, copper, uranium (world's fifth largest producer), gold, lead (world's second largest producer), tin, lithium, cadmium, zinc, vanadium, and natural gas, and there are thought to be deposits of oil, coal, and iron ore. Mining accounts for 25 percent of gross domestic product, this sector relying on the expertise of Namibia's small white population. More than half its African peoples depend on agriculture for a livelihood, working poor soils in an unfavorable climate. Livestock farmers produce beef and mutton. About half the country's food is imported, mainly from South Africa.

High-rise buildings in Pretoria, the South African capital (below). An elephant browsing in Kruger National Park (right page).

South Africa

Fact File

OFFICIAL NAME Republic of South Africa

FORM OF GOVERNMENT Republic with two legislative bodies (Senate and National Assembly)

CAPITAL Pretoria (administrative); Cape Town (legislative); Bloemfontein (judicial)

AREA 1,219,912 sq km (471,008 sq miles)

TIME ZONE GMT + 2 hours

POPULATION 43,648,000

PROJECTED POPULATION 2015 44,616,000

POPULATION DENSITY 35.8 per sq km (92.7 per sq mile)

LIFE EXPECTANCY 35.8

INFANT MORTALITY (PER 1,000) 61.8

OFFICIAL LANGUAGES Afrikaans, English, Ndebele, Pedi, Sotho, Swazi, Tsonga, Tswana, Venda, Xhosa, Zulu

OTHER LANGUAGES Indigenous and Indian languages

LITERACY RATE 85 %

RELIGIONS Christian 68 %, Hindu 2 %, Muslim 2 %, indigenous beliefs 28 %

ETHNIC GROUPS Indigenous 75.2 %, European 13.6 %, mixed 8.6 %, Indian 2.6 %

CURRENCY Rand

ECONOMY Services 62 %, industry 24 %, agriculture 14 %

GNP PER CAPITA US$ 9,400

CLIMATE Mainly semiarid; subtropical on southeast coast

HIGHEST POINT Njesuthi 3,408 m (11,181 ft)

MAP REFERENCE Pages 370–71

Occupying the southernmost tip of the African continent, South Africa comprises a central plateau or veld, bordered to the south and east by the Drakensberg Mountains and to the north by the countries of Namibia, Botswana, Zimbabwe and Mozambique. The Independent State of Lesotho is contained within South Africa's borders. European settlement in the seventeenth century culminated in white minority rule, and a controversial policy of racial segregation was officially implemented in 1948. After fifty years of deepening crisis and international isolation as a result of its racial policies, South Africa changed course in 1990, held democratic elections in 1994, and under a new government rejoined the international community. Always the economic powerhouse of southern Africa, it is now free from sanctions and able to renew normal trading relations. The abandonment of apartheid, and the freeing of long-term political prisoner (and then president)

Timeline

3 MYA Cave-dwelling Australopithecines in what is now Cape Province and Gauteng kill animals for meat and eat plants

120,000 BP "Modern" humans inhabit cave near Port Elizabeth; they eat shellfish, tortoises, and bird's eggs

25,000 BP Rock paintings on shelters show ceremonial dancers and animals, like antelope, which were hunted for food

c. 2000 BC Kalahari San (bushmen) inhabit the Kalahari Desert herding animals

4–500 AD Bantu people arrive from east Africa to find grazing for sheep and cattle and to plant crops. Displace Khoisan hunter-gatherers

c. 1000 Urban centers established; bone and ivory crafts; products traded between groups

1100 Different language groups emerge, such as the Xhosa and the Zulu

1488 First Portuguese vessels arrive at the Cape of Good Hope

1615 British settlement at Table Bay lasts only a few years

1652 Dutch East India Co. garrison at site of Cape Town supplies Dutch fleet; settlers granted land at Liesbeek River in 1657

1657 First slaves brought to the Cape from India, Indonesia, and West Africa as agricultural labor and to act as herders

1713 Khoikhoi pastoralists displaced by "trekboer" settlers in search of grazing land; numerous San people die of smallpox

1795–1802 British occupy Cape, a vital trade route supply post prior to opening of Suez Canal; more British settlers arrive

Nelson Mandela, have had an uplifting effect on national morale and provided a chance for a fresh start. Problems currently facing the nation include discrepancies between the educational level and skills of blacks and whites; vastly different income levels; increasing unemployment; high urban crime rates; and the ongoing conflict between Zulu groups and the ruling party, the African National Congress.

Physical features and land use

South Africa has three main geographic regions. First, there is the vast African Plateau of the interior. This slopes gradually north and west to form part of the semiarid and sparsely populated Kalahari basin, while to the east it rises to elevations of 2,000 m (6,500 ft). Second, the Great Escarpment, varying in height, structure, and steepness, forms a rim around the entire plateau from the mountains of the Transvaal Drakensberg in the northeast to Namibia in the northwest. Its highest peaks are in the Drakensberg along the Lesotho border. The third region consists of the narrow, fertile strips of land along the peripheral coastal plains.

Agricultural products include maize (a staple for many African farmers); apples, pears, stone fruit, grapes, and wine from Eastern Cape Province; wheat from Western Cape Province; and sugarcane from coastal KwaZulu-Natal. On the grasslands of the plateau large-scale pastoralism produces wool, mohair, skins, and meat. South Africa is geologically ancient—only a few superficial strata are less than 600 million years old. In the 1880s rocks of the Witwatersrand were found to contain gold and diamonds, and since then gold and diamond mining has been the basis of South Africa's national wealth.

Along the west coast, north of Cape Town, the cold Benguela current inhibits rainfall, producing the desert of the Namib. In the northeast there is dry savanna bushland. On the Mozambique border the best-known of South Africa's eight wildlife reserves, Kruger National Park, contains lions, leopards, giraffes, elephants, and hippopotamuses.

People and culture

First inhabited by San, or Bushmen, in the fifteenth century Southern Africa was occupied by a wave of cattle-keeping, grain-growing Bantu peoples from the north—their modern descendants being groups such as the Xhosa and the Zulu. Then in 1652 and 1688 two groups of settlers arrived from Europe—the first Dutch, the second French Huguenot, both firmly Protestant in their faith—and established a colony in the south at Cape Town. They became known as Boers (farmers) and later as Afrikaners (after their language, Afrikaans). The British established themselves on the Cape in 1806. Over the years a population of mixed Afro-European descent emerged who became known as "Cape Coloreds". In the nineteenth century laborers from India were brought in by the British, creating yet another large and distinct ethnic community. There are also a small number of Malays.

After 1948, under the ruling Afrikaners, apartheid (apartness) laws were drafted defining how each community should associate, where each should live, whether they could intermarry, and what work they could do. The entire population was to be organized in a hierarchy of privilege, with whites at the top and blacks at the bottom. Africans were to be confined to a series of internal Black States called "homelands", which were in practice mere labor pools, since the only way people could find employment was by leaving home and traveling to the South African mines. The impracticality, unreality, and injustice of the system aroused widespread international condemnation. The misery it created led to ongoing violent resistance.

Economy and resources

Although both the Bantu and the first Europeans to colonize South Africa were farming people, and agriculture formed the foundation of the economy for hundreds of years, during the nineteenth century gold and diamonds were the attractions that drew a new wave of settlers. Today, gold and precious stones still make up half the country's total exports, and over the last 100 years almost half the world's gold has come from South African mines. Other important minerals include asbestos, nickel, vanadium, and uranium (which can sometimes be found in old gold mines). In addition, South Africa is the world's largest producer of manganese, platinum, and chromium.

Energy conservation is a vital concern to the country as no petroleum deposits have yet been found. During the long period of South Africa's isolation and of trade boycotts, the state corporation Sasol extracted oil from coal. Though this is a expensive process, extensive deposits of coal make this a feasible supplementary supply. Many white South Africans enjoy a standard of living that is equal to the highest in the world. The challenge for the government in this century is to provide the circumstances and conditions in which less privileged social groups can have a share of the wealth. This is not an easy task: currently there are jobs for less than five percent of the 300,000 workers who enter the labor force each year.

PROVINCES

Eastern Cape • Free State • Gauteng • KwaZulu-Natal • Mpumalanga • Northern Province • Northern Cape • North West • Western Cape

Comoros

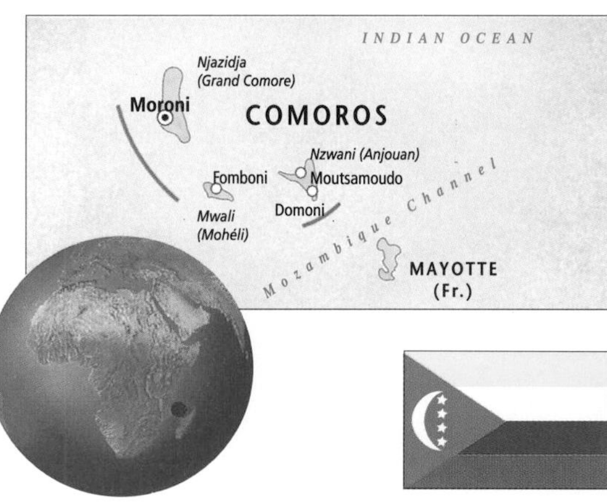

Fact File

OFFICIAL NAME Federal Islamic Republic of the Comoros

FORM OF GOVERNMENT Federal republic with single legislative body (National Assembly)

CAPITAL Moroni

AREA 2,170 sq km (838 sq miles)

TIME ZONE GMT + 3 hours

POPULATION 615,000

PROJECTED POPULATION 2015 876,000

POPULATION DENSITY 283.4 per sq km (733.9 per sq mile)

LIFE EXPECTANCY 60.8

INFANT MORTALITY (PER 1,000) 81.8

OFFICIAL LANGUAGES Arabic, French

OTHER LANGUAGE Comoran (blend of Swahili and Arabic)

LITERACY RATE 57.3 %

RELIGIONS Sunni Muslim 86 %, Roman Catholic 14 %

ETHNIC GROUPS Mixture of Malagasy, African, Malay and Arab groups

CURRENCY Comoran franc

ECONOMY Agriculture 80 %, government 3 %, other 17 %

GNP PER CAPITA US$ 710

CLIMATE Tropical, with wet season November to May

HIGHEST POINT Kartala 2,360 m (7,743 ft)

MAP REFERENCE Page 372

. 1800 Zulu nation ounded in today's waZulu-Natal, forcing hoshangane clan into waziland and Mzilika- i clan into Zimbabwe

1836–38 10,000 Boer settlers unhappy with British rule in Cape set out on Great Trek to seek new land in Natal and Orange River areas

1860 Laborers from India are imported by Natal farmers to work on farms and plantations

1870 Gold rush in the Kimberley area and discovery of diamonds transform the economic base from agriculture to mining

1880–81 British fail to bring Boer republics (Orange Free State, Transvaal) into federation—British defeated in First Boer War

1899 Gold-mining industry employs 110,000 workers; almost 100,000 are African laborers

1899–1902 British defeat the Boers (Afrikaners) in Second Boer War

1912 The African National Congress (ANC) founded by group of black Africans interested in obtaining political rights

1931 South Africa granted independence by Britain as a member of the Commonwealth

1948 National Party passes law restricting parliamentary representation to whites; "apartheid" official in 1950

1961 South Africa leaves Commonwealth and becomes a republic, without asking non-whites

1962 Nelson Mandela and other leading members of the ANC are imprisoned

1976 Black African protest over compulsory Afrikaans language lessons results in violence and the loss of 600 lives

1990 Mandela freed; apartheid abolished (1991); population 37 million (76 % black, 13 % white, 9 % mixed race, 2 % Asian)

1994 Mandela elected president in first non-racial general election—pronounces the new South Africa a "Rainbow Republic"

The Comoros are a group of islands in the Mozambique Channel, lying between northern Madagascar and the African coast. Some of the smaller ones are coral islets. The larger islands are volcanic, and three of the four largest constitute the Republic of the Comoros. (Another large island, Mayotte, chose to remain a French dependency but is claimed by the Comoros as indicated by the fourth star on the flag.)

For centuries, Indian and Arab traders have sailed across the Indian Ocean and worked their way along the coast of east Africa, visiting the Comoros as they went. The Comoran population reflects this history. There are large groups with African, Arab, Indonesian, and Madagascan backgrounds, and even a minority with Polynesian ancestors. France controlled the islands after declaring them a colony in 1912. They obtained their independence in 1975.

The island of Njazidja (formerly Grande Comore) consists mainly of a rocky lava plateau, rising at its southern end to the active volcano of Kartala. On the coast is the national capital, Moroni.

Because of the porous volcanic soils, rain quickly drains away, and despite heavy seasonal precipitation rainforests are only found on the mountain's upper slopes. On the island of Nzwani (formerly Anjouan) soils are more fertile, but clearing of land without proper terracing has led to serious erosion. The island of Mwali (formerly Mohéli) is the smallest of the group. It has dense forests and fertile valleys.

Comoros has few natural resources. Subsistence agriculture is the traditional way of life, the main food crops being cassava, mountain rice, and sweet potato. Nevertheless, the islands are not self-sufficient in food, and rice accounts for ninety percent of all imports. Cattle and goats are kept—the latter are another cause of erosion. There are a few small hydroelectric plants; otherwise, fuel must be imported. Revenue-earning exports are vanilla, cloves, perfume oil, and copra.

The government is trying to diversify exports, privatize industrial enterprises, and reduce the high population growth rate, but its authority has been weakened by chronic political instability and several attempted coups. Foreign aid is likely to be needed for some time.

Seychelles

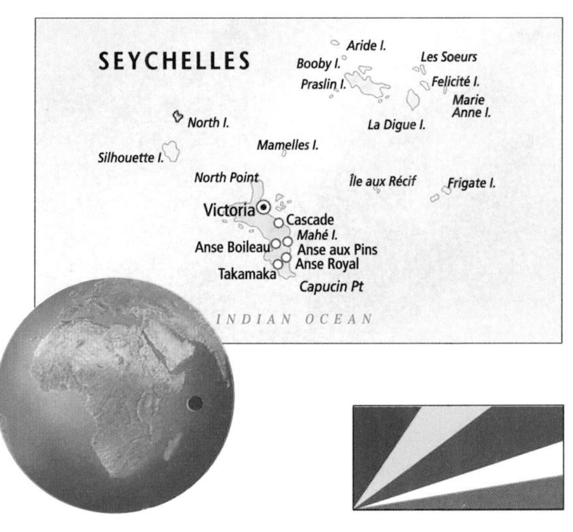

Fact File

Official name Republic of Seychelles

Form of government Republic with single legislative body (People's Assembly)

Capital Victoria

Area 455 sq km (176 sq miles)

Time zone GMT + 4 hours

Population 81,000

Projected population 2015 87,600

Population density 178 per sq km (460.2 per sq mile)

Life expectancy 71.5

Infant mortality (per 1,000) 16.0

Official languages English, French, Creole

Literacy rate 58 %

Religions Roman Catholic 90 %, Anglican 8 %, other 2 %

Ethnic groups Seychellois (mixture of Asian, African, European) 93.8 %, Malagasy 3.1 %, Chinese 1.6 %, British 1.5 %

Currency Seychelles rupee

Economy Services 80 %, agriculture 10 %, industry 10 %

GNP per capita US$ 7,800

Climate Tropical, with wet season December to May

Highest point Morne Seychellois 905 m (2,969 ft)

Map reference Pages 372, 373

The Seychelles are a group of four large and 36 small granite islands, plus a scattering of about 65 coralline islands, in the Indian Ocean northeast of Madagascar. Some 98 percent of the population live on the four main islands, the great majority on tropical and mountainous Mahé. Uninhabited when occupied by the French in 1742, the Seychelles were ceded to the British at the time of the Napoleonic Wars, and became a crown colony in 1903. After independence in 1976 the islands were ruled for fifteen years as a one-party socialist state, and North Korean military advisors were hired to guard against attempted coups. The first open elections were held in 1993 and the previous government party has since stayed in office.

The granite islands consist of a mountainous central spine—sometimes consisting of bare, eroded rock—surrounded by a flat coastal strip with dense tropical vegetation. In the areas cleared for farming vanilla, tobacco, tea, cinnamon and coconuts (for copra) are grown for export, along with food crops such as cassava, sweet potatoes, and bananas. Most food, however, is imported. The outer coralline islands are flat, waterless, and sparsely inhabited, having a total population of only 400. Short droughts periodically occur; though catchments collect some rainwater, there are no natural sources of supply. The Seychelles lie outside the cyclone belt, which is important for an economy depending on tourism.

The island's only natural resources are fish, copra, and cinnamon trees, which in earlier times provided a bare subsistence. Since independence in 1976, however, with the vigorous promotion of the tourist industry, per capita output has increased sevenfold. In recent years foreign investment has been encouraged in order to upgrade hotels and other services. Visitors find many attractions—the unique wildlife includes a rare giant land turtle and the colorful green sea turtle found on the coral reefs. The country's vulnerability in relying so heavily on tourism was shown during the Gulf War, when visitor numbers dropped sharply. The government is moving to reduce over-dependence on this sector by promoting farming, fishing, and small-scale manufacturing, including furniture-making, coconut-fiber rope-making, printing, and the re-export of petroleum products.

Madagascar

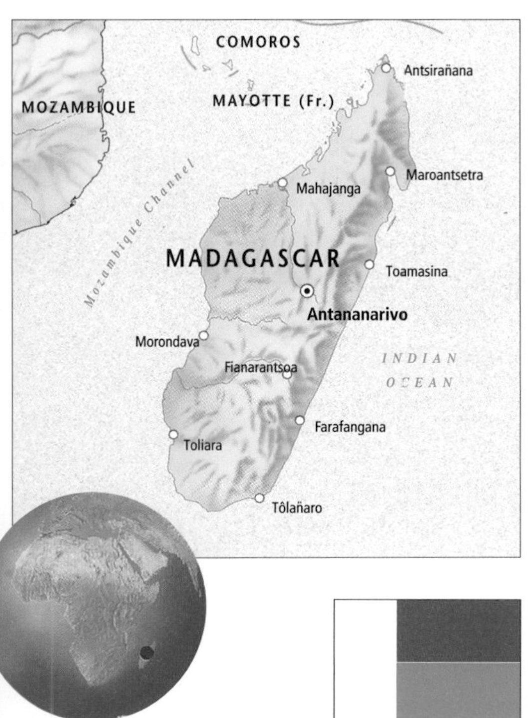

Fact File

Official name Republic of Madagascar

Form of government Republic with two legislative bodies (Senate and National Assembly)

Capital Antananarivo

Area 587,040 sq km (226,656 sq miles)

Time zone GMT + 3 hours

Population 16,474,000

Projected population 2015 24,072,000

Population density 28.1 per sq km (72.7 per sq mile)

Life expectancy 55.7

Infant mortality (per 1,000) 81.9

Official languages Malagasy, French

Literacy rate 80 %

Religions Indigenous beliefs 52 %, Christian 41 %, Muslim 7 %

Ethnic groups Chiefly Malayo-Indonesian inland (including Merina, Betsileo, Betsimisaraka) and mixed African, Arab, Malayo-Indonesian on coasts (including Tsimihety, Sakalava) 99%; other 1%

Currency Malagasy franc

Economy Agriculture 81 %, services 13 %, industry 6 %

GNP per capita US$ 870

Climate Tropical in coastal regions; temperate inland (wet season November to April); arid in south

Highest point Maromokotro 2,876 m (9,436 ft)

Map reference Page 372

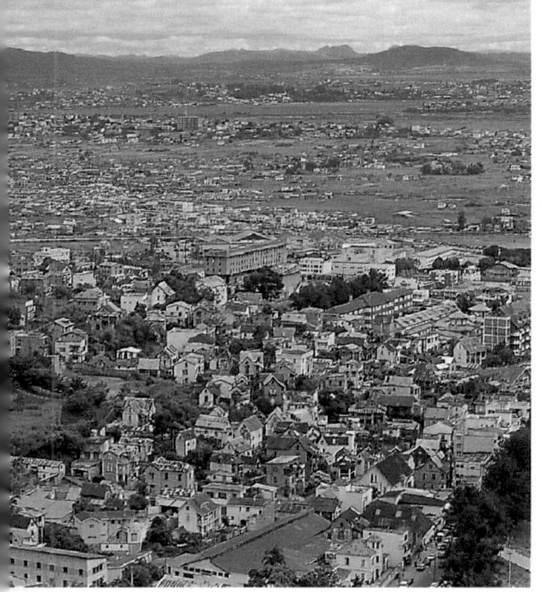

Larger than France, Madagascar is the world's fourth largest island. Located off the southeast coast of Africa, it contrasts sharply with the African mainland in its wildlife, people, culture, language, and history. In the center and the east live the Merina or Hova people who migrated to the island from the islands now known as Indonesia about 2,000 years ago. By the nineteenth century the Merinas, with their capital in Tanarive, ruled much of the country. In 1896 the island became a French colony. It won independence from France in 1960, following a bloody insurrection. From 1975 it was run as a one-party socialist state associated with the Soviet Union. In 1992 riots and mass demonstrations caused by deepening poverty forced the introduction of a multi-party democracy with elections in 1997 and 2002. The latter were contested and challenged legally and decided in court.

To the east the land drops precipitously to the Indian Ocean through forests dissected by rushing streams. Inland lies the mountainous central plateau, accounting for sixty percent of the island's total area, and rising in several places above 2,500 m (8,200 ft). Various geological eras are represented in the island's rugged topography, which features steep faulting, volcanic outcrops, and deep-cut valleys. On the western slopes of the plateau the land falls away more gently to broad and fertile plains. In the central highlands both the landscape and agriculture have a south Asian character, as rice farming is combined with raising cattle and pigs. Land usage is more African in style on the east coast and in the northern highlands, with fallow-farming of food crops such as cassava and maize, and the cultivation of coffee, sugar, and spices for export.

Separated from the African mainland for over 50 million years, Madagascar developed its own distinctive wildlife: three-quarters of the flora and fauna are found nowhere else. The island is known for its 28 species of lemur—dainty, large-eyed primates—and for the tenrec, a small, spiny, insect-eating mammal. Many of the island's 1,000 or so orchid species are endemic, and it is home to half the world's chameleon species.

Among the poorest countries in the world, Madagascar is not self-sufficient in food. The main staples are rice and cassava, but production is failing to keep pace with an annual population growth rate of around three percent. Additional problems derive from past government initiatives. When collective farming was introduced in 1975 it resulted in falling production and widespread resentment. Since 1993 corruption and political instability have accompanied economic confusion and a decay in the infrastructure.

Looking toward Silhouette Island in the Seychelles (left page top). Antananarivo, the capital of Madagascar (center). A street scene in Toliara, Madagascar (right).

Mauritius

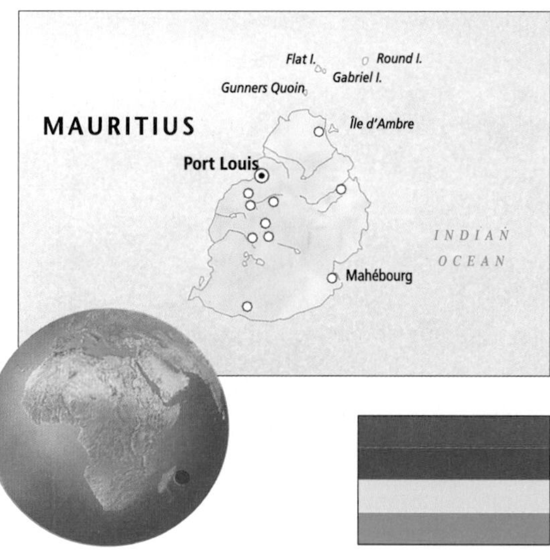

Fact File

Official name Republic of Mauritius

Form of government Republic with single legislative body (Legislative Assembly)

Capital Port Louis

Area 1,860 sq km (718 sq miles)

Time zone GMT + 4 hours

Population 1,201,000

Projected population 2015 1,301,000

Population density 645.7 per sq km (1,672.7 per sq mile)

Life expectancy 71.5

Infant mortality (per 1,000) 16.7

Official language English

Other languages Creole, French, Hindi, Urdu, Bojpoori, Hakka

Literacy rate 82.9 %

Religions Hindu 52 %, Christian (Roman Catholic 26 %, Protestant 2.3 %) 28.3 %, Muslim 16.6 %, other 3.1 %

Ethnic groups Indo-Mauritian 68 %, Creole 27 %, Sino-Mauritian 3 %, Franco-Mauritian 2 %

Currency Mauritian rupee

Economy Services 51 %, agriculture 27 %, industry 22 %

GNP per capita US$ 10,800

Climate Tropical, moderated by trade winds

Highest point Piton de la Petite Rivière Noire 828 m (2,717 ft)

Map reference Pages 372, 373

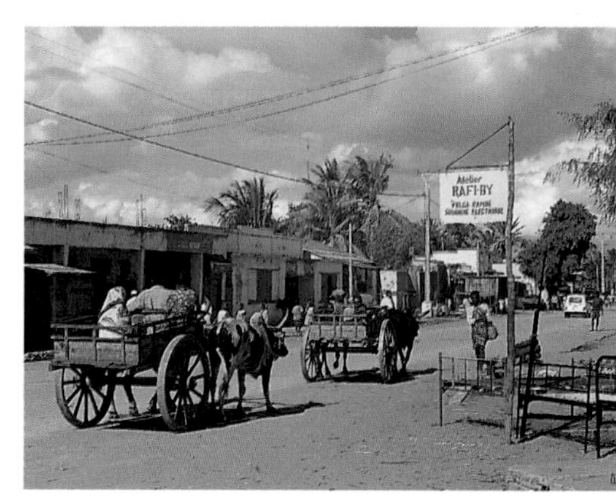

Famous as the home of the now-extinct flightless bird, the dodo, the Republic of Mauritius consists of one large and several smaller islands 800 km (500 miles) east of Madagascar. Mauritius was uninhabited when visited by the Portuguese and the Dutch between the fifteenth and seventeenth centuries. It was first settled by the French, after 1715, who brought African slaves for the sugar plantations. In 1810 it was taken over by the British, who brought in numerous indentured laborers from India. These colonial origins produced two distinct communities, one Afro-French Creole (27 percent), the other English-speaking and Indian (73 percent), who compete for influence and power. Independence within the British Commonwealth was granted in 1968 and Mauritius became a republic in 1992. Despite occasional unrest, the country has a record of political stability and economic growth. It attracts considerable foreign investment and has earned one of Africa's highest per capita incomes.

Fringed with coral reefs, the main island rises from coastal plains on its north and east to a plateau surrounded by rugged peaks—the remains of a giant volcano. The climate is tropical, but moderated by rain-bearing winds from the southeast. Sugarcane is grown on ninety percent of the cultivated land, and accounts, with derivatives such as molasses, for forty percent of export earnings. A by-product of the sugar industry, the cane-waste called bagasse, has been used to fuel power stations. Fast-flowing rivers descending from the plateau are used to produce hydroelectric power.

Industrial diversification (textile and garment manufacture now accounts for 44 percent of export revenue) and the development of a tourist industry (up to half a million visitors per year) have enabled Mauritius to transcend the low-income agricultural economy that existed at the time of independence. Since 1968 annual economic growth most years has been about five percent, life expectancy has been increasing and the infrastructure has improved.

Women agricultural workers walking beside a field of sugarcane in Mauritius (below left). Small town with a view of the Atlantic Ocean, Madeira (below right). The Pico de Teide on the island of Teneriffa (right page).

Dependencies in Africa

Mayotte

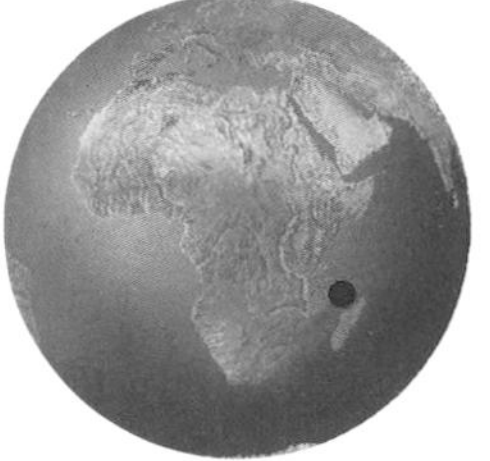

Fact File

Official name Territorial Collectivity of Mayotte

Form of government Territorial collectivity of France

Capital Mamoudzou

Area 375 sq km (145 sq miles)

Time zone GMT + 3 hours

Population 171,000

Life expectancy 60.2

Infant mortality (per 1,000) 67.8

Literacy rate Not available

Currency Euro

Economy Mainly agriculture and fishing

Climate Tropical, with wet season November to May

Map reference Page 372

Mayotte is a small island at the northern end of the Mozambique Channel, 34 km (21 miles) long, between Madagascar and the mainland. It is the easternmost of the four large islands of the Comoros group (a group first visited by Europeans ships in the sixteenth century) and was the first to be ceded to France in 1841. When, in the 1974 referendum, the other islands chose to become the Republic of the Comoros, Mayotte decided to become a territorial collectivity of France.

Volcanic in origin, Mayotte rises to 660 m (2,165 ft) at its highest point. The people are of African, Arab, and Madagascan descent. Agricultural products include coconuts, cocoa, and spices.

Réunion

Fact File

Official name Department of Réunion

Form of government Overseas department of France

Capital Saint-Denis

Area 2,510 sq km (969 sq miles)

Time zone GMT + 4 hours

Population 744,000

Life expectancy 73.2

Infant mortality (per 1,000) 8.3

Literacy rate 79 %

Currency French franc

Economy Services 49 %, agriculture 30 %, industry 21 %

Climate Tropical; cool and dry May to November, hot and rainy November to April

Map reference Page 373

Réunion is the largest of the Mascarene Islands which lie southwest of Mauritius and east of Madagascar. After the Portuguese had discovered the uninhabited island in 1513 the French settled them and brought in Africans, Chinese, Malays, and Malabar Indians. A fertile plain surrounds Réunion's rugged and mountainous interior. One of two volcanic peaks, Piton des Neiges rises to 3,069 m (10,069 ft) and is sporadically active. Plentiful rainfall comes with the winter trade winds.

On the intensively cultivated lowlands there are large sugarcane plantations which provide 75 percent of exports and are the island's only significant industry. Vanilla, perfume oils, and tea also produce revenue, while vegetables and maize are grown for local consumption. Tourism is growing, but unemployment is high. The population is divided over continued association with France, which uses Réunion as its main military base in the area.

The small, uninhabited islands of Bassas da India, Europa, Glorieuses, Île Juan de Nova, and Tromelin are associated dependencies.

Western Sahara

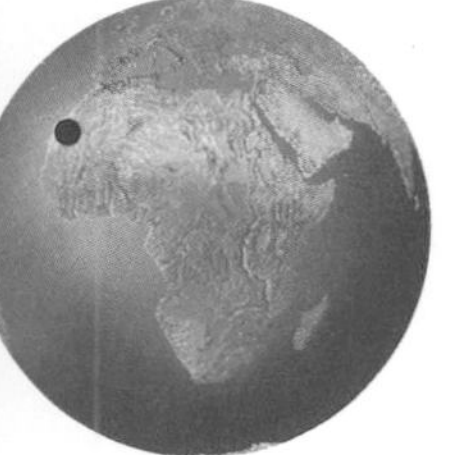

Fact File

Official name	Western Sahara
Form of government	Territory disputed by Morocco and Polisario Front independence movement
Capital	None
Area	266,000 sq km (102,703 sq miles)
Time zone	GMT
Population	257,000
Life expectancy	50
Infant mortality (per 1,000)	Not available
Currency	Moroccan dirham
Economy	Agriculture 50 %; fishing 25 %, mining 25 %
Climate	Mainly hot and arid
Map reference	Page 360

Western Sahara is a former Spanish possession. South of Morocco (and more than half the size of Morocco itself) it consists of the desert country lying between Mauritania and the Atlantic coast. The terrain is largely flat, with large areas of rock and sand, rising to low mountains in the northeast and the south. Possessing the world's largest known deposits of phosphate rock, it is a contested region of uncertain sovereignty, though since 1975 it has been occupied and administered by Morocco. Most of the indigenous people are Sahrawis, a mixture of Berber and Arab. Since 1983 a war has been waged on their behalf by the Polisario Front (Popular Front for the Liberation of the Saguia el Hamra and Rio de Oro) and by 1991 more than 170,000 Sahrawi refugees had fled the country and were living in camps in Algeria. Guerrilla activities continue, despite a United Nations-monitored ceasefire in 1991. Trade and other activities are controlled by the Moroccan government and most food for the urban population must be imported. Western Sahara's standard of living is well below that of Morocco.

St Helena

Fact File

Official name	St Helena
Form of government	Dependent territory of the United Kingdom
Capital	Jamestown
Area	410 sq km (158 sq miles)
Time zone	GMT
Population	7,320
Life expectancy	77.2
Infant mortality (per 1,000)	21.5
Literacy rate	97 %
Currency	St Helenian pound
Economy	Mainly fishing and agriculture
Climate	Tropical, moderated by trade winds
Map reference	Page 373

The island of St Helena lies about 1,950 km (1,200 miles) off the west coast of Africa. Together with Tristan da Cunha and Ascension Island, it is a British crown colony, and is Britain's main dependency in the South Atlantic. The crater rim of an extinct volcano, St Helena is marked by gorges and valleys, has many freshwater springs, and rises to an elevation of 824 m (2,703 ft).

Discovered by the Portuguese in 1502 and first visited by the English in 1588, St Helena was granted to the British East India Company in 1659. It acquired fame as Napoleon's place of exile from 1815 to 1821, but its importance as a port of call declined after the opening of the Suez Canal in 1869 . Today the island's main activities are fishing, livestock raising, and the sale of handicrafts, but it depends on aid from the UK. Tristan da Cunha, 2,000 km (1,243 miles) to the south, has a farming community. Ascension Island, a military base, the site of a US Air Force auxiliary airfield and communications center, has no resident population.

Autonomous communities

The municipalities of Ceuta and Melilla on the Moroccan coast and the Canary Islands, off southern Morocco, are autonomous communities of Spain. The islands of Madeira, to the north of the Canary Islands, constitute an autonomous region of Portugal.

Ceuta and Melilla

In 1912 the Sultan of Morocco signed a treaty with France making Morocco a French protectorate. At the same time the French, recognizing Spanish interests in the region, gave Spain several enclaves along the Moroccan coast. Two of these enclaves remain under Spanish administration—Ceuta and Melilla.

The high promontory of Jebel Musa at Ceuta, on the African side of the Strait of Gibraltar, stands opposite Gibraltar on the northern side. Legend has it that Jebel Musa and the Rock of Gibraltar were the two "Pillars of Hercules", set there by Hercules to commemorate his travels and achievements. Today, Ceuta is a military station and seaport with a population of about 125,000.

Canary Islands

The Canary Islands, grouped off southern Morocco, are an autonomous community of Spain. There are seven large islands and numerous smaller islands, the nearest of which are within 100 km (60 miles) of the African coast. The "inshore" islands of Lanzarote and Fuerteventura are low lying. The more mountainous outer islands of Gran Canaria and Tenerife include the volcanic cone of Pico de Teide (3,718 m; 12,198 ft).

With a subtropical climate and fertile soils, the islands support farming and fruit growing, and such industries as food and fish processing, boat building, and crafts.

Once known as the Fortunate Islands, the Spanish took control of the Canaries in 1479, subjugating the original Guanche and Canario inhabitants. Today, the islands' mild climate makes them a major tourist destination year round. They are divided into two provinces: Las Palmas de Gran Canaria, and Santa Cruz de Tenerife.

Madeira

Madeira is the largest of a group of volcanic islands forming an autonomous region of Portugal. A tourist destination, they are situated 550 km (340 miles) from the coast of Morocco, and 900 km (560 miles) southwest of Lisbon. The two islands of Madeira and Porto Santo are inhabited, unlike the barren islets of the Desertas and Selvagens. Madeira is 55 km (34 miles) long and 19 km (12 miles) wide, has deep ravines and rugged mountains, contains the group's capital, Funchal, and rises to Pico Ruivo (1,861 m; 6,106 ft) in the middle of the island. It was once heavily forested, but settlers cleared the uplands for plantation use. Produce includes wine (madeira), sugar, and bananas.

Africa: Physical

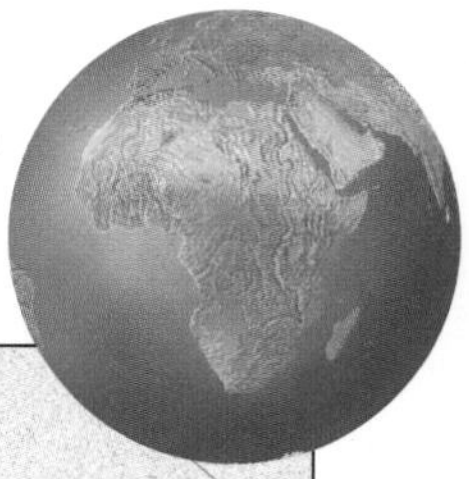

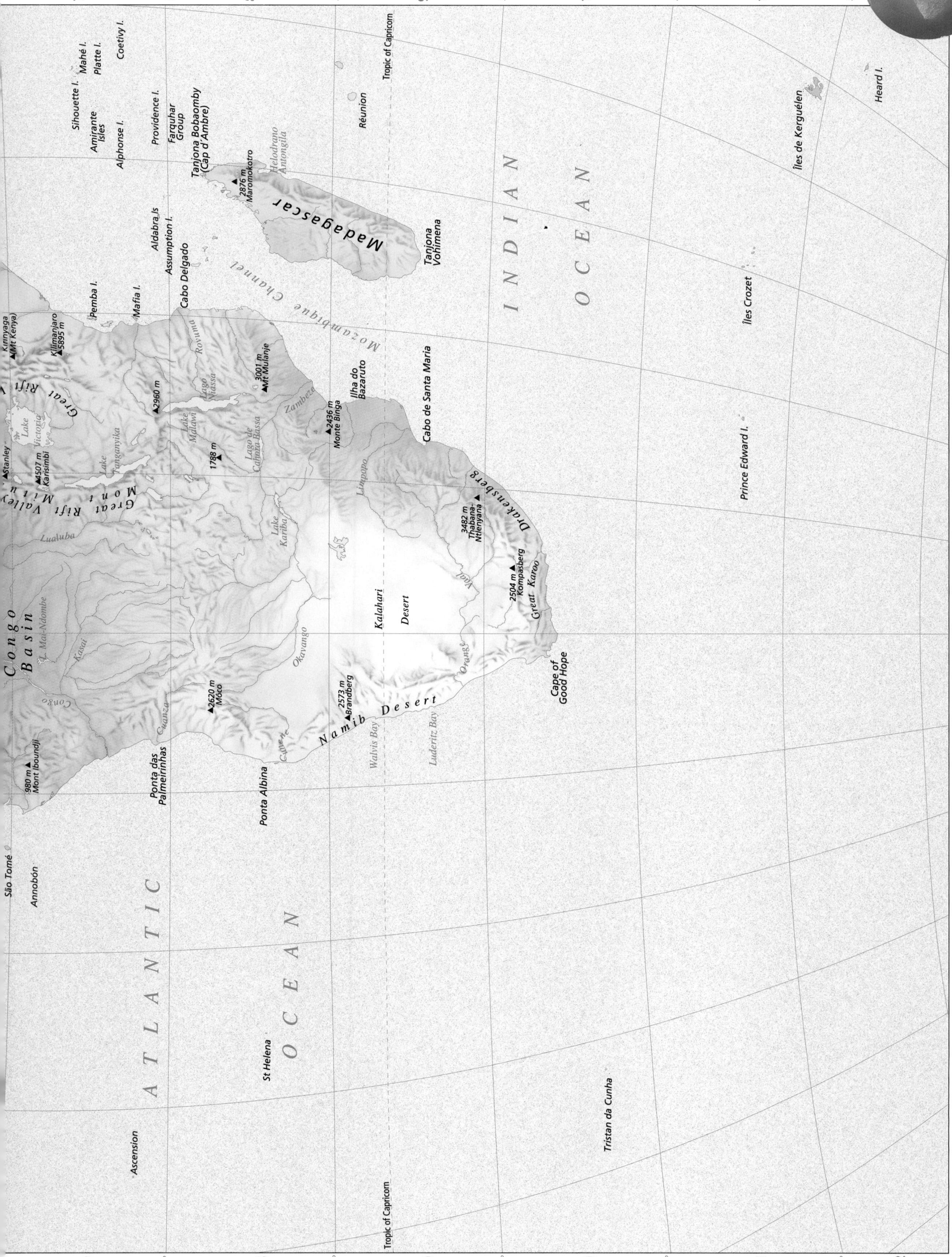

Africa
ATLANTIC OCEAN
INDIAN OCEAN
Madagascar
Mozambique Channel
Congo Basin
Great Rift Valley
Mitumba Mont
Kalahari Desert
Namib Desert
Drakensberg
Great Karoo
Cape of Good Hope
Cabo de Santa Maria
Ilha do Bazaruto
Tanjona Vohimena
Tanjona Bobaomby (Cap d'Ambre)
Cabo Delgado
Ponta das Palmeirinhas
Ponta Albina
Walvis Bay
Luderitz Bay
São Tomé
Annobón
Ascension
St Helena
Tristan da Cunha
Prince Edward I.
Îles Crozet
Îles de Kerguélen
Heard I.
Réunion
Tropic of Capricorn
Sihouette I.
Mahé I.
Platte I.
Coetivy I.
Amirante Isles
Alphonse I.
Providence I.
Farquhar Group
Aldabra Is
Assumption I.
Pemba I.
Mafia I.
Kirinyaga (Mt Kenya)
Kilimanjaro 5895 m
4507 m Karisimbi
Stanley
2960 m
1788 m
3001 m Mt Mulanje
2436 m Monte Binga
3482 m Thabana-Ntlenyana
2504 m Kompasberg
2573 m Brandberg
2620 m Môco
980 m Mont Iboundji
2876 m Maromokotro
Lake Victoria
Lake Tanganyika
Lake Malawi
Lago Niassa
Lago de Cahora Bassa
Lake Kariba
L. Mai-Ndombe
Lualaba
Congo
Kasai
Cuanza
Cunene
Okavango
Orange
Vaal
Limpopo
Zambeze
Rovuma
Helodrano Antongila
0° 10° 20° 30° 40° 50° 60° 70° 80°
A B C D E F G H J K L M N
7 8 9 10 11 12

0 400 800 1200 kilometers
0 200 400 600 miles
Scale 1:30,000,000 Projection: Azimuthal Equal Area

Africa: Political

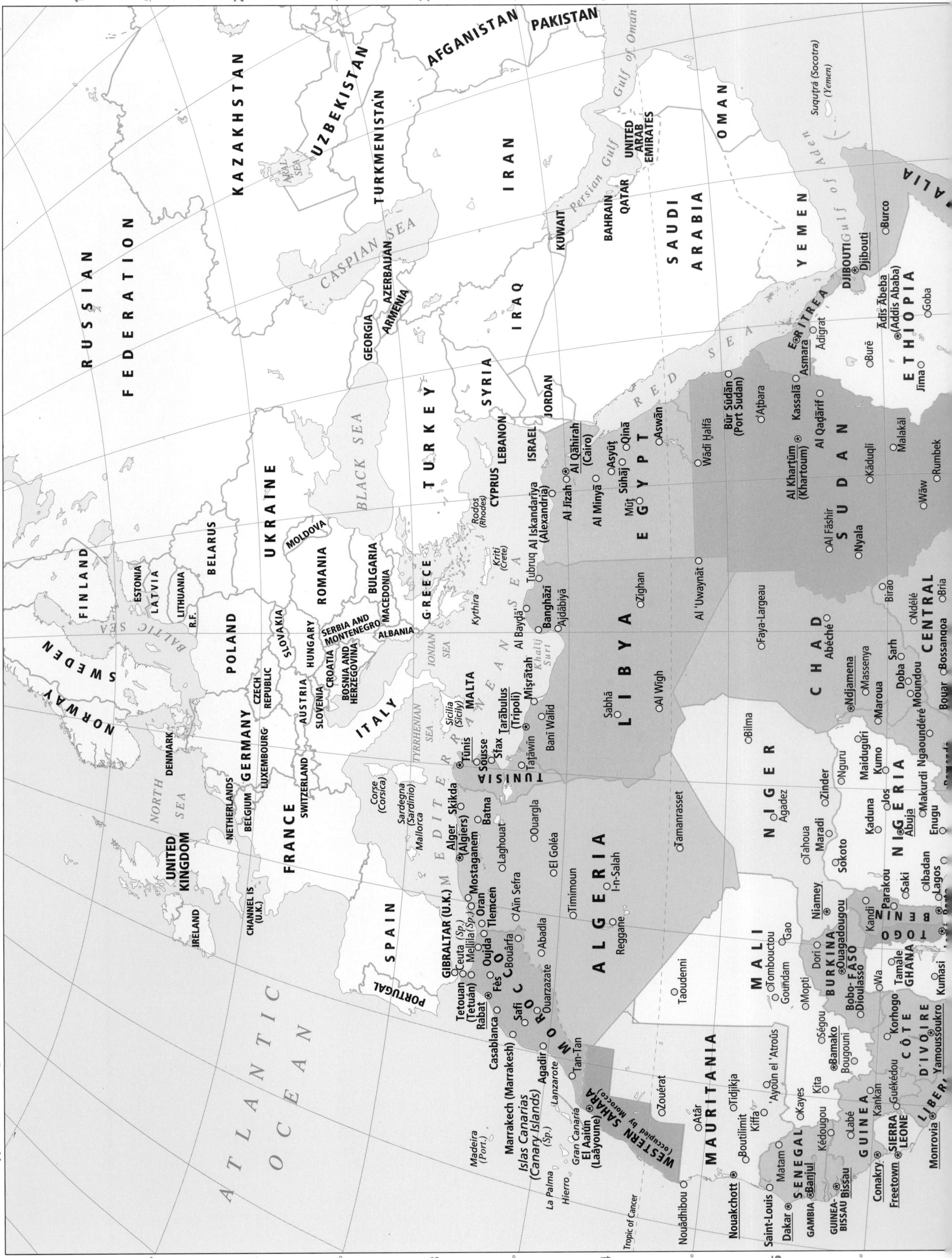

RUSSIAN FEDERATION
KAZAKHSTAN
UZBEKISTAN
TURKMENISTAN
AFGANISTAN
PAKISTAN
IRAN
IRAQ
SYRIA
TURKEY
GEORGIA
AZERBAIJAN
ARMENIA
SAUDI ARABIA
YEMEN
OMAN
UNITED ARAB EMIRATES
QATAR
BAHRAIN
KUWAIT
JORDAN
ISRAEL
LEBANON
CYPRUS
EGYPT
SUDAN
ERITREA
DJIBOUTI
ETHIOPIA
LIBYA
CHAD
NIGER
NIGERIA
MALI
ALGERIA
TUNISIA
MOROCCO
MAURITANIA
WESTERN SAHARA (occupied by Morocco)
SENEGAL
GAMBIA
GUINEA-BISSAU
GUINEA
SIERRA LEONE
LIBERIA
CÔTE D'IVOIRE
BURKINA FASO
GHANA
TOGO
BENIN
CENTRAL
FINLAND
SWEDEN
NORWAY
ESTONIA
LATVIA
LITHUANIA
BELARUS
UKRAINE
MOLDOVA
ROMANIA
BULGARIA
MACEDONIA
GREECE
ALBANIA
SERBIA AND MONTENEGRO
BOSNIA AND HERZEGOVINA
CROATIA
SLOVENIA
HUNGARY
SLOVAKIA
POLAND
CZECH REPUBLIC
AUSTRIA
GERMANY
DENMARK
NETHERLANDS
BELGIUM
LUXEMBOURG
SWITZERLAND
FRANCE
ITALY
MALTA
SPAIN
PORTUGAL
UNITED KINGDOM
IRELAND
CHANNEL IS (U.K.)
GIBRALTAR (U.K.)
ATLANTIC OCEAN
NORTH SEA
BALTIC SEA
BLACK SEA
CASPIAN SEA
ARAL SEA
MEDITERRANEAN SEA
TYRRHENIAN SEA
IONIAN SEA
RED SEA
Persian Gulf
Gulf of Oman
Gulf of Aden
Tropic of Cancer

ATLANTIC OCEAN

INDIAN OCEAN

DEMOCRATIC REPUBLIC OF THE CONGO
Kisangani
Mbandaka
Goma
Bukavu
Kindu
Lodja
Kananga
Kalemie
Mbuji-Mayi
Kamina
Kolwezi
Kinshasa

CONGO
Owando
Brazzaville
Pointe-Noire

GABON
Libreville
Port-Gentil
Mouila
Tchibanga

São Tomé
São Tomé
Annobón (Eq. Guinea)

ANGOLA
Luanda
Uíge
Saurimo
Luena
Dilolo
Benguela
Huambo
Menongue
Lubango
Namibe

ZAMBIA
Solwezi
Chingola
Luanshya
Mansa
Kasama
Mpika
Lusaka
Mongu

MALAWI
Lilongwe
Blantyre

KENYA
Nairobi
Garissa
Mombasa
Kismaayo

TANZANIA
Dodoma
Dar es Salaam
Zanzibar
Tanga
Moshi
Mwanza
Tabora
Mbeya
Iringa
Songea
Lindi
Mtwara
Pemba Island
Mafia I.

Kampala
Kigali
RWANDA
Bujumbura
BURUNDI

SEYCHELLES
Victoria
Mahé I.
Platte I.
Coetivy I.
Sihouette I.
Amirante Isles
Alphonse I.
Providence I.
Farquhar Group
Aldabra Is
Assumption I.

COMOROS
Moroni
MAYOTTE (Fr.)
Dzaoudzi

MADAGASCAR
Antsirañana
Sambava
Antsohihy
Mahajanga
Soanierana-Ivongo
Toamasina
Antananarivo
Antsirabe
Fianarantsoa
Morondava
Toliara
Vangaindrano
Tôlañaro
Tsiroanomandidy

MAURITIUS
Port Louis
REUNION (Fr.)
Saint-Denis
Tropic of Capricorn

MOZAMBIQUE
Nacala
Nampula
Lichinga
Quelimane
Chimoio
Beira
Ilha do Bazaruto
Inhambane
Chókwé
Maputo
Mozambique Channel

ZIMBABWE
Harare
Kariba
Gweru
Bulawayo
Thohoyandou

BOTSWANA
Francistown
Maun
Mahalapye
Gaborone

NAMIBIA
Windhoek
Rundu
Tsumeb
Otjiwarongo
Oshakati
Swakopmund
Keetmanshoop

SOUTH AFRICA
Pretoria
Johannesburg
Klerksdorp
Mbabane
SWAZILAND
Maseru
LESOTHO
Durban
East London
Port Elizabeth
Bloemfontein
Upington
De Aar
Beaufort West
Mossel Bay
Cape Town

Îles de Crozet (Fr.)
Prince Edward I. (S. Africa)
Îles de Kerguélen (Fr.)
HEARD AND MACDONALD IS (Aust.)
ST HELENA (U.K.)
ASCENSION ISLAND (ST HELENA)
TRISTAN DA CUNHA (St Helena)
Tropic of Capricorn

0 400 800 1200 kilometers
0 200 400 600 miles
Scale 1:30,000,000
Projection: Azimuthal Equal Area

Northwest Africa

Azores
(Port.)
Corvo
Flores
Graciosa
São Jorge
Terceira
Faial
Horta
Madalena
Pico
Praia da Vitória
Angra do Heroísmo
São Miguel
Ponta Delgada
Povoação
Santa Maria
ATLANTIC OCEAN
Madeira
(Port.)
1862 m
Funchal
Ilhas Desertas
Ilhas Selvagens
(Port.)
Islas Canarias
(Canary Islands)
(Sp.)
Alegranza
Graciosa
Lanzarote
Arrecife
Puerto del Rosario
Fuerteventura
807 m
Santa Cruz de la Palma
La Palma
Tenerife
Santa Cruz de Tenerife
Pico de Teide
3718 m
Gomera
1487 m
Hierro
1500 m
1949 m
Las Palmas de Gran Canaria
Gran Canaria
Leiria
PORTU
Lisboa
(Lisbon)
Grândola
Odemira
Lagos
Sagres
Faro
Mohammedia
Casablanca
Berrechid
Azemmour
El Jadida
Settat
Khourib
Safi
Youssoufia
Chemaïa
El Kelaa des S
Marrakech (Marrakesh)
Essaouira
Ounara
Imi-n-Tanoute
Jebel Toubkal
4165 m
Ouarzazate
Cap Rhir
Agadir
MOROCCO
Taroudannt
Oulad Teïma
2351 m
Tafraoute
Anti Atlas
Tata
Tiznit
Sidi Ifni
Bou Izakarn
Akka
Guelmim
Tan-Tan
Tisgui-Remz
Jebel Ouarkziz
Tarfaya
Tindouf
Hagunia
El Aaiún
(Laâyoune)
Semara
Bu Craa
Cabo Bojador
Tifariti
Aïn Ben Tili
Guelta Zemmur
Bîr Mogreïn
WESTERN SAHARA
(occupied by Morocco)
Sebkhet Oumm ed Droûs Telli
TIRIS ZEMMOUR
Bir Enzarán
Ad Dakhla
Punta Durnford
El Aargub
Sebkhet Oumm ed Droûs Guebli
El Hank
Tropic of Cancer
Sebkhet Ti-n-Bessaïs
Ausert
Fdérik
Zouérat
Kediet Ijill
915 m
Agûenit
Cabo Barbas
Adrar Sotuf
Tichla
Zug
Tmeimîchât
Choûm
Sebkhet Chemchâm
Ouadane
Nouâdhibou
Râs Nouâdhibou
Azeffal
Adrar
Atâr
Chinguettî
ADRAR
DAKHLET NOUÂDHIBOU
INCHIRI
Akjoujt
Oujeft
MAURITANIA
Râs Timirist
Nouâmghâr
TAGANT
Tidjikja
Tichît
Sebkha Narhamcha
Jreïda
Nouakchott
TRARZA
Aoukâr
Moudjéria
Oualâta
HOD
CHARG
Ponta do Sol
Santo Antão
Porto Novo
Mindelo
São Vicente
Pedra Lume
Sal
São Nicolau
Vila da Ribeira Brava
Boa Vista
Sal Rei
Curral Velho
CAPE VERDE
São Tiago
Tarrafal
Maio
Porto Inglês
Brava
Fogo
Praia
364

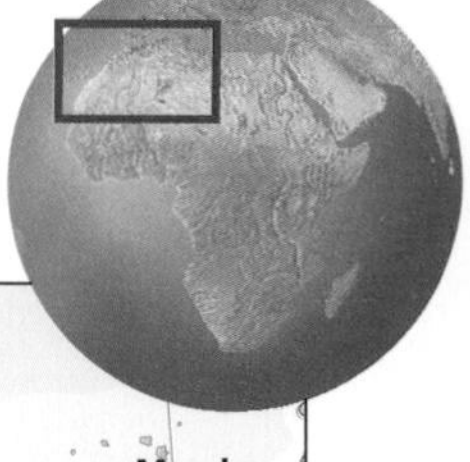

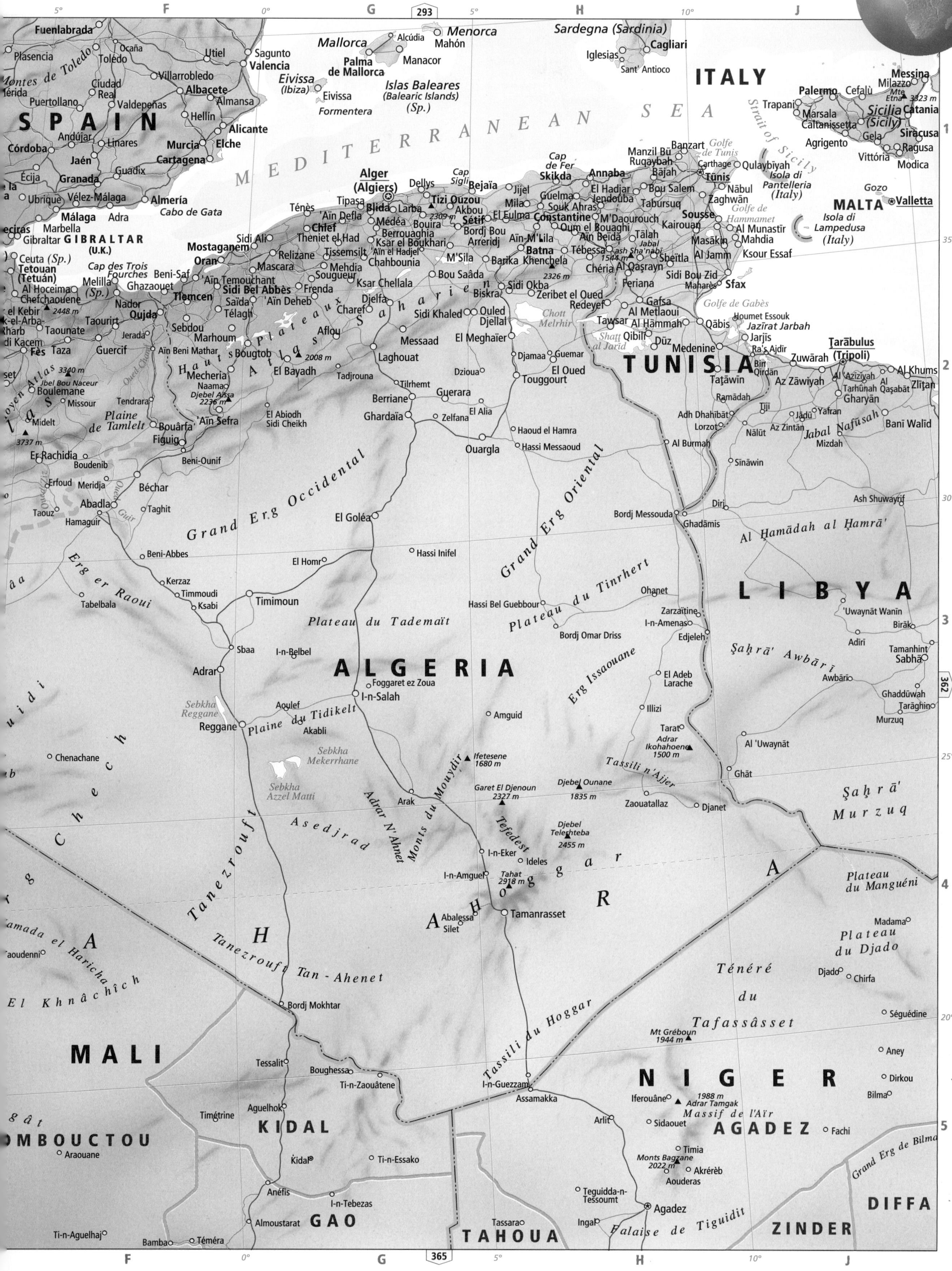

Scale 1:9,000,000 Projection: Azimuthal Equal Area

0 100 200 300 400 kilometers

0 100 200 miles

293
362
365

Libya • Egypt • North Sudan • North Chad

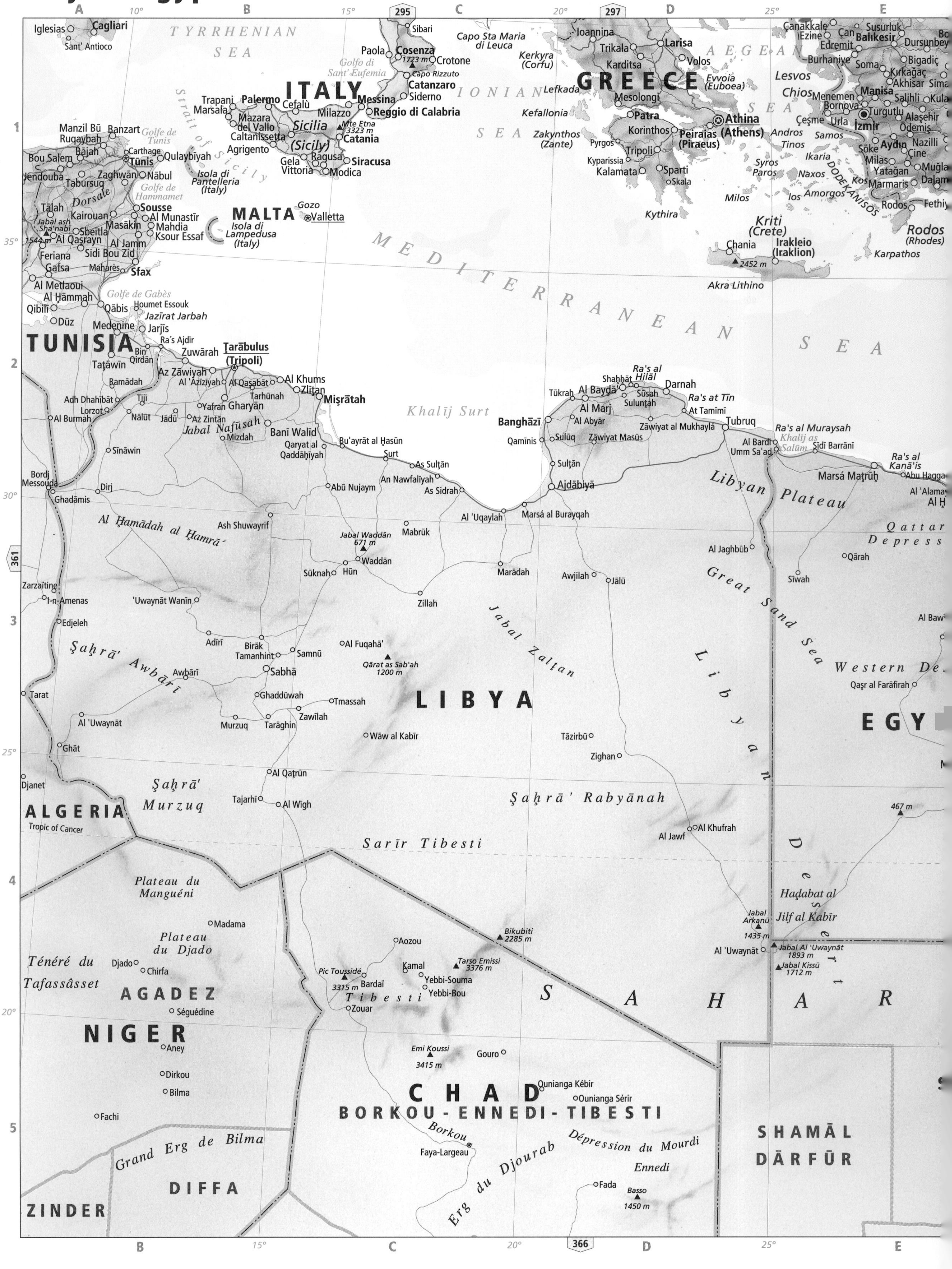

A 10° B 15° 295 C 20° 297 D 25° E

Iglesias Cagliari Sant' Antioco
TYRRHENIAN SEA
Sibari Paola Cosenza 1723 m Crotone Capo Sta Maria di Leuca
Golfo di Sant' Eufemia Capo Rizzuto Catanzaro Siderno
ITALY Trapani Palermo Marsala Cefalù Milazzo Messina Reggio di Calabria
Mazara del Vallo Sicilia (Sicily) Caltanissetta Mte Etna 3323 m Catania Agrigento
Gela Ragusa Siracusa Vittoria Modica
Strait of Sicily
Manzil Bū Ruqaybah Banzart Golfe de Tunis Bājah Bou Salem Carthage Tūnis Qulaybiyah Jendouba Zaghwān Nābul Tabursuq Golfe de Hammamet Dorsale
Isola di Pantelleria (Italy)
Tālah Kairouan Sousse Al Munastīr Masākin Mahdia Ksour Essaf Jabal ash Sha'nabī 1544 m Sbeitla Al Qaşrayn Al Jamm Sidi Bou Zid Feriana Gafsa Mahārès Sfax
MALTA Gozo Valletta Isola di Lampedusa (Italy)
Al Metlaoui Al Ḩammah Golfe de Gabès Qibili Qābis Houmet Essouk Dūz Jazīrat Jarbah Medenine Jarjīs
TUNISIA Ra's Ajdīr Bin Qirdān Zuwārah Taţāwīn Ţarābulus (Tripoli)
Ioannina Trikala Larisa Karditsa Volos Kerkyra (Corfu) GREECE Lefkada Evvoia (Euboea) Mesolongi Kefallonia Patra Athina Korinthos Peiraias (Athens) (Piraeus) Zakynthos (Zante) Pyrgos Tripoli Kyparissia Kalamata Sparti Skala Kythira
IONIAN SEA
AEGEAN SEA
Çanakkale Ezine Çan Susurluk Balıkesir Dursunbey Edremit Burhaniye Bigadiç Soma Kırkağaç Lesvos Akhisar Chios Menemen Manisa Bornova Turgutlu Salihli Kula Çeşme Urla İzmir Alaşehir Ödemiş Andros Samos Tinos Aydın Nazilli Söke Çine Syros Ikaria Milas Muğla Paros Naxos Yatağan Kos Marmaris Dalaman Milos Ios Amorgos DODEKANISOS Rodos Fethiye Rodos (Rhodes) Karpathos
Kriti (Crete) Chania Irakleio (Iraklion) 2452 m Akra Lithino
MEDITERRANEAN SEA
Az Zāwiyah Al 'Azīzīyah Al Qaşabāt Al Khums Zlīţan Tarhūnah Mişrātah Ramādah Adh Dhahībāt Tījī Gharyān Yafran Lorzot Nālūt Jādū Az Zintān Al Burmah Jabal Nafūsah Mizdah Banī Walīd Khalīj Surt
Qaryat al Qaddāḩīyah Bu'ayrāt al Ḩasūn Surt As Sulţān An Nawfalīyah As Sidrah Sīnāwin Abū Nujaym Bordj Messouda Dirj Ghadāmis
Ra's al Hilāl Shaḩḩāt Darnah Ţūkrah Al Bayḑā' Sūsah Sulunţah Ra's at Tīn Al Marj At Tamīmī Banghāzī Al Abyār Zāwiyat al Mukhaylā Ţubruq Qamīnis Sulūq Zāwiyat Masūs Ra's al Muraysah Khalīj as Salūm Al Bardī Umm Sa'ad Sīdī Barrānī Ra's al Kanā'is Abu Haggag Marsá Maţrūḩ Al 'Alamayn Al Ḩ Sulţān Ajdābiyā
Al 'Uqaylah Marsá al Burayqah Libyan Plateau Qattar Depression
Al Ḩamādah al Ḩamrā' Ash Shuwayrif Jabal Waddān 671 m Mabrūk Waddān Sūknah Hūn Marādah Awjilah Jālū Al Jaghbūb Qārah Siwah
361 Zarzaītine I-n-Amenas 'Uwaynāt Wanīn Zillah Edjeleh Great Sand Sea Al Bawītī
Adīrī Birāk Tamanhint Samnū Al Fuqahā' Qārat as Sab'ah 1200 m Jabal Zalţan
Şaḩrā' Awbārī Awbārī Sabhā Ghaddūwah Tmassah Tarat Al 'Uwaynāt Murzuq Tarāghin Zawīlah LIBYA Western Desert Qaşr al Farāfirah EGY
Ghāt Wāw al Kabīr Tāzirbū Zighan Libyan Desert
Djanet Al Qaţrūn Şaḩrā' Murzuq Tajarhi Al Wīgh Şaḩrā' Rabyānah 467 m
ALGERIA Tropic of Cancer Al Khufrah Al Jawf Sarīr Tibesti
Plateau du Manguéni Haḑabat al Jilf al Kabīr
Madama Plateau du Djado Aozou Bikubiti 2285 m Jabal Arkanū 1435 m Al 'Uwaynāt Jabal Al 'Uwaynāt 1893 m Jabal Kissū 1712 m
Ténéré du Tafassâsset Djado Chirfa Kamal Tarso Emissi 3376 m Pic Toussidé 3315 m Bardaï Yebbi-Souma Yebbi-Bou
AGADEZ Tibesti Zouar SAHARA
Séguédine NIGER Aney Emi Koussi 3415 m Gouro
Dirkou Bilma Ounianga Kébir Ounianga Sérir CHAD
Fachi BORKOU-ENNEDI-TIBESTI Borkou Faya-Largeau Dépression du Mourdi SHAMĀL DĀRFŪR
Grand Erg de Bilma Erg du Djourab Ennedi
DIFFA Fada Basso 1450 m
ZINDER

1 2 3 4 5
35° 30° 25° 20°
B 15° C 20° 366 D 25° E

Africa

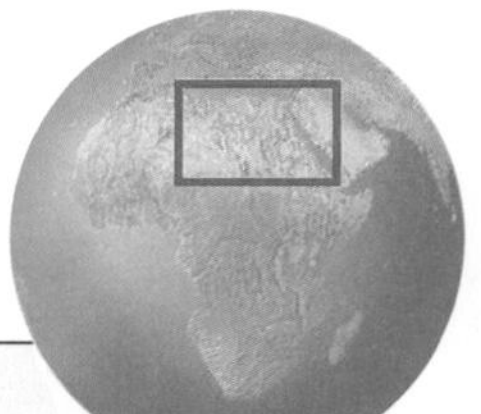

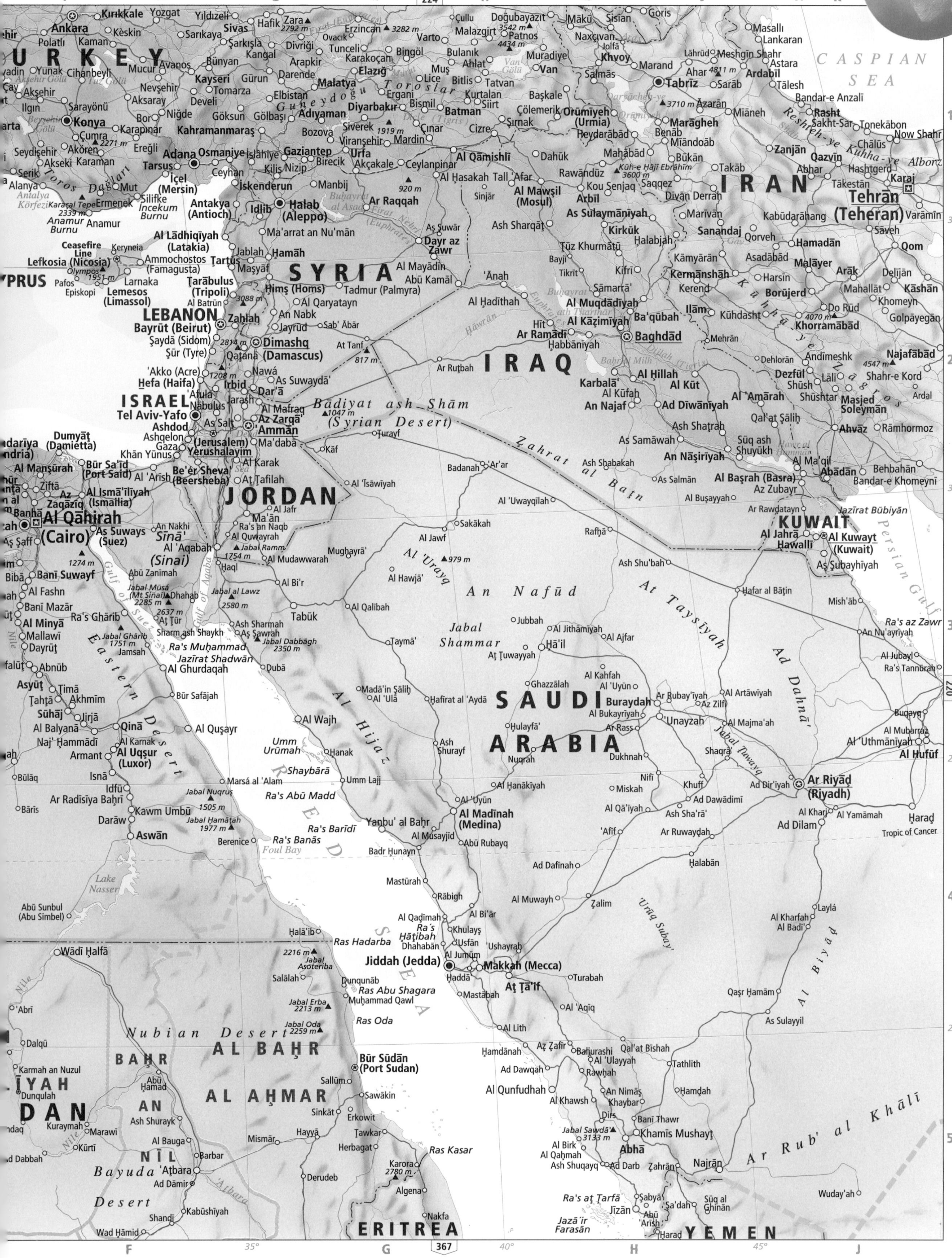

224

F 35° G 40° H 45° J 50° K

TURKEY

Ankara
Kırıkkale
Yozgat
Yıldızeli
Sivas
Hafik
Zara
Erzincan
Kangal
Divriği
Şarkışla
Kayseri
Gürün
Darende
Malatya
Elazığ
Tunceli
Bingöl
Muş
Bitlis
Tatvan
Van
Ahlat
Bulanık
Malazgirt
Patnos
Doğubayazıt
Iğdır
Maku
Polatlı
Kaman
Kırşehir
Cihanbeyli
Aksaray
Niğde
Bor
Konya
Karapınar
Ereğli
Karaman
Seydişehir
Akşehir
Ilgın
Sarayönü
Alanya
Silifke
Mersin (İçel)
Tarsus
Adana
Osmaniye
Kahramanmaraş
Göksun
Gölbaşı
Adıyaman
Diyarbakır
Batman
Siirt
Bismil
Ergani
Siverek
Viranşehir
Mardin
Çınar
Cizre
Şırnak
Gaziantep
Urfa
Birecik
Akçakale
Ceylanpınar
Kilis
Nizip
İslâhiye
İskenderun
Antakya (Antioch)
Ceyhan
Başkale
Çölemerik

Toros Dağları
Güneydoğu Toroslar

Antalya Körfezi
Anamur Burnu
İncekum Burnu

CYPRUS
Lefkosia (Nicosia)
Kyreneia
Ammochostos (Famagusta)
Larnaka
Lemesos (Limassol)
Pafos
Episkopi
Olympos 1951 m
Ceasefire Line

SYRIA
Halab (Aleppo)
Idlib
Al Lādhiqīyah (Latakia)
Jablah
Ţarţūs
Ḩamāh
Maşyāf
Ḩimş (Homs)
Tadmur (Palmyra)
Al Qaryatayn
An Nabk
Jayrūd
Sab' Ābār
Dimashq (Damascus)
Qaţanā
Dar'ā
As Suwaydā'
Manbij
Ar Raqqah
Dayr az Zawr
Al Mayādīn
Abū Kamāl
Al Qāmishlī
Al Ḩasakah
Ma'arrat an Nu'mān
Buhayrat al Asad

LEBANON
Ţarābulus (Tripoli)
Bayrūt (Beirut)
Zahlah
Şaydā (Sidon)
Şūr (Tyre)
Al Batrūn
3088 m

ISRAEL
Tel Aviv-Yafo
Hefa (Haifa)
'Akko (Acre)
'Afula
Nablus
Ashdod
Ashqelon
Gaza
Khān Yūnus
Be'ér Sheva' (Beersheba)
Yerushalayim (Jerusalem)
Dead Sea

JORDAN
'Ammān
Az Zarqā'
As Salt
Irbid
Jarash
Ma'dabā
Al Karak
Aţ Ţafilah
Ma'ān
Al Jafr
Ra's an Naqb
Al Quwayrah
Al 'Aqabah
Jabal Ramm 1754 m
Al Mafraq
Nawá
Al Mudawwarah

IRAQ
Baghdād
Al Mawşil (Mosul)
Arbīl
As Sulaymānīyah
Kirkūk
Dahūk
Tall 'Afar
Sinjār
Ash Sharqāţ
Tūz Khurmātū
Bayjī
Tikrīt
Sāmarrā'
Al Muqdādīyah
Ba'qūbah
Al Kāzimīyah
Al Ḩadīthah
'Ānah
Hīt
Ar Ramādī
Ḩabbānīyah
Ar Ruţbah
Karbalā'
Al Ḩillah
Al Kūfah
An Najaf
Al Kūt
Ad Dīwānīyah
Al 'Amārah
Ash Shaţrah
As Samāwah
An Nāşirīyah
Sūq ash Shuyūkh
Al Başrah (Basra)
Az Zubayr
Al Busayyah
Ash Shabakah
As Salmān
Ḩalabjah
Rawāndūz
Kifrī
Buhayrat ath Tharthār
Bahr al Milh

IRAN
Tehrān (Teheran)
Tabrīz
Orūmīyeh (Urmia)
Marāgheh
Mahābād
Bukān
Saqqez
Sanandaj
Kermānshāh
Hamadān
Qom
Arāk
Borūjerd
Malāyer
Khorramābād
Ilām
Dezfūl
Shūshtar
Ahvāz
Ābādān
Khorramshahr
Bandar-e Khomeynī
Rasht
Qazvīn
Zanjān
Ardabīl
Karaj
Kāshān
Najafābād
Shahr-e Kord
Andīmeshk
Masjed Soleymān
Rāmhormoz
Behbahān
Marand
Khvoy
Salmās
Ahar
Sarāb
Mīāneh
Bandar-e Anzalī
Tālesh
Chālūs
Now Shahr
Tonekābon
Sakht-Sar
Hashtgerd
Tākestān
Abhar
Kabūdarāhang
Qorveh
Kāmyārān
Asadābād
Harsīn
Kerend
Delījān
Varāmīn
Sāveh
Maḩallāt
Khomeyn
Golpāyegān
Kūh-e Hājī Ebrāhīm 3600 m
Rūd
Daryācheh-ye Orūmīyeh
Sahand 3710 m
Zagros
Reshteh-ye Kūhhā-ye Alborz
Kūhhā-ye Zāgros

ARMENIA / AZERBAIJAN
Goris
Sisian
Naxçıvan
Jolfa
Masallı
Lankaran
Astara

CASPIAN SEA

KUWAIT
Al Kuwayt (Kuwait)
Al Jahrā
Hawallī
Aş Şubayhīyah
Jazīrat Būbiyān

SAUDI ARABIA
Ar Riyāḑ (Riyadh)
Makkah (Mecca)
Jiddah (Jedda)
Al Madīnah (Medina)
Yanbu' al Baḩr
Tabūk
Al Jawf
Sakākah
Ḩā'il
Buraydah
'Unayzah
Al Hufūf
Aţ Ţā'if
Abhā
Khamīs Mushayţ
Najrān
Jīzān
Al Wajh
Umm Lajj
Al 'Ulā
Taymā'
Ḩafar al Bāţin
Rafḩā
'Ar'ar
Ţurayf
Al Qurayyāt
Al Jubayl
Ra's Tannūrah
Ad Dammām
Al Khobar
Ad Dir'īyah
Al Kharj
Ad Dilam
Ḩaraḑ
Rābigh
Al Līth
Al Qunfudhah
Tathlīth
Bīshah
Layla
Al Khafjī
As Sulayyil
Wādī ad Dawāsir
Ash Shu'bah
Badanah
Tabarjal
Duba
Ḩaql

An Nafūd
Ad Dahnā'
Al Ḩijāz
'Asīr
Tihāmah
Ar Rub' al Khālī
Bādiyat ash Shām (Syrian Desert)
Al 'Uwayqīlah
Aţ Taysīyah
Jabal Shammar
Al Ḩarrah
Najd
Ḩarrat Rahāţ
Ḩarrat Khaybar

Persian Gulf

EGYPT
Al Qāhirah (Cairo)
Al Jīzah
Al Iskandarīyah (Alexandria)
Bür Sa'īd (Port Said)
Al Ismā'īlīyah (Ismailia)
As Suways (Suez)
Az Zaqāzīq
Al Manşūrah
Dumyāţ (Damietta)
Banhā
Ziftā
Aş Şaff
Banī Suwayf
Al Fashn
Banī Mazār
Al Minyā
Mallawī
Dayrūţ
Abnūb
Asyūţ
Ţahţā
Sūhāj
Akhmīm
Jirjā
Al Balyanā
Qinā
Luxor
Isnā
Idfū
Kawm Umbū
Darāw
Aswān
Abū Sunbul (Abu Simbel)
Al Ghurdaqah
Būr Safājah
Al Quşayr
Marsá al 'Alam
Berenice
Ra's Banās
Foul Bay
Lake Nasser
Jabal Mūsá (Mt Sinai)
Sharm ash Shaykh
Sīnā' (Sinai)
Dhahab
Nuwaybi'
Aţ Ţūr
Ra's Ghārib
Eastern Desert
Gulf of Suez
Gulf of Aqaba

SUDAN
Būr Sūdān (Port Sudan)
Sawākin
Ţawkar
Sinkāt
Hayyā
Mismār
Derudeb
Karora
Wādī Ḩalfā
Abū Ḩamad
Karīmah
Marawī
Kūrtī
Ad Dabbah
Dunqulah
Barbar
'Aţbara
Ad Dāmir
Shandī
Kabūshīyah
Wad Ḩāmid
Bayuda Desert
Nubian Desert
AL BAHR AL AḨMAR
ASH SHAMALĪYAH
NAHR AN NĪL

RED SEA

Ras Hadarba
Ras Abu Shagara
Ras Kasar
Jazā'ir Farasān
Ra's Abū Madd
Ra's Barīdī

ERITREA
Nakfa
Algena

YEMEN
Şa'dah
Ḩaraḑ

Tropic of Cancer

220

367

F 35° G 40° H 45° J

0 100 200 300 400 kilometers

0 100 200 miles

Scale 1:9,000,000 Projection: Azimuthal Equal Area

West Africa

360

A
B
C
D
15°
10°
5°
0°
1
2
3
4
5
Nouakchott
TRARZA
Tidjikja
TAGANT
Tichît
Aoukâr
Moudjéria
MAURITANIA
Boutilimit
Magta' Lahjar
Tiguent
BRÂKNA
Aleg
Mederdra
Rosso
Tâmchekket
HODH ECH CHARGUI
Oualâta
Guérou
HODH EL GHARBI
Podor
Bogué
Bababé
ASSABA
Kiffa
'Ayoûn el 'Atroûs
Néma
Richard Toll
Dagana
Saint-Louis
Kaédi
GORGAL
Keur Momar Sar
Lagbar
Mbout
Tîntâne
Timbedgha
Dendâra
Louga
Koki
Linguère
Matam
Maghama
Kobenni
Kébémer
Méhké
Ranérou
Ould Yenjé
GUIDIMAKA
Touil
Djiguéni
Amourj
Bassikounou
Dara
Touba
Vélingara
Diamounguel
Kirané
Diandioumé
Nioro du Sahel
Cap Vert
Dakar
Pikine
Bambey
Mbaké
Fété Bowé
Bakel
Sélibabi
Rufisque
Thiès
Mbour
Diourbel
SENEGAL
Yélimané
Sandaré
Nara
Goumbou
Nampala
Joal-Fadiout
Fatick
Guinguinéo
Lour-Escale
Ambidédi
Kidira
Lakamané
MALI
Kaolack
Kaffrine
Koungheul
Kayes
Ségala
Diéma
Dioumara
Mourdiah
Sokolo
Ténenkou
Mopti
MOPTI
Koussanar
Goudiri
KAYES
KOULIKORO
Niono
Diafarabé
Bandiagara
GAMBIA
Farafenni
Banjul
Maka
Georgetown
Tambacounda
Bafoulabé
Didiéni
Massina
Koro
Brikama
Pata
Mahina
Markala
Djenné
Bankass
Dialakoto
Dialafara
Toukoto
Kolokani
Banamba
Diouloulou
Bignona
Sédhiou
Vélingara
Kolda
Ziguinchor
Médina Gounas
Ségou
San
Sirakorola
SÉGOU
Diembéreng
Wassadou
Saraya
Kédougou
Kita
Sébékoro
Nossombougou
Koulikoro
Tominián
Yangasso
Kimparana
Toucan
Nouna
GUINEA-BISSAU
Mansabá
Bafatá
Gabú
Koundâra
Kokofata
Négala
Kati
Fana
Bla
Cacheu
Mansôa
Massif du Tamgué
Mt du Tamgué 1538 m
Bamako
Mpessoba
Dioïla
Koutiala
Dédougou
Toma
BURKINA FASO
Bissau
Fulacunda
Xitole
Mali
Koumbia
Fouta Djalon
Baléya
Niagassola
Ouélessébougou
Zangasso
Réo
Ouagadougou
Koudougou
Arquipélago dos Bijagós
Bolama
Buba
MOYENNE-GUINÉE
Koubia
Dabatou
Kintinian
Kangaba
Massigui
Kignan
Mahou
Bondoukui
Orango
Catió
Cacine
Pita
Labé
Tougué
Sido
Bougouni
Kouka
Koundougou
Boromo
GUINÉE-MARITIME
Boké
GUINEA
Dinguiraye
Siguiri
HAUTE-GUINÉE
Sikasso
Kamsar
Cap Boffa
Cap Verga
Boffa
Mont Kavendou 1421 m
Dalaba
Bissikrima
Niandankoro
Kouroussa
SIKASSO
Kalana
Garalo
Kolondiéba
Orodara
Bobo-Dioulasso
Diébougou
Mamou
Kadiondola 1094 m
Banko
Mandiana
Filamana
Manankoro
Kadiolo
Toussiana
Fria
Kindia
Sougéta
Bèlèya
Faranah
Kankan
Saladougou
Tengréla
Banfora
Sidéradougou
Gaoua
Dubréka
Conakry
Coyah
Yana
Falaba
NORTHERN
Kabala
Moribaya
Komodou
Maninian
Mbengué
Niangoloko
Kampti
Forécariah
SIERRA LEONE
Kamaron
Tokouno
Odienné
Madinani
Ouangolodougou
Boundiali
Varalé
Kambia
Port Loko
Makeni
Kondembaia
Loma Mansa 1948 m
Kissidougou
Kérouané
Séguélon
Ferkessédougou
Téhini
Lungi
Lunsar
Magburaka
Yengema
Sefadu
Pic de Tibé 1504 m
Guékédou
Beyla
Bako
Korhogo
Bouna
Freetown
WESTERN
Macenta
GUINÉE-FORESTIÈRE
Sinko
Morondo
Borotou
Dianra
Dikodougou
Nyakaramandougou
Kotouba
Yawri Bay
Moyamba
Mano
Bo
EASTERN
Daru
Boola
Voinjama
Touba
Kani
CÔTE D'IVOIRE
Kakpin
Dabakala
Katiola
SOUTHERN
Matru
Kenema
Nzébéla
Zorzor
Nzérékoré
Gouéké
Lola
Woroflа
Bouandougou
Mankono
Séguéla
Biankouma
Sherbro Island
Pujehun
Bandajuma
Zimmi
Mano River
Belefuanai
Diecke
Sanniquellie
Nimba 1752 m
Man
Zuénoula
Béoumi
Bouaké
Bondoukou
Tanda
Dormaa
Berekum
Wenchi
Techiman
Nkoranza
Ahenkro
Sunyani
Ejura
Haindi
Robertsport
Gbatala
Gbarnga
Danané
Bangolo
Logoualé
Sakassou
Mbahiakro
Daoukro
Tubmanburg
Monrovia
Kakata
Totota
Sagleipie
Duékoué
Daloa 1002 m
Yamoussoukro
Bongouanou
Acnibilékrou
Goaso
ASHANTI
Agogo
Kumasi
Bouaflé
Sinfra
Dimbokro
Abengourou
Tapeta
Toulépleu
Guiglo
Toumodi
Mbatto
Arrah
Konongo
Harbel
LIBERIA
Issia
Gagnoa
Qumé
Afféri
Akoupé
Bibiani
Obuasi
Buchanan
Zwedru
Lakota
Hiré
Adzopé
Taï
Soubré
Divo
Tiassalé
Agboville
WESTERN
Dunkwa
Oda
Asamankese
Foso
CENTRAL
Zia Town
Guéyo
River Cess
Juazohn
Bingerville
Aboisso
Prestea
Aboso
Cape Coast
Tarkwa
Takoradi
Sekondi
Winneba
Saltpond
Fresco
Dabou
Abidjan
Bonoua
Grand-Bassam
Axim
Cape Three Points
Greenville
Sasstown
Grand Cess
Grabo
Sassandra
San-Pédro
Harper
Tabou
Cape Palmas
Grain Coast
Ivory Coast
Gold Coast
Accra
Tema
Araouane
TOMBOUCTOU
Ti-n-Aguelhaj
Lac Faguibine
Bamba
Téméra
Bourem
Râs el Mâ
Tombouctou
Gourma-Rharous
Goundam
Diré
Lerneb
Léré
Niafounké
Ngorkou
Ngouma
Doro
Gao
Gossi
Ansongo
Hombori
Boré
Konna
Douentza
Markoy
Gorom-Gorom
Aribinda
Djibo
Titao
Dori
Ouahigouya
Bani
Gourcy
Yako
Kongoussi
Kaya
Bogandé
Kombissiri
Zorgo
Koupéla
Tenkodogo
Manga
Ouargaye
Nebbou
Zabré
Ouessa
Léo
Pô
Sangha
Tumu
Bolgatanga
Bawku
UPPER WEST
UPPER EAST
Lawra
Nabolo
Wahabu
Fian
Wa
Gushiago
Savelugu
Tamale
Yendi
NORTHERN
Damongo
Bole
Bimbila
GHANA
Kintampo
Yeji
Salaga
Kpandae
BRONG-AHAFO
VOLTA
Atebubu
Mampong
Kpandu
Kpalimé
EASTERN
Koforidua
Somanya
Nsawam
Equator
ATLANTIC OCEAN

0 100 200 300 400 kilometers
0 100 200 miles

NIGER

CHAD

Massif de l'Aïr
AGADEZ
Grand Erg de Bilma
BORKOU - ENNEDI -
TIBESTI
Erg du Djourab

DIFFA

KANEM

ZINDER

MARADI

BATHA

LAC
Lac
Tchad

GUÉRA

SOKOTO

KATSINA

JIGAWA

YOBE

BORNO

CHARI-
BAGUIRMI

KANO

KEBBI

NIGER

KADUNA

BAUCHI

EXTRÊME-
NORD

MOYEN

CHARI

NIGERIA

FEDERAL
CAPITAL
TERRITORY

PLATEAU

ADAMAWA

MAYO-KÉBBI

TANDJILÉ

LOGONE
OCCIDENTAL

LOGONE
ORIENTAL

KWARA

OYO

OSUN

ONDO

KOGI

BENUE

TARABA

NORD

ADAMAOUA

Massif de l'Adamaoua

OUHAM-
PENDÉ

OUHAM

NANA-
GRÉBIZI

CENTRAL

OGUN

LAGOS

EDO

ANAMBRA

ENUGU

CROSS
RIVER

NORD-
OUEST

CAMEROON

OUEST

CENTRE

EST

NANA-MAMBÉRÉ

MAMBÉRÉ-
KADÉÏ

SANGHA-MBAÉRÉ

KÉMO

OMBELLA-MPOKO

AFRICAN
REPUBLIC

LOBAYE

Lagos
Porto-
Novo

ve Coast

Bight
of Benin

DELTA

RIVERS

AKWA
IBOM

ABIA

SUD-OUEST

LITTORAL

Bight of
Bonny

Isla
de Bioco

Guinea

EQUATORIAL

GUINEA

Príncipe

**SÃO TOMÉ
AND PRÍNCIPE**

São Tomé

Annobón
(Eq. Guinea)

SUD

WOLEU-NTEM

ESTUAIRE

Libreville

MOYEN-OGOOUÉ

OGOOUÉ-
MARITIME

Cap Lopez
Port-Gentil

GABON

NGOUNIÉ

LOLO

OGOOUÉ-
IVINDO

HAUT-
OGOOUÉ

NYANGA

NIARI

LÉKOUMOU

SANGHA

LIKOUALA

CONGO

CUVETTE

PLATEAUX

POOL

EQUATEUR

DEMOCRATIC
REPUBLIC
OF THE
CONGO

BANDUNDU

Scale 1:9,000,000 Projection: Azimuthal Equal Area

Sudan • Ethiopia • Somalia

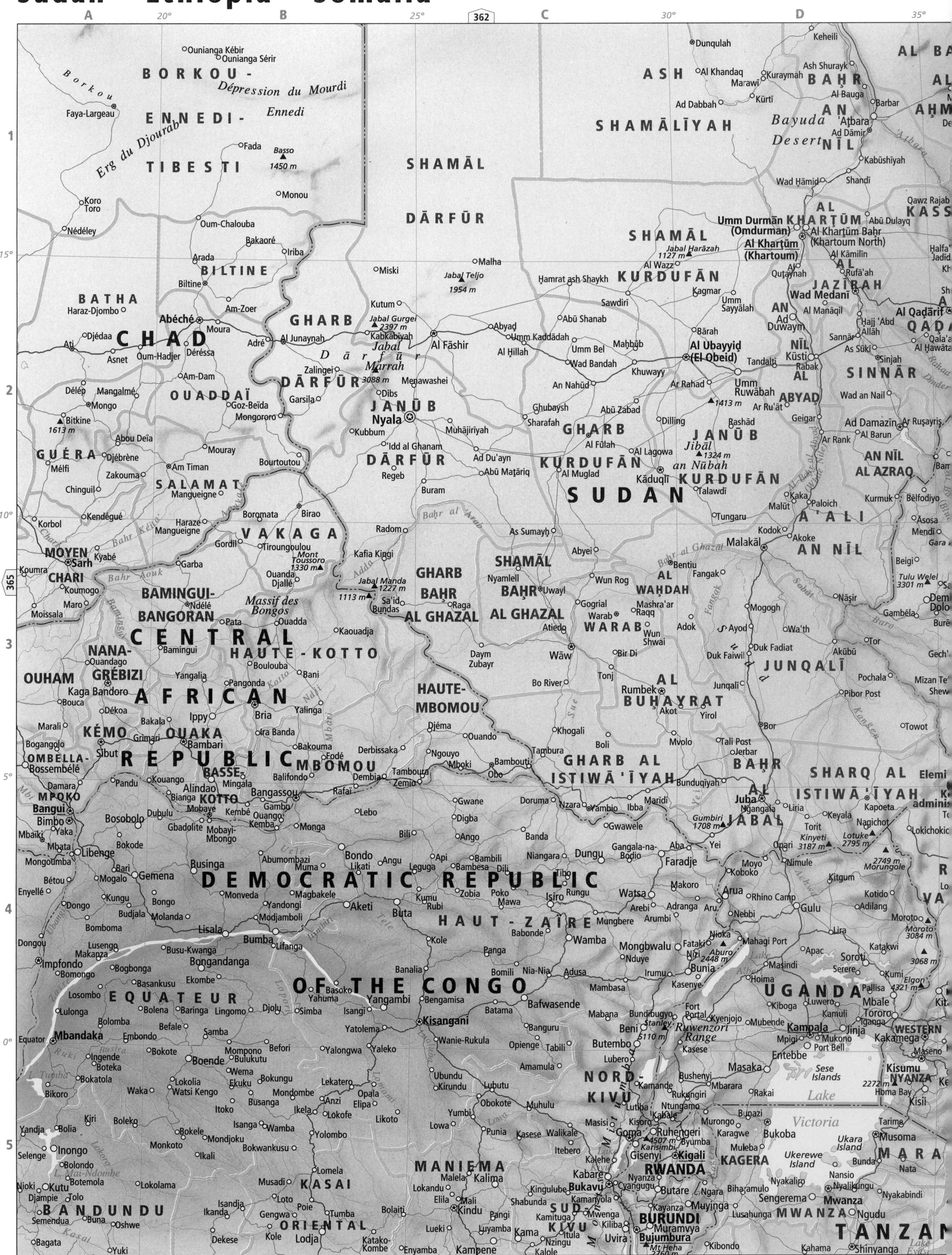
362
369
365
A
B
C
D
20°
25°
30°
35°
15°
10°
5°
0°
1
2
3
4
5
BORKOU-
ENNEDI-
TIBESTI
Dépression du Mourdi
Ennedi
Erg du Djourab
CHAD
BATHA
BILTINE
OUADDAÏ
GUÉRA
SALAMAT
MOYEN CHARI
SHAMĀL DĀRFŪR
GHARB DĀRFŪR
JANŪB DĀRFŪR
Jabal Marrah
ASH SHAMĀLĪYAH
Bayuda Desert
SHAMĀL KURDUFĀN
GHARB KURDUFĀN
JANŪB KURDUFĀN
Jibāl an Nūbah
SUDAN
Umm Durmān (Omdurman)
Al Kharṭūm (Khartoum)
Al Kharṭūm Baḥr (Khartoum North)
Al Ubayyiḍ (El Obeid)
Nyala
Al Fāshir
VAKAGA
BAMINGUI-BANGORAN
CENTRAL AFRICAN REPUBLIC
HAUTE-KOTTO
HAUTE-MBOMOU
MBOMOU
OUAKA
KÉMO
NANA-GRÉBIZI
OUHAM
OMBELLA-MPOKO
BASSE-KOTTO
Bangui
GHARB BAHR AL GHAZAL
SHAMĀL BAḤR AL GHAZAL
WARAB
AL WAḤDAH
AL BUḤAYRAT
JUNQALĪ
GHARB AL ISTIWĀ'ĪYAH
SHARQ AL ISTIWĀ'ĪYAH
BAḤR AL JABAL
Juba
Massif des Bongos
DEMOCRATIC REPUBLIC OF THE CONGO
HAUT-ZAÏRE
EQUATEUR
NORD-KIVU
SUD-KIVU
MANIEMA
KASAI ORIENTAL
BANDUNDU
Kisangani
Mbandaka
UGANDA
Kampala
RWANDA
Kigali
BURUNDI
Bujumbura
Lake Victoria
KAGERA
MWANZA
TANZANIA
Ruwenzori Range

363
SAUDI ARABIA
OMAN
YEMEN
ERITREA
DJIBOUTI
SOMALIA
ETHIOPIA
KENYA
Ar Rub' al Khālī
Al Qa'āmīyāt
Ramlat as Sab'atayn
Ḥaḍramawt
Al Mahrah
Jabal Mahrāt
Ẓufār
RED SEA
Gulf of Aden
INDIAN OCEAN
Bab el Mandeb
Golfe de Tadjoura
Massawa Channel
Dahlak Archipelago
Jazā'ir Farasān
Danakil Depression
Danakil Desert
Ogadēn
Haud
Suquṭrá (Socotra) (Yemen)
'Abd al Kūrī (Yemen)
Ghubbat al Qamar
Ṣan'ā'
Al Ḥudaydah
Ta'izz
'Adan (Aden)
Al Mukallā
Ash Shiḥr
Ṣalālah
Asmara
Mek'elē
Djibouti
Ādīs Ābeba (Addis Ababa)
Dirē Dawa
Hārer
Jijiga
Hargeysa
Berbera
Burco
Boosaaso
Garoowe
Gaalkacyo
Beledweyne
Baydhabo
Muqdisho (Mogadishu)
Marka
Kismaayo
Nairobi
Malindi
Lamu
Garissa
Meru
Embu
Kirinyaga (Mt Kenya) 5199 m
WOQOOYI GALBEED
SANAAG
BARI
TOGDHEER
NUGAAL
MUDUG
GALGUDUUD
HIIRAAN
BAKOOL
GEDO
BAY
SHABEELLAHA DHEXE
SHABEELLAHA HOOSE
BANAADIR
JUBBADA DHEXE
JUBBADA HOOSE
NORTH-EASTERN
EASTERN
COAST
Raas Caseyr
Raas Xaafuun
Equator
40° 45° 50°
E F G H
1 2 3 4 5
15° 10° 5° 0°
0 100 200 300 400 kilometers
0 100 200 miles
Scale 1:9,000,000
Projection: Azimuthal Equal Area

Africa

Central Africa • East Africa

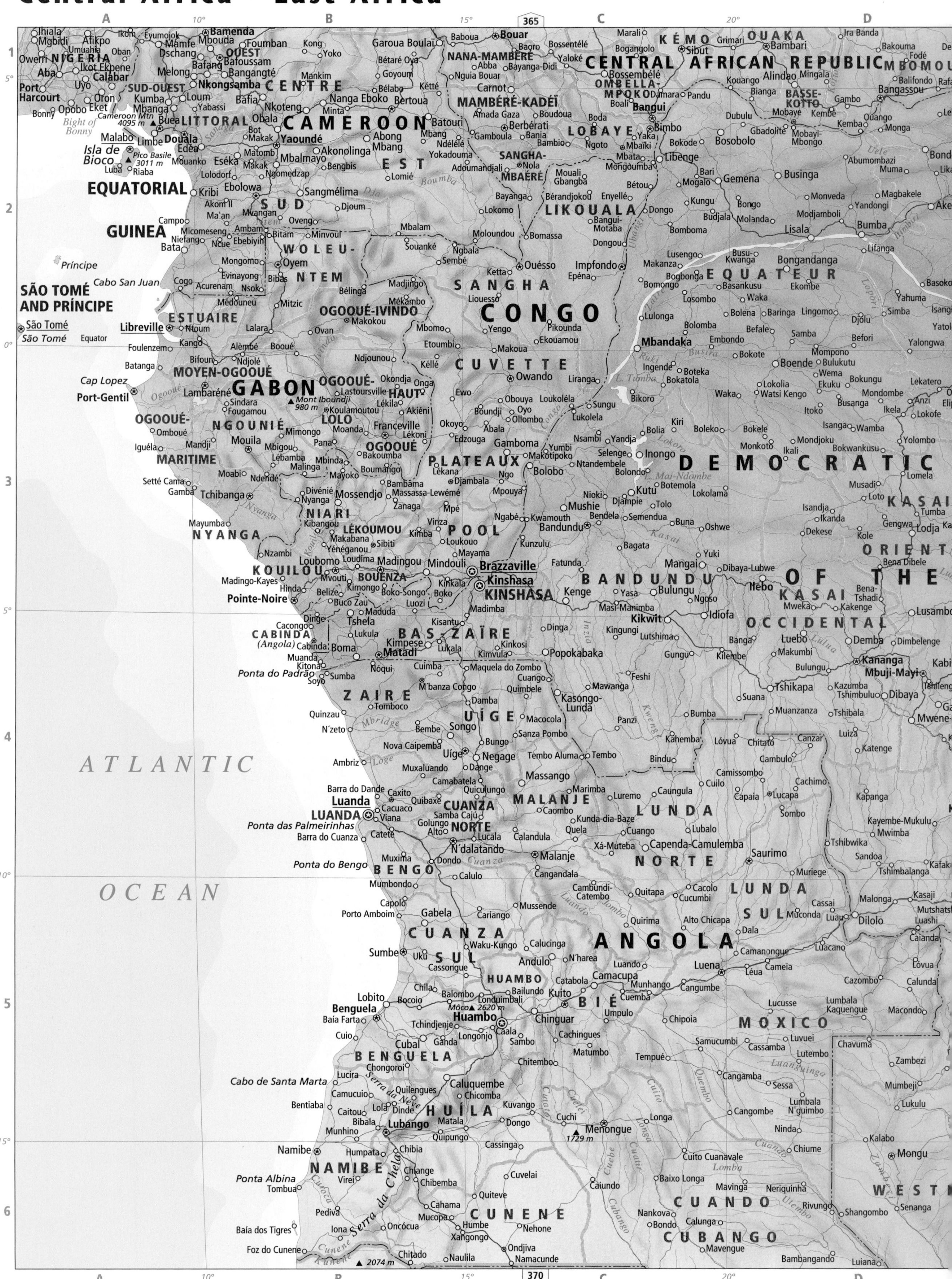

A
B
C
D
10°
15°
20°
5°
0°
10°
15°
1
2
3
4
5
6
365
370
NIGERIA
Calabar
Port Harcourt
Bonny
Bight of Bonny
Cameroon Mtn 4095 m
Malabo
Isla de Bioco
Pico Basile 3011 m
EQUATORIAL
GUINEA
Bata
Príncipe
Cabo San Juan
SÃO TOMÉ AND PRÍNCIPE
São Tomé
Equator
Bamenda
Foumban
OUEST
Bafoussam
SUD-OUEST
Nkongsamba
LITTORAL
Douala
Limbe
Edéa
CENTRE
CAMEROON
Yaoundé
Mbalmayo
Bertoua
Batouri
EST
SUD
Sangmélima
Ebolowa
Kribi
Garoua Boulaï
Bouar
Baboua
NANA-MAMBÉRÉ
MAMBÉRÉ-KADÉÏ
Berbérati
Carnot
Nola
SANGHA-MBAÉRÉ
LOBAYE
Mbaïki
Bangui
CENTRAL AFRICAN REPUBLIC
KÉMO
OUAKA
Bambari
Sibut
Bossembélé
OMBELLA-MPOKO
BASSE-KOTTO
Mobaye
Alindao
Libenge
Gemena
Businga
Lisala
Bumba
Bongandanga
Lulonga
Mbandaka
EQUATEUR
Boende
Ingende
Bolomba
Basankusu
Lusengo
Makanza
Impfondo
LIKOUALA
Dongou
Ouésso
SANGHA
CONGO
Ouesso
CUVETTE
Owando
Makoua
Mbomo
Etoumbi
PLATEAUX
Djambala
Gamboma
POOL
Brazzaville
Kinshasa
KINSHASA
BANDUNDU
Bandundu
Kikwit
Idiofa
Mushie
Inongo
DEMOCRATIC
Lac Mai-Ndombe
Kasai
KASAI ORIENTAL
OF THE
KASAI OCCIDENTAL
Kananga
Mbuji-Mayi
Tshikapa
Ilebo
Mweka
Luebo
Demba
Dibaya
WOLEU-NTEM
Oyem
Bitam
ESTUAIRE
Libreville
Ntoum
Cocobeach
Lambaréné
MOYEN-OGOOUÉ
GABON
OGOOUÉ-IVINDO
Makokou
OGOOUÉ-MARITIME
Port-Gentil
Cap Lopez
Omboué
NGOUNIÉ
Mouila
Mimongo
OGOOUÉ-LOLO
Koulamoutou
Mont Iboundji 980 m
HAUT-OGOOUÉ
Franceville
Moanda
Lastoursville
NYANGA
Tchibanga
Mayumba
NIARI
Mossendjo
Dolisie
LÉKOUMOU
Sibiti
KOUILOU
Pointe-Noire
BOUENZA
Madingou
Mindouli
CABINDA (Angola)
Cabinda
BAS-ZAÏRE
Matadi
Boma
Kimpese
Ponta do Padrão
Soyo
ZAIRE
M'banza Congo
UÍGE
Uíge
Negage
Maquela do Zombo
ATLANTIC
OCEAN
Ambriz
Luanda
LUANDA
Ponta das Palmeirinhas
Barra do Cuanza
CUANZA NORTE
N'dalatando
MALANJE
Malanje
LUNDA NORTE
Lucapa
Saurimo
LUNDA SUL
Dala
Dilolo
Ponta do Bengo
BENGO
Caxito
Porto Amboim
CUANZA SUL
Sumbe
Gabela
ANGOLA
HUAMBO
Huambo
Môco 2620 m
Kuito
BIÉ
Camacupa
Luena
MOXICO
Lobito
Benguela
Baía Farta
BENGUELA
Cabo de Santa Marta
HUÍLA
Lubango
Serra da Neve
Namibe
NAMIBE
Tombua
Ponta Albina
Baía dos Tigres
Foz do Cunene
Serra da Chela
CUNENE
Ondjiva
Menongue
1729 m
CUANDO CUBANGO
Cuito Cuanavale
Mavinga
2074 m
Namacunde
WEST
Mongu
Chavuma

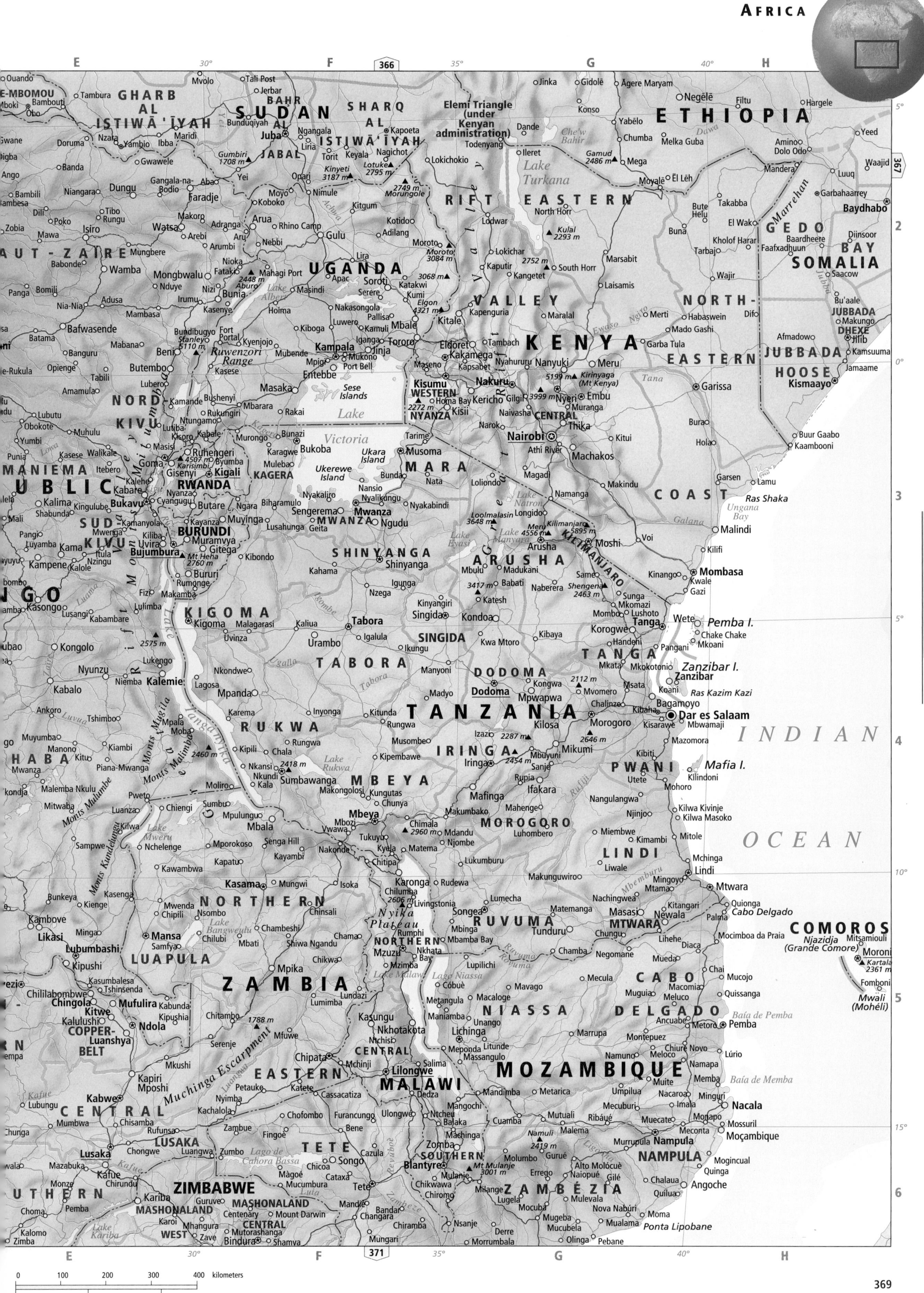

366
367
371

0 100 200 300 400 kilometers
0 100 200 miles
Scale 1:9,000,000 Projection: Azimuthal Equal Area

Southern Africa

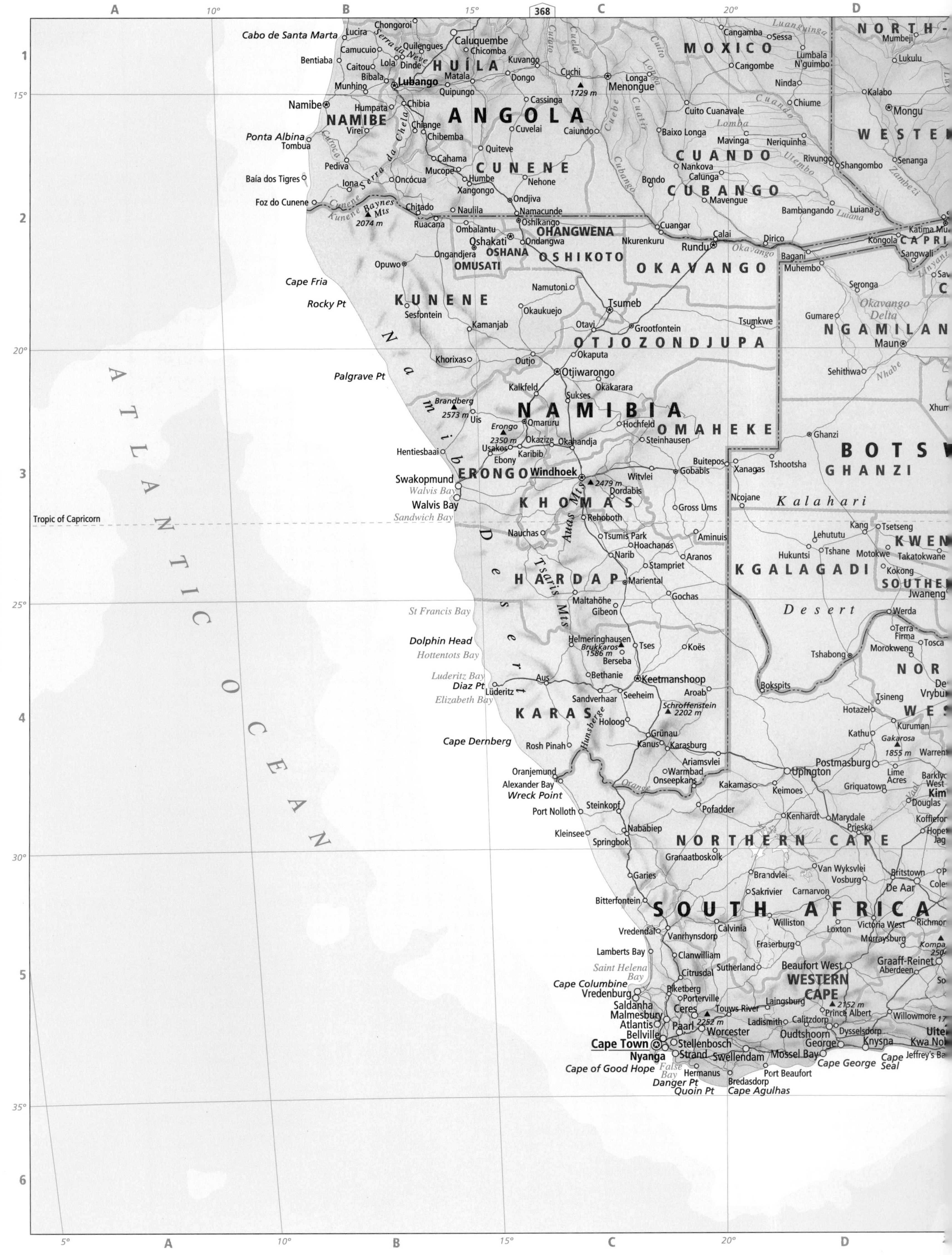
A
10°
B
15°
368
C
20°
D
1
2
3
4
5
6
15°
20°
25°
30°
35°
5°
ATLANTIC OCEAN
Tropic of Capricorn
ANGOLA
NAMIBIA
SOUTH AFRICA
BOTSWANA
HUÍLA
NAMIBE
CUNENE
MOXICO
CUANDO CUBANGO
OHANGWENA
OSHANA
OSHIKOTO
OMUSATI
OKAVANGO
KUNENE
OTJOZONDJUPA
OMAHEKE
ERONGO
KHOMAS
HARDAP
KARAS
NORTHERN CAPE
WESTERN CAPE
NGAMILAND
GHANZI
KGALAGADI
Namib Desert
Kalahari Desert
Cabo de Santa Marta
Lucira
Chongoroi
Caluquembe
Chicomba
Quilengues
Camucuio
Bentiaba
Caitou
Lola
Dinde
Bibala
Munhino
Lubango
Matala
Kuvango
Dongo
Quipungo
Cuchi
1729 m
Menongue
Longa
Namibe
Humpata
Chibia
Chiange
Chibembe
Virei
Ponta Albina
Tombua
Pediva
Baía dos Tigres
Iona
Oncócua
Mucope
Humbe
Xangongo
Cahama
Quiteve
Cuvelai
Caiundo
Cassinga
Nehone
Ondjiva
Namacunde
Foz do Cunene
Baynes Mts
2074 m
Chitado
Ruacana
Naulila
Oshikango
Ombalantu
Oshakati
Ondangwa
Ongandjera
Opuwo
Cape Fria
Rocky Pt
Sesfontein
Kamanjab
Namutoni
Okaukuejo
Tsumeb
Otavi
Grootfontein
Nkurenkuru
Rundu
Calai
Cuangar
Dirico
Bagani
Muhembo
Tsumkwe
Khorixas
Outjo
Okaputa
Otjiwarongo
Okakarara
Palgrave Pt
Kalkfeld
Sukses
Brandberg
2573 m
Uis
Erongo
2350 m
Omaruru
Hochfeld
Steinhausen
Okazize
Okahandja
Usakos
Karibib
Ebony
Hentiesbaai
Swakopmund
Walvis Bay
Windhoek
2479 m
Witvlei
Gobabis
Buitepos
Xanagas
Tshootsha
Dordabis
Gross Ums
Sandwich Bay
Rehoboth
Nauchas
Tsumis Park
Hoachanas
Aminuis
Narib
Aranos
Stampriet
Mariental
Gochas
Auas Mts
Tsaris Mts
Maltahöhe
Gibeon
St Francis Bay
Dolphin Head
Hottentots Bay
Helmeringhausen
Brukkaros
1586 m
Berseba
Tses
Koës
Luderitz Bay
Diaz Pt
Lüderitz
Elizabeth Bay
Aus
Bethanie
Keetmanshoop
Seeheim
Sandverhaar
Aroab
Schroffenstein
2202 m
Holoog
Huns berge
Cape Dernberg
Rosh Pinah
Grünau
Kanus
Karasburg
Ariamsvlei
Warmbad
Onseepkans
Oranjemund
Alexander Bay
Wreck Point
Port Nolloth
Steinkopf
Kakamas
Upington
Keimoes
Pofadder
Kleinsee
Nababiep
Springbok
Kenhardt
Marydale
Prieska
Granaatboskolk
Garies
Brandvlei
Van Wyksvlei
Vosburg
Sakrivier
Carnarvon
Britstown
De Aar
Bitterfontein
Williston
Victoria West
Richmond
Vredendal
Calvinia
Vanrhynsdorp
Loxton
Murraysburg
Fraserburg
Lamberts Bay
Clanwilliam
Saint Helena Bay
Citrusdal
Sutherland
Beaufort West
Graaff-Reinet
Aberdeen
Cape Columbine
Vredenburg
Saldanha
Malmesbury
Atlantis
Bellville
Cape Town
Nyanga
Piketberg
Porterville
Ceres
Touws River
2252 m
Paarl
Worcester
Stellenbosch
Strand
Swellendam
Laingsburg
Ladismith
Calitzdorp
Oudtshoorn
2152 m
Prince Albert
Willowmore
Dysselsdorp
George
Knysna
Mossel Bay
Cape George
Cape Seal
Jeffrey's Bay
Cape of Good Hope
False Bay
Hermanus
Danger Pt
Quoin Pt
Bredasdorp
Cape Agulhas
Port Beaufort
Cangamba
Sessa
Cangombe
Lumbala N'guimbo
Ninda
Chiume
Cuito Cuanavale
Baixo Longa
Mavinga
Neriquinha
Nankova
Calunga
Mavengue
Bondo
Rivungo
Shangombo
Bambangando
Luiana
Kalabo
Mongu
Senanga
Lukulu
Mumbeji
Katima Mulilo
Kongola
Sangwali
Seronga
Gumare
Okavango Delta
Maun
Sehithwa
Ghanzi
Ncojane
Kang
Tsetseng
Lehututu
Tshane
Hukuntsi
Motokwe
Takatokwane
Kokong
Jwaneng
Werda
Terra Firma
Tosca
Morokweng
Tshabong
Bokspits
Tsineng
Vryburg
Hotazel
Kuruman
Kathu
Gakarosa
1855 m
Postmasburg
Lime Acres
Griquatown
Douglas
Barkly West
Kimberley
Koffiefontein
Hopetown

369

E 30° F 35° G 40° H

ZAMBIA
CENTRAL
EASTERN
LUSAKA
SOUTHERN
Mkushi
Kapiri Mposhi
Kabwe
Lubungu
Mumbwa
Chunga
Lusaka
Chongwe
Luangwa
Zumbo
Rufunsa
Chisamba
Nyimba
Petauke
Katete
Kachalola
Chipata
Mchinji
Mazabuka
Kafue
Monze
Chirundu
Kariba
Choma
Pemba
Kalomo
Zimba
Maamba
Binga
Livingstone
Lake Kariba

MALAWI
CENTRAL
SOUTHERN
Lilongwe
Salima
Dedza
Mangochi
Balaka
Ntcheu
Machinga
Zomba
Chiradzulu
Blantyre
Mulanje
Chikwawa
Mt Mulanje 3001 m

MOZAMBIQUE
NIASSA
TETE
ZAMBÉZIA
NAMPULA
MANICA
SOFALA
INHAMBANE
GAZA
MAPUTO
Massangulo
Maúa
Namuno
Namapa
Memba
Baía de Memba
Muite
Umpilua
Nacaroa
Minguri
Nacala
Mossuril
Moçambique
Mandimba
Metarica
Cuamba
Mutuali
Mecuburi
Muecate
Monapo
Meconta
Nampula
Malema
Ribáuè
Murrupula
Namuli 2419 m
Gurué
Molumbo
Erego
Alto Molócuè
Naiopué
Gilé
Mogincual
Quinga
Chalaua
Angoche
Quilua
Milange
Lugela
Mugeba
Mulevala
Nova Nabúri
Moma
Ponta Lipobane
Mocuba
Mucubela
Mualama
Pebane
Olinga
Namacurra
Derre
Morrumbala
Namidobe
Quelimane
Mopeia
Marromeu
Chinde
Ponta Timbue
Chofombo
Fingoè
Furancungo
Ulongwé
Bene
Cazula
Lago de Cahora Bassa
Songo
Màgoè
Chicoa
Cataxa
Mucumbura
Tete
Mandie
Bandar
Changara
Chiramba
Nhamalábue
Mungari
Guro
Vila de Sena
Caia
Maringuè
Chiromo
Nsanje
Catandica
Nyanga
Inyangani 2592 m
Serra da Gorongosa 1862 m
Inhaminga
Gorongosa
Chimoio
Nhamatanda
Dondo
Beira
Buzi
Sofala
Monte Binga 2436 m
Chimanimani
Chipinge
Dombe
Espungabera
Hacufera
Chitobe
Divinhe
Machanga
Nova Mambone
Bartolomeu Dias
Ilha do Bazaruto
Jofane
Massangena
Mabote
Vilanculos
Mapinhane
Chicualacuala
Machaila
Pafuri
Mapai
Chigubo
Nhachengue
Funhalouro
Ponta da Barra Falsa
Massinga
Morrumbene
Homoine
Panda
Ponta da Barra
Inhambane
Mabalane
Massingir
Chókwé
Inharrime
Quissico
Mapulanguene
Macia
Chidenguele
Xai-Xai
Magude
Moamba
Matola
Marracuene
Maputo
Cabo de Santa Maria
Bela Vista
Catuane
Zambeze
Luia
Changane
Save
Limpopo

ZIMBABWE
MASHONALAND CENTRAL
MASHONALAND WEST
MASHONALAND EAST
MANICALAND
MIDLANDS
MATABELELAND NORTH
MATABELELAND SOUTH
MASVINGO
Guruve
Centenary
Mount Darwin
Karoi
Mhangura
Bindura
Shamva
Zave
Mutoko
Murewa
Chinhoyi
Concession
Harare
Chitungwiza
Chegutu
Kadoma
Marondera
Rusape
Wedza
Gokwe
Chakari
Kamativi
Msuna
Dete
Empress Mine
Lupane
Ngamo
Nkayi
Kwekwe
Chivhu
Redcliff
Mvuma
Gweru
Lalapansi
Shurugwi
Gutu
Buhera
Cashel
Mutare
Inyathi
Fort Rixon
Masvingo
Mashava
Nyamandhlovu
Bulawayo
Maitengwe
Tutume
Plumtree
Esigodini
Mbalabala
Filabusi
Zvishavane
Bikita
Zaka
Ngundu
Chiredzi
Kezi
Gwanda
West Nicholson
Mbizi
Mwenezi
Francistown
Mmadinare
Serule
Selebi Phikwe
Bobonong
Sefophe
Tuli
Mazunga
Beitbridge
Shashe
Bubi
Sebina
Kana

SOUTH AFRICA
NORTHERN PROVINCE
MPUMALANGA
GAUTENG
KWAZULU-NATAL
EASTERN CAPE
Messina
Alldays
Thohoyandou
Vivo
Mara
Louis Trichardt
Giyani
Tom Burke
Soekmekaar
Tzaneen
Phalaborwa
Ellisras
Pietersburg
Lebowakgomo
Thabazimbi
Nylstroom
Warmbad
Marble Hall
Tshokwane
Newington
Siyabuswa
Sun City
Pretoria
Mamelodi
Tembisa
Krugersdorp
Soweto
Johannesburg
Germiston
Heidelburg
Bethal
Evaton
Vereeniging
Vanderbijlpark
Carletonville
Klerksdorp
Sasolburg
Standerton
Ermelo
Barberton
Nelspruit
Mbabane
Mhlume
Siteki
Manzini
SWAZILAND
Big Bend
Hlatikulu
Lavumisa
Volksrust
Piet Retief
Ubombo
Kroonstad
Welkom
Virginia
Winburg
Bethlehem
Harrismith
Madadeni
Newcastle
Ozizweni
Vryheid
Dundee
Ulundi
Phuthaditjhaba
Ladysmith
Empangeni
Richards Bay
Lake St Lucia
Lejone
Maseru
Teyateyaneng
Mokhotlong
Estcourt
Greytown
Sundumbili
Stanger
Thabana-Ntlenyana 3482 m
Pietermaritzburg
Kwa Mashu
Roma
Mafeteng
LESOTHO
Umlazi
Durban
Mohale's Hoek
Quthing
Isipingo
Umzinto
Amanzimtoti
Scottburgh
Kokstad
Marburg
Barkly East
Port Shepstone
Uvongo
Elliot
Tsolo
Port St Johns
Umtata
Coffee Bay
Queenstown
Butterworth
Stutterheim
King William's Town
Bisho
East London
Mdantsane
Zwelitsha
Grahamstown
Port Alfred
Mochudi
Mokwena
Gaborone
Palapye
Mahalapye
Drakensberg

Mozambique Channel
Bassas da India (Réunion)
Île Europa (Réunion)
INDIAN OCEAN

MADAGASCAR
TOLIARA
Tambohorano
Maintirano
Reharaka
Masoarivo
Belo Tsiribihina
Tanjona Tsiribihina
Morondava
Andranopasy
Manja
Morombe
Tanjona Ankaboa
Ankazoabo
1348 m
Mahaboboka
Manombo Atsimo
Sakaraha
Toliara
Andranovory
Tongobory
Betioky
Soamanonga
Fotadrevo
Ejeda
Itampolo
Ampanihy
Androka
Beloha
Tanjona Vohimena
Mangoky
Linta

372

15° 20° 25° 30° 35°
1 2 3 4 5 6

E 30° F 35° G 40° H 45° J

0 100 200 300 400 kilometers
0 100 200 miles
Scale 1:9,000,000 Projection: Azimuthal Equal Area

Madagascar

40° A 45° B 50° C 55° D

1
2
3
4
5
6

Kilifi
Mombasa
Wete
Pemba I.
Chake Chake
Mafia I.
Praslin I.
Silhouette I.
La Digue I.
Victoria
Mahé I.
Amirante Isles
Platte I.
Alphonse I.
Coetivy I.
SEYCHELLES
Aldabra Is
Cosmoledo Group
Assumption I.
Astove I.
St Pierre I.
Providence I.
Farquhar Group
Agalega Is (Mauritius)
TANZANIA
Mtwara
Quionga
Cabo Delgado
Palma
CABO DELGADO
Mocimboa da Praia
Diaca
Chai
Mucojo
Quissanga
Muaguide
Baía de Pemba
Pemba
Lúrio
MOZAMBIQUE
Memba
Baía de Memba
Minguri
Nacala
Monapo
Mossuril
Moçambique
NAMPULA
Mogincual
Quinga
Mitsamiouli
Njazidja (Grande Comore)
Moroni
Kartala 2361 m
COMOROS
Nzwani (Anjouan)
Moutsamoudou
Domoni
Fomboni
Mwali (Mohéli)
MAYOTTE (Fr.)
Mamoudzou
Dzaoudzi
Mozambique Channel
Îles Glorieuses (Réunion)
Tanjona Bobaomby (Cap d'Ambre)
Andranovondronina
Ramena
Ambohitra 1475 m
Antsiranana
Bobasakoa
Anivorano Avaratra
Ampisikinana
Nosy Bé
Ambilobe
Iharaña
ANTSIRANANA
1785 m
Lohatanjona Angadoka
Ambanja
Marovato
Maromokotro 2876 m
Ampanefena
Bemarivo
Doany
Sambava
Analalava
Bealanana
Lohatanjona Maromony
Ampahana
Andapa
Antsohihy
Antalaha
INDIAN
Befandriana Avaratra
Leanja
Mahalevona
Ankavia
Mahajanga
Katsepy
Ambalakida
Boriziny
Maroantsetra
Ampanavoana
Vinanivao
Mitsinjo
Marovoay
Mampikony
Mandritsara
Tanjona Masoala
Tanjona Vilanandro
Soalala
Manarantsandry
Mananara Avaratra
Helodrano Antongila
Ambohipaky
Madirovalo
Ambato Boeny
1301 m
Tromelin I. (Réunion)
Besalampy
Sitampiky
Manompana
Île Juan de Nova (Réunion)
Mahabe
Maevatanana
Tsaratanana
TOAMASINA
Soanierana-Ivongo
MAHAJANGA
Betsiboka
Betrandraka
Andilamena
Tambohorano
Ikahavo
Kandreho
Ranobe
Fenoarivo Atsinanana
847 m
Andriamena
Vavatenina
Ampasafaravola
Mahavelona
Ambatomainty
Vatoloha 1575 m
Morafenobe
Maintirano
Ambatondrazaka
Beravina
Ankazobe
Andilanatoby
Didy
Toamasina
Reharaka
Fanandrana
ANTANANARIVO
Antsalova
Ambohidratrimo
Moroseranana
Tsiroanomandidy
Moramanga
Ampasimanolotra
OCEAN
Masoarivo
Miarinarivo
Antananarivo
MADAGASCAR
Anosibe an'Ala
Vatomandry
Miandrivazo
Ambatolampy
Antanambao Manampotsy
Belo Tsiribihina
Tanjona Tsiribihina
Tsiribihina
Antsirabe
Ibinty 2254 m
2119 m
Mahanoro
Mania
Marolambo
Morondava
Malaimbandy
Ambato-finandrahana
Fandriana
MAURITIUS
Port Louis
Curepipe
Mahébourg
Mahabo
Ambositra
Nosy-Varika
Amborompotsy
2052 m
Vohitrandriana
Matsiatra
Mandabe
Ikalamavony
Ambohimahasoa
Andranopasy
Saint-Denis
Manja
Fianarantsoa
Mananjary
Saint-Paul
RÉUNION (Fr.)
Morombe
Mangoky
Beroroha
FIANARANTSOA
Ifanadiana
Tanjona Ankaboa
TOLIARA
Ambalavao
Ampasimanjeva
Saint-Pierre
Vohilava
Zazafotsy
Ikongo
Ankazoabo
Ihosy
Boby 2658 m
Manakara
Mascarene Islands
1348 m
Satrokala
Vohipeno
Mahaboboka
Ranohira
Ivohibe
Manombo Atsimo
Sakaraha
Vondrozo
Farafangana
Tropic of Capricorn
Toliara
Andranovory
Betroka
1824 m
Lopary
Tongobory
Bezaha
Benenitra
Ranomena
Vangaindrano
Betioky
Belamoty
Ivakoany 1637 m
Midongy Atsimo
Manambondro
Soamanonga
Manankoliva
Befotaka
Fotadrevo
Beraketa
Ejeda
Bekily
Manantenina
Imanombo
Itampolo
Linta
Tranoroa
Tranomaro
Ampanihy
Antanimora Atsimo
Androka
Tôlañaro
Beloha
Amboasary
Tsiombe
Ambovombe
Tanjona Vohimena
Betanty

A 45° B 50° C 55° D 60°

kilometers 0 100 200 300 400
miles 0 100 200
Scale 1:9,000,000
Projection: Azimuthal Equal Area

369

Africa

Islands around Africa

A B C

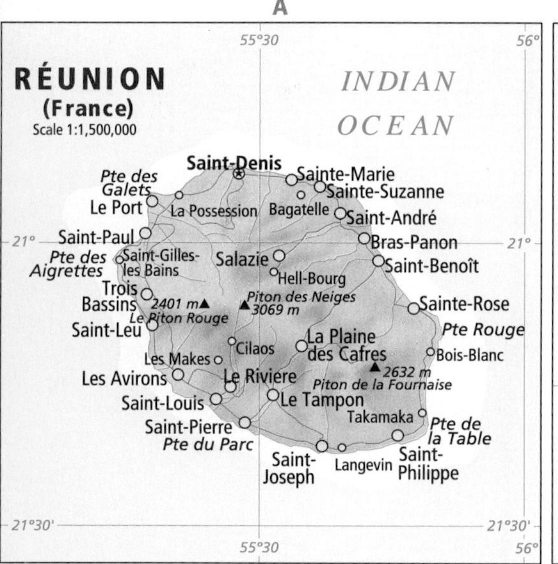
RÉUNION
(France)
Scale 1:1,500,000
INDIAN
OCEAN
55°30
56°
21°
21°30'
Saint-Denis
Sainte-Marie
Sainte-Suzanne
Pte des Galets
Le Port
La Possession
Bagatelle
Saint-André
Saint-Paul
Bras-Panon
Pte des Aigrettes
Saint-Gilles-les Bains
Salazie
Hell-Bourg
Saint-Benoît
Trois Bassins
2401 m
Le Piton Rouge
Piton des Neiges 3069 m
Sainte-Rose
Pte Rouge
Saint-Leu
La Plaine des Cafres
Cilaos
Bois-Blanc
Les Makes
2632 m
Piton de la Fournaise
Les Avirons
Le Rivière
Le Tampon
Saint-Louis
Takamaka
Pte de la Table
Saint-Pierre
Pte du Parc
Saint-Joseph
Langevin
Saint-Philippe

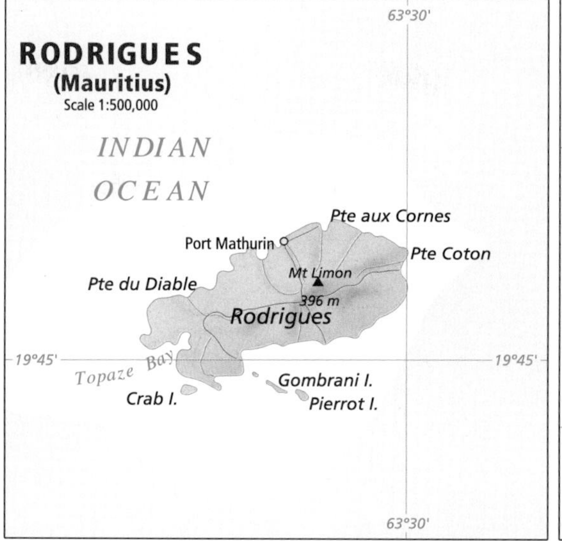
RODRIGUES
(Mauritius)
Scale 1:500,000
INDIAN
OCEAN
63°30'
19°45'
Pte aux Cornes
Port Mathurin
Pte Coton
Mt Limon
Pte du Diable
396 m
Rodrigues
Topaze Bay
Gombrani I.
Crab I.
Pierrot I.

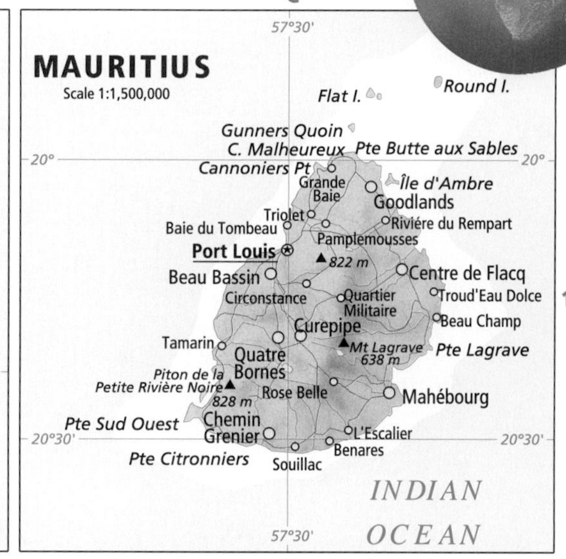
MAURITIUS
Scale 1:1,500,000
57°30'
20°
20°30'
Flat I.
Round I.
Gunners Quoin
C. Malheureux
Pte Butte aux Sables
Cannoniers Pt
Grande Baie
Île d'Ambre
Goodlands
Triolet
Rivière du Rempart
Baie du Tombeau
Pamplemousses
Port Louis
822 m
Centre de Flacq
Beau Bassin
Troud'Eau Dolce
Circonstance
Quartier Militaire
Beau Champ
Curepipe
Tamarin
Mt Lagrave 638 m
Pte Lagrave
Quatre Bornes
Piton de la Petite Rivière Noire
828 m
Rose Belle
Mahébourg
Chemin Grenier
Pte Sud Ouest
L'Escalier
Benares
Pte Citronniers
Souillac
INDIAN
OCEAN

1

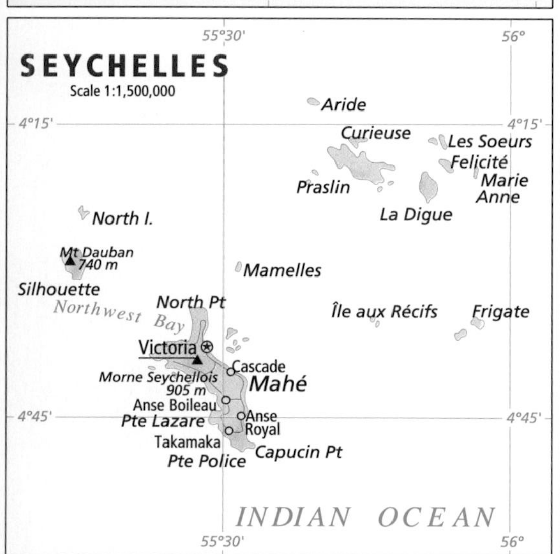
SEYCHELLES
Scale 1:1,500,000
55°30'
56°
4°15'
4°45'
Aride
Curieuse
Les Soeurs
Felicité
Praslin
Marie Anne
La Digue
North I.
Mt Dauban 740 m
Mamelles
Silhouette
Northwest Bay
North Pt
Île aux Récifs
Frigate
Victoria
Cascade
Morne Seychellois 905 m
Mahé
Anse Boileau
Pte Lazare
Anse Royal
Takamaka
Capucin Pt
Pte Police
INDIAN OCEAN

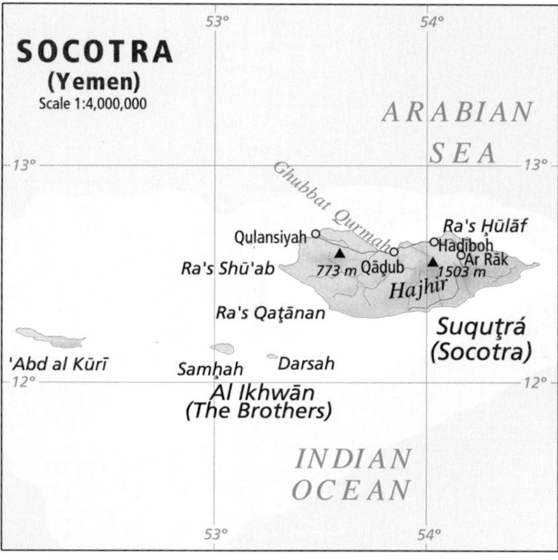
SOCOTRA
(Yemen)
Scale 1:4,000,000
53°
54°
13°
12°
ARABIAN
SEA
Ghubbat Qurmah
Ra's Ḥūlāf
Qulansiyah
Hadiboh
Ar Rāk
773 m
Qādub
1503 m
Ra's Shū'ab
Hajhir
Ra's Qaṭānan
Suquṭrá
(Socotra)
'Abd al Kūrī
Samḥah
Darsah
Al Ikhwān
(The Brothers)
INDIAN
OCEAN

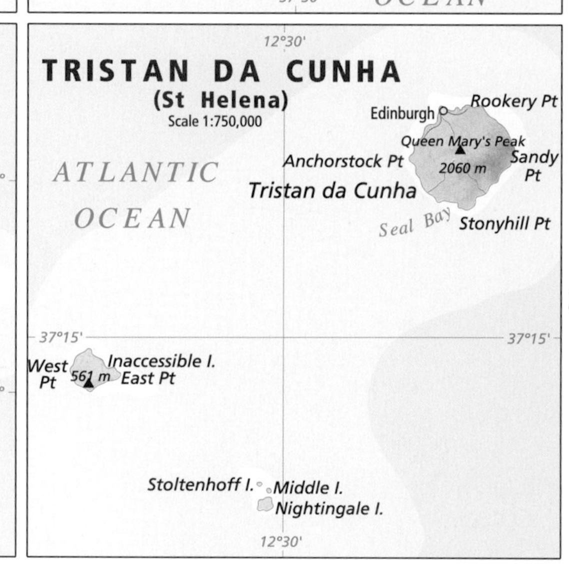
TRISTAN DA CUNHA
(St Helena)
Scale 1:750,000
12°30'
37°15'
Edinburgh
Rookery Pt
Queen Mary's Peak 2060 m
ATLANTIC
OCEAN
Anchorstock Pt
Sandy Pt
Tristan da Cunha
Seal Bay
Stonyhill Pt
Inaccessible I.
West Pt
561 m
East Pt
Stoltenhoff I.
Middle I.
Nightingale I.

2

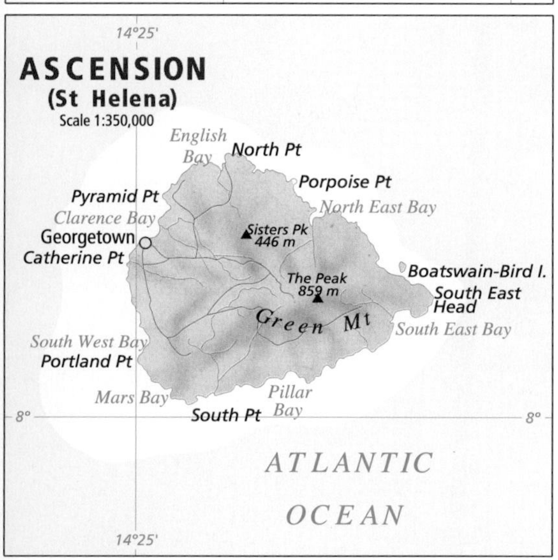
ASCENSION
(St Helena)
Scale 1:350,000
14°25'
8°
English Bay
North Pt
Pyramid Pt
Porpoise Pt
Clarence Bay
North East Bay
Georgetown
Sisters Pk 446 m
Catherine Pt
Boatswain-Bird I.
The Peak 859 m
South East Head
Green Mt
South West Bay
South East Bay
Portland Pt
Mars Bay
Pillar Bay
South Pt
ATLANTIC
OCEAN

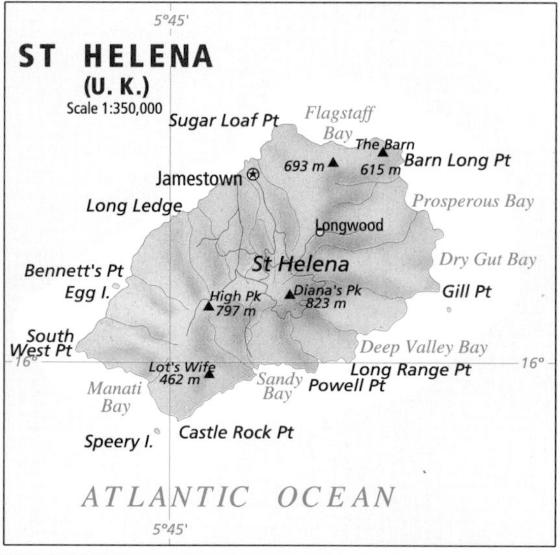
ST HELENA
(U. K.)
Scale 1:350,000
5°45'
16°
Sugar Loaf Pt
Flagstaff Bay
The Barn
693 m
615 m
Barn Long Pt
Jamestown
Long Ledge
Prosperous Bay
Longwood
Bennett's Pt
St Helena
Dry Gut Bay
Egg I.
High Pk 797 m
Diana's Pk 823 m
Gill Pt
South West Pt
Deep Valley Bay
Lot's Wife 462 m
Long Range Pt
Manati Bay
Sandy Bay
Powell Pt
Speery I.
Castle Rock Pt
ATLANTIC OCEAN

MADEIRA
(Portugal)
Scale 1:2,000,000
17°
33°
Porto Santo
517 m
Ilhéu de Ferro
Porto Santo
Ilhéu de Baixo
Porto Moniz
São Vicente
Santana
Pto do Pargo
1862 m
Faial
Calheta
Pico Ruivo de Santana
Pta de São Lourenço
Ribeira Brava
Machico
Madeira
Santa Cruz
Câmara de Lobos
Funchal
Deserta Grande
ATLANTIC
OCEAN
Ilhas Desertas
Ilhéu do Bugio

3

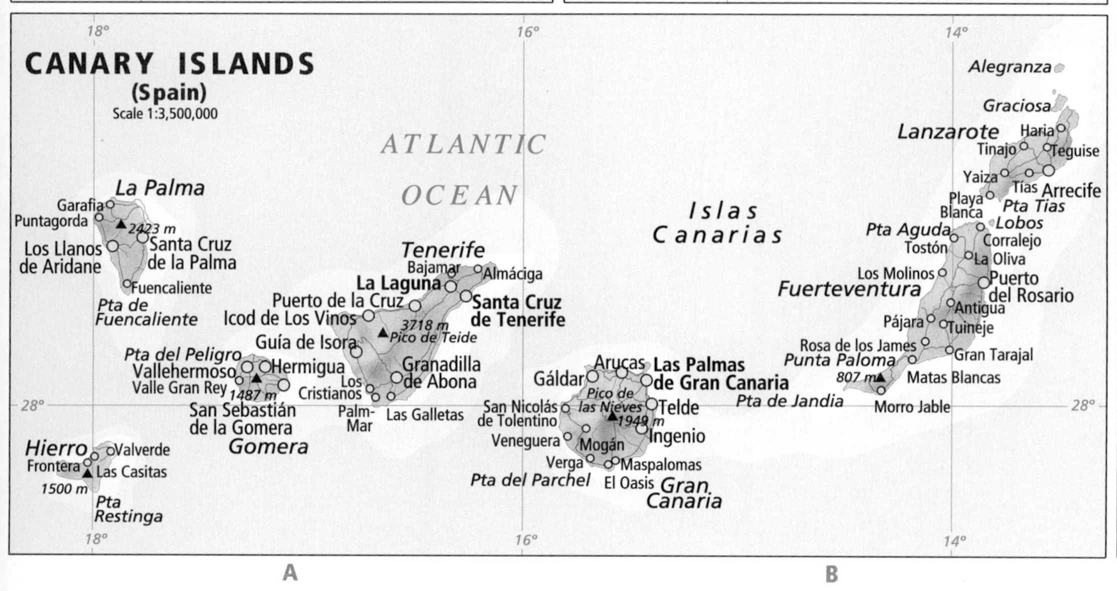
CANARY ISLANDS
(Spain)
Scale 1:3,500,000
18°
16°
14°
28°
ATLANTIC
OCEAN
Alegranza
Graciosa
Lanzarote
Haria
Tinajo
Teguise
Yaiza
Tías
Arrecife
Playa Blanca
Pta Tias
La Palma
Garafía
Puntagorda
2423 m
Islas Canarias
Pta Aguda
Lobos
Los Llanos de Aridane
Santa Cruz de la Palma
Tenerife
Tostón
Corralejo
Bajamar
Almáciga
La Oliva
Fuencaliente
La Laguna
Los Molinos
Fuerteventura
Puerto del Rosario
Pta de Fuencaliente
Puerto de la Cruz
Santa Cruz de Tenerife
Icod de Los Vinos
3718 m
Pico de Teide
Antigua
Pájara
Tuineje
Guía de Isora
Rosa de los James
Gran Tarajal
Pta del Peligro
Hermigua
Granadilla de Abona
Arucas
Las Palmas de Gran Canaria
Punta Paloma
Vallehermoso
807 m
Matas Blancas
Valle Gran Rey
1487 m
Los Cristianos
Gáldar
San Sebastián de la Gomera
Palm-Mar
Las Galletas
San Nicolás de Tolentino
Pico de las Nieves
1949 m
Telde
Pta de Jandía
Morro Jable
Gomera
Veneguera
Ingenio
Hierro
Valverde
Mogán
Frontera
Las Casitas
Verga
Maspalomas
1500 m
Pta del Parchel
El Oasis
Gran Canaria
Pta Restinga

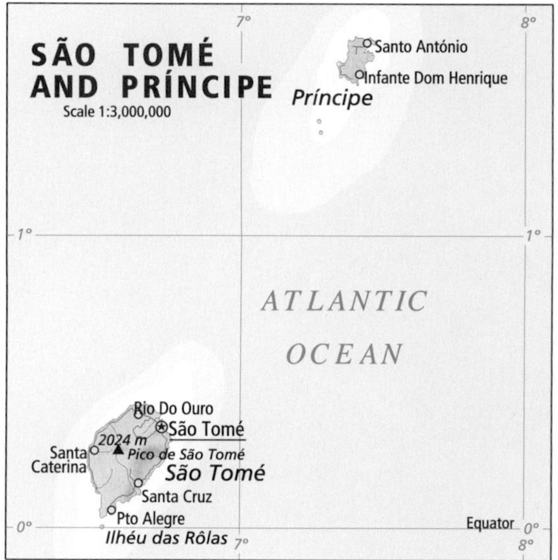
SÃO TOMÉ AND PRÍNCIPE
Scale 1:3,000,000
7°
8°
1°
0°
Santo António
Infante Dom Henrique
Príncipe
ATLANTIC
OCEAN
Rio Do Ouro
São Tomé
2024 m
Santa Caterina
Pico de São Tomé
São Tomé
Santa Cruz
Pto Alegre
Equator
Ilhéu das Rôlas

4

A B C

North and Central America

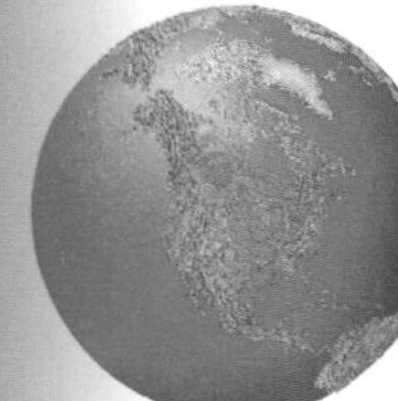

North America

The continent of North America covers an area of 25.3 million sq km (9.3 million sq miles). It is bounded by the Atlantic Ocean to its east and the Pacific Ocean to its west. Broadest toward the north, it tapers at its southern end, where a narrow isthmus connects it to South America.

The North American continent can be conveniently divided into temperate North America and the more tropical Central America. Central America consists of countries on the mainland and islands in the Caribbean Sea.

Infrastructure, provision of services, and quality-of-life indicators of Central American countries contrast markedly with those of Canada and the United States of America. In addition, a large cultural divide separates mainly English-speaking Canada and the USA from their predominantly Spanish-speaking southern neighbors. For these reasons, Central America is introduced separately.

North America consists of Canada and the United States, plus St Pierre and Miquelon (France) which lie off the east coast of Canada, and Bermuda (UK) which lies off the eastern coast of the USA.

Physical features

In North America there are both old and young mountains. Young folded mountains (the Cordillera) run along the western part of the continent from Alaska to the Central American isthmus and include a number of active volcanoes. This chain arose following the collision of the American and Pacific plates. In the USA, the Cordillera splits into the Rocky Mountains, which form the eastern arm, and the Sierra Nevada and other ranges, which form the western arm. Several peaks in the Rocky Mountains exceed 4,000 m (13,200 ft). The mountain ranges enclose basins such as the Mojave Desert and Death Valley, and a number of saline lakes. Death Valley lies below sea level at an altitude of -86 m (-282 ft).

The ancient Appalachian Mountains run along the eastern length of the USA; their highest peak, Mt Mitchell, has an altitude of 2,037 m (6,683 ft). An extensive coastal plain lies between this chain and the Atlantic Ocean. Plains and lowlands are found in the continent's interior. Glaciers, which covered much of this area during the ice ages, sculpted the rocky plateaus of Canada and deposited sediments as vast plains that straddle Canada and the USA.

Several important rivers flow through North America, primarily the Missouri, 4,088 km (2,540 miles) long and the Mississippi, 3,766 km (2,340 miles) long. The St Lawrence River links the Great Lakes of Canada and the USA to the Atlantic Ocean. There are several large lakes of which Lake Superior, which covers 82,100 sq km (31,699 sq miles), is the largest. The Rio Grande flows between the USA and Mexico. The Columbia River drains several states in northwestern USA.

Climate and vegetation

North America contains a broad range of temperate climates from warm temperate along the east coast and Mediterranean in southern California to cooler moist climates in northwest and northeast USA and southern Canada. Most of North America is humid, except for a dry belt across the southwest of the USA and basins within the Rockies. An extensive tornado zone is found in the continental interior of the USA. Tropical cyclones, known in this region as hurricanes, and mostly originating in the Caribbean Sea, often strike the southeastern parts of the USA.

Extensive forests occur in temperate North America, ranging from the predominantly deciduous forests found in eastern parts of the USA to the short-tree boreal forests of the subarctic. Tall trees such as redwoods and firs are found along the Pacific coastline. Other trees include maple, ash, and oak. Deer, brown and grizzly bears, lynx, and beavers are found in these forests. Boreal forests are home to migrating animals such as deer, elk, caribou, and moose.

In southern California, sclerophyllous shrubs thrive in the mild, wet winters and hot, dry summers. Eucalypt trees are an introduced species in this area and are a fire hazard during summer.

Extensive grasslands cover the interior of the continent. Tall-grass prairies occur where rainfall is over 750 mm (30 in), and short-grass prairies where precipitation is around 370 mm (15 in). Large herds of bison once roamed these areas, but they were practically eradicated by hunting.

In Alaska and Canada, north of the boreal forest, there is a belt of tundra where small shrubs, lichens, and grasses grow. Migrating herds of caribou, reindeer and lemmings live in this zone, along with bears, wolves, foxes, and lynx.

Population

North America had a population of 316 million in 2000. High living standards are reflected in the high life expectancies—74.5 years for males and

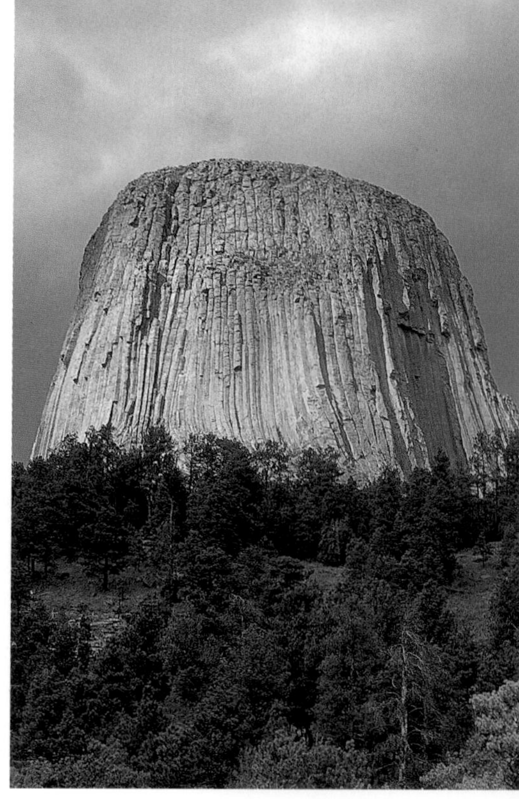

New York's Statue of Liberty; below vast cornfields in Colorado (left). Snow seems out of place on this pine in desert Utah (below). The magma core of an ancient volcano in Wyoming (above).

Nations

Dependencies

The crater of Haleakala Volcano, the world's largest dormant volcano, on Maui, Hawaii (above). Much further north, the beginning of the spring thaw in a town in Canada (right). Bermuda (above right), a tiny island off the USA east coast.

80.1 years for females (2000). The low population growth rate of one percent also reflects an advanced level of development. Approximately 77.4 percent of the population is urbanized.

Agriculture, forestry, and fishing

North America is well endowed with water resources, arable land, forests, and fishing areas. These favorable conditions, coupled with scientific farming practices, have enabled the establishment of highly productive agricultural industries. These include grain farming, such as wheat and maize; livestock for meat and dairying; cotton; and intensive farming of fruit and vegetables.

The extensive forests which still remain, following large-scale deforestation in the nineteenth century, are exploited for their valuable timbers. Large areas have been reforested in order to produce a long-term sustainable industry.

There are fishing grounds off both the Atlantic and Pacific coasts, especially along the east coast where the cold Labrador current flows.

Industrialization

Natural resources, technological innovation, and well-developed infrastructure facilities, including energy supplies, have combined to make North America the world's most important manufacturing region. Continuous innovation in computing, laser technology, optic fibers, and space science have enabled it to withstand strong competition from European and Asian industrial nations.

Manufacturing ranges from chemical industries, metal fabrication, automobiles, aircraft, and high-technology military equipment to books, films, computer software, and recorded music. Tertiary industries, which provide services to a relatively wealthy population, employ millions of people.

North America is well endowed with mineral wealth. Extensive deposits of iron ore and coal have been the cornerstone of the steel industry. However, metals such as chromium and manganese need to be imported. The Cordillera belt contains a large number of metallic ores including copper, zinc, molybdenum, gold, and silver. Nickel and iron ore are extracted from ancient plateau rocks in Canada. Among minerals used for energy supplies, coal, petroleum, and natural gas deposits are widespread. Although a large petroleum producer, the USA must also import large quantities because of heavy consumption.

Languages

English is the dominant language in North America, except in the Canadian province of Québec, where French is the main language. Some surviving American Indian languages are spoken by minority groups such as the Pueblo Indians of southwestern USA and the First Nations in western Canada. In southern states of the USA that were once parts of Mexico, such as California, New Mexico and Texas, Spanish is spoken among Hispanics. Considerable Hispanic migration to the USA, particularly from Mexico and Cuba, has made Spanish increasingly important in the USA, particularly in parts of the east coast, such as Florida and New York.

Boundary disputes and wars

There are no major boundary disputes in the region, nor has the region been directly affected by land war in recent decades. However, the terrorist attacks of 11 September 2001 have left a feeling of vulnerability, especially in the USA.

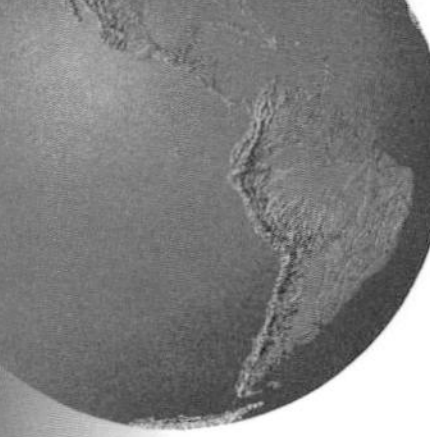

Central America

Central America, lying in the tropical zone between North and South America, consists of two distinct parts: a mainland area and a number of islands in the Caribbean Sea.

Mexico, Guatemala, Belize, Honduras, Nicaragua, Costa Rica, El Salvador, and Panama form the mainland. The two largest islands in the Caribbean Sea are Cuba and Hispaniola. The latter is divided into the Dominican Republic and Haiti. There are also several small island nations: Jamaica, Antigua and Barbuda, Dominica, Barbados, Trinidad and Tobago, Grenada, St Kitts and Nevis, St Lucia, St Vincent and the Grenadines, and the Bahamas.

Dependencies include Puerto Rico, the Virgin Islands and Navassa (USA), Aruba and the Netherlands Antilles (Netherlands), Anguilla, Montserrat, the British Virgin Islands, the Cayman Islands and the Turks and Caicos Islands (UK), and Martinique and Guadeloupe (France).

Physical features

Central America is a region of rugged mountains and volcanic peaks that were produced through the collision of several crustal plates. The Central American isthmus was formed by the interaction of the Caribbean and the Cocos Plates, while the Caribbean islands were the result of the Caribbean Plate moving against the North American Plate. Further north, in Mexico, the Pacific and North American Plates collided.

Volcanic activity is found in several sectors of these ranges, particularly in the area south of Mexico City, which contains volcanoes ranging in height from 3,000 to 4,000 m (10,000 to 14,000 ft). Volcanic eruptions have caused considerable damage through lava flows and ash deposits. Numerous islands in the Caribbean Sea, such as Martinique, with the famous active volcano Mt Pelée, and Antigua are volcanic. In contrast, the Bahamas are an example of coral islands.

Nelson's Harbour in Caribbean Antigua (below) contrasts with Mexican scenes, old and new: an ancient pyramid (right) and a woman washing radishes at the market (top).

Climate and vegetation

Central America lies within the tropics but because of its mountainous relief, climatic conditions vary with altitude. Such changes are notable in the narrow isthmus where variations in elevation are reflected in differences in vegetation. Low-lying areas, which are limited in extent, may have a hot, humid tropical climate with rainforest vegetation, while in elevated areas such as in the central Mexican Plateau the climate approaches temperate conditions. Mountain slopes facing rain-bearing winds are densely vegetated while, in contrast, northeastern Mexico is semiarid.

In areas of high rainfall there are large tropical evergreen forests, which provide cover for a dense undergrowth made up of smaller plants such as ferns and lianas. Animal life is abundant in these areas, but loss of habitat due to deforestation and hunting have caused several animal species to become endangered.

In drier areas, such as in the Yucatán region of Mexico, shrub vegetation dominates in areas previously farmed during the Mayan civilization.

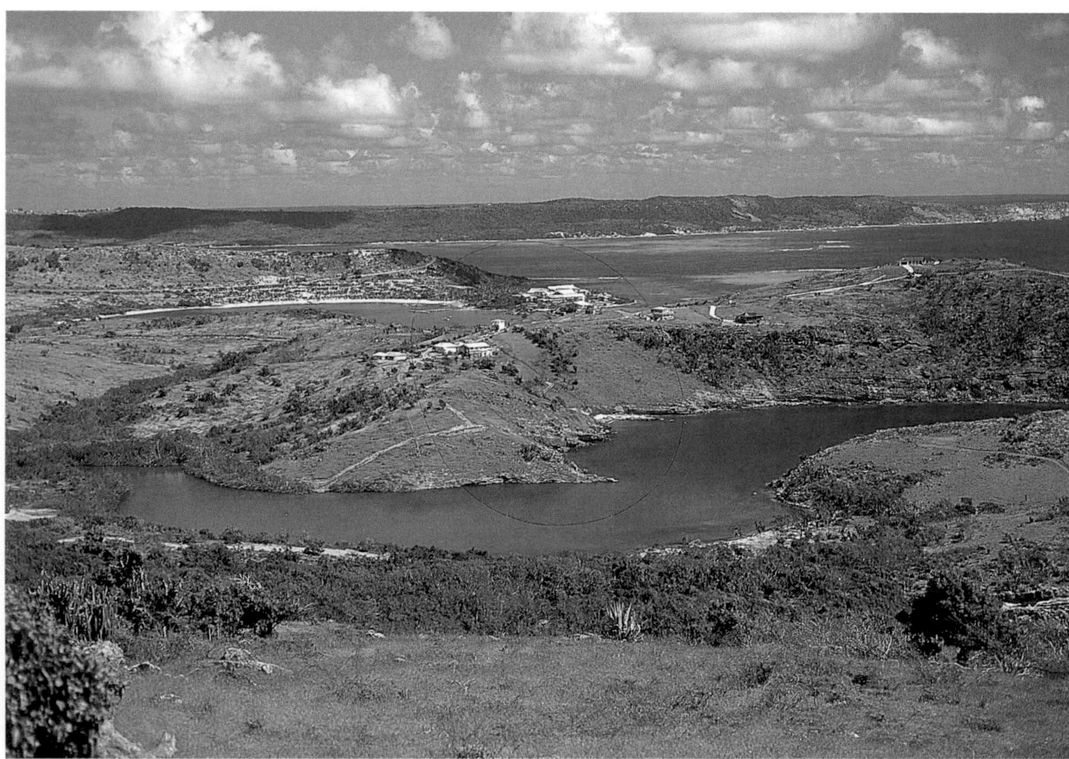

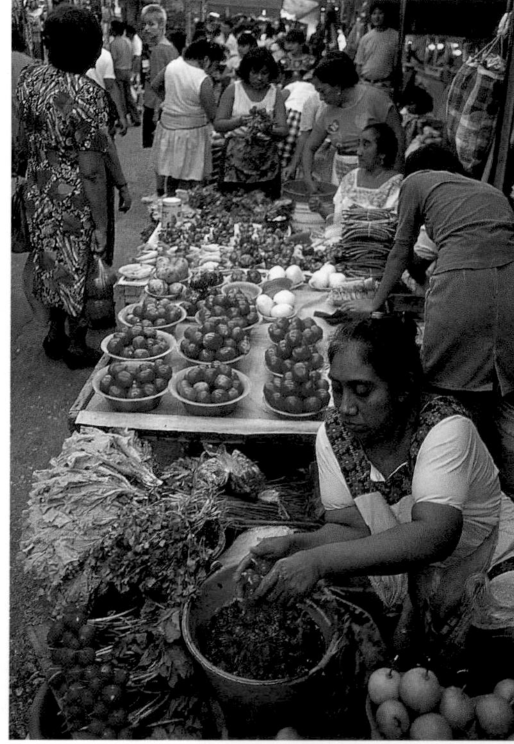

The region lies within a belt which is affected almost every year by hurricanes. In November 1998 a hurricane devastated the countries lying on the isthmus, particularly Honduras and Nicaragua.

Population

The population of the mainland is 135.2 million people while the Caribbean has 37.7 million inhabitants (2000). Life expectancies for the mainland are 69.5 years for males and 75.4 years for females, while in the Caribbean they are 64.9 years for males and 69 years for females. The mainland's annual population growth rate is 1.7 percent annually; that of the Caribbean is 0.9 percent. Urbanization is high—68.2 percent for the mainland and 63.1 percent for the Caribbean. Increasesin urban population, mainly as a result of rural to urban drift, have resulted in overcrowding and slum areas in many places. Mexico City is one of the world's largest cities.

Agriculture, forestry, and fishing

The economies of Central America are mainly agricultural. Maize, wheat, and rice are the principal cereals. The main livestock on the mainland are cattle, particularly where there are stretches of grassland; in the Caribbean, the main livestock are pigs. Extensive cattle ranches provide beef for export to North America.

Tropical plantation products such as sugarcane, coffee, cocoa, and bananas and other fruit are major export commodities, particularly to North America. Sugar is important in Cuba and Jamaica. Bananas are grown in several countries, such as Guatemala, Honduras, and Belize for export. Coffee is grown in some areas, including Honduras and Nicaragua.

Many of the countries are economically dependent on the USA, which is the principal buyer of their exports. Cuba is the sole exception; since the communist revolution of 1958, Cuba has been selling its sugar to the former Soviet Union (now to Russia). Citrus fruit are also grown in several areas. Coconuts are an important product of the coastal areas around the Caribbean Sea.

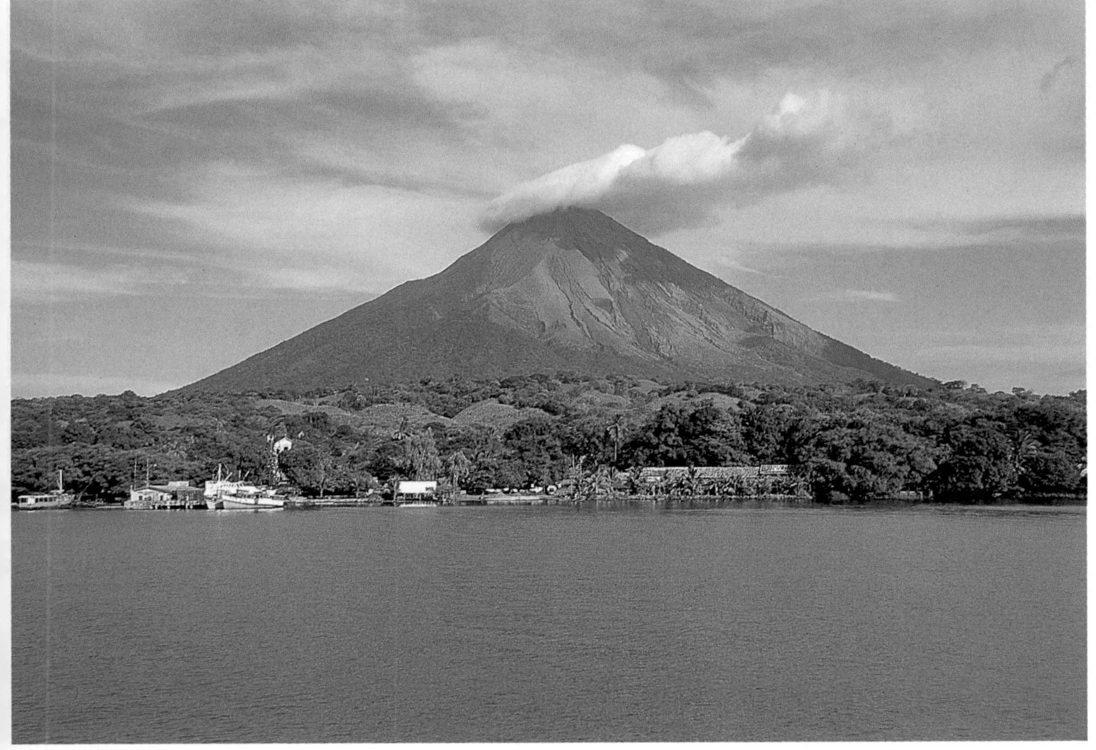

Coniferous and broad-leaf forests occur on mountain slopes; these have been exploited for timber and firewood. Tropical forests have been logged for valuable hardwoods such as mahogany. Mexico, Cuba, and Guatemala all have forest industries.

Marine resources are abundant around the Caribbean islands, and for many of these nations fishing is a key activity. Belize, for example, relies on lobster and shrimp fishing.

Industrialization

Several countries have been shifting their economies from agriculture to manufacturing. Mexico is the most industrialized of the Central American countries, producing iron and steel, transport equipment, chemicals, and clothing. Its main export market is the USA. In most countries, manufacturing is either based on locally produced raw materials, such as rum made from sugar or cigars and cigarettes from tobacco in Jamaica, or on other light industry.

Several countries have become tourist destinations, and for some Caribbean countries, with their attractive tropical environments, tourism is a mainstay.

Languages

Central America was carved up by colonial powers, resulting in the presence of four official languages: Spanish, English, French and Dutch. All the mainland countries, except for Belize, where English is important, are Spanish-speaking.

Cuba, Puerto Rico and the Dominican Republic are Spanish-speaking, although English is also spoken in Puerto Rico. There are several English-speaking Caribbean islands, the largest of which is Jamaica; others are Antigua, the Bahamas, and Barbuda. Martinique is French-speaking, and the tiny Antilles islands are Dutch-speaking.

A beautifully symmetrical Volcan Concepción appears in the background of this view of Moyogalpa in Nicaragua (above). A stone carving at Tegucigalpa, Honduras (below left), and a lush tropical rainforest in Grenada (below right).

Boundary disputes and wars

There have been no major boundary disputes in Central America, except for the Guatemalan claim to the former British Honduras, which is now the independent country of Belize. However, the region has been beset with a variety of insurgencies, often helped by external sources. The USA has several times intervened in the region, invading Grenada in 1983 and Panama in 1989, supporting right-wing opponents of leftist governments in Guatemala and Nicaragua, and imposing economic sanctions on Cuba. The communist revolution in Cuba, and its policy of exporting revolution, had a considerable effect on the region. Cuba received substantial support from the Soviet Union. A leftist guerilla movement succeeded in taking over Nicaragua in 1979 but its government lost office in the 1990 elections. An American Indian revolt took place in 1994 in the Chiapas region of Mexico.

Nations

Dependencies & territories

North America

Canada

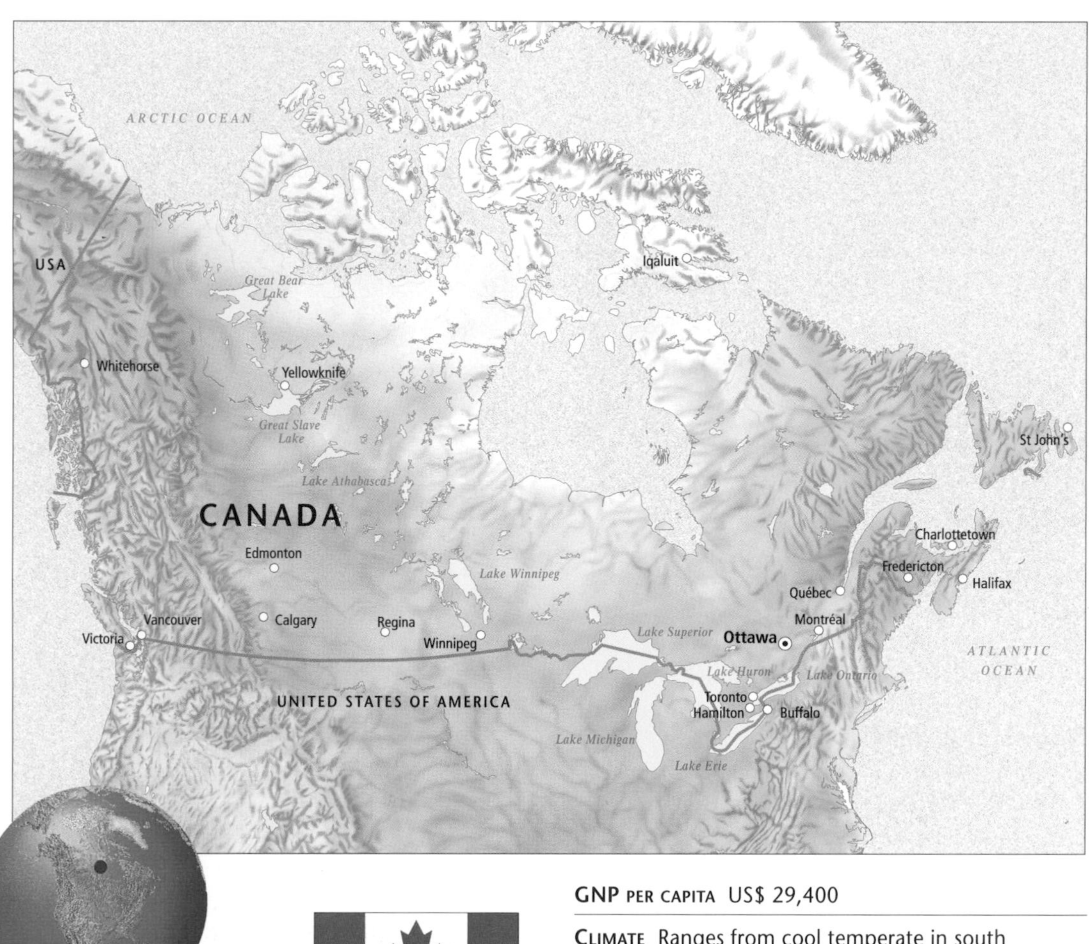

Fact File

Official name Canada

Form of government Constitutional monarchy with two legislative bodies (Senate and House of Commons)

Capital Ottawa

Area 9,976,140 sq km (3,851,788 sq miles)

Time zone GMT – 3.5/8 hours

Population 31,903,000

Projected population 2015 34,419,000

Population density 3.2 per sq km (8.3 per sq mile)

Life expectancy 79.7

Infant mortality (per 1,000) 7.5

Official languages English, French

Other languages Chinese, Italian, German, Polish, Spanish, Portuguese, Punjabi, Ukrainian, Vietnamese, Arabic, indigenous languages

Literacy rate 99 %

Religions Roman Catholic 45 %, United Church 12 %, Anglican 8 %, other 35 %

Ethnic groups British 40 %, French 27 %, other European 20 %, indigenous 1.5 %, other 11.5 %

Currency Canadian dollar

Economy Services 78 %, industry 19 %, agriculture 3 %

GNP per capita US$ 29,400

Climate Ranges from cool temperate in south to polar in north; long, cold winters; wetter and more temperate on coasts

Highest point Mt Logan 5,950 m (19,521 ft)

Map reference Pages 410–11, 412–13, 414–15, 416–17

Canada is the second-largest country in the world, with ninety percent of its population living close to the US border. Its citizens enjoy a standard of living second only to that of the US itself, but the huge scale of Canada's land area, the small, spread out population, and the division between the British and the French have made national unity more difficult to achieve.

Canada was initially populated by Inuit (Eskimo) and First Nation peoples (as indigenous Canadians are called). European settlement began in 1541 after Jacques Cartier's 1534 discovery of the St Lawrence River. Soon, French explorers pushed inland in search of furs and trade. The French were still in a majority when British victory in a war with France, in 1763, gave Britain control of French settlements in Québec. Following US independence in 1783, however, many British settlers came north, and this marked the start of the long-resented domination of a French minority by a larger English-speaking population. There have been various Francophone initiatives for the secession of Québec in recent years. A 1995 vote in the province failed by 50.6 to 49.4 percent to settle the matter.

Physical features and land use

There is much variety among Canada's geographic regions. In the east lie the Atlantic Provinces of New Brunswick, Nova Scotia, Prince Edward Island, and Newfoundland, as well as Québec. The geological foundation of the Atlantic Provinces is ancient worn-down mountains, along with sectors of the still older Canadian Shield. Although farming settlements are common, agriculture in this region has always been marginal (with the exception of such places as the Annapolis Valley in Nova Scotia and Prince Edward Island) and is in decline. Pulp and paper is produced from Québec's coniferous forests and the state is also a major producer of hydropower.

West and south lie the most temperate inland parts of Canada, the St Lawrence-Great Lakes lowlands, including the Ontario Peninsula. This fertile agricultural region reaches west from southern Québec along Lake Ontario and north from Lake Erie. Rural settlement is more dense here than elsewhere and, given the large urban concentrations of Toronto and Montréal, these lowlands are the most heavily populated part of Canada.

The Canadian Shield, or Laurentian Plateau, is an extensive, ancient region floored with some of the world's oldest known rocks. Centered on Hudson Bay, it covers nearly fifty percent of Canadian territory. Except for some low mountains in eastern Québec and Labrador, this is a rolling landscape typified by outcrops of rock and a great amount of surface water in summer. There

Timeline

35,000–12,000 BP Humans migrate to North American continent from Asia via land bridge across Bering Strait

5000 BP Communities in east survive by trapping caribou and bears and fishing; use fur clothing and build wood and skin kayaks

1200 BC Ancestors of today's Inuit spread east and north as far as Arctic Circle

AD 1100 Inuit meet Vikings in Greenland; as a result, more than one-third of Inuit die of such diseases as smallpox and measles

1497 John Cabot lands near the mouth of the St Lawrence River and claims land for England

1534 Jacques Cartier sails up St Lawrence River to site of present-day Montréal

1663 New France made a French colony by Louis XIV; French, English settler rivalry over fur trade; native population c. 200,000

1670 Hudson's Bay Company established in London

1791 British divic Canada into Uppe and Lower Canad French mainly i Lower Canada, alon lower St Lawrenc

are hundreds of thousands of water bodies, ranging in size from gigantic to tiny, connected by thousands of rivers and streams. The shield's southern half is covered by boreal forest, whereas the northern half (including the islands of the Canadian Arctic Archipelago) is beyond the tree line and has a cover of rock, ice, and ground-hugging tundra. The Arctic Archipelago islands range from high mountains in the east to low plains in the west.

West of the Canadian Shield lie the central plains. The southern portion of the "Prairie Provinces"—Saskatchewan, Manitoba, and Alberta—has a natural vegetation of prairie grasses. The northern part is forested. In the prairies the mechanization of wheat farming long ago reduced the need for rural labor, and population densities are low.

The Canadian Cordillera, reaching from the northern Yukon to southern British Columbia and southwest Alberta, dominates western Canada, and contains a number of national parks including Yoho, Banff, Jasper, and Kootenay. On the Pacific side the Coast Mountains run south through British Columbia, the coastline deeply embayed by fjords. Off the coast lies Vancouver Island, the peak of another mountain range, now cut off by the sea.

People and culture

With its major British and French components, its other Europeans who are largely from eastern and southern Europe, its Asians, and its indigenous First Nations, Métis, and Inuit, Canada is home to many peoples. Most now live in urban settings but this is quite a new development. At confederation in 1867, when Britain granted home rule, eighty percent of the population was rural, and only Montréal had more than 100,000 people. It was not until after the Second World War that rural and urban populations became about equal in size. The war years stimulated the economy, industrialization was rapid, people moved into the cities to work in factories, and Canada emerged from the conflict with a powerful industrial base. It was at this time that British influence began to decline and the USA became of increasing economic and cultural importance in Canadian life.

In the past twenty years Canada's ethnic mix has changed significantly, resulting from a move toward a less restrictive immigration policy that welcomes people with money and skills. Under this policy many Asians have come to settle. The government defines Canada as a "community of communities" within which each ethnic group is encouraged to maintain its own culture. While generally welcomed, these liberalization measures have also produced problems. Since the Supreme Court recognized "aboriginal title", First Nations land claims have been or are being negotiated with the governments concerned where prior treaties did not exist, and in some cases demands are being made for revision of existing treaties. Canada's most intractable political problem, however, remains the unsatisfied demand of many Québécois for autonomy.

Economy and resources

Canada's resource base includes nickel (Sudbury, Ontario usually provides some twenty percent of the western world's supply), and Canada is also a world leader in the output of zinc, potash, uranium, sulphur, asbestos, aluminum and copper. Alberta produces more than 75 percent of the nation's oil and is an important source of natural gas and coal. Hydroelectric power has led to the expansion of pulp and paper industries. Canada is one of the world's leading exporters of wood products.

Agriculture is an important activity, but it only employs around three percent of the labor force. Grain, dairying, fruit, and ranching all flourish. In addition to pigs and sheep, Canadian ranches support about 13 million head of cattle. Fruit-growing is found in British Columbia's irrigated southern plateau and the Fraser River delta. In addition to wheat other export crops include feed grains, oilseeds, apples, potatoes, and maple syrup.

The country's high taxes, regulatory structures, and low productivity have, however, led to ongoing problems. Starting the 1990s in recession, Canada's real rates of growth have averaged only one percent through much of the decade. A traditional commitment to high public service and welfare spending is proving hard to maintain. The current account deficit and national debt have led to the slashing of federal transfers to the provinces in the areas of health, education, and welfare. The continuing debate over Québec's future, and the possibility of a split in the confederation, also dampens investor confidence.

Bow Lake in Banff National Park in the Canadian Rockies (left). Ottawa, on the banks of the Ottawa River (top left). Niagara Falls, from the Canadian side (top right).

PROVINCES

Alberta • Edmonton
British Columbia • Victoria
Manitoba • Winnipeg
New Brunswick • Fredericton
Newfoundland • St. John's
Nova Scotia • Halifax
Ontario • Toronto
Prince Edward Island • Charlottetown
Québec • Québec
Saskatchewan • Regina

TERRITORIES

Northwest Territories • Yellowknife
Nunavut • Iqaluit
Yukon Territory • Whitehorse

1829 Welland Canal links Lakes Erie and Ontario, allowing ships to avoid Niagara Falls

1867 Britain creates Dominion of Canada, bringing together New Brunswick, Nova Scotia, Ontario, and Québec

1870 Dominion of Canada acquires the North West Territory from the Hudson's Bay Company

1871 British Columbia becomes sixth province; Prince Edward Island later made the seventh (1873)

1898 Yukon Territory added to Canada's official land area

1905 Saskatchewan and Alberta become provinces; Canada's population grows with European immigrants settling western prairies

1914 Canada fights alongside Britain and Allies against Germany in First World War

1930s Depression hits; new national bodies set up including Bank of Canada (1934) and Canadian Wheat Board (1935)

1939–45 More than 1 million Canadian troops aid Allies on European and Pacific fronts in Second World War

1945–55 Postwar migration from Europe boosts Canada's population by more than 1 million

1949 Newfoundland becomes tenth province; Canada joins North Atlantic Treaty Organization (NATO)

1959 Completion of St Lawrence Seaway creates waterway from Lake Superior to Atlantic of 3,767 km (2,340 miles)

1960 Demands for French-Canadian rights grow both peacefully and in form of terrorist attacks on public buildings

1982 Constitution Act, signed by Queen Elizabeth II, grants Canada sole power to amend its constitution

1988 Canada and USA sign free trade agreement ending wrangling over foreign investment, banking, and agriculture

1993 Parliament grants Inuit people (numbering around 30,000) self-governing homeland, Nunavut, effective 1 April 1999

United States of America (USA)

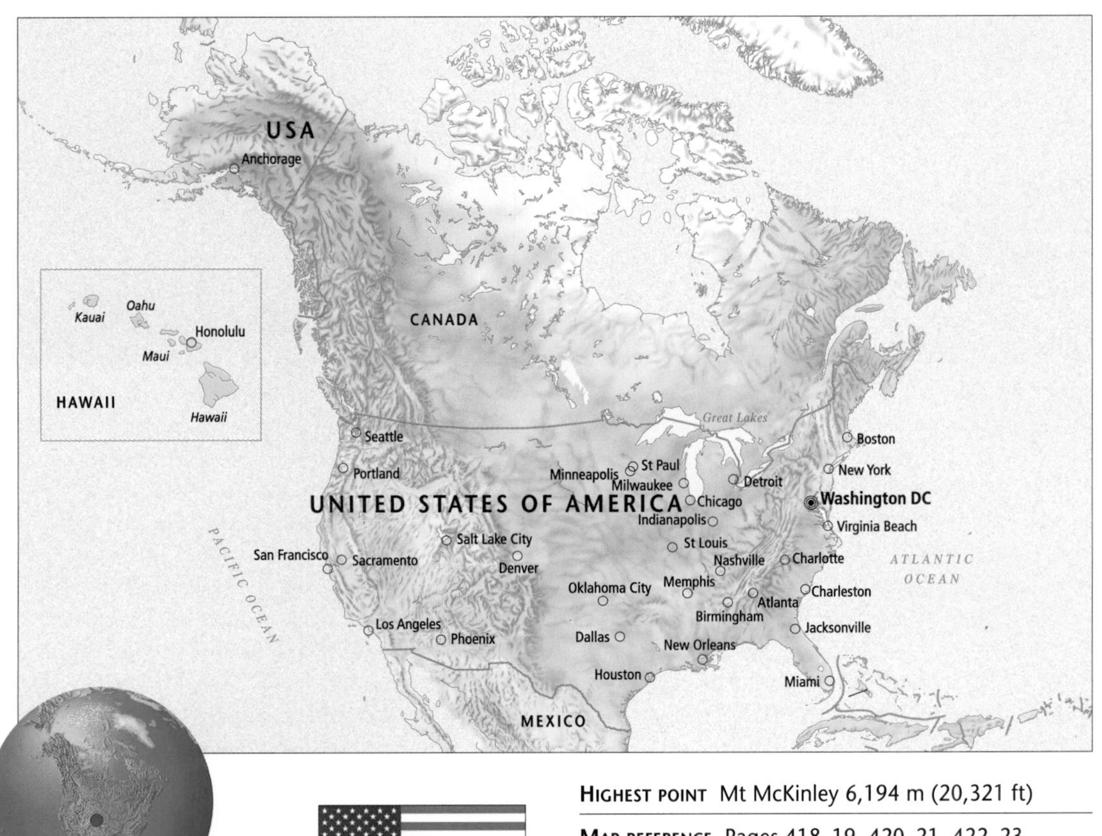

Highest point Mt McKinley 6,194 m (20,321 ft)

Map reference Pages 418–19, 420–21, 422–23, 424–25, 426

Fact File

Official name United States of America

Form of government Federal republic with two legislative bodies (Senate and House of Representatives)

Capital Washington DC

Area 9,372,610 sq km (3,618,765 sq miles)

Time zone GMT – 5/11 hours

Population 280,563,000

Projected population 2015 321,225,000

Population density 29.9 per sq km (77.5 per sq mile)

Life expectancy 77.4

Infant mortality (per 1,000) 6.7

Official language English

Other languages Spanish, German, French, Italian, Chinese, indigenous languages

Literacy rate 97 %

Religions Protestant 56 %, Roman Catholic 28 %, Jewish 2 %, other 4 %, none 10 %

Ethnic groups European 83.5 %, African 12.4 %, Asian 3.3 %, Native American 0.8 %

Currency US dollar

Economy Services 79 %, industry 18 %, agriculture 3 %

GNP per capita US$ 36,300

Climate Varied: eastern states are temperate, with warm summers and snowy winters in north and subtropical conditions in south; southwest is arid and semiarid; west coast is temperate but warmer in California and wetter in the Pacific Northwest; Hawaii is mainly tropical; Alaska is mainly polar but cooler and wetter on south coast

In the United States of America a variety of peoples, united by a shared belief in social and economic freedom, have built the most prosperous and powerful nation on earth. Abundant resources, a climate and soils ensuring plentiful food supplies, and an open society rewarding individual energy and initiative were all advantages from the beginning. In addition, huge oceans on both eastern and western coasts isolated America from the troubles of Europe and Asia, and its relations with Mexico to the south and Canada to the north were generally benign. Starting with these favorable conditions, and guided by the ideals of democracy and freedom, the United States of America—in this respect unique among nations—successfully invented itself according to its own political and social ideals.

The most serious danger to its existence was self-inflicted. From 1861 to 1865 the US was wracked by a civil war in which the implications of universal human liberty were played out in a struggle between slave-owners in the south of the country and slave-liberators in the north, but the nation survived. Later, in the face of widespread domestic opposition, the US entered the First World War in 1917, its military strength leading to Germany's defeat. Even more decisive was its role in the Second World War between 1941 and 1945, in alliance with Great Britain and the Soviet Union, when its industrial power and military might ensured victory over both Germany and Japan. After 1945, challenged for superpower supremacy by the Soviets, it engaged in a protracted trial of strength known as the Cold War. This ended in 1989 with the collapse of the USSR and its communist allies, leaving the United States stronger politically and economically than ever before.

The economy, already the most powerful, diverse, and technologically advanced in the world, continues to grow. But US prosperity is combined with a variety of problems: drug addiction, crime, long-term unemployment for some sectors of the population, racial tensions, a very low interest in politics and consequently very low voting rates, air and water pollution in some areas from automotive and industrial wastes, traffic congestion approaching "gridlock" in major cities, and rising medical costs. All these side effects appear to be the price of modernity on the American model. It is a price that most other developed countries have been prepared to pay, however, in order to establish high-tech, high-energy industrial societies.

Physical features and land use

Mainland United States can be divided into three major physical regions. The eastern part consists of the range of the Appalachian Mountains and the coastal plain that runs along the Atlantic Ocean. The broad basin of the Mississippi and Missouri Rivers comprises the central section. The western region is composed of mountain ranges, desert landscapes, and the land along the Pacific coast. In addition, there are two outlying sections of the country—Alaska and Hawaii.

In eastern North America the Appalachians, a band of sedimentary mountains and plateaus which are still widely forested, extend from northern Alabama to the Gulf of St Lawrence. They consist of a number of parallel ranges,

including the Blue Ridge Mountains in Virginia and the Great Smoky Mountains along the North Carolina-Tennessee border. For a long time these ranges constituted a barrier to inland settlement. In New York State the valley of the Mohawk River divides the mountains of the Appalachians from the Adirondacks, which are a southern extension of the ancient granite mass of the Canadian Shield. Traveling up this valley, from east to west, the early settlers were able to find a way through the range that led on to the land bordering the Great Lakes and the Ohio country beyond.

The original vegetation on these mountains was broadleaf deciduous forest of oak, ash, beech, and maple grading into yellow birch, hemlock, and pine towards the north. During the eighteenth and nineteenth centuries much of this forest area was cleared for farming, but declining agriculture in New England and the abandonment of farmland has brought widespread regeneration of tree growth. Flying across eastern America, much of the landscape still gives the impression of continuous woodland.

The coastal plain to the southeast through the Carolinas and Georgia is generally low-lying, and includes many areas of swamp. Nearly 1,700 km (more than 1,000 miles) of barrier islands and sandbars run parallel to the shore and are popular seaside resort areas for the inland population, despite being exposed to occasional hurricanes.

To the west of the Appalachian Range lies the enormous continental drainage basin of the Mississippi-Missouri river system. This basin is about 2,500 km (1,500 miles) wide, extending south from the Canadian border to the Gulf of Mexico. At its northern limit there are the hills along Lake Superior, a vestige of the Canadian Shield. What are called the Central Lowlands of this drainage basin are bounded on the east by the low plateaus of Kentucky and Tennessee. To the west of the Mississippi lie vast areas planted in wheat, and eventually grasslands, as the Great Plains reach 1,500 km (900 miles) across to the foothills of the Rocky Mountains.

Once the home of such tribes as the Mandan, the Omaha, and the Kansa Indians (settled farmers near the Missouri River), and the nomadic Blackfoot, Crow, and Arapaho further west, most of the plains had been taken by incoming ranchers and farmers by the end of the nineteenth century. Former range land was planted in wheat and maize. These crops were hugely productive at first, but overcropping and dry years led to severe soil deterioration in the first decades of the twentieth century. This reached a climax in the disasters of the 1930s, when a large part of the region became a "dustbowl." Although diversification of grain crops, contour plowing, and widespread irrigation have helped to restore agricultural productivity, some areas are still highly sensitive to climatic variation, especially where the original terrain was semidesert. Combined with fluctuations in grain prices, agriculture remains a risky business in a region where much of the land is marginal.

The mountain ranges of the western Cordillera, as it extends south from Canada, are divided by a number of high plateaus and deep valleys. There are two main systems, to the west and the east. The northern and central Rocky Mountains are the eastern arm facing out across the Great Plains, with the Grand Tetons forming spectacular ridges in Wyoming. The southern Rockies of Colorado and New Mexico—the remains of an ancient granite plateau—are also weathered into a series of striking peaks. In Colorado there are more than 1,000 mountains of 3,000 m (10,000 ft) or more. As with the mountains on the east of the continent, the Rockies were a major obstacle for westward-heading settlers. One major route lay through the Wyoming Basin, a rangeland where bison once grazed, and where yesterday's pioneer trails have become interstate highways.

On the lower slopes of the Rockies grow a mixture of piñon pines and juniper scrub, with ponderosa pine, spruce, and fir at higher altitudes. Wildlife includes elk, deer, moose, mountain sheep, bear, and a variety of smaller animals. National parks such as Yellowstone and Grand Teton provide an opportunity to see these animals in dramatic natural settings, and draw millions of visitors to the region every year.

High plateaus, rocky ranges, and desert basins extend westward across the states of Utah, Arizona, and Nevada, seamed in many places by vast, abrupt canyons, of which the Grand Canyon of the Colorado River is the most spectacular. On the Pacific side of these plateaus is the western branch of the cordillera. This forms a chain of mountains consisting of the Sierra Nevada in the south and the Cascade Range to the north. Stretching from Washington through Oregon to Lassen Peak in California (3,187 m; 10,456 ft), the Cascades include several large volcanoes, including Mt Saint Helens which erupted violently in 1980. The Sierra Nevada faces out over the fertile Central Valley of California, with its fruit and vegetable growing, viticulture, cotton, other crops, and livestock. In the early days long dry summers made farming difficult in the Central Valley. Meltwater from the snows of the Sierra Nevada, much of it diverted in lengthy canals, now provides summer irrigation.

Beyond the Central Valley on its western side rise the comparatively low Coast Ranges, running parallel to the Pacific shore all the way from the Mexican border to Canada. Together, the Coast Ranges, the Cascades, and the Sierra Nevada all serve to keep precipitation away from the interior plateaus and create its arid landscape. East of the Cascade Range in the Pacific Northwest lies the Columbia Basin. Here, the meltwaters of

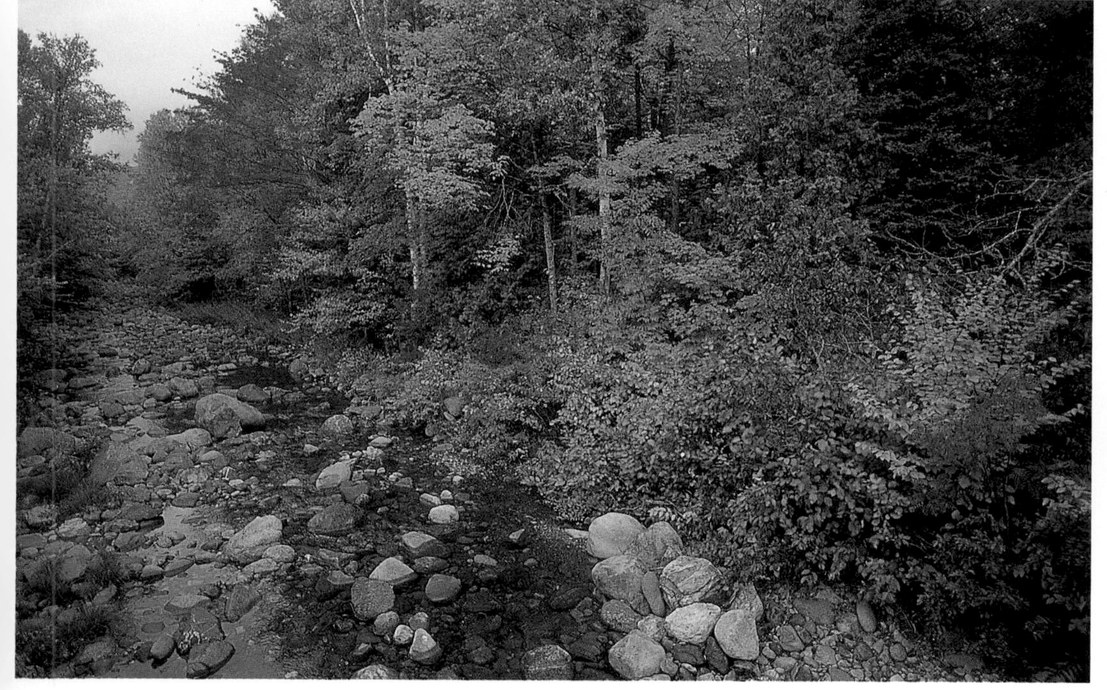

A desert landscape in Arches National Park, Utah (left page). Fall colors in northern Maine (left). Juneau, in Alaska, lies on the Inside Passage, a marine waterway that runs through the vast Tongass National Forest (above).

ancient glaciers have cut deep gorges in the land. In western Washington the most spectacular trees consist of Douglas fir, western hemlock, and Sitka spruce, some almost as tall as the giant redwoods of northern California. The wealth of the United States' Northwest was originally based on timber from the huge conifers that covered the Cascade Range.

The two non-contiguous parts of the United States have very different physical landscapes. The expansive state of Alaska is a mixture of massive glaciated mountains and broad river valleys, with a vegetation cover that varies from dense forest to sparse tundra. For much of the year large areas of Alaska are covered in snow. The Hawaiian islands mostly consist of the tops of prominent volcanoes which protrude above the sea, with a host of distinctive plants nurtured by the tropical climate.

History and settlement

The first peoples to settle North America probably crossed from Siberia to Alaska during the ice ages between 10,000 and 30,000 years ago. It is thought they became the ancestors of the many Indian tribes living in North America when the first Europeans arrived. Their cultures and languages varied widely, from the Iroquois who lived in bark lodges in the east, to the cliff-dwelling Pueblo peoples of the Southwest, to the salmon-fishing and whale-hunting Indians of Washington State and British Columbia on the Northwest coast who lived in large timber houses. Plains Indians such as the Sioux or the Comanche are sometimes depicted hunting bison on horseback, but this was only possible after horses had been introduced by incoming European traders and settlers from the fifteenth century onward.

The oldest authenticated European settlement in North America was made by Norse Vikings at the northern tip of the island of Newfoundland about AD 1000, but it was occupied for only a short time. The first successful English settlement was at Jamestown, Virginia, in 1607. Not long after this a party of religious dissenters, the so-called Pilgrim Fathers, arrived in 1620 to found the first of the New England colonies at Plymouth. Joined by other migrants later, this became part of the large Massachusetts Bay colony.

A Dutch colony on Manhattan Island that was founded in 1624 was captured by the British in 1664, who changed its name from Nieuw Amsterdam to New York. The Quaker William Penn founded one of the more successful of the early English colonies in 1682. Part of Pennsylvania later split off to become Delaware; North and South Carolina were established in 1663; Georgia, which was originally designed as a philanthropic alternative to a debtor's prison, in 1732. The defeat of the French, which ended the Seven Years War in 1763, brought huge territorial accessions to England: all of France's Canadian territories, the land west of the Mississippi River, plus Louisiana and Florida. The settlers throughout these areas became directly subject to the British Crown, and when London sought to recoup the huge expenses of the war (about £ 101,500,500) by imposing taxes, the cry of "No taxation without representation" was raised in Boston, and resistance to England began. When the American War of Independence broke out in 1776 George Washington commanded the rebel troops, and when it was won and the first elections were held in 1788 he became the inaugural president. In the aftermath, tens of thousands of British "loyalists" decided to leave and moved north to Canada.

The British government had forbidden westward expansion beyond the mountains of the Appalachians. After independence, however, this took place with a rush. Indian tribes were quickly dispossessed from the area and exiled, their land taken for farms, and throughout the nineteenth century there was a series of wars in the region to crush resistance. The last armed Indian defiance was crushed with the Ghost Dance Uprising of 1890.

But by far the most serious crisis for the new nation was the American Civil War of 1861 to 1865. This was both a clash of ideals (liberty versus servitude) and of ways of life (the industrializing, modern north versus the more traditionla, agrarian south). Led by the eloquent commonsense of Abraham Lincoln, the northern forces of the Union defeated the southern armies of the Confederacy, but the legacy of bitterness lasted for many decades and is still palpable at times in the South.

Meanwhile, westward expansion proceeded apace. Pioneers followed trails explored by men such as Meriwether Lewis and William Clark. Railroads spanned the continent, coal and iron were discovered and used, and new cities such as Pittsburgh and Chicago grew up in the interior. European migrants pouring in through the ports of Boston, Philadelphia, and New York substantially changed the nation's ethnic composition. Manufacturing cities, which were big markets in their own right, developed along the shores of the Great Lakes, while the mechanized farming of the Midwestern "corn belt" turned it into the granary of much of the Western world.

The history of California differed from that of the rest of the country in many ways, in that it was a part of Spanish conquest rather than of English settlement. The small, semi-nomadic hunting and seed-gathering Indian cultures of the area were little affected by the northward spread of Spanish forts and missions from New Spain (Mexico) in the 1760s. But by the middle of the nineteenth century pressures from land-hungry pioneers moving in from the eastern states were irresistible: by the end of the century the whole of the Southwest, including Texas, had been either ceded, purchased, or annexed. Since then the Pacific Coast economy has passed through various stages, from gold-prospecting and lumbering, through agriculture and the expansion of the aircraft industry after the Second World War, to the highest of high-tech today in Silicon Valley south of San Francisco Bay.

Once independence was established by the beginning of the nineteenth century, the United

Timeline

35,000–12,000 BP Modern humans *Homo sapiens sapiens* migrate to North America across Bering Strait land bridge and spread south

13,000 BP Settlements appear from south of Canadian border to Mexico; stone spearpoints in use in New Mexico

3500 BC Native Americans hunt bison; by 2500 BC squash, goosefoot, and sunflowers (seeds used as winter food) cultivated

1000 BC The Adena in eastern North America build ceremonial mounds; agriculture established in Southwest

300 BC Hohokam, Mogollon, and Anasazi people inhabit the South and Southwest; Anasazi build villages at Chaco, New Mexico

200 BC Hopewell culture takes over from Adena; Hopewell become first farmers in eastern North America (until AD 500)

AD 700 Start of Pueblo period in southwest; Native Americans of Hopi, Zuni, and other tribes live in villages built mainly of adobe

790 Vikings explore coasts of Europe and North America for the next 100 years, forming settlements in Greenland and Iceland

1492 Columbus reaches America while searching for route to Orient; later, French and English establish fur tracing posts in Canada

1539 Hernando de Soto reaches Florida and travels up the Mississippi; following year Coronado explores Southwest

1584 Sir Walter Raleigh claims Virginia for England, but no permanent settlement created until founding of Jamestown in 1607

1619 First slaves shipped from West Africa to USA

States kept Europe at arm's length, and the Monroe Doctrine warned Europe that the representatives of the old empires—Spanish, Portuguese, and British—were not to intervene in the Americas any more. Isolationism was the other side of this doctrine: the US had no wish to be entangled in Europe's troubles. But as the US developed into a major global power this disengagement was no longer possible. In two world wars in the twentieth century American military intervention was decisive, and with the onset of the Cold War, designed to contain the Soviet Union after 1945, it was prepared to intervene wherever it saw the need. However, subsequent action in Korea from 1950 to 1953, and in Vietnam from 1964 to 1975, both with heavy loss of US lives, has made the nation less enthusiastic about overseas military commitments and the risks and casualties of policing trouble-spots (Haiti, Somalia, the Persian Gulf) are often unpopular at home. Generally the American mood is inward-looking, more concerned with domestic than with foreign affairs. This, however, changed dramatically after the terrorist attacks on the World Trade Center in New York City and the Pentagon in Washington D.C. on 11 September 2001. Since then the government has pursued the strategy of actively reshaping the world, especially the Middle East, according to American ideals, interests and security concerns. As much opposition as this line of politics encountered in the rest of the world, large parts of the US population supported it, at least until after the toppling of Saddam Hussein's regime in Iraq, which was seen as a threat to stability in the Arab world as well as one of the main supporters of terrorist bands.

People and culture

The United States is a prosperous, industrial, capitalistic democracy, in which anyone with training and skills who is prepared to assimilate can usually find a place. It is the most open multicultural society on earth, which is the main reason why so many people from other countries want to live there. To keep this in check immense efforts are made to secure the long borders and other entry points into the country such as airports and ports. In addition to tremendous numbers of legal immigrants (the United States still has the highest legal immigration level of any country in the world) illegal entry is estimated to bring in up to 1 million people per year.

The descendants of the original Native American inhabitants are a small but not insignificant element of the population. People arriving from overseas were at first mainly English, and with those of Scottish and Irish descent dominated all other arrivals from the other side of the Atlantic until the middle of the nineteenth

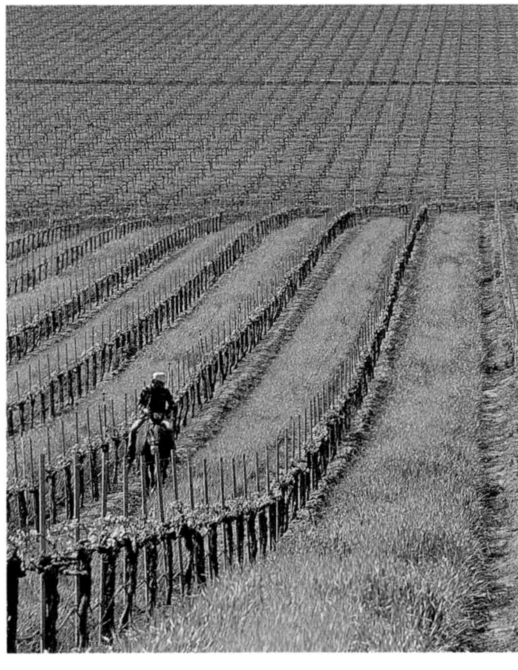

Rugged country in Great Basin National Park in Nevada (left page). One of California's numerous vineyards (above). The famous Empire State Building in New York City (far right). Undulating farming country in Idaho (below).

1776 USA founded, with American colonies adopting Declaration of Independence. Population 3 million

1804 Lewis and Clark explore the Missouri River then cross Rocky Mts and reach the Pacific near mouth of Columbia River

1805 The Louisiana Purchase acquires a large area of South from France, almost doubling the land area of the USA

1848 California gold rush. Within two years 90,000 people from San Francisco, the East, and overseas travel to diggings

1861–65 Civil War between southern (Confederate) and northern (Union) states; all slaves freed in Confederate states

1869 World's first transcontinental railroad is completed when the Union Pacific line and Central Pacific lines link up

1908 Ford launches Model T, a mass market automobile. It transforms US industry and economy; 15.5 million sold in 19 years

1917 USA enters First World War on the side of the Allies

1920 More Americans now living in industrial cities than on the land; women are given the vote in all elections

1929 Wall Street Crash ruins many investors and affects industry and farming; millions lose jobs in Depression

1936 Boulder Dam on Colorado River completed impounding Lake Mead; renamed Hoover Dam (1947)

1941 USA joins Allies in Second World War after Japan bombs Pearl Harbor; war ends 1945 after USA drops atomic bombs on Japan

1969 Apollo 11 mission opens a new chapter in space exploration by landing three astronauts on Moon

1992 Hurricane Andrew strikes Florida and Louisiana causing $25 billion damage and the loss of more than 50 lives

2001 On 11 September Arab terrorists fly three airplanes into the World Trade Center in New York and the Pentagon

century. During this period the only other major ethnic group to arrive were African slaves imported to work the plantations in the South. After the Civil War, however, mass immigration was encouraged, and a flood of migrants arrived from Italy, Scandinavia, Germany, the Balkans, and various troubled parts of Eastern Europe, including Russia. Many were Jews fleeing poverty and pogroms. In the sixty years between 1860 and 1920, 30 million people arrived, radically changing the ethnic composition of the country. Although there were national concentrations in specific neighborhoods (such as Little Italy in New York City) the ideal of assimilation ensured that by the middle of the twentieth century most of the new arrivals, or their children, had come to share the benefits of other citizens. More recently there has been an influx of Japanese, Chinese, Filipinos, Cubans, Vienamese, Koreans, and large numbers of Mexicans and Central Americans. In some places, Puerto Rican, Cuban, and Mexican groups provide a strongly Hispanic cultural orientation.

One group of long-term residents did not enjoy full participation in American life. These were the African-Americans descended from the slaves, who became increasingly concentrated in the cities. Long after the Civil War, deeply entrenched systematic discrimination barred them from jobs, and from equal access to housing, commercial premises, public facilities, and education—even forcing them to sit at the back of the bus in the old slave states. As a result of agitation and affirmative action, the second half of the twentieth century saw the legal rights of African-Americans secured. What remains, however, are inequalities which law alone seems unable to resolve. In the cities, many African-Americans remain part of an underclass plagued by unemployment, drug addiction, crime, and unstable family life. One of the consequences of this social imbalance is the fact that black African-American males constitute the vast majority of criminals sentenced to jail or even death.

Economy and resources

The US economy is the largest among the industrial nations, possessing an invaluable combination of skilled and unskilled labor and natural resources. Internationally, it is the most powerful, diverse, and scientifically advanced country. With the early application of research and technology, agriculture developed into a highly mechanized industry for food production and processing, with a distinct zonal pattern across the country. Dairy farming predominates in a broad belt from New England to Minnesota. Further west, where the climate is drier, wheat is grown. The corn (maize) belt, highly productive land which was once prairie and forest, consists of the maize-growing eastern and central states from Ohio to Nebraska. Maize is mainly used for feeding to cattle and pigs. In the warmer southern states where cotton and tobacco were once grown on plantations—the old "cotton belt"—a variety of other crops are now cultivated as well, from vegetables to fruit and peanuts. There has been a strong tendency for farming to move from small to large-scale operations and from labor-intensive to mechanized methods. Although agriculture's share of gross domestic product is only two percent, the US remains a leading producer of meat, dairy foods, soy beans, maize, oats, wheat, barley, cotton, sugar, and forest products.

Despite twenty years of strong competition from Japan and various other Asian economies, the giant United States economy remained resurgent throughout the 1990s. One reason for its success may be the greater flexibility of US capitalist enterprise when compared with either Asia or Western Europe. A labor market which is responsive to changing demands is another factor, and over the last twenty years there has been a huge shift in employment from manufacturing to services. The US unemployment rate remains one of the lowest in all the major industrialized states.

But the main reason for the health of the economy is probably its dynamic technological inventiveness. In every field, US firms are at or near the frontier of technological advance. This is especially true in computers, medical equipment, and aerospace. The advantages of this onrush of technology are obvious. But there are major social costs as well. What is called a two-tier labor market has evolved in which those at the bottom lack enough skills and education to compete, failing to get pay rises, health insurance coverage, and other benefits which are strongly tied to full-time employment.

Despite the economy's basic good health, marked by low inflation and low unemployment, debate continues on how a number of continuing problems should be addressed. These include low rates of personal and corporate saving, inadequate investment in infrastructure, the rising medical costs of an ageing population, large budget and trade deficits, and the stagnation of family income in the lower economic groups.

STATES

Alabama • Montgomery
Alaska • Juneau
Arizona • Phoenix
Arkansas • Little Rock
California • Sacramento
Colorado • Denver
Connecticut • Hartford
Delaware • Dover
District of Columbia • Washington DC
Florida • Tallahassee
Georgia • Atlanta
Hawaii • Honolulu
Idaho • Boise
Illinois • Springfield
Indiana • Indianapolis
Iowa • Des Moines
Kansas • Topeka
Kentucky • Frankfort
Louisiana • Baton Rouge
Maine • Augusta
Maryland • Annapolis
Massachusetts • Boston
Michigan • Lansing
Minnesota • St Paul
Mississippi • Jackson
Missouri • Jefferson City
Montana • Helena
Nebraska • Lincoln
Nevada • Carson City
New Hampshire • Concord
New Jersey • Trenton
New Mexico • Santa Fe
New York • Albany
North Carolina • Raleigh
North Dakota • Bismarck
Ohio • Columbus
Oklahoma • Oklahoma City
Oregon • Salem
Pennsylvania • Harrisburg
Rhode Island • Providence
South Carolina • Columbia
South Dakota • Pierre
Tennessee • Nashville
Texas • Austin
Utah • Salt Lake City
Vermont • Montpelier
Virginia • Richmond
Washington • Olympia
West Virginia • Charleston
Wisconsin • Madison
Wyoming • Cheyenne

OVERSEAS TERRITORIES

American Samoa
Baker and Howland Islands
Guam
Jarvis Island
Johnston Atoll
Kingman Reef
Midway Islands
Navassa Island
Northern Mariana Islands
Palmyra Atoll
Puerto Rico
Virgin Islands of the United States
Wake Island

Dependencies and territories

Virgin Islands of the United States

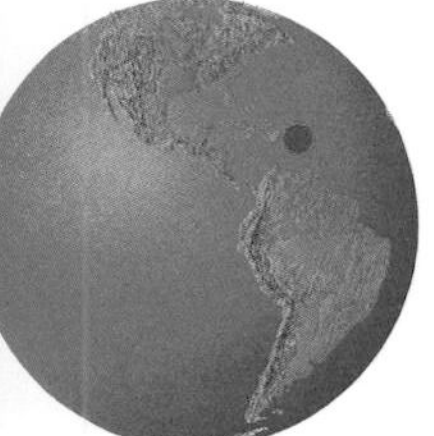

Fact File

Official name Virgin Islands of the United States

Form of government Unincorporated territory of the United States

Capital Charlotte Amalie

Area 352 sq km (136 sq miles)

Time zone GMT + 7 hours

Population 123,000

Life expectancy 78.4

Infant mortality (per 1,000) 9.2

Literacy rate Not available

Currency US dollar

Economy Tourism, light industry, agriculture

Climate Subtropical; wet season May to November

Map reference Page 427

The US Virgin Islands consist of 68 hilly volcanic islands east of Puerto Rico in the Caribbean. They are on a key shipping lane and were bought from Denmark by the USA in 1917 to protect the approaches to the Panama Canal. They contain one of the world's largest oil refineries on St Croix, but tourism is still the main economic activity, accounting for over seventy percent of the island's gross domestic product and seventy percent of employment. Manufacturing includes textiles, pharmaceuticals, electronics, and watch assembly. Business and financial services are also of growing importance. Agriculture is limited, and most food has to be imported.

Navajo Indians in Monument Valley, Arizona (left page).
Islands of the Great Sound in Bermuda (below).

Anguilla

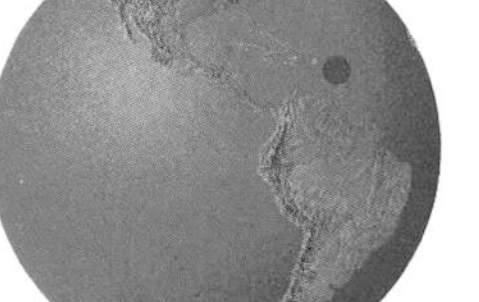
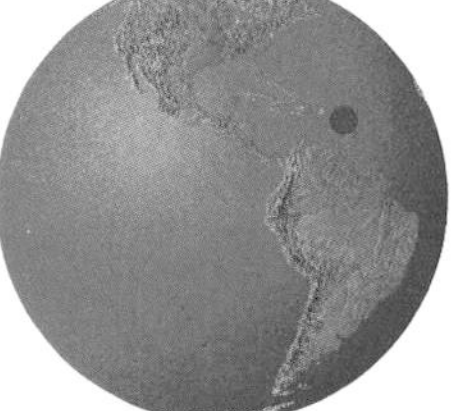

Fact File

Official name Anguilla

Form of government Dependent territory of the United Kingdom

Capital The Valley

Area 91 sq km (35 sq miles)

Time zone GMT – 4 hours

Population 12,400

Life expectancy 76.5

Infant mortality (per 1,000) 23.7

Literacy rate 95 %

Currency East Caribbean dollar

Economy Services 65 %, construction 18 %, transportation and utilities 10 %, manufacturing 3 %, agriculture 4 %

Climate Tropical, moderated by trade winds

Map reference Page 427

Anguilla's name comes from the Spanish *anguil* meaning "eel". The country is a long, thin, scrub-covered coral atoll in the Caribbean, north of St Kitts and Nevis. First colonized by Britain in 1690, its status as a UK dependent territory was formalized in 1980. While the governor is a crown appointee, a local assembly manages internal matters.

Anguilla has few natural resources and depends heavily on tourism, offshore banking, lobster fishing, and overseas remittances. Drawn by a subtropical climate tempered by trade winds, tourists have multiplied in recent years, reflecting the generally healthy economic conditions in both the USA and the UK. As a result, annual growth has averaged about seven percent, though it dropped to stagnation in 2003. The offshore finance sector was strengthened by comprehensive legislation enacted in 1994.

Aruba

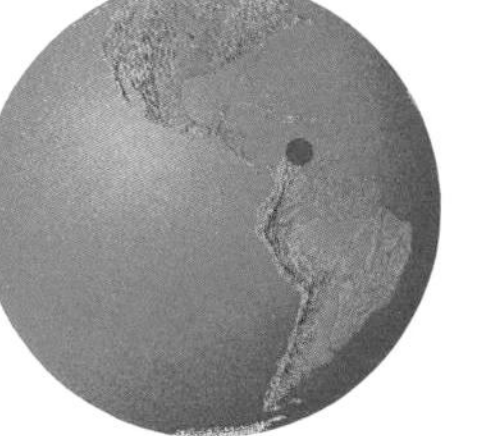

Fact File

Official name Aruba

Form of government Self-governing part of the Kingdom of the Netherlands

Capital Oranjestad

Area 193 sq km (74 sq miles)

Time zone GMT – 4 hours

Population 70,400

Life expectancy 78.7

Infant mortality (per 1,000) 6.3

Literacy rate 97 %

Currency Aruban florin

Economy Tourism, financial services

Climate Tropical

Map reference Page 427

Aruba is most unusual among the islands of the Caribbean in that it has a 0.6 percent unemployment rate, numerous unfilled employment vacancies, and a high gross domestic product. A flat, limestone island lying off the Venezuelan coast at the mouth of the Gulf of Venezuela, Aruba is barren on its eastern side and more lush on the west. It was once a part of the Netherlands Antilles, but since 1980 has been a separate but autonomous part of the Dutch realm. The population is mainly of African, European, and Asian descent.

Closed in 1985, the oil refinery on the island was reopened in 1993. This is a major source of employment and foreign exchange earnings and has greatly spurred economic growth. Tourism is extensive on the western side of the island, which is known as the Turquoise Coast, and its rapid development has led to an expansion of other activities.

Bermuda

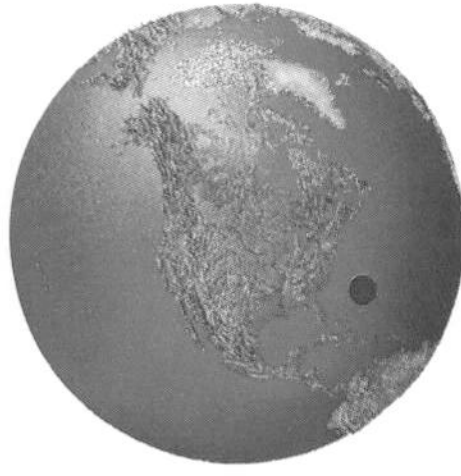

Fact File

Official name Bermuda

Form of government Dependent territory of the United Kingdom

Capital Hamilton

Area 50 sq km (19 sq miles)

Time zone GMT – 4 hours

Population 64,000

Life expectancy 77.3

Infant mortality (per 1,000) 9.3

Literacy rate 98 %

Currency Bermudian dollar

Economy Clerical 25 %, services 29 %, laborers 21 %, professional and technical 13 %, administrative 10 %, agriculture 2 %

Climate Subtropical; windy in winter

Bermuda is an island in the Atlantic Ocean 900 km (560 miles) off the coast of South Carolina, USA. It has one of the highest per capita incomes in the world, as its balmy location and lush vegetation draw tourists and its financial services offer tax-haven advantages. Bermuda also has one of the world's biggest flag-of-convenience fleets. The largest of some 360 low-lying coral islands which have grown atop ancient submarine volcanoes, it was discovered by the Spaniard Juan Bermudez in 1503, was later taken over by the British, and has a tradition of self-government going back to its first parliament in 1620. Its people are mainly descendants of former African slaves or British or Portuguese settlers. A move for full independence was rejected by 73 percent of voters in 1995, partly for fear of scaring away foreign business. With ninety percent of tourists coming from the US, links with that country are strong.

British Virgin Islands

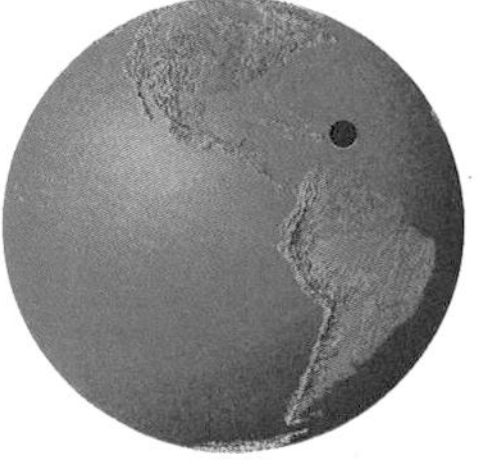

Fact File

Official name British Virgin Islands

Form of government Dependent territory of the United Kingdom

Capital Road Town

Area 150 sq km (58 sq miles)

Time zone GMT – 4 hours

Population 21,000

Life expectancy 75.9

Infant mortality (per 1,000) 19.6

Literacy rate 97.8 %

Currency US dollar

Economy Tourism, agriculture

Climate Subtropical, moderated by trade winds

Map reference Page 427

East of Puerto Rico in the Caribbean, the British Virgin Islands are the northernmost of the Lesser Antilles. There are four low-lying islands—Tortola, Anegada, Virgin Gorda, and Jost Van Dyke—and 36 coral islets and cays. Most are the peaks of a submerged mountain chain, and they share a subtropical climate moderated by trade winds. With the exception of Anegada, which is flat, the landscape is hilly, with sandy beaches and coral reefs around the coasts. Visited by Columbus in 1493, the British Virgin Islands were for 200 years pirate bases used by the English and the Dutch, until Tortola was annexed by the British in 1672. Today, they are a British dependency enjoying a large measure of self-government, and highly dependent on the tourism which produces some 45 percent of national income. International business makes use of offshore services, incorporation fees generating substantial revenues. Livestock raising is agriculturally important. Soil fertility is low and much food must be imported.

Cayman Islands

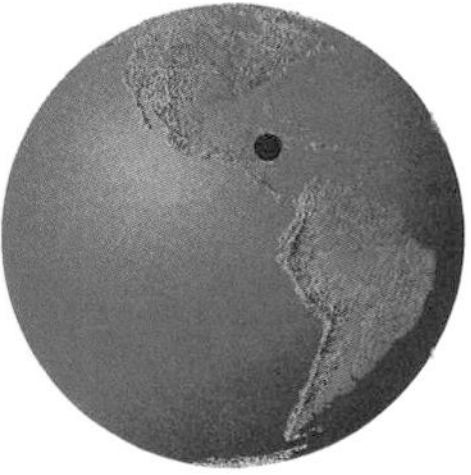

Fact File

Official name Cayman Islands

Form of government Dependent territory of the United Kingdom

Capital George Town

Area 260 sq km (100 sq miles)

Time zone GMT – 5 hours

Population 36,300

Life expectancy 79.2

Infant mortality (per 1,000) 9.9

Literacy rate 98 %

Currency Caymanian dollar

Economy Services 20 %, clerical 20 %, construction 13 %, finance and investment 10 %, directors and business managers 10 %, other 27 %

Climate Tropical, with cool, dry winters and warm, wet summers

Map reference Page 429

The largest of Britain's dependencies in the Caribbean, the Cayman Islands consist of three low-lying coral islands south of Cuba and 300 km (186 miles) west of Jamaica. Until the 1960s the main occupations were farming and fishing. Today the islands are one of the world's biggest offshore financial centers, offering a confidential tax haven to some 35,000 companies and several hundred banks. Tourism is also a mainstay, accounting for seventy percent of gross domestic product and 75 percent of foreign currency earnings. Tourism is aimed at the luxury end of the market and caters mainly to visitors from North America. The Cayman Islands were uninhabited when first discovered by Europeans. Most residents today are of mixed Afro-European descent, while an immigrant Jamaican labor force makes up about one-fifth of the population.

Greenland

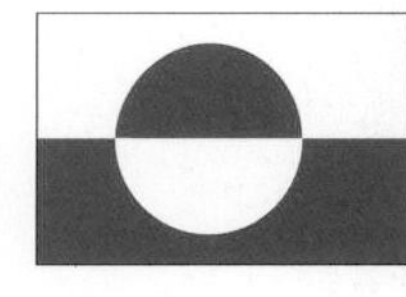

Fact File

Official name Greenland

Form of government Self-governing overseas administrative division of Denmark

Capital Nuuk (Godthab)

Area 2,175,600 sq km (839,999 sq miles)

Time zone GMT – 1/4 hours

Population 56,400

Life expectancy 68.7

Infant mortality (per 1,000) 17.3

Literacy rate Not available

Currency Danish krone

Economy Fishing

Climate Polar, with bitterly cold winters and cool to cold summers

Map reference Page 411

Greenland is nearly fifty times the size of its "mother country", Denmark, yet it has only one percent as much population. It is the biggest island in the world and about 85 percent of its land area is covered by an ice-cap with an average depth of 1,500 m (5,000 ft). Though there are a few sandy and clay plains in the ice-free areas of the island, settlement is confined to the rocky coasts.

It was named "Greenland" by the Viking Erik the Red during the tenth century, in the hope that the name would attract other adventurous Norsemen as settlers. The island became a Danish colony in 1721, an integral part of Denmark in 1973, and received full internal self-government in 1981. Most Greenlanders today are of mixed Inuit and Danish descent, and sometimes live uneasily between these two worlds. The social cost of this divide can be heavy; in the towns alcoholism, venereal disease, and suicide are prevalent.

Greenland's economic prospects are somewhat limited in that it is now almost completely dependent on fishing and fish processing. These constitute 95 percent of all exports, and there is the added problem of falling catches of shrimp—in recent years the Arctic fishing industry has contracted. Though it has a certain amount of mineral resources, the last lead and zinc mine was closed in 1990. There is some ship building and also potential for the development of adventure tourism. One problem is the large role of the public sector, which accounts for two-thirds of total employment. About half of government revenue comes from Danish government grants.

Guadeloupe

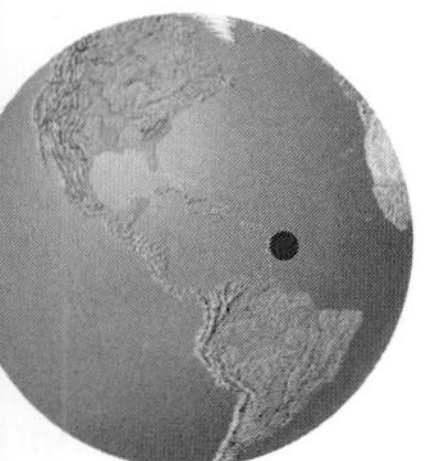

Fact File

Official name Department of Guadeloupe

Form of government Overseas department of France

Capital Basse-Terre

Area 1,780 sq km (687 sq miles)

Time zone GMT – 4 hours

Population 435,700

Life expectancy 77.4

Infant mortality (per 1,000) 9.3

Literacy rate 90 %

Currency Euro

Economy Services 65 %, industry 20 %, agriculture 15 %

Climate Subtropical, moderated by trade winds

Map reference Page 427

Guadeloupe consists of seven Caribbean islands in the Lesser Antilles, to the southeast of Puerto Rico. The biggest is the high, volcanic Basse-Terre (the active volcano of La Soufrière is the highest point in the Lesser Antilles) lying alongside the slightly smaller flat limestone island of Grande-Terre. A narrow sea channel separates the two. Arawak and Carib Indians were the original inhabitants. The first European settlers to arrive were the French, in 1635. Although there has been considerable agitation for independence, no vote in favor of it has succeeded, and the country is still governed by France—on which it is entirely dependent for subsidies and imported food. Tourism is important, most visitors coming from the USA. Sugar production is being phased out; bananas now supply about fifty percent of export earnings and the cultivation of other crops such as aubergines and flowers is being encouraged.

Jan Mayen

Fact File

Official name Jan Mayen

Form of government Territory of Norway

Capital None

Area 373 sq km (144 sq miles)

Time zone GMT – 1 hour

Population No permanent population

Economy Radio and meteorological stations

Climate Polar: cold, windy, and foggy

Map reference Page 411

The mountainous island of Jan Mayen lies in the Arctic Ocean about 900 km (560 miles)

Ice floes are visible in the water surrounding the town of Narsaruaq, Greenland (left page top). Chapel of Alto Vista on the eastern coast of Aruba (left page bottom). The former capital of Martinique, Saint-Pierre (above).

The colonial legacy

The Caribbean contains many small island states and a significant number of dependencies. This diversity in status is the legacy of centuries of engagement with colonial powers. After Columbus discovered the area at the end of the fifteenth century, Spain took possession of many islands, but Great Britain, France and the Netherlands also claimed, fought over and exploited the Caribbean. From the end of the fifteenth century to the middle of the eighteenth century the indigenous people were nearly wiped out and replaced by a much larger population of Europeans and African slaves, who were forcibly imported to work in the sugar, tobacco, and coffee plantations that dominated the local economies. The Caribbean has long served as an important trading route between North and South Americas and to Europe and the East. In recent years the United States has had a more direct influence on the economic and political developments and activities of some of the Caribbean regions.

The result of the history of the Caribbeans is a diversity of economic, social, and political interests. Some islands have retained their colonial or dependent status (Puerto Rico, for example, formerly a Spanish colony, has associated itself with the US and remains a dependent territory). Others chose independence, such as Cuba, which became independent from Spain in 1898 and severed its political ties to the United States in 1959. The mixture of races (Carib, African, and European) and cultures has created national identities marked by different peoples, languages, customs, and political systems.

Attempts to create larger political or economic entities out of the many small islands were not very successful. Nevertheless, in 1968 many of the islands agreed to the foundation of the Caribbean Free Trade Area. However, there are unifying forces that are responsible for a certain amount of common identity. One of these areas is sports. In cricket, for example, a heritage from British colonial rule, many of the former colonies unite to form one single national team: the team of the "West Indies".

west of Norway. It is volcanic, with the mighty active Beerenberg volcano rising 2,400 m (7,874 ft) straight out of the surf. From its ice-cap some 15 glaciers descend into the sea. Once an important base for Arctic whaling, Jan Mayen's only resources today are rich fishing grounds. These were the subject of a long dispute with Greenland over fishing rights, and possible oil and gas deposits. Mediated by the International Court of Justice, the two parties reached a compromise on this issue in 1993. The island's birdlife is spectacular and includes millions of fulmar, petrel, kittiwake, little auk, guillemot, and puffin.

Martinique

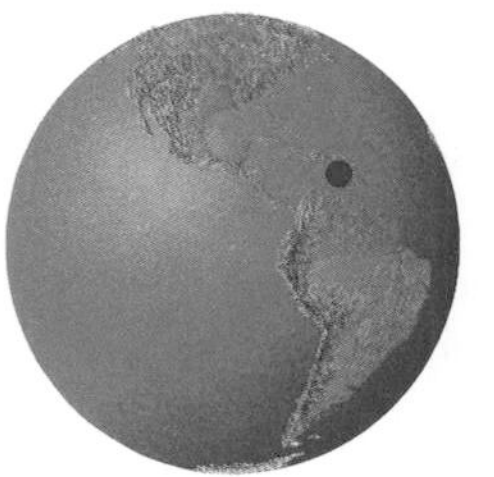

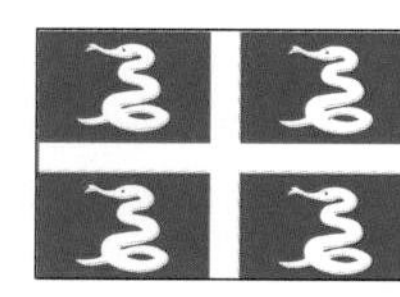

Fact File

Official name Department of Martinique

Form of government Overseas department of France

Capital Fort-de-France

Area 1,100 sq km (425 sq miles)

Time zone GMT – 4 hours

Population 422,300

Life expectancy 78.6

Infant mortality (per 1,000) 7.6

Literacy rate 93 %

Currency Euro

Economy Services 73 %, industry 17 %, agriculture 10 %

Climate Tropical, moderated by trade winds; wet season June to October

Map reference Page 427

Christopher Columbus described Martinique as "the most beautiful country in the world" when he laid eyes on it in 1493. This island in the eastern Caribbean was colonized by France in 1635 and has been French ever since. It consists of three groups of volcanic hills and the intervening lowlands, and is dominated by the dormant volcano Mt Pelée. Mt Pelée is famous for the eruption of 1902, when it killed all the inhabitants of the town of St-Pierre except one prisoner, who was saved by the thickness of his prison cell. The economy is based on sugarcane, bananas, tourism, and light industry, the export of bananas being of growing importance. Most sugarcane is used for making rum. The majority of the workforce is in the service sector and administration, tourism having become more important than agricultural exports as a source of foreign exchange.

Montserrat

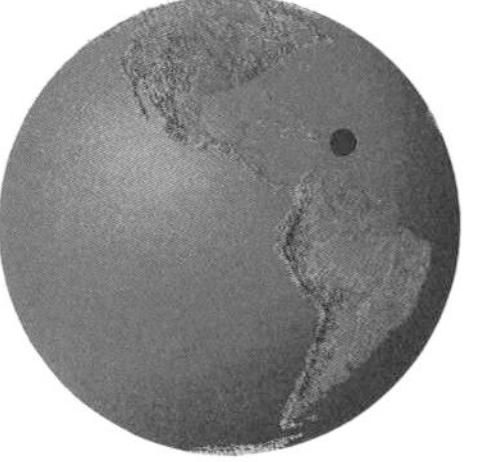

Fact File

Official name Montserrat

Form of government Dependent territory of the United Kingdom

Capital Plymouth

Area 100 sq km (39 sq miles)

Time zone GMT – 4 hours

Population 8,400 (a volcanic eruption in 1995 led to the evacuation of two-thirds of the population; before the eruption: 13,000, after the evacuation 4,000)

Life expectancy 78.2

Infant mortality (per 1,000) 8

Literacy rate 97 %

Currency EC (East Caribbean) dollar

Economy Tourism, industry, agriculture

Climate Tropical

Map reference Page 427

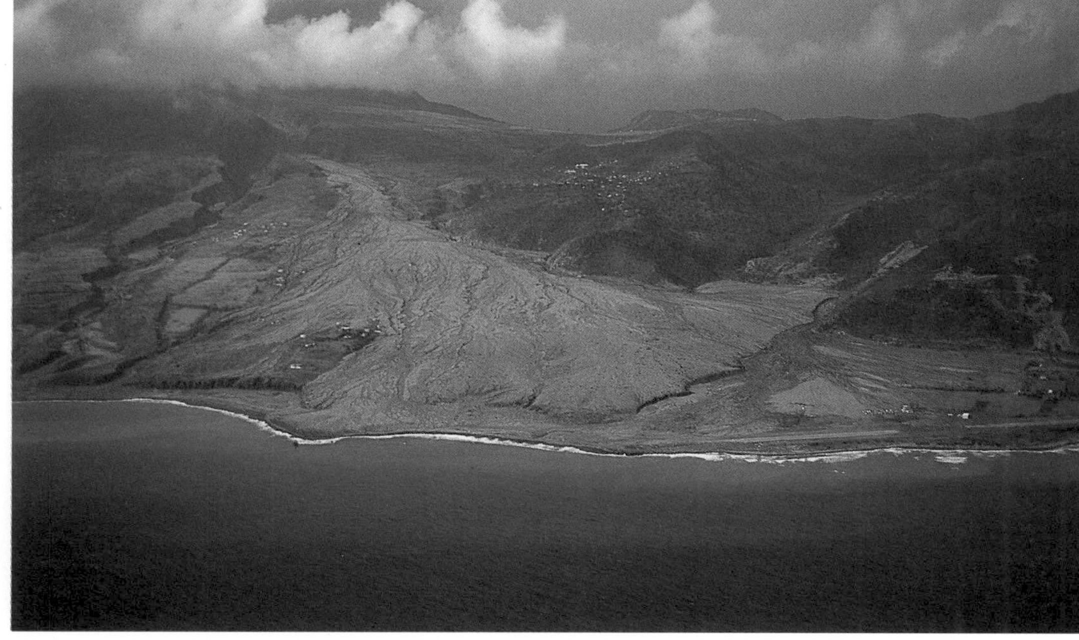

Montserrat is a Caribbean island with seven active volcanoes. In 1995 deep ash from one of them destroyed numerous crops and forced the evacuation of the capital, Plymouth. Montserrat was colonized in 1632 by the British, who at first brought in Irish settlers. (Together with its lush green foliage, this is why it is locally known as "the Emerald Isle".) Later, the island's sugar plantations were worked by African slaves. It has been a self-governing UK dependent territory since 1960. Tourism provides a quarter of the national income, other support coming from the export of electronic components which are assembled on the island, plastic bags, clothing, rum, hot peppers, live plants, and cattle. Data processing facilities and offshore banking are available.

Navassa

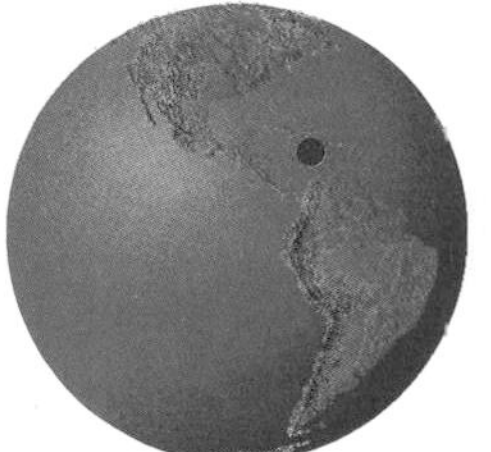

Fact File

Official name Navassa Island

Form of government Unincorporated territory of the United States

Capital None

Area 5.2 sq km (2 sq miles)

Time zone GMT – 5 hours

Population No permanent population

Climate Tropical, moderated by sea breezes

Map reference Page 429

Navassa Island is an uninhabited rocky outcrop in the Caribbean halfway between Cuba and Haiti. It is strategically located for the USA, since it is 160 km (100 miles) south of the Guantanamo Bay (Bahía de Guantánamo) naval base. The island is administered by the US Department of the Interior, which made it a natural reserve in 1999. The surface is mostly exposed rock but it has dense stands of fig-like trees, cacti, and enough grass to support goats. Its principal resource is guano.

Mud and lava from the 1995 volcanic eruption on Montserrat (left). The oceanfront in old San Juan, Puerto Rico (above).

Netherlands Antilles

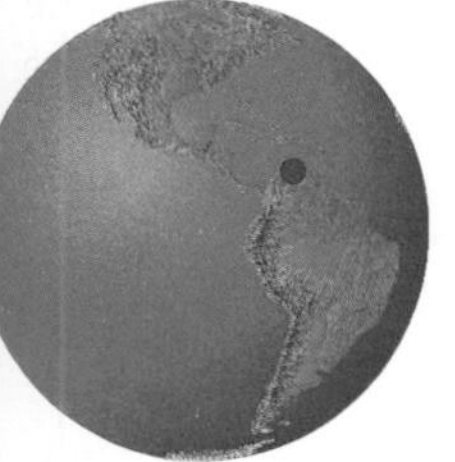

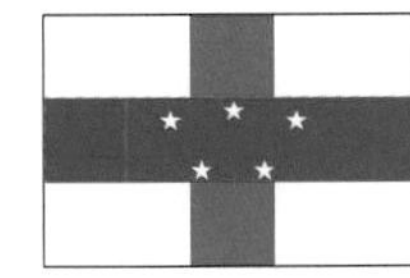

Fact File

Official name Netherlands Antilles

Form of government Self-governing part of the Kingdom of the Netherlands

Capital Willemstad

Area 960 sq km (371 sq miles)

Time zone GMT – 4 hours

Population 214,300

Life expectancy 75.2

Infant mortality (per 1,000) 11.1

Currency Netherlands Antillean guilder

Economy Tourism, offshore finance

Climate Tropical, moderated by trade winds

Map reference Page 427

The Netherlands Antilles consist of two very different island groups in two parts of the Caribbean. Curaçao and Bonaire are located off the coast of Venezuela, and while they may once have made money from the well-known orange liqueur, today 98 percent of their income comes from petroleum—either processed for products or for transshipment facilities. The other group, which lies east of the Virgin Islands, consists of the three islands of Saba, St Eustasius, and part of Sint Maarten (the other half belongs to French Guadeloupe and is called Saint-Martin). The people are largely of African and European descent, the original inhabitants having been killed in the sixteenth century by Spanish settlers. All told, the islands have a high per capita income and a well-developed infrastructure in comparison with others in the region. Nearly all consumer and capital goods are imported from the USA and Venezuela. Crops grown include aloes, sorghum, peanuts, vegetables, and tropical fruit, but poor soils and limited water make agriculture difficult.

Puerto Rico

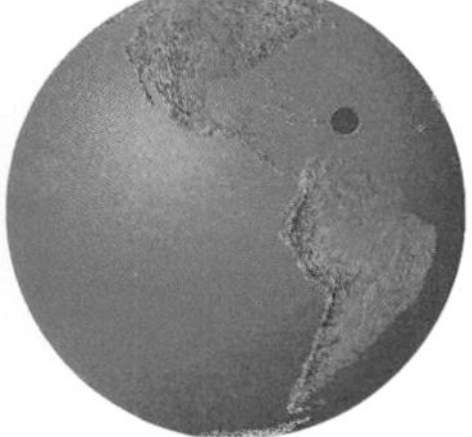

Fact File

Official name Commonwealth of Puerto Rico

Form of government Commonwealth associated with the United States

Capital San Juan

Area 9,104 sq km (3,515 sq miles)

Time zone GMT – 4 hours

Population 3,958,000

Life expectancy 76

Infant mortality (per 1,000) 9.3

Literacy rate 89 %

Currency US dollar

Economy Government 22 %, manufacturing 17 %, trade 20 %, construction 6 %, communications and transportation 5 %, other 30 %

Climate Tropical, moderated by sea breezes

Map reference Page 427

Puerto Rico is a large Caribbean island east of the Dominican Republic. Ceded by Spain to the USA in 1898, its citizens enjoy a number of privileges: full US citizenship, no federal taxes, and free access to the US. In 1998 the population again voted to continue their self-governing commonwealth status and forgo becoming either the 51st state of the USA or independent. Mountainous, with a narrow coastal plain, the little flat ground available for agriculture is used for growing sugarcane, coffee, bananas, and tobacco. The economy is essentially modern and industrialized. Tax relief and cheap labor have brought many businesses to the island and tourism is growing. Industries include petrochemicals, pharmaceuticals (the island produces over ninety percent of all US tranquillizers), and electronics. The standard of living in Puerto Rico is the highest in Latin America (outside the island tax havens), and is rising.

St Pierre and Miquelon

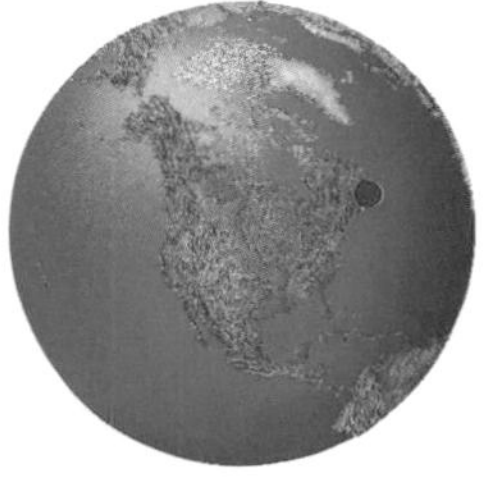

Fact File

Official name Territorial collectivity of St Pierre and Miquelon

Form of government Territorial collectivity of France

Capital St-Pierre

Area 242 sq km (93 sq miles)

Time zone GMT – 4 hours

Population 7,000

Life expectancy 77.9

Infant mortality (per 1,000) 8.2

Literacy rate 99 %

Currency Euro

Economy Mainly fishing and fish processing

Climate Cold, wet, and foggy

Map reference Page 417

St Pierre and Miquelon are islands in the North Atlantic Ocean, south of Newfoundland. They are cold and wet and have little vegetation. Surrounded by some of the world's richest fishing grounds, the islands were settled by French fishermen in the seventeenth century. Since then the inhabitants have earned a living from fishing and by servicing the foreign trawler fleets that operate off the coast. A dispute between Canada and France over fishing and mineral rights was settled in 1992. Since the French subsidize the islands, and their economy has been declining, the authorities are now trying to diversify by developing port facilities and encouraging tourism.

Turks and Caicos Islands

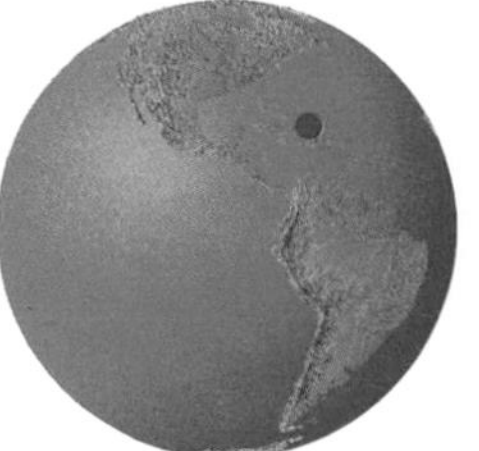

Fact File

Official name Turks and Caicos Islands

Form of government Dependent territory of the United Kingdom

Capital Grand Turk

Area 430 sq km (166 sq miles)

Time zone GMT – 5 hours

Population 18,800

Life expectancy 73.8

Infant mortality (per 1,000) 17.5

Literacy rate 99 %

Currency US dollar

Economy Fishing, tourism, agriculture

Climate Tropical, moderated by trade winds

Map reference Page 429

The Turks and Caicos Islands are a group of thirty islands, eight of them inhabited, north of Hispaniola. They are composed of low, flat, scrub-covered limestone with areas of marsh and swamp. There is little land for agriculture, though cassava, maize, citrus fruits, and beans are grown on Caicos by subsistence farmers. Today, the islands' economy is mainly based on tourism, fishing, and offshore financial services. Nearly all consumer and capital goods are imported. The islands have been British since 1766, and a crown colony since 1973. Although independence was agreed upon for 1982, the policy was reversed and the islands remain a British overseas territory.

Bahamas

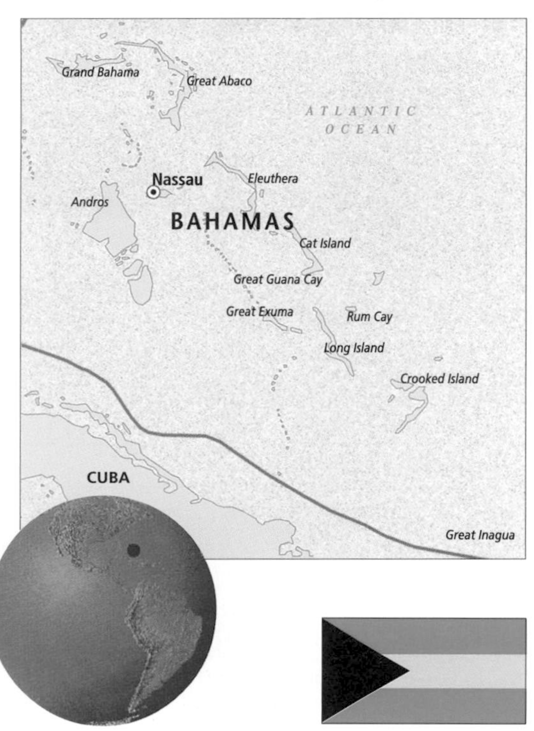

Fact File

Official name Commonwealth of the Bahamas

Form of government Constitutional monarchy with two legislative bodies (Senate and House of Assembly)

Capital Nassau

Area 13,940 sq km (5,382 sq miles)

Time zone GMT – 5 hours

Population 300,500

Projected population 2015 359,000

Population density 21.6 per sq km (55.8 per sq mile)

Life expectancy 69.9

Infant mortality (per 1,000) 17.1

Official language English

Other language Creole

Literacy rate 98.2 %

Religions Baptist 32 %, Anglican 20 %, Roman Catholic 19 %, Methodist 6 %, Church of God 6 %, other Protestant 12 %, other 5 %

Ethnic groups African 85 %, European 15 %

Currency Bahamian dollar

Economy Tourism 40 %, government 30 %, business services 10 %, agriculture 5 %, industry 4 %, other 11 %

GNP per capita US$ 16,800

Climate Subtropical, with warm summers and mild winters

Highest point Mt Alverina 63 m (207 ft)

Map reference Page 425

Off the southern tip of Florida in the western Atlantic, the Bahamas consists of 700 islands and about 2,400 cays. When Columbus landed here the islands were inhabited by Arawak Indians. The islands were claimed by Britain in 1690, but have had a checkered history since. A pirates' haven in the seventeenth century, they were held for short periods by the USA and Spain before Britain resumed control in 1783. They have been independent since 1983. The 25-year administration of Lynden Pindling ended in 1992 amid allegations of involvement in narcotics trafficking and money laundering. One of the most prosperous of the Caribbean's island states, the Bahamas has attracted many illegal immigrants from Haiti across the water. This influx has placed severe strain on government services. The increase of violent crimes also poses major problem.

All the islands are fragments of a large coralline limestone shelf. Most are only a few meters above sea level. Their coastlines are fringed with lagoons and coral reefs. Water is scarce. There are no rivers and rainfall disappears into the limestone. Much of the big islands are covered with pine forest. On the smaller islands people work mainly in fishing and agriculture.

Tourists come in large numbers: in 1995 there were more than 3,600,000 foreign arrivals. Tourism in turn has given rise to the manufacture of garments, furniture, jewelry, and perfume. All energy resources must be imported. Offshore banking, insurance, and financial services generate income and provide one of the region's highest standards of living. In addition, the Bahamas has a large open-registry fleet.

Cuba

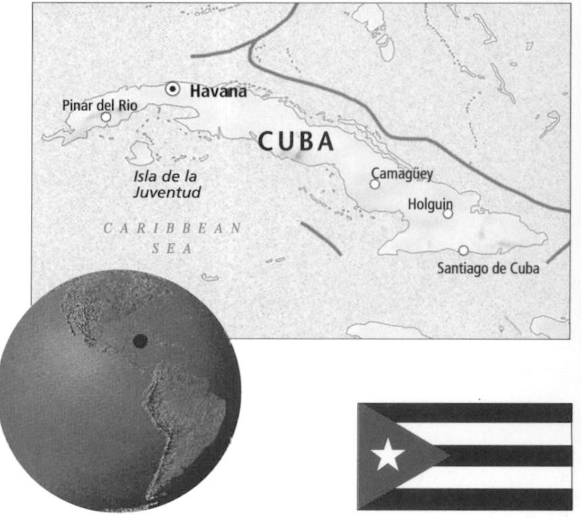

Fact File

Official name Republic of Cuba

Form of government Communist state with single legislative body (National Assembly of People's Power)

Capital Havana

Area 110,860 sq km (42,803 sq miles)

Time zone GMT – 5 hours

Population 11,225,000

Projected population 2015 11,664,000

Population density 101.3 per sq km (262.2 per sq mile)

Life expectancy 76.6

Infant mortality (per 1,000) 7.3

Official language Spanish

Literacy rate 96.2 %

Religions Roman Catholic 40 %, Protestant and African Spiritist 10 %, non-religious 50 %

Ethnic groups Mixed African-European 51 %, European 37 %, African 11 %, Chinese 1 %

Currency Cuban peso

Economy Services 47 %, industry 29 %, agriculture 24 %

GNP per capita US$ 2,300

Climate Tropical, moderated by trade winds; wet season May to October

Highest point Pico Turquino 1,974 m (6,476 ft)

Map reference Pages 428–29

The largest island in the Caribbean, Cuba is the size of all the others combined. Led by Fidel Castro, it is the only communist state in the Americas, and despite internal and external pressures remains politically unchanged after forty years. Cuba was visited by Columbus in 1492. It was at that time occupied by Arawak and Ciboney Indians. Under Spanish colonial rule sugar plantations worked by African slaves became the foundation of the island's economy—slavery was only abolished, under strong pressure from the Spanish government, in 1878. Gaining independence in 1898 but remaining under American tutelage until 1934, the country was run by a number of corrupt and gangster-ridden regimes until 1958, when Fidel Castro's

Hope Town on Elbow Cay, Abaco Island, Bahamas (left page). An aerial view of Havana, Cuba (above). Port Antonio on the northeast coast of Jamaica (below).

army captured Havana. In 1976 the de facto monopoly of the Communist Party was formalized, with Castro, supported by his brother, making all decisions. Since the collapse of the Soviet system, on which Cuba had become economically dependent, times have been hard.

Cuba is only 193 km (120 miles) across at its widest point, but it stretches over 1,200 km (745 miles) from the Gulf of Mexico, at its western extremity, to the Windward Passage between Cuba and Haiti in the east. In addition to the main island, the much smaller island of Isla de la Juventud lies off the southwest coast. Less mountainous than the other islands in the Greater Antilles group, Cuba nevertheless has three distinct ranges—the Oriental (Sierra Maestra), the Central, and the Occidental (Sierra de los Organos). These cover roughly 25 percent of the territory east to west. The remaining 75 percent of Cuba's surface area consists of lowlands and basins. On the more fertile soils sugar plantations, rice fields, coffee plantations, and tobacco fields are found; livestock is run on the central savanna. Cuba's irregular coastline is lined with mangroves, beaches, and coral reefs. Despite deforestation the island still has considerable areas of woodland, ranging from tropical near-jungle to pines growing in upland areas. Cuba has a mostly hot climate and experiences heavy seasonal rainfall and periodic hurricanes.

Sugarcane remains the country's main cash crop, as it has for more than 100 years. Cuba is the world's third-largest sugar producer, and sugar represents almost fifty percent of the country's exports by value. Other crops are tobacco, rice, potatoes, tubers, citrus fruit, and coffee. There are also extensive timber resources, including mahogany and cedar. Cuba has the world's fourth-largest nickel deposits, and production is rising as a result of a joint venture with a Canadian company.

Its situation as one of the world's few remaining communist states has left Cuba isolated and with few trading partners. In addition, because the government has been unwilling to hold multiparty elections, the country has been subject to a severe embargo imposed by the USA. Poor sugar harvests and falling prices for sugar, receding tourism, devastations by cyclones, insufficient funds to pay for fuel, and mounting deficits have added to the country's difficulties in recent times.

Jamaica

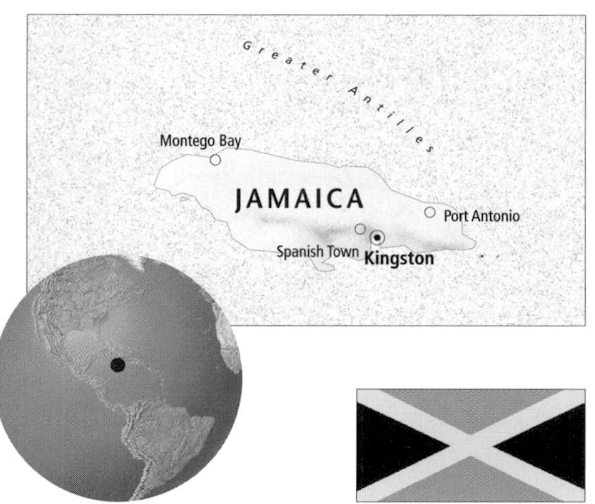

Fact File

OFFICIAL NAME Jamaica

FORM OF GOVERNMENT Constitutional monarchy with two legislative bodies (Senate and House of Representatives)

CAPITAL Kingston

AREA 10,990 sq km (4,243 sq miles)

TIME ZONE GMT – 5 hours

POPULATION 2,680,000

PROJECTED POPULATION 2015 2,957,000

POPULATION DENSITY 243.9 per sq km (631.6 per sq mile)

LIFE EXPECTANCY 75.6

INFANT MORTALITY (PER 1,000) 13.7

OFFICIAL LANGUAGE English

OTHER LANGUAGE Creole

LITERACY RATE 85 %

RELIGIONS Protestant (mainly Anglican, Presbyterian-Congregational, Baptist, Methodist) 70 %, Roman Catholic 7 %, other including Rastafari 23 %

ETHNIC GROUPS African 76.3 %, mixed African-European 15.1 %, East Indian and mixed African-East Indian 3 %, European 3.2 %, Chinese and mixed African-Chinese 1.2 %, other 1.2 %

CURRENCY Jamaican dollar

ECONOMY Services 63 %, agriculture 25 %, industry 12 %

GNP PER CAPITA US$ 3,700

CLIMATE Tropical; cooler inland

HIGHEST POINT Blue Mountain Peak 2,256 m (7,402 ft)

MAP REFERENCE Page 429

The Caribbean island of Jamaica lies 144 km (98 miles) south of Cuba and southwest of Haiti. Mountainous in the interior, it is the most populous of the English-speaking Caribbean islands. Arawak Indians were its first inhabitants. Columbus visited in 1494 and a slave-based sugar producing plantation society was established by the British after they seized the island in 1655. It won independence from Britain in 1962. An important contributor to world music, Jamaica is the home of reggae, a style originating in Kingston's tough urban environment. Also from Jamaica come the Rastafarians, followers of the one-time Emperor of Ethiopia. In September 1988 Jamaica was devastated by the fiercest hurricane to strike the island this century, causing widespread loss of life and leaving twenty percent of the people homeless.

In the northwest of the island is a limestone area of steep ridges and isolated basins, pitted with sink-holes. This "cockpit country" once gave refuge to escaped slaves. In the east the land rises to become the densely forested Blue Mountains. In the west the River Black is navigable upstream for about 30 km (19 miles). Sugar plantations dominate the densely populated and extensively cultivated lowland coastal fringe. Seasonal rains fall most heavily on the northeastern mountain slopes—still covered in the rainforest once found all over the island. In the rainshadow of the mountains, the southern lowlands support only savanna scrub.

Bauxite has been mined since 1952. Most of it is exported as ore, and about one-fifth as alumina, making Jamaica the world's third-largest producer. This accounts for more than fifty percent of exports. Tourism and bauxite production are Jamaica's two main industries, and comprise almost two-thirds of foreign earnings. Other export industries include printing, textiles and food processing, along with rum distilling and sugar production. In agriculture, sugarcane and bananas are the main cash crops, along with coffee, cocoa, and fruit. In recent years the government has removed most price controls and privatized state enterprises. Unemployment remains high. Jamaica's medium-term prospects depend largely on its ability to attract foreign capital and limit speculation against the Jamaican dollar.

Haiti

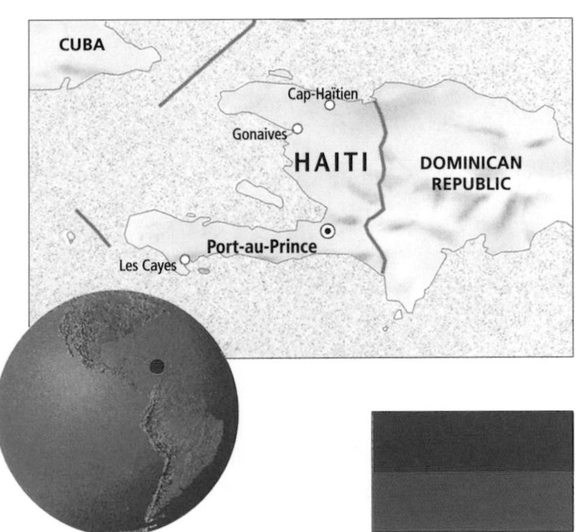

Fact File

Official name Republic of Haiti

Form of government Republic with two legislative bodies (Senate and Chamber of Deputies)

Capital Port-au-Prince

Area 27,750 sq km (10,714 sq miles)

Time zone GMT – 5 hours

Population 7,064,000

Projected population 2015 10,215,000

Population density 254.6 per sq km (659.3 per sq mile)

Life expectancy 49.6

Infant mortality (per 1,000) 93.4

Official language French

Other language French Creole

Literacy rate 45 %

Religions Roman Catholic 80 % (most of whom also practice Voodoo), Protestant 16 % (Baptist 10 %, Pentecostal 4 %, Adventist 1 %, other 1 %), other 4 %

Ethnic groups African 95 %, mixed African-European 5 %

Currency Gourd

Economy Agriculture 50 %, services 44 %, industry 6 %

GNP per capita US$ 1,700

Climate Mainly tropical; semiarid in eastern mountains; wet seasons April to June and August to November

Highest point Pic de la Selle 2,680 m (8,792 ft)

Map reference Page 429

Haiti lies in the Caribbean, east of Cuba. It is the western third of the island of Hispaniola, the Dominican Republic occupying the remainder. Visited by Columbus in 1492, it was used by the Spanish for sugarcane cultivation and was ceded to France in 1697. In the aftermath of the French Revolution it was the scene of a slave rebellion which led to the establishment, in 1804, of the world's first black republic. Since then the country has endured two centuries of instability, violence, dictatorship, military rule, and endemic poverty. Today Haiti is the poorest country in the western hemisphere. Under the brutal regime of the Duvalier family, between 1957 and 1986, it became a police state enforced by a private militia called the Tontons Macoute. Recent years have seen faltering steps toward electoral democracy and modest civil service reforms, but political killings are still occurring under an apparently corrupt and ineffective judicial system. Violent unrest and international pressure brought about a change of government in 2004.

Two peninsulas enclose the central plain of the Artibonite River, and the bight of the Golfe de la Gonâve beyond. Some 75 percent of Haiti's terrain is mountainous, the Massif du Nord providing the range which forms the northern peninsula, before extending east into the Dominican Republic where it becomes Hispaniola's Cordillera Central. The southern peninsula contains the Massif de la Hotte at its western end, and the Massif de la Selle in the east. The fertile lowland areas are densely populated, the largest of these being the Plaine du Nord. On the plains the major crop is sugarcane, coffee plantations being found on the higher land. The majority of the population is engaged in subsistence farming, growing cassava, bananas, and corn. Haiti's environmental problems are severe: one-third of its soil is seriously eroded, and extensive deforestation has occurred in the course of charcoal production.

Haiti is without strategic resources and, during a period of economic sanctions imposed to put pressure on the government in 1991, it was forced to find clandestine sources of oil. In addition to sugar refining, light industry includes flour and cement and the manufacture of textiles, shoes, and cooking utensils. The country's location, history, and culture proved attractive to tourists in the 1960s and 1970s, despite the repressive regime, but widespread crime has affected the industry in recent years.

Dominican Republic

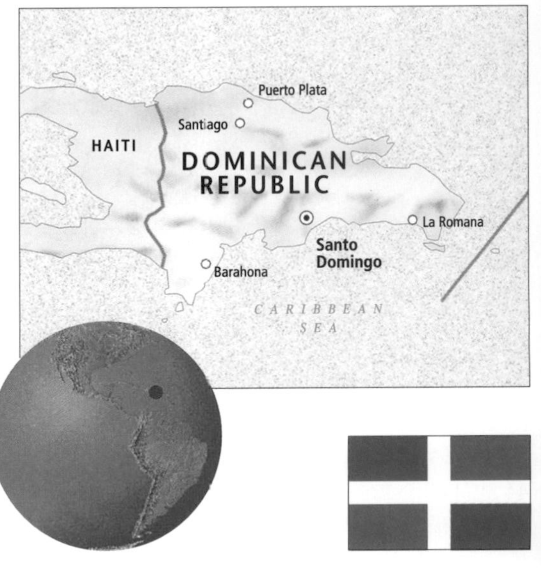

Fact File

Official name Dominican Republic

Form of government Republic with two legislative bodies (Senate and Chamber of Deputies)

Capital Santo Domingo

Area 48,730 sq km (18,815 sq miles)

Time zone GMT – 4 hours

Population 8,722,000

Projected population 2015 10,232,000

Population density 179 per sq km (463.6 per sq mile)

Life expectancy 73.7

Infant mortality (per 1,000) 33.4

Official language Spanish

Other language French Creole

Literacy rate 82.1 %

Religions Roman Catholic 95 %, other 5 %

Ethnic groups Mixed African–European 73 %, European 16 %, African 11 %

Currency Peso

Economy Agriculture 46 %, services 38 %, industry 16 %

GNP per capita US$ 5,800

Climate Tropical, with wet season May to November

Highest point Pico Duarte 3,175 m (10,416 ft)

Map reference Page 429

The second largest Caribbean nation in both area and population, the Dominican Republic occupies the eastern two-thirds of the island of Hispaniola. The island was visited by Christopher Columbus in 1492 and in 1496 his brother founded the city of Santo Domingo on its southern coast—the oldest Spanish city in the Americas. It was first colonized by Spain but the development of its sugar industry resulted from a period of French control. The country won independence in 1844 and since that time it has been ruled by a series of dictators with only short intervals of democracy. A bitter civil war in 1965 brought the intervention of the USA, which has kept a watch on Dominican affairs since then. Civil unrest continues. In 1996 President Balaguer had to resign after rigging the elections. The elections in 2000, however, were fair.

With a mountainous landscape, including the highest point in the West Indies, Pico Duarte, the Dominican Republic contains three considerable ranges—the Cordillera Septentrional in the north, the massive Cordillera Central, and the southern Sierra de Bahoruco. Between these ranges and to the east lie fertile valleys and lowlands. These include the Cibao Valley in the north, the Vega Real, and the coastal plains where sugar plantations are found. Because of the mountainous terrain there are wide variations in temperature and rainfall. Low-lying areas in the south and east support a dry savanna vegetation suitable for livestock raising. The Dominican Republic also has the lowest point in the West Indies—Lake Enriquillo, 44 m (144 ft) below sea level. The lake bisects the mountains in the southwest.

While still heavily dependent on its traditional agricultural base, in recent years the economy has been supplemented by industrial growth (making use of a vast hydroelectric potential), and a large increase in tourism. The Dominican Republic has good beaches and a hotel capacity of 30,000 rooms, the highest in the Caribbean. Sugar is still the leading agricultural export, followed by coffee, cocoa, tobacco, and fruit. Nickel and gold mining are increasing in economic importance. Subsistence farming provides most of the rural population with its livelihood, the staple crops being rice and corn. State-owned sugar plantations provide another source of employment. Illegal narcotics also play a part in the economy; the country is a transshipment point for drugs bound for the USA.

St Kitts and Nevis

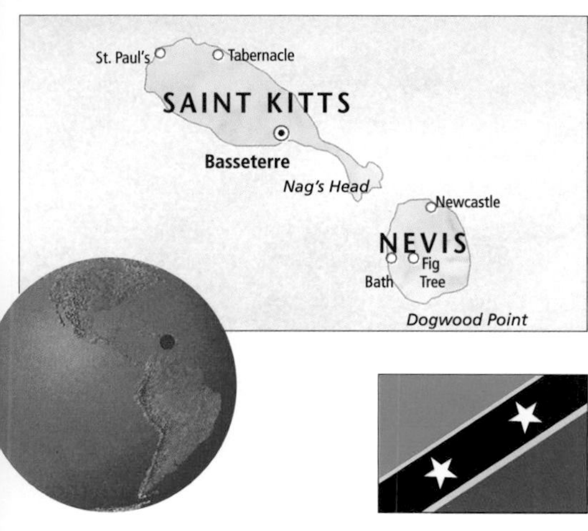

Fact File

Official name Federation of St Kitts and Nevis

Form of government Constitutional monarchy with single legislative body (House of Assembly)

Capital Basseterre

Area 269 sq km (104 sq miles)

Time zone GMT – 4 hours

Population 38,700

Projected population 2015 47,000

Population density 143.9 per sq km (372.1 per sq mile)

Life expectancy 71.3

Infant mortality (per 1,000) 15.8

Official language English

Other language English Creole

Literacy rate 97 %

Religions Anglican 36.2 %, Methodist 32.1 %, Roman Catholic 10.7 %, Pentecostal 5.5 %, Baptist 3.9 %, followers of the Church of God 3.9 %, other 7.5 %

Ethnic groups African 94.3 %, mixed African-European 3.3 %, European 0.9 %, other 1.5 %

Currency East Caribbean dollar

Economy Services 69 %, industry and agriculture 31 %

GNP per capita US$ 8,700

Climate Tropical, moderated by sea breezes

Highest point Mt Misery 1,156 m (3,793 ft)

Map reference Page 427

St Kitts and Nevis is a federation of two Caribbean islands in the Leeward Islands group. Each is well-watered and has a mountain of volcanic origin rising to about 1,000 m (3,300 ft). Once inhabited by Carib and Arawak Indians, St Kitts and Nevis were, in 1623 and 1628, the first West Indian islands to be colonized by Britain. Ownership of the islands was disputed with the French until 1783 when it was ceded to the United Kingdom. The islands became an associated state with full internal autonomy in 1967. The island of Anguilla rebelled and was allowed to secede in 1971. In 1983 the country became fully independent from Britain.

As on other Caribbean islands, African slaves were imported as labor for sugar and cotton plantations, this ceasing with the abolition of slavery in 1834. Most islanders today are descended from former slaves. The growing and processing of sugarcane remains important, though falling prices have hurt local industry in recent years. The government intends to revitalize this sector. Tourism and export-oriented manufacturing are of growing significance, in addition to manufactured products including machinery, food, electronics, clothing, footwear, and beverages. The main cash crops are sugarcane on St Kitts and cotton and coconuts on Nevis. Staple foods include rice, yams, vegetables, and bananas, but most food is imported.

Nevis claims it is starved of funds by its partner and is dissatisfied with its place in the federation. In 1996 Nevis announced its intention to seek independence from St Kitts. Nevis has the constitutional right to secede if two-thirds of the elected legislators approve and two-thirds of voters endorse it through a referendum. However, even though parliament decided accordingly to secede in 1998 the necessary popular support could not be mustered in the referendum.

Bananas are harvested on a plantation on Haiti (left page). Aerial view of the Antigua west coast (right).

Antigua and Barbuda

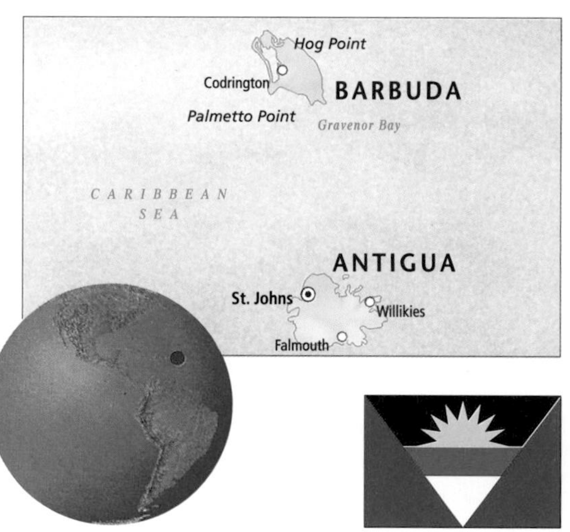

Fact File

Official name Antigua and Barbuda

Form of government Democracy with two legislative bodies (Senate and House of Representatives)

Capital St Johns

Area 440 sq km (170 sq miles)

Time zone GMT – 4 hours

Population 67,500

Projected population 2015 68,000

Population density 153.4 per sq km (397.1 per sq mile)

Life expectancy 71

Infant mortality (per 1,000) 21.6

Official language English

Other languages Indigenous languages

Literacy rate 89 %

Religions Protestant 90 %, Roman Catholic 10 %

Ethnic groups African 94.4 %, other 5.6 %

Currency East Caribbean dollar

Economy Services 67 %, industry 21 %, agriculture 12 %

GNP per capita US$ 10,000

Climate Tropical, moderated by sea breezes

Highest point Boggy Peak 405 m (1,328 ft)

Map reference Page 427

Antigua and Barbuda consists of three islands in the eastern Caribbean. In 1493 the largest of the group was visited by Christopher Columbus on his second voyage, who named it Antigua. It was first settled by the Spanish and the French, but became a British colony in 1667 and in the eighteenth century flourished under a plantation system using African slaves to produce sugar. This ended with the end of slavery in the British Empire in 1834. Originally populated by the Siboney in 2400 BC and later, when the Europeans arrived, by Arawak and Carib Indians, today the islands are peopled by Afro-Caribbean descendants of the plantation days. The islands were run by the Antiguan Labour Party and the Bird family, a combination that has held power almost constantly since 1956. Full independence was obtained in 1981. The elections of 2004, however, brought the former opposition under Baldwin Spencer to power.

Antigua rises to 405 m (1,328 ft) at Boggy Peak, a volcanic prominence in the southwest. Unlike the other Leeward Islands, to which it belongs, Antigua was denuded of forest long ago, and lacks both trees and rivers. In contrast, the flat coral-island game reserve of Barbuda, 40 km (25 miles) to the north, is fairly well wooded. Barbuda's one town is Codrington. The third island, Redonda, is an uninhabited islet southwest of Antigua. The tropical climate and palm-fringed beaches make Antigua and Barbuda an attractive tourist location. There is, however, little fresh water, and the region is hurricane-prone; one in 1995 caused extensive damage.

Since the sugar industry closed in 1971 the islands have relied almost entirely on tourism, with some income from two US military bases on Antigua. The Bird family's hold on power, and allegations of corruption and misuse of funds, plus a high level of external debt, are cause for concern.

The coastal town of Soufrière, Dominica (below). The spires of the Pitons tower above a small village on the southwest coast of St Lucia (above). Kingstown Harbor on the island of St Vincent (right page top).

Dominica

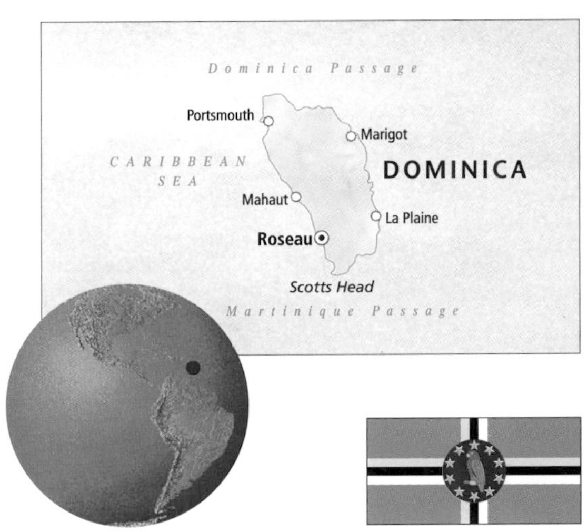

Fact File

OFFICIAL NAME Commonwealth of Dominica

FORM OF GOVERNMENT Parliamentary state with single legislative body (House of Assembly)

CAPITAL Roseau

AREA 750 sq km (290 sq miles)

TIME ZONE GMT – 4 hours

POPULATION 70,200

PROJECTED POPULATION 2015 70,000

POPULATION DENSITY 93.6 per sq km (242.1 per sq mile)

LIFE EXPECTANCY 73.9

INFANT MORTALITY (PER 1,000) 15.9

OFFICIAL LANGUAGE English

OTHER LANGUAGE French Creole

LITERACY RATE 94 %

RELIGIONS Roman Catholic 77 %, Protestant 15 %, other 6 %, none 2 %

ETHNIC GROUPS African 92 %, mixed 6 %, indigenous 1.5 %, European 0.5 %

CURRENCY East Caribbean dollar

ECONOMY Services 63 %, agriculture 25 %, industry 12 %

GNP PER CAPITA US$ 3,700

CLIMATE Tropical, moderated by trade winds

HIGHEST POINT Morne Diablatins 1,447 m (4,747 ft)

MAP REFERENCE Page 427

Fought over for years by the English and the French, the Caribbean island of Dominica was mainly occupied by the British after 1759. Locally it is known as the "nature island" because of its extensive forests and wildlife. It is unusual in still having a community of about 3,000 Carib Indians, whose fierce ancestors, protected by the forests in the interior, held off European colonization for 250 years. In the eighteenth century African slaves were brought to the island as labor and their descendants form the majority of the population today. Independence came to Dominica in 1978. Soon after, it was devastated by a series of hurricanes, while two coup attempts complicated its political life. Today, in free elections, power is contested between three parties in a stable democracy.

The most mountainous of the Lesser Antilles, Dominica is a volcanic island with fertile soils and the second largest boiling lake in the world. A high ridge forms the backbone of the island, from which several rivers flow to an indented coastline. There are many vents and hot springs. The rich volcanic soil supports dense tropical vegetation over 41 percent of Dominica's surface; only nine percent of the land is arable. The climate is warm and humid, with a risk of hurricanes during the rainy season from June to October. During 1995 hurricanes ruined ninety percent of the banana crop. The wildlife to be seen in the Morne Trois Pitons National Park is an important tourist attraction.

Dominica's only mineral resource is pumice and it has to import all its energy. There is hydroelectric potential in the rivers of the interior. Bananas, citrus fruits, and coconuts are the main cash crops—bananas accounting for 48 percent of exports, and coconut-based soaps 25 percent. Other exports include bay oil and vegetables. The country has to import much of its food and is depending on the development of luxury tourism for economic growth. Ecotourism is increasing, with visitors coming to view rare indigenous birds and volcanic sulphur pools. The lack of an airport able to service jetliners makes the country less accessible than its neighbors for mass-market tourism.

St Lucia

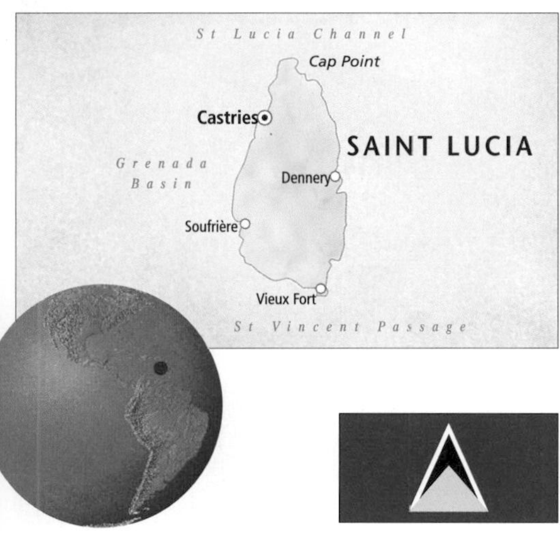

Fact File

OFFICIAL NAME St Lucia

FORM OF GOVERNMENT Constitutional monarchy with two legislative bodies (Senate and House of Assembly)

CAPITAL Castries

AREA 620 sq km (239 sq miles)

TIME ZONE GMT – 4 hours

POPULATION 160,100

PROJECTED POPULATION 2015 169,000

POPULATION DENSITY 258.2 per sq km (669.9 per sq mile)

LIFE EXPECTANCY 72.8

INFANT MORTALITY (PER 1,000) 14.8

OFFICIAL LANGUAGE English

OTHER LANGUAGE French Creole

LITERACY RATE 67 %

RELIGIONS Roman Catholic 90 %, Protestant 7 %, Anglican 3 %

ETHNIC GROUPS African 90.5 %, mixed 5.5 %, East Indian 3.2 %, European 0.8 %

CURRENCY East Caribbean dollar

ECONOMY Services 65 %, agriculture 26 %, industry 9 %

GNP PER CAPITA US$ 4,400

CLIMATE Tropical, moderated by trade winds; wet season May to August, dry season January to April

HIGHEST POINT Mt Gimie 950 m (3,117 ft)

MAP REFERENCE PAGE 427

An island in the Caribbean, St Lucia is one of the prettiest of the Windward Group of the Lesser Antilles. Tropical beaches and typical Caribbean towns like Soufrière have long drawn tourists to the island, who also come to see its varied plant and animal life. Once inhabited by Arawak and Carib Indians, St Lucia was wrangled over between France and Britain before finally being ceded to Britain in 1814. As elsewhere in the Caribbean, African slaves were imported to work sugar plantations until slavery was abolished in 1834. Most of the population are descended from slaves, though some are from South Asia. Internally self-governing from 1967, St Lucia has been fully independent since 1979.

The main features of the island are its forested mountains stretching north to south, cut by river valleys, and rising to Mt Gimie. In the southwest lies the Qualibou, an area with eighteen lava domes and seven craters. In the west, marking the entrance to Jalousie Plantation harbor, are the spectacular twin Pitons, two peaks rising steeply from the sea to a height of about 800 m (2,625 ft). The climate is tropical, with annual rainfall varying from 1,500 mm (59 in) in the lowlands to 3,500 mm (137 in) in mountainous areas.

While not poor, St Lucia still depends heavily on bananas (sixty percent of export income), a crop which is easily ruined by hurricanes and disease. Bananas are also a source of political tension: in recent years the USA has pushed for the abolition of the preferential treatment the EU accords banana imports from the Caribbean. The people of St Lucia have strongly objected to this. Other agricultural exports are coconuts, coconut oil, and cocoa. Clothing is the second largest export, and the free port of Vieux Fort has attracted modern light industry. Grande Cul de Sac Bay in the south is one of the deepest tanker ports in the region and is used for the transshipment of oil.

St Vincent and the Grenadines

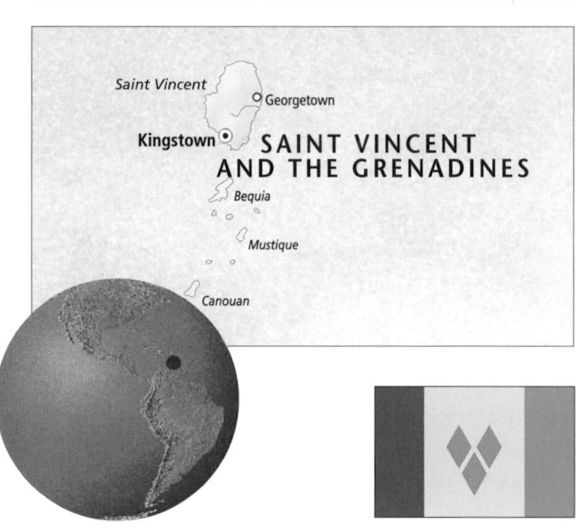

Fact File

OFFICIAL NAME St Vincent and the Grenadines

FORM OF GOVERNMENT Constitutional monarchy with single legislative body (House of Assembly)

CAPITAL Kingstown

AREA 340 sq km (131 sq miles)

TIME ZONE GMT – 4 hours

POPULATION 116,400

PROJECTED POPULATION 2015 123,000

POPULATION DENSITY 342.4 per sq km (888.5 per sq mile)

LIFE EXPECTANCY 72.8

INFANT MORTALITY (PER 1,000) 16.2

OFFICIAL LANGUAGE English

OTHER LANGUAGE French Creole

LITERACY RATE 96 %

RELIGIONS Anglican 42 %, Methodist 21 %, Roman Catholic 12 %, other 25 %

ETHNIC GROUPS African 82 %, mixed 14 %, European, East Indian, indigenous 4 %

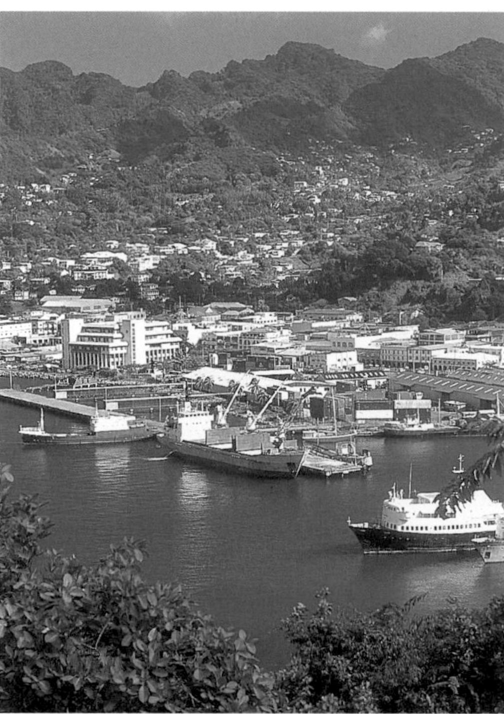

CURRENCY East Caribbean dollar

ECONOMY Agriculture 50 %, services 30 %, industry 20 %

GNP PER CAPITA US$ 2,900

CLIMATE Tropical, with wet season May to November

HIGHEST POINT Mt Soufrière 1,234 m (4,048 ft)

MAP REFERENCE Page 427

The mountainous, volcanic Caribbean island of St Vincent has 89 percent of the country's total land area and 95 percent of the population, the rest consisting of the islands of the Northern Grenadines—Bequia, Mustique, Canouan, and Union. St Vincent was visited by Columbus in 1498 but the fierce resistance of the Amerindian Caribs meant that settlement was slow. A long dispute with France (the French often being supported by the Caribs) finally led to it becoming a British colony in 1783. As St Vincent and the Grenadines the country became self-governing in 1969 and independent in 1979.

St Vincent is dominated by a north-south spur of densely forested mountains, cut east to west by numerous short, fast-running rivers and streams. In the north, volcanic Mt Soufrière is still very active. It caused serious damage in 1891 and in 1902 it killed 2,000 people. The 1979 eruption, which was followed by a hurricane the next year, devastated agriculture and caused a major setback in tourism.

The Northern Grenadines are coralline islets, extending south of St Vincent toward Grenada, some of them with picturesque names such as All Awash Island and The Pillories. The tropical climate is moderated by steady trade winds.

Agriculture, led by banana production, is the foundation of the country's economy, most of it small-scale or subsistence farming on the lower mountain slopes or terraces. Other crops exported include arrowroot starch used to make medicines and paper for computer printers. Tourism is of growing importance, with visitors drawn to the clear, clean waters of Mustique and Bequia. Attempts to develop various industries have so far had little success: unemployment stands at about thirty-five to forty percent.

Barbados

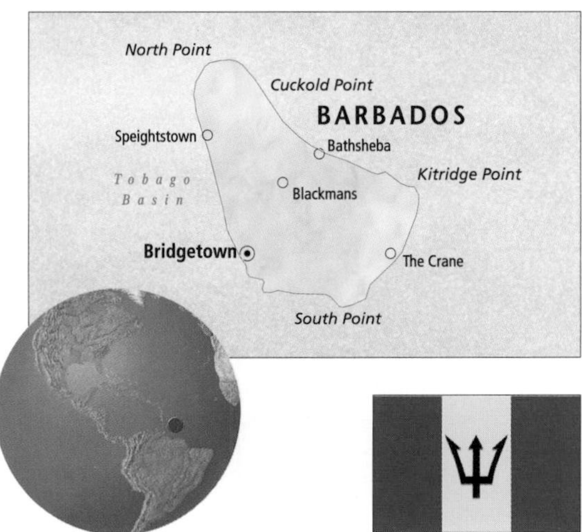

Fact File

Official name Barbados

Form of government Parliamentary democracy with two legislative bodies (Senate and House of Assembly)

Capital Bridgetown

Area 430 sq km (166 sq miles)

Time zone GMT – 4 hours

Population 276,600

Projected population 2015 281,000

Population density 643.3 per sq km (1,666.3 per sq mile)

Life expectancy 73.5

Infant mortality (per 1,000) 11.7

Official language English

Other language English Creole

Literacy rate 97.4 %

Religions Protestant 67 % (Anglican 40%, Pentecostal 8 %, Methodist 7 %, other 12 %), Roman Catholic 4 %, none 17 %, other 12 %

Ethnic groups African 80 %, European 4 %, other (mixed African-European, East Indian) 16 %

Currency Barbadian dollar

Economy Services 76 %, industry 18 %, agriculture 6 %

GNP per capita US$ 14,500

Climate Tropical, with wet season June to November

Highest point Mt Hillaby 336 m (1,102 ft)

Map reference Page 427

Northeast of Trinidad and 435 km (270 miles) off the coast of Venezuela, Barbados is the easternmost of the Caribbean Windward Islands. It is also one of the most orderly and prosperous. After becoming independent from the UK in 1966, power has alternated between two centrist parties, the Democratic Labour Party and the Barbados Labour Party. Both electoral results and freedom of expression are accepted features of Barbados life. Originally inhabited by Arawak Indians and later settled under the British in the seventeenth century, its population is mainly descended from African slaves brought to work on the sugar plantations. The governor-general of Barbados represents the British sovereign and the country has a strong colonial influence. Its neighbors sometimes refer to it as "little England."

The foundation of the island consists of coral deposits formed around a rocky core, and a fringe of coral reef has produced dazzling white beaches. Inland, the rolling terrain rises to hills in the north and center. About fifty percent of the land area is arable, sugar plantations accounting for 85 percent of the cultivated terrain. Barbados is sunnier and drier than many of its neighbors. There is a shortage of water. Surface water is negligible, though when it rains heavily gullies form natural reservoirs.

A small oil industry provides about one-third of the country's needs. Sugar refining is an important source of employment and revenue but has recently been overtaken by the rapid growth in tourism. Facilities are being upgraded to cope with the surge in visitors. Most arrive from Europe and North America and cruise-ship traffic is increasing. Recently, light industrial manufacture has been developed, much of it component assembly for export. The government has promised to build "a modern, technologically dynamic economy."

Grenada

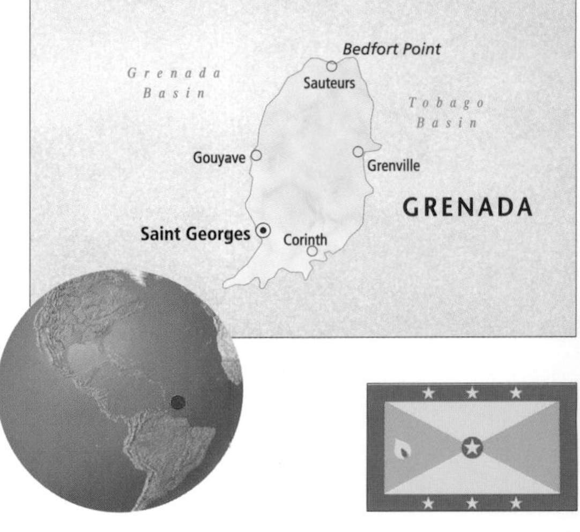

Fact File

Official name Grenada

Form of government Constitutional monarchy with two legislative houses (Senate and House of Representatives)

Capital Saint Georges

Area 340 sq km (131 sq miles)

Time zone GMT – 4 hours

Population 89,200

Projected population 2015 97,000

Population density 262.4 per sq km (680.9 per sq mile)

Life expectancy 64.5

Infant mortality (per 1,000) 14.6

Official language English

Other language French patois

Literacy rate 98 %

Religions Roman Catholic 64 %, Protestant (including Anglican, Seventh Day Adventist, Pentecostal) 27 %, other 9 %

Ethnic groups African 84 %, mixed 12 %, East Indian 3 %, European 1 %

Currency East Caribbean dollar

Economy Services 77 %, agriculture 14 %, industry 9 %

GNP per capita US$ 4,750

Climate Tropical, moderated by trade winds

Highest point Mt Saint Catherine 840 m (2,756 ft)

Map reference Page 427

The state of Grenada consists of the island of Grenada, lying off the coast of Venezuela not far from Trinidad, and two small islands of the Southern Grenadines—Carriacou and Petite Martinique. The islands were visited by Columbus in 1498 but the original Carib Indian inhabitants fought off all invaders until French settlers arrived in the 1650s. Grenada then became a typical sugar-producing Caribbean island, with plantations worked by slaves brought from Africa. British since 1762, English is its official language, though some Grenadans still speak a French patois. It won independence in 1974 and in 1979 the country became commun-

A street vendor in Bridgetown, Barbados (left page). Grenada is volcanic in origin and bisected by a mountain ridge; the coastal capital of St Georges, sheltered by hills (above). A view of one of Tobago's many bays (below).

ist after a bloodless coup. When the coup leader was murdered by fellow Marxists in 1983, the USA, with support from a number of other Caribbean countries, intervened to restore democratic elections. Since then power has been contested and has alternated between several different political parties, but the country has turned out to be a stable democracy. Economic recovery from the events of 1983, however, has been slow.

The most southerly of the Windward Islands, the main island of Grenada is volcanic in origin and has fertile soils. A forested mountain ridge runs north-south, cut by rivers, and there are a number of lakes, including the Grand Etang at an elevation of 530 m (1,739 ft). The western coastline is precipitous; the southern coastal landscape of beaches is gentler and includes some natural harbors. In recent years the government has become interested in developing ecotourism but protection of key environmental sites remains a concern. Large resort projects have resulted in serious beach erosion.

Grenada is known in the Caribbean as "the spice island" and is—after Indonesia—the world's leading producer of nutmeg and mace, its main crop. Other exports include cocoa and bananas, but attempts to diversify the economy from an agricultural base have so far been unsuccessful. The farming practised by the rural population is mostly small scale, with the exception of a few cooperatives. The small manufacturing sector is based on food-processing and makes products such as chocolate, sugar, alcoholic beverages, and jam. Garments and furniture are also produced, mainly for export to Trinidad and Tobago. Tourism had largely ceased after the crisis of 1983 but gradually recovered—until the attacks on 11 September 2001. It has since suffered severely from a drop in tourism.

Trinidad and Tobago

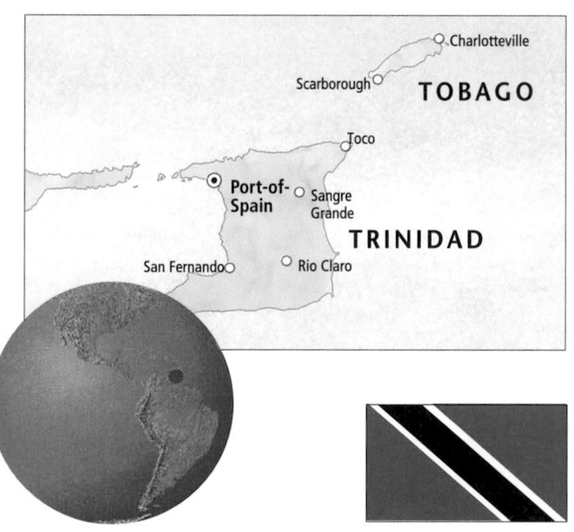

Fact File

OFFICIAL NAME Republic of Trinidad and Tobago

FORM OF GOVERNMENT Republic with two legislative bodies (Senate and House of Representatives)

CAPITAL Port of Spain

AREA 5,130 sq km (1,981 sq miles)

TIME ZONE GMT – 4 hours

POPULATION 1,164,000

PROJECTED POPULATION 2015 1,392,000

POPULATION DENSITY 226.9 per sq km (587.6 per sq mile)

LIFE EXPECTANCY 68.6

INFANT MORTALITY (PER 1,000) 24.2

OFFICIAL LANGUAGE English

OTHER LANGUAGES Hindi, French, Spanish

LITERACY RATE 94 %

RELIGIONS Roman Catholic 32.2 %, Hindu 24.3 %, Anglican 14.4 %, other Protestant 14 %, Muslim 6 %, other 9.1 %

ETHNIC GROUPS African 43 %, East Indian 40 %, mixed 14 %, European 1 %, Chinese 1 %, other 1 %

CURRENCY Trinidad and Tobago dollar

ECONOMY Services 73 %, industry 15 %, agriculture 12 %

GNP PER CAPITA US$ 9,000

CLIMATE Tropical, with wet season June to December

HIGHEST POINT El Cerro del Aripo 940 m (3,084 ft)

MAP REFERENCE Page 427

Trinidad is a square-shaped Caribbean island at the south end of the Windward Island chain, only 11 km (7 miles) off the coast of Venezuela. Along with Tobago it is the most prosperous island in the West Indies, oil and asphalt forming the basis of its wealth. It was visited by Columbus in 1498 and then held by the Spanish for three centuries before becoming a British possession after it was seized in 1797. The island's sugar plantations were initially worked by African slaves, and then after the abolition of slavery in 1834 East Indian and Chinese labor was imported. Today, in rural districts, some villages are mainly Afro-Trinidadian, some mainly Asian. Since gaining independence in 1962, Trinidad has been vexed by racial and ethnic complications, notably "Black Power" in 1970 and an attempted coup by black Muslim extremists in 1990. In 1995 the first prime minister from the Asian community was sworn in.

Unlike the Caribbean islands to the north, Trinidad is geologically an extension of South America across the Gulf of Paria. It is traversed by three mountain ranges (northern, central and southern) with El Cerro del Aripo in the Northern Range, and is drained by the Caroni, Ortoire and Oropuche Rivers. The Caroni Swamp is notable for the immense variety of its butterflies. The rest of the island is mostly low-lying, fringed with mangrove swamps. Tobago Island is a detached piece of the Northern Range, with volcanic uplands, that lies 34 km (21 miles) to the northeast of Trinidad. Tourism is concentrated on Tobago, which is renowned for its wildlife.

The strength of Trinidad's economy is its oil sector, and its large petroleum reserves. But living standards have fallen since the boom years of 1973 to 1982 and the country's prospects depend largely on the success of efforts towards diversification and on economic reforms. The floating of the exchange rate, capital market liberalization, and the partial privatization of such state operations as the main airline are among recent government initiatives.

Central America

Mexico

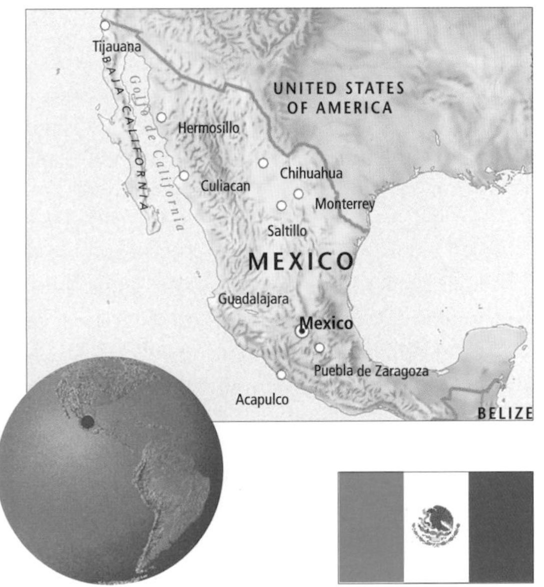

Fact File

Official name United Mexican States

Form of government Federal republic with two legislative chambers (Senate and Chamber of Deputies)

Capital Mexico City

Area 1,972,550 sq km (761,602 sq miles)

Time zone GMT – 6/8 hours

Population 103,400,000

Projected population 2015 119,115,000

Population density 52.4 per sq km (135.8 per sq mile)

Life expectancy 72

Infant mortality (per 1,000) 24.5

Official language Spanish

Other languages Indigenous languages (Nahuatl [Aztec] and 25 Mayan languages)

Literacy rate 89.6 %

Religions Roman Catholic 93 %, Protestant 4 %, other 3 %

Ethnic groups Mixed indigenous-European (mainly Spanish) 60 %, indigenous 30 %, European 9 %, other 1 %

Currency Mexican peso

Economy Services 57 %, agriculture 23 %, industry 20 %

GNP per capita US$ 9,000

Climate Tropical in south and on coastal lowlands; cooler and drier in central plateau and mountains

Highest point Vol Citaltepetl (Pico de Orizaba) 5,700 m (18,701 ft)

Map reference Pages 430–31

The story of Mexico is the story of Central American civilization itself. For thousands of years people have lived in the central valley, and when the Spanish arrived under Cortés in 1519 the population of the Aztec Empire may have numbered 15 million. The pattern of settlement established by Spain in Mexico, with large estates worked by Indians, was followed in many other Central and South American countries. Although most Mexicans are Roman Catholics, relations between Church and state have not always been easy, governments often viewing the Church's power as a challenge to their own. Mexico possesses major petroleum resources, is industrializing rapidly, and includes many traditional Indian cultures among its people from the Tarahumara in the northwest to the Maya of Quintana Roo.

Physical features and land use

The northern and less populated part of Mexico consists of the basin-and-range country of the Mesa Central. In this region desert scrub is the main plant cover, with grasses, shrubs, and succulents on higher ground. Cattle ranching is notable in this area. The land reaches heights of 2,400 m (7,900 ft) around Mexico City. South of the city three major peaks of the Sierra Volcanica Transversal reach elevations of more than 5,000 m (18,000 ft)—Citlaltepetl, Popocatepetl, and Ixtaccihuatl. An active earthquake zone, this is the most densely settled part of the country.

East of the Mesa Central the land falls steeply from the Sierra Madre Oriental to a broad coastal plain on the Gulf of Mexico fringed with swamps, lagoons, and sandbars. Further south is the isthmus of Tehuantepec, a neck of rainforested land dividing the mountains of the Sierra del Sur from the highlands rising toward the Guatemalan border. The Yucatán Peninsula to the east is a limestone plain lying only a little above sea level, marked by natural wells and sinkholes. Petroleum discoveries in the 1970s in Tabasco and Campeche, in the northwest Yucatán, have made Mexico one of the world's biggest oil producers.

The Mesa Central ends just as abruptly on its western frontier, falling from the pine-forested heights of the Sierra Madre Occidental to a narrow coastal strip extending north to the Californian border. In the far northwest is the long narrow, dry, mountain-spined peninsula of Baja California.

Contrasts in altitude and latitude produce wide climatic variations from the coasts, where temperatures are uniformly high, to the temperate land which prevails over much of the Mesa Central. Above 2,000 m (6,000 ft) lies what is known as the cold land, *tierra helada*, while on the higher slopes of the snow-capped volcanic cones is the frozen land where temperatures are usually below 10 °C (50 °F).

People and culture

Most Mexicans are descendants of the Amerindian peoples who lived in the region at the time of the Spanish conquest, and of the Spanish colonists. The Aztecs were one of a number of developed cultures in the region. Their capital, Tenochtitlan, featured monumental architecture in the form of pyramids, and their society was strongly hierarchic, with slaves at the bottom and an emperor at the top. Art, sculpture, and poetry were advanced and they had a form of writing. Aztec religious practices involved the annual sacrifice (and eating) of large numbers of slaves, prisoners, and captives taken in war.

The Maya in Yucatán were another major culture in the region but by the time the Spanish arrived the empire had already collapsed. Only their majestic stone monuments in the jungle remained, with settlements of corn-cultivating Mayan subsistence farmers nearby.

The Spanish brought Christianity and a system of large-scale estates using poorly paid (or unpaid) Amerindian labor. Colonial control was exercised by a form of serfdom under which Amerindians paid either tribute or labor in return for conversion to Christianity. This system was abolished in 1829. In 1810 the independence struggle began: in 1822 Mexico declared itself a republic and in 1836 Spain formally recognized the country's independence. A century of political chaos climaxed with the violent Mexican Revolution of 1910 to 1921.

Since 1929 Mexico has been dominated by one party, the PRI, which has ruled until recently in a corporatist and authoritarian fashion. There was widespread dissatisfaction with the political process and with the unsolved 1994 murders of two high-profile reformers within the ruling party. A peasant revolt in Chiapas in 1994 dramatized the problem of rural poverty and the poor understanding that Mexico's urban élite has of

Timeline

3500 BC Turkeys, corn, beans, and squash are domesticated for food

2600 BC Beginning of Mayan civilization in Yucatán Peninsula

1200 BC Rise of Olmec civilization on Mexico's Gulf Coast; it lasts until 300 BC

300 BC Completion of the Great Pyramid of the Sun Temple at Teotihuacán, in the Valley of Mexico

AD 325 Mayan civilization flourishes during its classic period (which lasts until 925); fine stone buildings with hieroglyphics

1000 Rise of Toltec Empire based in Tula, present-day Hidalgo, to the north of the Valley of Mexico; lasts around 200 years

1325 Aztecs establish their capital of Teotihuacán, a city housing 100,000–300,000 people

1519 Spanish explorer Cortés expelled by Aztec emperor Montezuma from Tenochtitlan; Cortés destroys city in 1520

1521 Spanish rebuild Tenochtitlan and it becomes new Spanish capital, Mexico City

1629 Floods kill 30,000 people in Mexico City; new drainage systems constructed

1810 Hidalgo y Costilla calls for rebellion against Spain; Hidalgo executed in 1811

1836 Mexico's independence is formally recognized by Spain

1847–48 US troops capture Mexico City in Mexican-American War until treaty grants large amounts of territory to USA

1876 Diaz becomes dictator; expands economy by building railways, developing industries, encouraging foreign investment

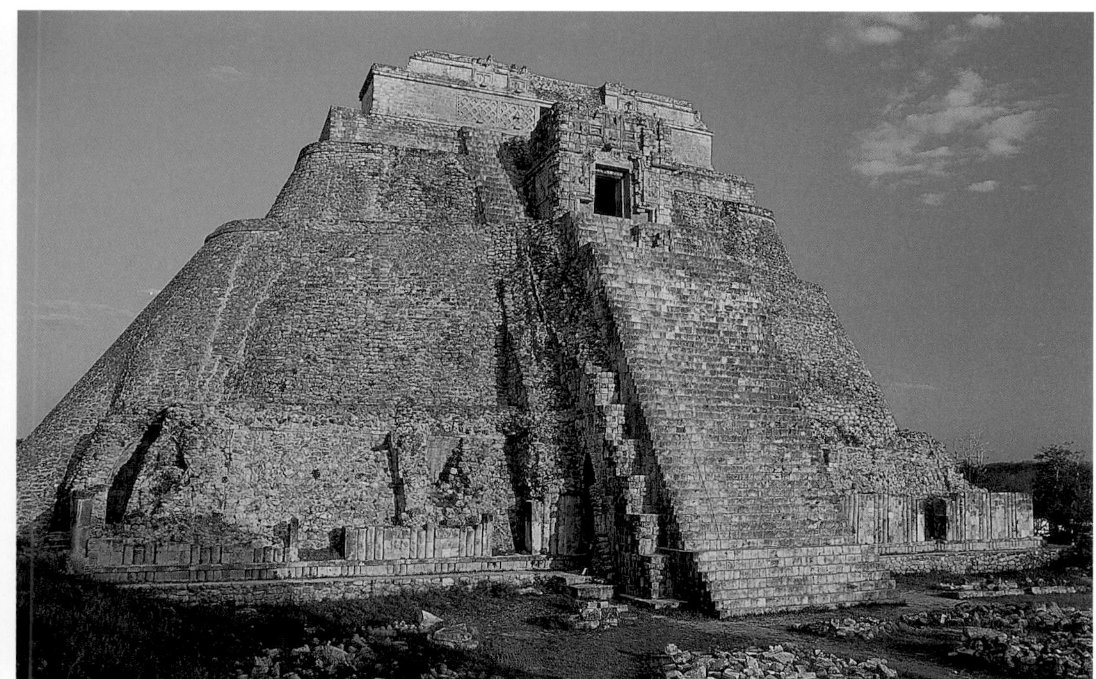

The Mayan Pyramid of the Magician, Uxmal, Mexico (above).

the world beyond the cities. The elections held in 2000 for the first time brought a politician from an opposing party into power.

Economy and resources

Agriculture occupies around a quarter of the population, many farmers living by growing maize, beans, and squash. The main export crops are coffee, cotton, and sugarcane. Some meat is exported from the north, while fish exports include tuna, anchovies, sardines, and shrimp. About one-fifth of Mexico is forested, producing hardwood and chicle, the base for chewing gum.

Mexico is one of the largest oil exporters outside OPEC, most oil coming from the Gulf of Mexico. Petrochemicals provide most of the country's export earnings and are the chief energy source. Mexico is the world's leading producer of silver. Only about twenty percent of the country's mineral reserves have so far been exploited. There are also sizeable deposits of coal and uranium. Hydroelectricity contributes approximately one third of all power used.

Although the economy is diverse, with food-processing, textiles, forestry, and tourism making contributions, it has been through a series of crises beginning with devaluation in 1994. Economic activity contracted by seven percent in 1995 and more than 1 million Mexicans lost their jobs. The health of the banking sector, investor confidence, drug-linked corruption, and the shaky grip of the ruling elite on power are matters of continuing concern.

1910–20 Mexican revolution; Madero overthrows Diaz government in 1911

1917 A new constitution is adopted making the revolution permanent

1934 Government begins major land reforms; in 1938 all foreign-owned oil company assets taken over by government

1970s Massive oil deposits discovered in the Gulf of Mexico

1985 Two earthquakes occur in south-central Mexico, including Mexico City, killing more than 10,000 people

1997 Paramilitary groups in Acteal massacre 45 Indian villagers

Guatemala

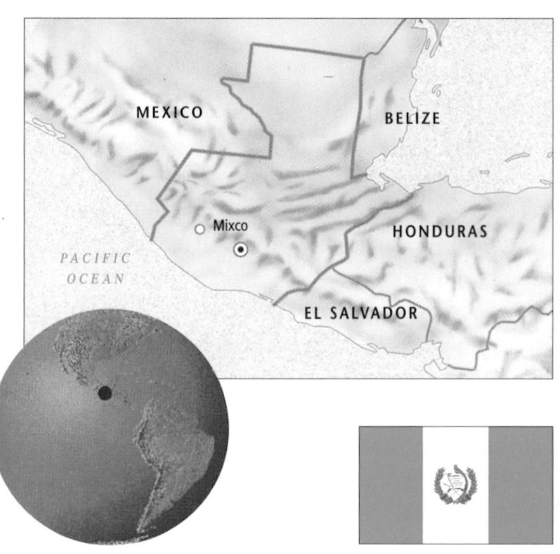

Fact File

OFFICIAL NAME Republic of Guatemala

FORM OF GOVERNMENT Republic with single legislative body (Congress of the Republic)

CAPITAL Guatemala

AREA 108,890 sq km (42,042 sq miles)

TIME ZONE GMT – 6 hours

POPULATION 13,314,000

PROJECTED POPULATION 2015 16,329,000

POPULATION DENSITY 122.3 per sq km (316.7 per sq mile)

LIFE EXPECTANCY 66.9

INFANT MORTALITY (PER 1,000) 44.6

OFFICIAL LANGUAGE Spanish

OTHER LANGUAGES 23 Maya Quiché languages

LITERACY RATE 63.6 %

RELIGIONS Roman Catholic 75 %, Protestant 25 %; some traditional Mayan beliefs

ETHNIC GROUPS Mixed indigenous-European 56 %, indigenous 44 %

CURRENCY Quetzal

ECONOMY Agriculture 50 %, services 38 %, industry 12 %

GNP PER CAPITA US$ 3,700

CLIMATE Tropical, but cooler in highlands

HIGHEST POINT Volcan Tajumulco 4,220 m (13,845 ft)

MAP REFERENCE Page 428

Guatemala lies just south of Mexico, and is the most populous of the Central American states. It was once part of the home of the Mayan civilization which reached its peak about AD 300–900. It has numerous volcanoes, including Tajumulco, the highest peak in Central America. In 1523 the region was overrun by Spanish conquistadors. As elsewhere in Central and South America, the newly arrived Spanish established large agricultural estates worked by Amerindian laborers, setting the social and economic pattern for 300 years. After becoming a republic in 1839, Guatemala has had a history of dictatorship, coups d'état, and guerrilla insurgency. Profound social divisions exist between the Amerindian majority, and an elite of mixed Spanish and Amerindian ancestry (called Ladinos) who run the government. Guatemala has had civilian rule since 1985. In 1996 a United Nations mediated accord was signed by President Alvaro Arzu and the members of the URNG guerrilla movement which it is hoped will bring an end to 36 years of armed struggle.

Two large mountain ranges cross the heart of the country. In the north are the older and more eroded Altos Cuchumatanes. To the south the geologically younger Sierra Madre Range includes 33 volcanoes, of which three are still active. Soil enriched with volcanic ash washed down from the Sierra Madre has created a narrow but fertile plain on the Pacific coast. This has been used for agriculture on a commercial scale only since the 1950s, when malaria was first brought under control and access roads were built. Now cattle and cotton are more important than this region's traditional banana crop. On the lower mountain slopes, up to about 1,500 m (5,000 ft), most of the country's highest quality coffee is grown. In the north of Guatemala the highlands fall away to the large, flat, forested Peten Tableland, where many ancient Mayan ruins are found, and to the plains along the Gulf of Honduras.

Guatemala's economy is largely agricultural. Coffee is the main crop and chief export, other exports being sugar, bananas, cardamom, and beef. From the forests, now reduced to about forty percent of the country's land area, come timber and chicle, the gum used for chewing gum. The country has few mineral or energy reserves, apart from small amounts of petroleum, and until recently guerrilla activity has hindered access to the wells. Industries include sugar refining, furniture, chemicals, metals, rubber, textiles and clothing, and tourism. Tourism, largely comprising visits to the Maya ruins, revived after the military activities of the 1980s but fell into decline again in 1994 and 1995 following attacks on foreigners. From 1990 the economy has shown mild but consistent growth though, given the extreme disparity of wealth, the government faces many difficulties in implementing its program of modernization and the alleviation of poverty.

Belize

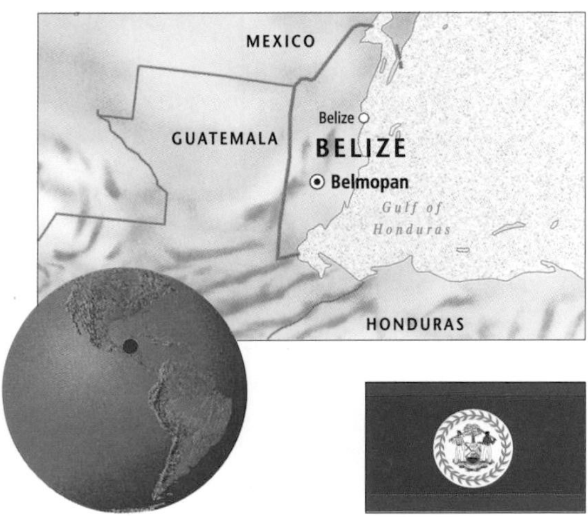

Fact File

Official name Belize

Form of government Constitutional monarchy with two legislative houses (Senate and National Assembly)

Capital Belmopan

Area 22,960 sq km (8,865 sq miles)

Time zone GMT – 6 hours

Population 263,000

Projected population 2015 287,000

Population density 11.5 per sq km (29.7 per sq mile)

Life expectancy 71.5

Infant mortality (per 1,000) 24.3

Official language English

Other languages Spanish, Mayan and Garifunan languages, German

Literacy rate 70.3 %

Religions Roman Catholic 62 %, Protestant 30 %, none 2 %, other 6 %

Ethnic groups Mixed indigenous-European 44 %, African 30 %, Maya 11 %, Garifuna 7 %, other 8 %

Currency Belizean dollar

Economy Services 60 %, agriculture 30 %, industry 10 %

GNP per capita US$ 3,250

Climate Tropical, with wet seasons June to July and September to January

Highest point Victoria Peak 1,160 m (3,806 ft)

Map reference Page 428

Belize lies on the eastern side of the Yucatán Peninsula. Bordering Mexico to the north and Guatemala to the west and south, it was the last country in the Americas to achieve independence. This came in 1981. Formerly known as British Honduras, its original inhabitants were Maya Indians, with a few Carib Indians along the coast. Though adjacent territory was conquered by the Spanish in the sixteenth century, the first recorded European settlers in the area were British woodcutters in the seventeenth century. At a later date sugar plantations worked by African slaves were established. When Guatemala became independent in 1821 it laid claim to British Honduras and the sovereignty issue strained relations between the two countries until Guatemala officially recognized Belize as an independent country in 1993.

The northern part of the country is a swampy plain. In the south the Maya Mountains continue from Guatemala in a northeasterly direction, dividing the coastal plain from the interior. Victoria Peak, on a spur of this range, is flanked by tropical forest, grasslands, and farming regions. Rainforests containing jaguar still cover nearly half the country and in the rivers there are crocodile and manatee. The world's second longest coral reef lies offshore. Belize is much affected by hurricanes. After the 1961 hurricane that destroyed Belize City the capital was moved inland to Belmopan.

Agriculture employs more than a quarter of the labor force, and is the mainstay of the economy. The main domestic staples are maize, rice, kidney beans, and sweet potatoes. Belize enjoyed a boom in the years following independence, citrus fruit processing and tourism helping to reduce the earlier dependence on timber, bananas, and sugar. Sugar still accounts for about thirty percent of export earnings. Timber has lost importance, but the forests still produce valuable rosewood, mahogany, and chicle used for chewing gum. Fisheries specialize in lobsters and shrimp.

Honduras

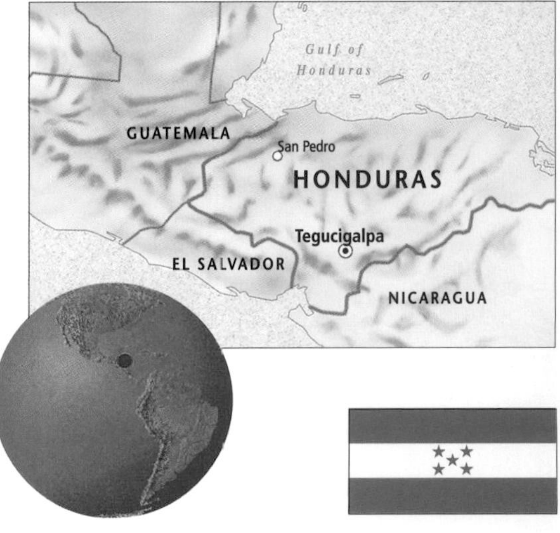

Fact File

Official name Republic of Honduras

Form of government Republic with single legislative body (National Congress)

Capital Tegucigalpa

Area 112,090 sq km (43,278 sq miles)

Time zone GMT – 6 hours

Population 6,561,000

Projected population 2015 8,703,000

Population density 58.5 per sq km (151.6 per sq mile)

Life expectancy 68.8

Infant mortality (per 1,000) 30.5

Official language Spanish

Other languages Indigenous languages, English Creole

Literacy rate 74 %

Religions Roman Catholic 97 %, Protestant and other beliefs 3 %

Ethnic groups Mixed indigenous-European 90 %, indigenous 7 %, African 2 %, European 1 %

Currency Lempira

Economy Agriculture 60 %, services 24 %, industry 16 %

GNP per capita US$ 2,600

Climate Tropical on plains, cooler in mountains

Highest point Cerro Las Minas 2,849 m (9,347 ft)

Map reference Page 428

Honduras is the second largest of the Central American countries. Its mountainous mass lies across the isthmus north of Nicaragua, with Guatemala to the west and El Salvador to the southwest. The Caribbean shoreline runs eastward from the Guatemalan border to the flat and almost uninhabited Mosquito Coast. In the west are the historic ruins of Copan, a site of the ancient Maya civilization which ended long before the Spaniards arrived in 1522. Gold first drew the Spanish to Honduras and when they discovered it in the west they founded Tegucigalpa in 1524. The Honduran mountains are highly metalliferous and silver is still an important export. Independent from Spain

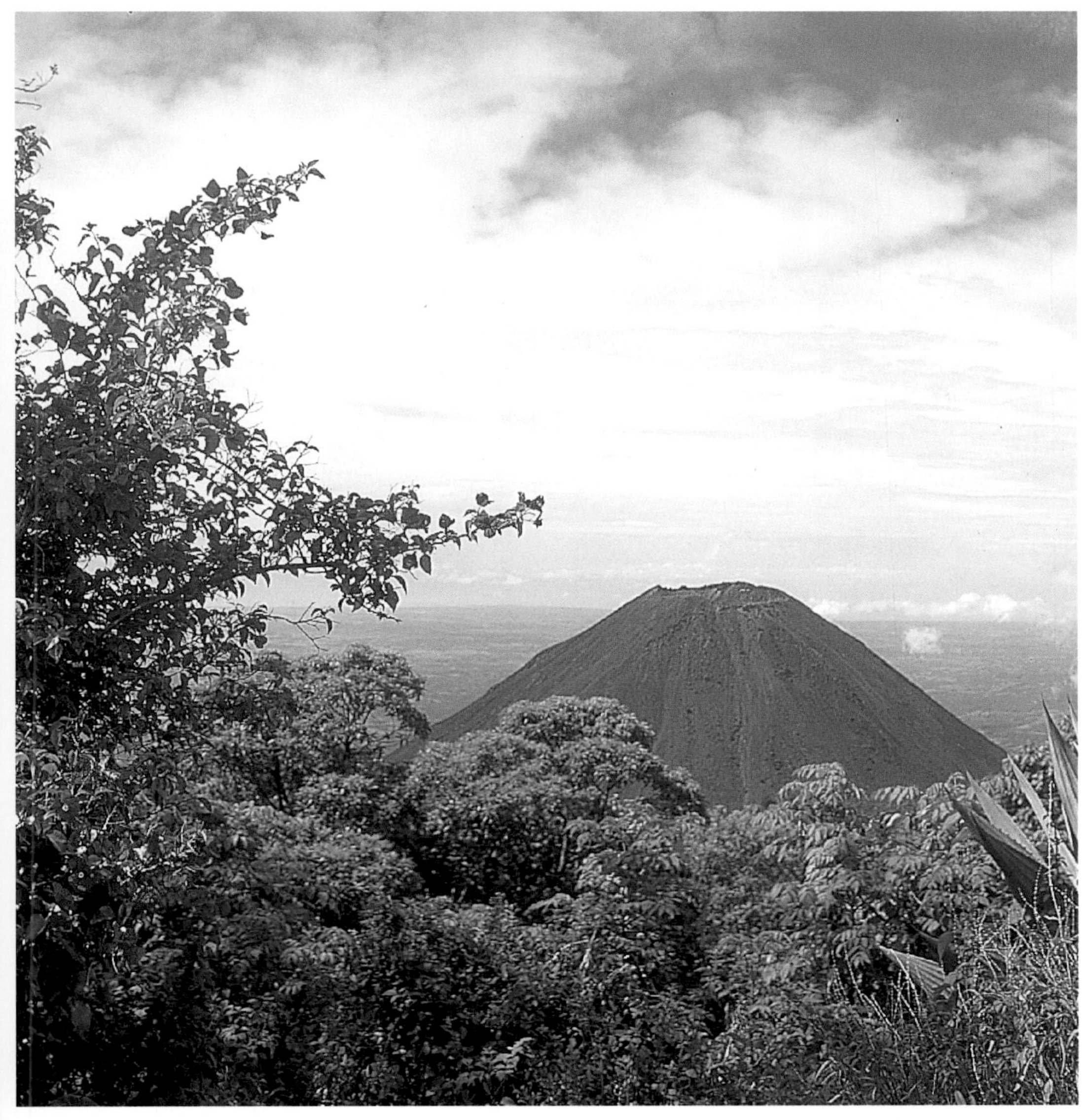

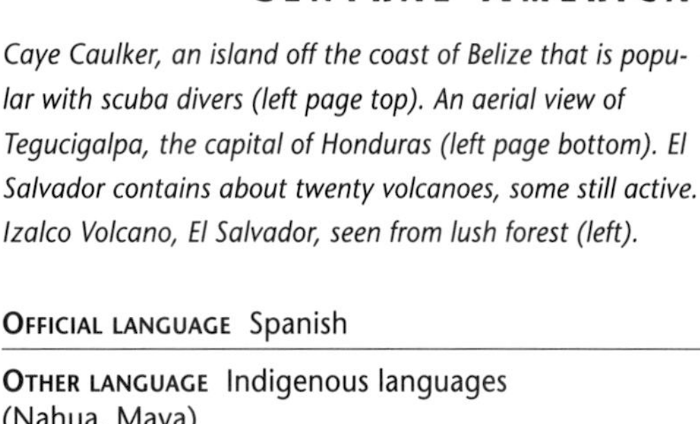

Caye Caulker, an island off the coast of Belize that is popular with scuba divers (left page top). An aerial view of Tegucigalpa, the capital of Honduras (left page bottom). El Salvador contains about twenty volcanoes, some still active. Izalco Volcano, El Salvador, seen from lush forest (left).

since 1821, the country has had decades of military rule with only the occasional elected government. The challenge for the present administration is to reduce the role of the military in political and economic life.

At least 75 percent of Honduras is mountainous. From the central highlands several river valleys run northwest to the coast, where the plains along the Caribbean shore broaden toward the east. The lower valleys have been reclaimed and the forests have been replaced by banana plantations. On the Pacific side there is a short stretch of coast in the Gulf of Fonseca. The adjacent lowlands are used for growing cotton. Rainforest in the northeast provides sanctuary for a great variety of wildlife.

The original "banana republic", Honduras was the world's leading exporter during the 1920s and 1930s. Bananas still account for nearly a quarter of all exports but coffee is now the largest earner. The country depends heavily on the USA for trade: fifty-three percent of its exports and fifty percent of its imports are with the USA. Most of the workforce are farmers, many of them at a subsistence level: food staples are corn, beans, and rice. Small-scale manufactures include furniture, textiles, footwear, chemicals, and cement. Subject to an International Monetary Fund (IMF) restructuring program in the 1990s, Honduras has faced difficulties, with its already poor people subject to sharp tax increases. In 1998, Hurricane Mitch killed more than 9,000 people in Central America, devastating crops and leaving thousands homeless.

El Salvador

Fact File

OFFICIAL NAME Republic of El Salvador

FORM OF GOVERNMENT Republic with single legislative body (Legislative Assembly)

CAPITAL San Salvador

AREA 21,040 sq km (8,123 sq miles)

TIME ZONE GMT – 6 hours

POPULATION 6,354,000

PROJECTED POPULATION 2015 7,979,000

POPULATION DENSITY 302 per sq km (782.2 per sq mile)

LIFE EXPECTANCY 70.3

INFANT MORTALITY (PER 1,000) 27.6

OFFICIAL LANGUAGE Spanish

OTHER LANGUAGE Indigenous languages (Nahua, Maya)

LITERACY RATE 71.5 %

RELIGIONS Roman Catholic 75 %, Protestant and other 25 %

ETHNIC GROUPS Mixed indigenous-European 94 %, indigenous 5 %, European 1 %

CURRENCY Colón

ECONOMY Services 70 %, industry 22 %, agriculture 8 %

GNP PER CAPITA US$ 4,600

CLIMATE Tropical, with wet season May to October; cooler in mountains

HIGHEST POINT Cerro El Pittal 2,730 m (8,957 ft)

MAP REFERENCE Page 428

El Salvador is the smallest, most densely populated country in Central America, and the only one without a coast on the Caribbean. It is in a seismic zone and has some twenty volcanoes, several of which are active. Once the home of the Pipil Indians and later a part of the Mexican Empire, the country won full independence in 1841 and established itself as the Republic of El Salvador in 1859. Over 100 years of civil strife and military rule followed.

From the 1880s about 75 percent of the land has been in the hands of 14 families, who farm huge plantations producing coffee, tobacco, and sugar. The potential for conflict between this landed oligarchy and the rural poor has been present since that time and in the 1970s left-wing disillusionment with the electoral process led to the formation of a number of guerrilla groups. Between 1979 and 1991 civil war raged, with the loss of 75,000 lives, and many people emigrated. The political and economic effects of this conflict are still evident.

Behind El Salvador's narrow Pacific coastal plain rises a volcanic range. Inland is a rich and fertile central plain, occupying 25 percent of the country's total land area. The urban and rural population in this area accounts for sixty percent of the country's total, and produces ninety percent of El Salvador's coffee and tobacco, along with most of its sugar and corn. Further inland still, along the frontier with Honduras, are mountain ranges. Once forested and unpopulated, they now draw poor farmers desperate for land.

El Salvador's economy has few strengths other than a large amount of cheap labor. Damage from the civil war is estimated at $2 billion and cotton and sugar cultivation declined significantly during the conflict. Coffee contributes about ninety percent of exports. Foreign aid remains important, much coming from the USA. Manufacturing is based on food and beverage processing, while other industries are textiles, clothing, petroleum products, and cement. The civil war brought tourism to a standstill but peace has resulted in visitors returning to the Pacific beach resorts of El Salvador's Costa del Sol.

Nicaragua

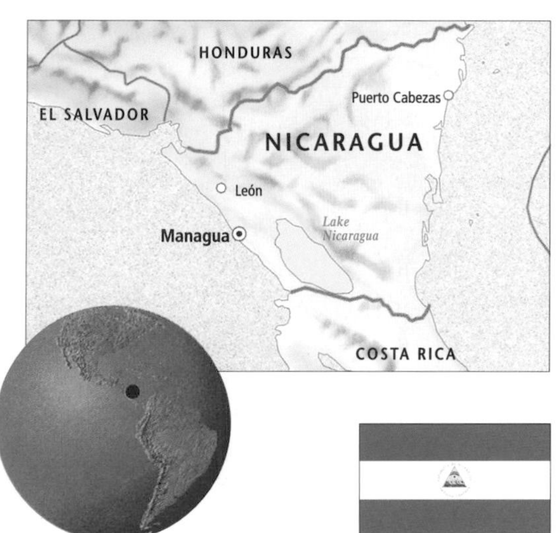

Fact File

Official name Republic of Nicaragua

Form of government Republic with single legislative body (National Assembly)

Capital Managua

Area 129,494 sq km (49,998 sq miles)

Time zone GMT – 6 hours

Population 5,024,000

Projected population 2015 7,216,000

Population density 38.8 per sq km (100.5 per sq mile)

Life expectancy 69.4

Infant mortality (per 1,000) 32.5

Official language Spanish

Other languages Indigenous languages (among them Chibcha, Miskito, Sumo), English

Literacy rate 68.2%

Religions Roman Catholic 95 %, Protestant 5 %

Ethnic groups Mixed indigenous-European 69 %, European 17 %, African 9 %, indigenous 5 %

Currency Córdoba

Economy Agriculture 47 %, services 37 %, industry 16%

GNP per capita US$ 2,500

Climate Tropical in lowlands, cooler in highlands; wet season May to January

Highest point Pico Mogoton 2,107 m (6,913 ft)

Map reference Page 428

The largest republic in the Central American isthmus, Nicaragua is also the least populated. The western half, including Lake Nicaragua, the largest lake in Central America, was settled by the Spanish in the sixteenth century, and the Caribbean shore was for two centuries the British protectorate of Mosquito Coast (Costa de Miskitos). Becoming independent from Spain in 1821, Nicaragua then experienced much instability. The 45-year right-wing rule of the Somoza family ended in 1979 when they were overthrown by the Marxist Sandinistas. Their left-wing rule provoked a US-backed insurgency known as the "contras." In free elections held in 1996 a right-of-

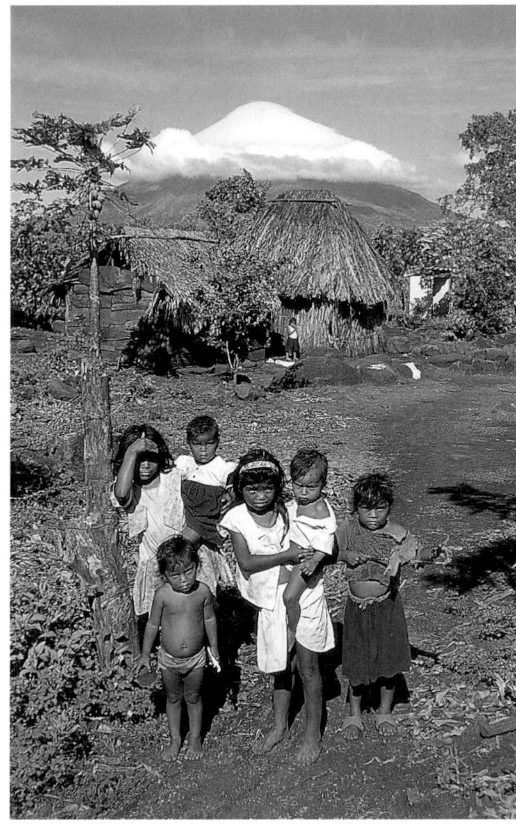

center party defeated the Sandinistas. President Arnoldo Alemán was excluded from the elections in 2001 because of claims of curruption. In 2002 he was convicted.

Nicaragua's broad plain on the Caribbean side leads to a coastal region of lagoons, beaches, and river deltas. Rainfall here is heavy and the tropical wildlife includes crocodile and jaguar. Inland, toward the east, there are mountain ranges broken by basins and fertile valleys. In the west and south a broad depression containing Lakes Managua and Nicaragua runs from the Gulf of Fonseca, on the Pacific coast, to the mouth of the San Juan del Norte River, on the Caribbean. Before the Panama Canal was built this was an important route across the isthmus. This is a region of cotton growing. Overlooking the lakes are forty volcanoes, among them the active Momotombo. An earthquake destroyed most of Managua in 1972.

Nicaragua is still reorganizing its economy—at one point under the Sandinistas inflation reached 3,000 percent. Large-scale confiscation of estates took place under the Sandinistas but the peasants to whom land was given have not always been able to live off their allotments, and some land has been resold. Coffee and cotton are the major export crops. Staples grown by the many subsistence farmers include maize, rice, and beans. Mineral production is led by silver and gold followed by tungsten, lead, and zinc. Falling prices for most of Nicaragua's export commodities, the loss of aid, and the impact of IMF policies reduced the nation's income in 1993 to close to Haiti's—the poorest in the Americas. There is a huge foreign debt. Conditions peculiar to Nicaragua include Sandinista "land reforms" in which luxury properties were seized and given to the movement's leaders and "privatized" state operations that are union-controlled. More than fifty percent of agricultural and industrial firms are state-owned.

Costa Rica

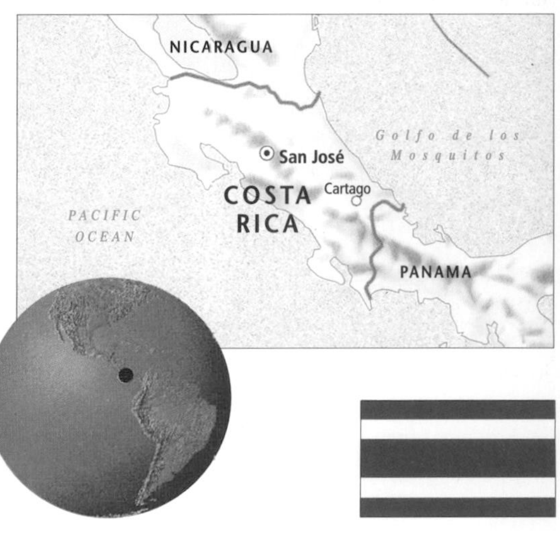

Fact File

Official name Republic of Costa Rica

Form of government Republic with single legislative body (Legislative Assembly)

Capital San José

Area 51,100 sq km (19,730 sq miles)

Time zone GMT – 6 hours

Population 3,835,000

Projected population 2015 5,233,000

Population density 75 per sq km (194.4 per sq mile)

Life expectancy 76.2

Infant mortality (per 1,000) 10.9

Official language Spanish

Other language English

Literacy rate 95.5 %

Religions Roman Catholic 95 %, other 5 %

Ethnic groups European and mixed indigenous-European 96 %, African 2 %, indigenous 1 %, Chinese 1 %

Currency Costa Rican colón

Economy Services 57 %, agriculture 25 %, industry 18 %

GNP per capita US$ 8,500

Climate Tropical, with wet season May to November

Highest point Cerro Chirripó 3,819 m (12,530 ft)

Map reference Page 428

Costa Rica lies on the Central American isthmus, between Nicaragua and Panama. Its rainforests and wildlife made it popular with tourists in the 1980s, but rising crime has recently reduced tourist interest. Like a number of other Central American countries it was historically influenced by the civilizations of the Maya and Aztec, and the earliest human settlements go back 10,000 years. It was named by Christopher Columbus in 1502, *costa rica* meaning "rich coast", and from the 1570s it was a Spanish colony. It gained its independence in 1821 and became a republic in 1848.

Costa Rica is known for its high standards of education, long life expectancy, democratic and stable system of government, high per capita gross domestic product, and a relatively small divide between the rich and the poor. It abolished its national army in 1948. This portrait, however, underestimates the economic role played by US aid in recent times. With aid now reduced, Costa Rican governments have had to take austerity measures, and this has led to unrest.

Three ranges form the mountainous skeleton of the country. From the border of Nicaragua the northern Cordillera de Guanacaste descends to meet the Cordillera Central. Between the Cordillera Central and the southern Cordillera de Talamanca lies the temperate Meseta Central, the valley where San José stands. The surrounding area is the main coffee-growing region, coffee production supporting more than fifty percent of the population.

The lowlands on the Caribbean and Pacific coasts are heavily forested and rich in wildlife. While the Pacific side is relatively dry, the Caribbean lowlands receive heavy rain. Both coasts have numerous mangrove swamps and white, sandy beaches. There are several volcanoes on the ranges, some of which are active. Cattle are raised in the dry northwest savanna region of Guanacaste.

Coffee is the country's largest export and along with bananas provides nearly half the country's export earnings. There are large bauxite deposits at Boruca, and aluminum smelting is a major industry. Minerals mined include small quantities of gold, silver, manganese, and mercury. Energy self-sufficiency is being pursued through the development of hydroelectric power.

Panama

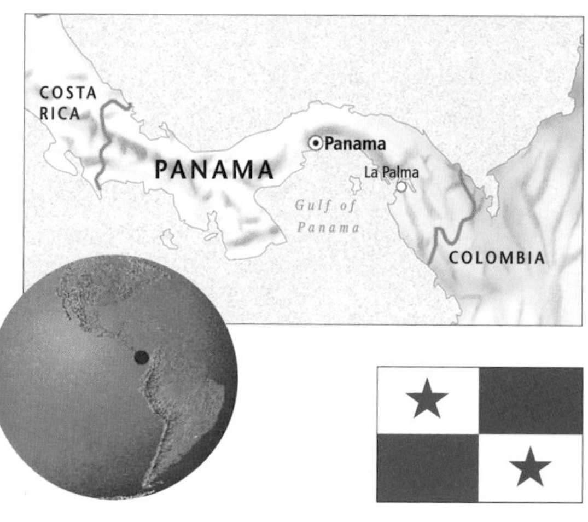

Fact File

OFFICIAL NAME Republic of Panama

FORM OF GOVERNMENT Republic with single legislative body (Legislative Assembly)

CAPITAL Panama

AREA 78,200 sq km (30,193 sq miles)

TIME ZONE GMT – 5 hours

POPULATION 2,883,000

PROJECTED POPULATION 2015 3,451,000

POPULATION DENSITY 36.9 per sq km (95.5 per sq mile)

LIFE EXPECTANCY 75.9

INFANT MORTALITY (PER 1,000) 19.6

OFFICIAL LANGUAGE Spanish

OTHER LANGUAGE Indigenous languages (Guaymi, Chibcha, and others), English

LITERACY RATE 90.8 %

RELIGIONS Roman Catholic 85 %, Protestant 15 %

ETHNIC GROUPS Mixed indigenous-European 70 %, African 14 %, European 10 %, indigenous 6 %

CURRENCY Balboa

ECONOMY Services 60 %, agriculture 27 %, industry 13 %

GNP PER CAPITA US$ 5,900

CLIMATE Tropical, with long wet season May to January

Nicaraguan children outside their thatched home on the island of Omotepe, with the volcano of Concepción in the background (left page top). The Pacuare River running through rainforest in Costa Rica (center). A cargo ship heading east through the Gatun locks on the Panama Canal (left).

HIGHEST POINT Volcán Barú 3,475 m (11,401 ft)

MAP REFERENCE Page 429

Panama joins two oceans and two continents. With Costa Rica to the west and Colombia to the east, it forms a narrow neck of land connecting Central to South America, while the Panama Canal links the Atlantic Ocean to the Pacific. The first proposal for a canal was made by the Spanish in the early sixteenth century. Later, at the time of the California Gold Rush, the USA began to press for action. In 1881 work began on a design prepared by de Lesseps, who was the builder of the Suez Canal, but malaria and yellow fever killed so many workers on the project that it had to be abandoned. Control of these diseases was one of the achievements of the later American builders, who eventually completed the canal in 1914.

Part of Colombia until 1903, Panama has been closely linked with the USA since the construction of the canal gave the latter rights over a 16 km (10 mile) wide Canal Zone. These rights ran out in 2000. A major upheaval took place in Panama during 1989 when the USA invaded and removed the country's self-proclaimed "maximum leader" General Manuel Noriega in order that he face drug charges in Miami, Florida. Electoral democracy was restored in the country, and Noriega was jailed, but the laundering of large amounts of drug money in association with cartels in neighboring Colombia continues to be a problem.

The 3,000 m (9,850 ft) tall mountains of the Serrania de Tabasara (Cordillera Central) run west of the canal along the isthmus, separated from the southern Peninsula de Azuera by a long stretch of plain. East of the canal two more mountain ranges form arcs parallel to the Pacific and Caribbean coasts. Most of the country, however, including 750 offshore islands, lies below 700 m (2,300 ft) and swelters in tropical heat and high humidity. Rainforests are extensive, and those of the Darien National Park, with their abundant wildlife, are among the wildest areas left in the Americas. Most Panamanians live within 20 km (12 miles) of the Canal Zone, a quarter of them in the capital itself.

Panama's economy is based on services, and is heavily weighted toward banking, commerce, and tourism. The country has the largest open-registry merchant fleet in the world. Along with the export of bananas (43 percent of total exports) and shrimp (11 percent), plus income derived from the USA's military installation, Panama has the highest standard of living in Central America. However, the country's commercial debt is also one of the highest in the world in per capita terms, and during the mid-1990s the country experienced an economic slow-down. When the United States withdrew their forces from Panama at the end of 1999 the effect on the contry's economy was very noticeable in 2000 and 2001, even though all revenues from the Canal remained in Panama.

North America: Physical

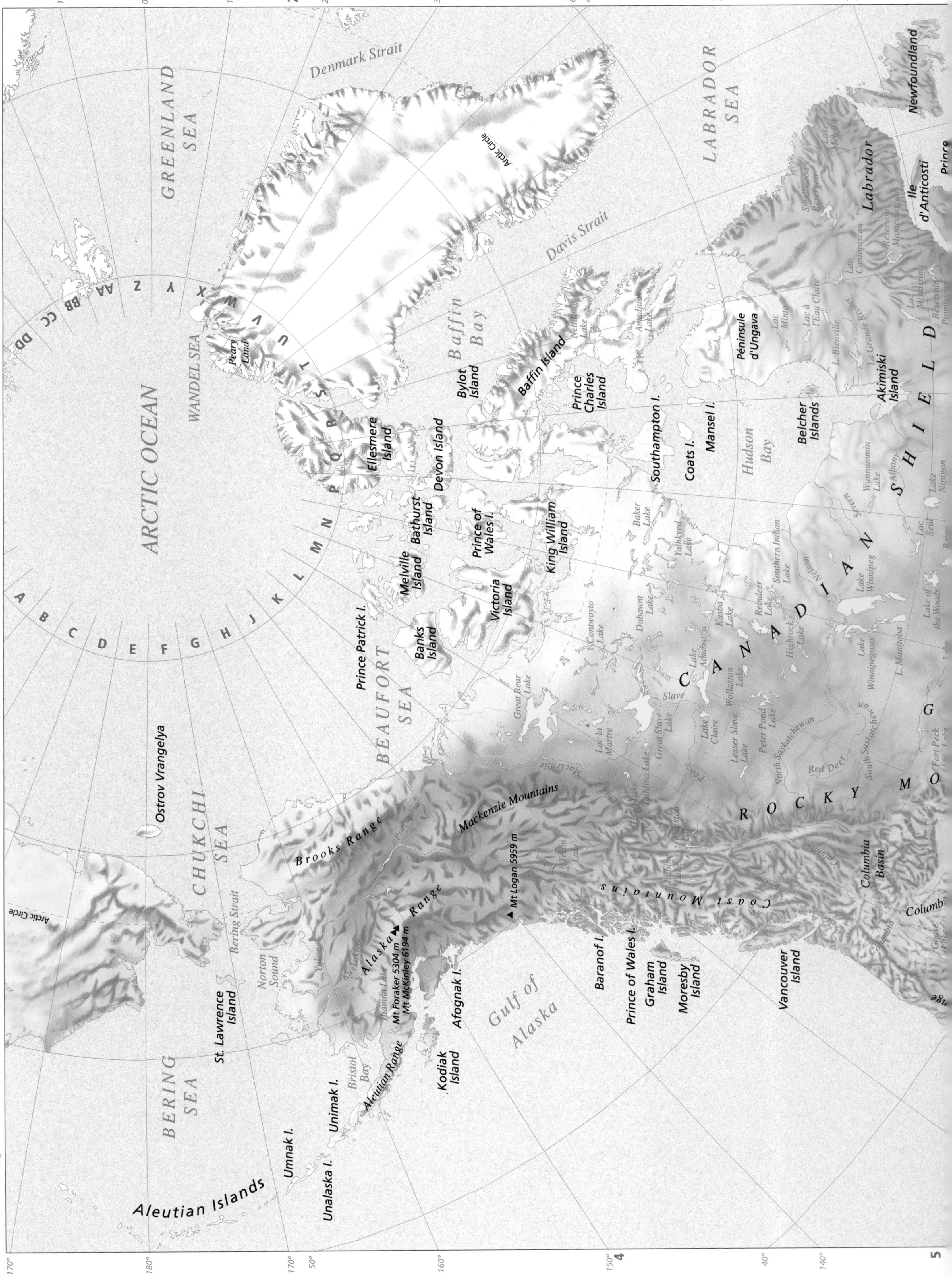

ARCTIC OCEAN
GREENLAND SEA
WANDEL SEA
Denmark Strait
Davis Strait
LABRADOR SEA
Baffin Bay
Hudson Bay
BEAUFORT SEA
CHUKCHI SEA
BERING SEA
Gulf of Alaska
Bering Strait
Norton Sound
Bristol Bay
Peary Land
Ellesmere Island
Devon Island
Bylot Island
Baffin Island
Prince Charles Island
Southampton I.
Coats I.
Mansel I.
Belcher Islands
Akimiski Island
Péninsule d'Ungava
Labrador
Newfoundland
Ile d'Anticosti
Bathurst Island
Prince of Wales I.
King William Island
Melville Island
Victoria Island
Prince Patrick I.
Banks Island
Ostrov Vrangelya
St. Lawrence Island
Unimak I.
Umnak I.
Unalaska I.
Aleutian Islands
Aleutian Range
Kodiak Island
Afognak I.
Baranof I.
Prince of Wales I.
Graham Island
Moresby Island
Vancouver Island
Brooks Range
Alaska Range
Mt Foraker 5304 m
Mt McKinley 6194 m
Mt Logan 5959 m
Mackenzie Mountains
Coast Mountains
ROCKY MOUNTAINS
Columbia Basin
CANADIAN SHIELD
Great Bear Lake
Great Slave Lake
Lake Athabasca
Lake Winnipeg
Lake Winnipegosis
Reindeer Lake
Wollaston Lake
Southern Indian Lake
Baker Lake
Dubawnt Lake
Contwoyto Lake
Lesser Slave Lake
Lake Claire
Lac la Martre
Nettilling Lake
Amadjuak Lake
Lac Mistassini
Arctic Circle

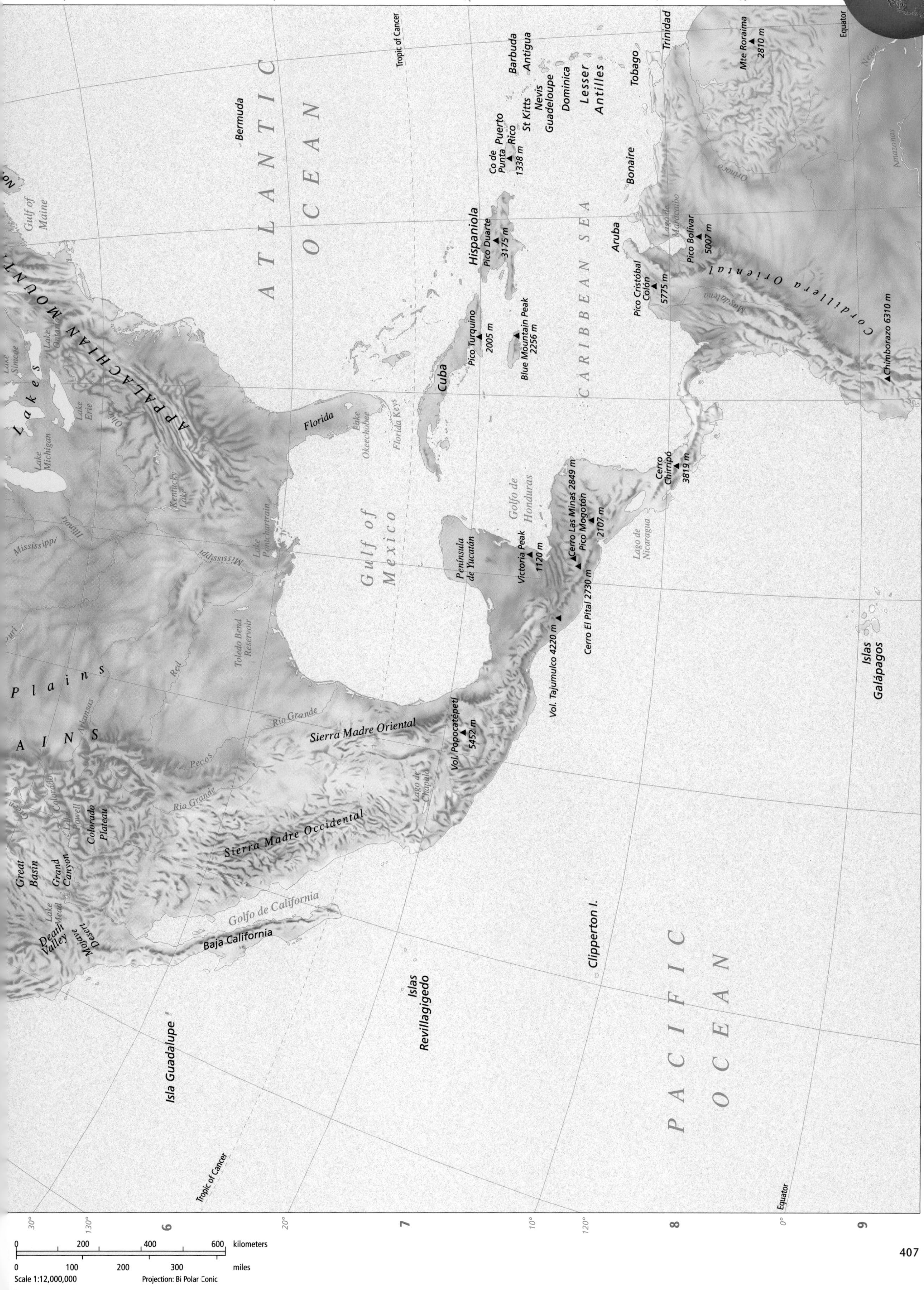

ATLANTIC OCEAN
Bermuda
Tropic of Cancer
Gulf of Maine
Lakes
Lake Simcoe
Lake Ontario
Lake Erie
Lake Michigan
APPALACHIAN MOUNT
Ohio
Kentucky Lake
Illinois
Mississippi
Plains
AINS
Florida
Lake Okeechobee
Florida Keys
Lake Pontchartrain
Toledo Bend Reservoir
Red
Arkansas
Rio Grande
Pecos
Gulf of Mexico
Cuba
Pico Turquino 2005 m
Blue Mountain Peak 2256 m
Hispaniola
Pico Duarte 3175 m
Co de Punta 1338 m
Puerto Rico
St Kitts
Nevis
Barbuda
Antigua
Guadeloupe
Dominica
Lesser Antilles
Tobago
Trinidad
Bonaire
Aruba
CARIBBEAN SEA
Lago de Maracaibo
Pico Bolívar 5007 m
Pico Cristóbal Colón 5775 m
Magdalena
Cordillera Oriental
Chimborazo 6310 m
Orinoco
Mte Roraima 2810 m
Amazonas
Negro
Equator
Península de Yucatán
Golfo de Honduras
Victoria Peak 1120 m
Cerro Las Minas 2849 m
Pico Mogotón 2107 m
Cerro El Pital 2730 m
Vol. Tajumulco 4220 m
Lago de Nicaragua
Cerro Chirripó 3819 m
Islas Galápagos
Sierra Madre Oriental
Vol. Popocatépetl 5452 m
Lago de Chapala
Sierra Madre Occidental
Great Basin
Grand Canyon
Lake Powell
Colorado
Colorado Plateau
Lake Mead
Death Valley
Mojave Desert
Golfo de California
Baja California
Isla Guadalupe
Islas Revillagigedo
Clipperton I.
PACIFIC OCEAN

North and Central America

0 200 400 600 kilometers
0 100 200 300 miles
Scale 1:12,000,000
Projection: Bi Polar Conic

North America: Political

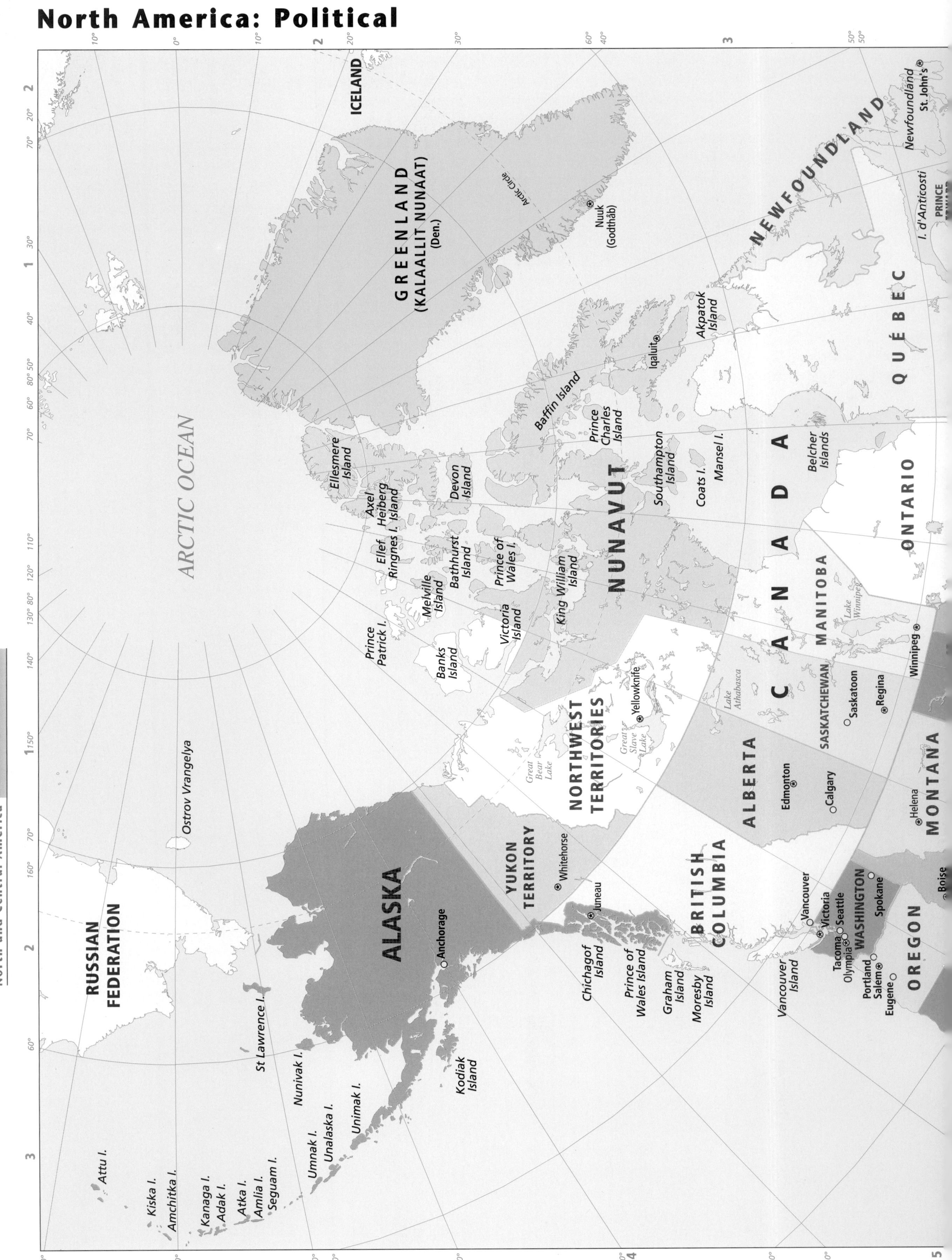

ICELAND
GREENLAND
(KALAALLIT NUNAAT)
(Den.)
Arctic Circle
Nuuk
(Godthåb)
NEWFOUNDLAND
Newfoundland
St. John's
I. d'Anticosti
PRINCE
QUÉBEC
ARCTIC OCEAN
Ellesmere Island
Axel Heiberg Island
Ellef Ringnes I.
Devon Island
Baffin Island
Iqaluit
Akpatok Island
Prince Charles Island
Southampton Island
Coats I.
Mansel I.
Belcher Islands
CANADA
NUNAVUT
ONTARIO
MANITOBA
Lake Winnipeg
Winnipeg
Prince Patrick I.
Melville Island
Bathurst Island
Prince of Wales I.
King William Island
Victoria Island
Banks Island
NORTHWEST TERRITORIES
Great Bear Lake
Great Slave Lake
Yellowknife
Lake Athabasca
SASKATCHEWAN
Saskatoon
Regina
ALBERTA
Edmonton
Calgary
MONTANA
Helena
Ostrov Vrangelya
RUSSIAN FEDERATION
ALASKA
Anchorage
YUKON TERRITORY
Whitehorse
Juneau
BRITISH COLUMBIA
Chichagof Island
Prince of Wales Island
Graham Island
Moresby Island
Vancouver Island
Vancouver
Victoria
Seattle
Tacoma
Olympia
WASHINGTON
Spokane
Boise
Portland
Salem
Eugene
OREGON
St Lawrence I.
Nunivak I.
Kodiak Island
Unimak I.
Unalaska I.
Umnak I.
Attu I.
Kiska I.
Amchitka I.
Kanaga I.
Adak I.
Atka I.
Amlia I.
Seguam I.

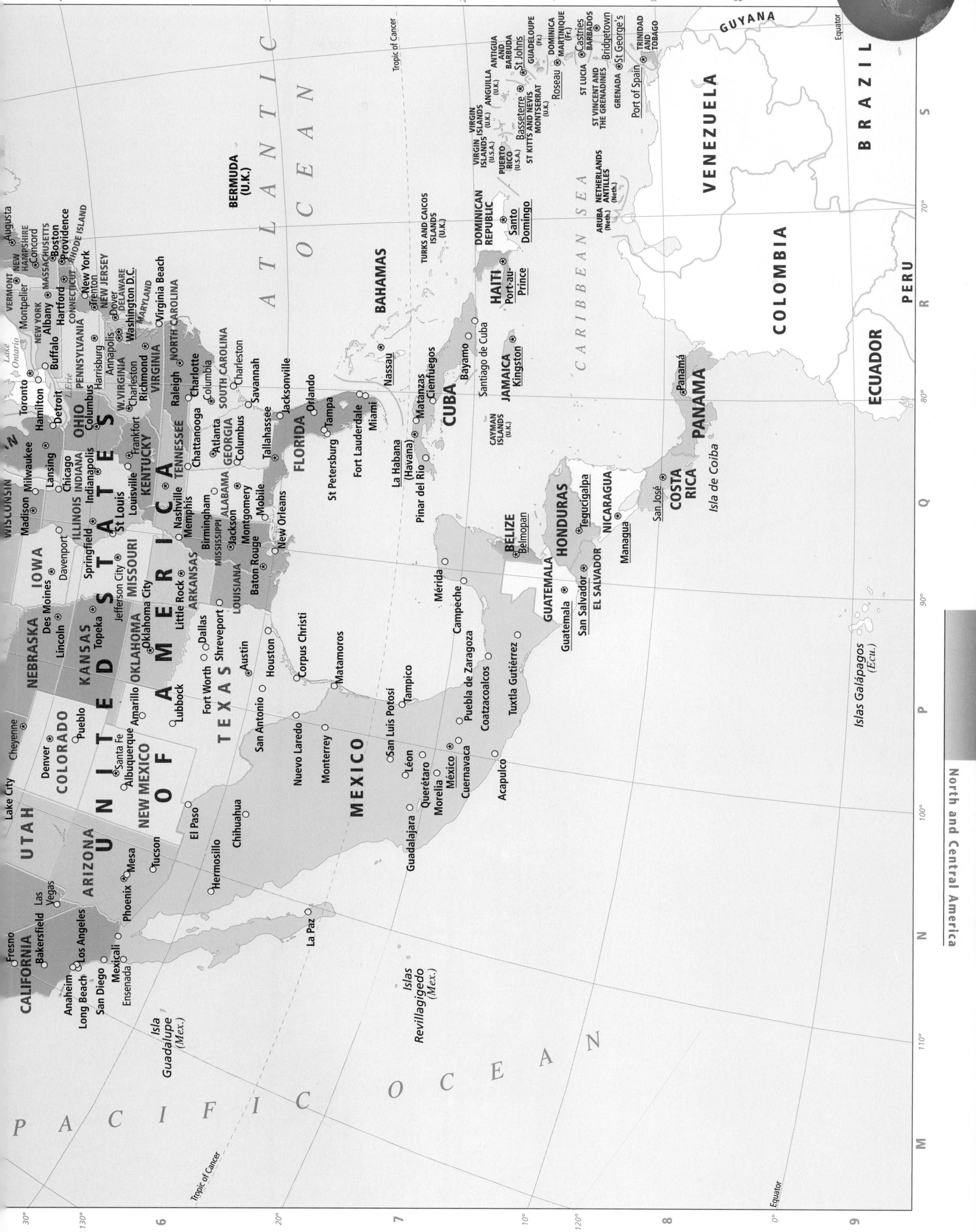

0 200 400 600 kilometers

0 100 200 300 miles

Scale 1:12,000,000

Projection: Bi Polar Conic

North Canada • Alaska • Greenland

RUSSIAN FEDERATION
U. S. A.
ALASKA
YUKON TERRITORY
NORTHWEST TERRITORIES
BRITISH COLUMBIA
ALBERTA
SASKATCHEWAN
WASHINGTON
BERING SEA
CHUKCHI SEA
BEAUFORT SEA
PACIFIC OCEAN
Gulf of Alaska
Bering Strait
Bristol Bay
Anchorage
Fairbanks
Juneau
Whitehorse
Yellowknife
Edmonton
Calgary
Vancouver
Victoria
Seattle
Saskatoon
Regina
Prince Rupert
Prince George
Kamloops
Dawson
Nome
Kotzebue
Barrow
Inuvik
Brooks Range
Alaska Range
Aleutian Range
Kuskokwim Mountains
Mackenzie Mountains
Selwyn Mountains
Ogilvie Mountains
Coast Mountains
Cassiar Mountains
Columbia Mountains
Banks Island
Alexander Archipelago
Queen Charlotte Is
Vancouver Island
Kodiak I.
Great Bear Lake
Great Slave Lake
Lake Athabasca
Mt McKinley 6194 m
Mt Logan 5959 m
Mt Waddington 4016 m
Mt Columbia 3747 m
Mt Olympus 2424 m
Keele Peak 2972 m
Mt Greenough 2207 m
Arctic Circle

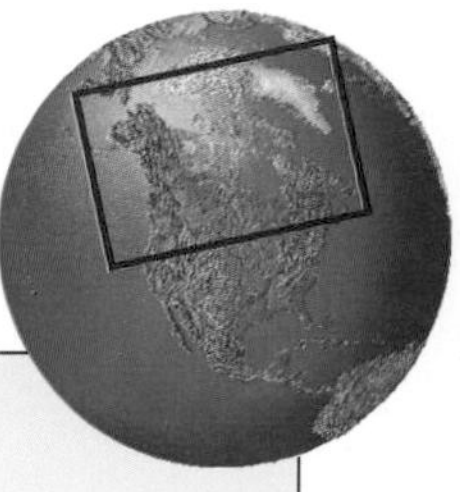

0 200 400 600 800 kilometers

0 200 400 miles

Scale 1:15,000,000

Projection: Azimuthal Equal Area

West Canada

YUKON TERRITORY
BRITISH COLUMBIA
ALASKA
U. S. A.
PACIFIC OCEAN
COAST MOUNTAINS
ROCKY
Whitehorse
Watson Lake
Juneau
Ketchikan
Prince Rupert
Prince George
Vancouver Island
Vancouver
Victoria
Queen Charlotte Islands
Alexander Archipelago
Skeena Mountains
Omineca Mountains
Cassiar Mountains
Stikine Plateau
Dixon Entrance
Hecate Strait
Queen Charlotte Sound
Strait of Georgia
Strait of Juan de Fuca
Mt Fairweather 4663 m
Mt Waddington 4016 m
Kamloops
Williams Lake
Quesnel
Fort Nelson
North and Central America

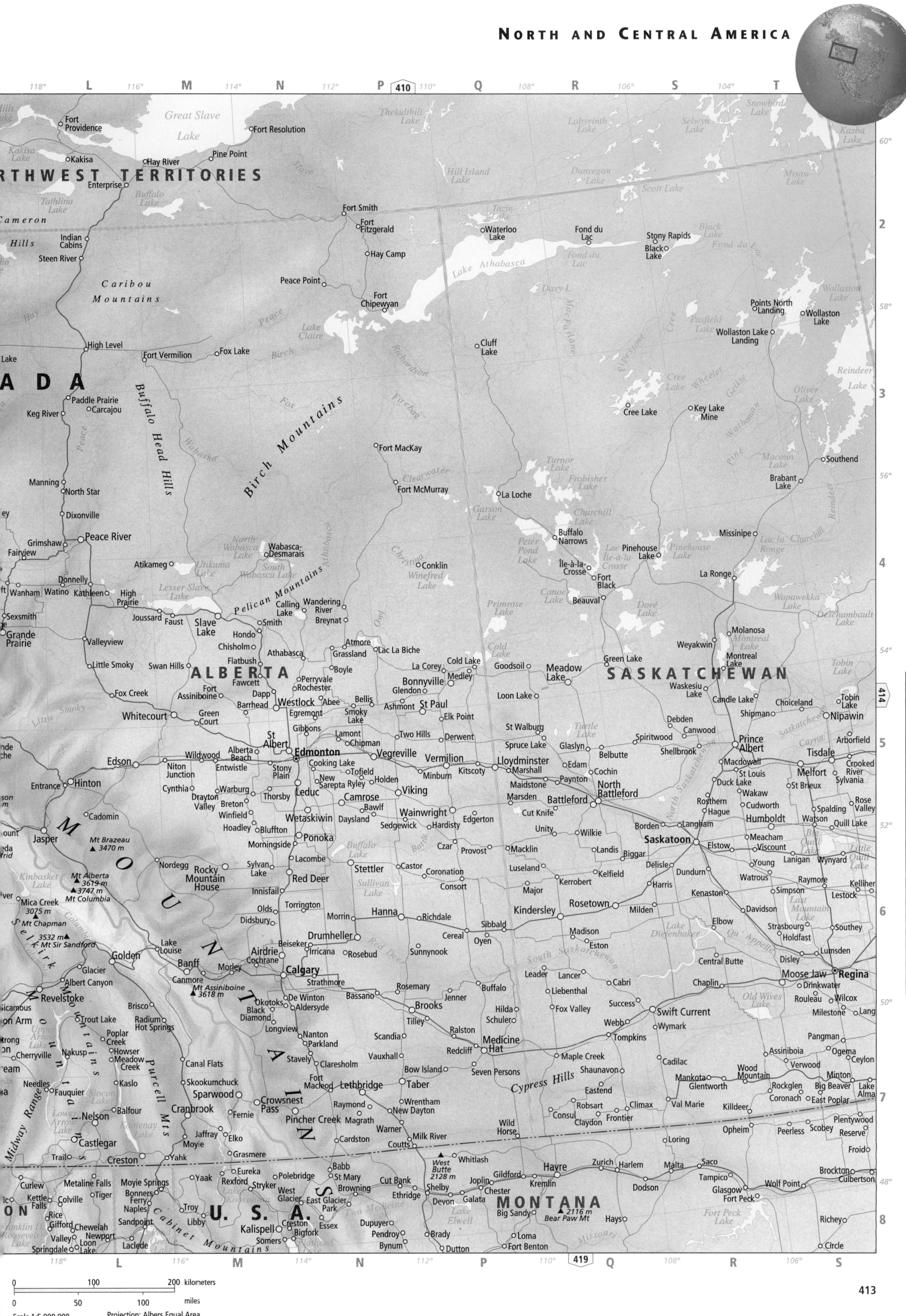

Central Canada

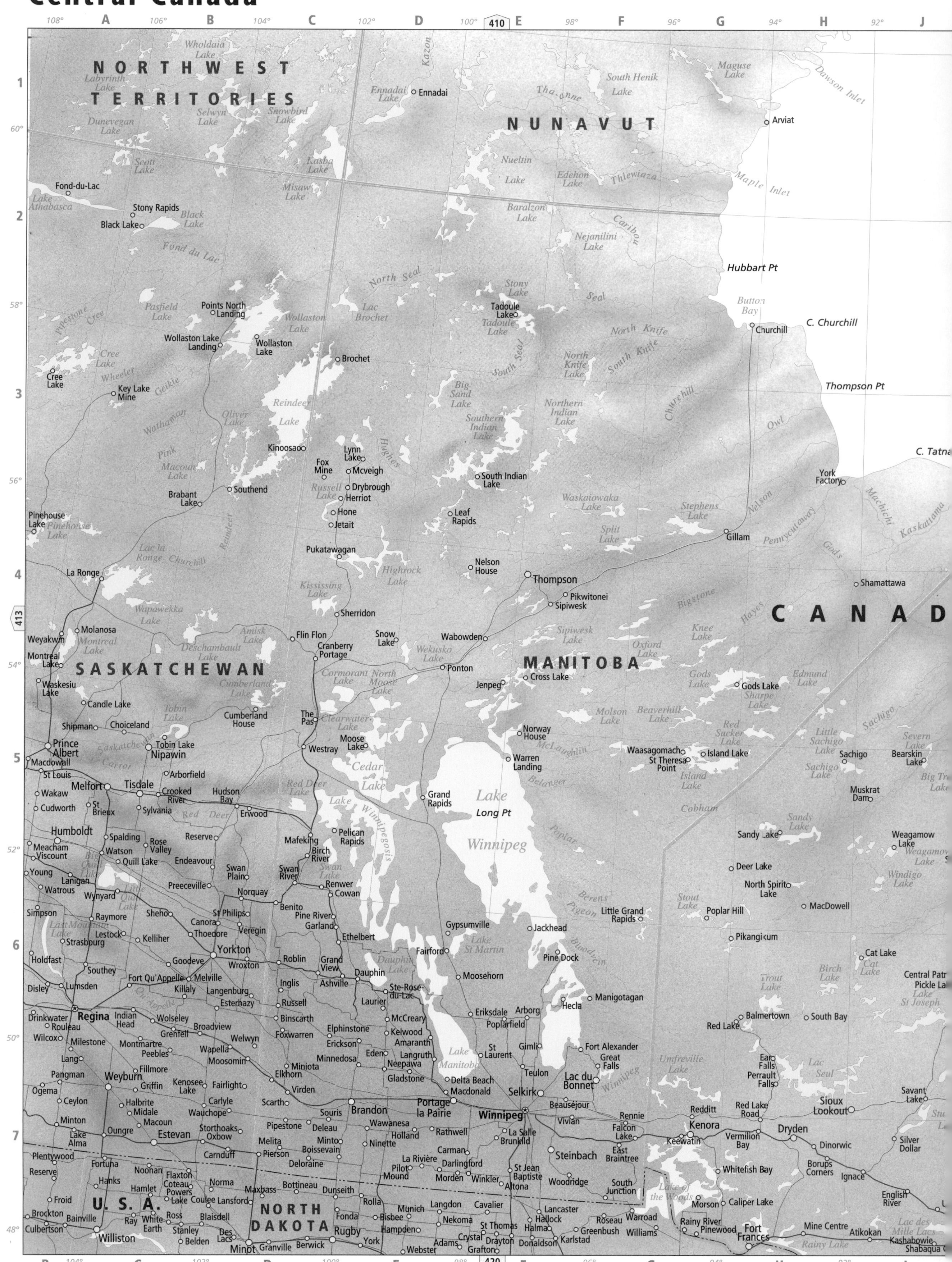
NORTHWEST TERRITORIES
NUNAVUT
SASKATCHEWAN
MANITOBA
CANADA
U. S. A.
NORTH DAKOTA
Lake Athabasca
Fond-du-Lac
Stony Rapids
Black Lake
Wollaston Lake
Reindeer Lake
Lake Winnipeg
Lake Winnipegosis
Lake Manitoba
Cedar Lake
Hubbart Pt
Churchill
C. Churchill
Thompson Pt
Arviat
Ennadai
Brochet
Thompson
Gillam
York Factory
Flin Flon
The Pas
Prince Albert
Regina
Brandon
Winnipeg
Kenora
Dryden
Sioux Lookout
Yorkton
Weyburn
Estevan
Selkirk
Steinbach
Portage la Prairie
Williston
Minot
Fort Frances
410
413
420

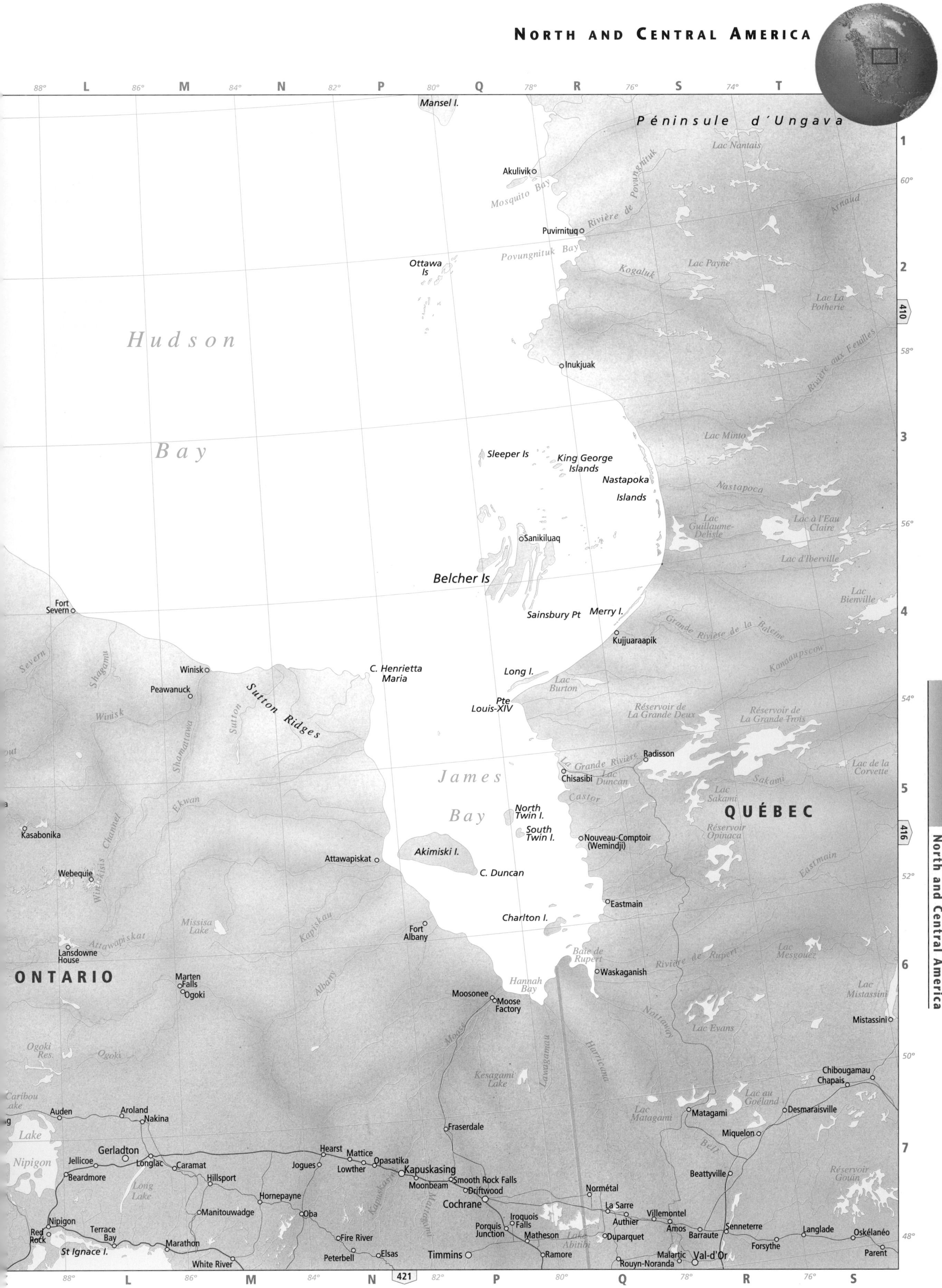

Hudson Bay
James Bay
Péninsule d'Ungava
QUÉBEC
ONTARIO
Mansel I.
Akulivik
Mosquito Bay
Puvirnituq
Rivière de Povungnituk
Povungnituk Bay
Ottawa Is
Lac Nantais
Arnaud
Kogaluk
Lac Payne
Lac La Potherie
Rivière aux Feuilles
Inukjuak
Lac Minto
Sleeper Is
King George Islands
Nastapoka Islands
Nastapoca
Lac Guillaume-Delisle
Lac à l'Eau Claire
Sanikiluaq
Lac d'Iberville
Belcher Is
Lac Bienville
Sainsbury Pt
Merry I.
Grande Rivière de la Baleine
Kujjuaraapik
Kanaaupscow
Fort Severn
Severn
Shagamu
Winisk
Peawanuck
Sutton Ridges
Sutton
Shamattawa
C. Henrietta Maria
Long I.
Lac Burton
Pte Louis-XIV
Réservoir de La Grande Deux
Réservoir de La Grande Trois
Radisson
La Grande Rivière
Chisasibi
Lac Duncan
Castor
Sakami
Lac Sakami
Lac de la Corvette
Ekwan
Winiskisis Channel
Kasabonika
Webequie
North Twin I.
South Twin I.
Nouveau-Comptoir (Wemindji)
Réservoir Opinaca
Akimiski I.
Attawapiskat
C. Duncan
Eastmain
Missisa Lake
Kapiskau
Attawapiskat
Lansdowne House
Eastmain
Charlton I.
Fort Albany
Baie de Rupert
Rivière de Rupert
Lac Mesgouez
Waskaganish
Marten Falls
Ogoki
Albany
Hannah Bay
Moosonee
Moose Factory
Nottaway
Lac Mistassini
Mistassini
Lac Evans
Ogoki Res.
Ogoki
Moose
Kesagami Lake
Lawagamau
Harricana
Chibougamau
Chapais
Caribou Lake
Auden
Aroland
Nakina
Lac au Goéland
Desmaraisville
Lac Matagami
Matagami
Fraserdale
Lake Nipigon
Gerladton
Jellicoe
Longlac
Caramat
Beardmore
Hearst
Mattice
Opasatika
Jogues
Lowther
Kapuskasing
Miquelon
Bell
Hillsport
Long Lake
Smooth Rock Falls
Moonbeam
Driftwood
Beattyville
Réservoir Gouin
Normétal
Hornepayne
Cochrane
La Sarre
Villemontel
Manitouwadge
Oba
Kapuskasing
Mattagami
Iroquois Falls
Authier
Amos
Nipigon
Porquis Junction
Barraute
Senneterre
Langlade
Red Rock
Terrace Bay
Matheson
Lake Abitibi
Duparquet
Forsythe
Oskélanéo
Marathon
Fire River
St Ignace I.
Peterbell
Elsas
Timmins
Ramore
Malartic
Val-d'Or
Parent
White River
Rouyn-Noranda
88° L 86° M 84° N 82° P 80° Q 78° R 76° S 74° T
88° L 86° M 84° N 82° P 80° Q 78° R 76° S
1 60° 2 58° 3 56° 4 54° 5 52° 6 50° 7 48°
410
416
421
0 100 200 kilometers
0 50 100 miles
Scale 1:5,000,000
Projection: Albers Equal Area

East Canada

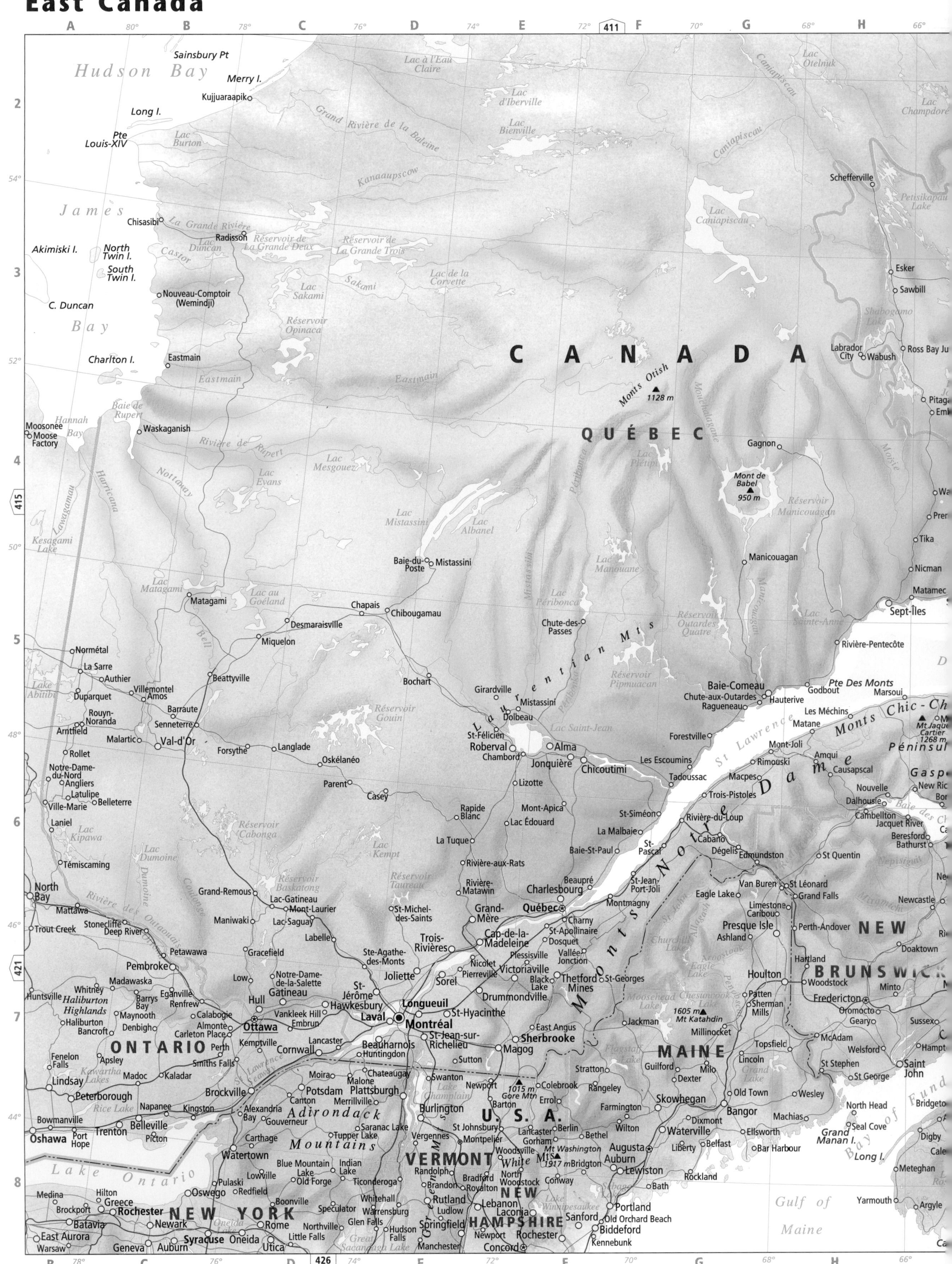
Hudson Bay
James Bay
CANADA
QUÉBEC
ONTARIO
NEW BRUNSWICK
MAINE
VERMONT
NEW HAMPSHIRE
NEW YORK
U. S. A.
Lake Ontario
Gulf of Maine
Laurentian Mts
Monts Notre Dame
Adirondack Mountains
Monts Otish
1128 m
Mont de Babel
950 m
Réservoir Manicouagan
Lac Mistassini
Lac Saint-Jean
St Lawrence
Kujjuaraapik
Chisasibi
Radisson
Eastmain
Waskaganish
Moosonee
Moose Factory
Schefferville
Labrador City
Wabush
Gagnon
Manicouagan
Sept-Îles
Baie-Comeau
Chibougamau
Chapais
Mistassini
Matagami
Val-d'Or
Rouyn-Noranda
Amos
La Tuque
Roberval
Alma
Jonquière
Chicoutimi
Rimouski
Matane
Québec
Trois-Rivières
Sherbrooke
Drummondville
Montréal
Laval
Longueuil
Ottawa
Hull
Gatineau
Cornwall
Kingston
Belleville
Peterborough
Oshawa
North Bay
Pembroke
Fredericton
Saint John
Edmundston
Rivière-du-Loup
Portland
Bangor
Augusta
Lewiston
Burlington
Montpelier
Concord
Manchester
Rochester
Syracuse
Utica
Watertown
Plattsburgh
Mt Washington
1917 m
Mt Katahdin
1605 m
Gore Mtn
1015 m
Mt Jacques Cartier
1268 m

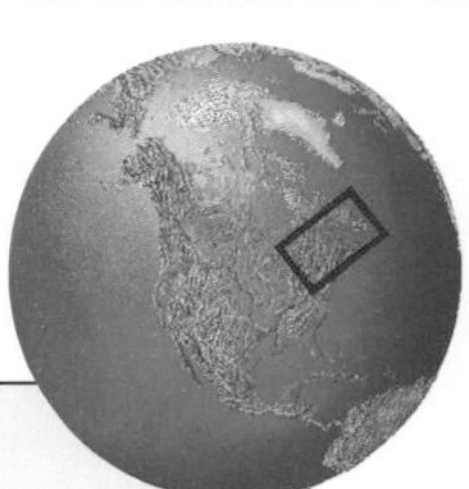

LABRADOR SEA
Labrador
Tunungayualok Island
Davis Inlet
Hopedale
C. Makkovik
C. Harrison
C. Turley
Mt Benedict 829 m
Holton
Groswater Bay
Kogaluk
Mistastin Lake
Kanairiktok
Snegamook Lake
Nipishish Lake
Naskaupi
Double Mer
Hamilton Inlet
Grand Lake
Lake Melville
Happy Valley - Goose Bay
Mealy Mts
Churchill
C. Porcupine
Grady Harbour
Cartwright
Sandwich Bay
Separation Point
Batteau
Comfort Bight
Sand Hill
Eagle
Square Islands
Port Hope Simpson
Alexis
St Lewis
St Paul
Little Mecatina
St-Augustin
Table Head
Belle Isle
Red Bay
C. Bauld
L'Anse aux Meadows
Strait of Belle Isle
Blanc-Sablon
Rivière-St-Paul
Forteaux
St Anthony
Main Brook
Hare Bay
St-Augustin
Brig Bay
Groais I.
Grey Is
Bell I.
St John I.
Northern Peninsula
Englee
Port aux Choix
Hawkes Bay
Williamsport
Horse Is
Long Range Mts
Mutton Bay
Romaine
Aguanus
Natashquan
Olomane
Lac Musquaro
Baie-Johan Beetz
Havre-St-Pierre
Natashquan
Kegaska
Gethsémani
Pointe-Parent
Détroit de Jacques-Cartier
Île d'Anticosti
Chicotte
Pte de l'Est
Daniel's Harbour
C. St John
La Scie
Baie Verte
Fogo
Fogo I.
Notre Dame Bay
White Bay
Westport
Sally's Cove
Rocky Harbour
Hampden
Springdale
Grose Morne 806 m
Musgrave Harbour
Cape Freels
Gander Bay
Wesleyville
Mt Gregory 674 m
Deer Lake
Sandy Lake
Grand Falls-Windsor
Gander
Bonavista Bay
Bonavista
Grand Lake
Badger
Gambo
Corner Brook
Buchans
Glover I.
Red Indian Lake
Summerville
Lewis Hills 815 m
Lourdes
Stephenville
Newfoundland
NEWFOUNDLAND
Musgravetown
Grates Cove
Cape St George
Victoria Lake
Meelpaeg Lake
Clarenville
Trinity Bay
Conception Bay
Middle Ridge
Goobies
Pouch Cove
St George's Bay
St Alban's
Milltown
Carbonear
St John's
Gulf of St Lawrence
C. Anguille
Bay Roberts
Mount Pearl
Bay Bulls
Avalon Peninsula
C. Ray
Rose Blanche
Burgeo
Harbour Breton
Hermitage Bay
Fortune Bay
Placentia
Placentia Bay
Channel-Port aux Basques
Garnish
Marystown
Ferryland
Grand Bank
Fortune
Cap aux Meules
Grand-Entrée
Îles de la Madelaine
Havre-Aubert
Miqeulon
ST PIERRE AND MIQUELON (Fr.)
St Pierre
St Lawrence
Branch
C. St Mary's
St Mary's Bay
Trepassey
Cape Race
Cape Pine
Cabot Strait
Cape North
Cape North
North Cape
PRINCE EDWARD ISLAND
Ingonish
Chéticamp
Summerside
St Peters
East Pt
Elmira
Margaree Forks
New Waterford
Glace Bay
Charlottetown
Inverness
Sydney
Montague
Port Hood
Whycocomagh
Main-à-Dieu
Cape Tormentine
Cape George
Bras d'Or Lake
Cape Breton Island
Amherst
Oxford
Tatamagouche
Port Hawkesbury
Fourchu
Cobequid Mts
New Glasgow
Monastery
Isle Madam
Stellarton
Arichat
Bolyston
Canso
Truro
St Mary's
Aspen
Tor Bay
NOVA SCOTIA
Windsor
Musquodoboit Harbour
Sheet Harbour
Halifax
Dartmouth
Sambro
ATLANTIC OCEAN

0 100 200 kilometers
0 50 100 miles
Scale 1:5,000,000
Projection: Albers Equal Area

Northwest United States

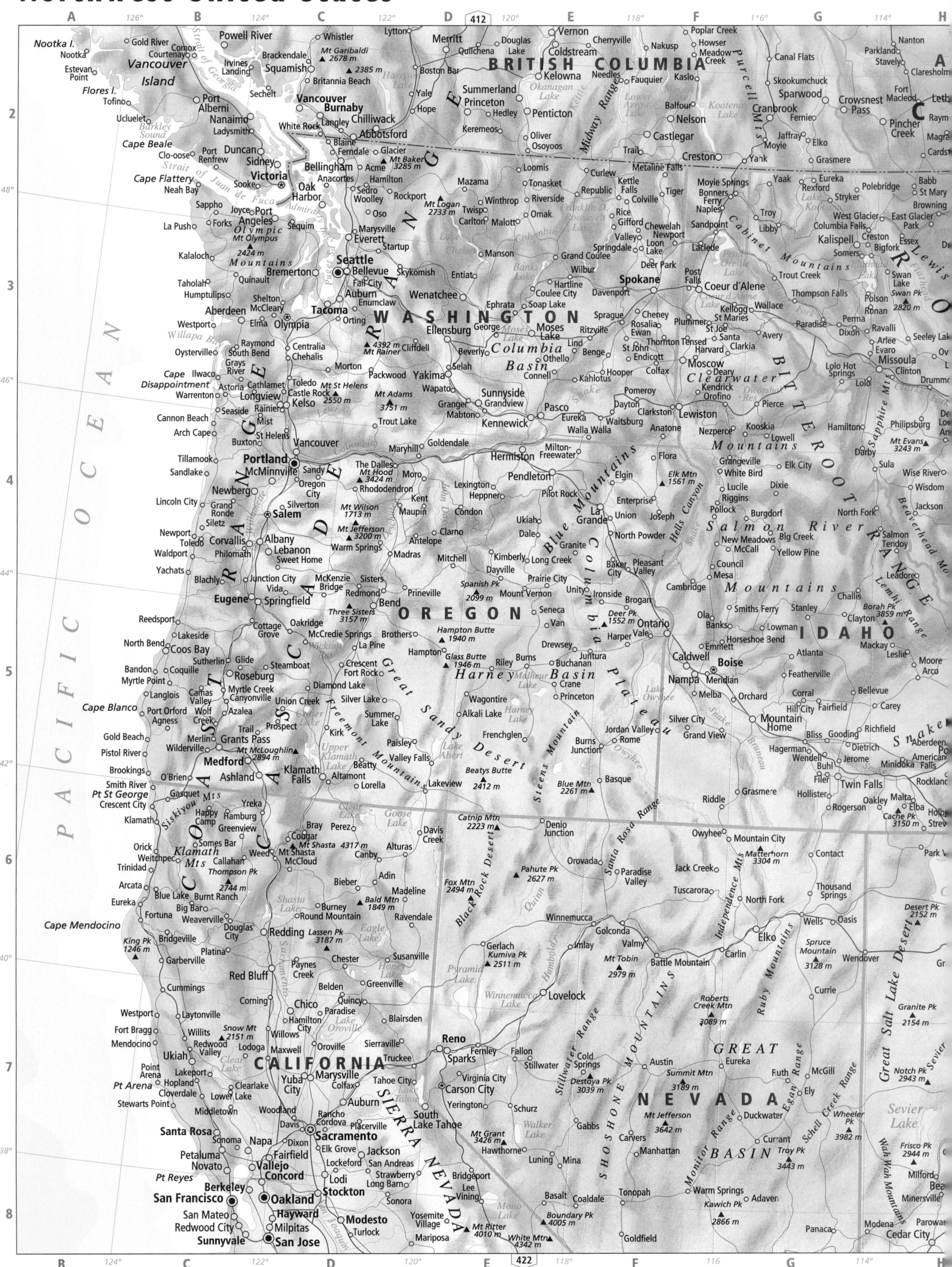

BRITISH COLUMBIA
WASHINGTON
OREGON
IDAHO
CALIFORNIA
NEVADA
PACIFIC OCEAN
Vancouver Island
Strait of Georgia
Strait of Juan de Fuca
Olympic Mountains
CASCADE RANGE
COAST RANGES
Columbia Basin
Blue Mountains
Columbia Plateau
Harney Basin
Great Sandy Desert
Freemont Mountains
Klamath Mts
Siskiyou Mts
Steens Mountain
Santa Rosa Range
Black Rock Desert
SIERRA NEVADA
SHOSHONE MOUNTAINS
GREAT BASIN
Salmon River Mountains
BITTERROOT RANGE
Clearwater Mountains
Purcell Mts
Cabinet Mountains
Ruby Mountains
Great Salt Lake Desert
Vancouver
Victoria
Seattle
Tacoma
Olympia
Spokane
Portland
Salem
Eugene
Medford
Boise
Reno
Carson City
Sacramento
San Francisco
Oakland
San Jose
Mt Rainier 4392 m
Mt Hood 3424 m
Mt St Helens 2550 m
Mt Shasta 4317 m
Mt Baker 3285 m
Mt Adams 3751 m
Lassen Pk 3187 m
412
422

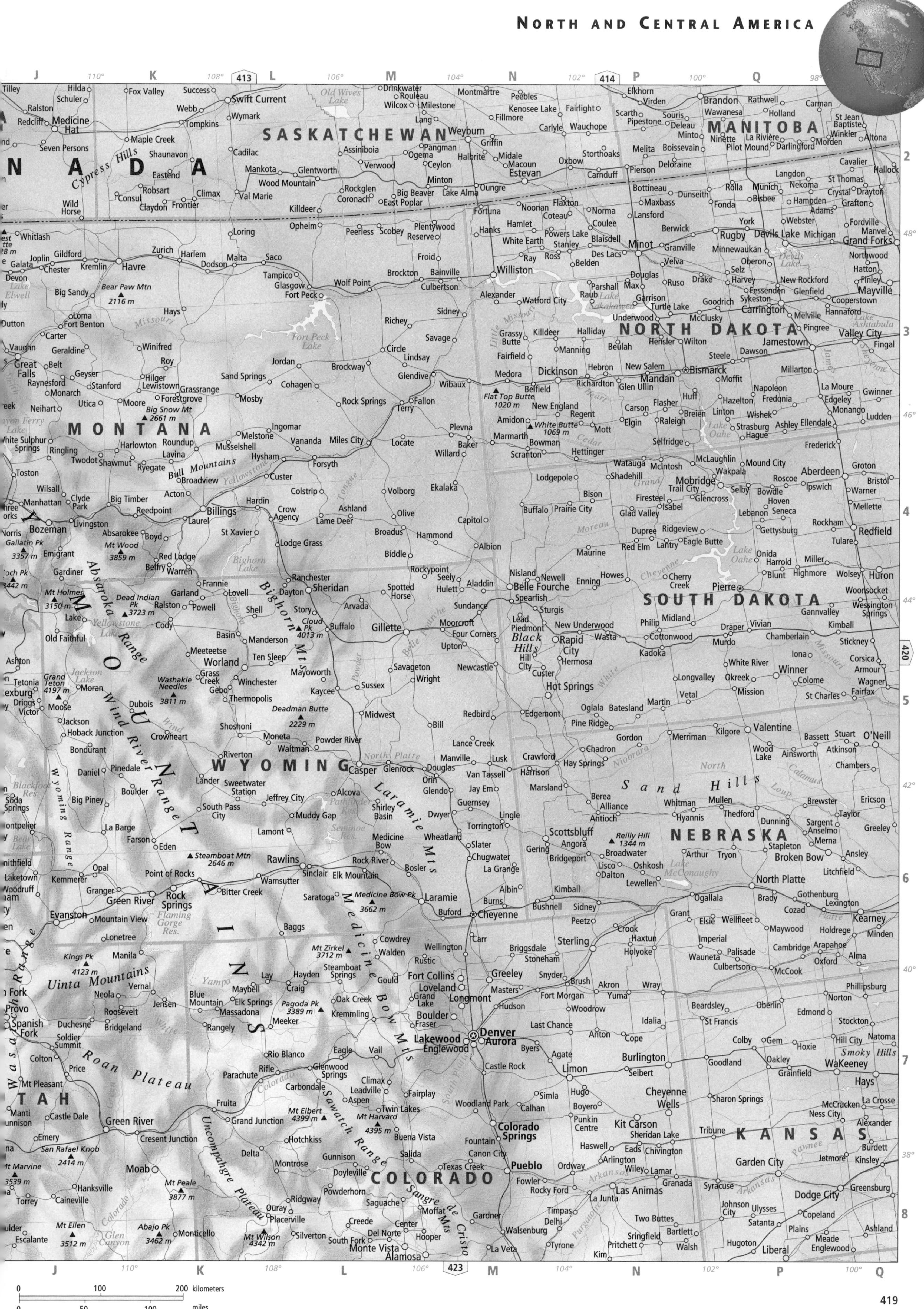

SASKATCHEWAN
MANITOBA
NORTH DAKOTA
SOUTH DAKOTA
MONTANA
WYOMING
NEBRASKA
COLORADO
KANSAS
ROCKY MOUNTAINS
Cypress Hills
Bighorn Mts
Absaroka Range
Wind River Range
Wyoming Range
Laramie Mts
Medicine Bow Mts
Uinta Mountains
Roan Plateau
Sawatch Range
Sangre de Cristo Mts
Uncompahgre Plateau
Sand Hills
Black Hills
Smoky Hills
Swift Current
Medicine Hat
Brandon
Weyburn
Estevan
Minot
Grand Forks
Williston
Bismarck
Mandan
Dickinson
Jamestown
Fargo
Aberdeen
Pierre
Rapid City
Great Falls
Havre
Billings
Bozeman
Miles City
Sheridan
Gillette
Casper
Rawlins
Laramie
Cheyenne
Rock Springs
Green River
Scottsbluff
North Platte
Fort Collins
Greeley
Boulder
Denver
Aurora
Lakewood
Colorado Springs
Pueblo
Grand Junction
Garden City
Dodge City
Hays
Mt Elbert 4399 m
Mt Harvard 4395 m
Kings Pk 4123 m
Grand Teton 4197 m
Cloud Pk 4013 m
Scale 1:5,000,000 Projection: Albers Equal Area
0 100 200 kilometers
0 50 100 miles
North and Central America

Central United States

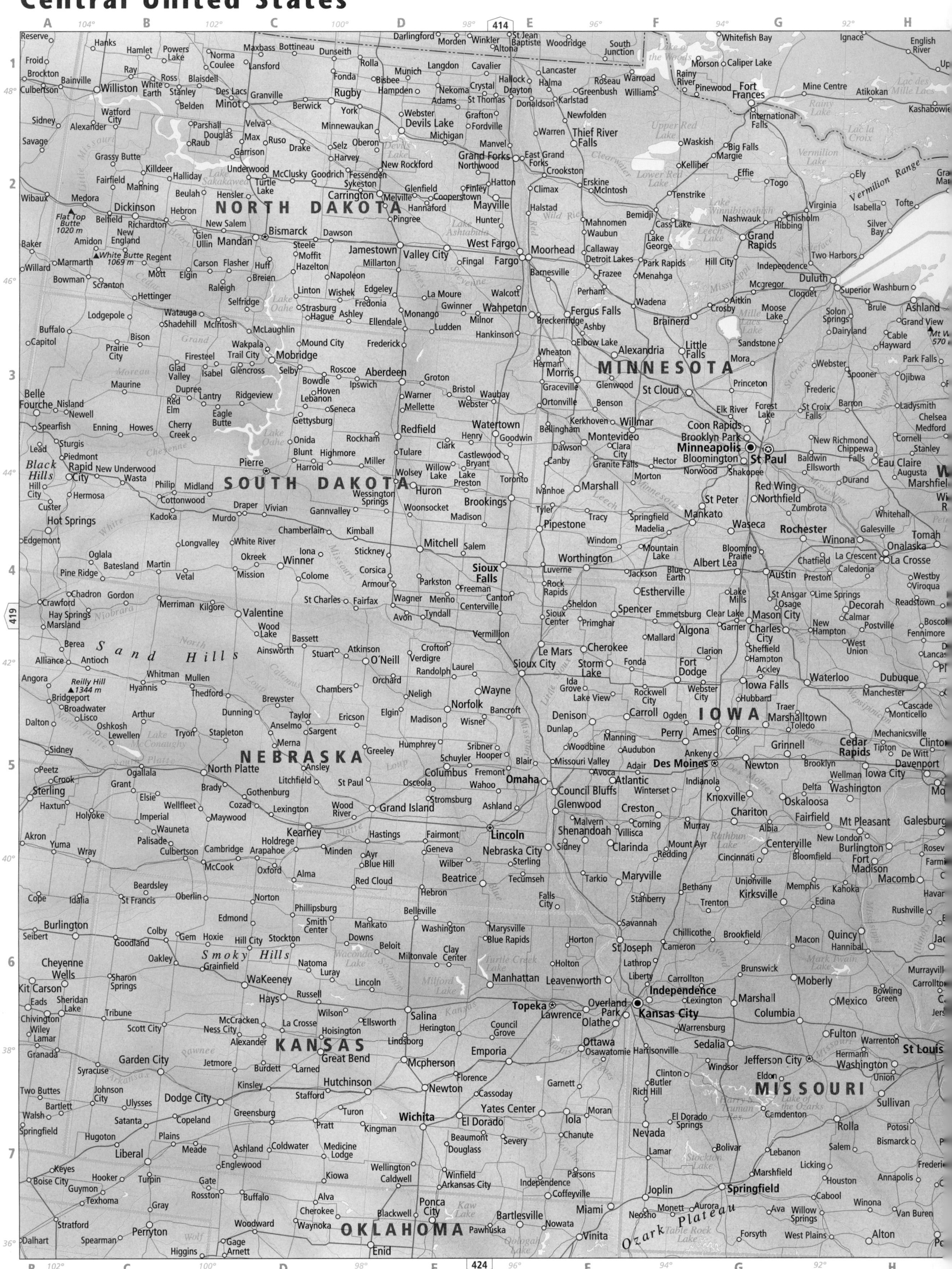
NORTH DAKOTA
SOUTH DAKOTA
NEBRASKA
KANSAS
OKLAHOMA
MINNESOTA
IOWA
MISSOURI
Bismarck
Pierre
Lincoln
Topeka
Des Moines
Jefferson City
Minneapolis
St Paul
Kansas City
Omaha
Wichita
Sioux Falls
Fargo
Duluth
St Louis
Springfield
Sand Hills
Smoky Hills
Ozark Plateau
Black Hills
Lake Sakakawea
Lake Oahe
Lake of the Woods
Upper Red Lake
Lower Red Lake
Mille Lacs Lake
Vermilion Range
Flat Top Butte 1020 m
White Butte 1069 m
Reilly Hill 1344 m

414
419
424

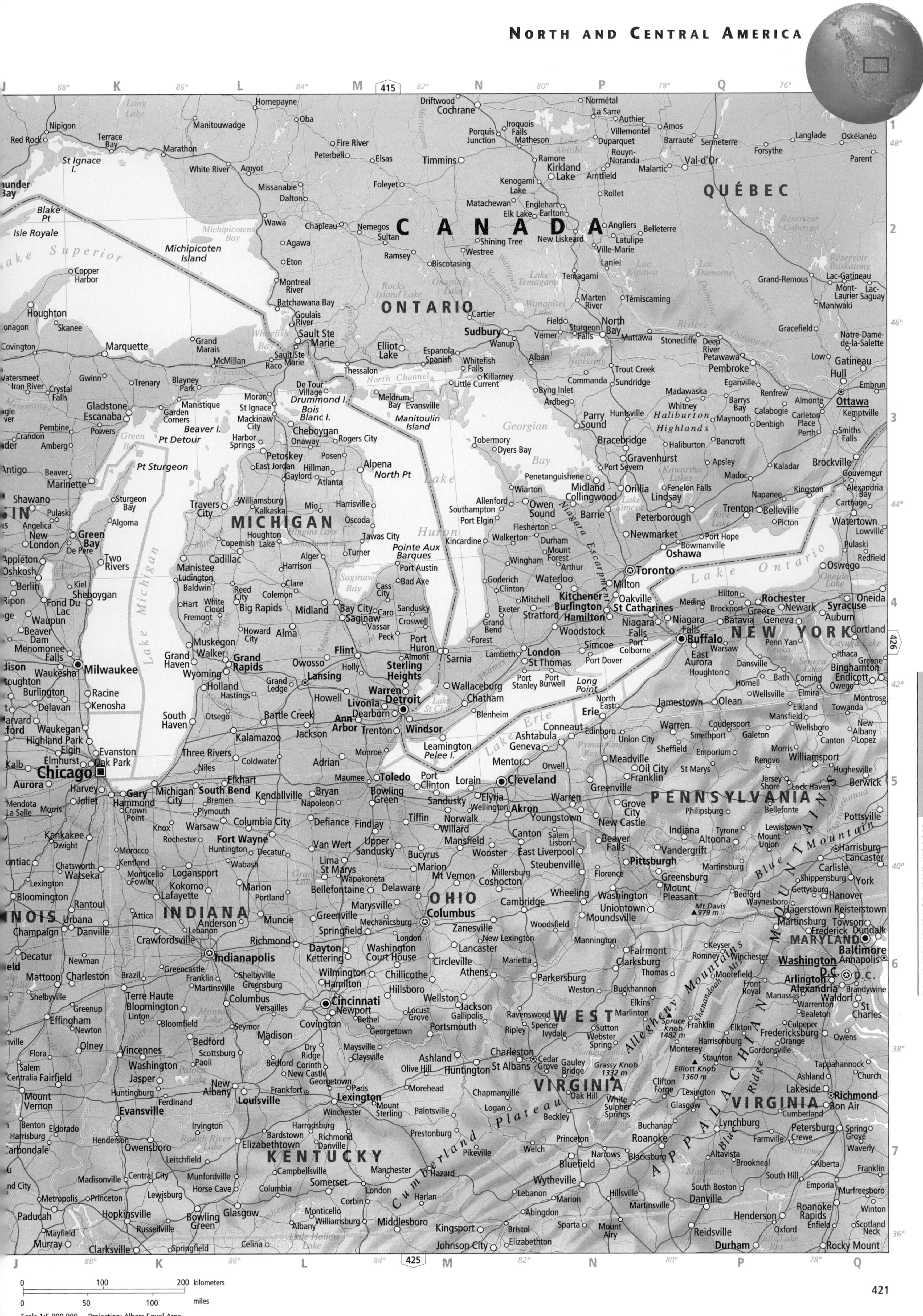

Scale 1:5,000,000 Projection: Albers Equal Area

Southwest United States

A
B
C
D
E
F
G
124°
122°
120°
118°
116°
114°
418
1
2
3
4
5
9
10
40°
38°
36°
34°
32°
Eureka
Fortuna
Big Bar
Weaverville
Shasta Lake
Burney
Bald Mtn 1849 m
Round Mountain
Cape Mendocino
Bridgeville
Douglas City
Redding
Lassen Pk 3187 m
Eagle Lake
Ravendale
King Pk 1246 m
Platina
Garberville
Red Bluff
Paynes Creek
Chester
Susanville
Honey Lake
Gerlach
Kumiva Pk 2511 m
Pyramid Lake
Winnemucca Lake
Winnemucca
Golconda
Imlay
Valmy
Elko
Carlin
Wells
Oasis
Spruce Mountain 3128 m
Wendover
Mt Tobin 2979 m
Battle Mountain
Independence Mts
Ruby Mountains
Cummings
Corning
Belden
Greenville
Lovelock
Roberts Creek Mtn 3089 m
Currie
Westport
Laytonville
Chico
Quincy
Paradise
Hamilton City
Lake Oroville
Blairsden
Fort Bragg
Willits
Willows
Snow Mt 2151 m
Mendocino
Redwood Valley
Ukiah
Lodoga
Maxwell
Oroville
Sierraville
Truckee
Reno
Sparks
Fernley
Fallon
Stillwater
Point Arena
Pt Arena
Lakeport
Clear Lake
Hopland
Lower Lake
Clearlake
Cloverdale
Yuba City
Marysville
Colfax
Tahoe City
Lake Tahoe
Virginia City
Carson City
Cold Springs
Destoya Pk 3039 m
Austin
Eureka
Summit Mtn 3189 m
Ruth
McGill
Ely
Stewarts Point
Middletown
Woodland
Auburn
South Lake Tahoe
Yerington
Schurz
GREAT
NEVADA
Mt Jefferson 3642 m
Santa Rosa
Sonoma
Petaluma
Napa
Davis
Rancho Cordova
Sacramento
Placerville
Dixon
Elk Grove
Jackson
Fairfield
Vallejo
Novato
Lockeford
San Andreas
Mt Grant 3426 m
Walker Lake
Hawthorne
Gabbs
Carvers
Manhattan
Duckwater
Currant
Wheeler Pk 3982 m
Sevier Lake
Pt Reyes
Berkeley
Concord
Oakland
Lodi
Stockton
Strawberry
Long Barn
Sonora
Bridgeport
Luning
Mina
BASIN
Troy Pk 3443 m
Frisco Pk 2944 m
Milford
San Francisco
San Mateo
Redwood City
Sunnyvale
Hayward
Milpitas
San Jose
Manteca
Modesto
Turlock
Lee Vining
Mono Lake
Yosemite Village
Mt Ritter 4010 m
Basalt
Coaldale
Tonopah
Warm Springs
Adaven
Boundary Pk 4005 m
White Mtn 4342 m
Kawich Pk 2866 m
Minersville
Parowan
Modena
Cedar City
Panaca
Caliente
Morgan Hill
Mariposa
Merced
Oakhurst
Goldfield
Lida
Bishop
Quartzite Mtn 2367 m
Alamo
Elgin
Enterprise
Santa Cruz
Gilroy
Los Banos
Monterey Bay
Watsonville
Madera
Friant
Fresno
Carp
Washington
St George
Hurricane
Marina
Salinas
Monterey
Gonzales
Sanger
Selma
Beatty
Amargosa Valley
Indian Springs
Mesquite
Littlefield
Moapa
Overton
Mt Bangs 2442 m
Soledad
Greenfield
King City
Hanford
Lemoore
Visalia
Mt Whitney 4418 m
Owens Lake
Panamint Springs
Big Sur
Lopez Pt
C. San Martin
San Ardo
Coalinga
Avenal
Porterville
Charleston Pk 3633 m
Las Vegas
Henderson
Lake Mead
Mt Trumbull 2447 m
Grand Canyon
Telescope Pk 3368 m
Little Lake
Boulder City
Cholame
Delano
Isabella Lake
Inyokern
Ridgecrest
Weldon
Cambria
Shandon
Lost Hills
Morro Bay
San Luis Obispo
Buttonwillow
Bakersfield
Caliente
Johannesburg
Nipton
Searchlight
Mt Tipton 2179 m
Chloride
Peach Springs
Valentine
Kingman
Grover City
McKittrick
Taft
CALIFORNIA
Baker
Santa Maria
Maricopa
Mojave
Mojave Desert
Lompoc
Grapevine
Barstow
Harvard
Bullhead City
Hualapai Pk 2566 m
Pt Arguello
Lancaster
Ludlow
Goffs
Needles
Topock
Santa Barbara
Goleta
Santa Paula
Simi Valley
Santa Clarita
Palmdale
Victorville
Amboy
Essex
Cadiz
Lake Havasu City
Bagdad
Alamo Lake
Ventura
Oxnard
Mt San Antonio 3068 m
Pasadena
Santa Cruz
San Miguel
Glendale
Beverly Hills
Los Angeles
Danby Lake
Twentynine Palms
Santa Monica
Santa Rosa
San Bernardino
Rice
Vidal
Parker
Congress
Inglewood
Anaheim
Riverside
Torrance
Santa Ana
Banning
Palm Springs
Indio
Desert Center
Palen Lake
Bouse
Long Beach
Irvine
Huntington Beach
Hemet
Sun City
Wenden
Channel Islands
Temecula
Pala
Palomar 1871 m
Bombay Beach
Salton Sea
Blythe
Quartzsite
San Nicolas
Santa Catalina
San Clemente
Oceanside
Escondido
Calipatria
Castle Dome Pk 1155 m
Carlsbad
Encinitas
Ocotillo Wells
Brawley
San Clemente
El Cajon
San Diego
El Centro
Calexico
Yuma
Dateland
Chula Vista
Tijuana
Tecate
Mexicali
San Luis Rio Colorado
Guadalupe
Ensenada
Cabo Punta Banda
Santo Tomás
El Golfo de Santa Clara
BAJA CALIFORNIA
San Vicente
Puerto Peñasco
San Telmo
San Felipe
Colonia Vicente Guerrero
El Socorro
San Quintin
Puertecitos
El Desemboque
El Rosario de Arriba
Punta Baja
Misión de San Fernando
Santa Catarina
Isla Ángel de la Guarda
Punta Prieta
Bahía de los Ángeles
Rosarito
GOLFO DE CALIFORNIA
PACIFIC OCEAN
Sierra de Juárez
Coast Ranges
Sierra Nevada
Santa Lucia Range
Diablo Range
San Joaquin Valley
Panamint Range
Death Valley
Shoshone Mountains
Stillwater Range
Monitor Range
Egan Range
Schell Creek Range
Great Salt Lake Desert
Wah Wah Mts
San Bernardino Mts
Chocolate Mts
Colorado Desert
Sonoran Desert
Black Mts
HAWAII
Hanalei
Kilauea
Anahola
Kapaa
Lihue
Mana
1598 m
Kekaha
Kauai
Lehua
Kii Landing
Puuwai
Niihau
Kaula
Kaulakahi Channel
Kauai Channel
Oahu
Kahuku
Waialua
Wahiawa
Waianae
Kaneohe
Makaha
Pearl City
Pearl Harbor
Honolulu
Diamond Head
Kaiwi Channel
Molokai
Kalaupapa
1515 m
Pailolo Channel
Kaunakakai
Wailuku
Maui
Lanai
Lanai City
Lahaina
Kahului
Wailea
Hana
3055 m
Kahoolawe
Alenuihaha Channel
HAWAIIAN ISLANDS (U.S.A.)
Hawi
Kapaau
Honokaa
Hawaii
Waimea
Mauna Kea 4205 m
Pepeekeo
Hilo
Kailua-Kona
Mountain View
Captain Cook
Mauna Loa 4169 m
Kilauea Crater 1247 m
Pahoa
Pahala
Milolii
Kauna Pt
Naalehu
Ka Lae
PACIFIC OCEAN
Q
R
160°
155°
20°
30°
116°
114°

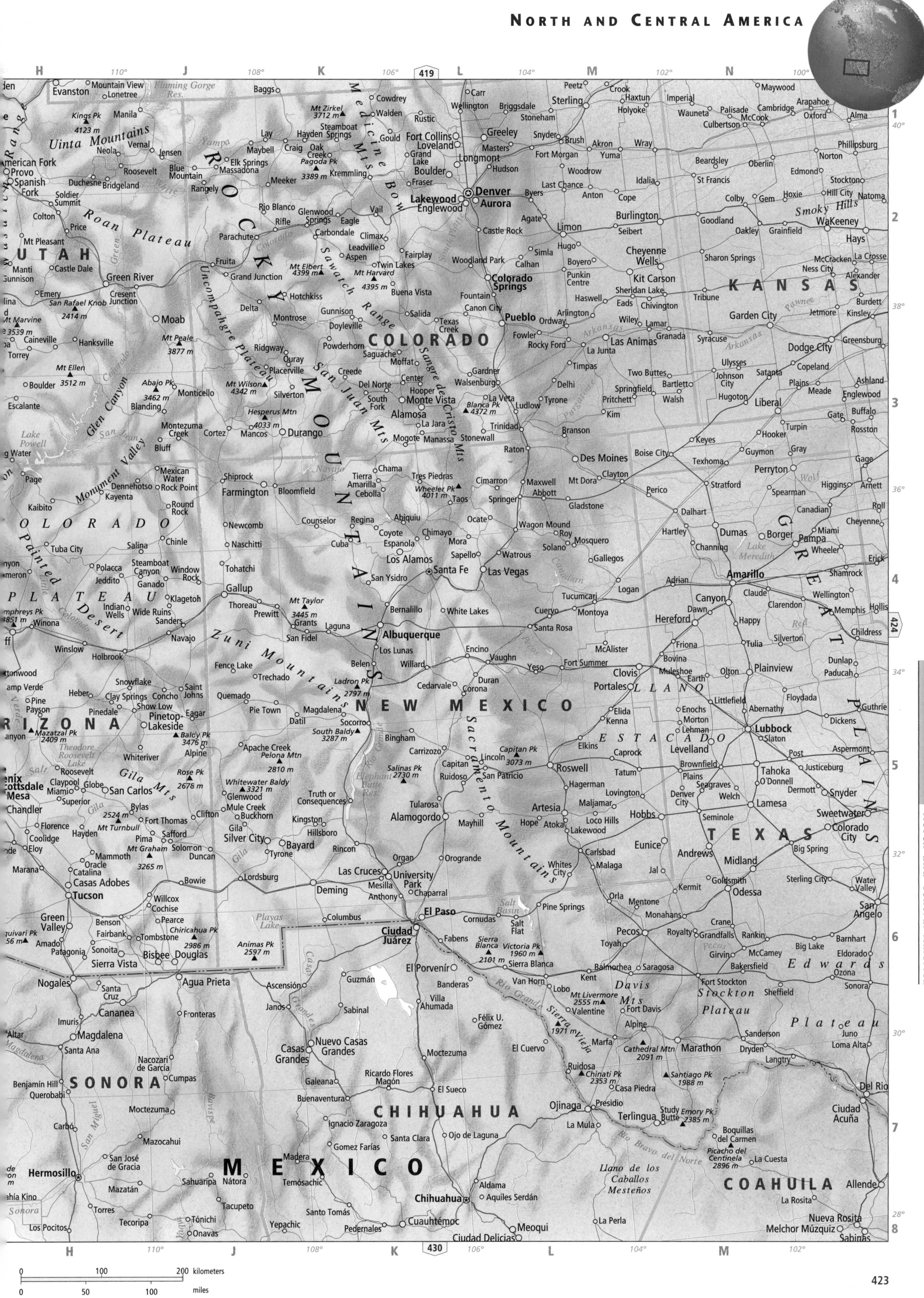

COLORADO
NEW MEXICO
UTAH
ARIZONA
KANSAS
TEXAS
MEXICO
CHIHUAHUA
SONORA
COAHUILA
ROCKY MOUNTAINS
GREAT PLAINS
LLANO ESTACADO
Uinta Mountains
Roan Plateau
Uncompahgre Plateau
Sawatch Range
Sangre de Cristo Mts
San Juan Mts
Medicine Bow Mts
Zuni Mountains
Sacramento Mountains
Gila Mts
Painted Desert
Glen Canyon
Monument Valley
Davis Mts
Stockton Plateau
Edwards Plateau
Smoky Hills
Llano de los Caballos Mesteños
Denver
Aurora
Lakewood
Englewood
Colorado Springs
Pueblo
Greeley
Fort Collins
Boulder
Grand Junction
Durango
Albuquerque
Santa Fe
Las Cruces
El Paso
Ciudad Juárez
Amarillo
Lubbock
Midland
Odessa
Roswell
Tucson
Hermosillo
Chihuahua
Mt Elbert 4399 m
Mt Harvard 4395 m
Blanca Pk 4372 m
Wheeler Pk 4011 m
Mt Taylor 3445 m
Kings Pk 4123 m
Rio Grande
Rio Bravo del Norte
Arkansas
Colorado
Pecos
Canadian
Gila
Scale 1:5,000,000 Projection: Albers Equal Area
0 100 200 kilometers
0 50 100 miles
North and Central America

Southeast United States

OKLAHOMA
TEXAS
ARKANSAS
MISSOURI
LOUISIANA
MEXICO
NUEVO LEÓN
TAMAULIPAS
GREAT PLAINS
Edwards Plateau
Balcones Escarpment
Ozark Plateau
Boston Mts
Ouachita Mts
GULF O
Oklahoma City
Tulsa
Dallas
Fort Worth
Houston
San Antonio
Austin
Amarillo
Lubbock
Abilene
Waco
Corpus Christi
Laredo
Nuevo Laredo
Monterrey
Guadalupe
Reynosa
Matamoros
Brownsville
Shreveport
Little Rock
Baton Rouge
Springfield
Galveston
Beaumont
Lake Charles
Texarkana
Wichita Falls
San Angelo
Padre I.
Matagorda I.
San Jose I.
Marsh I.
Salmon Pk 592 m
3205 m
North and Central America

421

426

H
J
K
L
M
N
KENTUCKY
TENNESSEE
NORTH CAROLINA
SOUTH CAROLINA
GEORGIA
ALABAMA
FLORIDA
CUMBERLAND PLATEAU
APPALACHIAN MOUNTAINS
BLUE RIDGE
Great Smoky Mts
Mt Mitchell 2037 m
Mt Guyot 2018 m
Brasstown Bald 1458 m
Nashville
Knoxville
Chattanooga
Atlanta
Birmingham
Montgomery
Huntsville
Mobile
Columbus
Macon
Augusta
Savannah
Charlotte
Columbia
Raleigh
Greensboro
Winston - Salem
Durham
Tallahassee
Jacksonville
Gainesville
Orlando
Tampa
St Petersburg
Clearwater
Fort Lauderdale
Hollywood
Hialeah
Miami
Pensacola
Wilmington
Charleston
Asheville
ATLANTIC
OCEAN
MEXICO
Long Bay
Onslow Bay
Apalachee Bay
Deadman Bay
Waccasassa Bay
Tampa Bay
Florida Bay
Lake Okeechobee
Florida Keys
Straits of Florida
Northwest Providence Channel
Grand Bahama Island
Bimini Islands
BAHAMAS
Cape Canaveral
Cape Romano
Ten Thousand Is
Sanibel I.
Knob I.
Key West
Key Largo
Chandeleur Is
Horn I.
Dauphin I.
St Joseph Point
Dog I.
St George I.
Ossabaw I.
St Catherines I.
Sapelo I.
St Simons I.
Cumberland I.
Hiton Head Island
Smith I.
North and Central America
0 100 200 kilometers
0 50 100 miles
Scale 1:5,000,000 Projection: Albers Equal Area

Northeast United States

CANADA
QUÉBEC
ONTARIO
NEW BRUNSWICK
MAINE
VERMONT
NEW HAMPSHIRE
MASSACHUSETTS
RHODE ISLAND
CONNECTICUT
NEW YORK
PENNSYLVANIA
NEW JERSEY
DELAWARE
MARYLAND
VIRGINIA
NORTH CAROLINA
Gulf of Maine
ATLANTIC OCEAN
Bay of Fundy
Lake Ontario
Adirondack Mountains
APPALACHIAN MTS
Green Mts
White Mts
Catskill Mts
Blue Mountain
Monts Notre Dame
Long Island
Cape Cod
Cape Sable
Québec
Montréal
Ottawa
Sherbrooke
Trois-Rivières
Kingston
Peterborough
Fredericton
Saint John
Edmundston
Bangor
Augusta
Portland
Lewiston
Burlington
Montpelier
Concord
Manchester
Boston
Worcester
Springfield
Providence
Hartford
New Haven
Bridgeport
Albany
Syracuse
Rochester
Binghamton
New York
Newark
Jersey City
Yonkers
Trenton
Philadelphia
Harrisburg
Allentown
Scranton
Baltimore
Washington D.C.
Annapolis
Dover
Richmond
Norfolk
Virginia Beach
Chesapeake
Atlantic City
Cape May Pt
Mt Katahdin 1605 m
Mt Washington 1917 m
Hatteras I.
Cape Lookout
Kitty Hawk
Scale 1:5,000,000
Projection: Albers Equal Area
kilometers 0 100 200
miles 0 50 100

416
421
425

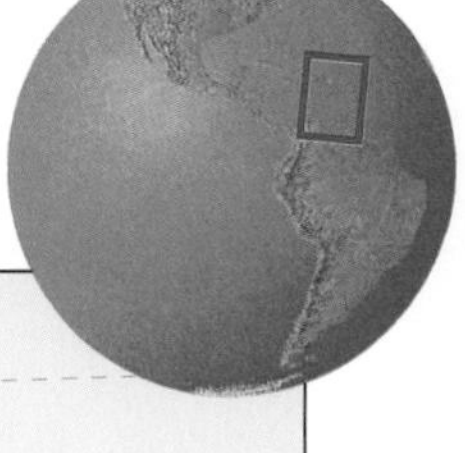

East Caribbean • North Venezuela

A 72° B 68° C 64° D 60°

Tropic of Cancer

1

TURKS AND CAICOS ISLANDS (U.K.)
Caicos Islands
Turks Islands
Cockburn Harbour
Grand Turk

ATLANTIC OCEAN

20°

Cap-Haïtien
Cabo Isabela
Puerto Plata
Monte Cristi
Cabrera
Fort Liberté
Santiago
Moca
Bahía Escocesa
San Francisco de Macorís
Hinche
La Vega
Bahía de Samaná
HAITI
DOMINICAN REPUBLIC
Pico Duarte 3175 m
Bonao
Monte Plata
Comendador
San Juan
Hato Mayor
El Seibo
Cabo Engaño
Dajabón
Neiba
San Pedro de Macorís
Port-au-Prince
Azua
San Cristóbal
La Romana
Santo Domingo
Barahona
Punta Salinas
Isla Saona
Pedernales
Cabo Beata
HISPANIOLA
GREATER ANTILLES

2

Aguadilla
Arecibo
San Juan
Carolina
Mayagüez
Cerro de Punta 1338 m
Fajardo
Caguas
San Germán
Ponce
Guayama
PUERTO RICO (U.S.A.)

LEEWARD ISLANDS
VIRGIN ISLANDS (U.K.)
Anegada
Road Town
Charlotte Amalie
St Croix
Frederiksted
VIRGIN ISLANDS (U.S.A.)
Anegada Passage
ANGUILLA (U.K.)
The Valley
Marigot
St Martin (Guad.)
St Maarten (Neth.)
Philipsburg
Saba
St Eustatius
Basseterre
ST KITTS AND NEVIS
Codrington
Barbuda
ANTIGUA AND BARBUDA
St John's
Antigua
Redonda
Plymouth
MONTSERRAT (U.K.)
Guadeloupe Passage
GUADELOUPE (Fr.)
Sainte-Rose
Pointe-à-Pitre
Basse-Terre
LESSER ANTILLES

16°

CARIBBEAN SEA

Dominica Passage
Portsmouth
Morne Diablotin 1447 m
DOMINICA
Roseau
La Plaine
Martinique Passage
Montagne Pelée 1397 m
Sainte-Marie
Le Lamentin
Fort-de-France
MARTINIQUE (Fr.)
St Lucia Channel
Castries
ST LUCIA
Micoud
Vieux Fort
St Vincent Passage
Soufrière 1234 m
ST VINCENT AND THE GRENADINES
Georgetown
Kingstown
BARBADOS
Speightstown
Bridgetown
The Grenadines
WINDWARD ISLANDS
Grenville
St George's
GRENADA

3

ARUBA (Neth.)
Oranjestad
LESSER ANTILLES
Pta Gallinas
Curaçao
Bonaire
Puerto Estrella
Península de Guajira
C. San Román
Pen. de Paraguaná
Willemstad
Kralendijk
Carrizal
Pueblo Nuevo
NETHERLANDS ANTILLES (Neth.)
Los Taques
Punto Fijo
Puerto Cumarebo
La Orchila
La Blanquilla
Golfo de Venezuela
Paraguaipoa
Coro
Píritu
Casigua
Pedregal
Jacura
San Juan de los Cayos
San Rafael
Dabajuro
Churuguara
Campo Mara
Maracaibo
Mene de Mauroa
Baragua
Santa Rita
Cabimas
Cerro El Cerrón 1990 m
Carora
Puerto Cabello
Catia La Mar
Caracas
Petare
Baruta
San Felipe
C. Codera
Higuerote
Maracay
Valencia
Los Teques
La Victoria
Lagunillas
Barquisimeto
Yaritagua
Barranquitas
Lago de Maracaibo
Mene Grande
El Tocuyo
Tinaco
San Juan de los Morros
Ortiz
Isla de Margarita
La Asunción
Porlamar
Carúpano
Río Caribe
Pen. de Paria
Güiria
La Tortuga
Puerto la Cruz
Barcelona
Cumaná
Caripe
Caripito
Maturín
Tobago
Charlotteville
Scarborough
Galera Pt
TRINIDAD AND TOBAGO
Bocas del Dragón
Arima
Port of Spain
Sangre Grande
Trinidad
Golfo de Paria
Rio Claro
San Fernando
Galeota Pt
Boca de la Serpiente

12°

4

Betijoque
Trujillo
Boconó
Acarigua
San Carlos
El Pao
San Antonio de Tamanaco
Aragua de Barcelona
Zaraza
El Sombrero
Anaco
Cantaura
San Carlos del Zulia
Valera
Guanare
Nueva Florida
Chaguaramas
Valle de la Pascua
El Chaparro
El Tigre
Pariaguán
San José de Guanipa
Las Mercedes
Calabozo
El Baúl
Guanarito
Portuguesa
El Vigía
Mérida
Barinas
Pico Bolívar 5007 m
Obispos
Santa María de Ipire
San Mauricio
Tucupita
Barrancas
Boca Araguao
Boca Grande
Tovar
VENEZUELA
El Toro
San José de Amacuro
Waini Pt
Morawhanna
Mabaruma
Boca del Pao
Soledad
Puerto Ordaz
Ciudad Guayana
Upata
El Palmar
La Horqueta
Port Kaituma
Baramanni
San Antonio de Caparo
Pedraza La Vieja
Puerto de Nutrias
Camaguán
Puerto Miranda
San Fernando de Apure
Orinoco
Parmana
Cabruta
Caicara de Orinoco
Mapire
Ciudad Bolívar
El Pao
Serranía de Imataca
Achaguas
Palmarito
Caparo
Mantecal
Ciudad Piar
El Miamo
Guasipati
El Callao
Matthews Ridge
Barama
Guasdualito
Arauca
Maripa
Co Turagua 1839 m
Embalse de Guri
Tumeremo
Arauquita
Arauca
Elorza
Capanaparo
La Urbana
Las Lajitas
Las Trincheras
San Pedro de Las Bocas
La Paragua
Cuyuni
Cinaruco
El Dorado
GUYANA
Tame
1320 m
Puerto Rondón
Casanare
Meta
Parguaza
Caura
Mazaruni
Cravo Norte
Puerto Páez
Puerto Carreño
Tumureng
Peter's Mine
COLOMBIA
Keweigek
Puerto Nuevo
Issano

8°

5

429
451

B 68° C 64° D 60° E

0 100 200 300 400 kilometers
0 100 200 miles

Scale 1:7,000,000
Projection: Lambert Conformal Conic

Central America • West Caribbean

A
B
C
D
431
96°
92°
88°
84°
20°
16°
12°
8°
2
3
4
5
GULF OF MEXICO
Bahía de Campeche
Golfo de Tehuantepec
PACIFIC OCEAN
Yucatán Channel
Golfo de Honduras
MEXICO
GUATEMALA
BELIZE
HONDURAS
EL SALVADOR
NICARAGUA
COSTA RICA
VERACRUZ
OAXACA
TABASCO
CHIAPAS
CAMPECHE
YUCATÁN
QUINTANA ROO
Península de Yucatán
Istmo de Tehuantepec
Sierra de Tamaulipas
Sierra de Miahuatlán
Sierra Madre de Chiapas
Maya Mts
Meseta de Zohlaguna
Cordillera Isabelia
La Pesca
Soto La Marina
Aldama
Gonzáles
Lomas del Real
Ebano
Ciudad Madero
Tampico
Pánuco
Tempoal
Ozuluama
Tantoyuca
Cabo Rojo
Naranjos
Huejutla de Reyes
Cerro Azul
Tuxpan de Rodríguez Cano
Poza Rica de Hidalgo
Papantla de Olarte
Tecolutla
Huauchinango
Nautla
Zacatlán
Martínez de la Torre
Teziutlán
Perote
Tlaxcala
Vol. Citlaltépetl (Pico de Orizaba) 5700 m
Jalapa Enríquez
Cardel
Puebla de Zaragoza
Tatutla
Veracruz
Orizaba
Soledad de Doblado
Ciudad Mendoza
Córdoba
Piedras Negras
Punta Roca Partida
Tlacotalpan
Tehuitzingo
Tehuacán
Ajalpán
Tierra Blanca
San Andrés Tuxtla
Acatlán de Osorio
3719 m
Tres Valles
Huajuapan de León
San Lucas Ojitlán
San Juan Bautista Tuxtepec
Acayucan
Coatzacoalcos
Minatitlán
Villa de Tamazulápan
Valle Nacional
Sayula de Alemán
Tlaxiaco
Ixtlán de Juárez
Putla
Oaxaca de Juárez
Zempoaltepec 3395 m
Zimatlán
Tlacolula de Matamoros
Matías Romero
Ejutla
San Pedro Totalapan
Ciudad Ixtepec
Santiago Pinotepa Nacional
Miahuatlán
Magdalena Tequisistlán
Juchitán de Zaragoza
Niltepec
San José del Progreso
Puerto Escondido
Salina Cruz
Santiago Astata
Puerto Ángel
Frontera
Paraíso
Cárdenas
Villahermosa
Huimanguillo
Macuspana
Emiliano Zapata
Candelaria
Teapa
Pichucalco
Vol. Chichón 2350 m
Tenosique de Pino Suárez
Amatán
Ococingo
Tuxtla Gutiérrez
Soyaló
San Cristóbal de las Casas
Teopisca
Cintalapa de Figueroa
San Pedro Tapanatepec
Arriaga
Villa Flores
Tonalá
Comitán de Domínguez
Puerto Arista
Tres Picos
Pijijiapan
Ciudad Cuauhtémoc
Escuintla
Huixtla
Tapachula
Ciudad del Carmen
Laguna de Términos
Isla de Aguada
Sabancuy
Champotón
Pital
Francisco Escárcega
Campeche
Seybaplaya
Hopelchén
Dzibalchén
Pixoyal
Silvituc
Hecelchakán
Calkiní
Maxcanú
Umán
Mérida
Sisal
Progreso
Telchac Puerto
Dzilam de Bravo
Río Lagartos
El Cuyo
Panabá
Tizimín
Temax
Tixkokob
Acancéh
Calotmul
Sotuta
Piste
Valladolid
Muna
Ticul
Tekax
Peto
Santa Rosa
Cabo Catoche
Cancún
Cozumel
Isla Cozumel
Vigía Chico
Felipe Carrillo Puerto
Punta Herrero
Chunhuhub
Valle Hermoso
Bacalar
Chetumal
Tomás Garrido
Corozal
Orange Walk
San Pedro
Belmopan
Belize
Turneffe I.
San Ignacio
Dangriga
1120 m Victoria Peak
San Antonio
Punta Gorda
Carmelita
Uaxactún
Paso Caballos
Ciudad Melchor de Mencos
La Libertad
Lago Petén Itzá
Flores
Sayaxché
Dolores
San Luis
Chinajá
Barillas
Huehuetenango
4093 m Vol. Tacaná
Vol. Tajumulco 4220 m
Cunén
Cobán
Salamá
San Marcos
Sololá
Quezaltenango
Mazatenango
Retalhuleu
Santa Lucía Cotzumalguapa
Mixco
Guatemala
Escuintla
Jalapa
Jutiapa
Puerto San José
Sipacate
El Progreso
Zacapa
Panzós
Quebradas
Livingston
El Estor
Morales
Puerto Barrios
Chiquimula
Santa Rosa de Copán
Gracias
Cerro Las Minas 2849 m
Ocotepeque
Cerro El Pital 2730 m
La Esperanza
Ahuachapán
Sonsonate
Santa Ana
Chalatenango
Cojutepeque
Sensuntepeque
Nueva San Salvador (Santa Tecla)
San Salvador
San Vicente
Usulután
San Miguel
Golfo de Fonseca
Punta Cosigüina
Puerto Cortés
Tela
La Ceiba
San Pedro Sula
Pico Bonito 2435 m
Savá
Olanchito
El Progreso
Santa Bárbara
Yoro
Trujillo
Limón
Islas de la Bahía
Roatán
Guanaja
Punta
Brus Laguna
Dulce Nombre de Culmí
Puerto Le
Siguatepeque
Comayagua
Juticalpa
Guaimaca
Azacualpa
Tegucigalpa
San Juancito
Waspán
Danlí
Bonanza
Siuna
Jalapa
Pico Mogotón 2107 m
Nacaome
Ocotal
Somoto
Condega
1650 m Cerro Saslaya
Choluteca
Potosí
Estelí
Jinotega
Somotillo
Darío
Matagalpa
Chinandega
Telica
El Jicaral
León
Lago de Managua
Boaco
Santo Domingo
Laguna de Perlas
Poneloya
Tipitapa
Juigalpa
Managua
Masaya
Granada
Acoyapa
Masachapa
Jinotepe
Lago de Nicaragua
Rivas
San Juan del Sur
San Carlos
Cabo Santa Elena
2028 m Vol. Miravalles
Liberia
Filadelfia
Altamira
Puerto Jesús
Alajuela
Puntarenas
San José
Cabo Blanco
Golfo de Nicoya
Parrita
Bahía de Coronado
Ciudad Co
Minas de Matahambre
Guane
Cabo San Antonio
La Fé
Cabo Corrientes
BAHAMAS
Grand Bahama
Cooper's Town
Marsh Harbour
Abaco
Freeport
High Rock
Cherokee Sound
Northwest Providence Channel
Northeast Providence Channel
Eleuthera Island
New Providence
Governor's Harbour
Nassau
Mastic Point
Staniard Creek
Andros Town
Rock Sound
Arthur's Town
Cat Island
Bannerman Town
Andros Island
Mangrove Cay
Kemps Bay
Port Howe
Cockburn Town
San Salvador
Great Exuma Island
George Town
Rum Cay
Port Nelson
Long Island
F
G
1
2
76°
24°

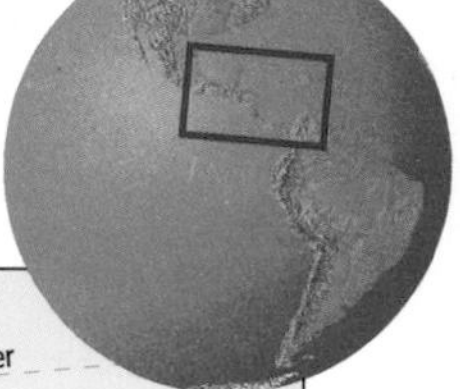

E 80° F 76° G 72° H

Tropic of Cancer

BAHAMAS

Mangrove Cay
Kemps Bay
Port Howe
Cockburn Town
San Salvador
Rum Cay
Port Nelson

Andros Island

Great Exuma Island
George Town
Long Island
Crooked Island

Clarence Town
Mortimers
Colonel Hill
Acklins Island
Snug Corner

Mayaguana Island
Little Inagua Island
Northeast Pt
Great Inagua Island
Matthew Town

TURKS AND CAICOS ISLANDS (U.K.)
Caicos Islands
Grand Turk
Cockburn Harbour
Turks Islands
Turks Island Passage

Guanabacoa
Matanzas
Güines
Cárdenas
Colón
Sagua la Grande
Caibarién
Artemisa
Santa Clara
Jagüey Grande
Pico San Juan 1156 m
Cabaiguán
Morón
Esmeralda
Cayo Romano
Cienfuegos
Sancti Spíritus
Ciego de Ávila
Nuevitas
Cayo Sabinal
Trinidad
Cabo de los Canarreros
Cayos Vertientes
Cinco Balas
Santa Cruz del Sur
Camagüey
Puerto Padre
Guáimaro
Gibara
Cabo Lucrecia
Banes
Cayo Largo
Cayo del Rosario
Archipiélago de los Jardines de la Reina
Las Tunas
Holguín
Cueto
Moa
Sagua de Tánamo
Golfo de Guacanayabo
Bayamo
Palma Soriano
Baracoa
Maisí
Manzanillo
Sierra Maestra
Pico Turquino 1974 m
Guantánamo

CUBA
GREATER

Cayman Brac
Little Cayman
Cabo Cruz
Pilón
Santiago de Cuba
Cabo Cruz

Grand Cayman
George Town
CAYMAN ISLANDS (U.K.)

ANTILLES

Île de la Tortue
Monte Cristi
Cabo Isabela
Puerto Plata
Cabrera
Bahía Escocesa
Cap-Haïtien
Port-de-Paix
Fort Liberté
Santiago
Moca
San Francisco de Macorís
La Vega
Gonaïves
Saint-Marc
Hinche
Comendador
Bonao
Monte Plata
El Seibo
Cabo Engaño
HAITI
Port-au-Prince
Pico Duarte 3175 m
San Juan
San Pedro de Macorís
Hato Mayor
La Romana
DOMINICAN REPUBLIC
Jimaní
Neiba
Azua
San Cristóbal
Santo Domingo
Isla Saona
Golfe de la Gonâve
Île de la Gonâve
Dame-Marie
Jérémie
Petit Goâve
Tiburon
Massif de la Hotte
Pic de la Selle 2680 m
Barahona
Punta Salinas
NAVASSA ISLAND (U.S.A.)
Port-à-Piment
Bainet
Jacmel
Pedernales
Les Cayes
Cabo Beata

Montego Bay
Falmouth
South Negril Pt
Ocho Ríos
Savanna-la-Mar
JAMAICA
Port Antonio
Mandeville
Blue Mtn Pk 2256 m
Black River
Spanish Town
Kingston
Portland Pt

Jamaica Channel
Windward Passage
Cayman Trench
Cayman Trench

HISPANIOLA

CARIBBEAN
SEA

Providencia (Col.)
San Andrés (Col.)

os Miskitos (Nic.)

ARUBA (Neth.)
Oranjestad
Curaçao
Willemstad
Pta Gallinas
Pen. de Paraguaná
Cabo de la Vela
Puerto Estrella
C. San Román
Península de Guajira
Pueblo Nuevo
Carrizal
Uribia
Los Taques
Punto Fijo
Puerto Cumarebo
Ríohacha
Maicao
Golfo de Venezuela
Coro
Piritu
Jacura
Santa Marta
Carraipía
Paraguaipoa
Churuguara
Barranquilla
Ciénaga
Tule
Casigua
Pedregal
Puerto Colombia
P. Cristóbal Colón
Barrancas
San Rafael Santa Rita
Dabajuro
Baragua
Baranoa
Soledad
5775 m
Villanueva
Campo Mara
Mene de Mauroa
Sabanalarga
Fundación
Agustín Codazzi
Maracaibo
Cerro El Cerrón 1990 m
Carora
Yaritagua
Cartagena
Valledupar
Rosario
Cabimas
Turbaco
Pivijay
La Jagua de Ibirico
Machiques
Barquisimeto
Arjona
Calamar
Lagunillas
Mene Grande
El Tocuyo
El Carmen de Bolívar
Plato
El Difícil
Chiriguaná
Barranquitas
Lago de Maracaibo
Trujillo
Acarigua
Sincelejo
Sincé
Mompós
El Banco
San Carlos del Zulia
Betijoque
Boconó
Guanare
Portobelo
Palenque
El Porvenir
Arch. de San Blás
Golfo del Darién
Tolú
Magangué
Tamalameque
Encontrados
Mérida
Valera
Barinas
Guanarito
Colón
Ailigandí
Lorica
Sucre
San Gil
Casigua
Pico Bolívar 5007 m
Obispos
Golfo de los Mosquitos
PANAMA
Lago Gatún
Chimán
Puerto Rey
Cereté
Sahagún
La Gloria
El Vigía
Obispos
Coclé del Norte
Panama Canal
Panamá
San Miguelito
Puerto Obaldía
Montería
Planeta Rica
Simití
Ocaña
San Carlos del Zulia
La Fría
Puerto de Nutrias
Volcán Barú 3475 m
La Chorrera
San Miguel
Acandí
Ayapel
Caucasia
Sardinata
Tovar
David
Penonomé
Antón
Isla del Rey
Yaviza
Turbo
Tierralta
Cáceres
Cúcuta
San Antonio de Caparo
Santa Catalina
Cordillera Central
Aguadulce
La Palma
El Real
Cáchira
San Cristóbal
Pedraza La Vieja
San Francisco
Chitré
I. San José
Garachiné
Zaragoza
Chinácota
Soná
Atalaya
Serr. de San Jerónimo
COLOMBIA
Pamplona
Palmarito
Los Santos
Jaqué
Chigorodó
Palo de las Letras
Dabeiba
Ituango
Segovia
Bucaramanga
Cubará
Mantecal
Golfo de Chiriquí
Las Tablas
Pedasí
Riosucio
Paramillo 3960 m
Yarumal
Amalfi
Zapatoca
Guasdualito
Arauquita
Punta Mala
Golfo de Panamá
Jurado
Antioquia
Floridablanca
Sierra Nevada del Cocuy 5493 m
Tame
Arauca
Isla de Coiba
Tonosí
Cupica
Anzá
Cisneros
Puerto Berrío
Socorro
El Cocuy
Puerto Rondón
Cravo Norte
Isla de Cébaco
Golfo de Cupica
Pta Logos
Medellín
Bello
San Gil
Puerto Nuevo
Punta Mariato

1:7,000,000

Projection: Lambert Conformal Conic

100 200 300 400 kilometers

100 200 miles

Mexico

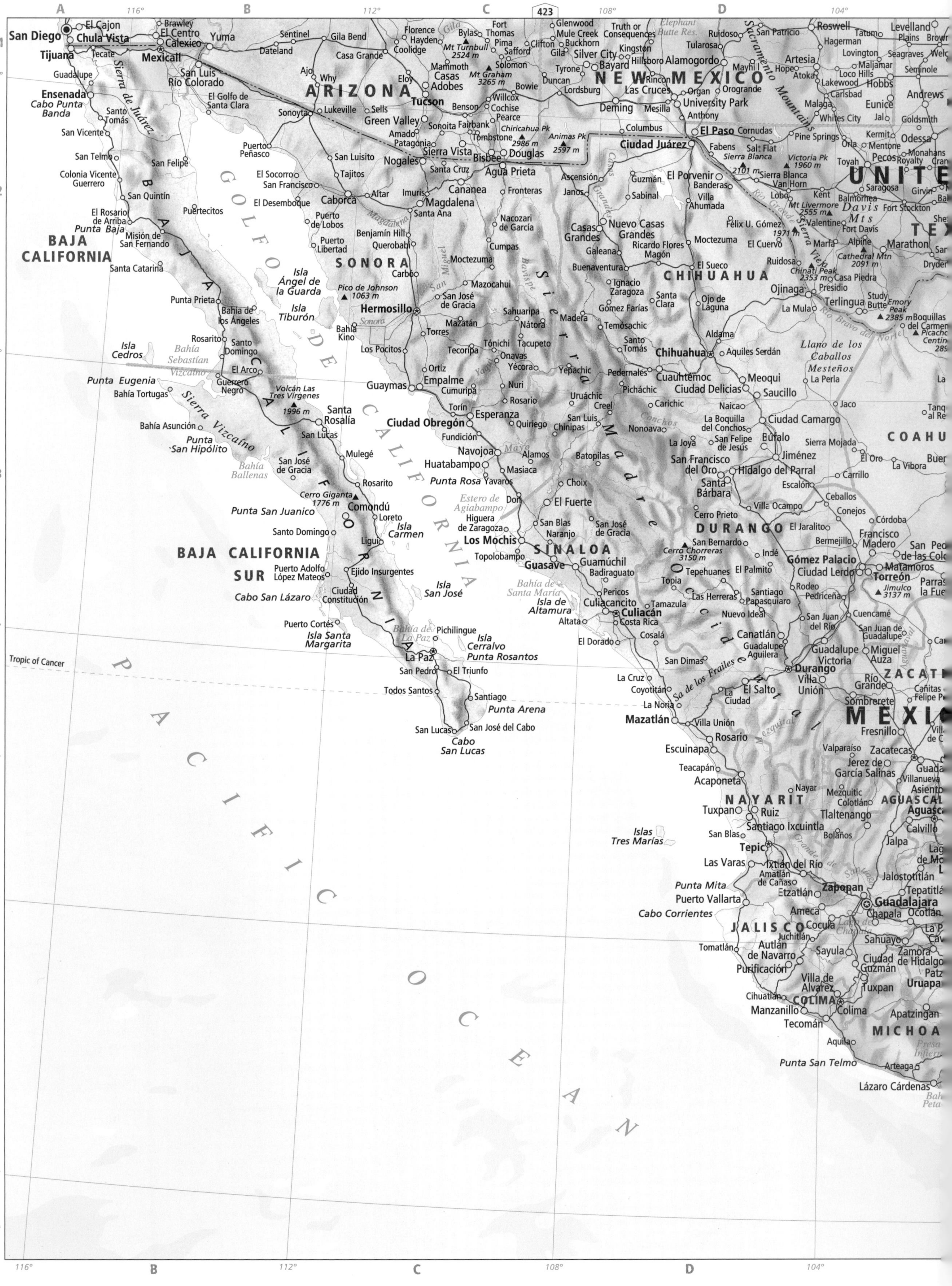

423

A B C D
116° 112° 108° 104°
32° 28° 24° 20° 16°
1 2 3 4 5 6

San Diego
Chula Vista
Tijuana
Tecate
El Cajon
Brawley
El Centro
Calexico
Mexicali
Yuma
San Luis Río Colorado
El Golfo de Santa Clara
Guadalupe
Ensenada
Cabo Punta Banda
Santo Tomás
San Vicente
San Telmo
San Felipe
Colonia Vicente Guerrero
San Quintín
El Rosario de Arriba
Punta Baja
Misión de San Fernando
Puertecitos
BAJA CALIFORNIA
Santa Catarina
Sierra de Juárez
Punta Prieta
Bahía de los Ángeles
Rosarito
Santo Domingo
Isla Cedros
Bahía Sebastián Vizcaíno
El Arco
Punta Eugenia
Guerrero Negro
Bahía Tortugas
Volcán Las Tres Vírgenes 1996 m
Santa Rosalía
San Lucas
Bahía Asunción
Sierra Vizcaíno
Punta San Hipólito
San José de Gracia
Mulegé
Bahía Ballenas
Rosarito
Cerro Giganta 1776 m
Comondú
Loreto
Isla Carmen
Punta San Juanico
Santo Domingo
Ligüí
BAJA CALIFORNIA SUR
Puerto Adolfo López Mateos
Ejido Insurgentes
Cabo San Lázaro
Ciudad Constitución
Isla San José
Puerto Cortés
Isla Santa Margarita
Bahía de La Paz
Pichilingue
Isla Cerralvo
Punta Rosantos
La Paz
San Pedro
El Triunfo
Todos Santos
Santiago
Punta Arena
San Lucas
San José del Cabo
Cabo San Lucas
Tropic of Cancer
GOLFO DE CALIFORNIA
PACIFIC OCEAN
Sentinel
Gila Bend
Dateland
Casa Grande
Florence
Hayden
Coolidge
Ajo
Why
Eloy
Mammoth
Casas Adobes
ARIZONA
Tucson
Lukeville
Sells
Sonoyta
Green Valley
Benson
Sonoita
Fairbank
Amado
Patagonia
Tombstone
Sierra Vista
Bisbee
Douglas
Nogales
Santa Cruz
Agua Prieta
Puerto Peñasco
San Luisito
Tajitos
El Socorro
San Francisco
El Desemboque
Caborca
Altar
Imuris
Cananea
Fronteras
Magdalena
Santa Ana
Puerto de Lobos
Puerto Libertad
Benjamín Hill
Querobabi
Nacozari de García
Cumpas
SONORA
Moctezuma
Carbó
Isla Ángel de la Guarda
Pico de Johnson 1063 m
Mazocahui
San José de Gracia
Isla Tiburón
Hermosillo
Bahía Kino
Sahuaripa
Nátora
Mazatán
Torres
Los Pocitos
Tecoripa
Tónichi
Tacupeto
Onavas
Yécora
Ortiz
Empalme
Guaymas
Cumuripa
Nuri
Rosario
Torín
Esperanza
Quiriego
Ciudad Obregón
Fundición
Navojoa
Álamos
Huatabampo
Masiaca
Punta Rosa
Yavaros
Estero de Agiabampo
Don
El Fuerte
Higuera de Zaragoza
San Blas
Naranjo
Los Mochis
Topolobampo
SINALOA
Guasave
Guamúchil
Badiraguato
Bahía de Santa María
Isla de Altamura
Pericos
Culiacancito
Culiacán
Tamazula
Altata
Costa Rica
Cosalá
El Dorado
San Dimas
La Cruz
Coyotitán
La Noria
Mazatlán
Villa Unión
Rosario
Escuinapa
Teacapán
Acaponeta
NAYARIT
Tuxpan
Ruiz
Santiago Ixcuintla
San Blas
Tepic
Islas Tres Marías
Las Varas
Ixtlán del Río
Amatlán de Cañas
Punta Mita
Puerto Vallarta
Cabo Corrientes
JALISCO
Tomatlán
Autlán de Navarro
Purificación
Cihuatlán
Manzanillo
COLIMA
Colima
Tecomán
Aquila
Punta San Telmo
Arteaga
Lázaro Cárdenas
Mt Turnbull 2524 m
Mt Graham 3265 m
Bylas
Fort Thomas
Pima
Safford
Solomon
Bowie
Willcox
Cochise
Pearce
Chiricahua Pk 2986 m
Animas Pk 2597 m
Glenwood
Mule Creek
Buckhorn
Clifton
Gila
Silver City
Bayard
Tyrone
Duncan
Lordsburg
Truth or Consequences
Kingston
Hillsboro
Deming
Columbus
NEW MEXICO
Las Cruces
Mesilla
Organ
Orogrande
University Park
Anthony
Alamogordo
Tularosa
Ruidoso
San Patricio
Elephant Butte Res.
Sacramento Mountains
Mayhill
Hope
Artesia
Roswell
El Paso
Ciudad Juárez
Fabens
Cornudas
Salt Flat
Sierra Blanca
Van Horn
Ascensión
Janos
Guzmán
Sabinal
El Porvenir
Banderas
Villa Ahumada
Casas Grandes
Nuevo Casas Grandes
Galeana
Ricardo Flores Magón
Moctezuma
Buenaventura
El Sueco
CHIHUAHUA
Ignacio Zaragoza
Gómez Farías
Santa Clara
Ojo de Laguna
Madera
Temósachic
Santo Tomás
Chihuahua
Aldama
Aquiles Serdán
Yepachic
Pedernales
Cuauhtémoc
Pichachic
Uruáchic
Creel
Carichic
Ciudad Delicias
Meoqui
Saucillo
San Luis
Chínipas
Nonoava
Naica
La Boquilla del Conchos
Ciudad Camargo
La Joya
San Felipe de Jesús
Búfalo
Batopilas
Jiménez
San Francisco del Oro
Hidalgo del Parral
Santa Bárbara
Choix
Villa Ocampo
Cerro Prieto
DURANGO
San Bernardo
Cerro Chorreras 3150 m
Tepehuanes
El Palmito
Indé
Topia
Las Herreras
Santiago Papasquiaro
Nuevo Ideal
Canatlán
Guadalupe Aguilera
Durango
Villa Unión
El Salto
La Ciudad
Sierra Madre Occidental
Sierra de los Frailes
Félix U. Gómez
El Cuervo
Ruidosa
Chinati Peak 2353 m
Presidio
Ojinaga
Casa Piedra
Terlingua
Study Butte
Emory Peak 2385 m
Boquillas del Carmen
La Mula
Llano de los Caballos Mesteños
La Perla
Jaco
Sierra Mojada
El Oro
La Vibora
Carrillo
Escalón
Ceballos
Conejos
Córdoba
El Jaralito
Bermejillo
Francisco I. Madero
Gómez Palacio
Ciudad Lerdo
Torreón
Matamoros
Rodeo
Pedriceña
Cuencamé
San Juan del Río
San Juan de Guadalupe
Guadalupe Victoria
Miguel Auza
Río Grande
Sombrerete
MEXICO
Fresnillo
Valparaíso
Zacatecas
Jerez de García Salinas
Nayar
Mezquitic
Colotlán
Tlaltenango
Bolaños
AGUASCALIENTES
Aguascalientes
Calvillo
Jalpa
Jalostotitlán
Tepatitlán
Zapopan
Guadalajara
Etzatlán
Ameca
Cocula
Chapala
Ocotlán
Juchitlán
Sayula
Sahuayo
Zamora
Ciudad Guzmán
Villa de Álvarez
Tuxpan
Uruapan
Apatzingán
MICHOACÁN
Hobbs
Carlsbad
Lovington
Eunice
Jal
Kermit
Odessa
Pecos
Toyah
Balmorhea
Davis Mts
Fort Davis
Marfa
Alpine
Marathon
Cathedral Mtn 2091 m
Mt Livermore 2555 m
Valentine
Victoria Pk 1960 m
Kent
Lobo
UNITED STATES
TEXAS

ARKANSAS
MISSISSIPPI
ALABAMA
LOUISIANA
UNITED STATES OF AMERICA
GULF OF MEXICO
Bahía de Campeche
Tropic of Cancer
NUEVO LEÓN
TAMAULIPAS
SAN LUIS POTOSÍ
VERACRUZ
HIDALGO
QUERÉTARO
MÉXICO
TLAXCALA
PUEBLA
MORELOS
GUERRERO
OAXACA
CHIAPAS
TABASCO
CAMPECHE
YUCATÁN
QUINTANA ROO
BELIZE
GUATEMALA
HONDURAS
Península de Yucatán
Golfo de Tehuantepec
Golfo de Honduras
Dallas
Houston
San Antonio
New Orleans
Baton Rouge
Corpus Christi
Monterrey
Matamoros
Ciudad Victoria
Tampico
Veracruz
México
Puebla de Zaragoza
Oaxaca de Juárez
Acapulco
Villahermosa
Campeche
Mérida
Cancún
Chetumal
Belmopan
Jackson
Montgomery
Mobile
Matagorda I.
Padre I.
Chandeleur Is
424
428
100°
96°
92°
88°
28°
24°
20°
16°
F
G
H
J
1
2
3
4
5
6
0 100 200 300 400 kilometers
0 100 200 miles
Scale 1:7,000,000
Projection: Lambert Conformal Conic

North and Central America

South America

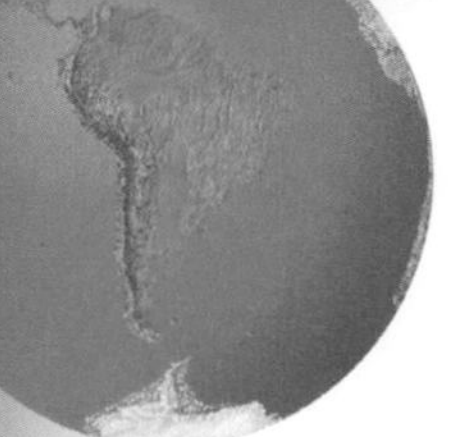

South America

South America has a land area of 17.6 million sq km (6.9 million sq miles). To its east lies the Atlantic Ocean and to its west is the Pacific. South America is triangular in shape, tapering southward.

The countries that make up the continent had their boundaries determined by the colonial powers that engulfed the entire continent from the sixteenth century onwards. Most of the continent was divided between Spain and Portugal. Portugal established the largest South American colony, Brazil, while Spain claimed most of the remaining area. The Spanish colonies were Venezuela, Colombia, Ecuador, Peru, Bolivia, Chile, Argentina, Uruguay, and Paraguay. In the north, three comparatively small countries were created by Britain, France, and the Netherlands: Guyana, French Guiana, and Suriname respectively.

Physical features

The Andes Mountains, which arose when the South American and Pacific plates collided, form an elongated zone along the continent's western margin. The range, which is prone to earthquakes and volcanic eruptions, is narrow in the north, broadens out into a high plateau at 4,000 m (13,000 ft) in the center, where Lake Titicaca is situated, and narrows again toward the south.

The basin of the Amazon River, which is 6,570 km (4,080 miles) long, covers 8 million sq km (3 million sq miles) in equatorial South America. It is bordered to the south by the Mato Grosso Plateau and the highlands of Brazil, and to the north by the Guyana Highlands. Angel Falls, which at 979 m (3,212 ft) is the world's highest waterfall, is in Venezuela.

Climate and vegetation

The continent stretches from the tropics to the sub-polar zones and is climatically diverse. The tropics cover a large area in the north, with the southern part being more temperate.

The broad humid tropical zone is characterized by extensive forests in Brazil, Guyana, and Venezuela, and includes the world's largest remaining rainforest, the Amazon. Vast areas of this zone have been cleared for agriculture—mainly sugarcane plantations and cattle ranches. Currently, the Amazon forests are under threat from logging and from the spread of agriculture and settlement, and are rapidly diminishing in size. The Amazon is rich in wildlife and contains a large number of plant species unique to the area.

In the north of the continent, where wet and dry seasons alternate, the forest trees are deciduous. In areas where there is little rainfall shrubs and thorny vegetation prevail. The subtropical and temperate areas in the south of the continent are marked by extensive grasslands, with dispersed trees, as in the pampas of Argentina and in Patagonia. Toward the west lie desert areas, where vegetation is sparse.

In the central Andes rainfall is concentrated on the eastern slopes, which are forested, though much deforestation has occurred. Along the arid western side, the sparse vegetation is generally thorny shrubs and animal life is limited. The driest region of all is the Atacama Desert in Chile. There are cool temperate rainforests in southern Chile.

South America has abundant wildlife, including llamas, anteaters, armadillos, and iguanas. The giant anteater and giant armadillo are endangered species. Several unique species inhabit the Galapagos Islands, including the giant tortoise and the marine iguana. The seas off the west coast of temperate South America are rich in marine life due to the nutrient-rich cold waters of the Peru Current.

Population

South America's population is about 347 million (2000). Its relatively high living standards are

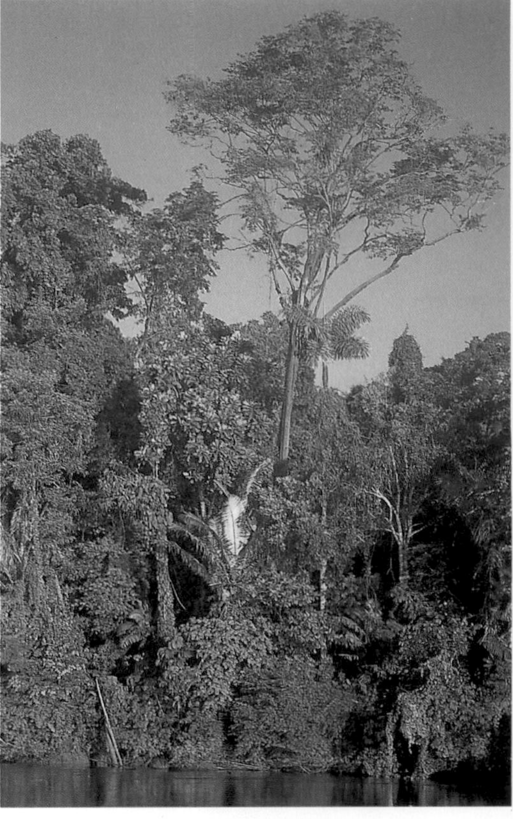

reflected by life expectancies of 66.5 years for males and 73.9 years for females. The current population growth rate is 1.4 percent per year.

The original inhabitants of the continent were Amerindians who, it is believed, migrated from Asia across the Bering Straits. From the seventeenth century, settlers from Portugal and Spain immigrated in considerable numbers, bringing in Africans to work as agricultural labor. In the twentieth century, while migration from Europe was predominant, migrants also came from Asia. People of Italian descent are significant in Argentina, and Japanese people form locally important groups in Brazil and Peru.

The continent is highly urbanized—79.6 percent of the population lives in urban areas. Within the last fifty years, large numbers of people have moved to cities such as São Paulo (population 18 million), Buenos Aires (12.7 million), Rio de Janeiro (10.6 million), and Lima (6 million). The result is urban congestion and the spread of shanty towns amid modern cities.

Agriculture

Several agricultural products, including maize, cashews, peanuts, avocadoes, and cacao, were grown in South America before the coming of the Europeans. Rubber-producing plants also grew there. Agriculture was extensively established when the continent was colonized, with crops including introduced species such as rice, wheat, sugarcane, coffee, bananas, and citrus fruits.

The tropical north of the continent produces sugar, bananas, mangoes, and rubber; wheat and temperate fruits are grown in the temperate south. Introduced animals provide the bulk of livestock; cattle are raised in a range of climate areas, and sheep are raised in the temperate grasslands. Among the indigenous animals reared are llamas and alpacas; alpacas are prized for their wool.

The Moreno Glacier in Argentina (left). An example of the richness of the diminishing Amazon jungle, in Ecuador (above). Tierra del Fuego, Argentina (previous pages).

Nations

Dependencies & territories

A view of the Lake District in Chile (above), and fishing boats of the minority Uru people, in Peru (left). The blue-footed booby (below), from the Galapagos Islands, and the statue carving site on Easter Island, off Ecuador (below, right).

Irrigation is important in certain regions, particularly in the west—Ecuador, Peru, and Chile. It is also of significance in Argentina.

Much of the forested areas of South America are logged for their timber. This is particularly the case in the Amazon, and conservationists worldwide are voicing their concern about the rate at which the forest is being lost. Tropical hardwoods are exported.

Illegal cultivation of narcotic drugs, particularly in Colombia, is also a matter of world concern.

Industrialization

South America is endowed with significant mineral deposits, such as tin in Bolivia, iron ore in Brazil, and petroleum in Venezuela. Large quantities of metallic ores are exported, though iron ore is used in Brazil for steel manufacture.

Industrialization has accelerated in South America since the 1950s, as a result of increased electricity generation; much of the continent's hydroelectric potential has been harnessed.

Manufacturing ranges from food processing to metal and chemical industries. Consumer items such as textiles, clothing, and footwear, as well as more expensive items such as automobiles, are manufactured both for the domestic market and for export.

Languages

The original inhabitants, the Amerindians, belong to various groups and have several languages. Although many no longer speak those languages, in some areas large numbers still do—Guaraní is widespread in Paraguay, for example. The official languages in South America are now those introduced by the colonial powers: Portuguese in Brazil, Spanish in most other countries, English in Guyana, Dutch in Suriname, and French in Guiana. In Guyana and Suriname, South Asian languages—principally Hindi—are also significant. Government, education, and the media predominantly use introduced European languages.

Boundary disputes and wars

There are currently no major boundary disputes or wars in South America; there was little conflict between the continent's countries during the twentieth century. However, there was considerable civil strife between guerilla groups and governments in several countries—Uruguay, Colombia, and Peru, for example. Armed drug cartels in Colombia also remain a major problem.

In some countries, notably Chile and Argentina, there have been periods of dictatorship during which the military have played a large role in government. During these periods there has been considerable loss of civilian lives.

In 1982 Argentina invaded the United Kingdom-ruled Falkland Islands (Islas Malvinas). After more than 1,000 people lost their lives in the ensuing war, and after international pressure, the islands were returned to United Kingdom rule.

South America

Colombia

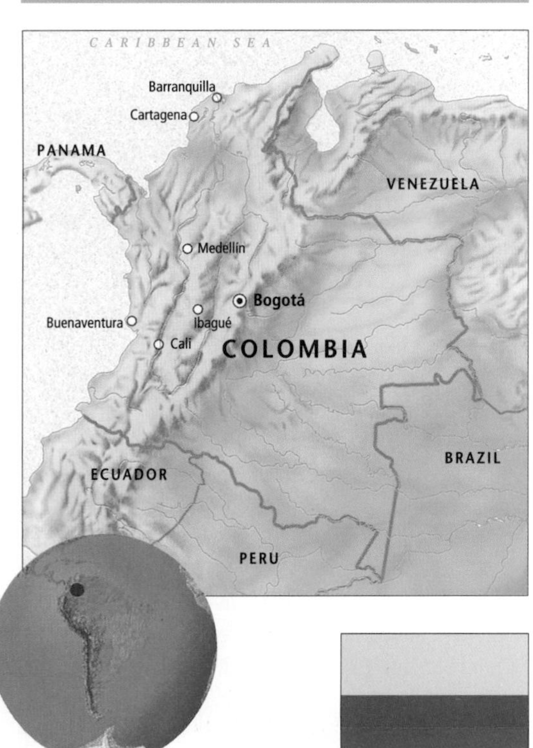

Fact File

Official name Republic of Colombia

Form of government Republic with two legislative bodies (Senate and House of Representatives)

Capital Bogotá

Area 1,138,910 sq km (439,733 sq miles)

Time zone GMT – 5 hours

Population 41,009,000

Projected population 2015 52,641,000

Population density 36 per sq km (93.3 per sq mile)

Life expectancy 70.9

Infant mortality (per 1,000) 23.2

Official language Spanish

Literacy rate 91.3 %

Religions Roman Catholic 95 %, other 5 %

Ethnic groups Mixed indigenous-European 58 %, European 20 %, mixed European-African 14 %, African 4 %, mixed indigenous-African 3 %, indigenous 1 %

Currency Colombian peso

Economy Services 46 %, agriculture 30 %, industry 24 %

GNP per capita US$ 6,300

Climate Tropical along coast and on plains, cool to sometimes cold in highlands

Highest point Pico Cristobál Colón 5,775 m (18,947 ft)

Map reference Pages 450–51

Visited by Hojeda and Vespucci in 1499 and named after Columbus, Colombia straddles the South American continent south of the isthmus of Panama. Once the home of the Chibcha Indians, the country came under Spanish control in 1544, after which it became their chief source of gold. Colombia achieved independence in 1819. From that time on the political and economic fortunes of the country have been contested by the anti-clerical free-trading Liberals and the Conservatives, upholders of protectionism and the Church. While Colombia is notorious for its drug cartels and exports of cocaine, it has a diversified and stable economy that has, for thirty years, shown Latin America's most consistent record of growth.

The country can be divided into three regions. The hot, wet Pacific lowlands run south from the Panamanian border; to the north they merge into drier lowlands along the Caribbean. The cities that face the Caribbean—Barranquilla, Santa Marta, and Cartagena—are tourist resorts. Inland, the parallel Andean ranges running north from the Ecuadorian border define the second region, the high valleys of the Cauca and Magdalena Rivers. This is where most people live. The third region comprises the foothills east of the Andes, where the land falls away into the forested basins of the Amazon and Orinoco Rivers. This region amounts to almost two-thirds of Colombia's area but only a few cattle ranchers and Indians live here.

With Latin America's largest proven reserves of coal, Colombia is the region's biggest coal exporter. Some eighty percent of the world's emeralds also come from here. Oil, however, remains the biggest legitimate revenue-earning export. Since 1990 growth in gross domestic product has averaged four percent annually, led by expanding construction and financial service industries, and inflows of foreign capital. Nevertheless, earnings from processed cocaine probably exceed all others. Problems include a poverty index of forty percent, and a continuing political crisis related to allegations of drug connections at high levels.

Venezuela

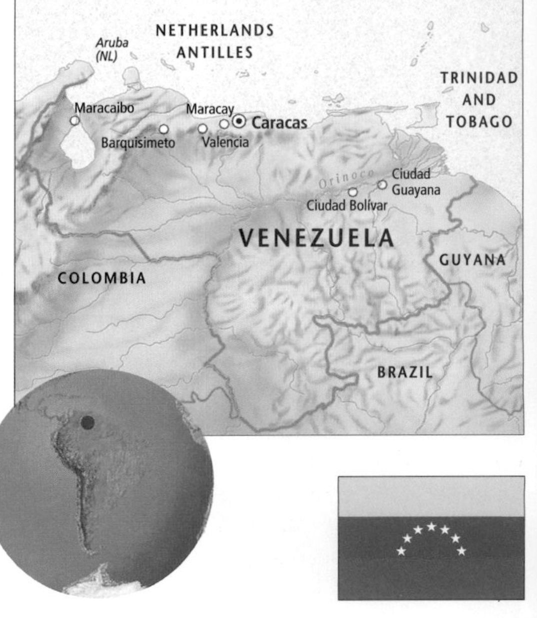

Fact File

Official name Republic of Venezuela

Form of government Federal republic with two legislative bodies (Senate and Chamber of Deputies)

Capital Caracas

Area 912,050 sq km (352,142 sq miles)

Time zone GMT – 4 hours

Population 24,288,000

Projected population 2015 30,877,000

Population density 26.6 per sq km (69 per sq mile)

Life expectancy 73.6

Infant mortality (per 1,000) 24.6

Official language Spanish

Other languages Indigenous languages

Literacy rate 91.1 %

Religions Roman Catholic 96 %, Protestant 2 %, other 2 %

Ethnic groups Mixed indigenous-European 67 %, European 21 %, African 10 %, indigenous 2 %

Currency Bolívar

Economy Services 63 %, industry 25 %, agriculture 12 %

GNP per capita US$ 6,100

Climate Tropical, with dry season December to April; cooler in highlands

Highest point Pico Bolívar 5,007 m (16,427 ft)

Map reference Pages 450–51

Venezuela is on the north coast of South America. When the first Spaniards arrived in 1499 they named it "New Venice" because the Indian stilt houses built in the water of Lake Maracaibo reminded them of the Italian city. The liberator Simon Bolivar was a Venezuelan general, the military campaign he led resulting in the country becoming independent in 1821. For the next century Venezuela's economy was largely based on agriculture, but in the 1920s it took a new direction with the development of a petroleum industry. In the last eighty years great wealth (unevenly shared) followed by industrialization have produced one of Latin America's most urbanized societies. Out of every twenty Venezuelans, seventeen are city-dwellers, and migration from the countryside left much of the interior depopulated.

Confident that oil revenues would never end, the Venezuelan government expanded the economic role of the state, even buying hotels. Falling oil prices in the early 1980s produced a fiscal crisis, and in 1991 a program of cutbacks and austerity measures triggered street riots in which hundreds died. Two attempted coups took place during 1992. Since that time there has been a concerted effort to achieve economic diversification and to cut back the state sector. In 1999 a new constitution was installed to create more stability, but a short-lived coup in 2002 and fights between government forces and opposition in 2003 shook the country.

The hot lowlands surrounding Lake Maracaibo in the far northwest comprise one of the areas of greatest population density. In this region abundant electricity from oil-fired generators provides power for light industry: food processing, pharmaceuticals, electrical equipment, and machinery. A spur of the northern Andes divides the Maracaibo Basin from the drainage system of the Orinoco to the east. Here are the lowland plains of the Llanos, savanna country used for cattle grazing. Much of the Llanos floods during the summer rains, especially in the west, though it is dry for the rest of the year. To the south is the vast granite plateau of the Guiana Highlands, and the highest waterfall in the world—Angel Falls (979 m; 3,212 ft).

Despite fluctuations in oil prices, petroleum continues to provide over seventy percent of Venezuela's export earnings and 45 percent of government revenue. Other minerals exported include iron ore, gold, and diamonds. The main cash crops are coffee, sugarcane, and tobacco; food crops include bananas, sorghum, and maize. Only five percent of arable land is cultivated, and agriculture supplies little more than seventy percent of the country's needs. In the 1990s, economic reforms proposed by the IMF were rejected by the president, who responded by defending exchange controls and other regulatory measures.

Guyana

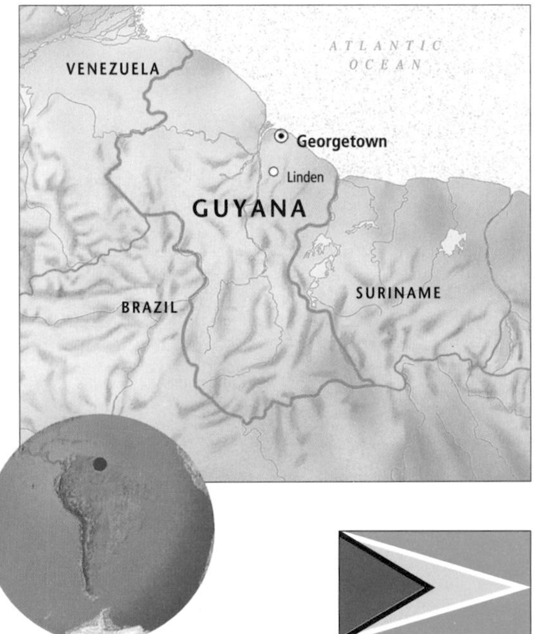

Fact File

Official name Cooperative Republic of Guyana

Form of government Republic with single legislative body (National Assembly)

Capital Georgetown

Area 214,970 sq km (83,000 sq miles)

Time zone GMT – 3 hours

Population 698,000

Projected population 2015 749,000

Population density 3.2 per sq km (8.4 per sq mile)

Life expectancy 62.6

Infant mortality (per 1,000) 38.4

Official language English

Other languages Amerindian languages, Hindi, Urdu

Literacy rate 97.9%

Religions Protestant 34 %, Hindu 34 %, Roman Catholic 18 %, Muslim 9 %, other 5 %

Ethnic groups East Indian 51 %, African and mixed indigenous-African 43 %, indigenous 4 %, European and Chinese 2 %

Currency Guyana dollar

Economy Industry 44 %, agriculture 34 %, services 22%

GNP per capita US$ 3,600

Climate Tropical with two rainy seasons (May to mid-August, mid-November to mid-January)

Highest point Mt Roraima 2,810 m (9,219 ft)

Map reference Page 451

Guyana means "the land of many waters". In 1616 it was settled by the Dutch, who built dikes, reclaimed coastal land, and planted sugarcane. When the indigenous people refused to work in the sugar plantations the Dutch, and later the British, imported slaves from Africa and indentured labor from India. The contrast between the communities descended from these two immigrant groups defines today's Guyanese political life. Beginning in 1953, and sharpened by independence in 1966, a struggle for dominance continues between the Afro-Guyanese and the numerically superior Indo-Guyanese. Until the early 1990s Guyana was ruled mostly by leftist governments. In the country's first free and fair elections in 1992 Cheddi Jagan was elected president. After his death in 1997 he was succeeded by his wife Janet who resigned in 1999 due to poor health. Her successor, Bharrat Jagdeo, was reelected in 2001.

Some 95 percent of the people live on the coastal strip, and there is concern about flooding because of poor dike maintenance. The savannas, river valleys, and forested plateaus of the interior are largely unpopulated. There are, however, settlements of two neglected minorities in the forests—blacks descended from escaped slaves; and Carib, Warrau, and Arawak Amerindians.

Numerous rivers, including the country's main river, the Essequibo, flow down from the mountains in the west through tropical forests inhabited by a rich assortment of wildlife including sloth, jaguar, tapir, and capybara. There is diamond dredging in many of the rivers, and in 1995 there was a major cyanide spill at the Omai gold mine near the Essequibo. The effects of mining activities on the wildlife is of major concern to conservationists.

The mining of high-quality bauxite and sugar production accounts for eighty percent of exports. Other resources include gold, diamonds, uranium, manganese, oil, copper, and molybdenum. Under successive governments, state ownership and government controls have stunted development and made adaptation to market fluctuations difficult. The bauxite industry remains a state monopoly. Recent deregulation has, however, shown benefits. Though weak infrastructure hampers tourist development, the spectacular scenery and wildlife of the interior is attracting visitors.

Riverboats in Puerto Colombia, Colombia (left page top). A view of Caracas, the capital of Venezuela (left).

Ecuador

The volcano Cotopaxi in Ecuador (top). Pigs for sale at the market at Otavalo, Ecuador (above).

Fact File

OFFICIAL NAME Republic of Ecuador

FORM OF GOVERNMENT Republic with single legislative body (National Congress)

CAPITAL Quito

AREA 283,560 sq km (109,483 sq miles)

TIME ZONE GMT – 5 hours

POPULATION 13,445,000

PROJECTED POPULATION 2015 16,329,000

POPULATION DENSITY 47.4 per sq km (122.8 per sq mile)

LIFE EXPECTANCY 71.6

INFANT MORTALITY (PER 1,000) 33

OFFICIAL LANGUAGE Spanish

OTHER LANGUAGES Indigenous languages, particularly Quechua and Chibcha

LITERACY RATE 90.1 %

RELIGIONS Roman Catholic 95 %, other 5 %

ETHNIC GROUPS Indigenous-European 55 %, indigenous 25 %, Spanish 10 %, African 10 %

CURRENCY Sucre

ECONOMY Services 42 %, agriculture 39 %, industry 19 %

GNP PER CAPITA US$ 3,000

CLIMATE Tropical on coast and plains, cooler in highlands

HIGHEST POINT Chimborazo 6,310 m (20,702 ft)

MAP REFERENCE Page 450

Ecuador is the smallest of the Andean republics, taking its name from the equator which divides it in half. Quito was briefly an Inca city before being conquered by the Spanish in the 1530s. The city is ringed by volcanoes, including Cotopaxi (5,896 m; 19,344 ft), the world's highest active volcano. The groups of Indians that form 25 percent of the population are pressing for recognition as distinct nationalities within the state.

Ecuador's agriculture is based on the coastal plains where more than half of the arable land can be found. Bananas, coffee, and cocoa are the main crops. Most production is on haciendas—huge estates established during the early years of Spanish occupation. Inland, among the Andes, are valleys where livestock is raised. The eastern slopes of the Andes give way to forested upland and the border with Peru. This region is so little known that hostilities between Peru and Ecuador in 1995 arose partly from uncertainty as to where the frontier should be. This conflict finally was resolved in 1999. Petroleum and natural gas from this area are piped over the Andes to the Pacific port of Esmeraldas.

Ecuador grows more bananas than any other country in the world. Until overtaken by petroleum and natural gas, bananas were its biggest export earner, and access to markets in the United States and the European Union is a continuing concern. The highland Indians survive through subsistence farming, growing maize and potatoes. Recent economic reforms have helped control inflation and increased foreign investment. Growth has been uneven, however, because manufacturing is seriously handicapped by a shortage of electricity.

Ecuador owns the Galapagos Islands, located about 1,000 km (621 miles) off the Pacific coast and home to many unique species of animals such as the giant tortoise, the marine iguana, the flightless cormorant as well as the tree finch. These islands are a popular ecotourism destination, with visitor numbers limited to 40,000 a year so as to protect the fragile ecosystem.

Suriname

Fact File

OFFICIAL NAME Republic of Suriname

FORM OF GOVERNMENT Republic with single legislative body (National Assembly)

CAPITAL Paramaribo

AREA 163,270 sq km (63,038 sq miles)

TIME ZONE GMT – 3 hours

POPULATION 437,000

PROJECTED POPULATION 2015 437,000

POPULATION DENSITY 2.7 per sq km (6.9 per sq mile)

LIFE EXPECTANCY 71.9

INFANT MORTALITY (PER 1,000) 23.5

OFFICIAL LANGUAGE Dutch

OTHER LANGUAGES English, Sranang Tongo (Surinamese), Hindi, Javanese, Chinese

LITERACY RATE 93 %

RELIGIONS Hindu 27.4 %, Muslim 19.6 %, Roman Catholic 22.8 %, Protestant 25.2 %, indigenous 5 %

ETHNIC GROUPS Hindustani (East Indian) 37 %, mixed European-African 31 %, Javanese 15 %, African 10 %, Amerindian 3 %, Chinese 2 %, European 1 %, other 1 %

Currency Suriname guilder

Economy Services 65 %, industry 22 %, agriculture 13 %

GNP per capita US$ 3,500

Climate Tropical: hot and wet year-round

Highest point Julianatop 1,230 m (4,035 ft)

Map reference Page 452

Formerly known as Dutch Guiana, Suriname is a small country on the northeastern coast of South America. In 1667 two colonial powers exchanged territory: the Dutch gave the British New Amsterdam, which became New York. In return the British gave Suriname to the Dutch. From the Low Countries the new proprietors brought their dike-building skills to reclaim a narrow coastal strip, and soon sugar plantations took the place of marshes and mangrove swamps. At first African slaves were imported to do the work; later labor was brought from India, China, and Java, and these three immigrant groups have determined both the ethnic composition of the country as well as its political fate.

Since 1954 Suriname has had the status of an equal partner in the "Tripartite Kingdom of the Netherlands". This has benefited those who have fled the continual military coups and civil disturbance in Suriname, using their Dutch citizenship to enter the Netherlands in large numbers. As was the case in nearby Guyana, escaped African slaves established isolated settlements in the hinterland. Guerrilla uprisings in both 1986 and 1994 have made the descendants of these people an urban political force.

Inland of the cultivated coastal strip lies a zone of sandy savanna, and south of this a vast area of dense forest begins (92 percent of the nation's total land area). Suriname has the world's highest ratio of forested country and it is still virtually untouched as timber is not among the nation's exports. The forests stretch inland to the Guiana Highlands, which are an extension of the Tumucumaque Mountain Range in northeastern Brazil. Over time, weathered soils have been washed from the uplands down to the alluvial valleys below, providing the foundation of the thriving bauxite industry.

Bauxite accounts for fifteen percent of Suriname's gross domestic product and more than 65 percent of export earnings. Other exports include shrimp, fish, rice, bananas, citrus fruits, and coconuts. For most people rice is the staple food, supplemented by tropical fruits and vegetables.

Both ethnic conflict and economic crises have damaged the country's prospects for some years, although the campaign by guerrillas against the urban political elite seems to have faded for the present. Inflation was running at 600 percent in 1994 but since has dropped considerably and was at seventeen percent in 2002. The resumption of economic aid by the Netherlands has led to a greater confidence in Suriname's economy, but substantial progress is unlikely without major economic reform.

Brazil

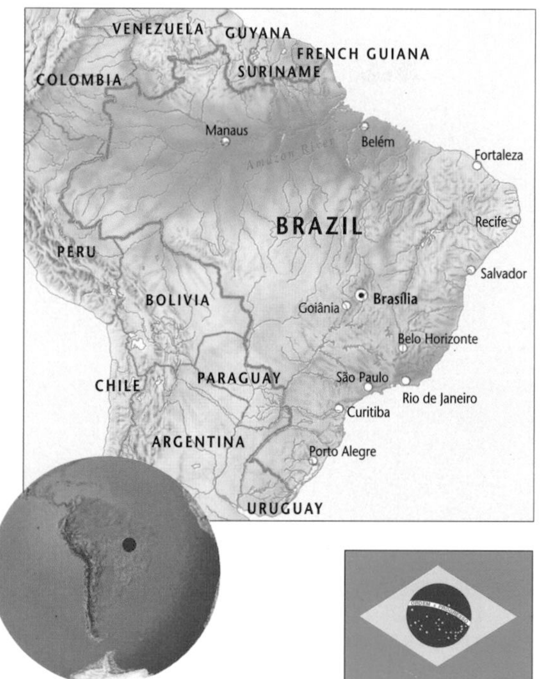

Fact File

Official name Federative Republic of Brazil

Form of government Federal republic with two legislative bodies (Senate and Chamber of Deputies)

Capital Brasília

Area 8,511,965 sq km (3,286,470 sq miles)

Time zone GMT – 3/5 hours

Population 176,030,000

Projected population 2015 201,393,000

Population density 20.7 per sq km (53.6 per sq mile)

Life expectancy 63.6

Infant mortality (per 1,000) 35.9

Official language Portuguese

Other languages More than 180 indigenous languages, Spanish, English, French

Literacy rate 83.3 %

Religions Roman Catholic 89 %, Protestant 7 %, other 4 %

Ethnic groups European 55 %, mixed European-African 38 %, African 6 %, other 1 %

Currency Real

Economy Services 55 %, agriculture 29 %, industry 16 %

GNP per capita US$ 7,400

Climate Mainly tropical, but temperate in south

Highest point Pico da Neblina 3,014 m (9,888 ft)

Map reference Pages 450–51, 452–53, 454–55, 456–57

Brazil is the fifth largest country in the world and comprises nearly half of South America. Originally the home of numerous Amerindian tribes, Brazil was ruled by the Portuguese after their arrival in 1500. Political independence of a sort came in 1822, but a form of monarchy, sponsored by Portuguese royalty and featuring a self-styled Emperor of Brazil, existed until the first republic was declared in 1889.

Today the well-being of the Amazon Basin is a cause of international concern, yet for most of Brazil's history this huge region was virtually ignored. In the eyes of the first settlers the most valuable land was the fertile coastal strip from Recife to Rio de Janeiro. In the north of this area they established huge sugarcane plantations, brought 4 million African slaves to do the work, and became so dependent on slavery that it was only abolished in 1888. In the south, around São Paulo (now the world's third largest city), a huge coffee-growing industry became established. Ethnically mixed and rich in resources, Brazil has the potential to play a major role internationally.

Physical features and land use

Brazil has two major and several minor regions. In the north is the vast tropical area—once an inland sea—drained by the Amazon River and its more than 1,000 tributaries. Occupying the entire northern half of the country, this river system passes through vast regions of rainforest. A greater variety of plant species grows here than in any other habitat in the world and the forest is home to a phenomenal range of animals and birds. More than 1,000 bird species are found here and as many as 3,000 species of fish swim in the rivers, along with other animals such as caiman (alligator), freshwater dolphin, and the endangered manatee—a large herbivorous mammal.

At present it is estimated that the rainforest is being reduced at a rate of between 1.5 and four percent per year as a result of logging, mining, ranching, and the resettlement of Brazil's many landless peasants. In early 1998 forest fires raged through the the northern state of Roraima. Ignited partly by traditional Amerindian slash-and-burn horticulture, partly by settlers clearing land, and aggravated by unusually dry conditions, they caused great devastation.

The second main region, the Brazilian Highlands, lies in the center and south of the country. This is an extensive plateau of hard, ancient rock in which weathering has formed deep river valleys. Much of the interior is covered by savanna woodland, thinning to semi-deciduous scrub in the northeast. There are spectacular waterfalls on the Uruguay River on the southern side of the plateau and on the Paraná River west of the coastal highlands.

The interior of the Nordeste (northeast) region is the most undeveloped and drought-stricken corner of Brazil, and it is from here that large numbers of subsistence farmers who can no longer make a living have emigrated to the industrial center of São Paulo, looking for work.

The swampy Pantanal, in the southwest, flooded for seven months of the year, is the largest area of wetland in the world and has a striking diversity of wildlife.

People and culture

As in the Caribbean countries, the sugar industry's demand for slaves strongly influenced the

Rio de Janeiro, in Brazil (above). The Igaçu Falls, from the Brazilian side (top). Llamas grazing on the plains at the foot of Mt Sajama, Bolivia (right page bottom).

ethnic composition of Brazil. But to a greater extent than in the slave-owning South of the USA, the result has been both economic and social integration. While Brazilian society shows extremes of wealth and poverty, the divisions are drawn along socio-economic rather than ethnic lines. Culturally, Brazil is a mixture of elements. This is particularly reflected in its religious life. Most people are Christian, mainly Roman Catholic. But a variety of African popular cults exist, such as candomblé, which are often mixed with Christianity.

Brazil also has the largest population of Japanese outside Japan. Arriving as poor farmers in the 1920s, 2 million of them now live in São Paulo and are prominent in commercial life. In the upper reaches of the Xingu, Araguaia, and Tocantins Rivers small groups of Indians such as the Tapirapé survive in forest refuges. Gold prospectors have driven off or killed Yanomami Indians in Roraima State who stood in their way.

Economy and resources

Traditional rural activities continue to be important, the rural sector employing 23 percent of the labor force. Brazil is the world's largest producer of coffee, but cocao, sugarcane, cotton, and maize are also major cash crops cultivated on large plantations. Brazilian livestock numbers are among the world's largest—mainly cattle and pigs—but trends show a steadily falling agricultural contribution to gross domestic product. Industry is increasing in importance, particularly manufacturing, with ninety percent of power coming from hydroelectric schemes. The enormous hydroelectric potential of the Amazon and Paraná, however, remains untapped. Despite some development of domestic sources, gasoline is still imported. Brazil attempted to substitute ethanol made from sugar for gasoline during the 1980s but falling oil prices made this uneconomical in the 1990s. There are enormous resources: iron ore and manganese, zinc, nickel, gold, and diamonds. The main mining regions can be found in the eastern state of Minas Gerais.

With South America's largest gross domestic product, Brazil has the potential to play a leading international role. Yet it must still be considered a developing country as it does not have a fully modern economy. Some difficulties have arisen from heavy state borrowing for unproductive projects; others stem from runaway inflation in the 1980s. Fiscal reforms are difficult to carry through politically—many require constitutional amendments. However, these problems are being addressed (consumer prices rose by 23 percent in 1995 compared to more than 1,000 percent in 1994) and investor confidence is returning.

Peru

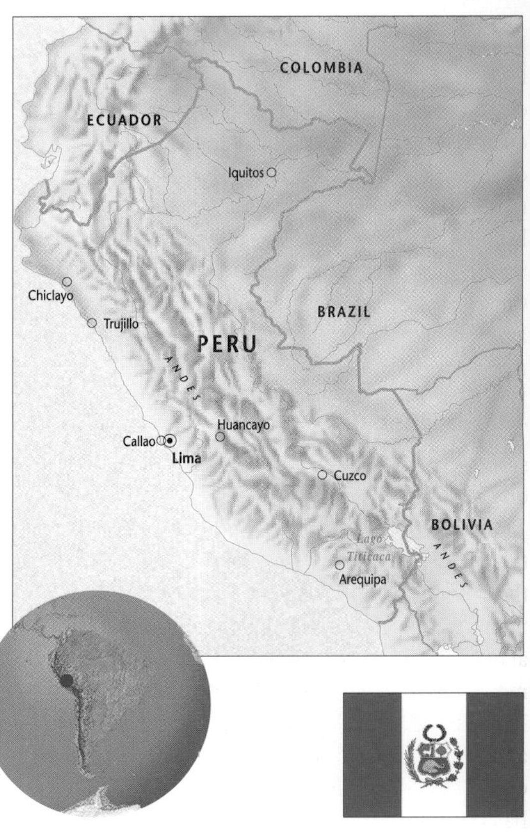

Fact File

Official name Republic of Peru

Form of government Republic with single legislative body (Congress)

Capital Lima

Area 1,285,220 sq km (496,223 sq miles)

Time zone GMT – 5 hours

Population 27,950,000

Projected population 2015 31,876,000

Population density 21.7 per sq km (56.3 per sq mile)

Life expectancy 70.4

Infant mortality (per 1,000) 41.4

Official languages Spanish, Quechua

Other language Aymara

Literacy rate 88.3 %

Religions Roman Catholic 90 %; others, including Anglican and Methodist 10 %

Ethnic groups Indigenous 45 %, mixed indigenous-European 37 %, European 15 %; others (mainly African, Japanese, Chinese) 3 %

Currency Nuevo sol

Economy Services 53 %, agriculture 35 %, industry 12 %

GNP per capita US$ 4,800

Climate Tropical in east, arid along coast, cold on high mountains

Timeline

12,000 BP Humans inhabit forests, living in small groups, hunting and fishing in rivers, and eating wild fruit and vegetables

3500 BC Amerindian people live in Amazon Basin, growing crops of potatoes and maize, and domesticating guinea pigs and llamas

AD 1500 Portuguese land in Brazil naming it after the *brasa* ("brazil-wood" in Portuguese); the native population is about 2 million

1530 Portuguese settle on Atlantic coast; establish sugarcane plantations, and grow tobacco and cotton for markets in Europe

1690 Prospectors find gold, diamonds in Minas Gerais and Mato Grosso; thousands of Portuguese settle in these regions

1790 Native peoples used as slaves on plantations; slaves also brought from Africa and elsewhere (slavery abolished 1888)

1808 John, ruler of Portugal, flees to Brazil, names Rio de Janeiro capital of Portuguese Empire; returns to Portugal 1821

1822 John's son Pedro declares independence and is Emperor until 1831; his son Pedro II rules 1841–89

1870 Rubber production soars in Amazon area, attracting migrants from the east and from Europe

1889 Dom Pedro II overthrown and Brazil is proclaimed a republic

1917 Brazil sides with the Allies in the First World War and declares war on Germany

1934 Republic ends; Vargas is President as Depression hits; he becomes dictator (1937) and embarks on major public works

1942 Brazil joins Allies in Second World War and sends 25,000 troops to fight in Italy

1946 New constitution creates democratic system

1950 Industrializati in southeast results rural depopulation; 1960 about 80 % of Brazilians are living near Atlantic coast

HIGHEST POINT Nevado Huascarán 6,768 m (22,204 ft)

MAP REFERENCE Pages 450, 454–56

Humans have been living in Peru for about 10,000 years, and by 3,000 years ago Peruvian civilization had emerged, featuring irrigation agriculture, fine pottery, and expertly woven textiles of striking design. The Incas, one of the many tribes that inhabited the highlands of Peru, established a great empire in the thirteenth century that extended from Ecuador south to central Chile. Accomplished engineers, the Incas built an extensive network of roads and bridges, and many fine cities. The most famous of these is Machu Picchu, high above the Urubamba Valley. The Spanish came to Peru in 1532, lured by stories of a "kingdom of gold", and rapidly destroyed Inca civilization.

Recently Peru has experienced serious political trouble. Deep social divisions gave rise in 1980 to the movement known as Sendero Luminoso, or Shining Path, a Maoist guerrilla group. By 1990 its activities had resulted in the loss of 23,000 lives—most of them members of its own constituency, the Indians and mixed Spanish–Indians of the Andes—along with damage to the economy in the order of US$ 20 billion. In recent years the government has been able to bring about greater stability.

Some forty percent of Peru's population live on its arid coastal plain, which merges in the south with the rainless Atacama Desert of northern Chile. Numerous rivers crossing the plain from the Andes have made fertile valleys where cotton, rice, and sugarcane are grown. Inland, in the valleys of two high ranges of the Andean Sierra, the western and the eastern cordilleras, about fifty percent of the people live, most of them Indians practicing subsistence agriculture. East of the Andes the land falls away into the almost uninhabited region of the Amazon Basin. Here, the Ucayali and Marañón Rivers flow through rainforest to Iquitos, the navigable port farthest inland on the Amazon River.

Peru's economy depends heavily on copper and petroleum exports. Agriculture is limited by the lack of arable land. Fishing for anchovies and sardines has been historically important in the cool Humboldt current offshore, but periodic warming of the ocean from the El Niño effect reduces the catch, as has occurred several times in recent years. In 1992 it fell by thirty percent.

The ruins of Machu Picchu are an incomparable spectacle for tourists, but poor facilities and guerrilla activities have discouraged visitors. Battered by hyperinflation, which reached 7,480 percent in 1990, Peru has recently undergone a series of economic reforms guided by the IMF and the World Bank. By 1995 inflation had been reduced to eleven percent, while growth in gross domestic product for that year was about seven percent, and in 2003 the inflation rate was 2.2 percent.

960 Capital moves om Rio de Janeiro Brasília, a new ty built in the ghlands of the terior

1982 Itaipú Dam on Paraná River, one of the world's largest, completed, provides hydroelectric power for growing industries

1992 Brazil hosts UN summit on global environmental issues, particularly global warming and greenhouse gas emissions

1973 Trans-Amazon Highway links remote western areas to the rest of the country

1975 Population reaches 108 million (rising from 53 million in 1950)

1998 Clearing of rainforest in Roraima attracts international attention—attempts are made to halt the process

Bolivia

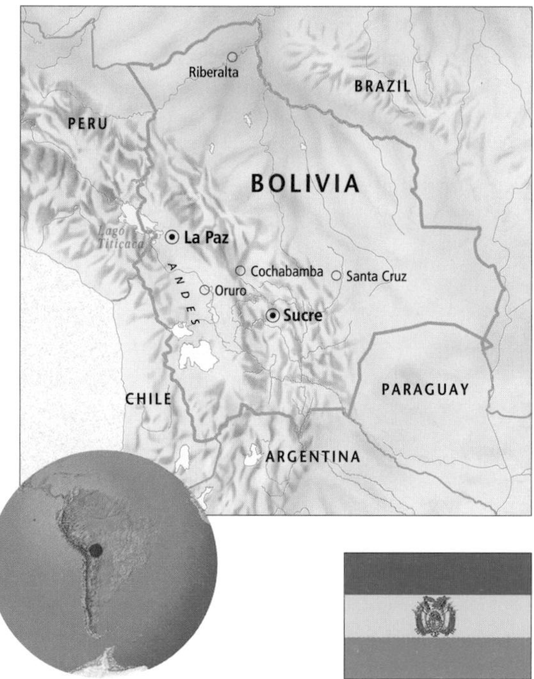

Fact File

OFFICIAL NAME Republic of Bolivia

FORM OF GOVERNMENT Republic with two legislative bodies (Senate and Chamber of Deputies)

CAPITAL Sucre (official); La Paz (administrative)

AREA 1,098,580 sq km (424,161 sq miles)

TIME ZONE GMT – 4 hours

POPULATION 8,445,000

PROJECTED POPULATION 2015 11,218,000

POPULATION DENSITY 7.7 per sq km (19.6 per sq mile)

LIFE EXPECTANCY 64.4

INFANT MORTALITY (PER 1,000) 57.5

OFFICIAL LANGUAGES Spanish, Quechua, Aymara

LITERACY RATE 83.1 %

RELIGIONS Roman Catholic 95 %, other 5 %

ETHNIC GROUPS Quechua 30 %, Aymara 25 %, mixed indigenous-European 30 %, European 15 %

CURRENCY Boliviano

ECONOMY Agriculture 50 %, services 36 %, industry 14 %

GNP PER CAPITA US$ 2,600

CLIMATE Tropical north and east; cold, arid west of Andes

HIGHEST POINT Nevado Sajama 6,520 m (21,391 ft)

MAP REFERENCE Page 455

High on the Altiplano, a plateau nearly 3,600 m (12,000 ft) above sea level, La Paz is the world's loftiest capital city. In the sixteenth century, when the Spanish conquistadores arrived in Bolivia, they found silver and the mine they established at Potosi soon became famous. But the silver boom passed, the prices for the minerals and metals that replaced it (mainly tin) have been volatile, and Bolivia is now South America's poorest nation. It is landlocked, and its rugged terrain makes it doubly inaccessible. Notorious for its political instability (192 coups between 1824 and 1981) and for the hyperinflation that rose to 11,700 percent in 1985, it now appears to have a democratic government that is trying to establish economic order.

Quechua and Aymara Indians together form 55 percent of the population. Subsistence farmers, they grow maize, potatoes, and coca on the Altiplano. This cold, treeless region runs 400 km (250 miles) north to south between two major Andean ranges. At its north, Indians still fish in Lake Titicaca from boats made of reeds. In the south are salt flats. The vegetation of the Altiplano is grassland which changes to scrubland at higher elevations. To the east lies the Oriente, reaching across the foothills and the plains. It includes the semi-arid Chaco of the southeast, the savanna of the center, and the plains of the northern forests whose rivers feed into the Amazon Basin.

The hyperinflation of the 1980s damaged the tin industry, causing the country to fall from first producer in the world to fifth. Government efforts reduced inflation to twenty percent by 1988, and to 9.3 percent by 1993. In the mid-1990s the state airline, railroad, and telephone companies were privatized, plus state mining and oil companies. Metals, natural gas, soybeans, and jewelry are the main exports but coca grown for cocaine may well surpass it—Bolivia is the world's second-largest cultivator of coca leaf. This affects foreign aid because the main donor, the USA, demands proof of Bolivian efforts to eradicate coca farms.

Chile

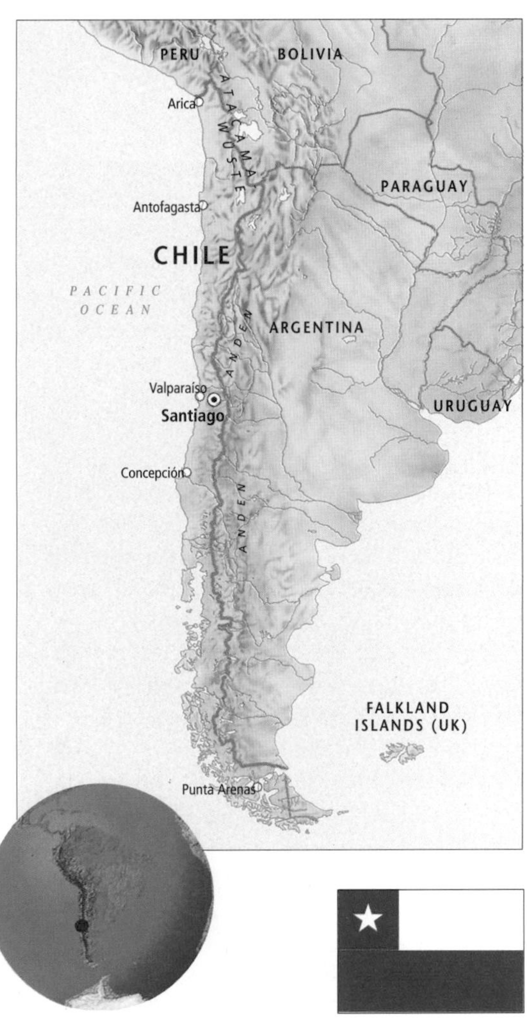

Fact File

Official name Republic of Chile

Form of government Republic with two legislative bodies (High Assembly and Chamber of Deputies)

Capital Santiago

Area 756,950 sq km (292,258 sq miles)

Time zone GMT – 4 hours

Population 15,499,000

Projected population 2015 17,912,000

Population density 20.0 per sq km (53 per sq mile)

Life expectancy 76.1

Infant mortality (per 1,000) 9.1

Official language Spanish

Literacy rate 95.2 %

Religions Roman Catholic 89 %, Protestant 11 %

Ethnic groups European and mixed indigenous-European 95 %, indigenous 3 %, other 2 %

Currency Chilean peso

Economy Services 63 %, agriculture 19 %, industry 18 %

GNP per capita US$ 10,000

Climate Arid in north, cold and wet in far south, temperate elsewhere

Highest point Ojos del Salado 6,880 m (22,572 ft)

Map reference Pages 458, 460

Chile lies between the Andes and the sea. It stretches 4,350 km (2,700 miles) along South America's Pacific coast, yet is never more than 180 km (110 miles) wide. In the fifteenth century, the Incas from Peru tried but failed to subjugate its Araucanian Indian population. This was gradually achieved by the Spanish, against strong resistance, after their arrival in the sixteenth century. The Spanish established mining in the north and huge estates in the Central Valley; by the nineteenth century produce was being exported to California, Australia and elsewhere. Today, fruit and vegetables remain important exports, along with wine.

The Atacama Desert (Desierto de Atacama), in the north, has one of the lowest rainfalls in the world. In the nineteenth century it was the world's main source of nitrate for fertilizer, an export which underwrote Chile's early economic development. Santiago and the port of Valparaíso form an urban cluster midway along the length of the country. Santiago lies in a sheltered, temperate valley between a coastal range of mountains to the west and the high Andes in the interior. This fertile 800 km (500 mile) valley is where Chile's main vineyards are located, and where sixty percent of the population live. It is also where most manufacturing industry is located. Volcanoes, active and inactive, mark the length of the Chilean Andes to the east. In the southern third of the country the coastal range disintegrates into a maze of islands, archipelagoes, and fiords.

In 1970 President Allende nationalized the copper industry and other large enterprises, raised wages, and fixed prices. By 1973 inflation had reached 850 percent. Fearing a Cubanization of Chile, the political right under General Pinochet staged a coup and ruled for the next seventeen years. During that time, over 2,000 political opponents "disappeared". Economically, the coup's effects were positive. The regime restored economic liberalism and dismantled state controls. Democracy was restored at a general election in 1989.

After two decades of political turmoil, Chile is now one of the more economically progressive of South America's democracies. It is the world's leading supplier of copper, and high copper prices remain vital to the nation's economic health. Growth in gross domestic product averaged more than six percent annually from 1991 to 1995, and in recent years an estimated 1 million Chileans have ceased to be classed as poor.

Argentina

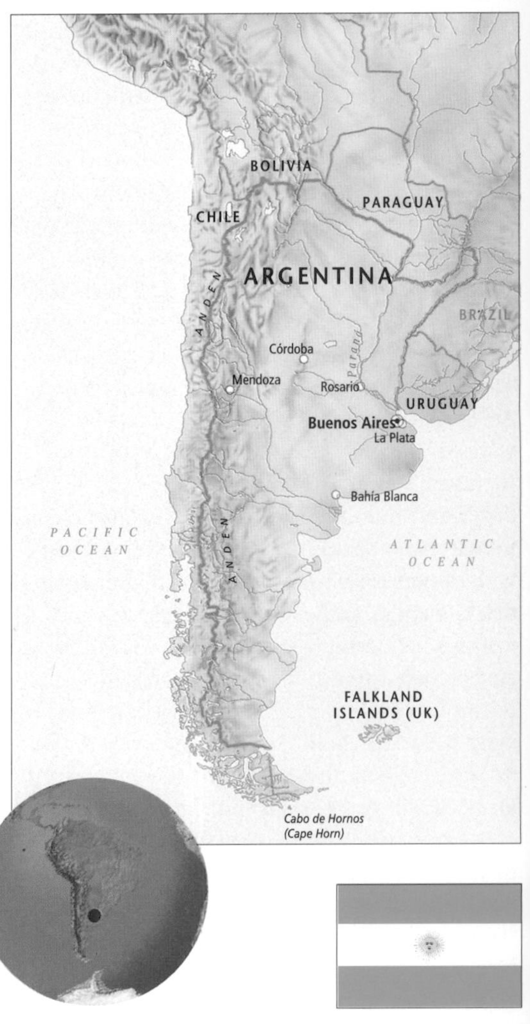

Fact File

Official name Argentine Republic

Form of government Federal republic with two legislative bodies (Senate and Chamber of Deputies)

Capital Buenos Aires

Area 2,766,890 sq km (1,068,296 sq miles)

Time zone GMT – 3 hours

Population 37,813,000

Projected population 2015 43,498,000

Population density 13.7 per sq km (35.4 per sq mile)

Life expectancy 75.5

Infant mortality (per 1,000) 17.2

Official language Spanish

Other languages English, Italian, German, French, indigenous languages

Literacy rate 96.2 %

Religions Roman Catholic 90 %, Protestant 2 %, Jewish 2 %, other 6 %

Ethnic groups European 85 %, indigenous, mixed indigenous-European, and other 15 %

Timeline

AD 600 Northwest settled by communities with complex social organizations—some have 10,000 to 20,000 members

12,000 BP Small human communities live by hunting and fishing in territory now known as Argentina

900 Native populations living in Andes in small-scale communities; culture has total population of 250,000–500,000

Currency Argentine peso

Economy Services 53 %, industry 34 %, agriculture 13 %

GNP per capita US$ 10,200

Climate Mainly temperate; subtropical in northern Chaco, cold and arid in Patagonia; snow on Andes

Highest point Aconcagua 6,960 m (22,834 ft)

Map reference Pages 458–59, 460

With its northern extremity just north of the Tropic of Capricorn, but lying mainly within the temperate zone, Argentina becomes narrower and colder as it tapers south to Tierra del Fuego. The largest Spanish-speaking country of Latin America, it is named for the silver deposits that were sought by early explorers (*Argentina* means "land of silver"). In the nineteenth century Argentina attracted many Spanish and Italian immigrants in search of a better life, and today it contrasts with some of its neighbors in having a population that is mainly middle-class, with cosmopolitan interests, and a strong European background and culture. Most Argentinians are of Spanish and Italian descent, but there are also people of German, Russian, French, and English background, as well as a Jewish community in Buenos Aires and a Welsh community in Patagonia.

Argentina's politics have been much influenced by the legacy of Colonel Juan Domingo Perón. A major force in Argentine politics from 1946 to 1976, "Perónism" was a mild form of fascism which combined military rule and statist economic policy with progressive labor legislation. After Perón's death in 1974, he was succeeded by his widow. That government was ousted by a military coup in 1976. A three-man junta was then installed. Under this government thousands of people "disappeared" in a violent campaign against left-wing elements. Their fate still haunts the present government.

Physical features and land use

There are four main regions. In the north lie the subtropical woodlands and swamps of the Gran Chaco, a zone that spills over the northeastern border into Paraguay. Swampy in parts, dry in others and covered with thorny scrub, the Chaco is known as "Green Hell". To the west are the wooded slopes and valleys of the Andes; in the far south is the cold, semiarid Patagonian Plateau. It was the temperate region to the west and south of Buenos Aires that made Argentina famous. Here are the plains of the pampas—moist and fertile near the capital, drier but still productive elsewhere. These grasslands, where the gauchos (part Indian, part Spanish cattleherders) once lived and worked, are the basis of Argentina's cattle industry.

The pampas was largely created by gravel and sand brought down by streams from the Andes. A large native clump-grass called pampas grass, with coarse gray blades and silvery plumes, provided stock feed when the Spanish settlers arrived. They brought horses and cattle, and began to fence off the more productive land for ranching and cultivation. While beef raising is still important, much of the fertile parts of the pampas are now used for growing wheat, maize, alfalfa, and flax.

Argentina has many lakes on the slopes of the Andes, and the alpine terrain attracts tourists and skiers from elsewhere in South America. The Andes are widely affected by volcanic activity and there are several active volcanoes along the border with Chile, as well as Aconcagua, the highest mountain outside the Himalayas. The huge Paraguay-Paraná-Uruguay river system, the second-largest on the continent, drains south from the Chaco and west from the highlands of Uruguay before emptying into the estuary of the River Plate (Río de la Plata). The three cities located here, two of them national capitals (the ports of Buenos Aires and Montevideo), mark the historic importance of this estuary.

People and culture

Hunters and fishermen occupied the Argentine region from 12,000 years ago, and in recent times the Yahgan and Ona people made their home in Tierra del Fuego, despite its bitter climate. In the sixteenth century Spanish settlers began moving into Argentina from Peru, Chile, and Paraguay, and in the nineteenth century a ferocious war cleared the pampas of its remaining Indians.

Today, more than one-third of the population is descended from Italian immigrants. Argentinians are overwhelmingly urban: 88 percent live in towns and cities, with forty percent in Buenos Aires itself (an urban agglomeration of around 11.5 million). The European orientation of cultural life is reflected in their art, music, and literature.

Mountains in the Torres del Paine National Park, Chile (left page bottom). Autumn colors in Tierra del Fuego, Argentina (top). Buenos Aires, Argentina (above).

Economy and resources

Although the rural sector remains important, today industry makes a major contribution to the economy. Roughly one-fifth of the workforce is in manufacturing, mainly in industries producing frozen meat, canned meat, tallow, and leather for export. Wheat and fruit are also major exports. Energy available for industry includes nuclear power, hydroelectric power, and petroleum. There are oilfields in Patagonia and in the Mendoza area near the Andes, directly west of Buenos Aires.

Argentina has varied mineral resources—lead, zinc, tin, copper, silver, and uranium. It has a well-educated workforce and a diversified industrial base. Buenos Aires has a thriving computer industry. Episodes of hyperinflation have shaken investor confidence but political stability and reduced inflation in recent years are attracting overseas investment. Reforms introduced by President Menem have seen a general restructuring. There are signs that the economy has begun a period of growth.

1516 Spanish explorer Juan Díaz de Solís, first European to land on what is now Argentine soil; killed by Querandi people

1553 Permanent settlements established in northwest by Spanish arriving from Peru in search of gold and silver

1573 Towns of Córdoba and Mendoza develop on trade routes between Chile and Argentina

1580 Spanish colonists establish settlement of Buenos Aires on La Plata Estuary

1816 Argentina declares independence from Spain

1830 Argentina lays claim to Islas Malvinas (the Falkland Islands), which are then occupied by Great Britain in 1833

1866 San Roque Dam built on the Primero River providing irrigation and hydroelectric power

1876 Exports of meat and grain to Europe grow rapidly following introduction of refrigerated shipping

1910 Large numbers of European migrants arrive to farm and work on estates in the southern Pampas region

1914 First World War followed by export-led boom in agricultural produce; Argentine population reaches 8 million

1944 Earthquake kills 5,000 people in San Juan province in the Andes

1946 Colonel Juan Perón is elected President and later assumes the powers of a dictator

1955 Perón dismissed in military coup; he flees the country with his first wife, Eva

1973–74 Perón returns, is re-elected, dies; his third wife, "Isabelita", governs until arrested in 1976 coup in which thousands die

1982 Argentina invades Falklands after talks with Britain over sovereignty break down—Britain retakes the islands

1990 Full diplomatic relations with Britain are restored

1994 Paraguay and Argentina jointly build Corpus Posados Dam on the Pananá River to create hydroelectric power

Uruguay

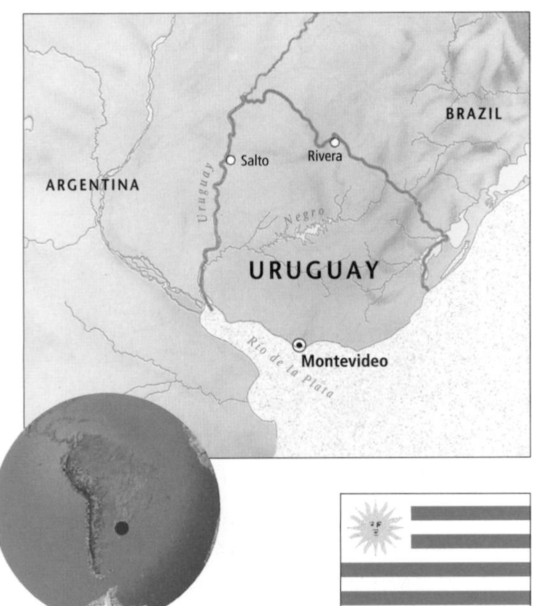

Fact File

Official name Eastern Republic of Uruguay

Form of government Republic with two legislative bodies (Senate and Chamber of Deputies)

Capital Montevideo

Area 176,220 sq km (68,038 sq miles)

Time zone GMT – 3 hours

Population 3,387,000

Projected population 2015 3,670,000

Population density 19.2 per sq km (49.8 per sq mile)

Life expectancy 75.7

Infant mortality (per 1,000) 14.3

Official language Spanish

Literacy rate 97.3 %

Religions Roman Catholic 66 %, Protestant 2 %, Jewish 2 %, unaffiliated 30 %

Ethnic groups European 88 %, mixed indigenous-European 8 %, African 4 %

Currency Uruguayan peso

Economy Services 67 %, industry 18 %, agriculture 15 %

GNP per capita US$ 9,200

Climate Temperate, with warm summers and mild winters

Highest point Cerro Catedral 514 m (1,686 ft)

Map reference Page 459

Uruguay, the second-smallest country in South America, lies northeast of Argentina on the estuary of the River Plate (Río de la Plata). Controlled for 150 years alternately by the Portuguese and the Spanish, Uruguay finally gained independence in 1828, after which came forty years of civil war. When peace was secured, waves of immigrants flocked to Uruguay from Spain and Italy, the cattle industry and meat exports expanded, investment poured in, and the country prospered. It may even have prospered too much: many benefits and welfare provisions were introduced in the days of prosperity which in poorer times have proved difficult to pay for. An urban guerrilla movement known as the Tupamaros paralyzed the cities during the 1960s, provoking a repressive military crackdown and dictatorship. Democracy was restored in 1984.

Most of Uruguay is temperate and mild: it never snows and frosts are rare, though the pampero, a wind coming off the pampas to the south, can be cold and violent. Most of the country is covered with rich grasslands, a continuation of the Argentine pampas, where cattle and sheep are raised. Although ninety percent of Uruguay's land is suitable for cultivation, only some ten percent is currently used for agriculture, but this is enough to ensure that the country is largely self-sufficient in food. Uruguay's main river is the Negro, flowing east-west across the center of the country. On either side of the Negro the land rises to a plateau that marks the southern limits of the Brazilian Highlands. Water from the uplands feeds down the Negro into a large artificial lake, Lake Rincón del Bonete, which is used for hydroelectric power.

Uruguay's rural economy is based on sheep and cattle raising, and its industries are mainly based on animal products: meat processing, leather, and wool and textile manufacturing. The country is the second largest wool exporter in the world. But Uruguay is not rich in other resources: it has no petroleum or minerals except for agate, amethyst, gold deposits, and small quantities of iron ore. It is entirely dependent on imported oil. The ample supplies of hydroelectricity that are available help to offset this disadvantage, and only governmental regulatory constraints prevent industrial expansion.

Uruguay is at present undergoing a program of modernization, the most prominent issue being the privatization of the extremely large state sector (25 percent of the country's employees are currently civil servants) inherited from its more prosperous past. Tourism is booming, consisting mainly of visitors to Montevideo.

The Palacio Legislativa in Montevideo, Uruguay (below). The mizzen mast of the Great Britain *on the harbor foreshore of Stanley in the Falkland Islands (right page top).*

Paraguay

Fact File

Official name Republic of Paraguay

Form of government Republic with two legislative bodies (Senate and Chamber of Deputies)

Capital Asunción

Area 406,750 sq km (157,046 sq miles)

Time zone GMT – 4 hours

Population 5,885,000

Projected population 2015 7,773,000

Population density 14.5 per sq km (37.5 per sq mile)

Life expectancy 74.2

Infant mortality (per 1,000) 28.8

Official language Spanish

Other language Guaraní

Literacy rate 92.1 %

Religions Roman Catholic 90 %; other (including Mennonite, Baptist and Anglican) 10 %

Ethnic groups Mixed indigenous-European 95 %; indigenous, European, Asian, and African 5 %

Currency Guaraní

Economy Agriculture 49 %, services 30 %, industry 21 %

GNP per capita US$ 4,600

Climate Subtropical; wet in east, semiarid in west

Highest point Cerro San Rafael 850 m (2,789 ft)

Map reference Pages 455, 458–59

A small landlocked country, Paraguay was originally the home of the Guaraní Indians. It was settled by the Spaniards in 1537 who hoped to use the Guaraní as laborers on their big estates. The strong influence of the Jesuits, however, largely prevented the exploitation of the indigenous people by settlers that occurred elsewhere in South America under Spanish Catholic rule, and a socially benign intermix took place. Today, 95 percent of the population are of combined Indian and Spanish descent.

Fully independent since 1813, Paraguay is best known in modern times for the severe regime imposed by General Stroessner between 1954 and 1989. Assuming power after a period of chronic upheaval—six presidents in six years and revolts that had left thousands dead—he brought economic and political stability, and greatly improved the national infrastructure. This was at the price of considerable repression, and the huge hydroelectric projects that were built on the Paraná River incurred sizeable foreign debts.

Across the plains, south of Asunción, the Paraná River becomes a highway to the sea. Paraguay has some 3,100 km (1,900 miles) of navigable waterways, the most important being the Paraguay River which bisects the country north to south. To the west of Paraguay are the marshy, insect-infested plains of the Gran Chaco, but as the land rises toward the Bolivian border the Chaco changes to semidesert scrub. East of the river the land rises to a plateau forested with tropical hardwoods.

The economy of Paraguay has long been based on agriculture, and large numbers of people still live by means of subsistence farming. Cattle raising and the production of meat products remain the leading agricultural activities but cash crops such as cotton, soybeans, and timber are of increasing importance as a source of export income. Moreover, Paraguay's excess electricity capacity enables it to export power to Brazil.

The informal sector of the economy is also important. Small enterprises and street vendors flourish by importing and re-exporting consumer goods such as electronic devices, alcoholic beverages, and perfumes. While tourism is poorly developed, day-trippers pour in from Brazil and Argentina to buy these goods.

Dependencies in South America

Falkland Islands

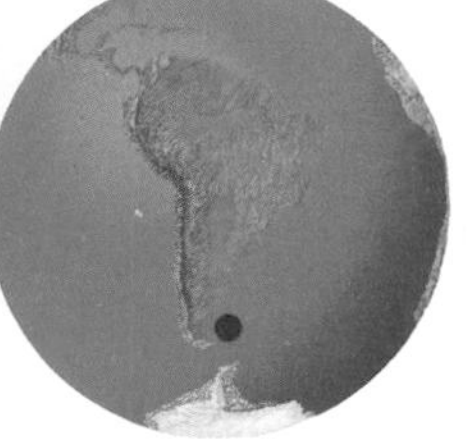

Fact File

Official name Colony of the Falkland Islands

Form of government Dependent territory of the UK

Capital Stanley

Area 12,170 sq km (4,699 sq miles)

Time zone GMT – 4 hours

Population 3,000

Currency Falkland Islands pound

Economy Agriculture 95 %, services and industry 5 %

Climate Cold, wet, and windy

Map reference Page 460

The Falkland Islands are in the South Atlantic. They were named for Lord Falkland, a seventeenth-century British Navy official. Lying 772 km (480 miles) northeast of Cape Horn, they consist of a hilly archipelago where rain falls on average 180 days a year. The area is known for the diversity of the bird life. East Falkland and West Falkland are the two main islands and there are about 200 islets. Most people are employed in sheep farming. Efforts to establish a fishing industry have failed. Sovereignty of the islands is disputed between the United Kingdom and Argentina, which in 1982 invaded, unsuccessfully, in an assertion of its claim. The resulting conflict lasted for three months. In 1995 the UK and Argentina launched a joint oil exploration program.

French Guiana

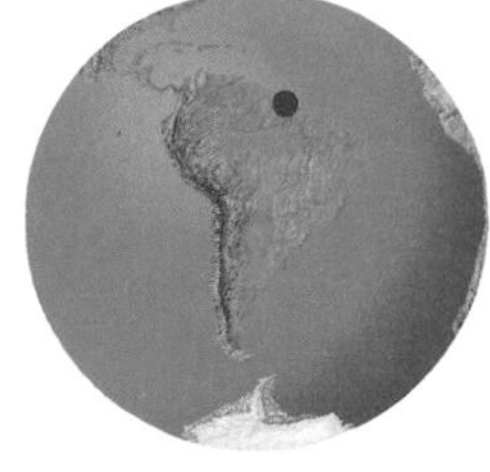

Fact File

Official name Department of Guiana

Form of government Overseas department of France

Capital Cayenne

Area 91,000 sq km (35,135 sq miles)

Time zone GMT – 3 hours

Population 183,000

Life expectancy 76.5

Infant mortality (per 1,000) 13.2

Literacy rate 83 %

Currency Euro

Economy Services 61 %, industry 21 %, agriculture 18 %

Climate Tropical with two wet seasons (December and June)

Map reference Page 452

Located along the northeast coast of South America, French Guiana has a narrow coastal plain and a largely unpopulated, forested hinterland. Brazil lies across its southern and eastern borders. After the French Revolution one of the islands became the French penal colony of Devil's Island (Île du Diable). Now French Guiana is the site of the European Space Agency's rocket base Kourou where the Ariane rockets lift off. Sugarcane plantations influenced its development; today, cash crops such as bananas and sugarcane grow on the coast, and the main exports are fish and fish products. Still, the country is highly dependent on France for its economic viability.

South Georgia and the South Sandwich Islands

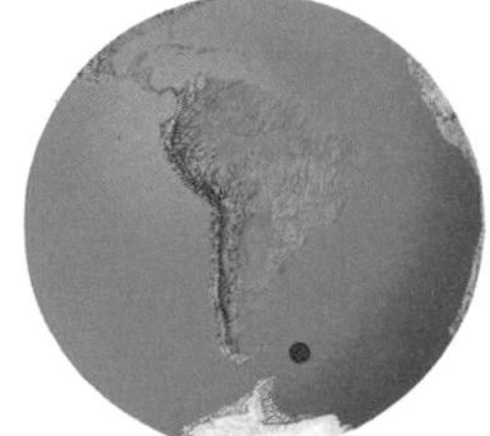

Fact File

Official name South Georgia and the South Sandwich Islands

Form of government Dependent territory of the UK

Capital None; Grytviken is garrison town

Area 4,066 sq km (1,570 sq miles)

Time zone GMT – 4 hours

Population No permanent population

Economy Biological station only

Climate Cold, wet, and windy

Map reference Pages 461, 476

South Georgia is a barren island in the South Atlantic 1,300 km (800 miles) southeast of the Falklands. Annexed by Captain Cook in 1775, the harbor of Grytviken was long used as a whaling base. Until the 1940s it had a population of up to 800 employed in the whaling industry. Its wildlife is now attracting increasing numbers of ecotourists. The military base entertained here was given up in 2001.

The South Sandwich Islands are six uninhabited volcanic cones to the southeast of South Georgia.

South America: Physical

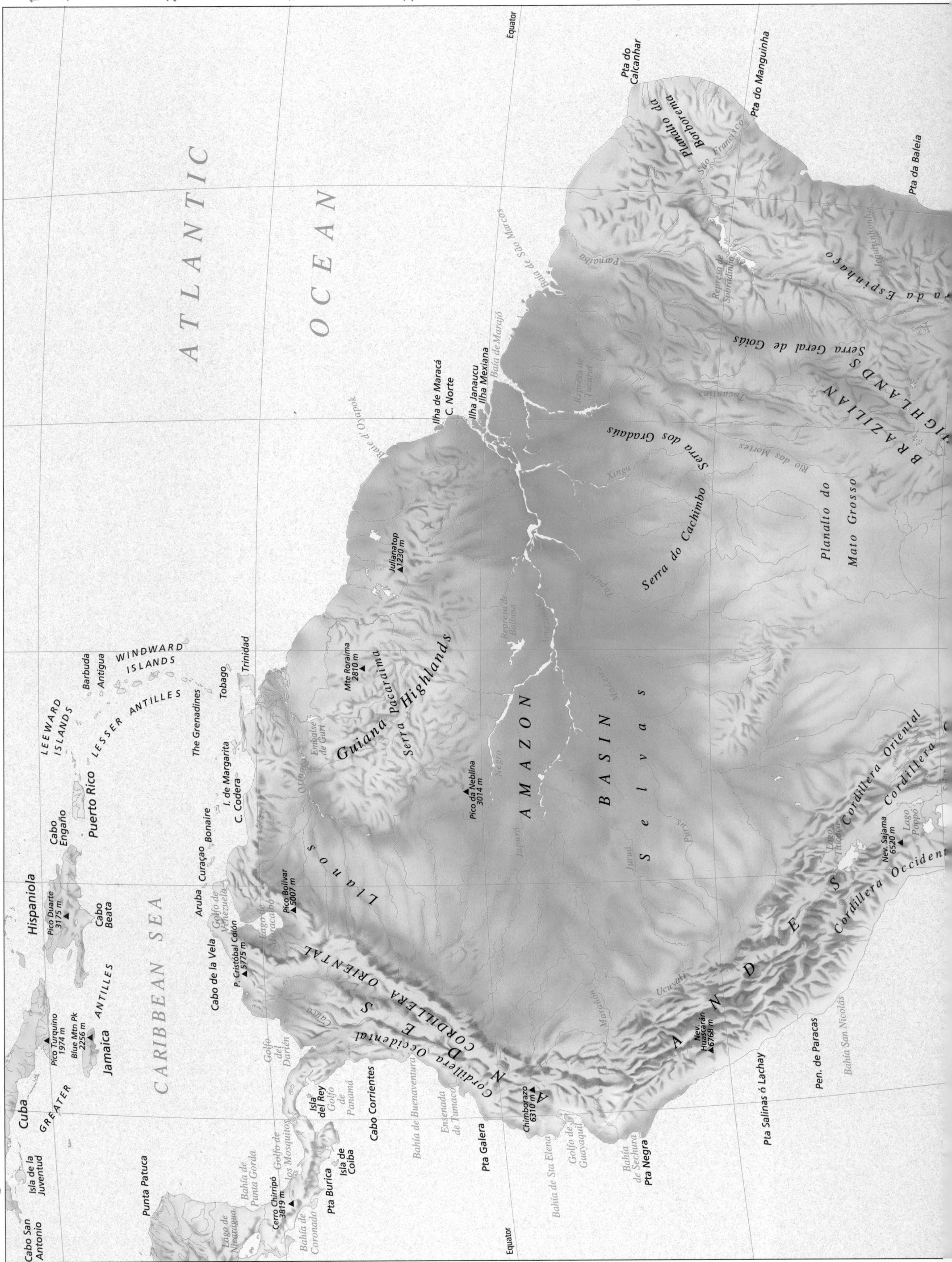

ATLANTIC OCEAN
CARIBBEAN SEA
Cuba
Hispaniola
Jamaica
Puerto Rico
GREATER ANTILLES
LESSER ANTILLES
LEEWARD ISLANDS
WINDWARD ISLANDS
Isla de la Juventud
Cabo San Antonio
Pico Turquino 1974 m
Blue Mtn Pk 2256 m
Pico Duarte 3175 m
Cabo Beata
Cabo Engaño
Barbuda
Antigua
The Grenadines
Tobago
Trinidad
Aruba
Curaçao
Bonaire
I. de Margarita
C. Codera
Cabo de la Vela
Golfo de Venezuela
Lago de Maracaibo
P. Cristóbal Colón 5775 m
Pico Bolívar 5007 m
Llanos
Embalse de Guri
Orinoco
Guiana Highlands
Serra Pacaraima
Mte Roraima 2810 m
Julianatop 1230 m
Pico da Neblina 3014 m
Punta Patuca
Lago de Nicaragua
Bahía de Punta Gorda
Golfo de los Mosquitos
Cerro Chirripó 3819 m
Bahía de Coronado
Pta Burica
Isla de Coiba
Isla del Rey
Golfo de Panamá
Golfo del Darién
Cabo Corrientes
Bahía de Buenaventura
Ensenada de Tumaco
Pta Galera
Chimborazo 6310 m
Bahía de Sta Elena
Golfo de Guayaquil
Bahía de Sechura
Pta Negra
Pta Salinas ó Lachay
Pen. de Paracas
Bahía San Nicolás
Nev. Huascarán 6768 m
Nev. Sajama 6520 m
Lago Titicaca
Lago Poopó
ANDES
CORDILLERA ORIENTAL
Cordillera Occidental
Cordillera Oriental
Cordillera Occidental
Cauca
Ucayali
Marañón
Juruá
Purus
Japurá
Negro
Madeira
Represa de Balbina
Tapajós
Xingu
AMAZON BASIN
Selvas
Serra do Cachimbo
Serra dos Gradaús
Planalto do Mato Grosso
Rio das Mortes
Tocantins
Represa de Tucuruí
BRAZILIAN HIGHLANDS
Serra Geral de Goiás
Serra do Espinhaço
Represa de Sobradinho
São Francisco
Jequitinhonha
Parnaíba
Planalto da Borborema
Baía de São Marcos
Baía de Marajó
Ilha Janaucu
Ilha Mexiana
Ilha de Maracá
C. Norte
Baie d'Oyapok
Pta do Calcanhar
Pta do Mangunha
Pta da Baleia
Equator

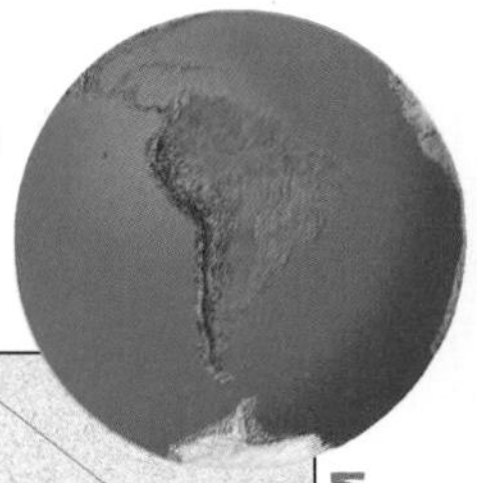

SOUTH ATLANTIC OCEAN

OCEAN

Tropic of Capricorn

São Sebastião

Ilha de Sta Catarina

C. de Sta Marta Grande

Serra Geral

Lagoa dos Patos

Lagoa Mirim

Cuchilla Grande

Represa del Rio Negro

Rio Negro

Uruguay

Paraguay

Rio de la Plata

C. Corrientes

GRAN C

Salado

L. Mar Chiquita

Sierras de Córdoba

PAMPAS

Salar de Arizaro

Vol. Llullaillaco 6723 m

Desierto de A

Co Aconcagua 6960 m

Colorado

Bahía Blanca

Bahía Anegada

Pta Rasa

Golfo San Matías

Península Valdés

Bahía Camarones

Golfo de San Jorge

C. Tres Puntas

Pta Medanosa

West Falkland

East Falkland

Bahía Grande

Pta Dungeness

Isla Grande de Tierra del Fuego

I. de los Estados

Islas Wollaston

Cabo de Hornos (Cape Horn)

I. Hoste

I. Londonderry

Península Brecknock

I. Santa Inés

Bahía Otway

I. Desolación

I. Diego de Almagro

I. Madre de Dios

Isla Wellington

I. Esmeralda

I. Patricio Lynch

Golfo de Penas

L. General Carrera

L. Buenos Aires

L. Viedma

L. Argentino

L. Colhué Huapi

L. Musters

Chubut

L. Nahuel Huapi

PATAGONIA

ANDES

Isla Grande de Chiloé

Canal de Chacao

Islas Guaitecas

Isla Magdalena

I. Benjamín

Pta Galera

Golfo de Arauco

Pta Curaumilla

Pta Lengua de Vaca

Bahía Salada

I. San Ambrosio

I. San Félix

Arch. Juan Fernández

South Georgia

South Orkney Is

South Shetland Is

Antarctic Peninsula

South America

0	200	400	600	800 kilometers
0	200	400		miles

Scale 1:21,000,000 Projection: Azimuthal Equal Area

South America: Political

ATLANTIC
OCEAN
CARIBBEAN SEA
CUBA
CAYMAN ISLANDS (U.K.)
JAMAICA
HAITI
DOMINICAN REPUBLIC
PUERTO RICO (U.S.A.)
VIRGIN ISLANDS (U.K.)
VIRGIN ISLANDS (U.S.A.)
ANGUILLA (U.K.)
ST KITTS AND NEVIS
ANTIGUA AND BARBUDA
MONTSERRAT (U.K.)
GUADELOUPE (Fr.)
DOMINICA
MARTINIQUE (Fr.)
ST LUCIA
BARBADOS
ST VINCENT AND THE GRENADINES
The Grenadines
GRENADA
TRINIDAD AND TOBAGO
Tobago
Trinidad
NETHERLANDS ANTILLES (Neth.)
ARUBA (Neth.)
Willemstad
HONDURAS
NICARAGUA
COSTA RICA
PANAMA
Isla de Coiba
Isla del Rey
Golfo de Panamá
VENEZUELA
COLOMBIA
ECUADOR
PERU
BOLIVIA
BRAZIL
GUYANA
SURINAME
FRENCH GUIANA (Fr.)
Barranquilla
Santa Marta
Cartagena
Valledupar
Maracaibo
Cabimas
Coro
Valencia
Caracas
I. de Margarita
La Asunción
Cumaná
Port of Spain
Barcelona
Maturín
Tucupita
Ciudad Bolívar
Ciudad Guayana
Barinas
San Fernando de Apure
Sincelejo
Montería
Cúcuta
San Cristóbal
Bucaramanga
Medellín
Tunja
Yopal
Quibdó
Pereira
Manizales
Bogotá
Armenia
Ibagué
Villavicencio
Puerto Inírida
Puerto Ayacucho
B. de Buenaventura
Cali
Popayán
San José del Guaviare
Florencia
Mitú
Pasto
Mocoa
Tulcán
Ibarra
Quito
Ambato
Riobamba
Guayaquil
Cuenca
Golfo de Guayaquil
Machala
Loja
Talara
Sullana
Piura
Bayovar
Moyobamba
Yurimaguas
Chiclayo
Cajamarca
Trujillo
Chimbote
Pucallpa
Cruzeiro do Sul
Iquitos
Leticia
Benjamin Constant
Cerro de Pasco
La Oroya
Huancayo
Callao
Lima
Ayacucho
Puerto Maldonado
Cuzco
Pisco
Ica
Sicuani
Marcona
Juliaca
Arequipa
Mollendo
Ilo
Tacna
Arica
La Paz
Cochabamba
Oruro
Punata
Huanuni
Sucre
Potosí
Montero
Santa Cruz
Trinidad
Costa Marques
Riberalta
Guayaramerín
Guajará-Mirim
Plácido de Castro
Rio Branco
Xapuri
Brasiléia
Bôca do Acre
Pôrto Velho
Ariquemes
Pimenta Bueno
Lábrea
Humaitá
Eirunepé
Manicoré
Tefé
São Gabriel da Cachoeira
Georgetown
New Amsterdam
Linden
Paramaribo
St-Laurent du Maroni
Cayenne
Normandia
Boa Vista
Calçoene
Ilha de Maracá
Macapá
Ilha Janaucu
Ilha Mexiana
Baía de Marajó
Baía de São Marcos
Santa Maria
Manaus
Parintins
Óbidos
Santarém
Altamira
Itaituba
Pôrto de Moz
Cametá
Belém
Abaetetuba
Castanhal
Bragança
São Luís
Parnaíba
Bacabal
Caxias
Teresina
Sobral
Fortaleza
Marabá
Imperatriz
Tocantinópolis
Barra do Corda
São Félix do Xingu
Carolina
Araguaína
Floriano
Picos
Mossoró
Natal
Juazeiro do Norte
Campina Grande
João Pessoa
Caruaru
Recife
Paulo Afonso
Garanhuns
Juazeiro
Maceió
Arapiraca
Aracaju
Senhor do Bonfim
Santa Maria das Barreiras
Gurupi
Barreiras
Bom Jesus da Lapa
Feira de Santana
Alagoinhas
Salvador
Jequié
Vitória da Conquista
Itabuna
Ilhéus
Canavieiras
Rio Branco
Cuiabá
Cáceres
Rondonópolis
Aragarças
Itaberaí
Brasília
Anápolis
Goiânia
São Francisco
Montes Claros
Grão Mogol
Teófilo Otoni
Jataí
Coxim
Corumbá
Araguari
Patos de Minas
Ituiutaba
Uberlândia
Governador Valadares
Equator
D
E
F
G
H
J
1
2
3
4
5
80°
70°
60°
50°
40°
20°
10°
0°

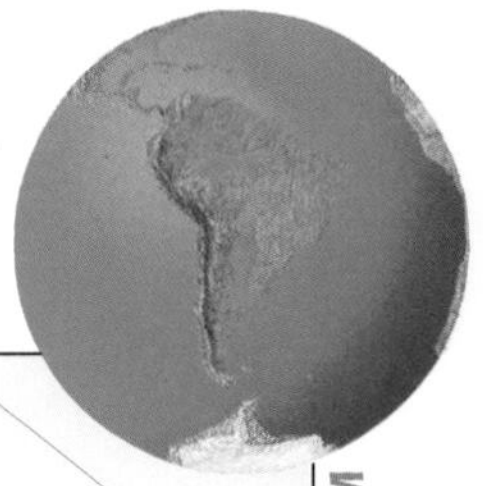

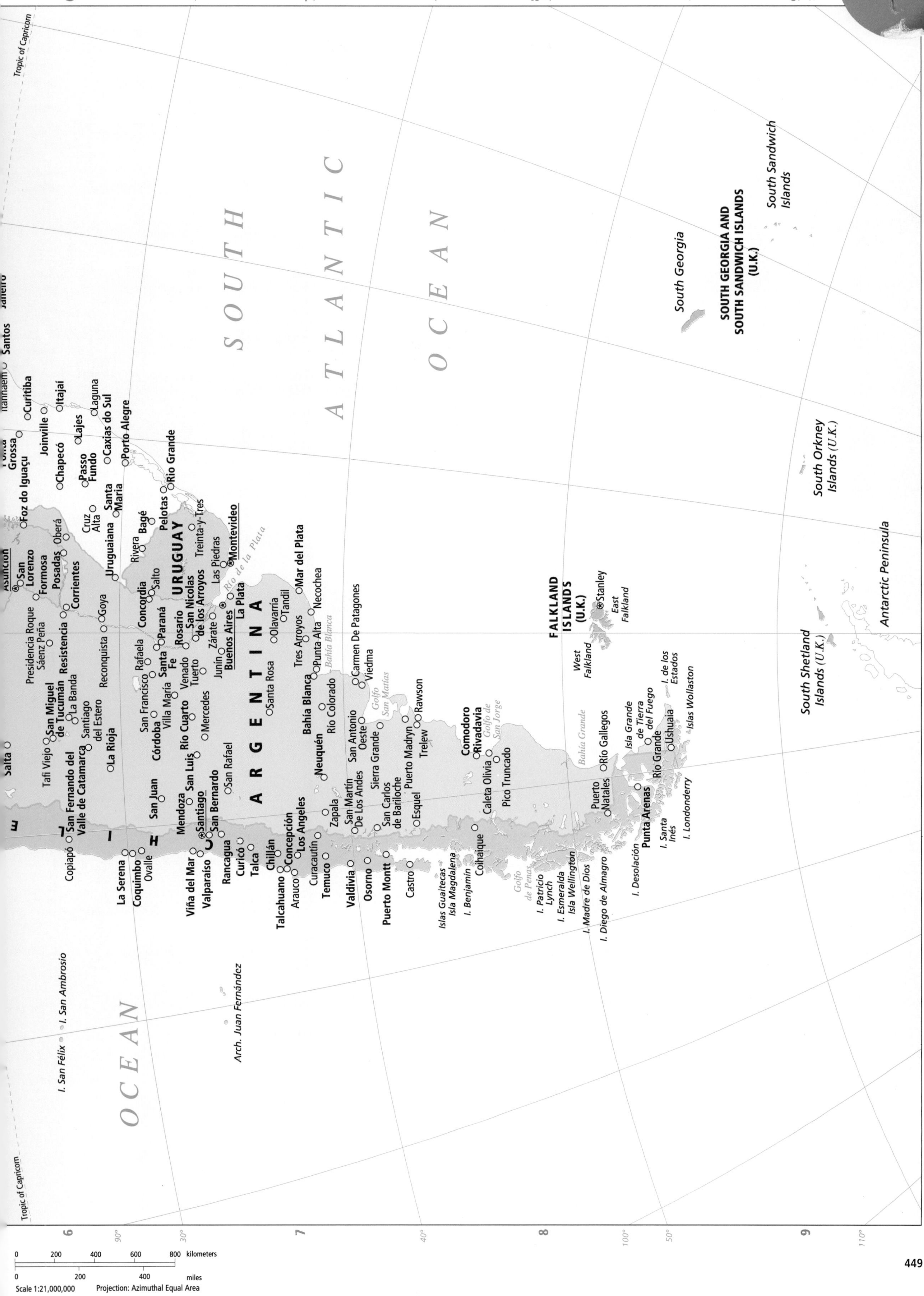

SOUTH ATLANTIC OCEAN

OCEAN

ARGENTINA

URUGUAY

FALKLAND ISLANDS (U.K.)

SOUTH GEORGIA AND SOUTH SANDWICH ISLANDS (U.K.)

South Georgia

South Sandwich Islands

South Orkney Islands (U.K.)

South Shetland Islands (U.K.)

Antarctic Peninsula

Buenos Aires

Montevideo

Santiago

Stanley

Río de la Plata

Arch. Juan Fernández

I. San Félix

I. San Ambrosio

Tropic of Capricorn

South America

0 200 400 600 800 kilometers

0 200 400 miles

Scale 1:21,000,000 Projection: Azimuthal Equal Area

Colombia • Venezuela • Ecuador • Guyana • Northwest Brazi

429

CARIBBEAN SEA

PACIFIC OCEAN

Santo Domingo
Juigalpa
Acoyapa
Laguna de Perlas
Bluefields

NICARAGUA

Lago de Nicaragua
Punta Gorda
San Carlos
Bahía de Punta Gorda
San Juan del Norte
Vol. Miravalles ▲ 2028 m
Altamira
Río Frío
Guápiles
Puerto Jesús
Alajuela Heredia
Puerto Limón
Puntarenas
Cartago

COSTA RICA

San José
Parrita
Cerro Chirripó ▲ 3819 m
Bribri
B. de Coronado
Dominical
Ciudad Cortés
Volcán Barú ▲ 3475 m
La Concepción Boquete
David
Tolé San Francisco
Puerto Armuelles
Santiago
Península de Osa
Pta Burica
Golfo de Chiriquí
Río de Jesús
Soná Parita
Atalaya Chitré
Las Tablas
Pedasí
Pta Mala
Tonosí
Golfo de Montijo
Península de Azuero
Isla de Coiba
Isla de Cébaco
Pta Mariato

Portobelo El Porvenir
Colón Palenque
Coclé
L. Gatún
Canal

PANAMA

La Chorrera **San Miguelito**
Penonomé
Antón
Aguadulce
Golfo de los Mosquitos
Santa Catalina
Ailigandí
Chimán
Isla del Rey
I. San José
San Miguel
La Palma
El Real
Yaviza
Garachiné
Jaqué
Golfo de Panamá
Golfo del Darién
Arch. de San Blás
Puerto Obaldía
Acandí
Juradó
Cupica
Golfo de Cupica
Pta Logos
El Valle
Bajo Baudó
Pta Charambirá
Puerto Colombia
Baranoa **Soledad**
Sabanalarga
Arjona Turbaco Calamar
Santa Marta
Ciénaga
Cabo de la Vela
Carrizal
Uribi
Ríohacha
Carraipía
Maicao
Valledupar
Fundación
P. Cristóbal Colón ▲ 5775 m
Villanueva
Maracai
Barrancas
Campo
El Carmen de Bolívar
Plato
Chiriguaná
El Difícil
Augustín Codazzi
Machiques
Ciuda
Sincelejo Tolú Sincé
Lorica
Montería
Puerto Rey Cereté
Sahagún
Magangué
El Banco
Mompós
Ocaña
Tamalameque
La Gloria
Chinácota
San
Planeta Rica Ayapel
Tierralta
Caucasia
Simití
Cáchira
Pedra
Zaragoza
Cáceres
Barrancabermeja
Puerto Berrio
Amalfi Segovia
Yarumal
Dabeiba
Ituango ▲ 3960 m
Paramillo
Antioquia
Anzá
Bolívar
Andes
Itagüí
Envigado
Quibdó
Cisneros
Cocorná
Santa Bárbara
Sonsón
Aguadas
Salamina
Manizales
Líbano
Pereira
Cartago
Armenia
Ibagué
Sevilla
Saldaña
Tuluá
Buga Chaparral
Buenaventura
B. de Buenaventura
Yumbo
Cali **Palmira**
Puerto Tejada Aipe
Naya Baraya
Santander
Pta Coco
Guapi
Mosquera
Co Munchique ▲ 3012 m
Popayán
Volcán Puracé ▲ 4646 m
Gigante
La Plata
Garzón
Altamira
Pitalito

Pamplona
Floridablanca
Zapatoca
Sierra Nevada del Cocuy ▲ 5493 m
San Gil
Socorro El Cocuy
Vélez Barbosa Belén Paz de Río
Chiquinquirá Duitama Sogamoso
La Dorada Honda
Armero
Tunja
Nev. del Ruiz ▲ 5399 m
Facatativá
Zipaquirá
Ubate Chocontá
Yopal
Soacha
Fusagasugá ▲ 4560 m **Villavicencio**
Agua de Dios
Cerro Nevado
San Martín Puerto López
Nev. de Huila ▲ 5750 m
Neiva
Campoalegre

COLOMBIA

Chafurray
Granada Pavón
Maní
Puerto La Concordia
San José del Gua
San Vicente del Caguán
Calamar
Florencia
Miraflo
Mesa de Iguaje
Macayari
Tres Esquinas
Santa Rita
Cerro Cumare ▲ 720 m
Macujer

Tumaco
Barbacoas
Sotomayor
La Unión
La Cruz
Florencia
Ensenada de Tumaco
B. de Ancón de Sardinas
San Lorenzo
Valdez
Esmeraldas
Punta Galera
Muisné
Cabo de San Francisco
Rosa Zárate
El Diviso Sandoná
Nev. de Cumbal ▲ 4764 m
Pasto
El Divoso
Túquerres
Ipiales
Tulcán
San Gabriel
San Lorenzo
Mocoa
Puerto Asís
Otavalo
Ibarra
Volcán Cayambe ▲ 5790 m
Cayambe
Lago Agrio
Cuyabeno
Hacha
La Tagua
Puerto Leguízamo
La Chorrera
Santo Domingo de los Colorados
Machachi
Quito ▲ 5704 m
Vol. Antisana ▲ 5704 m
Baeza
Puerto Francisco de Orellana
Araracuara
Co Maine Hanari ▲ 860 m
Vol. Cotopaxi ▲ 5897 m
B. de Caráquez
Bahía de Caráquez Chone
Rocafuerte
Latacunga Tena
Manta
Montecristi
Quevedo
Portoviejo
Santa Ana
Zapotal
Chimborazo ▲ 6310 m
Ambato
Puyo
Pantoja
Santa María
Jipijapa Balzar
Guaranda **Riobamba**
Villano
Arica
El Encanto
Paján Babahoyo
Vol. Sangay ▲ 5230 m

ECUADOR

Río Tigre
Santa Lucía
Alausí
Macas
Ayuy Montalvo
Arica
B. de Sta Elena
Morona
Puca Urco
Salinas
Guayaquil **Durán**
Santa Elena
Cañar Azogues
Morona
Puerto Tunigrama Andoas
Playas
Naranjal **Cuenca**
Girón Gualaceo
Santa Clotilde
Pebas
Golfo de Guayaquil
Isla Puná
Machala
Zarumilla Santa Rosa
Saraguro
Puerto Pardo
Intuto
Mazán
Francisco de Orellana
Tumbes
Zorritos
Piñas
Zamora
Borja
Santa María de Nanay
Canoas
Catacocha
Loja
Cariamanga
Puerto Pardo
Arica
Santa María
Mancora

PERU

Omaguas
Tamshiyacu
Lobitos
Macará Suyo
Talara
Concordia
Nauta
Pta Pariñas
Las Lomas San Ignacio
Barranca
Negritos
Sullana Tambo Grande
Chulucanas
La Huaca
Piura
Cahuapanas
Lagunas
Requena
Brasil
Paita
Catacaos
Castilla
Orellana

Bogotá

Quito

Panamá

Barranquilla

Medellín

Cali

Guayaquil

Cartagena

Bucaramanga

Cúcuta

Iquitos

Equator

454

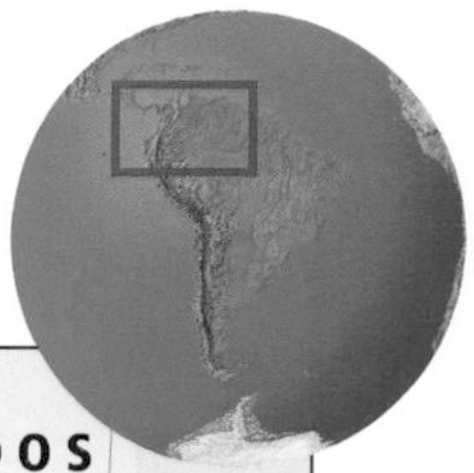

70° E 66° F 62° G

427

ARUBA (Neth.)
NETHERLANDS ANTILLES (Neth.)
Curaçao
Bonaire
Kralendijk
Willemstad
Oranjestad
Pen. de Paraguaná
Pueblo Nuevo
Puerto Cumarebo
Coro
Píritu
LESSER ANTILLES
La Orchila
La Blanquilla
The Grenadines
Grenville
St George's
GRENADA
BARBADOS
Tobago
Charlotteville
Scarborough
Galera Pt
TRINIDAD AND TOBAGO
Arima
Sangre Grande
Trinidad
Rio Claro
Galeota Pt
Port of Spain
San Fernando
Golfo de Paria
Pen. de Paria
Bocas del Dragón
Boca de la Serpiente
Boca Araguao
Boca Grande
Isla de Margarita
La Asunción
Porlamar
Carúpano
Río Caribe
Güiria
La Tortuga
Cumaná
C. Codera
Higuerote
Puerto la Cruz
Barcelona
Caripe
Caripito
Maturín
San Juan de los Cayos
Pedregal
Jacura
Churuguara
Baragua
Cerro El Cerron 1990 m
Puerto Cabello
Catia La Mar
Caracas
Petare
Baruta
Los Teques
Maracay
Valencia
San Felipe
La Victoria
Barquisimeto
Yaritagua
El Tocuyo
San Carlos
Tinaco
El Pao
Acarigua
San Juan de los Morros
Ortiz
Trujillo
Boconó
Guanare
Nueva Florida
El Sombrero
Chaguaramas
Calabozo
El Baúl
Las Mercedes
San Antonio de Tamanaco
Zaraza
Aragua de Barcelona
Anaco
Cantaura
Valle de la Pascua
El Chaparro
El Tigre
Santa María de Ipire
Pariaguán
San José de Guanipa
Tucupita
Barrancas
Barinas
Obispos
Guanarito
San Mauricio
Puerto de Nutrias
Camaguán
Puerto Miranda
San Fernando de Apure
Achaguas
Cabruta
Parmana
Caicara de Orinoco
Boca del Pao
Mapire
Soledad
Ciudad Bolívar
Ciudad Guayana
Puerto Ordaz
Upata
El Pao
El Palmar
El Toro
San José de Amacuro
Waini Pt
Morawhanna
Mabaruma
Palmarito
Mantecal
Arauca
Capanaparo
Elorza
La Urbana
Maripa
Ciudad Piar
Embalse de Guri
Co Turagua 1839 m
Las Lajitas
Las Trincheras
La Paragua
San Pedro de Las Bocas
El Callao
Guasipati
El Miamo
Tumeremo
Serranía de Imataca
La Horqueta
Port Kaituma
Baramanni
Matthews Ridge
Marlborough
Anna Regina
Charity
Suddie
Spring Garden
Georgetown
Parika
Enmore
Mahaicony
1320 m
VENEZUELA
El Dorado
GUYANA
Cuyuni
Barama
Cinaruco
Meta
Cravo Norte
Parguaza
Puerto Páez
Puerto Carreño
Sa de Parguaza
Casuarito
Puerto Ayacucho
Sierra Guanay
Co Yavi 2285 m
Co Guaiquinima 2100 m
Auyantepui 2585 m
Puerto Nuevo
Tomo
Samariapo
San Juan
Sierra Maigualida
Meseta del Co Jáua
Guiana Highlands
Sierra del Zamuro
Luepa
Equeipa
La Gran Sabana
Pakaraima Mountains
Mte Roraima 2810 m
Arabopó
Uacauyén
Santa Elena de Uairén
Keweigek
Tumureng
Peter's Mine
Bartica
Fort Wellington
Rosignol
New Amsterdam
Nieuw Nickerie
Linden
Mara
Corriverton
Issano
Malali
Paradise
Kangaruma
Tumatumari
Mahdia
Ituni
Orealla
Kwakwani
Epira
Apoera
Ventuari
Arabelo
Rejunya
Maihiá
Vichada
Sucuaro
José de Ocuné
Mituas
Puerto Inírida
San Fernando de Atabapo
Arrecifal
Co Marahuaca 2579 m
Co Duida 2404 m
La Esmeralda
San Antonio
Uaicás
Serra Pacaraima
Sa Tepequém
Tepequém
Orinduik
Maipuri Landing
Normandia
Apoteri
Annai
Yupukarri
Kabalebo stuwmeer
Co Guasacaví 668 m
Co Canapiare 692 m
Tomo
Inírida
Capibara
Boca Mavaca
Serra Parima
Uraricoera
Mucajaí
Boa Vista
Lethem
Kanuku Mts
Dadanawa
Aishalton
Isherton
Serra do Mucajaí
Sierra de Unturán
Serra Curupira
Orinoco
San Carlos
CLAIMED BY SURINAME
Caracaraí
RORAIMA
Biloku
Kamoa Mts
734 m
Serra Acaraí
502 m
Serra Iricoumé
Iutica
Cucuí
Pico Tamacuarí 2340 m
Pico da Neblina 3014 m
Pico Padauari 2755 m
Iauaretê
Içana
Taraquá
São Gabriel da Cachoeira
São José
Tapurucuara
Ilha Grande
Catrimani
Uberlândia
PARÁ
Equator
Boiaçu
Barcelos
Vila Bittencourt
Pedrera
Mamori
Japurá
Maraã
Carvoeiro
Moura
BRAZIL
Represa de Balbina
Santa Maria
Balbina
Novo Airão
Faro
Nhamundá
Urucará
Parintins
Santa Clara
Tarapacá
Tonantins
Jutaí
Fonte Boa
Uarini
AMAZONAS
Santo Antônio do Içá
São Paulo de Olivença
Amaturá
Alvarães
Tefé
Juruá
Manaus
Itapiranga
Silves
Urucurituba
Barreirinha
Itacoatiara
Manacapuru
Badajós
Codajás
Anori
Anamã
Careiro
Autazes
Ilha Tupinambarana
Ariaú
Maués
Sapucaia
Leticia
Tabatinga
Benjamin Constant
Coari
Lago de Coari
Beruri
Axinim
Novo Olinda do Norte
Canumã
Borba
Laranjal
Cantagalo
Carauari
Itaboca
Arumã
São Pedro
Vila Nova
Jutaí
Purus
Madeira
Novo Aripuanã
Lua Nova

1 2 3 4 5
10° 6° 2° 2°

452

E 66° F 62° G 58° H

455

0 100 200 300 400 kilometers
0 100 200 miles
Scale 1:7,000,000
Projection: Azimuthal Equal Area

Northeast Brazil • Suriname • French Guiana

58° B 54° C 50° D 46°

1

Georgetown
Parika
Enmore
Mahaicony
Fort Wellington
Rosignol
New Amsterdam
Linden
Mara
GUYANA
Corriverton
Malali
Paradise
Ituni
Orealla
Kwakwani
Epira
Apoera
Maipuri Landing
Apoteri
Nieuw Nickerie
Totness
Wageningen
Paramaribo
Alliance
Nieuw Amsterdam
Groningen
Boskamp
Onverwacht
Zanderij
Moengo
Albina
Corneliskondre
Sabana
Kwakoegron
Brokopondo
Njoeng Jacobkondre
Afobaka
W J van Blommestein Meer
Pokigron
Gramankondre
Aurora
Boslanti
Boto-Pasi
Djoemoe
694 m
SURINAME
Kabalebo stuwmeer
Julianatop 1230 m
Eilerts de Haan Gebergte
Pontoetoe
Cottica
Maripasoula
De Goeje Gebergte 658 m
Oranje Gebergte
Antecume Pata
Mana
Organabo
Iracoubo
Sinnamary
Malmanoury
St-Laurent du Maroni
Kourou
Cayenne
La Forestière
Apatou
Gare Tigre
Tonate
Rémire
St Elie
Montsinéry
Roura
Citron
Délices
Cacao
Kaw
FRENCH GUIANA (Fr.)
Régina
Guisanbourg
Grand-Santi
Bélizon
Ouanary
Cabo Orange
Ponta dos Índios
Baie d' Oyapock
Cormontibo
Patience
Mt Bellevue de l'Inini 851 m
Ouaqui
Saül
St-Georges
Oiapoque
Clevelândia do Norte
Clément
Bienvenue
Camopi
Oscar
Vila Velha
CLAIMED BY SURINAME
Mitaraka 690 m
Mt Saint-Marcel 635 m
Regina
Lourenço
Calçoene
Amapá
Ilha de Maracá
Serra Lombarda
CLAIMED BY SURINAME
Serra Tumucumaque
AMAPÁ
Cabo Norte
2
Biloku
Serra Acaraí
734 m
502 m
Serra Iricoumé
Tacalé
Yaripo
Merirumã
Aporema
Bailique
Ferreira Gomes
Ilha Curuá
Serra do Navio
Pôrto Grande
Maloca
Azauri
Ilha Janaucu
Ilha Caviana
Canal Perigoso
Ilha Mexiana
Cabo Maguarinho
Macapá
Mazagão
Pôrto Santana
Afuá
Chaves
Canal do Sul
Baía de Marajó
Equator
Arere
3
Planalto Maracanaquará
Barraca da Bôca
Itatupã
Ilha Grande de Gurupá
Ilha Anajás
Ilha de Marajó
Soure
Salvaterra
Anajás
Cachoeira do Arari
Marapanim
Salinópolis
Curuçá
Vigia
Maracanã
Colares
Igarapé-Açu
Bragança
Viseu
Mosqueiro
Castanhal
Capanema
Carut
Bôca do Jari
Curumu
Morro Grande 629 m
Almeirim
Gurupá
Ilha dos Macacos
Ilha da Breves
Ponta de Pedras
São Sebastião da Boa Vista
Belém
São Miguel do Guamá
Ourém
Cumiranga
Pôrto de Moz
Laguna
Melgaço
Portel
Curralinho
Bagre
Abaetetuba
Acará
Irituia
Monte Alegre 350 m
Mulata
Prainha
Oriximiná
Óbidos
Alenquer
Monte Alegre
Santa Maria
Faro
Juruti
Nhamundá
Juruti Velho
Santarém
Veiros
Carvalho
Bom Jardim
Cametá
São Joaquim
Badajós
Canindé
Mocajuba
Baião
Urucará
Parintins
Urucurituba
Barreirinha
Itapiranga
Silves
Belterra
Pacoval
Santa Cruz
Boim
Vitória
Belo Monte
Bertinho
PARÁ
Serra do Tapará
Altamira
Pindobal
Itacoatiara
Ariaú
Sapucaia
Maués
Aveiro
Brasília Legal
Ilha Tupinambarana
Autazes
Novo Olinda do Norte
Caima
Tucuruí
Represa de Tucuruí
Pindaré-M
Serra do Tiracambu
4
Canumã
AMAZONAS
Itaituba
Uxituba
Laranjal
Vila Nova
Pôrto Alegre
Sem Tripa
Jacundá
Rondon do Pará
Serra do Gurupi
Cantagalo
Paga Conta
Itupiranga
Marabá
São João do Araguaia
Açailândia
Imperatriz
Amarante do Maranhão
Lua Nova
Entre Rios
Serra dos Carajás
Araguatins
Montes Altos
São Sebastião
Parauapebas
Tocantinópolis
BRAZIL
Xambioá
Pôrto Franco
Araras
Nazaré
Araguanã
Jacareacanga
São Félix do Xingu
Xinguara
Babaçulândia
Araguaína
Carolina
Riachão
Manuelzinho
Pau d'Arco
Canudos
Cuiaba
Barra de São Manuel
Piacá
TOCANTINS
5
Redenção
Conceição do Araguaia
Couto Magalhães
Itacajá
Tupiratins
Serra dos Gradaús
Aldeia Velha
Serra do Estrondo
Recreio
Serra do Cachimbo
Santa Maria das Barreiras
Araguacema
Pedro Afonso
Alto Par
Campo Grande
Barracão do Barreto
Cachimbo
Miracema do Tocantins
Serra do Penitente

451
456

A 58° B 54° C 50° D 46°

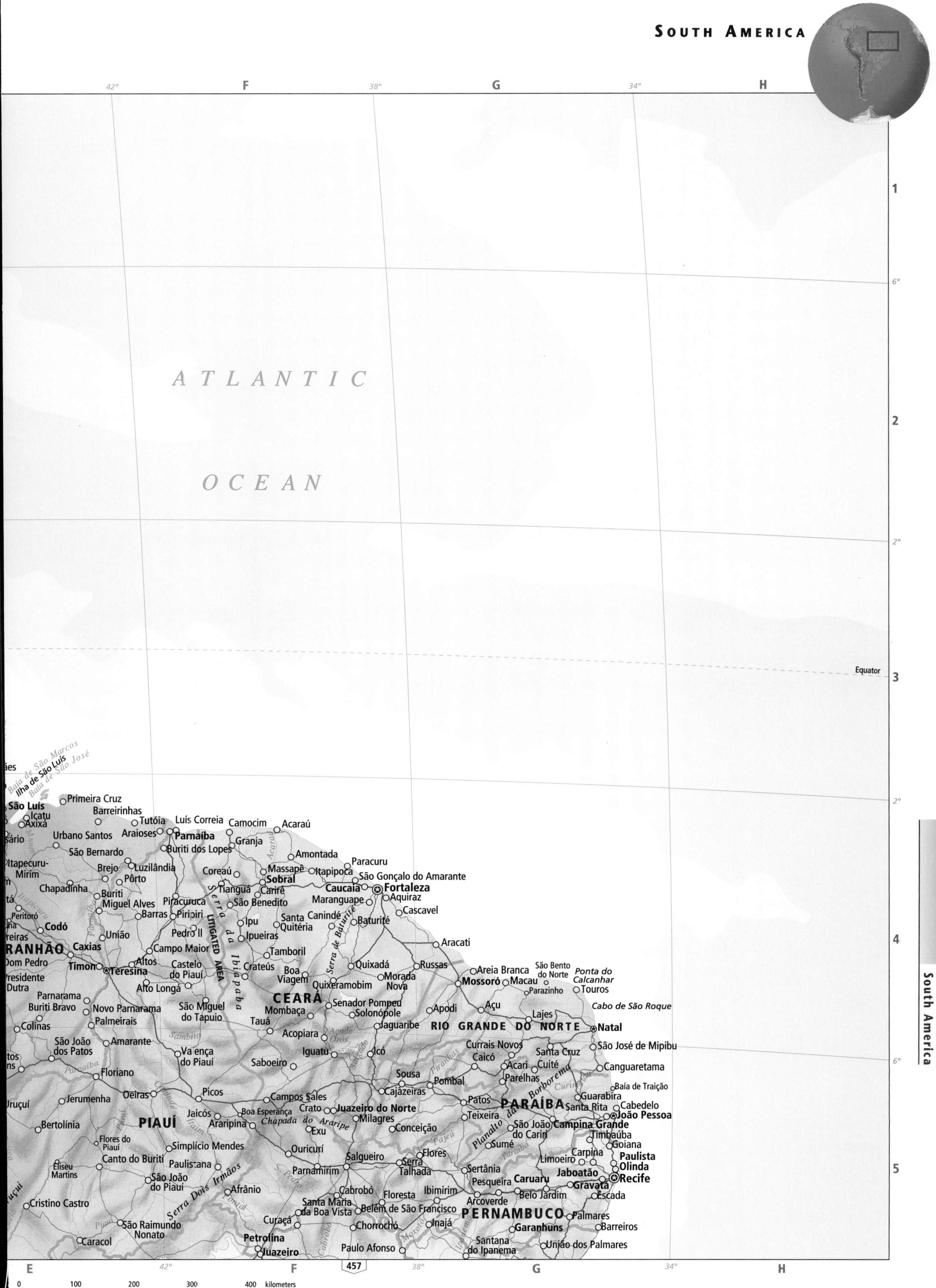

42° F 38° G 34° H

1

ATLANTIC

OCEAN

2

Equator

3

Baía de São Marcos
Ilha de São Luís
Baía de São José
São Luís
Primeira Cruz
Barreirinhas
Icatu
Axixá
Tutóia
Luís Correia
Camocim
Acaraú
Urbano Santos
Araioses
Parnaíba
Granja
São Bernardo
Buriti dos Lopes
Amontada
Itapecuru-Mirim
Brejo
Luzilândia
Coreaú
Massapê
Itapipoca
Paracuru
Pôrto
Sobral
São Gonçalo do Amarante
Chapadinha
Buriti
Tianguá
Cariré
Caucaia
Fortaleza
Miguel Alves
Piracuruca
São Benedito
Maranguape
Aquiraz
Peritoró
Barras
Piripiri
Serra da Ibiapaba
LITIGATED AREA
Ipu
Santa Quitéria
Canindé
Baturité
Cascavel
Codó
União
Pedro II
Ipueiras
Serra de Baturité
Aracati
Caxias
Campo Maior
Tamboril
4
Dom Pedro
Timon
Teresina
Altos
Castelo do Piauí
Crateús
Boa Viagem
Quixadá
Morada Nova
Russas
Areia Branca
São Bento do Norte
Ponta do Calcanhar
Presidente Dutra
Alto Longá
Quixeramobim
Mossoró
Macau
Touros
Parazinho
Parnarama
Buriti Bravo
Novo Parnarama
São Miguel do Tapuio
CEARÁ
Senador Pompeu
Apodi
Açu
Cabo de São Roque
Palmeirais
Mombaça
Solonópole
Lajes
Colinas
Tauá
Jaguaribe
RIO GRANDE DO NORTE
Natal
São João dos Patos
Amarante
Acopiara
Açude Orós
Currais Novos
São José de Mipibu
Valença do Piauí
Iguatu
Icó
Caicó
Santa Cruz
Saboeiro
Acari
Cuité
Canguaretama
Floriano
Sousa
Parelhas
Pombal
Baía de Traição
Oeiras
Picos
Campos Sales
Cajazeiras
Patos
Guarabira
Uruçuí
Jerumenha
Jaicós
Boa Esperança
Crato
Juazeiro do Norte
PARAÍBA
Santa Rita
Cabedelo
João Pessoa
PIAUÍ
Araripina
Chapada do Araripe
Milagres
Teixeira
São João do Cariri
Campina Grande
Bertolínia
Flores do Piauí
Exu
Conceição
Planalto da Borborema
Timbaúba
Simplício Mendes
Sumé
Goiana
Canto do Buriti
Ouricurí
Salgueiro
Flores
Carpina
Paulista
Eliseu Martins
Paulistana
Parnamirim
Serra Talhada
Sertânia
Limoeiro
Olinda
São João do Piauí
Serra Dois Irmãos
Pesqueira
Caruaru
Jaboatão
5
Afrânio
Cabrobó
Floresta
Ibimirim
Gravatá
Recife
Cristino Castro
Santa Maria da Boa Vista
Belém de São Francisco
Belo Jardim
Escada
Arcoverde
São Raimundo Nonato
Curaçá
Chorrochó
Inajá
PERNAMBUCO
Palmares
Garanhuns
Barreiros
Caracol
Petrolina
Juazeiro
Paulo Afonso
Santana do Ipanema
União dos Palmares

E 42° F 38° G 34° H

457

0 100 200 300 400 kilometers
0 100 200 miles
Scale 1:7,000,000
Projection: Azimuthal Equal Area

Bolivia • Peru • Southwest Brazil • North Paraguay

PACIFIC
OCEAN
PERU
CORDILLERA CENTRAL
CORDILLERA OCCIDENTAL
Cordillera Oriental
Cordillera Azul
Cordillera Vilcabamba
Cordillera Urubamba
Lima
Callao
Trujillo
Chiclayo
Piura
Sullana
Chimbote
Huancayo
Ayacucho
Cuzco
Pucallpa
Huánuco
Cajamarca
Ica
Nazca
Pisco
Huacho
Huaraz
Abancay
Moyobamba
Tarapoto
Yurimaguas
Cerro de Pasco
La Oroya
Huancavelica
Quillabamba
Cruzeiro do Sul
Bahía de Sechura
Desierto de Sechura
Pen. de Paracas
Pta Salinas ó Lachay
Nev. Huascarán 6768 m
Cerro Yerupaja 6634 m
Nev. Coropuna 6425 m
Nev. Auzangate 6384 m
Nev. Ampato 6310 m
Nev. Chachani 6075 m
Pumasillo 6246 m
Mollendo
Camaná
Marcona
Arequ
Moquegu
Ilo
Pta Coles
450
A
B
C
D
1
2
3
4
5
82°
78°
74°
6°
10°
14°
18°

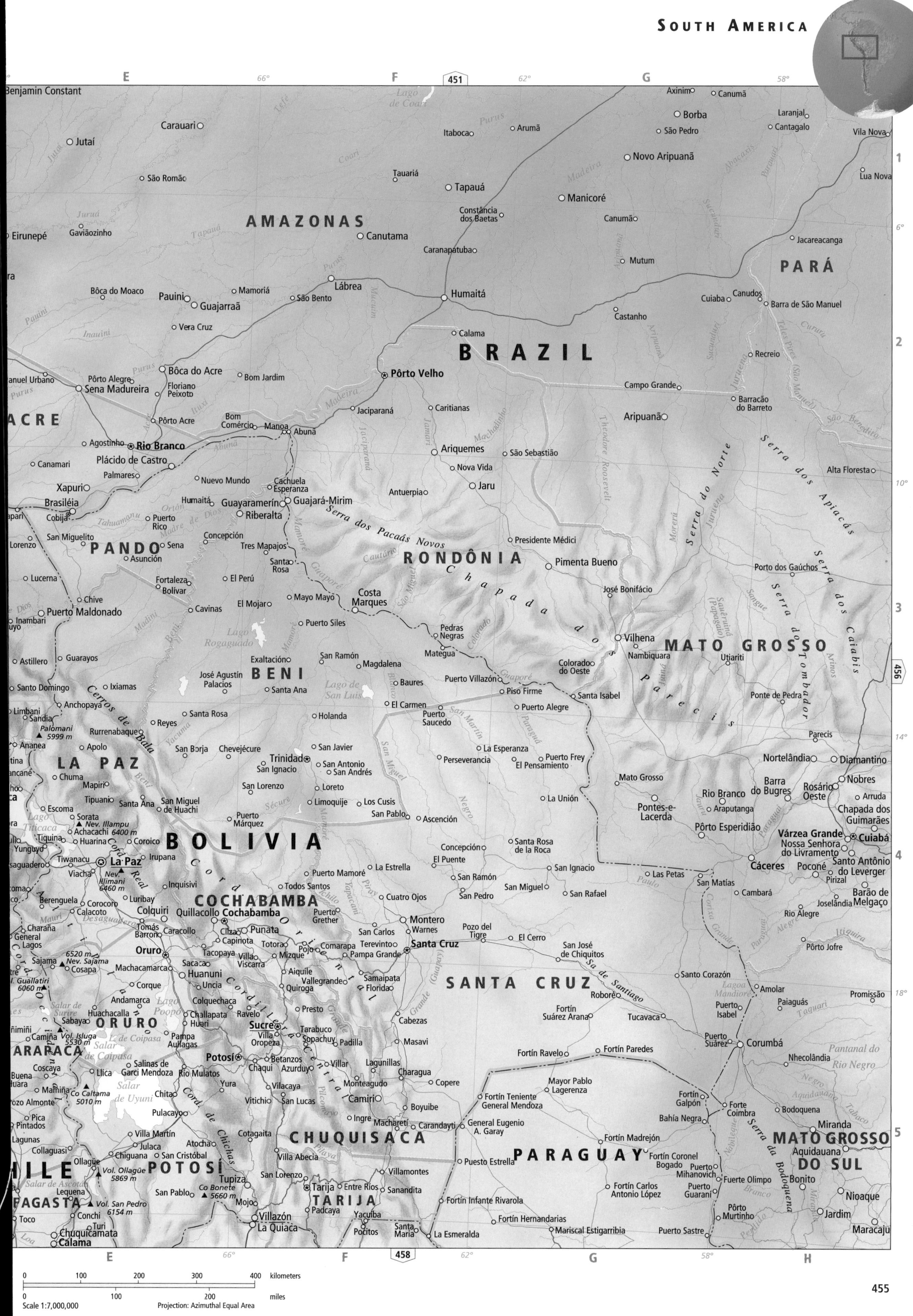
BRAZIL
AMAZONAS
RONDÔNIA
MATO GROSSO
PARÁ
ACRE
BOLIVIA
PANDO
BENI
LA PAZ
COCHABAMBA
ORURO
POTOSÍ
CHUQUISACA
SANTA CRUZ
TARIJA
PARAGUAY
MATO GROSSO DO SUL
Pôrto Velho
Rio Branco
La Paz
Sucre
Cochabamba
Santa Cruz

Itaboca
Arumã

Axinim
Canumã

Borba
São Pedro

Laranjal
Cantagalo

Vila Nova

São Romão

Tauariá
Tapauá

Novo Aripuanã

Lua Nova

Gaviãozinho

Constância
dos Baetas

Manicoré

Canumã

Jacareacanga

Eirunepé

Canutama

Mutum

Bôca do Moaco
Pauini
Guajarraã
Vera Cruz

Mamoriá
São Bento

Lábrea

Humaitá

Manuel Urbano
Pôrto Alegre
Sena Madureira

Bôca do Acre

Bom Jardim

Calama

Campo Grande

Barracão
do Barreto

Floriano
Peixoto

Jaciparaná
Caritianas

Aripuanã

Pôrto Acre

Bom
Comércio
Manoa
Abunã

Ariquemes

São Sebastião

Alta Floresta

Agostinho

Nuevo Mundo

Nova Vida

Plácido de Castro
Palmares

Cachuela
Esperanza

Jaru

Canamari

Humaitá
Guayaramerín
Guajará-Mirim

Antuerpiao

Xapuri
Brasiléia
Cobija

Riberalta

Presidente Médici

Pimenta Bueno

Porto dos Gaúchos

Lorenzo
San Miguelito
Sena
Asunción

Santa
Rosa

José Bonifácio

Lucerna

Fortaleza
Bolívar

El Perú

Mayo Mayó

Costa
Marques

Vilhena
Nambiquara

Chive
Cavinas

El Mojaru

Colorado
do Oeste

Puerto Maldonado

Puerto Siles

Pedras
Negras

Santa Isabel

Ponte de Pedra

Inambari
tuyo

Astillero
Guarayos

Exaltación

San Ramón
Magdalena

Matega

Puerto Villazón

Puerto Alegre

Parecis

Santo Domingo
Anchopaya

Ixiamas

Baures

El Carmen

Piso Firme

Nortelândia
Diamantino

Limbani
Sandia
Palomani
5999 m

Reyes

Santa Rosa

Santa Ana

Holanda

Puerto
Saucedo

La Esperanza

Puerto Frey
El Pensamiento

Barra
do Bugres

Rosário
Oeste

Nobres

Arruda

Ananea
Apolo

Rurrenabaque

San Borja

Chevejécure

San Javier

Perseverancia

Chuma

Mapiri

Trinidad
San Ignacio

San Antonio
San Andrés

La Unión

Pontes-e-
Lacerda

Pôrto Esperidião

Várzea Grande
Nossa Senhora
do Livramento

Cuiabá

Tipuani
Santa Ana

San Lorenzo

Loreto

Concepción

Santa Rosa
de la Roca

Cáceres

Poconé

Santo Antônio
do Levreger

Escoma
Sorata
Nev. Illampu

San Miguel
de Huachi

Puerto
Márquez

Limoquije
Los Cusis
San Pablo

Ascención

San Ramón

San Ignacio

Pirizal

Coroico

El Puente

San Miguel

San Rafael

Las Petas

Cambará

Barão de
Melgaço

Tiwanacu
Irupana

Rio Alegre

Joselândia

Achacachi 6400 m
Huarina

Nev.
Illimani
6460 m

Inquisivi

Puerto Mamoré

La Estrella

Cuatro Ojos

San Pedro

San José
de Chiquitos

Pôrto Jofre

Viacha

Todos Santos

Pozo del
Tigre

El Cerro

Santo Corazón

Berenguela
Corocoro

Luribay

Colquiri

Quillacollo Cochabamba

Puerto
Grether

San Carlos
Terevinto

Warnes

Montero

General
Lagos

Tomás
Barron

Caracollo

Punata
Capinota

Comarapa

El Cerro

Roboré

Amolar

Promissão

6520 m
Nev. Sajama

Totora
Mizque

Pampa Grande

Sajama
Cosapa

Machacamarca

Sacaca

Villa
Viscarra

Aiquile

Samaipata
Florida

Santa Rosa
de la Roca

Fortín
Suárez Arana

Tucavaca

Puerto
Isabel

Paiaguás

I. Guallatiri
6060 m

Andamarca
Corque

Huanuni
Uncia

Vallegrande
Quiroga

Colquechaca

Huari

Presto

Cabezas

Masavi

Fortín Ravelo

Fortín Paredes

Puerto
Suárez

Corumbá

Nhecolândia

Pantanal do
Rio Negro

Camiña
Vol. Isluga
5530 m

Sabaya

Challapata
Ravelo

Villa
Oropeza

Tarabuco
Sopachuy

Padilla

Lagunillas

Mayor Pablo
Lagerenza

Fortín
Galpón

Forte
Coimbra

Bodoquena

ARARACA

Huachacalla

Pampa
Aullagas

Betanzos

Villar

Charagua

Bahía Negra

Miranda

Coscaya

L. de Coipasa

Salinas de
Garci Mendoza

Chaqui
Azurduy

Montegudo

Copere

Fortín Teniente
General Mendoza

General Eugenio
A. Garay

Fortín
Bogado

Fuerte Olimpo

Aquidauana

Bonito

Buena

Salar
de Coipasa

Llica

Rio Mulatos

Yura

Vilacaya

Boyuibe

DO SUL

HILE

Mamiña
Pica

Co Caltama
5010 m

Chita

Pulacayo

Vitichio
San Lucas

Camiri

Ingre
Macharetí

Carandayti

Fortín Madrejón

Fortín Coronel
Bogado
Mihanovich

Puerto
Guaraní

Pôrto
Murtinho

Nioaque

Pozo Almonte

Lagunas
Collaguasi

Salar de Uyuni

Cotagaita

Villa Abecia

Villamontes

Puesto Estrella

Fortín Carlos
Antonio López

Jardim

Maracaju

Ollagüe
Vol. Ollagüe
5869 m

Tupiza

San Lorenzo

San Pablo

Entre Ríos

Sanandita

Fortín Infante Rivarola

San Cristóbal

Villazón

Co Bonete
5660 m

Mojo

Yacuba

Fortín Hernandarias

Conchi
Turi

Chiguana
Julaca

Atocha

Pocitos

Santa
María

La Quiaca

Padcaya

Mariscal Estigarribia

Puerto Sastre

Calama

Vol. San Pedro
6154 m

Toco

La Esmeralda

0 100 200 300 400 kilometers

0 100 200 miles

Scale 1:7,000,000
Projection: Azimuthal Equal Area
kilometers
miles

Southeast Brazil

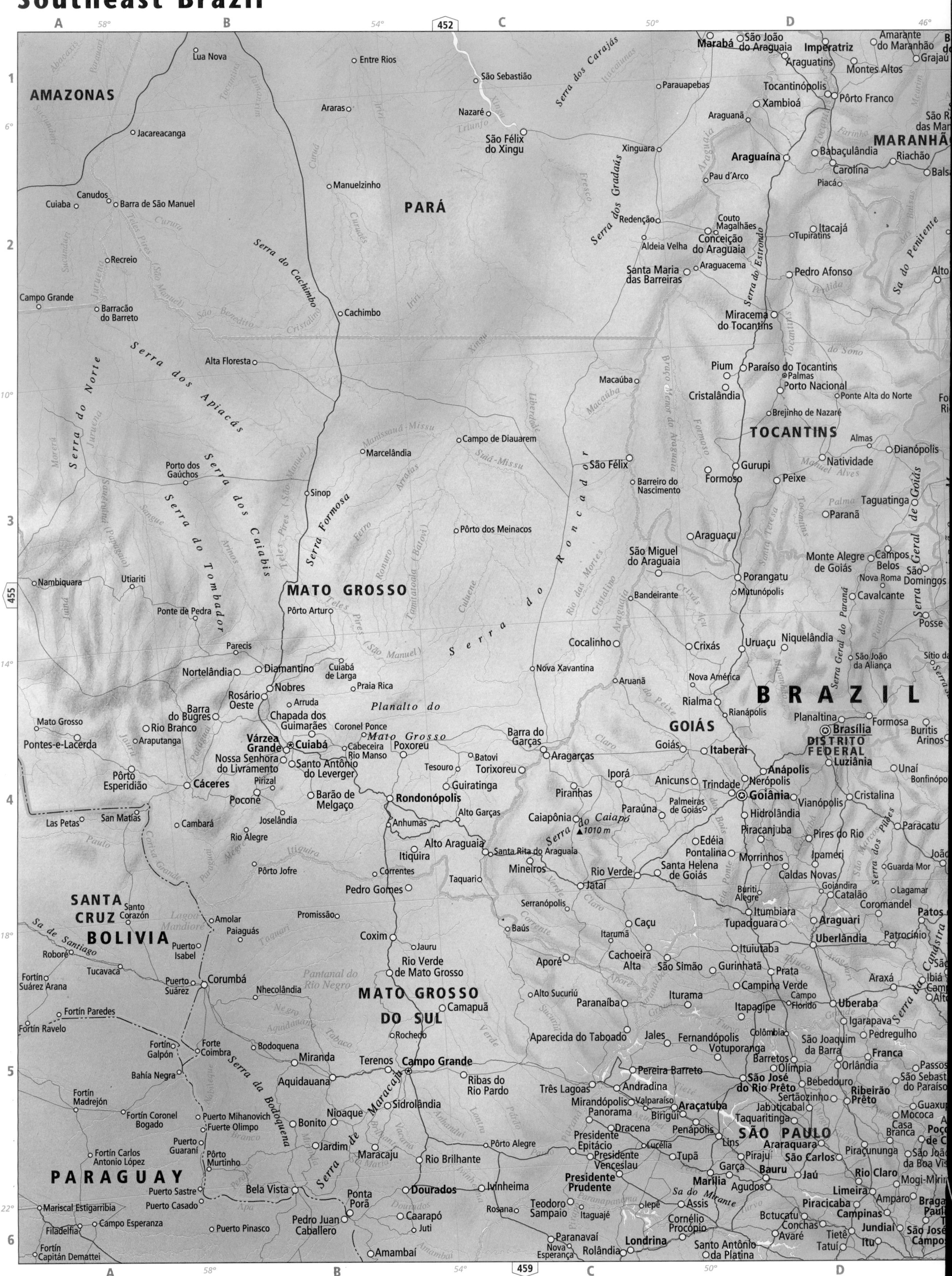
A
B
C
D
58°
54°
50°
46°
452
455
459
1
2
3
4
5
6
6°
10°
14°
18°
22°
AMAZONAS
PARÁ
MARANHÃO
TOCANTINS
MATO GROSSO
GOIÁS
BRAZIL
DISTRITO FEDERAL
MATO GROSSO DO SUL
SÃO PAULO
SANTA CRUZ
BOLIVIA
PARAGUAY
Lua Nova
Entre Rios
São Sebastião
Araras
Nazaré
São Félix do Xingu
Jacareacanga
Manuelzinho
Canudos
Cuiaba
Barra de São Manuel
Recreio
Campo Grande
Barracão do Barreto
Cachimbo
Alta Floresta
Serra do Cachimbo
Serra dos Apiacás
Serra do Norte
Serra dos Caiabis
Serra do Tombador
Serra Formosa
Serra do Roncador
Serra dos Carajás
Serra dos Gradaús
Serra do Estrondo
Marabá
São João do Araguaia
Imperatriz
Araguatins
Montes Altos
Amarante do Maranhão
Grajaú
Parauapebas
Tocantinópolis
Xambioá
Pôrto Franco
Araguanã
Xinguara
Araguaína
Babaçulândia
Riachão
Carolina
Balsas
Piacá
Pau d'Arco
Redenção
Aldeia Velha
Couto Magalhães
Conceição do Araguaia
Tupiratins
Itacajá
Santa Maria das Barreiras
Araguacema
Pedro Afonso
Miracema do Tocantins
Macaúba
Pium
Paraíso do Tocantins
Palmas
Porto Nacional
Cristalândia
Ponte Alta do Norte
Brejinho de Nazaré
Almas
Dianópolis
Campo de Diauarem
Marcelândia
São Félix
Barreiro do Nascimento
Gurupi
Formoso
Natividade
Peixe
Taguatinga
Paranã
Porto dos Gaúchos
Sinop
Pôrto dos Meinacos
Araguaçu
São Miguel do Araguaia
Porangatu
Mutunópolis
Monte Alegre de Goiás
Campos Belos
Nova Roma
São Domingos
Cavalcante
Posse
Nambiquara
Utiariti
Ponte de Pedra
Pôrto Arturo
Bandeirante
Parecis
Cocalinho
Crixás
Uruaçu
Niquelândia
São João da Aliança
Nortelândia
Diamantino
Cuiabá de Larga
Nova Xavantina
Rosário Oeste
Nobres
Praia Rica
Aruanã
Nova América
Rialma
Rianápolis
Planaltina
Formosa
Buritis
Arinos
Arruda
Planalto do Mato Grosso
Chapada dos Guimarães
Coronel Ponce
Barra do Bugres
Mato Grosso
Rio Branco
Pontes-e-Lacerda
Araputanga
Várzea Grande
Cuiabá
Cabeceira Rio Manso
Poxoreu
Barra do Garças
Goiás
Itaberaí
Brasília
Luziânia
Unaí
Nossa Senhora do Livramento
Santo Antônio do Leverger
Tesouro
Batovi
Torixoreu
Aragarças
Iporá
Anicuns
Trindade
Anápolis
Nerópolis
Goiânia
Vianópolis
Cristalina
Bonfinópolis
Pôrto Esperidião
Cáceres
Pirizal
Poconé
Barão de Melgaço
Guiratinga
Rondonópolis
Piranhas
Palmeiras de Goiás
Hidrolândia
Las Petas
San Matías
Cambará
Joselândia
Alto Garças
Caiapônia
Serra do Caiapó
1010 m
Paraúna
Piracanjuba
Pires do Rio
Paracatu
Anhumas
Rio Alegre
Itiquira
Alto Araguaia
Santa Rita do Araguaia
Edéia
Pontalina
Ipameri
Pôrto Jofre
Correntes
Mineiros
Rio Verde
Santa Helena de Goiás
Morrinhos
Caldas Novas
Guarda Mor
Pedro Gomes
Taquari
Jataí
Buriti Alegre
Goiandira
Catalão
Lagamar
Coromandel
Patos
SANTA CRUZ
Santo Corazón
Amolar
Paiaguás
Promissão
Serranópolis
Itumbiara
Tupaciguara
Araguari
Caçu
Baús
Itarumã
Uberlândia
Patrocínio
Roboré
Puerto Isabel
Coxim
Jauru
Cachoeira Alta
São Simão
Ituiutaba
Aporé
Gurinhatã
Prata
Araxá
Ibiá
Fortín Suárez Arana
Tucavaca
Puerto Suárez
Corumbá
Rio Verde de Mato Grosso
Nhecolândia
Pantanal do Rio Negro
Alto Sucuriú
Paranaíba
Iturama
Campina Verde
Campo Florido
Uberaba
Fortín Paredes
Fortín Ravelo
Camapuã
Itapagipe
Igarapava
Rochedo
Aparecida do Taboado
Jales
Fernandópolis
Votuporanga
Colômbia
São Joaquim da Barra
Pedregulho
Fortín Galpón
Forte Coimbra
Bodoquena
Miranda
Terenos
Campo Grande
Barretos
Olímpia
Orlândia
Franca
Serra da Bodoquena
Bahía Negra
Aquidauana
Ribas do Rio Pardo
Três Lagoas
Andradina
Pereira Barreto
São José do Rio Prêto
Bebedouro
Ribeirão Prêto
Passos
São Sebastião do Paraíso
Fortín Madrejón
Sidrolândia
Mirandópolis
Valparaíso
Araçatuba
Sertãozinho
Jaboticabal
Guaxupé
Fortín Coronel Bogado
Puerto Mihanovich
Fuerte Olimpo
Nioaque
Bonito
Serra de Maracaju
Panorama
Birigui
Taquaritinga
Mococa
Casa Branca
Puerto Guaraní
Jardim
Dracena
Penápolis
Lins
Araraquara
Presidente Epitácio
Lucélia
Pirajuí
São Carlos
Piracununga
São João da Boa Vista
Fortín Carlos Antonio López
Pôrto Murtinho
Maracaju
Rio Brilhante
Pôrto Alegre
Presidente Venceslau
Tupã
Garça
Bauru
Jaú
Rio Claro
Mogi-Mirim
Puerto Sastre
Bela Vista
Ponta Porã
Dourados
Ivinheima
Presidente Prudente
Marília
Agudos
Limeira
Amparo
Bragança Paulista
Mariscal Estigarribia
Puerto Casado
Teodoro Sampaio
Rosana
Iepê
Assis
Piracicaba
Campinas
Campo Esperanza
Puerto Pinasco
Pedro Juan Caballero
Caarapó
Juti
Itaguajé
Cornélio Procópio
Botucatu
Conchas
Avaré
Tietê
Jundiaí
Filadelfia
Paranavaí
Londrina
Santo Antônio da Platina
Tatuí
Itu
Fortín Capitán Demattei
Amambaí
Nova Esperança
Rolândia
Xingu
Teles Pires
Juruena
Araguaia
Tocantins
Rio das Mortes
Paraná
Paranaíba
Paranapanema
Pardo
Taquari
Paraguai
Sa de Santiago
Serra Geral de Goiás
Serra Geral do Paraná

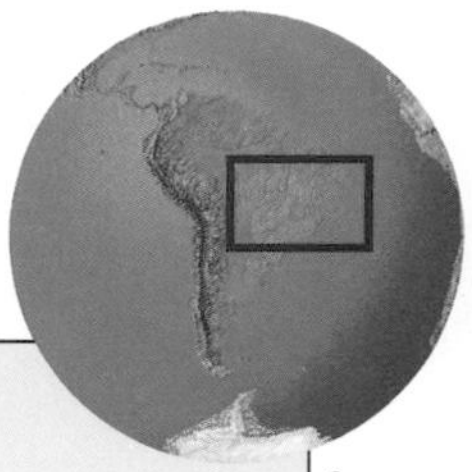

E 42° F 453 38° G 34° H

Parnaramá
Buriti Bravo
Novo Parnarama
Palmeirais
Colinas
São João dos Patos
Amarante
São Miguel do Tapuio
Mombaça
Tauá
Valença do Piauí
Floriano
Oeiras
Jerumenha
Uruçuí
Bertolínia
Picos
Jaicós
Araripina
Boa Esperança
Flores do Piauí
Simplício Mendes
Canto do Buriti
Paulistana
Eliseu Martins
PIAUÍ
São João do Piauí
Serra Dois Irmãos
Afrânio
Cristino Castro
São Raimundo Nonato
Caracol
Redenção de Gurguéia
Remanso
Pilão Arcado
Represa de Sobradinho
Sento Sé
Senador Pompeu
Solonópole
Acopiara
Jaguaribe
Iguatu
Icó
Saboeiro
CEARÁ
Campos Sales
Crato
Juazeiro do Norte
Milagres
Chapada do Araripe
Exu
Conceição
Cajàzeiras
Sousa
Pombal
Ouricurí
Salgueiro
Serra Talhada
Flores
Parnamirim
Cabrobó
Floresta
Ibimirim
Santa Maria da Boa Vista
Belém de São Francisco
Curaçá
Chorrochó
Inajá
Petrolina
Juazeiro
Paulo Afonso
Raso da Catarina
Uauá
Apodi
Açu
Lajes
RIO GRANDE DO NORTE
Natal
Cabo de São Roque
São José de Mipibu
Currais Novos
Caicó
Santa Cruz
Acari
Cuité
Canguaretama
Parelhas
Baía de Traição
Guarabira
Patos
PARAÍBA
Santa Rita
Cabedelo
João Pessoa
Teixeira
Planalto da Borborema
São João do Cariri
Campina Grande
Timbaúba
Goiana
Sumé
Carpina
Limoeiro
Paulista
Olinda
Sertânia
Jaboatão
Recife
Pesqueira
Caruaru
Gravatá
Arcoverde
Belo Jardim
Escada
PERNAMBUCO
Palmares
Barreiros
Garanhuns
União dos Palmares
Santana do Ipanema
Palmeira dos Índios
Atalaia
Rio Largo
Pão de Açúcar
ALAGOAS
Maceió
Arapiraca
São Miguel dos Campos
Jeremoabo
SERGIPE
Propriá
Coruripe
Nossa Senhora das Dores
Simão Dias
Maruim
Laranjeiras
Aracaju
Ponta do Manguinho
Lagarto
Estância
Itabaianinha
Senhor do Bonfim
Monte Santo
Euclides da Cunha
Campo Formoso
Queimadas
Tucano
Nova Soure
Conceição do Coité
Serrinha
Riachão do Jacuípe
Inhambupe
Esplanada
Conde
Palame
Irará
Alagoinhas
Jacobina
Morro do Chapéu
Buritirama
Xique-Xique
Jucara
Irecê
Barra
Santo Inácio
Copixaba
Morpará
Ipupiara
Santa Rita de Cássia
BAHIA
Mundo Novo
Ipirá
Feira de Santana
Cotegipe
Ibotirama
Oliveira dos Brejinhos
Palmeiras
Lençóis
Itaberaba
Chapada Diamantina
Ibitiara
Andaraí
Cachoeira
Maragogipe
Santo Amaro
Camaçari
Salvador
Iaçu
Santo Antônio de Jesus
Nazaré
Valença
Itaetê
Juraci
Iramaia
Chapada de Maracás
Sítio do Mato
Bom Jesus da Lapa
Macaúbas
Botuporã
Paramirim
Riacho de Santana
Livramento do Brumado
Gandu
Camamu
Jequié
Caetité
Guanambi
Brumado
Ipiaú
Maraú
Ubaitaba
Côcos
Carinhanha
Palmas de Monte Alto
Caculé
Aracatu
Anagé
Poções
Itabuna
Ilhéus
Manga
Urandi
Condeúba
Vitória da Conquista
Iguaí
Espinosa
Monte Azul
São João do Paraíso
Encruzilhada
Itapetinga
Arataca
Una
Januária
Rio Pardo de Minas
Porteirinha
Macarani
Canavieiras
Belmonte
Salto da Divisa
Jacinto
Itapebi
São Francisco
Brasília de Minas
Mirabela
Janaúba
Salinas
Pedra Azul
Almenara
Barrocão
Miralta
Francisco Sá
Planalto
Jequitinhonha
Santa Cruz Cabrália
Pôrto Seguro
Coração de Jesus
Grão Mogol
Itaobim
Montes Claros
Bocaiúva
Jequitaí
Virgem da Lapa
Itinga
Águas Formosas
Caraíva
Mte Pascoal 536 m
Itanhém
Minas Novas
Carbonita
Caraí
Pavão
Prado
Alcobaça
Pta da Baleia
Caravelas
Arquipélago dos Abrolhos
Teófilo Otoni
Capelinha
Carlos Chagas
Nanuque
Itamarandiba
Mucuri
Diamantina
Brasil
Itambacuri
Morro d'Anta
2033 m
P. de Itambé
Peçanha
Conceição da Barra
Nova Venécia
São Mateus
Curvelo
Sêrro
Guanhães
Governador Valadares
ESPÍRITO SANTO
Tarumirim
MINAS GERAIS
Conselheiro Pena
Linhares
Ipatinga
Coronel Fabriciano
Lagoa Santa
Belo Horizonte
Sabará
Itabira
Colatina
Barra do Riacho
Ibiraçu
Aracruz
Caratinga
Contagem
Nova Lima
Itabirito
Manhuaçu
2890 m
Cariacica
Serra
Vitória
Vila Velha
Ouro Prêto
Conselheiro Lafaiete
Carangola
Muniz Freire
Alegre
Guarapari
Viçosa
Cachoeira do Itapemirim
Itapemirim
Carandaí
Tombos
Barbacena
Ubá
Muriaé
Santos Dumont
Cataguases
Itaperuna
São Fidélis
Leopoldina
São João da Barra
Andrelândia
Além Paraíba
Campos
Cabo de São Tomé
Juiz de Fora
Três Rios
RIO DE JANEIRO
Nova Friburgo
Volta Redonda
Teresópolis
Macaé
Petrópolis
Barra Mansa
Nova Iguaçu
Duque de Caxias
São Gonçalo
Niterói
Cabo Frio
Itaguaí
Rio de Janeiro
I. Grande

ATLANTIC OCEAN

1 6° 2 10° 3 14° 4 18° 5 22° 6

E 42° F 38° G 34° H 30°

0 100 200 300 400 kilometers
0 100 200 miles
Scale 1:7,000,000
Projection: Azimuthal Equal Area

North Chile • North Argentina • Uruguay • South Paraguay

A 74° B 70° C 455 66° D 62°

1 22° 2 26° 3 30° 4 34° 5 38° 6

BOLIVIA
Chiguana
San Cristóbal
Ollagüe
Vol. Ollagüe 5869 m
Salar de Ascotán
Tupiza
San Pablo
Co Bonete 5660 m
San Lorenzo
Tarija
Entre Ríos
Sanandita
Villamontes
Fortín Infante Rivarola
Quillagua
Lequena
Vol. San Pedro 6154 m
POTOSÍ
Mojo
Villazón
La Quiaca
Sierra Sta. Victoria
TARIJA
Padcaya
Yacuiba
Pocitos
Santa María
La Esmeralda
Fortín Hernandarias
Tocopilla
Toco
Conchi
Turi
Chuquicamata
Calama
María Elena
Pedro de Valdivia
Michilla
Bahía de Mejillones del Sur
Mejillones
Loa
Atacama
Cord. Domeyko
Vol. Licancábur 5930 m
San Pedro de Atacama
Co Zapaleri 5655 m
JUJUY
Abra Pampa
Bermejo
Tartagal
Sierra Gorda
Carmen Alto
Baquedano
Toconao
Salar de Atacama
Salinas Grandes
Susques
San Ramón de la Nueva Orán
Humahuaca
Pichanal
Embarcación
Fortín Capitán Escobar
Puerto Irigoyen
Los Blancos
Tropic of Capricorn
Pta Tetas
Antofagasta
La Negra
Varillas
ANTOFAGASTA
Domeyko
Tilomonte
Tilcara
La Estrella
Ingeniero Guillermo N. Juárez
Augusta Victoria
Co del Rincón 5594 m
Nev. de Chañi 6200 m
San Salvador de Jujuy
San Pedro
Perico
Rivadavia
Teuco
Co Pular 6225 m
Escondida
Paso Socompa
San Antonio de los Cobres
General Martín Miguel de Güemes
Pta dos Reyes
Vol. Llullaillaco 6723 m
Desierto de Atacama
Salar de Arizaro
Nev. de Cachi 6720 m
Salta
Rosario de Lerma
SALTA
Lumbrera
Joaquín V. González
Nueva Pompeya
Paposo
Salinitas
Cachi
Guachipas
Metán
Taco Pozo
Monte Quemado
Taltal
Vol. Antofalla 6100 m
Sierra de Calalaste
Rosario de la Frontera
Altamira
Co Galán 6600 m
Antofagasta de la Sierra
Cafayate
Trancas
Quebracho Coto
San José del Boquerón
Pampa de los Guanacos
El Salvador
TUCUMÁN
SANTIAGO DEL ESTERO
Campo Gallo
Chañaral
Diego de Almagro
Sa Nevada 6400 m
Santa María
Tafí Viejo
San Miguel de Tucumán
Patay
Tintina
Presidencia Roque Sáenz Peña
Inca de Oro
CATAMARCA
Bella Vista
Las Cejas
Pozo Hondo
General Pinedo
Algarrobo
Vol. Copiapó 6080 m
Ojos del Salado 6880 m
Monteros
Otumpa
Caldera
Puquios
Concepción
Aguilares
Termas de Río Hondo
Copiapó
Tierra Amarilla
Fiambalá
Belén
Andalgalá
La Banda
Quimilí
Bahía Salada
La Guardia
Co Bonete 6872 m
La Cocha
Santiago del Estero
Fernández
Castilla
Las Juntas
Tinogasta
Totoral
San Fernando del Valle de Catamarca
Ciudad de Loreto
Carrizal Bajo
ATACAMA
Copacabana
Las Cañas
Añatuya
Colonia Dora
Miraflores
Co de Potro 5830 m
Aimogasta
Huasco
Freirina
Vallenar
Cord. de Oliva
Jagüé
Villa Mazán
Chumbicha
Frías
Bandera
Sarco
El Tránsito
Famatina
Mejicana 6250 m
Chilecito
San Antonio
Los Telares
Pinto
Tostado
C. Bascuñán
Domeyko
Co del Toro 6380 m
Sa de Famatina
Sa de Velasco
Sa de Ancasti
Recreo
PACIFIC
San Martín
Villa Unión
Famatina 6375 m
La Rioja
Villa Ojo de Agua
El Tofo
Guandacol
LA RIOJA
San Francisco del Chañar
Argentina
Ceres
Co Las Tórtolas 6332 m
Patquía
ARGENTINA
La Serena
Coquimbo
Rivadavia
Co de Olivares 6282 m
San José de Jáchal
Chamical
Quilino
Deán Funes
San José de la Dormida
San Cristóbal
Andacollo
Rodeo
Serrezuela
Mar Chiquita
Morteros
Pta Lengua de Vaca
SAN JUAN
San Agustín de Valle Fértil
Cruz del Eje
Ovalle
Tucunuco
Sa del Valle Fértil
Capilla del Monte
Jesús María
COQUIMBO
Malanzán
La Falda
Río Ceballos
Sunchales
Rafaela
Punitaqui
Castaño Viejo
Cosquín
Río Primero
Freyre
Maitencillo
Talacasto
Chepes
Desiderio Tello
Salsacate
Córdoba
San Francisco
Combarbalá
Mareyes
Mascasín
Chancaní
Alta Gracia
Villa del Rosario
San Carlos Centro
OCEAN
Barreal
San Juan
Caucete
Pampa de la Salinas
Co Champaquí 2880 m
Oncativo
Oliva
Las Varillas
San Jorge
Huentelauquén
Illapel
Salamanca
Co Mercedario 6770 m
Villa Dolores
Conlara
CÓRDOBA
El Trébol
Los Vilos
Sa de San Luis
Quines
Villa María
Dalmacio Vélez Sarsfield
Bell Ville
Marcos Juárez
La Ligua
Co Aconcagua 6960 m
Las Heras
Mendoza
Alto de Pencoso
San Antonio
Desaguadero
La Laguna
VALPARAÍSO
San Felipe
Godoy Cruz
Villa Nueva
La Toma
Río Cuarto
Chazón
La Calera
Quillota
Luján
Sa del Morro 1727 m
Viña del Mar
Pta Curaumilla
Valparaíso
Quilpué
Co Juncal 6060 m
Tupungato 5682 m
Rivadavia
Tupungato
Las Catitas
La Paz
San Luis
La Carlota
Arias
Firmat
Santiago
San Bernardo
Tunuyán
SAN LUIS
Beazley
Mercedes
Vicuña Mackenna
Venado Tuerto
San Antonio
Paine
Vol. San José 5830 m
San Carlos
Comandante Salas
Justo Daract
General Levalle
Laboulaye
Melipilla
SANTIAGO
Navidad
Graneros
Vol. Maipú 5290 m
Rancagua
MENDOZA
Villa Valeria
Rufino
Pta Topocalma
Rengo
San Rafael
Diamante
Monte Comán
Media Luna
Buena Esperanza
Villa Huidobro
Huinca Renancó
Buchardo
General Pinto
Pta de Lobos
LIBERTADOR
Pichilemu
Santa Cruz
San Fernando
Co Sosneado 5189 m
Emb. de Nihuil
General Alvear
General Villegas
Retén Llico
Vol. Tinguiririca 4300 m
El Sosneado
Carmensa
Nueva Galia
Parera
Realicó
Intendente Alvear
Timote
Nueve de Julio
Licantén
Curicó
Vol. Descabezado Grande 3830 m
Atuel
Sierra del Nevado
Canalejas
Rivadavia
Mataquito
Vol. Peteroa 4090 m
Co Nevada 3810 m
Malargüe
General Pico
Meridiano
Maule
Talca
San Clemente
Quemú-Quemú
Eduardo Castex
Pehuajó
San Javier
Trenque Lauquen
Chanco
Linares
Bardas Blancas
Campanario 4020 m
Victorica
Telén
Santa Isabel
Algarrobo del Aguila
Salazar
Henderson
Cauquenes
MAULE
Parral
Longaví 3242 m
Catriló
Tres Lomas
Daireaux
Quirihue
San Carlos
Co Payún 3680 m
LA PAMPA
Toay
Santa Rosa
Maza
Salliqueló
Guaminí
Chillán
Tomé
Vol. Domuyo 4709 m
Cord. del Viento
Grande
Quehué
Macachín
Huanguelén
Talcahuano
Concepción
Recinto
Sa Chachahuén 2065 m
Colorado
Limay Mahuida
Rivera
Carhué
General La Madrid
BÍO BÍO
Golfo de Arauco
Lota
Vol. Tromen 3980 m
General Acha
Puelén
Coronel Suárez
Pta Lavapié
Antuco
Chos Malal
Epu-pel
Darregueira
Puán
Pigüé
Saavedra
Arauco
La Laja
Los Angeles
Sa de Auca Mahuida 2253 m
Chadileo
Catriel
Bernasconi
Guatraché
Sa de la Ventana
Mulchén
Vol. Copahue 2969 m
Neuquén
Puelches
Tornquist
Co Tres Picos 1243 m
Saldungaray
Lebu
Cañete
Angol
Collipulli
Loncopué
Chihuido Medio 1494 m
Cuchillo-Có
Villa Iris
Cabildo
Purén
Curacó
Coronel Dorrego
Traiguén
Victoria
NEUQUÉN
Embalse Cerros Colorados
Gobernador Duval
Bahía Blanca
Curacautín
Las Lajas
L. Pellegrini
Colorado
Médanos
Punta Alta
Puerto Saavedra
Carahue
ARAUCANÍA
Vol. Llaima 3124 m
Zapala
Plaza Huincul
Cipolletti
RÍO NEGRO
Pichi Mahuida
Río Colorado
Bahía Blanca
Nueva Imperial
Temuco
Cutral-Có
Neuquén
General Roca
Chelforó
Choele Choel
Major Buratovich
CHILE
ANDES
PAMPAS

A 74° B 70° 460 C 66° D 62°

South America

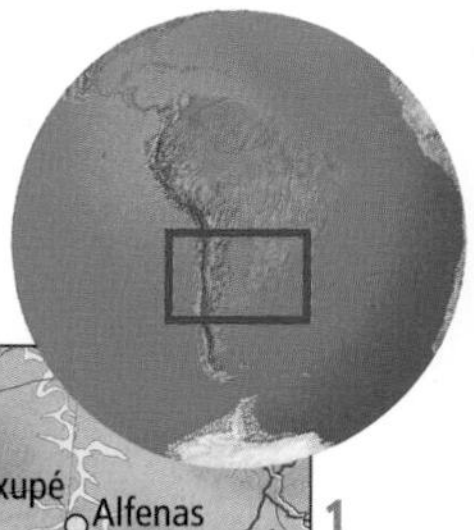

456

58° F 54° G 50° H

Fortín Carlos Antonio López
Puerto Guaraní
Pôrto Murtinho
Jardim
Maracaju
Mirandópolis
Valparaíso
Araçatuba
Birigüi
Bebedouro
Sertãozinho
São Sebastião do Paraíso
Panorama
Dracena
Jaboticabal
Taquaritinga
Ribeirão Prêto
Guaxupé
Alfenas
Varginha
Rio Brilhante
Pôrto Alegre
Presidente Epitácio
Presidente Venceslau
Lucélia
Penápolis
Lins
Araraquara
Mococa
Poços de Caldas
MINAS GERAIS
Piraçununga
Três Corações
Puerto Sastre
Puerto Casado
Bela Vista
MATO GROSSO DO SUL
Dourados
Tupã
Pirajuí
São Carlos
Casa Branca
São João da Boa Vista
Campo Esperanza
Puerto Pinasco
Ponta Porã
Ivinheima
Presidente Prudente
Marília
Garça
Bauru
Jaú
PARAGUAY
Pedro Juan Caballero
Caarapó
Juti
Rosana
Teodoro Sampaio
Itaguajé
Iepê
Assis
Agudos
SÃO PAULO
Rio Claro
Mogi-Mirim
Pouso Alegre
Puerto Cooper
Amambaí
Paranavaí
Cornélio Procópio
Botucatu
Piracicaba
Limeira
Americana
Amparo
Itajubá
Cruzeiro
Fortín Presidente Ayala
Pozo Colorado
Horqueta
Capitán Bado
Concepción
Coronel Sapucaia
Nova Esperança
Maringá
Rolândia
Londrina
Arapongas
Apucarana
Santo Antônio da Platina
Avaré
Conchas
Tietê
Campinas
Jundiaí
Bragança Paulista
Guaratinguetá
Taubaté
São José dos Campos
Nueva Germania
Puerto Antequera
San Pedro
Ypé-Jhú
Iguatemi
Umuarama
Cianorte
Angatuba
Itapetininga
Tatuí
Itu
Sorocaba
São Paulo
Jacareí
Mogi das Cruzes
Santo André
São Bernardo do Campo
Caraguatatuba
Rosario
Itacurubí del Rosario
Salto del Guairá
Guaíra
Puerto Adela
Goio-Erê
Campo Mourão
Venceslau Bras
Itapeva
Itararé
Capão Bonito
Santos
Guarujá
São Vicente
Itanhaém
Peruíbe
I. de São Sebastião
Dedo de Deus 1350 m
Juquiá
San Estanislao
Toledo
PARANA
Telêmaco Borba
Piraí do Sul
Jacupiranga
Iguape
I. Comprida
Cananéia
I. do Cardoso
Guaraqueçaba
I. das Peças
FORMOSA
Espinillo
Villa Hayes
Unión
Asunción
Coronel Oviedo
Caacupé
Clorinda
San Lorenzo
Hernandarias
Cascavel
Pitanga
Reserva
Ipiranga
Castro
Cêrro Azul
Ponta Grossa
Rio Branco do Sul
Curitiba
Laranjeiras do Sul
Prudentópolis
Pirané
Paraguarí
Caaguazú
Villarrica
Quiindy
Foz do Iguaçu
Ciudad del Este
Guarapuava
Irati
Palmeira
Lapa
São José dos Pinhais
Paranaguá
Guaratuba
Formosa
Alberdi
Iturbe
Caazapá
Capanema
Mangueirinha
União da Vitória
Rio Negro
Mafra
São Francisco do Sul
Herradura
Villa Florida
San Juan Bautista
Yuty
Co San Rafael 850 m
Eldorado
Montecarlo
San Pedro
Bernardo de Irogoyen
Clevelândia
Palmas
Canoinhas
Joinville
Jaraguá do Sul
Puerto Bermejo
Pilar
Humaitá
Desmochado
Paso de Patria
San Ignacio
Puerto Rico
General Artigas
MISIONES
São Carlos
Xanxerê
Chapecó
SANTA CATARINA
Caçador
Ibirama
Itajaí
Blumenau
Resistencia
San Luis del Palmar
Corrientes
Barranqueras
Encarnación
El Soberbio
Oberá
Posadas
Candelaria
Irai
Joaçaba
Curitibanos
Campos Novos
Rio Do Sul
Ituporanga
Pôrto Belo
Basail
Empedrado
Ituzaingó
Leandro N. Alem
Apóstoles
San Javier
Santa Rosa
Campo Novo
Palmeira das Missões
Sarandi
Erechim
Florianópolis
Ilha de Sta Catarina
São José
CORRIENTES
Saladas
Santo Angelo
Carazinho
Passo Fundo
Campo Belo do Sul
Lagoa Vermelha
Lajes
Bom Retiro
São Joaquim
Bella Vista
San Roque
Santo Tomé
São Borja
São Luis Gonzaga
Ijuí
Cruz Alta
Tapera
Casca
Vacaria
Pta Imbituba
Santa Lucía
Esteros del Iberá
BRAZIL
Bom Jesus
Tubarão
Laguna
C. de Sta Marta Grande
Turvo
Jaguaruna
Goya
Mercedes
La Cruz
Itaqui
Santiago
Tupanciretã
Soledade
Bento Gonçalves
Criciúma
Araranguá
Perugorría
Mariano Loza
Paso de los Libres
São Francisco de Assis
Jaguari
RIO GRANDE DO SUL
Garibaldi
Caxias do Sul
Tôrres
Curuzú Cuatiá
Uruguaiana
Alegrete
Santa Maria
Santa Cruz do Sul
Lajeado
São Francisco de Paula
Montenegro
Novo Hamburgo
São Leopoldo
Esquina
Sauce
Monte Caseros
Cacequi
São Sepé
São Gabriel
Rio Pardo
Cachoeira do Sul
Canoas
Porto Alegre
Osório
Palmares do Sul
San José de Feliciano
Bella Unión
Tomás Gomensoro
Artigas
Quaraí
Rosário do Sul
Guaíba
Barra do Ribeiro
La Paz
Chajarí
Caçapava do Sul
Encruzilhada do Sul
Tapes
Federal
Federación
Colonia Lavalleja
Rivera
Dom Pedrito
Lavras do Sul
Santa da Boa Vista
Camaquã
Lagoa dos Patos
Concordia
Salto
Tranqueras
Minas de Corrales
Bagé
Piratini
Canguçu
Boqueirão
São Lourenço do Sul
Mostardas
San Salvador
Villaguay
Villa San José
Rosario del Tala
Colón
Paysandú
Guichón
Tacuarembó
Ansina
Pinheiro Machado
Pelotas
Pedro Osorio
São José do Norte
Rio Grande
Represa del Rio Negro
Ervai
Arroio Grande
Jaguarão
Melo
Concepción del Uruguay
URUGUAY
Young
Paso de los Toros
Vergara
Gualeguaychú
Gualeguay
Fray Bentos
Mercedes
Treinta-y-Tres
Lagoa Mirim
Victoria
Arroyos
Durazno
Sarandí del Yí
José Pedro Varela
Dolores
Trinidad
Lascano
Santa Vitória do Palmar
Baradero
Carmelo
Cardona
Sarandí Grande
Zárate
Campana
Florida
Pilar
San Fernando
Colonia del Sacramento
San José de Mayo
Tala
Minas
Aiguá
Castillos
Buenos Aires
Avellaneda
Quilmes
Canelones
Las Piedras
Co Catedral 513 m
Rocha
La Paloma
Lomas de Zamora
Cañuelas
La Plata
Montevideo
San Carlos
Maldonado
Lobos
Alejandro Korn
Magdalena
Verónica
San Miguel del Monte
Chascomús
Río de la Plata
General Belgrano
Bahía Samborombón
Las Flores
Pila
Castelli
Dolores
General Lavalle
Pta Norte del Cabo San Antonio
General Guido
General Conesa
Rauch
Maipú
General Juan Madariaga
Pta Sur del Cabo San Antonio
Gardey
Tandil 500 m
Ayacucho
Villa Gesell
Coronel Vidal
Balcarce
San Agustín
Mar del Plata
C. Corrientes
Lobería
Miramar
Quequén
Necochea

ATLANTIC OCEAN

22° 26° 30° 34° 38°
46°
1 2 3 4 5 6
J

0 100 200 300 400 kilometers
0 100 200 miles
Scale 1:7,000,000
Projection: Azimuthal Equal Area

South Chile • South Argentina

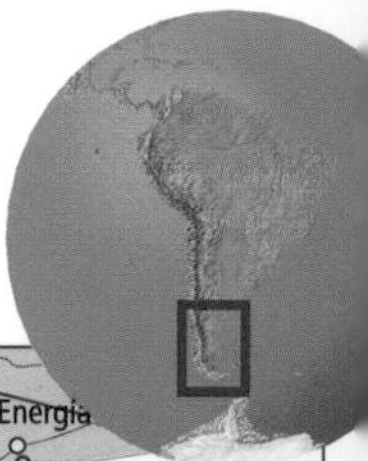

458

B 74° C 70° D 66° E 62° F

Nueva Imperial
Carahue
Puerto Saavedra
Curacautín
Temuco
Vol. Llaima 3124 m
ARAUCANÍA
Pitrufquén
L. Villarrica
Villarrica
Pucón
Vol. Villarrica 2840 m
Queule
Lanco
San José de la Mariquina
Vol. Lanín 3776 m
Panguipulli
L. Panguipulli
Valdivia
Riñihue
Pta Galera
Paillaco
Lago Ranco
La Unión
Río Bueno
Osorno
LOS LAGOS
Puyehue
Purranque
L. Rupanco
Vol. Osorno
C. Quedal
L. Llanquihue
2652 m
Puerto Varas
Puerto Montt
Co Tronador 3554 m
Maullín
Cochamó
Canal de Chacao
Calbuco
Ventisquero 2300 m
El Bolsón
Ñorquinco
Ancud
Chacao
Quemchi
G. de Ancud
Vol. Huequi 1050 m
Isla Grande de Chiloé
Castro
Minchinmávida 2470 m
Quellón
Chaitén
Quellón
Futaleufú
C. Quilán
Vol. Corcovado 2300 m
Boca del Guafo
Golfo Corcovado
I. Guafo
Islas Guaitecas
Palena
L. Palena
Mte Melimoyu 2400 m
Isla Magdalena
Canal Moraleda
I. Benjamín
Puerto Cisnes
I. James
Mte Macá 2960 m
Archipiélago de los Chonos
I. Melchor
I. Victoria
Puerto Aisén
Bahía Darwin
Coihaique
Bahía Anna Pink
Vol. Hudson 2500 m
Balmaceda
Península de Taitao
AISÉN
L. Presidente Ríos
Mte San Valentín 4058 m
C. Raper
L. General Carrera
Península Tres Montes
Co Arenales 3440 m
Golfo de Penas
Cochrane
Mte San Lorenzo 3700 m
Tortel
I. Campana
I. Prat
I. Patricio Lynch
I. Serrano
C. Mellizo Sur 3050 m
L. O'Higgins
I. Esmeralda
3380 m
Isla Wellington
Golfo Ladrillero
Pen. Wharton
Golfo Trinidad
Mte Fitz Roy 3375 m
I. Mornington
Co Murallón 3600 m
I. Madre de Dios
I. Duque de York
C. Santiago
Bahía Solvación
Canal Concepción
I. Diego de Almagro
Estrecho Nelson
I. Ramírez
I. Contreras
I. Pacheco
MAGALLANES
Mte Burney 1750 m
Archipiélago de la Reina Adelaida
I. Manuel Rodríguez
C. Pilar
Península Muñoz Gamero
Isla Riesco
Punta Arenas
I. Desolación
Bahía Otway
Península de Brunswick
Fuerte Bulnes
I. Santa Inés
I. Clarence
I. Cap Aracena
Bahía Stokes
Canal Cockburn
Península Brecknock
I. Stewart
I. Londonderry
Bahía Cook

CHILE
ANDES

Las Lajas
Embalse Cerros Colorados
Zapala
Cutral-Có
Plaza Huincul
Neuquén
NEUQUÉN
Picún Leufú
Catan Lil
Junín de los Andes
San Martín De Los Andes
Co Azul 2480 m
L. Nahuel Huapi
Pilcaniyeu
San Carlos de Bariloche
Cholila
Gualjaina
Esquel
Co Cónico 2270 m
Tecka
Corcovado
Co Steffen 2108 m
José de San Martín
Nueva Lubecka
Alto Río Senguer
L. Fontana
Río Mayo
Facundo
L. Musters
Sarmiento
L. Buenos Aires
Perito Moreno
Chile Chico
Las Heras
Deseado
Cerro Cojudo Blanco 1335 m
Bajo Caracoles
Meseta del Pedrero
Gran Altiplanicie Central
Gobernador Gregores
L. San Martín
L. Cardiel
SANTA CRUZ
L. Viedma
Tres Lagos
Chalía
Laguna Grande
Comandante Luis Piedrabuena
L. Argentino
Charles Fuhr
El Calafate
Co Pináculo 2160 m
Esperanza
Gobernador Mayer
Puerto Natales
El Turbio
Bella Vista
Villa Tehuelche
Río Verde
Cerro Sombrero
Sierra Balmaceda
Estrecho de Magallanes
Porvenir
Isla Grande de Tierra del Fuego
Camerón
Pico Nariz 822 m
L. Fagnano
Mte Darwin 2488 m
Ushuaia
Puerto Williams
I. Hoste
Pen. Rous
I. Navarino
Bahía Nassau
Península Hardy
Isla Hermite
Islas Wollaston
Cabo de Hornos (Cape Horn)

L. Pellegrini
Cipolletti
General Roca
Gobernador Duval
Villa Regina
Chelforó
Embalse Ezequiel Ramos Mexía
Cerro Policía
RÍO NEGRO
Santa Rosa
La Esperanza
Sierra Colorada
Los Menucos
Valcheta
Ingeniero Jacobacci
Maquinchao
El Caín
Meseta de Somuncurá
Cona Niyeu
Sierra Grande
Gastre
Sa Huancache
ARGENTINA
Gan Gan
Telsen
CHUBUT
Lomas Coloradas
Las Plumas
Paso de Indios
El Sombrero
Embalse Florentino Ameghino
Sierra Cuadrada
Meseta de Montemayor
Buen Pasto
L. Colhué Huapi
Pico de Salamanca
Pampa del Castillo
Pampa del Castillo
Comodoro Rivadavia
Golfo de San Jorge
Caleta Olivia
Bahía Langara
Pico Truncado
Fitz Roy
Las Martinetas
Mazarredo
Antonio de Biedma
PATAGONIA
Tres Cerros
Florida Negra
El Salado
Puerto San Julián
Pta Desengaño
C. San Francisco de Paula
Puerto Santa Cruz
Pta León
Bahía Grande
Puerto Coig
C. Buen Tiempo
Río Gallegos
Monte Dinero
Pta Dungeness
Punta Delgada
Pta de Arenas
Bahía San Sebastián
San Sebastián
Río Grande
C. Peñas
TIERRA DEL FUEGO
Bahía Thetis
Puerto Harberton
Península Mitre
I. Picton
I. Nueva
I. Lennox
Estrecho de Le Maire
I. de los Estados
C. San Juan
San Juan de Salvamento

Pichi Mahuida
Colorado
Lamarque
Choele Choel
Colonia Josefa
Negro
General Conesa
Salina Gualicho
Cinco Chañares
Aguada Cecilio
San Antonio Oeste
Salado
Verde
Golfo San Matías
Pta Sierra
Punta Pórfido
Puerto Lobos
Pta Norte
G. San José
Punta Norte
Puerto Pirámides
Península Valdés
G. Nuevo
Punta Delgada
Puerto Madryn
Pta Ninfas
Gaimán
Trelew
Rawson
Dolavón
Pta Castro
Florentino Ameghino
Dos Pozos
C. Raso
Cabo Raso
Camarones
Bahía Camarones
C. Dos Bahías
Bahía Bustamante
Puerto Visser
Bahía Solano
C. Tres Puntas
Cabo Blanco
Puerto Deseado
Pta Medanosa
Bahía Laura
C. Dañoso

Bahía Blanca
Médanos
Coronel Dorrego
Tres Arroyos
Energía
Oriente
Claromecó
Orense
Punta Alta
BUENOS AIRES
Bahía Blanca
Península Verde
Río Colorado
Major Buratovich
Villalonga
Bahía Unión
Stroeder
Bahía Anegada
Carmen De Patagones
Viedma
Pta Rasa
La Lobería
Pta Bermeja

SOUTH ATLANTIC OCEAN

FALKLAND ISLANDS (U.K.)
West Falkland
Pebble I.
C. Dolphin
King George Bay
Queen Charlotte Bay
Mt Adam 700 m
Mt Usborne 705 m
Darwin
Stanley
Weddell I
Port Stephens
Falkland Sound
Goose Green
Choiseul Sound
Lively I.
C. Meredith
Bay of Harbours
East Falkland

42° 46° 50° 54°

1 2 3 4 5

A 78° B 74° C 70° D 66° E 62° F 58° G

kilometers 0 100 200 300 400
miles 0 100 200
Scale 1:7 000 000
Projection: Azimuthal Equal Area

Islands around South America

A B C

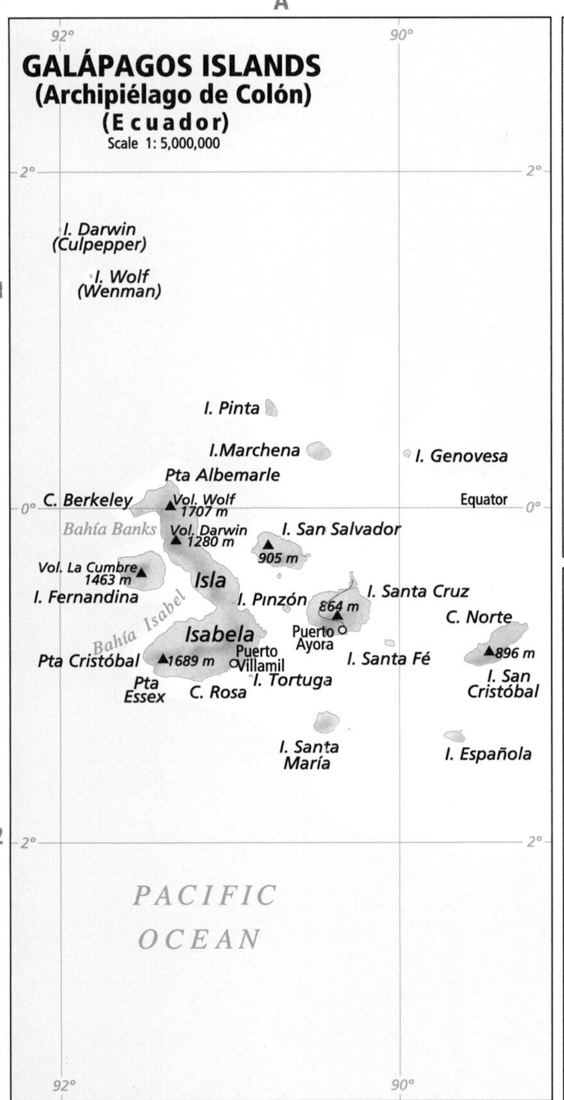
GALÁPAGOS ISLANDS
(Archipiélago de Colón)
(Ecuador)
Scale 1: 5,000,000
92°
90°
2°
0°
I. Darwin
(Culpepper)
I. Wolf
(Wenman)
I. Pinta
I.Marchena
I. Genovesa
Pta Albemarle
C. Berkeley
Vol. Wolf
1707 m
Equator
Bahía Banks
Vol. Darwin
1280 m
I. San Salvador
905 m
Vol. La Cumbre
1463 m
I. Fernandina
Isla
Isabela
Bahía Isabel
I. Pinzón
864 m
I. Santa Cruz
C. Norte
Puerto Ayora
Puerto Villamil
Pta Cristóbal
1689 m
I. Santa Fé
896 m
I. San Cristóbal
Pta Essex
C. Rosa
I. Tortuga
I. Santa María
I. Española
PACIFIC
OCEAN

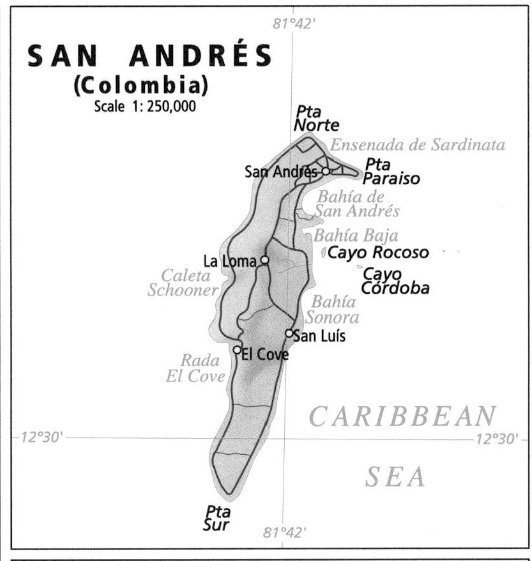
SAN ANDRÉS
(Colombia)
Scale 1: 250,000
81°42'
12°30'
Pta Norte
Ensenada de Sardinata
San Andrés
Pta Paraiso
Bahía de San Andrés
Bahía Baja
Cayo Rocoso
La Loma
Caleta Schooner
Cayo Córdoba
Bahía Sonora
San Luís
El Cove
Rada El Cove
CARIBBEAN
SEA
Pta Sur

PROVIDENCIA
(Colombia)
Scale 1: 200,000
81°22'
13°20'
Pta Bucanera
I. Santa Catalina
Santa Isabel
Bahía Catalina
Pueblo Viejo
San Felipe
Aguadulce
Providencia
Bogotá
La Paz
Casabaja
Aguamansa
CARIBBEAN
SEA

EASTER ISLAND
(Chile)
Scale 1: 350,000
109°20'
27°09'
C. Norte
Pta San Juan
Pta Rosalia
Terevaka
608 m
C. O'Higgins
Vol. Katiki
390 m
Motu Tautara
Vol. Puhi
470 m
C. Roggewain
270 m
Vol. Tangaroa
Pta Roa
Tuutapu
510 m
Pta Cuidado
Hanga-Roa
Mataveri
Vaihu
Pta Baja
Pta Redonda
PACIFIC
OCEAN
Motu Iti
Motu Nui

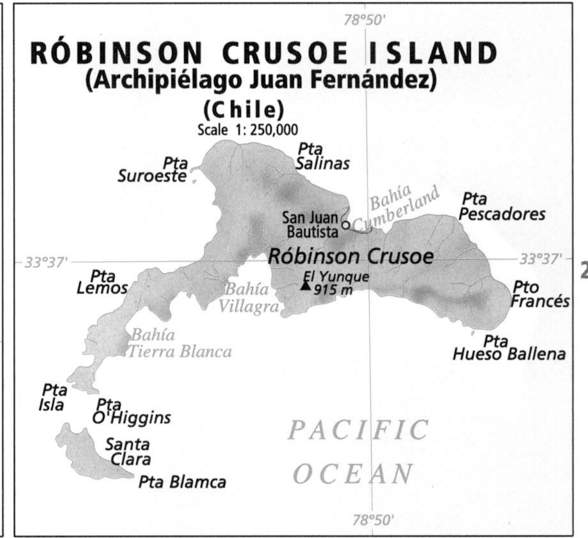
RÓBINSON CRUSOE ISLAND
(Archipiélago Juan Fernández)
(Chile)
Scale 1: 250,000
78°50'
33°37'
Pta Salinas
Pta Suroeste
Bahía Cumberland
Pta Pescadores
San Juan Bautista
Róbinson Crusoe
Pta Lemos
El Yunque
915 m
Bahía Villagra
Pto Francés
Bahía Tierra Blanca
Pta Hueso Ballena
Pta Isla
Pta O'Higgins
Santa Clara
Pta Blamca
PACIFIC
OCEAN

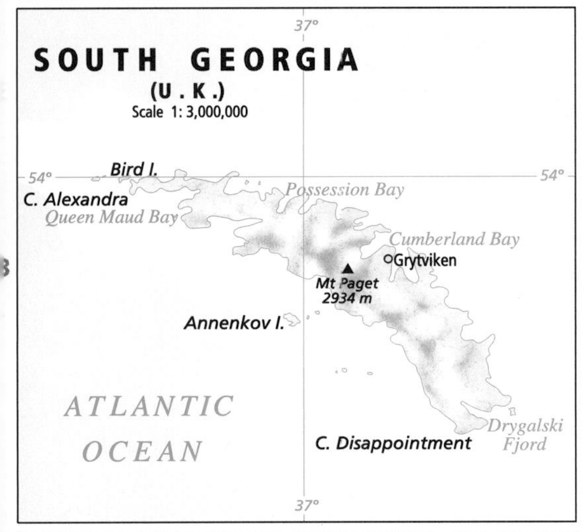
SOUTH GEORGIA
(U.K.)
Scale 1: 3,000,000
37°
54°
Bird I.
C. Alexandra
Queen Maud Bay
Possession Bay
Cumberland Bay
Grytviken
Mt Paget
2934 m
Annenkov I.
ATLANTIC
OCEAN
C. Disappointment
Drygalski Fjord

ARUBA
(Netherlands)
Scale 1:1,000,000
70°
12°30'
CARIBBEAN
SEA
Kudarebe
Alto Vista
71 m
Noord
Druif
Paradera
Oranjestad
Santa Cruz
Jamanota
188 m
Barcadera
Savaneta
Sint Nicolaas
Commanders Bay
Seroe Colorado
Pt Basora

CURAÇAO
(Netherlands Antilles)
Scale 1:1,000,000
69°
12°15'
Nordpunt
Westpunt
St Christoffelberg
372 m
CARIBBEAN
SEA
Santa Cruz
Barber
Soto
Santa Martabaai
Bocht Van Hato
Sint Willebrordus
Bullenbaai
Julianadorp
Santa Catharina
Otrabanda
Emmastad
Willemstad
Nieuw Poort
Oostpunt

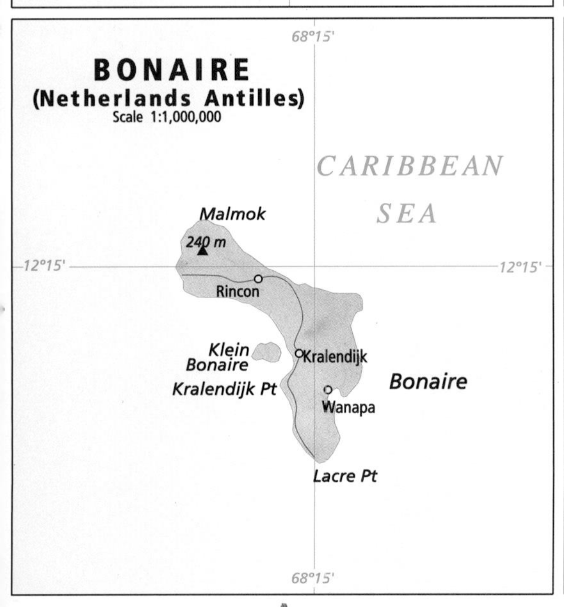
BONAIRE
(Netherlands Antilles)
Scale 1:1,000,000
68°15'
12°15'
CARIBBEAN
SEA
Malmok
240 m
Rincon
Klein Bonaire
Kralendijk
Kralendijk Pt
Bonaire
Wanapa
Lacre Pt

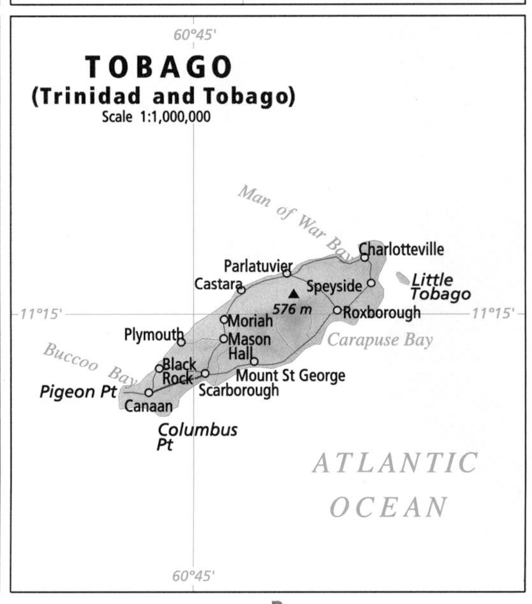
TOBAGO
(Trinidad and Tobago)
Scale 1:1,000,000
60°45'
11°15'
Man of War Bay
Charlotteville
Parlatuvier
Little Tobago
Castara
Speyside
576 m
Roxborough
Moriah
Plymouth
Mason Hall
Carapuse Bay
Buccoo Bay
Black Rock
Mount St George
Pigeon Pt
Scarborough
Canaan
Columbus Pt
ATLANTIC
OCEAN

TRINIDAD
(Trinidad and Tobago)
Scale 1: 2,000,000
61°
10°
ATLANTIC
OCEAN
Grande Rivière
Chupara Pt
Blanchisseuse
Toco
Galera Pt
Pta Peñas
Green Hill
Matelot
Redhead
Corozal Pt
El Cerro del Aripo
940 m
Northern Range
Macuro
Chaguaramas
Salibea
Saline Bay
Monos
Arima
VENEZUELA
Port of Spain
Tunapuna
Sangre Grande
Caroni
Manzanilla Pt
Chaguanas
Waterloo
Talparo
Golfo
de Paria
Biche
Cocos Bay
Planagin Town
Tabaquite
California
Guatuaro Pt
Rio Claro
San Fernando
Princes Town
Saint Joseph
La Brea
St. Marys
New Grant
Guapo Bay
Ortoire
Mayaro Bay
Point Fortin
Penal
Guayaguayare
Basse Terre
Icacos Pt
Bonasse
San Francique
Siparia
304 m
Trinity Hills
Galeota Pt
Moruga
Fullarton
Erin Pt
Boca de la Serpiente
VENEZUELA

A B C

Polar Regions

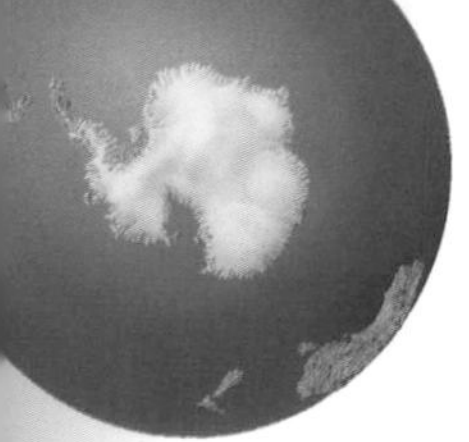

Polar Regions

The polar regions lie between 66.5° latitude and the North and South Poles. The continent of Antarctica, which is 14 million sq km (5.5 million sq miles) in area, is almost completely enclosed within the Antarctic Circle (66.5° S) and the South Pole. Antarctica is surrounded by the only continuous seas circling Earth, and during winter the seas freeze around it, making the continent appear larger than it actually is. Various nations have laid claim to certain parts of Antarctica, several of which overlap. Most non-claimant countries—and the United Nations—do not recognize these claims.

The region between the Arctic Circle (66.5° N) and the North Pole includes the Arctic Ocean and the northern fringes of the Eurasian and North American landmasses. The arctic lands are shared by several countries: Canada, the USA, Russia, Finland, Sweden, and Norway.

Physiography

Eastern Antarctica was once part of the ancient supercontinent of Gondwana, while the Western Peninsula is an island chain related to the geologically younger Andean ranges. Floating ice shelves cover the seas around the land areas, giving the appearance of one large ice-covered continent. Volcanic chains, such as the Scotia Arc, are found in the Antarctic Peninsula, and there are several active volcanoes. The highest point in Antarctica is Vinson Massif (4,897 m; 16,066 ft), while the average elevation of the continent exceeds 2,440 m (8,000 ft).

The Arctic Circle region encompasses the fringes of the North American, European, and Asian continents which surround the Arctic Ocean. The Arctic Ocean was formed when the Eurasian Plate moved towards the Pacific Plate, while the North American and Eurasian plates separated to form the Atlantic Ocean. The Arctic Ocean, reaching depths of 969 m (3,200 ft), is connected to the Atlantic and Pacific Oceans by several straits through which its cold waters move southward.

Climate

Very cold climates prevail in the polar regions. Because of Earth's axial tilt, the polar regions receive the Sun's rays obliquely, so although during the summer months there is practically no darkness, there is nevertheless little solar radiation. During the long polar winter "nights", which also last for months, there is no net solar radiation at all to warm the land surface.

Snow reflects a large proportion of solar radiation back to space. This is particularly true of Antarctica, which is covered by extensive ice sheets. Temperatures within the Arctic Circle are higher than those of Antarctica because of the presence of a warming ocean. Within Antarctica, temperatures fall as low as –89.2 °C (–128.6 °F). In contrast, the lowest recorded temperature on the ice sheet of Greenland is –68 °C (–90 °F). Temperatures during summer in the Arctic Ocean, when parts of the floating ice melt, are around 0 °C (32 °F) and during winter, when larger areas are covered by ice, they fall to –34 °C (–30 °F).

The polar areas are characterized by cold air masses which blow toward warmer, temperate latitudes. In Antarctica, strong, chilly winds blow

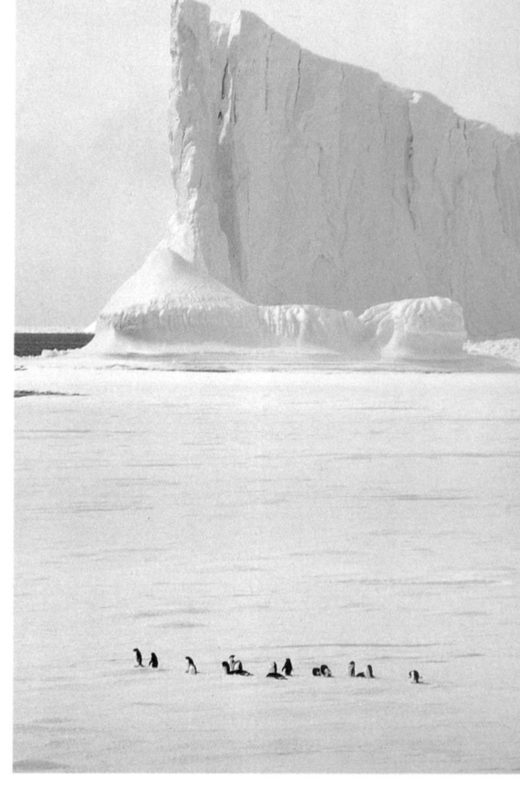

over the land surface. Winds blow continuously from west to east (the West Wind Drift) in the seas surrounding Antarctica; the seas are so often stormy that they have prevented explorers reaching the continent until relatively recently.

Winters within the Arctic Circle are windy, cold, and harsh; temperatures in northern Siberia can fall to –50 °C (–122 °F). During the arctic summer temperatures in the southern margins average around 10 °C (50 °F), with some short spells up to 30 °C (86 °F). In Antarctica, only the northern part of the Antarctic Peninsula becomes warm (up to 15 °C; 59 °F), the temperatures of the interior remaining below freezing.

Flora and fauna

Marine life thrives in the nutrient-rich waters around Antarctica. Phytoplankton abound, as do the tiny shrimp-like krill, which form part of an elaborate food chain that includes crustaceans, mollusks, fish, whales, porpoises, dolphins, and seals. Most of the fish are unique to the region. The ozone hole above the South Pole could adversely affect the phytoplakton of the Antarctic seas, which would disturb the food chain.

Around the Arctic lies the treeless tundra, south of which is boreal forest where firs, spruce, and larch grow. Lichens and mosses are common in the tundra; low-growing plants sprout in spring and blossom in summer.

There is marked contrast between the natural life of the Arctic Circle in summer and in winter. During summer there are large quantities of fish and whales in the sea, seals on the ice floes, and foxes, wolves, bears, caribou, and reindeer on land. There are also weasels, hares, and lemmings. Birds migrate to the Arctic during the summer in huge numbers; many birds and animals migrate to warmer lands and waters in winter.

Natural resources

The world's largest deposits of ice are in Antarctica. A large quantity of fresh water is frozen in these, but this water cannot easily be exploited.

Region

Dependencies & territories

Antarctic scenes: a summer night at Cape Bird (above), a Weddell seal (above right), and penguins galore—a crowd scene (below right), an inquisitive-looking Gentoo penguin (below left), and an Emperor penguin group (left).

Currently there is a concern that global warming could cause the ice sheets to melt, which would raise the levels of the world's oceans. Sea levels have risen in recent times but research indicates that the Antarctic ice sheets have not, to date, diminished in thickness.

As a large part of Antarctica was once part of Gondwana, minerals that occur in other parts of Gondwana, such as coal in Australia, might lie beneath the ice sheets. Likewise, because the Antarctic Peninsula can be considered an extension of the Andes, there is a possibility of metallic ore deposits being found in Antartica, as they have been in the Andes. In addition, the continental shelf around Antarctica could contain petroleum deposits. However, given the current state of technology, mining is not economically feasible in the harsh antarctic conditions.

International agreements which forbid mining and non-peaceful uses of Antarctica have been signed by claimant and non-claimant countries. These aim to ensure the conservation of its environment.

Polar bears (left) and people fishing under the ice (above left) in Arctic Siberia. An iceberg towers over this group of Adélie penguins in Antarctica (top).

Human habitation

Antarctica is uninhabited, except for several scientific research stations. The nearest human habitations lie on the subantarctic islands of Macquarie, Crozet, South Georgia, and Kerguelen. There is now a small amount of tourism developing in the area, mainly in the Antarctic Peninsula; tourists make short, supervized trips ashore from small cruise vessels. There are also tourist flights over the Antarctic.

In contrast, the Arctic region has been inhabited for thousands of years by indigenous groups such as the Inuit (Eskimo) in Canada, the Saami (Lapps) in Scandinavia, and the Nanets and Yakuts of Russia. Relationships have recently been discovered between these now scattered peoples—there is evidence that some of these indigenous groups migrated from Asia to North America, across the Bering Strait.

As the Arctic is not conducive to agriculture, its inhabitants have to gather food, and their ability to succeed in this is determined primarily by environmental conditions. Saami who live in the traditional way herd reindeer, taking their herds to high ground to graze in summer, then moving to woodlands in low mountain territory in winter. Caribou are hunted by the Nanets and Yakuts in the Russian tundra during spring and summer and in the forests during winter; both animals and people need to migrate with the seasons to survive. In Canada, the Inuit hunt seals along the coast during winter and move inland to hunt caribou during summer.

Polar exploration

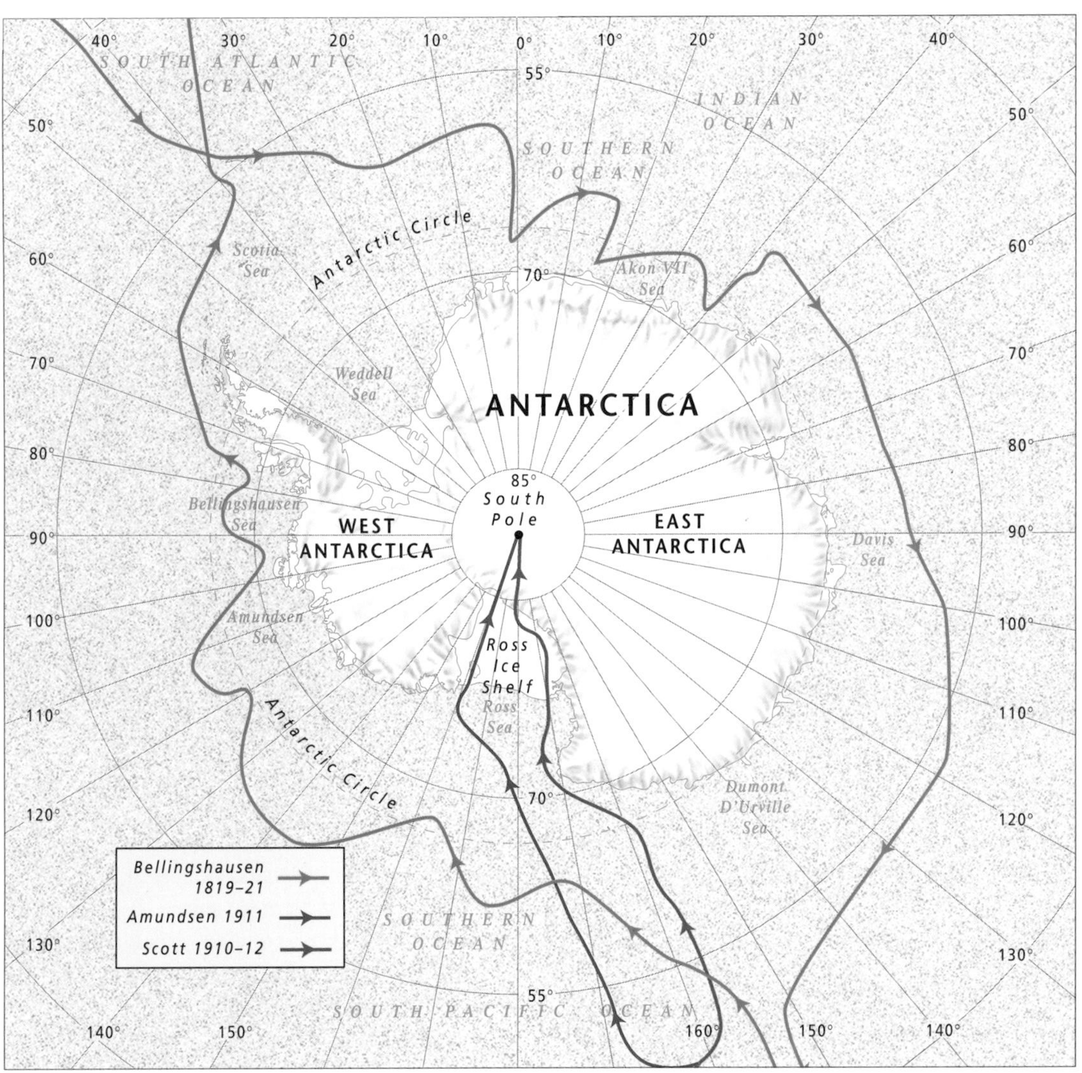

A number of motives have driven men to explore the frozen wildernesses at the uttermost ends of Earth—commerce, national glory, a personal desire for fame, and scientific discovery are just some of them. The long search for a better route from Europe to Asia through polar seas (either to the northwest or the northeast) combined political and commercial interests. The Norsemen had already discovered Iceland, Greenland, and northeast North America between the ninth and the twelfth centuries.

Then, in the sixteenth century, both English and Dutch seafarers began searching for a way through the Arctic to the riches of China and India. Looking for a Northwest Passage, the English mariner Martin Frobisher discovered and entered Hudson Strait in 1576, marched into the interior, and found a bleak landscape of mosses, juniper bushes, and stunted firs.

Davis Strait between Greenland and Baffin Island was explored by John Davis between 1585 and 1587. The Dutch navigator Willem Barents explored the west coast of Novaya Zemlya and Spitsbergen between 1594 and 1597, while he searched for a Northeast Passage around the top of Russia. He perished in the attempt—his possessions, including his flute, were found intact in a wooden hut 300 years later. With this episode, the search for a sailing route to Asia via the northeast came to an end.

In 1607, Henry Hudson navigated and explored the east coast of Greenland, discovering the island of Jan Mayen on his return. In 1610 he also discovered both the strait and the enormous bay in Canada which now bear his name. After enduring a freezing winter, however, his crew mutinied. Hudson and his son were abandoned in a little boat and never heard of again.

From Hudson's explorations until the nineteenth century, much pioneering navigation in this region was undertaken by agents of the Hudson's Bay Company, whose main interest was to buy furs. Samuel Hearne navigated the Coppermine River, and Alexander Mackenzie reached the mouth of the river which bears his name. Meanwhile, Russian merchants explored the Siberian coast, and at the direction of Peter the Great, in 1741, the Danish explorer Vitus Bering discovered a strait into the Arctic Ocean between Siberia and Alaska. His grave lies on Bering Island in the Aleutian chain.

Despite disaster, the famous expedition of Sir John Franklin in 1845 found a possible route around the top of North America. Although his party of 129 officers and men disappeared, more was probably learnt about the Arctic Archipelago by the forty relief expeditions that were sent to find him than had been discovered in all the years previously. Among the leaders of these searches, Sir James Ross (who located the position of the north magnetic pole), Captains Penny, Austin, and Ommaney, and Lieutenants M'Clintock, Collinson, and M'Clure all made valuable contributions to the world's knowledge of the Arctic region.

Following this period, the most famous polar explorer was the Norwegian Fridtjof Nansen. In 1893, believing that a polar current flowed beneath the ice from east to west, he forced his small wooden ship *Fram* into the ice on the eastern side of the Arctic. Three years later it emerged north of Spitsbergen. Previously, in 1888, he had crossed the Greenland ice cap on skis.

The Northwest Passage was first successfully traversed from 1903 to 1906 by the Norwegian explorer Roald Amundsen; the first person to reach the North Pole itself was the American explorer Robert Peary. Accompanied by a few companions, assisted by fifty Inuit, and with sleds pulled by 200 dogs, he reached the pole on 6 April 1909. His success was in part attributable to his use of dogs—an example the British failed to follow two years later in Antarctica. Peary located the North Pole on the frozen surface of a deep ocean with no land nearby. Soundings showed the depth of water below to be 2,743 m (9,000 ft) within only 8 km (5 miles) of the Pole. Research carried out much later has established a maximum depth for the Arctic Ocean of 5,450 m (17,880 ft).

Finding Antarctica

Unlike the Arctic, Antarctica was unlikely to be a route to anywhere, but the prospect it offered was even more attractive—the possibility of finding a new and humanly habitable continent. The notion of a vast Unknown South Land (*Terra Australis Incognita*) had been around since the time of the ancient Greeks, and was endorsed by the geographer Ptolemy (c. AD 100–160). It was believed to be a continuation of southern Africa, but Vasco da Gama's voyage round the Cape of Good Hope in 1498 showed this belief to be false. Nor could it be an extension of the South American continent: in 1578 Sir Francis Drake found himself blown by gales to latitude 57° S, far below Cape Horn, where he reported that the Atlantic and Pacific Oceans "meete in a most large and free scope".

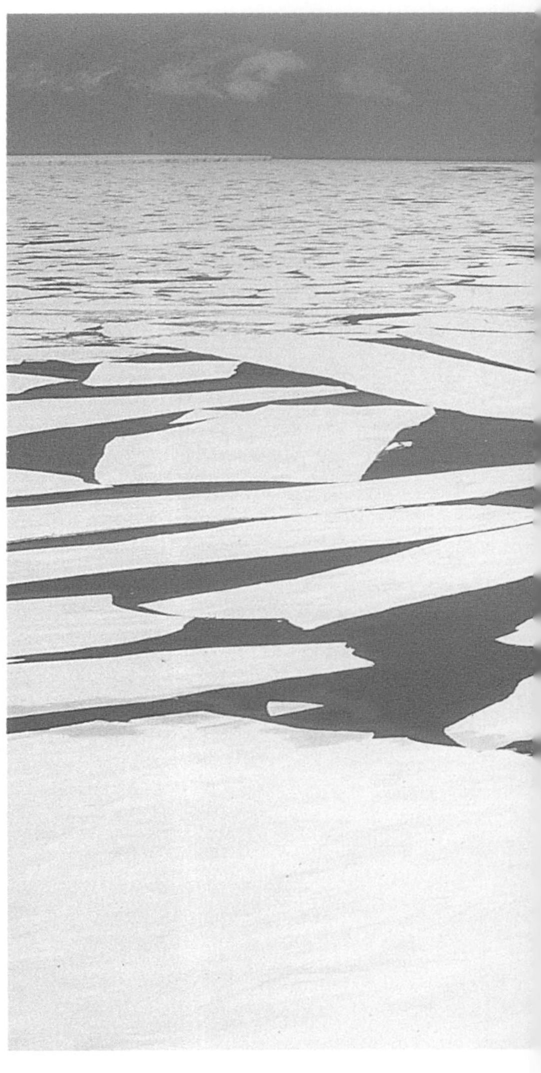

The British merchant Anthony de la Roche kept hopes alive when he sheltered at South Georgia in 1675, claiming to have seen "High Land" to the south, but this land was probably just the Clerke Rocks. When Captain James Cook circumnavigated Antarctica in the course of his second voyage (1771–75), it finally became clear that the age-old vision of a humanly habitable Great South Land had been only a dream.

During the nineteenth century a number of men from a range of nations expanded our knowledge of the land at the Antarctic perimeter. There were claims and counter claims to being the first to see the mainland (was it one of the Britons—Bransfield or Smith—in 1820, or the Russian Bellingshausen one year later?), and to being the first to step ashore (was it the American Nathanael Palmer in 1820 or the Norwegian Carsten Borchgrevink long after this in 1895?).

Borchgrevink was in fact the explorer to lead the first expedition to winter on the mainland of Antarctica, in 1899, by which time a number of scientific expeditions were being planned for the region, as well as more ventures to reach the South Pole for its own sake.

These plans led to the epic contest to be first to reach the South Pole, in the years 1910 to 1912, between the Englishman Robert Falcon Scott and the Norwegian Roald Amundsen. It was a clash between amateurism and professionalism, between a Royal Navy man who turned to expeditionary work to pass the time, and an experienced and hardened polar explorer who had spent twenty years preparing himself for the task.

Scott took ponies and mechanical tractors which had not been tried or tested; Amundsen took dog teams and experienced drivers, unsentimentally killing and eating the sled dogs as he went. Amundsen won the race, reaching the South Pole on December 14, 1911. Scott arrived almost a month later, on January 17, 1912. But the death of the British party during their return—exhausted, frozen, and out of food—plus Scott's moving journal of events, later found with his body, have ensured them a permanent place in the annals of polar exploration.

Polar research

Since the Second World War, the polar regions have very much become the preserve of scientists—mapping Antarctica and conducting oceanographic, geological, glaciological, and biological research programs. Environmental pollutants and global climate change are issues of particular concern. Today some 800 scientists and support staff from around 16 nations are based in Antarctica year-round. Key programs have included:

1947 US Operation Highjump and Operation Windmill map large parts of the Antarctic coastline and interior.

1954 Mawson Base (Australian) is set up. Over 25 years its scientists map 3,200 km (2,000 miles) of coastline and 1.3 million sq km (500,000 sq miles) of Antarctic territory.

1957–58 Scientists from 67 nations conduct research programs in both polar regions.

1961 The Antarctic Treaty (signed in 1959) comes into force, guaranteeing freedom of access and scientific research in all areas south of 60 ° S latitude.

1964–74 International Biological Programme contributes to understanding of Arctic ecology.

1986 2,000-m (6,500-ft) ice core recovered at the Russian Vostok Station provide information on climate change from 160,000 years ago.

1990 International Arctic Sciences Committee is set up to coordinate research programs.

1991 Arctic Monitoring and Assessment Program is set up by the eight Arctic rim nations and organizations representing indigenous peoples living in the region.

Antarctica: A Russian icebreaker (bottom left); the Cape Evans hut used by both Shackleton and Scott (top left); the inside of Scott's discovery hut (top, far right). Arctic: Remains of an ancient hut on the shore of the Arctic Ocean (bottom, far right).

Antarctica

Fact File

AREA 14,000,000 sq km (5,405,400 sq miles)

POPULATION No permanent population

ECONOMY Research stations

CLIMATE Extremely cold and windy

MAP REFERENCE Page 470

The fifth largest continent, Antarctica is the coldest and most inhospitable, and differs in important respects from the polar regions of the northern hemisphere. Whereas the Arctic consists of a frozen sea surrounded by land masses, the Antarctic consists of a foundation of continental rock surmounted by a massive ice cap thousands of meters thick, separated from all other major land masses by the wild and stormy waters of the Southern Ocean. Again in contrast to the northern polar region, which was inhabited by hunting peoples within the Arctic Circle, Antarctica had never seen a human being before around 1800. Even today only about 1,000 people, all of them temporary visitors, live there during the long, severe Antarctic winter. Although a number of countries active in the exploration of the continent made territorial claims to parts of it, all such claims were indefinitely deferred after the signing of the Antarctic Treaty in December 1959.

Several factors make the climate uniquely harsh. Although Antarctica receives plenty of sunlight in midsummer, eighty percent of this radiation is reflected back by the permanent cover of snow. Altitude also plays a part: Antarctica has by far the greatest average elevation of any of the continents—2,300 m (7,500 ft)—which helps produce the high winds prevailing over much of the region. Called katabatic (or downflowing) winds, these are gravity-driven, and consist of air pouring down at high speed from the elevated interior toward the coast. At one location the annual mean windspeed recorded was over 70 km/h (44 mph). Although some ninety percent of the world's fresh water is locked up in the ice cap (at places 4,800 m [15,700 ft] thick), Antarctica is also the world's driest continent, the very low temperatures limiting the moisture the air can hold. In fact only 120–150 mm (5–6 in) of water accumulates over the entire continent in the average year. Unique dry valleys, where the rock is exposed and rain has not fallen for about 2 million years, are the driest places in the world. Mummified animal carcases in these valleys have changed little in thousands of years.

The Transantarctic Mountains, which form a boundary between East and West Antarctica, are one of the world's great mountain chains, many peaks exceeding 4,000 m (13,000 ft). Geologically, East Antarctica consists mainly of an ancient continental shield with a history going back 3,000 million years. This was once part of the supercontinent known as Gondwana, from which Africa, South America, India, Australia, and New Zealand broke away. Many Antarctic rocks and fossils match up with those found in other southern continents, showing that the continents were once joined together. Ancient crystalline rocks of the shield are closely similar to those along the east coast of the Indian peninsula and Sri Lanka. Forming the base of the Transantarctic Mountains, and facing West Antarctica, is a belt of folded sediments 500 to 600 million years old.

It is a sedimentary formation dating from about 280 million years ago, however, that is most revealing. Up to 300 m (1,000 ft) thick, it is found in Australia, India, South Africa, and South America, as well as Antarctica. About 80 million years ago a series of earth movements accompanied extensive volcanic activity and it is thought that eruptions between 20 and 15 million years ago may be linked to the formation of the Transantarctic Mountains.

Plant life on the continent today consists almost entirely of mosses, lichens, and algae. Though soil mites and midges are able to survive, not a single land vertebrate can endure the winter. In contrast, life in the ocean is very rich, with a variety of seals and whales. Antarctica has five species of true or "earless" seals, including the predatory leopard seal, and both orcas and blue whales, the latter an ocean giant growing to a length of 30 m (100 ft). There are 43 species of bird, the best-known being the penguins. The Emperor Penguin, which breeds during the months of Antarctic darkness, is the only warm-blooded animal to remain on the continent during the bitter winter months. The most numerous birds are the Antarctic petrels, among which are the albatrosses.

The Antarctic Treaty of 1959 provides the legal framework for the management of Antarctica. This treaty superseded and indefinitely deferred the political partition of the continent among a number of separate nations. At present there are 42 treaty member nations, with 26 consultative nations and 16 acceding. Important articles of the treaty include No 1 (that the region is to be used for peaceful purposes only), No 2 (that freedom of scientific investigation and cooperation shall continue), and No 4 (that it does not recognize, dispute, or establish territorial claims, and that no new claims shall be asserted while the treaty is in force). Agreed-to measures adopted at consultative meetings include several conventions on the conservation of Antarctic flora and fauna.

The French Antarctic research station at Dumont d'Urville, built in 1956 (below). The Gerlache Strait on the western shore of the Antarctic Peninsula; this sheltered spot has allowed some ice to melt (bottom left). New Zealand's Scott Base, Antarctica (bottom right).

Dependencies in Antarctica

Bouvet Island

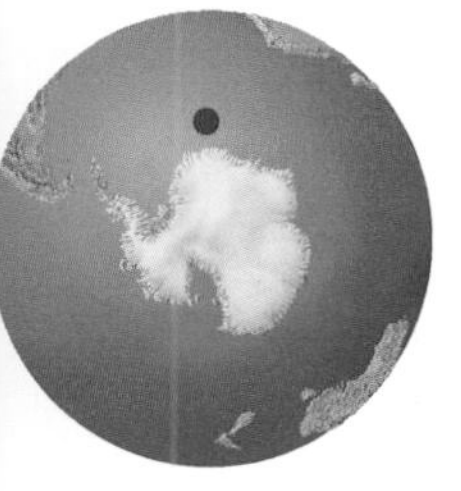

Fact File

OFFICIAL NAME Bouvet Island

FORM OF GOVERNMENT Dependent territory of Norway

CAPITAL None; administered from Oslo

AREA 58 sq km (22 sq miles)

TIME ZONE GMT

POPULATION No permanent population

ECONOMY Meteorological station

CLIMATE Cold and windy

MAP REFERENCE Page 470

Bouvet Island is named for its discoverer, Jean-Baptiste Charles Bouvet de Lozier, who came across it on 1 January 1739. Imagining that he had found a cape of the fabled Great Southern Land, he had in fact stumbled on the loneliest island on earth—the nearest land, in South Africa, being over 1,600 km (1,000 miles) away. Uninhabited except for occasional visiting meteorologists, it rises 935 m (3,068 ft) out of the Southern Ocean, and is largely covered with snow and ice.

French Southern and Antarctic Lands

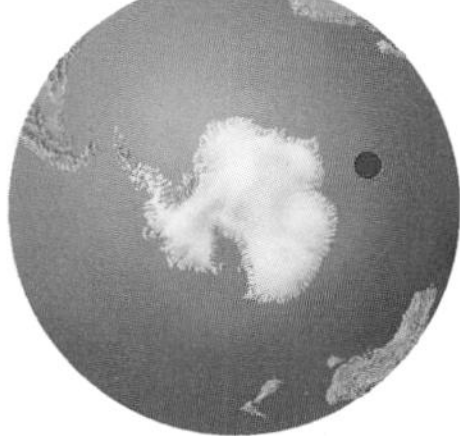

Fact File

OFFICIAL NAME Territory of the French Southern and Antarctic Lands

FORM OF GOVERNMENT Overseas territory of France

CAPITAL None; administered from Paris

AREA 7,781 sq km (3,004 sq miles)

TIME ZONE GMT + 3.5/6 hours

POPULATION No permanent population

ECONOMY None

CLIMATE Cold and windy

MAP REFERENCE Page 470

The French Southern and Antarctic Lands include Île Amsterdam, Île Saint-Paul, and Crozet and Kerguelen Islands in the southern Indian Ocean. Mean annual temperatures range from 4 °C to 10 °C (39 °F to 50 °F) and the islands are wet and stormy. The main island of Kerguelen is mountainous (Mt Ross is 1,960 m; 6,430 ft), with an irregular coastline and deep fiords, and there are snowfields in the central area. Vegetation consists of coastal tussock grass and peaty uplands. Breeding colonies of seals and penguins are found in summer. There are no permanent inhabitants; however, the islands are visited by researchers studying the native fauna.

Heard and McDonald Islands

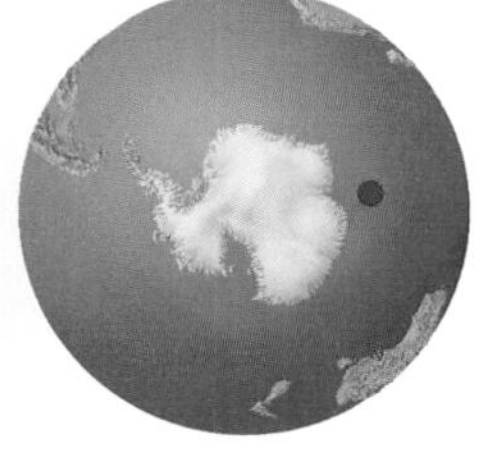

Fact File

OFFICIAL NAME Territory of Heard and McDonald Islands

FORM OF GOVERNMENT External territory of Australia

CAPITAL None; administered from Canberra

AREA 412 sq km (159 sq miles)

TIME ZONE GMT + 5 hours

POPULATION No permanent population

ECONOMY None

CLIMATE Cold and windy

MAP REFERENCE Page 470

The most inhospitable continent and one of the last regions on Earth to be explored, Antarctica is a long way from everywhere. This sign is at Scott Base, Antarctica (below left). Adélie penguin at Cape Bird, Antarctica (above right).

Heard and McDonald Islands are two bleak outposts in the Southern Ocean. Heard Island has the distinction of having the highest point in all Australian territory—2,750 m (9,021 ft). Classed as subantarctic islands, their mean annual sea level temperatures are between freezing and 3 °C (37 °F). They have ice caps, glaciers that descend to sea level, and furious gales. Vegetation consists of tussock grassland and small peaty fields. Seals and penguins breed ashore in summer.

Peter I Island

Fact File

OFFICIAL NAME Peter I Island

FORM OF GOVERNMENT Dependent territory of Norway

CAPITAL None; administered from Oslo

AREA 180 sq km (70 sq miles)

TIME ZONE GMT – 6 hours

POPULATION No permanent population

ECONOMY None

CLIMATE Cold and windy

MAP REFERENCE Page 470

One of the Antarctic maritime islands, Peter I Island lies off the continent near the Venable Ice Shelf. It was named by Bellingshausen in honor of the founder of the Russian Navy. Though moderated by the sea, the climate is basically that of the adjacent continent and the temperature rises above freezing only for short periods in summer. In winter the island is entirely surrounded by ice.

Antarctica

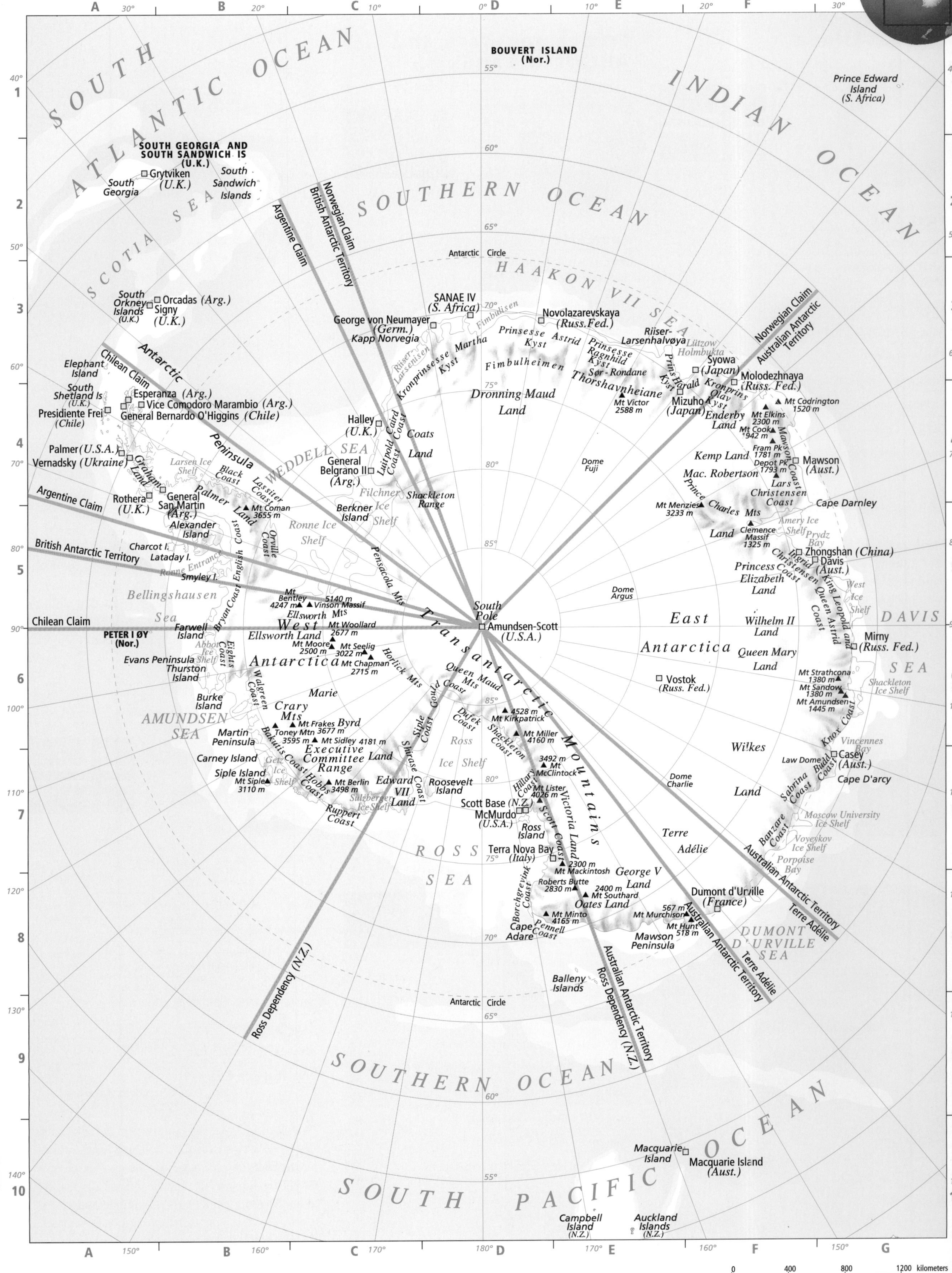
SOUTH ATLANTIC OCEAN
INDIAN OCEAN
SOUTHERN OCEAN
SOUTH PACIFIC OCEAN
BOUVERT ISLAND (Nor.)
Prince Edward Island (S. Africa)
SOUTH GEORGIA AND SOUTH SANDWICH IS (U.K.)
Grytviken (U.K.)
South Georgia
South Sandwich Islands
SCOTIA SEA
South Orkney Islands (U.K.)
Orcadas (Arg.)
Signy (U.K.)
Elephant Island
South Shetland Is (U.K.)
Esperanza (Arg.)
Vice Comodoro Marambio (Arg.)
General Bernardo O'Higgins (Chile)
Presidiente Frei (Chile)
Palmer (U.S.A.)
Vernadsky (Ukraine)
Rothera (U.K.)
General San Martin (Arg.)
Antarctic Peninsula
Graham Land
Palmer Land
Black Coast
Lassiter Coast
Orville Coast
English Coast
Bryan Coast
Eights Coast
Walgreen Coast
Larsen Ice Shelf
Mt Coman 3655 m
Alexander Island
Charcot I.
Lataday I.
Ronne Entrance
Smyley I.
Bellingshausen Sea
Farwell Island
PETER I ØY (Nor.)
Evans Peninsula
Abbot Ice Shelf
Thurston Island
Burke Island
AMUNDSEN SEA
Martin Peninsula
Carney Island
Siple Island
Mt Siple 3110 m
Getz Ice Shelf
Bakutis Coast
Hobbs Coast
Ruppert Coast
Sulzberger Ice Shelf
Edward VII Land
Marie Byrd Land
Crary Mts
Mt Frakes
Toney Mtn 3595 m
Mt Sidley 4181 m
Executive Committee Range
Mt Berlin 3498 m
3677 m
Siple Coast
Shirase Coast
Gould Coast
Roosevelt Island
Ross Ice Shelf
ROSS SEA
West Antarctica
Ellsworth Land
Ellsworth Mts
Mt Bentley 4247 m
Vinson Massif 5140 m
Mt Woollard 2677 m
Mt Moore 2500 m
Mt Seelig 3022 m
Mt Chapman 2715 m
Horlick Mts
Pensacola Mts
Queen Maud Mts
Dufek Coast
Shackleton Coast
Mt Kirkpatrick 4528 m
Mt Miller 4160 m
Mt McClintock 3492 m
Hillary Coast
Mt Lister 4026 m
Scott Coast
Victoria Land
Scott Base (N.Z.)
McMurdo (U.S.A.)
Ross Island
Terra Nova Bay (Italy)
Mt Mackintosh 2300 m
Roberts Butte 2830 m
Mt Southard 2400 m
Borchgrevink Coast
Oates Land
Mt Minto 4165 m
Cape Adare
Pennell Coast
George V Land
Mt Murchison 567 m
Mt Hunt 518 m
Mawson Peninsula
Balleny Islands
Dumont d'Urville (France)
DUMONT D'URVILLE SEA
Terre Adélie
Transantarctic Mountains
South Pole
Amundsen-Scott (U.S.A.)
Weddell Sea
Ronne Ice Shelf
Filchner Ice Shelf
Berkner Island
General Belgrano II (Arg.)
Halley (U.K.)
Luitpold Coast
Caird Coast
Coats Land
Shackleton Range
George von Neumayer (Germ.)
Kapp Norvegia
SANAE IV (S. Africa)
Riiser-Larsenisen
Kronprinsesse Martha Kyst
Fimbulisen
Novolazarevskaya (Russ.Fed.)
Prinsesse Astrid Kyst
Prinsesse Ragnhild Kyst
Fimbulheimen
Sør-Rondane
Thorshavnheiane
Dronning Maud Land
Mt Victor 2588 m
HAAKON VII SEA
Riiser-Larsenhalvøya
Lützow Holmbukta
Prins Harald Kyst
Syowa (Japan)
Mizuho (Japan)
Kronprins Olav Kyst
Molodezhnaya (Russ. Fed.)
Enderby Land
Mt Codrington 1520 m
Mt Elkins 2300 m
Mt Cook 1942 m
Fram Pk 1781 m
Depot Pk 1793 m
Mawson Coast
Mawson (Aust.)
Kemp Land
Mac. Robertson Land
Lars Christensen Coast
Cape Darnley
Prince Charles Mts
Mt Menzies 3233 m
Clemence Massif 1325 m
Amery Ice Shelf
Prydz Bay
Zhongshan (China)
Davis (Aust.)
Ingrid Christensen Coast
Princess Elizabeth Land
King Leopold and Queen Astrid Coast
West Ice Shelf
DAVIS SEA
Dome Fuji
Dome Argus
East Antarctica
Wilhelm II Land
Queen Mary Land
Mirny (Russ. Fed.)
Vostok (Russ. Fed.)
Mt Strathcona 1380 m
Mt Sandow 1380 m
Mt Amundsen 1445 m
Shackleton Ice Shelf
Wilkes Land
Knox Coast
Vincennes Bay
Casey (Aust.)
Law Dome
Budd Coast
Sabrina Coast
Cape D'arcy
Dome Charlie
Banzare Coast
Moscow University Ice Shelf
Voyeykov Ice Shelf
Porpoise Bay
Terre Adélie
Antarctic Circle
Norwegian Claim
British Antarctic Territory
Argentine Claim
Chilean Claim
Australian Antarctic Territory
Ross Dependency (N.Z.)
Macquarie Island (Aust.)
Campbell Island (N.Z.)
Auckland Islands (N.Z.)
Polar Regions

0 400 800 1200 kilometers
0 200 400 600 miles
Scale 1:30,000,000
Projection: Polar Azimuthal Equidistant

The Artctic

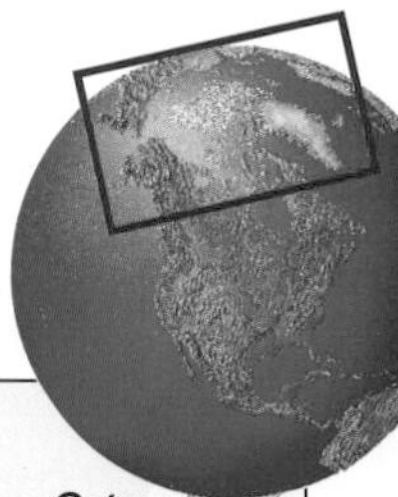

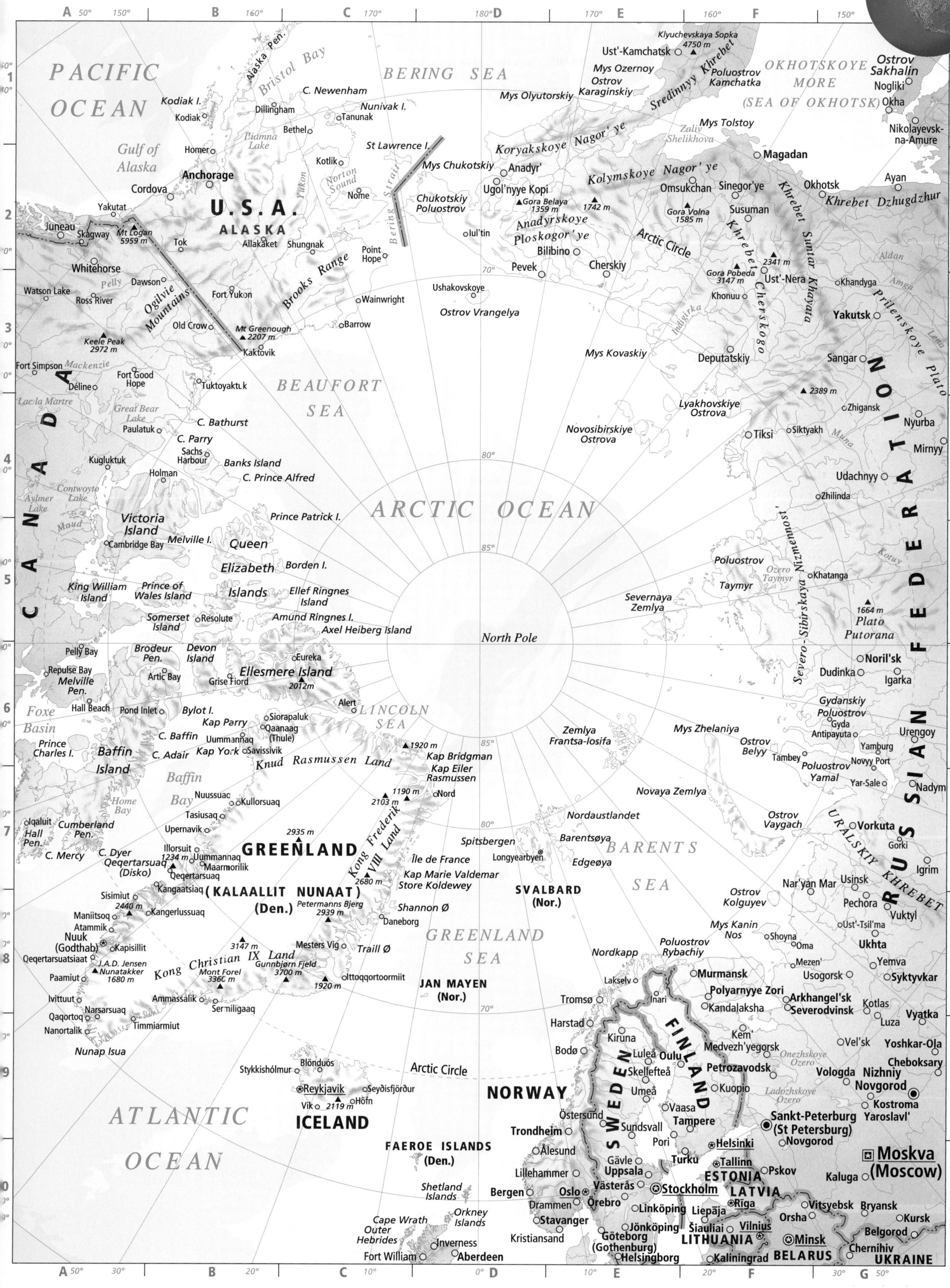

PACIFIC OCEAN
Gulf of Alaska
Bristol Bay
Alaska Pen.
Kodiak I.
Kodiak
Homer
Anchorage
Cordova
Yakutat
Juneau
Skagway
Mt Logan 5959 m
Dillingham
Iliamna Lake
C. Newenham
Nunivak I.
Tanunak
Bethel
Kotlik
Norton Sound
Nome
Yukon
U.S.A.
ALASKA
Allakaket
Shungnak
Tok
Point Hope
Brooks Range
Fort Yukon
Wainwright
Barrow
Mt Greenough 2207 m
Kaktovik
Old Crow
Ogilvie Mountains
Whitehorse
Dawson
Pelly
Watson Lake
Ross River
Keele Peak 2972 m
Fort Simpson
Mackenzie
Fort Good Hope
Déline
Tuktoyaktuk
Lac la Martre
Great Bear Lake
Paulatuk
C. Bathurst
C. Parry
Sachs Harbour
Banks Island
C. Prince Alfred
Kugluktuk
Holman
Contwoyto Lake
Aylmer Lake
Maud
Victoria Island
Cambridge Bay
Melville I.
Prince Patrick I.
Queen Elizabeth Islands
Borden I.
Ellef Ringnes Island
Amund Ringnes I.
Axel Heiberg Island
King William Island
Prince of Wales Island
Somerset Island
Resolute
CANADA
Pelly Bay
Repulse Bay
Melville Pen.
Brodeur Pen.
Devon Island
Artic Bay
Eureka
Ellesmere Island
Grise Fiord
2012 m
Alert
Foxe Basin
Hall Beach
Pond Inlet
Bylot I.
Prince Charles I.
Baffin Island
C. Baffin
C. Adair
Kap Parry
Siorapaluk
Qaanaag (Thule)
Uummannaq
Kap York
Savissivik
Knud Rasmussen Land
LINCOLN SEA
1920 m
Kap Bridgman
Kap Eiler Rasmussen
1190 m
Nord
2103 m
Baffin Bay
Home Bay
Nuussuaq
Kullorsuaq
Tasiusaq
Upernavik
Iqaluit
Hall Pen.
Cumberland Pen.
C. Mercy
C. Dyer
Qeqertarsuaq (Disko)
Illorsuit
1234 m
Uummannaq
Maarmorilik
Qeqertarsuaq
2935 m
GREENLAND
(KALAALLIT NUNAAT) (Den.)
Kong Frederik VIII Land
2680 m
Kangaatsiaq
Sisimiut
2440 m
Kangerlussuaq
Petermanns Bjerg 2939 m
Maniitsoq
Atammik
Nuuk (Godthab)
Kapisillit
Qeqertarsuatsiaat
J.A.D. Jensen Nunatakker 1680 m
Paamiut
Ivittuut
Narsarsuaq
Qaqortoq
Nanortalik
Nunap Isua
3147 m
Kong Christian IX Land
Mont Forel 3360 m
Gunnbjørn Fjeld 3700 m
1920 m
Mesters Vig
Traill Ø
Ittoqqortoormiit
Ammassalik
Sermiligaaq
Timmiarmiut
Shannon Ø
Daneborg
Île de France
Kap Marie Valdemar
Store Koldewey
GREENLAND SEA
JAN MAYEN (Nor.)
BERING SEA
Bering Strait
St Lawrence I.
Mys Chukotskiy
Chukotskiy Poluostrov
Iul'tin
Ushakovskoye
Ostrov Vrangelya
BEAUFORT SEA
ARCTIC OCEAN
North Pole
Ust'-Kamchatsk
Klyuchevskaya Sopka 4750 m
Mys Ozernoy
Ostrov Karaginskiy
Mys Olyutorskiy
Sredinnyy Khrebet
Poluostrov Kamchatka
OKHOTSKOYE MORE (SEA OF OKHOTSK)
Ostrov Sakhalin
Nogliki
Okha
Nikolayevsk-na-Amure
Zaliv Shelikhova
Mys Tolstoy
Magadan
Koryakskoye Nagor'ye
Anadyr'
Ugol'nyye Kopi
Gora Belaya 1359 m
1742 m
Kolymskoye Nagor'ye
Omsukchan
Sinegor'ye
Gora Volna 1585 m
Susuman
Anadyrskoye Ploskogor'ye
Bilibino
Pevek
Cherskiy
Arctic Circle
Khrebet Cherskogo
Khrebet Suntar Khayata
Okhotsk
Ayan
Khrebet Dzhugdzhur
Aldan
Gora Pobeda 3147 m
2341 m
Ust'-Nera
Khonuu
Khandyga
Amga
Indigirka
Yakutsk
Prilenskoye Plato
Lena
Mys Kovaskiy
Deputatskiy
Sangar
2389 m
Lyakhovskiye Ostrova
Novosibirskiye Ostrova
Zhigansk
Tiksi
Siktyakh
Muna
Nyurba
Mirnyy
Udachnyy
Zhilinda
RUSSIAN FEDERATION
Severo-Sibirskaya Nizmennost'
Poluostrov Taymyr
Ozero Taymyr
Khatanga
Kotuy
Severnaya Zemlya
1664 m
Plato Putorana
Noril'sk
Dudinka
Igarka
Gydanskiy Poluostrov
Gyda
Antipayuta
Urengoy
Yamburg
Novyy Port
Nadym
Yar-Sale
Poluostrov Yamal
Tambey
Ostrov Belyy
Mys Zhelaniya
Zemlya Frantsa-Iosifa
Novaya Zemlya
Nordaustlandet
Barentsøya
Edgeøya
Spitsbergen
Longyearbyen
SVALBARD (Nor.)
BARENTS SEA
Ostrov Vaygach
Uralskiy Khrebet
Vorkuta
Gorki
Igrim
Nar'yan Mar
Usinsk
Pechora
Vuktyl
Ust'-Tsil'ma
Ostrov Kolguyev
Mys Kanin Nos
Shoyna
Oma
Ukhta
Mezen'
Yemva
Usogorsk
Syktyvkar
Poluostrov Rybachiy
Nordkapp
Murmansk
Lakselv
Inari
Polyarnyye Zori
Kandalaksha
Arkhangel'sk
Severodvinsk
Kotlas
Luza
Vyatka
Tromsø
Harstad
Kiruna
Kem'
Medvezh'yegorsk
Onezhskoye Ozero
Vel'sk
Yoshkar-Ola
Bodø
Luleå
Oulu
Petrozavodsk
Cheboksary
Vologda
Nizhniy Novgorod
Skellefteå
Kuopio
Ladozhskoye Ozero
Kostroma
Yaroslavl'
Umeå
Vaasa
Tampere
Sankt-Peterburg (St Petersburg)
Novgorod
FINLAND
SWEDEN
NORWAY
Östersund
Sundsvall
Pori
Trondheim
Ålesund
Helsinki
Turku
Tallinn
ESTONIA
Pskov
Moskva (Moscow)
Kaluga
Lillehammer
Gävle
Uppsala
Västerås
Stockholm
LATVIA
Rīga
Bergen
Oslo
Drammen
Örebro
Linköping
Liepāja
Vitsyebsk
Bryansk
Orsha
Kursk
Stavanger
Kristiansand
Jönköping
Šiauliai
Vilnius
LITHUANIA
Minsk
Belgorod
Göteborg (Gothenburg)
Helsingborg
Kaliningrad
BELARUS
Chernihiv
UKRAINE
Blönduós
Stykkishólmur
Arctic Circle
Reykjavík
Seyðisfjörður
Höfn
Vík
2119 m
ICELAND
ATLANTIC OCEAN
FAEROE ISLANDS (Den.)
Shetland Islands
Orkney Islands
Cape Wrath
Outer Hebrides
Inverness
Fort William
Aberdeen

0 200 400 600 800 1000 kilometers
0 200 400 600 miles
Scale 1:26,000,000 Projection: Polar Azimuthal Equidistant

The Oceans

The Oceans

Oceans constitute one of Earth's great frontiers. Scientists, environmentalists, governments, industrialists and 'dreamers' all want to understand how oceans function in physical, chemical, ecological and economic terms. The role of oceans in military conflicts and for the security of nations is also still of concern, with many countries spending considerable sums of money on finding ways to exploit oceanic secrets to their advantage.

In stark contrast to all other known planets, oceans constitute approximately seventy percent of Earth. There are five main oceans of the world—the Atlantic, Pacific, Indian, Arctic, and Antarctic (also known as the Southern or South Polar Ocean). The biggest ocean is the Pacific, at about 170 million sq km (66 million sq miles), which occupies almost twice the area of the next biggest, the Atlantic.

Throughout history, these vast oceanic expanses and adjoining seas have challenged humans as to how they should be used. At least some 100,000 years ago, and especially over the last 10,000 years, successful efforts have been made to cross the oceans, allowing human migrations. Trade routes involving various kinds of ships have also developed, growing from local to transoceanic journeys. Today the sea is used, and at times abused, by oceanic craft transporting people and goods to form the connections vital for international commerce.

It is only in the past century or so that humans have really started to make an impact on oceanic environments. These environments have evolved and changed over billions of years. Ecosystems have become established and been modified by changes in atmospheric composition, sea-floor spreading, climatic and current patterns, the discharge of solutes and sediments from rivers, and the development of new life forms. Human interference and exploitation, including the pollution of ocean waters, has quickly altered conditions in many oceanic areas, leading to a decline in fish and mammal stocks, the destruction of habitats and even, potentially, to increased water temperatures. The challenge for the future will be to use our technological knowledge to protect oceanic environments, while allowing increased use of ocean resources by the world's growing population.

Ocean topography

Oceanographers have greatly expanded our knowledge of the sea floor over the past century. Using first primitive line soundings, then early echo sounders and now sophisticated electronic surveying techniques, it has been possible to build up detailed images of the bottom of the ocean. Submersibles have been used to photograph and document specific features, including remnants of wrecks like the Titanic which lie at great depths.

In recent decades there has been a great acceleration in the exploitation of ocean topography. In particular, the mapping of features such as faults, volcanic ridges and vents, slumps, and canyons, has enabled scientists to reconstruct the history of these features. The theory of plate tectonics has been greatly supported by geological and geophysical studies of the sea floor, especially the identification and interpretation of paleomagnetic strips contained in oceanic basalts. These form as new basalt moves away from mid-ocean spreading centers, and record the magnetic field of the period.

Typically, ocean floors are covered by thin, oozy sediment layers that form abyssal plains separated by ridges, seamounts and plateaus representing past geologic events. Continental margins descend steeply from bordering shelves down steep, often dissented, slopes to plains, the flattest surfaces on Earth. The plain may be as deep as 3,000 to 5,000 m (9840 to 16,400 ft). Beyond these depths there are relatively narrow trenches reaching 10,000 m (32,800 ft) below sea level, such as those found adjacent to the island areas and rising mountain chains of the Pacific.

A broad, rugged and near-continuous mountain range occurs in the centers of the Atlantic, Indian and South Pacific Oceans. This is the mid-oceanic ridge, now very clearly shown on all topographic maps of the ocean floor. Its crest is characterized by a rift valley which is the source area for new basaltic floors. Oceanographers have described deep gashes or fractures cutting the ocean floor at right angles to the crest of the ridge. These eventually become obscured, away from the ridge, by collections of sediment.

Islands and former islands or seamounts in ocean basins are often related to the oceanic ridge and its fractures. Active and dormant volcanoes provide the rocks that form the foundation of these islands. As oceanic basalt moves away from a volcanic "hot spot", the volcano dies and the island surface erodes and gradually subsides (as in the Emperor Seamounts near Hawaii). Corals colonize the shores of such islands in tropical areas, eventually forming atolls—the legacy of a once active volcanic system.

Ocean chemistry

The chemical composition of ocean waters is generally constant. Seawater is a solution containing a complex mixture of dissolved solids or solutes. Its evolution over time since the beginning of the Earth is little understood, but it is clearly linked to the development of a protective ozone layer in the atmosphere, to evolving life forms in shallow and deeper waters, to the gasses emitted by volcanoes or deepwater vents, and to run-off from the land. Many different minerals have accumulated in ocean waters, but about one billion years ago the concentration reached a steady-state position. In other words, new dry inputs were balanced by processes that removed the minerals, the most important of which was the deposition of minerals as sediments on continental shelves, slopes, and ocean floors.

The uniformity of ocean chemistry results from continuous mixing—the circulation of waters between oceans and seas—and numerous chemical reactions that take place over a comparatively restricted range of temperatures. Seven dominant elements form the dissolved solids in H_2O. They

The oceans support a vast diversity of marine life: southern right whales (left) live in the cold Antarctic Ocean, while shoals of Mao Mao (above) prefer warm tropical waters.

are chlorine (as chloride CE-), sodium (as Na+), magnesium (as Mg_2+), potassium (as K+), and bromide (as bromide Br-). Gases in a dissolved state, such as carbon dioxide, nitrogen and oxygen, are also present; the availability of oxygen is critical for many life forms. Other minor components of oceanic waters include trace elements, organic particles, and suspended matter.

Salinity is a term used to describe dissolved solids by volume in seawater. It is commonly expressed in parts per thousand (ppt), with the average value for oceanic waters being 35 ppt, varying between 34 and 37 ppt. Rainfall and ice melt tends to dilute the average salinity value; evaporation has the opposite effect, especially under the influence of hot, dry, subtropical high pressure systems.

One property of oceans that can vary quite widely is temperature. In polar regions, vast areas of oceans freeze to form sea ice and ice shelves. Seawater freezes at –2 °C (28.4 °F) at the surface of oceans. At the other end of the scale, tropical waters may have temperatures as high as 30 °C (86 °F). Ocean waters are typically layered, with marked differences in temperature and salinity between mixed surface waters and deeper zones, where temperatures approach freezing.

Ocean circulation

Differences in temperature and salinity between waters at varying depths, combined with Earth's rotational influence and wind forces, help drive ocean water masses within and between oceanic basins. At depth, the great movements of water are quite slow in comparison with the surface. This results in an upwelling of cold, nutrient-rich currents toward the margins of some continents, such as along the west coast of South America. Surface flows redistribute heat from the tropics to higher latitudes; the Gulf Stream flowing along the east coast of North America towards Europe is a classic example, helping to maintain milder temperatures in countries such as the Republic of Ireland, the United Kingdom and Denmark.

In some parts of oceans, water circulation is somewhat limited. This is the case at the centers of subtropical gyres (circular surface rotations of water), such as the gyre within the North Atlantic

Ocean, where the Sargasso Sea develops salinities up to 30 ppt.

During the Quaternary Period it is hypothesized that significant changes in oceanic circulation occurred. The so-called "conveyor belts" of surface and deeper currents moving masses of water between the basins would have been influenced by the spread of ice on and adjacent to continents. Microscopic organisms buried in sediments on the ocean floor have been used to determine in some detail shifts in temperature and salinity conditions over the past 2 million years.

Ocean exploration

The exploration of oceans can be described in three phases. First there was the pioneering period of great sea-going nations looking for new lands to exploit and colonize. From Europe the Vikings led the way, followed by the great voyages of the Portuguese, Spanish, Dutch, British and French. These were later joined by other nations, including Germany, Russia and the USA. From Asia and the Middle East came other maritime travellers, crossing the oceans for trade and also to promulgate religious beliefs.

The second phase consolidated the discoveries of the first and led to the establishment of ports and trading routes. Knowledge increased about hazards to shipping, climatic and current conditions, the best use of the sea for naval purposes, and the social and economic conditions of lands bordering the oceans.

The third phase encompasses the scientific exploration of the past five decades, including the use of satellites, permanent recorders, and surface and submerged survey techniques to greatly expand our knowledge of the oceanic realm. This includes an understanding of perhaps the largest mineral deposit on Earth—manganese nodules. It is estimated that about 2 billion tonnes of manganese nodules lie on the floor of our oceans.

Deep-sea drilling has proved invaluable in helping us determine the type of materials found on ocean floors and their age and modes of formation. Increasingly, this new knowledge is alerting scientists and decision-makers to our capacity to adversely affect ocean ecosystems.

Exploitation and pollution

The pressure to use large tracts of ocean and coastal waters for fishing and the extraction of minerals, including oil, has led in some cases to over-exploitation of our biggest natural resource, the sea. International conventions on rights to ocean use have become a mechanism to resolve disputes and to prevent the loss of endangered species. That differences of opinion still exist between nations—for instance, over whaling rights—indicate that serious issues remain unresolved. Two issues of global significance need to be considered by all countries of the world: water pollution and the impact of the greenhouse effect on ocean levels.

For a long time oceans have been considered a convenient dumping ground for human and chemical waste. It used to be thought that the oceans were big enough either to dilute the waste or at least to carry it conveniently out of sight. This is no longer the case—pollution by radioactive wastes in areas like the Arctic Ocean has proven that our planet is not big enough to absorb such toxic material. Urban industrial societies need to develop informed strategies for waste disposal before it is too late.

Oceans and the climate

It has been known for some time that oceans moderate the world's climate. Scientists are now able to use computers to model the interaction between oceans and the atmosphere, and are warning governments of potentially serious disturbances to climatic patterns. Phenomena such as El Niño already highlight the variability in ocean-climate patterns and the extreme climatic conditions (floods, droughts, storm surges) that can occur. Ocean warming due to the greenhouse effect also increases the possibility of extreme weather patterns and rising sea levels. These effects are particularly serious for low-lying nations built on coral reefs and coral debris. such as the Maldives.

Oceanic exploration includes the study of rich plant and marine life (top). Oil is a valuable oceanic resource (center). Lighthouses have ensured safe ocean travel for centuries (right).

Indian Ocean

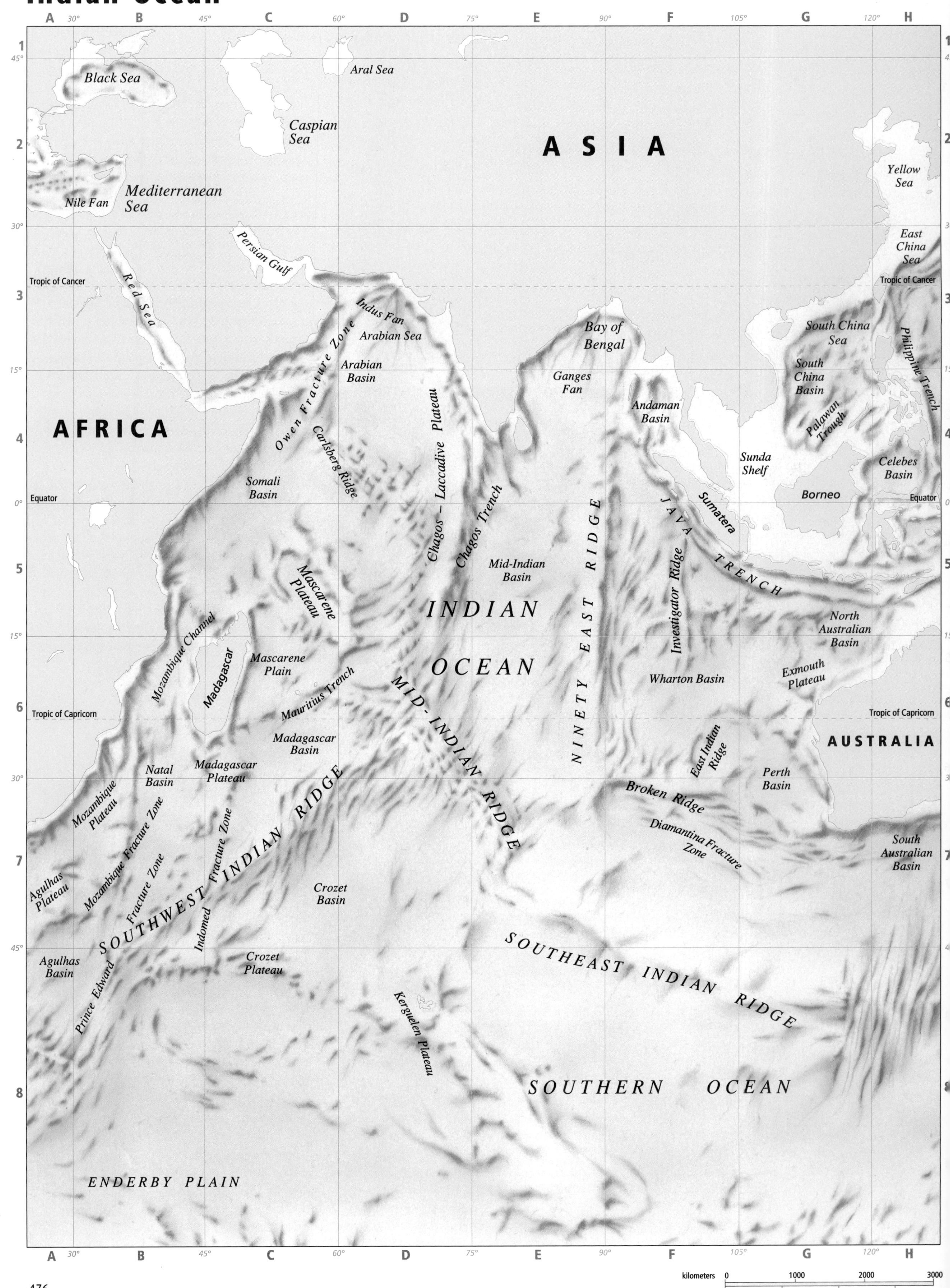
A
30°
B
45°
C
60°
D
75°
E
90°
F
105°
G
120°
H
1
2
3
4
5
6
7
8
45°
30°
15°
0°
Black Sea
Aral Sea
Caspian Sea
ASIA
Yellow Sea
Nile Fan
Mediterranean Sea
East China Sea
Persian Gulf
Red Sea
Tropic of Cancer
Indus Fan
Arabian Sea
Bay of Bengal
South China Sea
Philippine Trench
Arabian Basin
Ganges Fan
South China Basin
AFRICA
Owen Fracture Zone
Carlsberg Ridge
Chagos – Laccadive Plateau
Andaman Basin
Palawan Trough
Sunda Shelf
Celebes Basin
Somali Basin
Borneo
Equator
Chagos Trench
Sumatera
JAVA TRENCH
Mid-Indian Basin
NINETY EAST RIDGE
Investigator Ridge
Mascarene Plateau
INDIAN OCEAN
North Australian Basin
Mozambique Channel
Madagascar
Mascarene Plain
Mauritius Trench
Wharton Basin
Exmouth Plateau
Tropic of Capricorn
MID-INDIAN RIDGE
Madagascar Basin
East Indian Ridge
AUSTRALIA
Natal Basin
Madagascar Plateau
Perth Basin
Mozambique Plateau
Broken Ridge
Diamantina Fracture Zone
SOUTHWEST INDIAN RIDGE
Mozambique Fracture Zone
Indomed Fracture Zone
South Australian Basin
Agulhas Plateau
Fracture Zone
Crozet Basin
Agulhas Basin
Prince Edward
Crozet Plateau
SOUTHEAST INDIAN RIDGE
Kerguelen Plateau
SOUTHERN OCEAN
ENDERBY PLAIN
kilometers 0 1000 2000 3000
miles 0 500 1000 1500
Scale 1:60,000,000
Projection: Mercator

Atlantic Ocean

Baffin Bay
Greenland
Jan Mayen Ridge
Iceland
Faeroe-Iceland Ridge
Hudson Bay
Northwest Atlantic Mid-Ocean Canyon
Imarssuak Seachannel
Reykjanes Ridge
Maury Seachannel
North Sea
Baltic Sea
NORTH AMERICA
Charlie-Gibbs Fracture Zone
Porcupine Plain
EUROPE
ATLANTIC OCEAN
Grand Banks of Newfoundland
Biscay Plain
Azores-Biscay Rise
Laurentian Fan
MID-ATLANTIC RIDGE
Oceanographer Fracture Zone
Strait of Gibraltar
Mediterranean Sea
Mediterranean Ridge
Blake Plateau
Hatteras Plain
Bermuda Rise
Atlantis Fracture Zone
Gulf of Mexico
Tropic of Cancer
Kane Fracture Zone
Cape Verde Basin
Nares Plain
Peurto Rico Trench
AFRICA
Cayman Trench
Beata Ridge
Aves Ridge
Vema Fracture Zone
Caribbean Sea
Gambia Plain
Middle America Trench
Demerara Plain
Doldrums Fracture Zone
Amazon Fan
Sierra Leone Basin
Romanche Fracture Zone
Guinea Basin
Equator
Carnegie Ridge
Ceara Plain
Chain Fracture Zone
Pernambuco Plain
Ascension Fracture Zone
Peru-Chile Trench
SOUTH AMERICA
Brazil Basin
Angola Basin
Nazca Ridge
Tropic of Capricorn
PACIFIC OCEAN
Rio Grande Rise
Walvis Ridge
Cape Basin
ATLANTIC OCEAN
Agulhas Basin
Argentine Plain
Falkland Escarpment
Falkland Plateau
Humboldt Plain
South Georgia Ridge
South Sandwich Trench
ATLANTIC-INDIAN RIDGE
Drake Passage

A 90° B 75° C 60° D 45° E 30° F 15° G 0° H 15° J

0 1000 2000 3000 kilometers
0 500 1000 1500 miles
Scale 1:60,000,000
Projection: Mercator

Pacific Ocean

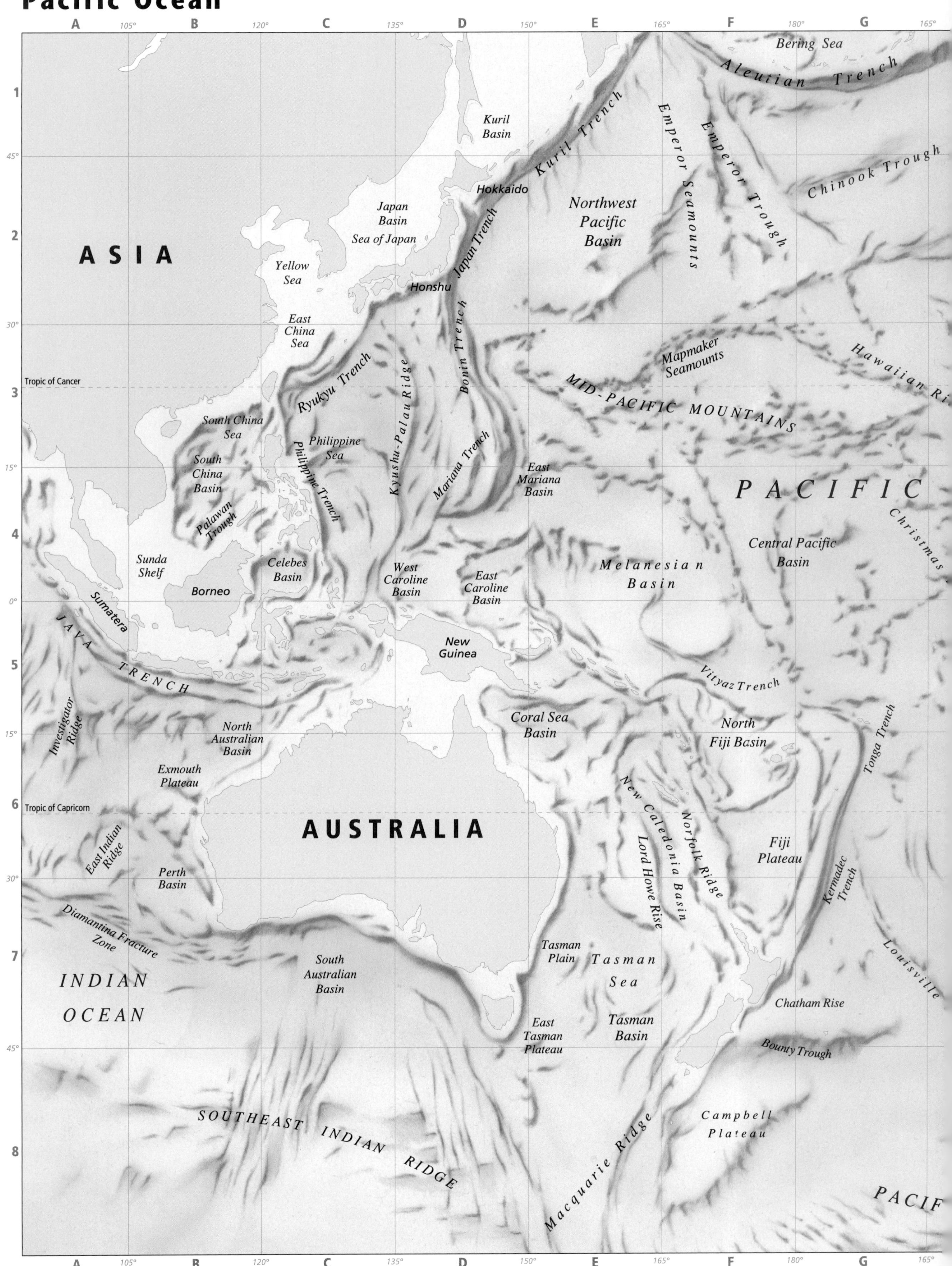

ASIA
Bering Sea
Aleutian Trench
Kuril Basin
Kuril Trench
Emperor Seamounts
Emperor Trough
Chinook Trough
Hokkaido
Japan Basin
Sea of Japan
Northwest Pacific Basin
Japan Trench
Yellow Sea
Honshu
East China Sea
Bonin Trench
Mapmaker Seamounts
Hawaiian Ri
Tropic of Cancer
Ryukyu Trench
Kyushu-Palau Ridge
MID-PACIFIC MOUNTAINS
South China Sea
Philippine Sea
Philippine Trench
South China Basin
Mariana Trench
East Mariana Basin
PACIFIC
Christmas
Palawan Trough
Sunda Shelf
Celebes Basin
West Caroline Basin
East Caroline Basin
Melanesian Basin
Central Pacific Basin
Borneo
Sumatera
JAVA TRENCH
New Guinea
Vityaz Trench
Investigator Ridge
North Australian Basin
Coral Sea Basin
North Fiji Basin
Tonga Trench
Exmouth Plateau
Tropic of Capricorn
AUSTRALIA
New Caledonia Basin
Norfolk Ridge
Lord Howe Rise
Fiji Plateau
Kermadec Trench
East Indian Ridge
Perth Basin
Diamantina Fracture Zone
South Australian Basin
Tasman Plain
Tasman Sea
Louisville
INDIAN OCEAN
East Tasman Plateau
Tasman Basin
Chatham Rise
Bounty Trough
SOUTHEAST INDIAN RIDGE
Macquarie Ridge
Campbell Plateau
PACIF

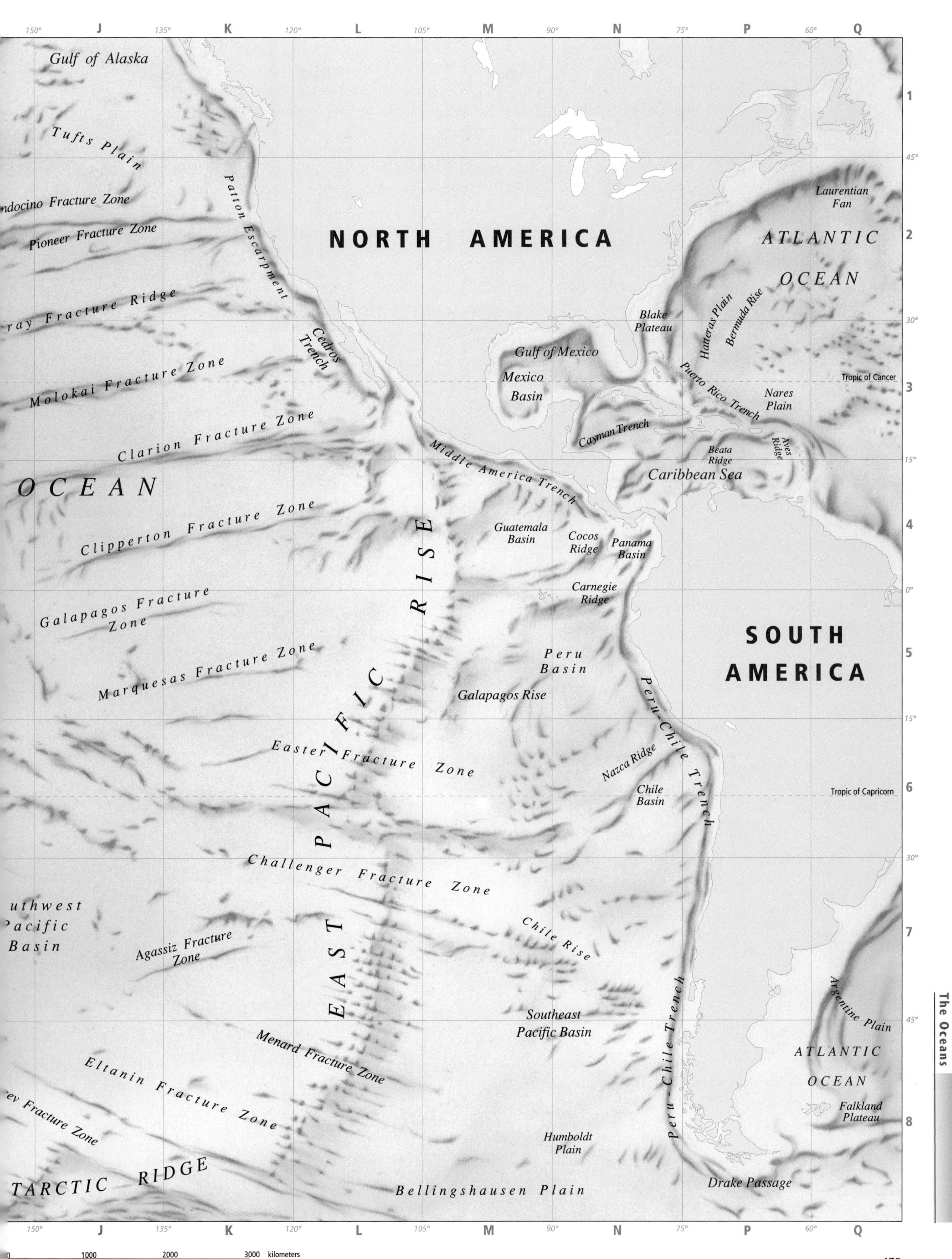
Gulf of Alaska
Tufts Plain
ndocino Fracture Zone
Pioneer Fracture Zone
Patton Escarpment
NORTH AMERICA
ray Fracture Ridge
Cedros Trench
Molokai Fracture Zone
Clarion Fracture Zone
OCEAN
Clipperton Fracture Zone
Galapagos Fracture Zone
Marquesas Fracture Zone
Easter Fracture Zone
EAST PACIFIC RISE
Challenger Fracture Zone
uthwest Pacific Basin
Agassiz Fracture Zone
Menard Fracture Zone
Eltanin Fracture Zone
ev Fracture Zone
TARCTIC RIDGE
Bellingshausen Plain
Humboldt Plain
Southeast Pacific Basin
Chile Rise
Middle America Trench
Guatemala Basin
Cocos Ridge
Panama Basin
Carnegie Ridge
Peru Basin
Galapagos Rise
Nazca Ridge
Chile Basin
Peru-Chile Trench
Gulf of Mexico
Mexico Basin
Cayman Trench
Caribbean Sea
Beata Ridge
Aves Ridge
Puerto Rico Trench
Nares Plain
Blake Plateau
Hatteras Plain
Bermuda Rise
Laurentian Fan
ATLANTIC OCEAN
Tropic of Cancer
SOUTH AMERICA
Tropic of Capricorn
Argentine Plain
ATLANTIC OCEAN
Falkland Plateau
Drake Passage
150° J 135° K 120° L 105° M 90° N 75° P 60° Q
1 2 3 4 5 6 7 8
45° 30° 15° 0° 15° 30° 45°
0 1000 2000 3000 kilometers
0 500 1000 1500 miles
Scale 1:50,000,000
Projection: Mercator

Part 4

Gazetteer

Abbreviations Used on Maps

Arch. Archipelago, Archipel, Archipiélago, Arquipélago
Arg. Argentina
Arm. Armenia
Aust. Australia
Azer. Azerbaijan
B. Bay, Baía, Baie, Bahía
B.-H. Bosnia and Herzegovina
Belg. Belgium
C.A.R. Central African Republic
C. Cape, Cabo, Cap, Capo
Co Cerro
Col. Colombia
Cord. Cordillera
Croat. Croatia
Cuch. Cuchillo
Czech Rep. Czech Republic
D.C. District of Columbia
Dem. Rep. of the Congo Democratic Republic of the Congo
Den. Denmark
E. East
Ecu. Ecuador
Emb. Embalse
Eq. Guinea Equatorial Guinea
Est. Estrecho
Fr. France
G. Gora
G. Gulf, Golfe, Golfo, Gulfo
G. Gunung
Germ. Germany
Harb. Harbor
Hung. Hungary
I. Island, Île, Ilha, Isla, Isola
Is Islands, Îles, Ilhas, Islas
Jez. Jezioro
K. Kolpos
Kep. Kepulauan
L. Lake, Lac, Lacul, Lago, Limni, Loch
Liech. Liechtenstein
Lux. Luxembourg
Mace. Macedonia
Mex. Mexico
Mt Mount, Mont
Mte Monte
Mti Monti
Mtn Mountain
Mts Mountains, Monts
N. North
N.Z. New Zealand
Neth. Netherlands
Nev. Nevado
Nor. Norway
P. Pic, Pico
P. Pulau
P.N.G. Papua New Guinea
Peg. Pegunungan
Pen. Peninsula, Péninsula, Péninsule
Pk Peak
Pk Puncak
Port. Portugal
Pt Point
Pta Ponta, Punta
Pte Pointe
Pto Porto, Pôrto, Puerto
R. River
Ra. Range
Rep. Republic
Res. Reservoir
Russ. Fed. Russian Federation
S. San
S. South
S.A. South Africa
Sa Serra
Sd Sound
Serr. Serranía
Slov. Slovenia
Sp. Spain
St Saint
Sta Santa
Ste Sainte
Sto Santo
Switz. Switzerland
Tel. Teluk
Tg Tanjong
U. Ujung
U.A.E. United Arab Emirates
U.K. United Kingdom
U.S., U.S.A. United States of America
Vol. Volcán
W. West

Foreign Geographical Terms

Açude (*Portuguese*) reservoir
Adası (*Turkish*) island
Adrar (*Berber*) mountains
Agios (*Greek*) saint
Akra (*Greek*) cape, point
Alpen (*German*) Alps
Alpi (*Italian*) Alps
Alta (*Spanish*) upper
Altiplanicie (*Spanish*) high plain, plateau
-älven (*Swedish*) river
Ao (*Thai*) bay
Archipel (*French*) archipelago
Archipiélago (*Spanish*) archipelago
Arquipélago (*Portuguese*) archipelago
Avtonomnaya Oblast' (*Russian*) autonomous region
Avtonomnyy Okrug (*Russian*) autonomous area

Bab (*Arabic*) strait
Bælt (*Danish*) strait
Bahía (*Spanish*) bay
Baḩr, Bahr (*Arabic*) lake, river, sea
Baía (*Portuguese*) bay
Baie (*French*) bay
Barajı (*Turkish*) dam
Barragem (*Portuguese*) reservoir
Bassin (*French*) basin
Beinn, Ben (*Gaelic*) mountain
Bjerg (*Danish*) hill, mountain
Bôca (*Portuguese*) river mouth
Boca (*Spanish*) river mouth
Bocht (*Dutch*) bay
Bodden (*German*) bay
Bogazi (*Turkish*) strait
Bögeni (*Kazakh*) reservoir
-bre/en (*Norwegian*) glacier
Bucht (*German*) bay
Bugt, -bugten (*Danish*) bay
Buḩayrat (*Arabic*) lake
Bukit (*Malay*) mountain
-bukten (*Swedish*) bay
Burnu, Burun (*Turkish*) cape, point
Buuraha (*Somali*) hill/s, mountain/s

Cabo (*Portuguese, Spanish*) cape
Canal (*Spanish*) channel
Cap (*French*) cape
Capo (*Italian*) cape
Cerro/s (*Spanish*) hill/s, peak/s
Chaîne (*French*) mountain range
Chapada (*Portuguese*) hills, upland/s
Chhâk (*Cambodian*) bay
Chott (*Arabic*) marsh, salt lake
Cima (*Italian*) mountain
Ciudad (*Spanish*) city
Co (*Tibetan*) lake
Colline (*Italian*) hill/s
Cordillera (*Spanish*) mountain range, mountain chain
Côte (*French*) coast, slope
Cù Lao (*Vietnamese*) island
Cuchilla (*Spanish*) mountain range

Dag/Dağı (*Turkish*) mountain
Dağlar/ı (*Turkish*) mountains
-dake (*Japanese*) peak
Danau (*Indonesian*) lake
Dao (*Chinese*) island
Dao (*Vietnamese*) island
Daryâcheh (*Persian*) lake
Dasht (*Persian*) desert
Denizi (*Turkish*) sea
Desierto (*Spanish*) desert
Détroit (*French*) strait
Djebel (*Arabic*) mountain, mountain range

-elva (*Norwegian*) river
Embalse (*Spanish*) reservoir
Ensenada (*Spanish*) bay
Erg (*Arabic*) sand dunes
Estrecho (*Spanish*) strait
Étang (*French*) lagoon, lake
ezers (*Latvian*) lake

Falaise (*French*) cliff
Feng (*Chinese*) peak
Fjeld (*Danish*) mountain
-fjell (*Norwegian*) mountain
-fjord/en (*Danish, Norwegian, Swedish*) fiord

Gang (*Chinese*) harbor
Gaoyuan (*Chinese*) plateau
Garet (*Arabic*) hill
Gebergte (*Dutch*) mountain chain, mountain range
-gebirge (*German*) mountain range
Ghubbat (*Arabic*) bay
Gjiri (*Albanian*) bay
Golfe (*French*) gulf
Golfo (*Italian, Portuguese*) gulf
Gölü (*Turkish*) lake
Gora (*Russian*) mountain
Góry (*Polish*) mountains
Gross/er (*German*) big
Gryada (*Russian*) ridge
Guba (*Russian*) bay, gulf
Gulfo (*Spanish*) gulf
Gunung (*Indonesian, Malay*) mountain

Haixia (*Chinese*) strait
-halvøya (*Norwegian*) peninsula
Har (*Hebrew*) mountain
Haut, Haute (*French*) high
Hawr (*Arabic*) lake
Hâyk' (*Amharic*) lake
Helodrano (*Malagasy*) bay
Höhe (*German*) height
Hora (*Belorussian, Czech*) mountain
-horn (*German*) peak
Hory (*Czech*) mountains
Hsü (*Chinese*) island, islet
Hu (*Chinese*) lake

Île/s (*French*) island/s
Ilha/s (*Portuguese*) island/s
Ilheu (*Portuguese*) islet
Isla/s (*Spanish*) island/s
Isola, Isole (*Italian*) island/s

Jabal (*Arabic*) mountain, mountain range
Jarv (Estonian) lake
-järvi (*Finnish*) lake
Jazīrat, Jaza'īr (*Arabic*) island/s
Jazīreh (Persian) island
Jbel (*Arabic*) mountain
Jezioro (*Polish*) lake
-jima (*Japanese*) island
-joki (*Finnish*) river

Kalnas (*Lithuanian*) mountain
Kangri (*Tibetan*) mountain
Kap (*Danish, German*) cape
-kapp (*Norwegian*) cape
Kepi (*Albanian*) cape, point
Kepulauan (*Indonesian*) islands
Khalij (*Arabic*) bay, gulf
Khao (*Thai*) peak
Khrebet (*Russian*) mountain range
Ko (*Thai*) island
Köli (*Kazakh*) lake
Kolpos (*Greek*) bay
Körfezi (*Turkish*) bay, gulf
Kray (*Russian*) territory
Kryazh (*Russian*) ridge
Kūh/hā (Persian) mountain/s
-kül (*Tajik*) lake
Kyst (*Danish*) coast
Kyun (*Burmese*) island

Lac (*French*) lake
Lacul (*Romanian*) lake
Lago (*Italian, Portuguese, Spanish*) lake
Lagoa (*Portuguese*) lagoon, lake
Laht (*Estonian*) bay
Lich (*Armenian*) lake
Liedao (*Chinese*) archipelago, islands
Limni (*Greek*) lake
Ling (*Chinese*) mountain range
Loch, Lough (*Gaelic*) lake
Lohatanjona (*Malagasy*) point
Loi (*Burmese*) mountain
Loma (*Spanish*) hill

Mae Nam (*Thai*) river
-man (*Korean*) bay
Mar (*Spanish*) lake, sea
Ma'abb (*Arabic*) river mouth
Massif (*French*) mountains, upland
Meer, -meer (*Dutch*) lake, sea
Mesa (*Spanish*) tableland
Meseta (*Spanish*) plateau, tableland
-misaki (*Japanese*) cape, point
Mont/s (*French*) mountain/s
Montagne/s (*French*) mountain/s
Monte (*Italian, Portuguese, Spanish*) mountain
Montes (*Spanish*) mountain
Monti (*Italian*) mountain/s
More (*Russian*) sea
Morne (*French*) mountain
Morro (*Portuguese*) hill
Munţii (*Romanian*) mountains
Mys (*Russian*) cape, point

-nada (*Japanese*) gulf, sea
Nagor'ye (*Russian*) upland
Nevado (*Spanish*) snow-capped mountain
Nieuw (*Dutch*) new
Nisoi (*Greek*) islands
Nizmennost' (*Russian*) lowland
Nord (*French, German*) north
Norte (*Portuguese, Spanish*) north
Nos (*Bulgarian*) point
Nosy (*Malagasy*) island
Nur, Nuur (*Mongolian*) lake
Nuruu (*Mongolian*) mountain range

Ø, Øer (*Danish*) island/s
-ö, -ön (*Swedish*) island
Oblast' (*Russian*) province
Odde (*Danish*) cape, point
Oros (*Greek*) mountain
Ostrov/a (*Russian*) island/s
Oued (*Arabic*) river, watercourse
-øy, -øya (*Norwegian*) island
Ozero (*Russian*) lake

Pantanal (*Portuguese*) marsh, swamp
Pegunungan (Indonesian) island
Pelagos (*Greek*) sea
Pendi (*Chinese*) basin
Pertuis (*French*) strait
Phnum (*Cambodian*) mountain
Phou (*Laotian*) mountain
Pic (*French*) peak
Pico (*Spanish*) peak
Pik (*Russian*) peak
Piton (*French*) peak
Pivostriv (*Ukrainian*) peninsula
Piz, pizzo (*Italian*) peak
Planalto (*Portuguese*) plateau
Planina (*Bulgarian, Macedonian*) mountains
Plato (*Russian*) plateau
Ploskogor'ye (*Russian*) plateau, upland
Pointe (*French*) point
Poluostrov (*Russian*) peninsula
Ponta (*Portuguese*) point
Porthmos (*Greek*) strait
Porto, Pôrto (*Portuguese*) port
Proliv (*Russian*) strait
Puerto (*Spanish*) port
Pulau (*Indonesian, Malay*) island
Puncak (*Indonesian*) mountain
Punta (*Italian, Spanish*) point

Qārat (*Arabic*) hill
Qooriga (*Somali*) bay
Qundao (*Chinese*) archipelago, islands
Qurnat (*Arabic*) peak

Raas (*Somali*) cape, point
Ras, Ra's (*Arabic*) cape, point
Ravnina (*Russian*) plain
Represa (*Portuguese, Spanish*) reservoir
Réservoir (*French*) reservoir
Reshteh (*Persian*) mountain range
Respublika (*Russian*) republic
Respublikasi (*Uzbek*) republic
-retto (*Japanese*) island chain
Rio, Río (*Portuguese, Spanish*) river
Rivière (*French*) river
Rubha (*Gaelic*) cape, point
Rudohorie (*Slovak*) mountains

Sāgar/a (*Hindi*) lake
Şaḩrā' (*Arabic*) desert
-saki (*Japanese*) cape point
Salar (*Spanish*) salt-flat, salt-pan
Salina/s (*Spanish*) salt-pan/s
Salto/s (*Portuguese, Spanish*) waterfall
-san (*Japanese*, Korean) mountain
San, Santa, Santo (*Spanish*) saint
-sanchi (*Japanese*) mountains
São (*Portuguese*) saint
Sarīr (*Arabic*) desert
Sebkha, Sebkhet (*Arabic*) salt-flat
See, -see (*German*) lake
Selat (*Indonesian*) strait
Serra (*Portuguese*) mountain range
Serranía (*Spanish*) mountain range
Shamo (*Chinese*) desert
Shan (*Chinese*) mountain/s
-shima (*Japanese*) island
-shotō (*Japanese*) islands
Shuiki (*Chinese*) reservoir
Sierra (*Spanish*) mountain range
Slieve (*Gaelic*) mountain
-spitze (*German*) peak
Steno (*Greek*) strait
Štít (*Slovak*) peak
Stretto (*Italian*) strait
Sud (*French*) south
Sul (*Portuguese*) south

Tanjona (Malagasy) cape
Tanjong (Indonesian, Malay) cape, point
Tao (*Chinese*) island
Tasek (*Malay*) lake
Tassili (*Berber*) plateau
Taungdan (*Burmese*) mountain range
Tekojärvi (*Finnish*) reservoir
Teluk (*Indonesian, Malay*) bay
Ténéré (*Berber*) desert
Tepe (*Turkish*) peak
Terara (*Amharic*) mountain
Tierra (*Spanish*) land
-to (*Japanese*) island

Ujung (*Indonesian*) cape, point
'Urûq (*Arabic*) dunes
Uul (*Mongolian*) mountain/s

väin (*Estonian*) channel, strait
-vatn (*Norwegian*) lake
-vesi (*Finnish*) lake, water
Voblasts' (*Belorussian*) province
Vodokhranilishche (*Russian*) reservoir
Vodoskhovyshche (*Ukrainian*) reservoir
Volcán (*Spanish*) volcano
Vozvyshennost' (*Russian*) plateau, upland
Vozyera (*Belorussian*) lake
Vrchovina (*Czech*) mountains

Wabē (*Amharic*) river, stream
Wādī (*Arabic*) watercourse
-wald (*German*) forest
Wan (*Chinese*) bay
-wan (*Japanese*) bay

Yam (*Hebrew*) lake, sea
Yang (*Chinese*) ocean
Yoma (*Burmese*) mountain range

-zaki (*Japanese*) cape, point
Zaliv (*Russian*) bay
Zangbo (*Tibetan*) river
Zatoka (*Polish*) bay, gulf
-zee (*Dutch*) sea
Zemlya (*Russian*) land
Zizhiqu (*Chinese*) autonomous region

Gazetteer

- The gazetteer contains the names shown on the continental and detailed regional maps at the end of each section.
- In the code given to locate a place, the bold number refers to the page on which the map is to be found, and the letter-number combination refers to the grid square formed by the lines of latitude and longitude on the map. Inset maps have their own letter-number combination.
- Where a name appears on more than one map, the gazetteer generally lists the largest scale map on which the name appears.
- Names that have a symbol (town or mountain peak) are given an area reference according to the location of the symbol. Names without a symbol are entered in the gazetteer according to the first letter of the name.
- Words in italics describe features in the gazetteer, e.g. island, point and mountain peak; numbers in italics refer to references in the text.
- All entries include the country or area in which the name is located.
- Features composed of a description and a proper name, e. g. Cape Hatteras, are positioned alphabetically by the proper name: Hatteras, Cape.
- Where a name contains a subordinate or alternative name in brackets on the map, the bracketed names are entered in the gazetteer with a cross-reference to the first name, e. g. Peking *see* Beijing, China, **210** G5.
- Words abbreviated on the map, e. g. C. or I., are spelt out in the gazetteer. If the word is English, the description in italics is not included. For example, if I. (standing for island) is abbreviated on the map and spelt out in the gazetteer, island is not added. However, if Island is not in English, e. g. Isla, island is added.
- The location (ocean, area of a continent) is included before the area reference when a place is part of a country but not located within the country, e. g. Madeira, Portugal, Atlantic Ocean; and Ceuta, enclave, Spain, N. W. Africa.

A

A Cañiza, Spain, **292** C1
A Coruña, Spain, **292** C1
A Estrada, Spain, **292** C1
A Fonsagrada, Spain, **292** D1
A Guardia, Spain, **292** C2
A Gudiña, Spain, **292** D1
Aachen, Germany, **288** C3
Aalen, Germany, **288** E4
A'ali An Nīl, *state*, Sudan, **366** D2
Aapua, Sweden, **285** L3
Aarau, Switzerland, **291** J3
Aare, *river*, Switzerland, **291** J3, *247*
Aasleagh, Ireland, **309** C4
Aba, China, **215** G2
Aba, Democratic Republic of the Congo, **366** D4
Aba, Nigeria, **368** A1
Abacaxis, *river*, Brazil, **452** A4
Abaco, *island*, Bahamas, **428** F1, *393*
Ābādeh, Iran, **220** F2
Abadla, Algeria, **361** F2
Abaeté, *river*, Brazil, **456** D5
Abaetetuba, Brazil, **452** D3
Abag Qi, China, **210** F4
Abagaytuy, Russian Federation, **210** G2
Abaji, Nigeria, **365** F3
Abajo Peak, *mountain*, U.S.A., **423** J3
Abakaliki, Nigeria, **365** F3
Abakan, *river*, Russian Federation, **223** M2
Abakan, Russian Federation, **223** N2
Abala, Niger, **365** E2
Abala, Congo, **368** C3
Abalak, Niger, **365** E3/F1
Abalessa, Algeria, **361** G4
Abancay, Peru, **454** D3
Abarkūh, Iran, **220** F2
Abashiri, Japan, **209** J2
Abatskiy, Russian Federation, **223** J1
Abau, Papua New Guinea, **140** C5
Abay, Aqmola, Kazakhstan, **212** A2
Abay, Qaraghandy, Kazakhstan, **212** B2
Abaza, Russian Federation, **223** N2
Abba, Central African Republic, **368** C1
Abbeville, Alabama, U.S.A., **425** K4
Abbéville, France, **290** E1
Abbeville, Louisiana, U.S.A., **424** F5
Abbeville, South Carolina, U.S.A., **425** L2
Abbeyfeale, Ireland, **309** C5
Abbeyleix, Ireland, **309** E5
Abborrträsk, Sweden, **284** J4
Abbot Ice Shelf, Antarctica, **470** B6
Abbots Langley, England, U.K., **305** G3
Abbotsbury, England, U.K., **304** E4
Abbotsford, Canada, **412** H7
Abbott, U.S.A., **423** L3
Abbottābād, Pakistan, **218** C2
'Abd al Kūrī, *island*, Suquṭrā (Socotra), Yemen, **373** B2
Abdelcader, Somalia, **367** F2
Abdulino, Russian Federation, **222** E2
Abéché, Chad, **366** B2
Abee, Canada, **413** N4
Abemama, *island*, Kiribati, **139** F4
Abengourou, Côte d'Ivoire, **364** D3
Åbenrå, Denmark, **286** D5
Abeokuta, Nigeria, **365** E3
Aberaeron, Wales, U.K., **304** C2
Aberchirder, Scotland, U.K., **308** G3
Aberdare, Wales, U.K., **304** D3
Aberdaron, Wales, U.K., **304** C2
Aberdeen, Idaho, U.S.A., **418** H5
Aberdeen, Mississippi, U.S.A., **425** H3
Aberdeen, Scotland, U.K., **308** G3, *276*
Aberdeen, South Africa, **370** D5
Aberdeen, South Dakota, U.S.A., **420** D3
Aberdeen, Washington, U.S.A., **418** C3
Aberdeen City, *local authority*, Scotland, U.K., **308** G3
Aberdeenshire, *local authority*, Scotland, U.K., **308** G3
Aberdyfi, Wales, U.K., **304** C2
Aberfeldy, Scotland, U.K., **308** F4
Aberfoyle, Scotland, U.K., **306** D1
Abergavenny, Wales, U.K., **304** E3
Abergele, Wales, U.K., **306** E4
Abernathy, U.S.A., **424** B3
Aberporth, Wales, U.K., **304** C2
Abersoch, Wales, U.K., **304** C2
Abert, Lake, U.S.A., **418** D5
Abertillery, Wales, U.K., **304** D3
Aberystwyth, Wales, U.K., **304** C2
Abhā, Saudi Arabia, **363** H5
Abhar, Iran, **222** D5
Abia, *state*, Nigeria, **365** F3
Abibe, Serranía de, *mountain range*, Colombia, **450** C2
Abide, Turkey, **297** G6
Abidjan, Côte d'Ivoire, **364** D3, *324, 325*
Abilene, U.S.A., **424** C3
Abingdon, England, U.K., **305** F3
Abingdon, U.S.A., **421** N7
Abington, Scotland, U.K., **308** F5
Abiquiu, U.S.A., **423** K3
Abisko, Sweden, **284** J2
Abitibi, Lake, Canada, **415** Q7
Ābīy Ādī, Ethiopia, **367** E2
Abkhazia, *autonomous republic*, Georgia, **222** C4, *190*
Abnūb, Egypt, **363** F3
Abohar, India, **218** C3
Aboisso, Côte d'Ivoire, **364** D3
Abomey, Benin, **365** E3
Abong Mbang, Cameroon, **368** B2
Abongabong, Gunung, *mountain peak*, Indonesia, **200** B1
Abooso, Ghana, **364** D3
Aborlan, Philippines, **204** B4
Abou Deïa, Chad, **366** A2
Aboyne, Scotland, U.K., **308** G3
Abra Pampa, Argentina, **458** D2
Abra, *river*, Philippines, **204** C2
Abrantes, Portugal, **292** C3
Abrī, Sudan, **363** F4
Abriès, France, **291** H4
Abrolhos, Arquipélago dos, *islands*, Brazil, **457** F4
Abrud, Romania, **296** D2
Abruka, *island*, Estonia, **287** L3
Abruzzi, *autonomous region*, Italy, **295** D4, *255*
Absaroka Range, *mountain range*, U.S.A., **419** J4
Absarokee, U.S.A., **419** K4
Abu aḍ Ḍuhūr, Syria, **225** D2
Abū 'Arīsh, Saudi Arabia, **363** H5
Abu Dhabi *see* Abū Zaby, United Arab Emirates, **221** F4, *176*
Abū Dulayq, Sudan, **366** D1
Abū Durbah, Egypt, **225** B5
Abu Haggag, Egypt, **362** E2
Abū Ḥamad, Sudan, **363** F5
Abū Ḥammād, Egypt, **225** A4
Abū Kamāl, Syria, **363** H2
Abū Maṭāriq, Sudan, **366** C2
Abū Madd, Ra's, *point*, Saudi Arabia, **363** G4
Abū Nujaym, Libya, **362** C2
Ābu Road, India, **218** C4
Abū Rubayq, Saudi Arabia, **363** G4
Abū Rudays, Egypt, **225** B5
Abū Rujmayn, Jabal, *mountain range*, Syria, **225** E2
Abu Shagara, Ras, *point*, Sudan, **363** G4
Abū Shanab, Sudan, **366** C2
Abu Simbel *see* Abū Sunbul, Egypt, **363** F4, *68, 88*
Abū Sunbul (Abu Simbel), Egypt, **363** F4, *68, 88*
Abu 'Ujaylah, Egypt, **225** C4
Abū Zabad, Sudan, **366** C2
Abū Zaby (Abu Dhabi), United Arab Emirates, **221** F4, *176*
Abū Zanīmah, Egypt, **225** B5
Abuja, Nigeria, **365** F3, *329*
Abulog, Philippines, **204** C2
Abumombazi, Democratic Republic of the Congo, **368** D2
Abunã, Brazil, **455** F2
Abunã, *river*, Bolivia/Brazil, **455** E2
Ābune Yosēf, *mountain peak*, Ethiopia, **367** E2
Aburo, *mountain peak*, Democratic Republic of the Congo, **366** D4
Ābuyē Mēda, *mountain peak*, Ethiopia, **367** E2
Åby, Sweden, **286** H3
Abyaḍ, Al Baḥr al (White Nile), *river*, Sudan, **366** D2, *336*
Abyaḍ, Sudan, **366** C2
Åbybro, Denmark, **286** D4
Abyei, Sudan, **366** C3
Åbyn, Sweden, **284** K4
Açailândia, Brazil, **452** D4
Acámbaro, Mexico, **431** E5
Acancéh, Mexico, **431** H4
Acandí, Colombia, **450** C2
Acaponeta, Mexico, **430** D4
Acapulco, Mexico, **431** F5
Acará, Brazil, **452** D3
Acará, *river*, Brazil, **452** D4
Acará-Mirim, *river*, Brazil, **452** D4
Acaraí, Serra, *mountain range*, Brazil, **452** B3
Acaraú, Brazil, **453** F4
Acaraú, *river*, Brazil, **453** F4
Acaray, Represa de, *reservoir*, Paraguay, **459** F2
Acari, Brazil, **453** G5
Acarigua, Venezuela, **451** E2
Acâș, Romania, **296** D2
Acatlán de Osorio, Mexico, **431** F5
Acayucan, Mexico, **431** G5
Acceglio, Italy, **294** A3
Accomac, U.S.A., **426** C6
Accra, Ghana, **364** D3, *325*
Aceh, *province*, Indonesia, **200** B1
Aceh, *river*, Indonesia, **200** A1
Achacachi, Bolivia, **455** E4
Achaguas, Venezuela, **451** E2
Achahoish, Scotland, U.K., **308** D5
Achalpur, India, **218** D5
Acheng, China, **211** J3
Acheryok, *river*, Russian Federation, **285** U3
Acheux-en-Amiénois, France, **305** K4
Achill Island, Ireland, **309** B4
Achill, Ireland, **309** C4
Achiltibuie, Scotland, U.K., **308** D2
Achinsk, Russian Federation, **300** L4
Achit, Russian Federation, **222** F1
Achnasheen, Scotland, U.K., **308** D3
Achwa, *river*, Uganda, **369** F2
Acigöl, *lake*, Turkey, **297** G7
Acıpayam, Turkey, **297** G7
Acireale, Sicilia, Italy, **295** E7
Ackley, U.S.A., **420** G4
Acklins Island, Bahamas, **429** G2
Acle, England, U.K., **305** J2
Acme, U.S.A., **418** C2
Acomayo, Peru, **454** D3
Aconcagua, Cerro, *mountain peak*, Argentina, **458** B4, *443*
Acopiara, Brazil, **453** F5
Acora, Peru, **455** E4
Acoyapa, Nicaragua, **428** D5
Acquasparta, Italy, **294** D4
Acqui Terme, Italy, **294** B3
Acre, *river*, Brazil, **455** E2
Acre *see* 'Akko, Israel, **225** C3, *173*
Acre, *state*, Brazil, **455** E2
Acri, Italy, **295** F6
Actéon, Groupe, *islands*, French Polynesia, **137** H3
Acton Point, New Zealand, **133** E5
Acton, U.S.A., **419** K4
Actopan, Mexico, **431** F4
Açu, Brazil, **453** G4
Acurenam, Equatorial Guinea, **368** B2
Ad Dabbah, Sudan, **363** F5
Ad Dafīnah, Saudi Arabia, **363** H4
Ad Dahnā', *desert*, Saudi Arabia, **363** J3
Ad Dakhla, Western Sahara, **360** C4
Aḍ Ḍāli', Yemen, **220** D6
Ad Damazīn, Sudan, **366** D2
Ad Dāmir, Sudan, **363** F5
Ad Dammām, Saudi Arabia, **220** F3
Ad Dāmūr, Lebanon, **225** C3
Ad Darb, Saudi Arabia, **363** H5
Ad Dawādimī, Saudi Arabia, **363** H4
Ad Dawḥah (Doha), Qatar, **220** F3, *177, 178*

B

C

D

E

G

H

I

J

K

L

M

N

O

P

R

S

T

U

V

W

X

Y

Z

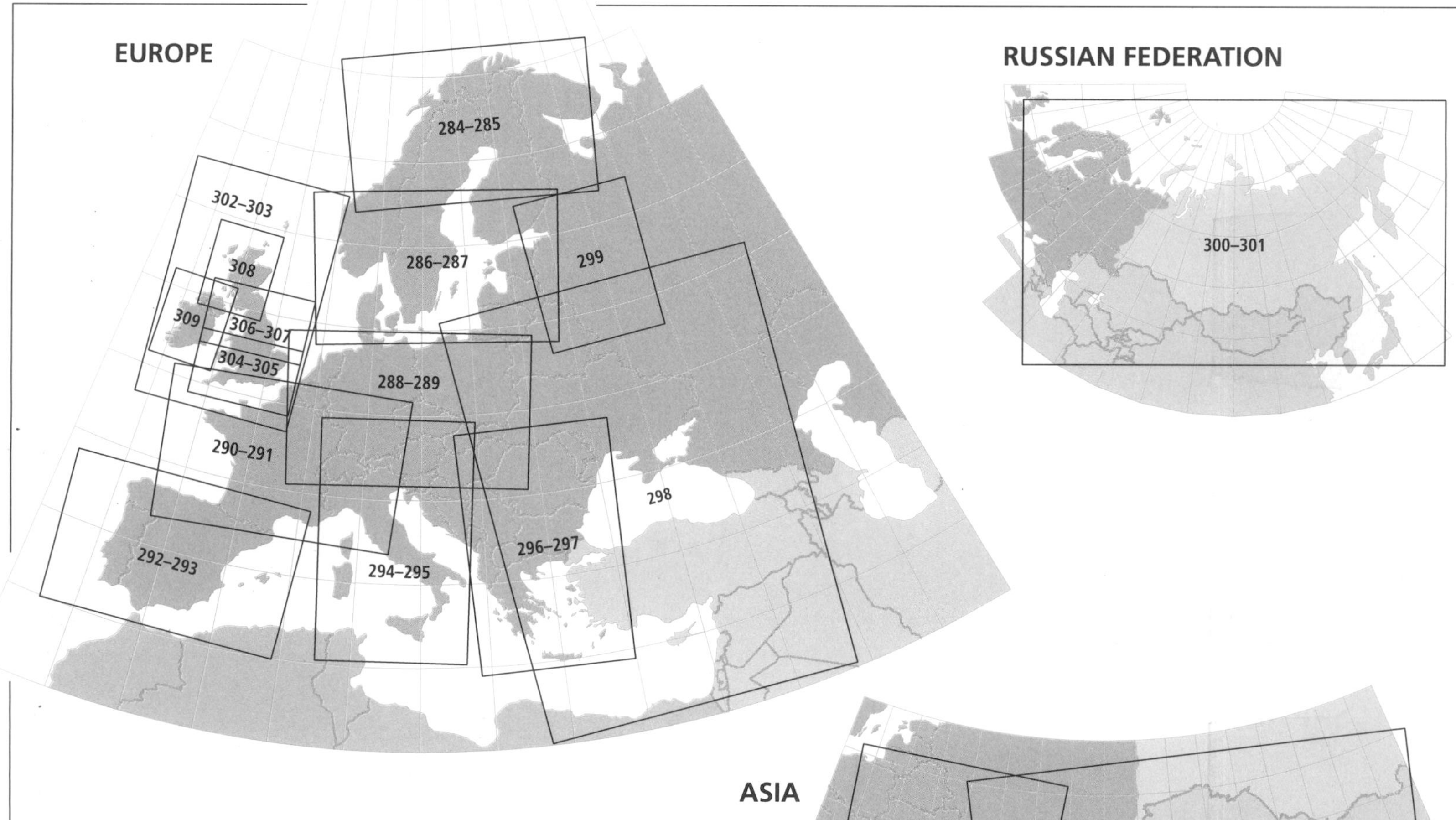

ASIA

222–223
224
225
218–219
220–221
216–217

OTHER MAPS

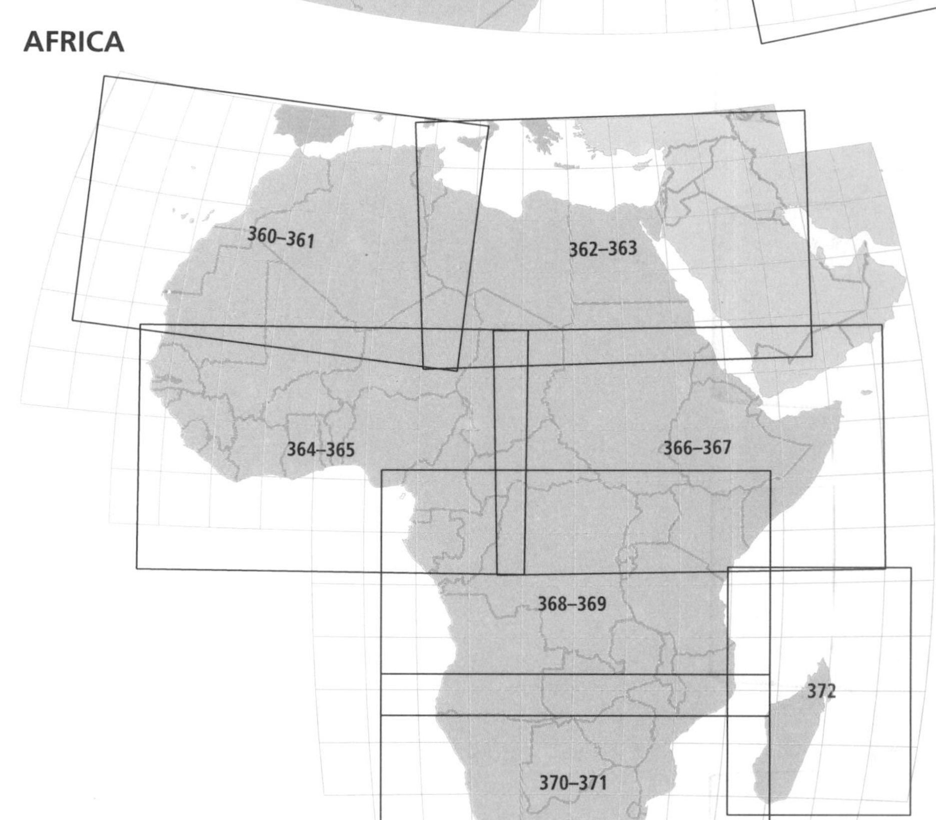

Key to Map Pages

Geographica

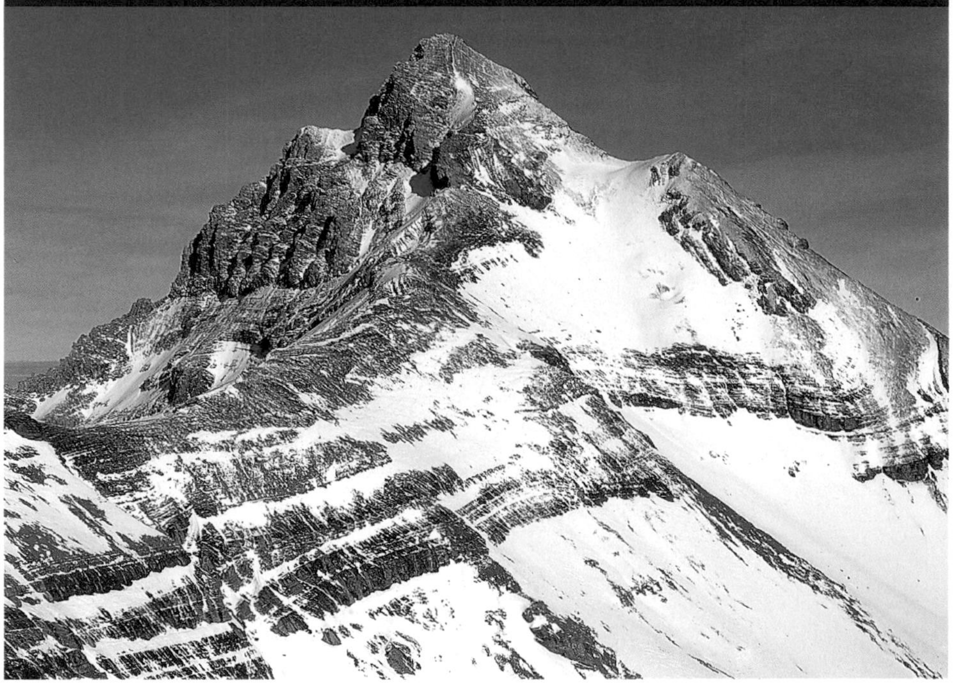

Geographica

The Complete Illustrated Atlas of the World

KÖNEMANN

Publisher: Gordon Cheers
Associate publisher: Margaret Olds
Managing editors: Philippe Sandall (text)
Valerie Marlborough (maps)
Editors: Scott Forbes
Sue Grose-Hodge
Gillian Hewitt
Siobhan O'Connor
Sarah Shrubb
Carolyn Beaumont
Anna Cheifetz
Clare Double
Kate Etherington
Denise Imwold
Heather Jackson
Oliver Rennert
Map editors: Janet Parker
Fran Church
Heather Martin
Marlene Meynert
Jan Watson
Chief designer: Clare Forte
Senior designer: Robert Taylor
Cover design: Bob Mitchell
Production designers: Deborah Clarke
Max Peatman
James Young
Cartographic manager: Graham Keane
Senior cartographer: Andrew Dunlop
Cartographers: Weimin Gu
Paul McDonald
David Morris
Melissa O'Brien
Clare Varney
Consultant for water areas: Tony Davidson
Thematic maps: John Frith
Contour shading: John Gittoes
Oliver Rennert
Ray Sims
Researchers: Derek Barton
Claudia Zipfel
Gazetteer: Valerie Marlborough
Heather Jackson
Janet Parker
Dee Rogers
Clare Double
Typesetting: Dee Rogers
Photo research: Gordon Cheers
Photo library: Susan Page
Production managers: Linda Watchorn
Angela Alegounarias
Publishing coordinator: Sarah Sherlock
Publishing assistants: Olivia Kleindienst
Anabel Pandiela

Layout (pages 105–461) and update of this edition:
Martin Sulzer-Reichel,
Agents–Producers–Editors Int'l,
Richmond, VA

Published by Random House Australia Pty Ltd
20 Alfred Street, Milsons Point, NSW Australia 2061

First published in 1999

Printed in Germany

ISBN 3-8331-1260-3

10 9 8 7 6 5 4 3 2
X IX VIII VII VI V IV III II I

page i: Rock layers in the Swiss Alps
pages ii–iii: The European Parliament building in Brussels, Belgium
page v: A Parisian sidewalk café, France
page xii: A farm at the foot of Mount Giestoso, Minho, Portugal
pages xiv–xv: View from Plaka towards the hill Lykavittos in Athens, Greece
pages xxii–1: Tongariro, volcano and crater, New Zealand
pages 52–53: An Aboriginal man fishing with spears in wetlands in the Northern Territory, Australia
pages 98–99: The countryside near Yangshuo in Guangxi Zhuangzu Zizhiqu Province, China
pages 106–07: A village on the Sepik River, Papua New Guinea
pages 142–43: Terrassed hills looking towards the Himalayas, Nepal
pages 226–27: The village Trebarwith Strand on the north coast of Carnwall, United Kingdom
pages 310–11: Rhinoceroses and calves in the waters of the Luangwa River in Zambia
pages 374–75: Grand Canyon, Arizona, USA
pages 432–33: Autumn colors in Tierra del Fuego, Argentina
pages 462–63: Polar bears in Arctic Siberia
pages 472–73: A whale shark in California waters
pages 480–81: Melting water in the Sharkiphu River Valley, Nepal

Consultants and Contributors

GENERAL EDITOR

Professor Ray Hudson BA, PhD, DSc (University of Bristol), DSc (Honoris Causa, University of Roskilde); Department of Geography, University of Durham

CONSULTANTS

Professor Tom McKnight BA, MA, PhD (University of Wisconsin); Professor Emeritus of Geography, University of California, Los Angeles

Professor Joan Clemons PhD (University of Minnesota); Visiting Professor, Graduate School of Education and Information Studies, University of California, Los Angeles

Professor John Overton MA, PhD (Cambridge); Professor, Institute of Development Studies, School of Global Studies, Massey University

Professor Toru Taniuchi BA, MSc, DSc, (University of Tokyo); Professor of Human Geography, University of Tokyo, Japan

Professor Bruce Thom BA, PhD (Louisiana State University), FIAG; Emeritus Professor of Geography, University of Sydney, Visiting Professor of Geography, University of New South Wales,

Professor William Wonders BA (Hons), MA, PhD (University of Toronto), Fil.Dr.h.c. (Uppsala); University Professor and Professor Emeritus of Geography, University of Alberta

CONTRIBUTORS

Part 1 Planet Earth

Professor Bruce Thom BA, PhD (Louisiana State University), F.I.A.G.

Dr John O'Byrne BSc, PhD (University of Sydney)
Dr Noel de Souza BSc (Hons), MSc., Doctorat de Specialité (University of Paris)

Dr Ron Horvath BA, MA, PhD (University of California, Los Angeles)

Dr Scott Mooney BSc (Hons), PhD (University of New South Wales

Part 2 People and Society

Dr Ron Brunton BA, MA, PhD (La Trobe University)

Associate Professor Sybil Jack MA, BLitt (Oxon), DipEd (University of New England)

Dr Ron Horvath BA, MA, PhD (University of California, Los Angeles)

Tess Rod BA (Hons), MA, BComm

Roger Sandall BA, MA (Columbia University)

Part 3 Regions of the World

Professor Bruce Thom BA, PhD (Louisiana State University), F.I.A.G.

Roger Sandall BA, MA (Columbia University)

Dr Noel de Souza BSc (Hons), MSc, Doctorat de Specialité (University of Paris)

Robert Coupe MA, DipEd

CARTOGRAPHIC CONSULTANTS

Henk Brolsma, Associateship in Land Surveying; Australian Antarctic Division, Tasmania, Australia
Antarctica

Dr John Cornell BA, PhD (University of London)
Papua New Guinea, Pacific Islands, Island Nations and Dependencies

Tony Davidson
Europe, Russian Federation, former Soviet Republics

Dr Noel de Souza BSc (Hons), MSc, Doctorat de Specialité (University of Paris)
India, Sri Lanka, Nepal, Bangladesh, Bhutan, Pakistan

Dr Joan Hardjono BA, LittB, PhD (University of New England); Padjadjaran State University, Bandung, Indonesia
Indonesia, Malaysia, Singapore

Dr Philip Hirsch BA, PhD
Thailand, Laos, Myanmar, Cambodia, Vietnam, Philippines

Professor Naftali Kadmon BA, MSc, PhD (University of Wales); Professor Emeritus, The Hebrew University of Jerusalem, Israel
Israel, Turkey, Iran, Cyprus, Afghanistan

Gerry Leitner
South America, Central America

Dr Zhilin Li BEng, PhD (University of Glasgow) Assistant Professor, The Hong Kong Polytechnic University, Hong Kong
China

Professor Tanga Munkhtsetseg; International Relations Institute, Ulan Bator, Mongolia
Mongolia

Chonghyon Paku MA BSc; Baito-Bunka University, Tokyo, Japan
Korea

Karen Puklowski NZCD/Survey; Massey University, New Zealand
New Zealand

Professor Chris Rogerson BSc (Hons), MSc, PhD (Queens), FSAGS; University of Witwatersrand, Johannesburg, South Africa
SubSaharan Africa

Dr Nasser Salma PhD (University of Washington, Seattle); Associate Professor, King Saud University, Riyadh, Saudi Arabia
Arabic speaking countries of the Middle East and Saharan Africa

Brian Stokes BBus (Tourism), AssDipCart
Australia

Professor Toru Taniuchi BA, MSc, DSc (University of Tokyo); Professor of Human Geography, University of Tokyo, Japan
Japan

Glenn Toldi BSc, DipCart&GIS
United States of America, Canada

Lillian Wonders BA, MA
Canada

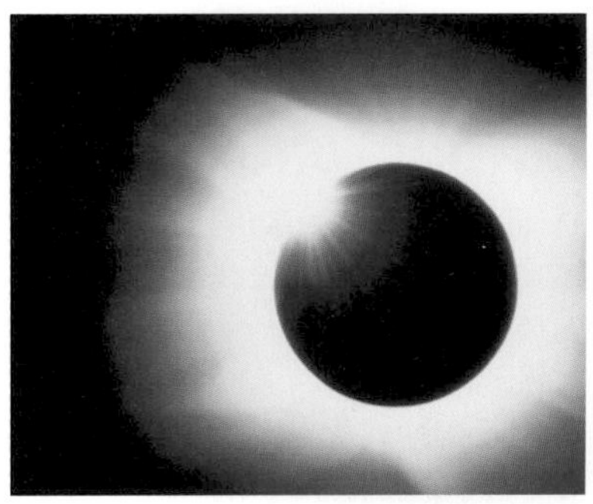

Content

Content

Content

Content

How This Book Works

Geographica is an authoritative, comprehensive and fully illustrated reference guide to the world. With maps, photographs, illustrations and text, *Geographica* will carry readers on a journey from outer space and Earth's place in the universe to the nations and cities, towns and even villages on the furthermost parts of the globe. An expert team of geographers, historians, anthropologists, astronomers, writers, editors and cartographers have worked together to create this reference.

The first part of the book is organized in topics which are each presented on a double-page spread for easy access to information. The text has been written by leading experts in their fields. The very best photographs have been chosen, and illustrations and thematic maps have been specially commissioned to complement the text. Many of the double-page spreads contain a feature box which looks at one aspect of the topic on the spreads in detail.

Geographica then moves on to the core of the book; this contains maps and detailed text on the world's 192 nations which are members of the United Nations and 65 dependencies and overseas territories. The world has been divided into major continents or regions (Oceania, Asia and the Middle East, Europe and the Russian Federation, Africa, North America and Central America, South America, Polar Regions, and Oceans). Each region starts with an introductory essay on the region in general and then moves on to entries for every country, territory or dependency. The country entries feature informative descriptions of the nation and its people, physical features and land use, culture, and economy and resources. Each country entry includes a locator map, the national flag, a locator globe, and a Fact File. Entries for the major nations also include a historical timeline. The entries for the dependencies and territories follow the country entries.

The Fact Files contain a wealth of carefully researched information for quick access to each nation's key indicators, such as form of government, infant mortality, literacy, ethnic diversity, religions and economy, as well as basic data

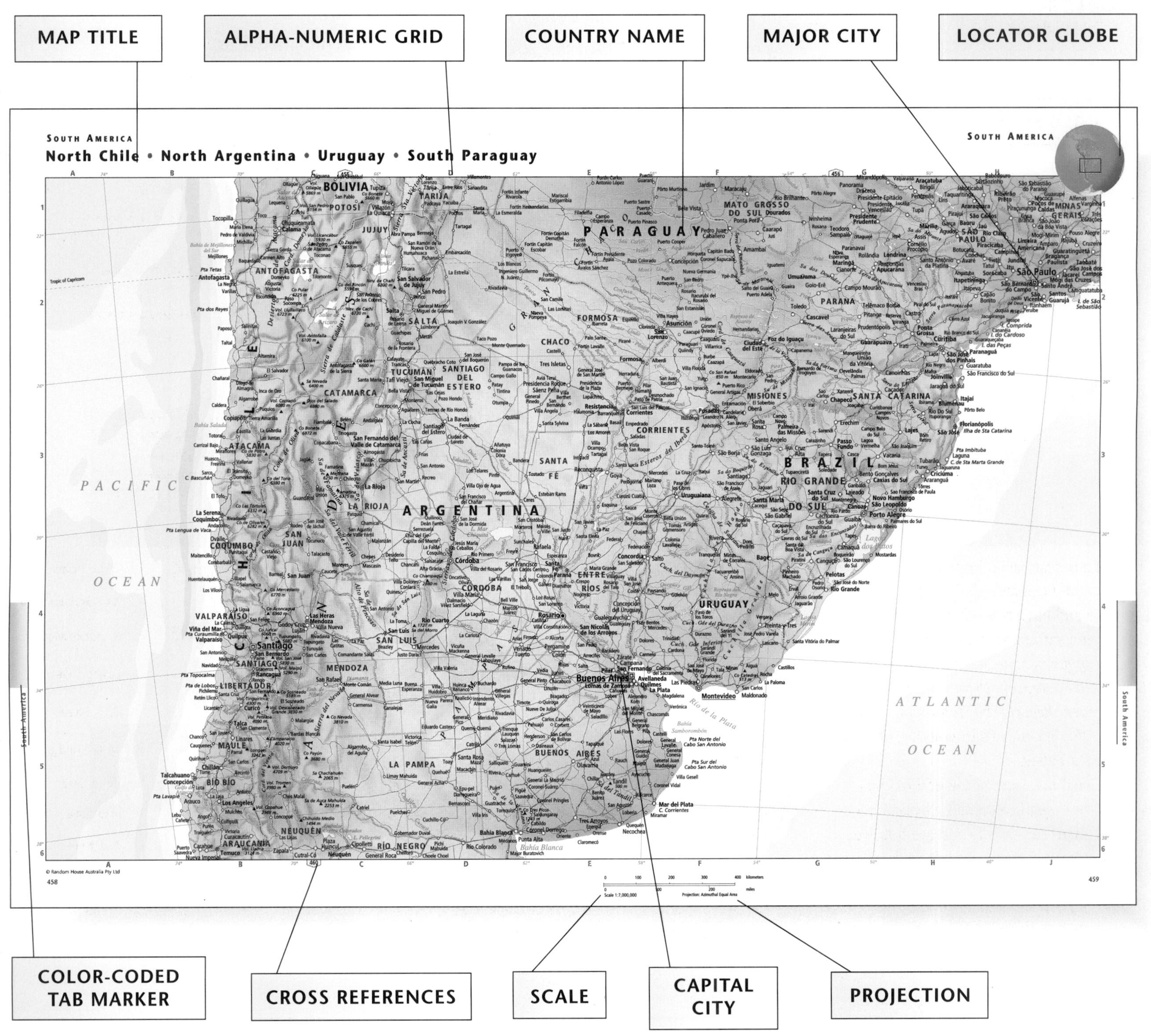

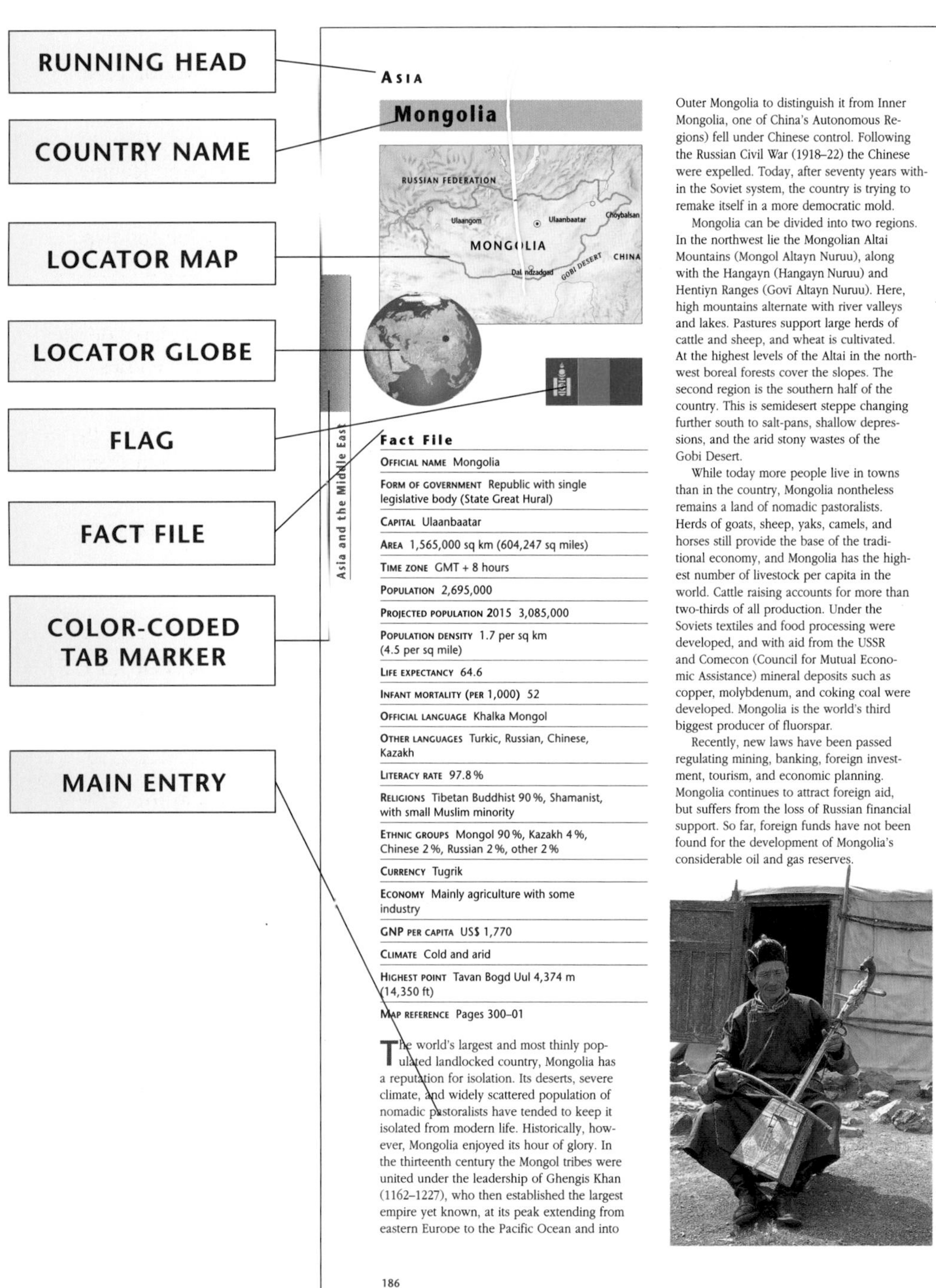

ASIA

Mongolia

Fact File

OFFICIAL NAME Mongolia

FORM OF GOVERNMENT Republic with single legislative body (State Great Hural)

CAPITAL Ulaanbaatar

AREA 1,565,000 sq km (604,247 sq miles)

TIME ZONE GMT + 8 hours

POPULATION 2,695,000

PROJECTED POPULATION 2015 3,085,000

POPULATION DENSITY 1.7 per sq km (4.5 per sq mile)

LIFE EXPECTANCY 64.6

INFANT MORTALITY (PER 1,000) 52

OFFICIAL LANGUAGE Khalka Mongol

OTHER LANGUAGES Turkic, Russian, Chinese, Kazakh

LITERACY RATE 97.8 %

RELIGIONS Tibetan Buddhist 90 %, Shamanist, with small Muslim minority

ETHNIC GROUPS Mongol 90 %, Kazakh 4 %, Chinese 2 %, Russian 2 %, other 2 %

CURRENCY Tugrik

ECONOMY Mainly agriculture with some industry

GNP PER CAPITA US$ 1,770

CLIMATE Cold and arid

HIGHEST POINT Tavan Bogd Uul 4,374 m (14,350 ft)

MAP REFERENCE Pages 300–01

The world's largest and most thinly populated landlocked country, Mongolia has a reputation for isolation. Its deserts, severe climate, and widely scattered population of nomadic pastoralists have tended to keep it isolated from modern life. Historically, however, Mongolia enjoyed its hour of glory. In the thirteenth century the Mongol tribes were united under the leadership of Ghengis Khan (1162–1227), who then established the largest empire yet known, at its peak extending from eastern Europe to the Pacific Ocean and into Outer Mongolia to distinguish it from Inner Mongolia, one of China's Autonomous Regions) fell under Chinese control. Following the Russian Civil War (1918–22) the Chinese were expelled. Today, after seventy years within the Soviet system, the country is trying to remake itself in a more democratic mold.

Mongolia can be divided into two regions. In the northwest lie the Mongolian Altai Mountains (Mongol Altayn Nuruu), along with the Hangayn (Hangayn Nuruu) and Hentiyn Ranges (Govi Altayn Nuruu). Here, high mountains alternate with river valleys and lakes. Pastures support large herds of cattle and sheep, and wheat is cultivated. At the highest levels of the Altai in the northwest boreal forests cover the slopes. The second region is the southern half of the country. This is semidesert steppe changing further south to salt-pans, shallow depressions, and the arid stony wastes of the Gobi Desert.

While today more people live in towns than in the country, Mongolia nontheless remains a land of nomadic pastoralists. Herds of goats, sheep, yaks, camels, and horses still provide the base of the traditional economy, and Mongolia has the highest number of livestock per capita in the world. Cattle raising accounts for more than two-thirds of all production. Under the Soviets textiles and food processing were developed, and with aid from the USSR and Comecon (Council for Mutual Economic Assistance) mineral deposits such as copper, molybdenum, and coking coal were developed. Mongolia is the world's third biggest producer of fluorspar.

Recently, new laws have been passed regulating mining, banking, foreign investment, tourism, and economic planning. Mongolia continues to attract foreign aid, but suffers from the loss of Russian financial support. So far, foreign funds have not been found for the development of Mongolia's considerable oil and gas reserves.

186

including offical name, population, language, currency, and climate. All figures are the latest available and have been drawn from internationally recognized sources such as the *US Bureau of the Census International Database*, *CIA World Factboook*, *United Nations Human Development Report*, *The Statesman's Yearbook*, *The SBS World Guide* (fifth edition), and *World Bank Data Tables.*

Regional maps are at the end of each section for ease of reference. Physical and political maps for each region are followed by more detailed mapping. Editorial policy on the spelling of place names was decided after researching a wide number of sources. The cartographic and editorial team used the *US Board of Geographic Names* database as a guide, and a team of international cartographic experts was consulted on maps for every region. Our editorial policy has been to use English for the names of countries (e.g., France), international bodies of water (e.g., Pacific Ocean, Black Sea) and regional features that cross international borders (e.g., Carpathian Mountains). Local name forms have been used for all other names, but for capital cities and for some major cities and features, the English name is also provided in brackets. These English names are cross-referenced in the gazetteer, which includes all names on the physical and political maps, as well as the regional maps.

Recent name changes and boundary changes are shown on the maps including, for example, the new territory of Nunavut in Canada. The contour shading used on the maps is based on a combination of altitude and vegetation and provides an idea of how the area would appear from space.

Legend

Boundaries

International border

Disputed or undefined border

Administrative border

Settlements

Capitals of a depicted administrative division

Beijing			Over 5 million
Sydney			1 million to 5 million
Swansea			100,000 to 1 million
Kindu			Under 100,000 (size of symbol and type indicates the relative importance and population.)
Ellora			
<u>Canberra</u>			National capital
			Antarctic research station

Communications

Major road

Other road

Railway

Physical features

River

Lake, dam or reservoir

Dry/intermittent lake

Mt Adams 3751 m — Peak (height in meters)

Sea depths

200 meters

2000 meters

4000 meters

6000 meters

Lettering styles

AUSTRALIA	Country name
TIROL	Administration name
MOUNTAINS	Mountain range name
Ivory Coast	Coastal name
VALLEY	Valley name
FLORIDA KEYS	Major island group
Comerong Island	Island name
Comerong Point	Point name
Thames	River name
Bodensee	Lake name
ATLANTIC	Ocean name
TIMOR SEA	Sea name
Small Bay	Bay name

Foreword

Geographica should be seen as a pathway for a journey of each reader's discovery of the world. Our journey commences with the origin of the universe and the birth of Earth, the planet of life. Land, water and the atmosphere provide sustenance for complex evolving life forms, culminating in the arrival of those dominant creatures, humans. Geological history, influenced by ever-changing natural forces, gradually turns into documented human history. Then our journey leads us into an understanding of how Earth has been transformed by the actions of countless millions of humans and their immediate ancestors over the past million years or so.

Geographica is about a world that has, and will continue to be, changed. It is designed to be a substantial reference of world information. Original maps convey a vast amount of place-names and boundaries, many of which have changed with the course of history. Timelines describe events that have influenced how humans relate to their environment and to each other. Fact Files for each country offer readers comprehensive descriptions of national identities as they have emerged in recent times, many of which are still undergoing change. (The breakup of Yugoslavia and the Kosovo conflict illustrate the potential savagery of this process.) A number of essays are used to highlight key characteristics of the way landscapes have evolved and how humans relate to each other. These features are documented by new maps on a world scale and also on national scales.

The journey *Geographica* offers readers is the exploration of a world often ravaged by war, pestilence, human suffering, and the degradation of the environment. But it is also a world where we can conquer great challenges, discover the unknown, and improve the quality of life of many people through the better use of natural and human resources. The future always holds great uncertainty; yet knowledge of the past and present geographical and historical conditions of our planet can only strengthen our ability to plan for a peaceful and ecologically sustainable world in which we and the generations to come can lead fulfilling lives.

This volume represents the combined efforts of many people. As geographers, cartographers, historians, illustrators and editors we seek to offer our readers a substantial educational experience—a journey into the past and an appreciation of the present as it has evolved.

PROFESSOR BRUCE G. THOM

BA, PhD (Louisiana State University), FIAG

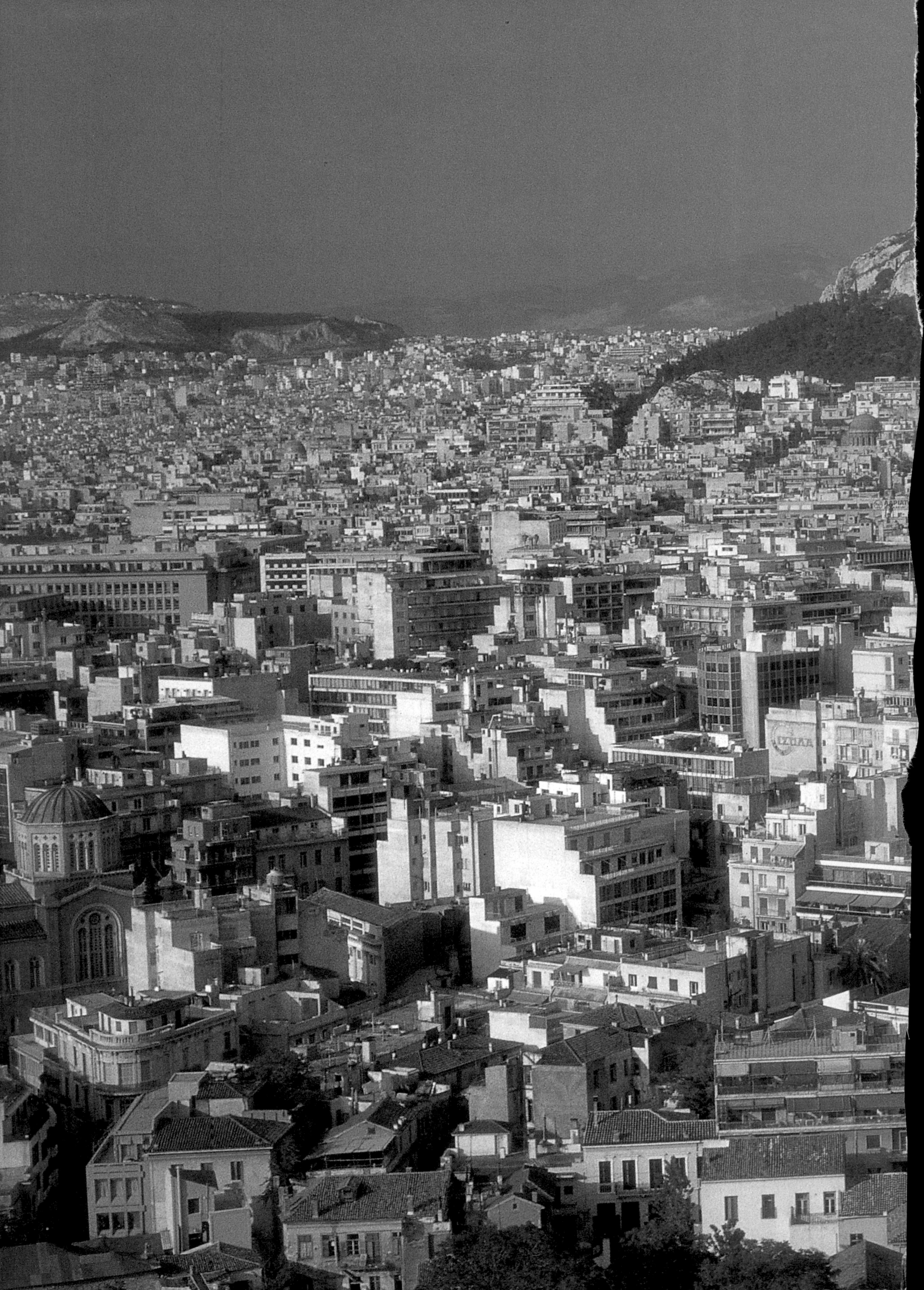

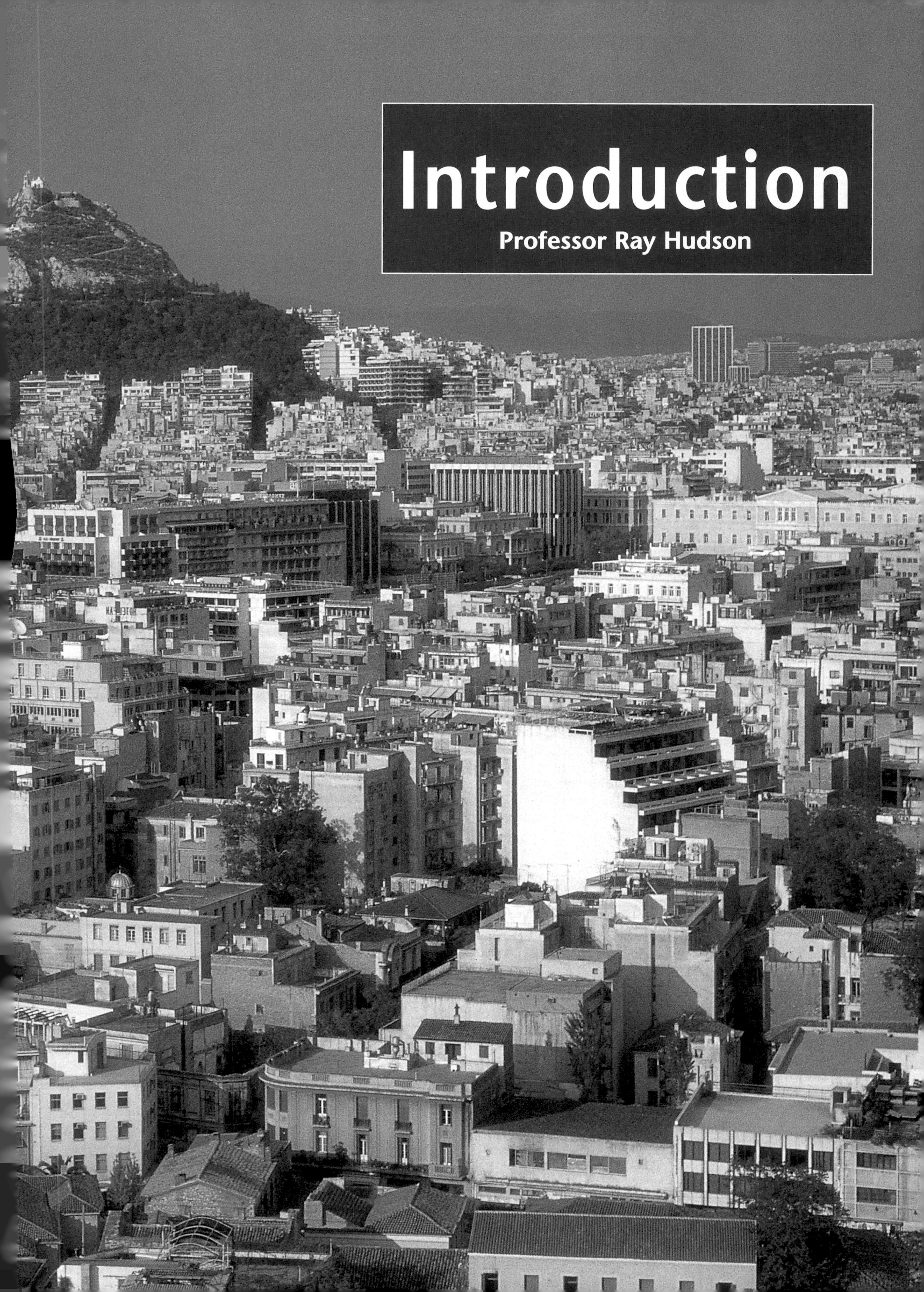

Introduction

Professor Ray Hudson

INTRODUCTION

Europe and the Russian Federation: The Changing Scene

The Mediterranean area is the birthplace of the ancient Greek and Roman civilizations. The Acropolis in Athens (above) bears the ruins of buildings from around 400 BC. Carcassone Castle, France (opposite), is an excellent example of medieval fortification.

If you look at Earth on a globe, the extent of the roughly triangular landmass covered by Europe and the Russian Federation is staggering—an enormous swathe of land extending almost around the world and from around 35° north of the equator to well into the Arctic Circle.

On two and a half sides, this large triangle is bounded by seas and oceans. This gives an initial indication of one of the many problems of defining precisely where the boundaries of Europe and the Russian Federation lie—many of the islands (of which arguably the most significant are those that make up the United Kingdom and the Republic of Ireland) lie off the coasts of Europe and the Federation. Furthermore, some European countries continue to have overseas territories that are colonies or dependencies, legacies of former empires, and a few have offshore islands that are an integral part of the national state—the Azores and Canary Islands in the Atlantic Ocean, parts of the territories of Portugal and Spain respectively, for example.

There are fairly clear physical boundaries to continental mainland Europe to the west (the Atlantic Ocean), to the north (the Arctic Ocean) and to the south (the Mediterranean Sea), although the southern boundary is less clear-cut around the eastern extremities of the Mediterranean Sea. Turkey, for example, is a member of NATO (the North Atlantic Treaty Organization) but is not generally regarded as a part of Europe.

In the same way, the Russian Federation has clear physical boundaries to the north, east and south, but at its western edge the European landmass slides into the Asian landmass without a precise border. Often the range of the Ural Mountains is taken as the boundary between European Russia to the west and the vast Siberian Plain and Asia to the east. In other respects, however, the boundary between Europe and Asia is more of a political and cultural divide than one that can be defined unambiguously by topography and physical geography.

THE NATURAL ENVIRONMENT

The natural environment of Europe and the Russian Federation is extremely diverse, as variations in latitude, longitude, and altitude combine to produce a great range of climatic and physical conditions and corresponding flora and fauna. Some of these environments have offered attractive possibilities for human settlement, influencing early patterns of habitation and also migration; others are harsh and unwelcoming, and have proved difficult to colonize even with the help of developments in contemporary technology.

The legacies of geology offer great opportunities in some parts of Europe and the Russian Federation, which have rich deposits of carboniferous and metallic minerals. Historically, these resources have been critical in influencing the pattern of economic development within these areas.

CLIMATE

Europe and the Russian Federation exhibit a vast latitudinal and longitudinal spread that is reflected in great climatic variation. The landmass extends almost around the globe, from a little more than 20°W at the westernmost tip of Ireland (though the western tip of Greenland is more than 70°W) all the way east (to around 170°E at the tip of the Bering Strait, which separates Asia from Alaska).

From its southernmost point, just below 35°N on the Greek island of Crete (although the Canary Islands lie not far north of the Tropic of Cancer in the Atlantic Ocean, just off the west African coast) Europe stretches northwards above the Arctic Circle, to North Cape in Norway. Much of Russia also lies well north of the Arctic Circle, extending almost to Alaska. Land in these latitudes is typically tundra, with the soil frozen for much of the year (permafrost) and a very short growing season.

The mean January temperature is below 0 °C (32 °F) over much of central, eastern and northern Europe and much of the Russian Federation; in inland Siberia it even falls below –50 °C (–58 °F). Few people live in these harsh environments.

In contrast, much of western and southern Europe has a more temperate climate and supports larger populations, though heavy urbanization means that distributions are uneven. The moderation of climatic extremes is especially noticeable in the west of the continent. Here, the effects of the Atlantic Ocean and the Gulf Stream soften the climatic extremes found in the continental interior in areas of eastern Europe and the Russian Federation. Mean July temperatures rarely exceed 30 °C (86 °F) even in the southernmost parts of Europe, but often exceed 20 °C (68 °F) over much of the inland continental areas of the Russian Federation. Given the longitudinal extent of Europe and the Russian Federation, the climatic contrast between maritime and inland continental areas is extremely pronounced.

The climate in the southern areas of Europe, around the Mediterranean Sea, is warm temperate with mild, wet winters and hot, dry summers—the classic Mediterranean climate in which much of European civilization and culture first took root during the classical Greek and Roman periods of history.

This broad climatic pattern generated by latitudinal and longitudinal variation is further complicated by altitudinal variation which adds another layer of complexity to the pattern of climatic variation.

LANDFORMS

The landscape of much of the area, and of Europe in particular, is the product of past (but in geological time, fairly recent) periods of orogenesis—when upward movements of the Earth's crust formed mountain ranges—especially during the Alpine period. Major mountain ranges stretch from the Iberian Peninsula through the Massif Central of France to the French, Swiss, Italian and Austrian Alps, to the Dynaric Alps and Apennines on either side of the Adriatic Sea in Italy and the former Yugoslavia respectively, and as far east as the Carpathian Alps, mainly in the eastern part of Romania. Most of Europe's major rivers, including the Danube, Rhine, Rhone, Loire and Po, originate in

these upland areas and drain to the various seas surrounding the continent.

To the southeast, the Caucasus form a land boundary on the bridge of land separating the Black Sea and the Caspian Sea, between Armenia and Azerbaijan and Turkey and Iran to their southeast. In the northwest, much of Scandinavia is also mountainous. A large part of these mountainous areas have been glaciated and processes of glaciation are ongoing.

To the north of the main mountain regions, most of Europe and the Russian Federation comprise the north European and Siberian plains. While some major rivers, such as the Ob and Yenisei, drain from the Siberian Plain to the Arctic Ocean, much of the drainage of the plain is to inland seas and lakes. The Volga River, for example, drains into the Caspian Sea, and other rivers drain into the Aral and Black Seas. The plains are periodically interrupted by ranges of mountain (such as the Urals) and by lower lying hills, bounded to the south by the hill and mountain ranges of Iran, Afghanistan, China and Mongolia.

In the far east, the Siberian Plain gradually rises in elevation and eventually gives way to the Verkoyhansk and then the Kolyma Mountains before the Russian Federation finally reaches its eastern boundaries in the Bering Sea and the Sea of Okhotsk.

Much of these plains was formed by various types of glacial deposits. In the north, much of Finland and southern Scandinavia also exhibit considerable evidence of glacial erosion, as in the numerous lakes of Finland.

VEGETATION

Much of Europe is forested, especially in the higher regions. The natural vegetation of the vast majority of Europe and a fair part of the Russian Federation is a mixture of broad-leafed deciduous and coniferous forest. Deciduous trees are generally more prevalent in the milder and wetter temperate areas, with conifers found further north in the colder regions; where the climate becomes too harsh for trees, tundra is dominant.

Around the Mediterranean region, evergreen trees and shrubs are the most common form of vegetation. As rainfall decreases with increasing distance eastwards, however, forested areas give way to steppe grassland. Within the milder temperate and Mediterranean areas, increasing altitude produces the same changes in vegetation as increasing latitude.

ENVIRONMENTAL TRANSFORMATION

While forest is the natural vegetation of much of Europe and Russia, the majority of this, especially in Europe, has been cleared for agriculture and other uses. Manufacturing industry, mining, and the expansion of cities and towns have all dramatically changed the landscape, and advances in technology have also allowed us to exploit the resources offered by the natural environment. Indeed, much of what is often thought of as the natural landscape is in fact a social product—the result of extended interactions between people and the environment. This process of environmental transformation has a very long history—it started when people first began to make the transition from peripatetic hunter-gatherers to become sedentary agriculturalists and farmers, establishing communities and settlements.

It is only in the last two or three hundred years, however, that dramatic technological advances in agriculture, combined with the developments of the Industrial Revolution, have allowed people to radically alter the natural environment in Europe. Irrigation and artificial fertilizers have permitted agriculture to flourish in formerly uncultivable regions, and the gradual process of removing natural vegetation and adding chemicals to the soil has altered the natural balance which had evolved over thousands of years.

While large-scale environmental processes remain beyond human control, the capacity to alter environmental conditions on a local or regional scale and to overcome environmental constraints has increased greatly in modern time, especially in wealthier countries. Such transformations have become integral to the development of industrial capitalism in Europe. One spectacular example of this is the reclamation of the Dutch polders and the subsequent development of intensive commercial glasshouse agriculture on this land which used to be part of the sea. Conquering nature was also an important preoccupation in the communist former USSR (Union of Soviet Socialist Republics), where it was seen as proof of the capacity of state socialism to triumph over a hostile environment for the collective good.

Thus in a whole variety of ways, and for a variety of motives, people have learned to modify their local environments so that they can live more comfortably, so that plants can be cultivated and animals reared.

It is also worth remembering, however, that human efforts to transform the natural environment and improve material living standards in turn have their own impact on the environment. One of the most spectacular—and unwanted—examples of this is the dramatic shrinkage of the inland Aral Sea in Kazakhstan in the Russian Federation. Another is the extensive soil erosion induced by large-scale agriculture in formerly fertile natural grassland transformed to cereal and cotton-growing areas. Manmade disasters

The agricultural and industrial revolutions gave considerable impetus to the economies of the leading European states, as industrial capitalism became established first in Britain and then in Belgium, Germany, France and other continental European countries. This diffusion was an uneven process, however, and many areas of Europe and Russia were virtually untouched by these new developments, remaining locked in a pre-industrial and pre-capitalist world until well into the twentieth century.

The rise of industrial powers within Europe increased the pressure among them to create empires. New colonies would provide European countries with cheap food and raw materials while also creating a new market, beyond the national markets, for the sale of industrial goods made in Europe. In the latter part of the nineteenth century European countries such as Belgium and Germany joined in the race to establish their own foreign empires. At the same time the struggle for supremacy within Europe intensified, as larger modern national states became established. This process of state building often led to people of different nations becoming citizens of the same state. People and places moved between states as national boundaries shifted (for example, Alsace and Lorraine moved between France and Germany on an almost regular basis). This process of economic and territorial competition finally culminated in the appalling destruction of the First World War, and the postwar settlement led to the creation of completely new states in the Baltic and the Balkans as the old Austro-Hungarian Empire was dismantled.

There followed a period of deep economic recession and dislocation, part of a wider global slump. This helped produce a resurgence of nationalist sentiment, most infamously in Germany, with the rise of fascism and its concepts of racial supremacy and *lebensraum* (living space), which were used to justify ethnic cleansing and territorial aggrandizement. Other parts of Europe followed a different path—most notably Russia. Here the October 1917 Revolution established a communist government and presaged the emergence of the USSR, dominated by Russia, in 1922. In 1939, the growing ambitions of fascist Germany culminated in the outbreak of the

can also have a devastating environmental impact—radioactive waste and smoke from the 1986 fire at the Chernobyl nuclear reactor, in Ukraine, spread widely over much of Russia and Europe as a result of westerly winds.

In addition, other human activities in the countries of Europe and the Russian Federation are a major contributing force to processes such as global warming which threatens possible climatic change and rising sea levels. Low-lying coastal areas and those that have been reclaimed from the sea (like the polders of the Netherlands) are particularly vulnerable to such changes.

A CHANGING POLITICAL-ECONOMIC MAP

For much of their history, the lands of Europe and the Russian Federation have been the arena for a succession of migrations and movements of people. As they gradually became settled, people sought to establish the boundaries of their own territories and armed conflict and wars became almost endemic as different groups sought to expand their territory, or to protect it from others seeking to take it from them. Empires were built, then declined within Europe—from the Roman to the Austro-Hungarian.

For several hundred years, this ebb and flow of political fortunes as an assortment of emperors, kings, queens and princes fought to consolidate and increase their territory, was accompanied by economic stagnation as European economies were predominantly organized around various forms of subsistence agriculture.

THE GROWTH OF EMPIRES

Towards the end of the fifteenth century, a number of European states began to explore the possibilities of creating empires outside Europe. This added a new dimension to the political struggle between states, and a new source of economic dynamism, as new subtropical and tropical crops and products began to arrive in Europe.

A number of European states sought to establish new empires in the "New World", and there was much competition between the British, Dutch, French, Portuguese and Spanish. By the nineteenth century, however, Britain had emerged as the dominant power (despite the loss of its colonies in North America). Trade began to allow the accumulation of capital and, in due course, that capital was channelled into economic development within Europe.

The church of Sveti Jovan Bogoslov Kaneo, on the shores of Ohrid Lake, Macedonia (right). Blaenau Ffestiniog in Wales, where the houses are dwarfed by the slate mine workings (above).

Second World War, leading to further devastation and carnage in Europe.

AFTER THE SECOND WORLD WAR

The immediate postwar period was to reshape the map of Europe for the next fifty or so years—in ways that had global implications—until the de facto collapse of socialism in Europe in 1989 and the formal break-up of the USSR in 1991. At the end of the Second World War, the USSR occupied most of eastern Europe. The partitioning of Berlin between East and West in 1948 and the creation of two Germanies (the Federal Republic of Germany and the German Democratic Republic) confirmed that postwar Europe would be divided into two ideologically opposed blocs, a capitalist West and communist East. The "Cold War" had descended on Europe.

In 1949 NATO was established as a common defense organization in the west. The USSR developed a series of buffer satellite states between itself and Western Europe, and became the center of both economic (COMECON) and defense (the Warsaw Pact) alliances. In these ways, the USSR sought to prevent the spread of capitalism into the East and to limit the ambitions of the USA, with which it vied to become the dominant global power.

There were also significant moves to redraw the political map within Western Europe—in large part stimulated by a wish to avoid future European wars—by creating new supranational institutions. Thus in 1951 the European Coal and Steel Community (the ECSC) was established with the signing of the Treaty of Paris by Belgium, France, Germany, Italy, Luxembourg and the Netherlands. This sought to guarantee the future peace of Europe by inextricably binding together the coal and steel industries of France and Germany, then seen as the key to the capacity to wage war. Plans for a greater degree of political unification and the creation of a common European Defense Force foundered.

In response, the six signatories of the Treaty of Paris then signed the Treaty of Rome (in 1957) creating the European Economic Community (EEC). The aim of the EEC was to promote democratic political systems and economic growth and the free movement of capital and labor within the territory of the member countries. This posed problems for those Western European states that had not signed the Treaty of Rome. In 1960 Austria, Denmark, Portugal, Norway, Sweden, Switzerland and the United Kingdom signed the Stockholm Convention, which established the European Free Trade Area (EFTA). This effectively divided Western Europe into two free trade areas, EFTA and the EEC. Much of the next thirty or so years witnessed a redefinition of the boundaries between these two groupings.

In the late 1950s and 1960s the countries of the EEC enjoyed sustained high rates of economic growth—so much so that they drew in migrant workers from Mediterranean Europe and North Africa as a way of avoiding labor shortages. Other Western European countries began to gaze with envious eyes at the economic growth rates of the six signatories to the Treaty of Rome, and to consider whether their interests would not be better served by joining the EEC. In 1973 Denmark, Ireland, and the UK became members of the EEC, significantly shifting the balance between it and EFTA.

In the 1960s and 1970s, the EEC concluded a series of trade treaties with a number of southern European, Mediterranean and North African states and former colonies in other regions of the developing world. These trade and aid agreements tied these countries closely into the EEC's economy in various ways—as markets for their agricultural produce and migrant workers and as suppliers of technology, especially that needed for industrial development.

Several of the southern European states actively sought full membership of the EEC but failed to meet a key condition for entry to the club—Greece, Portugal and Spain had dictatorial rather than democratic political systems. With a return to democracy in the mid-1970s in these countries, however, the way was clear for full membership—Greece joined the EEC in 1981, Portugal and Spain in 1986. The reunification of the two Germanies in 1990 further enlarged the European Community, while in 1995 Austria, Finland and Sweden also joined. The EEC now had 15 members.

There are strong pressures for further expansion, predominantly south and east, with Cyprus, the Czech Republic, Estonia, Hungary, Poland and Slovenia signing on in 2004. Thus former members of COMECON became members of the European Union following the breakup of the USSR and the emergence of the looser federation of the Commonwealth of Independent States (CIS) in 1991.

This is seen as a way of underwriting capitalism and democracy throughout Eastern Europe in the twenty-first century, much as the Mediterranean enlargement of the 1980s was seen as a way of underpinning democracy and ensuring the end of dictatorships in Greece, Portugal and Spain.

At the same time as extending territorially, there have also been processes of deepening integration, leading to a transition from the EEC to the European Union following the 1992 Maastricht Treaty. There have been significant moves to complete the Single European Market and towards economic and monetary union, with eleven of the member states signing up to a common currency (the Euro) from 1 January 1999 (the non-participants are Denmark, Greece, Sweden and the UK).

There has been a complex process of political change throughout Europe since the 1950s, with tendencies towards the creation and collapse of supranational organizations. Of particular significance has been the collapse of the former USSR and, related to this, of the federal Yugoslav Republic. Here, ethnic and religious tensions which had been kept in check for many decades were suddenly released with devastating and tragic consequences. Much of the Balkans and many of the republics in the southeastern European part of the Commonwealth of Independent States erupted into violence as a range of national groups sought to secure their own territorial states. They often pursued this goal using savage military force and ethnic cleansing on a scale not seen in Europe since the horrors of the Holocaust in the 1930s.

At the the beginning of the twenty-first century, as at the start of the twentieth century, much of Europe has again been engulfed in war, centered on the Balkans. Unlike the early years of the last century, however, developments in the global media now ensure that individuals worldwide are kept informed of events in the European arena as televisions broadcast pictures (transmitted in real time) of the damage wrought by missile attacks and "smart" bombs, and of refugees forced to flee their homes under threat of death.

ECONOMIC DIVERSITY: VARIETIES OF CAPITALISM

With the formal dissolution of the USSR in 1991, the economic landscape was no longer one of competition between capitalism and socialism but rather one of competition between varieties of capitalism found over Europe and the Russian Federation.

One immediate consequence of the collapse of socialism was to increase poverty and inequality within this new shared space. Attempts to establish thriving capitalist economies over much of Eastern Europe and Russia and its republics failed initially, as the cultural and institutional requirements for such a change were simply not present. Moreover, the social welfare supports of the former socialist system were swept away.

Economic transition was reasonably smooth in the more economically advanced countries of the former COMECON in which forms of private property ownership had survived in the socialist period or emerged well before 1989 (in the Czech Republic, Hungary and Poland).

Elsewhere, however, economies simply collapsed, while in Russia and several of the other member states of the Commonwealth of Independent States, black markets, gangsterism and crim-

inal capitalism of a sort associated with the Mafia became the norm. Where economic collapse went hand-in-hand with the devastation of war and forced population movements, problems of poverty, ill health and death became even more acute.

In contrast, over much of the European Union, economic fortunes have become more assured and lifestyles correspondingly more comfortable. There are differences in the forms of capitalism (for example, Germany and Sweden remain much more committed to corporatist approaches, the UK to a neo-liberal market approach), but even these differences have been reduced by the need to conform to the criteria for entry to the European Monetary Union. This is not to deny that considerable inequalities remain within the European Union—at national, regional and local scales and between people—but these are insignificant compared with the situation in much of Eastern Europe, Russia and the rest of the CIS.

There are marked variations in population densities within the European Union, with people heavily clustered in urban areas, which typically rely on service-based economies. There are similar variations in output and income per capita and also in the sectoral structure of economies, with the more developed and affluent regions generally relying less upon agriculture and more upon advanced services. National economies vary greatly in size and structure, but the pattern and variation at subnational scales is more complex still.

The scope of welfare state provision has certainly been reduced over much of Western Europe, often as a direct response to the need to meet the fiscal and macroeconomic requirements for entry to the European Monetary Union. Nevertheless, the welfare net still remains in place to an extent no longer found over much of the remainder of Russia and the CIS and parts of southern and eastern Europe.

This provision, along with the perception of more and better job opportunities in the West, has encouraged fears of floods of economic migrants (as opposed to political refugees) from Eastern Europe and the Russian Federation (as well as possibly from North Africa). One consequence of this has been concern about both immigration polices into the European Union and the status of individuals of varied ethnic origins who have lived in Europe for decades, after arriving as temporary migrant workers, but who still lack citizenship rights.

We began with a question—where is Europe? However, more important questions to consider for the future are perhaps who are Europeans now, what does it mean to be European, and what are the rights and responsibilities of each putative European citizen?

The mild climate of Madeira makes these Portuguese islands a popular resort all year round (left). An aerial view of the old city of Salzburg (top) on the south bank of the Salzach River, in Austria. Dubrovnik (above), in Croatia, is another city that retains its Old Town charm; here the Franciscan belltower is featured.